PSYCHOLOGY
SCIENCE, BEHAVIOR AND LIFE

PSYCHOLOGY

SCIENCE, BEHAVIOR AND LIFE

ROBERT L. CROOKS

OREGON HEALTH SCIENCES UNIVERSITY, PORTLAND COMMUNITY COLLEGE

JEAN STEIN

HOLT, RINEHART AND WINSTON, INC.

NEW YORK   CHICAGO   SAN FRANCISCO   PHILADELPHIA   MONTREAL   TORONTO   LONDON   SYDNEY   TOKYO

Editor-in-Chief: Ted Buccholz
Publisher: Susan Meyers
Developmental Editor: Laura Pearson
Project Management: Caliber Design Planning, Inc.
Art Direction: Caliber Design Planning, Inc.
Illustrations: Caliber Design Planning, Inc.
Design Concept: Koppel and Scher
Cover, Part, and Chapter Illustrations: Koppel and Scher
Field Editor: Jim Lizotte

Library of Congress Cataloging-in-Publication Data
Crooks, Robert, 1941–

    Psychology: science, behavior, and life/Robert L. Crooks, Jean Stein.
       p.   cm.
    Bibliography: p.
    Includes index.
    ISBN 0–03–006758–8: $26.50
    1. Psychology.   I. Stein, Jean, 1947–   II. Title.
BF121.C675 1988   87–35600
150—dc19   CIP

ISBN 0-03-006758-8

Printed in the United States of America

8 9 0 1   032   9 8 7 6 5 4 3 2 1

Holt, Rinehart and Winston, Inc.
The Dryden Press
Saunders College Publishing

Photo Credits

Chapter 1: page 7, © Kathy Talbot/The Image Works; page 8, AP/Wide World Photos; page 10, The Bettmann Archive; page 11, The Bettmann Archive; page 12, (top) The Bettmann Archive; (bottom) © Larry Mulvehill/Photo Researchers, Inc.; page 14, Stephen R. Brown/The Stock Market; page 16, © Nancy Bates/The Picture Cube; page 17, © Ken Robert Buck, 1980/The Picture Cube; page 18, © E. Simonsen/H. Armstrong Roberts, Inc.; page 19, © 1983 Will McIntyre/Photo Researchers, Inc.

Chapter 2: page 25, P. Davidson/The Image Works; page 30, (bottom photos) Professor Philip Zimbardo, Stanford University; page 32, © Jeff Albertson/The Picture Cube; page 34, UPI/ Bettmann Newsphotos; page 35, (top) © Roy Morsch/The Stock Market; (bottom) George W. Gardner/The Image Works; page 37, (top) © 1982 De Sazo—Rapho/Photo Researchers, Inc.; (bottom) © Suzanne Szasz/Photo Researchers, Inc.; page 38, AP/Wide World Photos

Chapter 3: page 49, Courtesy of Dr. John C. Mazziotta et al., UCLA School of Medicine; page 50, © Ulrike Welsch, 1981/Photo Researchers, Inc.; page 56, © Therese Frare/The Picture Cube; page 62, (top 2 photographs) © 1984 Lester V. Berg-man and Associates; (bottom) © John Coletti/ Stock Boston; page 67, © Brownie Harris/The Stock Market; page 75, © Jean-Claude Lejeune/ Stock Boston; page 77, © Jim Amos/Photo Researchers, Inc.; page 78, © Alexander Tsiaras/ Photo Researchers, Inc.; page 79, (left) © Bill Gallery/Stock Boston; (right) © Alexander Tsiaras/ Photo Researchers, Inc.; page 82, © Frank Siteman/Stock Boston

Chapter 4: page 91, © Jeff Rotman/The Picture Cube; page 92, © A. I. Parnes, 1978/Photo Researchers, Inc.; page 98, © Lennart Nilsson, from *Behold Man*, Little, Brown and Company, Boston;

(continued following indexes)

For my children.
    BOB CROOKS

For Phil.
    JEAN STEIN

PREFACE

Why would anyone choose to write an introductory psychology textbook? There were moments during the writing of *Psychology* when we wondered why we had been unbalanced enough to tackle a project of this magnitude. Imagine sitting at a great table literally strewn with notes and articles, knowing that the pressure of a deadline is upon you. Further imagine that the table is located in front of a vast window overlooking the country at sunset, with a view of picturesque waters dimpled only by feeding trout. Finally imagine looking wistfully from those waters to the fly rod poised for action at the front door, and you can *begin* to imagine how difficult writing a textbook can be.

Both of us have had prior experience with writing textbooks, and we entered this project fully aware of how our lives would be regimented by the demands of production deadlines. Our previous experience did help get us through "vacations" when we peered over the tops of our computer monitors while family members departed for the ski slopes or the beach. However, it was not experience alone that provided us with the motivation we needed to make this project an ongoing priority; rather, it was our vision for the kind of book we felt we could write. Our goal was to write a textbook that offered a unique array of features that would truly distinguish it from the dozens of other textbooks available, and we believe that *Psychology* represents the fulfillment of that goal.

OUR GOALS FOR WRITING THIS TEXT

Despite the enormity of the project, three goals motivated us. First, we wanted to show students the science of psychology. Second, we hoped to make the content of *Psychology* challenging but accessible to students of varying levels of academic ability. Third, we believed that we could create a textbook that would encourage students to *think* about and, as a result, better *remember* the principles of psychology. Each of these goals deserves a more detailed explanation.

THE SCIENCE OF PSYCHOLOGY

Beginning students often think of psychology as a discipline based on common sense. We believed that it was important to show students *how* we know what we know; that is, to show that psychology is actually based on the dynamic process of doing research. To demonstrate that psychology is indeed a science, a full chapter on research methods is included (Chapter 2.) More importantly, as you flip through the pages of *Psychology,* you will see that we have described hundreds of classic and contemporary research studies in detail. There are over 2,000 references to published research and over 500 of them discuss research published in 1986 and 1987. We are confident that this textbook represents the most balanced and the most current information available for introductory psychology.

Of course, many textbooks are well grounded in psychological research. What makes *Psychology* special is the *way* in which the research is presented. We have attempted to tell the stories of psychological researchers: the questions they asked, the studies they conducted to answer the questions, and the theories they developed as a result of those studies. Where appropriate, illustrations of the experimental apparatus are included to make our descriptions even more vivid for students. Also, we have attempted to show that psychological research is an ever-evolving process, and that our knowledge is constantly changing as a result.

Finally, throughout *Psychology* you will find coverage of the biological bases of behavior. Because contemporary research is discovering some amazing links between chemical and neurological processes and behavior, we felt it was important to integrate these findings throughout the text.

CHALLENGING BUT ACCESSIBLE COVERAGE

Our second goal, to make the content of *Psychology* interesting and accessible to students at varying levels of preparedness and academic ability, stemmed directly from the teaching experience of one of the authors, Bob Crooks. Bob has taught introductory psychology for over 20 years at both the community college and university levels. During that time, he has interacted with students of virtually every age, from a wide variety of backgrounds, and with vastly different levels of academic preparedness and ability. In writing *Psychology,* we have drawn on that experience and have tried to reach and motivate as wide a range of students as possible. Three features of the textbook deserve special mention: the range and use of examples, the diversity of the examples chosen, and the elimination of boxes.

Use of Examples   Wherever possible, we have used concrete examples to better explain psychological concepts. We believe (and reviewers concur) that the use of such examples in *Psychology* will make the content more enjoyable and more understandable for students. While each chapter provides evidence of this goal, examples in the Learning chapter (Chapter 6) are perhaps most noteworthy in this regard.

Diversity of Examples   There is no "typical" introductory psychology student, and therefore we have avoided "typical" examples wherever possible. Throughout each chapter you will find examples that relate to older students, working students, and parents, as well as to the traditional 18 year old. *Psychology* is unique in this regard.

Elimination of Boxes   In our experience of teaching introductory psychology, we have noticed that virtually every introductory textbook includes important research studies or interesting highlights in *boxes* throughout the text. We have also realized that most students find these boxes distracting and annoying. Even worse, students believe that boxes are ancillary to the text material, and often skim over important information. To make *Psychology* as readable as possible and to ensure that students read *all* the content, we have virtually eliminated boxes. Examples, highlights, and research are presented in the body of the text. Only practical suggestions in the form of Health Psychology and Life sections are in boxes, because we think students want these practical suggestions and tips set off from the primary material.

PEDAGOGY THAT ENCOURAGES THINKING

Our third and final goal for writing *Psychology* was perhaps the most challenging: We believed that we could write a textbook that would be totally designed to encourage students to *think* about the subject matter, to apply it to their lives and, as a result, to better remember the principles of psychology. In addition to showing students the thought processes of researchers, we have developed three types of pedagogy that are designed to achieve our goal: Critical Thinking questions, First-Person accounts, and Health Psychology and Life discussions.

Critical Thinking Questions   This feature is integrated directly into the body of the text and is set off by a tan bar. Each question is designed to make students stop and think about the topic they are reading in an attempt to encourage higher order processing of information and learning. Critical Thinking questions challenge them to think like psychological researchers by making hypotheses, by predicting experimental results, and by working toward answers to some key issues surrounding human behaviors.

First-Person Accounts   One of the most exciting facts about taking a psychology course is that students can directly relate the concepts to their own experiences. In our teaching experience, we have realized that students enjoy thinking about and relating their experiences to one another, and that theory and research becomes much more memorable when they do so. To encourage students to think about how the content of *Psychology* relates to them, First-Person accounts are included in the text margins. We have used these accounts to stimulate in-class discussion, and have found them to be quite valuable.

Health Psychology and Life Features   Perhaps no area of psychology is receiving more research attention or is more inherently interesting to students than the area of health psychology. It encompasses and incorporates virtually every other area of psychology, and because of this we decided to integrate coverage of health psychology into each chapter. These features show the practicality and relevance of the science of psychology, and provide tips, techniques, and suggestions for applying psychology to deal with problems in the students' own lives.

Writing *Psychology* was a difficult but rewarding process. We have worked to achieve the goals outlined above, and we hope that this textbook will help *you* to achieve your goals for the introductory psychology course.

SUPPLEMENTS

FOR THE STUDENT

To help students better master the subject matter and to help in that inevitable quest for a better grade, a Study Guide is available with this textbook. Each chapter of the Study Guide contains learning objectives, a programmed review of the chapter, multiple choice and matching exercises, and review diagrams and matrices. Two unique features of the Study Guide are designed to promote critical thinking. First, application exercises challenge students to apply chapter content to answer questions or problems. Second, critical thinking problems encourage them to analyze and evaluate research according to a framework given in the Study Guide.

FOR THE INSTRUCTOR

A complete ancillary package is available upon adoption of *Psychology*, which is designed to help both new and experienced instructors introduce critical thinking and discussion into the classroom. Elements include an Instructor's Manual, two Test Banks (one specifically designed with questions that encourage critical thinking), Computerized Test Banks available in IBM and Apple II formats, software, videos, and transparency acetates. For additional information on these items, contact your local Holt, Rinehart and Winston representative.

ACKNOWLEDGMENTS

Psychology reflects a combination of talents, insights, and perspectives that range well beyond those of the authors. Whatever valued qualities a reader may perceive in its pages are due, in large part, to the invaluable contributions of the reviewers who evaluated our manuscript, the staff of Holt, Rinehart and Winston, the thousands of students whose collective thoughts, experiences, and wisdom have enriched our book, and our families and friends who provided us with much needed support.

While each of us brings a somewhat different perspective to our writing, we share a common appreciation for the indispensable value of the review process. Fortunately, our editors were committed to securing reviews from a broad array of psychologists representing a variety of specializations and perspectives. These individuals reviewed the manuscript at various stages during its development. Their comments and suggestions are reflected throughout the book. We deeply appreciate the efforts of these reviewers, whose names are listed at the end of this section.

The task of writing a textbook can be a lonely and somewhat arduous endeavor at times. However, it has been our good fortune that the staff of Holt, Rinehart and Winston consistently supported us in ways that eased our burden and made the process of writing a less burdensome and, at times, even delightful experience. Space does not allow us to describe the many important contributions of all of those who have been involved in this project. However, we would like to express our heartfelt appreciation to three very special people.

Our sponsoring editor, Susan Meyers, provided a broadly faceted vision for our book that helped to shape its features and guide its production. In addition, Susan offered unwavering support, acted as our advocate, provided a wealth of publishing savvy, and maintained an attitude of infectious enthusiasm that helped to see us through some difficult times. Our multitalented developmental editor, Laura Pearson, gave us so much that it is difficult to summarize her accomplishments in a few words. Among her many contributions are selecting all the illustrative photographs, providing the kind of organization essential to the success of a project of this magnitude, responding to and resolving innumerable issues pertaining to manuscript development, maintaining sharp attention to details, and perhaps most important, providing the kind of empathic listening and warm friendship that can lighten the darkest of times. Special thanks are extended to Crystal Riley, consummate journal researcher. The extremely current nature of our text is due in considerable part to Crystal's exhaustive search of the recent journal literature in psychology. Through it all, even during those lazy Sundays when she was the recipient of frantic calls asking for an immediate search for information on some late breaking development, Crystal never stopped smiling.

We would also like to give special thanks to Michael Raulin who prepared the Statistics Appendix; to William Titus who wrote the Industrial/ Organizational Psychology Appendix; and to Jack Kirschenbaum, who creatively and determinedly wrote the Instructor's Manual, Study Guide, and Test Bank.

Finally, we owe special thanks to the following reviewers for their criticisms and helpful suggestions:

Charles T. Allen, University of Wisconsin—Stout
John Anson, Stephen F. Austin University
Gilbert Atnip, Indiana University Southeast
Amy Baldwin, Northern Arizona University
Barbara Basden, California State University—Fresno
Richard Bauer, Middle Tennessee State University
Ltc. Johnston Beach, USMA—West Point
William Calhoun, University of Tennessee—Knoxville

Douglas Chute, Drexel University
Debra Clark, SUNY—Cortland
Stephen Cooper, Glendale Community College
Frank Costin, University of Illinois—Champaign/Urbana
Jacqueline Cuevas, Midwestern State University
Steve Davis, Emporia State University
Mitzi Doane, University of Minnesota—Duluth
James Dougan, Indiana University
Richard Griggs, University of Florida
J. H. Grosslight, Florida State University
James R. Haines, Indiana University
Marty Haraway, Northeast Louisiana University
Philip Hartley, Chaffey College
Christine Jazwinski, St. Cloud State University
Fred A. Johnson, University of the District of Columbia
John P. Keating, University of Washington—Seattle
Melvyn B. King, SUNY—Cortland
Jack Kirschenbaum, Fullerton College
Stephen Mark Kopta, University of Evansville
Joan F. Lorden, University of Alabama—Birmingham
Al J. Mayer, Portland Community College
Linda Musun-Miller, University of Arkansas—Little Rock
John Nezlek, College of William and Mary
Merrill E. Noble, Pennsylvania State University
Robert Ochsman, University of Arkansas—Little Rock
John Orlosky, Jackson Community College
David Payne, SUNY—Binghamton
Robert Provine, University of Maryland—Baltimore County
Antonio E. Puente, University of North Carolina—Wilmington
Donald Ragusa, Bowling Green State University
Michael Raulin, SUNY—Buffalo
Richard Sanders, University of North Carolina
Rickard Sebby, Southeast Missouri State University
David A. Schroeder, University of Arkansas—Fayetteville
Paul Stager, York University
Harry Tiemann, Mesa College
William Titus, Arkansas Technical University
Pat Tuntland, Pima County Community College
W. Larry Ventis, College of William and Mary
Doris Ward, San Jacinto College South
Carol West, Western Piedmont Community College
Fred Whitford, Montana State University
Joan Wilterdink, University of Wisconsin—Madison
Loren C. Wingblade, Indiana University
Tae Woo, Millersville University
William Zachry, University of Tennessee—Martin

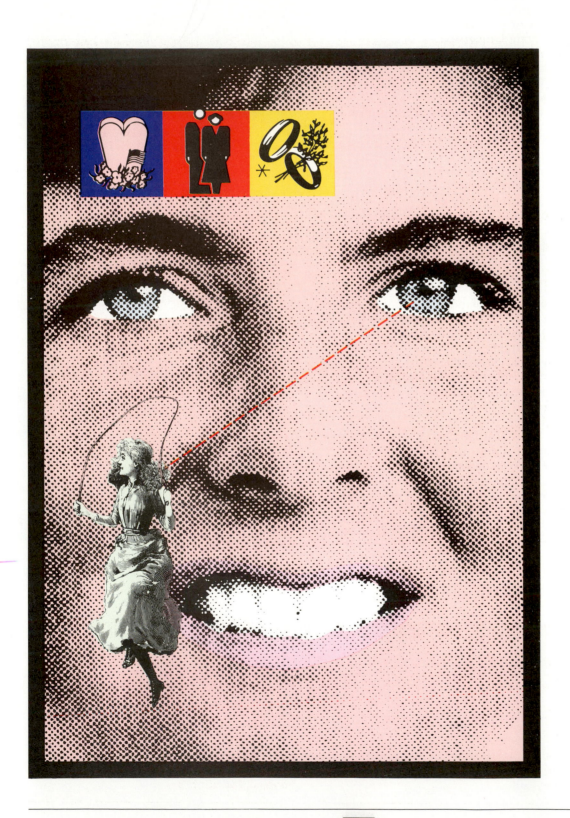

CONTENTS
IN BRIEF

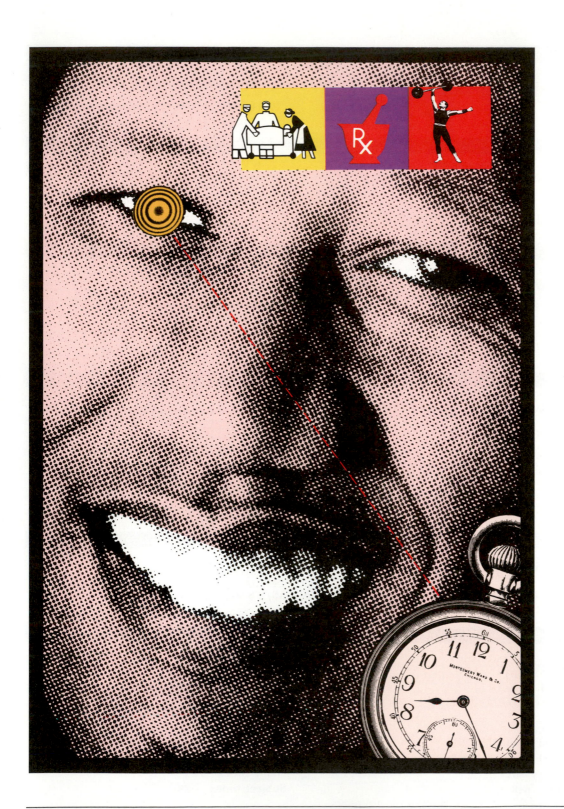

CONTENTS

CONTENTS

APPENDIX C

FEATURES

HEALTH PSYCHOLOGY AND LIFE

PSYCHOLOGY
SCIENCE, BEHAVIOR AND LIFE

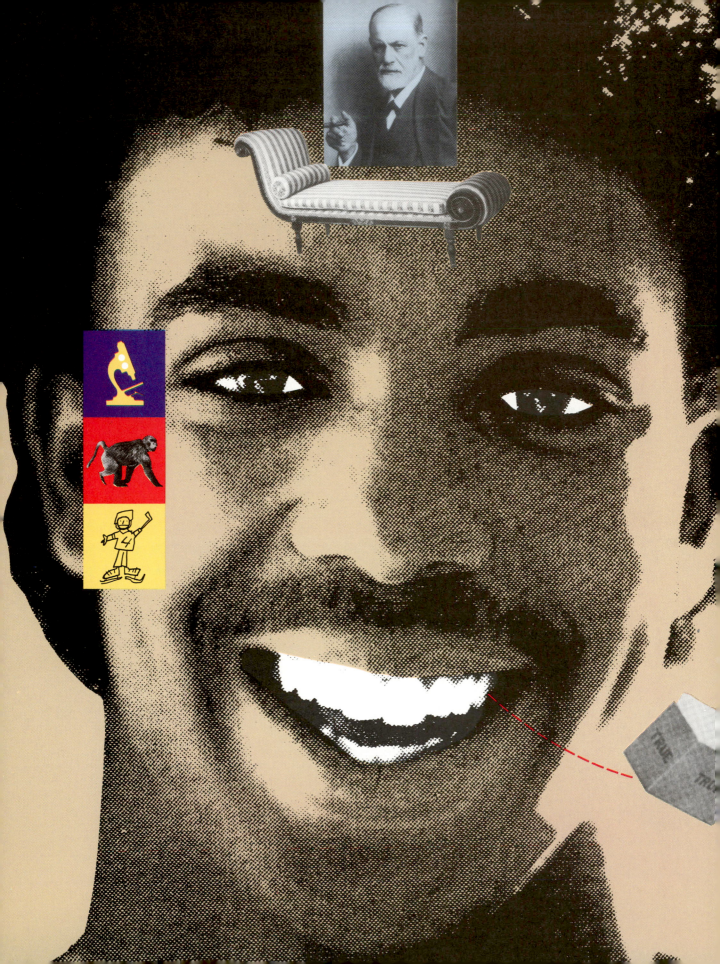

PART 1

NATURE, ORIGINS, AND METHODS OF PSYCHOLOGY

1
THE NATURE AND ORIGINS OF PSYCHOLOGY

2
THE METHODS OF PSYCHOLOGY

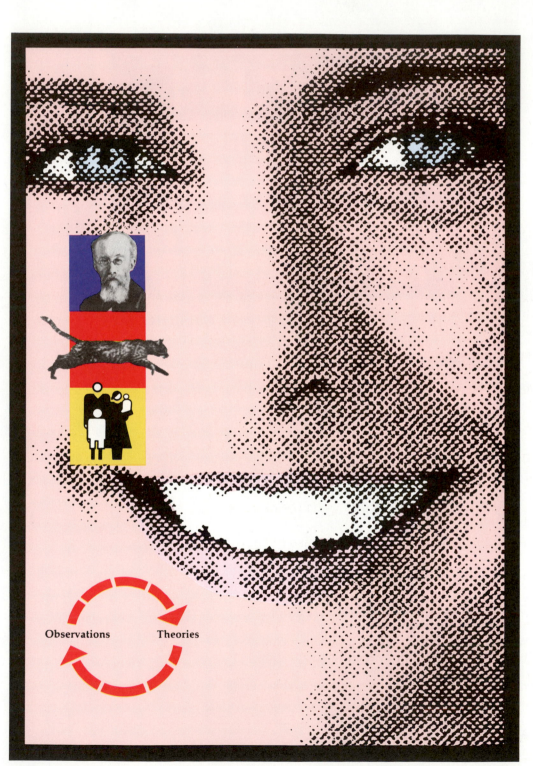

Observations Theories

1

The Nature and Origins of Psychology

Welcome to the study of psychology. For many of you, this may be your first formal exposure to a science that is central to our lives. Perhaps you have wondered, as you have explored some other subjects, "What has this to do with my life?" Psychology has everything to do with your life.

The authors admit to some bias, but we do believe that a knowledge of psychology is helpful even to people who do not plan to pursue it as a career. Studying psychology provides insights into why people behave as they do. It also helps us better understand our own thoughts, feelings, behaviors, and attitudes, and hopefully, it can strengthen our appreciation of and tolerance for the wide differences that exist among people.

Psychology investigates a wide variety of questions and attempts to answer them using scientific methods. Among the questions that will be explored in this book are:

Is there a relationship between psychological disorders and brain biochemistry?

Do intelligence tests provide accurate data?

What causes people to overeat, and what can be done to overcome obesity?

Why do people dream, and what happens if they aren't permitted to dream?

Can human abilities be artificially enhanced by chemical or electrical stimulation of the brain?

What techniques are effective in changing people's attitudes?

Psychology also helps us evaluate the many "psychological facts" we encounter every day in popular media. When was the last time you read a newspaper or magazine article or heard a talk-show host present the latest findings on the meaning of dreams, the effects of marijuana on memory, or why men behave differently from women? Many people accept such "scientifically based facts" without questioning whether they are founded on reliable evidence. An understanding of psychology can help us think critically and carefully evaluate such claims.

PSYCHOLOGY DEFINED

Formally defined, **psychology** is *the scientific study of the behavior and mental processes of humans and other animals.* This definition can be broken down into three parts. It is a scientific study; it studies both behavior and mental processes; and it includes the study of other animals as well as humans.

PSYCHOLOGY AS A SCIENCE

The first part of our definition states that psychology is a scientific study. Indeed, the theories and facts of psychology emerge from the careful application of scientific methods. This may contradict many people's views of psychology, for it is often assumed that psychology is just a matter of common sense. After all, are we not "applying psychology" when we mix enough praise with criticism to make a child feel good about changing bad habits or when we carefully discuss relationship problems with our partners rather than keeping those concerns within us? If syndicated advice columnists in the daily paper can provide psychological advice for dealing with people, what sets psychology apart as a science?

Psychology certainly involves knowing how to deal with people effectively, but it involves a great deal more than common sense. For example, take a minute to consider the following issue. (Throughout this text, we will periodically ask you to take a few moments to think about a variety of issues that arise from our discussion of the subject matter of psychology.)

INTELLIGENCE AND ADJUSTMENT

How would you expect people with genius-level intelligence (IQs above 135) to compare with people of average intelligence in areas such as general life satisfaction, social competence, physical health, and mental health? Relying on your own common sense and experience, try to formulate an answer before reading on.

There is a widespread view that people of genius-level intelligence are more likely to be socially and emotionally maladjusted than are people of average intelligence. Thus, when asked the above question, many students predict that very high intelligence is often counterbalanced by difficulties in other areas of functioning. Evidence gathered from psychological research indicates otherwise, however. The classic research is a long-term study of 1,528 gifted children that was initiated in the early 1920s by Stanford University psychologist Lewis Terman. After his death, this study was continued by Stanford University psychologists Robert Sears and Pauline Sears, so that these "whiz kids" have been evaluated at regular intervals since the 1920s. Now in their seventies, most of the subjects are still providing information about their lives. This research has provided a wealth of information about the impact of superior intelligence on life satisfaction and development. The findings indicate that as a group, highly intelligent people tend to be happier with their lives, more socially adept, physically healthier, and less inclined to develop emotional disorders than are people of average intelligence (Sears, 1977; Sears & Barbee, 1977; Terman, 1925, 1954).

Psychological research using scientific methods often provides enlightening and reliable information about behaviors and mental processes that we might not otherwise learn. In contrast, relying on common sense produces subjective opinions that may have little basis in fact. As the first-person account in the margin illustrates, what is "common sense" to one person may make no sense at all to another. Throughout this book, such accounts express firsthand views or experiences of individuals, many of them students, that were provided to us either in the form of written personal reflections (minor changes have been made to preserve anonymity) or verbal reports. These anecdotes help to demonstrate the many dimensions of psychology.

Psychology uses scientific methods to investigate its subject. Many of these methods are discussed in detail in Chapter 2. Despite its careful meth-

FIRST PERSON 1.1

Sometimes it amazes me how different my husband's approach to childrearing is from my own. I tell my young son to ignore it when kids tease him about wearing glasses; my husband tells him to give them a taste of their own medicine. I think it's ok for my 10-year-old daughter to play with makeup on the theory that she'll outgrow it; he's just as logical about reasoning that she shouldn't be encouraged to grow up too quickly. It's like the old song "I say tomato, you say tomato"—we each have our own views about what is right. (*Authors' files*)

odology, however, many questions about behavior and mental processes remain unanswered by the science of psychology, and much of psychologists' understanding of people and behavior is subject to constant review and revision. You will see in this book that very few psychological principles are "carved in stone"; new theories as well as new technological developments are constantly providing new directions and methods for expanding knowledge.

THE STUDY OF BEHAVIOR AND MENTAL PROCESSES

The second part of our definition of psychology states that it studies both behavior and mental processes. There have been times in the history of the discipline, as you will see later in this chapter, when psychology has focused almost entirely on internal mental processes. At other times, psychologists have been concerned only with behaviors that can be observed.

Both these perspectives provide an incomplete picture. To illustrate why behavior and mental processes must both be the subject matter of psychology, imagine that you are riding your bike when a car suddenly goes out of control and veers toward you. You would react instantly in several ways. First, your body would become alert, preparing for an emergency response: your heart rate would quicken and you would experience a "rush" of epinephrine (commonly referred to as adrenalin). At the same time, thoughts would flash through your mind, directing you to get out of the way as quickly as possible. Finally, you would take action to avoid an accident, turning your handle bars and peddling quickly or perhaps even jumping off your bike if necessary. An onlooker would observe reactions such as the expression on your face, your actions as you got out of the car's way, and perhaps an expletive you might have uttered. The observer, however, would have no way of knowing about your "invisible" reactions, such as your heart rate and your thoughts.

Psychology does not simply study behaviors that can be observed directly by onlookers or research scientists (although those observations are an important part of psychology). Nor, contrary to some people's assumptions that all psychologists are interested in analyzing dreams and probing for repressed memories, does psychology confine itself only to the inner workings of the mind. Instead, contemporary psychology studies both behavior—either observable behaviors or internal physiological responses—and mental processes.

WHY STUDY ANIMALS?

The third part of our definition of psychology states that it is the study of humans and other animals. Psychologists study rats, dogs, cats, and pigeons, among other animals; even insects have provided information about behavior.

LEARNING ABOUT PSYCHOLOGY FROM NONHUMAN ANIMALS

Students are often less than pleased to discover that the subject matter of psychology includes the behavior of all animals, not just humans. How can psychologists generalize from rats to people? Why study nonhumans, when there are so many pressing problems threatening the quality of human lives? Try to formulate at least a few answers to this question before reading on.

There are at least five major reasons why psychology includes the study of animal behavior as well as human behavior. One is the need to find a simpler model. Scientists in all fields generally attempt to understand a particular phenomenon by first studying the simplest example available in nature. For instance, to understand respiration, metabolism, and other cel-

The study of psychology includes nonhuman animals and even computers, both of which help to unlock the mysteries of the human mind.

FIRST PERSON 1.2

I hear you psychologists spend a lot of time studying rats running in mazes. I hope we aren't going to spend all our time talking about rats in this class. I want to learn about people and a human is certainly a lot more than an oversized rat! (*Authors' files*)

lular processes, a biologist might first examine them in a simple, one-celled amoeba as opposed to a more complex multicelled organism. Similarly, scientists seeking to understand neurological processes underlying behavior can benefit from examining neuronal activity in a relatively simple organism, like a cockroach, rather than by beginning their investigations with more complex mammals.

A second reason to study animal behavior is the greater control that it provides. In a typical experiment, a number of different factors or variables may influence the outcome. The more control the experimenter has over these variables, the more precise the conclusions can be. For instance, suppose you wanted to study the relationship between environmental noise levels and problem-solving behavior. You might anticipate that a number of variables (such as how rested, hungry, or relaxed a subject is) could also influence problem solving. If you used human subjects, it would be hard to control precisely the events occurring in their lives in the 24-hour period before they arrived at your laboratory for testing. In contrast, the life of an experimental animal, such as a monkey, can be controlled 24 hours a day. Thus, by using animal subjects, you could carefully monitor important conditions such as levels of hunger, rest, and stress.

Ethical considerations are a third reason for studying animals. Psychologists often ask questions that for ethical reasons cannot be addressed initially in research with humans. For example, over the last four decades psychologists involved in brain research have conducted experiments in which they have sunk electrodes into the brain to stimulate or record brain activity. Can you imagine the ethical questions that would surface if we were limited to human subjects in these pioneer efforts? Just as medical researchers must test experimental drugs extensively with nonhumans before they can begin clinical testing on people, research psychologists cannot apply new laboratory procedures to human subjects until they have ruled out the possibility of harmful effects.

The fact that psychologists conduct experiments on nonhuman animals that may be unethical to conduct on humans does not mean that ethical guidelines are not followed in animal research. Quite the contrary, virtually everywhere that research is conducted in the United States, ethics committees review all proposed studies to ensure that the welfare of subjects (human or otherwise) is safeguarded. In fact, the growing momentum of

When five-year-old Levan Merritt fell 20 feet into the gorilla pit at the Jersey Zoo in St. Helier, the Channel Islands, terrified parents looked on helplessly. Curiously, the gorillas inspected the boy but did nothing to harm him. Why didn't the gorillas attack the boy? Incidents such as these continue to encourage psychologists to study animals and their behavior.

the animal rights movement in America has underscored the importance of rigorous review procedures currently in place at research centers throughout our country. The vast majority of scientists conducting animal research are "aware of their responsibilities regarding humane treatment of their subjects and work within the confines of these limitations" (Pincus et al., 1986, p. 1586). The 1981 update of the American Psychological Association's *Ethical Principles of Psychologists* affirms the commitment of psychologists to ensuring the welfare of animals involved in research and to treating them humanely.

Another reason for using nonhuman subjects is a practical one. Animals are readily available for experimentation, often at minimal cost. White rats, for instance, are generally in plentiful supply at a price well within most researchers' budgets. In addition, some experiments require frequent testing of subjects, often over a protracted period. Few humans would commit to any kind of research that requires more than a few hours conveniently extracted from their daily routines. Laboratory animals, on the other hand, are available night and day for as long as is necessary.

Finally, psychologists often wish to examine the relative contributions of heredity versus environment to a given behavioral pattern. This question, commonly known as *"nature versus nurture,"* has been a classic controversy among psychologists trying to explain traits and behaviors. Are we what we are because we have inherited characteristics (such as social competence, quick tempers, musical abilities, and so forth) or because our environment has provided the learning tools we need to develop these traits? One way to gain some insight into the role of heredity is to study how a given trait is passed on over several generations. While the long life span of humans makes such research difficult at best, several generations of rats can be studied in a few years. With the increasing prominence of *behavior genetics,* the study of how heredity influences behavior (see Chapter 10), this is no small advantage.

Even if you may acknowledge that animal research has some advantages, you may still not be convinced that such research is worthwhile. If so, the findings of research psychologist James Olds (1973) may persuade you to modify this view somewhat, for they illustrate how animal studies can have direct value for humans. Olds identified an area within a rat's brain that produces intense pleasure when stimulated electrically (see Chapter 3). This pioneer work encouraged researchers to look for similar "pleasure centers" in human brains. Their discovery in humans has had many important applications, including pleasure-center stimulation to provide relief for severely disturbed psychiatric patients and to counteract debilitating pain in terminally ill patients (Heath, 1972; Olds & Forbes, 1981). Now that the rewarding effects of electrical stimulation of various sites within the brain have been established, researchers are attempting to discover what mechanisms underlie these effects (Gallistel, 1986; Mora & Ferrer, 1986; Velley, 1986). We can expect that this exciting area of research will continue to yield important clues about the intricate workings of our brains.

We have defined psychology as the scientific study of behavior and mental processes, yet this definition represents only a contemporary view of psychology. In its short history (the discipline had its formal beginnings only a little over a century ago), the answer to the question "What is psychology?" has varied considerably, depending on the era in which it was asked. The following section presents a brief overview of the history of the discipline.

PSYCHOLOGY'S HISTORY

Although psychology is a very young science, its roots go back to antiquity. Since early civilization, people have been concerned about issues considered central to present-day psychology. This was particularly true of *philosophers* such as Plato, Aristotle, Descartes, and Locke, who raised provocative questions about human thoughts, feelings, and behaviors. However, as later discoveries were to reveal, their reasoning often led to inaccurate conclusions. (Aristotle, for example, believed that mental processes occurred in the heart.)

Physiology, the systematic study of bodily processes, has also contributed to the discipline of psychology. The physiologists of the mid-nineteenth century provided important new insights into how the brain and the rest of the nervous system influence behavior. For example, in the mid-1800s a group of German scientists led by Hermann von Helmholtz (1821–1894) pioneered a series of experiments in which they measured the speed of conduction of a nerve impulse and assessed the nature of neural communication within the nervous system. By 1870, researchers at the University of Berlin had begun to study the exposed brains of laboratory animals and found that electrical stimulation of certain locations caused specific bodily movements. Studies such as these marked the way for later laboratory research that has helped reveal the relationship between brain processes and behavior.

Thus, psychology has roots in both philosophy, which posed many of the important questions, and physiology, which provided the tools for a careful, scientific examination of these questions. The next logical step in the evolution of psychology was to take the questions about behavior and mental process into the laboratory.

Aristotle believed that mental processes occurred in the heart.

WUNDT'S LABORATORY

This is exactly what Wilhelm Wundt (1832–1920), a German scientist trained in physiology, did in the late 1800s. The establishment of Wundt's small laboratory at the University of Leipzig in 1879 marks the formal beginning of psychology as a scientific discipline.

Wundt defined the task of psychology as the systematic study of the structure of the conscious adult mind. He believed that the conscious mental processes involved in such things as perceiving colors, reacting to stimuli, and experiencing emotions could be best understood by breaking them down into their basic elements and then analyzing how the elements interacted with one another. In this sense, he hoped to pattern psychology after the physical sciences of chemistry, physics, and physiology.

Wundt borrowed a tool of philosophy, *introspection* ("looking inward") for studying mental processes. For example, a subject listening to music might be asked to break the perceptual experience down into its basic elements of pitch, volume, timbre, and so forth. Subjects were trained in introspection, so that they could provide clear, "scientific" reports of their sensations. Wundt also believed that introspection needed to be supplemented by experiments. Therefore, he would systematically vary some physical dimension of a stimulus, such as the volume of a particular sound, to see how conscious awareness changed. This approach came to be known as *experimental self-observation.* Throughout Wundt's career, he continued to emphasize gaining information about the mind from observable, measurable events.

Wilhelm Wundt

STRUCTURALISM

Many of the pioneers of American psychology got their training in Wundt's Leipzig laboratory. One of these students, Edward Titchener (1867–1927), brought his mentor's particular brand of psychology to America when he established a psychology laboratory at Cornell University in 1892. Like Wundt, Titchener thought the proper goal of psychology was to specify mental structures. He introduced the label **structuralism** to describe his approach.

Structuralism attempted to develop a kind of "mental chemistry" by breaking experience down into its basic elements or structures in the same way that a substance such as water could be broken down into particles of hydrogen and oxygen. It enjoyed only short-lived popularity. Psychologists soon discovered that the major research tool of structuralism, introspection, often altered the nature of the conscious mental processes they wished to analyze. The next time you find yourself entranced by an exquisite sunset or a haunting melody, stop and pay attention to your sensations, thoughts, and feelings. You will probably find, as did many of the early introspectionists, that analyzing what you are experiencing changes the experience.

An even more damaging flaw became apparent when a number of researchers who were using introspection independently of one another discovered that their results were often different. Finally, many American psychologists criticized structuralism as impractical; they thought psychology should offer solutions to the problems of everyday life. This movement toward a more pragmatic psychology culminated in the functionalist school.

FUNCTIONALISM

The distinguished American psychologist William James (1842–1910) agreed with the structuralists that psychology should study mental processes. However, he felt that the science would be better served by attempting to understand the fluid, functional, continually changing, personal nature of conscious experience. He was particularly interested in trying to understand mental processes that helped humans and other animals adapt to their environments. Because of his emphasis on the functional, practical nature of the mind, his conception of psychology's proper task became known as **functionalism.**

James was greatly influenced by Charles Darwin's theory of *natural selection,* which said that characteristics that help ensure the survival of a species are passed on from one generation to the next. For instance, the protective coloration of some types of moths or the opposable thumbs of humans are traits that were preserved because they helped these species adapt to their environments. The functionalists concluded that consciousness also evolved because it served a functional purpose, namely guiding the activities of the individual. Functionalists wanted to learn how various mental processes, such as perceiving, learning, and thinking, helped people adapt. To accomplish this purpose, they continued to use introspection in their investigations. However, they also introduced another focus to psychology, collecting data from observations of human and animal behavior.

Both structuralism and functionalism served important functions in the development of psychology as a science. Structuralism brought psychology to the laboratory by demonstrating that mental processes are a legitimate focus for scientific research. Functionalism broadened psychology to include the study of nonhuman animals, expanded the data of psychology to include observations of behavior, and encouraged the application of psychology in areas such as education. Having served these functions, these early schools of psychology were eventually replaced by several newer approaches, including behaviorism, Gestalt psychology, psychoanalysis, humanism, and cognitive psychology.

William James emphasized the functional, practical nature of the mind, and his conception of psychology's proper task became known as functionalism.

BEHAVIORISM

Behaviorism was founded in the first few decades of this century by John B. Watson (1878–1958). Although trained as a functionalist, Watson ultimately came to believe it was impossible to study the mind objectively. He especially opposed the use of introspection, which he considered unscientific, and he chastised the functionalists for not going far enough in their rebellion against structuralism. Watson proclaimed a new psychology, free of introspection, whose task was simply to observe the relationship between environmental events (*stimuli*) and an organism's responses to them. This

John B. Watson, believing it was impossible to study the mind objectively, founded a new approach to psychology—behaviorism.

stimulus–response (S–R) approach to psychology was a radical departure from Watson's predecessors' focus on mental processes, establishing a new emphasis on objectively verifiable phenomena.

Behaviorism quickly caught on in the 1920s, and soon most younger American psychologists were calling themselves behaviorists. Behaviorism continues to exert a profound influence on contemporary American psychology, due in part to the monumental contributions of Harvard's B. F. Skinner. We shall have much to say throughout this book about the behaviorist approach to psychology.

GESTALT PSYCHOLOGY

At about the same time as behaviorism was catching hold in America, a group of German psychologists were conducting important investigations of human perceptual processes. These scientists, most notably Max Wertheimer (1880–1943), Wolfgang Köhler (1887–1967), and Kurt Koffka (1886–1941), disagreed with the principles of both structuralism and behaviorism. They argued that it was a mistake to try to break psychological processes into basic components like elementary sensations or stimuli and responses, for the whole of an experience (*Gestalt* means "whole" in German) is different from the sum of its parts. This approach became known as **Gestalt psychology.**

Consider a simple example of the Gestalt approach. Suppose you took four 12-inch rulers and placed them at right angles to each other so that they formed an unbroken structure, with each ruler touching two other rulers. You would have a square. If you rearranged the rulers in one continuous sequence so that no angles were formed between them, you would have a straight line instead. Both a straight line and a square have the same components, but the two are different. It is therefore the relationship between the parts rather than the parts, themselves, that is the critical ingredient in what we see. Gestaltists focused on these relationships and on the way we perceive patterns and organize experiences.

Because many of our experiences as humans cannot be broken down into separate pieces, Gestalt psychology remains an active force in our present-day investigation of perceptual processes and learning. In fact, it is enjoying renewed popularity among some contemporary psychologists who prefer to emphasize the "whole person" rather than isolated aspects of how people function.

As in the construction of a puzzle, Gestalt psychology emphasizes the sum of the parts rather than the individual parts themselves.

PSYCHOANALYTIC PSYCHOLOGY

During the period when psychology was struggling to become more objective and scientific, an Austrian physician, Sigmund Freud (1856–1939), was gradually developing a highly subjective approach to understanding human personality. Freud based his theories on extensive experiences treating emotionally disturbed individuals. His theories, which ultimately became known as the **psychoanalytic approach,** are more widely recognized among nonpsychologists than is any other school of psychological thought. This is not to say that Freud's analytic approach has been at the forefront of scientific psychology since it was first introduced to America in the early 1900s. Quite the contrary, much of the impact of psychoanalysis lies in the critical reactions it has generated. Psychoanalysis has been widely criticized, in part because its assertions cannot be tested in the laboratory.

Many of Freud's views, particularly his belief that sexual urges were powerful energizers of human behavior, shocked both professionals and laypeople. His emphasis on the *unconscious mind,* with its irrational urges and drives beyond the control of conscious, rational processes, upset many people: it was a blow to human pride to be told that we are often not the masters of our own lives.

Despite these criticisms, Freud's impact upon psychology was profound. He provided important insights into understanding the emotional lives of humans. He encouraged psychologists to consider the impact upon behavior of processes not immediately available to conscious inspection. He also helped to legitimize the study of human sexuality. We will discuss Freud's views more thoroughly in several places throughout the book, particularly Chapter 13.

Sigmund Freud developed the psychoanalytic approach to psychology, which emphasized the unconscious mind with its irrational urges and drives.

HUMANISTIC PSYCHOLOGY

Humanistic psychology differs from both the psychoanalytic approach and behaviorism in that it does not view humans as being controlled by either events in the environment or by internal, irrational, unconscious forces. Humanist psychologists, most notably Abraham Maslow (1908–1970) and Carl Rogers (1902–1987), de-emphasize the influence of both stimulus–response events and unconscious processes in determining human behavior. Instead, they emphasize the role of *free choice* and our ability to make conscious rational choices about how we live our lives. Humanists also believe that people have a natural inclination to strive to fulfill their potential, a process called *self-actualization.*

Although many of humanism's major tenets are just as difficult to test objectively as are the concepts of psychoanalysis, many psychologists respond favorably to this movement's optimism. Humanism has increased psychologists' awareness of the importance of such things as love, feeling needed, personal fulfillment, and self-esteem. In this sense, its contributions are of great value.

COGNITIVE PSYCHOLOGY

Although "internal" mental processes were considered important in the days of structuralism and functionalism, these processes received little attention while psychology was dominated by behaviorism. Now **cognitive psychology** is refocusing our attention on processes such as thinking, language, problem solving, and creativity.

Cognitive psychology considers behavior to be more than a simple response to a stimulus. For example, a small child observes his mother reacting fearfully when the neighbors' dog wanders into their yard. Later, he responds fearfully when a friend brings his new dog by for a visit. You smell the delightful aroma of newly baked bread just removed from the oven, and then, 10 minutes later, at just the right time for the bread to be sliced, you happen to wander into the kitchen. Both of these acts involve more than simple reflexive or automatic responses to stimuli: the actions of both the small child and you are influenced by a variety of mental (cognitive) processes including perceptions (interpreting dangerous images or delectable smells), memories of previous experiences (a frightened mother, or the taste of fresh-baked bread), and expectations for future events (the dog may bite, and the bread will taste good). Cognitive psychologists are interested in learning about these mental processes that intervene between stimuli and responses and in analyzing how we process information.

RECENT TRENDS: INFORMATION PROCESSING AND NEUROPSYCHOLOGY

In the past few decades, psychology has developed some new perspectives, partly as a result of technological advances. One of the most exciting areas has been **information processing,** which uses computers to help develop models of cognitive processing of information. In a sense, the human brain is like a computer, although infinitely more complex. When we are presented stimuli, our brains assimilate the information, match it to existing memory systems, and instigate appropriate responses. Cognitive psychologists are now using computers to seek better understanding of how this information processing works. (Interestingly, computer scientists are also drawing upon knowledge of how the brain processes information in the hope that this understanding may be applied in designing computers [Abu-Mostafa & Psaltis, 1987].)

Computers are powerful tools for examining a variety of psychological phenomena. They have some limitations, however, particularly in some types of information-processing tasks. For instance, even a young child has no trouble identifying a tree in a picture of a farm scene, yet this same task presents a serious challenge to the most powerful of available supercomputers. One reason for this is that the task of recognizing a tree requires knowledge of essentially every conceivable variation of what a tree can be, including myriad shapes and sizes as well as variations in leaves (or needles), bark, color, seasonal phases, and so forth. For a computer to solve such a pattern-recognition task, it would need to have stored (memorized) a set of all possible solutions, and then be able to compare input data with this stored memory and quickly select the best possible solution. In this type of information processing, even the most sophisticated programs running on the most powerful supercomputers "cannot match the memorization and recollection capability of the human brain, which regularly and effortlessly conquers pattern-recognition problems" (Abu-Mostafa & Psaltis, 1987, p. 88).

A second recent development in the field of psychology is **neuropsychology,** the study of the brain and the rest of the nervous system. Scientists are now able to record the activity of a single *neuron* (nerve cell) within the central nervous system (the part of the nervous system consisting of the brain and spinal cord), modify behavior by electrical stimulation of the brain, and determine precisely the effects of certain drugs on the nervous system. These and a host of other advances have led to an explosion of knowledge about the relationships between biological and neurological events, mental processes, and behavior. Neuropsychology, or physiological psychology, will be discussed further in the following section.

Computers are powerful tools for examining a variety of psychological phenomena.

FIELDS OF SPECIALIZATION IN PSYCHOLOGY

During its brief history, psychology has grown by leaps and bounds. The American Psychological Association (APA), the major professional organization of psychologists in this country, was founded in 1892 by 31 charter members. The APA now has approximately 100,000 members, and countless numbers of professional psychologists are not listed in its membership (Howard et al., 1986). As the APA's ranks have increased, so have the num-

TABLE 1.1 *The Divisions of the American Psychological Association and Membership Statistics*

Division*	Total	Men	Women	% Men	% Women
1. General Psychology	5,052	3,498	1,554	69.2	30.8
2. Teaching of Psychology	1,933	1,492	441	77.2	22.8
3. Experimental Psychology	1,472	1,248	224	84.8	15.2
5. Evaluation and Measurement	1,226	998	228	81.4	18.6
6. Physiological and Comparative Psychology	794	672	122	84.6	15.4
7. Developmental Psychology	1,254	680	574	54.2	45.8
8. Personality and Social Psychology	3,233	2,488	745	77.0	23.0
9. SPSSI (The Society for the Psychological Study of Social Issues)	2,832	1,858	974	65.6	34.4
10. Psychology and the Arts	437	304	133	69.6	30.4
12. Clinical Psychology	5,418	4,133	1,285	76.3	23.7
13. Consulting Psychology	937	788	149	84.1	15.9
14. Industrial and Organizational Psychology	2,499	2,119	380	84.8	15.2
15. Educational Psychology	2,093	1,568	525	74.9	25.1
16. School Psychology	2,261	1,288	973	57.0	43.0
17. Counseling Psychology	2,588	1,968	620	76.0	24.0
18. Psychologists in Public Service	980	796	184	81.2	18.8
19. Military Psychology	621	562	59	90.5	9.5
20. Adult Development and Aging	1,049	648	401	61.8	38.2
21. Applied Experimental and Engineering Psychology	583	535	48	91.8	8.2
22. Rehabilitation Psychology	974	744	230	76.4	23.6
23. Consumer Psychology	422	357	65	84.6	15.4
24. Theoretical and Philosophical Psychology	519	438	81	84.4	15.6
25. Experimental Analysis of Behavior	1,317	1,085	232	82.4	17.6
26. History of Psychology	622	525	97	84.4	15.6
27. Community Psychology	1,653	1,220	433	73.8	26.2
28. Psychopharmacology	1,043	864	179	82.8	17.2
29. Psychotherapy	4,684	3,303	1,381	70.5	29.5
30. Psychological Hypnosis	1,352	1,142	210	84.5	15.5
31. State Psychological Association Affairs	559	423	136	75.7	24.3
32. Humanistic Psychology	788	574	214	72.8	27.2
33. Mental Retardation	836	584	252	69.9	30.1
34. Population and Environmental Psychology	466	335	131	71.9	28.1
35. Psychology of Women	2,203	116	2,087	5.3	94.7
36. PIRI (Psychologists Interested in Religious Issues)	1,193	922	271	77.3	22.7
37. Child, Youth, and Family Services	1,465	870	595	59.4	40.6
38. Health Psychology	2,507	1,837	670	73.3	26.7
39. Psychoanalysis	1,949	1,112	837	57.1	42.9
40. Clinical Neuropsychology	1,785	1,346	439	75.4	24.6
41. Psychology and Law Society	1,018	797	221	78.3	21.7
42. Psychologists in Independent Practice	5,020	3,719	1,301	74.1	25.9
43. Family Psychology	998	737	261	73.8	26.2
44. Society for the Psychological Study of Lesbian and Gay Issues	458	233	225	50.9	49.1
Total Division Memberships	71,093	50,926	20,167	71.6	28.4
No Divisional Affiliation	24,529	14,774	9,755	60.2	39.8

*There are no Divisions 4 and 11.

Source: From American Psychological Association, 1985.

bers of fields within the profession. There are some generalists, just as there are general practitioners in medicine. However, most psychologists find that as their careers evolve they become increasingly specialized in both their interests and professional activities. Table 1.1 lists all the divisions within the APA. The following paragraphs outline some of these areas of concentration.

CLINICAL AND COUNSELING PSYCHOLOGY

More than half of the psychologists in America are engaged in either of two closely related fields: clinical psychology and counseling psychology (see Figure 1.1). Both of these groups of psychologists are involved in the diagnosis and treatment of psychological problems, including such things as developmental disorders, substance abuse, relationship difficulties, vocational and educational problems, and antisocial behavior.

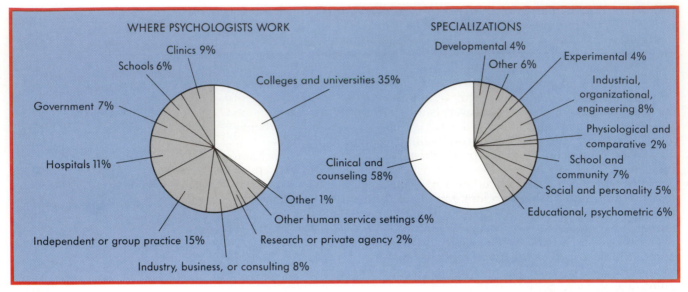

WHERE PSYCHOLOGISTS WORK

Clinics 9%
Schools 6%
Government 7%
Hospitals 11%
Colleges and universities 35%
Clinical and counseling 58%
Other 1%
Other human service settings 6%
Independent or group practice 15%
Research or private agency 2%
Industry, business, or consulting 8%

SPECIALIZATIONS

Developmental 4%
Other 6%
Experimental 4%
Industrial, organizational, engineering 8%
Physiological and comparative 2%
School and community 7%
Social and personality 5%
Educational, psychometric 6%

FIGURE 1.1   **Places where psychologists work and areas of specialization within the field.**

While it is difficult to precisely distinguish between clinical and counseling psychology, it is generally accurate to state that individuals specializing in **counseling psychology** tend to focus on less serious problems of adjustment than their counterparts in **clinical psychology.** Thus a counseling psychologist in a high school, college, or university setting might assist students with problems of social or academic adjustment or provide guidance in the area of career decisions. In contrast, clinical psychologists are more likely to work in mental health clinics, mental hospitals, juvenile and adult courts, medical schools, and prisons. Specialists in both areas often see clients in private practice.

Clinical psychology and psychiatry are often confused since professionals within these respective fields often perform comparable functions, such as providing psychotherapy. However, these occupations differ in several important ways. Most clinical psychologists obtain a doctor of philoso-

Although both clinical and counseling psychologists see clients in private practice, counseling psychologists tend to focus on less serious problems of adjustment than their counterparts in clinical psychology.

phy degree (Ph.D.) in training that is likely to consist of three to five years of university graduate school instruction in psychological theory, research methods, techniques of clinical diagnosis, and psychotherapy strategies, followed by a one-year clinical internship in an institutional setting. In contrast, a *psychiatrist* is a medical doctor who undergoes several years of specialized training in psychiatry after earning an M.D. degree. Of the two, only psychiatrists can prescribe medical treatments, such as drugs, in treating psychological disorders. However, clinical psychologists generally obtain a more intensive education on the psychological determinants of behavior problems and the methods of conducting research.

Clinical psychologists and psychiatrists may also differ somewhat in their perspectives about the causes of psychological problems and appropriate treatment for such difficulties (Kingsbury, 1987). For example, psychiatrists are more inclined to look for physical causes such as abnormal brain chemistry or hormonal imbalances, and to use medical or biological therapies as remedies for disorders. In contrast, clinical psychologists tend to emphasize psychosocial causes such as inappropriate learning, faulty attitudes, and disturbed interpersonal relationships, and to focus on psychotherapy as the best road to improvement. Exceptions to these generalizations, however, are not uncommon.

EXPERIMENTAL PSYCHOLOGY

Psychologists in every area of specialization usually conduct experiments at some point in their careers. Thus, it may be a bit misleading to call **experimental psychology** a separate field. Nevertheless, approximately four percent of the profession classify themselves as experimental psychologists whose primary activity involves conducting research.

In Chapter 2 we shall discover that psychologists use a number of research methods in their efforts to understand the nature and causes of behavior. Most experimental psychologists prefer to conduct research in a laboratory setting where they have precise control over the varied factors that influence behavior. For example, an experimental psychologist might investigate the relationship between sexual response and alcohol consumption by precisely measuring sexual arousal to erotic stimuli under different levels of alcohol consumption. (The results of these experiments are discussed in Chapter 2.)

Most experimental psychologists prefer to conduct research in a laboratory setting where they have precise control over the varied factors that influence behavior.

PHYSIOLOGICAL PSYCHOLOGY

Still another field, **physiological psychology** (or neuropsychology), studies the relationship between physiological processes and behavior. Neuropsychologists investigate such things as the association between behavior and drugs, hormones, genes, and brain processes.

Physiological psychology often captures the attention of the public, for over the years we have seen countless cases in which irrational and sometimes violent behavior has been linked to abnormal biological processes. In one widely discussed event in 1966, Charles Whitman, a student at the University of Texas, climbed a tower and opened fire on the campus with a high-powered hunting rifle. Before he was killed by police, Whitman managed to murder 14 people and wound 24. While a number of explanations were suggested to account for Whitman's behavior, a postmortem exam did reveal a large, malignant tumor in a region of the brain that physiological psychologists have shown to be involved in aggressive behavior.

EDUCATIONAL AND SCHOOL PSYCHOLOGY

Many important discoveries of psychology have direct application to the educational process. **Educational psychology** involves the study and application of learning and teaching methods. Psychologists in this field conduct research on ways to improve educational curricula, and they often help train teachers. They may work in primary or secondary schools, but more often they are found in a university's school of education.

School psychologists work in elementary or secondary schools, dealing primarily with individual children, teachers, and parents in an effort to evaluate and resolve learning and emotional problems. They often administer and interpret personality, interest, and ability tests. School psychologists are a valuable resource both for troubled students and for concerned teachers trying to cope with the stresses of classroom problems.

INDUSTRIAL/ORGANIZATIONAL PSYCHOLOGY

The field of **industrial/organizational (I/O) psychology** is concerned with using psychological concepts to make the workplace a more satisfying environment for both employees and management. I/O psychologists may work with businesses either as company employees or as consultants, designing programs to improve morale, increase job satisfaction, foster better communication within the corporation, enhance productivity, and increase workers' involvement in decision making. They are also frequently involved in designing job-training programs and in selecting the most suitable people for a particular job.

ENGINEERING PSYCHOLOGY

Engineering psychologists (sometimes called human factors psychologists) focus on creating optimal relationships among people, the machines they operate, and the environments they work in. For example, engineering psychologists have helped design the lighting and instrumentation within the cockpits of sophisticated aircraft to maximize pilot efficiency. These professionals have also been involved in America's space program, helping to develop optimal functional efficiency within the severely limited confines of spacecraft.

DEVELOPMENTAL PSYCHOLOGY

Another important field is **developmental psychology.** Psychologists in this field are interested in factors that influence development and shape

Engineering psychologists have been increasingly concerned about the lighting, instrumentation, and other conditions within cockpits.

behavior throughout the life cycle, from conception through old age. These specialists typically focus on a particular phase of the growth process, such as adolescence or old age, and examine how a particular ability or trait unfolds during that phase of development. For example, a developmental psychologist might investigate the role that viewing television violence plays in the development of aggressive behavior in children.

Developmental psychologists typically focus on a particular phase of the growth process and examine how an ability or trait unfolds during this phase of development.

SOCIAL PSYCHOLOGY

Social psychology is concerned with understanding the impact of social environments and social processes on the individual. Social psychologists are interested in attitude formation and change, social perception, conformity, social roles, prejudice, interpersonal attraction, and group processes.

PERSONALITY PSYCHOLOGY

Personality psychology focuses on exploring the uniqueness of the individual and on describing the key elements that provide the foundation for human personalities. There is considerable diversity of opinion among personality theorists as to what are the major components of personality. For example, do our personalities consist of three interacting and sometimes conflicting forces (the id, ego, and superego) described by Sigmund Freud, or are we better characterized as a composite of 16 primary traits, as suggested by Raymond Cattell? Perhaps as you read Chapter 13 you will form your own opinion on this matter. Many personality psychologists devote their professional careers to investigating how personality develops, evolves, and influences people's activities.

NEW AREAS OF SPECIALIZATION

In recent years a number of exciting new areas of specialization have begun to emerge. With the increasing number of environmental issues confronting the world's population, a number of **environmental psychologists** have turned their major research efforts toward assessing the effects on behavior of such things as noise pollution and overcrowding. Like engineering psychologists, environmental psychologists are interested in designing psychologically optimal environments for both work and leisure.

Forensic psychology is another emerging specialty that works hand in hand with the legal, court, and correctional systems. Forensic psychologists assist police in a variety of ways, from developing personality profiles of criminal offenders to helping law-enforcement personnel understand problems like family conflict and substance abuse. They may also assist judges and parole officers in making decisions about the disposition of convicted offenders.

In recent years there has been a mounting interest in achieving and maintaining good health, both physical and psychological. Psychologists have known for many years that emotional conditions such as stress or depression often play a major role in the development of physical ailments such as ulcers, skin diseases, stomach disorders, and probably even cancer and the common cold. There is also growing evidence that psychological factors have a great deal to do with prevention of and recovery from illness. This growing body of data pertaining to the interaction between physical and psychological health factors has led to the emergence of a dynamic new area of specialization known as **health psychology.** In recognition of the importance of this new field of study, the National Institutes of Health (NIH) recently designated health psychology as a priority training area and allocated funds for developing training programs within psychology departments throughout the country.

Health psychologists are currently active in such diverse areas as assessing the psychological and physical effects of stress, developing programs to help people reduce stress in their lives, studying coping strategies for dealing with serious or catastrophic illness, evaluating the impact of psychological factors on diseases such as cancer and cardiovascular illness, devising ways to test people for susceptibility to disease, and seeking to identify the factors that motivate people to engage in health-threatening activities such as smoking and over- and undereating (Taylor, 1986). Recognizing the importance of this emerging field, we have included several health psychology discussions throughout the text under the heading "Health Psychology and Life." In addition, Chapter 17 deals specifically with several important health-related topics.

A fourth new area of specialization, **quantitative psychology,** uses mathematical techniques and computer science to aid in understanding human behavior. Quantitative psychologists may focus on developing mathematical models to reflect complex relationships between behavior and its causes.

A recent report by a committee commissioned by the American Psychological Association expressed some concerns about "the changing face of American psychology" (Howard et al., 1986). The authors of this report noted that in recent years there has been a marked increase in the number of psychologists who obtain doctorates in applied areas such as clinical, counseling, and school psychology, coupled with a pronounced decline in doctorates in such research-oriented subfields as physiological, experimental, social, and personality psychology. Commensurate with this shift toward more human-service-provider specializations, there has been a significant decline in the number of psychologists employed full time in academic settings (see Table 1.2).

On the one hand, these changes may be seen as positive in that the greater number of psychologists working as clinicians has helped to meet growing demands for mental-health services. However, there is also a somewhat unsettling side to these recent trends. The decline in both the number of psychologists trained in research-oriented specialties and in those who work in academic settings, where most research is conducted, coupled with evidence that individuals trained in clinical, counseling, and school psychology tend to spend little time conducting research (Gottfredson, 1987), suggests the possibility of a reduction in future research efforts. Though these changes are cause for concern, it is unlikely that psychology will forsake its commitment to quality research in the rush to meet escalating demands for health care.

We have considered in some detail the nature, scope, and origins of the science of psychology. In Chapter 2, we look more closely at some of the methods psychologists have developed for exploring the many questions posed by the richly varied behaviors of humans and other animals.

TABLE 1.2 *Percentages of Doctoral-level APA Members Employed Full Time by Primary Employment Setting: 1976, 1982, and 1985*

Primary Employment Setting	1976	1982	1985
Academic settings	46.8	38.1	33.9
Schools and school systems	4.0	4.1	3.7
Organized human service settings	24.8	25.0	24.5
Independent practice	12.2	15.8	22.0
Business, government, and other	12.1	15.9	13.0
Unspecified	0.1	1.1	2.9

Note: Data are from (Employment settings of 1976 and 1985 APA members) by G. Pion, 1985b, unpublished analyses, and from "The Employment of APA Members: 1982" by J. Stapp and R. Fulcher, 1983, *American Psychologist, 35,* 1298–1320.

Source: From Howard et al., 1986.

SUMMARY

PSYCHOLOGY DEFINED

1. Formally defined, psychology is the scientific study of the behavior and mental processes of humans and other animals.
2. The theories and facts of psychology emerge from the careful application of scientific methods.
3. Psychology includes the study of animal behavior as well as human behavior because of, among other reasons, the need to find a simpler model, the benefits associated with greater control afforded by nonhuman subjects, ethical considerations, time and cost factors, and the advantages of short life spans in assessing genetic contributions to behavior.

PSYCHOLOGY'S HISTORY

4. Psychology has roots in both philosophy, which posed many of the important questions, and physiology, which provided the tools for careful, scientific examination of these questions.
5. The establishment of Wilhelm Wundt's laboratory at the University of Leipzig in 1879 marks the formal beginning of psychology as a scientific discipline.
6. Wundt employed the methods of introspection and experimental self-observation to pursue what he considered to be the task of psychology—the systematic study of the structure of the conscious adult mind.
7. Edward Titchener, who brought Wundt's brand of psychology to America, introduced the label structuralism to describe his attempt to develop a kind of "mental chemistry" by breaking experience down into its basic elements or structures.
8. Structuralism soon gave way to the more practical psychology of William James, who emphasized the functional, practical nature of the mind. His conception of psychology's proper task became known as functionalism.
9. In the first few decades of this century a new force in psychology emerged called behaviorism. This approach, championed by John B. Watson, defined the task of psychology as one of simply observing the relationship between environmental events (stimuli) and an organism's response to them.
10. At the time behaviorism was catching hold in America, a group of German psychologists decried the principles of both structuralism and behaviorism. They argued that it was a mistake to try to break psychological processes into basic components like elementary sensations or stimuli and responses, for the whole of an experience is different than the sum of its parts. This approach became known as Gestalt psychology.
11. During the period when psychology was struggling to become more scientific and objective, Sigmund Freud traveled a different road as he developed his highly subjective psychoanalytic approach with its emphasis on the unconscious mind and repressed irrational urges and drives.
12. Freud's impact on psychology was profound, particularly the impetus he provided for psychology to con-

sider the impact upon behavior of processes not immediately available to conscious inspection.
13. Humanistic psychology de-emphasizes the impact of both stimulus–response events and unconscious processes in determining human behavior. Instead, it focuses on the role of free choice and our ability to make conscious rational choices about how we live our lives.
14. In recent years the emergence of cognitive psychology as an important force in psychology has led to a refocusing of attention on processes such as thinking, language, problem solving, and creativity.
15. Two other important areas in psychology that are achieving increasing prominence in the field are information processing, which uses computers to help develop models of cognitive processing of information, and neuropsychology, the study of the brain and the rest of the nervous system.

FIELDS OF SPECIALIZATION IN PSYCHOLOGY

16. Both clinical and counseling psychologists are involved in the diagnosis and treatment of psychological problems. Individuals specializing in counseling psychology tend to focus on less serious problems of adjustment than their counterparts in clinical psychology.
17. While psychologists in every area of specialization usually conduct experiments at some point in their career, individuals who classify themselves as experimental psychologists devote their primary efforts to conducting research.
18. Physiological psychologists (or neuropsychologists) study the relationship between physiological processes and behavior.
19. Educational psychologists focus their efforts on the study and application of learning and teaching methods.
20. School psychologists work in elementary or secondary schools where they seek to evaluate and resolve learning and emotional problems of students.
21. Industrial/organizational psychology is concerned with using psychological concepts to make the workplace a more satisfying environment for both employees and management.
22. Engineering psychologists focus on creating optimal relationships among people, the machines they operate, and the environments they work in.
23. Developmental psychologists investigate the factors that influence development and shape behavior throughout the life cycle.
24. Social psychologists seek to understand the impact of social environments and social processes on the individual.
25. Personality psychologists focus on exploring the uniqueness of the individual and describing the key elements that provide the foundation for human personalities.
26. Relatively new areas of specialization include environmental psychology, forensic psychology, health psychology, and quantitative psychology.

2 The Methods of Psychology

Examine the following statements and decide whether they are true or false (chapter references are provided, if you wish to review the evidence):

1. The best way to ensure that a desired behavior will persist after training is completed is to reward the behavior every time it occurs throughout training rather than to provide rewards only once in a while (Chapter 6).

2. Under hypnosis, people can perform feats of physical strength or mental prowess that they could not otherwise perform (Chapter 5).

3. A small minority of people rarely or never dream while sleeping (Chapter 5).

4. Couples who cohabit (live together) before marriage generally experience happier and more stable marriages than couples who do not live together before getting married (Chapter 11).

5. Humans are the only organisms that can use abstract language symbols to communicate (Chapter 8).

Most students evaluate all or most of these statements incorrectly when they first begin studying psychology; you also may be surprised to find that they are all false. Many of the things people presume to be true about behavior are in fact fallacies. To safeguard against the fallibility of relying on common sense, psychologists have developed a number of tools or methods for systematically collecting data about behavior. These scientific methods have disproven many widely held beliefs about behavior and mental processes; they have also verified some other common assumptions. In this chapter we discuss the reasons for psychological research and outline the methods that psychologists use.

REASONS FOR CONDUCTING RESEARCH

Chapter 1 discussed an important research finding of the 1950s, but it did not tell you the story of how that finding was made. James Olds and a fellow researcher at McGill University, Peter Milner, were investigating the ways in which electrical stimulation of the brain affected exploratory behavior in rats. As they implanted electrodes in the rats' brains, one electrode was placed incorrectly, and Olds and Milner stumbled onto an important finding (Olds, 1956). When electrodes were placed in sites within the hypothalamus and the septal areas (discussed in Chapter 3), the rats seemingly could not get enough stimulation. They preferred stimulation of these brain areas even to food when they were hungry. This unexpected finding led to a series of experiments with animals and humans that clearly indicated that there are "pleasure centers" within the brain.

Some psychological studies have their origins in *serendipity,* or a lucky discovery such as this one, but this is not typical. Most psychological research is carefully planned and conducted with a specific end in mind. In this section we look at three of the most common reasons why psychologists conduct research: to test a hypothesis, to solve a problem, and to confirm findings of previous research.

RESEARCH TO TEST A HYPOTHESIS

A **hypothesis** is a statement proposing the existence of a relationship between variables. Hypotheses are typically offered as tentative explanations for relationships or events, and they are often designed to be tested by research. For example, a clinical psychologist who notes an unusual number of obese individuals among clients she has treated for depression and anxiety disorders might hypothesize that excess weight increases people's susceptibility to certain emotional disturbances.

Hypotheses frequently emerge from psychologists' observations of behavior or from the results of previous investigations. For example, psychologists Robert Hicks and Eliot Garcia (1987) noted that people often complain about not sleeping well when they are under stress, an observation consistent with previous research reports linking insomnia to the stressful effects of anxiety and worry (Kales et al., 1984). This information prompted Hicks and Garcia to hypothesize that during periods of high stress people sleep less than normal, while during periods of low stress they increase their sleep time. To test this hypothesis they asked a group of college students to keep diaries of sleep and stress levels for a four-month period. All subjects maintained a daily record of overall level of stress and total sleep duration (including naps). Hicks and Garcia found that, consistent with their hypothesis, sleep was reduced significantly during periods of high stress, while sleep increased during intervals of low stress.

RESEARCH TO SOLVE A PROBLEM

A second reason to conduct research is to find a solution to a problem. For example, diverse lines of investigation have sought a way to prevent or at least to relieve the symptoms of Alzheimer's disease, a very destructive form of senility that can affect middle-aged and occasionally young people, as well as the elderly. This illness systematically robs a person of the capacity to remember, think, relate to others, and care for oneself.

Although we presently do not know the cause(s) of this disease, researchers have uncovered a few promising clues. First, there is evidence that Alzheimer's victims may lack a specific brain enzyme necessary for the proper utilization of acetylcholine, a chemical substance important in transmitting nerve impulses from one neuron to another in the brain (Tamminga et al., 1987). If researchers can find a way to correct this enzyme deficiency, it is possible that at least some of the symptoms of this destructive disease might be controlled. Another promising clue is the identification of a gene that causes a familial or inherited form of Alzheimer's disease (St. George-Hyslop, 1987). (About 10 percent of cases of this disease are hereditary.) A third clue is the recent identification of another gene that causes the build-up of tangled fibers (known as *amyloid webs*) that ultimately choke the life out of the infected brain cells of Alzheimer's victims (Goldgaber et al., 1987). The identification of a defective gene or genes associated with

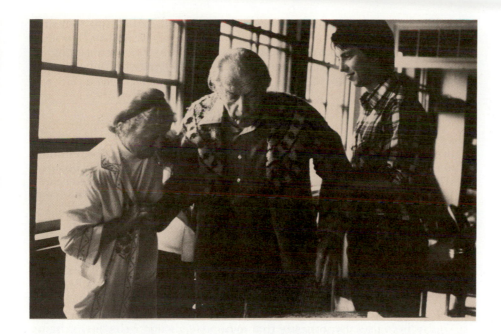

Problem solving is one reason to conduct research—in this case, to find a cure for Alzheimer's disease, which robs a person of the capacity to remember, think, relate to others, and care for oneself.

this dread disease opens up exciting possibilities of better understanding its cause and perhaps even preventing the illness through use of the emerging technology of genetic engineering (sometimes called gene therapy) to correct the genetic defect. (More detailed discussions of genetic engineering and Alzheimer's disease are contained in Chapters 10 and 11, respectively.)

RESEARCH TO CONFIRM PREVIOUS FINDINGS

Another reason for conducting research is to verify previous findings. When psychologists publish new research findings, they typically publish details about the research so that others may repeat the experiment to verify their results. This **replication** of prior research is the backbone of good science. Sometimes an especially controversial experiment is repeated in laboratories all over the world. This was the case many years ago when researcher James McConnell (1962) published a study suggesting that memory could be transferred from one organism to another by cannibalism (that is, one eating the other!). This amazing experiment generated countless replication efforts, some successful and others not (Gaito, 1974). Because the results of these follow-up investigations were inconsistent, the controversy surrounding memory transfer studies has never been fully resolved.

In many cases, the results of replication studies are less ambiguous. For example, a number of studies conducted over 30 years ago revealed that *identical twins* (siblings with identical genes) raised in different environments are more similar in intelligence as measured by IQ scores than are *fraternal twins* (siblings born at the same time whose genes are not identical) who are raised in the same environment (Erlenmeyer-Kimling & Jarvik, 1963). These early findings met with considerable criticism from a number of psychologists, particularly those who believed that environment is more important than heredity in shaping human intelligence, and so numerous replication studies were conducted. A sizeable number of these more recent studies have confirmed the early findings (Hendersen, 1982; Plomin & Defries, 1980), and because of these successful replications, most psychologists consider the IQ data obtained from twin studies to be reliable. However, not all psychologists interpret the data in the same way. (See Chapter 12 for a discussion of the relative impact of heredity and environment on tested intelligence.)

Replication is important because the results of a study can vary considerably, depending on experimental conditions and the research method used. As we shall see in the following section, psychologists use a number of techniques to collect data, and a specific research method may not always be appropriate for a specific task.

RESEARCH METHODS

The goals of psychological research are to describe behavior, explain its causes, and, hopefully, to predict the circumstances under which certain behaviors are likely to occur. Although a researcher may ultimately be interested in accomplishing all these goals, they often require different research methods. For example, a researcher interested in understanding the role of aggression in children's play might begin by simply observing children at play in a variety of natural settings. Later, the investigator might test out some hypotheses arising from those observations by modifying the setting or circumstances in specific ways—for instance, by denying the children access to favored toys to see if their behavior becomes more aggressive. This kind of research might reveal a certain cause-and-effect relationship between frustration and aggression, perhaps allowing the researcher to predict circumstances under which aggression is likely to occur.

Psychologists use a number of methods to study behavior, ranging from measuring responses in controlled laboratory environments to detailed case studies of specific individuals. Other research methods include conducting surveys based on questionnaires or interviews, observing behavior in a natural setting, and assessing statistical relationships between two traits, events, or behaviors (such as the relationship between exercise and stress levels). Each of these strategies has advantages or disadvantages for investigating different types of questions about behavior.

SELECTING A RESEARCH METHOD

Many people believe that a few drinks get them "in the mood" and enhance sexual pleasure. If you were a psychologist trying to determine whether alcohol really does have a positive effect on sexual response, what method would you use to test this relationship? See what you can come up with before reading on.

One approach would be to use a questionnaire to ask a large number of people how alcohol consumption affects their sexual response. In fact, this method was used in the early 1970s. In a survey of 20,000 middle-class and upper-middle-class Americans, 60 percent of respondents reported that drinking increased their sexual pleasure (Athanasiou et al., 1970). There was a pronounced sex difference, with significantly greater numbers of women reporting this effect. However, this research might be questioned because it relies on subjective reports: what people believe to be true may not always be the case. There is sometimes considerable discrepancy between actual behavior and the way people report it.

Another approach might be to conduct in-depth studies of people who drink considerable amounts of alcohol. Many studies of chronic alcoholics have revealed that these people often report reduced sexual interest and arousability, but here again, the evidence is difficult to interpret. It is unclear whether this reduced sexual interest is a direct result of drinking or a generalized side effect of the physical deterioration often associated with chronic alcoholism.

A third possible approach would be to have people keep personal diaries in which they record their daily alcohol intake along with some measure of sexual interest, such as frequency of orgasm or occurrence of sexual fantasies. We might then determine if a relationship exists between these two measures. Here again, however, the results might be clouded by a number of factors, such as inconsistent record keeping. In addition, some people might alter their normal behavior patterns simply because they are keeping records. And finally, even if alcohol intake were found to be related to sexual response, could we be certain that this was a cause-and-effect relationship? For example, if sexual activity and drinking both increase during the summer, is the increased drinking the cause of the sexual activity? It might be—but it is also possible that the summer heat is the cause of both of these phenomena. People are more thirsty in hot weather; they may also sleep less on hot nights, so there are increased opportunities for sexual activity.

The problem with all of these research methods is that they do not allow for precise control over the various factors that may influence the behavior being investigated. One research technique that does allow this control is the experimental method. All things considered, this is often the research approach preferred by psychologists. Also, as we shall see, it is the method that provides us with a clear answer to the question, "How does alcohol affect sexual response?"

THE EXPERIMENTAL METHOD

In **experimental research,** subjects are confronted with specific stimuli under precisely controlled conditions that allow their reactions to be reliably measured. The major advantage of the experimental method is that it allows the researcher to control conditions, ruling out all possible influences on subjects' behaviors other than the factors that are being investigated. A research psychologist using this method directly manipulates a particular set of conditions, then observes the effect on behavior. The purpose of the experimental method is to discover relationships among *variables*—conditions or behaviors that can take on different values.

Independent and Dependent Variables   There are two kinds of variables in psychological experiments: independent and dependent. An **independent variable** is a condition or factor that the experimenter manipulates; the resulting behavior that is measured and recorded is called the **dependent variable.**

For example, in a recent experiment, psychologists Barbara Kaplan and Francis Weisberg (1987) sought to determine whether grade-school children's performance on *visual-spatial tasks* (tasks requiring one to perceive relationships among objects and shapes) would improve as a result of receiving *feedback,* or information about the accuracy of their performance. All subjects in this experiment were first pretested to assess their visual-spatial performance. Next, half of the subjects received some feedback on how they performed on the visual-spatial tasks in the pretest, while the other half received no feedback. Finally, both groups were posttested on visual-spatial ability. The results revealed that receiving feedback did not significantly affect posttest scores. In this study, the independent variable controlled by the experimenters was the condition of either receiving or not receiving feedback. The resulting behavior (the performance on the posttest) was the dependent variable.

In many experiments, such as the one just described, the **experimental groups** (various groups of subjects exposed to different varieties of independent variables) provide a sufficient source of comparison to arrive at a reasonably sound conclusion about the relationship between the independent and dependent variables. In some cases, however, merely being exposed to a controlled laboratory environment may change behavior. In such circumstances, it is necessary to use a control group.

Control Groups   A **control group** is a group of subjects who experience all the same conditions as subjects in the experimental group except for the key factor the researcher is evaluating.

For example, consider an experiment conducted to discover how electroconvulsive shock (ECS) affects memory in rats. (ECS is electric current delivered to the brain that causes convulsions and temporary loss of consciousness.) In this study, a number of different experimental conditions were used to test white rats in a maze. Some rats were given a series of shocks and then trained on a learning task requiring *short-term memory* (the immediate recollection of stimuli that have just been perceived); others were trained in the same maze, but under conditions in which the learning trials were widely spaced, thereby drawing upon *long-term memory* (memory retained for longer than about 20 seconds). All animals in the various experimental groups were periodically removed from their cages and placed in the "shock box" where shocks were administered.

It was important to rule out the possibility that maze performance might be influenced simply by the rats' being handled, clipped with electrodes, and stuck in a strange environment. Consequently, each experimental group was matched with a control group of rats who experienced all the same conditions as experimental subjects except for the key factor, ECS. These control groups thus provided a source of comparison, allowing the researcher to assess how ECS affected memory as reflected in maze performance. The major finding of this experiment was that ECS markedly impaired long-term memory formation in these experimental animals (Crooks, 1972). The implications of this finding for treatment of behavioral disorders will be discussed in Chapter 15.

Examples of the Experimental Method   Now that we have some understanding of the experimental method, let us return to the question of how alcohol affects sexual response. Recall that in an earlier survey, a majority of respondents had reported that alcohol enhanced their sexual pleasure. However, a survey is limited to asking people what they *think* happens when they drink, and these subjective assessments may not match up with what actually happens. Two subsequent experimental studies revealed that there was good cause to be wary of the survey's findings.

Both investigations were conducted at Rutgers University's Alcohol Behavior Research Laboratory. The first experiment involved 48 male college students between the ages of 18 and 22 (Briddell & Wilson, 1976). During an initial session the researchers obtained baseline data on flaccid (nonerect) penis diameter for all subjects. The participants were then shown a 10-minute erotic film of explicit sexual interaction between male and female partners. Penile tumescence (engorgement) was measured continuously during the film, using a flexible rubber-band-like device. This measurement provided information about these men's level of sexual arousal when they were not under the influence of alcohol.

A second session was held a week later. Here, subjects drank measured amounts of alcohol prior to viewing a somewhat longer version of the erotic film. The 48 men were assigned to four experimental groups, with 12 subjects in each group. Depending on his group assignment, each subject consumed 0.6, 3, 6, or 9 ounces of alcohol. Thus the independent variable in this experiment consisted of the various levels of alcohol intake. After a 40-minute rest period, the subjects viewed the film, during which sexual arousal was again precisely measured. The results indicated that alcohol significantly reduced sexual arousal, especially at higher intake levels.

The second investigation was conducted with 16 college women between the ages of 18 and 22 (Wilson & Lawson, 1976). Here, a group of 16 women participated in weekly experimental sessions under varying conditions. Each received four different doses of alcohol (0.3, 1.4, 2.9, and 4.3 ounces) on different occasions, and then watched either a control film or an erotic film. The control film was a boring 12-minute review of the computer facilities at Rutgers University; the erotic film portrayed explicit heterosexual interaction. Vaginal changes reflecting sexual arousal were measured continuously during film viewing by use of a vaginal photoplethysmograph, a device designed to measure increased vaginal blood volume in a sexually aroused female. As expected, "subjects showed significantly more arousal in response to the erotic than the control film" (p. 493). More importantly, there was clear evidence that alcohol significantly reduced sexual arousal, especially at higher dosages.

Both of these experiments tend to refute the belief that alcohol enhances erotic experiences; they also reveal the advantages of controlled laboratory conditions for measuring behavior. Clearly, the experimental method provided a more accurate indication of how alcohol affects sexual arousal than did the survey.

Limitations of the Experimental Method   Laboratory experiments offer researchers the advantage of being able to control variables, and they often allow direct conclusions to be drawn about cause-and-effect relationships between variables. The experimental method also has some limitations, however.

First, the somewhat artificial nature of the laboratory setting may influence subjects' behaviors. The very fact that people know they are in an experiment can cause them to respond differently from the way they might normally behave. For instance, a classic experiment conducted in the early 1960s demonstrated that children who observed adults acting aggressively were more likely to show similar aggressive behaviors in a laboratory environment than were children who either observed adults behaving nonaggressively or did not see any adult models (Bandura et al., 1961). These results suggested that children might learn aggressive behavior by imitating the adults. However, several psychologists urged caution in interpreting these results, pointing out that children's behavior in a contrived laboratory situation might be quite different from their actions in the real world. Perhaps the children who observed adult models behaving aggressively might have assumed it was all right to copy these behaviors within the "permissive" laboratory environment, even though they would not behave in this fashion outside of the laboratory.

A second limitation of the experimental method is simply that not all questions posed by psychologists lend themselves to experimental investigation. For instance, you might be interested in finding out whether children of two-career families are as emotionally secure as children of families where one parent stays at home during the day. This kind of data could not be gathered by manipulating variables in a laboratory setting. Instead, you would need to take your investigation to real families and collect data about them.

The appropriateness of the experimental method has sometimes been questioned for another reason besides the type of data it provides: a number of experimental studies have been criticized on ethical grounds. This complex issue is discussed below.

Are Some Psychological Experiments Unethical? Four Examples   In past years, several controversial studies have prompted serious questions about the ethics of some psychological experiments. Consider the following examples and decide whether you think any ethical principles were violated.

The Milgram Obedience to Authority Study   In the 1960s, social psychologist Stanley Milgram (1963) used deception in a widely discussed study of obedience to authority. Milgram's goal was to determine whether subjects would administer painful electric shocks to others merely because an authority figure instructed them to do so. Milgram's subjects, all male, thought they were participating in a study of how punishment affects learning. They were told to use an intercom system to present problems to a learner who was strapped in a chair in another room, out of sight, and to administer a shock each time the learner gave the wrong answer to a problem. Labeled switches on the "shock apparatus" ranged from a low of 15

In Milgram's obedience study, subjects were instructed to administer painful electrical shocks to "learners" in another room. In spite of protests and cries from the other room, most of the subjects delivered what they believed to be a full range of these shocks. (The learners actually felt nothing.) (*Source:* © 1965 by Stanley Milgram. From the film OBEDIENCE, distributed by the New York University Film Division and the Pennsylvania State University, PCR)

volts to a high of 450 volts; subjects were instructed to increase the voltage with each successive error the learner made.

In spite of protests and cries from the other room, most of the subjects delivered what they believed was a full range of these painful shocks. Although they followed the experimenter's instructions, the task was not easy for them. Virtually all of the subjects exhibited high levels of stress and discomfort as they administered the shocks. Later, these subjects were told that the experiment was merely a contrived situation in which they had been deceived, and that no shocks had actually been given. How would you feel about yourself if you had been one of Milgram's subjects? Do you think Milgram violated ethical principles by placing people in a position where they might feel compelled to engage in hurtful behavior? Was deception appropriate in this experiment, or, for that matter, in any psychological research with human subjects?

The Stanford University Prisoner Study A second controversial study, the now famous Stanford University prisoner study, was conducted some years ago by social psychologist Philip Zimbardo and his colleagues (Haney & Zimbardo, 1977; Zimbardo, 1975). These investigators created a simulated prison environment to study how incarceration influenced the behavior of healthy, well-adjusted people. Student recruits played the roles of either guards or inmates.

No one anticipated the profoundly disturbing impact of this experi-

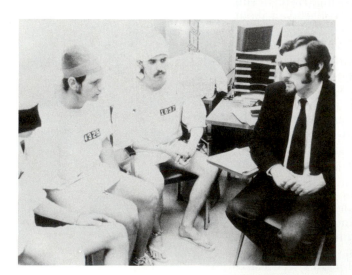

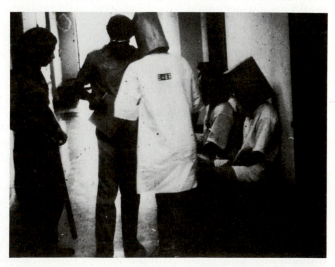

In the Stanford University prisoner study, students played the roles of either the guards or the inmates. The "guards" soon became so cruel that several of the "prisoners" suffered severe emotional reactions, and consequently, the experiment was terminated before it had run its course.

ence on students cast in either of the roles. The "guards" soon became so cruel that several of the "prisoners" suffered severe emotional reactions ranging from depression to anxiety and even extreme rage (not unlike the responses of many inmates in genuine penal institutions). As soon as Zimbardo and his associates became aware of the severe impact their study was having upon their subjects, they terminated the experiment—even before it had run its course. Should this experiment have been conducted? Was it unethical to put subjects in positions of "Keeper" and "Kept?" Was it unethical to place humans in a situation the researchers might have anticipated could lead to hostile confrontations?

Replication of the Stanford Prisoner Study   In 1983 the press widely reported a repeat of the Zimbardo research conducted by a high-school teacher who used volunteer students. This researcher obtained permission from both parents and school officials to conduct the investigation. The results were similar to those obtained by the Stanford group a decade earlier, and many of the students were severely upset by their participation in this follow-up study. Needless to say, parents were irate, school officials were chagrined, and the press had a field day. Were ethical principles violated in this repeat of Zimbardo's earlier research?

Stroke Simulation in Monkeys   A fourth controversial study was conducted a few years ago by a prominent researcher. In an effort to find ways of helping stroke victims regain use of their limbs, this investigator experimented with monkeys. Nerves in one of each monkey's arms were cut to simulate the loss of feeling that might result from a stroke. The undamaged arms were then bound to the monkeys' bodies to force them to use their nerve-dead limbs. Unfortunately, the surgically altered arms were susceptible to injury because they lacked feeling; some monkeys even treated their damaged arms as foreign objects and inflicted further damage by chewing on their fingers.

Some time after the initial surgery was conducted, the researcher went on vacation. While he was away, an animal-welfare activist who had volunteered to work in that laboratory became concerned about the monkeys' deteriorating physical condition. He contacted local authorities and the research scientist was ultimately charged with a variety of criminal acts, including cruelty to animals. The researcher maintained that his investigation was appropriate and that the physical condition of the monkeys was the fault of workers who had not properly cared for the animals during his absence. Do you believe that he was guilty of violating ethical principles in his research?

Ethical Guidelines for Research   These four examples present complex ethical issues. Perhaps the most controversial is Milgram's research, which generated a great deal of criticism. Many psychologists questioned the ethics of exposing unsuspecting people to a situation that might cause them considerable stress and might even have lasting harmful effects. Psychologist Diana Baumrind (1964), for example, argued that subjects' feelings and rights had been abused. She suggested that many would have trouble justifying their willingness to administer high levels of shock and that their self-respect would be damaged. Milgram pointed out, however, that all subjects had gone through extensive debriefing after the study, in which they were told that they had not actually shocked anyone and were reassured that many other subjects had responded in the same way. He documented the success of these debriefing sessions, citing results from a follow-up questionnaire returned by 92 percent of the original subjects. A large majority, 84 percent, said they were glad to have participated in the study. Fifteen percent indicated neutral feelings and only one percent reported being sorry they had participated in the experiment (Milgram, 1964).

Some researchers seemed relatively satisfied by Milgram's response to his critics. One psychologist recently commented that Milgram "seems to have employed little more deception in his work than is used regularly on TV programs such as 'Candid Camera'" (McConnell, 1983, p. 629). Nevertheless, studies such as this have generated a debate about ethics in research that ultimately culminated in the American Psychological Association's adopting, in 1973 (subsequent revisions have been published in 1979 and 1981), a list of ethical guidelines requiring, among other things, that researchers avoid procedures that might cause serious physical or mental harm to human subjects. If an experiment involves even the slightest risk of harm or discomfort, investigators are required to obtain informed consent from their subjects. Researchers must also respect a subject's right to refuse to participate at any time during the course of a study, and special steps must be taken to protect the confidentiality of the data and maintain participants' anonymity unless they agree to be identified.

The issue of deception in research remains controversial. Some studies would lose their effectiveness if participating subjects knew in advance exactly what the experimenter was studying. The APA's guideline is that if deception must be used, a postexperiment debriefing must thoroughly explain to participants why it was necessary. At such time, subjects must be allowed to request that their data be removed from the study and destroyed.

With these guidelines in mind, how would you now evaluate the other three research examples? Most psychologists believe that Zimbardo's simulated prison study did not violate ethical principles: the researchers were as shocked as anyone by the effect of their experiment on subjects, and the study was terminated as soon as it became clear that some subjects were experiencing severe emotional reactions. Also, all subjects had voluntarily participated in the study after being well informed about its nature.

The third example is a different case entirely. Unlike Zimbardo's group, the high-school teacher who replicated the prisoner study had access to previous research results which strongly indicated the possibility of psychological harm to subjects. These findings were ignored, however, and the experiment was recreated in clear violation of research ethics.

The final research example presents very complex ethical issues. A considerable amount of important medical and behavioral research, some with potentially great benefits for humans, could not be conducted without animal experimentation. The mere fact that nonhumans are used, however, does not justify an "any treatment goes" attitude, and researchers must ensure that animals are treated humanely. Despite the monkey researcher's claim that others were responsible for laboratory conditions during his vacation, the court determined that his role as primary investigator made him ultimately responsible for the animals' welfare. He was found guilty of cruelty to animals and fined (Holden, 1981).

Sometimes it is hard for researchers to weigh objectively the potential benefits of a study against the possibility of harming its subjects. Recognizing the difficulty of this task, virtually every institution conducting research in the United States has established ethics committees that review all proposed studies. If they perceive that subjects' (human or otherwise) welfare is insufficiently safeguarded, the proposal must be modified or the research cannot be conducted.

The APA's list of ethical principles, together with the activities of institutional ethics committees, makes it very unlikely that research along the lines of Stanley Milgram's study could be conducted today. Researchers who do not adhere to this strict code of ethics risk serious professional and legal consequences.

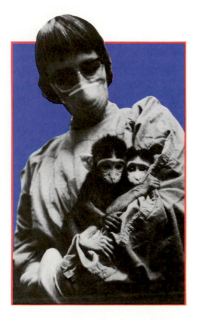

There are strict ethical standards regarding the treatment of animals in research experiments.

SURVEYS

A second important research method is the **survey,** in which a representative group of people are questioned about their behaviors or attitudes. Psychologists use this method when they are interested in obtaining information from more people than it is practical to study in the laboratory—for instance, to find out how college students feel about men and women sharing domestic chores at home, or to determine whether publicity about AIDS (acquired immune deficiency syndrome) has changed people's sexual practices in the past few years.

Since such questions cannot be put to everybody in a population, psychologists may elect to survey a representative sample group. A carefully constructed questionnaire may show trends that exist in the general population even though only a relatively small percentage of that population is surveyed.

How Samples Are Selected   Most research questions relate to a population much too large to be studied in its entirety. For example, if you wished to find out how the use of marijuana affects adolescent problem-solving ability and scholastic achievement, your relevant population would include teenagers from all over the world. Even if you decided to limit your observations to American adolescents, your target group would still be prohibitively large: you could never evaluate all its members.

Psychologists get around this difficulty by gathering data from a relatively small **sample** or selected segment of the entire population that interests them. Our ability to draw inferences or conclusions confidently about a much larger population rests chiefly on the techniques we use for selecting subjects for the sample study group.

The ideal sample is called a **representative sample;** that is, a sample in which critical subgroups are represented according to their incidence in the larger population that we wish to draw conclusions about. In such a sample, every individual in the total population of interest has a chance of being included in the limited sample actually studied.

SELECTING A REPRESENTATIVE SAMPLE

How would you go about selecting a representative sample that you could use to investigate what proportion of adolescents use marijuana? In order to draw broad conclusions about the general population (all American adolescents), your sample would need to be representative of that group. How could you ensure this? Take a few moments to consider what procedures you might use before reading on.

You might begin by obtaining the rosters of all high-school students in a variety of geographic areas throughout the United States. You would need to select these regions very carefully to reflect the actual distribution of the population you are studying. For instance, if 30 percent of American adolescents live in the western states, 30 percent of your sample would be drawn from the West. Likewise, if 20 percent of western adolescents live in rural environments, 20 percent of the subjects selected from this area must be country dwellers.

Once the rosters were compiled in this systematic fashion, the next step would be to select the actual participants by some method that would ensure equal probability of inclusion, such as using a table of random numbers to generate random picks from the rosters. Provided that your final sample was sufficiently large, you could be reasonably confident in generalizing your findings to all American adolescents.

Another kind of sample, called a **random sample,** is not necessarily the same as a representative sample. A random sample is selected by randomization procedures, which alone do not ensure a representative sample. For example, suppose you have an opportunity to buy into a café on campus. The café has been only marginally profitable, and you think that converting to a health-food-oriented menu may help to increase profitability.

You decide to survey students' attitudes about patronizing a health-food restaurant on campus. Since summer provides you the most free time, you decide to conduct your poll during this period. A friend who works in the registrar's office supplies you with the roster of summer session enrollees, and you randomly select your survey sample from this group.

Assuming that your question about patronizing a health-food restaurant is clearly stated, and that a large percentage of the sample respond to your poll, can you be confident that your findings reflect the views of the entire student body at your school? The answer is no, for a reason you may already have guessed. Students enrolled in summer classes are not necessarily representative of all students at your college or university. For example, if more graduate students enroll in the summer program, the average age will be higher than that of students in the fall and winter sessions. Differences such as this could contribute to somewhat different attitudes toward health food. For instance, there is evidence that people become more aware of the importance of healthful dietary habits as they grow older.

Thus, while randomization is an important tool, the sample will not be truly representative unless it includes members of specific groups (for instance, students enrolled during all seasons of the year), or proportionate numbers of individuals with certain characteristics (such as age, sex, or race).

Representative samples generally represent the total population they are designed to reflect more accurately than do mere random samples. Nevertheless, random samples are often quite adequate for many kinds of investigations. A decision whether or not to add systematic representation to randomization depends both on the questions(s) the psychologist seeks to answer and on how precisely she or he wishes to generalize the findings to a larger population.

Survey Methods   Once a sample is selected, survey data may be obtained in two major ways: either orally, through a face-to-face interview, or in written form, using a paper-and-pencil questionnaire. Questionnaire design can vary tremendously: questionnaires may range from a few questions to over a thousand; they may be multiple-choice, true–false, or discussion questions; respondents may fill out the questionnaire either alone or in the presence of a researcher.

Each of the two major survey methods has both advantages and shortcomings. Because questionnaires are more anonymous, some people may be less likely to distort information about their lives by boasting, omitting facts, and so forth. (The presence of an interviewer sometimes encourages such false responses.) Questionnaires have another advantage in that they are usually cheaper and quicker than interview surveys. However, interviews have the advantage of flexibility. The interviewer may clarify confusing questions and vary their sequence in order to meet the needs of the participant. A competent interviewer can establish a sense of rapport that may encourage more candor than that produced by an impersonal questionnaire. On the other hand, data obtained through oral interviews may be subject to bias if the researcher interprets them inaccurately.

Limitations of the Survey Method   The survey is effective for gathering a large amount of data, but, like the experimental method, it has limitations. An important caution has to do with sample selection: researchers need to be wary of demographic bias. In a famous example illustrating the danger of demographic bias, a 1936 survey poll of more than two million people led to a prediction that Republican presidential candidate Alf Landon would defeat Democratic incumbent Franklin Roosevelt by a landslide. In fact, the reverse happened.

The poll was dead wrong because the survey sample was selected by picking names from telephone directories. In those depression years few people but the well-to-do had telephones, and the wealthy favored Landon.

In 1936 a survey poll of more than two million people led to a prediction that Republican presidential candidate Alf Landon would defeat Democratic incumbent Franklin Roosevelt by a landslide. Here, newly elected President Franklin Roosevelt enjoys his victory. Names drawn from a limited demographic sample resulted in this erroneous survey.

Political survey techniques have been refined so that such errors no longer happen. However, surveys conducted by psychologists sometimes are compromised by a tendency to weight samples with Caucasian, middle-class, educated respondents.

For instance, much of what we know about human behavior is gathered from college students. This population is not completely representative of the general population in terms of age, socioeconomic status, and education, and these variables might well influence a subject's responses. Although the segment of the population from which subjects are drawn may have little impact on the results of some research (for instance, the study of how receptors in the eye respond to different colors), it may have an important influence on some other types of research. Thus, we need to be very careful in generalizing from a sample of college students to a broader population. This caution applies to experiments and some other research methods as well as to surveys.

Another potential bias in sample selection is sex bias. Males are used as subjects for psychological investigation far more commonly than are females (Holmes & Jorgensen, 1971; Rohrbaugh, 1979). This has led some people to suggest that our data reflect a psychology of men more than of people in general. This preference for male subjects can have a serious biasing effect upon research. For example, a substantial majority of investigations of human aggressive behavior have studied only male subjects—a fact that suggests that psychologists have been influenced by our society's tendency to view males as more active and aggressive than females. This assumption would have little chance of being proven false by research that systematically ignored women.

Fortunately, research psychologists are becoming more aware of the implications of sex bias in research. Recent investigations of aggressive behavior, using subjects of both sexes, have revealed that under some circumstances women may behave just as aggressively as men. As psychological research continues to reduce sex biases, we can expect less scientific support for some of our society's common gender stereotypes.

Still another caution in using the survey method concerns the design of the questions themselves. Psychologists have learned, often to their dismay, that even very minor changes in the wording of a question can alter people's responses. For example, Elizabeth Loftus (1975) found that subjects who were asked, "Do you get headaches occasionally and if so how often?" reported an average of 0.7 headaches a week, while a comparable group of subjects asked "Do you get headaches frequently and if so how often?" reported a weekly average of 2.2 headaches. Clearly, a considerable amount of thought and careful attention must be applied in constructing survey questions.

Finally, surveys, like experiments, are not appropriate for every research project. A survey can provide a broad profile of attitudes and behaviors of a large group, but it cannot look closely at specific individuals to understand their behaviors or attitudes. Psychologists must use other methods, such as the observational method or the case study, to provide that kind of information.

THE OBSERVATIONAL METHOD

A third research method is the **observational method.** Here, researchers observe their subjects as they go about their usual activities. This often takes place in a natural setting, and when it does the research method is called **naturalistic observation.**

Like the survey, the observational method provides descriptive information. For instance, in the study of children's aggressive behavior discussed earlier in this chapter, researchers might observe that when children become aggressive, adults pay more attention to them. This observation might lead to the hypothesis that aggressive behaviors in children are likely

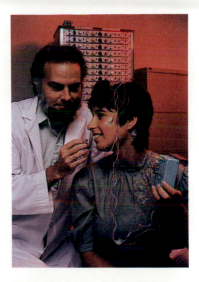

Much of what we know about human behavior is gathered from college students. We need to be very careful in generalizing from this sample of students to a broader population.

A substantial majority of studies of human aggressive behavior have studied only male subjects. How could the assumption that males are more aggressive than females be proven false if research systematically ignored women?

to increase commensurate with the amount of adult attention they produce. This hypothesis could not be tested using the observational method, since it does not provide any way of controlling variables. Nevertheless, such observations could serve as an excellent starting point for further research in a more controlled environment.

Another example of the observational method is a study by Daniel Stern of the Cornell Medical School and his associates (1986). Interested in discovering how the interaction between parents and infants affects personality development, researchers in this study periodically videotaped normal everyday interactions between mothers and infants over a span of about two years. They found that the innumerable small interchanges that take place—for instance, when an infant makes a squealing sound and the mother echoes it back, or when the infant seeks eye contact and the mother rewards it with a smile—influence how the infant will interact with other people.

Limitations of the Observational Method   Like the experimental method and the survey, direct observation is not appropriate for every research question. One potential problem is the risk of subjectivity, or **observer bias:** an observer may read more into a situation than is actually there. For instance, a psychologist observing children's play may be tempted to record that a child is "frustrated" upon finding a favored merry-go-round temporarily out of order, when in reality all that is observed is a period of suspended activity. Far from sulking in frustration, the child might simply be considering alternative things to do.

Observer bias may also take the form of investigators seeing what they expect to see. In one study, for instance, teachers were asked to observe and rate children who had been labeled normal, emotionally disturbed, or intellectually impaired (Foster & Ysseldyke, 1976). As you might guess, the labels were assigned arbitrarily in an effort to induce observer bias artificially. The researchers found that the teachers rated the children in markedly different ways that were clearly influenced by the labels applied to each child. This is a rather sobering finding, considering the widespread tendency of American educators to evaluate students as disruptive, cooperative, and so forth, and to enter these evaluations into permanent records that future teachers rely on. Psychologists conducting observational research generally try to avoid making biased interpretations by keeping very careful records of their observations. Sometimes audiovisual records that can be evaluated by independent observers are also used in the effort to minimize observer bias.

Another potential problem is that the presence of a human observer may affect the behavior being observed. For example, children on a playground may behave less aggressively simply because they are being watched by a strange adult. This problem of **observer effect** may require special attention when researchers take the observational method into the laboratory. For instance, when William Masters and Virginia Johnson (1966) used direct observation to document male and female sexual response patterns in the laboratory, many people questioned the validity of their findings.

Actually, in much of Masters' and Johnson's work no one directly observed the volunteer subjects. When investigators did use direct observation, they were as unobtrusive as possible, observing from a peripheral location or from behind one-way glass, or using videotapes to be viewed later, and so forth. According to a subsequent report, "the vast majority of volunteers found it surprisingly easy to respond sexually in the laboratory in much the same way as they responded at home in private" (Brecher & Brecher, 1966, p. 56). Although there may be some merit to the concern about the artificial nature of Masters' and Johnson's laboratory observations, time has demonstrated that their research findings are accurate enough to be beneficially applied to such areas as sex therapy, infertility counseling, conception control, and general sex education. (Masters' and

Johnson's findings will be discussed at greater length in Appendix C.)

Thus, despite its potential disadvantages, direct observation often produces valuable information when it is carefully conducted. In addition, there are some clear advantages to seeing and measuring behavior firsthand instead of relying on subjective reports of past experiences. Firsthand direct observation virtually eliminates the possibility of data falsification, either through a subject's inaccurate recollections or through deceptive reporting. In addition, direct observation can provide some important insights into relationships that may exist in a particular behavioral area.

CASE STUDIES

Still another form of research is the **case study,** an in-depth exploration of either a single case or a small group of subjects who are examined individually. People often become subjects for case studies because they have some physical or emotional disorder or because they have manifested a specific atypical behavior. In fact, much of our current information about criminal behavior, incest victims, disorders such as multiple personality, and other unusual conditions has been obtained using this approach.

A number of methods can be used to gather data in a case study, including direct observation, testing and experimentation (to see, for instance, if other conditions such as memory loss or a poor sense of balance are associated with a particular disability), and interviews or questionnaires. Because of this flexibility, case studies often provide opportunities to acquire insight into specific behaviors. Highly personal, subjective information about how individuals actually feel about their behavior represents an important step beyond simply recording activities. And case studies have another advantage. Because of their clinical nature and because they may continue for long periods of time (months or even years), the researcher is able to explore important variables, and possible relationships among them, in some detail.

Limitations of the Case Study   There are some important limitations to the case-study method, however. One of these is lack of investigative control. A set of circumstances typically gives rise to the research investigation, rather than the other way around. Thus, the researcher's role is to gather as much information as possible from a given situation, but the variables are beyond his or her control.

A second limitation—one that the case study shares with the observational method—is the potential for subjective bias on the researcher's part. Since the case study usually arises out of a rare case, it is often impossible to get objective verification such as is provided when experiments are replicated, and unlike surveys, proper sampling techniques are rarely used with this method (how could they be?). Thus, it is hard to generalize from one subject to the rest of the population.

Finally, case studies often include data that are not directly observed by the researcher. Since an individual's past usually does not become a target of research interest until that person develops some sort of problem, the researcher must often reconstruct the subject's earlier history in order to gather data (Bradburn et al., 1987). For example, suppose we want to evaluate Sigmund Freud's theory that *agoraphobia* (an intense fear of being in open, public places) is related to *separation anxiety,* which is an underlying fear of being separated from parents. According to this view, certain individuals are predisposed to develop agoraphobia as a result of incidents of traumatic separation from their parents during early childhood. The case-study method would be a logical way to evaluate this hypothesis: people with agoraphobia might be asked to recall events from early childhood in which they were separated from their parents; then the frequency of these experiences could be compared to a control sample of nonagoraphobic people matched with the agoraphobic group on other variables. Unfortunately,

What causes people to act the way they do? Research methods attempt to explain some of these phenomena.

How would you describe this child: happy, bored, depressed, fearful? What caused you to come to your conclusion? Your opinion of what this child is thinking and feeling is an example of observer bias.

Case studies are of a clinical nature and may continue for long periods of time. In April of 1987, presidential assailant John Hinkley, Jr., is escorted away after a hearing for a bid for a pass from St. Elizabeth's hospital to visit his family. A psychiatrist testified that Hinkley had written a sympathetic letter to convicted mass murderer Theodore Bundy and was encouraged by another would-be assassin to write to Charles Manson.

however, many subjects might have trouble remembering these early experiences accurately, especially if they are inclined to repress or block them from conscious memory. Thus, the recall of past events in the case-study method is subject to errors in memory and sometimes to intentional efforts to distort or repress facts.

These general cautions can be applied to the first-person accounts throughout this book. We believe these examples represent especially relevant experiences, attitudes, and feelings, and they are included so that readers may draw perspectives from them, not conclusions.

THE CORRELATIONAL METHOD

Some types of questions cannot be answered by experiments, surveys, direct observation, or case studies. For instance, suppose that you wanted to determine how high-school seniors' Scholastic Aptitude Test (SAT) scores related to their grade point averages (GPAs) during the first year of college. The best approach would be simply to collect the SAT scores and first-year GPAs of a large sample of college freshmen and use a statistical technique to determine the relationship between these two variables. This research technique is called the **correlational method,** and the statistic used to describe the amount and type of relationship is a **coefficient of correlation.**

A coefficient of correlation always falls somewhere between +1.00 and −1.00. (A minus sign is used to signify negative correlations, but the plus sign is usually omitted from positive correlations.) If it is around zero, this indicates a weak or nonexistent relationship between the two variables in question. A positive correlation indicates that the variables vary together in the same direction, so that increases in one measure are accompanied by increases in the other and decreases are similarly matched by decreases. For instance, it is known that SAT scores are positively correlated with college GPAs, because students who obtain high SAT scores tend to achieve high

GPAs and those with low SAT scores tend to have lower grades. This relationship is far from a perfect 1.00, however. In the real world, correlations between variables are virtually never perfect.

It is important to note that a high positive correlation between two variables does not mean that the matched scores are nearly identical in value. It simply means that a generally consistent proportional relationship exists. For example, suppose we find a strong positive correlation of .90 among scores on variables X and Y. We further note that for every increase of one point in variable X, there is typically a corresponding increase of approximately two points in variable Y. This is what is meant by the expression "a generally consistent proportional relationship." The nature of the relationship between variables is determined not by their actual numerical values but rather by the consistency of the relationship between them. Thus, if variable Y increased an average of 10 points for every increase of one point in variable X, we would still be dealing with a positive correlation of the same magnitude as our first example.

A negative correlation indicates that increases on one measure are associated with decreases on the other. If you have ever followed the stock market, you may have noted that as interest rates go up, market averages tend to come down. This relationship is by no means a perfect −1.00, but it indicates a definite trend. Another example of a negative correlation is the relationship between adult age and physical strength: all other things being equal, the older an adult is, the lower he or she is likely to score on measures of physical strength. Table 2.1 helps clarify the proportionate relationships that exist under various degrees of correlation.

Knowing the type and degree of relationship that exists between variables may be especially helpful to psychologists and others who wish to make predictions about behavior. For example, if you know that a high-school senior scored high on the SAT test, you can predict with some confidence that she or he is likely to earn good grades in college.

Limitations of Correlational Studies   Correlational studies help us discover relationships between variables, but it is important not to read more into them than is there. One of the most common mistakes people make in interpreting correlational studies is to conclude that because two factors are related, one causes the other. This is sometimes the case, however. For instance, observations of drivers negotiating obstacle courses under the influence of alcohol reveal a positive correlation between error scores and blood alcohol levels (the higher the level, the greater the number of errors). We can be assured that this correlational relationship is a causal one since

TABLE 2.1   Four Sets of Data Indicating Various Degrees of Correlational Relationships Between Scores on Two Variables

Subject	Set A X	Set A Y	Set B X	Set B Y	Set C X	Set C Y	Set D X	Set D Y
1	1	2	1	3	1	7	1	12
2	2	4	2	2	2	8	2	10
3	3	6	3	4	3	6	3	8
4	4	8	4	7	4	4	4	6
5	5	10	5	5	5	3	5	4
6	6	12	6	6	6	1	6	2
	$r = +1.00$		$r = +.58$		$r = -.76$		$r = -1.00$	

Each data set comprises the scores of six subjects on two variables X and Y. The product-moment correlation coefficient (r) has been calculated for each set. The formula for calculating r is included in the Statistics Appendix.

alcohol is known to impair the brain's ability to perceive, interpret, and respond to stimuli.

On the other hand, a consistent relationship between two factors is not always causal. In some cases a third factor, related to each of the other two, may account for the apparent causal relationship. For instance, there is a positive correlation between soft-drink sales and average daytime temperature: as temperatures rise, so do soft-drink sales. It is tempting to presume that this correlation also reflects a cause-and-effect relationship: hot weather makes people more thirsty, and so they are more likely to consume soft drinks. However, it is also possible that this relationship simply reflects a third common factor, vacation time. Perhaps people consume more soft drinks during vacations, which occur most commonly during the summer when temperatures climb. In sum, it is dangerous to read too much into findings of correlational studies.

DESCRIBING AND INTERPRETING RESEARCH FINDINGS

Regardless of the research method used, psychologists generally end up with data that must be described and interpreted. Usually the data are in the form of numbers that can be analyzed by **statistics**—mathematical methods for describing and interpreting data. There are essentially two kinds of statistics: descriptive and inferential. The Statistics Appendix provides detailed information about using statistics to make sense out of research findings; this section provides only a brief overview.

DESCRIPTIVE STATISTICS

Suppose that you are enrolled in a psychology class attended by 200 students. On the first exam, you receive 41 points out of a possible 50. Naturally, you want to know how your score compares with the class as a whole. Your instructor announces that the top score is 48. This still does not provide sufficient information for you to evaluate your score: 41 may be well above average, but it is also possible that most of the class scored higher than you. What you need is a succinct statistical description of the overall class performance that will allow you to make sense out of a relatively large amount of data. This is what **descriptive statistics** is about—reducing a quantity of data to a form that is more understandable. There are two major ways of describing a distribution of scores such as the grades on your psychology exam: measures of central tendency and measures of variation.

Measures of Central Tendency   A **measure of central tendency** is a value that reflects the middle or central point of a distribution of scores. There are three measures of central tendency: the mean, the median, and the mode. The **mean** is an arithmetic average obtained by adding the scores and dividing by the number of scores. The **median** is the score that falls in the middle of a distribution of numbers that are arranged from lowest to highest. The **mode** is the score that occurs most frequently in a distribution of numbers.

In a **normal distribution** (sometimes called a *bell-shaped curve*), in which scores are distributed similarly on both sides of the middle value, the mean, median, and mode will be quite close together (see Figure 2.1). This is not true for distributions where the scores are **skewed** or unbalanced (for example, scores on a difficult test that most people fail but a few "curve breakers" ace). In such situations, a person needs to decide which measure most accurately reflects central tendency. All things considered, the mean is generally the most commonly used measure of central tendency.

Returning to our previous example, suppose you find out that 36 is the mean score on the psychology exam. You now know that your 41 is at least above average. With only this information, however, you still do not have a sense of how your score ranks. That average of 36 could result from the fact that, aside from your 41, half of the class scored 48s and the other

FIGURE 2.1

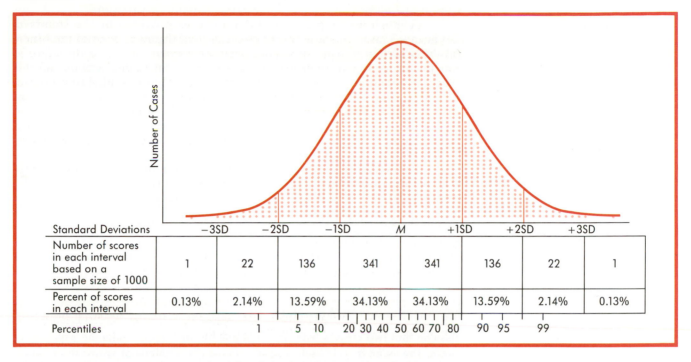

	−3SD	−2SD	−1SD	M	+1SD	+2SD	+3SD
Standard Deviations							
Number of scores in each interval based on a sample size of 1000	1	22	136	341	341	136	22	1
Percent of scores in each interval	0.13%	2.14%	13.59%	34.13%	34.13%	13.59%	2.14%	0.13%
Percentiles		1	5 10	20 30 40 50 60 70 80	90 95	99	

This figure portrays a perfectly symmetrical distribution of 1,000 scores. Each dot represents an individual score. The horizontal axis shows the amounts of whatever variable is being measured, such as height, IQ, or reaction time. The vertical axis represents the number of individuals who obtain a particular score. Actual distributions of scores are never quite as balanced as this hypothetical curve. However, some come quite close to it (for example, IQ scores obtained from a large sample of randomly selected people).

Certain key features of the normal distribution provide very useful information. For instance, we know that in any large random sample of scores that are approximately normal in their distribution, a certain percentage of scores will fall in a given segment of the distribution. You will note that in the provided example about 68 percent of normally distributed scores fall in the middle third portion (between plus and minus one standard deviation from the mean). In a normal distribution all but a few scores fall within three standard deviations above and below the mean.

Percentile ranks, shown on the figure, are a convenient way to determine the standing of a given score relative to others in the distribution. For example, a percentile rank of 95 indicates that 95 percent of the scores in the total distribution fall below this point.

half scored 24s, or it could result from most of the class scoring in the 33–39 range. Your rank would be very different in these two situations. What you need to know is the measure of variability.

Measures of Variability A measure of central tendency, such as the mean, tells us only part of the story about a group of scores. Often we need to know whether scores are clustered closely around their average or whether they are widely spread out. Measures that indicate the spread of a distribution of scores are called **measures of variability.**

One measure of variability is the **range**—the difference between the highest and lowest score. This is the easiest measure of variation to calculate. However, it may provide a misleading indication of how dispersed scores are. For example, suppose that all but one student in your psychology class received a test score somewhere between 26 and 48. Excluding this one exception, the range would be 22 (48 − 26). However, the one score outside the spread, a 4, had the effect of doubling the range to 44 (48 − 4). As you can see, whenever there are extreme scores at either end of a distribution, the range will provide a biased, inflated estimate of variation.

A much better measure of variability is provided by the **standard deviation.** This measure is a rough indication of the average extent to which all the scores in a distribution vary from the mean. Standard deviation is much more sensitive than the range because it takes into account all the scores in a data set, not just the extreme values at either end. The standard deviation effectively describes whether a distribution of scores varies widely or narrowly around the mean. If the standard deviation is small, we know that individual scores tend to be very close to the mean. If it is large, we know that the mean is less representative because the scores are much more widely dispersed around it.

Knowing the mean and standard deviation allows us to make relatively precise judgments about how a particular score relates to other scores. For instance, if the standard deviation on your psychology test was 5, this would place you exactly one standard deviation unit above the mean, which was 36. Assuming that your class's test scores were fairly normally distributed, you would know that roughly 4 out of 5 of your classmates scored below your score of 41. This conclusion is derived from known properties of the normal distribution, discussed in the Statistics Appendix.

APPLYING STANDARD DEVIATION

Assume that two classes with an equal number of students take the psychology exam. The mean is 36 in both classes, and the distributions of scores are normal. However, the standard deviations are different: in class A it is 8, while in class B it is 4. Assuming that your score is four points above the mean and that your instructor grades on a "curve" (i.e., assigns grades based on relative standing in the overall distribution of scores), which class would you prefer to be enrolled in? Think about your answer before reading on.

If you selected class B, you are correct. In this class a standard deviation of 4 indicates scores are clustered much more closely around the average than in class A, where the variation is much greater. This greater dispersion of scores would place more people above you in class A, thereby lowering your relative rank.

Central tendency and variability are just two kinds of statistics psychologists use to summarize and characterize data. The coefficient of correlation, discussed earlier, is another important descriptive statistic, as are **percentiles** (numbers from a range of data that indicate percentages of scores that lie below them) and **standard scores** (a number that indicates how far a score deviates from the average in standard units). These and other descriptive measures are discussed in the Statistics Appendix.

INFERENTIAL STATISTICS

The descriptive phase is often just the first step in analyzing and interpreting research results. Once data have been described, psychologists often wish to draw inferences or conclusions about their findings. The process of using a variety of mathematical procedures to draw conclusions about the meaning of data is called **inferential statistics.**

As we have seen in this chapter, research often begins with some type of hypothesis about how things are related. For example, you may believe that people who use special relaxation techniques are likely to have lower anxiety levels than those who do not use such techniques. To test this hypothesis, you might begin by selecting a group of subjects, none of whom have been trained in relaxation techniques, who are matched on a number of important variables that might influence anxiety (things such as age, socioeconomic status, profession, health factors, etc.). Subjects might then be randomly assigned to one of two groups—one group trained in relaxation techniques (the independent variable), and the other receiving no training. You would then collect data on the subjects' anxiety levels for *x* number of weeks or months.

Anxiety, the dependent variable, could be measured in a number of ways, depending on how you define it for the purposes of your study. Many of the variables studied by psychologists (such as anxiety, hunger, intelligence, or aggression) cannot be investigated until we specify precisely what we mean by the term. This is accomplished by providing an **operational definition** that specifies the operations we use to measure or observe the variable in question. For instance, you might use physical measures such as blood pressure or muscle tension to measure anxiety, or you could use a score on a psychological test that measures anxiety levels.

At the completion of your experiment you would have lots of data to analyze. Suppose you find that after eight weeks the relaxation training group scores significantly lower on your measure of anxiety than does the control group. This difference seems meaningful. However, whenever you evaluate the performance or characteristics of two or more groups of subjects, it is likely there will be some differences based on chance alone. The problem for the researcher is to determine whether differences between research groups reflect a true difference due to the experimental condition or whether the difference is simply a chance result.

How can you assess whether the difference in anxiety levels of the two groups is genuine rather than a chance result? A variety of tests have been devised to accomplish this. Such procedures are called measures of statistical significance. When scientists conclude that a research finding is statistically significant, they are merely stating, at a high level of confidence, that the difference is attributable to the experimental condition being manipulated by the researcher. The Statistics Appendix discusses this topic in more detail.

WHAT TO BELIEVE: A STATEMENT OF PERSPECTIVE

We have seen in this chapter that psychological research can be hindered by a number of factors, including difficulties in obtaining representative samples, ethical considerations, experimenter bias, subject bias, and a variety of other problems. We have also seen that research psychologists have shown remarkable versatility in their efforts, collecting data in many different ways. Thus, a major strength of psychological research is its reliance on a wide assortment of methodological techniques.

It is important that any serious student of psychology learn to differentiate between nonscientific polls and opinions and the results of scientific research conducted by serious investigators. However, even carefully planned investigations should be evaluated critically: a good rule of thumb is to avoid the tendency to believe something just because it is "scientific." You may find the following checklist of questions useful in evaluating any particular piece of research:

1. Who conducted the research? Are they considered to be reputable professionals?

2. What type of methodology was used? Were scientific principles adhered to?

3. How large was the sample group, and is there any reason to suspect bias in the selection of subjects?

4. Can the results be applied to individuals other than those in the sample group? How broad can these generalizations be and still remain legitimate?

5. Is it possible that the method used to obtain information may have biased the findings? (Did the questionnaire promote false replies?

Is it likely that the artificial nature of the laboratory setting influenced subjects' responses? And so forth.)

6. Have there been any other published reports that confirm or contradict the particular study in question?

Keeping questions like these in mind is helpful in finding a middle ground between absolute trust and offhand dismissal of a given research study.

SUMMARY

REASONS FOR CONDUCTING RESEARCH

1. Three of the most common reasons why psychologists conduct research are to test a hypothesis, to solve a problem, and to confirm findings of previous research.
2. A hypothesis is a statement proposing the existence of a relationship between variables. Hypotheses are typically offered as tentative explanations for relationships or events, and they are often designed to be tested by research.
3. When psychologists publish new research findings they include details so that others may repeat the experiment to verify the results. The replication of prior research is the backbone of good science.

RESEARCH METHODS

4. Psychologists use a number of methods to study behavior. These techniques include the experimental method, surveys, the observational method, case studies, and the correlational method.
5. In experimental research, subjects are confronted with specific stimuli under precisely controlled conditions that allow their reactions to be reliably measured. The purpose of the experimental method is to discover relationships among independent and dependent variables.
6. An independent variable is a condition or factor that the experimenter manipulates; the resulting behavior that is measured and recorded is called the dependent variable.
7. Many experiments utilize both experimental groups, which consist of various groups of subjects exposed to different varieties of independent variables, and a control group composed of subjects who experience all the same conditions as subjects in the experimental group except for the key factor the researcher is evaluating.
8. Special advantages of the experimental method include control over relevant variables and opportunities to draw conclusions about cause-and-effect relationships.
9. Limitations of the experimental method include the artificial nature of the laboratory setting, which may influence subjects' behaviors, and the fact that some questions posed by psychologists do not lend themselves to experimental investigation.
10. The APA has adopted ethical guidelines for research that require, among other things, that researchers avoid procedures that might cause serious physical or mental harm to human subjects, that they protect confidentiality of the data, and that they respect a subject's right to refuse to participate at any time during the course of a study.
11. Another important research method is the survey, in which a representative group of people are questioned, via face-to-face interviews or written questionnaires, about their behaviors or attitudes.
12. Surveys are often conducted with a representative sample—that is, a sample in which critical subgroups are represented according to their incidence in the larger population that one wishes to draw conclusions about.
13. Another kind of sample, called a random sample, is selected by randomization procedures, which alone do not ensure a representative sample.
14. Potential limitations of the survey method include demographic and sex bias, improperly worded questions that bias responses, and a tendency to provide only limited insights about factors that contribute to behaviors and attitudes of specific individuals.
15. Researchers employing the observational method observe their subjects as they go about their usual activities. This often takes place in a natural setting, and when it does the research method is called naturalistic observation.
16. A potential problem with the observational method is the risk that an observer may read more into a situation than is actually there, a phenomenon called observer bias.
17. Another possible limitation of the observational method is the problem of observer effect, in which the presence of a human observer may affect the behavior being observed.
18. The case study is an in-depth exploration of either a single case or a small group of subjects who are examined individually.
19. Shortcomings of the case-study method include lack of investigative control of important variables, a potential for subjective observer bias, and a tendency for subjects to report earlier experiences inaccurately.
20. The correlational method utilizes statistical methods to assess and describe the amount and type of relationship between two variables of interest, such as the SAT scores of high-school seniors and their GPAs during the first year of college.
21. One major limitation of the correlational method is that this technique, considered alone, does not provide sufficient evidence to determine if a demonstrated correlational relationship between scores on two variables is reflective of a causal relationship or merely indicative of another factor(s) related to each of the variables.

DESCRIBING AND INTERPRETING RESEARCH FINDINGS

22. There are two kinds of statistics: descriptive and inferential. Descriptive statistics provide succinct descriptions by reducing a quantity of data to a form that is

more understandable. Inferential statistics include a variety of mathematical procedures to draw conclusions about the meaning of data.

23. Measures of central tendency—descriptive statistics that reflect the middle or central point of a distribution—include the mean, median, and mode. The mean is the arithmetic average; the median is the score that falls in the middle of a distribution; and the mode is the most frequent score.

24. Measures of variability—descriptive statistics that indicate the spread of a distribution of scores—include the range and the standard deviation. The range is the difference between the highest and lowest score, and the standard deviation is an approximate indication of the average extent to which all scores in a distribution vary from the mean.

25. Inferential statistics allows researchers to make judgments about whether their research findings are statistically significant. When scientists conclude that a research finding is statistically significant, they are merely stating, at a high level of confidence, that obtained differences in the performances of different groups of subjects is attributable to the experimental condition being manipulated by the researcher.

PART 2

BIOLOGICAL FOUNDATIONS, PERCEPTION, AND CONSCIOUSNESS

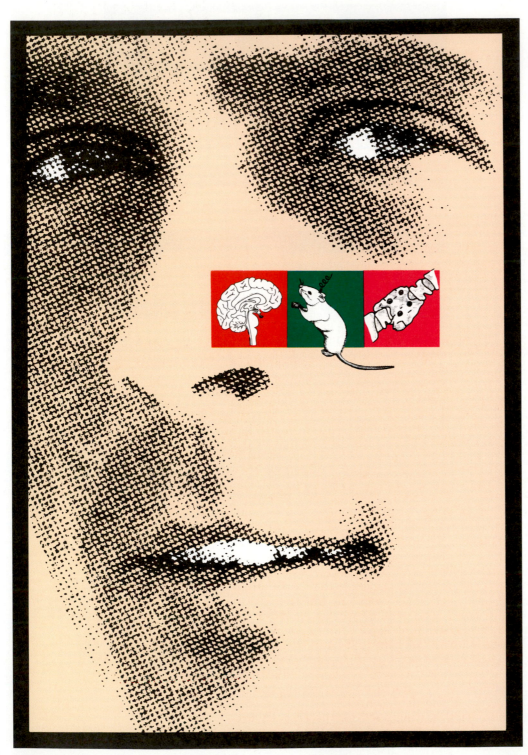

3 Biological Foundations of Behavior

The two photographs shown here are PET (positron emission tomography) scans of a live human brain. Both are views of the top of the head, with the front of the head at the top of the picture and the back of the head at the bottom. In the photograph on the left the subject's ears have been blocked, so he hears nothing. In the right photograph the subject is listening to a Sherlock Holmes story with a music background (one of Bach's Brandenburg Concertos).

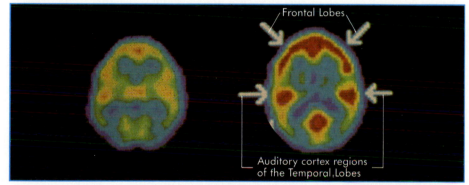

Frontal Lobes

Auditory cortex regions
of the Temporal Lobes

The different patterns in the photographs are related to activities within the brain. When we hear a sound, as in the right photograph, the neurons in a special area of our brains called the *auditory cortex* region of the *temporal lobes* become active, for they are busy processing information about the sound. (In the PET scan, a bright red or orange "glow" indicates high activity areas.) If the sounds we are listening to include the narration of a mystery story, we may try to piece together the clues—an intellectual activity that involves regions of the *frontal lobes*, another area of the brain. The PET scan lets us "see" such functions as thinking or listening by revealing areas of high activity in the brain (Mazziotta et al., 1982). It is one of several new techniques that physiological psychologists use to learn about the relationship between behavior and biological functions. (The method by which these photographs were produced will be discussed later in this chapter, along with other techniques for studying the brain.)

The PET scan provides a good starting point for this chapter, for it illustrates the basic concept of physiological psychology: that human behaviors, thoughts, memories, emotions, and even qualities such as intelligence and creativity are based on biological processes that take place within and between cells. We still do not have a clear picture of where or how each of these functions happens. New techniques and new discoveries are being made every year, however, and many scientists believe that it is only a matter of time before even complex behaviors and emotions can be understood at the cell level.

This chapter provides a very broad overview of what we know about the biological foundations of behavior. Biological structures—individual neurons, the central and peripheral nervous systems, and the endocrine systems—are examined to see how they influence or regulate behaviors. We begin with a look at the nervous system.

OVERVIEW OF THE NERVOUS SYSTEM: ORGANIZATION AND FUNCTION

All of our activities—sensing, perceiving, moving, feeling, thinking, or remembering—depend upon the functioning of our nervous systems. Although the brain is the hub of the nervous system, it is by no means its sole component. The nervous system of humans and all other vertebrates (organisms with a spinal cord encased in bone) consists of two major parts: the central nervous system (CNS) and the peripheral nervous system (PNS). The PNS is further subdivided into the somatic and autonomic nervous systems. These components are all shown in Figure 3.1. We shall examine each of these parts in depth after a preliminary overview.

The **central nervous system (CNS)** consists of the brain and the spinal cord, which are the most protected organs of the body. Both are encased in bones and surrounded by protective membranes called *meninges*. The CNS plays a central role in coordinating and integrating all bodily functions. It acts as an intermediary between stimuli we receive and our responses. For example, if your bare foot comes in contact with something hairy and wiggly when you pull on a shoe, this alarming message will travel through nerves in your legs, enter your spinal cord, reach your brain, and trigger a rapid response.

In the situation just described, the CNS acts as a processor of incoming and outgoing messages. But the brain also sends commands directly to various parts of our bodies without first receiving an incoming stimulus. For instance, the decision to put on your shoes in the first place may have been the result of an urge to go outdoors that was unrelated to any immediate stimulus.

Our brains can also send commands to glands or organs. For instance, if we are dressed too warmly in an overheated classroom, we will probably begin to perspire. This response is mediated by the hypothalamus, a small structure in our brains that serves many critical functions including temperature regulation. When our bodies become too hot, the hypothalamus signals our sweat glands to perspire, a process that helps to lower our body temperature.

Although the CNS occupies the commanding position in the nervous system, it could neither receive stimuli nor carry out its own directives without the **peripheral nervous system (PNS),** which transmits messages to and from the central nervous system. The peripheral nervous system is subdivided into two functional parts, the somatic nervous system and the autonomic nervous system, both of which will be discussed later in this chapter. Before looking further at both the central and peripheral nervous systems, it is helpful to have an understanding of the building blocks that are the basis of the entire nervous system—neurons.

All of our activities—sensing, perceiving, moving, feeling, thinking, or remembering—depend upon the functioning of our nervous systems.

NEURONS: BASIC UNITS OF THE NERVOUS SYSTEM

Our bodies are made up of trillions of living cells including blood cells, skin cells, muscle cells, and bone cells. The cells of particular interest in this

FIGURE 3.1   DIVISIONS OF THE NERVOUS SYSTEM

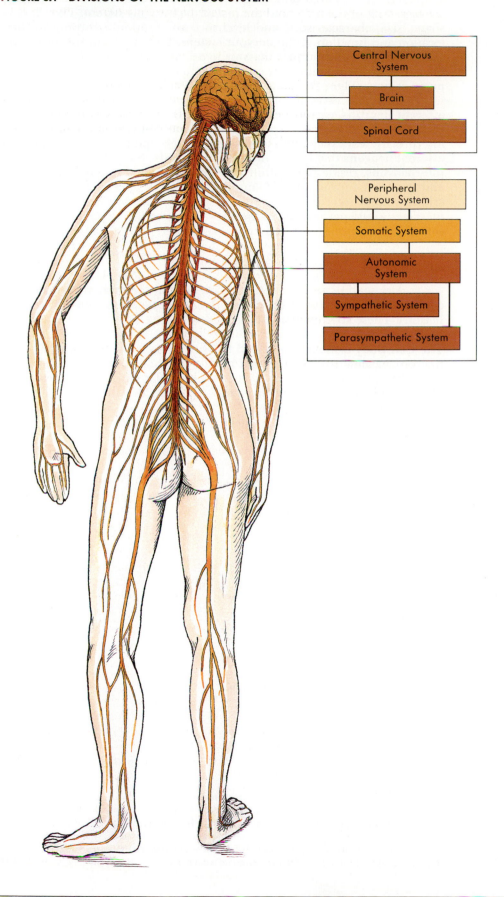

Central Nervous System

Brain

Spinal Cord

Peripheral Nervous System

Somatic System

Autonomic System

Sympathetic System

Parasympathetic System

chapter are the cells of the nervous system. These cells, called **neurons,** are the basic unit of the brain and the rest of the nervous system. They vary in shape, size, characteristics, and level of concentration according to their location and function in the nervous system. The brain, for instance, contains the most concentrated mass of neurons. It is impossible to say how many neurons it contains, but estimates range from around 10 billion to as many as one trillion (Nauta & Feirtag, 1979).

There are three major classes of neurons. Some, called **sensory** or **afferent neurons,** carry messages to the CNS from receptors in the skin, ears, nose, eyes, and so forth. The brain and sometimes the spinal cord interpret these messages and send appropriate responses through **motor** or **efferent neurons** that lead to muscles and glands. A third class of neurons, **interneurons,** reside only within the central nervous system. Since motor and sensory neurons rarely communicate directly, interneurons play the critical role of intermediary. Without these connecting neurons, sensory messages would never result in the appropriate bodily responses. Interneurons also communicate directly with each other.

NEURON STRUCTURE

Although neurons vary in size, shape, and function, they share four common structures: the cell body, the dendrites, the axon, and the terminal buttons. These structures are illustrated in Figure 3.2.

The Cell Body or Soma　The **cell body** or soma is the largest part of the neuron. It contains structures that handle metabolic functions; it also contains the nucleus, which holds genetic information. The cell body can receive impulses from other neurons, although the dendrites are the primary receptors.

FIGURE 3.2　A SCHEMATIC DRAWING OF A NEURON

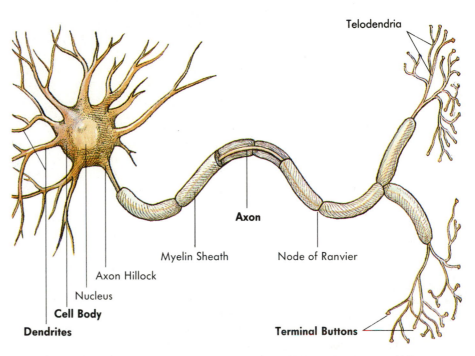

Telodendria

Axon

Myelin Sheath

Node of Ranvier

Axon Hillock

Nucleus

Cell Body

Dendrites

Terminal Buttons

Neural messages from surrounding neurons are typically received by branched fibers called dendrites and then passed down to the cell body, the portion of the neuron where metabolic functions take place. The neural signal then moves on through the axon, an elongated, slender fiber that is the transmitting end of the neuron. Terminal buttons at the branched endings of the axon release chemical substances (neurotransmitters) that enable the nerve impulse to cross to adjacent neurons.

The Dendrites   Neurons typically receive neural messages at one end and pass them on at the other end. The part of the neuron that receives most transmitted signals is a collection of fibers called **dendrites** that extend out from the cell body like branches of a tree. (The word dendrite comes from the Greek word for tree.) Dendrites may receive information from a few to thousands of surrounding neurons. The more extensive the neuron's network of dendrites, the more connections can be made with other neurons. (Interneurons in the brain typically contain far more dendritic fibers than neurons in the spinal cord or the peripheral nervous system.) Signals received by the dendrites pass down the dendritic branches to the cell body, which in turn passes them through the axon.

The Axon   The **axon** is a slender, extended fiber that takes a signal from the cell body and conducts it along its entire length, which may range from two or more feet in spinal cord and PNS neurons to a tiny fraction of an inch in brain neurons. (The axon may divide into two or more major branches called *collaterals*, thereby increasing its capacity to communicate with other neurons.)

The Terminal Buttons   The transmitting end of the axon consists of small branches called *telodendria* that end in swollen bulblike structures known as **terminal buttons.** The terminal buttons release chemical substances that enable nerve impulses to cross from one neuron to adjacent neurons, in a complex process that we will look at next.

HOW NEURONS COMMUNICATE

People often think of the nervous system as a vast, complex network of interconnected wirelike structures. However, the multitude of neural circuits or pathways within the central nervous system are not at all like electric wires. Instead of a continuous filament, these circuits are made up of perhaps hundreds of thousands of individual neurons, and in order for a message to travel from neuron to neuron, it must move from the terminal buttons at the end of one neuron's axon to the dendrites or cell body of an adjacent neuron. The process by which impulses are transmitted in the CNS is not just electrical, as in a wire. It also involves chemical substances.

Within the peripheral nervous system, messages are transmitted along the extended axonal fibers of both motor and sensory neurons that are contained within bundles of neural fibers called *nerves*. These fibers extend as continuous structures from sensory receptors or muscles to the CNS. For example, a sensory message from a pain receptor in the skin of your finger is transmitted along a single axonal fiber that extends the length of your arm to a point where it enters the spinal cord and transfers its message to an interneuron.

NEURON ELECTRICAL ACTIVITY

Like all cells, neurons are surrounded by a membrane. This membrane acts as a kind of skin that permits the cell to maintain an internal environment different from the fluid outside the membrane. On both sides of the cell membrane are many particles called *ions* which carry either a positive or a negative electrical charge. Ions that are particularly important in electrical conduction are negatively charged organic ions (An−) and chlorine ions (Cl−) and positively charged sodium ions (Na+) and potassium ions (K+). If the cell membrane did not act as a barrier, these ions would be equally distributed both inside and outside of the neuron. However, some charged particles, such as the negative organic ions, are too large to pass through the cell membrane to the surrounding fluid. The membrane is semipermeable to other, smaller ions, although some pass through more freely than others. (For instance, potassium ions pass through more easily than do sodium ions.)

Thus, the negative and positive charges are unequal on either side of the membrane, and its interior has a negative electrical potential with respect to its exterior. This is due primarily to a high concentration of positively charged sodium ions outside the membrane. A neuron "at rest" (that is, not transmitting a nerve impulse) contains a net negative charge of about −70 millivolts (70/1,000 of a volt) relative to the outside environment. The membrane is said to be in a *polarized state*.

This differential charge gives the "resting" neuron a state of potential energy known as the **resting potential.** In other words, it is in a constant state of readiness to be activated by an impulse from an adjacent neuron. Maintaining this resting potential allows the neuron to store the energy that it utilizes when it transmits an impulse (Kolb & Whishaw, 1985).

The resting potential is disturbed when an impulse is received from another neuron. What happens then? Perhaps the best way to understand what happens when a neuron fires is to break this event down into two processes. First, the impulse is transmitted within the neuron from the dendrites on one end to the terminal buttons on the other. Second, the impulse passes from one neuron to another neuron. The first process is primarily electrical; the second, primarily chemical.

WHAT HAPPENS WHEN A NEURON FIRES? ELECTRICAL PROCESSES

When the dendrites or cell body of a neuron receive an impulse from neighboring neurons, the cell membrane undergoes a change in permeability at the point of stimulation. This change allows more positive sodium ions to flow into the cell. The result is that the resting potential, usually measured at −70 millivolts, is disturbed. The membrane is *depolarized* at the point where the signal was received, and the depolarization remains local until the charge changes to about −60 millivolts. At this point, the depolarization begins to spread along the dendrite or cell body away from the point of stimulation.

These voltage changes are called **graded potentials,** and the graded potentials sent along the dendrites vary in strength with the intensity of stimulation received. All fade with increasing distance from the point of stimulation, and unless they are combined with other graded potentials (as when a neuron receives several impulses simultaneously), it is unlikely that the neuron's voltage change will become sufficient to cause the impulse to be transmitted to other neurons.

The determination of whether or not a graded potential is sufficient to transmit an impulse through an axon is made at the *axon hillock,* a specialized region of the cell body near the base of the axon (see Figure 3.3). Like a tiny computer, the axon hillock combines and totals all the graded potentials that reach it. If the sum of these graded potentials reaches a sufficient magnitude or *threshold* (the minimum voltage change sufficient to activate a response), the axon hillock triggers a sudden depolarization of the axon membrane, allowing charged ions to flow across its surface. This generates an electrical signal that flows along the entire surface of the axon to the telodendria and terminal buttons (Wang & Freeman, 1987). This electrical signal is called an **action potential,** and it has been defined as "the event that initiates the release of transmitter substances from the terminal buttons, thus making them 'talk' to the receiving cells" (Carlson, 1981, p. 47).

Unlike the graded potential, the strength of an action potential does not vary according to the degree of stimulation. Once a nerve impulse is triggered within an axon, it is transmitted the entire length of the axon with no loss of intensity. Partial action potentials or nerve impulses do not occur; thus, an axon is said to conduct *without decrement*. Because of this, the nerve impulse in the axon is said to follow the **all-or-none law.** According to this

FIGURE 3.3   PASSAGE OF AN ELECTRICAL IMPULSE THROUGH A NEURON

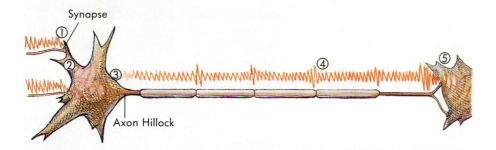

Synapse

Axon Hillock

(1) Impulses are received. Membrane at receptor site is depolarized. (2) When depolarization at receptor point reaches −60mv., graded potential is sent along dendrite. (3) Combined charge of graded potential signals at axon hillock triggers depolarization of entire axon membrane. (4) Action potential flows along surface of axon to terminal buttons. (5) Terminal buttons release transmitter substances which convey neural impulse to adjacent neurons.

law, if the sum of the graded potentials reaches a threshold, there will be an impulse; if the threshold is not reached, an action potential will not occur.

QUESTIONING THE ALL-OR-NONE LAW

According to the all-or-none law, a neuron fires at only one level of intensity. How, then, is it possible to distinguish between different levels of stimulus intensity (for instance, a loud noise and a soft sound, or a light or heavy touch)? Consider this question before reading on.

The answer to this question lies in the fact that even though a single neuron's impulse level is always the same, two important variables may still change: the number of neurons affected by an impulse, and the speed with which neurons fire. Very weak stimuli may trigger impulses in only a few neurons, whereas very strong stimuli may cause thousands of neurons to fire. The rate at which neurons fire can also vary greatly, from fewer than 100 times per second for weak stimuli to as often as 1,000 times per second. Thus, the combination of how many neurons fire and how often they fire allows us to distinguish different intensities of stimuli.

The speed with which an impulse travels through a neuron varies with the properties of the axon, ranging from less than one meter per second to as fast as 100 meters per second (roughly 224 miles per hour). At least two important factors affect speed. One is the resistance to current along the axon: there is an inverse relationship between resistance and impulse speed, so that speed is reduced as resistance increases. Resistance is most effectively decreased by an increase in axon size, which helps explain why large axons such as those in PNS neurons tend to conduct impulses at a faster rate than do small axons.

However, if the nervous system had to depend only on axon size to transmit impulses quickly, there would not be enough room in our bodies for all the large axons we would need. Fortunately, a second property also helps to speed the transmission of nerve impulses. Specialized cells, called **glia cells,** wrap around some axons, forming an insulating cover called a **myelin sheath.** (One type of glia cells, the *oligodendrocytes*, forms the myelin within the CNS. In the PNS the insulating sheaths are built from another type of glia cells known as *Schwann cells*.) Between each glia cell the axon membrane is exposed by a small gap called a **node of Ranvier,** as shown in Figure 3.2.

A person with multiple sclerosis often experiences a weakness or loss of control over the limbs caused by the progressive breakdown of the myelin sheaths. Fortunately, modern technology has provided ways for people with this disease to live productive, fulfilling lives.

In these myelinated neurons, nerve impulses do not travel smoothly down the axon. Instead, they jump from node to node, in a process called *saltatory conduction* (from the Latin *saltare*, meaning to leap). Saltatory conduction is extremely efficient in that a small myelinated axon can conduct a nerve impulse just as quickly as an unmyelinated axon 30 times larger. Given the critical importance of myelin in the nervous system, you can better understand the devastating effects of certain diseases, such as multiple sclerosis (MS), that involve progressive breakdown in these insulating sheaths. In MS, the loss of myelination may short-circuit or delay the transmission of signals from the brain to the muscles of the arms and legs. As a consequence, a person with MS often experiences a weakness or loss of control over the limbs.

WHAT HAPPENS WHEN A NEURON FIRES? NEUROTRANSMITTERS AND SYNAPSES

The transmission of an electrical impulse from one end of a neuron to the other provides only a partial explanation of how messages are transmitted. When an electrical nerve impulse reaches the end of an axon, it cannot flow directly into other neurons. That is because there is a space between neurons, known as the *synaptic gap* or *cleft*. The space is minuscule, generally no more than five-millionths of an inch across, but the electrical impulse does not bridge it alone. A chemical process is necessary in bridging the synaptic gap.

The synaptic gap is part of the **synapse,** a larger area that also includes the parts of both the sending and receiving neurons' membranes that are involved in transmitting the impulse (see Figure 3.4). With few exceptions, synapses transmit messages in only one direction, from the terminal buttons of one neuron to the dendrite or cell body of the next. Therefore, different terms are used to describe the membranes on each side of the synapse: the membrane around the terminal button of the transmitting neuron is called the *presynaptic membrane*, while that of the receiving neuron is called the *postsynaptic membrane*.

Many years ago some scientists speculated that impulses were transmitted from neuron to neuron when something like an electric spark jumped the synaptic gap. We now know that this is not the case: neurons communicate primarily through the release of chemicals. These chemical messengers, called **neurotransmitters,** are contained within tiny sacs in the axon terminal buttons called *synaptic vesicles*. When the axon fires, some of the synaptic vesicles migrate to the presynaptic membrane, where they release their contents into the synaptic gap (Cooper et al., 1986; Wang & Freeman, 1987). The total amount of neurotransmitters released is a function of how many times the axon fires. More intense stimulation produces a greater frequency of signals, which in turn increases the amount of neurotransmitters released.

What keeps the supply of neurotransmitters from being exhausted? There are three answers to this question. First, the raw materials used in the manufacture of neurotransmitters are constantly being replenished by the cell body. Second, some neurotransmitters are broken down by enzyme action once they have accomplished their function. Their breakdown products then reenter the terminal buttons to be recycled for further use. Finally, in many cases the transmitter substance is retrieved intact, in a process called *reuptake*.

The neurotransmitters interact with receptors in the postsynaptic cell membrane to change its electrical potential. If the change is sufficient to depolarize the cell membrane, a graded potential is initiated, thus beginning the cycle outlined earlier in Figure 3.3.

As much as scientists know about the electrochemical process of transferring nerve impulses, the neurotransmitters themselves have been hard to identify. Table 3.1 presents a list of substances believed to be neurotransmitters, as well as the functions they are believed to perform. Although this list is not definitive, all of the substances it identifies meet the following criteria:

They are contained in the synaptic vesicles of an axon's terminal buttons.

They are known to be released into the synaptic gap when the neuron fires.

They attach to receptor sites on the postsynaptic membrane.

New neurotransmitters and other brain chemicals are still being discovered and investigated, a trend that has been central to the development of the science of *molecular neurobiology*, a field devoted in part to a study of the molecular bases of behavior. Accompanying this new field has been an important shift in the way many scientists think about the brain. Until recently, both laypersons and many brain scientists viewed things like thinking, feeling, and remembering as something more than a complex interplay among a variety of brain chemicals. However, many researchers are becoming increasingly convinced that molecular neurobiology will eventually explain most if not all complex brain processes in molecular terms.

HOW DOES THE BRAIN AVOID OVERLOAD?

We have learned that individual neurons in our bodies can receive and transmit impulses to hundreds or perhaps thousands of neighboring neurons, and that the greatest concentration of neurons is located in the brain. Why doesn't the brain become overloaded with impulses that are transmitted and retransmitted from neuron to neuron in its close quarters? Before reading on, see if you can think of a plausible explanation for how the brain avoids overload.

The answer to this question lies in the fact that neurotransmitters may act in more than one way. You may have noticed in Table 3.1 that different neurotransmitter substances seem to have different effects. Instead of transmission of a signal from one area to another, the function of some neurotransmitters is listed as *inhibition* (that is, they restrain or suppress the transmission of neural impulses). This may seem contrary to logic, especially since we have just seen that neurotransmitters are essential for the transmission of neural impulses. Sometimes, however, neurotransmitters have just the opposite effect, as we will see in the following discussion.

FIGURE 3.4   A SYNAPSE

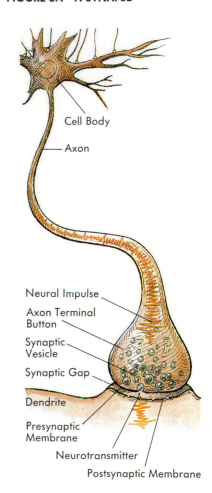

Cell Body

Axon

Neural Impulse

Axon Terminal Button

Synaptic Vesicle

Synaptic Gap

Dendrite

Presynaptic Membrane

Neurotransmitter

Postsynaptic Membrane

Neurons communicate primarily through the release of chemical messengers called neurotransmitters into the synaptic gap. The synaptic gap is part of the synapse, an area that also includes parts of both the sending and receiving neurons' membranes. When a neural message reaches the axon terminal button of the transmitting neuron, some of the synaptic vesicles migrate to the presynaptic membrane where they release their contents (neurotransmitters) into the synaptic gap. The neurotransmitters then interact with receptors in the postsynaptic membrane of the receiving dendrite to change its electrical potential, thus initiating a continuation of the neural message.

TABLE 3.1 *Chemicals Believed To Be Neurotransmitters*

Probable Neurotransmitter	Location	Indicated Effects
Acetycholine	Brain, spinal cord, and target organs activated by parasympathetic nervous system	Excitation in brain. Excitation or inhibition in target organs. Appears to be essential for movement of muscles. Also important in learning and memory.
Biogenic Amines		
Dopamine	Brain	Inhibition. Found in brain regions involved in voluntary movement, emotional arousal, memory, and learning.
Histamine	Throughout CNS and PNS	Unclear. Has been implicated in severe depression.
Norepinephrine	Brain, spinal cord, and certain target organs activated by sympathetic nervous system	Inhibition in brain. Inhibition or excitation in target organs. Located in brain circuits involved in emotional arousal, wakefulness, eating, memory, and learning.
Serotonin	Brain and spinal cord	Inhibition or excitation. Found in brain regions that regulate sleep and influence emotional arousal.
Amino Acids		
Aspartic Acid	Brain and spinal cord	Excitation.
Gamma-amino-butyric acid (GABA)	Brain and spinal cord	Inhibition. Appears to be the primary inhibitory neurotransmitter in the brain.
Glycine	Spinal cord	Inhibition. Appears to be the primary inhibitory neurotransmitter in the spinal cord.
Neuropeptides (perhaps hundreds of these small chains of amino acids involved in neuro-transmission)	Brain	Mostly inhibitory, but excitatory in some regions. Believed to influence such things as eating, drinking, sexual behavior, sleep, temperature regulation, pain reduction, and responses to stress.

EPSPs AND IPSPs: TRANSMISSION AND INHIBITION OF IMPULSES

The postsynaptic membrane of the receiving neuron contains specialized receptor sites that respond to a variety of neurotransmitters. Neurotransmitters act on these receptor sites to produce a rapid change in the permeability of the postsynaptic membrane. Depending on the receptor site and the type of neurotransmitter, this change in permeability can either excite or inhibit action potentials in the receiving neuron.

In simplified terms, neurotransmitters exert their effects by opening "gates" or "channels" in the postsynaptic membrane, letting ions of one kind or another pass through. If positive-charged sodium ions enter, the membrane is excited or depolarized and graded potentials are released. Neurotransmitters that cause these changes are called *excitatory neurotransmitters*, and their effects are referred to as **excitatory postsynaptic potentials,** or **EPSPs.** Conversely, if positive-charged potassium ions pass to the outside of the postsynaptic membrane or negatively charged chloride ions enter, the membrane is inhibited from releasing a graded potential (a process called hyperpolarization). Neurotransmitters that act in this way are called *inhibitory neurotransmitters*, and their effects are called **inhibitory postsynaptic potentials,** or **IPSPs.**

Since hundreds or even thousands of axon terminals may form synapses with any one neuron, EPSPs and IPSPs may be present at the same time. The combination of all these excitatory and inhibitory signals determines whether or not the receiving neuron will fire. For an action potential to occur, EPSPs must not only predominate; they must do so to the extent of reaching the neuron's threshold. To prevent this from happening, there merely need to be enough IPSPs present to prevent the algebraic sum of EPSPs and IPSPs from reaching the threshold of depolarization.

Some neurotransmitters seem to be exclusively excitatory or inhibitory, while others seem capable of producing either effect under different circumstances. When transmitters have both capabilities, the postsynaptic receptor site determines what the effect will be, so that these neurotransmitters may have an inhibitory effect at one synapse and an excitatory effect at another.

NEUROTRANSMITTERS AND BEHAVIOR

Although the information about cell structures that we have discussed so far may seem like a collection of dry facts, it relates directly to our behavior. The behavioral changes that are associated with schizophrenia, depression, and the use of some drugs provide some of the clearest illustrations of this relationship.

Schizophrenia *Schizophrenia* is a severe psychological disorder characterized by disturbed thought processes, delusions, hallucinations, and emotional distortions. In many cases, the most bizarre symptoms of schizophrenia can be controlled by drugs such as chlorpromazine and reserpine, both of which have a similar effect: they inhibit the effects of *dopamine*, a neurotransmitter found in the brain (Davison & Neale, 1986; Lipper, 1985). This finding has led some psychologists to hypothesize that the disorder may be linked to excessive levels of dopamine or above-normal reactivity to this neurotransmitter (Carlsson, 1977; Langer et al., 1981)—an argument that was supported by one study that found an abnormal number of dopamine receptors in the brains of some schizophrenics (Crow et al., 1978).

Neurotransmitter systems are complex, and no conclusions have been reached about the relationship of schizophrenia to dopamine (Davison & Neale, 1986; Goldstein et al., 1986; Kolb & Whishaw, 1985). Nevertheless, it seems possible that at least some symptoms of this disorder may be related to neurotransmitter levels.

Depression Other studies have linked another disorder, *depression*, to two other neurotransmitters: *norepinephrine* and *serotonin*. A group of drugs called tricyclics, among the most successful in relieving depression, are believed to increase the availability of both these neurotransmitters in certain areas of the brain (Colusanti, 1982a). Recent research suggests that the antidepressant effects of these drugs may be related to increased sensitivity of the receptors for these two neurotransmitters rather than a mere change in the actual levels of these brain chemicals (Charney et al., 1984; Heniger et al., 1983). Since studies (Carlson, 1981) have linked norepinephrine and serotonin to people's positive feelings, it seems possible that either insufficient brain levels of these chemicals or decreased responsivity to these neurotransmitters may be related to depression. As with theories about dopamine and schizophrenia, however, the evidence is far from conclusive. Chapter 14 explores the evidence linking neurotransmitter abnormalities to depression, schizophrenia, and some other psychological disorders.

Drug-related Behaviors   A wide variety of commonly used drugs have the effect of changing thought processes, emotional states, or behavior (Snyder, 1986). Solomon Snyder, an expert on neurotransmitters, recently stated that "Virtually every drug that alters mental function does so by interacting with a neurotransmitter system in the brain" (1984, p. 23). This may happen in a variety of ways. Some drugs increase neural activity by releasing neurotransmitters from the presynaptic vesicles; some actually mimic certain excitatory transmitters. Other drugs may prevent transmission of neural impulses by binding or attaching themselves to receptors on the postsynaptic membrane, thus preventing the kind of contact between excitatory transmitters and postsynaptic receptors that is necessary to trigger EPSPs. Still other drugs interfere with the reuptake of intact chemicals or the recycling of their breakdown products. Chapter 5 considers how several widely known drugs modify the activity of neurotransmitters.

NATURAL BRAIN OPIATES

One of the most interesting groups of druglike substances is produced in the brain itself. In 1975 an English research team published a paper announcing their discovery of two morphinelike factors produced by the brain (Hughes et al., 1975), and since this time, other similar substances have been discovered. In recent years all these natural opiates have been collectively labeled **endogenous opiates** (endogenous meaning from within). These natural brain opiates, which include *endorphins*, *enkephalins*, and *dynorphins*, are part of a family of neurotransmitters known as *neuropeptides*. They act as neurotransmitters, and they also act to inhibit or increase the activity of other transmitters (Snyder & Childers, 1979).

Receptors for endogenous opiates are widely distributed throughout most of the brain, suggesting that many brain functions are influenced by the actions of these substances (Panksepp, 1986). Extensive research has linked the brain opiates to an array of behavioral and mental processes, including inducing a sense of well-being and euphoria, counteracting the influence of stress, modulating food and liquid intake, facilitating learning and memory, and reducing pain (Olson et al., 1986; Panksepp, 1986). Medical science is particularly interested in the pain-reducing properties of endogenous opiates, some of which may be as much as 100 times stronger than morphine. Researchers are hopeful that one day a synthetic version of these powerful brain chemicals will be developed for use in pain-control programs.

THE BRAIN AND SPINAL CORD

Suppose you are in an accident that causes traumatic injuries, leaving you brain-dead (incapable of higher mental processes such as consciousness and thinking). Another person being treated in the same hospital is in the terminal stages of a cancer that has ravaged the body but left the brain intact. Suppose also that medical science has advanced to the point that whole brain transplants are possible. A decision is reached to replace your useless brain with the healthy brain of the other patient, which is preserved at the moment of death. Operation successfully completed, you recover and are discharged from the hospital.

Are you still *you*, or are you now the other patient? Or are you a composite of the two? Consider what would happen if you ran into an old friend on the street after the operation. Your friend would recognize you, but to your new brain, your friend would be a stranger. Furthermore, your home, your parents, all your previous life experiences would be alien to you. In addition, you would take on the personality of the brain donor, including his or her intellectual abilities. Who are you, then?

This question was recently addressed to a group of students who concluded (with our agreement) that the transplant patient would be the cancer victim and not some composite, hybrid person. If your brain were transplanted to another body, you would still retain your memories, your style of relating to others, your personality traits—everything that makes you a unique human being. We are our brains. (By the way, as outlandish as the idea of a brain transplant may sound, research on grafting healthy tissue into diseased brains has already begun. See the following Health Psychology and Life discussion, "Brain Grafts.")

BRAIN GRAFTS

Diseases or injuries that destroy vital brain tissue can have a devastating effect on people's ability to function normally. Once damaged, brain cells usually do not regain their capacity to guide vital functions. Therefore, unless damaged neurons can be trained to take over impaired functions, the long-term prospects for recovery are often poor. However, a new line of research has provided some startling results suggesting that there may soon be help for some brain-damaged patients.

Until recently, many brain scientists might have dismissed the idea of grafting healthy tissue into damaged brains. Actually this idea is not at all far-fetched, considering that most areas of the brain are protected from attack by the body's immune system. (Something called the *blood-brain barrier* provides this protection.) In the last few years, evidence from several investigations has raised the possibility that such grafts may provide at least a partial remedy or cure for disorders such as Parkinson's disease or Alzheimer's disease, both of which are associated with the death of brain cells.

Most of the brain-graft studies thus far have been conducted with nonhuman animals. In one study, dopamine-producing cells in the brains of mice were destroyed, producing a loss of motor control similar to that in Parkinson's disease (a common illness characterized by difficulties in movement, body rigidity, and tremors, caused by a progressive deterioration of dopamine-producing cells in the brain). Researchers obtained healthy dopamine-producing cells from the brains of mouse embryos and grafted them adjacent to destroyed cells in the damaged brains. These grafted cells were not rejected, and they soon began to produce dopamine. The mice recovered from their artificially induced Parkinson's disease. In a related study, rats with frontal lobe damage received grafted tissues obtained from the brains of rat fetuses. Here again, the impaired functions showed remarkable recovery (Labbe et al., 1983).

Recently a research team at Emory University headed by neurosurgeon Ray Bakay (1985) reported success in reversing Parkinson's disease symptoms in monkeys by grafting cells from monkey fetuses into the brains of affected animals.

There have been efforts to apply these same techniques to humans. For example, a team of Swedish researchers grafted dopamine-producing cells into the brains of some Parkinson's disease patients. To avoid the ethical implications of using human fetal cells, this team grafted dopamine-producing cells from their patients' own adrenal glands. While the symptoms of these patients were not reduced, there was an apparent slowing of the progression of the disease (Backlund et al., 1985).

More recently, a team of Mexican medical researchers used a surgical technique different from that of the Swedish group and reported marked improvements in two young men suffering from incapacitating Parkinson's disease. Both of these individuals were also provided grafts of dopamine-producing tissue from their own adrenal glands (Madrazo et al., 1987). One of the Mexican patients, who was wheelchair-bound prior to receiving the brain graft, was able to play soccer with his young son 10 months after the surgery.

The Mexican researchers' success has stimulated interest in this new approach among American researchers, who are anxious to test the validity of this method (Moore, 1987). At the time of this writing, neurosurgical teams at four major medical centers in the United States have recently completed surgical grafting procedures based on the model provided by the Mexican team (Lewin, 1987). We wait with cautious optimism to see if the results of these operations—and those that will follow—will ultimately confirm the benefits of grafting healthy tissue into damaged brains.

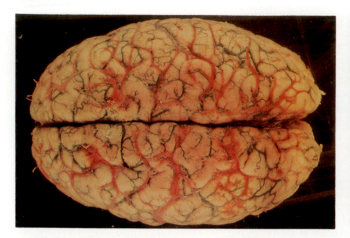 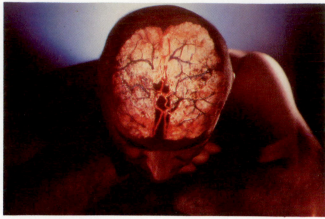

FIGURE 3.5   THE HUMAN BRAIN   Viewed from this perspective, with the top of the skull removed, only the cerebral cortex covering of the two cerebral hemispheres is visible.

A LOOK AT THE BRAIN

The average human brain weighs roughly three pounds and is about the size of a grapefruit. Yet it can store more information than many great libraries combined, and its communication network has more potential interconnections between cells than the number of atoms in our solar system. How does the brain work? How do electrical impulses and chemical transmissions translate to memories, creative insights, intelligence, and feelings? The answers to these questions are still far from complete, but we are piecing more and more clues together. Much of what we know has to do with the brain's physical structure.

If the top of a person's skull were removed so that you could look straight down on the brain, you would see something like Figure 3.5. In its natural state, the human brain looks much like a soft, wrinkled walnut, its outer surface filled with crevices and folds. The left and right sides appear to be separated by a long, deep cleft (called the *longitudinal fissure*) that runs from the front to the back. The area of the brain visible from the top is known as the **cerebrum,** and it is divided into two sides or **cerebral hemispheres** which, while not precisely identical, are almost mirror images of each other.

Under the cerebrum are many other structures, as shown in Figure 3.6. Starting from the spinal cord and working roughly upward through the base of the brain, these include the medulla, the pons, the cerebellum, the reticular formation, the structures of the limbic system, the hypothalamus, and the thalamus.

THE SPINAL CORD

The *spinal cord* is often overlooked in discussions of the biological bases of behavior, since the brain occupies the commanding position in the CNS. However, the spinal cord fills the very important function of conveying messages to and from the brain.

Housed within a hollow tubelike structure composed of a series of bones called *vertebrae*, the spinal cord looks something like a long, white, smooth rope extending from the neck to the small of the back. Along the length of the spinal cord are spinal nerves that branch out between pairs of vertebrae. These nerves connect with various sensory organs, muscles, and glands served by the peripheral nervous system. The spinal nerves occur in 31 matched pairs, with one nerve of each pair connected to the right side of the spinal cord and its counterpart connected to the left side. Thus, the spinal cord can help coordinate the two sides of your body.

Kicking your leg when your knee is tapped is a rapid automatic reflex controlled by centers within the spinal cord and does not require brain processing.

FIGURE 3.6   THREE VIEWS OF THE HUMAN BRAIN SHOWING THE LOCATION OF MAJOR STRUCTURES AND AREAS

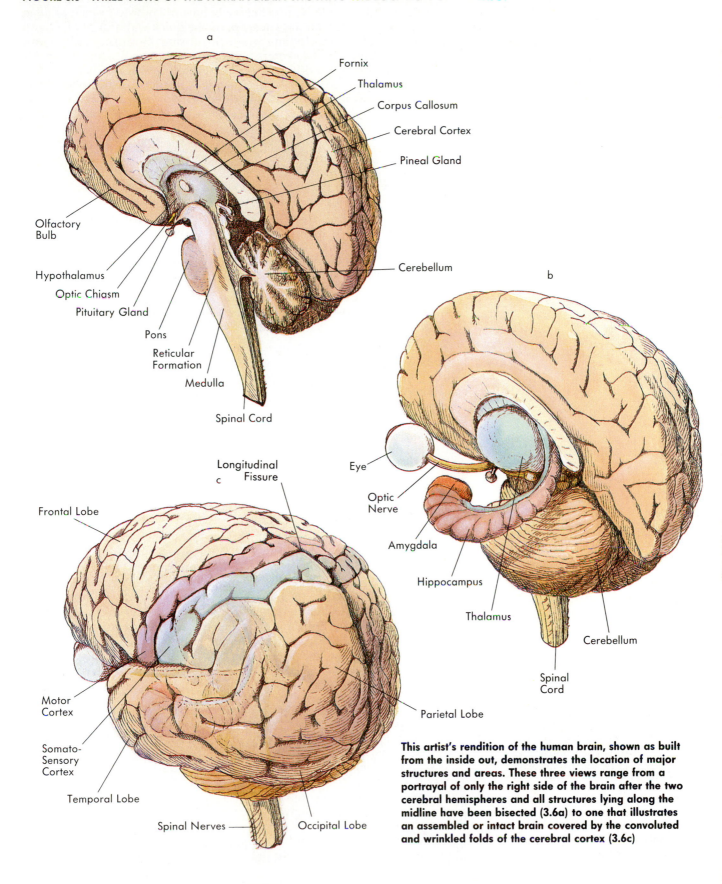

a

Fornix
Thalamus
Corpus Callosum
Cerebral Cortex
Pineal Gland

Olfactory Bulb

Hypothalamus

Optic Chiasm

Pituitary Gland

Pons

Reticular Formation

Medulla

Spinal Cord

Cerebellum

b

Longitudinal Fissure

c

Eye

Optic Nerve

Amygdala

Hippocampus

Thalamus

Cerebellum

Spinal Cord

Frontal Lobe

Motor Cortex

Somato-Sensory Cortex

Temporal Lobe

Spinal Nerves

Occipital Lobe

Parietal Lobe

This artist's rendition of the human brain, shown as built from the inside out, demonstrates the location of major structures and areas. These three views range from a portrayal of only the right side of the brain after the two cerebral hemispheres and all structures lying along the midline have been bisected (3.6a) to one that illustrates an assembled or intact brain covered by the convoluted and wrinkled folds of the cerebral cortex (3.6c)

All complex behaviors require integration and coordination at the level of the brain. Certain basic reflexive behaviors, however (such as a leg jerk in response to a tap on the kneecap, or the quick withdrawal of a hand from a hot stove), do not require brain processing. Both are rapid, automatic reflexes controlled by centers within the spinal cord. Different parts of the spinal cord control different reflexes: hand withdrawal is controlled by the upper spinal cord, whereas the knee-jerk response is controlled by an area in the lower cord. The brain is not directly involved in controlling these simple reflexive responses, but it is clearly aware of what action has transpired.

THE MEDULLA

The **medulla** is the lowest part of the brain, located just above the spinal cord. This structure is in a well-protected location, deep and low within the brain—which is fortunate, since it contains centers that control many vital life-support functions such as breathing, heartbeat, and blood pressure. Even the slightest damage in a critical region of the medulla can cause death. The medulla also plays an important role in regulating other reflexive, automatic physiological functions such as sneezing, coughing, and vomiting.

THE PONS

The **pons** is a large bulge in the lower brain core, just above the medulla. In addition to containing the reticular formation (to be discussed shortly), which runs though its central core, the pons plays an important role in fine-tuning motor messages as they travel from the motor area of the cerebral cortex down through the pons to the cerebellum. Species-typical behaviors (such as the feeding patterns of a particular breed of animals) have been shown to be strongly influenced by the pons, which seems to "program" the patterns of muscle movement that produce these behaviors.

The pons also seems to play a role in processing some sensory information, particularly visual information. In addition, the pons contains specialized nuclei that help control respiration and influence facial expression.

THE CEREBELLUM

The **cerebellum** is a distinctive structure about the size of a fist tucked beneath the back part of the cerebral hemispheres. It consists of two wrinkled hemispheres covered by an outer cortex. The cerebellum's primary function is to coordinate and regulate motor movements (Stein, 1986) that are broadly controlled by higher brain centers. The cerebellum fine-tunes and smooths out movements, particularly those required for rapid changes in direction. Damage to the cerebellum results in awkward, jerky, uncoordinated movements. Activities such as running, walking, or even standing may be accomplished, but often only with great concentration on each component motion.

THE RETICULAR FORMATION

The **reticular formation** consists of a set of neural circuits that extend from the lower brain, where the spinal cord enters, up to the thalamus (see Figure 3.6). Research has demonstrated that the reticular formation plays a critical role in controlling arousal or alertness. For this reason, it has become common to refer to this weblike collection of nerve cells and fibers as the **reticular activating system,** or **RAS.**

Some of the neural circuits that carry sensory messages from the lower regions of the brain to the higher brain areas have ancillary or "detouring" fibers that connect with the reticular system. Impulses from these fibers prompt the reticular formation to send signals upward, making us more responsive and alert to our environment. Experiments have shown that mild electrical stimulation of certain areas within this network causes sleeping animals to awaken slowly, whereas stronger stimulation causes animals to awaken rapidly, with greater alertness.

The reticular formation also seems to be linked to sleep cycles. When we fall asleep, our reticular systems cease to send alerting messages to our brains. While sleeping, we may screen out all extraneous stimuli, with the possible exception of critical messages like the sounds of a thunder clap or a baby's cough. The role of the reticular formation in sleep is still not fully understood. We do know, however, that serious damage to this structure may cause a person to be extremely lethargic or to enter into a prolonged comalike sleep (Kalat, 1981). Research also suggests that the reticular formation may play an important role in dreaming (Hobson & McCarley, 1977). The impact of the RAS on sleep and dreaming patterns is considered further in Chapter 5.

THE LIMBIC SYSTEM

The **limbic system** is the portion of the brain most closely associated with emotional expression; it also plays a role in motivation, learning, and memory. The limbic system is a collection of structures located around the central core of the brain, along the innermost edge of the cerebral hemispheres. Figure 3.7 shows some key structures of the limbic system, including the amygdala, the hippocampus, the septal area, and parts of the hypothalamus. Damage to or stimulation of sites within this system may

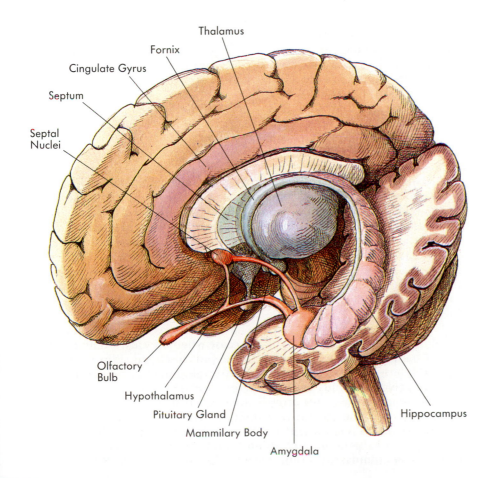

Thalamus
Fornix
Cingulate Gyrus
Septum
Septal Nuclei
Olfactory Bulb
Hypothalamus
Pituitary Gland
Mammilary Body
Amygdala
Hippocampus

FIGURE 3.7   THE LIMBIC SYSTEM

Key structures include the amygdala, hippocampus, the septum and septal nuclei, fornix, cingulate gyrus, and portions of the hypothalamus, which play a regulating role.

profoundly affect emotional expression, either by causing excessive reactions to situations or by greatly reducing emotional responses.

The **amygdala,** a small structure next to the hippocampus, plays an important role in the expression of anger, rage, and aggressive behavior (Chozick, 1986). Electrical stimulation or surgical damage to some areas of the amygdala may cause an animal to go into a blind rage, attacking everything in sight, while on other parts of the amygdala the same procedures may produce extreme passivity, even in threatening situations. In one study, experimenters were easily able to handle normally aggressive wild rats after surgically altering their amygdalas (Galef, 1970).

Results such as these have prompted some law-and-order activists to suggest that criminals with histories of repeated violent crimes should undergo surgery on their amygdalas. Indeed, voluntary amygdala surgery has occasionally been performed to alleviate uncontrollable rage in some psychiatric patients. Understandably, the ethical implications of such a radical treatment prevent it from being used except in voluntary cases.

Another limbic-system structure, the **hippocampus,** seems to be important for memory (Bureš et al., 1987). Individuals who experience damage to this structure have difficulty storing new information in memory. In one sad case, a man whose hippocampus was completely removed from both sides of his brain was unable to retain any new information in memory. He remembered skills and information learned prior to the surgery but was unable to store memories of anything that happened after the surgery. We shall discuss the implications of this finding in Chapter 7.

Still another area of the limbic system, the **septal area**, is associated with the experience of pleasure. This was demonstrated in the 1950s in James Olds' series of experiments on brain stimulation in rats, which were mentioned in Chapters 1 and 2. Olds implanted electrodes in various regions of rats' limbic systems and wired the electrodes in a way that allowed the rats to stimulate their own brains by pressing a lever. When the electrodes were placed in sites within the hypothalamus and the septal area, the rats seemingly could not get enough stimulation. They would press the lever several thousand times per hour, often to the point of exhaustion. Because the animals labored so incessantly to produce this experience, such behavior was interpreted as meaning they "liked" the feeling. In fact, it seemed as though they were experiencing something akin to intense pleasure, which led to the label "pleasure center" (Olds, 1956).

Researchers have been more reluctant to study the effects of stimulating human limbic systems, although a similar procedure has been used in a few instances to achieve therapeutic effects. Robert Heath (1972), a Tulane University researcher, is one of the pioneers in this area. In the early 1970s he experimented with limbic system stimulation on two subjects, a female epileptic and a man troubled with emotional problems. Heath hypothesized that the pleasure associated with such stimulation would be of therapeutic value to these patients. When stimulation was delivered to the septal area, both individuals reported intense pleasure. The male patient, in fact, used a self-stimulating transistorized device to stimulate himself incessantly (up to 1,500 times per hour). According to Heath, "he protested each time the unit was taken from him, pleading to self-stimulate just a few more times" (p. 6).

In other kinds of motivated behavior, such as eating, drinking, and sexual responding, organisms typically cease when they are satiated, but this did not happen in experiments like those just described. Why? This question and related questions have led to the development of a separate area of psychoneurological study called *intracranial self-stimulation* (Olds & Forbes, 1981). Researchers are now actively involved in seeking to understand the mechanisms that underlie the reinforcing effects of electrical stimulation of various brain sites (Gallistel, 1986; Mora & Ferrer, 1986; Velley, 1986).

It is also possible to produce aversive rather than pleasurable responses by stimulating certain areas of the limbic system (Sem-Jacobsen,

1968). Earlier we mentioned that rage could be induced by electrode stimulation in the amygdala. Stimulation of areas in the middle and back of the hypothalamus produces unpleasant emotions such as fear, often disturbing the subject's overall tranquility. In some cases, surgical destruction of these sites has produced a calming, sedative effect in anxious, overagitated psychiatric patients (Sano, 1962).

THE HYPOTHALAMUS

As its name indicates (*hypo* means below), this grape-sized structure lies below the thalamus. Although it is small, the **hypothalamus** has an important impact on several bodily functions and behaviors; it has thus been a major focus of many investigations (some of which will be discussed in later chapters). The hypothalamus contains control mechanisms that detect changes in body systems and correct imbalances to restore *homeostasis*, the maintenance of a relatively constant internal environment. Shivering when we are cold and perspiring when we are hot are both homeostatic processes that act to restore normal body temperature, and both are controlled by the hypothalamus. The hypothalamus is also critical to motivation. It contains nuclei (densely packed concentrations of specialized cell bodies) that govern eating, drinking, and sexual behavior.

The hypothalamus is also the hub of the neuroendocrine system, which will be discussed later in this chapter. This system, composed of the hypothalamus, the pituitary gland, and the various other hormone-secreting endocrine glands, is essential to a variety of behaviors, including sexual expression, reproduction, aggression, and reactions to stress. You may have heard the brain's pituitary gland described as the master gland, since it secretes substances that control the activity of other glands throughout the body. However, the term "master" is somewhat of a misnomer, since the pituitary gland itself takes directions from the hypothalamus.

Finally, the hypothalamus plays a role in controlling emotional expression. When it is removed from experimental animals, emotional arousal may be completely absent. The hypothalamus is not responsible for a full range of emotional expression. It plays an integrative role instead, partly through interacting with the endocrine system and partly as a key member of the limbic system.

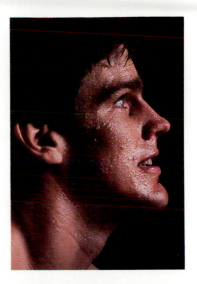

Sweating when we are hot is a homeostatic process that acts to restore normal body temperature. The hypothalamus contains control mechanisms that detect changes in body systems and correct imbalances to maintain a constant internal environment.

THE THALAMUS

Buried beneath the cerebrum are two egg-shaged structures that lie side by side, one in each hemisphere. These are the left and right halves of the **thalamus,** a structure that has often been referred to as the brain's "relay station" because of the role it plays in routing incoming sensory information to appropriate areas within the cerebral cortex. Many of the cell nuclei in the thalamus also perform initial data processing before relaying information to the cortex.

Distinct regions in the thalamus are specialized for certain kinds of sensory information. For example, when you hear a sound, the message transmitted from your ears passes through specialized neurons in an auditory area of the thalamus and is then relayed to the auditory cortex, an area in the cerebral cortex specialized for processing sound impulses. With the sole exception of the sense of smell, all sensory information is routed through specialized regions of the thalamus.

In addition to this function, the thalamus also appears to work in conjunction with the reticular formation to help regulate sleep cycles.

THE CEREBRAL CORTEX

The major structure of the brain is the **cerebral cortex,** the thin outer layer of the cerebrum. The Latin translation of cortex is bark, and the cortex covers the cerebrum in much the same way as bark covers a tree trunk. This portion of the brain is also called the *neocortex*, or "new cortex," since it was the last part of the brain to develop during evolution.

You may wonder why the cortex is wrinkled and convoluted. The answer has to do with the economics of space. The cortex's folds and wrinkles are nature's solution to the problem of cramming the huge neocortical area into a relatively small space within the skull. In the same way that crumpling a piece of paper allows it to fit into a smaller container than will a flat sheet, the cortex's folds permit it to fit into the fixed space of the skull.

The cortex is gray in color, which is why it is often referred to as the "gray matter" of the brain. The gray color comes from the lack of the whitish myelinated coating that insulates the neural fibers of the inner part of the cerebrum. (The inner core of the cerebrum is often called the "white matter" because it contains three kinds of myelinated neural fibers; *commissural fibers*, which pass from one hemisphere to another; *projection fibers*, which convey impulses to and from the cortex; and *association fibers*, which connect various parts of the cortex within one hemisphere.) The cortex is composed of the unmyelinated fibers and cell bodies of billions of neurons, and it is the part of the brain responsible for higher mental processes such as perceiving, thinking, and remembering.

The cortex is where our memories are stored, where we make decisions, where we "see" a sunset or recognize and appreciate a melody, and where we organize our worlds and plan for the future. Without a cortex, we would cease to exist as unique, functioning individuals. This is not to say that the cortex acts alone in running our lives. Instead, it functions like an executive, interpreting incoming information and making decisions about how to respond. As we go about our daily lives, our cerebral cortexes constantly analyze a vast array of incoming messages, evaluating them against stored information about past experiences and then making decisions that are translated into messages that are sent to the appropriate muscles and glands.

Although we know the cortex functions in this manner, we are far from understanding precisely how it controls our lives. For example, while we know that memory is largely a cortical function, science has yet to explain exactly how the brain initiates a command to search and retrieve a specific recollection. Nor are we even sure where specific memories are stored, nor how the cortex can spontaneously generate new ideas and insights. Investigations of the higher mental processes of the cortex are likely to remain at the frontier of psychology for many years to come, and only time will tell if the cortex is capable of unraveling and understanding all the complex mechanisms that govern its operation. Let us examine, however, what we do know about how the cortex functions.

Localization of Cortical Functioning As Figure 3.5 illustrated earlier in this chapter, the two hemispheres of the cerebrum are approximately symmetrical, with areas on the left side roughly matched by areas on the right. To some degree, researchers have been able to localize a variety of functions within various regions of the two cortical hemispheres. Approximately 25 percent of its total area is involved in receiving sensory messages or transmitting movement messages to our muscles. These regions are called the **sensory cortex** and the **motor cortex,** respectively. The remaining 75 percent of the cerebral cortex, called the **association cortex,** is involved in integrating sensory and motor messages, and in processing such higher mental functions as thinking, interpreting, remembering, and planning.

To facilitate studying and describing the brain, researchers have found it convenient to divide each of the cortical hemispheres into four separate regions called lobes. These four regions, the frontal, parietal, occipital, and temporal lobes, are shown in Figure 3.8. Two long, shallow fissures within the surface of the cortex serve as landmarks separating these

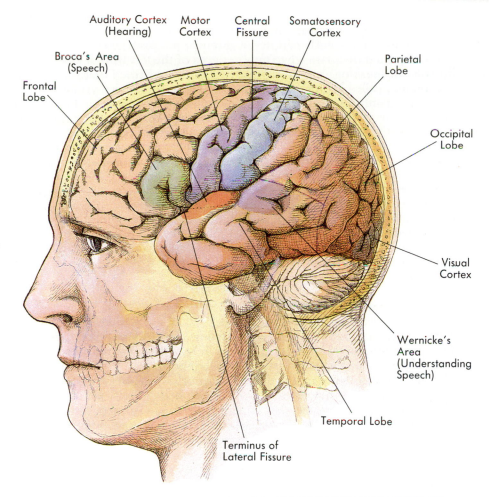

Auditory Cortex (Hearing)
Motor Cortex
Central Fissure
Somatosensory Cortex
Broca's Area (Speech)
Parietal Lobe
Frontal Lobe
Occipital Lobe
Visual Cortex
Wernicke's Area (Understanding Speech)
Temporal Lobe
Terminus of Lateral Fissure

FIGURE 3.8   LOCALIZATION OF CORTICAL FUNCTIONS IN THE FOUR LOBES OF THE LEFT CEREBRAL CORTEX

four lobes. The frontal lobe includes everything in front of the *central fissure* except the forward tip of the temporal lobe. The parietal lobe lies behind the central fissure, above the *lateral fissure*. The temporal lobe lies under the lateral fissure, and the occipital lobe lies at the back of the brain.

    The Frontal Lobe   The **frontal lobe** is the largest of the four lobes in each hemisphere and is an important center for both the motor and association cortex. A narrow strip just in front of the central fissure along the back of the frontal lobe, the motor cortex contains areas that control the hundreds of muscles in our bodies that carry out intentional actions. Virtually all intentional body movement, from throwing a ball to wiggling a small toe, is directed by precise regions within the motor cortex.

    The body is represented in an upside-down fashion along the motor cortex, in that neurons that control facial muscles are at the bottom of the motor cortex, whereas those that control movement of the toes are at the top part (see Figure 3.9). Larger areas of the motor cortex are devoted to the muscles involved in talking and moving the fingers, reflecting the critical role of speech and tool use in human behavior. Nerve fibers that descend from the motor cortex on one side of the brain activate muscles on the opposite side of the body. Thus, the left hemisphere controls the right side of the body and vice versa.

In the nineteenth century a French neurosurgeon, Pierre Paul Broca, reported that damage to another area of the left frontal lobe caused difficulty in speaking. Subsequent research has confirmed that this frontal lobe region, called **Broca's area** after its discoverer, is the primary brain center for controlling speech (see Figure 3.8). People who have been injured in this critical area typically have trouble articulating the right words to describe things, even though their comprehension of what they hear or read is unaffected. This condition is called *motor or expressive aphasia*.

The association areas of the frontal lobes seem to be important in making decisions, solving problems, planning and setting goals, and adapting to new situations. If the association area were damaged, we would probably have trouble understanding complex ideas and planning and carrying out purposeful behavior. A considerable amount of our emotional lives is also probably influenced by our frontal lobes. There are extensive, reciprocal connections between the association areas in the frontal lobes and certain lower brain structures (such as those in the limbic system) known to be involved in emotional expression.

The Parietal Lobe   The **parietal lobe** lies just behind the central fissure and above the lateral fissure. At the front of the parietal lobe, directly across from the motor cortex in the frontal lobe, is an area called the **somatosensory cortex.** This portion of the parietal lobe receives sensory information about touch, pressure, pain, temperature, and body position. Like the motor cortex, the somatosensory areas in each hemisphere receive sensory input from the opposite sides of the body. Thus, when you stub your left toe, the message is sent to your right somatosensory cortex. As in the motor cortex, the body is represented in an upside-down fashion, with the largest portions receiving input from the face and hands, as is shown in Figure 3.9. Each of the primary somatosensory areas in the parietal lobes lies directly across the central fissure from the corresponding area in the frontal lobe's motor cortex.

The Occipital Lobe   At the rear of each hemisphere lies the **occipital lobe.** This lobe consists primarily of the **visual cortex,** a complex network of neurons devoted to the business of seeing. Most people think they see with their eyes, but although the eyes receive sensory information, it is the visual cortex that integrates this information into electrical patterns that the brain translates into vision. The visual cortex of each hemisphere receives sensory messages from both eyes. Nerve fibers from the right side of each eye go to the right hemisphere, whereas fibers from the left side send impulses to the left hemisphere. Damage to the occipital lobe results in varying degrees of visual impairment, ranging from partial to complete blindness (Aldrich et al., 1987).

The occipital lobes are not solely responsible for vision. Some visual messages are transmitted to the temporal lobes; and, although the visual association areas are located primarily within the occipital lobes, they also extend to portions of the temporal and parietal lobes (Baylis et al., 1985; Rolls et al., 1987).

The Temporal Lobe   A primary function of the **temporal lobe** is hearing. The **auditory cortex,** located on the inner surface of the temporal lobe in a region below the lateral fissure, receives information directly from the auditory system. These auditory signals are then transmitted to an adjacent structure, known as **Wernicke's area,** which is involved in interpreting sounds, particularly the sound of human speech (see Figure 3.8). Association areas within the temporal lobes also appear to be involved in memory.

Recall that Broca's area in the left frontal lobe was found to control the expression of speech. Some years after this discovery, another European

FIRST PERSON 3.1

Several years ago I was holding my infant son in the passenger seat of a car when a speeding car slammed against us. The impact forced the door into my baby's head. He recovered from his injuries, except for one lasting effect: he is permanently blind. It turns out that the accident produced damage to the visual cortex in his occipital lobe, an injury that there is still no remedy for. (*Authors' files*)

FIGURE 3.9   PRIMARY AREAS OF THE MOTOR CORTEX AND SOMATOSENSORY CORTEX

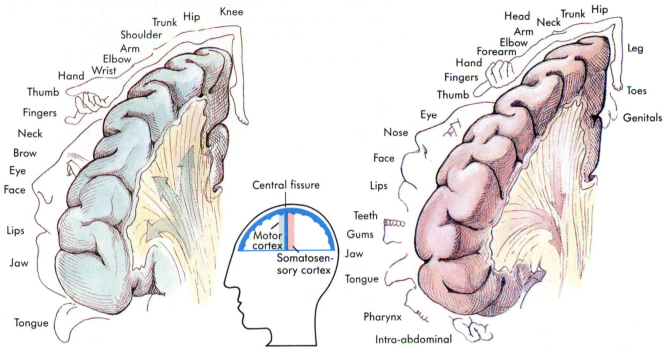

Motor Cortex (cross section just in front of central fissure)

Somatosensory Cortex (cross section just behind central fissure)

The body is represented in an upside-down fashion along the motor cortex and the somatosensory cortex. Neurons that control facial muscles as well as those that respond to stimulation of the facial area are located at the bottom of the motor and somatosensory cortex regions, respectively, whereas those neurons that activate movement and respond to stimulation of the toes are at the top part of these respective regions. You will note a disproportionate allocation of cortex area to the various motor and sensory functions of the body, with a marked exaggeration of the size of the motor and somatosensory regions devoted to the face and hands.

researcher, Germany's Carl Wernicke, reported that patients who were injured in the rear portion of the left temporal lobe, just below the lateral fissure, often had trouble understanding the speech of others. This condition is known as *sensory* or *receptive aphasia*. Subsequent research has confirmed that this temporal lobe region is the brain's primary area for understanding speech (Naeser et al., 1987).

Lateralization of Function   You may have noticed in the preceding discussion that both Broca's area and Wernicke's area were identified in the left hemisphere. Indeed, in most people (95 percent of right-handed people and about 70 percent of left-handers), verbal abilities such as the expression and understanding of speech are governed more by the left hemisphere than the right hemisphere, and there are other differences as well. Furthermore, the right side of the brain seems to be more specialized for spatial orientation, including the ability to recognize objects and shapes and to perceive relationships among them (Gordon, 1986).

The term **lateralization of function** is used to describe the degree to which a particular function is controlled by one rather than both hemispheres. If, for example, a person's ability to deal with spatial tasks is controlled exclusively by the right hemisphere, we would say that this ability in this person is highly lateralized. In contrast, if both hemispheres contribute equally to this function, the person would be considered bilateral for spatial ability.

Studies have shown that the two hemispheres are asymmetrical, differing in anatomical, electrical, and chemical properties (Woods, 1986). For example, autopsies reveal that one hemisphere, usually the left, is larger than the other about 95 percent of the time (Geschwind & Levitsky, 1976).

Although each hemisphere is specialized to handle different functions, they are not entirely separate systems. Rather, our brains function mostly as an integrated whole. The two hemispheres constantly communicate with each other through a broad band of millions of connecting nerve fibers called the **corpus callosum** (Cook, 1986; Gazzaniga, 1987), shown earlier in Figure 3.6a. And while in most people a complex function like language is primarily controlled by regions in the left hemisphere, interaction and communication with the right hemisphere also play a role. Furthermore, if a hemisphere that is primarily responsible for a particular function is damaged, the remaining intact hemisphere may take over the function. For example, if a young child experienced an injury to the language-processing area of the left hemisphere, the right hemisphere might develop a greater capacity to handle verbal functions (Rudel et al., 1974). As people grow older, however, it becomes increasingly difficult to switch cortical control from one hemisphere to another.

Split-Brain Research   Many important discoveries about how each hemisphere influences behavior have come from "split-brain" research, which began in the 1950s with Roger Sperry's investigations of cats whose brains had been bisected. Initially, Sperry and his colleagues made the startling discovery that the left hemisphere of a split-brain cat could learn something, while the right hemisphere remained ignorant of what had been learned, and vice versa (Sperry, 1968). In the decades since this landmark study, additional experiments with split-brain subjects have added greatly to our knowledge about hemispheric lateralization of function.

Some of these studies have involved split-brain research with human subjects. This radical surgery is not performed for experimental purposes but is occasionally performed to control very severe cases of epilepsy that have become incapacitating and even life threatening. During an epileptic seizure, neurons in the site of a damaged area begin to fire wildly, and the abnormal activity can spread from one hemisphere to the other through the corpus callosum. Although drugs are often effective in localizing the abnormal brain activity, the medication is not always effective, and in these cases the only recourse may be to sever the corpus callosum. This procedure is usually very effective in controlling the seizures, and the patients appear to be virtually unchanged in intelligence, personality characteristics, and behavior. However, their brains do not function in entirely the same manner after the surgery. After being disconnected, the two hemispheres operate independently. Their motor mechanisms, sensory systems, and association areas can no longer exchange information.

The difference makes itself felt in a variety of ways. For instance, the right hand might arrange some flowers in a vase, only to have the left hand tear it apart. Occasionally, people with split brains may be embarrassed by the left hand making inappropriate gestures, or perhaps doing some bizarre thing like zipping down the fly on a pair of trousers after the right hand has zipped it up. With time, such symptoms usually subside as the person learns to compensate for and adjust to the independent functioning of the two hemispheres.

Scientists have developed a number of procedures for detecting the effects of split-brain surgery. For instance, in one study a woman recently recovered from split-brain surgery sat in front of a screen with a small black dot at its center (see Figure 3.10). She was asked to stare continuously at the

FIGURE 3.10 STUDYING THE EFFECTS OF SPLIT-BRAIN SURGERY

The subject focuses on images that are projected through the screen to the left or right of a central black dot.

dot while pictures were flashed to either the left or the right of her visual field. Information presented to her left visual field was transmitted only to her right hemisphere, and vice versa. Each stimulus appeared on the screen for only about one-tenth of a second, so that the subject did not have time to shift her eyes to get a better look. Her task was to identify verbally what she was shown, and then to reach under the screen and select the object solely by touch from a collection of objects (LeDoux et al., 1977).

TESTING THE EFFECTS OF SPLIT-BRAIN SURGERY

In the experiment just described, do you think that the woman was able to identify correctly, both verbally and by touch, objects projected in the left and right visual field? If yes, why? If no, why not? What differences, if any, do you think were noted between her responses to left versus right visual field images? Take some time to reason out the probable results of this experiment before reading on.

Images in the right visual field fall on the left side of each retina (the image-recording part of the eye), and images in the left visual field fall on the right side of each retina. Half of each retina sends information to the occipital cortex on the same side of the brain, while information from the other half of each retina crosses over to the cortex on the opposite side of the brain. This means that if a person stares straight ahead, information from the entire left visual field will reach the right hemisphere and vice versa.

Normally, this information is transferred between the two hemispheres through the corpus callosum, so that both hemispheres have information about both the left and right visual fields. In split-brain people, however, this is no longer possible (see Figure 3.11); and in this particular experiment researchers made sure, by flashing the image for such a short period of time, that each hemisphere received only the information in the opposite visual field. (In one-tenth of a second the subject would not have time to shift her eyes, enabling her to perceive the image in both hemispheres.)

The results of the experiment showed a difference in the subject's responses. When a picture of a cup was projected to the right of the dot (and

FIGURE 3.11 PASSAGE OF VISUAL INFORMATION IN BRAINS WITH INTACT AND SEVERED CORPORA CALLOSA

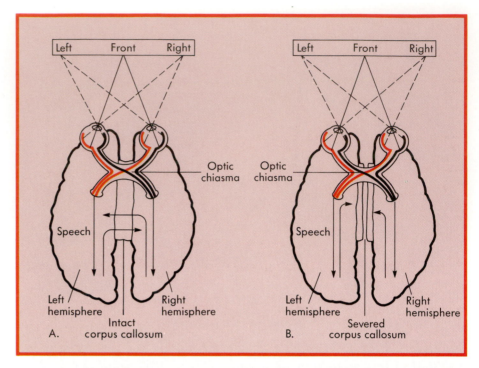

In A, the corpus callosum is intact. Visual information in the right visual field is focused on the left half of each retina; it then passes through the optic nerve to the left hemisphere. (The opposite process takes place for information in the left visual field.) Information in either hemisphere is passed through the corpus callosum to the opposite hemisphere.

In B, the process is identical up to the point where information reaches the brain. Information from the right visual field reaches the left hemisphere but, since the corpus callosum is severed, it cannot be passed to the right hemisphere; the reverse is also true.

thus projected to her left hemisphere), the subject was able to quickly name the object; and she had no trouble locating the cup by touch. (She could locate the object with her left hand, since naming the object out loud conveyed information about its nature to her right hemisphere via auditory input from her ears.) Additional objects presented to her right visual field presented no problems. However, when a picture of a spoon was flashed to the left side of the dot, the results were quite different. The subject reported seeing nothing. Despite this reply, the researchers pressed her into trying to pick out the object from the articles on the table. After feeling the various objects with her left hand, she held up the spoon—a result she dismissed as a lucky guess. When asked to identify it verbally, she called it a "pencil." Time after time her sense of touch allowed her to identify objects presented to her right hemisphere, even though she insisted that she saw nothing each time a new image was flashed.

In a variation of this test, a sexually suggestive picture of a nude was flashed to the left side of the dot. The subject giggled and blushed, but when she was asked what she saw, she replied "Nothing, just a flash of light." When the experimenter pressed further and asked why she was laughing, she exclaimed, "Oh, doctor, you have some machine!"

These results reveal that in this individual (as well as in the majority of people) the left hemisphere is primarily responsible for language and speech. People who have intact brains have no problem with tasks such as the one just described, since the two hemispheres work together in perceiving and naming things. However, after a split-brain operation, each side of the bisected brain is cut off from the other side. Therefore, even though the subject of this study was able to identify the spoon with her hand, she could not name it. Her right hemisphere, with its undeveloped language and speech areas, was essentially mute. Her response to the picture of the nude is similar. Even though her left hemisphere did not know what had happened, her blushing and giggling revealed that her right hemisphere had processed the information and produced an emotional response.

Would she have been able to identify the spoon with her right hand after its image had been projected to the right side of her brain? The answer is no, since her right hand is governed by the left hemisphere, and her left hemisphere knew nothing about the object.

A Dominant Hemisphere? Studies like the one just discussed support the theory that the left hemisphere is dominant in verbal ability. It is also specialized in other areas, such as logic and mathematics. Because of this special role, the left hemisphere has sometimes been called the dominant hemisphere, and the right has in turn been called the minor or nondominant hemisphere.

These distinctions are being used less frequently in recent years, however, for a few reasons. For one, lateralization of function may not be quite as clear-cut as some studies have indicated. Working with split-brain subjects, researcher Eran Zaidel (1975) demonstrated that the right hemisphere is capable of some language function. Zaidel's study involved a special instrument, called the Z lens, that permits prolonged viewing of a stimulus while ensuring that only one hemisphere receives visual input. Zaidel worked with split-brain subjects whose left hemisphere was dominant for language. The results revealed that the right hemisphere could understand more about words than was previously thought. On vocabulary tests, for instance, the right hemisphere's comprehension vocabulary, while inferior to that of the left, was nevertheless roughly equivalent to that of a 10-year-old.

Another reason why the idea of "dominant hemispheres" is being reevaluated is because research continues to demonstrate that the right hemisphere is itself critical or dominant in a number of functions. For example, several studies have demonstrated that the right hemisphere is superior in perceiving spatial relationships and in manipulating objects.

Consequently, you might expect that the right hemisphere would be better at constructing geometric and perspective drawings. In one experiment designed to test this hypothesis (Gazzaniga, 1970), a split-brain subject was able to copy three-dimensional designs with the left hand (guided by the right hemisphere), but could not reproduce the designs with the right hand (see Figure 3.12).

Studies of subjects with intact brains do tend to confirm lateralization of function, at least for verbal and spatial skills. For example, in one experiment, recordings of EEG brain waves revealed that electrical activity increases in the right hemisphere when a person is performing a spatial task, and that activity picks up in the left hemisphere when the subject performs a verbal task (Ornstein, 1977).

The right hemisphere is also superior at synthesis, or the ability to generalize the whole from segments. A number of studies have shown that this side of the brain is particularly good at putting isolated elements together to perceive things as a whole (Kempler & Van Lancker, 1987). For example, in one study, split-brain people were better able to match portions of circles to completed circles when guided by their right rather than left hemispheres (Nebes, 1972). Some writers have argued that the right hemisphere is also superior in governing musical and artistic abilities, pointing to evidence that a much larger percentage of music and art students (as opposed to science majors) are left-handed (Peterson, 1979). Presumably, being left handed may indicate that the right hemisphere is playing a more dominant role.

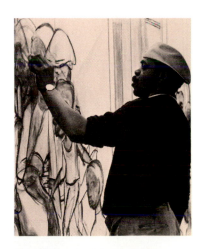

Do you have a "dominant hemisphere"? Some studies suggest that the right hemisphere is superior in governing artistic abilities. This left-handed artist would probably agree.

FIGURE 3.12 COPIES OF THREE-DIMENSIONAL DESIGNS BY A SPLIT-BRAIN SUBJECT

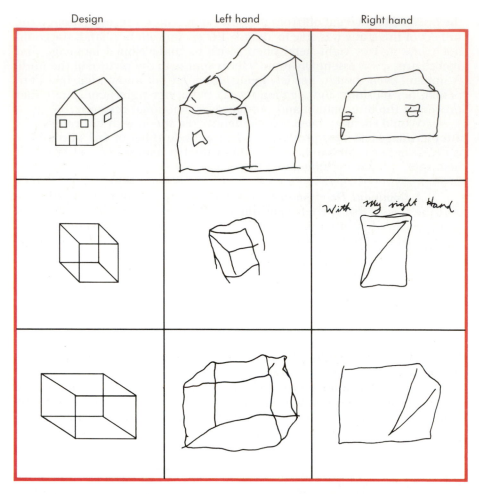

Design Left hand Right hand

With my right Hand

A split-brain subject was able to copy three-dimensional designs with the left hand, guided by the right hemisphere (although somewhat crudely, since the subject is right-handed). However, the subject could not accurately reproduce these designs with the right hand, guided by the left hemisphere. (*Source:* From Gazzaniga, 1970)

In view of the right brain's greater ability to perceive spatial relationships and produce perspective drawings, it seems reasonable to attribute artistic functions more to right than to left hemisphere control. However, evidence linking musical functions to the right brain is less convincing, and "neither studies of musical abilities after brain damage nor studies of music perception in persons with normal brains have established the localization of musical ability in one or the other hemisphere" (Bloom et al., 1985, p. 220).

Information about lateralization of function provides only general guidelines about how the brain functions. While some highly lateralized people do show rather striking differences between the two hemispheres, this is not universal. In less lateralized people, language skills in the right brain may be almost as good as those in the left, and spatial abilities may be present in the left as well as the right. In fact, some fascinating recent evidence suggests that individuals with extremely high mathematical and verbal reasoning abilities and spatial skills may demonstrate an unusually low amount of lateralization or hemispheric specialization of these abilities (Benbow, 1987). In such individuals, these cognitive functions appear to be represented bilaterally across both hemispheres, a condition that may be associated with a more extensive anatomical connection through the corpus callosum (Witelson, 1985). A lack of notable differences in hemispheric function has also been found recently in some split-brain subjects (Myers,

Electrical stimulation of these monkeys' amygdalas causes them to go into a blind rage, attacking everything in sight. The same procedures on other parts of the amygdala may produce extreme passivity, even in threatening situations.

1984; Zaidel, 1983). All of these findings remind us not to generalize too broadly from a few split-brain studies. In most of us, our brains function as unified structures.

The information presented in this chapter has only touched on what scientists know about the brain. Although there are still many unanswered questions, new methods developed in recent years have added greatly to our knowledge. In the next section we look at some techniques used to study the brain.

HOW THE BRAIN IS STUDIED

Some of the earliest clues about how the brain functions came from observations of people with head injuries, as investigators attempted to link specific behavioral deficits with specific locations of brain damage. For example, if a person's vision was impaired by a blow to the back of the head, the natural conclusion was that the injured region of the brain was responsible for vision. This way of learning about the brain has provided some valuable insights, but it has some serious drawbacks. One is the impracticality of waiting for the right kind of injury to occur so that the role of a specific brain site can be assessed. It is also often difficult to determine the precise location and amount of damage inflicted by a given injury. Because of such limitations, researchers concluded that it might be more efficient to create the injuries with surgical techniques. The areas of brain damage created by such procedures are called *lesions*, and the technique is called **lesion production.**

For obvious ethical reasons, lesion production is used with nonhuman subjects (although in some cases, lesions have been produced in human brains for therapeutic purposes, for example, to destroy an area in the amygdala that is responsible for abnormal cellular activity associated with uncontrollable rage). Typically, an animal is anesthetized, a small hole is drilled in its skull, and a specific part of the brain is destroyed. A special device called a *stereotaxic apparatus* (see Figure 3.13), allows researchers to insert a fine wire into a specific brain area. Enough electric current is then passed through the wire to destroy a small amount of brain tissue at its tip. This refined lesioning technique has allowed researchers to identify the relationship of specific behaviors to precise locations in the brain.

A second technique, **brain stimulation,** involves stimulating precise regions with a weak electric current. A stereotaxic device is used to implant

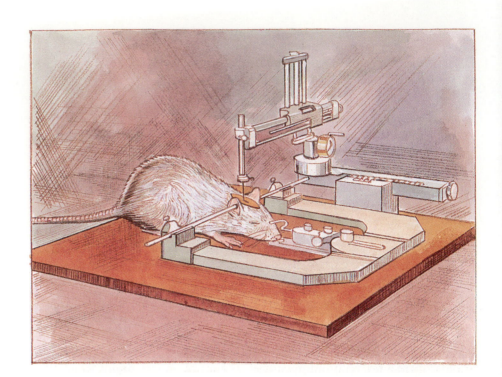

FIGURE 3.13   A STEREOTAXIC APPARATUS

Brain researchers use this device to insert fine wires into precise regions of the brain.

In electroencephalography (EEG), electrodes are placed on the scalp and the electrical activity of the cortex is recorded on paper in patterns called brain waves. The EEG has been used to diagnose such conditions as epilepsy, brain tumors, and a variety of other neurological disorders.

tiny wires called microelectrodes at specific brain sites. Stimulation of the targeted area often results in some kind of behavioral response, such as the pleasure response that results from stimulating the septal area. Results like this provide researchers with valuable information about where certain behavioral functions are localized within the brain. Because brain stimulation is generally painless, and because measures can be taken to avoid tissue damage, this method may be used with human as well as animal subjects.

Another technique used for studying the brain is **electrical recording.** Here, tiny wires implanted in the brain are used to record the electrical activity of neurons. Scientists using this technique have been able to record the responses of a single brain neuron to a stimulus such as a beam of light. In some studies, electrical activity is transmitted through several implanted electrodes while the subject engages in various behaviors. The electrical messages are then fed into a computer, which analyzes the complex relationships between the behaviors and patterns of neuron activity.

Lesion production, electrical stimulation, and electrical recording are all *invasive* in that they require surgery. Fortunately, technology has made possible a variety of brain study methods that do not require surgery and are *noninvasive.* One technique, **electroencephalography** (EEG) has been around for quite some time. Because the brain constantly generates electrical activity, electrodes placed on the scalp can be used to record the electrical activity of the cortex. The electroencephalograph amplifies these very small electrical potentials thousands of times and records them on paper in patterns called brain waves. Brain waves vary according to a person's state— alert and mentally active, relaxed and calm, sleeping, or dreaming. The EEG has been used to diagnose such conditions as epilepsy, brain tumors, and a variety of other neurological disorders that generate abnormal brain wave patterns.

Although the EEG provides overall information about a person's mental state, it can tell us little about responses to specific stimuli. Typically, there is so much "background noise" (in the form of ongoing spontaneous brain waves) that it is difficult to identify what brain wave changes result from a specific stimulus. A relatively new variation of the EEG uses computers to extract the background noise so that brain wave responses can be identified. These wave patterns associated with specific stimuli are called *evoked potentials*.

Brain scientists have recently developed some effective techniques for observing living brains. The first of these, **computerized axial tomography** (CAT), was developed in the early 1970s. It is a refined X-ray technique that provides an accurate image of the brain. An X-ray scanner is rotated in a circular path around the skull, sending a thin beam of X-rays through the brain. A detector measures the amount of radiation that reaches the other side. Because different brain tissues absorb different amounts of radiation, the CAT scanners produce excellent pictures that can be used to locate tumors, lesions, and a variety of neurologic abnormalities—information that in the past could only be obtained by autopsy.

A second technique, the PET scan **(positron emission tomography),** was introduced at the beginning of this chapter. The PET scan takes advantage of the fact that glucose sugar is the primary source of energy for brain cells (like all other body cells). Each time a neuron fires, it expends tremendous energy, so active brain cells metabolize a great deal of glucose. The scientists who developed the PET scan reasoned that if they could find a way to measure glucose utilization, they could tell what parts of the brain are active at different times in response to different stimuli. The use of radioactive isotopes paved the way.

The technique works as follows: A patient receives an intravenous injection of a glucoselike sugar that has been tagged with a radioactive fluoride isotope. Active brain cells metabolize the sugar, but they cannot metabolize the radioactive component. Thus, the isotope accumulates within the cells in direct proportion to their activity level. As it decays, it emits charged particles called positrons. Instruments scanning the brain detect the radioactivity and record its location, and a computer converts this information into colored biochemical maps of the brain, like those shown at the beginning of the chapter.

The PET scan has proved to be an extremely useful tool in mapping the brain, pinpointing locations involved in movement, sensation, thinking, and even memory (Altman, 1986; Fox et al., 1986; Restak, 1984). There is also some evidence suggesting that PET scans may be helpful in both the diagnosis and treatment of various behavioral disorders. Some researchers report that the brains of schizophrenics and severely depressed people reveal a different pattern from those of healthy people (Buchsbaum et al., 1987).

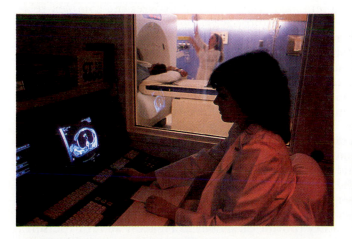

The computerized axial tomography (CAT) scanner is rotated in a circular path around the skull, sending a thin beam of X-rays through the brain. The CAT scanners produce excellent pictures that can be used to locate tumors, lesions, and a variety of neurologic abnormalities.

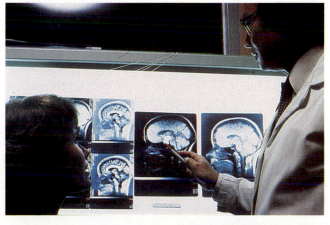

Providing much sharper and more detailed images than the CAT scan, the nuclear magnetic resonance (NMR) procedure can pinpoint the tiniest tumors, locate the slightest reduction in blood flow in an artery or vein, and even distinguish between cancerous and noncancerous cells.

A third technique, **nuclear magnetic resonance** (NMR), is so new that it is still being developed (Kim & Haynie, 1987; Prichard, 1986). This procedure uses harmless radio waves to excite hydrogen protons in the brain tissue, creating a magnetic field change that is detected by a huge magnet that surrounds the patient. The information is fed into a computer, which compiles it into a highly detailed three-dimensional colored picture of the brain. The images created are much sharper and more detailed than those provided by the CAT scan. The NMR can pinpoint the tiniest tumors and locate even the slightest reduction in blood flow in an artery or vein. It can also provide biochemical information, distinguishing between cancerous and noncancerous cells. In addition, NMR has been shown to be particularly helpful in diagnosing various diseases associated with brain abnormalities, such as multiple sclerosis (a degenerative disease of the CNS characterized by tremors and impaired speech [Geisser et al., 1987]), spinal cord abnormalities in children (Bale et al., 1986), and brain lesions associated with epilepsy (Jabbari et al., 1986).

Researchers are hopeful that the NMR will ultimately pinpoint the precise location of neurotransmitters and other important brain chemicals. It is also possible that this powerful tool will help clarify differences in physiological processes between people with healthy brains and those who have physical and emotional disorders.

THE PERIPHERAL NERVOUS SYSTEM

The peripheral nervous system consists of all the nervous system structures located outside the central nervous system. Its primary purpose is to serve the CNS by transmitting information to and from the spinal cord and brain. The PNS has two divisions, the somatic and autonomic.

THE SOMATIC NERVOUS SYSTEM

The **somatic nervous system** contains nerves that serve the major skeletal muscles, such as the arm and leg muscles. These muscles, often called striated because they appear striped or striated when seen under a microscope, carry out intentional movements directed by messages from higher brain centers. The somatic nervous system also contains nerves that transmit sensory information from the skin, muscles, and various sensory organs of the body.

THE AUTONOMIC NERVOUS SYSTEM

The other division of the PNS, the **autonomic nervous system,** controls the glands and the smooth muscles of the heart, lungs, stomach, intestines, blood vessels, and various other internal organs. This division of the PNS is named for the fact that the muscles and glands it serves operate reflexively, without intentional or voluntary control. Thus, they are autonomous or self-regulating. (In some cases, however, people can be trained to exert conscious control over these so-called involuntary processes. See the discussion of biofeedback in Chapter 17.)

The autonomic nervous system is itself subdivided into two branches, the **sympathetic** and the **parasympathetic.** In most cases, each internal organ serviced by the autonomic nervous system has a separate set of connections with the sympathetic and the parasympathetic branches. These two distinct sets of connections operate quite differently, often having opposing effects on the organs they control, as shown in Figure 3.14. For example, the sympathetic system increases heart rate, dilates the pupils, and inhibits digestive activity; the parasympathetic system has the opposite effect in each case.

The sympathetic and parasympathetic systems do not operate in a counterproductive fashion, however. Instead, they work together to allow

FIGURE 3.14 FUNCTIONS OF THE SYMPATHETIC AND PARASYMPATHETIC DIVISIONS OF THE AUTONOMIC NERVOUS SYSTEM

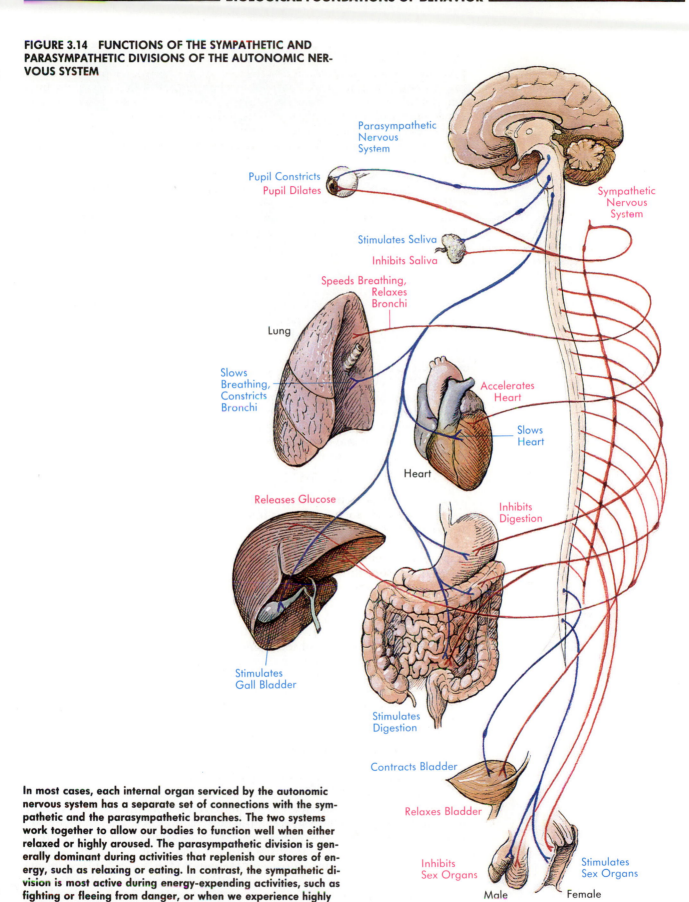

Parasympathetic Nervous System

Pupil Constricts
Pupil Dilates

Sympathetic Nervous System

Stimulates Saliva

Inhibits Saliva

Speeds Breathing, Relaxes Bronchi

Lung

Slows Breathing, Constricts Bronchi

Accelerates Heart

Slows Heart

Heart

Releases Glucose

Inhibits Digestion

Stimulates Gall Bladder

Stimulates Digestion

Contracts Bladder

Relaxes Bladder

Inhibits Sex Organs

Stimulates Sex Organs

Male   Female

In most cases, each internal organ serviced by the autonomic nervous system has a separate set of connections with the sympathetic and the parasympathetic branches. The two systems work together to allow our bodies to function well when either relaxed or highly aroused. The parasympathetic division is generally dominant during activities that replenish our stores of energy, such as relaxing or eating. In contrast, the sympathetic division is most active during energy-expending activities, such as fighting or fleeing from danger, or when we experience highly arousing emotions such as fear and anxiety.

If you have ever been chased by a dog, or caught in an emergency situation of any kind, then you know what it feels like when the sympathetic nervous system activates certain organs, such as your heart, to operate at their upper limits.

our bodies to function well when either relaxed or highly aroused. Our normal state, somewhere between extreme excitement and complete relaxation, is maintained by the balance between these two systems. However, there are times when we need an emergency source of energy—as when we are stressed or feeling strong emotion—and at these times our sympathetic nervous systems come into play.

For instance, imagine that you are hiking in the wilderness when you are suddenly confronted by a bear. The result will probably be the classic response that prepares you (and probably the bear, too) for "fight or flight": your pupils dilate, your heart pumps like mad, and epinephrine (commonly called adrenalin) pours into your blood vessels. These effects produce distinct sensations in your body, but they also serve a critical function. Under the influence of the sympathetic nervous system, organs such as the heart operate at their upper limits. This response serves us well in emergencies, whether we need to escape from a bear in the woods or to rescue a child from a burning house, but our bodies cannot continue at this pace for very long. If they did, we would soon be exhausted. This is when the parasympathetic nervous system comes into play, providing a braking mechanism for each of the organs activated by the sympathetic nervous system. This countersystem helps us conserve energy and resources and is active in restoring our bodies to normal.

Sympathetic and parasympathetic responses take place in different ways. The parasympathetic nervous system tends to affect specific glands and organs independently of one another, often one at a time. In an emergency, however, there is no time to waste. As a result, the sympathetic nervous system acts as a unit, mobilizing most or all of the various sympathetic effects outlined in Figure 3.14 at once.

THE ENDOCRINE SYSTEM

Up to this point in this chapter we have covered only the nervous system. However, the nervous system is not the only biological system that governs behavior. To be complete, a discussion of biological foundations of behavior should also consider the role of the endocrine system.

The **endocrine system** consists of several glands located throughout the body. (Glands in the endocrine system are ductless; that is, they have no external excretory ducts but rather secrete internally directly into the bloodstream or lymph fluid.) The major endocrine glands include the pituitary,

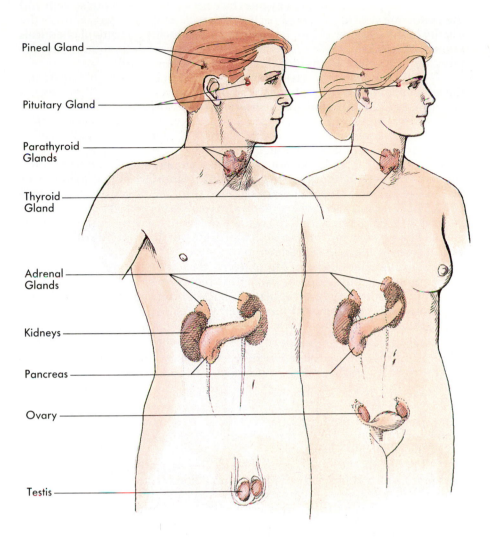

Pineal Gland

Pituitary Gland

Parathyroid Glands

Thyroid Gland

Adrenal Glands

Kidneys

Pancreas

Ovary

Testis

FIGURE 3.15   THE MAJOR GLANDS IN THE ENDOCRINE SYSTEM

the thyroid, the parathyroids, the adrenals, the pancreas, and the gonads. The location of the various endocrine glands is shown in Figure 3.15. Each of these glands produces **hormones,** which are secreted directly into the bloodstream. A single gland may produce several quite different hormones that perform virtually the same function. An entire series of related hormones is often referred to as one hormone, for example, the androgens and estrogens produced by male and female gonads.

Like neurotransmitters, hormones act as chemical messengers. In fact, some important chemicals within the body can function as both neurotransmitters and hormones. Norepinephrine, for example, acts as a hormone when released by the adrenal glands and as a neurotransmitter when released by a neuron. There is, however, a key difference in the way these two classes of chemicals act. Because neurotransmitters need to travel only across a synaptic gap (a fraction of the distance that most hormones travel through the bloodstream), they have a much more immediate effect upon behavior than does the endocrine system.

The endocrine system often works in tandem with the nervous system. For example, when a person is suddenly exposed to a fearful stimulus, such as the bear in the earlier example, heart rate increases instantly in response to sympathetic nervous system input. At the same time, the adrenal glands secrete epinephrine, which has a similar effect on heart rate. In this fashion, the two major regulating systems of the body often work together.

The hypothalamus is a key interface between the nervous system and the endocrine system. As noted earlier, this region of the brain controls the activity of the pituitary gland. It does this by producing a group of chemicals known as *hypothalamic-releasing factors*. These chemicals in turn stimulate the pituitary to produce hormones that stimulate other glands.

Once an endocrine gland releases a hormone into the bloodstream, the substance travels throughout the body. However, each hormone exerts its primary influence only on certain specific organs and cells, often referred to as *target organs*. Some hormones, called trophic hormones, affect only the activity of another endocrine gland. For example, hormones called gonadotropins stimulate only the gonads.

Endocrine glands do not produce a steady stream of hormones. Instead, target organs signal the secreting glands to either increase or decrease secretions. Hormones are secreted until the target organ is stimulated; at this point, the target organ releases another substance that circulates back through the system to regulate hormonal activity in the initiating gland. This *negative-feedback mechanism* provides an internal control that limits extremes of hormonal production.

Through these general mechanisms, the endocrine system influences many important physiological functions, mental processes, and behavior patterns, including disease regulation, metabolism, emotional responses, and motivation. A number of these effects are of particular interest to psychologists.

THE PITUITARY GLAND

Located in the brain below the hypothalamus, the **pituitary gland** produces the largest number of different hormones, some of which trigger other glands to release hormones. For these reasons, the pituitary gland is sometimes called the "master gland," but, as we have seen, it is itself controlled by the hypothalamus.

One of the key hormones released by the pituitary is the **growth hormone,** which controls a number of metabolic functions, including the rate of growth of the bones and soft tissues (Rechler et al., 1987). If too little of this hormone is produced, the result will be dwarfism, whereas too much growth hormone can cause a person to attain giant stature.

The pituitary also produces a number of huge protein molecules called neuropeptides, mentioned in our earlier discussion of endogenous opiates. Each neuropeptide consists of a long chain of amino acids that are broken down by enzyme action into various lengths of small chains. These substances act as neurotransmitters, and they influence a number of functions such as eating and drinking, sexual behavior, sleep, temperature regulation, pain reduction, and responses to stress.

THE THYROID GLAND

The **thyroid gland,** located within the neck, responds to pituitary stimulation by releasing the hormone *thyroxine*. This substance affects a number of biological functions, the most important of which is the regulation of metabolism. Because metabolism is in turn closely linked to motivational and mood states, the thyroid has an important impact on behavior. For example, if too little thyroxine is produced (a condition known as *hypothyroidism*), a person will behave in a lethargic manner, with little motivation to accomplish tasks. Excessive thyroxine output (*hyperthyroidism*) may have just the opposite effect, causing hyperactivity and excessive tension. An undersecretion of thyroxine early in life produces *cretinism*, a condition characterized by low intelligence and various body defects such as dwarfed stature and dry, wrinkled skin. Fortunately, all of these conditions can be prevented or remedied by medical treatments.

THE ADRENAL GLANDS

The **adrenals** are a pair of glands, located just above each kidney, that influence our emotional state, level of energy, and ability to cope with stress. They consist of two distinct parts, an inner core called the *adrenal medulla* and an outer layer called the *adrenal cortex*. The medulla produces epinephrine and norepinephrine, both of which prepare the body to respond to emergencies by making the heart beat faster, diverting blood from the stomach and intestines to the voluntary muscles (so a person can run faster or fight better), and enhancing energy resources by increasing blood-sugar levels. The adrenal medulla is able to act quickly in threatening situations because it is stimulated directly by neural impulses.

As suggested earlier in the discussion of the peripheral nervous system, epinephrine and norepinephrine act in a way that is similar to the sympathetic nervous system. In fact, these hormones and the nervous system perform basically the same work. The sympathetic nervous system works more quickly, producing its effects almost instantly. Yet the effects of the adrenal hormones can persist much longer. It is the lingering effects of hormones that explain why it often takes time for strong emotional arousal to subside after the cause for anxiety has been removed.

At times of stress, the hypothalamus causes the pituitary to release ACTH, *adrenocorticotropic hormone*, which in turn stimulates the adrenal cortex to increase its secretion of a number of hormones that influence metabolism. The higher metabolic rate makes the stressed person more active, and therefore more able to cope with an emergency. Prolonged stress, however, can have a debilitating effect on mind and body. A chronic state of tension, nervousness, fear, or even panic can take a terrible toll on one's emotional and physical well-being. Furthermore, abnormally high metabolic rates deplete vital body resources, and over time this can lead to exhaustion and increased susceptibility to illness. Stress-related problems and stress-management techniques will be discussed in Chapter 17.

THE GONADS

The **gonads,** ovaries in the female and testes in the male, produce several varieties of sex hormones. The ovaries produce two classes of hormones: the *estrogens* (the most important of which is estradiol), which influence development of female physical sex characteristics and regulation of the menstrual cycle, and the *progestational compounds* (the most important is progesterone), which help to regulate the menstrual cycle and prepare the uterus for pregnancy. The primary output of the testes are the *androgens*. The most important of these is testosterone, whose function is to influence the development of both male physical sex characteristics and sexual motivation. In both sexes, the adrenal glands also secrete sex hormones, including small amounts of estrogen and greater quantities of androgen.

Around the onset of puberty, the sex hormones play a critical role in initiating changes in the primary sexual systems (the growth of the uterus, vagina, penis, and so forth) and the secondary sex characteristics, including body hair, breast development, and voice changes. They also exert strong influences on the fertility cycle in women, and they seem to contribute to sexual motivation. Chapter 9 discusses the relationship of sex hormones to sexual motivation in some detail.

SUMMARY

OVERVIEW OF THE NERVOUS SYSTEM: ORGANIZATION AND FUNCTION

1. The nervous system of humans and other vertebrates consists of two major parts: the central nervous system (CNS) and the peripheral nervous system (PNS).

2. The CNS consists of the brain and the spinal cord. It occupies the commanding position in the nervous system as it coordinates and integrates all bodily functions.

3. The PNS transmits messages to and from the CNS. It is subdivided into the somatic nervous system and the autonomic nervous system.

NEURONS: BASIC UNITS OF THE NERVOUS SYSTEM

4. There are three major classes of neurons: sensory neurons that carry messages to the CNS; motor neurons that transmit messages from the CNS to muscles and glands; and interneurons that act as intermediaries between sensory and motor neurons.

5. Neurons have four common structures: the cell body, which handles metabolic functions; the dendrites, which receive neural messages; the axon, which conducts a message to the end of the neuron; and the terminal buttons at the end of the axon, which release transmitter substances.

6. The transmission of a neural message involves both electrical and chemical aspects. Electrical processes are activated when the dendrites (or cell body) of a neuron respond to an impulse from neighboring neurons by undergoing a change in permeability of their cell membranes. Voltage changes then occur, due to an influx of positive sodium ions through the more permeable membrane. These voltage changes are called graded potentials. When the sum of graded potentials reaches a sufficient magnitude, an electrical signal or action potential is generated that flows along the length of the neuron.

7. Neural impulses are transmitted from one neuron to another, across the synaptic gap, via chemical messengers called neurotransmitters. These neural transmitters may act to either excite or inhibit action potentials in the receiving neuron.

8. Variations in neurotransmitter levels or in responsivity to these chemical messengers has been linked with various psychological disorders and the action of numerous drugs.

9. Endogenous opiates, which are part of a family of neurotransmitters known as neuropeptides, have been linked to a range of behavioral and mental processes, including inducing euphoria, counteracting stress, modulating food and liquid intake, facilitating learning and memory, and reducing pain.

THE BRAIN AND SPINAL CORD

10. The spinal cord conveys messages to and from the brain, helps coordinate the two sides of the body, and mediates certain basic reflexive behaviors (such as the quick withdrawal of a hand from a hot stove).

11. The medulla, the lowest part of the brain, contains centers that control many vital life-support functions (breathing, heartbeat, and blood pressure).

12. The pons, a large bulge in the lower brain core, plays a role in fine-tuning motor messages and in processing some sensory information.

13. The cerebellum, tucked beneath the back part of the cerebral hemispheres, coordinates and regulates motor movements.

14. The reticular formation, a set of neural circuits extending from the lower brain up to the thalamus, plays a role in controlling levels of arousal and alertness.

15. The limbic system, a collection of structures located around the central core of the brain, is closely associated with emotional expression. It also is active in motivation, learning, and memory.

16. The hypothalamus, located beneath the thalamus, helps to maintain homeostasis within the body's internal environment. In addition, it plays a key role in controlling emotional expression and serves as the hub of the neuroendocrine system.

17. The thalamus, located beneath the cerebrum, plays a role in routing incoming sensory information to appropriate areas within the cerebral cortex.

18. The cerebral cortex, the thin outer layer of the cerebrum, is the part of the brain responsible for higher mental processes like perceiving, thinking, and remembering.

19. To some degree, researchers have been able to localize a variety of functions within various regions or lobes of the cortex of the two hemispheres. The frontal lobe contains the motor cortex, a narrow strip of brain tissue that controls a wide range of intentional body movements. The primary brain center for controlling speech is also in the frontal lobe. The parietal lobe contains the somatosensory cortex, which receives sensory information about touch, pressure, pain, temperature, and body position from various areas of the body. The occipital lobe consists primarily of the visual cortex, devoted to the business of seeing. A primary function of the temporal lobe, hearing, is localized in the auditory cortex.

20. Split-brain research, in which the primary connection between the two hemispheres (the corpus callosum) is severed, has revealed important information about the degree to which a particular function is controlled by one rather than both hemispheres (lateralization of function). This research has supported the interpretation that in most people the left hemisphere is primarily responsible for language and speech, logic, and mathematics. In contrast, the right hemisphere appears to be more important in perceiving spatial relationships, manipulating objects, synthesizing (generalizing the whole from segments), and artistic functions.

21. A number of techniques are employed to study the brain, including lesion production, brain stimulation and electrical recording via implanted wires, electroencephalography (EEG), computerized axial tomography (CAT), positron emission tomography (PET), and nuclear magnetic resonance (NMR).

THE PERIPHERAL NERVOUS SYSTEM

22. The PNS, which transfers information to and from the CNS, has two divisions: somatic and autonomic.

23. The somatic nervous system serves the major skeletal muscles that carry out intentional movements. It also contains nerves that transmit sensory information from the skin, muscles, and sensory organs of the body.

24. The autonomic nervous system controls the glands and smooth muscles of internal organs. The two subdivisions of the autonomic nervous system, the sympathetic and parasympathetic systems, operate in an integrative fashion to allow the body to function optimally when either relaxed or highly aroused. The sympathetic system is particularly active during emotional emergencies. The parasympathetic system, which provides a braking mechanism for organs activated by the sympathetic system, is more involved during relaxation and body restoration.

THE ENDOCRINE SYSTEM

25. The endocrine system is composed of several ductless glands that secrete hormones directly into the blood-

stream. The endocrine system often works in tandem with the nervous system to regulate a variety of bodily responses. The hypothalamus functions as a key interface between the nervous system and the endocrine system.

26. The endocrine system influences many important physiological functions, mental processes, and behavior patterns, including disease regulation, metabolism, emotional responses, and motivation.

27. The pituitary gland produces hormones which trigger other glands to release their products. Among other important products of the pituitary are growth hormone, which controls a number of metabolic functions, including the rate of growth, and neuropeptides, which act as neurotransmitters that influence such things as eating and drinking, sexual behavior, sleep, pain reduction, and responses to stress.

28. The thyroid gland produces thyroxine, which helps to regulate metabolism. Lethargy and hyperactivity are related to too little or too much thyroxine, respectively.

29. The paired adrenal glands produce a variety of hormones, including epinephrine and norepinephrine, that prepare the body to respond to emergencies and cope with stress.

30. The gonads secrete several varieties of sex hormones which influence development of physical sex characteristics, sexual reproduction, and sexual motivation.

4 Sensation and Perception

The first-person account in the margin illustrates three things. First, **sensations** (the basic, immediate experiences that a stimulus such as a sound or a touch elicits in a sense organ, such as the ears or the sensory receptors in the skin) provide an important input that directly affects our behavior. We react to the things we see, hear, smell, taste, and feel. Thus, an understanding of sensory experiences and processes is basic to our understanding of psychology.

The second point that the account illustrates is that the input of sensory organs only partly explains our behavioral responses to stimuli. There is much more to the story—for we interpret, organize, and often elaborate on the raw materials of sensation. This process, called **perception,** involves complex processes within the brain. Perception may be influenced by a variety of higher mental processes, such as memories, motivations, and expectations. This is illustrated by the fact that the pressure of someone else's fingers against our skin can set off uncontrollable giggles, while the same pressure caused by our own fingers does not feel ticklish at all. Our awareness that we are in control of the stimulus allows us to perceive pressure instead of tickles.

A third point illustrated by the account is the difference between sensation and perception. Whereas sensation occurs at the level of sensory receptors, perception is a cognitive process. Other evidence of this difference between sensation and perception is supplied by Figure 4.1. If you look at the figure, you probably see a spiral curving round and round until it reaches its innermost part. At least that is how most people perceive this image, known as *Fraser's spiral*. In actuality, there is no spiral at all—only concentric circles. One image (a pattern of circles and pinwheel-like lines) is projected onto your retinas, but your brain's interpretation of this information is quite different.

This chapter is concerned with both the sensory processes that bring us information about our environments and the mental activity that gives this information meaning. Although many of the processes described in this chapter may seem to be physiological, not psychological, it is important to remember that our sensations and perceptions form the raw material on which much of our behavior is based.

FIRST PERSON

I was very ticklish as a child, and my older brother was unmerciful in exploiting this weakness. He would hold me down and tickle away as I would holler and squirm. One day my uncle took me aside and told me that being ticklish was all in my head. Of course I didn't believe him at first, but he suggested I try tickling myself the same way my brother did.

What a revelation! The sensations produced by my own fingers were only mildly ticklish and easy to tolerate. My uncle told me to relax, close my eyes, and just pretend it was my own fingers the next time my brother tried his torture act. It worked. My perception of the sensations changed from intolerable to only mildly unpleasant simply as a result of changing my thoughts about what was occurring. (*Authors' files*)

FIGURE 4.1   FRASER'S SPIRAL

Fraser's "spiral" illustrates the difference between sensation and perception. Our perception of this figure as a spiral is an illusion—trace carefully and your finger will always come back to its starting point.

PRINCIPLES OF SENSATION AND PERCEPTION

All perceptions begin with a *stimulus*, some type of physical energy such as a sound or a flash of light, to which we can respond. The stimulus produces a physiological change in our sensory receptor cells, and this information is then transmitted to the brain, where it is organized and interpreted as psychological perceptions. Psychologists have coined the term **psychophysics** to describe the study of the relationship between the physical aspects of external stimuli and our own perceptions of them.

Five major senses provide us with important information about the outside world. These senses are vision, hearing, smell, taste, and the skin senses (pressure, temperature, and pain). In addition, the so-called body senses allow us to detect movement and the position of our bodies. Although the messages differ, the process by which sensory information reaches our brains is the same. It is called transduction.

TRANSDUCTION

In order for us to sense and perceive the surrounding world, information about external events must reach our brains. This information comes in many forms: mechanical energy for hearing and the skin senses; chemical energy for smelling and tasting; and light energy for seeing. However, the brain is only able to respond to the electrochemical events that are generated by neurons firing. Therefore, before we can perceive our environment, all sensory input must be transformed into electrochemical energy that may be processed by the brain. The process by which sensory organs transform mechanical, chemical, or light energy into neural firing is called **transduction.**

Each sense receptor has specialized cells designed to respond to a particular kind of energy. For example, our eyes contain chemicals called photopigments that change their shape when they are hit by light. These shape changes initiate a series of events that ultimately culminate in the transmission of an electrical impulse to the brain. Likewise, other kinds of receptors change other kinds of energy into electrical impulses.

DISTINGUISHING TYPES OF SENSORY IMPULSES

We know that the brain cannot respond directly to physical energy such as pressure or light: this information must first be transduced into electrochemical signals. If all sensory messages are converted to electrochemical signals, how does the brain distinguish among them? How can it differentiate among the impulses that represent sight, sound, taste, and smell? Take a moment to formulate your answer to this question before reading on.

Perhaps the best clue comes from some discoveries made in brain surgery, when various sites on the surface of an alert patient's cortex have been electrically stimulated. Such stimulation may produce vivid sensations. For example, stimulation of the occipital cortex at the back of the brain can create sensations of flashing lights, and stimulating the auditory region on the side of the brain can cause the patient to hear tones (Penfield & Perrot, 1963).

As this evidence reveals, the ability to distinguish sensations does not depend on differences between the sense organs but, rather, on that part of the brain that is activated by the sensory messages. Chapter 3 pointed out that sensory nerves travel to particular target sites within the brain. It is now widely believed that the distinctiveness of sights, sounds, smells, and so forth is related to unique properties of tissue in various parts of the brain (Sekuler & Blake, 1985).

WHY DO WE NOT PERCEIVE EVERYTHING?

The fact that sensations result from the transduction of physical energy in the environment into neural impulses raises an interesting question. Since we are surrounded by noises, smells, sights, and sounds, why are we not equally aware of all these sensations? For instance, suppose you end a summer evening stroll by sitting on a log near the edge of a mountain lake. The sun has long since set behind some nearby mountains, and the air is beginning to carry a chill. Somewhere close by a cricket chirps, and there are other sounds, sights, smells, and tactile sensations. Your world is full of different kinds of physical energy.

Although many of these physical events are transformed into sensations and ultimately perceptions, many go unheeded. What variables determine whether or not we perceive the things happening around us? There are several factors; the most important are sensory thresholds, attention, and adaptation.

Sensory Thresholds The psychological worlds constructed by our brains are much simpler than the physical complexity of the world around us. This is because our sense organs do not inform our brains about all of the events that take place. Our perception of various sensory inputs can occur only when the strength of a stimulus reaches a minimal or **threshold** level of intensity sufficient to activate a sensory process. For example, our sense of smell is activated only when an adequate number of chemical molecules are present in the air.

One of the most important reasons why we do not respond to many stimuli, therefore, is simply the biological limitations of our senses. If our senses responded to all the sights, sounds, smells, and other stimuli around us, we would be overwhelmed by too much stimulation. Two kinds of sensory thresholds operate to limit our perception of sensations: absolute thresholds and difference thresholds.

Absolute and Difference Thresholds Assume that you are still sitting on your log in the darkness. On the far shore of the lake, a camper strikes a match to light a pipe. You see a brief flicker, then only darkness. Your eyes

Sensory thresholds are different for different life forms. For example, sharks are able to sense one drop of blood in thousands of gallons of water.

As this girl smells the flower, its odor is transformed to chemical energy that causes neurons to fire, the brain to respond to the electrochemical events, and the girl to enjoy the wonderful scent.

remain fixed on this spot, and in a moment you see another light that you perceive to be brighter than the first. This second light is produced by the beam of a small flashlight being used to search for a dropped book of matches. How bright did the light from the match have to be before you could see it, and how much brighter did the second light from the flashlight have to be in order for you to realize it was brighter than the first light? Both of these questions are about sensory thresholds. The first pertains to what psychologists call an absolute threshold, and the second refers to a difference threshold.

An **absolute threshold** is defined as the minimum physical intensity of a stimulus that can be perceived by an observer 50 percent of the time. Figure 4.2 demonstrates some absolute thresholds for the five major senses. (Note that absolute thresholds for various sensory modalities differ significantly from person to person [Satow, 1987]. These values are averages for most humans; your sensory organs may be more or less efficient.) These averages represent ideal conditions; obviously, you will not be able to hear a watch ticking 20 feet away on New Year's Eve in Times Square.

The ability to discriminate relative differences between stimuli in a particular stimulus category is an important part of the sensory/perceptual process. For example, you were able to distinguish between the light of the match and that of the flashlight. A considerably weaker flashlight beam (or a much brighter match) might have made the difference indistinguishable. The minimum difference in intensity that you can distinguish between two stimuli 50 percent of the time is called the **difference threshold,** or the **just noticeable difference (jnd).**

Unlike the absolute threshold, the difference threshold is variable. How we experience a particular stimulus is always relative to its background level or its context. Thus, the degree of increase or decrease in intensity that is necessary to produce a jnd depends upon the original strength of the stimulus. In 1834 a German scientist, Ernest Weber, conducted a classic experiment that revealed one of the first major principles of sensation. He discovered that, for various stimulus intensities, the difference threshold tends to be a constant fraction of the stimulus. This means that as the strength of the original stimulus increases, the magnitude of the change

FIGURE 4.2   AVERAGE ABSOLUTE SENSORY THRESHOLDS OF HUMAN SENSES

Average absolute sensory thresholds for the five senses have been established by laboratory experiments. These are portrayed in the form of environmental stimuli comparable to those presented in the laboratory.

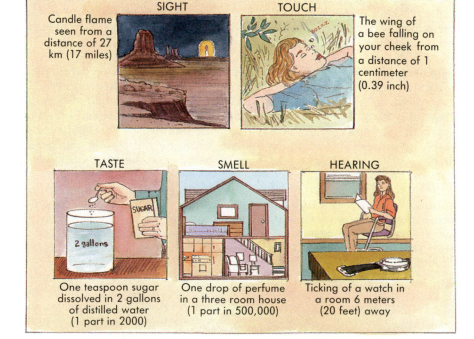

SIGHT
Candle flame seen from a distance of 27 km (17 miles)

TOUCH
The wing of a bee falling on your cheek from a distance of 1 centimeter (0.39 inch)

TASTE
One teaspoon sugar dissolved in 2 gallons of distilled water (1 part in 2000)

SMELL
One drop of perfume in a three room house (1 part in 500,000)

HEARING
Ticking of a watch in a room 6 meters (20 feet) away

must also increase in order for a jnd to be perceived. This relationship is known as **Weber's Law.**

Attention   Another factor influencing how much of the outside world we perceive is **attention.** In most situations, it is impossible to be aware of all the stimuli around us, even if we are biologically capable of responding to them. Instead, we pay attention to some but not to others (Johnston & Dark, 1986). For example, returning to your summer evening stroll, you may not have been aware of the mosquito buzzing around your bare leg because you were listening to the cricket. After feeling its sting, however, your attention might shift so that future mosquito sounds would be quickly detected.

Attention is a psychological selection mechanism that overrides mental processing of unimportant stimuli. It does not block the physical and biological response of our sense organs to these stimuli; it simply alters our psychological perception of these events. Of course, some stimuli are difficult to overlook, for example, someone mentioning your name in a conversation at the next table. The *Stroop effect*, portrayed in Figure 4.3, illustrates how difficult it is to ignore some kinds of stimuli. Later in this chapter we shall consider several characteristics of stimuli that are particularly effective in capturing our attention.

Adaptation   **Adaptation** describes the decrease in the response of sensory receptors when they are exposed to continual, unchanging stimulation. Adaptation occurs in all of the sensory organs, but some adapt more quickly than others. Our receptors for smell are the quickest to adapt, which is fortunate for people who live near industrial plants or have jobs requiring them to work in foul-smelling environments.

Most of our other senses adapt fairly quickly to constant stimulation. For example, you are probably not aware of the sensation of a belt around your waist even though you felt it when you put it on. You can conduct a simple experiment to demonstrate adaptation to yourself. Place ice-cold

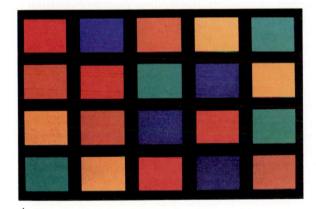

A.

B.

C.

FIGURE 4.3   THE STROOP EFFECT

This figure illustrates how difficult it is to ignore some kinds of stimuli. To demonstrate this to yourself, begin by naming the colors of the boxes in A. Next, read the words describing different colors in B. Up to this point, you should be able to respond quickly and with ease. Now, name the colors of the words in C. You will probably find that you proceed much more slowly, and perhaps make some errors. This reveals how difficult it is to ignore the meaning of the words. (*Source:* Adapted from Stroop, 1935)

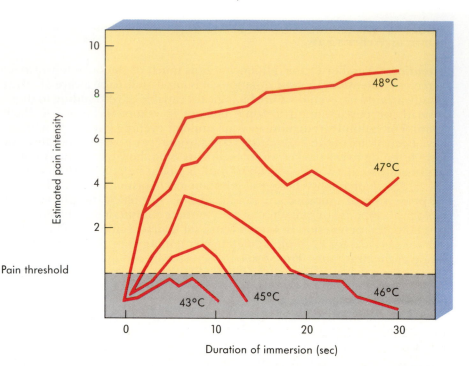

FIGURE 4.4   PAIN ADAPTATION

Averaged estimates of intensity of pain from different durations of hand immersions in hot water of varied temperatures. (*Source:* Adapted from Hardy et al., 1968)

water in one container, lukewarm water in another, and water so hot you can barely stand it in a third. Put your right hand in the ice water and your left hand in the very hot water. After a couple of minutes, put both hands into the container of lukewarm water. Since your right hand was previously adapted to ice water, the lukewarm water will feel very hot. Conversely, your left hand will feel cold, because it has adapted to the high temperature.

Unfortunately, the one sense modality that adapts very slowly (and usually only to a slight degree) is pain. People who are faced with chronic pain may learn to live with their discomfort, but seldom do they experience anything resembling acceptable adaptation. Research has demonstrated that while we often adapt somewhat to mild pain, we may not adapt to extremely painful stimuli (Coren et al., 1984). In one experiment, subjects rated the pain they felt from immersing their hands in hot water over a period of time. Figure 4.4 shows the results: adaptation was complete for lower temperatures, but it diminished with increasing pain to the point where there was no adaptation to the most painful stimulus level (Hardy et al., 1968).

The principles we have just discussed relate to all sensations, but each sense also has unique properties that we respond to in unique ways. The following sections explore the major senses: vision, hearing, taste, smell, and senses of touch and of body position.

VISION

In many ways, vision is our most important sense. It contributes enormously to our awareness of the surrounding environment, and it provides extremely valuable information that we can use to change our location or actions (Cutting, 1987). Much of what we do depends upon an adequately functioning visual system. When a person is deprived of his or her vision, as in an accident, the adjustment is often long and arduous. Vision's primary importance is reflected in the fact that a greater portion of our brains is devoted to vision than to any of the other senses.

Our visual systems are composed of three major parts: the eyes, which capture and respond to light energy; the neural circuits that transmit signals from the eye to the brain; and visual centers within the brain that interpret these messages.

FIGURE 4.5   THE ELECTROMAGNETIC SPECTRUM

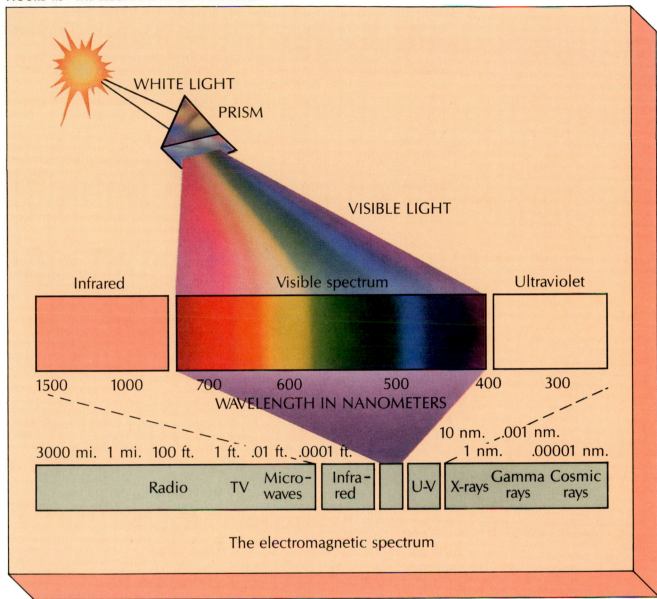

This figure shows the full range of the electromagnetic spectrum. The colors of the visible spectrum, which is only a small portion of the entire electromagnetic spectrum, may be obtained by passing a source of white light (such as sunlight) through a prism. Note that visible light ranges from roughly 400 nm to 750 nm.

LIGHT: THE STIMULUS FOR VISION

We see things because they reflect light. Light is a form of electromagnetic radiation. Virtually all matter consists of oscillating, electrically charged particles that discharge many forms of electromagnetic radiation, only one of which is light. Other varieties include cosmic rays, gamma rays, X-rays, ultraviolet rays, infrared rays, microwaves, and TV and radio waves. Electromagnetic radiation travels in waves, and different forms of this energy have different wavelengths. A *wavelength* is precisely defined by how far the radiation travels between oscillations. Wavelength is measured in nanometers, abbreviated *nm*. A nanometer is equal to a billionth of a meter.

Figure 4.5 shows the full range of the electromagnetic spectrum. Note that visible light ranges from roughly 400 to 750 nm—only a small portion of the electromagnetic spectrum. Our blindness to other segments of the full spectrum is not shared by all living things. For example, some insects can discern ultraviolet light, and some predators use infrared radiation to detect prey.

Brightness, hue, and saturation are three properties of light that are particularly important in the psychological study of vision. **Brightness,** or the intensity of light, is measured by the number of *photons* (particles of electromagnetic radiation that we see as light). In general, the more intense the light source, the more photons are emitted, and the brighter a light will appear.

Hue, or the color we perceive, is determined partly by the wavelength of light. In normal eyes, wavelengths of 400 nm are perceived as violet, 500 nm appear blue-green, 600 nm appear yellow-orange, and 700 nm look red. The perception of color is not just a matter of wavelength, however. Several colors, such as brown, purple, and white, are not even in the spectrum of visible light. Such colors are produced by a complex process in which the visual system mixes various wavelengths to produce a broad variety of colors.

A third dimension of light, **saturation,** determines how colorful light appears. White corresponds to a completely colorless state; the more white is present in color, the less saturated it is. If you slowly added white paint to red paint, the color red would undergo a gradual transition from a saturated deep red to a shade of pink, which is unsaturated red. Saturation may therefore be viewed as the proportion of colored (chromatic) light to non-colored (achromatic) light.

THE EYE

Brightness, hue, and intensity describe the stimulus of light, but our primary concern is how we receive that stimulus. For that, we must have some understanding of how our eyes work.

Figure 4.6 illustrates several key structures of the human eye. Two components of the eye are most relevant to our discussion. One is the image-focusing part, roughly comparable to a camera. Major structures within this unit are the cornea, lens, iris, and pupil. The other primary component of the eye's visual system is the image-recording part, called the retina. The film in a camera is roughly analogous to the retina.

Visual sensations result when patterns of light that enter the eye are focused on the light-sensitive retina. (Images focused on the retina are inverted, as shown in Figure 4.7.) When a light beam first enters the eye, it passes through the *cornea*, a thin, transparent membrane that bends or refracts light waves to bring them into sharper focus on the retina. Light then passes through the *aqueous humor*, a watery fluid that helps nourish the cornea.

Light next passes through a small opening in the *iris* called the *pupil*. The iris is a pigmented set of muscles that constrict or expand to control the amount of light that can enter. The pupil dilates (opens wide) to let more light in when illumination is low; and it constricts (becomes smaller) in response to bright light. Eye color is determined by the amount of pigmentation in the iris. Heavy pigmentation produces brown eyes, while little or no pigment results in blue eyes.

After light passes through the pupil, it enters the *lens*, an oblong elastic structure that further refracts and focuses the light beam into an image that is projected through the *vitreous humor* (a clear fluid that supplies nutrients to the interior of the eye) onto the retina. The focusing power of the lens resides in its ability to adjust its shape from flat to more rounded, depending on the distance between the object viewed and the eye. This focusing process is called **accommodation.** If the lens is functioning properly, a clear image is projected onto the retina. However, abnormalities in eye shape often make it impossible for the lens to accommodate correctly.

FIGURE 4.6   STRUCTURE OF THE EYE

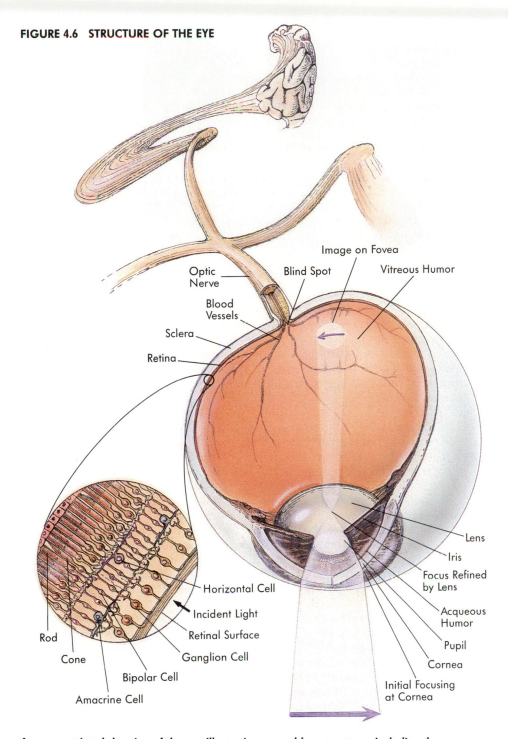

A cross-sectional drawing of the eye illustrating several key structures, including the image-focusing structures—the cornea, lens, iris, and pupil—and the image-recording part, the retina. The inset is a magnified portion of the retina which shows the key cells within this structure in greater detail. Visual information that converges on the retina is passed through a three-cell chain, from the primary receptor cells, the rods and cones, to bipolar cells to ganglion cells. The axons of the ganglion cells travel across the inner surface of the retina and converge to form the optic nerve, which carries visual messages to the brain.

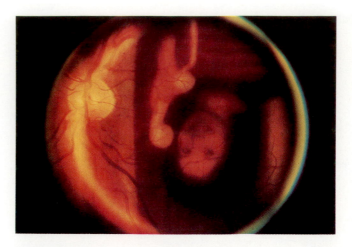

FIGURE 4.7   INVERTED RETINAL IMAGE

A specially designed camera allowed this photograph of a person's retina as the individual viewed a woman talking on the telephone. Notice that the image of the viewed person is inverted (images focused on the retina are inverted). The round blob of yellow at the right of the photo is the optic disk region, or blind spot, where the optic nerve exits the eye.

When this happens, a person may be either nearsighted or farsighted. (A nearsighted person is able to see distinctly for only a short distance, while someone who is farsighted can see distant objects clearly but cannot see near objects in proper focus.)

The Retina   Most of the structures of the eye function to focus light onto the **retina,** a thin layer of tissue at the back of the eye that records images. The insert in Figure 4.6 shows the key parts of the retina: rods, cones, bipolar cells, and ganglion cells. Light focused on the retina passes through several layers of neurons en route to the primary *photoreceptor cells*, the **rods** and **cones.** There are approximately 120 million rods and 8 million cones in each of our eyes (Sekuler & Blake, 1985).

The rods and cones are distributed in an orderly fashion across the inner layer of the retina. The most dense concentration of cones occurs in a region of the retina called the *fovea* (see Figure 4.6). Because our vision is sharpest when images are focused on the fovea, we move our eyes around until the image is projected to the fovea when we wish to focus clearly on an object.

Both the rods and the cones contain photopigments that respond to light. Their chemical response transduces light energy into neural signals (Pugh, 1987; Pugh & Miller, 1987). Neural signals are passed on from the rods and cones to the *bipolar cells*, which in turn pass information to the *ganglion cells*. The axons of the ganglion cells travel across the inner surface of the retina and converge to form the *optic nerve*, which carries visual messages to the brain (Shatz & Sretavan, 1986).

The part of the retina where the optic nerve exits the eye is known as the *optic disk*. There are no photoreceptor cells at this point. Consequently, the optic disk region is a blind spot: an image that is projected there will not be recorded. We are usually unaware of our blind spot, for a number of reasons. For one, our eyes are constantly moving, allowing us to pick up the image in another part of the retina. Furthermore, an image that hits the blind spot in one eye is focused somewhere else in the other eye, thus compensating for the momentary blindness. To see your blind spot in action, try the exercise in Figure 4.8.

In summary, visual information is passed through a three-cell chain, from rods and cones to bipolar cells to ganglion cells. Two other kinds of retinal cells, *horizontal cells* and *amacrine cells*, do not transmit visual signals toward the brain. Instead, they transmit signals laterally across the retina,

FIGURE 4.8 FINDING YOUR BLIND SPOT

There are no photoreceptors where the optic nerve leaves the eye. This creates a blind spot in our vision. To demonstrate this, close your left eye, fix your right eye on the cross, and move the book slowly toward your face. At a viewing distance of about 14 inches the obnoxious person will disappear but the vertical lines will not.

allowing interaction between adjacent photoreceptor, bipolar, and ganglion cells. This lateral communication is primarily inhibitory in nature, preventing visual signals from spreading out across the retina (Bloom et al., 1985; Coren at al., 1984).

Our perception of color depends largely on the cones (Nathans, 1987). Different cones respond to different-colored light. However, the cones are relatively poor light sensors as compared to the rods. A considerable amount of light must be projected on a cone before it responds by converting this energy to neural signals. Thus, the cones are not much good at night—which is why your friend's colorful sweater will be hard to see in a dark theater and why that classy new paint job on your car will hardly be noticeable at night.

Rods are extremely sensitive photoreceptors, allowing us to see in dim light. Our peripheral vision (vision away from the center of focus) depends primarily upon the rods, which are concentrated around the edges of the fovea and elsewhere on the surface of the retina. (No rods are in the fovea and only a relatively few cones are located outside the fovea.)

You can demonstrate for yourself some of the distinguishing features between the rods and cones next time you are outside on a clear night. Pick out a distant object that is barely discernible, like a faint star. If you look slightly to the side of the object, it will be easier to detect. This is because you have moved the image away from your fovea to the outer part of your retina, which is filled with light-sensitive rods.

Dark and Light Adaptation   You have probably had the experience of walking out of the light of your home or apartment into the dark of night. At first, you may not be able to see anything. In a short time, however, dim outlines of objects begin to appear, and you can find your way about fairly easily. This process is called **dark adaptation,** and it is due to a slow chemical change within the cones and the rods as they gradually become more sensitive to minimal levels of light. As Figure 4.9 shows, the rods reach full sensitivity about 30 minutes after you enter darkness, compared to 10 minutes for the cones.

When you return from the dark to your well-lit home, just the opposite process takes place. **Light adaptation** is a much faster process than dark adaptation. However, after your eyes have become completely dark-adapted, a brief exposure to bright light will not entirely reverse the process. For example, if you look into the bright lights of an approaching car for a

FIGURE 4.9   DARK ADAPTATION

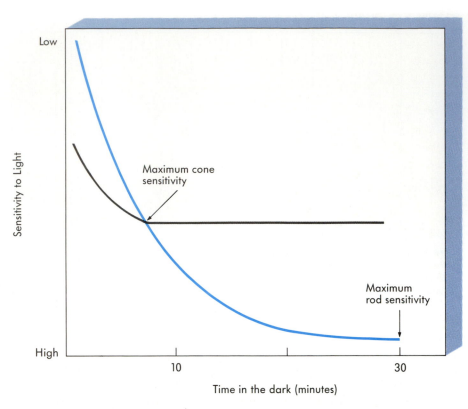

Low

Sensitivity to Light

Maximum cone
sensitivity

Maximum
rod sensitivity

High

10   30

Time in the dark (minutes)

This figure demonstrates that the amount of light necessary for detection is a function of the amount of time a person spends in the dark. The major dark adaptation occurs within the rods, which reach their full sensitivity to minimal light in about 30 minutes. The cones, which adapt less to darkness, reach maximum sensitivity in about 10 minutes.

few seconds, your dark adaptation will be only slightly lessened for a brief moment or two.

A few specialized techniques can help you maintain your night vision if you must use a light for a short period of time. One suggestion is to avoid exposure to white light. If you must read a road map while driving at night, for example, use a flashlight with a red filter. In the absence of a colored light device, cover one eye with the palm of your hand while reading the map. This way, you can maintain night vision in one eye even though you lose it in the other. (Simply closing one eye is not sufficient, since a considerable amount of light can penetrate our rather thin eyelids.)

In poor lighting, our eyes are most responsive to light in the 550–650 nm range, which corresponds to yellow-green. Other colors, particularly reds and blues, are difficult to detect in dimly lit surroundings. This is why many emergency vehicles such as fire engines are now often painted a lime or yellow-green color.

Projecting Visual Signals to the Brain   Visual signals from the retina are projected to the brain along the optic nerve. Before reaching the visual cortex at the back of the brain, visual information from the two eyes converges in a region of the thalamus called the *lateral geniculate nucleus.* As discussed in Chapter 3, the thalamus acts as a relay station, directing incoming sensory information to appropriate areas within the cortex. The two lateral geniculate nuclei, located in the left and right hemispheres of the thalamus, combine information from both eyes before sending it on to the cortex. From the lateral geniculate nuclei, this information is then sent to the visual cortex in the right and left hemispheres of the occipital lobe.

FIGURE 4.10   PICTURES AS COMPOSITES OF DOTS

You may be surprised to learn that this painting is actually composed of a multitude of tiny dots. When we look at a small area of this painting, highly magnified (lower left), it is impossible to decipher the overall image. However, at a lower magnification, the dots become indistinguishable as they merge to form a recognizable image. Information may enter the visual system in this form, to be analyzed by a "dot-detection system" in the visual cortex.

Research has yet to determine exactly how these neural signals are translated into visions of the things that we see. Perhaps the most revealing research to date has been conducted by David Hubel and Thorsten Wiesel (1979), who received the Nobel Prize in 1981 in recognition of their work. Hubel and Weisel inserted electrodes into the visual cortexes of anesthetized cats in order to study the responses of single cells to a variety of visual stimuli. They discovered that many cortical cells respond only to specific stimuli, such as movement in one direction, or lines, or contours in particular orientations. From the responses of single cells, the visual cortex seems to be able to extract information about size, shape, and movement. But how do all these individual signals yield the solid images that we see?

If you used a powerful magnifying glass to examine a photograph in this book, you would discover that the image is composed of dots, as Figure 4.10 illustrates. The dots are closely packed in dark areas and farther apart in light areas. When we look at only a small area of the dots, highly magnified, it is impossible to decipher the overall image. However, when we back off, the individual dots become indistinguishable. Our perception of particular patterns and shapes may result from highly specialized detector cells in the cortex operating in a similar fashion. Thus, you might say that the visual cortex is the brain's "dot-detection system" (Bloom et al., 1985).

DO WE SEE WITH OUR EYES OR OUR BRAINS?

What do we actually see with, our eyes or our brains? What type of sight-eliminating injuries would rule out the possibility of recovering sight through treating the eyes? Is it possible that a person could "see" without functioning eyes? If so, how might this miracle be accomplished? Try to generate some answers to these questions before reading on.

As marvelous as they are for detecting light energy, our eyes are merely devices for gathering and sending visual messages. Visual perception occurs in the brain. We see only when our brains allow us to interpret incoming signals. If the visual cortex were destroyed, we could no longer see even though our eyes would continue to gather and transmit visual signals. Consequently, brain damage is the one type of sight-destroying injury medical intervention cannot yet overcome. In contrast, many abnormalities of the eyes can often be treated by surgery or corrective devices.

The idea of a person seeing without functioning eyes might strike you as absurd. Until recently, most vision researchers would have agreed that the eyes are indispensable to the experience of vision. However, in the mid–1970s, a fascinating new line of research began to provide evidence that contradicts this assumption.

Visual Help for Blind People   Many totally blind people cannot see because defects in the retina or optic nerve prevent neural signals from reaching the visual cortex. A team of researchers, headed by William Dobelle, reasoned that if they could by-pass the affected area by sending signals to electrodes on the surface of the visual cortex, such patients might be able to have some kind of visual experience. After all, what is vision other than an intricate interrelationship of neurons within the visual cortex?

Applying this rationale, Dobelle and his co-workers implanted 64 electrodes in the visual cortex areas of totally blind volunteers' brains (see Figure 4.11). Stimulation of the cortex by a single electrode created some primitive visual experiences, causing a subject to "see" a *phosphene*—a tiny spot of glowing light that seemed to be located several feet in front of the viewer's face. Dobelle's team discovered that if a number of electrodes were activated at the same time, subjects could discern meaningful patterns among simultaneously occurring phosphenes. For example, one subject who had been accidentally blinded several years earlier was able to see various patterns and shapes, and even to differentiate letters of the alphabet (Dobelle, 1977).

Researchers are currently working to develop a more sophisticated visual prosthesis, such as the apparatus shown in Figure 4.11. A blind person might be provided with an artificial eye that consists of a highly miniaturized TV camera mounted in a glass enclosure. The camera would convert light images from the environment into a pattern of electrical signals that would be relayed to a tiny computer, which in turn would process the information and transfer it to the visual cortex through implanted electrodes.

Many problems must be solved before an effective working model of this system is developed. For example, since an array of only 64 electrodes is not adequate to process complicated visual information, researchers are trying to develop a 512-electrode system that would let people respond more naturally to their changing environments (Goldstein, 1984).

COLOR VISION

Among mammals, only primates (humans, apes, and monkeys) are able to perceive a full range of colors. Cattle have no color vision (the colorful cape of the matador is merely a prop for human observers). Most

FIGURE 4.11   ARTIFICIAL VISION: ELECTRICAL STIMULATION OF THE VISUAL CORTEX

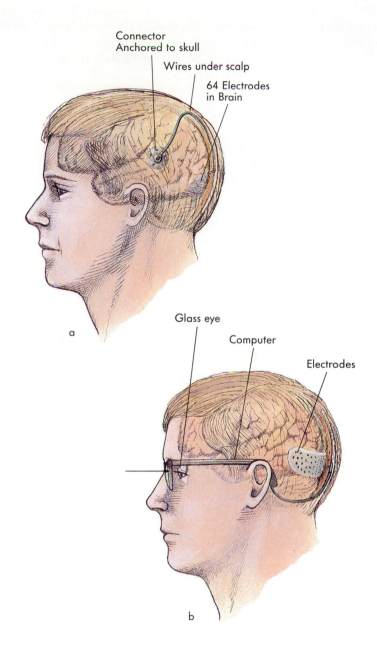

The illustration on the top portrays the procedure used by William Dobelle and his associates to create primitive visual experiences in blind volunteers. An array of 64 electrodes was implanted in the visual cortex. Wires from the implanted electrodes exited through a small opening in the back of the skull, and then passed beneath the scalp to a point where they terminated in a connector attached to the skull. An external source of electrical current was then attached to the connector, and stimulation was introduced via a single electrode or a pattern of several electrodes activated simultaneously. Dobelle found that stimulation of a single electrode caused a subject to "see" a phosphene (see text for description). The activation of several electrodes at the same time allowed subjects to discern meaningful patterns among simultaneously occurring phosphenes.

   Researchers are hopeful that a more sophisticated visual prosthesis, such as the apparatus shown in the illustration on the bottom, will allow a more refined variety of artificial vision. See the text for a description of how this apparatus might work.

The colorful cape of the matador may impress human observers, but the bull would not react differently if the cape were grey or brown.

color-vision experts think that dogs do not see color either, although some recent evidence suggests that they may have some limited capacity to discern colors (Jacobs, 1983). Surprisingly, simpler organisms like fish, birds, reptiles, and insects have excellent color vision (Nathans, 1987). Before examining what is known about how we perceive colors, let us briefly consider how colors are mixed to produce all the various hues.

Additive and Subtractive Color Mixing Color is a psychological phenomenon in that it is determined by our brains as they perceive light reflected from objects. The potential for color perception is not inherent in the objects themselves; instead, it is determined by the reflected beams of light. Most light, including light from incandescent lamps and from sunlight, is called *white light*. We do not perceive it as being colored, yet it contains all the wavelengths for the various colors within the visible spectrum. The grass growing outside your front door appears green because it absorbs most of the wavelengths in the white light falling on it but reflects those within a limited range that send "green" signals to your brain. Thus the perception of different colors depends on different sets of wavelengths being absorbed and reflected.

From working with pigment agents, such as paints or crayons, you probably know that all the hues are produced by different mixtures of the primary colors, red, blue, and yellow. Interestingly, when colored lights rather than pigments are mixed, the primary colors are red, green, and blue. Physicists who have experimented with mixing different colors of light report that all the various hues can be obtained by mixing red, green, and blue lights. Combining this information about primary pigments and light colors leads us to conclude that humans with normal color vision are able to distinguish a vast array of colors formed from various combinations of four basic hues—red, blue, yellow, and green—and two hueless colors, white and black (Hurvich, 1981).

EXPLAINING SUBTRACTIVE AND ADDITIVE COLOR MIXING

You probably know that if you mix yellow and blue paints, the result is green. However, when yellow and blue light are combined, the result is gray. Why is this so? Take a moment to formulate an answer before reading on.

Explaining the difference between subtractive and additive color mixing provides an answer to this question. Most if not all of your experience mixing colors has probably been of the subtractive variety. **Subtractive color mixing** occurs when paint or other pigments are mixed. When light falls on a colored object, some wavelengths are absorbed (subtracted) and others are reflected. The wavelength of the reflected light determines the hue we perceive. For example, when yellow and blue paint are mixed, these two pigments subtract or absorb nonyellow and nonblue wavelengths. The result is a pigment that reflects only those wavelengths that are between yellow and blue, which is green.

Additive color mixing occurs when lights with different wavelengths simultaneously stimulate the retina. Our resulting color perception is based on the adding or combining of these respective wavelengths. Unlike subtractive color mixing, which takes place in the object we are viewing, additive mixing is done by our visual systems. The colors you perceive on your television screen are products of additive color mixing. If you were able to magnify this picture many fold, you would see that images are composed of tiny red, green, and blue dots. A close examination of a yellow object would reveal that it consists of red and green dots.

Theories of Color Vision Two major theories have been proposed to explain how we see colors. They are the trichromatic theory and the opponent-process theory of color vision.

The Trichromatic Theory of Color Vision In 1802 Thomas Young, an English physicist and physician, demonstrated that various combinations of red, green, and blue can produce all the other colors in the spectrum. He suggested that the human eye contains three types of color receptors corresponding to these three distinct hues, and that the brain somehow creates our perception of color by combining the information transmitted by each type of receptor. Half a century later, Young's theory was modified and expanded by the German physiologist Hermann von Helmholtz. Their combined theory became known as the **Young-Helmholtz theory,** or the **trichromatic theory of color vision.**

Neither Young nor Helmholtz was aware that the retina contained distinct photoreceptor cells. Over a century later, their theory was supported when research revealed that there are three distinct kinds of cones in the human retina, each containing a different photopigment. These cones are maximally sensitive to light of three wavelengths: 435, 540, and 565 nm (Nathans, 1987). Figure 4.5 reveals that these wavelengths correspond to blue, green, and yellow-green. However, to be consistent with earlier convention, researchers continue to refer to these receptors as blue, green, and red cones. Although the photopigments in each of these types of cones respond most effectively to light in the wavelengths listed above, light of a particular wavelength stimulates more than one type of receptor (Ohtsuka, 1985).

The trichromatic theory explains the effects of mixing colors of different wavelengths. However, it does not explain some other phenomena, such as negative afterimages (discussed in the following section) and the fact that color-blind people almost always fail to distinguish pairs of colors rather than just one color. A second theory, the opponent-process theory, helps to explain these phenomena.

The Opponent-process Theory of Color Vision In the 1870s a German physiologist, Ewald Hering, proposed a theory of color vision asserting that yellow is as basic a color as red, blue, and green; that is, that yellow is not a mixture of other colors. Hering believed we see six primary colors rather than the three proposed by Young and Helmholtz: red, green, blue, yellow, black, and white. He further theorized that these six colors are grouped into three pairs, which form three types of receptors: one receptor, the black-

FIGURE 4.12   A TEST FOR COLOR BLINDNESS

A person with red-green color blindness will not be able to see the number 6 in the top illustration, and the number 12 in the bottom illustration will not be visible to a person with yellow-blue color blindness. (Please note that these reproductions of color plates employed in tests for color blindness cannot be used to screen for these defects.)

white pair, contributes to our perception of brightness and saturation; and the other two receptors, a red-green and a blue-yellow pair, are responsible for our perception of color.

Hering believed that the two members of each pair tend to work in opposition to each other, one inhibiting the other (hence the name **opponent-process theory**). According to this viewpoint, if our eyes are struck by light containing more red wavelengths than green, the red inhibits the green and we perceive red. The blue-yellow system works similarly. This is why we never perceive such shades as greenish red or bluish yellow.

Hering's opponent-process theory is consistent with what we know about color blindness. Approximately eight percent of males and one-half percent of females exhibit some form of color blindness (Nathans, 1987), but only rarely are individuals totally blind to color. Most people with color-vision problems have difficulty detecting pairs of colors. Red-green color blindness is the most common (see Figures 4.12 and 4.13). People with red-green color blindness cannot see either red or green, but they can see other colors. Yellow-blue color blindness is much less common.

Hering was also intrigued with the phenomenon of *negative after-images*. Figure 4.14 provides a demonstration. If you stare for about a minute at the dot in the middle of the oddly colored American flag, then turn your gaze on the dot in the adjacent white space, you will see the flag appear in the form of a negative afterimage in the familiar red, white, and blue of Old Glory.

This fits in nicely with the opponent-process theory. When you stare at the green stripes, the green component of the red-green receptor becomes fatigued. However, the red component does not tire since it is not being stimulated. When you shift your eyes to the white surface, the light it reflects stimulates the red and green components equally. Since the overloaded green component is fatigued, it responds only minimally. This imbalance in the opponent pair produces the faint red afterimage. A similar rationale explains why blue appears in the place of yellow and white in the place of black.

Most contemporary vision experts believe that both the trichromatic theory and the opponent-process theory may be at least partly correct. In fact, our color perception may be a product of both mechanisms. The trichromatic system may operate at the level of the photoreceptors, with three kinds of light-sensitive pigments in the cones. At the same time, the "on and off" type of process described by Hering has been identified in ganglion cells of the retina and in the lateral geniculate nuclei (DeValois & DeValois,

FIGURE 4.13   COLOR BLINDNESS

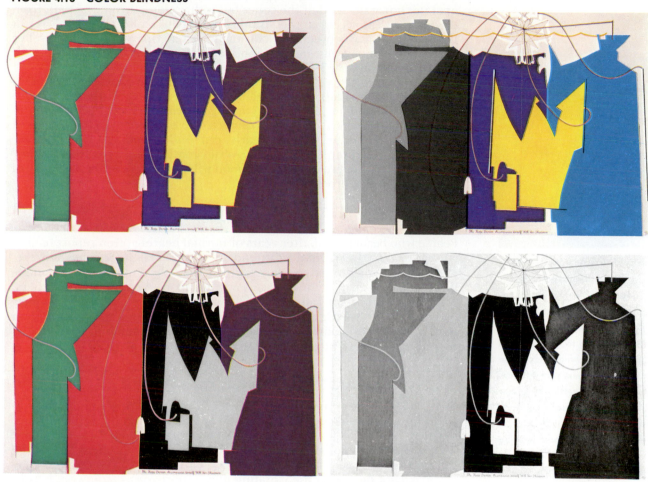

The painting in the upper left panel—"The Rope Dancer Accompanies Herself With Her Shadows," by Man Ray—appears as it would to a person with normal color vision who can see all the colors in the visible spectrum. In the upper right panel the painting is reproduced as it might look to someone with red-green color blindness. Similarly the reproductions in the lower left and right panels reflect how the painting would appear to individuals with yellow-blue and total color blindness, respectively. (Painting by Man Ray, Museum of Modern Art, New York. Gift of G. David Thompson)

FIGURE 4.14   DEMONSTRATION OF NEGATIVE AFTERIMAGES

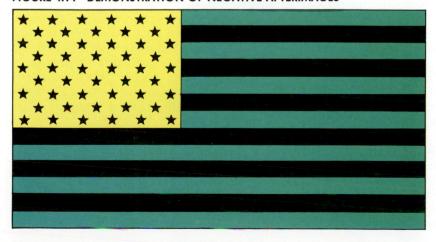

Stare at the center of the flag for about 45 seconds. Then shift your gaze to a sheet of white paper. You will see a faint image of the more familiar red, white, and blue of Old Glory. This is a negative afterimage.

1975, 1980). These findings suggest that the opponent-process mechanism operates not at the level of the cones but rather along the neural path from the photoreceptor cells to the visual cortex. Thus, color vision may result from an interplay between a trichromatic system operating at the level of the photoreceptor cells and an opponent-process mechanism working at later stages (Hurvich, 1978).

In the last few years, researchers have begun to explore the possibility that the trichromatic cone system might even interact in an opponent-process manner. This speculation was supported by a recent discovery that red and green cones are directly connected to each other in the retinas of turtles (Norman et al., 1984). Clearly, our understanding of how we see color is far from complete. New discoveries continue to be made, and many researchers are hopeful that science soon will provide a complete picture of how this complex process works.

HEARING

People who become deaf after years of normal hearing often report feeling a great deal of stress and a profound sense of isolation (Sekuler & Blake, 1985). Hearing allows us to enjoy perhaps the richest form of communication. A deaf person cannot easily engage in conversation with others, whereas a blind person can converse with people either person-to-person or over the phone. Thus, while our ears may bring us less information than our eyes, they do convey a special type of social communication that is exceedingly important to our appreciation of life.

SOUND: THE STIMULUS FOR HEARING

Most of the sounds we hear consist of physical energy in the form of rhythmic pressure changes in the air. When an object vibrates to produce sound, it sets air molecules in motion. The vibrating motion of the sound source alternately pushes air molecules together and pulls them apart. The forward thrust of the vibrating object as it moves toward you *compresses* the air, making it denser; as the vibrating object moves away from you, it pulls the molecules farther apart, thus *rarefying* the air, making it thinner. These changes in air pressure constitute sound waves, and they travel at a speed of approximately 1,100 feet per second.

When the compressed-air portion of the sound wave arrives at your ear, it bends the tympanic membrane (your eardrum) inward. The negative pressure of the following rarefied portion of the sound wave causes your eardrum to bend out (see Figure 4.15). These movements or vibrations of the eardrum begin the complex process of transducing the energy of sound waves into the neural signals that carry auditory messages to the brain.

Sound waves most commonly travel through the medium of air. However, other media such as the ground, water, wood, or metal also convey sound waves. Perhaps you have listened to a conversation in the next room with your ear against the wall, have heard an approaching train by pressing your ear against a metal rail, or have heard sounds while swimming under water. In outer space, where no atmosphere exists to provide a medium for sound waves, all events occur in total silence. When the astronauts walked on the moon, they were able to communicate because radio waves were converted into sound waves within the artificial atmospheres of their helmets.

Three characteristics of sound waves influence our perception of sound: loudness, pitch, and timbre. The amplitude or intensity of a sound wave determines the **loudness** of a sound. Loudness is measured in *decibels* (db). A decibel is not a linear unit like a pound or an inch; rather, it is a point on a sharply rising curve of intensity. For example, 10 db is 10 times greater than 1 db, but 30 db is 1000 times greater than 1 db, and 100 db is approximately 10 billion times greater than 1 db. To most people, a sound at 10 db

My loss of hearing [which took place in this woman's early adulthood] degraded the quality of my life more than I ever would have imagined. Aside from the general problems of trying to function in a silent world, my deafness has made interaction with others very difficult.

I used to enjoy getting together for gab sessions or spending hours on the phone talking with friends. Now I can't do any of that. Reading lips is not a perfected skill, at least not for me. Can you imagine what it would be like to be surrounded by people, concentrating on one person's lip movements, and not be able to hear any of the activity around you? For me, deafness produces a profound sense of isolation. Sometimes I almost think it would be better to be blind than deaf. At least then I could talk with people and feel more connected to them. (*Authors' files*)

The movie *Children of a Lesser God* gives us a firsthand account of what it's like to be deaf. Here, actress Marlee Matlin communicates her deepest feelings to actor William Hurt through sign language. Marlee Matlin, who is deaf in real life, won an Oscar for her performance in this film.

In outer space, where no atmosphere exists to provide a medium for sound waves, astronauts are able to communicate through the artificial atmospheres created within their helmets.

is quite soft, whereas one as loud as 130 db is painful. Figure 4.16 shows the decibel levels of a number of common sounds.

A second important property of a sound wave is its frequency, which determines the **pitch** that we perceive. Sound wave frequency is measured in *Hertz* (Hz), or cycles per second. The higher the pitch, the shriller we perceive a sound to be. The average human ear can perceive sound waves within the range of 20 to 20,000 Hz. We are most sensitive to sound waves in the 100–3,500 Hz range, which is, conveniently, the range where most human speech falls. The lowest pitched note on a piano, at 27.5 Hz, is barely audible to us. The highest sound a piano can make has been recorded at 4,180 Hz.

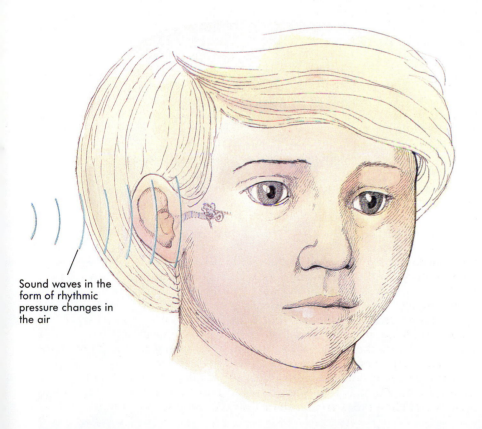

Sound waves in the form of rhythmic pressure changes in the air

FIGURE 4.15   THE STIMULUS OF SOUND

Sound waves composed of changes in air pressure as air molecules are alternately compressed and pulled farther apart.

FIGURE 4.16 THE DECIBEL LEVELS OF A NUMBER OF COMMON SOUNDS

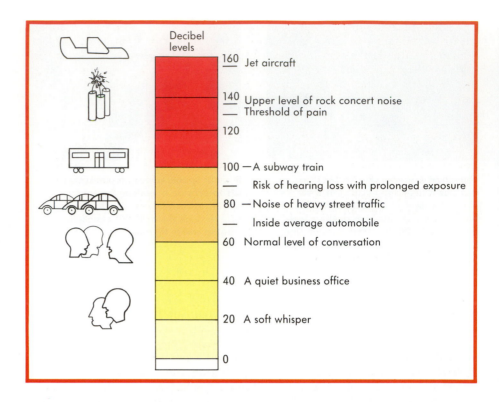

FIGURE 4.17 PHYSICAL PROPERTIES AND PERCEPTUAL DIMENSIONS OF SOUND WAVES

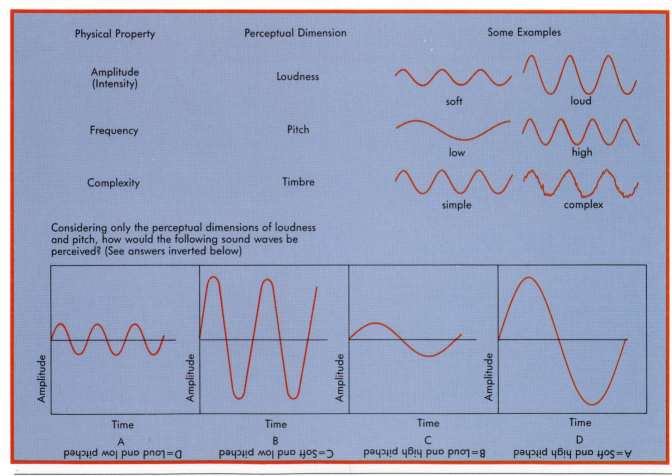

Nonhuman animals can perceive sound wave frequencies well above the upper limits for humans. For example, dogs can hear up to about 80,000 Hz, which is why you can use a special whistle to call your dog in the middle of the night without awakening other members of your family. The upper limits of the audible pitch range are even higher for dolphins, extending well beyond 100,000 Hz.

DISTINGUISHING DIFFERENT SOUNDS OF THE SAME PITCH

You may have noticed that the same notes sound different when produced by different instruments. Middle C played on the piano sounds quite different from the same note played on the violin, in spite of the fact that both instruments produce sound waves with exactly the same frequency. What explains this distinction? Try to formulate an answer before reading on.

Neither the violin nor the piano produces a pure note of a single frequency. In fact, very few of the sounds we hear are pure tones. Most are a combination of a *fundamental frequency* and a unique set of additional frequency components called *overtones*. Combined with the fundamental frequency, these overtones add a characteristic quality called **timbre** to complex sounds. Our ability to distinguish between the sounds of various musical instruments depends on differences in timbre. If sound filters were used to screen out all overtones, it would be impossible for a person to identify various instruments just by hearing them play.

Figure 4.17 summarizes the three characteristics of sound waves. Before reading on, see if you can tell how samples A, B, C, and D would be perceived.

THE EAR

The ear has three major parts: the outer ear, the middle ear, and the inner ear (see Figure 4.18). What most of us call our ears are merely the *pinnas*, the odd-shaped, flesh-covered cartilage that protrudes from the sides of our heads. The function of the pinna is to collect and funnel sound waves down the *auditory canal*, which, along with the pinna, forms the outer ear.

At the end of the auditory canal, sound waves strike the eardrum, or **tympanic membrane**, and start it vibrating. The eardrum, which serves as the opening to the middle ear, is connected to a set of three tiny linked bones called **ossicles**. The ossicles act like a system of levers that transfer and amplify the intensity of a sound stimulus. When the eardrum vibrates, it nudges the first bone in the series, the *malleus* (hammer), which in turn moves the *incus* (anvil), which moves the *stapes* (stirrup).

When the ossicles vibrate in response to sound waves, the last bone in the series, the stapes, pounds against an opening to the inner ear called the oval window. The inner ear consists of a snail-shaped, coiled chamber called the **cochlea**, which is filled with fluid. The cochlea consists of three wedge-shaped chambers: the *vestibular canal*, the *cochlear duct*, and the *tympanic canal* (see Figure 4.19). The tympanic canal and cochlear duct are separated by the **basilar membrane**.

Except for two locations, where it is covered by flexible, elastic material, the walls of the cochlea consist of hard bone. The two flexible spots are the *oval window* and the *round window* at the base of the tympanic canal. These two flexible surfaces allow pressure waves to be generated within the fluid that fills the vestibular and tympanic canals.

When the oval window is pushed inward by the action of the stapes, the round window compensates by bulging outward. These mechanical displacements are translated into pressure waves that flow through the vestibular and tympanic canals, causing ripples in the flexible basilar membrane.

FIGURE 4.18 ANATOMY OF THE HUMAN EAR

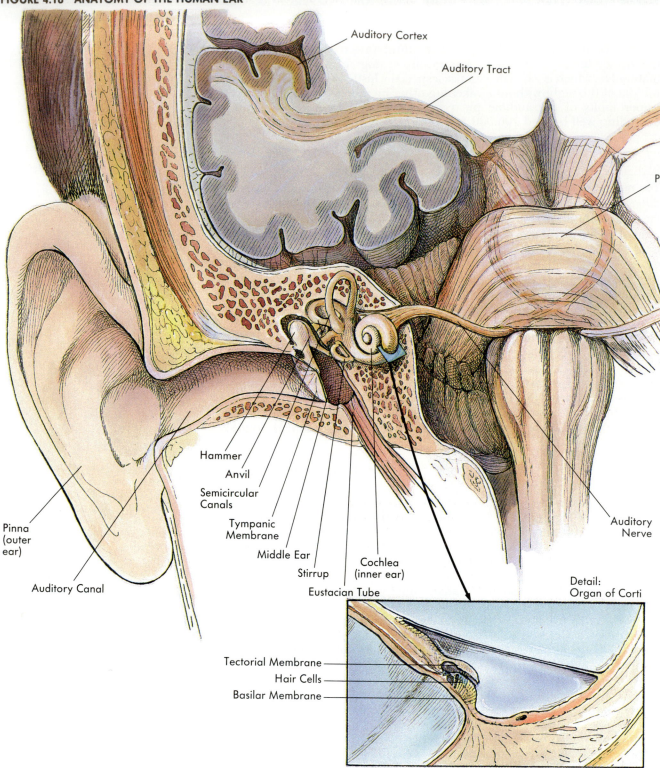

Auditory Cortex

Auditory Tract

Pons

Hammer

Anvil

Semicircular Canals

Tympanic Membrane

Middle Ear

Stirrup

Cochlea (inner ear)

Eustacian Tube

Auditory Nerve

Pinna (outer ear)

Auditory Canal

Detail: Organ of Corti

Tectorial Membrane

Hair Cells

Basilar Membrane

The outer ear, consisting of the pinna and auditory canal, collects and funnels sound waves to the eardrum which cause it to start vibrating. The eardrum, which serves as the opening to the middle ear, is connected to a set of three tiny linked bones called ossicles which act as a system of levers that amplify the intensity of a sound stimulus as it is transmitted to the inner ear. The last bone in the series, the stapes, pounds against an opening to the inner ear called the oval window. The resulting vibrations of the oval window generate pressure waves within the fluid of the cochlea that flow through its confines, causing ripples in the flexible basilar membrane. The sound message is then transduced, via the organ of Corti, into a neural message transmitted to the brain along the auditory nerve.

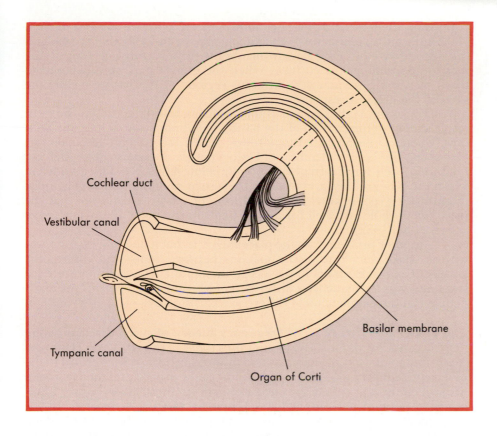

Cochlear duct

Vestibular canal

Tympanic canal

Organ of Corti

Basilar membrane

FIGURE 4.19   THE THREE CHAM-BERS OF THE COCHLEA

Another structure, the **organ of Corti**, sits on top of the basilar membrane. It consists of a layer of supporting cells resting on the basilar membrane, rows of specialized neurons known as auditory hair cells that project upward, and a *tectoral membrane* that hangs over the basilar membrane like an awning. The hair cells terminate in tiny hairlike protrusions called *cilia*. When the basilar membrane ripples in response to pressure waves, the cilia are moved against the relatively stationary tectoral membrane, bending "like tiny clumps of seaweed swept back and forth by invisible underwater currents" (Sekuler & Blake, 1985, p. 311). This bending of the cilia causes the hair cells to release neurotransmitters that activate adjacent neurons of the *auditory nerve*, which carries messages to the auditory cortex in the brain.

In summary, then, sound waves are converted into mechanical movements of the ossicles in the middle ear, which in turn act on the inner ear to produce pressure waves that travel through the fluid of the cochlea, flexing the basilar membrane and activating hair cells of the organ of Corti, which in turn activate neurons of the auditory nerve. In this complex manner, the physical energy of sound waves is converted into neural impulses that our brains translate into sounds.

THEORIES OF PITCH DISCRIMINATION

How can we distinguish between high- and low-pitched sounds, so that we can automatically tell a child's voice from an adult's voice or hear the differences among the notes of a scale? There are two major theories explaining how we discriminate pitch: the place theory and the frequency theory.

The Place Theory   The **place theory of pitch discrimination** was developed primarily by Georg von Békésy, who was awarded the Nobel Prize in recognition of his monumental contributions to the science of hearing. Békésy theorized that sound waves of different frequency displace different regions on the basilar membrane, allowing us to perceive varying pitches. He conducted experiments with guinea pigs to test this theory, using a microscope to observe the basilar membrane through tiny holes cut in various locations along the cochlea. When the guinea pigs were exposed to tones of varying frequencies, different regions of the basilar membrane showed the greatest response.

For example, Békésy noted that high-pitched tones caused the most displacement in the portion of the basilar membrane close to the oval window, whereas intermediate-range tones caused the greatest response farther along the basilar membrane. Unfortunately, Békésy's theory did not hold up as well for low-frequency tones, below 4,000 Hz. The manner in which tones below this level displace the basilar membrane is largely indistinguishable (von Békésy, 1960). Subsequent research confirms that the place theory holds up well for all but tones in the lower frequency range (Lewis et al., 1982).

Another problem with the place theory is that it does not explain how we can make very fine discriminations between tones that differ only slightly. The displacement in the basilar membrane is virtually identical for two tones whose frequencies differ by as little as 1 or 2 Hz, and yet many people can discriminate tonal differences this small.

The Frequency Theory   The **frequency theory of pitch discrimination** helps account for our ability to distinguish tones in the 20–4,000 Hz range. According to this interpretation, first advanced by Ernest Rutherford in the nineteenth century, our perception of low tones depends on the frequency with which the hair cells trigger firing of fibers in the auditory nerve. Thus, our perception of pitch in the lower frequency range is determined by the frequency of impulses traveling up the auditory nerve. Research has demonstrated that fibers in the auditory nerve actually do fire in rhythm with tones in the low-frequency range (Rose et al., 1967). Thus, if we listen to middle C on a piano (262 Hz), our auditory nerve fibers will fire at a rate of 262 times per second.

PERCEIVING PITCH IN THE 1,000–4,000 Hz RANGE

Single auditory neurons are capable of firing up to 1,000 times per second. How, then, can we account for the pitch perception in the 1,000–4,000 Hz range? (Remember, place theory does not adequately explain our perception of tones below 4,000 Hz.) See if you can come up with a possible explanation before reading on.

Since one hair cell can fire no more than 1,000 times per second, researchers have theorized that groups of interrelated neurons fire in a staggered fashion to convey frequencies above 1,000 Hz. This conception of a group of neurons working together is a version of the frequency theory appropriately named **volley theory**. For example, three neurons working in concert, each firing at 1,000 impulses per second, could produce a perception of a 3,000 Hz tone if their respective messages were appropriately integrated.

The best available evidence suggests that pitch is determined by both the *place* of maximal excitation of the basilar membrane and the *frequency* with which auditory nerve fibers fire. Place theory seems to explain how we discriminate among higher pitched tones above 4,000 Hz, whereas the frequency theory, with the volley principle, seems to offer the best explanation of pitch discrimination among lower frequencies.

AUDITORY LOCALIZATION

People are usually able to locate the origins of sounds rather well. Even infants do a good job of locating sounds in their environments (Castillo & Butterworth, 1981). This ability, called **auditory localization**, is the result of the difference in the sounds that arrive in each of our two ears. One key difference is in the intensity of loudness of the sounds. If someone sitting to the left of you blows a whistle, the sound wave reaching your left ear will be more intense than the sound striking your right ear. This occurs because a large object like the human head does not transmit high-frequency sounds very well; your right ear is in a "sound shadow." By the time the sound wave circumnavigates your head to reach your right ear, its intensity diminishes somewhat. Our brain uses this information about differing intensities to determine the origin of the sound (Semple & Kitzes, 1987).

In addition to intensity difference, another important auditory localization cue has to do with the time a sound arrives. As we learned earlier, sound waves travel through the air at the relatively slow rate of 1,000 feet per second. Thus, sound originating from our left will strike the left eardrum fractions of a second before it completes the somewhat longer journey to our right ear. Here again, our brains utilize information about these minuscule time differences to help us localize sounds.

HEARING LOSS

Roughly 20 million people in the United States suffer some hearing loss, which makes this the most common of all physical disabilities. Hearing loss can have a number of causes, including prolonged exposure to loud noises, infections, head injuries, and excessive wax build-up. Regardless of the causes, all hearing difficulties can be divided into two classes: sensorineural hearing loss and conduction hearing loss.

Sensorineural Hearing Loss   Damage to either the hair cells of the inner ear or the auditory nerve can cause **sensorineural hearing loss**. The most common example of this type of impairment is the gradual loss of sensitivity to high frequencies that occurs with aging, a condition called *presbycusis*.

Research has shown that high-frequency deafness begins at a surprisingly early age: most 30-year-olds are unable to hear tones above 15,000 Hz, and by ages 50 and 70 the upper limit of the average person's hearing range drops to 12,000 Hz and 6,000 Hz, respectively (Davis & Silverman, 1960). Some medical researchers believe that presbycusis is due, at least in part, to a lessening of blood flow to the inner ear, which destroys some of the critical neural elements in this structure.

Exposure to excessively loud noises can also cause permanent damage to the sensitive structures of the inner ear. This type of hearing loss is often accompanied by an annoying condition called *tinnitus*, a continuous ringing in the ears. The effects of exposure to loud noises may accumulate over a person's life, thereby contributing to a steady loss of hearing with advancing age. Hearing loss is not just age related, however. Brief exposure to extremely loud noises can produce similar damage. In one study, extremely high-decible noises tore the cilia off the hair cells of experimental animals (Smith, 1947).

Most people do not willingly stand next to a jet as it takes off or expose themselves to some other equally intense sound that can cause permanent damage. However, many people go to rock concerts and discos where noise levels are often measured in the 100–300 db range. Ear specialists warn that a person risks hearing loss with more than a two-hour exposure to 95–100 decibels (Murray, 1985). The ringing in your ears you may have experienced after attending a rock concert may indicate damage to the hair cells of your inner ear. You may not notice any change in your hearing after one concert because the damage is often quite minimal. However, the effects are cumulative: in a few years you may notice that you no longer hear the phone ringing in the back bedroom or that people complain that the volume on your TV set is too loud.

If your ears ring after a rock concert, it may indicate damage to the hair cells of your inner ear. As many as 60 percent of college students have some form of hearing impairment.

Young people who spend a great deal of time listening to loud music can suffer permanent damage to the hair cells. Hearing tests conducted among college students have shown that as many as 60 percent have some form of hearing impairment (Sekuler & Blake, 1985). The following Health Psychology and Life discussion, "Protecting Your Hearing," provides some suggestions for reducing your chances of hearing loss.

Conduction Hearing Loss   The role of the outer and middle ear is to conduct sound energy to the receptors of the inner ear. When they fail to function properly, the result is called **conduction hearing loss**. This loss may simply be due to a build-up of ear wax in the auditory canal, a condition that is usually easy to remedy. Sometimes an ear infection can cause so much pressure in the middle ear that the eardrum ruptures, resulting in impaired hearing.

A fairly common cause of conduction deafness is a disease called *otosclerosis*, in which a spongy substance around the base of the stapes hardens, cementing the bone in a locked position. This disease, which tends to occur in young adults, can be surgically repaired by replacing the stapes with a plastic substitute.

Conduction hearing loss does not produce total deafness, as is often the case with severe forms of sensorineural impairment. One reason for this is that sounds can be transmitted directly through the bones of the skull to the inner ear. (This is the reason why a tape recording of your voice probably sounds funny to you. When you talk, the sound of your voice is transmitted not only through the air to your outer ear receptacles, but also directly through your skull to your inner ear. Since you are accustomed to hearing this blending, the tape-recorded sound of your voice sounds different.) Many hearing aids, designed to amplify sound transmission via bone conduction, can markedly reduce the effects of conduction hearing loss.

HEALTH PSYCHOLOGY AND LIFE

PROTECTING YOUR HEARING

Exposure to loud noises can have many serious consequences, from hearing loss to heightened stress that can affect behavior. In our society, however, loud noise is often unavoidable. The following guidelines suggest ways of reducing its effects.

Wear earplugs   If you are forced to work around loud noises, or if you engage in recreational pursuits such as target shooting or attending car or motorcycle races, you can wear special protective earplugs or muffs. Although this may seem an inappropriate measure if you are attending a loud rock concert, you can provide yourself with some protection by stuffing some cotton or a piece of tissue paper into the opening of the auditory canals. (Be careful not to insert these "plugs" too deeply.)

Use care with stereo headsets   Stereo headsets can be especially harmful to hearing, because the sound from a Walkman on high volume can be more intense than the sound you hear at a rock concert. Some manufacturers of personal stereos are adding a light that flashes when the volume exceeds safe limits; you can help protect your hearing by exercising care in adjusting the volume.

Use care with cordless phones   Some common devices such as cordless telephones present a potential hazard. A recent article in a medical journal reported several cases of hearing loss resulting from improper use of cordless phones. For instance, some phones will produce a loud blast of noise when the user converts from "standby" to "talk"; if the phone is held to the ear when this occurs, it can easily damage the ear. If you have a cordless phone, be sure to exercise care in using it—and not to experiment while holding it to your ear.

Your fingers can provide protection   Finally, if you are unexpectedly exposed to excessive noise, stick a finger in each ear until you can get away from the sound. Enduring the social implications of "looking silly" is probably better than risking damage to your sensitive hearing system.

THE CHEMICAL SENSES: TASTE AND SMELL

The senses of taste, or **gustation**, and smell (**olfaction**) are classified as chemical senses because both are activated by chemical substances in the environment. Taste and smell are often called minor senses because, relatively speaking, vision and hearing provide considerably more information about our worlds. We may not rely as much on the senses of smell and taste as do many other animals. However, these "minor senses" contribute greatly to our experience. The smell of the air after a spring rain, meat sizzling on the barbecue, the exciting aromas during and after love-making, all contribute immeasurably to our zest for life. Sometimes smells and flavors provide crucial information. Odors like the smell of gas or smoke signal danger, for instance, and a bad taste may warn us of spoiled food.

TASTE

The sense of taste is somewhat limited in humans. Our taste receptors can distinguish among only four different sensations: sweetness, saltiness, sourness, and bitterness. These four qualities may seem too simple to explain how we can distinguish between spicy and mild mustards or vanilla, chocolate, and strawberry milk shakes—and they are. The sense of smell also contributes greatly to our ability to perceive differences in tastes. In fact, without the sense of smell, you could not distinguish many of the tastes you recognize. You have probably noticed that things taste flat when you have a bad head cold that plugs up your nose.

The receptors for taste are located in the little bumps on the tongue called *papillae*. Each papilla contains as many as 200 *taste buds*, which in turn contain a number of receptor cells called *microvilli*. The microvilli are hairlike projections that extend into the saliva that coats the tongue. When we

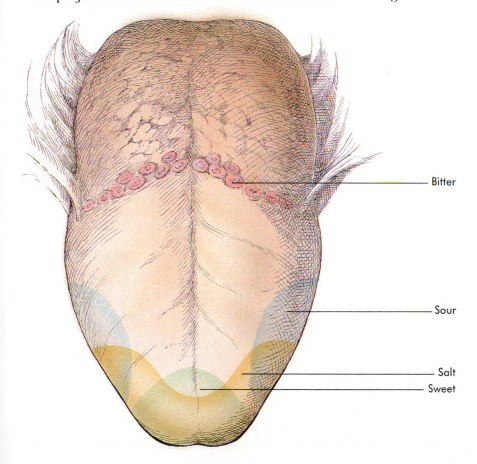

Bitter

Sour

Salt

Sweet

FIGURE 4.20   DISTRIBUTION OF THE TASTE BUDS

Certain areas of the tongue are particularly sensitive to different tastes.

Humans do not rely on certain senses as much as some animals. In many instances, we are able to use their superior sensory ability to our advantage, such as this dog being trained to locate bombs.

FIRST PERSON 4.4

I particularly enjoy going to the home of a new friend. The first time I walked into her house, I suddenly felt very upbeat. It was more than just feeling good about spending time with a friend. Something about that house made me unusually happy. I thought about it and decided it was the way the place smelled. It reminded me of the home of an aunt and uncle that I visited frequently during my childhood. I would have great times during those visits, and I guess it is the good feelings associated with those happy days that are triggered by the good smells in my friend's house. (*Authors' files*)

take ingestible material into our mouths, chemicals that are dissolved by saliva stimulate the receptor cells, which transduce this chemical energy into neural signals that are transmitted to the brain (Travers et al., 1987).

As Figure 4.20 shows, different parts of the tongue are most sensitive to different taste qualities. The tip of the tongue is most responsive to sweet tastes; the tip and forward portion of each side respond to salty substances; the sides to sour substances; and the back or base to bitter tastes. These regional differences only reflect zones of greatest sensitivity. Actually, all areas that have taste buds can sense all four of the primary taste qualities. (The middle of the tongue is devoid of taste receptors.)

There is evidence that taste sensitivity undergoes considerable change over the course of our lives, which may account, in part, for changes in taste preferences (Cowart, 1981). For example, most children prefer sweetness to other tastes, but this preference often does not hold up in the adult years. Unfortunately, as we grow oder, our taste buds become less sensitive, which is why many older people often complain that food does not taste as good as it once did.

SMELL

Unlike many other animals, we do not depend on our sense of smell to identify friends, repel enemies, and attract mates. Nevertheless, odors do enhance our enjoyment of life, particularly those smells connected with the foods we eat. Odors enter the nasal cavity as airborne molecules, either through the nostrils or through the back of the oral cavity. The receptor cells for odors lie in the *olfactory mucosa*, or mucous membrane that lines the nasal cavity (see Figure 4.21). Tiny hairlike projections (cilia) extend outward from the receptor cells, catching the airborne molecules (Getchell, 1986; Lancet, 1986).

We do not know exactly how the chemical energy of various odors is converted to neural signals that carry differing smell messages to the brain (Lancet, 1986). However, one widely held theory is that the cilia on the olfactory receptor cells are specialized to accommodate odor molecules with particular shapes. This viewpoint suggests that substances have different odors because they have different molecular shapes. There is not yet enough evidence to substantiate this theory fully, but research demonstrates that there is a relationship between the shape of a molecule and its odor (Amoore, 1970, 1982). Presumably, odor molecules and the receptor cells interact in some fashion that causes the receptor cells to fire, transmitting neural messages to the olfactory tract and on to the brain.

Although people can typically name only a few basic odors, such as floral, pepperminty, musky, or putrid, most of us are able to differentiate among as many as 80 different odors (Cain, 1981). Researchers have exerted considerable effort to identify primary odors that would serve the same role as primary hues in color vision. Although it would be convenient to be able to explain the multiplicity of odors we perceive as mixtures of primary scents, efforts to distinguish primary odors have not yet succeeded (Lancet, 1986).

Odors have a powerful ability to stimulate recall of old memories and to elicit feelings connected with experiences well removed in time. Because of this, odors are often used to sell products. It is difficult to pass by the delectable odors emanating from the chocolate-chip cookie franchise in a local shopping mall. Car dealerships often spray a "new car" scent into used vehicles. The outsides of bread wrappers may be infused with a fresh-baked smell, and inexpensive vinyl-covered furniture is sometimes moistened with a leather scent.

Some perfume manufacturers have implied—sometimes not so subtly—that their product contains an aphrodisiac-like product that will attract a potential mate. Odors that attract sexual interest, called *pheromones*, do exist among a variety of animals. The females of many species secrete

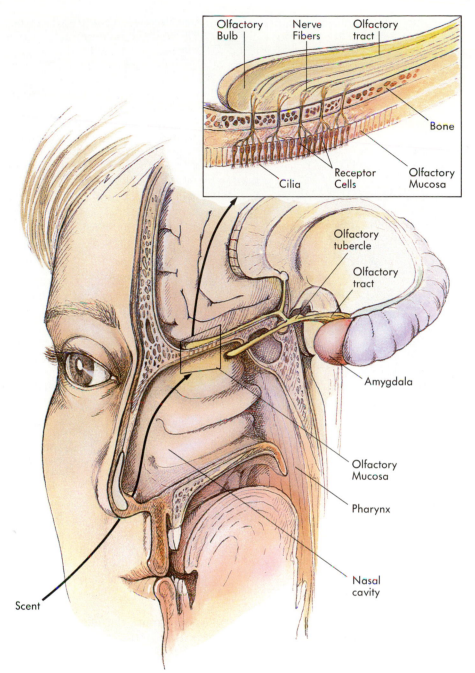

Olfactory Bulb
Nerve Fibers
Olfactory tract
Bone
Receptor Cells
Olfactory Mucosa
Cilia

Olfactory tubercle
Olfactory tract
Amygdala
Olfactory Mucosa
Pharynx
Nasal cavity
Scent

FIGURE 4.21   THE SENSE OF SMELL

When we smell a substance, molecules of its fragrance enter the nasal passage from the nose and/or the throat. Receptor cells in the olfactory mucosa transduce these stimuli into messages transmitted to the olfactory cortex.

pheromones during their fertile periods. However, evidence supporting the existence of such odors among humans is far from conclusive.

THE SKIN SENSES

The fourth type of sensation is the sense of touch. As Figure 4.22 shows, our entire skin surface is embedded with receptors for the various skin sensations. All of these various receptors are the dendrites of neurons: unlike vision, hearing, and taste, our skin senses use no specialized receptor cells other than neurons. These neurons do have specialized dendrite endings, however, which modify the manner in which they transduce physical energy into a neural firing.

Receptors for different kinds of skin senses are distributed unevenly over the body. For example, our faces are much more sensitive to touch

FIGURE 4.22 A CROSS-SEC-TIONAL DRAWING LOCATING SPECIALIZED RECEPTORS FOR THE VARIOUS SKIN SENSATIONS

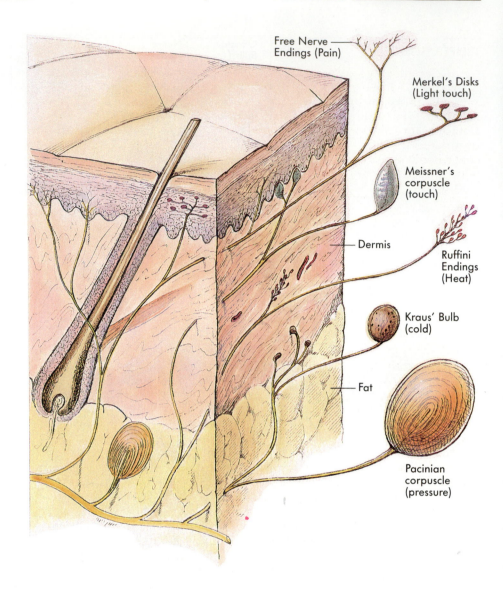

Free Nerve Endings (Pain)

Merkel's Disks (Light touch)

Meissner's corpuscle (touch)

Dermis

Ruffini Endings (Heat)

Kraus' Bulb (cold)

Fat

Pacinian corpuscle (pressure)

than are our backs, because the receptors are more densely packed in the skin of the face than the back. Researchers have attempted to link particular kinds of skin receptors to specific sensory experiences, with only limited success.

The sense of touch is actually a composite of three different senses: pressure, temperature, and pain. More complex sensory experiences such as tingling, itching, tickling, or wetness are produced from combinations of these three basic sensations.

PRESSURE

We experience the sensation of pressure when a mechanical force causes a displacement of the skin. Sensory adaptation occurs very quickly, which is why we are soon unaware of the pressure of tight-fitting pants or snug shoes. (If you continue to be aware of your tight shoes, it is probably because you are feeling the sensation of pain rather than pressure.) Some parts of our bodies are much more sensitive to pressure than others. The most sensitive regions are the face and fingers; the least sensitive are the back and the legs.

TEMPERATURE

Certain very localized areas of the skin seem to be sensitive to cold but not warmth, while other spots show just the opposite sensitivity. This observation is consistent with general agreement among researchers that different specialized dendrite endings respond to cold and heat (Spray, 1986). Detectors for cold appear to be located closer to the skin's surface than are heat detectors. This may explain why you experience a brief sensation of cold when you place your hand in a stream of hot water while checking the temperature of your morning shower.

PAIN

As much as we dislike pain, it is essential. It acts as a warning that something is harming us, and it drives us to seek necessary medical attention. Despite its importance (and despite the fact that nearly one third of the American adult population experience persistent or recurrent chronic pain), very little is known about what causes it and how to relieve it. A recent survey of 17 standard textbooks on surgery, medicine, and cancer found that only 54 out of 22,000 pages provided information about pain (Wallis, 1984).

Theories about the mechanisms involved in pain sensation and perception have been highly controversial (Besson & Chaouch, 1987). One thing that makes understanding pain so difficult is that no specific physical stimulus exists for pain as it does for the other sensory processes we have been discussing. A sound that is too loud, a light too bright, or a temperature too hot or too cold can all produce pain sensations. Some pain researchers maintain that pain results from overstimulation of any sensory receptors; others believe that pain results when damaged tissue releases chemicals that stimulate specialized nerve endings in the skin, which then transduce the chemical energy to neural signals that carry pain messages to our brains. Chemicals believed to be involved in this process include prostaglandins, bradykinins, and something called substance P (for pain).

Researchers have identified nerve fibers that transmit pain signals from the point of injury to the spinal cord and then on to the brain (Besson & Chaouch, 1987). One set of rapidly transmitting, myelinated fibers convey a message of localized, sharp, pricking pain—probably the only sensation we feel when the pain begins and ends quickly (as when our skin is pierced by a needle). However, if the pain stimulus is more severe, as might result from a burn or a damaging body blow, we will perceive a second sensation within a second or two. This message, which is conveyed by unmyelinated "slow" nerve fibers, induces an awareness of a burning, searing, throbbing, or aching pain that is usually more diffuse.

One widely discussed attempt to explain some of the phenomena associated with pain perception is called the **gate-control theory** (Melzack & Wall, 1965, 1983; Melzack, 1973, 1980). It suggests that when nerve fibers that convey pain messages are activated, neural "gates" in the spinal cord are opened to allow passage of pain signals on their way to the brain. However, these pain gates can be closed by the firing of other nonpain nerve fibers if they are activated simultaneously with the pain fibers. Thus, this theory suggests that competition from other sensations may block our perception of pain.

Research support for the gate-control theory has been inconsistent, and not all of its propositions have fared equally well under the close scrutiny of research scientists. Nevertheless, some of its major tenets, particularly its emphasis on pain as a perceptual as well as a sensory phenomenon, have been widely supported by experimental evidence (Turk & Rudy, 1986; Warga, 1987). A number of phenomena make this interpretation seem particularly plausible. For example, we know that pain relief can be induced in both humans and other animals by electrical stimulation of certain areas within the spinal cord (Besson & Chaouch, 1987). Presumably, such stimulation inhibits the spinal transmission of pain messages, perhaps by closing pain gates.

The gate-control theory also suggests an explanation for why people are often unaware of pain when they are injured under conditions of high stress and intense emotions (Amit & Galina, 1986). For instance, a woman who cuts herself while rescuing a child from a broken window may not notice her own injury until the crisis has passed. It seems plausible that intense emotions can create competing stimuli that overload the neural circuits, thereby blocking the pain pathways.

THE BODY SENSES

Try closing your eyes and moving your hand to various positions. You will have no trouble keeping track of where your hand is. With your eyes still closed, try touching your nose. Again, you will have no problem. Finally, eyes closed, try standing on one foot. This is a little tougher, but you will probably find you can maintain your balance reasonably well.

All of these simple tasks are accomplished without the aid of the senses discussed so far in this chapter. Rather, these tasks are aided by two interrelated sensory systems called kinesthesis and equilibrium. These two **body senses,** working in concert, tell us the orientation of our bodies in space, the relative position of the various body parts, and the movement of any parts of the body.

The sense of **kinesthesis** is diffuse throughout the entire body. It consists of specialized nerve endings embedded in the muscles, tendons, and joints that tell the brain whether muscles and tendons are being stretched, contracted, or relaxed. The cortex translates this sensory information into perceptions about locations of the various parts of the body in relation to the other parts. Kinesthesis allows us to throw a ball without watching what our arms are doing, and it helps us to take appropriate corrective action when we stumble or slip.

The sense of **equilibrium,** or balance, is localized within the inner ear. It comprises two sets of sensory receptors: the semicircular canals and the vestibular sacs. The **semicircular canals** are three ring-shaped structures, oriented at right angles to each other so that they lie roughly in each of the three dimensions of space (see Figure 4.18). Each is filled with a fluid that moves when the head is rotated. The lining of the semicircular canals contains hair cells that bend in the direction of the fluid flow. When you move your head, the fluid flows in the canal along the plane in which your head is moving. This movement is transduced to neural messages which tell your brain how your head is moving.

Another source of information is the **vestibular sacs,** located at the junction of the semicircular canals and the cochlea. These sacs contain hair cells weighted with crystals of calcium carbonate. When the head is tilted, gravitational forces cause the weighted cilia to shift, and this in turn triggers neural activity in adjacent nerve fibers. This information, in conjunction with information received from the semicircular canals (as occurs in a swaying car or a boat on a rough sea) sometimes produces motion sickness.

Body senses allow us to detect movement and the position of our bodies.

PERCEIVING THE WORLD

To this point in this chapter, we have been looking at the processes by which we receive sensations. Our perceptions are much more than what we see, hear, smell, taste, or sense with our skin and body senses, however. Our brains organize and give meaning to the constant input of sensory messages through an active process of selecting, ordering, synthesizing, and interpreting. In the remaining pages of this chapter we consider some of the basic principles that govern our perceptions. We focus mainly on visual perception, since this is the area psychologists know most about.

FIGURE 4.23   PERCEPTUAL ORGANIZA-TION

Perceptual organization is the process whereby we structure elementary sensations (in this case, meaningless dots and lines) into logical objects.

PERCEPTUAL ORGANIZATION

Look at the illustration in Figure 4.23. Rather than meaningless dots, lines, and colors, you no doubt perceive a familiar animal. Virtually everything we perceive with our eyes is made up of elementary sensations in the form of points, lines, edges, brightness, and varied hues. The process by which we structure these elementary sensations into the objects we perceive is called **perceptual organization.**

The major principles of perceptual organization were identified in the first half of this century by the Gestalt psychologists. This group of influential German psychologists included Max Wertheimer, Kurt Koffka, and Wolfgang Köhler. As mentioned in Chapter 1, they theorized that we perceive figures and forms as whole patterns that are different from the simple sum of individual sensations. They outlined several principles that influence how people organize sensations into whole patterns, called *Gestalts*. These include figure and ground, perceptual grouping, and closure.

Figure and Ground   One feature of perceptual organization identified by the Gestalt psychologists is our tendency to differentiate between **figure** (the part of an image that we focus our attention on) and **ground** (the background against which the figure stands). For example, the black words on this page stand out as figure against the white background.

Figure 4.24 illustrates an ambiguous figure-ground relationship. At first glance, you may see either two green face profiles as a figure against a blue ground, or a blue vase as the figure against a green ground. This figure further demonstrates the distinction between sensation and perception. The pattern of sensory receptors activated in our retinas remains constant while our perceptions shift between the two figure-ground patterns. The manner in which our brains organize these constant sensory stimuli allows us to perceive either the faces or the vase, but not both at the same time.

The figure and ground organization principle also applies to senses other than vision. For example, when you listen to music, the melody may stand out as the figure against a background of chords that serve as ground. However, a sudden change in tempo, rhythm, or volume may suddenly bring a chord to the forefront, where it becomes the central figure. Perhaps you are listening to a friend describe some important political event when a voice on the TV set behind you mentions your favorite athletic team. Suddenly the TV announcement becomes the focal point of your attention, and your friend's voice becomes background noise. You cannot focus on your

FIGURE 4.24   THE RUBIN VASE

The Rubin vase is widely employed to illustrate the figure-ground principle of perceptual organization. The illustration is ambiguous, with neither blue nor green clearly representing either figure or ground.

FIGURE 4.25 PERCEPTUAL GROUPING PRINCIPLES

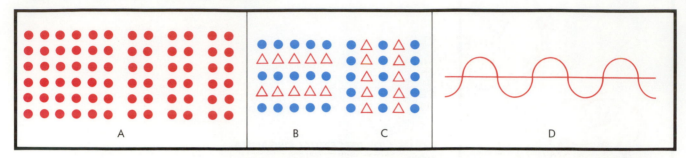

A illustrates the principle of proximity. The pattern on the left can be seen as either columns or rows since the circles are spaced equally. The pattern on the right is perceived as three pairs of columns because the horizontal spacing has been altered. B and C demonstrate grouping by the principle of similarity (in B we see rows and in C we see columns). D illustrates the principle of continuity or good continuation (stimuli that flow smoothly into one another are perceived as forming a single group). It is easier for us to perceive smooth, continuous patterns rather than discontinuous ones. Thus, we are inclined to perceive this pattern as a wavy line superimposed on a straight line rather than as an alternating series of semicircles.

friend's voice and the TV announcer at the same time: one must be figure, and one must be ground.

Perceptual Grouping Gestalt psychologists also demonstrated the role of **perceptual grouping** to explain how we organize sensory input into meaningful wholes. Patterns of stimuli are grouped into larger units in three major ways: by proximity, similarity, and good continuation.

Figure 4.25 illustrates these three perceptual grouping principles. The principle of **proximity** suggests that, all else being equal, we tend to organize our perceptions by grouping elements that are the nearest to each other. The principle of **similarity** suggests that we group elements that are similar to each other. A final grouping principle, **good continuation,** suggests that we are more likely to perceive stimuli as a whole or single group if they flow smoothly into one another as opposed to being discontinuous.

Closure Another powerful organizing principle is our inclination to perceive incomplete figures as complete, a process known as **closure.** A careful examination of Figure 4.26 reveals that what appears to be two overlapping triangles are actually incomplete figures. Furthermore, the solid white triangle does not exist; it is merely an illusion. We see these figures because of our mental set to fill in the gaps and achieve closure.

THE ROLE OF ATTENTION IN PERCEPTUAL PROCESSING

Another basic principle of perceptual processing is **selective attention,** the process of focusing on one or a few stimuli of particular significance while ignoring others. As was shown earlier in this chapter, in the discussion of the mosquito bite on your evening stroll by the lake, we never attend equally to all the stimuli we receive at any given point in time. If we did, our nervous systems would become hopelessly overloaded. Instead, we select certain stimulus inputs to focus on, and the other events fade into the background (Johnston & Dark, 1986). Through this process of selective attention our perceptual ability is enhanced (Moran & Desimone, 1985).

To some extent, we control our attention. For example, at this moment your attention is focused on the printed words of this book. Hopefully, your desire to understand the principles discussed here is sufficient inducement to allow you to screen out a variety of background stimuli. However, a number of possible changes in these background stimuli might

FIGURE 4.26 THE PRINCIPLE OF CLOSURE

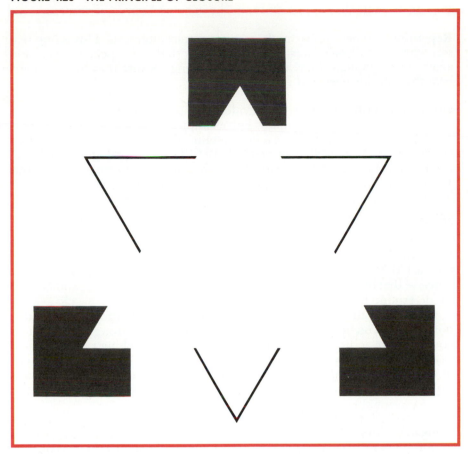

If you see two overlapping triangles in this illustration, it is because of your tendency to fill in perceptual information. The solid white triangle is merely an illusion induced by the incomplete structures in the figure.

cause your attention to shift suddenly. Psychologists have discovered that certain characteristics of stimuli, described below, tend to capture attention almost automatically:

Sudden Change   A sudden change generally causes a shift in attention. For example, if your roommate studying in the next room suddenly gets up and starts dancing, your attention will probably shift to his or her actions; or, if you have been dozing off at the movie theater and the sound suddenly stops because the projectionist forgot to start a new reel, the change may arouse you.

Contrast and Novelty   Contrast and novelty also tend to capture our attention. For example, a brightly lit neon sign along a dark stretch of highway often diverts our attention because it contrasts with its surroundings. Things that are new or unusual also tend to attract our attention. For instance, if someone drove through campus in a vehicle shaped like a giant hot dog, you would probably take notice.

Stimulus Intensity   Another way of getting our attention is to vary the intensity of a stimulus. This is why TV commercials may increase their volume slightly above the sound of normal TV programming and why they often use very bright and colorful images. Sudden reduction of stimulus intensity can also command attention. If your friends talking on the other side of the room suddenly begin whispering, you may prick up your ears in the effort to hear what they are saying.

   Some professors may use this perceptual concept in their lectures. To cause their students to pay attention to a point, they may lower their voices

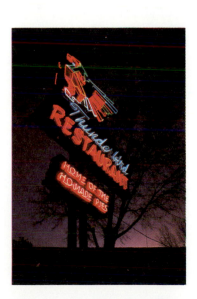

This neon sign captures our attention because it contrasts with the dark sky.

to a level that is barely audible. As a result, students often lean forward in their seats while they concentrate on the ensuing "words of wisdom."

Repetition   Repetition is another way to attract attention. This is one reason why TV and radio ads often use jingles that are repeated again and again. Many popular tunes are attention getting because they have a catchy beat that repeats over and over again.

Difficult Stimuli   There is also evidence that stimuli that are difficult to process may command attention. For example, some of the complex illustrations in this chapter require a fair amount of effort to comprehend. Psychologists believe that the more energy we focus on one category of stimuli, the less is left over for responding to other stimuli (Norman & Bobrow, 1975).

PERCEIVING DISTANCE

Earlier in this chapter, we learned that visual images are focused on the retina, which is essentially an image-recording sheet of tissue that lines the back of the eye. Since retinal images are two-dimensional, how can we perceive that objects in our environment are three-dimensional, and how do we determine how close or far away they are?

Clearly, these types of discrimination are essential for healthy functioning. Can you imagine what it would be like to walk through a busy city if you could not accurately estimate how far away approaching cars happened to be? A variety of perceptual cues allows us to judge accurately the distance of objects. Some of these cues, called **binocular cues,** depend on both eyes working together; others, called **monocular cues,** can be used with just one eye.

Binocular Cues   The fact that most of us see with both our eyes provides important binocular cues for distance perception (Foley, 1985). Perhaps the most accurate of these is **binocular** or **retinal disparity.** Binocular disparity is based on the fact that since the eyes are a couple of inches apart, each has a slightly different view of the world. You can demonstrate this to yourself by staring at this page and alternately closing one eye at a time. You will note that the page appears to shift its position slightly. Normally our brains fuse these two images into a single, three-dimensional image (O'Shea, 1987). At the same time, the brain analyzes the differences in the two images to obtain information about distance.

There is greater binocular disparity when objects are close to our eyes than when they are far away. You can demonstrate this by holding the index finger of one hand very close to your face and aligning it with the same finger of the other hand held as far away as possible. Now alternately close each eye. Your closest finger will seem to leap back and forth, while the far one will shift only slightly. Figure 4.27a shows why close objects create more significant disparity, while those that are far away create only minor disparity: the difference in the angle of the two eyes to the far object is much slighter than the difference for the close object.

Another important binocular distance cue is a phenomenon called **convergence.** When we look at an object that is no more than 25 feet away, our two eyes must converge (rotate to the inside) in order to perceive it as a single, clearly focused image. This rotation of the eyes is necessary to allow them to focus on the same object, but it creates tension in the eye muscles. As Figure 4.27b shows, the closer the object, the greater the tension. (Objects far away require no convergence for sharp focusing.) With experience, our brains learn to equate the amount of muscle tension with the distance between our eyes and the object we are focusing on. Consequently, muscular feedback from converging eyes becomes an important cue for judging the distance of objects within roughly 25 feet of our eyes.

FIGURE 4.27 BINOCULAR (RETINAL) DISPARITY AND CONVERGENCE

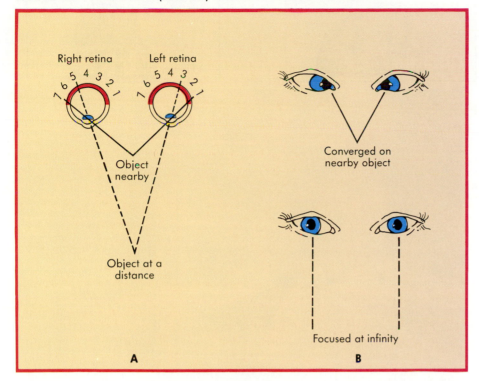

Right retina   Left retina

Object nearby

Object at a distance

A

Converged on nearby object

Focused at infinity

B

A illustrates that the closer a viewed object is, the greater the binocular disparity. B illustrates the convergence of the eyes that is necessary to view a nearby versus distant object. Both binocular disparity and convergence are important binocular cues for depth perception.

Monocular Cues If objects that are far away create little retinal disparity and no convergence, how can we judge their distance? A number of one-eye, or monocular, cues provide that information.

Figure 4.28 illustrates several important monocular cues for distance perception. One of these is **height on a plane.** Note that the objects in the photo that appear to be the farther away are higher on your plane of view. This cue is always present. If you look around your room or gaze out the window, you will see that the farther away an object is, the higher it will be on your plane of view and the more you have to lift your gaze to perceive it.

Another distance cue, called **overlap** or **interposition,** describes the phenomenon in which objects close to us tend to block out parts of objects that are farther away from us. If you look around your room again, you will notice that your textbook blocks your view of the desk under it, that the desk in turn blocks your view of the floor, and so forth. A third distance cue, called **linear perspective,** is based on the fact that parallel lines converge when stretched into the distance. For example, when you look at a long stretch of road or railroad tracks, it appears that the sides of the road or the parallel tracks converge on the horizon.

If we know how large objects are, we can judge their distance by their apparent size in relation to each other. If you look out your window and see two people, one 50 yards away and the other 200 yards away, you will notice a great difference in their **relative size.** Instead of concluding that one person is a pygmy and the other a giant, you will take this cue as evidence that the smaller person is a greater distance from you.

Another monocular cue, **texture gradients,** has to do with perceived changes in the texture of surfaces as they extend farther from our eyes. For example, if you look at a textured surface such as an expanse of grassy lawn or a rock-strewn field, the elements close to you will seem to be farther apart or less dense than those that are farther away. The close elements will also be clearer. A striking illustration of this is provided in Figure 4.29.

Objects that are far away from us appear to be more fuzzy than those close by because as distance increases, smog, dust, and haze reduce the

FIGURE 4.28 MONOCULAR CUES FOR DEPTH PERCEPTION

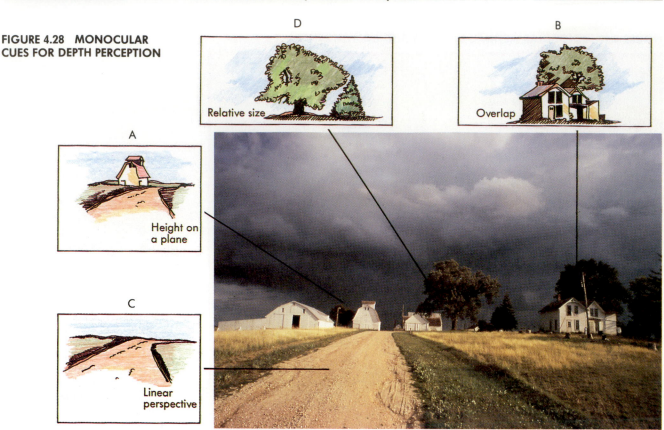

Many cues help us perceive depth: A) Height on a Plane. Objects farthest away are higher on our plane of view. B) Overlap. Objects close to us tend to block out parts of objects that are farther away. C) Linear Perspective. When you look at a long stretch of road, it appears that the sides of the road converge on the horizon. D) Relative Size. Closer objects appear larger than objects which are farther away.

The day after I arrived in the high country of Ecuador, I decided to climb a small peak located close by to get a better view of the surrounding countryside. I guessed the peak was only a few miles away. When I mentioned my plans to my host, he smiled as if he were privy to some kind of inside joke. When I had walked most of the morning and still didn't seem to be any closer to my destination, I realized who the joke was on. As it turned out, the peak was almost 15 miles away. Its extreme clarity in the crystal-clear air fooled me into thinking it was very close. (*Authors' files*)

clarity of the projected image. This depth cue, called **aerial** or **atmospheric perspective,** can sometimes cause us to judge distance inaccurately, especially if we are accustomed to the smoggy atmosphere of urban areas.

A final monocular cue for distance may be demonstrated if you gaze at the scene outside your window and move your head from side to side. You will notice that objects nearby seem to move a much greater distance than objects farther away. This cue, called **relative motion** or **motion parallax,** is particularly noticeable when you look out the window of a moving car and observe nearby objects moving much more rapidly than distant ones.

Perceiving Depth: The Visual Cliff   There can be little doubt that many distance cues are enhanced by experience. In fact, before a classic experiment almost 30 years ago, many psychologists believed that distance or depth perception depended upon learning. However, Eleanor Gibson and Richard Walk (1960) provided convincing evidence that some aspects of depth perception are inborn or innate, at least in some species.

The device created by Gibson and Walk is called the **visual cliff,** and it is illustrated in Figure 4.30. The visual cliff is an elevated glass surface. A checkerboard-patterned plane lies just under half of the glass surface, while there is nothing under the other half except for the checkerboard painted on the floor, roughly three and one-half feet below. This design produced the illusion of a deep side and a shallow side.

Babies of many species that can walk immediately after birth were tested on the apparatus. All of these newborn animals, including kittens, puppies, lambs, chickens, piglets, and kids, refused to cross over to the deep

FIGURE 4.29 TEXTURE GRADI-
ENTS

This expansive desert appears to
be furrowed up close and smooth
in the distance. This is because
surfaces of objects become less
defined the farther away they are.

side, indicating that depth perception is innate in these species. Even chicks
whose initial visual experience occurred on the visual cliff would not step
over the "deep side."

Since human babies could not be tested until they were able to crawl
(usually around the age of six months), their depth perception was more
difficult to interpret. Obviously, a lot of learning can take place in the first
six months of life. Most of the infants tested would not spontaneously crawl
onto the deep side—something that infants of other species would never do.

Some researchers argue that by the time human infants can be tested
on the visual cliff, they may have already learned to avoid drop-offs (Campos et al., 1978). Others have argued that the kind of depth perception that

FIGURE 4.30   THE VISUAL CLIFF APPARATUS

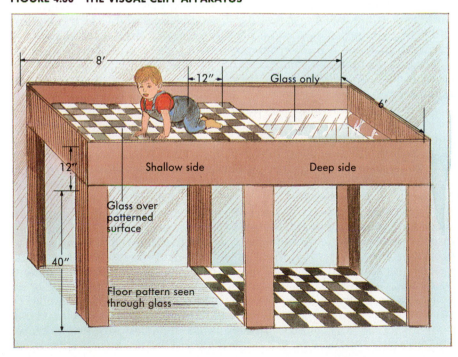

The illusion of a deep side and a
shallow side produced by the visual cliff apparatus discourages
this infant from crossing over to
her mother.

When you look at this photograph, you do not think that the hot-air balloons are all different sizes. Rather, you know that the balloons are different distances from each other, and you automatically account for this difference.

is required for the cliff is an innate capacity in humans that is not triggered until about six months of age (Radar et al., 1980; Richards & Rader, 1981). Which explanation is correct? At this point, we can say with confidence that depth perception is clearly an innate ability in many species of animals, and that in humans it is either innate or is learned very early in life.

PERCEPTUAL CONSTANCY

When you bid farewell to friends at the dock and see them sail off into the distance, you do not assume that their boat is shrinking. Rather, you know the boat is staying the same size in spite of the fact that the image projected onto your retinas gets smaller and smaller. Your perception of the boat adjusts automatically, taking into consideration changes in the distance between you and it. This perceptual phenomenon, known as **size constancy**, is but one of several forms of **perceptual constancy** that allow us to adjust for varying conditions and changing patterns as we perceive the world (Rock & DiVita, 1987).

Research strongly suggests that size constancy is learned rather than innate. Most babies seem to master this perceptual process by six months of age (Yonas et al., 1982). It appears that we learn to use a variety of distance cues to estimate the true size of objects. In a classic study, A. H. Holway and Edwin Boring (1941) found that subjects were able to make extremely accurate judgments of the size of a circle located at varied distances from their eyes, under conditions that were rich with distance cues. As distance cues were progressively eliminated, however, subjects' judgments of circle size became increasingly dependent on the size of the retinal image. Thus, the subjects' perception of the size of the circle increased when it was moved closer and decreased as it was moved away—a complete breakdown in size constancy.

A recent experiment conducted by Bernice Rogowitz (1984) demonstrated that illumination is important in determining some types of perceptual constancy. Under conditions where there is no constant illumination, size constancy breaks down dramatically. When a scene is viewed under stroboscopic illumination (disco-type lighting), it becomes impossible to judge distance accurately. Maybe this is one reason why frequent collisions occur on disco floors.

Brightness constancy and **color constancy** also help us perceive our world as constant. When you look out your window at night, the trees, grass, and bushes do not appear to be the same color or brightness as they are during the daytime. Since you already know that the leaves of the bushes are a dark green and the grass and trees are brighter green, however, you perceive these qualities to be constant even under conditions of different illumination.

Another element of perceptual constancy is **shape constancy.** When we look at objects from different angles, the shape of the image projected to our retinas is different in each instance. Nevertheless, we perceive the object as unchanged. This is illustrated in Figure 4.31. When we view the door from straight on, it appears rectangular in shape. When the door is opened, we still perceive it as rectangular despite the fact that the image projected on our retinas is trapezoidal.

How do we manage to perceive the actual size, brightness, color, and shape of objects under highly variable environmental conditions? There are at least two possible explanations. The fact that these processes seem to occur automatically has led some psychologists to suggest that perceptual constancies are based largely on mechanisms that operate below conscious awareness. When we know the true size, shape, color, or brightness of an object, we make *unconscious inferences* to adjust for changes in the object's appearance under varying conditions. Thus, since we know that objects that are close cast a larger image on our retinas than those farther away, we unconsciously use this information to judge their size.

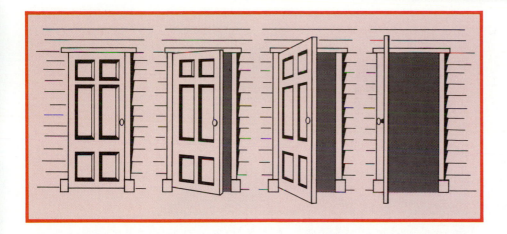

FIGURE 4.31 SHAPE CONSTANCY

We perceive the opening door as being rectangular in shape despite the nonrectangular images projected on our retinas.

An alternative viewpoint suggests that we analyze the relationships between *environmental cues* to achieve perceptual constancies. According to this theory, a person walking away from us remains constant in size because the relationship between his or her size and the surrounding trees, buildings, and so forth remains the same. We perceive all the sizes as remaining constant despite variations in projected retinal images. We process such cues so rapidly that our perceptual adjustments may appear to result from unconscious inferences.

The first theory, that of unconscious inferences, is difficult to demonstrate through experiments, but it seems likely that it plays a role in our perception of size constancy. The second point of view, that environmental cues provide perceptual constancy, has been easier to demonstrate. Perhaps one of the most vivid illustrations is provided by the *Ames room*, shown in Figure 4.32. A person standing on one side of the room appears to be a giant, while someone on the other side appears to be a dwarf. Even more amazing is that when people cross the Ames room, they steadily appear to grow or shrink, depending on the direction in which they are walking. These illusions are produced by environmental cues.

The Ames room was designed to fool the observer into thinking it is shaped like a normal rectangular room. However, as you can see from the diagram in the figure, the room is definitely not rectangular. Both windows are trapezoidal, and one is much larger than the other. In addition, the floor is uneven so that one end of the Ames room is higher on the plane than the other. The relationships between the various objects in the room were altered in this manner to change relationships that we are accustomed to perceiving between people and their environments. Since we have not experienced this kind of arrangement before, however, our perceptual constancy processes cause us to perceive the room as rectangular and the windows as equal in size and rectangular in shape. Recent research has shown that the Ames-room illusion persists (although in somewhat diminished form) even when subjects are allowed to leave the viewing point indicated in the figure and move about the room (Gehringer & Engel, 1985).

Without the operation of perceptual constancies, we would depend largely upon the characteristics of images projected on our retinas in our efforts to perceive objects. Perceptual constancies help us to interpret accurately the world we live in. However, they can also be the basis for illusions that can fool the viewer, as in the Ames-room example.

PERCEPTUAL ILLUSIONS

An **illusion** is a perception that is false in that it differs from the actual physical state of the perceived object. Some illusions, like the distorted images seen in carnival mirrors, are physical; that is, they result from

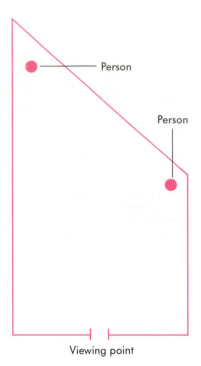

FIGURE 4.32   THE AMES ROOM

In the Ames room people appear to change sizes. In reality, the woman is much taller than the boy. As you can see from the diagram, the person on the left is almost twice as far from the viewer, and since this distance is not apparent to the viewer, the illusion results.

an actual distortion in the image projected on our retinas. Other illusions are perceptual in nature.

This second type of illusion interests psychologists because such illusions provide insights into the way the perceptual system operates. Visual illusions have been explored the most extensively, and it seems clear that our visual perceptions are not just copies of retinal images. Instead, we construct perceptions from sensory information, and sometimes this creative process misleads us.

EXPLAINING THE MULLER-LYER ILLUSION

One of the most widely analyzed visual illusions is the *Muller-Lyer illusion*, illustrated in Figure 4.33. Ignoring the angled lines (arrowheads) at the ends of each vertical line, decide which line is longer. Most people see the line on the right as longer, but actually the two are of equal length. How can the Muller-Lyer illusion be explained? Think back to what you have learned about perceptual constancy in this chapter and try to formulate an answer before reading on.

Actually, psychologists do not all agree about why the Muller-Lyer illusion fools us. According to one interpretation that enjoyed popularity for a period of time, the illusion is created by the fact that the outward-turned angles draw the viewer's eyes farther out into space, while the inward-turning angles draw the eyes back toward the center.

A recent study has cast serious doubt on this interpretation, however. In this experiment, an apparatus was designed to hold a subject's eyes and head very still while the lines of the Muller-Lyer illusion were flashed into one eye and the arrowheads into the other. When these sensations were combined in the subject's brain, the same illusion resulted (Gillam, 1980). This finding indicates that the illusion is created by something more than the movement of the eyes.

A British psychologist, R. L. Gregory (1978), has proposed a more likely interpretation—that the Muller-Lyer illusion is the result of size constancy. According to Gregory, the angled lines provide linear perspective cues. As Figure 4.34 shows, the vertical line on the left, enclosed by the inward-turned angled lines, is perceived as being closer than the line with the outward-turned angled lines. We have already learned that if two objects appear to be the same size, and we think one is closer, then size constancy will cause us to assume that the farther one is bigger.

Gregory's theory is supported by research that demonstrates that the Muller-Lyer illusion is either very weak or absent in cultures where people have little exposure to angles (Seagall et al., 1966). For example, the Zulus of southeast Africa, who live in circular huts with few straight lines and corners (see Figure 4.35), do not judge distance from such linear cues as effectively as we do. These people respond only minimally to the Muller-Lyer illusion.

An illusion you are probably familar with is the *moon illusion* (see Figure 4.36). Most people have had the experience of looking at a full moon on the horizon and thinking how huge it looks. When the moon is low on the horizon, it appears larger than when it is overhead, yet the actual size of the moon's image on the retina is the same regardless of its position in the sky. Why does this occur?

The moon illusion also seems to result from size constancy, When the moon is low, it appears to be farther away than when it is overhead. This effect results from the presence of visual cues for distance, such as overlapping structures and relative size. Compared to the trees or buildings on the horizon, we perceive the moon to be very far away. In contrast, when we look at the moon overhead, we have no visual cues for distance. Consequently, we tend to underestimate its distance. As in the Muller-Lyer illusion, we assume that the moon on the horizon is larger because distance cues tell us it is farther from us than the identically sized moon overhead.

One last illusion is the *Poggendorff illusion*, shown in Figure 4.37a. It appears that if the diagonal lines were continued toward each other, the one on the right would pass above the left line. In reality, they would join—as you can determine by laying a straight edge along their projected paths. Many psychologists believe this illusion results from our inclination to maintain shape constancy. Figure 4.37b illustrates one possible example of some-

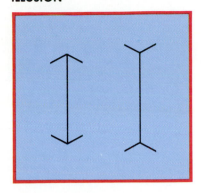

FIGURE 4.33 THE MULLER-LYER ILLUSION

The two vertical lines are equal in length.

FIGURE 4.34 DOES THE MULLER-LYER ILLUSION RESULT FROM SIZE CONSTANCY?

This illustration demonstrates that the figures in the Muller-Lyer illusion may provide cues for depth, which may be the basis for the illusion (see explanation in text).

FIGURE 4.35   THE CIRCULAR CULTURE OF THE ZULUS

The Zulus of southeast Africa live in an environment in which there are few straight lines and corners. Since they do not become accustomed to judging depth from these cues, they are less likely to be fooled by the Muller-Lyer illusion than are people from Western cultures where rectangular architecture is common.

thing we have experienced that influences our perception of the Poggendorff illusion. Clearly, if lines A and B were the leg and back support, respectively, of an overturned chair, they could never meet.

PERCEPTUAL SET

In addition to the many cues that we have been discussing, our perceptions are also influenced by many subjective factors. Such factors include our tendency to see (or hear, smell, feel, or taste) what we expect or what is consistent with our preconceived notions of what makes sense.

This phenomenon is known as **perceptual set,** and it is illustrated in Figure 4.38. You can try this demonstration out on two friends. Show one friend picture A (keep B and C covered) and ask what is seen. The response will probably be an old woman. Then show picture C while covering A and B. Again, an old woman is likely to be seen. Next, repeat the procedure with a different friend, but this time start with picture B followed by C. In this situation, your friend is likely to report seeing a young woman in both pictures. The difference is explained by the fact that the particular image seen in picture C depends on the viewer's previous experience. Since the

FIGURE 4.36   THE MOON ILLUSION

The greater number of visual cues provided by the earth's terrain create the illusion that the moon is larger on the horizon than when it is higher in the sky.

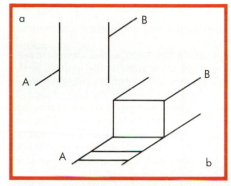

FIGURE 4.37   THE POGGENDORFF ILLU-SION

The illusion created in part *a* of this figure may convince a casual observer that if the two diagonal lines were extended, they would pass one above the other. In fact, they would meet, as you can see by laying a straight edge along their projected paths. This illusion may result from our inclination to maintain shape constancy. For example, if lines A and B in part *b* of the illustration were the back and leg support, respectively, of an overturned chair, they could never meet.

first friend was initially exposed to the picture of the old lady, he or she developed a perceptual set to see an old lady in picture C. In contrast, the second friend's perceptual set was geared toward seeing the youthful image in picture B.

Motivational state can also have a strong impact on how we perceive our environments, presumably by the mechanism of establishing perceptual sets. For example, if you drive down a main throughfare while feeling hunger pangs, you will probably notice almost every sign advertising food. You may even misread signs so that an ad in the window of the local garden store seems to say "steaks" instead of "stakes."

Another form of perceptual set is the tendency to perceive stimuli that are consistent with our expectations or beliefs, and to ignore those that are inconsistent. This phenomenon is frequently referred to as **selective perception.** For example, if you believe that all neatly dressed elderly women are honest, you might not even think twice about the elderly woman at the next table when your wallet disappears in a restaurant, even if she is the most obvious suspect. Likewise, people who distrust groups of people because of their appearance, religion, or ethnic background are unlikely to recognize the good qualities of an individual who is a member of one of those groups.

FIGURE 4.28   A DEMONSTRATION OF PERCEPTUAL SET

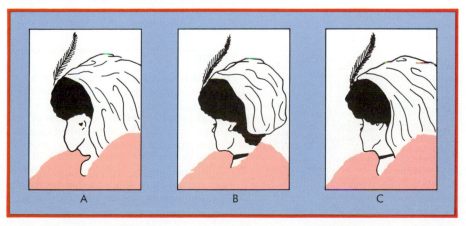

SUMMARY

PRINCIPLES OF SENSATION AND PERCEPTION

1. Sensations are basic, immediate experiences that a stimulus elicits in a sense organ. Perception refers to the process of interpreting, organizing, and elaborating on the raw materials of sensation. Sensation occurs at the level of sensory receptors, whereas perception is a cognitive process.
2. The process by which sensory organs transform mechanical, chemical, or light energy into neural firing is called transduction.
3. The ability to distinguish sensations does not depend on differences between the sense organs, but rather on what part of the brain is activated by the sensory messages.
4. Many of the physical events surrounding us go unheeded. The most important variables determining whether or not we perceive things happening around us are sensory thresholds, attention, and adaptation.
5. Our perception of various sensory inputs can occur only when the strength of a stimulus reaches a minimal or threshold level of intensity sufficient to activate a sensory process.
6. Attention is a psychological selection mechanism that reduces our awareness of surrounding events by overriding mental processing of unimportant events.
7. Adaptation refers to the decrease in the response of sensory receptors when they are exposed to continual, unchanging stimulation.

VISION

8. Our visual systems consist of three major parts: the eyes, which capture and respond to light energy; the neural circuits that transmit signals from the eye to the brain; and visual centers within the brain that interpret these messages.
9. Visible light, the stimulus for vision, has three particularly important properties: brightness, or the intensity of light; hue, or the color we perceive; and saturation, which is the proportion of colored light to noncolored light.
10. Two key components of the eye are the image-focusing part, consisting of the cornea, lens, iris, and pupil, and the image-recording part, called the retina.
11. The primary photoreceptor cells in the retina, the rods and cones, contain photopigments that respond to light. Our perception of color is largely dependent on the cones, whereas the rods are extremely sensitive photoreceptors that allow us to see in dim light.
12. Two major theories of color vision have been proposed: the trichromatic theory and the opponent-process theory. Most vision experts believe that color vision may result from an interplay between a trichromatic system operating at the level of photoreceptor cells and an opponent-process mechanism working at later stages.

HEARING

13. Most of the sounds we hear consist of physical energy in the form of rhythmic pressure changes in the air.
14. Three characteristics of sound waves that influence our perception of sound are loudness (amplitude), pitch (frequency), and timbre (a combination of a fundamental frequency and additional frequency components called overtones).
15. Auditory perception results when sound waves are converted into mechanical movement of the ossicles in the middle ear, which in turn act to produce pressure waves within the fluid of the inner ear that stimulate hair cells that transduce the physical energy of sound waves into neural impulses that our brains translate into sounds.
16. The best available evidence suggests that our perception of pitch is determined by both the place of maximal excitation on the basilar membrane and the frequency with which auditory nerve fibers fire.
17. Auditory localization is the result of differences in both the loudness and the time of arrival of sounds reaching each of our ears.
18. Hearing loss may result from either damage to the neural structures that transmit auditory messages to the brain (sensorineural hearing loss) or inability of the outer and middle ear to conduct sound energy to the receptors in the inner ear (conduction hearing loss).

THE CHEMICAL SENSES: TASTE AND SMELL

19. Our taste receptors, located on little bumps on the tongue called papillae, can distinguish only four different sensations: sweetness, saltiness, sourness, and bitterness.
20. The receptors for odors lie in the mucuous membrane that lines the nasal cavity.

THE SKIN SENSES

21. The sense of touch is a composite of three different senses: pressure, temperature, and pain.
22. The sensation of pressure occurs when a mechanical force causes a displacement of the skin.
23. Different specialized dendrite endings respond to cold and heat.
24. Some pain researchers maintain that pain results from overstimulation of any sensory receptor, whereas others believe that pain occurs when damaged tissue releases chemicals that stimulate specialized nerve endings in the skin.

THE BODY SENSES

25. The two body senses of kinesthesis and equilibrium, working in concert, tell us the orientation of our bodies in space, the relative position of the various body parts, and the movement of any parts of the body.

PERCEIVING THE WORLD

26. The process by which we structure elementary sensations into the objects we perceive is called perceptual organization.
27. Three important principles that influence how people organize sensations into whole patterns, called Gestalts, are figure and ground, perceptual grouping, and closure.
28. Figure and ground refers to our tendency to differentiate between the part of an image we focus on (figure) and the background against which the figure stands (ground).

29. According to the principle of perceptual grouping, we tend to group patterns of stimuli into larger units in three major ways: by proximity, similarity, and good continuation.

30. Another organizing principle is our inclination to perceive incomplete figures as complete, a process known as closure.

31. Selective attention refers to the process of focusing on one or a few stimuli of particular significance while ignoring others.

32. Characteristics of stimuli that tend to capture attention almost automatically include sudden change, contrast and novelty, intensity, repetition, and difficulty in processing.

33. Binocular cues for perceiving distance include retinal disparity and convergence.

34. Important monocular cues for distance perception include height on a plane, interposition, linear perspective, relative size, texture gradients, aerial perspective, and relative motion.

35. Research has revealed that depth perception is clearly an innate ability in many species of animals, and that in humans it is either innate or is learned very early in life.

36. Perceptual constancy allows us to adjust for varying conditions and changing patterns as we perceive the world. When we look at objects at different distances and angles and under different levels of illumination, we are able to make the necessary adjustments to maintain a degree of constancy in our perception of size, shape, brightness, and color.

37. A perceptual illusion is a perception that is false in that it differs from the actual physical state of the perceived object.

38. A tendency to perceive what we expect or are inclined to see, a phenomenon known as perceptual set, may have a strong impact upon how we perceive our environments.

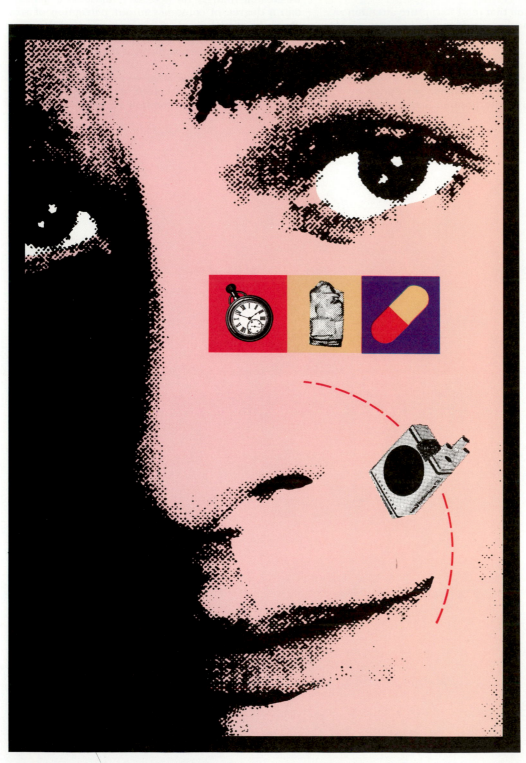

5 States of Consciousness

You are sitting in the library trying to concentrate on your studies, but your mind just isn't picking up the words that your eyes are tracking. Instead, it wanders to that gorgeous person in your psychology class, and you begin to fantasize a situation in which you both feel drawn to each other. Then you are stopped short by the realization that that gorgeous person likes someone else anyway . . . and speaking of psychology, you are behind on your homework. You focus in on your studies again, but it is only a moment before your mind begins to wander once more, this time to consider whether you should lose some weight.

Sound familiar? If you are like most people, you spend a great deal of time manufacturing fantasies and mulling over issues of similarly grandiose proportions. Such *daydreams* are mild shifts from a state of alert consciousness in which your thoughts move from external focal points to internal stimuli. When you daydream, you create "pictures in the mind's eye" that are akin to waking dreams. Most of us spend a significant portion of our waking hours daydreaming (Singer, 1975, 1978)—according to one study, about one-third of our time (Bartusiak, 1980). The vividness of daydreams waxes and wanes over a 90-minute cycle, with peak vividness occurring roughly every 90 minutes (Kripke & Sonneschein, 1978).

Interestingly, this cycle is remarkably similar to the cycle of dreaming in our sleep, discussed later in this chapter. It is a natural variation in consciousness that occurs without our attempting to regulate it and often without our even being aware that we are drifting in and out of daydreams. This chapter looks at other variations in consciousness—both natural states, such as sleeping and dreaming, and states that are deliberately induced by meditation, hypnosis, and consumption of drugs—as it explores what consciousness is, how and why it varies, and how different states of consciousness affect our abilities and behavior.

THE NATURE OF CONSCIOUSNESS

A key component of consciousness is **awareness**—our own subjective sense of self, our actions, and the world around us. Awareness includes the perceptions, thoughts, feelings, and memories that we are processing at any given moment. However, there are varying degrees of awareness, and consciousness also includes things we may be only dimly aware of until our attention is directed to them.

Most of us drift in and out of daydreams without being aware we are doing so, even though some studies suggest we spend up to one-third of our waking hours daydreaming.

An example of these varying degrees of awareness is a human interest story that was broadcast on the radio not long ago. It concerned the actor Robert Redford, who stopped in at an ice cream parlor near a location where he was filming. A woman walked in for an ice cream and noticed the famous actor. Trying her best to act nonchalant, she made her purchase and left. She returned immediately, however, when she discovered she did not have her cone. When she asked where it was, Redford looked up. "It's there in your purse," he said, "right where you put it."

At some level, the woman had probably been aware of putting the ice cream in her purse, but her attention had been so focused on her unusual situation that she was not conscious of her own actions. Things we focus attention on become central in our consciousness, whereas things we ignore either do not become part of our consciousness or occupy an area of dim or vague awareness.

CONSCIOUS, UNCONSCIOUS, AND PRECONSCIOUS

Psychologists have found it helpful to distinguish between consciousness and two other mental states, the preconscious and the unconscious. (There is also a fourth state, **nonconscious**, that psychologists use to classify events that cannot be called into conscious awareness, such as the flow of blood through your veins or the chemical changes that take place in the photoreceptors in your eyes.)

The term **consciousness** describes our awareness of processes that are going on inside or outside our bodies. The conscious mind can contain only a limited amount of thoughts, perceptions, and memories at any given time. However, a number of thoughts and memories exist on the fringe of awareness, in what is called the **preconscious.** These thoughts and memories can be pulled into consciousness fairly easily. For instance, you may not think about where you left your car keys last night until you need them and find that they are not in their usual location. By mentally reconstructing what you did after you last used the car, you may be able to shift your memory of where you left the keys from your preconscious to conscious awareness.

A more controversial mental state is the **unconscious.** Sigmund Freud popularized the notion that certain ideas, feelings, and memories are *repressed,* or banished to the unconscious because they are too painful or traumatic to deal with at a conscious level. Freud believed that even though these repressed memories and thoughts are not easily accessible, they may still influence people to behave in irrational or neurotic ways. Later chapters will look more closely at this view.

STATES OF CONSCIOUSNESS

Virtually all psychologists agree that consciousness is not a singular state of mind but rather encompasses a wide range of highly subjective, constantly changing states. Right now, you are presumably alert and concentrating on these printed words. You are in what psychologists would call a **"normal" state of consciousness**. However, as you read on, your mind may begin to wander and you may daydream. Many psychologists consider daydreaming to be an **alternative state of consciousness**. Later, when you go to bed and dream, you will be experiencing two more alternative states of consciousness, sleep and dreaming.

All the states classified as alternative consciousness are natural states of consciousness. In contrast, **altered states of consciousness** result from deliberate efforts to change our state of consciousness. If you go to a party tonight, have a few drinks, and get mildly "high," you will experience an altered state of consciousness. Other altered, nonnatural states of consciousness include states produced by meditation, hypnosis, and drugs.

Characteristics of Alternative and Altered States of Consciousness
Although alternative and altered states of consciousness differ in the way they are produced, both share differences from normal consciousness. The distinction between normal and nonnormal states is more qualitative than quantitative: When we move from normal awareness to an alternative or an altered state of consciousness, the changes in mental state are more of *kind* than *degree*. In other words, these transitions involve more than simply becoming more or less alert, responsive, or emotional. Rather, we may note that we are thinking in a manner not typical of our usual state of consciousness or that we are aware of things around us that we normally do not notice.

A number of general characteristics help distinguish alternative or altered states of consciousness from a normal state of consciousness. One is a change in body awareness. This altered awareness of our bodies may be no more than a sense of feeling very heavy, as when falling asleep. Drugs or hypnosis may produce more extreme shifts in body image, to the extent that we may feel as though we are out of our bodies or floating in space.

A second characteristic is altered perception. Perceptual processing of sensory input may simply be reduced, as when your professor interrupts your daydreaming to ask you a question and you have no idea what is going on. More extreme forms of altered perception may involve heightened awareness (such as colors that seem more vivid than usual) or *hallucinations*—seeing things, hearing voices, and other false perceptions.

The ability to pay attention, concentrate, and think clearly may also change significantly as we shift from a normal state of consciousness. Things that would usually seem illogical, such as flying like a bird, may seem perfectly natural in a dream state. More extreme alterations of consciousness, such as those produced by drugs, may result in difficulty distinguishing between what is and is not real.

Emotional changes may also accompany altered or alternative states of consciousness. When people daydream, meditate, or enter a hypnotic state, they may express little or no emotion. Certain drugs may also curb emotional expression and cause a person to become withdrawn, while other drugs may induce a profound sense of ecstasy or cause outbursts of emotion. Finally, altered and alternative states may distort a person's sense of time, making it seem to pass either more quickly or more slowly. A dream may seem to go on forever, when in reality it may have taken only 20 or 30 minutes.

Most of our waking hours are spent in a normal state of awareness. The things we do in this alert state—sensing, perceiving, learning, remembering, thinking, feeling, and relating to others—constitute the primary subject matter for most of the other chapters in this text. This chapter focuses primarily on what occurs in alternative and altered states of consciousness. We will look first at alternative states of consciousness, focusing on sleep cycles and dreams. Then we will examine altered states of consciousness including meditation, hypnosis, and the effects of drugs.

SLEEP AND DREAMING

At least once every day, we experience a dramatic shift in consciousness when we go to sleep; and we experience still another state of consciousness if we dream while sleeping. We spend roughly one-third of our lives sleeping, and the question of what happens when we sleep and dream has fascinated people for ages. As far back as 4,000 years ago Egyptians were interpreting dream symbols (a distant crowd, for example, was seen as a warning of death), and dream diaries existed long before the emergence of psychology as a science. Systematic sleep and dream research was not possible, however, until the technological breakthroughs of the past half century.

Sleep is a natural, periodically recurring state of rest characterized by reduced activity, lessened responsiveness to stimuli, and distinctive brain wave patterns. In 1937, Loomis, Harvey, and Hobart used the recently invented *electroencephalogram (EEG)* to demonstrate that brain waves change in form when a person shifts from a waking to a sleeping state. These researchers also observed further systematic changes in brain waves throughout the sleep period, and this discovery ultimately provided the basis for distinguishing between different stages of sleep.

STAGES OF SLEEP

In the early 1950s, Eugene Aserinsky, a graduate student working with sleep researcher Nathaniel Kleitman at the University of Chicago, observed systematic changes in the eye movements of sleeping infants. He noted periods of sleep when the eyes moved very rapidly, followed by intervals of little or no eye movements. This provided the distinction between **REM** (rapid eye movement) and **NREM** (nonrapid eye movement) **sleep**. These researchers found that when adult subjects were awakened during REM sleep, they almost invariably reported dreaming but that they rarely reported dreams when awakened after NREM sleep (Aserinsky & Kleitman, 1953).

Research since the 1950s has confirmed the connection between REM sleep and dreaming. However, we have also learned that dreaming is not limited to REM sleep and that REM is not synonymous with dreaming (Williamson et al., 1986). People awakened during REM sleep do not always report dreams. Likewise, people awakened from NREM sleep sometimes report having some kind of mental activity (such as a vague recall of some event), although they do not consistently label such activity dreaming (Herman et al., 1978; Webb, 1975). For this reason, it is difficult to estimate the exact proportion of NREM dreaming to REM dreaming. However, there is widespread agreement among sleep researchers that NREM sleep is considerably more dream-free than REM sleep and that dreams reported during REM sleep are usually much more vivid, tend to last longer, and are more visual than the "thoughtlike" mental processes that occur during NREM sleep (Foulkes & Schmidt, 1983).

Further distinctions between various stages of sleep have been made possible by sophisticated measuring devices such as the EEG, the *electrocu-*

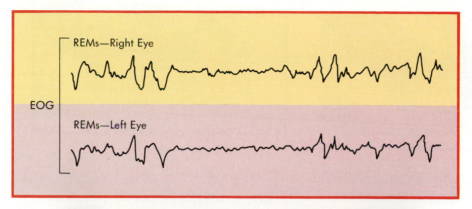

FIGURE 5.1 ELECTROCULO-GRAM RECORDINGS OF EYE MOVEMENTS DURING SLEEP

This illustration shows the left and right eye movements of a person during REM sleep, as measured by an EOG.

logram (EOG), which measures movements of the eye, and the *electromyograph (EMG)*, which measures electrical activity in the muscles. Figure 5.1 shows the left and right eye movements of a person during REM sleep, as measured by an EOG. Research using these and other devices has revealed systematic changes in brain wave patterns, muscular activity, levels of breathing, and heart rate during the course of a night's sleep. These measures have not only clarified the differences between REM and NREM sleep; they have also allowed researchers to identify four distinct stages of sleep in addition to REM sleep. Figure 5.2 demonstrates characteristic brain wave patterns of each of these stages as well as REM sleep and wakefulness.

Characteristics of Waking and Sleeping States   When we are awake and alert, the EEG reveals low-amplitude, high-frequency waves called *beta waves*. (The two key characteristics of brain waves are their *amplitude*, or height, and their *frequency*, measured in cycles per second.) When we are relaxed and drowsy, just before falling asleep, our brain waves show an *alpha* rhythm of higher amplitude and slower frequency (8 to 12 cycles per second). In this drowsy state, breathing and heart rate also slow down, body temperature drops, and muscles relax.

The light sleep that occurs just after dozing off is known as **Stage 1 sleep**. It is characterized by low-frequency (3 to 7 cycles per second), low-amplitude brain waves called *theta waves*. Stage 1 sleep may be accompanied by some slow eye movements, irregular breathing, and muscle relaxation. People are easily awakened during Stage 1 sleep—and often they do not realize they have been sleeping.

Stage 1 sleep normally lasts only a few minutes. We gradually drift into the deeper **Stage 2 sleep**, characterized by brief bursts of brain activity called *sleep spindles* (12 to 14 cycles per second) as well as another brain wave pattern called the *K complex*—a low-frequency, high-amplitude wave that occurs in response to either an external stimulus, such as the sound of a voice, or an internal stimulus, such as stomach cramps. Eye movements are minimal during Stage 2 sleep, and muscular activity often decreases to an even lower level.

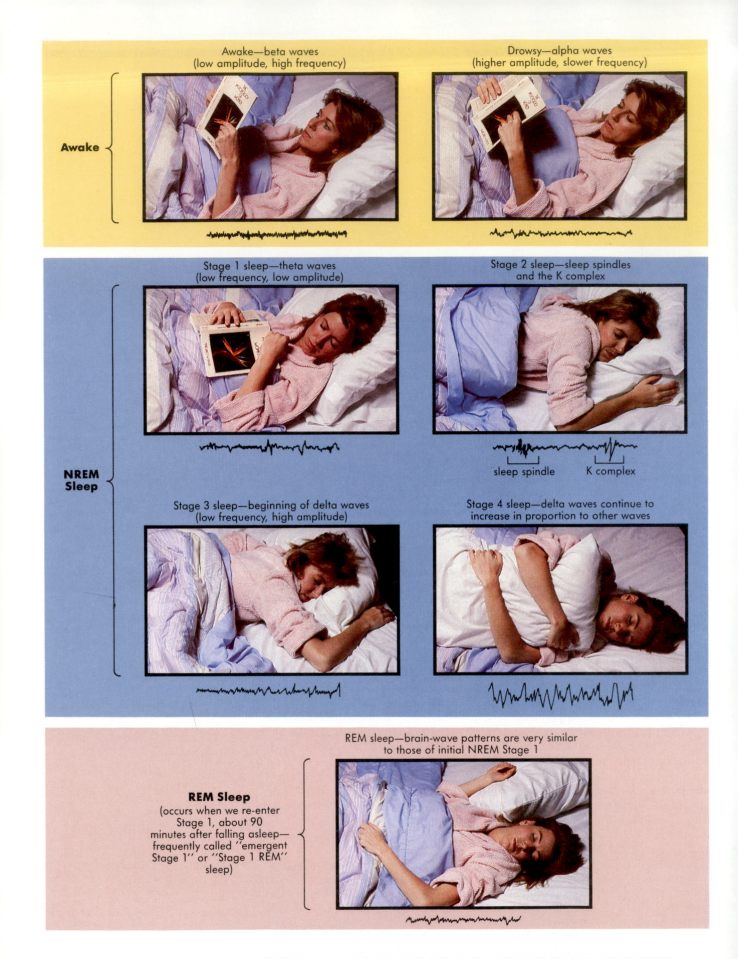

Awake—beta waves
(low amplitude, high frequency)

Drowsy—alpha waves
(higher amplitude, slower frequency)

Awake

Stage 1 sleep—theta waves
(low frequency, low amplitude)

Stage 2 sleep—sleep spindles
and the K complex

sleep spindle   K complex

Stage 3 sleep—beginning of delta waves
(low frequency, high amplitude)

Stage 4 sleep—delta waves continue to
increase in proportion to other waves

**NREM
Sleep**

REM sleep—brain-wave patterns are very similar
to those of initial NREM Stage 1

REM Sleep
(occurs when we re-enter
Stage 1, about 90
minutes after falling asleep—
frequently called ''emergent
Stage 1'' or ''Stage 1 REM''
sleep)

FIGURE 5.2   STAGES OF SLEEP AND CHARACTERISTIC BRAIN WAVE PATTERNS

As the cycle progresses into an even deeper level of sleep, there is a gradual increase in the incidence of low-frequency (0.5 to 2 cycles per second), high-amplitude *delta waves*. When these waves account for 20 percent to 50 percent of the EEG tracing, a person is in **Stage 3 sleep**. As sleep continues, delta waves continue to increase in proportion to other brain waves. When they exceed 50 percent, a person is said to be in **Stage 4 sleep**, the deepest level of sleep. It is difficult to arouse a person from Stage 4 sleep. If your alarm clock rings at this point, you will probably be disoriented and confused when you awaken. During Stages 3 and 4 there are virtually no eye movements.

The Sleep Cycle   It takes roughly 15 to 30 minutes to reach Stage 4 sleep after first dozing off. People typically remain in Stage 4 for about 30 to 40 minutes, then return gradually through Stages 3 and 2 to Stage 1 again. The first period of REM sleep occurs when we reenter Stage 1, about 90 minutes after falling asleep. During this period, which is frequently called "emergent Stage 1" or "Stage 1 REM" sleep, brain wave patterns are very similar to those of the initial NREM Stage 1.

In a night's sleep, we move through successive cycles, drifting up and down between the various phases of REM and NREM sleep. These cycles are about 90 minutes long, and we generally complete about five of them during the course of the night. The first episode of REM sleep may last only 5 to 10 minutes. However, with each subsequent cycle, the REM periods become progressively longer and deep sleep stages become shorter (Lavie, 1987). In later cycles, we may go only to Stage 2 and then back to REM. The final episodes of REM sleep before awakening may last 40 minutes or more. Figure 5.3 demonstrates the typical sequence of sleep stages.

REM SLEEP

Early sleep researchers reported an apparent relationship between dream content and eye movements during REM sleep (Dement & Kleitman, 1957). One subject, awakened just after a REM period with many side-to-side eye movements, reported watching a tennis game in his dream. Recent research suggests, however, that at least some REM activity may have little to do with dream content. For example, people who have been blind for over 50 years and cats raised in the dark who have never seen anything still show normal rapid eye movements during sleep (Webb & Bonnet, 1979). Some researchers believe that the rapid eye movements may be comparable to the occasional muscle twitches that occur during dreaming, in that both of these processes reflect a kind of overflow from a nervous system activated by dream activity.

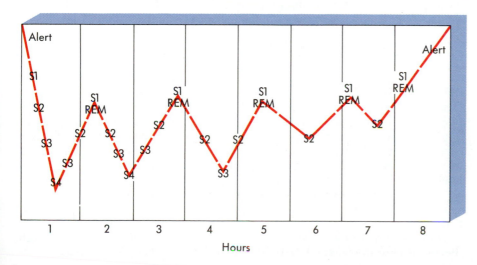

FIGURE 5.3   TYPICAL SEQUENCE OF SLEEP STAGES

Sleep grows progressively less deep throughout the sleep cycle of humans, and the dream or REM periods tend to lengthen as the night wears on (S1 = Stage 1, S2 = Stage 2, and so on.)

Of course, our eyes are not the only part of our bodies to show activity as we sleep. During a night's sleep, body activity may vary from lying very still to thrashing and twisting in bed. In extreme cases, some people may sleepwalk.

AT WHAT STAGE DOES SLEEPWALKING OCCUR?

You know that dreams generally take place during REM sleep. Based on this information, together with commonsense logic, can you predict during which phase of the sleep cycle the greatest amount of body movements occur? Do you think sleepwalking is most likely to occur during REM sleep, or during one of the stages of NREM sleep?

It seems logical that sleepwalking would take place when people dream, during REM sleep. When we are dreaming, our sympathetic nervous system causes an increase in breathing and heart rate as well as an elevation of blood pressure. Certain hormones associated with emergency situations may be released, and genital tissues may become engorged with blood, resulting in penile erection or vaginal lubrication. All of these signs of activation and arousal, together with brain waves similar to those of the waking state, suggest that the greatest amount of body movement takes place during REM sleep.

However, the true state of affairs is just the reverse. Typically, the only part of the body to move vigorously during dreams is the eyes. Muscular activity is inhibited during REM sleep by activity in a network of cells called the *pontine reticular formation*, located in the pons of the brain. When these cells become active, the body experiences a profound loss of muscle tone, making it almost impossible for a dreaming person to move. Thus sleepwalking almost invariably occurs during NREM sleep. One study of cats demonstrated the link between the pons and the loss of muscle tone during dreaming. When researchers destroyed a small portion of the region of the pons that produces *atonia* (loss of muscle tone), cats became very active during REM sleep (Morrison, 1983). Sometimes the inhibitory processes of REM sleep lessen for a moment. When this occurs, the nerve fibers in our muscles fire sporadically, resulting in jerks and twitches (Chase & Morales, 1983).

It seems puzzling that the least movement during sleep occurs when the eyes and brain are the most active. However, it is probably a good thing that our movements are inhibited when we dream. Can you imagine how battered and bruised we might be if we physically acted out all of our dreams?

CHANGES IN SLEEP PATTERNS WITH AGE

Sleep patterns are not stable throughout our lives. The percentage of the night's sleep that is spent dreaming decreases throughout the life cycle. Newborn babies sleep an average of 16 hours per day, with roughly 50 percent of that time spent in REM sleep. Adults in their twenties sleep about 8 hours, of which about 20 percent is REM sleep. Throughout middle age, there is further decline in both the time spent sleeping and the proportion of sleep spent in the REM phase, until at the age of 60 to 70, a person is likely to sleep only about 6 hours and dream only 15 percent of this time.

The amount of time spent in Stage 4 sleep also changes with age, so that by the time we are in our sixties, deep sleep is likely to disappear altogether. As a consequence, older people are more easily awakened: It is not uncommon for an older person who was accustomed to sleeping through the night now to awaken five or six times.

FIRST PERSON 5.1

I am now 76 years old, and I sleep fewer hours than at any other time in my life. During the years when I was raising my family, I would usually go to bed around 11 p.m. and sleep until 7 the next morning. Now I rarely go to bed before midnight, and it is almost impossible to sleep beyond 6 a.m. I usually lie in bed for a while after awakening to see if I can get back to sleep, but often I am too wide awake to doze off again. I also seem to wake up during the night a lot more than I did when I was younger. I don't like this, because I usually end up getting up and going to the bathroom, and I hate getting out of my warm bed. If I could just stay asleep, I wouldn't feel the need to get out of bed. (*Authors' Files*)

IS SLEEP NECESSARY?

In a widely reported "personal experiment" in 1959, New York disc jockey Peter Tripp staged a "wakeathon": He managed to stay awake for 200 hours. It was not easy. Halfway through his wakeathon, he began to hallucinate. His ability to think and reason deteriorated dramatically, and by the end of his ordeal he was unable to distinguish between fact and fantasy. He also became increasingly paranoid: He was convinced that a physician who had arrived to examine him was planning to haul him off to jail (Luce, 1965).

Sleep Deprivation Studies   Peter Tripp's experience, though fascinating, took place in an uncontrolled environment. Several subsequent studies have been carefully controlled, and they provide more reliable findings. In one experiment, for instance, six volunteers were deprived of sleep for 205 consecutive hours (Kales et al., 1970). By the end of the third day, subjects were hallucinating and experiencing *delusions* (false or distorted beliefs). They also developed hand tremors, double vision, and reduced pain thresholds. Surprisingly, however, their reflexes were largely unimpaired. In addition, physiological functions such as heart rate, respiration, blood pressure, and body temperature showed little change from normal throughout the course of the experiment. After the experiment was over, no long-term effects were evident. Subjects slept a few days, then awoke feeling fine.

In another controlled experiment conducted by famed sleep researcher William Dement (1972), a 17-year-old subject stayed awake for 268 consecutive hours, after which he needed only 14 hours of sleep to recover a normal state of consciousness. In contrast to Peter Tripp, this young man remained lucid and coherent throughout his vigil.

Findings such as these caused some researchers to question the importance of sleeping in our lives. A few even speculated that people might learn to get by without any sleep, particularly if scientists could isolate the factor that makes us sleepy and find a way to counter it. With this in mind, a team of researchers at the University of Chicago devised an inge-

This scene from the film *They Shoot Horses, Don't They?* depicts a dance marathon popular in the 1940s and 1950s, where the contestants who danced the longest won the prize. Competitors often fell unconscious into the arms of their partners, exhausted from lack of sleep. Delusions and hallucinations sometimes occur during long periods of sleep deprivation.

FIGURE 5.4 THE EXPERIMENTAL APPARATUS FOR MEASURING THE EFFECTS OF SLEEP DEPRIVATION IN RATS

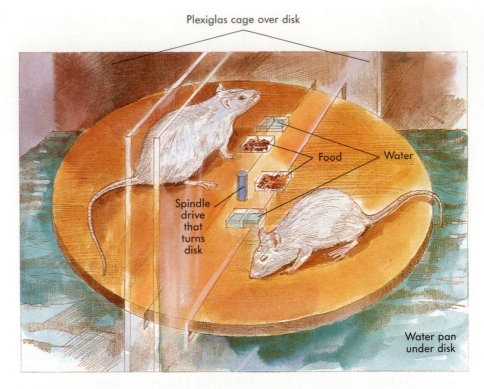

Plexiglas cage over disk

Food   Water

Spindle drive that turns disk

Water pan under disk

Both rats were placed on a plastic disk located above a water pan. If the disk rotated, both rats had to walk to avoid falling into the water. Each animal was connected to an EEG that monitored its brain waves. Whenever the sleep-deprived rat fell asleep, the EEG registered the change and opened a circuit, causing the disk to rotate. The control rat, who was not to be sleep-deprived, could sleep when the other rat was awake. However, the sleep-deprived rat could never sleep because it was jarred awake at each lapse of consciousness by the rotation of the disk.

nious device to study the effects of sleep deprivation in rats. Rats were studied in pairs: One was deprived of sleep, and the other acted as a control. Both rats were placed on a plastic disk located above a water pan, as shown in Figure 5.4. If the disk rotated, the rats had to walk to avoid falling into the water. The rats were connected to an EEG that monitored their brain waves. Whenever the sleep-deprived rat fell asleep, the EEG registered the change and opened a circuit, causing the disk to rotate. Both rats would have to walk to avoid falling into the water. The control rat could sleep when his counterpart was awake, but the sleep-deprived rat was jarred awake at each lapse of consciousness. The sleep-deprived rats lasted as long as 33 days, but they all eventually died. In contrast, all the control animals survived, apparently no worse for the experience. Autopsies of the sleep-deprived rats revealed no single cause of death. They died from a variety of causes, including stomach ulcers, imbalance of body chemistry, and internal hemorrhages (Rechtschaffen et al., 1983).

Explaining Sleep   From the studies just described, it seems evident that sleep is necessary, but why it is necessary is not clear. A number of theories have been suggested to explain why we need sleep.'

Sleeping to Conserve Energy   One explanation for why we sleep roughly one-third of every 24-hour period is that sleep conserves energy, thus preventing exhaustion. We burn more calories while awake than asleep. Perhaps in our distant history, when food resources were scarce, sleeping 8 hours a day may have been a helpful mechanism for limiting the use of scarce energy resources.

Sleeping to Restore Depleted Resources According to a second theory, sleep restores resources that we deplete in our daily activities. This explanation is supported by studies that show that people often sleep longer after particularly tiring events. In one study, for example, subjects' sleep was monitored after they ran a 57-mile race. Not only did they sleep longer than normal, but their sleep also contained an unusual amount of deep, Stage 4 sleep (Shapiro et al., 1981).

We still do not know exactly what restorative processes occur during sleep, or what (if any) kinds of physiological processes or energy sources are depleted when we are awake. There is tentative evidence that certain kinds of tissue restoration, such as cell repair, may occur during sleep (Adam & Oswald, 1977). Some researchers also believe that certain brain chemicals such as neurotransmitters are restored during sleep and that the amount of sleep we need is related to the levels of these chemicals that are present when we fall asleep. This condition may be genetically influenced (Hartman, 1973; Webb & Campbell, 1983).

Sleeping to Clear the Mind Recently, Francis Crick and Graeme Mitchison (1983) proposed another explanation: People sleep to clear their minds. According to this theory, our brains accumulate a great deal of extraneous, largely useless information during the course of each day. If these varied memories and mental associations were allowed to remain, they would clutter our brains, interfering with the learning and recall of new information. Crick and Mitchison suggest that the heightened electrical activity typical of REM sleep acts as an eraser, wiping away this extraneous information and leaving the brain more receptive to new learning.

Sleeping to Dream Finally, it has been proposed that people sleep so that they can dream. Although a few people claim they never dream, virtually every subject ever studied has reported dreams when awakened during REM sleep. The fact that we all dream suggests that this alternative state of consciousness serves some important function in life. Perhaps we *need* to dream during the course of a night's sleep.

IS DREAMING NECESSARY?

What happens when people are permitted to sleep but not to dream? An experiment designed by William Dement (1960) attempted to answer this question by using both an EEG and an EOG to register the beginning of REM sleep. For seven consecutive nights, subjects were able to sleep during other stages but were awakened as soon as they entered REM sleep. The total amount of REM sleep they could experience was reduced by about 75 percent. A control group was awakened the same number of times as the REM-deprived subjects, but only during NREM sleep. Both groups were monitored throughout the course of the experiment.

Dream-deprived subjects demonstrated a number of effects not shown by the control group. They became increasingly irritable, anxious, hostile, and aggressive as the experiment progressed; they also had trouble concentrating on tasks. They also became increasingly "dream starved," entering REM sleep almost as soon as they dozed off. Over the course of the one-week experiment, Dement found it increasingly difficult to prevent REM sleep. On the first night, subjects had to be awakened an average of 12 times. By the seventh night, this figure had more than doubled to an average of 26 awakenings. When Dement's subjects were allowed to sleep without interruption on the eighth night, most (but not all) showed a *REM rebound* effect, spending about 50 percent more time dreaming than they had prior to the onset of the experiment. The REM rebound effect has recently been shown to occur immediately after a period of forced wakefulness during a night's sleep. Subjects who were awakened and asked to sit quietly in an illuminated room for varying periods of time demonstrated a marked increase in the length of their first and second REM episodes after returning to sleep (Campbell, 1987).

Such results have been interpreted as supporting the theory that we sleep to dream, and Dement's findings have been cited by some psychologists as evidence that dream deprivation can produce severe emotional consequences. To investigate this possibility, researchers turned to animal studies. In one study, rats were placed on tiny platforms over water where the only possible way to sleep was standing up (Morden et al., 1967). As mentioned earlier, muscle tone is lost when REM begins. Consequently, whenever REM sleep began, the rat's legs would collapse, toppling it off the platform. The rats were able to experience NREM sleep because their muscle tone allowed them to sleep standing up. Contrary to what Dement's earlier findings seemed to suggest, the rats did not show any significant behavioral or emotional difficulties.

Not surprisingly, this research model has not been used on humans. However, some studies have been able to test the effects of REM deprivation through such techniques as drugs that prevent REM sleep. Two extensive reviews of the literature (Vogel, 1975; Webb, 1975) revealed no serious emotional or behavioral consequences associated with lack of REM sleep, although some evidence suggests that REM-deprived subjects may have difficulty learning complex things (Greenberg & Pearlman, 1974; Webb & Bonnet, 1979). Other than consistent evidence for the REM rebound effect, researchers have not found support for the claim that REM deprivation might threaten a person's emotional or physical health. There is even some evidence that too much REM sleep may be a cause of some forms of depression, and that some depressed people may show improvement after exposure to several nights of controlled REM deprivation (Arehart-Treichel, 1977; Joffe & Brown, 1987; Lechin & Van der Dijs, 1984).

Explaining Dreams A number of theories attempt to explain why we spend roughly 1½ hours dreaming each night. It is possible that dreaming has more than one cause; thus several of the following viewpoints may help explain this alternate state of consciousness. Note, however, that to date none of these theoretical explanations of why we dream has been conclusively confirmed or disconfirmed by research (Chase, 1986).

Dreaming as the Brain's Explanation for Stimuli One theory suggests that dreams are the brain's attempt to make sense out of random bursts of neuronal activity. Studies of REM sleep in cats indicate that certain cells in the brain stem region of the reticular formation produce random spikes of electrical activity during REM sleep and that this activity arouses adjacent neurons that influence eye movements, balance, and actions such as walking and running (Hobson & McCarley, 1977). Although most of these body movements are blocked during REM sleep, these cells still send signals to higher cortical centers. The brain has to reconcile the inconsistency between signals that indicate movement and the fact that the body is still. To accomplish this, it searches through its existing "file" of memories and manufactures a dream. Dreams are thus the brain's solution to an absence of logical connections in the stimuli reaching the cortex.

This theory is known as the *activation-synthesis hypothesis*, and it seems to fit many common dreaming experiences. Thus dreams of falling, flying, or floating might be the brain's interpretation of messages from cells involved in balance; and sexual dreams might reflect an effort to fit a logical explanation to physiological arousal of the genital tissues. Table 5.1 lists the most common dream experiences of college students. See how many of these can be explained by the activation-synthesis hypothesis.

TABLE 5.1 *A Sample of the 20 Most Common Dreams of College Students*

Type of Dream	Percentage of Students
Falling	83
Being attacked or pursued	77
Trying repeatedly to do something	71
School, teachers, studying	71
Sexual experiences	66
Arriving too late	64
Eating	62
Being frozen with fright	58
A loved person is dead	57
Being locked up	56
Finding money	56
Swimming	52
Snakes	49
Being dressed inappropriately	46
Being smothered	44
Being nude in public	43
Fire	41
Failing an examination	39
Flying	34
Seeing self as dead	33

Source: From Griffith, Miyago & Tago, 1958.

After a mentally tiring day, people and other animals may need a greater amount of REM sleep. Perhaps this young woman has been studying all day for a psychology exam; maybe her feline friend has been developing strategies to catch that mouse that keeps sneaking into the house.

Dreaming as Mental Reprogramming Another theory explains dreams as a form of mental "reprogramming" in which the brain reorganizes its memory systems to accommodate new information. From this perspective, the REM sleep of humans and other animals should increase following activities requiring unusual mental efforts.

A number of studies have supported this theory. In one, subjects wore special lenses so that they saw things upside down, a situation that demands great mental adjustments. After this experience, they spent more time in REM sleep (Zimmerman et al., 1970). Subjects in other experiments who have worn lenses that severely distort the visual field have also shown increased REM sleep (Herman & Roffwarg, 1983). In still other experiments, subjects asked to perform particularly complex or frustrating tasks have been shown to spend more time in REM sleep (Lewin & Gambosh, 1973; McGrath & Cohen, 1978). Even rats exposed to new learning show increased REM sleep (Leconte et al., 1972), and kittens and rats placed in stimulating environments spend more time in REM sleep than control animals in sterile environments (McGinty, 1969).

The fact that older people spend less time in REM sleep seems to fit in nicely with this mental reprogramming viewpoint. Presumably, as people grow older, they assimilate less new information. This theory also seems consistent with the experience of many college students who report that they dream more after a marathon study session.

Dealing with Problems in Dreams A third explanation of dreaming sees dreams as a relatively safe, low-stress way to deal with problems that occur during waking hours. Dream researcher Rosalind Cartwright (1975) conducted an experiment to test this theory. She presented student subjects with stories about common problems faced by young adults, none of which included a solution. The subjects then spent the night in a laboratory where their sleep was monitored. Some were allowed to dream and others were not. In the morning, subjects who had dreamed were able to suggest more realistic solutions to the problems than those who had not been permitted to dream. This finding suggests that dreams may well help people resolve problems that occur when they are awake—an explanation that is supported further by evidence that people spend more time in REM sleep when they are experiencing relationship conflicts, problems at work, or other emotionally stressful events (Hartmann, 1973; Monroe, 1967).

FIRST PERSON 5.2

I dream like crazy after hitting the books hard, studying for a major exam. Do you think it just seems this way because I am tense and that makes me wake up more so I remember my dreams more? Or do I actually dream more? I bet that I actually do dream more. (*Authors' Files*)

Why do we dream? Research shows that we all have a definite need to dream, though many theories attempt to explain why. Freud believed that dreams were the disguised expressions of repressed desires and aptly called them "the royal road to the unconscious."

Dreams as Expressions of the Unconscious Finally, there is the Freudian interpretation of dreams. In his classic *Interpretation of Dreams* (1900), Freud called dreams the "royal road to the unconscious"—that is, disguised expressions of wishes that have been repressed. For example, a person who is sexually frustrated might dream repeatedly about sexual themes. Freud noted that these dreams might not seem to be sexual to the untrained observer, however. The reason for this is that we recall only the **manifest content** of our dreams. The manifest content is a disguised version of the **latent** (hidden) **content**, which is the true meaning of our dreams. Thus a train passing though a tunnel in a dream might be the manifest representation of a penis entering a vagina. If the person having this dream also reported other dreams in which umbrellas, rifles, or swords (all representing the male organ) and boxes, chests, and ovens (female representations) appeared, Freud would be convinced that the dreams expressed a sexual conflict.

Why do we dream about manifest representations instead of the real thing? Freud believed that if people expressed their true desires directly in dreams, the result would be such startling, upsetting dreams that they would awaken immediately. Thus our unconscious minds tame things down to ensure a good night's sleep.

Lucid Dreaming Although we may not all agree with Freud, most of us are intrigued by the content of dreams at some time or other. To some groups of people, dream experiences are regarded as highly significant. Australian anthropologist Kilton Stewart has written about an isolated society of people in Malaysia, the Senoi, who make dreams the central feature in their culture. The Senoi spend a great deal of time discussing their dreams. They also practice **lucid dreaming**, in which dreamers are aware that they are dreaming and actually influence the content of their own dreams. When frightening or negative dreams occur, the Senoi redream the event in a way that makes it pleasant or positive.

Stewart reported that this society runs like a well-oiled wheel and is remarkably free of acts of overt aggression, conflict, or emotional illness. Although a number of factors might contribute to this, both Stewart and the Senoi believe that the major source of their societal health is the practice of lucid dreaming and the emphasis on daily discussion of dreams (Stewart, 1969).

Although lucid dreaming is uncommon in our society, some people claim not only that they know when they are dreaming but also that they can influence their dreams. Although researchers were inclined to dismiss these claims, a recent study has supported them. Stephen LaBerge and his associates at the Stanford University Sleep Research Center trained volunteers to signal in a prearranged manner when they became aware that they were dreaming. For example, they were instructed to make upward eye movements or to make a fist with each hand (in the dream) in a prearranged pattern. Corresponding muscle changes in the wrist were electrically recorded. Many of LaBerge's subjects were able to register these signals during their dreams, a finding that supports the concept of lucid dreaming (LaBerge et al., 1981).

You may wish to learn more about lucid dreaming. Stephen LaBerge believes that lucid dreaming is a learnable skill. He has written an article in which he outlines an easy-to-follow routine for learning to increase lucid dreaming. You can find this article in most university libraries. The reference is "Lucid Dreaming as a Learnable Skill: A Case Study," *Perceptual and Motor Skills*, 1980, *51*, 1039–1042.

SLEEP DISORDERS

Most people relish their sleep. However, a sizable minority (perhaps one in five adults) find little comfort in the night. These children and adults suffer from a variety of **sleep disorders** including insomnia, sleep apnea, night terrors and nightmares, and sleepwalking.

Insomnia   People with **insomnia** have difficulty going to sleep. Less commonly, they may experience frequent awakenings. Figures released in the early 1980s by the U.S. Department of Health and Human Services suggest that approximately 25 million Americans are insomniacs; approximately twice as many women as men seem to be affected (Cirignotta et al., 1985; Kripke & Simons, 1976).

Insomnia may have a variety of causes, including stressful events, health problems, emotional disturbances, and drug use. The most common form of insomnia, *temporary* or *situational insomnia*, is related to stress associated with a particular situation—loss of a job, death or illness of a loved one, a relationship that falls apart, and so on. Such events cause stress or worry that may produce heightened physical arousal, which inhibits sleep. Stress may be the most common cause of sleep loss among college students, who have been found to experience marked reductions in sleep during periods of high stress (Hicks & Garcia, 1987).

People who suffer from long-lasting sleep loss, or *chronic insomnia*, are more likely to report a serious erosion of the quality of their lives. Although we are not sure exactly what causes chronic insomnia, this condition seems to be associated with anxiety or depression (Kales et al., 1976; Nicassio et al., 1985). Some chronic insomniacs have been found to have irregular sleep patterns (Monroe, 1967).

Sleeping potions (usually barbiturates) are often prescribed to relieve insomnia. These drugs may be helpful in small doses for a brief period. However, they often have an effect that is just the opposite of that desired. Sleeping potions erode the quality of sleep by reducing the amount of REM sleep and Stage 4 sleep. In addition, people quickly develop a tolerance to these drugs, requiring ever-increasing dosages to produce a sedative effect. (Barbiturate tolerance and dependency are discussed later in this chapter.) The result is a kind of drug dependence insomnia. Nonprescription, over-the-counter drugs are not the answer either, for they have little or no sleep-inducing capability. People who find these substances helpful are probably demonstrating a placebo effect, experiencing relief simply because they believe the drugs will work (Webb & Bonnet, 1979).

Since drugs tend to be ineffective at best and potentially damaging at worst, psychologists have developed a number of behaviorally based remedies for poor sleepers. One or more of these suggestions, outlined in the Health Psychology and Life discussion "Suggested Remedies for Insomnia" may prove helpful.

Sleep Apnea   A second sleep disorder is a disturbing condition known as **sleep apnea.** People with this disorder do not breathe regularly during sleep. In fact, their breathing actually stops for as long as a few seconds to a minute or two (Brouilette et al., 1982; Guilleminault, 1979; Guilleminault & Dement, 1978; Hall, 1986). As the need for oxygen becomes acute, the person briefly awakens, gulps in air, and then settles back to sleep, only to repeat the cycle when breathing stops again. A person with this disorder is unlikely to be aware that he or she wakes up to breathe as often as several hundred times a night. In one extreme case, a man monitored in the sleep laboratory could not sleep and breathe at the same time. Fortunately, most cases are not so severe. It has been estimated that about 5 percent of the general population and as many as 1 out of 10 men over age 40 have this disorder (Raymond, 1986).

Sleep apnea seems to occur when the brain stops sending signals that trigger the breathing response. It may also be caused by a blockage in the upper air passage. (Some apnea victims are older, obese men whose airways may become blocked by their overly thick necks.) Some researchers believe that sleep apnea may be one cause of *sudden infant death syndrome (SIDS)*,

SUGGESTED REMEDIES FOR INSOMNIA

Psychologists have developed a number of behaviorally based remedies for insomnia. Perhaps one or more of the following suggestions may be helpful to you or someone you care for.

1. Adopt a regular schedule. Go to sleep and get up at the same time every day, even on weekends. Many insomnia sufferers have erratic sleep patterns. A regular schedule can establish a predictable rhythm that will greatly improve sleep. Avoid spending excessive time in bed, since this behavior can perpetuate insomnia (Spielman et al., 1987).
2. Try to engage in a relaxing, soothing activity before going to bed. Some people find that a warm bath is helpful; others prefer reading or listening to soothing music. Avoid high-stress activities such as discussing money with your partner or trying to debug a computer program.
3. A number of procedures are designed to relax your body; these may be helpful before retiring. (See the Health Psychology and Life discussion "Techniques for Producing the Relaxation Response" on page 157.) You can learn about relaxation techniques from several books that are easily found in bookstores.
4. A daily exercise routine can help promote a good night's sleep. It is probably not a good idea to engage in this activity just before going to sleep, however, since exercise can be very energizing.
5. Avoid drinking large quantities of beer, wine, or distilled spirits before retiring. These substances may help you fall asleep, but they are likely to interfere with your ability to stay asleep once their sedative effect wears off. In addition, avoid all stimulants after midday. One of the most commonly consumed stimulants, caffeine, is found in chocolate, coffee, tea, and many carbonated soft drinks. Caffeine-free forms of these products are available.
6. Avoid engaging in anything other than sleep in your bed. Do not read, watch TV, eat, or even think in bed. In this way, only sleep becomes associated with retiring to bed.
7. Make your bedroom environment as sleep-compatible as possible. Use curtains or shades that shut out external light. If you must sleep in a noisy area, try using ear plugs or turning on a fan or air conditioner to drown out the noise.
8. Finally, try not to get upset about not sleeping. This is often easier said than done. However, remember that anger will only energize you more, thus adding to your problem. It would probably be much better to get up and read a book until you feel sleepy enough to doze off.

commonly called crib death. There is speculation that immature breathing centers in the brain stem malfunction, causing susceptible infants to stop breathing (Hales, 1980).

Extreme cases of apnea may be relieved by a *tracheostomy*, an operation in which a valve is surgically inserted into the throat. In recent years, medical researchers have developed a nonsurgical approach to treating severe sleep apnea in which a continuous flow of air is applied to the nostrils through a nose mask. This technique, called *continuous positive airway pressure (CPAP)*, is now often the treatment of choice for this disorder (Miller, 1986).

Narcolepsy A peculiar sleep disorder called **narcolepsy** manifests itself as uncontrollable sleep attacks in which a person falls asleep suddenly, perhaps while talking, standing, or driving. The attack may last only a few minutes, or it may last half an hour or more. EEG monitoring reveals that these sleep attacks involve the immediate onset of REM sleep. Since REM sleep produces a loss of muscle tone, most victims collapse the moment they lapse into sleep. For this reason, narcoleptic attacks can endanger a person's life, particularly if they occur while driving or operating dangerous machinery.

We still do not know why narcolepsy occurs. The fact that many narcoleptics seem most likely to have sleep attacks during periods of high anxiety or tension suggests that narcolepsy may be some kind of defense against stress. However, many researchers link narcolepsy to an inherited abnormality in the brain mechanisms that control sleep and waking. This deficiency may involve inadequate production of the neurotransmitter dopamine, which is believed to play a role in arousal (Mefford et al., 1983). Recent research has also linked structural brain abnormalities with this condition (Erlich & Itabashi, 1986). Although physicians sometimes prescribe stimulant drugs to reduce the frequency of sleep attacks, there is no effective treatment yet.

Nightmares and Night Terrors   A **nightmare** is a bad dream that occurs during REM sleep (Kellerman, 1987). Nightmares typically leave a strong impression on the dreamer; people often awaken after a nightmare with vivid recall of the dream. Sometimes nightmares are repetitive. Many dream theorists believe that repetitive nightmares may reflect areas of conflict or sources of emotional turmoil in a person's waking life. Some research suggests that people who have frequent nightmares tend to be sensitive and open persons with creative interests and greater than normal tendencies to exhibit symptoms of psychological disorder (Belicki & Belicki, 1982; Hartmann et al., 1987; Hartmann et al., 1981).

People often confuse night terrors with nightmares. **Night terrors**, like nightmares, are frightening experiences associated with sleep, but night terrors occur during Stage 4 sleep. A sleeper suddenly awakens in a state of blind panic. Typically, a person experiencing a night terror will sit up, stare unseeingly, and perhaps gasp or hyperventilate. Occasionally he or she will scream or jump out of bed. People awakened by a night terror usually do not report any frightening dreams or thoughts. They go back to sleep easily and do not recall the experience when they awaken the next morning. Night terrors seem to be more a function of being suddenly awakened from a deep sleep than a manifestation of some underlying psychological problem.

Sleepwalking   For many years, it was believed that people who **sleepwalk** (called somnambulists) are acting out dream events. We now know that sleepwalking occurs during Stage 3 or 4 of NREM sleep, when the body is capable of movement. Sleepwalkers negotiate obstacles, although they move quite clumsily and often fall down or bump into things. Occasionally sleepwalking may subject a person to extreme danger. In one case reported in a news account, a man sleepwalked out the door of a travel trailer as it was being pulled along a highway.

Sleepwalking seems to be most prevalent among children, who usually outgrow it. Parents can reduce the possibility of their child being injured during sleepwalking by adjusting the environment, for instance, putting gates across windows and at the top of stairs. Sometimes sleepwalking may reflect conflicts that remain unresolved during a person's waking state. Since the normal constraints are not present during sleep, a person may occasionally act out conflicts during sleepwalking that would be unacceptable in a waking state.

Practically everyone talks during sleep on occasion. The only connection between sleepwalking and sleeptalking is that both occur during Stage 3 or 4 of NREM sleep. In contrast to sleepwalking, talking while asleep is usually purposeless and unrelated to events that occur during the waking state.

Whereas sleep and dreaming are natural variations of consciousness, other states result from deliberate efforts to force alterations of consciousness. The remaining discussions in this chapter look at the altered states of consciousness produced by meditation, hypnosis, and drugs.

MEDITATION

Meditation is the practice of deliberately altering consciousness in an effort to achieve a state of tranquillity, relaxation, and inner peace. It has been practiced by monks, mystics, and yogis since ancient times, and since the 1960s many Americans have practiced it.

My husband received his draft notice at the height of the Vietnam War, a few weeks after graduating from college. This came as a shock; we had a painful talk in which he said he thought we should move to Canada. I was opposed, and my husband finally agreed to report to basic training. For the first few weeks he wrote about how he hated boot camp and how his drill instructor was always on his case. One day he called and said he had had it, and that he was going to go AWOL and head for Canada. This panicked me. After several frantic phone calls, he was persuaded to tough it out.

Then suddenly he was given a medical discharge; we found out the details when he came home. He had begun to sleepwalk shortly after his call about going AWOL. At first, all he did was get up and start walking off the base. But then his sleepwalking made an abrupt shift. One night he went into the hated drill instructor's room and tried to strangle him. He swears he had no awareness of what he was doing until the commotion woke him up. At this point, the Army had had enough, and he got his walking papers. The sleepwalking stopped when he was back home. (*Authors' Files*)

Meditation has become a popular way to reduce stress, although many researchers believe the same benefits can be derived through effective resting and relaxation techniques.

For some people, prayer can act as an effective relaxation technique, reducing stress and filling the person with a sense of peace and well-being.

There is no single technique for meditation. Perhaps the most commonly practiced form of meditation in America is *concentrative*. It involves focusing on a single, unchanging stimulus, such as a repeated word with a smooth, full sound like *hum* or *om*. A less popular form of meditation uses *opening up*, a technique in which the meditator attempts to broaden his or her awareness to include all forms of sensations.

Meditation has been linked to a range of physiological changes. Many studies have shown that meditators exhibit alpha brain waves typical of the relaxed state that occurs just before dozing off (Anand et al., 1961; Wallace & Benson, 1972). Metabolism also slows down: Oxygen consumption decreases, as do respiration and heart rate, and blood chemistry changes (Wallace & Benson, 1972). These metabolic changes account for some of the amazing feats of yogis—for example, being buried alive and surviving for a much longer time on limited oxygen than would normally be possible.

Many researchers believe that in spite of the mystical aura surrounding many forms of meditation, there is nothing unique about this state. In fact, it has been suggested that the effects of meditation are virtually indistinguishable from those of merely resting. In the last few years, many studies have compared meditating subjects with resting subjects. No significant differences were found in heart and respiration rates, skin temperature, muscle tone, rate of oxygen consumption, or blood pressure (Holmes, 1984).

This observation is not meant to contradict the benefits attributed to meditating. It is clear that many people achieve a serenity and sense of well-being from daily meditation. A number of clinics have successfully used meditation programs to reduce anxiety, lower stress, decrease blood pressure, reduce chronic pain, ease insomnia, and diminish dependency on tobacco, alcohol, and other drugs (Kanellakos, 1978; Raskin et al., 1980).

However, it is possible that these same benefits might be achieved by merely learning to relax or rest effectively during brief intervals once or twice a day. Harvard's Herbert Benson (1977), one of the leading investigators of the physiology of meditation and relaxation, has developed a simple procedure for producing what he calls the *relaxation response*, which is a composite of the physiological effects attributed to meditation. A general outline of Benson's techniques is presented in the Health Psychology and Life discussion "Techniques for Producing the Relaxation Response" on the next page.

TECHNIQUES FOR PRODUCING THE RELAXATION RESPONSE

1. Sit in a confortable, relaxing position in a quiet room where distractions are minimized. Close your eyes.
2. Slowly and progressively, relax your muscles, beginning with your feet and moving upward to your head.
3. Concentrate on your breathing, which should be steady and rhythmic. Each time you breathe out, repeat the word one silently to yourself.
4. Maintain a passive attitude. Do not attempt to force relaxation or become disturbed if you are distracted or have

difficulty letting go. Allow relaxation to happen in its own time.
5. If thoughts or distractions come into your consciousness, pay them little heed and continue repeating one.

With time, you will probably find that these procedures allow you to achieve a deep state of relaxation in a very few minutes. One or two daily sessions of approximately 20 minutes each should be sufficient. These episodes of controlled rest should not be attempted during the two hours after eating, since digestion appears to inhibit the relaxation response.

HYPNOSIS

Hypnosis is a fascinating phenomenon that has aroused considerable controversy within the discipline of psychology. It is also an area that most psychologists consider worthy of research. Much of its credibility stems from the thoughtful research and writings of renowned psychologist Ernest Hilgard.

It has been suggested that hypnotized people are experiencing an altered level of consciousness similar to a dreaming state. In fact, the word *hypnosis* was derived from Hypnos, the Greek god of sleep. Hypnosis is not a state of sleep, however. Hypnotized people are very relaxed and calm, but EEG recordings demonstrate that they are not asleep. Efforts to differentiate between the brain waves, heart rates, and respiration of hypnotized and nonhypnotized people have been largely unsuccessful.

Research does strongly suggest, however, that hypnosis is qualitatively different from a normal waking state. For example, one study compared the responses of six hypnotized subjects with six who were pretending to be hypnotized. All subjects were told to tap their feet in time to imaginary music. Then a power failure was simulated, causing the light to go off and the tape to stop. The experimenter left the room but continued to monitor the subjects' responses. Of the six fakers, five stopped tapping their feet as soon as the experimenter left and resumed faking when the power went back on. In contrast, five of the six hypnotized subjects continued to tap their feet to the imaginary music, seemingly oblivious to either the power failure or the experimenter's absence. These results suggest that the hypnotized subjects were in a demonstrably unique state of consciousness (Evans & Orne, 1971).

But in what way is a hypnotic state unique? Observations of countless hypnotized people indicate that hypnosis is characterized by total relaxation and a strong sense of detachment. Hypnotized people are alert and particularly attentive to the hypnotist's words, appearing to have few or no independent thoughts. In this passive state, a hypnotized person does not initiate activity but rather waits for instructions. In a very deep trance state, a person may become largely oblivious to stimuli other than the hypnotist's voice.

Although psychologists have not agreed on a precise definition of this state, a functional working definition is that **hypnosis** is a state of heightened suggestibility in which a person is unusually willing to comply with the hypnotist's directives, including those that alter perceptions of self and the environment.

While in a hypnotized state, people are totally relaxed, particularly attentive to the hypnotist's words, and generally aware of surrounding stimuli. However, in a very deep trance state, a person is oblivious to almost all stimuli other than the hypnotist's voice. Here, Dr. David Spiegel, of Stanford University, monitors the brain activity of a hypnotized subject.

PHENOMENA ASSOCIATED WITH HYPNOSIS

Hypnosis has been linked to a number of phenomena, sometimes accurately and sometimes with a fair amount of hyperbole. Its reputed effects include improved athletic performance, symptomatic relief of physical ailments, pain reduction, enhanced memory, age regression, imaginary sensory experiences, and posthypnotic suggestions that subjects carry out as if they were their own ideas. The evidence is evaluated in the following paragraphs.

Hypnosis and Athletic Ability   You may have heard reports about people demonstrating amazing feats of strength or other outstanding athletic performances, allegedly as a direct result of hypnotic suggestion. Although many of these stories are true, a caveat must be kept in mind: there is no evidence that hypnosis can increase a person's capacity to perform beyond natural limits. It may act as a powerful motivator, providing the extra impetus to close the gap between potential and actual performance. In this sense, its effects may be similar to the emergency reponse that enables a 150-pound salesman to lift a 500-pound steel pipe off an injured child.

Hypnosis and Relief of Physical Ailments   Well-documented evidence shows that suggestions given to hypnotized people can help relieve the symptoms of a variety of stress-related illnesses, including asthma, ulcers, and colitis. Hypnotism has also been used to help clear up warts, psoriasis, and a variety of other skin ailments (Smith, 1985). Hypnosis has not been so effective in treating self-initiated addictive disorders such as alcoholism, smoking and overeating (Wadden & Anderton, 1982).

Hypnosis and Pain Relief   In the nineteenth century, before anesthesia was discovered, a few surgeons used hypnosis to block surgical pain. However, most of the medical community looked on this practice with suspicion, and it was even suggested that hypnotized patients were "faking" pain relief. Today, most medical practitioners acknowledge that hypnosis can be very effective in reducing the pain associated with childbirth, back problems, arthritis, dental procedures, burns, and even major surgery. One study found that hypnosis was more effective than aspirin, acupuncture, or morphine in reducing pain (Stern et al., 1977). One particularly noteworthy

I didn't believe the stories I had heard about hypnosis enhancing people's athletic abilities until an event that occurred in an upper level psychology class I was enrolled in several years ago. As part of our segment on hypnosis, our teacher gave us an unusual assignment: to use self-hypnosis to achieve some goal. One of my classmates was an athlete who had won several regional weight-lifting competitions; he was also a pretty good student. For his goal, he decided he would set a new American weight-lifting record. Believe it or not, he succeeded! (*Authors' Files*)

recent development in pain control has been the use of hypnotic suggestion to augment the effectiveness of chemical painkillers (Davidson, 1984).

Hypnosis and Memory Enhancement in Criminal Investigations   For a time, claims about the memory enhancement capabilities of hypnosis led to its widespread use by police departments, often to help witnesses recall criminal acts. Certainly, some limited benefits are associated with its use in law enforcement—for example, as a way to calm a frightened, traumatized victim of an assault so that he or she can concentrate on the events surrounding the crime. However, there is little substance to claims that it can enhance a person's recall of a criminal act. Furthermore, there may actually be dangers to relying too heavily on hypnosis. Recent findings have shown that when hypnotized subjects are pressed to recall specific events, they will report many things that are not true (Dywan & Bowers, 1983). For these reasons, there is now a strong trend to bar testimony from hypnotized witnesses (Stark, 1984).

Hypnosis and Age Regression   One of the most widely reported phenomena associated with hypnosis is **age regression**, in which a hypnotized subject is instructed to move back in time to an earlier age. In one demonstration of age regression, a young woman was systematically moved backward through the years of her youth, in an effort to trace her dislike of eggs. At each suggested age, she described her experiences on the farm where she was raised. As he regressed his subject backward in increments of two years, the hypnotist asked the same question: "Do you like eggs?" At each level, she responded "no" until it was suggested that she was six. At this point, she indicated that she did eat eggs. The hypnotist then moved her forward to age seven, and she described her daily task of collecting eggs from the chicken house. She reported that she was appalled at how dirty the eggs were—apparently the cause of her dislike for eggs. The hypnotist then explained to her, as he would to a child, that nature put a shell around the egg so that the inside would remain pure; and he suggested that she would no longer dislike eggs when she awoke from the trance. In the weeks that followed, people who knew this woman reported that she was eating eggs.

EVALUATING AGE REGRESSION IN HYPNOSIS

What really happened in this situation? Is age regression a legitimate phenomenon in which a person actually visits an earlier age? Take a moment to try to answer these questions before reading on.

The best available evidence suggests that age-regressed subjects behave in a manner consistent with their *present* conception of past behavior. In other words, such subjects are playing a role rather than actually reliving events that occurred many years ago. Many observations of logical incongruities in what age-regressed subjects say have led psychologists to draw this conclusion (Orne, 1972).

Posthypnotic Suggestion   Posthypnotic suggestions motivate people to perform a variety of actions after they return to a normal state of consciousness. Subjects typically carry out these suggestions without any recall of the instructions they received, and they often attempt to justify or rationalize the behavior in other ways. For example, in one classroom demonstration, a hypnotized student volunteer was given a posthypnotic suggestion to open a window when she observed her instructor loosen his tie. Right on cue, she raised her hand and asked if it would be OK to open a window since the room seemed "stuffy."

WILL HYPNOTIZED SUBJECTS CARRY OUT ALL INSTRUCTIONS?

Can hypnosis be used to make you do something you would not ordinarily do? Could it be used to get you to commit a crime, disrobe in front of strangers, or engage in some type of act that you would normally consider unacceptable? Take a moment to evaluate this question based on what you have already learned about hypnosis before reading on.

A common misconception is that hypnosis cannot be used to motivate behavior that a person would not ordinarily engage in. It is true that most hypnotized people would not comply with direct suggestions to behave in an antisocial or inappropriate way. However, a hypnotist can alter the perceptions or awareness of a susceptible subject in such a way that such behaviors seem necessary or appropriate.

For example, a software designer might be induced to give away corporate secrets when hypnotized by a "friend" operating in the guise of an amateur hypnotist trying to liven up a party. The unsuspecting victim, who might go along with the stunt just to be a good sport, could be told that he was appearing before the board of directors to explain his latest design innovations. As we have learned, hypnotic suggestions can sometimes alter a subject's sensory and perceptual experiences. Consequently, the software designer might actually reveal secrets in the mistaken belief that the other partygoers were board members. There are numerous accounts in the literature of unscrupulous hypnotists using such strategies to induce subjects to engage in inappropriate or unacceptable behavior. This potential negative application of hypnotic suggestion, together with other possible deleterious effects, suggests that this consciousness-altering technique is not without risks when it is employed by someone other than a clinician who is well versed in the proper use of hypnosis (Echterling & Emmerling, 1987; Kleinhauz & Eli, 1987).

EXPLAINING HYPNOSIS

A number of theories have been offered to explain hypnosis. Perhaps the most widely held explanation is Ernest Hilgard's (1977) **neodissociation theory**. According to Hilgard, a hypnotized person operates on more than one level of consciousness, which allows some behaviors to become divorced or *dissociated* from conscious awareness. This theory evolved from an unexpected discovery that a part of a hypnotized person's mind (which Hilgard calls the *hidden observer*) is observing and remembering all that goes on, even though the person is not consciously aware of this process. Hilgard discovered this hidden observer during a classroom demonstration in which he suggested that his subject would be unable to hear anything until Hilgard touched his shoulder. The suggestion worked, and the subject ceased responding to any verbal stimuli. A student then asked if the subject really could not hear. Hilgard asked his subject if some part of him could hear, and if so, he was to signal by raising a finger. The finger rose. Everybody in the room was surprised, including Hilgard (and the subject, who asked why he had raised his finger).

Hilgard touched the subject's shoulder (so that he could "hear" again), then asked him what he had experienced. The subject said that the room had suddenly grown very quiet and that he had let his mind wander when suddenly he felt his finger move. Hilgard asked the part of the man that had made his finger rise to explain what had happened. This second part of the subject's mind, the so-called hidden observer, accurately reported everything that had transpired (Hilgard, 1977).

This account indicates that two separate states of consciousness can occur concurrently—which, incidentally, is how Hilgard defines the hypnotic state. There is nothing mystical about this: All of us have had experiences in which our consciousness seems divided or dissociated. An example of this is driving your car while thinking about a complex problem and then suddenly realizing that you have arrived at your destination without consciously navigating.

A second theory of hypnosis is offered by Theodore Barber (1970, 1975), who argues that hypnosis is not a special state of consciousness. According to Barber, all of the phenomena associated with hypnosis can be demonstrated in people who are not hypnotized: hypnosis works because the subject is willing to go along with the hypnotist's suggestions uncritically. Barber compares being hypnotized to becoming a vicarious participant in the story line of a good novel or movie. To support this viewpoint, Barber and others have demonstrated that many "hypnotic" phenomena can be shown by nonhypnotized subjects who are instructed to think along with the hypnotist or merely to pretend they are hypnotized.

In one experiment, 66 nurses were divided into three matched groups. Subjects in one group were hypnotized using traditional techniques. Subjects in a second group were encouraged to focus their imaginations uncritically on whatever suggestions were provided. The third group, acting as a control, received no special instructions. All subjects were asked to perform the same tasks, such as watching an imaginary TV program, drinking imaginary water, and hearing nonexistent music. Comparisons of the scores obtained by subjects in the different groups revealed that those in the "think along with" group actually obtained somewhat higher scores, on the average, than those in the hypnotized group (Barber & Wilson, 1977).

DRUGS THAT ALTER CONSCIOUSNESS

It is not uncommon for people in our society to have a few glasses of wine at a party, then follow through the next morning with a few cups of coffee or tea to "help clear the cobwebs." Most of us regularly consume a variety of chemicals (such as alcohol and caffeine) that alter our state of consciousness. Such substances, as well as nicotine, marijuana, sleeping pills, cocaine, and other drugs, share a common effect: They alter perceptions and behavior by changing conscious awareness. These drugs are called **psychoactive drugs**.

Continued use of many of the psychoactive drugs tends to lessen their effects, so that the user develops a *tolerance* for the drug. For example, repeated injections of opiates such as heroin cause the body to produce natural antiopiates (Snyder, 1984). The slow buildup of these antiopiates causes tolerance to develop, so that a person must increase intake of the drug in order to achieve the same effects. Eventually this may lead to a **physiological dependence** on the drug. The person becomes *addicted* so that withdrawal symptoms such as cramps, nausea, tremors, headaches, and sweating occur in the drug's absence. Physiological dependence seems to be related to the fact that excessive, chronic levels of the drug in the body deplete certain vital body substances such as neurotransmitters. One of the most ironic things about drug addiction is that the original reason for taking the substance (for example, to go to sleep more easily at night) may be replaced by a desperate need to maintain adequate levels of the drug just to avoid withdrawal symptoms.

Not all psychoactive drugs produce physiological dependence. Sometimes a person merely finds that a drug is so pleasurable or helpful in coping with life that a kind of **psychological dependence** develops. In this sense, a person can become either dependent on or addicted to a wide range of drugs. The addiction often involves both physiological and psychological components. It is important to note that drugs that induce psychological dependence may be just as harmful and addictive as those that produce physiological dependence.

Repeated injections of opiates, such as heroin, cause tolerance to develop so that a person must increase intake of the drug in order to achieve the same effects.

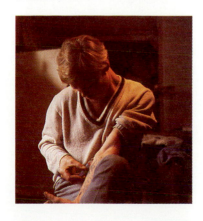

The three major groups of drugs, classified by their effects, are depressants, stimulants, and hallucinogens. The remainder of this chapter looks at these types of drugs and their effects on people.

DEPRESSANTS: SEDATIVES, OPIATES, AND ALCOHOL

Drugs that tend to slow or depress activity in the central nervous system are classified as **depressant drugs**. Substances in this category include sedatives, opiates, and alcohol.

Sedatives Sedatives are drugs that induce relaxation, calmness, and sleep. This group of drugs include *tranquilizers*, such as Librium and Valium, *barbiturates* such as Nembutal and Seconal, and the *nonbarbiturates* Miltown and Quaalude. Many of these drugs are widely prescribed by physicians as remedies for emotional and physical complaints such as anxiety, insomnia, gastrointestinal disorders, and respiratory problems. Tranquilizers are some of the most widely prescribed drugs in the world. Chapter 15 discusses some of their therapeutic uses for treating psychological disorders.

All the sedative drugs, particularly barbiturates (also known as "barbs" or "downers") are prime candidates for drug abuse. Tolerance for barbiturates develops quite rapidly, and abusers of these drugs often increase their consumption to the point where respiratory function, memory, judgment, and other mental and physical processes are seriously impaired. Barbiturate abusers soon develop a physiological addiction that makes withdrawal an arduous, traumatizing experience. Recent statistics reveal that roughly one out of every three reported cases of drug-caused death is due to barbiturate overdose. The effects of depressant drugs taken in combination can be volatile: Combining a nonlethal dose of alcohol with a nonlethal dose of barbiturates can cause death.

As Chapter 3 indicated, virtually every drug that alters mental functions does so by interacting with a neurotransmitter system in the brain. The sedative drugs are no exception. Research suggests that barbiturates inhibit the activity of norepinephrine, a neurotransmitter linked to emotional arousal, although the precise mechanism by which this occurs is unknown (Kolb & Whishaw, 1985).

Opiates Opiates, or **narcotics**, are another category of depressant drugs. *Opium* is derived from a sticky resin secreted by the opium poppy. Two of its natural ingredients, *morphine* and *codeine*, have been widely used as painkillers. A third derivative, *heroin*, is obtained by chemically treating morphine. It is the strongest of all known narcotics.

Heroin in snorted (inhaled through the nostrils) or injected directly into the veins. When it is injected, the almost immediate effect is a "rush," which users describe as an overwhelming sensation of pleasure akin to sexual orgasm. This may be the closest many heroin addicts come to this experience, however, as regular use of opiates often significantly decreases sexual interest and activity (Abel, 1984). Shortly after it is injected, heroin decomposes into morphine, which produces other effects commonly associated with opiate usage: a sense of well-being, contentment, insulation from dangers or challenges, and drowsiness.

Increasingly larger doses are needed to produce these effects, however, and the user quickly acquires a physiological and psychological dependence. The long-term effects of this addiction can be devastating. People addicted to heroin will do almost anything to ensure their supply of the drug—cheat, steal, or prostitute themselves. William Burroughs, a writer and former addict, calls heroin the ultimate merchandise. "The client will crawl through a sewer and beg to buy" (In White, 1985, p. 149).

What happens when an addict tries to break the habit? After a few hours without heroin, the user begins to experience symptoms such as vomiting, running nose, aching muscles, and abdominal pain. These symptoms are very uncomfortable, but they are probably less painful than withdrawal from some other drugs, including alcohol and barbiturates.

Opiates themselves rarely produce physical damage to the user. In rare cases, chronic opiate use may damage the body's immune system, thus increasing the addict's susceptibility to disease (McDonough et al., 1980). However, recent research indicates that the mortality rate among narcotics addicts is approximately seven times greater than that of the general population (Joe & Simpson, 1987). There are a variety of reasons for this. Addicts often cause harm to themselves because of drug-related habits, such as using nonsterile needles, obtaining contaminated heroin, or not eating properly. Carelessness about using sterile drug paraphernalia increases the risk of potentially life-threatening infectious diseases such as hepatitis (a liver infection) and endocarditis (inflammation of a membrane in the heart). Recently, AIDS (acquired immune deficiency syndrome) has taken an alarming toll on heroin users who have shared needles with infected people.

Another source of heroin-related problems comes from the mix of the drug itself. When heroin is manufactured for street use, it is often cut (diluted) to make it go farther. This can have two potentially tragic consequences. First, heroin is sometimes cut with impure substances that can be deadly. Second, high grade, only moderately diluted heroin occasionally finds its way to the street. An addict accustomed to shooting large amounts of weak heroin can easily overdose on the more potent variety.

Alcohol   Like other depressants, **alcohol** retards the activity of neurons in the central nervous system, particularly in the cerebral cortex. It is an extremely potent drug that affects behavior in a highly variable manner. Some people become more communicative and expressive under its influence, perhaps even boisterous and silly. Others become aggressive, abusive, and sometimes violent. People under the influence of alcohol may engage in behaviors they normally keep in check, probably because alcohol suppresses the inhibitory mechanisms of the cerebral cortex.

These behavioral effects may be evident at relatively low levels of alcohol consumption. As intake increases, it is accompanied by more pronounced impairments of coordination, reaction time, thinking, and judgment (Ward & Lewis, 1987). When the blood alcohol content reaches 0.10 percent (the equivalent of four to six beers or three to four 1.5-ounce shots of 80-proof alcohol), a person's chance of having a severe accident—behind the wheel of a car or otherwise—may be as much as five or six times greater than normal.

Alcohol is the nation's number one drug problem and, after heart disease and cancer, the third largest health problem. More than 200,000 alcohol-connected deaths occur each year. Alcohol is also linked to two-thirds of all incidents of domestic violence and a third of all child abuse cases (Ziegler, 1984). Despite these facts, alcohol is the leading rcreational drug in America, among teenagers as well as adults. Two mid-1980s surveys of teenagers in both Oregon (grades 9–12) and New York (grades 7–12) showed very similar results: 83 percent of both samples reported that they had tried alcohol. In Oregon, 16 percent were weekly users; in New York, 20 percent stated that they had five or more drinks at least once a week. Approximately 10 percent of the New York survey said they were "hooked" on alcohol (Oreskes, 1984). A recent study of substance abuse in a sample of 424 college students found the prevalence of alcohol abuse to be 8.2 percent (Deykin et al., 1987).

Like the other depressants, alcohol is physiologically addictive. Withdrawal is often accompanied by severe symptoms, including nausea, vomiting, fever, the "shakes," and sometimes the "d.t.'s" (*delirium tremens*, bizarre visual hallucinations). Occasionally, withdrawal from alcohol produces such a profound shock to the body that death may result.

Prolonged and excessive use of alcohol can have disastrous physical effects. Liver and heart disease are commonly associated with alcohol abuse

Some people enjoy drinking because they feel it makes them more communicative and expressive. Others become more aggressive, abusive, and sometimes violent. Do you notice a change in your behavior when you drink?

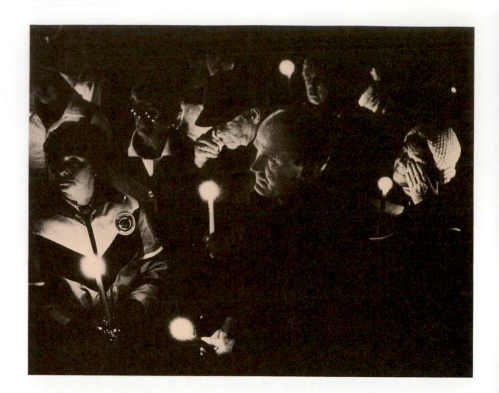

More than 200,000 alcohol-related deaths occur each year. This abuse of alcohol has led to the formation of many protest groups, including Mothers Against Drunk Drivers (MADD), shown here at a vigil for people killed by drunk drivers.

Alcohol is both the most popular recreational drug in America and also the nation's number one drug problem. People who are depressed or anxious about the future will often drink to ease their anxieties.

(Cunningham, 1986; Davidson, 1986; Novick et al., 1986). Malnutrition is also a problem: Alcoholics typically eat poorly, since their daily consumption of liquor provides hundreds of calories. In addition, alcohol interferes with the proper absorption of B vitamins, so vitamin B deficiency is common. A prolonged deficiency of these essential vitamins can lead to brain damage, a complication that occurs in about 10 percent of alcoholics (Johnson et al., 1986). Alcoholic brain damage, which can include cerebral and cortical atrophy and reduced brain weight, has been associated with a variety of cognitive and behavioral impairments (Carlen et al., 1986; Johnson et al., 1986).

Heavy drinking during pregnancy causes further complications. Because alcohol passes from the mother's body to the fetus, the infant may be born with an alcohol addiction. Drug withdrawal in a baby can be fatal. Offspring of mothers who drink heavily while they are pregnant may suffer from *fetal alcohol syndrome*, which is characterized by retarded physical growth, intellectual development, and motor coordination as well as abnormalities in brain metabolic processes and liver functioning (Coles et al., 1987; Golden et al., 1982; Singh et al., 1986; Vingan et al., 1986; Wright et al., 1983).

Why People Drink   A great deal of research has investigated the question of why people drink excessively. As you might guess, there is no single answer. Poor self-image and other personal problems are often factors, for people who are anxious or depressed may feel that alcohol provides temporary relief. Another explanation strongly supported by research suggests that certain genetically linked biological abnormalities may play a decisive role in at least some forms of alcoholism (Baribeau et al., 1986; Begleiter et al., 1984; Blum, 1983; Cadoret et al., 1987; Cloninger, 1981; Goodwin, 1981; Pollock et al., 1983; Tarter, 1984). Finally, our own society creates pressure to drink, and this pressure undoubtedly plays a role in alcohol abuse. Billboards and glossy advertisements portray drinking as something that is sophisticated and glamorous; these images are especially appealing to teenagers, who are anxious to enter the adult world. In light of the mounting evidence that some people may be biologically predisposed to become alcohol abusers, it is important to balance these images with a realization that alcohol is a drug to be wary of.

Stopping Drinking   The leading approach to stopping drinking has been through Alcoholics Anonymous, which sees total abstinence as the only way to stop drinking. The AA creed, that one drink is an invitation to disaster, has been the cornerstone of one of the most successful programs for dealing with alcoholism.

AA's approach remained virtually uncontested until Mark and Linda Sobell's highly controversial study, which reported successfully teaching a group of male alcoholics to drink in moderation (1973). The Sobells contend that total abstinence is not necessarily the key to overcoming alcoholism. Instead, they taught a variety of specific **controlled-drinking** skills that would allow subjects to drink in moderation. They found that the controlled-drinking training produced better long-term results than did total abstinence.

The Sobells' study has been controversial, and some claimed that its research was fraudulent (Pendery et al., 1982). However, a review panel has exonerated the Sobells of fraud (Boffey, 1982), and a number of psychologists consider their conclusions to be largely valid. This interpretation is strengthened by a number of recent studies indicating that at least some alcoholics can acquire controlled-drinking skills that allow them to make the transition to social drinking (Elal-Lawrence et al., 1987; Nordstrom & Berglund, 1987).

Another approach teaches alcoholics and other drug abusers coping behavior to respond to stress—a process called **skill training intervention** (Marlott, 1983 & 1984). This approach is based on findings that reformed alcoholics are more likely to resume drinking under conditions of environmental or social stress than in response to some internal craving. Through modeling and role playing, clients are taught to deal more effectively with environmental stress situations, as when friends are drinking and pressuring the client to join in.

The results are encouraging. Subjects who have been trained are just as likely to take a drink in the year following treatment as those in a control group who have not been trained. However, one study showed that trained clients drank only one-quarter as much alcohol, and they demonstrated an ability to stop drinking more quickly once drinking started (Marlott, 1984). In this sense, they behaved in a fashion similar to the men in the Sobells' research.

STIMULANTS: CAFFEINE, NICOTINE, AMPHETAMINES, AND COCAINE

Drugs that stimulate the central nervous system by increasing the transmission of nerve impulses are called **stimulants**. The most widely consumed of these drugs are caffeine and nicotine, both of which are mild stimulants. Amphetamines and cocaine are the most frequently used of the stronger stimulants.

Caffeine   Found in a variety of products including chocolate, coffee, tea, and many carbonated soft drinks such as colas, **caffeine** has long provided people with a "quick lift." Caffeine acts quickly. Within a few minutes after it is consumed, heart and respiration rates and blood pressure increase.

People experience these physical effects in a variety of ways. Most feel mentally stimulated; some experience a brief burst of energy. People who consume a large amount of caffeine (for example, six or more cups of coffee) may feel more pronounced effects: irritability, headaches, the jitters, difficulty concentrating, nausea, and sleep disturbances. A recent study revealed that adult subjects who received moderate doses of caffeine demonstrated increased scores on scales measuring anxiety, depression, and hostility, unlike control subjects who were administered placebos (Veleber &

Are you a "chocoholic"? You might not think of a chocolate bar as being a stimulant, but, in fact, its caffeine content provides the same sort of "lift" as caffeinated coffee and colas.

Templer, 1984). Caffeine has been implicated in anxiety disorders and learning difficulties in children (Dusek & Girdano, 1980). People can become psychologically dependent on caffeine, as evidenced by the countless numbers of people who "just cannot function" without their daily quota of coffee, tea, or cola.

Nicotine   **Nicotine** is second only to caffeine on the list of widely used stimulants. Found in tobacco, nicotine increases heart rate, blood pressure, and stomach activity, and constricts blood vessels. Paradoxically, it may have either a relaxing or a stimulating effect on the user, depending on the circumstances and the user's expectations. Nicotine is physiologically addictive, and people who stop smoking may experience a variety of withdrawal symptoms including craving for tobacco, increased appetite, stomach cramps, headaches, restlessness, irritability, insomnia, anxiety, and depression (Hughes et al., 1987). Long-term effects of smoking have been well publicized: Hundreds of thousands of people die every year from cancer caused by smoking. It has been estimated that as many as one-third of heavy smokers will die before age 85 from various diseases caused by smoking (Mattson et al., 1987). There is also evidence that women who smoke while pregnant have a higher incidence of miscarriages, stillbirths, and low-birthweight babies than do women who do not smoke (Fox et al., 1987; Schwartz-Bickenbach et al., 1987).

Many programs are available to help people stop smoking, running the gamut from aversive conditioning (for instance, administering an electric shock when a person tries to smoke) to hypnosis, to peer support groups and counseling, to medications. Unfortunately, about four out of every five people who use a formal program to quit smoking resume within a year (Leventhal & Cleary, 1980; Rzewnicki & Forgays, 1987). Many smokers seem to be more successful at kicking the habit on their own. One study found that 64 percent of a sample of smokers who had tried to stop smoking on their own were successful (Schachter, 1982), and more recent research has found that since the late 1960s, approximately 35 million American adults have stopped smoking, most without the help of clinical intervention (Flay, DPhil, 1987) (sic).

Amphetamines   **Amphetamines** are much more powerful stimulants, sold under the trade names Benzedrine, Dexedrine, and Methedrine and known on the street as "uppers" or "speed." These drugs tend dramatically to increase alertness, counteract fatigue, and promote feelings of euphoria and well-being.

These effects are probably due to the way the neurotransmitter dopamine reacts to amphetamines. Dopamine is linked to feelings of emotional well-being, and amphetamines seem to increase its level in the brain. Amphetamines also enhance the activity of the neurotransmitter norepinephrine—exactly the opposite of the effect that sedatives have on this chemical. This is why some students who take amphetamines to get through an all-night study session find it difficult to "come down" when they are ready to rest.

People use amphetamines for a variety of reasons: to stay awake, to feel good, to improve energy levels, to increase confidence, and to lose weight (amphetamines are appetite suppressants). Most users take the drug orally, but some inject it directly into a vein. When amphetamines are used in excess, they can cause muscle and joint aches, tremors, feelings of paranoia, and, in extreme cases, a kind of *amphetamine psychosis*, which combines paranoia with hallucinations and difficulty recognizing people.

Users seem to develop a tolerance to the euphoric effects of amphetamines but not to its "antisleep" effects (Blum, 1984). In addition, they often develop a profound psychological dependence on the drug. Until recently, it was believed that no physiological dependence developed among users. However, by the mid-1980s, researchers had accumulated enough evidence to suggest that the amphetamine "hangover" (depression, extreme fatigue, prolonged sleep, irritability, disorientation, and agitated motor activity) is a strong indicator of physical dependence (Blum, 1984).

In the 1970s, a chemical relative of speed, **MDMA** (3,4-methylene-dioxymethamphetamine), made its street debut. Known also as "ecstasy," MDMA is one of a new breed of "designer drugs"—drugs produced by basement chemists who fiddle with the chemical structure of a controlled substance to produce just enough molecular change to avoid legal regulations without reducing the drug's potency (Gallagher, 1986). (Under federal drug laws, a drug is legal until declared otherwise.) In light of growing evidence that even short-term use of the drug can cause long-term and sometimes irreversible effects on the brain, the federal Drug Enforcement Administration (DEA) placed MDMA on its list of controlled substances in 1975.

Cocaine   Cocaine is a powerful central nervous system stimulant that is extracted from leaves of the coca shrub. It is usually sniffed ("snorted") through a straw into the mucous membranes of the nasal passages. A solution of the drug may also be injected into a vein. In a somewhat different form, cocaine may also be smoked in a process called "freebasing."

In 1985, a new form of freebase cocaine entered American drug culture. **"Crack"** is the street name given to cocaine that has been processed from cocaine hydrochloride (the crystalline derivative of the coca leaf that is sold on the street as "coke") into freebase by using ammonia or baking soda and water and heating the mixture. (It is believed that the baking soda causes a crackling sound when the base is heated, thus giving rise to the street name.) It is difficult to estimate the extent of crack use in America. However, since individual packages of crack may be purchased for as little as $5 or $10 and since its effects are produced more rapidly than through snorting, many drug experts predict that crack will soon replace the powdered form of cocaine as the most common form of cocaine abuse (SADAP Summary, 1986).

No matter which form is used, many of cocaine's effects are similar to those of amphetamines. They include increased alertness, an abundance of energy, feelings of euphoria, and a sense of well-being. Cocaine increases heart and respiration rates, constricts blood vessels, and dilates the pupils. It is metabolized very quickly, so its effects often last only 20 to 30 minutes. Thus to maintain a high, a user must take the drug frequently—one reason why a cocaine habit can become very costly.

Like other drugs, cocaine seems to derive its effects by altering normal patterns of neurotransmitter activity. There is good evidence that cocaine blocks the reuptake of serotonin, dopamine, and norepinephrine, increasing the time these chemicals actively stimulate emotional arousal.

Cocaine abuse can lead to severe problems, both physical and mental. It has been linked to heart and lung damage, anemia, damage to the nasal tissues, immune system impairment, and, in rare cases, sudden death (McCarthy, 1985; Smith, 1986; Wetli & Wright, 1979). In large doses, cocaine can impair judgment, create anxiety attacks, and induce paranoid reactions; it can also depress centers in the brain's medulla that control breathing and heartbeat. The result may be sudden death due to cardiac or respiratory arrest (Blum, 1984; Wetli & Wright, 1979). This tragic consequence of cocaine abuse caused the death of superstar basketball player Len Bias in 1986. There is evidence that cocaine used during pregnancy may have an adverse effect on prenatal development (Bingol et al., 1987).

Cocaine users do not typically develop a tolerance to the euphoric effects of the drug. Drug authorities have generally assumed that although chronic cocaine use produces profound psychological dependence, it does not result in physiological dependence in the sense that alcohol or heroin

Because "crack" is less expensive and produces effects faster than the powdered form of cocaine, it has become increasingly popular on the streets and in the schools and is becoming the most common type of cocaine abuse.

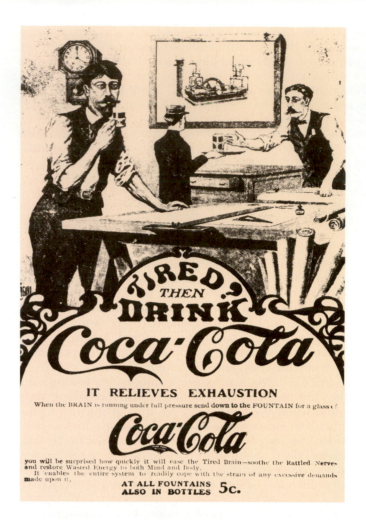

When Coca-Cola first appeared on the market in 1885, it contained cocaine (which remained an active ingredient until its use in soft drinks was banned in 1903).

does (Blum, 1984; Gawin & Kleber, 1984). However, a number of drug researchers maintain that it is not possible to distinguish clearly between physiological and psychological dependence on cocaine. These authorities point out that after "crashing" (coming down off the drug), the user often experiences a variety of withdrawal symptoms including fatigue, depression, irritability, aches and pains, and a restless protracted sleep (Cohen, 1986; Gold, 1984).

Despite these facts, cocaine use is growing rapidly in America. A federal agency reported that the amount of high quality cocaine in this country is at an all-time high. With increased supplies, the price of the drug is going down—a trend with important implications. Many people who previously might not have been able to afford it are now experimenting with cocaine (Smith, 1986). Lower costs have also brought cocaine into the schools. In a government survey of public schools, 6 percent of high school seniors reported regular cocaine use (Heckler in Kronholm, 1985). In a national survey of high school seniors in 1985, 17 percent reported having used cocaine at least once (SADAP Summary, 1986).

As the price of cocaine has tumbled, emergency room admissions for severe cocaine reactions have more than doubled (Stein, 1984). This is a result of both a swelling in the ranks of users and an increase in drug purity, which increases the possibility of overdose. Although most people outside the medical profession associate overdoses with narcotic drugs and barbiturates, hundreds of cocaine users die of overdoses each year in America (Anderson, 1983; Blum, 1984).

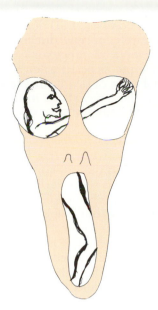 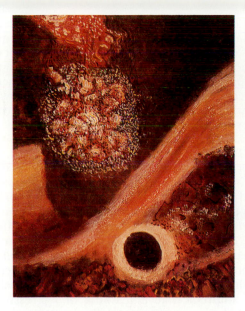 

Three examples of art produced under the influence of LSD. People who use hallucinogenic drugs claim that the drugs enhance their creativity, though research does not support these claims. What do you think?

HALLUCINOGENS: LSD, PCP, AND MARIJUANA

Drugs in a third group, **hallucinogens,** produce changes in sensory perceptions, thinking processes, and emotions. Under their influence, a person's sense of time and space may be altered. Other effects include delusions, impaired judgment, and visual, auditory, and tactile hallucinations. Some hallucinogenic drugs, such as LSD (lysergic acid diethylamide) and psylocybin (derived from a mushroom) appear to produce their hallucinogenic effects by interfering with the actions of the neurotransmitter serotonin. Other hallucinogens, including mescaline (derived from the peyote cactus) and possibly marijuana, affect the way the brain reacts to norepinephrine.

LSD   Derived from the ergot fungus that grows on rye grass, **LSD** became recognized for its psychoactive properties in the 1940s. Throughout the 1950s and early 1960s, researchers experimented with it as a tool for treating behavioral and emotional disorders, as a pain reliever in people suffering from terminal disease, and as a drug that might have possible military applications (Neill, 1987). Eventually, LSD fell into disrepute, largely because of its unpredictable effects. However, this did not curtail its growing popularity as a street drug used to alter and "expand" consciousness. In recent years, LSD's popularity has declined as other drugs such as cocaine and marijuana have become more common.

LSD is one of the most powerful known hallucinogens. A tiny amount can produce profound distortions of sensations, feelings, time, and thought. Some users describe an LSD "trip" as spiritual, mind expanding, and a source of ecstasy. Some claim that the drug adds to their creativity, but this assertion is not supported by research (Dusek & Girdano, 1980). Others have painful, frightening experiences in which they may feel that they have lost control, that their body is disintegrating, or that they have died. Having a "good trip" one time is no guarantee that the next LSD experience will not turn into a nightmare.

Despite some early claims that the drug produces chromosomal damage, the evidence is not convincing. Nor has other long-term damage been linked to its use. For some undetermined reason, however, LSD does seem to impede reproductive processes, since women rarely conceive during periods of heavy use of the drug. People do not develop a tolerance for LSD. It is not physically addictive, and no withdrawal symptoms occur when a user stops using the drug. There are no documented cases of deaths due to the direct effects of the drug on the body. However, there have been instances in which people on a "trip" have jumped from a building or been struck as they wandered through traffic.

PCP   Phencyclidine hydrochloride, **PCP**, or "angel dust," has become more popular in recent years. We have placed PCP in the category of hallucinogens since one of its more pronounced effects is sensory distortions and hallucinations. However, it also has stimulant, depressant, and painkilling properties. PCP was originally used as an anesthetic, but its legal use was barred in medical practice when its side effects became know.

People take PCP because it sometimes produces euphoria, heightened awareness, relaxation, and occasionally a sense of invincibility. However, it also produces many dangerous effects, including loss of contact with reality, memory distortions, severe depression, anxiety and paranoia, and the unpredictable unleashing of aggressive, violent behavior. Disrupted thought processes, mood disturbances, and aggression may persist for weeks after a single dose of the drug, and convulsions and coma may also result. In rare cases, people experience convulsions or respiratory failure that can cause death. PCP is not physiologically addictive, but there is evidence that users may become psychologically dependent on it (Bolter et al., 1976).

Marijuana   As a recreational drug, **marijuana**, the most widely used of the illegal psychoactive drugs, is second in popularity only to alcohol. It is derived from the flowering top of *Cannabis sativa*, a hemp plant once known primarily as an excellent material for making ropes.

The mind-altering component of marijuana is the chemical *THC* (delta 9-tetrahydrocannabinol). Marijuana is classified as a hallucinogen because relatively high doses of THC can produce hallucinations. Sometimes marijuana is classified as a depressant because in low doses it often has a sedative effect. However, in higher doses it acts as a stimulant, which further complicates any efforts to categorize it.

Marijuana seems to alter neurological activity in the brain by influencing the action of neurotransmitters, including norepinephrine. Two predictable physiological effects are increased heart rate and enhanced appetite. Small doses often produce euphoria and enhance some sensory experiences, such as listening to music. Marijuana impairs reaction time and the ability to concentrate on complex tasks, and some people become confused, agitated, or extremely anxious under its influence (Relman, 1982). Recall may be impaired due to use of marijuana (Miller & Branconier, 1983). Large doses of marijuana may induce frightening hallucinations.

Medical practitioners have discovered that marijuana can be therapeutic in some situations. For example, it may be helpful in treating asthma, epilepsy, and glaucoma (a disease that can cause blindness), and it has been shown to reduce the nausea that often accompanies chemotherapy treatments for cancer patients (Cohen, 1978; Relman, 1982).

There is currently a debate over the relative merit of legalizing marijuana. This controversy is fueled by many issues, not the least of which is the cost of the drug. Americans spend an estimated $44 billion annually for marijuana (White, 1985), and many people would like to see the price drop. Another key issue is whether or not long-term use of the drug produces harmful effects. We do know that marijuana is not physically addictive, although some people become psychologically dependent on it. Claims that it causes brain damage or irreversible intellectual impairment do not appear to be supported by research (Schaffer et al., 1981). There is some evidence that marijuana may have disruptive effects on the reproductive systems of both sexes—for example, decreased testosterone levels and disruption of the menstrual cycle (Relman, 1982; Smith et al., 1983).

Many health professionals have been concerned about potential lung damage, since most people who smoke "joints" (marijuana cigarettes) inhale deeply and hold the smoke in their lungs. At a recent meeting of the American Lung Association, UCLA researcher Donald Tashkin reported results of an ongoing study of 200 young adults who smoked an average of one or two joints daily for five years. He said that the lungs and air passages of these individuals resembled those of heavy cigarette smokers and that 24 of 25 subjects who allowed tissue to be taken from their bronchial tubes had precancerous cells (Sternberg, 1984).

SUMMARY

THE NATURE OF CONSCIOUSNESS

1. The term "consciousness" describes our awareness of processes that are going on inside or outside our bodies. Only a limited amount of thoughts, perceptions, and memories can be contained in the conscious mind at any given time.

2. Thoughts and memories that exist on the fringe of awareness but that can be pulled into consciousness fairly easily are said to reside in the preconscious.

3. The unconscious is believed to contain ideas, feelings, and memories that are too painful to deal with at a conscious level.

4. Psychologists distinguish between alternative and altered states of consciousness. The former refer to natural states of consciousness (such as sleep and dreaming) that differ from the normal state of alert consciousness. In contrast, altered states of consciousness refer to nonnatural states of consciousness that are produced by drugs, meditation, or hypnosis.

5. A number of general characteristics distinguish alternative and altered states of consciousness from a state of normal, alert consciousness. These include changes in body awareness, altered perception, shifts in concentration and thinking, emotional changes, and a distorted sense of time.

SLEEP AND DREAMING

6. Sleep is a natural, periodically recurring state of rest, which is characterized by reduced activity, lessened responsiveness to stimuli, and distinctive brain wave patterns.

7. Researchers distinguish between REM (rapid eye movement) and NREM (nonrapid eye movement sleep). Dreaming is more likely to occur in REM than in NREM sleep. However, dreaming is not limited to REM sleep, and REM is not synonymous with dreaming.

8. During a normal night's sleep we pass through four stages of sleep in naturally recurring, successive cycles. These stages range from very light sleep, characteristic of Stage 1, through Stage 4, the deepest level of sleep. Dreaming occurs most commonly during Stage 1 sleep.

9. During dreaming muscular activity is inhibited. Sleepwalking almost invariably occurs during NREM sleep.

10. As people grow older there is a decline in both the time spent sleeping and the proportion of sleep spent in the REM phase.

11. Research suggests that sleep is necessary but why it is necessary is not clear. A number of theories have been suggested to explain why we need sleep, some of which are that sleeping conserves energy, that it restores depleted resources, that it helps to clear the mind of useless information, and that it allows us the opportunity to dream.

12. People deprived of dreaming tend to increase their time spent dreaming in subsequent uninterrupted sleep periods, a phenomenon known as REM rebound.

13. To date research has not provided a definitive answer as to why we dream. Some theories put forth to explain dreaming are that dreams are the brain's attempt to explain random bursts of neuronal activity, that dreams are a form of mental "reprogramming" in which the brain is reorganized to accommodate new information, that dreaming provides a low-stress solution to dealing with problems, and that dreams are disguised expressions of unconscious wishes.

14. People who practice lucid dreaming maintain that they are aware when they are dreaming and that they are actually able to influence the content of their own dreams.

15. Sleep disorders include insomnia, sleep apnea, narcolepsy, night terrors and nightmares, and sleepwalking.

MEDITATION

16. Meditation is the practice of deliberately altering consciousness in an effort to achieve a state of tranquility, relaxation, and inner peace.

17. Meditation has been linked to a range of physiological changes including an increase in alpha brain waves and reduced metabolism, respiration, and heart rate.

18. Some researchers have suggested that the effects of meditation are virtually indistinguishable from those of merely resting.

HYPNOSIS

19. Hypnosis is a state of heightened suggestibility in which a person is unusually willing to comply with the hypnotist's directives.

20. Hypnosis can act as a powerful motivator, but it cannot increase a person's capacity to perform beyond natural limits.

21. Evidence suggests that hypnosis can help to alleviate pain and relieve the symptoms of a variety of stress-

related illnesses. However, it has been shown to be only marginally beneficial when used in criminal investigations.

22. The best available evidence suggests that age-regressed subjects behave in a manner consistent with their present conception of past behavior.

23. A hypnotist can alter the perceptions or awareness of a susceptible subject in such a way that a hypnotized person operates on more than one level of consciousness, which allows some behaviors to become dissociated from conscious awareness.

DRUGS THAT ALTER CONSCIOUSNESS

25. Drugs that alter perceptions and behavior by changing conscious awareness are called psychoactive drugs.

26. Psychoactive drugs may produce physiological dependence, psychological dependence, or both.

27. Drugs that tend to slow down or to depress activity in the central nervous system are classified as depressant drugs. Included in this category are sedatives, opiates, and alcohol.

28. Sedatives induce relaxation and calmness, probably by inhibiting the activity of norepinephrine.

29. The opiates, or narcotics, include three major derivatives of opium: morphine, codeine, and heroin. Chronic users of the opiates quickly acquire a physiological and psychological dependency.

30. Alcohol, the nation's number one drug problem, impairs coordination, reaction time, thinking, and judgment by retarding the activity of neurons in the central nervous system. Alcohol abuse produces physiological dependency, and prolonged use can have disastrous physical effects, including liver and heart disease.

31. Alcohol abuse has been linked to psychological problems, genetically linked biological abnormalities, and social pressures.

32. Strategies for reducing alcoholism include membership in AA, with its emphasis on abstinence, and teaching alcoholics controlled drinking skills and coping behavior so that they can respond more effectively to stress—a process called skill training intervention.

33. Drugs that stimulate the central nervous system by increasing the transmission of nerve impulses are called stimulants. Substances included in this category are caffeine, nicotine, amphetamines, and cocaine.

34. Caffeine increases heart rate, respiration, and blood pressure. In large doses it may cause problems such as irritability, headaches, and sleep disturbances.

35. Nicotine may have either a relaxing or a stimulating effect on the user, depending on the circumstances and the user's expectations.

36. Most people who stop smoking do so without clinical intervention.

37. Amphetamines dramatically increase alertness and promote feelings of euphoria and well-being, probably by increasing the activity of both dopamine and norepinephrine in the brain.

38. When amphetamines are used in excess, they can cause muscle and joint aches, feelings of paranoia, and, in extreme cases, amphetamine psychosis.

39. Cocaine, which is a stimulant, seems to derive its effects by blocking the reuptake of serotonin, dopamine, and norepinephrine, increasing the time these neurotransmitters actively stimulate emotional arousal.

40. Cocaine abuse has been linked to heart and lung damage, anemia, immune system impairment, and sudden death due to cardiac or respiratory arrest.

41. Hallucinogens are drugs that produce changes in sensory perceptions, thinking processes, and emotions. Drugs included in this category are LSD, psylocybin, mescaline, PCP, and marijuana.

42. LSD, one of the most powerful known hallucinogens, produces profound distortions of sensations, feelings, time, and thought by interfering with the neurotransmitter serotonin.

43. PCP has stimulant, depressant, and painkilling properties as well as hallucinogenic effects. Dangerous side effects associated with its use include reality and memory distortions, severe depression, anxiety, paranoia, and violent aggression.

44. Marijuana, the most widely used of the illegal psychoactive drugs, appears to alter neurological activity in the brain by influencing the action of neurotransmitters, particularly norepinephrine.

45. In small doses, marijuana often produces euphoria and enhanced sensory experiences. It also impairs reaction time, concentration, and recall. Large doses may induce frightening hallucinations.

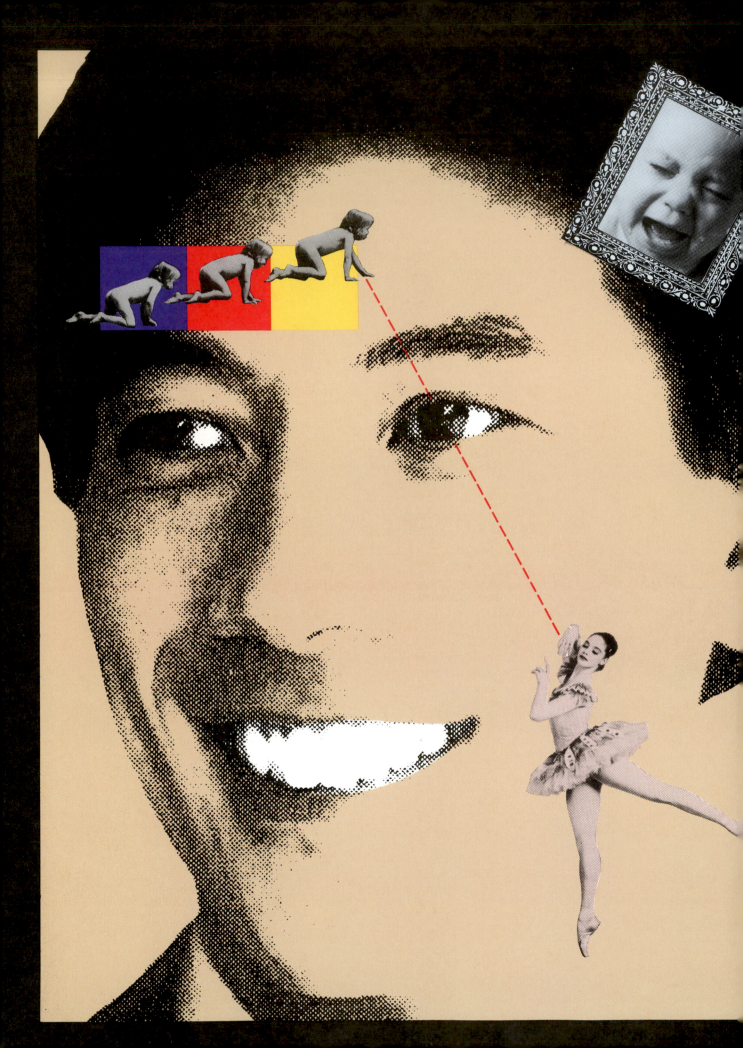

PART 3

LEARNING, MEMORY, THINKING, MOTIVATION, AND EMOTION

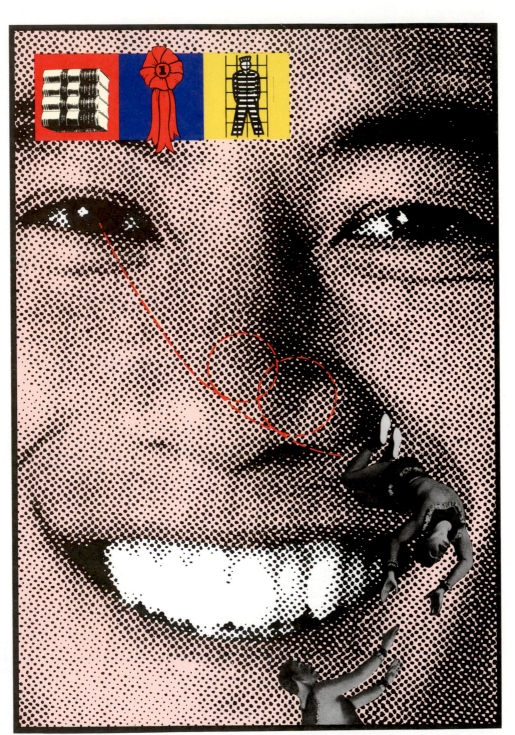

6 Learning

In recent years there has been mounting concern that grizzly bears may become extinct. Trying to protect a species that many people consider just plain ornery, however, has presented some special problems for conservationists.

These problems are particularly evident in the Yellowstone and Glacier National Parks regions of Montana. After years of living close to civilization (and foraging through civilization's garbage dumps), the bears in these areas have lost their fear of humans. In the past, before these regions were as heavily populated, the bears avoided human contact whenever they could. But bears that have become accustomed to humans react differently—with the result that in recent years a number of people have been injured. Bears that injure humans must be destroyed; thus, rangers have been put in the position of bringing this endangered species even closer to extinction.

Most efforts to protect the grizzlies have been remarkable for their lack of success (Chadwick, 1986). For instance, when grizzlies are trapped and transported deep into the wild, they often return to human habitats, where the "living is easy." Recently, however, wildlife officials have begun a new program that looks far more promising. The goal of this program is to reestablish fear of humans in these animals. The bears are trapped and caged; then a human delivers electric shocks to the animals. (The shocks produce pain for a brief time, but there is no lasting injury.) The bears associate humans with pain, and thus they learn to fear people. Later, when they are released in the wilderness, they are more likely to stay away from people (Peacock, 1983).

Protecting endangered species may seem to be far from the topic of this chapter, but it illustrates some of the principles that are basic to learning processes not just in grizzly bears, but in humans and other animals. As we will see, much of our learning takes place by associating events, just as the bears learned to associate pain with the presence of humans.

An understanding of learning is relevant to many other fields that seem to have little to do with psychology, from designing employee incentive programs in industry to raising children to be responsible adults. The pages that follow present at least a portion of what psychologists have learned about learning, and they help to explain how we can apply this knowledge to our lives. Before we discuss the applications of learning, we begin with a definition.

After years of living close to civilization, grizzly bears have lost their fear of humans. This has caused them to react differently around humans, with the result that some people have been injured and the bears that caused the injuries have had to be destroyed. How can we reestablish the grizzly's fear of humans, for their own protection?

We often wonder where certain behaviors are learned, and what the long-lasting effects will be.

LEARNING DEFINED

Learning may be defined as *a relatively enduring change in potential behavior that results from experience.* This definition contains three important elements. First, it excludes changes in behavior that result from anything other than experience. (Behavior can be modified by nonexperiential events like injuries, diseases, or maturation.)

Second, this definition speaks of *potential* behavior. Although learning causes changes in behavior, it is not always reflected directly in performance. The absence of observable behavior change does not necessarily mean that no learning has taken place.

For example, a young boy often sees his father strike his mother during arguments. For the time being, this has no apparent effect on the boy's behavior. When the boy becomes an adult, however, he strikes his wife during an argument. During the boy's childhood, we would have had no reason to believe that he had learned to be physically violent when frustrated. However, the potential for this behavior clearly was acquired; it simply required the necessary circumstances for it to occur.

Another example of learning that cannot be observed immediately is demonstrated by rats in a maze. If there is no reward (such as food) at the end of the maze, rats will wander aimlessly, with no indication that learning is taking place. When food is placed at the end of the maze, however, they quickly negotiate the twists and turns to reach it. Learning had taken place during the "aimless" wandering, but it required a proper incentive to be reflected in actual performance.

The third element of our definition of learning is that most learning tends to produce lasting changes in the learner. We hope that the grizzly bears in the opening example of this chapter will continue to associate humans with the discomfort they experienced in captivity.

HOW LEARNING TAKES PLACE

You should now have an understanding of what learning is. But how does it take place? The best starting point in answering this question is to think of an example of learning. For instance, you get up early one day to catch a plane. At 5:45 in the morning, it is dark outside and there is no other traffic, so you slow down rather than coming to a complete halt at a stop sign. No other traffic? Well, just one other car—the police car waiting around the corner.

It has now been months since you received your expensive ticket and missed your plane, but the lesson has stuck. No matter what time of day or night, you carefully pull to a complete stop at that intersection.

This kind of learning is called **associative learning.** It describes the process by which we make a connection or association between two events, such as driving through a stop sign and getting a ticket. Associative learning may take place in two primary ways: through classical conditioning and through operant conditioning.

Classical conditioning involves learning a connection between two stimuli. For example, a small child learns to associate the sight of a physician's syringe with the discomfort of an injection. In **operant conditioning,** people or other animals learn to associate their own behavior with its consequences. Thus, a child learns that pressing a button brings an elevator, a college student learns that answering questions in a certain class produces praise, a porpoise learns that jumping through a hoop results in a tasty morsel of fish—and you learn that driving through a stop sign produces a ticket.

Not all learning can be described solely as classical and operant conditioning. Certain kinds of learning involve more complex processes, such as thinking, reasoning, and memory. This kind of learning is labeled **cognitive learning.** In this chapter we also examine cognitive learning in some detail. First, however, we turn our attention to the classical and operant conditioning models.

CLASSICAL CONDITIONING

Some years ago, one of the authors' psychology students came to him with a problem. She was enrolled in a biology class in which students spent much of their time in a laboratory. When she entered the lab early in the term she suddenly felt an overwhelming state of anxiety bordering on terror. She was unable to remain in the laboratory; consequently, she could not complete her assignments. Perplexed and concerned, she tried a number of times to return to the lab, but she could not shake her feeling of terror.

This whale has learned that performing a certain behavior, such as jumping to touch a ball, results in a reward of its favorite fish. This is an example of operant conditioning.

EXPLAINING A FEAR RESPONSE

Here are some of the facts in the case just described:

> The student had completed two previous terms of biology without experiencing any discomfort in the laboratory segments.
>
> Between her previous biology class and the present term was a one-year absence from college, during which she gave birth to her first child.
>
> Her problem in the biology laboratory commenced immediately after returning to resume her studies.

Take a moment to consider the facts and try to explain the woman's fear response before reading on.

If you guessed that the student had some terrible experience during her year's absence from college that somehow became associated with the environment of the biology laboratory, you are correct. Because of complications during the delivery of her baby, her physician decided to perform a caesarean section (surgical removal of the baby through an incision in the abdomen and uterus). There was no time for her to be psychologically prepared, and she panicked. She found herself unable to breathe when she received an injection of anesthesia (a rare response during this type of medical procedure, probably related to stress). For a few terrible moments she was convinced she would die. Fortunately, the feeling subsided quickly and the operation proceeded smoothly.

Later, looking back, she did not associate this very brief experience with her present anxiety in the biology laboratory. But the two were definitely associated. By explaining classical conditioning, we can better understand the connection.

The trigger for this woman's original fear response was her experience on the operating table. Because this experience took place in an environment with medical smells, the woman associated these smells with the awful experience at the hospital. The odors of antiseptic and anesthetic agents in the biology laboratory were similar enough to the medical smells of the operating room to trigger the same fear response that the woman had developed while receiving anesthesia for her operation.

The connection was not a conscious one. In fact, the woman was not aware that she had been conditioned. Yet it followed a classical model that was first recognized around the turn of the century by the Russian physiologist, Ivan Pavlov (1849–1936).

PAVLOV'S DISCOVERY

Ivan Pavlov's real interest was the physiological mechanisms involved in digestion. (He never associated himself with psychology, insisting that he was dealing only with physiological mechanisms.) Toward this end, he was investigating the salivation responses of dogs. Pavlov placed his dogs in the harnesslike apparatus shown in Figure 6.1. A surgical procedure exposed each dog's salivary glands, which were connected directly to a device that measured the flow of saliva. Pavlov then presented a stimulus, meat powder. When food entered the dog's mouth, the immediate result was the natural, reflexive response of salivation.

However, Pavlov soon noted an unexpected occurrence. His dogs began to salivate to stimuli other than food in their mouths. For example, an animal might start salivating at the mere sight of the experimenter. The sound of Pavlov's footsteps or the sight of the food dish also caused salivation.

This discovery changed the course of Pavlov's study, for Pavlov now began to investigate how other stimuli could cause dogs to salivate. His

Ivan Pavlov

FIGURE 6.1 PAVLOV'S CLASSICAL CONDITIONING APPARATUS

Saliva was collected via a tube attached to the dog's salivary glands and measured by the revolving drum apparatus pictured at the left. During a typical procedure, a laboratory assistant, sitting behind the mirror, rang a bell (the CS) and then presented meat (the UCS) to the dog. Initially the animal salivated only in response to the food (the UCR). However, after several pairings of the bell with the meat, the dog salivated in response to the bell alone (the CR).

experiments are generally recognized as the first systematic study of learning, and the processes that he outlined came to be called classical (as in "the first") conditioning. A basic outline of this relatively simple model of learning follows:

A hungry dog, secured in Pavlov's apparatus, hears a bell. It probably looks around a bit, but it does not salivate. A moment later, the dog is given meat powder; copious salivation results. This procedure is repeated several times, with one stimulus (the sound of the bell) followed consistently by another stimulus (food). Eventually, the dog salivates when it hears the bell, even when no food follows. The dog has learned to *associate* the bell with food.

The fact that a previously *neutral* stimulus (a stimulus that has no effect on the animal, such as the sound of the bell) eventually produces a response (salivation) ordinarily associated with another stimulus (food) is clear evidence that learning has taken place. Pavlov identified four key events or elements in this classical conditioning model.

1. *The unconditioned stimulus (UCS).* Meat causes dogs to salivate. This occurs automatically, without learning or conditioning. A stimulus that elicits an unlearned response is called an **unconditioned stimulus (UCS).** Therefore, meat is a UCS.

2. *The unconditioned response (UCR).* Salivating at the presentation of meat is an automatic response that does not require learning. An unlearned response is called an **unconditioned response (UCR).** Thus, salivation in response to meat is a UCR.

3. *The conditioned stimulus (CS).* The bell initially is a neutral stimulus in that it has no effect on the animal. It causes salivation only

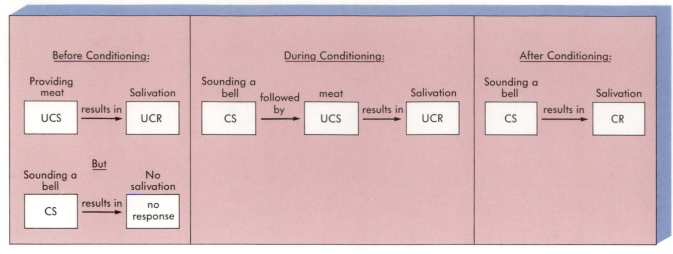

FIGURE 6.2 PAVLOV'S BASIC CONDITIONING MODEL

when the dogs learn to associate it with the unconditioned stimulus, the food. A stimulus that an organism must learn to respond to is called a learned or **conditioned stimulus (CS).** Therefore, the bell is a CS.

4. *The conditioned response (CR).* Pavlov's dogs were taught, or conditioned, to salivate when a bell sounded. Such a learned response is called a **conditioned response (CR).**

Figure 6.2 summarizes the steps by which conditioning took place in Pavlov's model.

While the conditioning in Pavlov's dogs was clearly measurable, it is interesting to note that classical conditioning may also take place on an "invisible" physiological level that may take even psychological researchers by surprise. The Health Psychology and Life discussion, "Classically Conditioning the Immune System," describes some intriguing findings that could have far-reaching medical implications.

DIFFERENTIATING BETWEEN THE UCR AND THE CR

At first glance, the unconditioned response and conditioned response often appear to be identical. The UCR in Pavlov's experiments occurred when the dogs salivated in response to meat; the CR was also salivation, but this time in response to the sound of a bell. Do you think there might be a difference between the CR and the UCR besides the stimulus that causes these responses to occur? Take a moment to think about this question before reading on.

Although they are usually similar, the unconditioned response and the conditioned response are rarely identical. An unconditioned response is generally more intense than is a response that has been conditioned. For example, dogs salivate more copiously when meat is actually placed in their mouths than they do when they either hear a bell or see the person who feeds them.

What do dogs salivating to a sound have to do with our lives as humans? We can best put this question in perspective by returning to the case of the biology student. The same elements that Pavlov traced in his dogs can be found in this conditioning experience. The unconditioned response is fear, a natural response to the frightening event in the hospital room (the UCS). Fear is also the learned or conditioned response. (Remember, the CR and the UCR are essentially similar in classical conditioning.)

CLASSICALLY CONDITIONING THE IMMUNE SYSTEM

A few years ago, researchers Robert Ader and Nathan Cohen (1982) observed a curious effect as they were studying classically conditioned taste aversion. In their experiment, rats were given drinks of a saccharin-flavored water (the CS) followed immediately by injections of a drug that made them nauseous (the UCS). As you might predict, the animals immediately acquired a taste aversion that caused them to avoid or reduce their consumption of the sweet solution. The rats were then exposed to several extinction trials in which they were presented with the sweet solution but no toxic drug. (Extinction is a process designed to reduce the strength of the association between the CS and UCS through repeated presentations of the CS alone without the UCS.)

During this stage of the study something unexpected happened. For no apparent reason, some of the rats died. Ader and Cohen considered a variety of possibilities to explain what had happened. One of their primary clues was that the drug they used to induce nausea, cyclophosphamide, is also known to suppress the body's immune system.

Ader and Cohen reasoned that perhaps the saccharin water had become a conditioned signal that suppressed the rats' immune systems in the same way as the drug that it had been paired with. If this were the case, the repeated exposures to the sweetened water alone during the extinction trials may have suppressed their immune systems so much that they fell victim to disease-bearing microorganisms in the laboratory.

To test this possibility, they conditioned other rats, using the original design with one modification. Before the extinction trials in which rats received only the CS of sweet water, they were injected with red blood cells from sheep—foreign bodies that would normally trigger the rats' immune systems to produce high levels of defensive antibodies. The researchers' hypothesis was supported: the conditioned animals produced significantly fewer antibodies than control animals for whom the sweet water was not a CS.

Ader and Cohen also tested the immune-system responses of mice who had been classically conditioned to respond to the sweet water. They found that if these conditioned mice received only half the usual dosage of cyclophosphamide, together with exposure to the CS, their immune systems were suppressed as completely as if they had been given a full dosage of the toxic drug.

What are the health implications of these findings? Certainly they extend our knowledge of how the mind and body interact to reduce or increase our vulnerability to disease. But beyond this, they may lead to a practical medical application in the future. Consider, for instance, that a major problem associated with many drugs used to combat disease is that they often produce serious side effects. For example, although cyclophosphamide is toxic enough to have been selected as the nausea-inducing UCS in Ader and Cohen's experiment, it has a legitimate and very valuable medical use as treatment for lupus, an immune-system disorder in which the body turns against itself. If classical conditioning could be used to trick the body of a lupus victim into responding to a significantly lowered dosage of the drug, a diseased person might be able to benefit from cyclophosphamide without having to experience its debilitating side effects. The same kinds of benefits might be obtained with drugs used to treat cancer. Hopefully, in the years to come these psychological principles can be applied to alleviate suffering and improve the treatment of many victims of disease.

Just as Pavlov's dogs learned to associate the bell with food, the young woman learned to associate medical smells (the CS) with the hospital event.

There is a difference, however. Unlike the dogs, the young woman needed to be exposed to only one conditioning event. This is true of many learned fears. One profoundly frightening event can establish a conditioned fear that may last a lifetime.

The difference between the repeated pairing that Pavlov used on his dogs and the single experience of the young woman illustrates one way in which classical conditioning experiences may vary. The following discussions will deal with other variations on the same theme, exploring both the ways in which learning is acquired and the ways in which it can be "unlearned," or extinguished.

ACQUISITION IN CLASSICAL CONDITIONING

The period during which an organism learns to associate the conditioned stimulus with the unconditioned stimulus is known as the **acquisition** stage of conditioning. Each paired presentation of the two stimuli is called a *trial*. In cases such as Pavlov's conditioning experiments, these repeated trials strengthen, or reinforce, the association between the CS and the UCS.

Several factors influence how easily a classically conditioned response will be acquired. For example, conditioning takes place more easily when the neutral or conditioned stimulus is clearly different from other stimuli. Had Pavlov signaled the arrival of food by quietly humming a Russian ballad, his dogs might never have perceived the connection—such sounds are commonplace and might not have been noticed. In contrast, Pavlov's dogs could hardly overlook a ringing bell.

Another factor influencing acquisition is the frequency with which the CS and UCS are paired. Infrequent pairings are likely to retard conditioning. If bells were only occasionally accompanied by feeding, Pavlov's dogs would have been less likely to be conditioned.

Finally, and perhaps more importantly, the order and timing with which the CS is paired with the UCS is critical. This point demands extra attention.

Timing and Conditioning   Ideally, the CS is presented just moments before the UCS appears, and it is continued until the learner responds to the UCS. For example, the bell rings before food is presented to Pavlov's dog, and it continues until the animal begins to salivate as food enters its mouth. This timing sequence is called **delayed conditioning.** The ideal CS–UCS interval in delayed conditioning depends somewhat on the associations to be learned (Carew & Sahler, 1986). Conditioning occurs most readily when the CS precedes the UCS by less than two seconds, with about .5 second being optimal.

Conditioning may still take place when timing is varied. For instance, **simultaneous conditioning** takes place when the conditioned stimulus is presented at the same time as the unconditioned stimulus. Another variation in timing is known as **trace conditioning.** Here, the conditioned stimulus begins and ends before the unconditioned stimulus is presented. Finally, in **backward conditioning** the UCS is presented prior to the CS. Figure 6.3 illustrates all four variations in timing.

Delayed conditioning generally yields the most rapid rate of learning (Hulse et al., 1980). In contrast, the least effective sequence, backward conditioning, usually results in little or no learning (Keith-Lucas & Guttman, 1975).

APPLYING CONDITIONING PRINCIPLES

Joey is a typical one-year-old who explores everything within reach by poking, squeezing, and, if possible, mouthing. To protect Joey from dangerous objects such as electrical outlets, Joey's parents must teach him the meaning of the word "no." Like many parents, they do this by associating the verbal command "no" with a slap on the hand. From what you know about timing and conditioning, what is the most effective way for them to pair the slap on the hand with the verbal command? Take a moment to answer this question before reading on.

The next time you see a toddler handling a prized household item, watch the parents to see how they respond. Most frequently, they will pounce on the child, slap a hand, and then talk about "no-no's." They may wonder why their child has such a hard time figuring out what "no" means. To a psychologist, the answer is clear: it is because they are applying backward conditioning. Instead of delivering the unconditioned stimulus (the

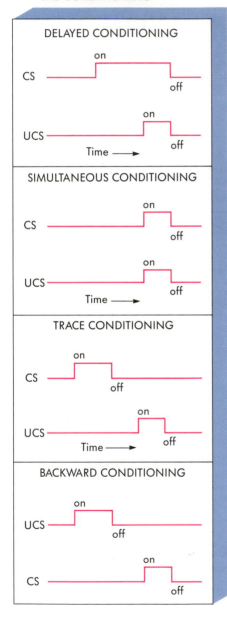

FIGURE 6.3   PAIRING OF THE CS WITH THE UCS: FOUR TEMPORAL RELATIONSHIPS IN CLASSICAL CONDITIONING

DELAYED CONDITIONING

SIMULTANEOUS CONDITIONING

TRACE CONDITIONING

BACKWARD CONDITIONING

Delayed conditioning generally yields the most rapid rate of learning. Backward conditioning, the least effective sequence, usually results in little or no learning.

FIGURE 6.4   EFFECTIVE AND INEFFECTIVE CONDITIONING MODELS

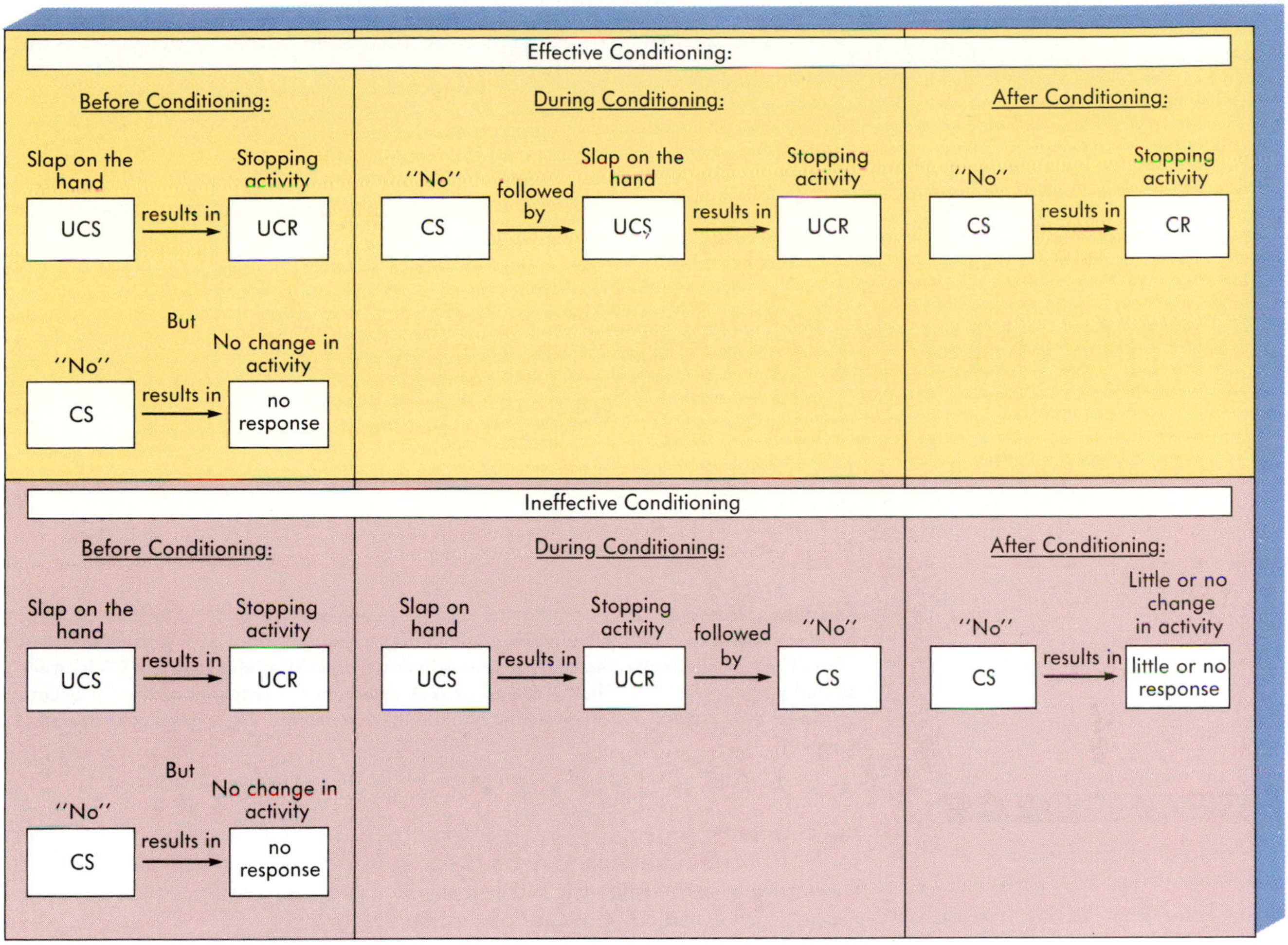

Effective Conditioning:

Before Conditioning:

Slap on the hand
UCS →results in→ Stopping activity
UCR

But

"No"
CS →results in→ No change in activity
no response

During Conditioning:

"No"
CS followed by Slap on the hand
UCS →results in→ Stopping activity
UCR

After Conditioning:

"No"
CS →results in→ Stopping activity
CR

Ineffective Conditioning

Before Conditioning:

Slap on the hand
UCS →results in→ Stopping activity
UCR

But

"No"
CS →results in→ No change in activity
no response

During Conditioning:

Slap on hand
UCS →results in→ Stopping activity
UCR followed by "No"
CS

After Conditioning:

"No"
CS →results in→ Little or no change in activity
little or no response

slap on the hand) before the conditioned stimulus (the "no"), they would achieve more effective training if the "no, no" preceded and accompanied the slap on the hand. Figure 6.4 demonstrates the key elements involved in the ineffective and effective ways to conduct this form of classical conditioning.

EXTINCTION AND SPONTANEOUS RECOVERY

Would Pavlov's dogs have continued to salivate at the sound of the bell if it were no longer accompanied by food? The answer, of course, is no. They would salivate less and less at the sound until, without any reminders of the association between food and the bell, they would cease salivating altogether.

This process is called **extinction.** Extinction occurs in classical conditioning when the CS is repeatedly presented alone, without the UCS. Extinction does not mean that a response is totally stamped out, however. Once extinguished, a conditioned response can be reactivated in much less time than it took to acquire it in the first place. For instance, the classically conditioned response of salivating to a bell may have been established only after several pairings or trials. But after extinction, the conditioned response could be reestablished after only one or two pairings of the bell and the food.

In fact, a conditioned response will sometimes reappear spontaneously after extinction. For example, we might thoroughly extinguish the

FIGURE 6.5   ACQUISITION, EXTINCTION, AND SPONTANEOUS RECOVERY

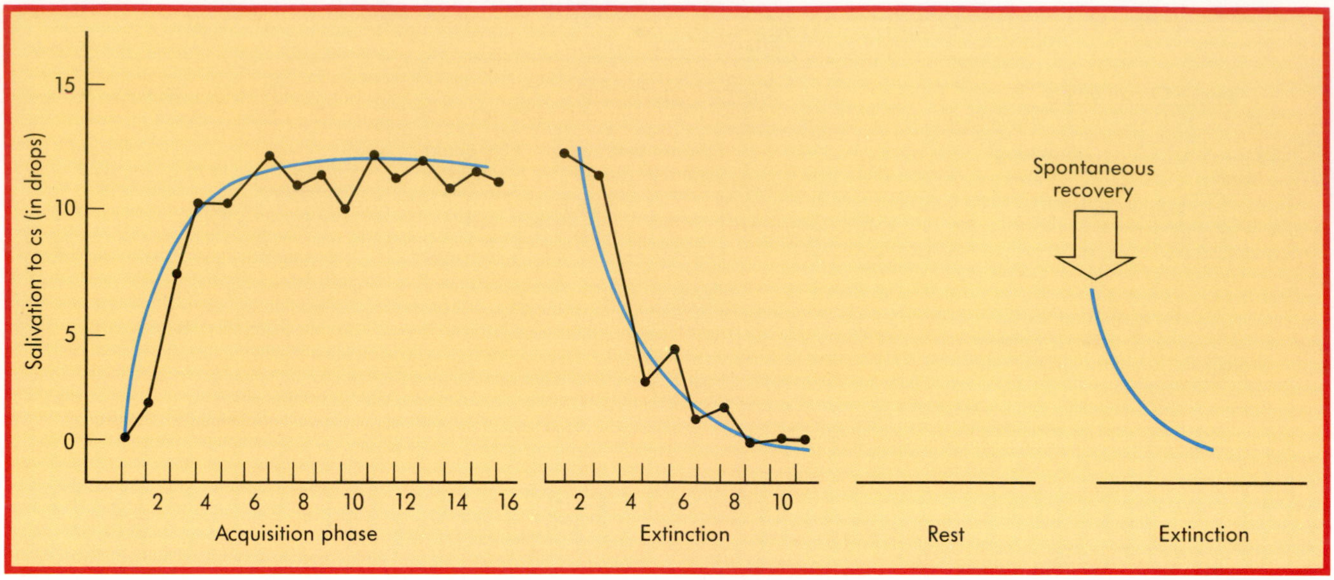

This figure, based on data from Pavlov (1927), demonstrates rapid acquisition of the CR (dog salivating to a bell) after a few trials in which the bell (the CS) is paired with meat (the UCS). Subsequently, the CR is extinguished in about 10 trials when the CS is presented without the UCS. After a period of rest, spontaneous recovery of the CR occurs followed by a second set of extinction trials during which the CR is more rapidly extinguished.

FIRST PERSON 6.1

The concept of generalization reminds me of the day my brother came home from his first day in medical school. We were standing in the kitchen, talking about his experiences. His wife was sitting on a stool listening to our conversation, when all of a sudden, she passed out.

It turned out that the explanation for her behavior had to do with the white coat my brother was wearing. As a child, my sister-in-law had been subjected to many painful procedures administered by a physician wearing a white coat. Apparently, she had generalized her anxiety response to her husband's lab coat. Fortunately, my brother didn't stick a needle in her arm every time he wore his white coat, so she soon learned to distinguish between a loving husband who wore a white coat to school and physicians who sometimes do painful things while dressed in white. (*Authors' files*)

salivation response and then, after keeping the dog away from the experimental procedures for a day or two, again present the bell. Even without food to help reestablish the old connection, the dog might salivate to the bell alone. This is called **spontaneous recovery.**

As Figure 6.5 demonstrates, spontaneous recovery is not a complete recovery. A response does not come back at full strength; it also extinguishes more rapidly if the CS is once more repeatedly presented alone.

GENERALIZATION AND DISCRIMINATION

When a response has been conditioned to a particular stimulus, other stimuli may also produce the same response. For example, a war veteran who has been conditioned to dive for cover at the sound of gunfire may show the same response at the sound of a car backfiring. The more similar a new stimulus is to the original CS, the more likely it is to elicit the CR.

This principle is called **generalization,** and it explains why people and other animals respond to many related stimuli without undergoing training for each specific stimulus. For example, a child who has just learned to call the family pet "doggy" may use the same term to describe a sheep during a subsequent visit to a farm.

Just as a learned response may generalize to similar situations, it may also be restricted through the process of **discrimination.** Early in the conditioning process, generalization may cause a learner to respond to a variety of similar stimuli. However, with time he or she will learn that only one of these stimuli, the CS, is consistently associated with the UCS. Once the learner discriminates between stimuli, he or she will respond only to the CS. For example, if the war veteran experienced a variety of jarring loud noises, without the accompaniment of bullets whizzing through the air, he would soon learn to discriminate between noises like a car backfiring and gunshot.

HIGHER ORDER CONDITIONING

We have seen that, through classical conditioning, an organism learns to respond to a previously neutral stimulus, the CS, in a similar way as to the UCS. You might wonder whether the process can be carried one step further. With its newly acquired strength, can the CS be used to condition the same response to other stimuli?

The answer is yes. For example, Pavlov's dog might first learn to salivate to a bell. Once the connection is firmly established, a tone might then be paired repeatedly with the bell, with no food present, until the tone alone elicits salivation. This process is called **higher order conditioning,** and it is illustrated in Figure 6.6.

Higher order conditioning can greatly extend the impact of classical conditioning on our lives. We have a virtually unlimited capacity to make associations between events. This is one reason why therapists treating such things as classically conditioned phobias (persistent, irrational fears) often trace convoluted processes by which everyday stimuli come to produce unreasonable fear in a person.

FIGURE 6.6   HIGHER ORDER CONDITIONING

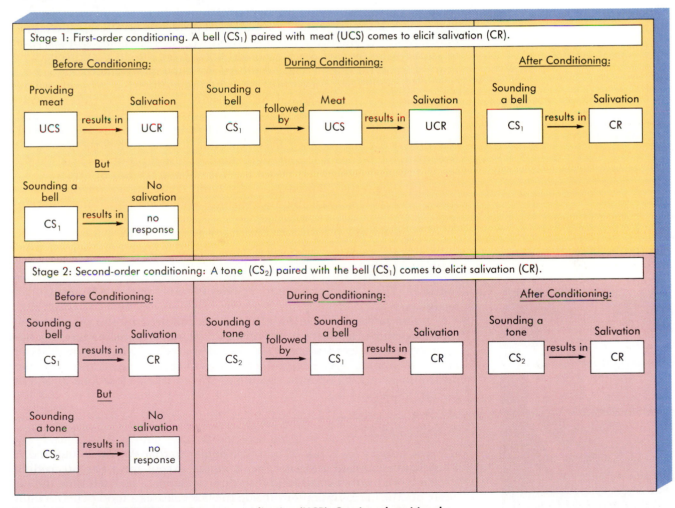

In stage 1, giving food (UCS) to a dog causes salivation (UCR). Consistently pairing the sound of a bell (CS) with the food produces a conditioned salivation response (CR). In stage 2, the first CS (or CS_1, the bell) can be paired with a second CS (or CS_2, in this case a tone) so that the tone will eventually be sufficient to produce the salivation response.

We have seen that classical conditioning is a relatively simple form of associative learning that accounts for certain types of behaviors. However, classical conditioning does not explain all forms of learning. For instance, why are you diligently (we hope) reading this textbook? What is the UCS that automatically causes you to study? Obviously, there is none. To learn why you study and why you engage in a host of other voluntary behaviors, we must examine the second kind of associative learning, called operant conditioning.

OPERANT CONDITIONING

Operant conditioning takes place when behavior is influenced by its consequences. We can trace the origins of this model of learning to the American psychologist, Edward Thorndike (1911). At about the same time that Pavlov was investigating involuntary, reflexive responses, Thorndike was analyzing the effect of stimuli or events that are produced by voluntary behavior.

Thorndike believed that animals learn to make voluntary responses that help them adapt to their environments. To test his theory, he designed a device called a puzzle box. He placed hungry cats in wooden boxes latched from the inside. Outside he dangled a piece of fish in full view. The cats howled, meowed, clawed, and frantically explored in the attempt to get out of the box. Eventually, they accidentally tripped the latch and gained access to the food. The next time a cat found itself inside the box, it repeated some of the same trial-and-error behavior as before, but it generally took less time to escape from the box. With each additional trial, the cat's actions became more purposeful until it learned to trip the latch immediately.

Thorndike explained his results by suggesting that behavior will be strengthened if it is followed by a positive consequence. Alternatively, behavior that does not lead to a satisfying consequence will be eliminated. Thus, some of the cat's antics, such as clawing at the walls and howling, ceased to occur because they did not produce food. On the other hand, the latch-tripping behavior was strengthened because it produced fish. On the basis of these observations, Thorndike formulated the **law of effect,** which held that behavior followed by a satisfying consequence (effect) will be strengthened. This law is the underlying foundation of operant conditioning.

Thorndike's puzzle box illustrates why the term *operant* has been applied to this type of learning. His cats learned to *operate* on their environment in a manner that resulted in satisfaction. Another way of saying the same thing is that their behaviors were *instrumental* in achieving a positive outcome. Thus, this conditioning model is sometimes called *instrumental conditioning*.

Thorndike's pioneering efforts were followed by the monumental contributions of Harvard psychologist B. F. Skinner. Skinner's research has spanned several decades, and it has provided much of what we know about operant conditioning. Perhaps the best way to become acquainted with the principles governing operant conditioning is to take a close look at one of Skinner's basic models.

SKINNER'S MODEL

A hungry rat is placed in a box similar to that shown in Figure 6.7. This chamber, called a *Skinner box,* is empty except for a bar protruding from one wall with a small food dish directly beneath it. Each time the rat depresses the bar, a dispenser outside the box releases a food pellet. A light above the bar can be activated at the experimenter's discretion.

Left alone in a Skinner box, the rat begins to examine its surroundings. As it explores randomly, it eventually presses the bar. A food pellet clinks into the dish. The next bar-press occurs after some more random exploration. Soon the bar-pressing occurs in a less random fashion, and

B.F. Skinner

**FIGURE 6.7 A SKINNER BOX—
AN APPARATUS USED FOR OPER-
ANT CONDITIONING**

before long the rat spends most of its time hanging around the bar. The operant response of bar-pressing is strengthened by the food it produces, and the rate of pressing steadily increases.

You may have wondered about the light above the bar. Skinner used this to introduce a new variable, setting the dispenser to deliver food only when the bar is pressed *and* the light is on. When the light is off, no food is delivered. Under these conditions of *differential reinforcement* (that is, reinforcement that takes place only under certain circumstances), the rat soon learns to make the appropriate discrimination: it presses the bar only when the light is on. In this circumstance, the light serves as a **discriminative stimulus,** that is, a stimulus that controls the response by signaling the availability of reinforcement.

Skinner's experiment illustrates the primary features of the operant model of learning. An animal learns to act upon its environment to achieve a satisfying consequence. Unlike classical conditioning, in which the learner passively waits for a stimulus to trigger a response, operant conditioning occurs when the learner acts on the environment to produce desired consequences. How do researchers measure the strength of operant responses?

Measuring the Strength of Operant Behavior   Perhaps the most common measure of operant strength is *rate of response*. Simply stated, the more frequently an operant response (that is, the behavior that leads to reinforcement) is made during a designated time interval, the greater the operant strength.

Skinner designed a device called a *cumulative recorder* (see Figure 6.8) that is used to measure the strength of operant behavior in a laboratory environment. A recording pen rests on paper that moves slowly at a fixed rate. Each time an animal makes an operant response, such as pressing a bar, the pen moves up a fixed distance and then continues on its horizontal path. The more frequently an animal responds, the more rapidly the pen climbs up the chart. The result, called a **cumulative curve** (see Figure 6.9), is a reliable measure of operant strength. Steep curves indicate strong response strength; horizontal lines indicate lack of response.

FIGURE 6.8 A CUMULATIVE RECORDER

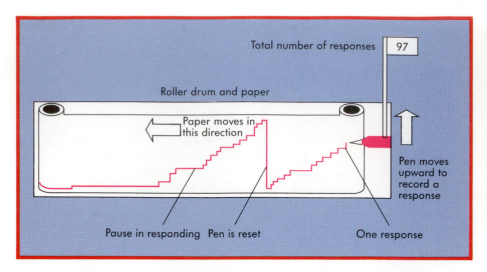

A recording pen rests on paper that moves slowly at a fixed rate as the roller drum turns. The pen is rigged so that it can only move upward and never downward. Each time an animal makes an operant response, such as pressing a bar, the pen moves up a fixed distance and then continues on its horizontal path. The more frequently an animal responds, the more rapidly the pen climbs up the chart. When the pen reaches the top of the paper, it is automatically reset to the bottom.

FIGURE 6.9 CUMULATIVE CURVES DURING ACQUISITION

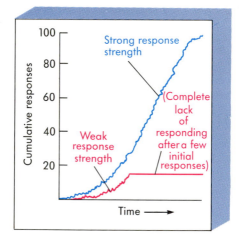

Another way to measure operant strength is to record the total number of responses made during extinction. For example, how many times will a rat continue to press the bar in a Skinner box when food is no longer delivered? In a laboratory, this can be measured with a cumulative recorder. Outside the laboratory, a trainer might observe how many times a circus dog will jump through a hoop without receiving any reinforcement.

REINFORCEMENT

Operant conditioning stresses consequences of behavior, and under this model consequences are synonymous with reinforcers. Reinforcement is the most important aspect of operant conditioning because it establishes which behavior will be increased.

Reinforcement is defined as any event that increases the probability that a response will occur. In studying operant conditioning, researchers have experimented with different types of reinforcers and different schedules for delivering reinforcement. Their findings help to explain how and why operant conditioning takes place.

Positive and Negative Reinforcers Psychologists distinguish between positive and negative reinforcers. A **positive reinforcer** is any stimulus presented following a response that increases the probability of the response. A **negative reinforcer** is a stimulus that increases the probability of a response through its removal when the desired response is made. Introductory psychology students frequently misunderstand negative reinforcement, often confusing it with punishment and assuming that it is used to stop a behavior (Deater & Tauber, 1987). In fact, quite the opposite is true: Negative reinforcement is used to strengthen or increase the occurrence of a desired behavior. Since the previous examples in this chapter have illustrated positive reinforcement, we will look here at some examples of negative reinforcers.

A rat is placed in a Skinner box, the floor of which is a metal grid that can be electrified. A mild current is activated and, as the rat tries to escape, it bumps into a bar and the shocking current immediately ceases. The pattern is repeated several times until the rat remains poised by the bar, ready to slam it down at the first jolt.

This form of learning, called **escape conditioning,** clearly involves a negative reinforcer. The shock, an unpleasant stimulus, may be terminated only by the appropriate bar-press response. The removal of the shock thus strengthens the correct response.

Escape conditioning can be taken one step further by introducing a warning signal. This allows the rat to avoid the shock altogether. If light goes on a few seconds prior to each shock, the rat will soon learn to respond to this discriminative stimulus by pressing the bar in time to avoid the shock. This type of learning is called **avoidance conditioning.**

These examples bring to mind many parallels in our own lives. For instance, people who live in Oregon are accustomed to carrying umbrellas. Out-of-staters or optimistic natives have had to experience getting drenched while running back to fetch an umbrella (escape conditioning) before learning to have one always on hand on a cloudy day (avoidance conditioning).

People often use the term *reward* interchangeably with reinforcement. The two are not necessarily synonymous. While reward and positive reinforcement are one and the same, negative reinforcers like an electric shock or a cloudburst are certainly not rewards.

Two other terms that are frequently confused are **punishment** and negative reinforcement. Again, the two are not the same. A negative reinforcer, by virtue of its removal, strengthens a response. Thus, a rat learns to press a bar to escape a shock. On the other hand, punishment decreases the probability of a response by virtue of its presentation. For instance, if a rat trained to press a bar for food began to be shocked after each bar-press, the response would be weakened. Punishment will be discussed later in this chapter.

Primary and Secondary Reinforcers Just as psychologists distinguish between positive and negative reinforcers, they also distinguish primary and secondary reinforcers. A **primary reinforcer** is a stimulus that satisfies a biologically based drive or need, such as hunger, thirst, sex, or sleep.

It is obvious why food, water, sex, or sleep are reinforcing. But why are such things as money reinforcing? The answer lies in the concept of **secondary** or **conditioned reinforcers.** A variety of neutral stimuli associ-

Have you ever been caught in a rainstorm without an umbrella? If you have, you probably carried an umbrella on the next cloudy day!

FIGURE 6.10   A "CHIMP-O-MAT"

In a classic experiment, chimpanzees learned to perform a variety of tasks to earn tokens (secondary reinforcers) that could be inserted into a vending machine to obtain primary reinforcers in the form of goodies like grapes or raisins.

ated with primary reinforcers can also become secondary reinforcers. Much of our behavior is influenced more by secondary reinforcers than by biologically significant primary reinforcers. Words of praise, pats on the back, good grades, and money are some of the secondary reinforcers that influence our lives.

Humans are not the only animals who are influenced by secondary reinforcers such as money. In a classic experiment conducted in the 1930s, chimpanzees learned that putting a coin (actually a token) into a "chimp-o-mat" vending machine produced goodies like grapes or raisins (see Figure 6.10). Through their association with food, the coins became secondary reinforcers. The chimps were then trained to perform a variety of tasks just to get a coin. The coins soon acquired considerable reinforcing properties: the chimps worked hard to get them, often hoarded them, and sometimes they even tried to steal them from each other (Wolfe, 1936).

We have seen that secondary reinforcers acquire their reinforcing properties through their association with a primary reinforcer, but what is the critical element that determines this association? For many years, psychologists believed that the strength of a secondary reinforcer depended simply on the frequency with which it had been paired with a primary reinforcer.

Recent research suggests otherwise. Instead of the frequency of pairings, the crucial factor seems to be the reliability with which the secondary reinforcer predicts the availability of the primary reinforcer (Fantino, 1977; Rose & Fantino, 1978). For example, a coin that always produces raisins when inserted in a chimp-o-mat will quickly become a strong secondary reinforcer, while coins that have less predictable results may be much weaker secondary reinforcers, no matter how often they have been paired with raisins.

The Premack Principle   It is evident that many different stimuli can serve as reinforcers. Is it possible to determine which of several available reinforcers would be the most effective in strengthening a given behavior? For example, is it better to reward an employee's good performance with a cash bonus, more vacation time, or greater opportunities to participate in management decisions? You might expect that different employees would rank the desirability of these rewards in different ways. This leads us to a consideration of the work of psychologist David Premack (1962, 1965).

According to Premack, reinforcers can be viewed as responses or behaviors the learner engages in. From this perspective, it is not food that reinforces a rat for bar-pressing, but rather the act of eating it. Premack further stated that the desirability of potentially reinforcing behaviors varies from one individual to the next and from time to time. Thus, one employee might prefer receiving extra cash for good work, while another would rather have opportunities to participate in company policy making.

Premack summarized these notions by stating that individual reinforcement hierarchies exist for all humans and other animals. Reinforcers at the top of the list are those behaviors most likely to be engaged in, given the opportunity. Premack further stated that for a given individual, any behavior in the hierarchy may reinforce any of the behaviors listed below it and may itself be reinforced by any behaviors listed above it. This latter point has come to be known as the **Premack principle.**

Premack has supported his views in research with both rats and humans. In one study, he gave thirsty rats the opportunity to choose between drinking or running in an activity wheel. As expected, these thirsty rats drank more than they ran, suggesting that drinking was above running on the hierarchy of reinforcing behaviors. Premack then used drinking to reinforce running. Rats learned to run in the wheel in order to drink water. Next he demonstrated a reversal of the hierarchy. Rats who were no longer thirsty preferred running to drinking. With these rats, running could be used as a reinforcer to increase their drinking behavior.

Premack performed similar experiments with children, who were offered the choice of eating candy or playing pinball. Children who preferred playing pinball would increase their candy consumption if this increased their chance to play pinball. Conversely, those who preferred candy increased their pinball playing in order to get more candy.

APPLYING THE PREMACK PRINCIPLE

You may have observed parents telling a child that he or she can watch only one TV program before tackling a homework assignment. Given what you know about the Premack principle (and what you know about most children's preference for TV versus homework), do you think that this is an effective way to encourage children to complete their homework? Take a moment to answer this question before reading on.

Applying the Premack principle to this question, the answer becomes clear. Since most children prefer watching TV to doing homework, the former activity can be used as a reinforcer to persuade children to tackle their assignments. Thus, TV watching should be made contingent upon completing homework, rather than offered as a treat before starting an assignment.

Continuous Versus Partial Reinforcement In addition to the type of reinforcer that is used, another factor that determines how effective operant conditioning will be is the consistency with which a behavior is reinforced.

In laboratory demonstrations of operant conditioning, a behavior may be reinforced every time it occurs. This is called a **continuous reinforcement schedule.** For instance, a rat receives a food pellet each time it presses a bar.

Outside the laboratory, particularly in the everyday lives of humans, continuous reinforcement is unusual. For example, smiling at the food server in your college cafeteria does not always produce an extra large helping of food, nor does getting out of the house 20 minutes early always ensure your favorite parking space on campus. But these behaviors persist because they are sometimes reinforced. A **partial reinforcement schedule** exists when behavior is reinforced only part of the time. There are startling differences in how continuous and partial reinforcement schedules affect behavior.

Continuous reinforcement schedules almost always produce the highest rate of acquisition of a new behavior. For example, a rat learns to bar-press most rapidly when it receives food each time it makes the appropriate response. However, what happens when reinforcement is withdrawn? Extinction begins, and the rat quickly ceases its bar-pressing behavior.

Behaviors that are acquired on partial instead of continuous schedules of reinforcement are slower to be established, but they are remarkably more persistent when no reinforcement is provided (Bitterman, 1975; Tarpy, 1983). For example, a rat accustomed to only intermittent reinforcement for bar-pressing will continue to press long after the food dispenser has run dry. This is particularly true when the partial reinforcement is delivered in an unpredictable fashion. This phenomenon is known as the **partial reinforcement effect.** There are four possible variations in partial reinforcement schedules.

Partial Reinforcement Schedules Partial reinforcement can be delivered in either of two basic ways: ratio or interval schedules. On a *ratio schedule,* a certain percentage of responses receive reinforcement. For instance, a slot machine in a casino might be programmed to provide some kind of payoff on 10% of all plays. An *interval schedule,* in contrast, is time-based: subjects are reinforced for their first response after a certain amount of time has passed, regardless of how many responses might occur during that period. An example of an interval schedule is finally getting to speak to your friend after repeated dialings of her phone number resulted in busy signals.

Both ratio and interval schedules may be either variable or fixed. *Variable schedule* reinforcement is delivered unpredictably, with the amount of time or number of responses required varying randomly around an average. In contrast, *fixed schedule* reinforcement is always delivered after a constant number of responses or a fixed interval of time. These categories combine to form four basic partial reinforcement schedules: fixed ratio, variable ratio, fixed interval, and variable interval (see Figure 6.11).

Fixed Ratio Schedule On a **fixed ratio (FR) schedule,** reinforcement occurs after a fixed number of responses. For example, a rat receives a food pellet after 12 bar-presses and a strawberry picker receives $1.00 after filling 12 small boxes with berries. Both are on an FR-12 schedule. This schedule tends to produce rather high rates of responding: the faster the rat

FIGURE 6.11 SCHEDULES OF RE-INFORCEMENT

	Ratio	Interval
Fixed Schedules	Fixed Ratio (FR)	Fixed Interval (FI)
Variable Schedules	Variable Ratio (VR)	Variable Interval (VI)

bar-presses, the more pellets it gets, and the quicker the strawberry picker works, the more money she or he will earn.

This fact explains why some factories and businesses pay their workers on a piecework basis (like the strawberry picker). However, there are some limitations to this practice. For example, if workers in an automobile assembly plant were paid only according to the number of cars they ran through the assembly line, quality might suffer. Another potential limitation of the fixed ratio schedule is that people and other animals often pause briefly after reinforcement is delivered, probably because they know that their next few responses will not be rewarded. This may be one reason why payday typically occurs on Friday.

Variable Ratio Schedule   A **variable ratio (VR) schedule** of reinforcement also requires the occurrence of a certain number of responses before reinforcement is delivered. Unlike a fixed ratio schedule, however, the number of responses required for each reinforcement will vary. For example, a rat on a VR-6 schedule will receive a food pellet on the average of every six bar-presses, but any given reinforcement may require fewer or more than six responses.

Variable ratio schedules produce high response rates. Furthermore, because of the unpredictable nature of reinforcement, there is typically no pause after a reward, for it is possible that a reward will occur on the very next response. Behavior that is acquired on this schedule is often very slow to extinguish.

Gamblers are very familiar with variable ratio schedules. For example, a person who always bets on 13 at the roulette wheel is on a VR-38 schedule (the wheel has 36 numbers plus 0 and 00). On the average, 13 will come up every 38 spins. However, during a hot streak 13 might occur three times in 20 spins (of course, it also might not occur at all). Similarly, a slot machine may be rigged to pay off once every 20 times a coin is deposited, on the average (a VR-20 schedule). The gambler does not know when it will return a few of the coins it has swallowed. It is the unpredictable, highly variable nature of these payoffs that makes gambling so compelling to some people.

Fixed Interval Schedule   On a **fixed interval (FI) schedule,** reinforcement is provided for the first response after a specified period of time has elapsed. For example, a rat on an FI-30 schedule, whose bar-press has

People pause briefly after reinforcement is delivered, probably because they know that their next few responses will not be rewarded. This may be one reason why payday typically occurs on Friday.

These gamblers do not know when the slot machines will return some coins—maybe the next pull of the handle, or the *next!* This highly variable nature of payoffs is what compels many people to gamble.

One of my favorite places to fish is a lake where the trout feed in a highly erratic manner. They tend to bite in flurries. Sometimes the action is fast and furious for 30 minutes and then nothing happens for hours. One day they are biting at 10 A.M., 2 P.M., and again just before dark; the next day the only good time might be just after sunup. At other lakes, where the feeding pattern is more predictable, I might fish only in the early morning or perhaps only in the evening. But at this particular lake I stay most of the day because I don't want to miss any of the periods when the bite is on. (*Authors' files*)

just produced a food pellet, will receive its next reinforcer the first time it bar-presses after 30 seconds have elapsed.

An animal placed on this schedule quickly learns to adjust its response rate. Since no reinforcements occur for a period of time, no matter how often it responds, it typically stops working after reinforcement is delivered and then begins to respond toward the end of the interval. Thus, this pattern of reinforcement tends to produce regular, recurring episodes of inactivity followed by short bursts of responding.

This schedule is not very effective in maintaining consistent behavior, but it is quite common in everyday life. For instance, college students who are accustomed to being tested every two weeks might avoid studying until the end of the second week, when the anticipation of the reinforcement of a good grade (or the threat of failure) is strongest. This last-minute cramming is less common in classes where instructors give unannounced exams.

Variable Interval Schedule Finally, a **variable interval (VI) schedule** involves variable time intervals between opportunities for reinforcement. Thus, an animal on a VI-45 schedule might receive a reward for a response after 30 seconds have elapsed, then after 60 seconds, and then after 45 seconds. This averages out to a reward every 45 seconds.

As you might guess, the random, unpredictable occurrence of the reinforcements on this schedule tends to produce more steady rates of responding than fixed interval schedules. However, the rate of responding may be quite slow when there is a long average interval between reinforcements.

Applying Reinforcement Schedules We have seen that partial reinforcement affects behavior differently from continuous reinforcement, and that reinforcement schedules may further influence performance. What are the practical implications of these findings?

Assume that you are the parent of a young boy who has not yet learned to clean his room each day. The best way to establish this behavior would be to use a continuous reinforcement schedule. You would reward your son each time he completed his task during the initial stages of his training—perhaps with points that could be turned in either for "little" payoffs (like a short back-rub) or accumulated for more sizeable prizes, like a trip to the zoo. It would also be important to praise the boy for each good job. Associating praise with other reinforcers allows praise to become a more powerful reward itself.

You cannot monitor and reward this behavior indefinitely, however. Once the room-cleaning behavior is established, you could begin shifting to a partial reinforcement schedule, rewarding the behavior only some of the time. A variable ratio schedule would be the logical choice since it is most resistant to extinction. Gradually, you would make the schedule more demanding until just a few words of praise delivered now and then would be sufficient.

Partial reinforcement can be a good way to encourage a child's room-cleaning, but it also has a flip side. For example, a father might tell his young daughter that she cannot leave her yard unless accompanied by an adult. Since children typically test the limits, the little girl will probably sneak over to her friend's house at the first opportunity. The father may punish this behavior the first few times it occurs, but he may sometimes overlook it because he is too busy. In this manner, a pattern of inconsistency is established, with the child discovering she can get away with inappropriate behavior at least some of the time. These unpredictable victories over the system can be powerfully reinforcing. In essence, parents who inconsistently enforce rules are training their children to be gamblers. Like Atlantic City slot players, these children are conditioned to keep "pushing the button" until the inevitable payoff is provided.

The reinforcement schedules we have been discussing share a common assumption: that the learner will produce the desired behavior so that it can be reinforced. In operant conditioning, however, it is sometimes difficult to get an animal (humans included) to make the initial correct response so that it can be rewarded. The next section discusses several methods for increasing the probability that a desired response will occur.

OBTAINING INITIAL OPERANT RESPONSES

In operant conditioning, many responses occur spontaneously. For example, rats placed in Skinner boxes invariably get around to pressing the bar during the course of their explorations. In other circumstances, however, the behavior may not occur without some additional help. For instance, no matter how many times you say "roll over" to your untrained dog, the odds are very remote that it will perform the trick so that you can reward it. Some special techniques can be used to encourage the desired response, however.

Physical Guidance   The best strategy for training a dog to roll over would be to guide compliance to the command by gently manipulating the animal. As the dog scrambles back on its feet, you would reinforce it with a piece of meat or a pat on the head. After several sequences of command, manipulation, and reinforcement, the animal should begin to roll over on command without any manipulation required.

This same technique might be used to train a child to drink from a cup. A parent's hand, over a child's hand holding a cup, can guide the child through the appropriate sequence of lifting the cup to the mouth. Each response is then rewarded by both the parent's praise and the act of drinking (it is a good idea to offer an especially tasty liquid in this initial training).

Shaping   **Shaping** is another technique for establishing desired behavior. It involves a systematic process whereby responses that are increasingly similar to the desired behavior are reinforced step by step until finally the desired behavior occurs.

Shaping is especially effective for establishing novel behaviors. For instance, one of the authors remembers a county fair at which a popular attraction was a chicken who "played" a piano each time an observer fed a quarter into a slot outside its cage. This operant behavior was shaped in the following fashion: Initially, the chicken was reinforced any time it faced the piano. Next, it was required to move a few steps toward the piano before getting corn. Then it had to stand beside the piano; then move its head toward the keyboard, and so forth. Eventually the chicken received corn only when its beak struck the keys with sufficient force to make sounds.

Once this behavior was established the chicken learned to discriminate when reinforcement was available by watching a light. No reinforcement was provided when the light was off, but whenever the light was on, pecking produced corn. Once the discriminative stimulus, the light, was attached to the coin slot, the trainers could open a bank account.

Many therapists use shaping to obtain desirable behavior in emotionally disturbed children and adults. An example of this is the case of a nine-year-old boy with autism, a profound emotional illness that blocks normal patterns of social interaction. His parents consulted a behavior therapist, who used shaping to establish social behavior.

At first, the boy learned to obtain candy from a machine activated remotely. (Since no social pressures were imposed, this procedure was nonthreatening.) The next step was more complex. The boy was placed in a room that contained a variety of toys, the candy machine, and another boy about his age, a confederate of the therapist. The ensuing behavior was viewed through a one-way glass.

The disturbed youth made no overtures to the other boy. However, each time he looked at him, the therapist activated the candy dispenser. Once this behavior was established, the next step was to reward the boy when he took a step toward the other boy. In this fashion the autistic boy gradually learned to stand next to his would-be playmate, then to interact with him. (Even a normally undesirable act like grabbing a toy from him was acceptable at first, for it represented an interaction.) Gradually, over a period of weeks, a number of social behaviors were shaped, and eventually the candy machine became a less important reinforcer than the other boy.

Modeling   Another technique for producing a desired operant response is **modeling.** Modeling involves demonstrating the desired behavior to the learner. Many athletic skills, such as diving, hitting a tennis ball, or riding a skateboard, are learned by watching someone else. In cases like these, the reinforcement is the acquisition of the skill. Modeling teaches a wide range of behaviors, undesirable as well as desirable. For instance, a young child who admires an older youth who hates school may himself begin grumbling that he wants to quit school. Modeling will be discussed later on in this chapter, under the heading "Observational Learning."

Verbal Instruction   Sometimes desired behavior can be established by simply describing the appropriate response. Parents and educators often use this method. When you learned to drive, most of your instruction was probably verbal, as someone sat next to you and told you when to turn, brake, and accelerate.

Increasing Motivation   Finally, we can sometimes increase the probability that a first operant response will occur by increasing the motivation to make the response. For example, hungry cats are more likely than are cats that are not hungry to find their way out of a puzzle box to get a fish dangling outside.

COMPARING CLASSICAL AND OPERANT CONDITIONING

As we have seen, both classical and operant conditioning involve associative learning—the establishment of a relationship between two events. Each learning process produces a new behavior, whether it be the conditioned response of salivating when a bell rings or an operant response such as bar-pressing in a Skinner box. However, classical and operant conditioning use very different procedures to reach their goals. Two key differences help distinguish between these two learning models.

First, in classical conditioning there is always a specific stimulus (the UCS) which elicits the desired response. (For example, food elicits salivation.) However, in operant conditioning there is no such stimulus: it is up to the learner to emit the appropriate response, which is then reinforced.

Second, in classical conditioning the occurrence of the UCS does not depend upon the response of the learner. Thus, Pavlov's dogs received meat regardless of how they reacted to the bell. In contrast, in the operant model, reinforcement is contingent upon the learner's behavior. Thus, Skinner's rats are rewarded with a food pellet only when they press a bar. In essence, then, in the operant model the learner actively operates on its environment, while under the classical model the learner simply responds to the environment.

TWO-PROCESS LEARNING

Some learning situations combine both classical and operant conditioning in what is called **two-process learning.** For instance, let us return to the case of the biology student, discussed earlier in this chapter. This example was originally presented to illustrate classical conditioning, and classical conditioning was indeed the first learning process that took place in this case: through pairing with the frightening experience at the hospital, the medicinal odors became the CS that triggered a fear response.

A second learning process also took place, however. Since fear is unpleasant, any responses that reduce or eliminate fear are strengthened through negative reinforcement. When the young woman avoided the biology lab, she was operating on her environment to alleviate her fear. Therefore a second process, operant conditioning, became a factor. The student's avoidance behavior kept her far from the biology lab. And since she was never exposed to the laboratory long enough to find out that the UCS would not occur, her conditioned fear was maintained.

Many human phobias are products of two-process learning. An understanding of the principles underlying this kind of conditioning provides a clue for treating such fear responses. In order to extinguish conditioned phobias, a person must be exposed to the CS in the absence of the UCS. To do this, the operant avoidance behavior must be prevented. One possible way to accomplish this would be initially to expose a relaxed subject to a very mild version of the feared stimulus (for example, a mildly medicinal odor in a nonthreatening situation). Gradually, more intense versions of the conditioned fear stimulus would be introduced. This technique, called *systematic desensitization*, is discussed in Chapter 15.

IDENTIFYING DIFFERENT TYPES OF LEARNING

It is sometimes difficult to distinguish different types of learning: the line between operant and classical conditioning and two-process learning is often fuzzy, and the various elements (the UCS, UCR, CS, CR, and operant response) are not always easy to pinpoint. One way to improve our understanding of these differences is to apply what we have learned to specific examples. The following paragraphs describe a few examples of conditioning. For each example, try to identify what kind of learning took place—classical, operant, or two-process.

EXAMPLES

Example A   In an experiment designed to explore the origins of *fetishism* (sexual behavior in which an individual becomes sexually aroused by focusing on an inanimate object or a part of the human body), male subjects are repeatedly shown a photograph of women's boots followed by erotic slides of nude females. The subjects soon begin to show sexual response to the boots alone (Rachman, 1966).

Example B   A child repeatedly wets the bed (a condition called *enuresis*) because he has not learned to wake up in response to the tension of a full bladder. To condition this response, a device is installed in his bed that causes a loud buzzer to sound as soon as the child begins urinating. He awakens and completes voiding in the bathroom. After several trials of pairing the bladder tension with the loud buzzer, he begins to awaken prior to wetting the bed. Success is achieved when bladder tension alone is sufficient to awaken him.

Example C   Because social interaction can be therapeutic for emotionally disturbed people, a loud noise is used to increase conversation among residents at a treatment facility. Each time a silence lasts longer than one minute, a speaker hidden in an air-conditioning vent emits an obnoxious, loud noise. As soon as the residents begin to talk, the noise stops. Very quickly, there is a marked increase in the amount of conversation these individuals engage in (Heckel et al., 1962).

FIRST PERSON 6.3

When I was a youngster, about eight or nine, my parents acquired a large doghouse for our pet. One day several friends and I made it our headquarters in a war game. At least five of us had crowded in through the small door when along came my older brother. With nothing better to do, he decided it would be great fun to block the door and trap us inside. I still have a visual image of him backing in part way and bracing himself, taunting us with the words "You can't get out, you can't get out." There was pandemonium in those cramped quarters. Five panicked kids fought to squeeze by my brother's behind.

By the time we finally got out, my claustrophobia was well established. From that point on, I avoided all small enclosures. I refused to walk into closets and preferred to climb ten flights of stairs rather than ride in an elevator. It took years to overcome this irrational, consuming fear. (*Authors' files*)

Example D A horse is taught to come when its handler whistles. This is accomplished by the handler's first approaching to within a few feet of the horse, whistling and holding a bucket of oats. The horse approaches and eats. Gradually, the distance between the handler and the horse is expanded. Eventually, the horse learns that approaching its handler, after hearing a whistle, will generally result in a reward. The animal also learns that when there is no whistling, approaching will not result in reinforcement.

Example E The grizzly bears that we discussed in the opening pages of this chapter learned to associate humans with pain. It is hoped that their conditioned fear of people will keep them far from civilization.

SOLUTIONS

In the cases described above, Example A illustrates classical conditioning. Initially, the photograph of women's boots is a neutral stimulus in that it does not elicit sexual arousal. However, through its association with erotic slides (the UCS), it eventually acquires the capacity to stimulate sexual response. It therefore becomes a conditioned stimulus.

Example B illustrates two-process learning. The classical conditioning part involves conditioning the child to wake up in response to bladder tension (the CS) by pairing this initially neutral stimulus with a loud buzzer (the UCS).

If you have difficulty picturing this classical conditioning process, it may be helpful to refer to the diagram in Figure 6.12. Once this classically conditioned response is established, the child continues to wake up in the future, even when the training apparatus is removed, presumably to avoid the unpleasantness associated with a wet bed. Thus, operant avoidance conditioning takes over.

Example C shows operant conditioning. The emotionally disturbed patients learn very rapidly to increase their communication efforts (operant behavior) because these efforts have the effect of silencing the unpleasant sound, which is a negative reinforcer.

Example D also illustrates operant conditioning. The horse learns the conditioned response of going to its handler to obtain food reinforcement. Furthermore, this operant behavior comes under the control of a discriminative stimulus, the sound of a whistle.

Finally, Example E illustrates two-process learning. Initially, the fear elicited by the shock (the UCS) becomes associated with humans (the CS)

FIGURE 6.12 CLASSICAL CONDITIONING AND BEDWETTING

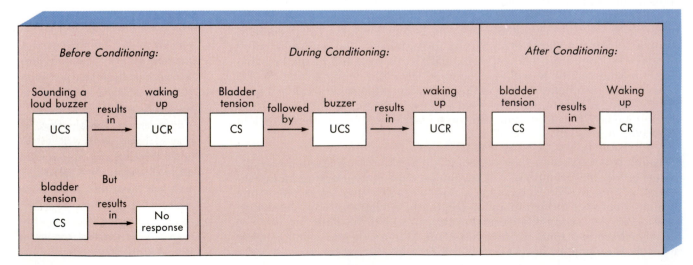

through a process of classical conditioning. This conditioned fear response causes the grizzly to avoid future contacts with humans (operant behavior). Hopefully, the conditioned fear of humans will continue to motivate these avoidance behaviors in the future.

Before we turn our attention to the influence of cognitive factors on learning, one important issue deserves attention. That is the practical application of learning techniques in everyday life, and particularly the application of punishment.

PUNISHMENT: IS IT EFFECTIVE?

So far in this chapter we have discussed the use of reinforcers to strengthen desired behavior. From observing our society, however, one might conclude that punishment is the most effective learning technique. Certainly its use is widespread, from spanking misbehaving children to keeping pupils after school, meting out traffic fines, and incarcerating people in prisons.

However, the fact that many people and institutions rely on punishment to control behavior does not necessarily mean that it is more effective than rewards. People have long debated the relative advantages and disadvantages of rewarding good behavior versus punishing undesirable acts. There is no simple answer. Nevertheless, research has provided ample data that can help us make more reasoned choices as we confront this issue in our own lives. We begin by defining punishment.

Punishment can be defined as a consequence that decreases the probability that a given behavior will occur. We often think of a punishment as an unpleasant or aversive stimulus, such as a spanking. However, punishment may also involve the withdrawal of positive reinforcers such as playtime, watching TV, or the use of the family car. Students sometimes confuse this second form of punishment with the process of extinction discussed earlier. The two are quite different. For example, if we wished to stop a child's temper tantrums through extinction, we would simply withhold our attention (which presumably is the reinforcer of this behavior). In contrast, modifying this behavior through punishment might be accomplished by withdrawing TV-watching privileges each time a temper tantrum occurred.

LIMITATIONS OF PUNISHMENT

Punishment often brings about a change in behavior, at least temporarily (Fantino, 1973). However, its effectiveness is reduced by a number of limitations and negative side effects (Newsom et al., 1983).

Temporary Suppression Instead of Extinction   One limitation has to do with punishment's effectiveness over the long term. In most cases, punishment suppresses the unwanted behavior for a short time, but does not extinguish it (Clarizio & Yelon, 1974). In fact, there is ample evidence that suppressed behavior may reemerge, stronger than ever, when the prospect of punishment is eliminated or sharply curtailed.

For example, a child who is punished by a parent each time she raids the cookie jar will probably learn to suppress this behavior. However, when her "understanding" grandparents come to provide child care for a weekend while her parents are away, a cookie feast may result.

In contrast to the typically temporary effects of punishment, rewarded behavior tends to be remarkably persistent, especially if a variable ratio schedule has been used. One reason for this is that punishment fails to provide the punished individual with an alternative. In effect, it says "stop it!" but does not provide a clear picture of what behavior should be substituted. In contrast, rewards say "continue with your behavior." Thus, the learner is provided with a clear direction for which course of action to pursue.

Threat of punishment seems to control this crowd's behavior, but are punishments for unacceptable behavior more effective than rewards for good behavior?

When I was in the 10th grade, I was put in a math class where the teacher took an instant dislike to me. He constantly put me on the spot, ridiculed me in front of my classmates, and found fault with my work. Eventually, things got so rough that I began to skip his class.

My attitude toward my other classes also turned sour, and my studies went downhill fast. Before long, I dropped out of school. I hated that place so much that I went out of my way to avoid passing it on my way to work. It took a lot of years, and a good experience working on my high-school equivalency certificate at the community college, to overcome my hatred of the educational process. (*Authors' files*)

Emotional Side Effects of Punishment   Another potential problem is that punishment may produce undesirable emotional side effects such as fear, hostility, anger, and even hatred. This is particularly true when punishment is severe or unjust. For example, a child who receives constant, severe punishment from a parent may learn to fear and even hate that parent, and this negative interactive pattern may generalize to other relationships. Sometimes punishment may induce counteraggression against the punisher.

Another side effect of punishment may be anxiety. If the punishment is harsh, it may produce anxiety that interferes with a person's ability to cope with daily events. The combination of constant punishment in an environment where escape is difficult or impossible (for example, in a home where parents are highly punitive) may cause a person to withdraw psychologically (Seligman et al., 1969). The result may be extreme passivity, a defeatist attitude, or perhaps retreat into a fantasy world.

The negative emotional effects of punishment are often generalized to related behaviors. Thus, a child who is singled out for harsh punishment in one class may begin to react negatively to school in general. In contrast, people who are rewarded for desirable behavior generally feel good about themselves, are motivated to perform well, and are optimistic about future endeavors that they anticipate will lead to additional positive consequences.

Physical Punishment and Modeling   Children are often punished by physical means, such as slapping or spanking. Considerable evidence suggests that youngsters who are punished physically learn to model or imitate these aggressive acts and often become more aggressive in their interactions with others (Bandura & Walters, 1959; George & Main, 1979). Thus, parents who "tan the hides" of misbehaving children may be teaching them a different lesson than intended—namely, that physical aggression is acceptable.

MAKING PUNISHMENT MORE EFFECTIVE

While it is important to be aware of the limitations of punishment, most psychologists do not advocate total abolition of all punishment for controlling or modifying behavior. Although rewards are preferable in most cases, punishment is sometimes essential—for example, as a way to suppress undesirable actions temporarily so that a desirable alternative behavior may occur.

For instance, assume you are the parent of the young child discussed earlier in this chapter, who constantly strays out of your yard. To avoid establishing a pattern of partial reinforcement caused by inconsistent punishment, you might decide to wait until the day occurs when she stays home, so you can reward her. Theoretically, this is a good idea, but the behavior might not occur spontaneously, and in the meantime your child might be hit by a car.

In cases like this, it makes sense to apply sufficient punishment to suppress an unwanted behavior temporarily. At the same time, you would also reinforce the desired behavior with an appropriate reward. What other principles can be applied to help ensure that punishment is as effective as possible?

Immediate Application of Punishment   Punishment works best when it immediately follows an undesirable behavior (Parke, 1969; Schwartz, 1984). Perhaps one of the more common violators of this rule is the parent who says to a misbehaving child, "Wait until Dad/Mom comes home." Not only does this long delay dramatically reduce the effectiveness of punishment, it also forces the other parent to "play the heavy."

Sometimes, however, punishment cannot be delivered immediately. For instance, punishing a child who intentionally emits distracting noises during a church service would disrupt the service for everyone. In cases like this, it is desirable to restate the past indiscretion before administering punishment, perhaps after returning to the scene of the crime.

Consistent Application of Punishment   A second point that should be remembered in applying punishment is that it loses effectiveness if it is inconsistent (Schwartz, 1984). Inconsistencies may occur over time or from one person to another. In the first variety, inappropriate behavior may be punished in one instance and ignored the next. As we saw earlier in this chapter, such inconsistencies place the learner on a variable ratio schedule of reinforcement, a practice that can produce remarkable persistence of undesirable behavior.

Inconsistencies from person to person are quite common. Two parents often have differing concepts of discipline. Children in these home environments frequently learn to play one parent against the other, a situation that can teach the child to manipulate others for personal gain.

Moderation   Punishment should be just strong enough to accomplish the desired goal of suppressing undesirable behavior, but it should not be too severe. You probably know some people who believe that if a little bit of punishment works, a lot will work even better. Unfortunately, this philosophy often results in negative side effects such as fear and hostility. Moderate punishment, especially when it is designed to be informative, can redirect behavior so that new responses can be rewarded. When punishment is severe, however, the intent is more likely to be retribution than positive redirection of behavior.

In most circumstances, physical punishment should be avoided. For example, instead of getting a spanking, a misbehaving child could be sent to a "time-out" room for 15 minutes. (A time-out room is a boring but safe place, like a laundry room with nothing but a stool for the child to sit on.) Sometimes even this type of punishment can be too severe. Fifteen minutes is usually ample time for a young child to be alone in a time-out room; one or two hours would be unreasonable.

Avoid Withholding Love   Another way to avoid some of the problems associated with punishment is to be sure that love is not treated as a reinforcer that is contingent upon desired behavior. Love should never be withheld. All of us have a strong need to feel wanted and loved. When love is withheld, the results can be devastating. Not uncommonly, people treated in this fashion experience feelings of rejection and lowered self-esteem, which can result in further behavior problems.

Interestingly, research has shown that punishment administered by warm, loving, and accepting people such as parents and teachers does not disrupt affectional bonds between the individual providing punishment and the person on the receiving end (Parke & Walters, 1967; Walters & Grusec, 1977).

Reinforce Positive Behaviors   Probably the most important rule in applying punishment is always to reward acceptable alternatives to the punished behavior. Unfortunately, this may also be the one rule that is most often violated. Some people reason that if punishment is working, why "rock the boat" by rewarding appropriate alternative behaviors? Others may believe that good behavior does not require special recognition. Still others may simply be unaware of the powerful motivating impact of positive reinforcers.

This is illustrated by a case that one of the authors became familiar with several years ago at a mental health clinic. A teenager whom we will call Mary was referred by the local juvenile authorities after a series of shoplifting offenses. She did not steal because she needed to: she was well provided for by her upper-middle-class parents, and most of the things she stole were either given to friends or discarded.

Why did she steal, then? Her father was a strict disciplinarian who was raised with frequent trips to the woodshed and no pats on the back. Mary was a typical teenager who tested the limits on occasion. She felt his punishments were unfair. For example, she was once grounded for a month after coming home 30 minutes late from a date. She resented such punishments and showed it by shirking her household responsibilities, such as doing dishes and providing child care for her siblings. The result, of course, was a vicious cycle. Her father reacted with more severe punishments, and Mary's behavior got worse and worse.

Mary was hurt and angered, but she was unable to confront her father directly. To get even, she instead set out to disobey the law so flagrantly that her behavior would come to the attention of the authorities. Her father was well respected in the community, and Mary knew he would be devastated if one of his children became known as a criminal. She was right—but she had hurt herself as well as her father, and she was depressed and confused at the time she entered therapy.

The vicious cycle was broken by working with both the father and Mary. Although her father loved her, he believed that children do not need to be praised for behaving "like any decent kid should." Therefore, he rarely counterbalanced his criticisms with praise and rewards for good behavior. When it was suggested that he make an effort to provide positive reinforcement, he reluctantly agreed—although he was not convinced it would do any good. It did, however. Over time, their relationship improved and so did Mary's behavior.

EXTINCTION AS AN ALTERNATIVE TO PUNISHMENT

Sometimes the most effective way to stop undesirable behavior is simply to withhold the rewards that are maintaining the behavior. This technique for modifying behavior can be applied only when one has control over the reinforcement contingencies. For instance, parents have a great deal of control over their young children's actions. When parents simply refuse to show interest in their children's mild misbehaviors (and at the same time provide plenty of reinforcement for good behavior), behavior problems often disappear.

Practical applications of this extinction technique are not limited to parent-child interaction. For example, consider the case of a woman known to the authors who invariably turned conversations toward her self-perceived inadequacies. Others would often respond by praising her good qualities and strengths. Although she seemed to have some genuine self-esteem concerns, it also seemed clear that her friends' reactions provided her with reinforcement. A friend chose to respond differently. Each time she put herself down, he would listen, offer no comments, and change the subject at the first opportunity. Conversely, whenever she had something positive to say about herself, he would provide effusive support, encouraging her to talk more. In time, she focused much more on the positive rather than the negative in conversations with this friend.

In all, it seems that punishment can be useful for modifying behavior under certain circumstances. When punishment is used, however, it should be applied in moderation, in combination with incentives for desirable behavior.

COGNITIVE INFLUENCES ON LEARNING

To this point, we have focused on associative learning through either classical or operant conditioning. These conditioning models do not account for all forms of learning, however, nor can we reduce all learning to conditioned associations.

Up until recently, my two children fought all the time. I tried everything to stop them, including telling them how bad it made Mommy feel, scolding them, threatening them, and occasionally punishing them. Nothing worked. Then I happened to attend a lecture on child psychology. The idea was presented that children fight mainly to get the attention of their mother. The suggested remedy was to ignore this behavior. This is easier said than done, especially when they are going after each other right at your feet. However, the lecturer had a solution. He suggested going into the bathroom when the fighting starts and locking the door.

It was hard at first. My children carried on their battles right outside the bathroom; sometimes their bodies would crash into the door. I turned the radio on loud, but I could still hear them. The big breakthrough came one day when I heard a knock on the door, turned down the radio, and heard my oldest say, "Mommy, you can come out now. We are all finished fighting!" That moment marked the beginning of better times around our house. (Authors' files)

Many contemporary psychologists (including learning theorists) have argued that the conditioning models provide too mechanistic an interpretation: there is more to learning than the mere association of events. As they were originally proposed by Pavlov, Thorndike, Skinner, and others, the conditioning theories do not take into account mental processes that cannot be observed, such as perception, thinking, and memory. Another theoretical perspective, **cognitive learning theory,** attempts to clarify the role these mental or cognitive processes play in learning.

As you might guess, cognitive theorists stress the individual's active participation in the learning process. They suggest that we learn by forming a *cognitive structure* in memory that preserves and organizes information pertaining to the key elements in a situation. Thus, instead of simply responding to a stimulus, as conditioning theories might suggest, we make conscious choices that allow us to adapt to our environment.

Cognitive learning theories did not become an important force in psychology until the late 1960s, but their roots go back many years. Two important early influences were Wolfgang Köhler's work with insight in chimpanzees and Edward Tolman's research on latent learning in rats.

INSIGHT

An **insight** is a sudden recognition of relationships that leads to the solution of a complex problem. Almost 60 years ago, German psychologist Wolfgang Köhler (1925) demonstrated the importance of insight in the problem-solving behavior of chimpanzees.

Köhler's research included two classic experiments. In one, the "box problem" (see Figure 6.13), chimps had to solve the problem of reaching a tantalizing bunch of bananas that hung just beyond their grasp. After some trial-and-error behavior, they suddenly arrived at the solution: they stacked the boxes on top of each other. In the second experiment, the "stick problem," the fruit was placed out of reach outside a chimp's cage. A short stick

FIGURE 6.13 KÖHLER'S "BOX PROBLEM"

In Köhler's "Box Problem," chimps had to solve the problem of reaching a tantalizing bunch of bananas that hung just beyond their grasp. After some trial-and-error behavior, they came up with the solution: If they stacked the boxes they would be able to reach the fruit.

(too short to reach the fruit) was well within the chimp's reach, while a longer stick lay outside the cage. Here is Köhler's description of how one of his chimps, Sultan, solved the problem:

> Sultan tries to reach the fruit with the smaller of the two sticks. Not succeeding, he tears at a piece of wire that projects from the netting of his cage, but that, too, is in vain. Then he gazes about him (there are always in the course of these tests some long pauses, during which the animals scrutinize the whole visible area). He suddenly picks up the little stick once more, goes up to the bars directly opposite to the long stick, scratches it towards him with the "auxiliary," seizes it, and goes with it to the point opposite the objective (the fruit), which he secures. From the moment that his eyes fall upon the long stick, his procedure forms one consecutive whole (Köhler, 1925, pp. 174–175).

The solution to both of these problems involved more than simple trial-and-error or associative learning. Rather, after pondering the problem for some period of time, the chimpanzees suddenly seemed to perceive the important relationships among the key elements.

We all know that such insight is typical of human learning. Who has not experienced the exhilaration of having the pieces of a problem suddenly come together in one insightful moment? As psychologists continue to study insight in human learning, we can expect to gain an expanded awareness of the role it plays in our daily lives.

LATENT LEARNING

A fundamental principle of operant conditioning theory is that reinforcement is essential to "stamp in" new behavior. However, over 50 years ago psychologist Edward Tolman and his associates demonstrated that rats will learn a maze even when they are not reinforced. He called this **latent** (or hidden) **learning** because it is not demonstrated by an immediately observable change in behavior at the time of learning. Such learning typically occurs in the absence of a reinforcer, and it is not demonstrated until an appropriate reinforcement appears.

In a classic latent-learning experiment, three groups of rats were run for 16 consecutive days in the complex maze shown in Figure 6.14. An error was recorded each time a rat entered a blind alley in the maze. Rats in one group, the reward group, received food when they reached the goal box at the end of the maze on each of the 16 days. A second group, the nonreward group, also explored the maze each day, but they did not receive food when they reached the end. Rats in a third group, the latent-learning group, received no reward for the first 10 days and then were rewarded for the remaining six days.

Over the first 10 days, rats in the reward group showed considerably more improvement than animals in either of the other groups. In fact, the animals in the nonreward group showed very little improvement in performance over the entire 16 days. However, after food was introduced on day 11 for rats in the latent-learning group, they immediately began to perform as well as animals in the reinforcement group. This clearly demonstrated that Tolman's rats were learning something about the maze even with no reinforcement (Tolman & Honzik, 1930).

This latent-learning experiment demonstrates the distinction between learning and performance, for learning can take place even when it is not demonstrated by performance. The experiment also poses a question: if no responses can be observed, what is being learned? Tolman answered this question by claiming that his rats were developing a **cognitive map,** or mental picture, of the maze in the absence of rewards. Later, when reinforcement was introduced, the map allowed the animals to reach a high level of performance immediately.

Tolman and his associates conducted a number of additional experiments that demonstrated how cognitive maps work in problem solving. For

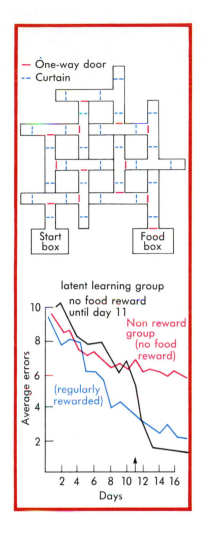

— One-way door
-- Curtain

Start box   Food box

latent learning group
no food reward
until day 11

Non reward group
(no food reward)

(regularly rewarded)

Average errors

2 4 6 8 10 12 14 16
Days

FIGURE 6.14   A CLASSIC LATENT-LEARNING EXPERIMENT: APPARATUS AND RESULTS

In this experiment three groups of rats were run for 16 consecutive days in the complex maze shown at the top of the illustration. You will note in the graphical portrayal of the results of the experiment that after reinforcement was introduced on day 11, rats in the latent-learning group performed as well as (even a little better than) those animals in the regularly reinforced reward group. (*Source:* Adapted from Tolman & Honzik, 1930)

example, once rats had learned how to get through a complex maze to reach food, obstructions were placed in their way and new routes introduced. Tolman suggested that these complications were quickly mastered because the rats were able to resort and rearrange the mental picture of the maze, and thereby find the new route with ease (Tolman et al., 1946).

Cognitive maps have become a very important concept in contemporary learning theory. Research suggests that a variety of organisms, including rats, chimpanzees, birds, and bees, use cognitive maps in adapting to their environments (Gould & Marler, 1987; Olton, 1979; Shettleworth, 1983; Whitam, 1977). Humans also tend to create mental composites of their environments that allow them to function more effectively (Evans, 1980).

A fascinating new application of cognitive map theory is the study of **behavioral geography** (Parfit, 1984). Geographers who specialize in this area ask people to indicate where they think important places and landmarks are located within a city. This helps them construct maps that are more closely aligned with the mental maps that people have of their city.

Research in this area has revealed a number of interesting findings. For example, most people think that undesirable locations in a city are smaller and farther away than they actually are, while places people like to visit are seen as closer and bigger than they actually are. (Now you know why your favorite restaurant, in that nice neighborhood across town, always seems closer than it actually is.)

The kinds of cognitive maps people construct also seem to reflect different life experiences. For instance, people in low-income groups typically think things are farther away than do their more affluent counterparts. This may be due, in part, to the fact that a more limited transportation budget makes it harder to get around: a bus can take much longer than a car. Thus, even locations that are fairly close as the crow flies are psychologically more distant.

COGNITIVE PROCESSES IN CONDITIONING: THE ROLE OF EXPECTANCY

We have presented cognitive learning as separate from the associative types of learning. This is the traditional way of viewing learning. Pavlov, for instance, stressed the importance of *temporal contiguity* (that is, closeness in time) of the CS and the UCS as being essential for classical conditioning, and most learning theorists after Pavlov continued to view classical conditioning as a relatively "automatic" form of learning that is "stamped in" through repeated pairings of the CS and the UCS.

Recent evidence has caused some psychologists to question this view, however. According to their interpretation, cognitive processes are involved even in classical conditioning.

This is what they think happens during classical conditioning: First, the learner observes that the CS and UCS typically occur together, and stores this information in memory. Later, when the CS appears by itself, the learner retrieves the information from memory and makes the conditioned response in anticipation that the UCS will occur. In other words, what is learned in classical conditioning is not a mere contiguity between the CS and UCS, but rather an *expectancy* that the UCS will follow the CS. From this perspective, then, it appears that the CS and UCS become associated "not simply because they occur contiguously in time, but rather because the CS provides information about the UCS" (Rescorla, 1987, p. 121).

A number of experiments support this view. In one study, two groups of rats were exposed to an equal number of pairings of a tone (CS) and a shock (UCS). However, one group also received an equal number of shocks that were not accompanied by a tone. This caused the predictive relationship between the CS and the UCS to be different in these two groups. Conditioning was quite rapid in the group where shocks were always paired with the tone, whereas conditioning did not occur in the other group (Rescorla, 1968). This experiment suggests that the most important factor in classical conditioning may not be how many CS–UCS pairings there are, but rather how predictably the UCS follows the CS.

Studies of a phenomenon known as *blocking* also support the cognitive interpretation. In such experiments, subjects are exposed to repeated CS–UCS pairings (for example, a light with a shock). Later, after conditioning is established, a second stimulus (such as a tone) is added to the original CS so that both stimuli now occur prior to the UCS. According to Pavlov, the second stimulus should quickly become conditioned since it is regularly paired with the UCS. However, this does not occur (Halas & Eberhardt, 1987; Kamin, 1969). Apparently, the previous conditioning of the response to the light somehow interferes with or "blocks" the tone from becoming an effective CS.

Cognitive theorists refer to the expectancy concept to explain these results. They argue that since the original stimulus already predicts the occurrence of the UCS, the new stimulus is irrelevant because it provides no new information that subjects can use to predict the UCS.

Today, more and more learning theorists believe that the predictability of the relationship between the CS and UCS is probably more important than either the timing or the frequency of pairings (Fantino & Logan, 1979; Fuhrer & Baer, 1965). We now know that CS–UCS pairings, while necessary for classical conditioning, are not sufficient by themselves to ensure that learning will occur. Unless the CS also can be predicted, conditioning will not occur.

Cognitive factors are important in operant as well as classical conditioning. Although the operant model emphasizes the consequences of behavior, those consequences do not automatically strengthen or weaken responses. Rather, they provide the learner with important information about the probable consequences of a given behavior under certain circumstances (Colwill & Rescorla, 1986; Rescorla, 1987). Cognitive theorists view individuals as information-processing systems that store this relevant information about consequences. Later, when confronted by similar circumstances, the learner retrieves this information from memory, and acts accordingly. Thus, from the cognitive perspective, operant behavior is guided by expectations of probable outcomes (Bolles, 1979; Greeno, 1980).

The cognitive theorists have made a good case for the argument that the events that occur in classical and operant conditioning do not automatically "stamp in" behavior. Instead, they provide relevant information that helps individuals to establish expectancies—and it is these expectancies that form the basis for subsequent behavior.

OBSERVATIONAL LEARNING

While cognitive factors play a role in both classical and operant conditioning, there is another kind of cognitive learning that does not involve physical responses or reinforcers. Sometimes we learn by watching others, a process called **observational learning.**

One of the major findings of observational-learning research is that children tend to behave in a manner similar to their parents, both during their childhood and later on in life. This is why child abuse and other maladaptive behaviors are often passed on from one generation to the next—just as are warm, nurturant behaviors.

There are strong cognitive components in learning by observation. People observe the behaviors of others, then store cognitive images of these acts in memory, where they remain until the right influence triggers the individual to enact that behavior.

The role of observation and imitation in learning is explained in **social learning theory,** and Albert Bandura (1977, 1986) of Stanford University is probably the leading proponent of this theory. Bandura and his colleagues have peformed a number of studies that demonstrate the importance of observational learning in our lives. In one widely cited experiment, children observed adults beating on a five-foot inflated "BoBo" doll and were then placed in a similar situation. The researchers found that children who had observed this aggressive behavior were more likely to act aggressively when placed in the same situation than did children in control conditions who had observed a quiet model (Bandura et al., 1963). These results would not have been predicted by classical or operant conditioning theory since neither responses nor reinforcement played a role in the learning process.

Social learning theorists use the term *models* to describe the people whose behaviors we observe and often imitate. These models can range from parents (usually the most influential models in our lives) to people we see on television or in movies. Humans have a great capacity to store mental images. In this fashion we learn from the examples of others.

Some of the behaviors we observe become part of our own behavioral repertoire, but we also observe many responses that we never imitate. (For instance, watching another diner chew gum at an elegant restaurant may cause you to resolve never to do such a thing.) Our brains process all these stored memories of previously observed behaviors, selecting out those that seem appropriate in a given situation. Once we allow an observed behavior to become part of our own response system, it becomes subject to the rules

Being able to learn by watching (modeling) allows us to profit from the experience of others.

of reinforcement discussed earlier. In this fashion, imitative behaviors become either stamped in or stamped out.

Bandura (1977) has identified four key steps in observational learning. The first is simply having our attention drawn to a modeled behavior. Second, we store a mental image of the behavior in our memories. Third, a specific type of situation triggers us to convert the remembered observation into actions. Finally, if our actions are reinforced, we add the behavior to our repertoire of responses.

Learning by observation, or *modeling*, can exert a powerful influence on our lives. Being able to learn by watching is extremely useful. Can you imagine how tedious it would be to acquire all our behaviors by trial and error? Modeling allows us to profit from the experiences of others.

In some circumstances, modeling may be even more effective than operant conditioning in shaping our behavior. For example, in one study researchers tried a variety of strategies to increase the sociability of nursery-school children who normally kept to themselves. The most effective strategy turned out to be to have these youngsters watch a film showing sociable children. It was even a faster agent of social change than a shaping process that involved praising and paying attention to children when they behaved sociably (O'Connor, 1972).

Cognitive learning, then, plays a role in a number of ways, through insight, through the formation of cognitive maps or structures that play a role in latent learning, through the establishment of expectancies, and through observational learning. Most importantly, cognitive learning does not operate separately from the classical and operant conditioning models discussed earlier in this chapter. Instead, all three forms of learning interact in a complex fashion.

SUMMARY

LEARNING DEFINED

1. Learning may be defined as a relatively enduring change in potential behavior that results from experience.
2. Associative learning, the process by which we make a connection or association between two events, may take place in two primary ways: through classical conditioning and through operant conditioning. Classical conditioning involves learning a connection between two stimuli. In operant conditioning, people or other animals learn to associate their own behavior with its consequences.

CLASSICAL CONDITIONING

3. The four key elements in classical conditioning are the unconditioned stimulus (UCS), the unconditioned response (UCR), the conditioned stimulus (CS), and the conditioned response (CR). In the conditioning model the learner associates a previously neutral stimulus (CS) with a stimulus (UCS) that automatically elicits an unlearned response (UCR). As a result of this learning by association the CS acquires the capacity also to elicit a response (CR) that is similar to but not identical to the UCR.
4. Factors which facilitate the acquisition of a classically conditioned response include a CS that is clearly different from other stimuli, frequent pairings of the CS and the UCS, and the order and timing with which the CS is paired with the UCS.
5. The rate of acquisition in classical conditioning is generally most rapid when the CS is presented before the

UCS appears and is continued until the learner responds to the UCS, a process called delayed conditioning.
6. Extinction, or cessation of the CR, occurs in classical conditioning when the CS is repeatedly presented alone, without the UCS.
7. A CR will sometimes reappear spontaneously after extinction, a process called spontaneous recovery.
8. When a response has been conditioned to a particular stimulus, other stimuli may also produce the same response. This principle is called generalization.
9. Early in the conditioning process, a learner may respond to a variety of similar stimuli (generalization). However, with time he or she learns that only one of the stimuli, the CS, is consistently associated with the UCS. This process of learning to make distinctions between the CS and similar but not identical stimuli is called discrimination.
10. A classical conditioning variation in which a neutral stimulus becomes a CS through association with an already established CS is referred to as higher order conditioning.

OPERANT CONDITIONING

11. In operant conditioning humans and other animals learn to operate on the environment in a manner that results in satisfying or reinforcing consequences.
12. A discriminative stimulus in the operant model of conditioning serves to control the response by signaling the availability of reinforcement.
13. Reinforcement is defined as any event that increases the probability that a response will occur.

14. A positive reinforcer is any stimulus presented following a response that increases the probability of the response. A negative reinforcer is a stimulus that increases the probability of a response through its removal when the desired response is made.

15. In escape conditioning a human or other animal learns to produce a response that will allow termination or escape from an aversive stimulus (negative reinforcer). In avoidance conditioning the individual learns to respond to a signal and emit an appropriate avoidance response, thereby averting any exposure to the aversive stimulus.

16. A primary reinforcer is a stimulus that satisfies a biologically based drive or need. Secondary reinforcers are stimuli that acquire reinforcing properties through association with primary reinforcers.

17. It has been suggested that a reinforcement hierarchy exists for any given human or other animal. Reinforcers at the top of the list are those behaviors most likely to be engaged in, given the opportunity. According to the Premack principle any behavior in the hierarchy may reinforce any of the behaviors listed below it and may itself be reinforced by any behaviors listed above it.

18. A continuous reinforcement schedule exists when behavior is reinforced every time it occurs. A partial reinforcement schedule exists when behavior is reinforced only part of the time.

19. Behaviors that are acquired on partial instead of continuous schedules of reinforcement are slower to be established, but they are remarkably more persistent when no reinforcement is provided.

20. Four varieties of partial reinforcement schedules include those based on a percentage of responses that are reinforced (fixed ratio and variable ratio) or passage of a certain amount of time before a response is reinforced (fixed interval and variable interval).

21. Methods used to encourage the occurrence of an initial desired operant response include physical guidance, shaping, modeling, verbal instruction, and increasing motivation.

TWO-PROCESS LEARNING

22. Some learning situations combine both classical and operant conditioning in what is called two-process learning.

23. Many human phobias are by-products of two-process learning. First an individual acquires a fear of a neutral stimulus (classical conditioning), and then acts to reduce or eliminate this fear by learning to avoid the frightening stimulus (operant avoidance conditioning).

PUNISHMENT: IS IT EFFECTIVE?

24. Punishment can be defined as a consequence that decreases the probability that a given behavior will occur.

25. The effectiveness of punishment in producing a desired change in behavior is often compromised by a number of limitations and negative side effects, including the fact that it merely suppresses rather than extinguishes unwanted behavior, that it may produce undesirable emotional side effects (fear, hostility, anger, hatred, anxiety), and that individuals who are subjected to physical punishment may learn to model or imitate these aggressive acts.

26. Principles which may improve the effectiveness of punishment include immediacy, consistency, moderation, and combining it with positive reinforcement (always rewarding acceptable alternatives to the punished behavior).

COGNITIVE INFLUENCES ON LEARNING

27. Cognitive learning theory attempts to clarify the role that mental or cognitive processes, such as perception, thinking, and memory, play in learning.

28. Cognitive theorists suggest that we learn by forming a cognitive structure in memory that preserves and organizes information relevant to a given situation.

29. The roots of cognitive learning theories go back many years to studies of insight in chimpanzees and latent learning in rats.

30. Insight is a sudden recognition of relationships that leads to the solution of a complex problem. Latent learning refers to learning that is not demonstrated by an immediately observable change in behavior at the time of learning.

31. Cognitive theorists suggest that what is learned in classical conditioning is not a mere contiguity between the CS and UCS, but rather an expectancy that the UCS will follow the CS.

32. From the cognitive perspective, operant behavior is also viewed as being guided by expectations of probable outcomes.

33. Cognitive theorists believe that there are strong cognitive components in learning by watching and imitating others, a process called observational learning.

34. The role of observation and imitation in learning is explained in social learning theory. In some circumstances, learning by observation, or modeling, may be even more effective than operant conditioning in shaping our behavior.

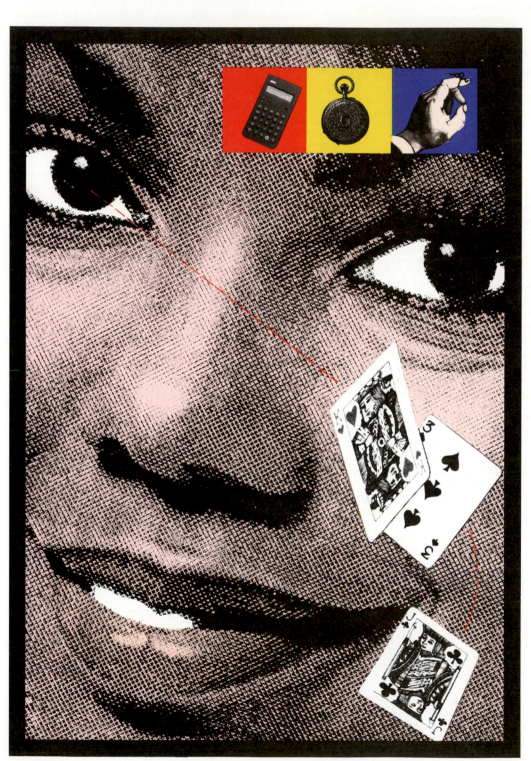

7 Memory

Bob was sitting outdoors watching the sun slowly disappear. When only a few golden streaks could be seen on the horizon, he saw something that transported him back 30 years. There, walking with an odd, shuffling gait, was his father. Of course, it wasn't—he had sat dejected through his funeral several years ago—but the connection was powerful, and for a moment he was a boy of 14 again, watching his father return from an evening hike. The same night sky, the chill of fall in the air, the odd gait. He almost expected his father to call out to him. He could actually hear his father's words: "Put another log on the fire; it's cold in these hills!"

The hiker continued on his way, heading toward some other warm house. It was a bittersweet experience. For a few moments Bob's father was with him again. The passing stranger's resemblance triggered a flood of memories. For several minutes he sat and recalled some of the experiences they had shared. He could no longer talk to him, but Bob still carried his father with him in memories that, on occasions like this, he cherished.

It has been said that memory is the most important function of our brains. Can you imagine what life might be like if you could not remember your experiences? Without memory you would have no history and thus no identity. You would have no skills, for all knowledge is based on memory. All but the most primitive human responses require memory. Perceiving, thinking, learning, feeling—they all depend on our ability to store information that we processs each day.

Psychologists have studied memory for years, but in many ways it is still a mystery. What changes take place in our brains that allow us to store memories, sometimes for a lifetime? By what process do we retrieve these memories from a brain cluttered with information? We shall explore questions like these in this chapter. Although we do not have all the answers, we will see that there is much that we do understand about what we remember, how we remember, why we forget, and even what we can do to improve memory. We begin by describing what memory is.

WHAT IS MEMORY?

The term **memory** has a dual meaning. When someone asks you how good your memory is, he or she is probably referring to your efficiency at storing new information for later recall. In this sense, memory refers to the *process or processes whereby we store and preserve newly acquired information for later recall.*

Many of us would feel as though we had no identity if we did not have the ability to remember. Memories of important events are often cherished over a lifetime.

However, we also use the term memory to describe *recall for a specific experience or the total collection of remembered experiences stored in our brains.* In other words, the term "memory" describes either putting information into storage or pulling it back into conscious awareness.

AN INFORMATION-PROCESSING PERSPECTIVE

Psychologists once viewed humans and other animals as organisms that merely experience and respond to stimuli. They did not concern themselves with the mental events that govern complex processes such as learning and memory.

This has changed in the last two decades. Most psychologists have come to view the human brain as an information-processing system (Houston, 1986). That is, information is not simply stored in the brain and then later retrieved; instead, it is shaped or modified in some way to fit the brain's storage system. In other words, people actively participate in the assimilation of their experiences. For example, if we introduced you to a man named Harry who had prominent ears, you could increase your probability of remembering his name by associating the name with the ears. (You might form a mental image of long black hairs growing out of his ears.) This kind of information-processing mental event must be included in any explanation of how we remember, learn, and think.

The information-processing model is particularly helpful in conceptualizing memory processes. In the following pages we examine the various stages that are part of the memory process.

THREE MEMORY PROCESSES

You are sitting quietly at your desk, studying for an exam. From somewhere in your apartment complex you hear a muffled scream. This is not particularly unusual; you live in a big housing unit, and you often hear strange noises, including an occasional scream or loud shouting. Nevertheless, your attention is diverted. A few moments later, you hear an engine start in the parking lot below. You hear the sound of an engine being revved, then of a car speeding through the parking lot. You rush to the window, and catch a fleeting glimpse of a low-slung red sports car. Could there be a connection between the scream and this vehicle? Maybe you will end up as a key witness in a murder trial. Your imagination runs rampant for a minute or two, then you return to your books.

Will you accurately remember what you have just seen and heard if a violent incident *did* occur on this day? The chances are very good that you will remember something. The accuracy of your recall will depend on three separate processes (Murdock, 1974). First, you had to *encode* or translate incoming information into a neural code that your brain could process. Second, you put the encoded information into *storage* so that it could be retained over time. Finally, you must be able to find and recover this stored information when you need it later on, through the process of *retrieval*.

Encoding Encoding involves first perceiving some particular stimulus event, like the sound of a scream or a revving engine, and then translating or coding the information so that it can be more easily stored. This process involves categorizing or organizing information in some meaningful way. Is the information a sight, a sound, a smell, some tactile sensation? You would classify the scream as a sound and further categorize it as a signal of distress. When we encode material, we try to establish associations or links between the new facts and what we already know. For instance, you code the fact that the car has a manual transmission because you already know that glitches in the sound of acceleration indicate shift points. Memories that we can connect to information already stored in our brains are much easier to retain.

Storage   **Storage** is the process by which encoded material is retained over time in our brains' "memory banks." Exactly how this happens is the topic of some of the most important current research in psychology. We know that memories do not just float around in our brains waiting to be retrieved: some changes must take place in the brain to allow memories to be stored for later use. We will investigate this topic in some detail later in this chapter.

The efficiency of the storage process is greatly influenced by the effort we put into encoding or orgainizing what we file away. Suppose your roommate asks you to order a pizza by calling 234-4454. This number is easy to remember because it is organized in two clusters; after one or two rehearsals, you have it memorized—at least for a few moments. If your roommate asks you to call and check on the order ten minutes later, however, you will probably need to ask her to repeat the number.

Now, assume that you meet someone interesting at a party. That person gives you a telephone number, 245-5565, and says "call me sometime." Of course, nobody seems to have a pen at critical moments like this. Chances are you will choose a much more effective method for encoding and storing this number than the one for Joe's Pizzeria. Perhaps you will note the logical progression of 10 units in the sequence 45, 55, 65, and use this as a meaningful way to code and store this information. You are likely to remember this number for a longer period.

Retrieval   The final step in the process of remembering is **retrieval.** If you properly encoded and stored your new friend's telephone number, or information about the "getaway car" in the earlier example, you will be able to retrieve this information from memory at a later time. Generally speaking, the more effort we put into preparing information for storage, the more efficiently we can retrieve it.

A THREE-SYSTEM MODEL OF MEMORY

Psychologists distinguish between memories that stay with us, such as an important phone number, and those that are quickly lost. In fact, most psychologists today believe that there are three distinct memory systems that allow us to process, store, and recall information. This perspective, articulated by Richard Atkinson and Richard Shiffrin (1968, 1971), suggests that information that first comes to us through our senses is stored for a fleeting moment within **sensory memory (SM).** Because of the highly transitory nature of this memory system, we usually are not consciously aware of it, nor do we actively organize or encode this information. The function of this memory system seems to be to hold or preserve impressions of sensory stimuli just long enough for important aspects of this information to be transferred to the next system, short-term memory.

Short-term memory (STM) comprises our immediate recollection of stimuli that we have just perceived. The amount of information that this memory system can store is much more limited than that of sensory memory. Unless we repeatedly reinstate the information transferred to short-term memory, it will probably be retained only momentarily, perhaps for no more than about 20 seconds (Brown, 1958; Muter, 1980; Peterson & Peterson, 1959). For example, you have probably forgotten the number of Joe's Pizzeria by now. Unless you repeatedly rehearse the phone number, it is likely to fade from memory very quickly.

Information that we transfer from short-term memory into **long-term memory (LTM)** may remain for minutes, hours, days, or perhaps even a lifetime. When we retrieve information from long-term memory, it passes through short-term memory, which acts as a port of both entry and exit for long-term memories. (Figure 7.1 presents a theoretical model of how information flows into and among these three memory systems.)

When I mix the ingredients for a recipe, after having just read the instructions in a cookbook, it doesn't seem like I am using my memory. These instructions are actively in my mind. I have just read them. They don't go away. I haven't needed to remember them because they never left my thoughts. Now, if I can repeat the recipe tomorrow without looking up the instructions in my cookbook, *that's* memory. (*Authors' files*)

FIGURE 7.1 A THEORETICAL MODEL OF THE HUMAN MEMORY SYSTEM

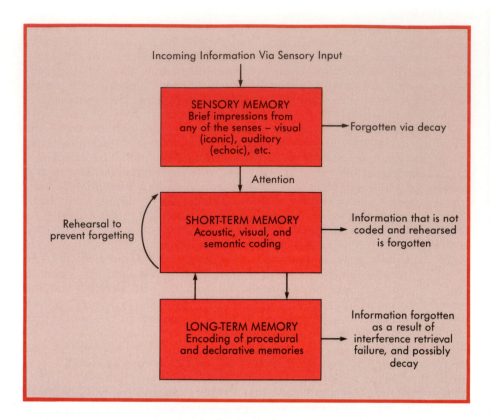

According to this model, human memory is comprised of three systems. Information, in the form of sensory inputs, is first fleetingly stored within sensory memory. If we attend to these brief impressions, they are transferred into short-term memory. Otherwise, they are forgotten within a second or two. Unless we pay special attention to the information transferred to short-term memory, or repeatedly reinstate it through rehearsal, it will probably fade within 20 seconds or less. Things we remember for longer than 20 seconds enter long-term memory, where they are encoded and stored. When we retrieve information from long-term memory, it passes through short-term memory, which acts as both a port of entry and exit from long-term memory. Long-term memories may last indefinitely. However, material that is poorly encoded or subjected to interference may be quickly forgotten.

Long-term memory is what most people mean when they talk about memory. For some people, the concept of short-term memory does not correspond to their preconceived notion of what memory is. Information that is immediately put to use, like a phone number or instructions given in exercise class, are not in memory, they say. Instead, such information is simply "in my mind." Psychologists would disagree with this contention. What else are thoughts "in your mind" *but* memories? Any time we can recall information, no matter how recently it passed through our sensory/perceptual systems, we are tapping memory. Let us look more closely at how these three memory systems work.

SENSORY MEMORY

Sensory memories, sometimes called *sensory registers*, are brief impressions from any of our senses. We are surrounded by sights, sounds, smells, tactile sensations, and countless other stimuli. When we first receive a particular stimulus, it is held momentarily in sensory memory. These fleeting impressions appear to be largely accurate reproductions of the original sensory inputs. For example, when you glance out the window, for a fraction of a second your brain absorbs the entire visual panorama with the varied colors, shapes, and patterns. A similar process occurs when you walk into a

While we play our weekly card game and take note of which cards have been played and by whom, we are exercising our short-term memory skills. Remembering how to play the game itself illustrates long-term memory.

cafeteria: your nose captures a variety of odors and you hear a different set of noises from those you heard on the street.

Unless they are successfully transferred to short-term memory, these sensory impressions disappear within a second or two. That is because the only coding that takes place in sensory memory appears to be the physiological processes of our sensory systems—for instance, the translation of sound and light waves to messages that are transmitted to our brains (see Chapter 4). Sensory memory is a very primitive type of memory storage in which no organization or categorization of information takes place.

There are as many kinds of sensory memories as there are different sense modalities. However, research psychologists interested in sensory memory have concentrated primarily on visual and auditory memories.

Iconic (Visual) Memory Visual sensory memory is called **iconic memory** (*icon* means "image") (Neisser, 1967). It includes images of what we see. For many years, researchers thought that visual memory held only limited information. They based this assumption on evidence from research that had measured the storage capacity of visual sensory memory. Such studies would flash a grid of letters or numbers such as those shown here on a screen for a fraction of a second:

H	C	N	M
P	O	X	U
S	J	T	B

Subjects would then be asked to recall as many of the items as possible. When this *whole report procedure* was used, most people could remember only four or five items, no matter how many were shown in the grid.

One researcher, George Sperling (1960), was convinced that subjects in these studies actually registered more than just four or five items; the problem was simply that they forgot the rest while they were reporting the first few items. To test his theory, he designed a new research strategy called the *partial report procedure.* Subjects were told that they would view a grid for 1/20 of a second, then hear a tone. They would only have to report part of what they had seen. If they heard a high-pitched tone, they were to report only on the top row of four letters. A medium-pitched tone meant they were to report on the middle row, and a low tone meant the bottom row. The point at which a subject heard the tone varied from immediately after the letters disappeared to a maximum delay of one second. Figure 7.2 illustrates this partial report procedure.

As Figure 7.3 shows, subjects' recall was best when the tone sounded immediately after the image disappeared—an average of 3.3 letters out of 4. Since subjects did not know what row they would be reporting until the image had disappeared, Sperling reasoned that they must have had 9 or 10

FIRST PERSON 7.2

Some years ago my children and I were camping out in western Wyoming. One night our sleep was interrupted by a severe storm. I was looking out a window flap when a flash of lightning illuminated the surrounding area. My brain took an instant "flash photo" of the entire scene.

Only after darkness had returned did I recognize a critical element in what I had seen. A small creek, located a short distance from our tent, was flowing over its banks, and its waters were dangerously close to our tent. Had that instantaneous image not stayed in my mind, I would never have recognized our danger (which fortunately became no worse, as the rain soon abated). (*Authors' files*)

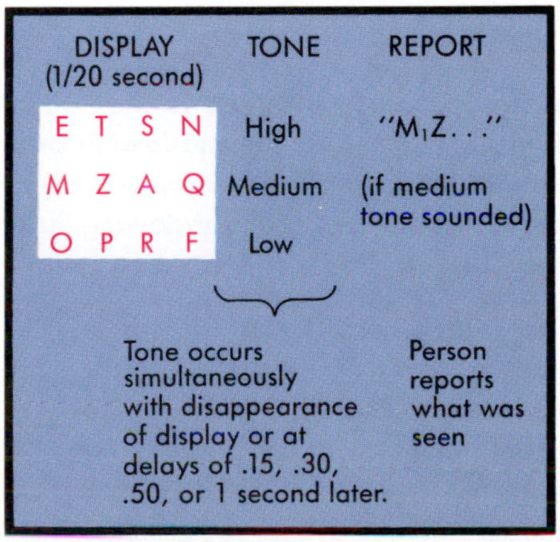
DISPLAY (1/20 second)
TONE
REPORT
E T S N
M Z A Q
O P R F
High
Medium
Low
"M, Z. . ."
(if medium tone sounded)
Tone occurs simultaneously with disappearance of display or at delays of .15, .30, .50, or 1 second later.
Person reports what was seen

FIGURE 7.2 SPERLING'S PARTIAL REPORT PROCEDURE

Subjects viewed a grid of 12 letters for 1/20 of a second, then heard a tone after a short delay that varied from a fraction of a second to a second. If a high tone sounded, subjects were instructed to report the top row of the grid; a medium tone meant they reported the middle row, and so forth.

FIGURE 7.3 RESULTS OF SPERL-ING'S PARTIAL REPORT PROCE-DURE

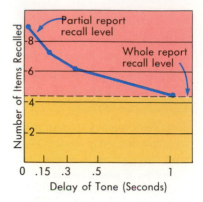

The solid line represents average number of items recalled (for four subjects) by the partial report method at varying intervals between the presentation of the memory set and the sound of the tone; the dotted line represents the average recall level when the whole report procedure was used. (*Source:* Adapted from Sperling, 1960)

items available for immediate recall (3 rows times 3.3 per row)—roughly twice the earlier estimates of what we can register in iconic memory. The later the tone sounded, the less subjects remembered.

Sperling concluded that his subjects were actually reading the letters from a brief afterimage, or iconic reproduction, of the original stimulus pattern. This image fades quite rapidly. From Sperling's research as well as other evidence, we know that an image stored in iconic memory generally fades from usefulness within approximately 0.3 seconds (Irwin & Yeomans, 1986; Yeomans & Irwin, 1985).

Echoic (Auditory) Memory   You may have noticed an auditory afterimage or echo when you have turned off the radio and the voice of a commentator seems to linger momentarily. This auditory sensory memory is called **echoic memory:** After the physical sound stimulus ceases, an auditory afterimage or echo persists for a second or two. Like iconic memory, echoic memory functions to hold information temporarily for possible further processing.

We are constantly bombarded by sounds. Most of these "go in one ear and out the other," which is to say that only a few selected sounds of importance are passed to our short- and long-term memory systems. It appears that we use echoic memory to analyze all incoming sounds quickly and to determine which (if any) are important enough to be transferred to short-term memory.

For example, suppose you are sitting alone in a crowded airport. Every sound that is loud enough to be heard—talking voices, laughter, loudspeaker announcements, shuffling feet, background music—is temporarily stored in echoic memory. These unimportant auditory messages register fleetingly in your sensory memory system, but they are unlikely to be transferred into short-term memory. However, at some level you are aware of these sounds and they are being processed. If you find something important among these inputs—for example, if you hear your name in a loudspeaker message—your attention is captured and you transfer this information into short-term memory.

Are the auditory messages that we do not pay attention to actually lost, or is there an afterimage similar to the iconic afterimage? To find out, a number of researchers, most notably Anne Treisman (1960, 1964), have used a technique called *shadowing*. In this procedure, a subject wears headphones and is exposed simultaneously to two different recordings, one presented to each ear. To ensure that the subject will pay attention to only one of the two messages, he or she is asked to "shadow" or repeat the message presented to one ear. This task is extremely demanding, so much so that subjects typically repeat the words in a dull monotone. Figure 7.4 demonstrates the experimental procedure. When questioned at the end of a shadowing task, subjects are unable to provide any information about the message they did not repeat.

FINDING OUT WHAT HAPPENS DURING SHADOWING

Do you think that subjects' inability to repeat material presented to the "other ear" means that this channel of sensory input is blocked by the shadowing process? Or, do words that enter through the unattended ear register momentarily in echoic memory? If you were conducting an experiment that used shadowing, how would you answer these questions? See if you can devise a procedure before reading on.

To see if the information that subjects did not repeat was really lost, Treisman added one additional task to her experiment. Although subjects had been instructed to concentrate all their attention on the shadowing task, they were also told that when the recordings stopped and they heard a signal, they were to try to recall anything they could of the unattended

College students often experience . . .

Right ear

Left ear

the car with the . . .

Um, college students often . . .

FIGURE 7.4   THE SHADOWING TASK

The subject is exposed to two messages, one in each ear. The message in the right ear must be repeated as soon as the subject hears it. Since all attention is focused on the right ear, the message in the left ear is ignored. Is it completely lost?

message. This additional task provided interesting results: if the subjects' attention was switched soon enough, it was possible for them to "rehear" some of the last words of the other message in the form of an echo.

Research indicates that auditory sensory memory for language stimuli can last up to two seconds. This is considerably longer than the estimated 0.3-second capacity of iconic memory. This difference makes sense, however, when we consider the nature of the sensory messages received by our eyes and ears. When we look around us, we can almost always look back if we fail to process something important through our iconic memories. In contrast, if we miss something in an auditory message, we cannot "listen back." Therefore, there seems to be a good functional reason why auditory afterimages should last longer than visual afterimages.

We also seem to recall information better if we hear it rather than see it (Crowder, 1970, 1976). This phenomenon, known as the *modality effect*, probably reflects the fact that an echo lasts longer than a visual image in sensory memory. Have you ever noticed that you can remember a telephone number or items on a grocery list better if you read them aloud? Auditory afterimages give us more time to transfer this important information over into short-term memory for further organizing and processing.

SHORT-TERM MEMORY

Short-term memory provides a temporary resting place for information from sensory memory that we have attended to. It is an intermediate memory process sandwiched between sensory memory and long-term memory. STM is often referred to as our working memory, because it is the memory system within which we actively process information, both as we transfer it from sensory memory and as we retrieve it from long-term storage.

As its name suggests, short-term memory has a short duration. If you look up a term in this book's index and see that it is included on pages 342 and 563, you will probably find that after searching page 342, you must check again for the second page reference. Unless we make active efforts to hold information in consciousness, it fades from STM in about 20 seconds or less. However, we can retain information in our working memories for as

Many of us routinely chunk telephone numbers by grouping the first three digits together and treating the last four as two chunks.

long as we wish by active *rehearsal*—for example, by repeating the index references over and over.

Short-term memory has a limited capacity. You can test your STM capacity by reading the following list of numbers once, covering them, and writing down as many as you can in the order in which they appear.

9 2 5 7 6 1 3 7 8 4 5 6

If your short-term memory is like most people's, you probably recalled about seven of these numbers. The capacity of STM is about seven items or chunks of unrelated information if the information has been encoded on the basis of how it sounds (acoustic coding), and about three chunks when items are encoded based on what they look like or what they mean (visual and semantic coding) (Miller, 1956; Yu et al., 1985; Zhang & Simon, 1985). Note that this STM capacity does not necessarily refer to seven numbers or letters. It refers to seven pieces of information—which can be letters, words, or even meaningful sentences. The term **chunk** describes a meaningful unit of short-term memory. One important way that we can increase the limited capacity of our STM systems is through chunking.

Chunking   **Chunking** is the process of grouping items into longer, meaningful units to make them easier to remember (Frankish, 1985; Miller, 1956). For example, the sequence 1, 9, 4, 1 consists of four numbers which could be treated as four chunks. This would leave room for about three more chunks in STM. However, we could combine these four digits into one meaningful chunk—1941, the year America went to war with Japan. This would leave space for at least five or six more chunks of information.

You were probably unable to recall all 12 of the numbers in the previous short-term memory test. However, you might find it relatively easy to recall all 12 numbers by grouping or chunking them into four groups, a process that yields four individual numbers (925, 761, 378, 456). Many of us routinely chunk telephone numbers by grouping the first three digits together, and then treating the final four as separate chunks, thereby reducing the original seven numbers into five chunks. We may further improve our retention of the last four digits by chunking them by twos—for example, remembering 39 and 15 instead of 3-9-1-5.

We can also organize or chunk information held in STM according to its personal meaning, or we can match it with codes already stored in long-term memory. For instance, try reading once through the following list of letters and then recalling as many as possible from memory.

C P A N O W M A D D N B A

If you tried to recall these items as 13 separate letters, you probably remembered no more than seven. However, if you coded them into four well-known chunks (CPA, NOW, MADD, NBA), you would have no trouble recalling them in proper sequence.

How Information Is Coded in Short-Term Memory   Most of the information that is placed in STM is held there in an acoustic form, according to how it sounds. This seems to be true even when the information comes through our visual rather than our auditory sense. For example, suppose you are walking along the edge of a wheat field with a friend, and suddenly a pheasant explodes out of the grass nearby. Your immediate recall of the name of the species of bird you just saw would probably be coded in your STM by the sound of the word pheasant, not by a visual image of the bird in flight.

We know that *acoustic coding* is important from a number of studies. In one (Conrad, 1964), subjects were asked to recall lists of letters immediately after they saw them. When errors occurred, they were likely to involve confusions of letters that sounded alike (for example, confusing T for

B or D for E) rather than those that looked alike, such as F and E or D and O.

Not all of the encoding we do in STM is acoustic. If it were, profoundly deaf people would be unable to store information in short-term memory. It appears that people with this handicap rely heavily on *visual coding,* in which information is identified and stored as visual images of letters, words, shapes, and so on. For instance, the pheasant that flew out of the field a minute ago would be coded by its image or perhaps by the way its name appears in writing. Hearing-impaired people also use *semantic coding,* in which objects they see are categorized by class. For example, the pheasant is a bird, its size is about the same as a chicken's, and so forth. We know this from research that shows that the STM-recall errors of hearing-impaired people tend to result from confusing items that are similar in appearance or meaning rather than items that sound similar (Frumkin & Anisfeld, 1977). People who are not hearing-impaired may also use visual or semantic encoding at times (Conrad, 1972).

LONG-TERM MEMORY

The third memory system, long-term memory, is like a giant storehouse that never quite fills up with the facts, feelings, images, skills, and attitudes that we keep on accumulating. Long-term memory allows us to do more than simply store information from past experiences. Faced with new problems and situations, we can pull chunks of information from LTM into short-term memory to help us deal with and process new information.

For example, suppose you are walking down the street and see a person lying prone next to a downed power line. In an instant, you would search your LTM to determine the significance of the scene. You have heard enough about the effects of high-voltage shock to guess that the person may be in cardiac arrest. Suppose this is confirmed by a pulse check. What next? If the person is lucky, your LTM also contains a knowledge of cardiopulmonary resuscitation (CPR). You transfer this information into short-term memory and administer CPR. Then you search your long-term memory for information you can use to keep the victim from going into post-trauma shock. This new information would displace the CPR information in short-term memory, which you no longer need. It is this constant, ongoing interaction between short- and long-term memory that allows us to reason, solve problems, follow schedules, see relationships between events, ride a bike, and so forth.

Two Types of Long-Term Memory   The abilities just mentioned are diverse, including not only what we can do but what we know. Most psychologists categorize long-term memories along these lines, as either procedural or declarative memories.

Procedural memories are memories for how to perform skills. These memories can be highly complex. Suppose you enter a local golf competition. Before teeing off, a friend provides you with some specific information about course conditions. As you play your round, you draw upon a storehouse of knowledge about how to adjust your strokes to accommodate all these factors: the proper follow-through on a sand shot, how much muscle to put behind a stroke on wet turf, how to adjust for wind at the third hole, and so forth. All of these actions are specific skills acquired through practice and reinforcement, and they constitute procedural memory.

Not all memory, of course, is based on recalling how to execute specific skills or procedures. For instance, your memory of what you have learned so far in psychology class is based primarily on lecture notes and your readings in this book. Recall of specific facts such as these is made possible by **declarative memory.**

Procedural memories are often hard to acquire. It may have taken months to perfect your golf swing. Once established, however, these skill

The ongoing interaction between long-term and short-term memory enables this firefighter to deal effectively with the present crisis.

Riding a bike is an example of procedural memory and draws upon skills acquired through practice and reinforcement. (Am I balanced? How do I adjust for a wet or bumpy road? What signals do I use to warn motorists of my intentions?, etc.)

memories can be remarkably persistent. Facts stored in declarative memory are often established more quickly, but they are much more susceptible to forgetting.

Another difference between procedural and declarative memory seems to be the location of their storage areas in the brain. One especially interesting source of information about this is a case in which a fencing foil was thrust through a young man's nostril into the left side of his thalamus. Since his injury, this person, known in the literature as N.A., has been unable to store virtually any new declarative knowledge in LTM. It is impossible for him to read a textbook and remember information on a previous page that the author might refer back to. Even watching TV is hopelessly confusing, since plots are never registered in LTM. Interestingly, however, N.A. is still able to store procedural knowledge. He can learn how to do things like riding a horse, swinging a golf club, or swimming (Kaushall et al., 1981). These observations strongly suggest that fact knowledge and skill knowledge must be stored in different parts of the brain. We will return to N.A. later in this chapter.

Procedural and declarative memories seem to develop at different rates. Infants from a variety of species, including humans, develop the ability to remember skills well before they are able to remember facts. For example, in one study three-month-old monkeys were just as proficient in a skill task as mature adult monkeys. In contrast, tasks requiring memory for facts could not be totally mastered until they were two years old (Mishkin, 1982).

Until recently, many psychologists divided declarative memory into two distinct categories, episodic memory and semantic memory—a categorization that was proposed by Endel Tulving (1972, 1983). **Episodic memory** represents essentially autobiographical facts about a person's experiences, stored in roughly chronological order. This type of memory would include your memories of your first kiss, the day you graduated from high school, what you had for breakfast this morning, and the sequence in which you consumed these food items. **Semantic memory** contains general, nonpersonal knowledge about the *meaning* of facts and concepts without reference to specific experiences. Knowledge about the principles of grammar, mathematical formulas, different kinds of food, and the distinction between afferent and efferent nerves are all examples of facts stored in semantic memory.

However, several recent efforts to test the hypothesis that episodic and semantic memory represent distinct memory subsystems have, for the most part, failed to support this distinction (Dosher, 1984; Neely & Durgunoglu, 1985). This has led to criticisms of the semantic-episodic distinction (McKoon et al., 1986; Ratcliff & McKoon, 1986), which prompted Tulving to modify his theoretical framework. Tulving now conceptualizes episodic memory as a subsystem of semantic memory (1986).

FIGURE 7.5   A TEST OF VISUAL MEMORY

A Dual-Code Model of Semantic Memory   Semantic memory is equivalent to an encyclopedic collection of facts about our world. In what form is this information stored in long-term memory? One widely discussed theory, the **dual-code model of memory** (Paivio, 1983), argues that memories may be stored either in *sensory codes* (for example, as visual images or sounds) or *verbal codes* (as words).

Study the photo in Figure 7.5 for 20 or 30 seconds and then look away and see how many items you can recall and write down. How did you remember the objects? Did you name them while studying the figure, or did you categorize them according to the use you would put them to? If the objects were stored as words, you employed a verbal code. However, perhaps you were able to retain a visual image of the picture and to use this sensory code to aid your recall of specific items.

Some people appear to be able to use visual codes so efficiently that they can retain a vivid image of large amounts of visual material for several minutes. Research subjects with this ability, called **eidetic imagery** (photographic memory), claim they can close their eyes and see an entire picture or printed page from a book as if they were looking directly at it rather than scanning their memory. Eidetic imagery is a very rare talent (some question whether it even exists [Lieblich, 1979]) that is more common among children than adults (Gray & Gummerman, 1975; Haber, 1969; Richardson, 1986). This difference may reflect the fact that children's memory storehouses are less cluttered with extraneous facts, thus allowing for clearer, less encumbered images.

Which type of coding, verbal or sensory, is most common? Do we even use two codes to store declarative memories? These questions have been the subject of much debate in psychology. To complicate matters further, it appears that we store some memories in the form of abstract codes that are neither strictly verbal nor sensory. For example, if you describe a movie you have just seen to a friend, you will not repeat word for word what you heard the actors say. Instead, you will have abstracted your impressions of the movie into a commentary that is your own creation, including your views on the cinematography, the acting, the plot, and the mood.

Since most of us do not use eidetic imagery to remember everything we see, we often have trouble extracting information from long-term memory. Some bits of information can be maddeningly elusive. Our ability to access information depends largely on the care with which we encode it for storage. There are several strategies for efficient encoding, which we will examine in the following section.

Encoding in Long-Term Memory Many memory experts draw an analogy between long-term memory and a set of file cabinets or the card catalog in a library. Encoding information for storage is like numbering books or files, storing them in specified places, and using index cards to provide cues or access codes. The better we organize our file systems, the more quickly we can access information and the longer we can remember it. Therefore, a key to efficient long-term memory is meaningful organization of material. A number of memory systems or **mnemonic devices** can help us to do this (Nield, 1987). The appropriateness or effectiveness of the various mnemonic devices outlined below vary from task to task (Merrman, 1987). You may want to experiment with more than one approach for a given memory task.

Clustering **Clustering** is one mnemonic device; it involves grouping items into categories (Bousfield, 1953; Buschke, 1977; Forrester & King, 1971; Thompson et al., 1972). For example, suppose you want to memorize the following shopping list:

toilet paper	hamburger	asparagus
corn	green beans	bacon
chicken	broom	matches
milk	sour cream	cheese

These 12 items, if treated separately, are about five too many chunks for your short-term memory. Thus, you can probably forget trying to hold them in STM by repeatedly rehearsing the list all the way to the grocery store. If you treat the items as separate, without trying to organize the list in some meaningful way, your LTM recall is also likely to prove inadequate for the task. A far easier method is to group the items under four subcategories: dairy items, meat, vegetables, and household products. Remembering four categories, each with three items, is a much more manageable task.

Method of Loci This method, developed by the early Greeks, involves forming mental associations between items you wish to recall and specific locations along a designated route you might travel (*loci* means locations or places in Latin).

Many memory experts draw an analogy between long-term memory and filing systems. The better we organize our filing systems, the more quickly we can access information and the longer we will remember it.

The first step is to develop a route you are familiar with. Imagine, for example, that you are walking from the campus library to your apartment. Pick out specific locations along the way that are easy to remember, such as a bus-stop bench, a flagpole, a large oak tree, a broken-down van parked on the street, the sidewalk leading to your apartment house, and so forth. Then create a series of images that will associate each item on your list with a specific location along your route.

For example, to use the loci method to remember a grocery list in the clustering discussion, you might imagine toilet paper strewn on the bus-stop bench, cornstalks leaning against the flagpole, a chicken sitting in the oak tree, and so forth. Picture these associations as vividly as possible. Later, when you need to remember the list, take a mental walk along your route.

Narrative Story Another way to remember information is to organize it into a narrative (Wall & Routowicz, 1987). The story does not need to be particularly logical or plausible; it simply has to place items within a meaningful framework. For example, suppose you want to remember the five explanations for why we forget outlined later in this chapter. (They are interference, organic amnesia, decay of the memory trace, retrieval failure, and motivated forgetting.) The following narrative provides one possible way to encode this information (the key words describing explanations for forgetting are italicized).

> The rotten odor emanating from his duffle bag was sufficient to run *interference* as Sam weaved his way through the crowded corridors. "Phew!" exclaimed his buddy Bill. "It smells like something *organic* is *decaying* in your duffle bag." "Oh, that is just the remnants of a crummy brown bag lunch that my Mom *failed to retrieve* from my bag because she wants me to overcome my *motivation to forget* about the little details in my life," responded Sam.

An experiment by Gordon Bower and Michael Clark (1969) demonstrated how powerful this mnemonic device can be. Subjects inexperienced in this technique were asked to try to memorize 12 lists, each containing 10 nouns. Half the subjects were instructed to make up 12 brief stories, each containing the 10 words. The other half of the subjects merely spent an equivalent amount of time attempting to memorize the lists with whatever technique they chose. When tested later, subjects who had used the narrative story technique recalled an average of 94 percent of the words, while those who did not remembered only an average of 14 percent.

The Peg-Word System This encoding system involves first learning a series of words that correspond to a sequence of numbers (Miller et al., 1960). Each word and corresponding number represents a peg in the system. The following 10 rhyming pairs is a popular example of this approach:

One is a bun	Six is sticks
Two is a shoe	Seven is heaven
Three is a tree	Eight is a gate
Four is a door	Nine is wine
Five is a hive	Ten is a hen

Once you have memorized these associations, you can use them to recall a list of one to 10 items. You do this by creating a series of visual images that allow you to "hang" the item you wish to remember on the appropriate peg. For instance, to remember the following list of building supplies—nails, masking tape, saw, electric sander, electric drill, wire, hammer, tape measure, pliers, and vise grips—you would imagine each item on your list interacting with one peg-word. Thus, you might imagine a hamburger bun stuffed with nails, two shoes taped together with masking tape, a large saw embedded in your mother's favorite fruit tree, and so forth.

Acrostics **Acrostics** are sentences in which the first letter of each word serves as a cue for recalling specific information. For example, suppose you need to remember the last six presidents of the United States, starting with the Reagan administration and moving sequentially back in time. Here is a sentence that would help you accomplish this task: "Rotten Canned Fruit Never Justifies Killing." The names are Reagan, Carter, Ford, Nixon, Johnson, and Kennedy. If you took piano lessons at some point in your life it is a good bet that you used another acrostic, the sentence "Every Good Boy Does Fine" to help you memorize the keys on the lines of the treble clef.

Acronyms Still another memory system is **acronyms,** meaningful arrangements of letters that provide cues for the recall of material. For example, many people have learned the colors on a color wheel, in their order of appearance, by remembering Roy G. Biv (red, orange, yellow, blue, indigo, and violet). Another acronym, FACE, is often used by piano teachers to help students remember the spaces in the treble clef.

Do memory systems really work? One experiment demonstrates not only that they do but also that they seem to be something we learn to use at a fairly young age. Sixth-grade children were shown to be much better at remembering lists than were third-graders (Ornstein & Naus, 1978). This difference reflected a difference in strategy: the younger children used **maintenance rehearsal** to try to remember the list, while the older subjects applied **elaborative rehearsal.** Maintenance rehearsal is simply repeating the words without any attempt to find meaning in them. In contrast, elaborative rehearsal involves organizing strategies such as clustering. When the younger children in this study were taught how to organize material, their recall improved to the level of the older subjects.

Retrieval from Long-Term Memory The reason why the memory systems just described work so well is that they provide cues or "handles" that help us to access information. The more retrieval cues that we can link to information, the more likely we are to recall it later on.

This was revealed in an experiment conducted by Fergus Craik and Endel Tulving (1975). In the first phase of the study, subjects were given index cards containing single sentences with a word missing. After reading the sentence, they viewed a word flashed on a screen and pressed either a "yes" or "no" button to indicate whether or not the word fit the sentence. The sentence complexity varied from simple ("She cooked the _____") to complex ("The great bird swooped down and carried off the struggling _____").

Subjects saw a given word once. In some instances the word did not fit the sentence. In other cases it fit into a simple, medium, or complex sentence. For example, the word "chicken" could fit both of the sample sentences, while "house" could fit neither. Subjects were told that the experiment was concerned with perception and speed of reaction time, so they made no special effort to store the words in their long-term memory.

After completing this phase of the experiment, subjects had a short rest period. They were then given the cards containing the sentences and asked to recall the word associated with each sentence.

PREDICTING RECALL WITH CUES

Based on your understanding of memory processes described thus far, what kind of performance would you expect the subjects to exhibit on these retention tests? Would you predict that their ability to recall words was influenced by whether or not they matched with a sentence? Do you think that sentence complexity influenced recall, and if so, in what direction and why? Take a moment to formulate your answer before reading on.

FIGURE 7.6 RESULTS OF THE CRAIK AND TULVING EXPERIMENT

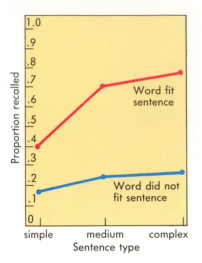

Subjects were much more likely to recall words that fit a sentence than those that did not. They were also considerably more likely to remember a word if it fit a complex sentence than if it fit a simple sentence. (*Source:* Adapted from Craik & Tulving, 1975)

Figure 7.6 demonstrates the results of this experiment. Subjects were much more likely to recall words that fit a sentence than those that did not. They were also considerably more likely to remember a word if it fit a complex sentence than if it fit a simple sentence.

It seems, then, that we remember things better if they are associated with specific cues. For example, we are more likely to remember the item "watch" if we can associate it with a visual cue, as suggested by the sentence, "He dropped the watch." We are even more likely to remember the item when it is used in a more complex sentence such as, "The old man hobbled across the room and picked up the valuable watch from the mahogany table." This complex sentence provides considerably more visual cues that can aid our retention.

Association Networks   Another key to retrieving information is the way it is stored in memory. Many psychologists believe that much of the information in our declarative memories is stored in the form of networks of associations between concepts or fragments of knowledge we have about things in our worlds (Anderson, 1983a; Chang, 1986; Collins & Loftus, 1975; Norman & Rumelhart, 1975).

An example of such a network is shown in Figure 7.7. Each knowledge fragment or concept is represented as a *node* in the association network. Properties or characteristics of the nodes are linked directly to them. For example, the direct link between the property "reduce anxiety" and the node "tranquilizers" means that a person with this knowledge network would have stored the information that tranquilizers reduce anxiety. However, other facts may not be linked directly in memory. For example, the fact that tranquilizers are substances dispensed by pharmacists must be inferred from information stored higher in the network. The lines between the nodes in the figure represent *associations* between concepts. These associations allow us to retrieve facts from our memories by drawing upon our knowledge of the kinds of relationships that link nodes together.

This interpretation of declarative memory suggests that we retrieve facts from LTM through a process of *spreading activation* (Anderson, 1983b; Balota & Lorch, 1986; Jones & Anderson, 1987). When a specific node or concept in the memory hierarchy is triggered, activation spreads along the interlinking pathways to associated concepts. For example, if you heard the word "psychedelics," this information node would be activated and mental energy would spread to related concepts such as "illegal" or "alter physiological processes."

The concept of spreading activation is supported by a number of studies. In one experiment, subjects were asked to watch as a string of letters was flashed on a screen and then to decide if the letters constituted a word. Response speed provided an indication of the amount of time necessary for retrieval from memory. Subjects were able to recognize more quickly that a second word in a series (for example, salmon) was in fact a word if it was related to the previous word (fish) than if it was unrelated (bird). Presumably, the first word in the list activated a specific node in a network of associations, and this activation spread to related concepts. Consequently, when a related word appeared, it took less time to recognize it (Schvaneveldt & Meyer, 1973).

In another study (Collins & Quillian, 1969), subjects were presented with simple sentences and asked to judge their accuracy by responding "yes" or "no." For example, referring to the network in Figure 7.7, a subject might be given a sentence like "Tranquilizers reduce anxiety," or "Amphetamines alter physiological processes." The researchers theorized that the length of time required to judge the accuracy of sentences is influenced by how far apart the concepts are stored in an association network in memory. Presented with the two sentences above, a subject would respond most rapidly to the first since the concepts of "tranquilizers" and "reduce anxiety" are directly linked. The response to the second would be slower because "am-

FIGURE 7.7   A HYPOTHETICAL THREE-LEVEL NETWORK

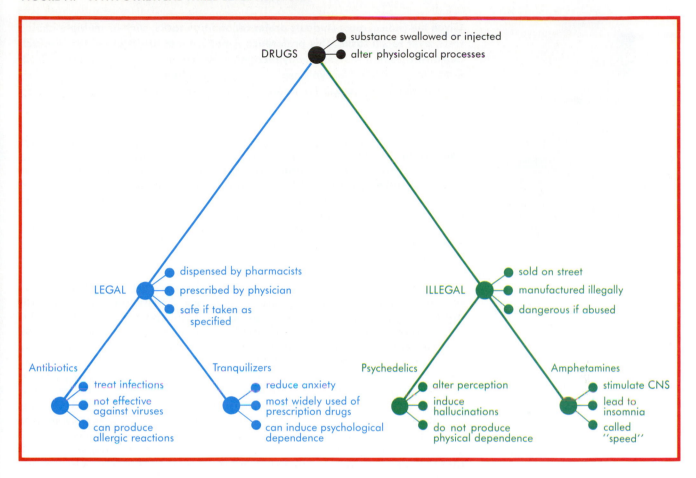

phetamines" and "alter physiological processes" are two steps apart in the hierarchy. Indeed, the researchers found that a sentence containing facts stored together requires less time to judge than one in which facts are stored one or more steps apart in the network.

Testing Long-Term Memory   A number of methods have been used to measure our ability to store new material in long-term memory. The three most common techniques are recall tasks, recognition tasks, and relearning.

Recall   In a **recall** task, the subject is asked to reproduce information he or she was previously exposed to. For example, a recall question designed to test your knowledge of the material in this chapter might ask you to name the three memory processes. Fill-in-the-blank or essay questions are other examples of recall tasks.

Recognition   A **recognition** task presents possible answers from which the subject must pick the correct one. Instead of having to pull information from memory, a recognition test simply involves realizing whether you have been previously exposed to a particular bit of information. The previous question on three memory processes, in a recognition format, might read "What are the three primary memory processes: (1) encoding, networking, activation; (2) elaboration, storage, retrieval; (3) encoding, storage, retrieval; (4) association, networking, retrieval." This is the familiar multiple-choice format often used in classrooms. True-false questions are another example of recognition tasks.

Herman Ebbinghaus

Actors use the technique of overlearning by rehearsing their lines over and over after already mastering them.

COMPARING RECALL AND RECOGNITION TASKS

Given the choice, most students prefer recognition tasks, such as multiple-choice tests, over recall tasks. This preference is not without justification, for research demonstrates that we can usually recognize much more than we can recall (Craik & McDowd, 1987). Can you explain why recognition tests yield better performances than recall tasks? Try to answer this question by yourself before reading on.

A recognition test simply requires you to perform one memory task: you search through your memory to see if stored information matches the new information. The test stimulus is typically rich with retrieval cues that help you gain access to stored information. In contrast, a recall test requires you to perform two tasks, both of which are more difficult than the recognition task. First you must search through your memory and reconstruct possible answers from information that is not presented to you in the test. Then you must identify the correct answer from the varied possibilities and describe it well enough to demonstrate that you truly recall it.

Relearning A third method of measuring memory, relearning, is perhaps the most sensitive measure of memory. Relearning is infrequently used today, however, mostly because it is so time-consuming.

Relearning involves measuring how much more quickly a person can relearn material that was learned at some previous time. For example, you might be asked to memorize a list of *nonsense syllables* (meaningless combinations of two consonants and a vowel, such as *ZUD* or *XUT*). The number of trials it took you to master the list would be recorded to measure your initial performance. The list would then be put aside for a period of time, and at a later point you would be asked to relearn it. If there is no memory trace of the nonsense syllables previously learned, it should take as much effort to relearn the list the second time as it did the first, which is to say there would be no *savings* due to memory. However, if at least some recall for the nonsense syllables is prompted by your LTM, relearning should be faster than the original learning. For instance, if it takes 10 trials for you to master the original list but only five to relearn it, there will be a savings of five trials due to memory. This would yield a savings score of 50 percent (5 trials saved ÷ 10 original trials, or 50 percent).

The relearning method was used by Herman Ebbinghaus (1885) in the first systematic studies of human memory. He used the most reliable subject he could find, himself. He memorized countless lists of nonsense syllables, set them aside for varied periods of time, and then relearned the lists using savings scores as a measure of retention. Ebbinghaus invented the concept of nonsense syllables because he felt that people vary in their ability to make associations with real words like *dog, gun,* or *pit.*

Ebbinghaus' systematic studies of memory had a great impact on the then infant discipline of psychology. He is perhaps best remembered for *curves of forgetting,* which were derived from his accumulated data on savings scores. As Figure 7.8 shows, forgetting is strongly influenced by the passage of time. It occurs very rapidly at first: within 20 minutes after mastering a list of nonsense syllables, Ebbinghaus had forgotten about 40 percent of it. However, after this initial rapid loss, the rate of forgetting declines significantly. Note that the savings score after 20 days was almost the same as the 10-day score.

Ebbinghaus found that when he used meaningful material in place of nonsense syllables, forgetting took place more gradually. Furthermore, he discovered that he could greatly improve his savings scores by rehearsing a list after he had already mastered it. This technique, called **overlearning,** is an extremely valuable approach to memorizing material that you wish to retain.

FIGURE 7.8   THE EFFECTS OF TIME ON RETENTION

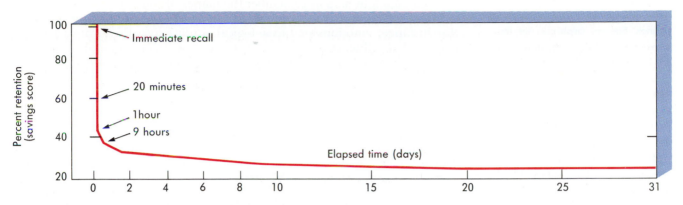

As the curve demonstrates, the drop in retention is initially very rapid after learning and then it slows down markedly. (*Source:* From Ebbinghaus, 1913)

SOME FACTORS THAT INFLUENCE WHAT WE REMEMBER

As we have seen in this chapter, we are most likely to remember information that is meaningful to us. We can increase the meaning of material by organizing and categorizing it and by developing strong associations that serve as retrieval cues. This section explores some additional factors that influence how well we remember material.

THE SERIAL POSITION EFFECT

Have you ever noticed that when you memorize a list of formulas, terms, or grocery items, you are most likely to remember those items at the beginning and end of the list? This phenomenon is called the **serial position effect.**

Why is it easier to remember items at the beginning and end of a data set? One possible explanation draws upon our knowledge of short- and long-term memory. Presumably, items at the beginning of a list move successfully into long-term memory because there is no competing information. As additional items move into memory, however, they may displace previously processed items because short-term memory can hold only a limited number of chunks. Items at the end of the list are remembered better than those in the middle because they have not been bumped or replaced by any additional material. In contrast, items in the middle of a list encounter interference from both preceding and subsequent items. A typical serial position effect curve is shown in Figure 7.9.

The serial position effect shows up in a variety of situations. For example, when children learn the alphabet, letters in the middle are most difficult to remember. Similarly, students are more likely to miss test questions drawn from material in the middle of a lecture than information at the beginning or end (Holen & Oaster, 1976).

In practical terms, this means that we should give extra attention to information in the middle of a list or sequence of material that we are trying to learn. Furthermore, it may be helpful to vary the order in which material is structured and recited (as long as this change does not disrupt the logical sequence). Perhaps when we become familiar with the overall framework of information, we can approach it effectively in varied sequences.

THE IMPACT OF CONTEXT ON MEMORY

Another factor that influences memory is context. Research reveals that it is often easier to recall a particular event or experience if we are in the same location or context in which the information was first encoded (Estes,

FIGURE 7.9   THE SERIAL POSITION EFFECT

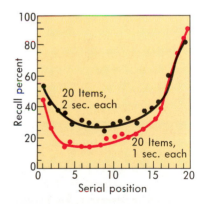

Subjects in this experiment were shown a list of 20 words, one at a time, and asked to remember as many as they could. Some saw each word for only one second, and others for two seconds. Under both conditions subjects were most likely to remember the words at the beginning and end of the list, a phenomenon known as the "serial position effect." (*Source:* From Murdock, 1962)

I often play twenty-one in Nevada casinos. Several strategies for improving a player's advantage over the house are commercially available. I have almost mastered one of these complex systems. It involves assigning numerical plus or minus values to cards and keeping track of the "running count." Certain basic strategies for playing the game are modified as the running count changes. For example, whether or not you split a pair of 9's will be influenced by both the dealer's up card and the running count. My system requires me to master several sets of strategies, including rules governing splitting pairs of 9's, 8's, and so on down to 3's and 2's.

When I first tried to remember these rules, I had little trouble with those governing the combinations at either end of the set (for example, what to do with a pair of 9's or 2's). It was the items in the middle of the set that gave me the most trouble. This was true of other strategy sets, also. It was always the strategies for the values smack in the middle of the sets that were the hardest to remember. (*Authors' files*)

I recently underwent a painful breakup of a long-term relationship. It was my partner's decision to end our involvement. Shortly after he announced he was moving out, all kinds of bad memories from a breakup with a former boyfriend came flooding back. As if it wasn't enough to have to cope with the present pain, I had to deal with feelings and memories that I thought had been buried five years earlier with the end of the previous relationship. (*Authors' files*)

1972; Watkins et al., 1976). Thus, a return to the classrooms of our elementary school might help us remember the names of some of our classmates in the first and second grades. Some research suggests that our internal state (for instance, emotions or physiological conditions) also forms a kind of context that influences recall. For example, research has demonstrated that recall of information learned while under the influence of a drug (such as alcohol or marijuana) occurs more easily in the same drug state versus a nondrug state (Deutsch & Folle, 1973; Goodwin et al., 1969; Horton & Mills, 1984; Swanson & Kinsbourne, 1976).

This phenomenon, known as **state-dependent memory,** also appears to encompass emotion—that is, people may remember things better when they are in the same mood or emotional state as when the information first entered their memories (Blaney, 1986; Bower, 1981; Clark & Teasdale, 1982; Johnson & Magaro, 1987; Rholes et al., 1987; Riskin, 1983; Riskin et al., 1982). However, the evidence for state-dependent memory associated with mood state is less convincing and certainly more controversial than the data demonstrating a drug-induced, state-dependent memory effect. Some studies indicate that emotion-based, state-dependency effects are small (Gage & Safer, 1985; Schare et al., 1984) or nonexistent (Bower & Mayer, 1985; Wetzler, 1985). Further research is needed to clarify how influential mood state is upon state-dependent memory effects.

FLASHBULB MEMORY

If you ask virtually any American who was an adolescent or older in 1963 what they were doing when they heard about John F. Kennedy's assassination, the odds are very good that they will be able to tell you an amazing number of details—where they were, what the weather was like, perhaps even what they were wearing. You may have a similar recall of what you were doing the moment you heard of the explosion of the space shuttle Challenger in January of 1986.

This kind of vivid recall for earlier events associated with extreme emotion has been called **flashbulb memory** (Brown & Kulik, 1977; Winograd & Killinger, 1983). Such memories are so vivid that it is as if our brains have recorded them like a scene caught in the sudden glare of a camera's flashbulb. Our recall for such occurrences is not so precise for factual details surrounding the event itself, but rather for the specific setting and manner in which we first heard about the event. For example, you may have trouble remembering the exact date of Challenger's explosion, even though you may never forget the image of the explosion on the TV news broadcasts.

Flashbulb memories may be triggered by any sudden shocking event that has great personal significance to an individual. Researchers Roger Brown and James Kulik (1977) surveyed 80 people, aged 20 to 40 (40 blacks and 40 whites), asking them to recall the circumstances in which they first heard about nine major events that had occurred during the previous 15 years. Included in these events were the successful or attempted assassinations of seven prominent Americans, including John Kennedy, Martin Luther King, and Robert Kennedy. In addition, subjects were asked if they had flashbulb memories for any shocking event of a personal nature, such as the death of a relative or friend or diagnosis of a life-threatening disease.

Of the 80 subjects, 73 reported flashbulb memories associated with a personal shock, most commonly the sudden death of a relative. Many of the accounts were rendered in stunning detail, including specifics about the color of the sky, what they were wearing, and vivid anecdotes such as "I was carrying a carton of Viceroy cigarettes, which I dropped." All but one subject had flashbulb memories for John Kennedy's assassination. However, while 75 percent of the blacks reported flashbulb memories for the death of Martin Luther King, only 33 percent of the white respondents recorded such vivid memories associated with this event. Brown and Kulik interpreted this racial difference as evidence that a link exists between the personal importance of an event and flashbulb memories.

Ask friends what they were doing when the news broke that the space shuttle Challenger had exploded. You will probably be surprised at the amount of detail they recall about the event. When you first looked at these photographs, you may have experienced strong emotional memories about the incident as well.

MEMORY AS A CONSTRUCTIVE PROCESS

You may remember many details about the moment when you first heard about Challenger's explosion, but a good friend who was in the same room with you may have a different memory. Our memories often vary significantly from the actual facts. Why does this occur?

Some psychologists suggest that vivid, photolike flashbulb memories may actually represent our tendency to go back and fill in the details of an event after the fact (Neiser, 1982). This makes sense if we view memory as a *constructive* process in which information that we have already stored affects the way we remember an event. From this perspective, our information processing is not limited to efforts to store facts as accurately as possible. Rather, we frequently add or delete details to make new information more consistent with the way we already conceive our world. Thus, remembering is often a process of mentally "reconstructing" an event rather than simply searching long-term memory for a perfect copy of it. As a result, many of our memories are not necessarily accurate representations of what actually occurred. Instead, they may be accounts of what we think happened, or perhaps what we believe should have happened.

Serious investigations of constructive processes in memory did not catch on in psychology until the last couple of decades. However, this research was pioneered over 55 years ago by an English psychologist, Sir Frederick Bartlett (1932), who tested college students' memories of simple stories set in unfamiliar cultures. One story read by his subjects was an American Indian folktale titled "The War of the Ghosts." This story, along with a student reproduction of it, is shown in Figure 7.10.

Bartlett found that his subjects never recalled the material exactly as it had been presented. Rather, they stored a few primary facts and organized the rest of the story around these central themes. Bartlett's subjects tended to modify their memories of the original stories in any of three ways: by shortening and simplifying the story (a process called *leveling*); by focusing on and overemphasizing certain details (*sharpening*); and by altering certain details to make the story fit their own views more closely (*assimilation*). For example, in the student's rendition of "The War of the Ghosts," certain words have been changed and the supernatural theme has been minimized.

SCHEMAS

This tendency to change details to fit our own cultural perspectives is consistent with recent findings on the impact of **schemas** on reconstructive

FIRST PERSON 7.5

I can remember in vivid detail the moment I heard that President John Kennedy had been shot. I was studying for a statistics exam. The phone rang; I answered it, and the woman who lived in an apartment above mine said "Have you heard the President has been shot!" I can still hear that voice as if I had answered that call only a few moments ago. Other details of that day are also etched in my mind—a criminology professor beginning to cry uncontrollably in the middle of a lecture, the haunted expression on Jackie Kennedy's face as the camera zoomed in for a close-up. I remember my sense of disbelief followed by rage and then a profound sense of loss. (*Authors' files*)

FIGURE 7.10   THE ORIGINAL VERSION OF "THE WAR OF THE GHOSTS" AND AN EXAMPLE OF A SUBJECT'S REPRODUCTION OF IT

(*Source: From Bartlett, 1932*)

The War of the Ghosts

One night two young men from Egulac went down to the river to hunt seals, and while they were there it became foggy and calm. Then they heard war-cries, and they thought: "Maybe this is a war party." They escaped to the shore, and hid behind a log. Now canoes came up, and they heard the noise of paddles, and saw one canoe coming up to them. There were five men in the canoe, and they said:

"What do you think? We wish to take you along. We are going up the river to make war on the people."

One of the young men said: "I have no arrows."

"Arrows are in the canoe," they said.

"I will not go along. I might be killed. My relatives do not know where I have gone. But you," he said, turning to the other, "may go with them."

So one of the young men went, but the other returned home.

And the warriors went on up the river to a town on the other side of Kalama.

The people came down to the water, and they began to fight, and many were killed. But presently the young man heard one of the warriors say: "Quick, let us go home: that Indian has been hit." Now he thought: "Oh, they are ghosts." He did not feel sick, but they said he had been shot.

So the canoes went back to Egulac, and the young man went ashore to his house, and made a fire. And he told everybody and said: "Behold I accompanied the ghosts, and we went to fight. Many of our fellows were killed, and many of those who attacked us were killed. They said I was hit, and I did not feel sick."

He told it all, and then he became quiet. When the sun rose he fell down. Something black came out of his mouth. His face became contorted. The people jumped up and cried.

He was dead. (p. 65)

Sample Reproduction

Two youths were standing by a river about to start seal-catching, when a boat appeared with five men in it. They were all armed for war.

The youths were at first frightened, but they were asked by the men to come and help them fight some enemies on the other bank. One youth said he could not come as his relations would be anxious about him; the other said he would go, and entered the boat.

In the evening he returned to his hut, and told his friends that he had been in a battle. A great many had been slain, and he had been wounded by an arrow; he had not felt any pain, he said. They told him that he must have been fighting in a battle of ghosts. Then he remembered that it had been queer and he became very excited.

In the morning, however, he became ill, and his friends gathered round; he fell down and his face became very pale. Then he writhed and shrieked and his friends were filled with terror. At last he became calm. Something hard and black came out of his mouth, and he lay contorted and dead. (p. 72)

memory processes. Schemas are conceptual frameworks that we use to make sense out of our world. Because schemas provide us with preconceived expectations, they help make the world seem more predictable. However, they can also lead to significant distortions in our memory processes, in that they often exert a strong impact on the manner in which memory for a particular event is encoded (Brewer & Nakamura, 1984; Johnson & Hasher, 1987; Thorndyke, 1984). In fact, many memory distortions occur because we interpret events in the context of established schemas.

This was demonstrated in a classic study conducted over 40 years ago, in which subjects were shown a picture of two men engaged in an argument (see Figure 7.11). One man was black and the other was white; the white man held a razor in his hand. After briefly viewing the picture, subjects were asked to describe the scene to someone who had not seen the picture, who in turn passed the information on to someone else, and so on. As the information was passed from person to person, some of its features were altered. Most notably, the razor ended up in the hand of the black man (Allport & Postman, 1947). These findings suggest that the subjects' schemas (that is, their assumption that blacks were more prone to violence than whites) caused them to distort the way they constructed and stored this information.

Some more recent studies have demonstrated another interesting point: When people remember information that is not consistent with their schemas, they are likely to distort the facts to make them fit better with their conceptual frameworks. For instance, in one study (Spiro, 1976) subjects read one of two different versions of a story about an engaged couple. In both versions, the male partner did not want to have children. The difference between the stories was that in one version the woman did not want

FIGURE 7.11 SCHEMAS CAN ALTER WHAT WE REMEMBER

In this classic study, subjects were shown this picture of two men engaged in an argument. The better dressed man is black and the man with a razor in his hand is white. As subjects described this scene to others, it became distorted as some of its features were altered. Most notably, the razor ended up in the hand of the black man. These findings suggest that the subjects' schemas (that is, their assumption that blacks are more violent than whites) caused them to distort the way they constructed and stored this information. (*Source:* From Allport & Postman, 1947)

children either, whereas in the other version she was upset because she wanted children. Subjects were asked to read the story; then when they were finished they did some paperwork. Then a postscript was added to the story: Some of the subjects were told that the couple married and lived together happily, while others were told that they broke up and never saw each other again. Subjects were then asked to recall the story at a later date.

FITTING STORIES INTO SCHEMAS

Can you predict the outcome of this experiment? Do you think that the relationship between the story version and the postscript influenced the way subjects remembered the story later on? Apply what you have learned about schemas and constructive memory processes to formulate a prediction before reading on.

If you predicted that subjects modified the story to fit their own views about men's and women's roles in the family, you were right. Subjects who heard a postscripted ending that did not seem to fit the rest of the story tended to "remember" information that resolved that contradiction. For example, those who read a version in which the couple disagreed about having children did not expect the couple to "live together happily." When they remembered the story, they were likely to "recall" other "facts" that would make the ending fit with the story—such as a compromise in which the couple had agreed to adopt a child instead of having one of their own.

Similarly, subjects who were told that the couple who agreed not to have children had broken up were likely to "remember" that this pair had other difficulties, such as parents who opposed the relationship. In contrast, subjects who read stories that matched the postscripted endings did not add new facts to the story. They had no reason to, for the stories were consistent with their schemas.

Although schemas can lead to memory distortions, they also provide important association cues that can aid recall. This was shown in an experiment in which subjects were asked to study a list of behaviors of a hypothetical person. Some participants were told that they were subjects in a memory experiment and that they should attempt to remember as many of the behaviors as possible. Other subjects were told that they were in an experiment designed to evaluate how people form impressions of others, and they were asked to try to form an impression (a schema) of the person. A later recall test revealed that subjects who attempted to fit the information into a schema demonstrated better recall than those who had merely attempted to memorize a list of behaviors (Hamilton et al., 1980).

We have seen that our memories may sometimes involve fiction as well as facts. This may result from our tendency to fill gaps in our knowledge of previous events or to modify memories to match existing schemas. Such active constructive processes, which may occur in both the storage and retrieval stages of memory, may have profound impact on a number of areas of human experience, one of which is eyewitness testimony.

EYEWITNESS TESTIMONY

The legal system places great value on the testimony of eyewitnesses. Police officers who file automobile accident reports, criminal investigators, and juries all tend to give considerable credence to the accounts of people who were on the scene. In recent years, however, new findings raise questions about the reliability of eyewitness testimony.

Psychologist Elizabeth Loftus has been the leading investigator in this area of research. The accumulating evidence of memory as a constructive process prompted Loftus to wonder to what degree eyewitness testimony might be influenced by people's tendency to reconstruct their memory of events to fit their schemas. She also wondered whether information received after the fact might be integrated into witnesses' memories of what they had seen. Is it possible that subtle differences in the way questions are worded might cause a witness to remember the event in a different light? Can witnesses be misled into remembering things that did not actually occur?

A number of studies by Loftus and other researchers have investigated such questions. In one, subjects watched a film of a two-car accident and then filled out a questionnaire about what they had seen. There were four versions of the wording of one critical question. Some subjects were asked "About how fast were the two cars going when they *contacted* each other?" In the three other versions the words *hit, bumped,* or *smashed* were substituted for *contacted.* The word *contacted* yielded an average speed estimate of 32 mph, whereas the words *hit, bumped,* and *smashed* produced estimates of 34, 38, and 41 mph, respectively (Loftus & Palmer, 1974). The words used to describe the collision clearly influenced the way these subjects reconstructed their memory of the accident (see Figure 7.12). From this, it seems clear that the way witnesses remember an event can be influenced by the kinds of questions they are asked about the event.

After-the-fact information may do more than merely change our recollections. In some cases, it may cause people to incorporate completely false information into their memories. This was suggested in another study in which subjects watched a videotape of an automobile accident, then were asked questions designed to introduce false information (Loftus, 1975). Half the subjects were asked "How fast was the white sports car going when

FIGURE 7.12 DESCRIPTIVE LANGUAGE CAN ALTER WHAT WE REMEMBER

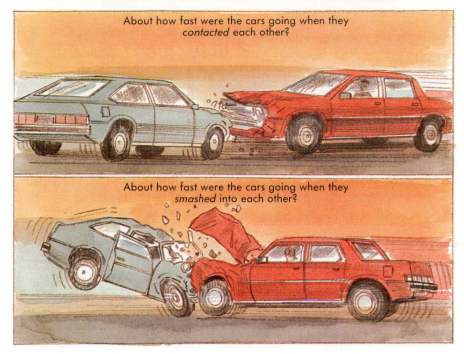

About how fast were the cars going when they *contacted* each other?

About how fast were the cars going when they *smashed* into each other?

Subjects who viewed a film of an accident were more likely to "remember" that the cars were traveling faster if the words "*smashed* into each other" were used to describe the accident instead of the words "*contacted* each other." (*Source:* Adapted from Loftus and Palmer, 1974)

it passed the barn while traveling along the country road?" The other half of subjects were asked the same question, but without the words "when it passed the barn."

In point of fact, there was no barn in the videotape. When subjects were questioned again about the accident a week later, however, 17 percent of those who heard "when it passed the barn" did report seeing a barn in the videotape. In contrast, only 3 percent of the subjects who had heard nothing about a barn remembered seeing the barn.

In another study, Loftus and her colleagues showed subjects a series of color slides depicting the sequence of events in an automobile accident. Each subject saw one of two possible versions of a critical slide in the series. In one version, a car was stopped at an intersection posted with a stop sign. In the other, a yield sign was substituted for the stop sign. Immediately after viewing the slide series, subjects were asked follow-up questions that presumed the existence of either a stop or yield sign. (Sometimes this was consistent with what they had seen; in other cases it was not.) Then, 20 minutes after completing the questionnaire, they were shown several pairs of slides and asked to pick which one out of each pair they had seen before.

When the follow-up questions presumed that subjects had seen the same sign as they had actually seen, subjects identified the correct slide in the retest 75 percent of the time. In contrast, when the questions had mentioned a sign not present in the original scene, the misled subjects identified the correct slide only 41 percent of the time (Loftus et al., 1978). This same research team has also demonstrated that the longer the time interval between observing an event and later exposure to inaccurate information, the less accurate recall is likely to be.

Such findings are alarming when we consider what often happens to eyewitnesses. First a witness may be questioned repeatedly by police officers, some of whom may introduce erroneous information by asking leading questions. Friends and family members also ask questions and introduce new information. Later (probably much later), an attorney may question a witness on or off the stand. If intelligent college students can be misled into "remembering" erroneous information in controlled experiments such as those just described, how reliable are eyewitness accounts of real-world crimes and accidents?

Although questions like this are valid, recent evidence suggests that a flaw in the Loftus team's research techniques may have biased their findings, creating a high probability that misled subjects would exhibit poorer recall than control subjects even when the misleading information had no effect on memory for the original event (Zaragoza et al., 1987). Several recent studies that corrected for this methodological flaw reported that misleading postevent information does not impair recall of the original event (McCloskey & Zaragoza, 1985a, 1985b; Zaragoza et al., 1987). Thus, it may be that the misleading information to which eyewitnesses are often exposed may not be as damaging as the original research of Loftus and her associates suggested.

A number of studies indicate that people exposed to violent events are especially likely to incorporate misinformation into their memory. This may be because shocking events interfere with our ability to store details accurately, even though we may have vivid "flashbulb" memories of what we were doing or feeling at the time. Since an eyewitness' recall of a violent event may lack many details, he or she may be inclined to fill in the gaps with subsequent misinformation (Loftus & Burns, 1982).

An example of this was a series of armed robberies committed in Delaware several years ago. The local media circulated a composite sketch of the robber that looked like a priest, Father Bernard Pagano. As unlikely as it might seem that a priest could be an armed robber, investigators suspected the father since many victims had said the robber was very polite and neatly dressed. Eventually, seven eyewitnesses identified Father Pagano, and he was taken to trial. Fortunately, court proceedings were halted when another man, Robert Clouser, confessed.

From the photographs of Pagano and Clouser, shown in Figure 7.13, you might wonder how seven witnesses could confuse two men who look so different. Why did the mistake occur? Apparently, criminal investigators

FIGURE 7.13   WOULD YOU BE LIKELY TO CONFUSE THESE TWO MEN?

Father Bernard Pagano (left) would probably have been convicted for a series of armed robberies, based on the testimony of seven eyewitnesses who identified him as the culprit, if Robert Clouser (right), the actual perpetrator, had not confessed to the crimes.

working on this case had mentioned to witnesses that the robber might be a priest. In the pictures of suspects that the witnesses examined, Father Pagano was the only suspect photographed wearing a clerical collar. In mentioning the possibility that the robber was a priest, the investigators seem to have influenced the eyewitnesses' memories. Had Pagano been dressed in lay clothes in the photo, it is unlikely that he would ever have been singled out.

It is clear from these cases that memory is a constructive process, involving much more than merely placing bits of data in storage and then retrieving them later on. Another issue is the *destructive* process that often interferes with our ability to remember things at all. What makes us forget?

WHY WE FORGET

There is no single answer to the question, "Why do we forget?" Forgetting seems to occur for many reasons. Among the explanations that psychologists have put forward to explain forgetting are the decay of the memory trace, problems with interfering material, a breakdown in the retrieval process, emotional and motivational conditions, and organic factors.

DECAY OF THE MEMORY TRACE

One explanation of why we forget is that the *memory trace* (the neurochemical and/or anatomical changes in the brain that encode memories) for some information simply deteriorates, fading away with the passage of time. For example, Ebbinghaus may have forgotten many of his nonsense syllables because the memory trace grew gradually dimmer until it faded altogether.

A number of psychologists believe that decay is at least partially responsible for forgetting. Some suggest that decay may cause us to lose material in short-term memory, but that any information in long-term memory is stored permanently and failure to recall it is due to a retrieval difficulty (Shiffin & Atkinson, 1969; Tulving, 1977). Other psychologists do not agree that long-term information storage is forever. They maintain that some memories may decay over time and become lost (Loftus & Loftus, 1980). Since long-term memories must be stored through some type of physical changes in the brain, it seems possible that these physical codes can sometimes break down with the passage of time.

The difficulty with proving that decay is ever the cause of forgetting lies in the need to rule out other possible explanations. To accomplish this, we would have to ensure that no mental activity occurs between initial learning and later recall that could interfere with establishing the memory trace. This is a virtually impossible task in the case of both short- and long-term memory, since people's minds cannot be held in a "blank" state during such intervals. Consequently, it is virtually impossible to either prove or disprove the decay theory of forgetting.

INTERFERENCE

There is evidence that forgetting is probably influenced more by what we do before or after learning than by the passage of time. According to the *interference* interpretation of forgetting, experiences that occur either before or after we learn something new interfere with our memory. There may be two types of interference: retroactive and proactive.

Retroactive (or backward) **interference** occurs when a later event interferes with recall of earlier information. Suppose, for instance, you look up a telephone number, and as you pick up the phone and prepare to dial, your roommate distracts you by asking what time it is. When you return to the call, you discover that you no longer remember the number. This is an example of retroactive inhibition of memory.

In **proactive** (forward acting) **interference,** earlier learning disrupts memory for later learning. For example, if you learn a list of new vocabulary terms in your English class this afternoon, you may find that it is difficult to remember the psychology terms you review tonight. Figure 7.14 illustrates how psychologists study both types of interference effects.

You can put your knowledge of interference to practical use. For example, if you must study more than one subject in the same time period, you should choose subjects that are as dissimilar as possible since similarity of information increases interference (Dempster, 1985; Underwood, 1983). Sleeping after you study material is the best way to reduce the possibility of retroactive interference. Even relatively brief naps (an hour or so after a study session) can help you remember new material.

RETRIEVAL FAILURE

Suppose you are having trouble recalling the title of an old love song you heard last week. A friend drops by and announces that it is a "splendid" day today. Suddenly you remember the title—"Love is a Many Splendored Thing." It is clear that your memory for the song title was intact, but it was just out of reach, waiting for the right retrieval cue.

Failure to recall a memory does not necessarily mean it is not there. It may simply be inaccessible because it was poorly encoded in the first place or because we have inadequate retrieval cues. Forgetting of long-term memories often reflects a failure of retrieval cues rather than decay or interference. Even memories that seem impossible to retrieve may pop into mind when the right cues are used.

MOTIVATED FORGETTING

Sometimes we forget long-term memories because we do not want to remember them. Psychologists call this *motivated forgetting:* People often push certain kinds of memories out of conscious awareness because they are too embarrassing, frightening, painful, or degrading to recall.

Sigmund Freud's concept of repression is an example of motivated forgetting. Freud believed that we *repress* or forget certain ideas, feelings, and experiences because they are too painful to deal with on a conscious level. Repression thus lets us maintain a sense of self-esteem and avoid

FIGURE 7.14 DESIGN OF EXPERIMENTS FOR STUDYING THE EFFECTS OF RETROACTIVE AND PROACTIVE INTERFERENCE

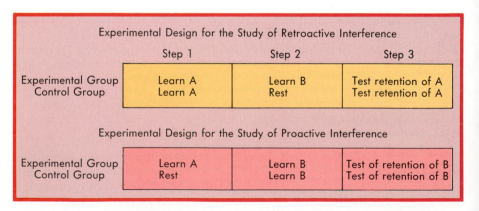

When retroactive interference occurs, later learning (learning task B) interferes with the recall of information learned earlier (recall of task A information). In proactive interference, earlier learning (learning task A) disrupts memory for later learning (recall of task B information). A better performance registered by the control group at step 3 of this experimental design would provide clear evidence of interference effects.

anxiety that would result if this information surfaced in our awareness. As discussed in Chapter 13, there is some disagreement over how viable Freud's concepts of repression and the unconscious mind are as explanations of human behavior. However, psychologists agree that motivated forgetting does play a role in blocking at least some material stored in long-term memory (Davis & Schwartz, 1987).

ORGANIC CAUSES OF FORGETTING

Forgetting is not usually caused by organic pathology. However, certain physical illnesses or accidents can alter the physiology of the brain. Memory deficits caused by this condition are referred to as **organic amnesia.** There are many types of organic amnesia; in this section, we look at three main types: amnesia caused by disease, retrograde amnesia, and anterograde amnesia.

Amnesia Caused by Disease Some diseases produce actual physical deterioration of brain cells, impairing memory as well as a variety of cognitive functions. For instance, cardiovascular disease is characterized by decreased blood circulation, which sometimes limits the oxygen supply to the brain to the point that some brain cells die. Strokes are another common physical cause of memory impairment. Here, a vessel in the brain ruptures, with resulting damage to cells. Alzheimer's disease is another illness that produces progressive widespread degeneration of brain cells. This devastating disease produces severe memory deficits and other impairments of mental functioning. Alzheimer's disease is discussed in some detail in Chapter 11.

Retrograde Amnesia Sometimes a blow to the head may cause loss of memory for certain details or events that occurred prior to the accident. This condition is called **retrograde amnesia.** In many of these cases, lost memories return gradually after time, with older memories tending to come back first. (In almost all cases investigated, memories for recent events have been shown to be more susceptible to disruption than older memories [Gold, 1987].) This suggests that the amnesia reflects a temporary loss of access to information rather than an actual destruction of the memory trace.

Retrograde amnesia is more likely to impair declarative memory, particularly the episodic type, than to interfere with procedural memory. This is exhibited in accident victims who may not remember who they are or what they were doing prior to the accident but who can remember old skills such as playing a musical instrument or speaking a foreign language.

Anterograde Amnesia Amnesia can also work in the opposite direction. Some victims of brain damage may be able to recall old memories established before the damage, but cannot remember information processed after the damage occurred. This condition is called **anterograde amnesia.** It may be caused by injury to a specific area of the brain; it may also be associated with certain surgical procedures and chronic alcoholism. Unlike retrograde amnesia, anterograde amnesia is often irreversible. The following section provides some clues about how and why injuries may be associated with memory loss.

THE PHYSICAL BASES OF MEMORY

We know that memories are not transitory mental events that float freely within our brains. When you learn the name of your psychology professor, your sweetheart's address, or how to play golf, some lasting changes must take place within your brain. For decades researchers have tried to understand the nature of these changes and to identify where they take place. A number of recent discoveries suggest that they are closing in on the answer. As the following Health Psychology and Life discussion, "Chemical En-

FIRST PERSON 7.7

When I regained consciousness after my motorcycle accident, I had no recall at all of what had happened. I couldn't even remember getting on my motorcycle and heading for school. Gradually, some bits and pieces of memory began to return. The first thing I remembered about the day of the accident was being in a good mood, appreciating the fact that it wasn't raining, and just taking my time cruising along the backroads to the college. It was weeks before I could visualize the car coming out of the long driveway and remember thinking that the crazy fool wasn't going to stop, and trying to decide if I should hit the deck or try my luck with the ditch. I still haven't been able to recall the instant before impact. Maybe I am blotting that part out since I suspect I had more terror at that moment than at any other time in my life. (*Authors' files*)

hancement of Memory," points out, we may even be on the verge of discovering some substances that can increase people's ability to remember things.

Years ago, physiological psychologist Donald Hebb (1949) suggested that short- and long-term memory have different physical bases. Short-term memory, he proposed, is maintained by the firing of a collection of neurons arranged in a specific circuit labeled a "cell assembly." Our recall of a telephone number when we put down a phone book and begin to dial is thus

HEALTH PSYCHOLOGY AND LIFE

CHEMICAL ENHANCEMENT OF MEMORY

If someone handed you a nasal spray while you were studying for a test and told you that a few whiffs would enable you to remember much more material than you normally can, you probably would not take them seriously. However, recent findings suggest that there may be drugs that can do just that.

Several years ago a research team led by David de Wied discovered that rats injected with the pituitary hormone *vasopressin* learned faster and remembered what they learned longer than did rats who did not receive the drug (de Wied et al., 1976). Once it was discovered that vasopressin can be put in a nasal spray and sniffed, experiments with humans followed rapidly. In 1978 a team of Belgian and Swiss researchers tested vasopressin on a group of older men, ages 50 to 65, who had experienced various degrees of memory loss. Some of the men received vasopressin three times daily; the remaining subjects sniffed a placebo spray an equal number of times. Subjects who were exposed to vasopressin significantly outperformed the control group on tests of attention, learning, and memory (Legros et al., 1978).

A few years later Herbert Weingartner and his colleagues tested a synthetic form of vasopressin on healthy college students, middle-aged depressed women, and older senile subjects. As in the earlier research, some subjects received vasopressin while others took a placebo. Each day for three weeks, their ability to learn and remember was evaluated. In all three categories, subjects who took the real thing showed significant learning and memory improvements, but those who took the placebo did not. The improvement was particularly marked in the depressed women (Weingartner et al., 1981).

How does vasopressin produce this effect? We know that this hormone stimulates the sympathetic nervous system and that learning rates and memory are often improved by substances that stimulate the nervous system, particularly hormones such as epinephrine that are associated with stress (Gold, 1987; McGaugh, 1983). This led several early researchers to theorize that vasopressin's effects result from stimulating the nervous system rather than acting directly on memory processes. However, later research does not support this theory. When vasopressin is broken down into its component parts, some of these substances enhance learning and memory even though they do not act as stimulants (Burbach et al., 1983). Thus, vasopressin seems to have some kind of direct effect on memory independent of stimulating the nervous system. Just what this effect might be remains to be learned.

In an exciting new line of research, Paul Gold (1987) and his colleagues at the University of Virginia have demonstrated that glucose may also enhance memory. Older subjects in their seventies were asked to drink a glass of lemonade prepared with either saccharin or glucose; shortly thereafter, they were administered a variety of memory tests. Of the two groups, those subjects who had ingested glucose performed better than those who had received saccharin. Gold and his associates have also found an apparent connection between poor memory and inadequate regulation of blood glucose in elderly subjects.

Many memory researchers are confident that very powerful memory-boosting substances will be available in the near future—and in fact, some of them are calling for serious dialogue about the possible impact of such substances on society (Rosenzweig, 1984). Although we would welcome the availability of chemicals to relieve victims of strokes, senility, and Alzheimer's disease, should they be available to people whose memories function normally? If substances were available that could double or triple our memory capacity, should everyone have access to them? (If so, should everyone have *equal* access to them?) These are difficult, thought-provoking questions that may pose complex moral and ethical issues for society in the years to come.

kept alive by neurons firing in a repeated pattern that forms a briefly held memory trace. Hebb maintained that this brief electrical activity does not bring about changes in the physical structure of the brain; that is why short-term memory is transitory. Long-term memory is a different matter. Hebb suggested that information is transferred to LTM when physical changes take place, in the form of new connections between neurons. These physical changes were thought to involve structural changes in the synapses between neurons as a cell assembly is repeatedly activated.

Hebb's conception of short- and long-term memory as distinct phenomena has been supported by research. So has the idea that memory is transferred from short-term electrical activation of neuronal circuits to a more lasting long-term memory coded by physical changes in cells. This process is called **consolidation,** and it has been the subject of a great deal of research. Three questions that have been investigated are how long-term memory is stored, where it is stored, and where long-term memories are processed.

HOW IS LONG-TERM MEMORY STORED?

Hebb's idea that experiences are recorded and memories stored via changes in brain neurons remained novel and even controversial for many years. However, "today, most neuroscientists would unquestionably agree with this hypothesis" (Byrne, 1987, p. 330). Of particular interest is evidence from several sources indicating that structural changes take place in the synapses between neurons when long-term memories are coded (Byrne, 1987; Schwartz & Greenberg, 1987). Repeated firings of nerve circuits (Hebb's cell assemblies) appear to induce structural changes in some synaptic connections. Recall from Chapter 3 that the synapse is the region where neural messages, in the form of chemical neurotransmitters, are passed from the axons of neurons to the dendrites of other neurons. The dendrites contain thornlike projections called *dendritic spines* that respond to transmitter substances.

Several investigators have conducted postmorten examinations, comparing the brains of animals reared in enriched environments (for instance, rats raised in cages with many toys) with those of animals raised in environments with few learning opportunities. The brains of the animals from enriched environments have been found to contain far more dendritic spines and more synapses with larger areas of contact (Crick, 1982; Hubbard, 1975; Rosenzweig, 1984; Rosenzweig et al., 1972; Sokolov, 1977). Changes in dendritic branching of certain groups of neurons have also been shown to result from specific kinds of training (Greenough, 1984).

Why do dendritic spines change as a result of experience? To find out, researcher Gary Lynch administered high-frequency electrical stimulation to neurons in a specific region of rats' brains. When these same neurons were later stimulated with low-frequency currents, they responded more extensively than they did before the high-frequency bursts (Lynch & Baudry, 1984). Lynch explains these results as follows: Stimulation causes neurotransmitters to flow across the synaptic gap to the dendrites, where they cause calcium ions to enter the dendritic spines. This triggers the release of an enzyme called *calpain* that in turn triggers growth of additional spines that act like "catchers' mitts," enabling neurons to receive messages more efficiently (Lynch, 1984).

Lynch's interpretation fits nicely with Hebb's original conception of how memory is transferred from STM to LTM. New information is held briefly in assemblies of firing neurons. As these cells fire, neurotransmitters flow across the synapses. If this information is held long enough in these circuits, structural changes take place in the dendrites of the receiving neurons. They become more sensitive to neurotransmitters, thus preserving a particular circuit or memory trace. The next question is, where are these memory traces for specific experiences stored?

WHERE ARE LONG-TERM MEMORIES STORED?

Physiological psychologist Karl Lashley (1929, 1950) spent most of his research career searching for the *engram,* the place where memories are stored. His technique was to train rats in a variety of tasks, then surgically destroy selective regions of the cortex, and then later test the rats' memories for the tasks. He never did succeed in pinpointing specific brain sites where memory is stored, which led him to report humorously, "I sometimes feel, in reviewing the evidence on the localization of the memory trace, that the necessary conclusion is that learning is just not possible" (1950, p. 477).

In a more serious vein, Lashley concluded that memories do not reside in precise locations in the brain but, rather, involve large areas of cortical tissue. This conclusion has been supported by extensive evidence collected over the last several decades, suggesting that memory is represented by large networks of neurons distributed over broad portions of the brain (Black et al., 1978; Squire & Butters, 1984; Woody, 1986, 1984, 1982). However, some memory researchers continue to believe that at least some memories may be localized within precisely defined brain regions.

For instance, recent research by Richard Thompson (1985) has isolated the location of a memory trace for a specific experience. Rabbits were classically conditioned to blink one eye in response to a tone. (The conditioning procedure involved sounding a tone followed by a puff of air to the eye.) After this conditioned response was established, Thompson was able to obliterate it entirely by creating a lesion in the cerebellum. His finding: "Destruction of as little as one cubic millimeter of neuronal tissue in a region of the cerebellar deep nuclei on the left side permanently abolishes the learned eyelid response, and it can never be relearned" (Thompson, 1985, p. 300). (While Thompson's research is noteworthy in its demonstration of a localized brain site for a specific memory, it should not be interpreted as evidence that the cerebellum is an important center for memory storage. Researchers continue to focus on the cortex as the primary brain structure where memories are stored.)

WHERE ARE LONG-TERM MEMORIES PROCESSED?

We know more about where long-term memories are processed than about the site in the brain where they are stored. Much of this information comes from studies of people who have experienced memory impairment through brain damage or through electroconvulsive shock therapy. We will examine some of this evidence.

The Case of H.M. In one famous case in the mid-1950s, a young man, identified as H.M., suffered from a severely debilitating epileptic condition. To ease his violent seizures, a neurosurgeon removed most of two limbic system structures, the hippocampus and amygdala (see Chapter 3). The operation was successful in reducing the seizures. However, it had the unfortunate side effect of virtually eliminating his ability to store newly acquired facts in long-term memory. H.M. remembers events that occurred up to three years before his surgery. Since he can learn new skills, it is also clear that his procedural memory is still intact (Milner, 1966). However, his declarative memory is virtually destroyed, so that he is unable to consolidate new factual information.

If you were introduced to H.M. and visited with him for a few minutes, he would seem quite normal to you. However, if you left the room and returned a few minutes later, you would again be a total stranger to him. It is difficult to imagine what it would be like to have no sense of a past other than very old memories. H.M. expressed his frustration and confusion in an interview some years ago:

Right now, I'm wondering. Have I done or said anything amiss? You see, at this moment everything looks clear to me, but what happened just before? That's what worries me. It's like waking from a dream. I just don't remember. (Thompson, 1985, p. 305)

Since H.M. was able to recall his earlier life after his hippocampus and amygdala were removed, we can deduce that long-term memory is not stored in either of these two structures. It does appear, however, that these structures are involved in transferring information from short-term to long-term memory. H.M.'s experience also suggests that the process of consolidation may continue for several years. Since he lost much of his memory for events within the three years preceding his surgery, these memories were probably not completely consolidated when portions of his brain were removed. Finally, the fact that H.M. could acquire new skills, such as playing tennis, suggests that procedural memory and declarative memory are distinct memory systems that involve processing by different portions of the brain.

The Case of N.A.   Another famous case, mentioned earlier in this chapter, is that of N.A., the young man whose thalamus was damaged by a fencing foil. N.A.'s memory impairment was similar to that of H.M., although his retrograde amnesia affected only recent events dating back about one year. Like H.M., his ability to consolidate new information acquired after his injury is markedly impaired. The left portion of his thalamus was the part affected, and his impairment is most obvious when the material to be learned is verbal (recall from Chapter 3 that the left side of the brain is typically more involved in verbal tasks than the right side). For example, he quickly forgets items on lists of words, but he is better at nonverbal tasks, such as remembering faces or learning how to negotiate mazes (Bloom et al., 1985). From this case, it seems likely that the thalamus plays an important role in consolidation.

Korsakoff's Syndrome   In the late 1800s a Russian physician, S. S. Korsakoff, called attention to a condition that often accompanies chronic, long-term alcoholism. The most pronounced characteristic of *Korsakoff's syndrome* is severe anterograde and retrograde amnesia. Not only are alcoholics with this condition unable to form new memories; their memories of events earlier in their lives are also impaired (Kolb & Whishaw, 1985). There is evidence of widespread brain damage associated with this disease. Perhaps most noteworthy is damage to the thalamic nucleus—the same damage that N.A. experienced in his fencing accident (Bloom et al., 1985).

Electroconvulsive Shock   In the late 1930s, psychiatrists began using *electroconvulsive shock therapy* (ECT) to treat some severe mental illnesses. (The origins and rationale for this treatment method are discussed in detail in Chapter 15.) In ECT, electrodes are placed against each temporal lobe and a current is sent through the brain, causing an epileptic-like seizure.

Research psychologists became interested in ECT when it was noted that patients experienced retrograde amnesia for events immediately preceding the shock. For example, Subin and Barrera (1941) asked psychiatric patients to learn lists of words before receiving ECT. Their subjects could not remember words they had learned immediately before the treatment, but they could remember words memorized some minutes earlier.

Similar findings have been reported in animal studies. In one experiment, rats learned that when they stepped off a platform onto a floor consisting of a metal gridwork, they would receive a foot shock. Typically, animals trained in this fashion will remain on the platform when they are placed there the following day. This did not happen when rats received ECT within a few seconds after experiencing the foot shock. When tested on the platform the following day, they stepped right off as if they had never received a foot shock before (Chorover & Schiller, 1965).

Such findings lead us to conclude that ECT produces retrograde amnesia only for events immediately preceding the treatment. Presumably, the electrical activity induced by the treatment disrupts the specific patterns of neural firing that provide the code for short-term memory. Researchers are not certain which areas of the brain are involved in this disruption of short-term memory. However, the hippocampus and the amygdala are the brain structures most sensitive to seizures, and it is likely that the insult to these structures is involved in the memory loss associated with ECT (Kolb & Whishaw, 1985).

These various causes of amnesia tell us a number of things about the physical bases of memory. The case of H.M., together with ECT research, strongly suggests that the hippocampus and amygdala are necessary for memory consolidation, particularly when it involves the transfer of declarative information from short- to long-term memory. The thalamus is also involved in memory consolidation, as revealed by the case of N.A. and studies of alcoholics with Korsakoff's syndrome. The thalamus may play a primary role in the initial coding of verbal material.

Other studies have provided further clues. Recently, Mortimer Mishkin and his associates have demonstrated two distinct memory circuits in limbic system structures. In one circuit, which seems to be involved in processing memories for things we see, visual messages are relayed from the occipital cortex to the hippocampus, which in turn directs the thalamus to begin the encoding necessary for long-term memory. Emotional events or experiences seem to be processed by a second circuit, this one mediated by the amygdala (Mishkin et al., 1984).

In sum, memory researchers are beginning to identify specific areas of the brain that play a role in placing new memories in storage. What is the final resting place of memories for things more complex than a simple conditioned eyeblink? We still cannot answer this question, although it seems likely that these memories are stored somewhere in the cerebral cortex in the form of networks of interrelated neurons.

SUMMARY

WHAT IS MEMORY?

1. The term memory describes either putting information into storage or pulling it back into consciousness.

2. The information-processing perspective on human learning and memory suggests that people actively participate in the assimilation of their experiences.

3. Memory consists of three separate processes: encoding or translating incoming information into a neural code that the brain can process; storage of information over time; and finally, the process of retrieval whereby stored information is located and recovered.

A THREE-SYSTEM MODEL OF MEMORY

4. One widely held perspective suggests that there are three distinct memory systems that allow us to process, store, and recall information: sensory memory (SM), short-term memory (STM), and long-term memory (LTM).

5. Sensory memories are brief impressions from any of our senses. Visual sensory memory and auditory sensory memory are referred to as iconic memory and echoic memory, respectively.

6. STM, frequently referred to as our working memory, is an intermediate memory process, sandwiched between SM and LTM, within which we actively process information.

7. STM has both a short duration and a limited capacity. Chunking, the process of grouping items into longer meaningful units, is an effective way to increase the limited capacity of STM.

8. Most of the information placed in STM is held there in an acoustic form, according to how it sounds. Information is also stored in STM based on what it looks like or what it means (visual and semantic coding).

9. Long-term memories are composed of both procedural memories and declarative memories. Procedural memories are memories for how to perform skills. Recall of specific facts is made possible by declarative memory.

10. It has been suggested that declarative memory may be further subdivided into episodic memory (autobiographical facts about a person's experiences stored in roughly chronological order) and semantic memory (general, nonpersonal knowledge about the meaning of facts and concepts without reference to specific experiences). It has recently been suggested that episodic memory may be best conceptualized as a subsystem of semantic memory.

11. A number of memory systems or mnemonic devices can improve encoding of information in LTM. These include clustering, the method of loci, using narrative sto-

ries, the peg-word system, acrostics, and acronyms.

12. The more retrieval cues that can be linked with information stored in LTM, the more likely we are to recall it later on.

13. Many psychologists believe that much of the information in our declarative memories is stored in the form of networks of associations between concepts or fragments of knowledge we have about things in our worlds.

14. The three most common techniques for testing LTM are recall tasks, recognition tasks, and relearning.

15. Research by Herman Ebbinghaus revealed that forgetting tends to occur very rapidly during the initial period after learning and that the rate of forgetting declines significantly thereafter.

SOME FACTORS THAT INFLUENCE WHAT WE REMEMBER

16. When we memorize a list of items we are most likely to remember those items at the beginning and end of the list, a phenomenon known as the serial position effect.

17. It is often easier to recall a particular event or experience if we are in the same context in which the information was first encoded. Context includes external environment and internal state (physiological conditions, emotions, etc.). This phenomenon is referred to as state-dependent memory.

18. Flashbulb memory refers to a kind of vivid recall for earlier events associated with extreme emotion.

MEMORY AS A CONSTRUCTIVE PROCESS

19. Remembering is often a process of mentally "reconstructing" an event rather than simply searching LTM for a perfect copy of it.

20. People may change details to reconstruct memories to be consistent with their schemas, which are conceptual frameworks that they use to make sense out of their worlds.

21. Research has called into question the reliability of eyewitness testimony. Considerable evidence suggests that eyewitness testimony may be flawed by people's tendency to reconstruct their memory of events to fit their schemas.

22. A number of studies indicate that people exposed to violent events are especially likely to incorporate misinformation into their memory.

WHY WE FORGET

23. Among the explanations put forth by psychologists to explain forgetting are the decay of the memory trace, interference, retrieval failure, motivated forgetting, and organic causes of forgetting.

24. Psychologists are not in agreement as to whether or not some memories may decay over time and become lost.

25. According to the interference interpretation of forgetting, experiences that occur either before or after we learn something new interfere with our memory. Retroactive interference occurs when a later event interferes with recall of earlier information. Proactive interference occurs when earlier learning disrupts memory for later learning.

26. Failure to retrieve memory may occur because it was poorly encoded in the first place or because we have inadequate retrieval cues.

27. Sometimes we forget long-term memories because we do not want to remember them, a process called motivated forgetting.

28. Memory deficits caused by organic factors may be of three kinds: amnesia caused by disease (impaired brain circulation, Alzheimer's disease, etc.); retrograde amnesia (loss of recall for events occurring just before a brain trauma); and anterograde amnesia (inability to recall information processed after brain damage).

THE PHYSICAL BASES OF MEMORY

29. Evidence from several sources indicates that structural changes take place in the synapses between neurons when long-term memories are coded.

30. Changes in dendritic branching of certain groups of neurons have been shown to result from specific kinds of training.

31. Extensive evidence suggests that memories are, in the main, represented by large networks of neurons distributed over broad portions of the cortex.

32. Evidence from a variety of sources strongly suggests that the hippocampus and amygdala are necessary for memory consolidation, particularly when it involves the transfer of declarative information from STM to LTM. The thalamus also appears to be involved in memory consolidation.

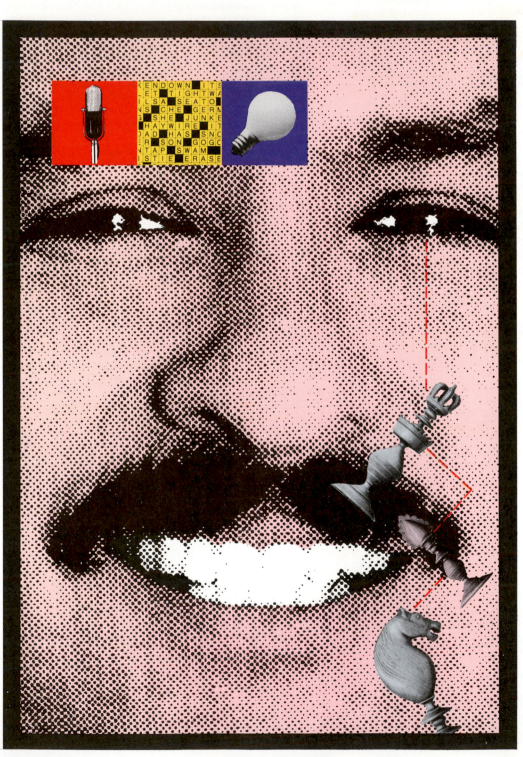

8 Thinking and Language

In Germany, around the turn of the century, there was a famous horse named Hans who performed amazing intellectual feats. When asked to solve spoken arithmetic problems such as "What is the sum of 5 plus 1?" he consistently signed the correct answer by tapping his hoof. Some cynics declared that Hans was a hoax and that his trainer was somehow cueing the right answer to the horse, but these assertions were dispelled when the horse provided the correct answer even when his trainer was not present.

Many people view abstract thought, problem solving, and language as qualities that set humans apart from other animals. Does Hans provide evidence disproving this belief? To answer this question, let us return to the story of Hans. After the critics had seemingly been disproved, someone noticed an odd pattern. Hans had trouble answering questions if the person who was asking them either did not know the answer or was standing out of sight. What did this mean?

Hans was clever, but, as the saying goes, a horse is a horse. He did not understand either the words or the math problems; instead, he had learned to respond to body language. This is what Hans had learned: Whenever his trainer or another questioner said something to him in an expectant tone of voice, then leaned forward and tensed up, Hans knew that he should start tapping his hoof on the ground. He would keep striking the ground until the trainer relaxed and stopped leaning forward. Hans knew that if he stopped tapping his hoof at this point, he would receive a carrot as a reward (Fernald, 1984).

We started this chapter with the story of "Clever Hans" because it illustrates something about our topic. Perhaps more than any other chapter in this book, our subject matter here deals with attributes that many view as unique to humans (at least to the extent to which these skills or abilities are developed within humans). In the following pages, we will explore what thought is, how we solve problems, how we reason and make decisions, and what are the special qualities of human language. We begin with the most fundamental of this chapter's topics, thought.

The concept of thinking has always fascinated humans.

THOUGHT

The term *think* means a variety of things to us. For example, we might remark to a companion, "I can't think of the name for that architectural style" or "I think that car is a terrific buy." Or if a neighbor asks your opinion

"Clever Hans" with his owner, Mr. van Osten.

on how best to deal with the problem of cars driving too fast along your quiet street, you may respond, "Let me think about it for a while."

In the first two instances the word "think" is synonymous with remembering and belief, respectively; in the third example it implies a process of reasoning about a particular situation with the intent of solving a problem. Psychologists who study thought are primarily interested in this latter meaning. Thus, we may define **thought** or thinking as a collection of internal processes directed toward solving a problem. When we use symbols or concepts to imagine something internally, and to solve problems mentally, we are said to be thinking. (Note that this is a somewhat narrow definition of the term *thinking*. Broader definitions of thinking include diverse cognitive processes, including such things as understanding language, memory retrieval, and perceiving patterns in sensory inputs [Houston, 1986; Oden, 1987].)

Thinking is the process that lets us make sense out of our perceptions. Our ability to think also allows us to put what we have learned to use to give meaning to our memories. Perhaps most importantly, thinking allows us to manipulate objects mentally, so that we can solve problems without actually going through any physical motions. For example, an architect working on a design for a new home on a hilltop does not have to draw several sets of plans to determine which will best take advantage of the view. Instead, he or she mentally manipulates various design features in order to arrive at a best solution before even getting out the drafting paper.

Cognitive psychologists who study thought are interested in determining how people transform and manipulate information to solve problems and make decisions. Before examining what research has revealed about how we accomplish these goals, we first consider a fundamental question: What are the basic components of thought?

COMPONENTS OF THOUGHT

About half a century ago, many psychologists believed that thinking was essentially a matter of talking to ourselves. The leading proponent of this view was John Watson (1930), the founder of behaviorism. Like other behaviors, Watson argued, thinking involves specific motor reactions; the only difference is that the muscular movements involved in thinking are much more difficult to observe than those of other kinds of behavior. Watson maintained that tiny movements of the tongue and throat, which he called *subvocal* or *implicit speech*, occur when we think.

Thinking gives us the ability to manipulate objects mentally and to solve problems.

Some early evidence supported Watson's view. For example, when researchers used sensitive recording devices, they were able to record very subtle movements of the tongue and throat muscles that occurred when subjects were silently thinking about various problems (Jacobson, 1932). One noteworthy study found that deaf people, who were accustomed to communicating with sign language rather than speech, exhibited muscular activity in their fingers when asked to solve problems (Max, 1937). Such results certainly indicated some relationship between thought and motor action, a relationship you may have noted yourself if you have ever observed people scratching their heads or furrowing their brows as they think. Watson, however, argued that there was more than just a relationship, and that subvocal speech was essentially equivalent to thinking.

This assertion was put to the test in an interesting experiment. A member of the research team acted as the subject; he was injected with curare, a drug that temporarily paralyzes all of the skeletal muscles. Since the paralyzed subject could not move any muscles, he was unable to engage in subvocal speech, to breathe, or even to blink. His research associates provided artificial respiration and other vital support services while their colleague was temporarily immobilized. When the drug wore off, the subject reported that his mind had remained clear during the entire procedure, and that he had been able to think about questions put to him and about what was going on throughout the experiment (Smith et al., 1947). These results indicate that thinking is an internal mental activity that can indeed be entirely independent of motor action.

Mental Images   If thought is not talking to ourselves, what is it? One component is mental images of visual scenes, sounds, or tactile sensations that we manipulate in some systematic or logical fashion (Richardson, 1983; Shepherd & Cooper, 1982).

For example, suppose you are trying to figure out how to assemble a new lawn mower after removing all the parts from the packing crate. You are likely to think about this task by manipulating visual pictures or mental images of the various parts. You might also use mental imagery to associate sounds as you try to recognize a melody, to picture the components of a perfect tennis swing, or to figure out the fastest route from your dorm to the laundromat.

It is clear that mental images are an element of thought, but there is more to thought than images of sights, sounds, and touches. Most cognitive psychologists believe that there is another, more abstract or symbolic form of thinking that involves the use of *concepts* (Medin & Smith, 1984).

Concepts   Suppose you are a parent of a six-year-old who asks "Where do babies come from?" You respond as well as you can by providing a simplified version of a very complex set of emotional and biological processes. This may not be the easiest task you have ever performed, but imagine how difficult it would be to answer this question if your child had not already acquired a mental representation or cognitive conception of the meaning of the terms you used to answer the question—terms like *love, feeling good, little,* or *seeds*?

In order to think and communicate about the objects, living things, activities, physical properties, relationships between things, and mental states we encounter in our daily lives, we learn to simplify and provide order to our world by mentally grouping events, objects, and so forth into general cognitive categories called **concepts** (Houston, 1986). Concepts thus represent categories or kinds of things, not just individual cases. Most of our knowledge is in the form of concepts rather than independent, specific items or instances (Bourne et al., 1986).

A concept may represent a category to which all varieties of one kind of physical object belong. For example, our concept of a car encompasses everything from a Model-T to a Rolls Royce. Concepts also represent kinds

FIGURE 8.1   A HURDY-GURDY

You probably recognize certain elements that lead you to categorize this object as a musical instrument.

of living things (such as a dog or a person); types of activities (reading and jogging); physical properties (little, pungent, or square); and relationships between things (such as taller than or prettier than). Concepts may also represent more abstract cognitive states, such as feeling good, love, or morality.

Our ability to think and to function efficiently would be greatly impaired if we were not able to form concepts. Without the general concept of a car, we could never give our children simple instructions such as "Watch out for cars when you cross the street." Instead, we would have to list every name of every automobile. Without the concepts of happy or sad, we could not describe someone's mental state without a drawn-out description of facial expressions, vocal inflections, and the nature of communicated messages.

Concepts provide a sense of order to a world filled with unique things and events, allowing us mentally to group things that share certain features even though they are not identical. They also allow us to categorize most of the new objects or activities that we encounter, even though they may be quite novel. Since we can relate these new situations to objects or events we are already familiar with, we can immediately understand something about them even though they are new. For instance, chances are that you have never seen a hurdy-gurdy before, as shown in Figure 8.1. However, you probably recognize certain elements—the drum, the crank at the base, and the guitarlike shape—that lead you to categorize this as a musical instrument.

Concepts may be either broad or very specific. Examples of specific, narrow concepts are socks, golden retrievers, and red balls. Examples of broader concepts are footwear, dogs, and balls. We tend to organize concepts into hierarchies, ranging from very broad to very specific. Thus, airplanes represent a broad category which may be subdivided into more specific lower-level categories, such as propeller aircraft and jet aircraft. Furthermore, jet aircraft may be subdivided into more specific groupings such as jet fighters, commercial passenger jets, and so forth.

There seems to be an optimal or **basic level** in each concept hierarchy that we naturally use when we think about objects or events. For example, look at the two objects pictured in Figure 8.2. What were the first labels for each of these objects that came to your mind? The odds are that you probably said "a *house* and a *car*." Certainly it would have been correct to classify them as a *colonial-style house* and a *two-door coupe*. However, these lower-level-category responses provide more detail than you need to think optimally about the objects. You could also have classified the objects in the picture as an *architectural structure* and a *motorized vehicle*, respectively, but this would not have been efficient, either, because such categorizations are too imprecise.

Research has supported the idea that we rely on basic-level categories most of the time. When subjects are shown a picture of an object and are asked to verify (yes or no) that it illustrates a particular concept, they tend to react fastest at the basic level (Rosch, 1978; Rosch et al., 1976). For example, when shown a picture of a kitchen chair, subjects consistently classify it more quickly at the basic level (a chair) than at either a subordinate level (a kitchen chair) or at a superordinate level (a piece of furniture). As children develop and learn to think conceptually about their environments, basic-level categories are probably the ones they use first as they acquire the ability to name and classify events and objects (Mervis & Crisafi, 1982). Many cognitive psychologists now believe that this dependence on basic levels of concepts continues to be a fundamental aspect of human thought throughout our lives.

Formal Concepts and Natural Concepts   Some concepts are logical and well defined. These **formal concepts** have clear, unambiguous rules specifying what features belong to that category. Examples of such well-defined

FIGURE 8.2

What are the first labels for each of these objects that come to your mind?

concepts are a red baseball hat and a spouse. In the first case, which is known as a *conjunctive concept,* all of the specified features—a hat, baseball style, the color red—must be present for an article to be included in the conceptual category. In the second case, which represents a *disjunctive concept,* the category is specified by an either/or rule (a spouse is either a husband or a wife).

Formal concepts are typically used by researchers as they conduct laboratory investigations of how people form concepts. However, in real life most of the **natural concepts** we use to think efficiently about past and present experiences tend to be more ambiguous. For example, how would you distinguish between crying and sobbing, or between a breeze and wind? We know what crying is and we can recognize sobbing when we hear it. Similarly, we can distinguish between a breeze and wind. It is difficult, however, to specify logical distinctions between the two items.

This can sometimes cause confusion. For example, the concept *bird* makes us think of animals that fly in the sky, build nests, and lay eggs. However, if we used these attributes to define a conjunctive concept of a bird, that concept would exclude turkeys, ostriches, penguins, and several other members of this species. Considering the fuzzy nature of this concept, it is quite understandable that many children do often exclude turkeys, ostriches, and penguins from their conceptualization of what a bird is (Rosch, 1977).

Try thinking about how you would clarify the natural concept *game.* We all know what a game is, but it is not easy to specify exactly what attributes are shared by board games, card games, video games, Olympic games, and contact-sport games. Since there are no specific rules that designate all members of a natural-concept category, we typically learn by experience what events or objects should be encompassed by a natural-concept category.

HOW DO WE FORM CONCEPTS?

A number of different theories have been proposed to explain how people form concepts. These include association theory, hypothesis-testing theory, and exemplar theory.

This three-year-old quickly identifies the seagull as a bird but has much more difficulty identifying the penguin as a bird.

Association Theory   One theory of how we form concepts was proposed by the early behaviorist Clark Hull (1920), who described concept formation as the acquisition of stimulus–response (S–R) associations. According to this view, we learn to associate a single response (the concept) with a set of stimuli that share one or more common elements. Thus, we associate the concept response *bird* with a pattern of stimuli (has wings, flies, lays eggs, etc.). We form a mental representation of a concept that is broad enough to allow us to generalize the response to many different instances of the concept. When we encounter a novel instance of the concept, such as an exotic bird we have never seen before, we respond correctly ("it is a bird") on the basis of stimulus generalization (see Chapter 6).

Hypothesis-Testing Theory   Another view, originally proposed by Jerome Bruner and his Harvard colleagues, suggests that we acquire formal concepts in a more or less systematic fashion by forming and testing hypotheses. Thus, we develop some type of strategic, hypothesis-testing plan for identifying members of a particular category or concept. This typically takes the form of speculating about what attribute or attributes are critical for determining whether an item belongs in a particular concept category, generating a hypothesis about how the attribute(s) determines the concept, and maintaining the hypothesis if it leads to a correct decision. If an hypothesis is proved wrong, another one is formed until the concept is learned (Bruner et al., 1956; Medin & Smith, 1984).

   Although subjects often seem to use hypothesis testing in laboratory settings, many psychologists have questioned whether this model applies to real life. Laboratory studies are typically based on artificial tasks, using arbitrarily selected attributes that bear little resemblance to the kind of natural concepts that we encounter in ordinary life (Bourne et al., 1986). Eleanor Rosch (1973, 1978) proposed an alternative explanation of how we form concepts in everyday life.

Exemplar Theory   According to Rosch's **exemplar theory,** the natural concepts that we learn in everyday life are represented in our memories by examples rather than by abstract rules. Thus, our concept of *fish* may be based on images of salmon, trout, or bass—all examples of fish that we have seen—rather than arbitrary rules such as "have fins," "breathe through

TABLE 8.1 *Furniture Items Ranked by Goodness of Example*

Member	Goodness of Example Rank	Member	Goodness of Example Rank	Member	Goodness of Example Rank
chair	1.5	vanity	21	mirror	41
sofa	1.5	bookcase	22	television	42
couch	3.5	lounge	23	bar	43
table	3.5	chaise lounge	24	shelf	44
easy chair	5	ottoman	25	rug	45
dresser	6.5	footstool	26	pillow	46
rocking chair	6.5	cabinet	27	wastebasket	47
coffee table	8	china closet	28	radio	48
rocker	9	bench	29	sewing machine	49
love seat	10	buffet	30	stove	50
chest of drawers	11	lamp	31	counter	51
desk	12	stool	32	clock	52
bed	13	hassock	33	drapes	53
bureau	14	drawers	34	refrigerator	54
davenport	15.5	piano	35	picture	55
end table	15.5	cushion	36	closet	56
divan	17	magazine rack	37	vase	57
night table	18	hi-fi	38	ashtray	58
chest	19	cupboard	39	fan	59
cedar chest	20	stereo	40	telephone	60

Source: From Rosch, 1975.

gills," "live in water," and so forth. Rosch pointed out that most natural concepts, such as furniture, fish, bird, and game, are not easily described as some well-defined combination of discrete attributes; nor are all instances of a natural concept equally good examples of their respective categories. For any given concept category, some examples are more typical and some less typical. Rosch suggests that we often structure our concepts around best instances, or most typical representatives of the category, which she calls **prototypes**. The more closely objects or events match our prototypes for a concept, the more readily we will include them in the category (Armstrong et al., 1983).

Suppose, for example, you were asked "Is a robin a bird?" and "Is a penguin a bird?" You would respond yes to both questions, but you would probably be slower to respond to the second question (Rips et al., 1973). The reason is that a robin is more typical of a bird than is a penguin. (It may, in fact, be the prototype around which you have organized your concept of bird.)

Rosch demonstrated this in an experiment in which she asked people to rank different instances of a given category according to the degree to which they typified the concept. For example, when subjects were asked to rank various examples of furniture, a chair and a sofa received the highest ranks (most prototypical), a lamp and a stool received the intermediate rank, and a fan and a telephone were ranked as the least typical examples of furniture (see Table 8.1). These rankings correlated with reaction time, with the most typical examples producing the fastest yes/no responses and the least typical examples resulting in the slowest responses (Rosch, 1975).

PROBLEM SOLVING

Imagine that you and a friend have just hiked the last leg of a week-long backpacking trip. You arrive at your parked car hot, thirsty, and anxious to get back to civilization, but when you try to start your car, the motor will not turn over. You quickly diagnose the problem—a dead battery. A few other vehicles are parked at the trail head but nobody is around to provide help. The nearest town is 10 miles away on an absolutely flat country road. You have to be home in six hours for an important engagement, and it is a three-hour drive to your home. You have a problem.

A problem exists when there is a discrepancy between your present status and some goal you wish to obtain, with no obvious way to bridge the gap. The essence of a problem is that you must figure out what can be done to resolve a predicament and to achieve some goal. In this example, your goal is to start your car so that you can get home on time, but the dead battery is preventing you from reaching that goal.

Problem-solving is different from simply executing a well-learned response or a series of behaviors, as a rat might do when it negotiates a maze to reach a food reward. It is also distinct from learning new information. For instance, you would not be problem solving if some hikers fortuitously returned to their car and told you they could take you to the nearest service station. The essence of all problems is that they require you to supply the new knowledge that will allow you to achieve your goal.

Problems consist of three components: (1) the *original state* of the situation as it exists at the moment, as perceived by the individual; (2) the *goal state,* which is what the problem solver would like the situation to be; and (3) the *rules or restrictions* that govern the possible strategies for moving from the original state to the goal state. To return to the dead battery problem, your perception of the original state might be, "My car won't start because of a dead battery and I am 10 miles from the nearest garage." Your goal would be, "I want to be home in six hours." The rules or restrictions might include, "Walking to the nearest town is unacceptable because it would take too long" and "There are three other cars at the trail head but no people to provide help."

How would you go about solving a problem like this? To treat this topic fairly, we have to admit that there is no one ideal solution. Instead, there are a number of possibilities—ranging from hitchhiking to borrowing a battery from one of the parked cars so that you can drive your own battery to a service station for recharging. Each of these strategies, however, has its own risks. The solution to this problem (and other problems we will be discussing) is not really the issue in this section. Instead, our concern is the way we approach problems, the strategies that can make problem solving easier, and potential stumbling blocks that can get in the way of problem solving. We explore these issues in the next several pages.

STAGES OF PROBLEM SOLVING

Problem-solving behavior generally involves three logical steps or stages: representing or defining the problem, generating possible solutions, and evaluating how well a given solution works.

Representing the Problem Logically, the first step in problem solving is to determine what the problem is and to conceptualize it in familiar terms that will help us better understand and solve it. Consider the following problem:

> Two train stations are fifty miles apart. At 2:00 P.M. one Saturday afternoon two trains start toward each other, one from each station. Just as the trains pull out of the stations, a bird springs into the air in front of the first train and flies ahead to the front of the second train. When the bird reaches the second train it turns back and flies toward the first train. The bird continues to do this until the trains meet. If both trains travel at the rate of twenty-five miles per hour and the bird flies at one hundred miles per hour, how many miles will the bird have flown before the two trains meet? (Posner, 1973)

The manner in which you represent this problem in your mind will significantly influence the ease with which you can generate solutions. Some problems can be represented visually. Thus, you might be tempted to draw a diagram showing the paths of the two trains and the zig-zagging path of the bird as it goes back and forth between them. Unfortunately, this strategy will probably serve to complicate this problem for you, rather than making it easier to solve. A much more logical approach is to represent the problem mathematically.

Thus, you know that the bird flies at 100 miles per hour and that it will keep flying until the trains meet. All you have to do is figure out how long it will take the trains to meet and translate this figure into the bird's flying rate. Since the stations are 50 miles apart, and since each train travels at 25 miles per hour, they will meet at the halfway point between the stations in exactly one hour. This means the bird will have to fly for one hour, and since it flies 100 miles per hour, it will fly a total of exactly 100 miles.

Our understanding of a problem is influenced not only by how we represent it in our minds, but also by how the problem is presented to us. The following problem illustrates this point: Assume you are sitting at the table shown in Figure 8.3; on it are a few candles, several matches, and a box containing some tacks. The table is flush against a corkboard wall. You are told to attach a candle to the wall so that no wax will drip on either the table or the floor when the candle is lit. Try to solve this problem, and then check your solution by looking at Figure 8.4.

REPRESENTING THE CANDLE PROBLEM SO IT IS EASY TO SOLVE

Research has shown that this problem is often quite difficult to solve when the elements (candle, matches, etc.) are presented in the fashion illustrated in Figure 8.3. Now that you know what the solution is, can you think of a different way to present the elements that would make the problem easier to solve? Give some thought to this question before reading on.

Only one minor variation in how the candle problem is represented can make it much easier to solve. When the tacks are removed and scattered on the table, and the box is thus presented empty, most people have no trouble solving the problem (Glucksberg & Weisberg, 1966). When the box is shown holding tacks, people have a hard time visualizing it as a separate object that may be used as a platform to mount the candle.

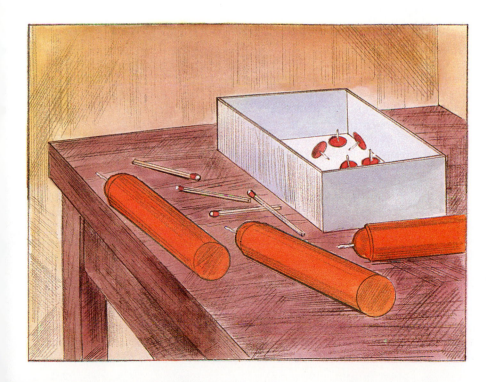

FIGURE 8.3   MATERIALS AVAILABLE IN THE CANDLE PROBLEM

How can you attach a candle to the wall so that it will drip on neither the floor nor the table? (*Source:* Adapted from Bourne et al., 1971)

FIGURE 8.4   SOLUTION TO THE CANDLE PROBLEM

(*Source:* Adapted from Bourne et al., 1971)

Generating Possible Solutions   Once we have a clear idea what the problem is, the next step is to generate possible solutions. Sometimes these solutions are easy. For example, if you sit down to begin studying and discover that your notes are missing, you might only need to search your long-term memory: "Ah yes, I remember lending the notes to my roommate, who missed yesterday's lecture." Assuming your roommate is handy, your problem is solved. Other more complicated problems may require you to generate more complex strategies. Consider the following problem:

> Find a number such that if 3 more than 4 times the number is divided by 3, the result is the same as 5 less than 2 times the number. (Mayer, 1982, p. 448)

One approach to this problem is through trial-and-error, testing different numbers at random. However, this approach would be highly inefficient. A person who understands algebra might elect to apply an algebraic strategy. This approach would lead to the formula $(3 + 4X)/3 = 2X - 5$. Solving for X yields the correct answer, 9. This example illustrates once again how representing a problem makes all the difference in the ease with which we can solve it. Subjects who represented the problem as a mathematical formula were able to solve it more readily than those who represented it as a word problem (Mayer, 1982).

Evaluating the Solution   The final stage in problem solving is to evaluate your solution. In some cases, this is a simple matter. For example, solving for X in the previous problem and then plugging the obtained value into the original formula would quickly reveal whether or not the solution was correct. That is because the problem is clear cut, with only one possible solution.

With some other types of problems, the solution may be much more difficult to evaluate. For example, college students often have trouble evaluating their answer to the problem "What should I major in?" The reason for this difficulty has to do with the vague nature of the problem itself. Many students have not yet defined what their goals are, and have only a vague notion of their options. As a result, many students are not certain that they have made the best choice even after they have selected a major. Problems that are unclear or poorly defined are almost always difficult to evaluate.

STRATEGIES FOR PROBLEM SOLVING

Whether a problem is clear cut or vague, the way we approach it makes a critical difference in our ability to find a workable solution. A number of different strategies can be applied. This section considers four common approaches: trial-and-error, testing hypotheses, algorithms, and heuristics.

Trial-and-Error   Some problems have such a narrow range of possible solutions that we decide to solve them through **trial-and-error.** For example, suppose you return to campus late Sunday after a weekend trip, and an acquaintance in your dorm tells you that you had a call from a woman who sounded distraught, insisting that you call immediately upon your return. Unfortunately, your acquaintance cannot find the slip of paper with her name and phone number, and has forgotten her name. The list of women who call you is somewhat limited, so you decide to call them one by one until you find out which one left the message. This trial-and-error process is not a bad strategy for solving the problem of the mystery caller, since the likely solutions are probably few in number.

Testing Hypotheses   A somewhat more systematic approach to problem solving is provided by the strategy of **testing hypotheses.** Assume that the list of possible woman callers is rather lengthy (you are a very social person) and that calling each one on a trial-and-error basis would be too time consuming. Instead, you may formulate specific hypotheses that will generate a more efficient approach to solving your problem. For example, it sounds to you as though the person who called is going through some difficult emotional times. Based on this information, you may narrow your choices to those friends who you know have recently been distressed or agitated. Thus, your first calls would be to a friend whose father has been ill and to another whose romance has been on shaky grounds lately.

Algorithms   A third possible problem-solving strategy is the **algorithm.** Algorithms involve a systematic exploration of every possible solution until the correct one is found. This strategy originated in the field of mathematics, where its application can produce guaranteed solutions. Algorithms are especially well suited to computers, which can rapidly sort through hundreds, thousands, even millions of possible solutions without growing tired or suffering from boredom (both shortcomings of the human data processor).

Algorithms guarantee a correct solution if you are aware of all the possibilities—but in real life that is a big if. For instance, you could not apply an algorithm in solving the problem of the unknown caller, since the caller might have been someone you have never met, or it might be a voice from the distant past that you would never think to include in your list of possibilities. In addition, humans (unlike computers) will try to find shortcuts when faced with complicated problems: often algorithms simply require too much effort. One type of shortcut strategy we commonly use is called a *heuristic.*

Heuristics   **Heuristics** refer to a variety of rule-of-thumb strategies that may lead to quick solutions but are not guaranteed to produce results. We all have a repertoire of "quick-fix" methods for dealing with problems, based on both experiences with strategies that have worked in the past and our own personal storehouse of accumulated knowledge.

For example, suppose you are watching TV and your picture suddenly becomes a tangled jumble of random lines. Your strategy for solving this problem is to adjust the horizontal control knob. This strategy, which is probably based on previous experiences with your TV set, may lead to a quick solution. But there is also the possibility of failure: The lost picture might be caused instead by interference from some other electrical appliance or by some defect in your set unrelated to the horizontal control function.

We use several kinds of heuristic strategies. One of the most common, **means-ends analysis,** involves first identifying the difference between the original state and the desired goal state, and then choosing a set of operations that will reduce this difference by progressing through a series of subgoals that systematically move you closer to the final solution (Newell & Simon, 1972). For instance, you would probably use means-ends analysis to solve the anagram *teralbay*, rather than using the algorithmic strategy to combine and recombine its eight letters 40,300 times.

To use means-ends analysis, you might begin by defining some subgoals that would help you move to a solution. Perhaps your accumulated knowledge about the English language would first prompt you to focus on certain common letter combinations (such as *ra, be, bay, able,* and *tray*) from the 8-letter anagram and to exclude combinations that rarely or never occur (such as *aa, lbya, yblt, rtbl*). With these subgoals accomplished, you could then manipulate common letter combinations to seek a final solution. Do words with the combination *bay* in them work? No such luck. How about *able*? Again, no cigar. What about *tray*? This is the one: the answer is betrayal.

Another common heuristic strategy is **working backward** from a clearly defined goal to the original state (Newell & Simon, 1972). For example, suppose that you decide to stay on campus over the Thanksgiving holiday to study for a major biology exam scheduled for the following week. On Thanksgiving Day you discover that both your textbook and lecture notes are missing. After searching your memory, you remember leaving them in the biology laboratory, which is locked up for the holidays. You also recall that your lab partner is a good friend of the young man who is performing custodial duties in the Science Building. This young man was taking some time off from school to earn money to continue his education, and he lives close to campus. If you can find him, he can probably help you gain access to your textbooks.

You have now defined your goal as getting into the biology lab. The best way to reach it is to work backward from that goal. The final step that will lead to this goal is phoning the janitor and asking if he would kindly take a few minutes to drive to campus and let you into the laboratory. What has to be done before this step? You must get the janitor's phone number from the telephone directory, but to do this you must have his name. You can get his name from your lab partner, who is home for the holidays. Thus, you must begin by calling your lab partner at home. You now have a reasonable strategy for solving your problem.

WHY WE HAVE DIFFICULTY SOLVING SOME PROBLEMS

Most of us are reasonably successful at solving the kinds of problems we encounter in the classroom, in the laboratory, and in our everyday lives. However, a number of relatively common situations can create obstacles to effective problem solving. Some of these obstacles have to do with the problem itself; others are the result of the way we approach the problem.

Characteristics of Difficult Problems   Problems come in many forms and vary greatly in difficulty. Two characteristics that can make a problem difficult to solve are lack of definition and complexity.

Ill-Defined Problems   According to cognitive psychologists, problems exist on a continuum ranging from well defined to ill defined. *Well-defined problems* are those in which the original state and goal state are clearly specified, as are rules for allowable problem-solving operations. Assembling a lawn mower from parts that arrive in a crate, putting together pieces of a jigsaw puzzle, and solving a mathematical problem are all examples of well-defined problems.

As we have already seen in our discussion of evaluating solutions, *ill-defined problems* are often more difficult. With these problems, we usually have a poor conception of our original state and only a vague notion of where we are going and how we can get there; there is also no obvious way of judging whether a solution we might select is correct (Houston, 1986). For example, it is not uncommon to reach the goal of graduating from college only to face a new problem of vast dimensions: what to do with the rest of our lives. Before we can work effectively toward solving such problems, we need to define our goals more clearly and have a better idea of what means are available to us.

Complex Problems   Try to solve the following two problems:

> Orcs are monsters who eat small humanlike dwarfs called hobbits (characters from Tolkien's *Lord of the Rings*). Three orcs and three hobbits are stranded on one side of a river. They have a small boat that will hold a maximum of two creatures. The problem is to transport all six safely to the other side. If at any time orcs outnumber hobbits (on either side of the river), the orcs will dine on the outnumbered hobbits(s). How can all six get across in one piece?

> A man and his two sons want to use an available boat to get across a river. The boat has a maximum capacity of 200 pounds. The father weighs 200 pounds and each son tips the scales at 100 pounds. How can all three safely cross the river?

The solutions to these problems are provided in Figure 8.5. If you were able to solve one of these problems successfully, you probably found it relatively easy to solve the other, since both require the same kind of strategy. However, observations of people who work on only one or the other of these problems, but not both, generally reveal that the "man and his sons" version is solved more quickly than the "orcs and hobbits" version. The reason for this difference is related to the number of steps required to solve each version. The father and his sons get across the river in only five steps, compared to 11 steps to get all the orcs and hobbits across. In sum, complex problems with numerous steps are generally more difficult to solve than problems whose solutions involve fewer steps.

Perceptual Obstacles That We Create   Although complex and ill-defined problems tend to be inherently difficult, sometimes we have only ourselves to blame for the trouble we have solving problems. Three common obstacles that we often create for ourselves are mental set, functional fixedness, and confirmation bias.

Mental Set   Suppose you have three containers that have a maximum capacity of 21 ounces, 127 ounces, and 3 ounces, respectively, and a tap to draw water from. Your task is to use these three containers to obtain exactly 100 ounces of water. Attempt to solve this problem, as well as the other problems listed in Table 8.2.

How well did you do on these problems? Did you overlook a simpler solution on the sixth water-container problem and perhaps get temporarily stymied by the seventh problem? If you answered yes, you have just experienced firsthand how a mental set can inhibit or block effective problem solving. A **mental set** is a tendency to approach a problem in a set or predetermined way regardless of the requirements of the specific problem. When we operate under the influence of a mental set, we apply strategies that have previously helped us solve similar problems, instead of taking the time to analyze the current problem carefully.

FIGURE 8.5 SOLUTIONS TO RIVER-CROSSING PROBLEMS

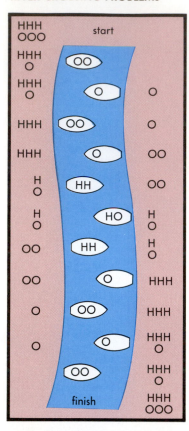

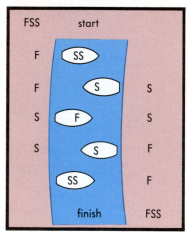

TABLE 8.2 *Water-Container Problems*

Problem No.	Containers with Capacity in Ounces			Obtain Exactly These Amounts of Water
	Container A	Container B	Container C	
1	21	127	3	100
2	14	163	25	99
3	18	43	10	5
4	9	42	6	21
5	20	59	4	31
6	23	49	3	20
7	10	36	7	3

Source: From Luchins and Luchins, 1959.

Mental sets often facilitate problem solving, but they can also get in the way. This is illustrated by the way most people perform on the water-container problems in the figure. The chances are good that you figured out that the way to obtain 100 ounces is to fill the *B* container with 127 ounces and pour 21 ounces into the *A* container, then fill *C* with 3 ounces twice. Once you solved this problem, you probably applied the same strategy (mathematically represented by the formula $B - A - 2C$) to the next several problems. Thus, this mental set helped you to solve these problems readily. But what about item six? If you are like most people, you probably applied the same formula to this problem as well. This worked, but problem six can also be solved by a simpler and more efficient method, expressed by the formula $A - C$.

It is interesting to note that when these problems are presented to students in a classroom demonstration, many dash along to item seven, at which point they often get stuck and sometimes even declare that it cannot be solved. Even though they are never told to solve all problems in the same way, the $B - A - 2C$ strategy has worked so well that the resulting strong mental set keeps them from considering another approach.

Functional Fixedness A second common obstacle to solving problems is functional fixedness. To see how this factor operates, consider the problem illustrated in Figure 8.6. You are brought into a room where two strings dangle from the ceiling. Your task is to tie the two strings together. Unfortunately, they are just far enough apart so that it is impossible to hold on to one and to stretch out and grasp the other. Several objects are present in the room, as pictured in the figure. Before reading on, take some time to search for a solution to the problem (or solutions, since there is more than one).

One possible solution is illustrated in Figure 8.7. You could attach the pliers to the end of one string and swing the pliers and string like a pendulum. This would allow you to grasp the stationary string in one hand and simply to wait until the swinging string comes within easy reach of your free hand. If you did not think of this, you may be kicking yourself now for overlooking such a simple solution. However, you may take consolation in knowing that many people faced with this problem also overlook this solution. This may be due to what psychologists call **functional fixedness**—the tendency to be so set or fixed in our perception of the proper function of a given object that we are unable to think of using it in a novel way to solve a problem. Thus, we may be so fixed in considering that the function of pliers is to hold on to things that we do not consider this tool as a potential pendulum weight.

Confirmation Bias Another relatively common obstacle to problem solving is our inclination to seek out evidence that will confirm our hypothesis, while at the same time overlooking contradictory evidence. This phenomenon, known as **confirmation bias,** was demonstrated in investigations

FIGURE 8.6 THE TWO-STRING PROBLEM

conducted by British researcher Peter Wason (1968). Wason asked his sub-jects to discover what rule applied to a three-number series. Initially the subjects were provided with one example of a positive instance of the rule to be discovered, such as 2, 4, 6. They were then told to propose additional series to the experimenter, who would indicate whether each did or did not conform to the rule.

> ### FINDING THE OBSTACLE IN WASON'S NUMBER-SERIES PROBLEM
>
> **Many of Wason's subjects tackled the problem we have just described by hypoth-esizing a specific rule, such as "numbers increasing by 2." They then proposed additional series, such as 4, 6, 8; 8, 10, 12; or 1, 3, 5, to verify their hypothesis. Wason responded that each of these series conformed to the rule. On this basis, many of Wason's subjects concluded that their hypothesis was correct—and they were visibly frustrated when told that "numbers increasing by 2" was not the general rule the experimenter had in mind. Can you figure out what they failed to do as they put their hypothesis to the test? Take a moment to consider this ques-tion before reading on.**

The fact is, Wason's unknown rule was very general—"numbers in increasing order of magnitude." Thus, if you had been a subject and your initial hypothesis had been "numbers increasing by two," any series that you proposed (4, 6, 8; 10, 12, 14; or 1, 3, 5), would also have conformed to the unknown rule. The point is that you would never be able to solve this prob-lem if you continued to search only for evidence that would confirm your initial hypothesis. The only way you could discover Wason's general rule would be to seek evidence that would disprove your hypothesis. For instance, you might have proposed 4, 6, 7 to disconfirm your "increasing by 2" hypothesis. Discovering that this series also conformed to the rule would allow you to shift your thinking and quickly discover the correct solution.

People often have trouble with problems such as this because they are more anxious to find instances that verify rather than disprove hypoth-eses. We can all benefit from being aware that finding solutions may require us to look not only for what might be correct, but also for what is incorrect.

FIGURE 8.7   SOLUTION TO THE TWO-STRING PROBLEM

REASONING AND DECISION MAKING

Life constantly presents us with problems and decisions: how to get to class on time when the car will not start, what to major in, what political candidate to support, how to get an A in psychology, what to do about an uncomfortable relationship. Our ability to solve problems successfully and make good decisions is greatly influenced by the reasoning processes we use. In this section we consider the ways in which people reason when they make a decision. We also examine some of the common thinking errors that can cloud our reasoning process. We will end the section by examining certain aspects of decision making.

LOGICAL REASONING

We often attribute a poor decision or failure to solve a problem to faulty reasoning, implying that there are normative standards for proper or correct reasoning. Such standards are available. In fact, they emerged ages ago from the discipline of formal logic, a branch of philosophy.

You may have already been exposed to the basic tenets of logic in your prior studies. If so, you know that there are two basic types of reasoning: deductive and inductive. When we engage in **deductive reasoning,** we begin with certain general assumptions or premises that we believe to be true, and we use these assumptions as the basis for drawing conclusions that apply to specific instances. For example, we know that all dogs have shorter natural life spans than humans. Therefore, we deduce that a two-year-old child will outlive the puppy she received on her second birthday. As long as we begin with valid assumptions and follow certain rules of logic, we can be confident that our deductions are valid (Skyrms, 1986).

In **inductive reasoning,** we reach a general conclusion by generalizing from specific instances. For example, suppose that every male acquaintance expresses an interest in watching TV broadcasts of football games. This might lead us to conclude that men in general enjoy this activity. With inductive reasoning, however, we can never be absolutely certain that we have reached a correct conclusion: some day we might meet a man who hates watching TV football.

In real life, most of us tend to use both deductive and inductive reasoning (Halpern, 1984). However, the discipline of formal logic has placed its emphasis primarily upon deductive reasoning, providing a set of rules and systematic methods for reaching valid conclusions. A classical model for studying deductive reasoning is provided by the syllogism.

Syllogisms   A **syllogism** is an argument consisting of two (or more) presumably true statements, called *premises,* and a statement of conclusion that may or may not follow logically from the premises. Once the form of a syllogism is established, a person is not asked to decide if the premises are true or if the conclusion is factually valid. Rather, the task is to determine whether or not the conclusion follows necessarily from the premises. Consider the following examples:

> All men are humans.
> All humans are animals.
> Therefore, all men are animals.

> All women are child abusers.
> All child abusers are highly intelligent.
> Therefore, all women are highly intelligent.

The conclusion in the first example follows logically from the two premises; therefore, it is true. Very few people have a problem with this kind of argument since its statements seem reasonable and consistent with our collective knowledge of the world. In contrast, the bizarre statements in the second example may have caused you to question the validity of the argument. If you rejected the second argument after accepting the first, you were not consistent in applying the principles of formal logic to your reasoning process.

As this example illustrates, the psychological content of verbally expressed arguments can misdirect our reasoning processes and lead to faulty conclusions. This is one reason why logicians prefer to express syllogisms in a more abstract way by substituting letters for real words. If we abstract the previous two examples of syllogisms in this fashion, we will see that both follow the same form, shown below:

> All As are Bs.
> All Bs are Cs.
> Therefore, all As are Cs.

To apply the principles of formal syllogistic reasoning correctly, we must meet the following three requirements: (1) each premise must be considered in terms of all its possible meanings (most premise statements are ambiguous in that they may refer to more than one possible relationship); (2) all of the varied meanings of the premises must be combined in every conceivable way; and (3) a conclusion may be judged to be valid only if it applies to every conceivable combination of all possible meanings of the premises. If we can come up with at least one combination of the premise meanings that is inconsistent with the conclusion, we may judge the syllogism to be erroneous. Figure 8.8 diagrams how these three principles may be applied in logically analyzing the syllogistic form above.

SOME COMMON CAUSES OF REASONING ERRORS

If we were able to apply the rules of formal logic consistently and systematically to our reasoning, we would be remarkably successful in solving problems and making decisions. However, even students of logic probably find it difficult to apply these principles with total accuracy to everyday life. Instead, we often err because we are too quick to accept faulty premises, because we misinterpret a premise, or because our attitudes or experiences interfere with our ability to think logically.

FIGURE 8.8 LOGICAL ANALYSIS OF A SYLLOGISM

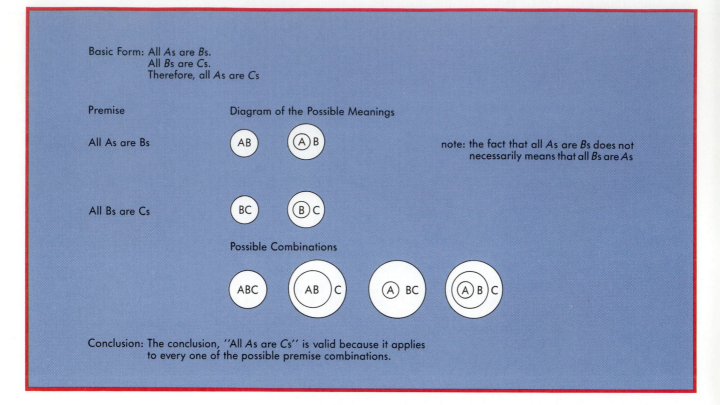

Basic Form: All *A*s are *B*s.
All *B*s are *C*s.
Therefore, all *A*s are *C*s

Premise   Diagram of the Possible Meanings

All As are Bs   note: the fact that all *A*s are *B*s does not
                                                                    necessarily means that all *B*s are *A*s

All Bs are Cs

Possible Combinations

Conclusion: The conclusion, "All *A*s are *C*s" is valid because it applies
to every one of the possible premise combinations.

Faulty Premises Consider the following syllogisms:

> The job applicant comes from a broken home.
> People who come from broken homes are social misfits.
> Therefore, the job applicant is a social misfit.

> All women experience mood swings.
> No one with mood swings becomes a corporate president.
> Therefore, no women are corporate presidents.

In both of these examples the conclusions are false in spite of the fact that the actual syllogisms are logically valid. The problem lies in the fact that both arguments are based on faulty premises: many people from broken homes are not social misfits, and not all women experience mood swings (in addition, some corporate presidents surely do experience mood swings). Unfortunately, we are often inclined to make bad judgments not because we reason incorrectly, but rather because our initial assumptions or premises are false.

Misinterpreting a Premise A second common cause of error can be our own misinterpretation of a premise. Instead of considering all possible meanings of a premise statement, we may incorrectly conclude that it has just one meaning. One of the most common premise misinterpretation errors is to assume that if the premise is true, so is its converse. For example, given the premise "All *B*s are *A*s," people commonly interpret this statement to mean that "All *A*s are *B*s" is also true. When these misinterpreted premises are then combined, erroneous conclusions may follow. For example, consider the following syllogism:

> All *B*s are *A*s.
> All *C*s are *B*s.
> Therefore, ____?____

As you can see in Figure 8.9, when all possible meanings of each of these premises are combined, there is only one valid conclusion: "Some *A*s are *C*s." However, if you misinterpreted the premises to mean that their converses are also true (i.e., that "All *A*s are *B*s" and that "All *B*s are *C*s"), you would have been led to the logically invalid conclusion that "All *A*s are *C*s."

Belief-Bias Effect   A third possible source of trouble is the tendency to rely on cherished beliefs rather than logical analysis. This **belief-bias effect** may be stated as follows: people tend to accept conclusions that conform to their beliefs and reject conclusions that do not conform, regardless of how logical these conclusions are (Bourne et al., 1986).

A recent study demonstrates this phenomenon. Subjects were asked to evaluate several syllogisms and to decide whether or not the conclusions followed from the premises. The conclusions were sometimes logically valid and sometimes not; in addition, their believability (the key variable in the experiment) varied greatly. Some conclusions were quite believable (for example, "some good ice skaters are not professional hockey players") and others were unbelievable ("some professional hockey players are not good ice skaters"). The results indicated that many subjects succumbed to the belief-bias effect, accepting believable but invalid conclusions and rejecting unbelievable but valid conclusions (Evans et al., 1983). We often face conflict between principles of logic and what we believe about the world. This research suggests that too much reliance on preexisting beliefs can impair our ability to think logically and make valid judgments.

RATIONAL APPROACHES TO DECISION MAKING

We have considered a number of situations in which the rules of formal logic allow us to decide whether or not a conclusion follows from the given facts, and, assuming that we have correctly applied the principles of logic, our true or false decisions have been relatively straightforward. However, our lives are shaped by many everyday decisions in which the facts as we know them do not dictate a single, logical conclusion. For example, you know of several approaches to losing weight, and you have to select one option on the basis of the evidence at your disposal. *Decision making* is a process that occurs whenever we are faced with an array of alternative

FIGURE 8.9   PREMISE MISINTERPRETATION LEADING TO REASONING ERROR

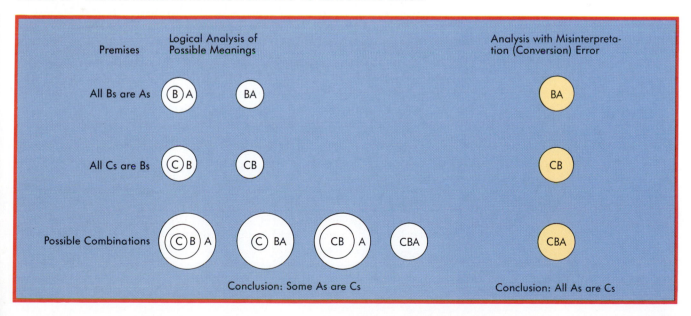

choices and we choose one option while rejecting others (Hammond & Arkes, 1986; von Winterfeldt & Edwards, 1986).

This section outlines a few rational approaches or models for making important decisions; then the following section examines some of the approaches we use for making quick decisions each day.

Compensatory Models   Decisions are often quite complex, including both desirable and undesirable dimensions on either side. **Compensatory models** of decision making allow us to evaluate how desirable potential outcomes stack up against (or compensate for) undesirable potential outcomes. We consider two such models: the additive model and the utility-probability model.

Additive Model   The *additive model* allows us to weigh potential positive and negative features for each alternative. The decision maker starts by listing common features of the various alternatives, and assigning arbitrary units that reflect the value of a given feature to the decision maker (higher numbers indicate greater value). These numbers are then added up to arrive at a total score for each alternative.

For example, suppose you must make a career decision that has been narrowed down to three alternatives: college biology teacher, physician, or the family business. Each alternative has both attractive and unattractive dimensions. Table 8.3 indicates arbitrary quantitative values (on a scale of -2 to $+2$) that you might assign to each dimension relative to each of the three alternatives. Using the additive model of decision making, it appears that you should definitely reject the family business alternative, and that you would probably be more satisfied working as a college biology teacher than as a physician.

The additive model is relatively easy to implement, but a second, more complex model of compensatory decision making is generally more accurate. This is the utility-probability model.

Utility-Probability Model   People often make important decisions by weighing the desirability of each available option on two scales: (1) its *utility*, which is the value you place on potential positive or negative outcomes; and (2) its *probability*—the likelihood that the choice will actually produce the potential outcome. For example, suppose you are faced with the following decision: You have a year of college left, but you and your sweetheart are considering marriage right now, rather than waiting until graduation. This is a very serious decision and not one that you want to take lightly or make too hastily.

Table 8.4 shows how you would approach this decision using the *utility-probability model*. First you would list several potential outcomes and assign a utility to each on some scale, say -10 to $+10$. For instance, you might assign a value of $+10$ to being happy, -8 to having financial difficulties, and so forth. These potential outcomes and their corresponding utility values would be listed under each choice (get married, do not get married). Next, you would assign a best-guess probability to each potential

TABLE 8.3   *The Additive Model Applied to a Hypothetical Decision-Making Process*

	Biology Teacher	Physician	Family Business
Interest	+1	+2	−1
Personal autonomy	+1	+1	+1
Income	0	+2	+2
Vacation time	+2	−1	0
Stress	+1	−2	−2
Satisfaction	+2	+2	−2
	+7	+4	−2

TABLE 8.4 *Utility-Probability Model Applied to Hypothetical Decision: Whether or Not to Get Married While Still in College*

	Choice: Get Married				Choice: Do Not Get Married		
Potential Outcome	Utility (on a scale of −10 to +10)	Probability (0 to 1.0)	Expected Utility (utility × probability)	Potential Outcome	Utility (−10 to +10)	Probability (0 to 1.0)	Expected Utility (utility × probability)
Happy	+10	.7	+7	Happy	+10	.2	+2
Good study habits	+5	.8	+4	Good study habits	+5	.3	+1.5
Ample alone time (personal space needs)	+6	.2	+1.2	Ample alone time (personal space needs)	+6	.9	+5.4
Financial difficulties	−8	.8	−6.4	Financial difficulties	−8	.1	−.8
Friendships limited	−4	.7	−2.8	Friendships limited	−4	.1	−.4
Lowered motivation to stay trim	−3	.4	−1.2 +1.8	Lowered motivation to stay trim	−3	0	0 +7.7

outcome. For instance, you have an 80 percent chance of running into financial difficulties if you marry now, as opposed to a 90 percent chance of not having money troubles if you wait. Once you have assigned utilities and probabilities to each outcome, you multiply the probabilities by the appropriate utility values to determine expected utilities. The final step would be to sum all expected utility values under each option, and to select the alternative that yields the highest value. Given the values assigned in the figure, you would probably choose to postpone your marriage—if your decision were completely governed by rationality, that is.

Noncompensatory Models   Not all approaches to decision making involve carefully weighing all the pros and cons. In **noncompensatory models** of decision making, not all features of each alternative may be considered, and features do not compensate for each other. There are a number of noncompensatory strategies; let us see how we might apply four of them in deciding what car to buy.

Table 8.5 lists the choices: Ford Escort, Toyota Corolla, Honda Civic, and Dodge Colt. All purchase options are comparably priced, so the decision models are applied to five other features: mechanical reliability, crash test rating, leg room, noise level, and resale value. All four vehicles are assigned a hypothetical rating on each of these five dimensions on a scale of 1 to 10.

The first strategy, the *maximax strategy*, is a very basic model. It simply involves comparing the choice options on their best features, and then selecting the alternative with the strongest best characteristic. For instance, if we used this strategy to choose a car, we would select the Toyota Corolla since its best feature, mechanical reliability, is the strongest of best features.

An equally simple approach is the *minimax strategy*. Here, we compare the weakest features of each option and select the alternative whose weakest

TABLE 8.5 *Hypothetical Values for Decision Task: Which Car to Buy?*

	Ford Escort	Toyota Corolla	Honda Civic	Dodge Colt
1. Mechanical reliability	6	10	9	5
2. Crash test rating	4	9	6	1
3. Leg room for occupants	5	5	4	3
4. Noise level	5	3	3	6
5. Resale value	5	4	7	3

feature is most highly rated. If we used this approach, we would select the Ford Escort, because its lowest rating, a 4, is higher than any other car's lowest rating.

A third strategy, the *conjunctive strategy*, sets minimally acceptable values for features. For instance, we might set the minimum criteria at "four or higher on every feature." We would then rule out any alternative that did not meet or exceed these criteria. If we were to apply this strategy to selecting a car, the Ford Escort would once again be our choice.

One final noncompensatory strategy described by Amos Tversky (1972) is called *elimination by aspects*. Tversky believes that when we are faced with complex decisions, we often proceed by eliminating undesirable alternatives step by step. We have certain criteria that each feature must meet; when an alternative does not meet those criteria, we eliminate it. We begin with one minimum criterion and we use it to test the various alternatives. If more than one alternative remains after applying our minimum criteria, we use a second criterion to eliminate additional alternatives, and so forth until just one alternative remains.

To apply this strategy to the car-choice problem, we might begin by deciding not to buy any car with a mechanical reliability rating of less than six. This eliminates the Dodge Colt and narrows our choice to three candidates. Next we decide not to accept any car with a crash rating below five. This eliminates the Escort, leaving two alternatives. Next we decide that the leg-room rating must be five or better. This eliminates the Honda Civic, leaving us with one choice, the Toyota Corolla.

HEURISTIC APPROACHES TO DECISION MAKING

If we made all of our decisions in a rational, systematic manner such as those just described, we might find that our friends would begin to call us "wise one," "learned one," "Socrates," or some other suitably laudatory title. However, it is also possible that we would not have any friends, since we would be so bogged down in charting options or calculating probabilities that we would have no time to socialize.

We took the time to outline some of these rational decision-making strategies because important life choices should be approached in a systematic fashion that will increase the odds for making good choices. However, for the dozens of lesser decisions we must make every day, we need to be able to choose quickly. Consequently, we often concentrate on only a few relevant facts, relying on intuition and certain heuristic, or "rule-of-thumb," approaches (Thorngate, 1980). Heuristics often work rather well, as we saw earlier in the discussion of problem-solving strategies. The time they save, however, can sometimes be offset by costly errors of judgment (Hogarth, 1981). To gain a better sense of the potential benefits and costs of these short-cut approaches, we will consider two common rule-of-thumb decision-making strategies identified by psychologists Amos Tversky and Daniel Kahneman (1974, 1984): the representative heuristic and the availability heuristic.

The Representative Heuristic Consider the following description of a friend of one of the authors and decide which of the following two occupations she is most likely to be involved in: police officer, or host of a local radio talk show oriented to solving relationship problems.

> She is petite, soft spoken, and very gentle. She almost never displays any aggressive or hostile behavior, although she is moderately assertive. She likes to read about psychology and enjoys dealing with people on a personal-emotional level. She is sensitive to others' needs and always willing to listen to viewpoints that may not be her own.

If you were not expecting to be tripped up, you probably guessed that the mystery person earns her living in radio because the description is more representative of your preconceived notion of a person who solves personal problems than of a police officer. When we use the **representative heuristic** strategy, we judge the likelihood of something by intuitively comparing it to our preconceived notion of a few characteristics that represent a given category to us.

For example, most people probably have a prototype image of a police officer. You might associate characteristics such as "tough," "aggressive," and "nonemotional" with this job. The extent to which our mystery person fits these stereotypes indicates how representative she is of this category: clearly, the fit is quite poor. On this basis alone, many people would be unlikely to guess that she is indeed a police officer. On the other hand, traits such as "sensitive," "good listener," "likes psychology," and "assertive but not aggressive" do match many people's image of someone who hosts a talk show that focuses on solving relationship problems.

A SHORTCOMING OF THE REPRESENTATIVE HEURISTIC METHOD

The representative heuristic strategy can be useful: because it allows us to concentrate on only a few relevant variables, it helps streamline our decision making. However, sometimes this selective strategy blinds us to relevant information. For example, what extremely useful piece of information is likely to be overlooked in the occupation decision problem you just considered? Think about this question before reading on.

Do you think you might have made a different choice if we had suggested that you consider the relative proportion of police officers and talk-show hosts in the general population? In the greater metropolitan area of Portland, Oregon, there are over 100 police officers for every talk-show host. This information might have influenced you to decide that the woman is probably a police officer (as indeed she is). On the other hand, it might have had no influence at all on your decision.

In one study, college-student subjects were presented with a series of brief personality profiles allegedly drawn at random from a sample of 100 attorneys and engineers (Kahneman & Tversky, 1973). They were asked to assign each profile to one job category or the other. Before the task began, they were told the relative proportions of attorneys to engineers in the sample—a proportion that the researchers varied with different groups of subjects, so that it might be 70:30 in some trials and 30:70 in others. Although you might expect this information about proportions to influence their decisions, it had virtually no impact. If a description stated that a person was politically active, argumentative, and articulate, subjects were likely to assign the profile to the attorney category no matter what the ratio. The subjects overlooked the information about probabilities, basing their decisions instead on how well the profiles matched their own stereotypes.

The Availability Heuristic   Another heuristic strategy bases decisions primarily on the degree to which we can access information from our memories. This approach, called the **availability heuristic,** is based on two assumptions: first, that the probability of an event is directly related to how frequently it has occurred in the past; and, second, that events that occur more frequently are usually easier to remember than less common events.

The availability heuristic strategy probably serves us well most of the time. For example, our decision to serve hamburgers rather than calamari (squid) to a group of teenagers at a Sunday picnic is no doubt a wise choice based on past experiences with teenagers who enjoy hamburgers but dislike exotic seafood. Similarly, we decide to carry an umbrella on a gray, overcast day because we remember that clouds often bring rain.

On the other hand, the easiest events to remember are not always the most common ones. For example, a person who lives near a nuclear power plant may seriously consider relocating in order to reduce the risk of becoming a victim of a nuclear disaster similar to the one that occurred in 1986 in Chernobyl, U.S.S.R., despite the fact that the chances of that happening are statistically minute. Considering the extensive media attention to the risk of nuclear accidents, it is understandable that many people might decide to move away from the shadows of a nuclear plant. We are not suggesting that this would necessarily be an irrational move. It does, however, illustrate decision making that is influenced by vivid media images rather than by the logical evaluation of probabilities.

Although heuristic strategies sometimes lead to bad decisions, these intuitive strategies can often help us make accurate decisions with little intellectual effort. Perhaps now that you are more aware of the potential shortcomings of these rule-of-thumb strategies, you will be less inclined to apply them inappropriately. Maybe the next time you decide to buy a car your decision will not be dictated by Uncle Bill's enthusiastic testimony about the virtues of a Buick. Instead, you may elect to do some research to obtain reliable estimates of the probability of mechanical problems, structural integrity in a crash, and so forth, and then base your decision on a systematic evaluation of these facts.

LANGUAGE

The processes that we have considered so far in this chapter—thinking, abstract problem solving, and reasoning and decision making—set humans apart from animals like Clever Hans, the horse we met at the beginning of this chapter, and indeed from all other animals. Our last topic, the ability to use language, is perhaps the most profound indicator of the power of human cognition (Miller, 1981). Without language, our ability to communicate our thoughts would be limited to the basic kinds of meanings that we could indicate by nonverbal gestures. We would not be able to establish complex social structures and pass on knowledge from generation to generation. Our ability to remember, to reason, and to solve problems would also be severely curtailed since so much of human information processing and thinking occurs at the abstract level of language symbols.

Language is the primary means by which we communicate with one another. This is not to say that language and communication are the same thing. An animal in the forest who emits a cry of warning as a predator approaches, or a dog who drops a ball at its master's feet, are communicating messages. However, it is the ability to use abstract symbols to convey messages that lifts communication to its heights.

Psycholinguistics is the psychological study of how we translate sounds and symbols into meaning, and of what cognitive processes are involved in the acquisition and use of language. Psycholinguists have devoted considerable effort to studying the structure and rules of language. We begin our discussion at this level.

THE STRUCTURE AND RULES OF LANGUAGE

The people we talk to each day are able to make sense out of what we say to them because we all string sounds together according to a common set of rules. There are actually four levels of rules—phonemes, morphemes, syntax, and semantics—and psycholinguists analyze languages at each of these four levels.

Phonemes The basic structural elements of language are called **phonemes.** All languages are made up of individual sounds that are recognized as distinct or different. The English language has about 45 phonemes, while other languages may have as few as 15 or as many as 85 (Houston, 1986). Most of the phonemes in the English language correspond to the consonant and vowel sounds. For example, in the word *tap* we may identify three

Psycholinguistics is the psychological study of how we translate sounds and symbols into meaning. All human languages follow four levels of rules—phonemes, morphemes, syntax, and semantics.

separate phonemes, corresponding to the consonant sounds of *t* and *p* and the vowel sound of *a*. (The letter *a* makes four different vowel sounds, *a* as in *tap*, *a* as in *pray*, *a* as in *care*, and *a* as in *water*.) Some phonemes are produced by letter combinations, such as the *th* sound in *the* and the *sh* in *shout*. In some cases different letters produce the same sounds, such as the *a* in *bay* and the *ei* in *sleigh*. Thus, phonemes are not identical to the letters of the alphabet, even though individual letters do generate many of the sounds unique to our language.

In order to represent ideas in our thought processes or to convey meaningful information, we must combine phonemes according to rules we all understand. For instance, you will quickly recognize that *thnkng* and *lngg* are not acceptable words. The rule that has been violated is that words in the English language must contain both consonants and vowels. If we add the missing vowels to the two letter groupings, we can form the legitimate words *thinking* and *language*.

Morphemes A **morpheme** is the smallest unit of meaning in a given language. In the English language almost all morphemes consist of combinations of two or more phonemes (exceptions are the pronoun *I* and the article *a*). Many morphemes, like *book*, *learn*, and *read*, are words that can stand alone. Other morphemes must be attached as prefixes or suffixes to root words. For example, the word *replays* is a word that consists of three morphemes: *play*, which can stand alone, the prefix *re*, meaning "again" or "anew," and the suffix *s*, which indicates "more than one."

The manner in which morphemes are formed and used also follows distinct rules. In the English language, for example, no more than three consonant sounds can be strung together in one morpheme. Rules also govern the manner in which suffixes can be added to form plurals. Thus, the plural forms of *hat* and *bus* are *hats* and *buses*. Morphemes also have fixed positions in the structure of language: A football broadcaster who repeats a critical play for home viewers is presenting a *replay*, not a *playre*.

Syntax Besides learning how to recognize phonemes and use morphemes, we also learn to use **syntax** (commonly known as grammar), the set of language rules that governs how words can be combined to form meaningful phrases and sentences. The sentence, "She purchased the dog small" is immediately recognizable as an improper sentence because one of the rules of English syntax is that adjectives generally precede the nouns they modify ("small dog"). If a Spanish-speaking person read this same sentence, translated into Spanish, he or she would consider it to be grammatically correct, since adjectives normally come after nouns according to Spanish rules of syntax.

Semantics   Finally, language is also characterized by a system of rules that help us determine the meaning of words and sentences. (The study of meaning in language is called **semantics**.) For example, you know immediately that there is something wrong with the sentence, "People who engage in regular daily exercised are often able to keep their levels of stress to a minimum." Adding *d* to the word *exercise* conveys the meaning of something that happened in the past. However, since the semantic intent of this sentence is to describe exercise as a present or future activity, the *d* should obviously be omitted. Sentences may be syntactically correct but semantically incorrect. For example, the grammatically correct sentence "The dorm food is emotionally disturbed" violates our knowledge of semantics, for food cannot be emotionally disturbed (although some dorm food can lead to disturbed emotions!).

THEORIES OF LANGUAGE ACQUISITION

How do we learn all of these rules? A number of theories have been proposed to explain how we acquire language. These explanations vary considerably in their emphasis on environment versus innate biological mechanisms.

The Learning Perspective   At one end of the continuum are theories that emphasize the role of learning. According to behaviorist B. F. Skinner (1957) and social learning theorist Albert Bandura (1971), children learn to shape sounds into words and words into sentences through processes of selective reinforcement and imitation.

This learning perspective is supported by some evidence. For example, babies whose parents reinforce their early attempts at meaningful sounds do tend to vocalize more than institutionalized children who receive less attention (Brodbeck & Irwin, 1946). Small children often imitate the words they hear their parents say, and this behavior is often reinforced. Selective reinforcement and behavioral modeling techniques have also been successful in teaching language to emotionally disturbed or developmentally delayed children (Lovass, 1973).

However, the learning perspective does not explain all aspects of human language acquisition. For example, many of the words children spontaneously utter are their own inventions, not imitations of a model: where do they come from if they are not learned? Again, children typically do not verbally imitate exactly what they hear. Instead, they put words together in their own, often unique, way. Furthermore, even though parents seldom correct their children's syntax, children usually begin to form grammatically correct sentences before formal schooling begins (Stine & Bohannon, 1983; Tartter, 1986). Most importantly, it has been demonstrated that language acquisition follows an invariable sequence among children all over the world, under highly variable conditions (Brown, 1973; Nelson, 1981; Tartter, 1986). This suggests that there is something innate about language, which is exactly the position championed by psycholinguist Noam Chomsky.

The Nativistic Perspective   Just as children are genetically programmed or "prewired" to follow the developmental sequence of sitting, crawling, and walking. Chomsky (1965, 1968, 1980) maintains that the human brain is also programmed to learn speech according to a sequential pattern. This view of language acquisition, sometimes referred to as *nativism*, does not

Babies whose parents reinforce their early attempts at meaningful sounds tend to vocalize more than children who receive less attention.

Twins often communicate with meaning and clarity in their own private language, unintelligible to anyone but themselves. Originally these twins were believed to be severely retarded, but later it was discovered that their "meaningless gibberish" was intelligent and that they actually understood English and German.

suggest that our brains are programmed to learn a specific language such as English or French. Instead, it says that a newborn's brain is prewired with the ability to recognize phonemes and morphemes and to learn the basic rules of grammar and semantics. Chomsky labeled this innate ability to learn language the **language acquisition device (LAD).** He believes that without this innate mechanism we would be overwhelmed by the virtually unlimited number of possible variations in how sounds might be combined, and thus would be unable to understand the rules of language.

This genetic or nativist position has been supported by a variety of data, and "there is strong evidence that the process of learning human speech is largely guided by innate abilities and tendencies" (Gould & Marler, 1987). Certainly, the fact that all normal children progress through the same sequence of language acquisition suggests some basic, genetically shaped biological program. (According to the learning position, in contrast, we should find considerable individual differences in patterns of language development because of the wide variations that occur in learning histories of people from widely divergent environments.) Further support for the nativist position is provided by evidence that human infants recognize virtually all of the consonant sounds characteristic of human speech (Eimas, 1985).

Have you ever had an occasion to listen to preschool-age identical twins communicate with each other? One of the authors attended graduate school with the father of identical twin daughters. These girls, approximately age four, had developed a language that was completely unintelligible to anyone else. Nevertheless, observations of the animated way they carried on conversations with their strange lingo indicated they were clearly communicating thoughts that had meaning and clarity for both. Psycholinguists have frequently observed this phenomenon among sets of twins (Carelli & Benelli, 1986; Malmstrom & Silva, 1986). The key finding of these observational studies is that these special languages are not a mere variation on the common language(s) spoken by others in their environments. Furthermore, the private language of twins appears to have the characteristics of other languages, including nouns, verbs, and a definite syntax. Psycholinguists, such as Noam Chomsky, interpret these findings as supporting the view that humans are born with a prewired knowledge of syntax. How else might we explain why the private language of twin sets contains a structure comparable to all known languages?

Although it helps explain many questions that the learning perspective leaves unanswered, the nativistic position does not explain all aspects of language acquisition. Most notable is the question of how we acquire language. Some learning must take place for a child to acquire the rules of English rather than the rules of some other language. Chomsky's theory does not explain what this process is.

Thus, most contemporary psychologists look to both the learning position and the nativistic approach to supply pieces for the puzzle of human language. The learning position helps explain how children learn specific rules of grammar, and it also explains why language acquisition may be retarded among children raised in environments that offer few opportunities to observe, imitate, and receive reinforcement. At the same time, the nativistic view explains not only the universal developmental sequence of language acquisition, but also the ease with which children acquire one or more languages despite the enormous complexity of language rules. It seems, then, that genetics and environment interact in some complex fashion—what Vivien Tartter (1986) calls a "tuneable blueprint"—to provide us with the necessary foundations for learning language.

THE SEQUENCE OF LANGUAGE ACQUISITION

That "tuneable blueprint" can be traced through several stages in a universal developmental sequence in which children learn language. This section presents a typical timetable. Note that there is considerable individual variation within the normal range of the stages outlined below.

Early Evidence of Prewiring A large body of evidence indicates that human infants are prewired to understand and process human speech sounds (Eimas, 1985; Flavell, 1985; Gibson & Spelke, 1983). Even in the earliest stages of infancy, children are able to distinguish speech from non-speech sounds, and they seem particularly tuned in to speech (de Villiers & de Villiers, 1979). Thus, a one-day-old baby will rhythmically move her or his body in accordance with the surrounding speech sounds (Condon & Sander, 1974), and a three-day-old can distinguish the voice of mother from strangers (DeCasper & Fifer, 1980).

By the age of one month, infants are able to distinguish between phonemes and other sounds, even when they are physically and acoustically almost the same (Eimas, 1975; Aslin et al., 1983). This apparently innate perceptual ability, called *categorical speech perception*, may be the portion of Chomsky's language acquisition device that allows children to understand the phonological code of whatever language they are exposed to.

All children typically progress through the same stages of sound production during their first year (Tartter, 1986). Initially, newborns emit only one sound: crying (Hopkins & Palthe, 1987). Even though crying is clearly a very rudimentary form of communication, research has shown that parents of both sexes are generally able to distinguish between taped cries of their own offspring and those of other infants (Roberts, 1987). Some people, particularly parents, also believe that they can distinguish between cries of hunger, pain, or anger by noting different patterns of pitch and intensity. If this were true, we would have to conclude that cries at an early age exhibit *semanticity*, or special meaning.

TESTING WHETHER BABIES USE DIFFERENT CRIES FOR DIFFERENT MESSAGES

You have probably observed parents remarking, in response to the cries of their babies, that "he sounds hungry" or "she is mad because I am ignoring her." Can parents actually determine when a cry means "I'm hungry," "I hurt," or "I'm annoyed"? How would you investigate this question? Can you think of another explanation for why parents often seem able to determine the reasons for their infants' cries? Give these questions some thought before reading on.

One simple way to determine whether parents can distinguish cries in different contexts would be to record the cries of infants in situations where they are clearly hungry, frustrated, or in pain, and then to play the tapes for parents and ask them to identify their baby's mental state. An experiment that used this methodology demonstrated that parents could not distinguish between different prerecorded cries (Dale, 1976). Under natural conditions, however, they are likely to make much better judgments because they have considerable additional information: they know how long it has been since the last feeding, or that the infant is due for a diaper change, and so forth.

Early Vocalizations   Sometime between four and six weeks, infants enter the second stage of vocalization, called *cooing*, in which they emit sounds of pleasure when they are happy. At about six months, sometimes earlier, there is another significant stage referred to as *babbling*. The baby begins to utter repeatedly a variety of simple, one-syllable consonant and vowel sounds like "da-da-da," "ba-ba-ba," or "ma-ma-ma." In the first few months of this stage, the babbling consists both of sounds that are used in the adult language and those that are not. Vivien Tartter (1986) concludes that infants at this stage appear "to be playing with the sounds, enjoying the tactile and auditory feel of vocalization" (p. 337).

At about nine or ten months the babbling becomes intelligible as babies begin to imitate more purposefully the sounds of the speech of others, even though they may not yet understand them. At this point in language development, these vocalizations begin to approximate the phonemes of the language they hear every day. Thus, cooing and babbling provide babies with a basic repertoire of sounds, laying the foundation for real speech.

First Words   Children usually produce their first one-word utterances sometime around their first birthday. They have already learned that sounds can be associated with meanings, and now they begin to use sounds to convey meaning. First words are usually very simple, and they often refer to concrete things like familiar people ("mama," "dada"), toys ("ball"), consumables ("juice"), common implements ("cup"), animals ("da" or "dog"), words for greeting ("hi"), and a few action words ("eat," "up," "more") (Clark, 1983). These words may be an oversimplification of the actual words, but they nevertheless qualify as words if they are used consistently to refer to a particular object or event (thus, "ba" for bottle or "nana" for banana).

A child may also use single words in a way that indicates much more. For example, a toddler who tugs on your leg and pleads "up" is probably conveying the meaning "Pick me up," just as a child who points to a balloon and says "ba" with a rising inflection at the end is asking "Is that a ball?" These single-word utterances designed to express a complete thought are call *holophrases*.

Telegraphic Speech   Within about six months after the first word is spoken, children develop a vocabulary of about 50 words. Sometime between 18 and 24 months they generally produce their first "sentences," which usually consist of two-word utterances like "More milk" or "There ball." These early primitive sentences typically leave out articles (such as "a" and "the"), prepositions ("to," "on"), conjunctions ("and"), and auxiliary verbs ("can," "will") (Flavell, 1985). This pattern of condensed or *telegraphic speech* is typical of the first sentences spoken by children all over the world (Brown, 1973)—evidence that tends to support the theory of genetic prewiring. Young children also seem to express similar meaning in their short utterances, no matter what culture they belong to (Flavell, 1985).

Harvard's Roger Brown (1973) has extensively reviewed data from a number of diverse cultures to determine what early meanings are expressed

TABLE 8.6 *Common Semantic Relations in First Sentences*

agent–object	e.g., "daddy ball," when the child wants daddy to do something with the ball
action–object	"hit ball"
agent–action	"daddy hit"
entity–locative	"ball box"
action–locative	"lie bed"
entity–attributive	"little doll"
demonstrative–entity	"that baby"
possessor–possession	"mommy coat"

in children's two-word sentences. He concludes that most two-word sentences are designed to express any of eight common semantic or meaning relations, as shown in Table 8.6.

Expanded Language From age two, language development progresses rapidly. Children expand their vocabulary at the rate of several hundred words for every six months of age. Children seem to be remarkably adept at determining the meaning of new words they hear from the context in which the word was spoken (Markman, 1987). Two-word sentences give way to meaningful sentences that may lack absolutely correct grammatical structure but nevertheless display a syntax that approximates proper language structure (Valian, 1986). Children begin to make a shift from simple sentence grammar to a more complex syntax sometime between ages two and three (Bloom & Capatides, 1987). By age four or five, most children have learned most of the basic grammatical rules for combining nouns, adjectives, and verbs into meaningful sentences.

As they learn to combine morphemes into more complex words and into still more complex sentences, a number of errors typically occur regardless of what language is being learned. For instance, when children first learn the basic rules of grammar (such as that plurals are formed by adding an *s*, and the past tense of many verbs is formed by adding a *d* sound to the end) they may tend to *overgeneralize* these rules to instances where they do not apply. Thus, *oxs* may be used instead of *oxen*, *deers* instead of *deer*, and "I sleeped in the bed" instead of "I slept in the bed." Children may also overgeneralize by applying concept words too broadly. For instance, a child who learns to recognize police officers by their uniforms may call every person in uniform "police."

Another common error in the early stages of sentence usage is *oversimplification*—using just enough words to convey a message, without being syntactically correct. For example, when a three-year-old wants to play in the park she might say to her mother, "I go park." Later on she will learn to add in the articles, prepositions, and other parts of speech that are necessary to form grammatically correct sentences such as "I want to go to the park." Most children are quite successful at mastering these refinements: By the time they enter school, they usually have a good comprehension not only of the general rules of their language, but also of the exceptions.

IS LANGUAGE UNIQUE TO HUMANS?

We have been discussing human language, but nonhuman animals also have methods of communicating. A walk in any forest is likely to produce a cacophony of bird calls that communicate danger. Monkeys have been shown to produce different sounds to indicate danger approaching from above, such as an eagle, versus danger from below, such as a prowling panther (Marler, 1967). Bees communicate with each other about the nature and location of food sources by engaging in an intricate "waggle dance" (von Frisch, 1974) (see Figure 8.10). Do these methods of commu-

FIGURE 8.10   THE BEE'S DANCE

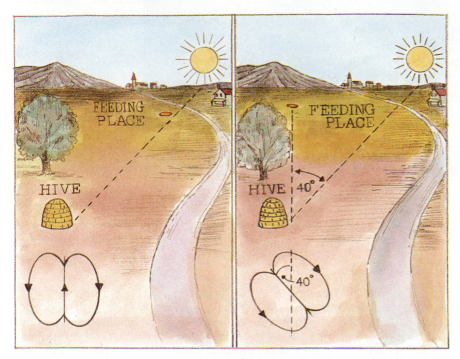

Bees have a complex system of communicating to each other about the location, quantity, and quality of food. For example, to indicate the location of food, a bee engages in an elaborate "dance" that is mimicked by other bees who dance with her until they "understand" and fly off in the direction of the food. A variation in the nature of the dance provides information on the direction and the distance of the food. A dance in a circle indicates a nearby source, whereas a dance in a "figure eight" pattern signifies a more distant source. Indications of direction are particularly important in the case of a distant source. As shown in the figure, the bees determine the direction in which they must fly from the hive to the food by "interpreting" the angle that the figure eight forms with respect to the sun's position and the vertical axis of the hive.

nicating qualify as a "true language" in the sense that they contain the same features as human language? To answer this question, we first need to identify the primary criteria or attributes of all human languages: generativity, specialization, arbitrariness, displacement, and novelty. Table 8.7 defines these five criteria.

TABLE 8.7   *Attributes of Human Languages*

1. *Generativity:* The ability to provide for a huge variety of meanings in an unlimited number of utterances.
2. *Specialization:* The only purpose of the language is to communicate information to others.
3. *Arbitrariness:* The combinations of sounds selected to refer to objects or events is purely arbitrary. Thus our English word *book* might just as well have been *zock.*
4. *Displacement:* Language can be generated in the absence of any eliciting stimulus. Thus, humans can talk about dangerous dogs when no dogs are present, whereas a monkey vocalizes a sound indicating danger only when a predator is observed. Displacement also refers to the ability to communicate about things in the past and future, not just the present.
5. *Novelty:* Humans are able to express themselves with novel phrases and sentences that they have never heard before. Thus, human language is more than mere memorization and repetition of word strings.

Source: Adapted from Hockett, 1960.

Although their sounds cannot be construed as language in the strictest sense of the word, whales and other nonhuman animals have definite methods of communication.

If we strictly interpret the criteria in the table, it is quite clear that bird calls, monkey vocalizations, dolphin whistles, or bee dances do not qualify as language. But this does not rule out the possibility that nonhuman animals have the ability to learn to use language to communicate abstract thoughts and ideas. Considerable research with apes, in fact, has challenged the view that only humans can communicate with abstract symbols.

Some of the earliest research attempted to teach chimpanzees to talk. These experiments were essentially failures, although one chimpanzee did learn to vocalize four words: "mama," "papa," "cup," and "up" (Hayes, 1951; Kellogg & Kellogg, 1933). Later experiments used another strategy. Speculating that chimpanzees simply did not have the vocal apparatus to communicate verbally, Allen and Beatrice Gardner (1969, 1975) took another route: they taught American Sign Language (ASL) to a chimpanzee named Washoe.

The Gardners began training Washoe when she was eight months old. They used a variety of methods, including modeling and physical guid-

The bee carrying the red pollen is communicating with the others about the nature and location of food sources by engaging in an intricate "waggle dance."

ance (actually moving her hands) and applying operant reinforcement. Washoe spent all of her waking hours with a trainer who communicated with her only through ASL. After four years of training, she could use 132 signs.

Not only was Washoe adept at imitating her trainer's signs, but she also seemed to create her own communications. For example, when she was menaced by an aggressive rhesus monkey, she signed "dirty monkey," and when she saw a swan for the first time, she signed "water bird." Since she already knew the signs for "water" and "bird," her trainer speculated that she understood the meaning of the words and was thus able to combine them creatively. Washoe was never exposed to training in syntax, but she occasionally produced syntactically meaningful phrases like "gimme tickle" (chimpanzees enjoy being tickled). Washoe even seemed to be able to string words together in a creative and meaningful fashion, as evidenced by such requests as "You me go out please."

Other studies have used varying approaches, also with success. Psychologist David Premack (1971) used operant and classical conditioning to teach a chimpanzee named Sarah to associate pieces of plastic with different aspects of her environment. The plastic pieces, which differed in size, shape, and color, had magnetic backing so that they could be placed on a metal "language board" to form vertical sentences (see Figure 8.11). Sarah learned a large number of symbols indicating names of trainers, objects, properties of objects (like "color of"), and prepositions; she also learned to string words together in an apparently meaningful fashion (such as "Mary give apple Sarah"). Premack and his associates believed that Sarah could also learn concepts. For example, when she was asked to compare a banana and a yellow ball, she arranged symbols on the magnetic board to indicate

FIGURE 8.11 SARAH AND THE "LANGUAGE BOARD"

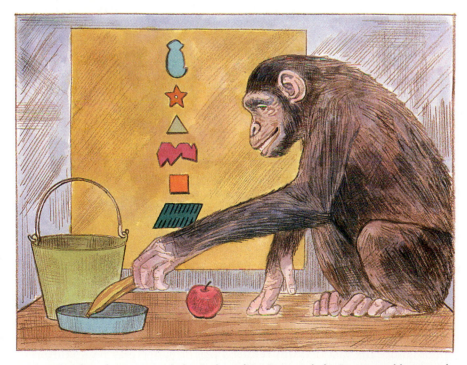

Using principles of operant and classical conditioning, psychologists were able to teach Sarah to understand the meaning of symbols strung together in a meaningful fashion on a "language board." In this example, the message tells Sarah to put the apple in the pail and the banana in the dish.

FIGURE 8.12 CHIMPANZEES AT THE YERKES PRIMATE RE-SEARCH CENTER IN ATLANTA, GEORGIA, LEARN TO USE THE COMPUTER TO TYPE REQUESTS AND ANSWER QUESTIONS

"the same." (This correct answer requires an appreciation of the concept of color.)

At the Yerkes Primate Research Center in Atlanta, Georgia, another study attempted to teach chimpanzees "Yerkish," a computer language. The star pupil of this study, Lana, was raised in a room with a computer that she learned to use to obtain food, drink, and so forth (see Figure 8.12). Each key was labeled with a particular symbol that stood for an object or action. (For example, a circle with a dot inside signified juice.) Lana and other chimpanzees learned to use the computer to type requests, answer questions, and even to engage in a complex game with another chimpanzee which required them to use the computer symbols to make statements. Some of Lana's keyboard talk was quite amazing. For example, one day she observed that her trainer had an orange that she wanted, but Lana did not have a symbol for orange in her language repertoire. So Lana improvised and keyboarded "Tim give apple which is orange" (Rumbaugh, 1977; Savage-Rumbaugh et al., 1980, 1983).

IS LANGUAGE UNIQUE TO HUMANS?

The evidence we have just discussed, as well as findings from several other studies, seems to suggest that language is not unique to humans. From your reading of the ape studies and a review of Table 8.7, what is your conclusion? Take a moment to consider this question before reading on.

To do justice to this question, we must return again to the horse that we met at the beginning of this chapter, Clever Hans. According to some critics of ape language studies, the impressive results that we have just described simply show that chimpanzees can learn to respond to trainers in a manner similar to Clever Hans. Some support for this contention is provided by the frequent observation that when apes are tested by people who either are not familiar with the particular language symbols being used or do not know the correct answers, they consistently perform far more poorly than when they are tested by familiar trainers (Tartter, 1986). However, we cannot ignore the fact that this reduced performance may be no different from the common tendency of children to perform worse for strangers than for people they know.

Evidence that chimpanzee's signs may be nothing more than imitations of a trainer's signs was provided by Herbert Terrace (1979) who care-

Nim Chimpsky is shown here learning the sign for "drink" from his trainer, Joyce Butler. Nim learned combinations of 125 basic signs.

fully analyzed videotapes of chimpanzees signing. Terrace concluded that his top performer, a chimpanzee named Nim Chimpsky, was able to use an impressive number of combinations of 125 basic signs, but only in imitative response to his trainer, and not as a means of creatively communicating new information.

It has also been suggested that language researchers, anxious to be vindicated for their enormous investments in time and effort in training their chimpanzees, may fall victim to what has been called the "generous interpretation pitfall" (Tartter, 1986). We all have a tendency to interpret the words of others as if we were emitting them ourselves. Thus, when Washoe signed "water bird" it was natural for a human observer to assume that she was being creative in naming a novel stimulus, a swan, by combining two other words. It has been pointed out, however, that a less generous interpretation would need to acknowledge the possibility that Washoe was first naming the *water* the swan was swimming in and then naming the animal, *bird,* both words that she was familiar with (Terrace et al., 1979).

You may agree that the accomplishments of Washoe and Sarah can probably be explained by the Clever Hans phenomenon or by their trainers' generous interpretations, but significant questions are still raised by the Yerkes Primate Research Center studies of computer communications. How can these results be explained? According to behaviorists such as B. F. Skinner and his colleagues at Harvard, the so-called language-driven behaviors of chimpanzees may be explained simply by common principles of learning, such as imitation and reinforcement. They see little difference between pigeons pushing buttons in sequence to get a grain reward and chimpanzees stringing together a series of symbols to obtain a payoff of juice or a tickling session. Epstein, Lanza, and Skinner (1980) used operant conditioning to train two pigeons, Jack and Jill, to perform languagelike behaviors in which one pecked colored keys to answer a question selected by the pecks of its partner. These researchers noted that "We have thus demonstrated that pigeons can learn to engage in sustained and natural conversation without human intervention, and that one pigeon can transmit information to another entirely through the use of symbols" (p. 545).

In all, much of the data obtained from the ape language studies can be explained by simpler principles, such as the Clever Hans phenomenon or learning principles—none of which require us to assume that apes have language capabilities. Certainly if we confine our conception of true language ability to the criteria in Table 8.7, we must conclude that humans alone possess language. However, if we define language as the ability to convey meaning through the use of symbols, it is clear that apes also have this ability.

SUMMARY

THOUGHT

1. We may define thought or thinking as a collection of internal processes directed toward solving a problem.
2. Research has demonstrated the inaccuracy of John Watson's early contention that subvocal speech was essentially equivalent to thinking.
3. One component of thought is mental images of visual scenes and sounds that we manipulate in some systematic or logical fashion.
4. A more abstract or symbolic form of thinking involves the use of concepts. Concepts represent general categories into which we mentally group things (objects, activities, kinds of animals, and so forth) that share certain features even though they are not identical.
5. We tend to organize concepts into hierarchies, ranging from very broad to very specific. There seems to be an optimal or basic level in each concept hierarchy that we naturally use when we think about objects or events.
6. Formal concepts, employed by laboratory researchers, are logical and well defined with clear, unambiguous rules specifying what features belong to that category.
7. In real life most of the natural concepts that we use to think efficiently about past and present experiences tend to be more ambiguous than formal concepts.
8. A number of different theories have been proposed to explain how people form concepts. These include association theory, hypothesis-testing theory, and exemplar theory.

PROBLEM SOLVING

9. A problem exists when there is a discrepancy between your present status and some goal you wish to obtain, with no obvious way to bridge the gap.
10. Problems consist of three components: the original state of the situation as it exists at the moment; the goal state, which is what the problem solver would like the situation to be; and the rules or restrictions that govern the possible strategies for moving from the original state to the goal state.
11. Problem-solving behavior generally involves three logical stages: representing or defining the problem, generating possible solutions, and evaluating how well a given solution works.
12. Four common strategies for problem solving are trial-and-error, testing hypotheses, algorithms, and heuristics.
13. A trial-and-error approach is often applied to problems whose likely solutions are probably few in number.
14. When potential solutions to a given problem are more extensive, people often formulate specific hypotheses that generate a more efficient approach to solving a problem.
15. Algorithms involve a systematic exploration of every possible solution to a problem until a correct one is found.
16. Heuristics refer to a variety of rule-of-thumb strategies that may lead to quick solutions but are not guaranteed to produce results. Two commonly employed heuristic strategies are means-ends analysis and working backward.
17. Two characteristics that can make a problem difficult to solve are lack of definition and complexity.
18. Common obstacles that we often create for ourselves when engaged in problem solving are mental set, functional fixedness, and confirmation bias.
19. Mental set is a tendency to approach a problem in a set or predetermined way regardless of the requirements of the specific problem.
20. Functional fixedness is the tendency to be so set or fixed in our perception of the proper function of a given object that we are unable to think of using it in a novel way to solve a problem.
21. Confirmation bias refers to our inclination to seek evidence that will confirm our hypothesis, at the same time that we overlook contradictory evidence.

REASONING AND DECISION MAKING

22. There are two basic types of reasoning: deductive and inductive. Deductive reasoning involves beginning with certain assumptions that we believe to be true and using these assumptions as the basis for drawing conclusions that apply to specific instances. In contrast, in inductive reasoning we reach a general conclusion by generalizing from specific instances.
23. A classical model for studying deductive reasoning is provided by the syllogism, which is an argument consisting of two (or more) presumably true statements, called premises, and a statement of conclusion that may or may not follow logically from the premises.
24. We often err in our deductive reasoning processes because we are too quick to accept faulty premises, because we misinterpret a premise, or because our attitudes or experiences interfere with our ability to think logically.
25. Decision making is a process that occurs whenever we are faced with an array of alternative choices and we choose one option while rejecting others.
26. Compensatory models for decision making allow us to evaluate how desirable potential outcomes stack up

against (or compensate for) undesirable potential outcomes. Two compensatory models are the additive model and the utility-probability model.

27. In noncompensatory models of decision making, not all features of potential choices may be considered, and features do not compensate for each other. Noncompensatory models include the maximax, minimax, conjunctive, and elimination-by-aspects strategies.

28. Two common rule-of-thumb or heuristic approaches to decision making include the representative heuristic and the availability heuristic.

LANGUAGE

29. The ability to use language is perhaps the most profound indicator of the power of human cognition.

30. Psycholinguistics is the psychological study of how we translate sounds and symbols into meaning, and of what cognitive processes are involved in the acquisition and use of language.

31. The basic structural elements of language are called phonemes.

32. A morpheme is the smallest unit of meaning in a given language.

33. Syntax refers to the set of language rules that govern how words can be combined to form meaningful phrases and sentences.

34. Language is also characterized by a system of rules that help us to determine the meaning of words and sen-

tences. The study of meaning in language is called semantics.

35. Theories of language acquisition include the learning perspective, which emphasizes the role of experience in language acquisition, and the nativistic perspective, which maintains that the human brain is genetically programmed to learn speech. Most contemporary psychologists believe that genetics and environment interact in a complex fashion to provide us with the necessary foundations for learning language.

36. There appears to be a universal developmental sequence in which children learn language by progressing from crying to cooing to babbling to one-word utterances to two-word utterances, and finally to expanded language in which two-word sentences give way to more complex sentences.

37. Much of the data obained from the ape language studies can be explained by simpler principles, such as the Clever Hans phenomenon or learning principles—none of which requires us to assume apes have language capabilities.

38. If we confine our conception of true language ability to the criteria of generativity, specialization, arbitrariness, displacement, and novelty, then we must conclude that humans alone possess language. However, if we define language as the ability to convey meaning through the use of symbols, it is clear that apes also have this ability.

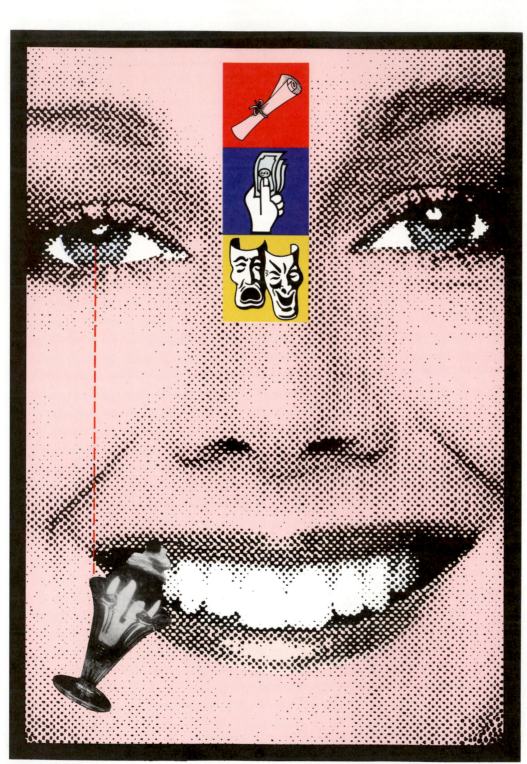

9 Motivation and Emotion

I was smitten by "love" for the first time at the tender age of 16. A few dates and a couple of exciting interludes at the local lovers' lane, and I was "in lust," which of course I interpreted as love. Then disaster struck. An automobile accident, which was my fault, prompted my father to declare that the family Buick was no longer available for my use. I was shattered. My sweetheart attended a different school and we lived five miles apart with no bus service between our homes. I had to see her, so I did something very unusual for teenagers. I walked the 10 miles round trip to her house. (*Authors' files*)

This example of highly motivated behavior reveals something about the role of motivations and emotions in determining our behaviors. Because these two concepts are very closely related, they have been combined in this chapter. Motivation is a general term for the forces that prod us to do something, whereas emotion refers to our subjective feelings or moods.

As we will see in this chapter, both of these processes are considerably more complex than these brief descriptions imply, and our behavior is often a combination of the two processes. For example, emotions often act as primary motivating forces for our actions, as when the strong emotion of first love motivated the young man in the opening anecdote to walk 10 miles to his girl friend's house. Indeed, without emotions, our motivated behavior would reflect an air of indifference. Can you imagine how boring dating would be if it were not colored by feelings of excitement, happiness, and possibly love? Similarly, think how hard it might be to become motivated for a test if you never experienced fear of failure or the anticipation of success.

In this chapter we examine the nature, causes, and manifestations of human motivation and emotion. We begin by exploring motivation, some theories that try to explain motivation, and a few specific motivational forces that influence our behavior; then we discuss what emotions are and how they are aroused.

What motivates people like Mother Theresa to help needy children in Calcutta? What motivated Lenny Skutnik to jump into the icy Potomac River on January 15, 1982, to rescue a passenger from certain death after the jetliner crashed into the river?

THE NATURE OF MOTIVATION

A Vietnam veteran attracts national media attention by housing himself inside a cage and refusing to eat. A college graduate with great promise for an academic career gives up everything to work as a missionary under extremely impoverished conditions in a poor, undeveloped country. You might ask the same question about each of these two accounts: Why would someone do such a thing?

This question raises the issue of motivation, the *why* of behavior. In a sense, the entire study of psychology is concerned with the underlying causes of behavior. Thus far in this text, we have explored the neurological foundations of behavior and the role that such processes as sensation, perception, learning, and thinking play in influencing our activities. However, these explanations still leave questions unanswered about our behavior.

One such question concerns inconsistencies or variations in behavior. Why do you dress to the hilt one day and go to class in a baggy sweatshirt the next? Why do two people with comparable ability and training tackle the same job and one excels while the other fails? Motivation helps to explain both inconsistencies in a person's behavior over time and also variations between people's performance in the same situation, when these discrepancies cannot be attributed to differences in basic ability, skills, or environmental conditions.

Besides explaining such inconsistencies, motivational concepts help to explain the distinction between learning and performance. Learning does not always lead directly to behavior. Recall the latent-learning experiment discussed in Chapter 6, in which rats learned how to move through a complex maze but did not demonstrate this behavior until they were motivated by food. In a similar vein, if you learn to imitate the voice of Ronald Reagan, you probably will not use this voice to communicate with your dog, your professors, or your parents. You are likely to express this behavior only when you have an appreciative audience. Motivation is what often translates learning into overt behavior.

Rich Little has learned to impersonate many people and, here, a chimpanzee. However, he probably would not impersonate either people or chimpanzees without the motivation of an appreciative audience.

DEFINING MOTIVATION

Motivation can include physiological factors, such as the body signals that tell us we are hungry or tired, but there is more to motivation than the simple translation of body needs into action. Motivation also includes cognitive conditions such as a desire to achieve or an urge to be with friends. In fact, **motivation** can be defined as any condition that might energize and direct our actions.

To illustrate, suppose you are reading this chapter late at night and are becoming increasingly aware of a familiar urge. Finally, you close your book and decide to do something about your mounting need. It is time to get something to eat, but will any old food satisfy your need? Not when the best 24-hour doughnut shop in town is only a few blocks away. So off you go into the night in mouth-watering anticipation of lemon-filled doughnuts and chocolate eclairs.

This example of one of the most familiar motives, hunger, illustrates that motivation not only energizes or *activates* us to behave in a certain way but also *directs* or defines the direction of the resulting behavior. Motivation also has a direct impact upon how *vigorous* or intense our behaviors are. If you had skipped dinner earlier in the evening, your trip to the doughnut shop might be characterized by brisk walking rather than a leisurely stroll—and you might consume all of the goodies you purchased rather than saving one or two for the morning.

In all, we might say that it is motivation that makes our behavior more than the sum of parts such as physiology, learning, sensation, and perception. However, what explains motivation? As we will see in the following discussion, this question has not been an easy one to answer.

Motivation can be defined as any condition that might energize and direct our actions.

EXPLAINING MOTIVATION: THEORETICAL PERSPECTIVES

Since its beginnings, psychology has attempted to conceptualize and explain motivation. These explanations have not all been equally successful. Yet each of the approaches we consider here—instinct theory, drive-reduction theory, Maslow's need hierarchy, and the cognitive perspective—help contribute to our understanding of motivation.

INSTINCT THEORY

One of the earliest attempts to explain motivation was based on the notion of **instincts,** innate patterns of behavior that occur in every normally functioning member of a species under certain set conditions. For example, a salmon may swim thousands of miles through ocean waters and up a river system to reach the exact spot in a gravel bed where it was spawned several years earlier. An arctic tern, born in the northland, will depart for the southernmost portion of South America when the arctic days grow shorter. Such behaviors occur in virtually identical fashion among all members of a species, generation after generation.

The attempt to explain human behavior in terms of instincts was the dominant force in psychology in the late 1800s and early 1900s, due in large part to Charles Darwin's emphasis on the similarity between humans and other animals. William James (1890), a highly influential early psychologist, argued that humans are even more influenced by instincts than are lower animals because they are motivated not only by biological instincts but also by a variety of psychosocial instincts such as jealousy, sympathy, and sociability. James proposed a list of 15 instincts, which he suggested account for much of human behavior (see Table 9.1). Other psychologists suggested their own lists. Predictably, by the early 1920s, almost 15,000 instincts had been proposed to account for virtually every kind of human behavior imaginable (Houston, 1985).

Eventually, psychologists realized that there was a basic flaw to instinct theory: Instincts did not explain behavior; they simply provided another way of labeling it. Today, psychologists do not totally discount the idea that there are inborn or inherited factors in human behavior. In fact, the concept that genetic factors influence our behaviors is very much alive. However, since our behaviors are so profoundly influenced by learning, it is

The influence of instincts is reflected in the behavior of salmon who may swim thousands of miles through ocean waters and up a river system to reach the exact spot in a gravel bed where they were spawned several years earlier.

TABLE 9.1 *Fifteen Instincts Proposed by William James That Account for Much of Human Behavior*

Cleanliness	Playfulness
Constructiveness	Pugnacity
Curiosity	Rivalry
Fearfulness	Secretiveness
Hunting	Shyness
Jealousy	Sociability
Modesty	Sympathy
Parental love	

essentially impossible to find one example of human behavior that fits the literal definition of instincts as proposed by the early psychologists.

DRIVE-REDUCTION THEORY

Just as instinct theory reflected the late-nineteenth-century interest in Darwin's evolutionary theory, a second explanation of motivation fits well with behaviorist theory. According to the *drive-reduction theory,* motivation originates with a need or drive, such as hunger or loneliness, that is experienced as an unpleasant, aversive condition. This internal need motivates us to act in a way that will reduce the aversive condition. For instance, if we feel thirsty, we find something to drink; if we feel lonely, we seek company.

The drive-reduction theory explains motivation in these terms. According to this viewpoint, proposed by Clark Hull (1943), drives are any unpleasant internal conditions that motivate an organism to engage in behaviors that reduce this unpleasant state of tension. Hull postulated that there are two kinds of drives. *Primary drives* are induced by internal biological needs, such as water or food deprivation, and they do not depend on learning. In contrast, *secondary* or *acquired drives* are derived from experience.

The concept of acquired drives is directly linked with the idea of secondary reinforcement, discussed in Chapter 6. Any neutral stimuli associated with primary reinforcers can acquire the power to motivate behavior. For instance, the motive of *affiliation,* the desire to be with others, would be explained as a secondary drive acquired through the process of associating primary need gratification (eating, being warm, and so forth) with a secondary reinforcer, the presence of other people.

While the drive-reduction theory seems to explain some motivation, it does not explain all motivation. A major problem with this approach is that a large number of events can serve as reinforcers. If we presume that these events are reinforcing because they reduce a drive, then we are left with the question, "What drive does this behavior reduce?" For example, some people enjoy catching fish in a mountain stream. Does this mean that there is a fishing drive that is reduced by catching fish?

Another difficulty with the drive-reduction theory is that sometimes stimuli in our environments can energize or motivate us to behave in a certain way in the absence of an internal drive state. For instance, have you ever found yourself sampling home-baked cookies because they smell so good, even though you are not at all hungry? A number of studies have demonstrated that external stimuli, which psychologists call **incentives,** can motivate behavior even when no internal drive state exists. In one experiment, for instance, it was shown that a substance such as saccharin, which has no food value and does not satisfy hunger, will reinforce learning and motivate subsequent performance of animals just because it tastes good (Sheffield, 1966).

Still another problem with the drive-reduction theory has to do with the fact that many motivated behaviors do not decrease as they are expressed. According to the drive-reduction hypothesis, an internal need directs us to a goal, and reaching that goal reduces the tension of the drive.

The drive-reduction theory states that motivation originates with a need that causes us to act in a way to reduce that need.

It follows, then, that when the drive is reduced, the motivated behavior should cease. However, sometimes a motivated behavior seems to be self-perpetuating. An example is the desire to explore or master our environments. When humans and other animals have the opportunity to explore their surroundings, these reinforcing experiences often motivate further exploration rather than less. Similarly, other motives, such as the need to achieve and the need for power, typically continue to grow and expand as they are expressed rather than diminish, as drive theory would predict.

For these and other reasons, the drive-reduction theory is inadequate to deal with the entire range of human motivation, particularly more complex motives involving psychological and social factors. A number of other theoretical perspectives offer different explanations for motivation. One of the more influential of these models is Abraham Maslow's hierarchy of human needs.

MASLOW'S HIERARCHY OF NEEDS

Humanistic psychologists have looked toward the role of motives such as love, personal fullfillment, the need to belong, and self-esteem in arousing and directing human behavior. The most influential of these humanistic perspectives was provided by a theory of human motivation developed by Abraham Maslow (1970). Maslow proposed that human needs exist on a multilevel hierarchy consisting of five stages, ranging from the "lowest," most basic biological needs to the "highest" need to fulfill one's own unique potential (see Figure 9.1).

According to Maslow, we all start our lives at the lowest level of the motivational hierarchy. As infants we are dominated by basic *biological needs* for food, water, sleep, and so forth. (Drive-reduction theory operates at this level.) Relatively soon, however, we become concerned with our need to feel physically and psychologically safe, and so we are motivated by *safety needs* to secure some control over our environments. As we continue to develop, we move into the next two stages or levels on the hierarchy, where more complex psychosocial motives become more important. We need to love, to be loved, and to feel a sense of belonging. These socially based *love and belongingness needs* are satisfied both by our family involvement and by the relationships we form with others outside the family. As we express our social affiliation with others we are also likely to become motivated by *esteem needs*. These include the need to achieve and see ourselves as competent, and the desire to be recognized, appreciated, and held in esteem by others.

Finally, if we are successful in satisfying all of these needs, some of us may progress to the highest level in Maslow's hierarchy, where the need for *self-actualization* may become a dominant motivating force in our lives. Self-actualization is a complex concept, perhaps best described as the need to reach our own highest potential and to do the things we do best in our own unique way. Maslow characterized the self-actualized person as someone who is self-aware and self-accepting, striving to help others reach their goals, open to new experiences and challenges, and engaging in activities that are commensurate with that individual's highest potential (for example, a musician making music or a poet writing). Figure 9.1 illustrates each of Maslow's need levels.

Maslow's conception that we must fulfill our basic needs before we can pursue needs at higher levels makes some sense. For example, if you are lost in the hills for days without food and then stumble upon a small mountain community, your desire to find food is likely to be much more powerful and immediate than your need to establish a sense of belonging. However, once your lower needs are satisfied, you are likely to be more concerned with higher needs such as those for belonging.

Yet Maslow's theory has also been criticized, especially his view that people's needs are precisely ordered in a five-level hierarchy with successive needs being satisfied only after those on a lower level have been met. This

FIGURE 9.1 MASLOW'S HIERARCHY OF NEEDS

Maslow proposed that human needs exist on a multilevel hierarchy that consists of five stages ranging from the "lowest," most basic biological needs to the "highest" need to fulfill one's own unique potential.

theoretical assumption is difficult to demonstrate by empirical research. Beyond the lowest level of the hierarchy, there is little evidence that human motives or needs are ordered in the exact sequence that Maslow proposed (Wahba & Bridwell, 1976).

Research-oriented psychologists have also criticized Maslow's theory because many of his major precepts, particularly the concept of self-actualization, are so vague that it is virtually impossible to define them operationally. Without operational definitions, Maslow's theory cannot be experimentally tested. Consequently, the need hierarchy theory has remained largely an unproven conceptualization of the various forces that motivate human behavior.

THE COGNITIVE PERSPECTIVE

A fourth explanation of motivation is offered by the cognitive perspective. According to this view, our cognitions—thoughts, beliefs, and other mental processes—play an important role in motivating our actions (Bandura, 1982; Deci, 1980). This is exemplified by the role of expectations in both classical and operant conditioning. Recall from Chapter 6 that the cognitive viewpoint sees expectations as important in both classically conditioned responses and operant behaviors. For example, when we study for an exam (operant behavior), a consequence occurs (hopefully a good grade) that serves as a reinforcer. We form a mental association between the behavior and the reinforcement that follows. This association then generates an *expectation* that if the behavior is repeated, it will again produce positive consequences.

The idea that expectations are important motivators was championed in the 1950s and 1960s by Julian Rotter (1954, 1966). Rotter maintained that our likelihood of engaging in a given behavior depends upon two factors: our expectations that that behavior will lead to a desired goal, and the value that we assign to that goal. Thus, the likelihood that you will gather your courage and ask that exciting person you just met for a date is determined to some degree by your past experiences in asking people out. If your last several overtures have all resulted in rejection, you are less likely to try again. However, if you assign great value to the goal of having a date for the dance Friday night, you may overcome your expectations of failure.

THE RANGE OF HUMAN MOTIVATION

Whether we attribute motivation to inherited behavior patterns, to the need to reduce drives, to a humanistic striving toward self-fulfillment, or to learned expectations, it seems clear that no one theory explains all aspects of motivation. This is probably because the range of human motivation is so broad. Certain behaviors, such as drinking a glass of water after exercising, can be explained predominantly by drive-reduction theory. Yet other behaviors, such as cultivating the habit of smoking despite the fact that it makes you cough, have more complex explanations. It seems, then, that to understand motivation we must first determine what type of motivation is in question. In general, it is useful to classify human motives under four categories: biologically based motives, sensation-seeking motives, multifactor motives, and complex psychosocial motives.

Biologically based motives are rooted primarily in body tissue needs, such as those for food, water, air, sleep, temperature regulation, and the avoidance of pain. Psychologists generally use the term **drive** to refer to motives that are based on tissue needs: in both humans and other animals, such basic biological drives as hunger and thirst must be satisfied in order to ensure survival. (You will recall that Clark Hull made a distinction between primary or biological drives and secondary or learned drives. Today most psychologists apply the term drive only to motives induced by internal biological needs.)

While the underlying needs behind biological drives are inborn, the expression of these drives is often learned. For example, a hungry person is motivated by a state of physiological food deprivation. Consequently, that person learns how to search the environment effectively for food that will satisfy this basic need.

In addition to tissue needs, humans and other animals seem also to have an innate need for certain levels of stimulation. These **sensation-seeking motives** are perhaps most evident in the way people attempt to create their own sensations when they are placed in sensory isolation. As we will see later in this chapter, some people even begin to hallucinate, apparently to compensate for a lack of external stimulation.

Some human motives are based upon a combination of biological, psychological, and cultural factors. One of the best examples of **multifactor motives** is the complex array of conditions that give rise to human sexual behavior, which will be discussed later in this chapter.

Finally, our behaviors are energized and directed by a variety of **complex psychosocial motives** that seem to demonstrate little or no relationship to biological needs. These motives are determined by learning, and they are aroused and satisfied by psychological and social events rather than body tissue needs. Unlike the biological drives, these motives do not need to be satisfied to ensure survival. However, much of human happiness and misery is associated with the satisfaction or thwarting of these important motives. This category includes such motives as the desire to be with others, the need to achieve, the need for power, the need for social approval, and the need to control or master our environments.

In the remainder of this chapter's discussion of motivation, we will explore examples of these four types of motivation: a biological drive, *hunger; sensation-seeking motives;* a multifactor motive, *sexuality;* and a complex psychosocial motive, the *need for achievement.*

HUNGER AND EATING

What processes let us know we are hungry, and how do we know when we have eaten enough? Researchers have tried to answer these seemingly basic questions since the beginning of this century. In spite of extensive research, however, we are still a long way from a complete understanding of this extremely complicated biological drive. The following discussion examines what we have learned about many of the factors that influence hunger and eating; it also considers two related topics, obesity and eating disorders.

BIOLOGICAL BASES OF HUNGER

Hunger performs a critical biological function: It tells us when our bodies require more nutrition. What are the mechanisms that tell us we are hungry? Although the obvious answer to this question is that our empty stomachs tell us, the picture is actually more complicated than this. Attempts to explain the possible biological bases of hunger have focused on a number of areas, including the stomach, monitoring mechanisms in the brain, and other body organs such as the liver and intestines. We will consider the evidence in each of these areas of investigation.

The Stomach We have all experienced hunger pangs and growling stomachs when we have not eaten for some time. We are also familiar with the feeling of a full stomach when we have completed a meal. From our own experience, then, it seems logical that the contractions of an empty stomach are what makes us hungry and that the pressure of food against the stomach walls tells us to stop eating.

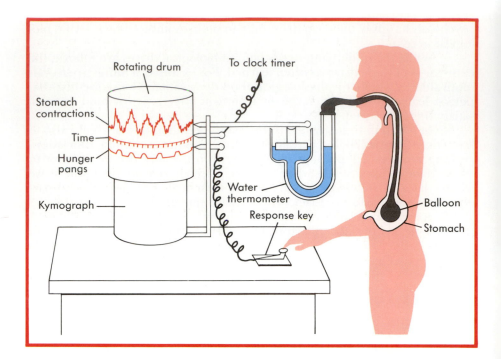

FIGURE 9.2 CANNON AND WASHBURN'S APPARATUS

The subject (Washburn) swallowed a small balloon, which was then inflated. Each contraction of the stomach forced air out of the balloon, which then activated a recording device. Washburn also pressed a key whenever he felt a hunger pang.

A classic study conducted by Cannon and Washburn (1912) tested this hypothesis. One of the investigators, Washburn, trained himself to swallow a small balloon. Once in the stomach, the balloon was inflated by air introduced through an attached tube. Each stomach contraction forced air out of the balloon, activating a recording device. Washburn also pressed a key whenever he felt a hunger pang. (Figure 9.2 demonstrates the apparatus used in this experiment.) These investigators found a close relationship between stomach contractions and reports of hunger, seemingly confirming their hypothesis that the hunger motive is caused by stomach contractions.

However, later investigations raised some serious questions. For instance, one line of research investigated what happens when the nerves that carry messages from the stomach to the brain are severed, so that stomach sensations can no longer be felt. If the messages from our stomachs can't reach our brains, we should be unaware that we are hungry—yet these experiments did not eliminate hunger either in rats (Morgan & Morgan, 1940) or in humans (Grossman & Stein, 1948). Even more serious questions were raised by the discovery that people whose cancerous stomachs have been entirely removed continue to experience normal hunger drives (Wangensteen & Carlson, 1931; Janowitz & Grossman, 1950).

Despite this evidence, however, most hunger researchers believe that stomach sensations do contribute to our overall feelings of hunger and satiety (fullness). For example, there is strong evidence that the stomach contains pressure detectors that are activated when the stomach is distended with food and/or fluids. These sensors seem to play a role in signaling satiety and thus inhibiting further eating. Nevertheless, research has made it clear that stomach contractions are not necessary for hunger, and that we must look elsewhere for a complete explanation. One primary line of research has focused on the hypothalamus.

Dual Hypothalamic Control Theory It has long been suspected that the hypothalamus is somehow involved in hunger motivation. A number of different studies have identified two specific regions within the hypothalamus that may possibly serve as control centers for eating. One is the **ventromedial hypothalamus (VMH),** located in the front center portion of this brain structure. When the VMH is electrically or chemically stimulated, feeding behavior in animals in inhibited (Hess, 1957; Wyrwicka, 1976); and when the VMH is destroyed, the result in many species is extreme overeating and obesity, a condition called *hyperphagia* (Cox et al., 1968; Hetherington & Ranson, 1940; Tokunago et al., 1986). These findings suggest that the VMH serves as a "satiety center" that inhibits eating by somehow signaling an organism when it has had enough to eat.

Just as the VMH seems to act as an "off switch" to inhibit eating, another structure in the hypothalamus seems to act as an "on switch" or feeding center. Damage to the **lateral hypothalamus (LH),** an area on the sides of the hypothalamus, produces just the opposite effect of that caused by lesions in the VMH. When the LH is destroyed, animals will dramatically reduce food consumption or stop eating altogether, a condition known as *aphagia.* Conversely, electrical or chemical stimulation of the LH feeding center causes animals to eat even if they are already satiated (Anand & Brobeck, 1951; Bloom et al., 1985; Fukuda et al., 1986).

These findings led to the formulation of the **dual hypothalamic control theory** (Stellar, 1954). This theory suggests that these structures in the hypothalamus operate together to maintain a relatively constant state of satiety, much as a thermostat maintains a constant temperature in a house. The VMH satiety center monitors the status of our bodies' energy resources. Most of the time, when we are not eating, the satiety center suppresses activity of the LH feeding center. When our fuel reserves are low, however, the VMH activates the LH, releasing it from its inhibited state. The result is a feeling of hunger.

This interpretation is appealing but, like the stomach contraction theory, it still leaves questions unanswered. What internal bodily changes stimulate the feeding and satiety centers to trigger hunger and to regulate how much we eat? To answer this question, we need to know what internal biological conditions the VMH monitors. The search for this information has led to the formulation of the glucostatic theory.

The Glucostatic Theory   The glucostatic theory, originally proposed by Jean Mayer (1955), tries to pinpoint what body conditions are monitored by the feeding and satiety centers. Because one of the most important body fuels is glucose, this theory sees glucose levels as the key. It seems logical that hunger might occur as time passes since our last meal and levels of glucose in the blood become lower.

The **glucostatic theory** suggests that levels of glucose are monitored by *glucoreceptors* (cells sensitive to glucose in the bloodstream). Another substance, *insulin* (a hormone secreted by the pancreas), is also monitored, for insulin must be present in order for glucose to be used by cells. (That is why people with untreated *diabetes mellitus,* or sugar diabetes, are chronically hungry despite high blood-sugar levels.) Thus, hunger results whenever the glucoreceptors detect that glucose is unavailable, either because of low blood-sugar levels or because there is not enough insulin present to enable cells to use the glucose in the bloodstream. Support for this theory was provided by evidence that insulin injections and other treatments that lower blood-sugar levels stimulate hunger and eating (Epstein & Teitelbaum, 1967; Thompson & Campbell, 1977).

Where are the glucoreceptors located? For a time it was thought that they were in the VMH satiety center—an idea that has been supported by some research. It has been found, for instance, that when glucose is injected into the VHM, the firing rate of cells in this area is increased (Oomura, 1976). However, there has also been contradictory evidence. For example, direct injections of glucose into the VMH do not inhibit eating (Epstein, 1960) as one would expect according to the glucostatic theory. Perhaps one of the biggest shortcomings of this theory is related to the fact that unless mealtime is spread over an unusually long period, most of us stop eating before blood glucose levels have risen appreciably as a result of food intake (Geen et al., 1984).

This rat's ventromedial hypothalamus has been destroyed, resulting in extreme overeating and obesity, a condition known as hyperphagia.

During the 1970s researchers began to consider the possibility that glucoreceptors were located in another part of the body than the hypothalamus. Mauricio Russek (1971) demonstrated that while intravenous injections of glucose directly into a dog's bloodstream do not seem to influence a dog's eating behavior, comparable injections directly into the abdominal cavity cause it to stop eating quickly.

Russek concluded that the glucoreceptors must be somewhere in the abdomen rather than the brain. The liver seemed a likely candidate, since the bloodstream carries nutrients directly from the intestines to the liver. To test this hypothesis, Russek surgically implanted a small tube in the major blood vessel that carries nutrients from the intestines to the liver, then deprived the dog of food long enough to induce hunger. Just before presenting food, Russek injected a small amount of glucose into the blood vessel that supplies intestinal nutrients to the liver. The result was a sudden and dramatic loss of hunger: the dog was not interested in eating. To control for the possibility that any kind of fluid injections might produce this effect, Russek repeated this same procedure several times, substituting a variety of nonnutritive solutions. In all cases the hungry animal continued to eat. These findings led Russek to conclude that glucoreceptors in the liver are important in regulating hunger and eating behavior. Other studies have confirmed Russek's findings (Novin, 1976; Schmitt, 1973; Vanderweele & Sanderson, 1976).

The picture that emerges, then, is that the liver glucoreceptors detect changes in blood glucose levels, then send this information to the hypothalamus along the vagus nerve. This view has been supported by findings that when the vagus nerve is severed, injections of glucose into the liver's blood supply do not inhibit eating.

There is evidence that the liver can initiate as well as suppress eating behavior. In one study a substance that prevents cells from absorbing glucose was injected into the vein that carries nutrients to the liver. The result was a sudden stimulation of eating behavior. Apparently, the liver's temporary inability to utilize glucose caused it to react as though glucose levels were low. The authors of this experiment theorized that this message was then communicated along the vagus nerve to the feeding center in the lateral hypothalamus, which in turn triggered the feeding behavior (Novin, 1976; Novin et al., 1973).

Research also suggests that there may be glucoreceptors at another site, in the *duodenum,* the upper portion of the intestinal tract. When glucose solutions are injected directly into this structure, rats stop their feeding behavior (Campbell & Davis, 1974). The duodenum also secretes a variety of hormones that may help signal satiety. There is especially strong evidence linking the hormone cholecystokinin (CCK) to appetite suppression (Cox, 1986; Gibbs et al., 1973; Maddison, 1977; Smith & Gibbs, 1976). CCK is released when food enters the duodenum; it then seems to travel through the bloodstream to the brain where it acts to inhibit eating behavior. In one study, investigators found that brain levels of this hormone were significantly lower in obese rats than in normal rats, suggesting that the overweight rats consumed excessive food because their CCK levels were not sufficient to suppress their eating behavior (Straus & Yalow, 1979). A number of other investigations (such as Cox, 1986) have shown that injections of CCK inhibit motivation to eat.

All of this research, as well as much more that we have not considered, suggests that several processes are involved in regulating hunger and eating. We have seen that specialized cells in the liver, and probably the duodenum, respond to the presence of nutrients, particularly glucose. These sensors appear to send messages through the nervous system to specialized control centers within the hypothalamus. It also appears that chemical messages, in the form of hormones secreted by the duodenum, help to regulate hunger. As research continues, other receptor sites and specialized messages may also be implicated.

So far, we have been exploring only the hour-to-hour control of hunger and eating. In addition, there must also be some long-term control mechanism that allows most of us to maintain our weight at a relatively constant level over time. We investigate this topic next.

Long-Term Weight Regulation   Although some people seem to be perpetually losing and regaining the same 10 or 20 pounds, most of us maintain a relatively constant weight that may fluctuate only a few pounds up or down over the long term. How do we manage to do this?

Lipostatic Theory   The lipostatic theory helps explain why our weight usually stays constant. Just as blood glucose levels are the key to the glucostatic theory, stored fats, or lipids, are the key to the **lipostatic theory.** Fat acts as long-term storage that is not typified by the rapid changes characteristic of glucose levels. The average adult consumes somewhere between 2,000 and 2,500 calories each day, much of which is immediately metabolized and used. Excess energy is stored as fat, or lipids.

According to the lipostatic theory of long-term eating control, our bodies monitor the amount of fat they contain and use this as a barometer to regulate food intake, so that fat levels are held relatively constant. This constant level, of course, varies from person to person. Many researchers now believe that our bodies may be preprogramed in some fashion to maintain a specific body weight (Keesey & Powley, 1986; Keesey et al., 1976). This physiologically preferred level of body weight for each individual is known as the **set point.**

Perhaps the most widely supported explanation of how we maintain a certain body weight is the theory that regions within our brains, most likely regulatory centers within the hypothalamus, respond to some kind of signal indicating the level of fat in our bodies at any given time (Houston, 1985). The question is, what might this signal be? Some researchers have theorized that it might be some blood component, such as glycerol (a component of triglycerides, the major form of stored fat). A positive correlation exists between glycerol levels in the blood and the size of a person's fat cells (Geen et al., 1984). Thus, it seems possible that increased body weight might lead to increased blood glycerol, which in turn would trigger the hypothalamus to send signals that would reduce food consumption until the set-point weight is reestablished.

This interpretation has received some support from research findings that daily injections of glycerol reduce food intake and body weight in rats (Davis & Wirtshafter, 1978; Wirtshafter & Davis, 1977). The excess glycerol in the rats' bloodstreams seems to have triggered some mechanism in the rats' brains, causing them to eat less.

Other Mechanisms in Long-Term Weight Regulation   Earlier in this chapter we examined the dual hypothalmic control theory, which postulated that the LH feeding center triggers eating behavior when not restrained by the VMH satiety center. We saw that rats with VMH or LH lesions demonstrate dramatic shifts in food intake in the period following surgery. The story does not end there, however.

Several studies have shown that lesions in the satiety and feeding centers do not necessarily destroy a rat's capacity to regulate eating and body weight over the long term, although that may be the immediate effect. Rather, rats with VMH lesions or LH lesions who are provided with free access to food after surgery eventually establish new set points adjusted upward or downward, respectively, in which they maintain a new constant higher-than-normal or lower-than-normal body weight (Geen et al., 1984; Hoebel & Feitlebaum, 1966; Powley & Keesey, 1970). These findings suggest that the VMH and LH are not absolutely essential for regulating hunger and eating. However, the fact that lesions in these two structures do appear to adjust the set point of body weight up or down certainly implicates both of these structures in long-term weight control.

Some researchers believe that the hunger-regulating processes attributed to the LH and VMH may actually be mediated, at least in part, by nerve tracts that pass through the hypothalamus (Almli, 1978). In fact, one study demonstrated that obesity resulted not from destruction of cells within the VMH, but rather from damage to axonal fibers passing through this region (Gold et al., 1977).

OBESITY

We are a nation that seems obsessed both by food and losing weight. Television commercials besiege us with images of beautiful bodies and athletic-looking people engaging in energetic aerobic exercises. At the same time we see ads for ice cream, doughnuts, "Big Macs," and "whoppers." How many people do you know who are on a diet? Perhaps you are one. According to recent estimates, approximately 34 million Americans are **obese,** weighing 20 percent or more above the desirable weight for their height, as shown in Table 9.2. By midlife, more than half of the people in this country are overweight (Brody, 1985; NOVA, 1983).

Most health professionals agree that obesity places a person at greater risk of developing one or more health problems. Obesity greatly increases the risk of high blood pressure, high blood cholesterol, diabetes, several types of cancer, heart disease, gall bladder disease, menstrual abnormalities, respiratory problems, and arthritis (Brody, 1985; Manson et al., 1987; Simopoulos, 1987; Wolff, 1987). Still another frequent consequence is the psychological burden of obesity, which may be its most severe side effect. A number of studies have linked obesity with such negative psychological states as poor body image, low self-esteem, and depression (Davis et al., 1987; Leon & Roth, 1977; Mayer, 1968).

People try to get rid of excess weight by starving or sweating it off, but the grim fact is that in most cases fat wins. This is not to say that people cannot lose weight. Quite the contrary, many people lose and regain the same 10 or 20 pounds over and over again. Studies demonstrate that of those people who go on fad diets, approximately 95 percent regain all of their lost weight within one year. Furthermore, as many as 75 percent of individuals placed on medically supervised diets regain most if not all of their lost weight (Haney, 1983; NOVA, 1983). This seemingly never-

TABLE 9.2 Weights and Heights for Men and Women

	Men					Women			
Height Feet	Height Inches	Small Frame	Medium Frame	Large Frame	Height Feet	Height Inches	Small Frame	Medium Frame	Large Frame
5	2	128–134	131–141	138–150	4	10	102–111	109–121	118–131
5	3	130–136	133–143	140–153	4	11	103–113	111–123	120–134
5	4	132–138	135–145	142–156	5	0	104–115	113–126	122–137
5	5	134–140	137–148	144–160	5	1	106–118	115–129	125–140
5	6	136–142	139–151	146–164	5	2	108–121	118–132	128–143
5	7	138–145	142–154	149–168	5	3	111–124	121–135	131–147
5	8	140–148	145–157	152–172	5	4	114–127	124–138	134–151
5	9	142–151	148–160	155–176	5	5	117–130	127–141	137–155
5	10	144–154	151–163	158–180	5	6	120–133	130–144	140–159
5	11	146–157	154–166	161–184	5	7	123–136	133–147	143–163
6	0	149–160	157–170	164–188	5	8	126–139	136–150	146–167
6	1	152–164	160–174	168–192	5	9	129–142	139–153	149–170
6	2	155–168	164–178	172–197	5	10	132–145	142–156	152–173
6	3	158–172	167–182	176–202	5	11	135–148	145–159	155–176
6	4	162–176	171–187	181–207	6	0	138–151	148–162	158–179

Source of basic data: 1979 Build Study Society of Actuaries and Association of Life Insurance Medical Directors of America, 1980. Copyright 1983 Metropolitan Life Insurance Company.

ending struggle against obesity has been labeled "the rhythm method of girth control" by Tufts University nutritionist Jean Mayer. The following account is one woman's description of her experience with this distressing yo-yo cycle of weight:

> Since age 12, I have easily lost 1,200 to 1,400 pounds and gained them all back. There probably has not been a week of my life that I wasn't dieting or gaining weight back. I always thought I was a very good dieter. I lost weight time and time and time again. Every time that I really set my mind to it, I lost weight. And then, I gained it back, even though I did not want to. I tried not to. I never understood the concept of maintenance. I just always gained it back. I felt out of control. (NOVA, 1983, pp. 8–9)

Such extraordinary rates of failure have prompted researchers to study why people are obese, what the effects of obesity are, what happens when we lose weight, and how we can more effectively manage weight problems.

Possible Causes of Obesity There are many theories about why people become overweight. Blame has been placed on genes, conditions of early development, metabolic factors, and learned responses to emotional stress. We will briefly consider the evidence for each of these viewpoints.

Genetic Causes Several studies have demonstrated that a child whose parents are both of normal weight has less than one chance in ten of becoming obese. When one or both parents are overweight, however, the odds jump to approximately two out of five and four out of five, respectively (Haney, 1983). Of course, just because obesity runs in families is no proof that a genetic predisposition is involved. An equally logical explanation is that obese parents overfeed their children as well as themselves, thereby establishing a habit of excessive eating.

To control for these environmental factors, researchers have compared the concordance rate of obesity in identical twins who have the same genes, with that of fraternal twins who do not share the same genes. (*Concordance* refers to the degree of agreement in the expression of a given trait in both members of a twin pair. Concordance is usually expressed as a correlation coefficient.) Investigators have also compared the weight correlations between adopted individuals and their biological parents with correlations between the weights of adopted individuals and their nonbiological, adopting parents. Data from both of these kinds of studies have led obesity researcher Albert Stunkard to conclude that "genetic influences have an important role in determining human fatness in adults" (Stunkard et al., 1986, p. 193).

Early Childhood Experience It has been found that the fat cells of obese people are as much as 50 to 100 percent larger than those of lean people. In addition, overweight people may have as many as five to ten times the normal number of fat cells (Hirsch, 1983; Hirsch & Knittle, 1970). Many researchers believe that eating patterns during childhood and adolescence strongly influence the number and size of fat cells in the body of an adult, and this theory has been supported by some studies. For instance, rats placed on a fattening diet during early development have been found to produce a significantly increased number of fat cells (Knittle & Hirsch, 1968). In a similar way, it seems likely that obesity during a child's early development may cause an increase in fat cells that will make it difficult to maintain an ideal weight during adulthood. There is ample research evidence that obesity is a common problem among children and that childhood obesity is associated with an increased risk of adult obesity (Dietz, 1986; Epstein & Wing, 1987; Epstein et al., 1987). An obvious implication of these findings is that adults are not doing children a service when they urge them to "have another helping of Grandma's good cooking."

Rewarding children with high-caloric foods helps them to associate overeating with love and acceptance, and could be partly responsible for their weight problems later on in life.

FIRST PERSON 9.1

I have a good friend who I enjoy doing all kinds of things with— except eating. In the food department the guy really bugs me. I have to watch everything I eat, but I don't think my friend has ever counted a calorie in his life. I sit down for lunch with my salad and a small bowl of soup and here he comes with his tray loaded with a cheeseburger, large order of fries, king-sized coke, a salad smothered with blue cheese dressing, and pie topped with ice cream. The way he eats, he should be dead. Instead, he is tall, slim, and athletic looking. There is no justice in the world. (*Authors' files*)

FIRST PERSON 9.2

I try to limit my food, as much as possible, to items that must be cooked before they can be consumed. This way, when I open the refrigerator I see fresh vegetables, like asparagus or cauliflower, that must be steamed before I can eat them. I keep on hand a good supply of eggs, rice, pastas, fish, chicken, soups, and other foods that must be cooked or at least heated up. I am not tempted to grab foods like these and shove them into my mouth. If I have to work to eat, I usually am inclined to wait for mealtime. (*Authors' files*)

Metabolic Factors   Metabolic disturbances have often been blamed for obesity. Some people do seem to convert food into body tissue, primarily fat, at a faster rate than others, and they are likely to have trouble maintaining a desirable weight. Several studies have demonstrated that at least some obese people do not eat more than people of average weight (Ries, 1973; Rodin, 1978; Stunkard, 1980). In fact, it has been shown that when pairs of subjects are matched for weight, height, age, and activity, one of the pair may consume on the average as much as twice the intake of his or her counterpart (Rose & Williams, 1961).

Reactions to Emotional Stress   Many of us have a tendency to overeat when we are under stress. Campus cafeterias and local pizzerias seem to do a lot of business just before and during finals week. Some people who are chronically under stress, depressed, or anxiety-ridden tend to overeat as a matter of course (Bruch, 1961; Mayer, 1968; Rodin, 1978). This may be due to a number of factors.

One possible cause is experience. Unfortunately, some parents reward their children's good behavior with high-calorie goodies such as cookies or cake. This kind of experience helps a child learn to associate eating with feeling good, and food may also take on the symbolic meaning of love and acceptance. Again, parents often praise their children for eating lots of food—another experience that strengthens the association between food and feeling good. Later in life, these early experiences may show up as craving for food whenever a person feels rejected, depressed, disappointed, or unhappy.

Why Weight Is Hard to Keep Off   Regardless of the cause, it is often very difficult for overweight people to take weight off and keep it off. Many dieters have had the experience of losing a great deal of weight and then discovering, much to their chagrin, that they regain the weight while eating much less than before they started their diet. Why does this happen?

When people go on a diet, especially a starvation diet, there is a pronounced reduction in their *resting metabolic rate*—the energy the body uses when in the resting state (Keys, 1983). This change in metabolic rate occurs because the body actually resists the weight loss. Ironically, the dieter and his or her body are working toward opposite goals. While the dieter wants to take off extra pounds and inches, the body reacts to the sharp reduction in food intake as if it were protecting itself from starvation. It slows down its metabolic rate to conserve energy, thus ensuring that the brain, heart, and other vital organs will have sufficient fuel.

This change in metabolic rate produces highly inconvenient results for the dieter. For instance, assume that you normally consume 3,000 calories per day and you suddenly begin an 800-calorie diet. At first, you may experience a dramatic weight loss. Then your body will eventually lower its resting metabolic rate to conserve its fat stores—with the result that you will likely hit a plateau. If you tough it out, however, you will be able to reach your weight goal.

At this point, you will want to begin eating a more reasonable diet again—but beware. Your body is now likely to play one of its cruelest tricks. Used to conserving energy, your metabolism will continue running in low gear. Thus, even a modest increase in calorie consumption (often well below your prediet level) may result in gaining the pounds back. It may take weeks or months for your metabolism to readjust to a normal level, and by then you may have given up in disgust.

This sounds discouraging, but, as with everything else, there are right ways and wrong ways of dieting. The following Health Psychology and Life discussion, "Some Suggestions for Overcoming Obesity," provides additional information to keep in mind if you are trying to lose weight.

SOME SUGGESTIONS FOR OVERCOMING OBESITY

Countless solutions have been proposed to deal with weight problems. Nevertheless, the great majority of obese people who try to reduce and maintain a lower weight ultimately fail. This discussion presents a few suggestions based on the clinical experiences and experimental findings of weight loss specialists. Note that it is a good idea to consult a physician before embarking on a weight loss program.

1. *Determine your calorie intake.* Many people are convinced they are overweight not because they eat too much, but rather because they have metabolic problems. Most normal-weight adults consume around 2,000 to 2,500 calories each 24-hour period, depending on their size, sex, and activity level. If you are overweight and convinced that you eat no more than your skinny friends, try keeping a record of everything you eat and drink for a period of a week or so. You can buy a convenient calorie counter to help you convert items consumed into average calories per day. Some people are shocked at the number of calories they consume without thinking about what they are doing.

2. *Reduce food intake, if necessary.* We added the disclaimer "if necessary" because for some obese people, whose food consumption is in fact moderate, exercise without dieting may be more effective than eating less. However, if you are consuming more than a normal allotment of calories, it will be helpful to reduce the amount you eat, particularly food high in fat and sugar content. Consult a physician, dietician, or authoritative textbook to be sure your reduced food intake provides a healthy, balanced diet.

Avoid crash diets that may reduce calories to only a few hundred a day. Your odds for success are much better if you cut back only moderately on daily calorie consumption. Research clearly demonstrates that a slow, steady weight loss, of perhaps only a pound or two per week, will increase your chances of keeping excess pounds off once you reach your desired weight.

Several tips may help you moderately lower food consumption. First, try stocking up on nutritious food that does not inspire lust in your taste buds. Get rid of cookies, candies, ice cream, porterhouse steaks well marbled with fat, potato chips, cream cheese, soft drinks, or anything else you love to consume. It is a good idea to allow for some interesting variety in your diet so that you will not end up feeling so deprived that

you lose all control and binge. Occasionally reward yourself for a job well done by eating small portions of desired food.

Second, commit yourself to eating only at mealtime, and always in the same place. This will help eliminate the urge to snack that often results from learned associations between certain activities and food (for example, raiding the refrigerator during TV commercials). It can also be helpful to reduce access to foods that require no preparation. It is all too easy to nibble from an open box of crackers or cookies without even thinking about what you are doing.

3. *Exercise.* When used in conjunction with reduced food intake, regular, moderate exercise is probably the best strategy for losing weight (Belko et al., 1987; Keesey & Powley, 1986; Thompson et al., 1982). Unfortunately, however, some people make the mistake of thinking they will drop all their excess weight in a herculean exercise program. Like crash diets, this strategy often fails, due to physical burnout, injury, or boredom.

Moderation is the key for most people. If you can burn off 200 to 300 calories each time you exercise, you will obtain noticeable results in a reasonable amount of time (assuming, of course, that your food intake is held to a moderate level). Most specialists recommend exercise sessions that last a minimum of 20 to 30 minutes and occur at least three times a week. The activities you choose should be strenuous enough to raise your heart rate appreciably and to allow you to burn 200 to 300 calories per session. All kinds of exercise possibilities exist. Choosing one that is relatively enjoyable, or at

Avoid crash diets that may reduce calories to only a few hundred a day. Your odds for success are much better if you cut back only moderately on daily calorie consumption.

least not unpleasant, will pay dividends in greater perseverance. Studies indicate that 30 minutes of brisk walking burns off about 150 calories, 30 minutes of bicycling on normal terrain burns off 200 calories, swimming 275 calories, and jogging 370. For many people, exercise actually seems to decrease the appetite (Stunkard, 1983).

Recent research demonstrates that people who exercise either very intensively or for very long periods may experience an increase in their metabolic rate that can last for two or three days after cessation of exercise (Kolata, 1987). In addition, the more muscle tissue a person has relative to fat, the greater his or her metabolic rate. This is because muscle tissue consumes more caloric energy than fat (Kolata, 1987). Such findings suggest that an exercise regimen that combines muscle building with extended periods of cardiovascular exercise (such as jogging, bicycling, or swimming for a couple of hours several times a week) may be the optimal strategy for weight control. However, such a rigorous exercise program poses the risk of burnout or perhaps injury for individuals who do not build slowly into a program in accordance with the rate of improvement in their physical fitness.

4. *Keep Records and Reward Yourself.* Research indicates that people who keep records of how much they eat, when they eat, and what they were doing before and during eating are more likely to benefit from a weight loss program than those who do not record this information. This is because these records may reveal certain patterns that you were unaware of, such as a tendency to eat more in the company of a certain friend or to raid the refrigerator when you are feeling depressed.

It may be helpful to include others in your efforts to lose weight. Sometimes the first five or ten pounds are the toughest because nobody seems to notice. However, having someone around to praise you for the pound or two you have lost can be very reinforcing. Setting up little rewards along the way can also be helpful. Perhaps you can treat yourself to a professional massage after you drop the first five pounds. Maybe after 10 or 15 pounds you can take yourself to a beach resort where you can show off your gorgeous new body.

EATING DISORDERS

Two types of eating disorders are quite common among certain segments of society, particularly young women. The first of these disorders is anorexia nervosa, a form of self-starvation; the second is bulimia, in which a person may eat a full meal and then purge the stomach and intestines of food by inducing vomiting or using a laxative.

Both of these conditions seem to have increased in frequency in recent years. Many health professionals and psychologists think that our society's emphasis on thinness and perfect bodies is at least partly to blame. Young women seem particularly susceptible to the media-induced equation of "beautiful is thin." There are also indications that both conditions may be linked to psychological and physiological disturbances.

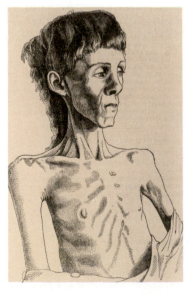

Anorexia is characterized by a prolonged refusal to eat adequate amounts of food and may affect as many as one in every 100 teenage women.

Anorexia Nervosa **Anorexia nervosa** may affect as many as one in every 100 teenage women (Wooley, 1983). In recent years, there has been increasing recognition that this disorder often demonstrates an early onset in prepubertal children age 14 or younger (Fosson et al., 1987). This eating disorder is characterized by a prolonged refusal to eat adequate amounts of food. The result may be emaciation and even death in extreme cases. Most recorded cases of anorexia occur among women in their teens or early 20's, although males, children, and middle-aged adults may also be afflicted.

The causes of anorexia are still being investigated. Social influence, via the media, probably plays a significant role in many cases (Bemis, 1978; Wooley, 1983). People with anorexia nervosa often have an extremely disturbed body image in which they perceive themselves as attractive only when pathetically thin (Striegel-Moore et al., 1986). In addition, it has been suggested that this disease may be linked to a variety of physical abnormalities including a malfunctioning hypothalamus or an endocrine disorder (Bemis, 1978; Gwirtsman & Gerner, 1981; Muuss, 1985; Russel, 1979; Walsh et al., 1978).

Bulimia **Bulimia** is a disorder in which a person, most commonly a young woman in her teens or 20s, engages in periodic episodes of binge eating, then uses either vomiting or a laxative to purge the body (Pope & Hudson, 1984). Some bulimics maintain normal weight, and others are also anorexic. In one study, approximately half of the patients hospitalized for anorexia indicated that they periodically resorted to bulimic purges (Casper et al., 1980). Estimates of the incidence of bulimia on college campuses run as high as 20 percent (Wooley, 1983).

Many people with bulimia frequently manifest depression, anxiety, poor body image, inadequate communication with family members, and guilt (Hinz & Williamson, 1987; Krueger & Bornstein, 1987; Pope & Hudson, 1984; Striegel-Moore et al., 1986; Williamson et al., 1985). In addition to these psychological problems, they may have a variety of physical complications including gastrointestinal difficulties, extensive tooth decay and enamel deterioration, and hair loss.

Both anorexia and bulimia are serious disorders that are showing up with increasing frequency. As a result, many campus health or counseling centers, and a growing number of urban hospital centers, have added specialists to their staff who are experienced in treating eating disorders. If allowed to continue unchecked, both of these conditions can seriously erode psychological and physical health.

SENSATION-SEEKING MOTIVES

Humans and other animals seem to require a certain amount of stimulation in order to feel good and function effectively. The need to manipulate and explore the environment and the need for sensory stimulation both fall under the category of sensation-seeking motives. These urges seem to be natural to a broad range of mammals. Observations of infants of many species, including humans, reveal a strong inclination to explore and manipulate the environment as soon as they are able. Animals have been shown to expose themselves willingly to various kinds of stimulation in the apparent effort to raise their level of physiological arousal. For example, young monkeys provided with mechanical puzzles, such as metal clasps used to seal a door, will tirelessly manipulate this object with no apparent reward beyond the opportunity to manipulate something (Harlow et al., 1950—see Figure 9.3).

FIGURE 9.3 YOUNG MONKEYS TIRELESSLY MANIPULATE MECHANICAL OBJECTS IN A PROBLEM-SOLVING SITUATION

(*Source:* Harry F. Harlow, University of Wisconsin Primate Laboratory)

Arousal level is directly related to how we feel. Most people prefer an intermediate level of arousal; however, some seek an extremely complex and novel level of stimuli.

We can see this same drive in ourselves. Very few of us, if any, are content with constant, never changing environments. Sometimes we seek quiet and solitude, but after a time we are likely to seek the sounds and sights of people and activity. We turn on the television, jog, play tennis, talk on the phone, and so forth. We may thrive on challenging games, complex puzzles, or the opportunity to explore new things.

Some psychologists believe that the motivation to seek stimulation evolved in many species because of its survival value: organisms that explore and manipulate their environment will become more aware of its parameters of safety and danger. Beyond these evolutionary implications for survival of the species, sensation-seeking motives also seem to be related to how we feel. The optimum level of arousal theory is one attempt to link sensation-seeking behavior with how we feel.

OPTIMUM LEVEL OF AROUSAL

Arousal is a general concept referring to a state of mind and body; we experience arousal as the ability to process information effectively and to engage in motivated behavior. A certain minimum level of arousal is essential in order to express goal-directed behavior. Conversely, too much arousal may leave us overstimulated, overloaded, and temporarily incapable of effective action. A number of researchers, most notably Donald Hebb (1955), have theorized that people have an **optimum level of arousal,** which is the level at which their performance will be most efficient.

According to Hebb's optimum level of arousal theory, our performance on a task will improve as arousal increases up to an optimal level. Further increases will begin to interfere with our efficiency. This theory has been generally supported by research, but with some exceptions (Houston, 1985). For example, low levels of arousal have frequently been shown to hinder performance, but not under all experimental conditions (Orne & Scheibe, 1964).

The Yerkes-Dodson Law The optimum level of arousal seems to vary according to the type of task a person is performing. For instance, the high arousal level you need to compete successfully in a 100-yard race would be inappropriate and even counterproductive for some other tasks such as writing a book report.

According to the **Yerkes-Dodson law,** the optimum level of arousal for peak performance will vary somewhat depending on the nature of the task (Yerkes & Dodson, 1908). If you are doing something quite easy, you will probably perform best if your arousal level is relatively high. Conversely, you are likely to do better on a difficult task if your arousal level is somewhat lower. Figure 9.4 demonstrates the relationship between arousal and performance, as predicted by the Yerkes-Dodson law. It is now generally recognized that the Yerkes-Dodson law somewhat oversimplifies the complex relationship between arousal and performance. Nevertheless, data from diverse studies have generally supported Yerkes and Dodson's formulation (Houston, 1985).

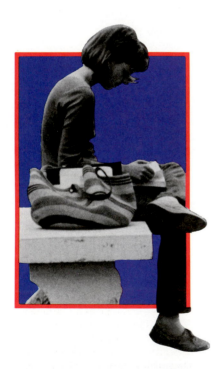

Some of us have low-level arousal needs and are perfectly happy to be alone and read a book.

Arousal and Emotions Just as arousal affects performance, it also affects how we feel. A number of researchers have suggested that extremes of arousal, either very low or high, produce unpleasant feelings in most people, while intermediate levels of arousal are preferable (Berlyne, 1970, 1971). One experiment evaluated people's feelings as they reacted to a variety of stimuli, ranging from very simple and familiar to extremely complex and novel. Most of the people in this study indicated a preference for stimuli of moderate complexity and newness (Berlyne, 1970).

Our own experience usually bears this out. Most of us prefer to be moderately aroused during the better part of our waking hours. We may enjoy attending a campus political rally or watching an athletic contest (both

FIGURE 9.4   THE YERKES-DODSON LAW APPLIED TO THE CONCEPT OF OPTIMUM LEVEL OF AROUSAL

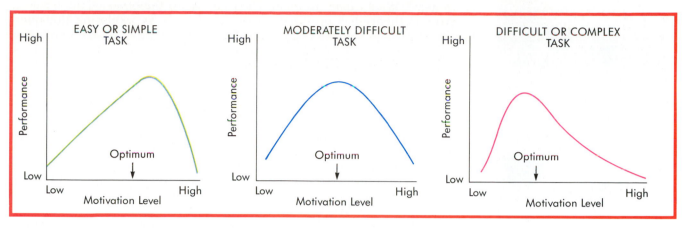

The optimum level of arousal seems to vary according to the type of task that a person is performing. As task complexity or difficulty increases, the optimum level of arousal (that which induces the best performance) decreases.

moderately arousing), but we probably prefer not to be leading the rally or providing a solo rendition of the national anthem at the start of the game (too arousing). Similarly, most of us will probably start to feel rather depressed if illness forces us to lie in bed, alone in our rooms for several days (too little arousal). On the other hand, a visit from friends (moderate arousal) is likely to provide a lift.

On an intuitive level, then, it does seem that we usually prefer moderate levels of arousal. What about those times, however, when we enjoy high levels of arousal, such as while riding a roller coaster or zooming down a ski slope, or when we want nothing more than to relax?

Questions like these led Walters, Apter, and Sveback (1982) to propose two curves to reflect the relationship between arousal and emotions (see Figure 9.5). According to these theorists, there are two preferred levels of arousal, one low and one high, and we switch back and forth between these two states. When we want to be excited, we are likely to be bored or frustrated if we are unable to find something arousing to do; when we want

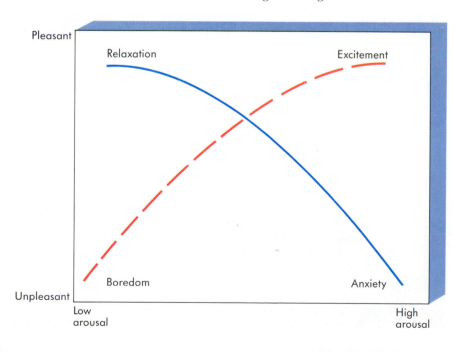

FIGURE 9.5   TWO KINDS OF AROUSAL CURVES

According to Walters, Apter, and Sveback (1982), there are two preferred levels of arousal, one low and one high (relaxation and arousal curves, respectively), and we switch back and forth between these two states. When we want to be excited, we are likely to find low arousal states to be boring and unpleasant. Conversely, when we wish to be relaxed, we are likely to find a low state of arousal to be pleasant.

Psychologist Marvin Zuckerman (1979) would probably describe this person as a "sensation-seeker"—someone who seeks out high levels of stimulation through adventurous activities.

to relax, even a visit from talkative friends is likely to be experienced as aversive. What causes us to switch from one to the other of these states? Arousal theory has provided a theoretical basis for exploring this question.

EXPLAINING WHY AROUSAL PREFERENCES VARY

According to the optimum level of arousal theory, we seek out stimulating experiences in order to maintain our arousal level within an optimal range. When we are overstimulated, negative feelings and/or lowered performance efficiency motivate us to seek out a more quiet environment; just the opposite happens when we are understimulated.

A variety of physical and cognitive consequences of arousal may cause us to switch from one preferred arousal level to the other. For example, we might be motivated to switch from high arousal to low arousal because we have become overloaded, physically fatigued, or fully satiated. Conversely, we may be motivated to switch from low to high arousal preference because we are feeling nonproductive, uninspired, or physically sluggish.

Different people seem to prefer a different mix between these two states (Farley, 1986; Weiss, 1987). Some prefer to work alone or live alone: their idea of a good time might be to curl up with a book. Other people seem motivated to seek out high levels of stimulation provided by crowded, vibrant work environments and adventurous activities. Psychologist Marvin Zuckerman (1979) has coined the term "sensation-seeker" to describe this latter type of individual who prefers a very high level of arousal. Most of us probably fall somewhere between these two extremes.

PREDICTING RESPONSES TO SENSORY DEPRIVATION

Perhaps the best examples of how arousal needs motivate sensation-seeking behavior are developed in **sensory deprivation** studies. The classic experiment in this area was conducted by a group of Canadian psychologists at McGill University who paid male student volunteers to stay as long as possible in an isolation room like that shown in Figure 9.6. Subjects were asked to lie motionless when not eating, drinking, or using the bathroom; gloves and cardboard cuffs

FIGURE 9.6 SUBJECT IN A SENSORY-DEPRIVATION STUDY

In a classic experiment conducted in the 1950s by Canadian psychologists at McGill University, student volunteers were paid to stay as long as possible in an isolation room. They wore coverings over their eyes, gloves, and cardboard cuffs over their hands and lower arms, and the hum of a fan drowned out all other sounds. The participants quickly became bored, and they developed a strong craving for any kind of stimulation. Many of them quit the experiment within the first two days. Some of those who stayed on began to hallucinate after two or three days of continuous sensory deprivation.

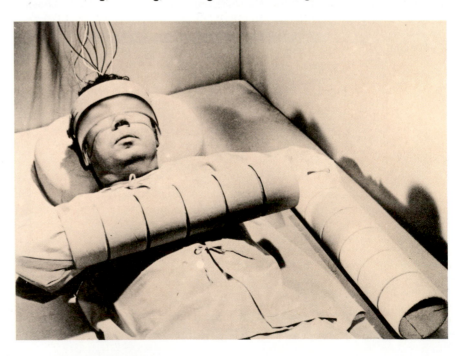

over their hands and lower arms prevented tactile sensations. Translucent coverings over their eyes reduced vision to a dim haze, and the hum of a fan drowned out all other sounds. Based on what you have learned about sensation-seeking motives and optimum levels of arousal, how do you think these subjects responded to this "easy way to make money"? Make your predictions before reading on.

Many of the subjects quit the experiment within the first couple of days. Of those who did not find the experience intolerable, nearly all said that it was unpleasant. Why did they respond in this way? Perhaps part of the answer is related to the stress of social isolation, but it also seems likely that experiencing a level of sensory stimulation dramatically below their optimal arousal level played an important role. The subjects seemed to develop such a strong need for sensory stimulation that they resorted to almost any kind of stimulation to raise their level of arousal. For example, when given a chance to listen to boring taped lectures, such as a report on the evils of alcohol written at a six-year-old level, they would repeatedly press a button that activated the tape. Furthermore, some subjects began to hallucinate after two or three days of sensory deprivation. Perhaps they were trying to generate their own sensory experiences to cope with the absence of external stimulation (Bexton et al., 1954).

These findings have been confirmed by subsequent studies. Of particular interest is the finding that prolonged sensory deprivation often reduces a person's performance on a variety of mental tasks (Goldberger, 1982). This information has been applied by engineering psychologists and other design professionals to provide enriched sensory experiences to individuals forced to work in monotonous environments for long periods of time, from astronauts in space to workers on assembly lines.

SEXUAL MOTIVATION

Another important type of motivation is human sexual motivation. For a time, sexual motivation was thought to be primarily a physiological drive, mostly because of the dominant role of physiology in animal sexual behavior. In nonprimate mammals such as rats, for instance, hormones appear to be essential to sexual arousal and function. However, there is now general agreement that learning, emotions, and social norms become more important as the complexity of the organism increases. In humans, sexual interest and expression are controlled less by hormones and more by the cerebral cortex, reflecting a complex combination of biological, psychological, and cultural factors.

All this is not to say that biology is irrelevant to sexual motivation in humans. In the following sections we compare the effects of biological and psychosocial factors to see what roles they play in sexual motivation and arousal.

BIOLOGICAL FACTORS: THE ROLE OF HORMONES

It is extremely difficult to distinguish between the effects of strictly physiological processes such as hormone production and those of psychosocial processes such as early socialization, peer group learning, and emotional needs. In recent years, however, a number of well-designed, carefully implemented studies have yielded information about the complex relationship between hormones and sexual activity. As we shall see, the evidence linking hormones to sexuality is considerably more substantial for males than females.

Hormones in Male Sexual Motivation   The general term for the male sex hormones is **androgens.** About 95 percent of these androgens are secreted by the testes in the form of testosterone; the remaining 5 percent are produced by the adrenal glands. A number of studies have linked androgens with sexual activity, with some of the best evidence coming from studies of the effects of castration, androgen-blocking drugs, and reduced gonadal function.

Castration Studies A number of studies of *castration* (removal of the testes) have provided somewhat inconsistent evidence of the connection between androgens and sexual function. One major investigation of a large group of castrated Norwegian males found significantly reduced sexual interest and activity among a substantial majority within the first year after the operation (Bremer, 1959). A more recent study of 39 sex offenders in West Germany, who voluntarily agreed to surgical castration while in prison, obtained similar results (Heim, 1981). However, the effects were varied. While 16 of the subjects reported that their sexual behavior was extinguished soon after castration, the remaining 11 continued to engage in sexual activity throughout the next several years, although with diminished frequency.

These studies, together with numerous other investigations, have generally shown that sexual interest and activity diminish after castration, but that the amount of reduction is highly variable. The fact that this diminution effect has occurred in so many studies suggests that hormones play an important role in instigating sexual interest. However, we cannot rule out the possible impact of feelings, attitudes, and beliefs. Psychological factors that may inhibit sexual functioning after castration include embarrassment due to a sense of physical mutilation, the self-fulfilling belief in the myth that castration abolishes erectile response, or perhaps a combination of these and other factors.

Androgen-Blocking Drugs Another source of information about the effect of hormones has been androgen-blocking drugs. In recent years a class of drugs known as antiandrogens has been used experimentally in Europe and America to treat sexual offenders. Antiandrogens drastically reduce the amount of testosterone circulating in the bloodstream. One of these drugs, medroxyprogesterone acetate (MPA, also known by its trade name, Depo-Provera), has received a great deal of media attention in America in the last few years. Although a number of studies have found that Depo-Provera and other antiandrogens may be effective in reducing both sexual interest and activity in human males (Crooks & Baur, 1987), altering the sex hormones provides no guarantees for treating sex offenders, especially when the assaultive acts stem from nonsexual motives such as the need to express anger or to exert control over another person.

Reduced Function of the Testes A third source of evidence about androgens and sexual motivation is studies of **hypogonadism**—a state of androgen deprivation that results from certain diseases of the endocrine system. If this condition occurs before puberty, maturation of the primary and secondary sex characteristics is retarded and the individual may never develop an active sexual interest.

The results are far more variable if androgen deficiency occurs in adulthood. However, extensive studies conducted by a number of researchers, including Scottish endocrinologist John Bancroft (1984) and Stanford University physiologist Julian Davidson (1984), provide strong evidence that androgens play an important role in male sexual motivation. For example, it has been shown that when hypogonadal men receive hormone replacement treatments to replace androgens in the bloodstream, they often experience a return of normal sexual interest and activity. If the treatments are temporarily suspended, however, sexual motivation and activity decline within two or three weeks.

A recent investigation provided very strong evidence of a link between androgen levels and sexual motivation and behavior in adolescent males (Udry et al., 1985). This study found that the higher the androgen level in the bloodstreams of teenage subjects, the more time they spent thinking about sex and the more likely they were to have engaged in coitus, noncoital sex play, and masturbation.

Hormones in Female Sexual Behavior   Many people assume that **estrogens** play a major role in female sexual motivation and behavior. We do know that these hormones help maintain the elasticity of the vaginal lining and contribute to production of vaginal lubricant. However, their role in female sexual motivation is far from clear.

There is some evidence that estrogens are an insignificant factor in female sexual activity. For instance, studies of postmenopausal women (Masters & Johnson, 1966) and women who have had their ovaries removed for medical reasons (Kinsey et al., 1953) show no significant change in sexual interest. This conclusion has recently been challenged, however. Two well-designed studies showed that estrogen replacement therapy improved not only vaginal lubrication but also sexual motivation, pleasure, and orgasmic capacity (Dennerstein et al., 1980; Dow et al., 1983). Findings such as these suggest that some estrogen is necessary to maintain a normal sexual interest, just as testosterone is needed to maintain a male's sexual interest (Bancroft, 1984).

It has long been assumed that androgens produced by adrenal glands are important for female sexual motivation. Much of the evidence supporting this viewpoint comes from reports of gynecologists and endocrinologists, including numerous references to cases in which women undergoing androgen therapy report increased sexual interest and activity (Dorfman & Shipley, 1956; Kupperman & Studdiford, 1953). Reduced sexual arousal has also been experimentally linked to androgen deprivation. Two studies have reported marked decreases in sexual desire in women who have undergone surgical removal of the adrenal glands (Schon & Sutherland, 1960; Waxenberg et al., 1959).

Recently, however, a different picture has begun to emerge. Three systematic investigations compared the effect of androgens on female sexuality with that of a placebo, with no significant difference (Mathews, 1981). Future research may clarify what relationship, if any, exists between sex hormones and female sexual interest and behavior. Even in the case of male sexuality, where the role of hormones is now becoming clearer, we must continue to be aware that human sexual behavior is so tremendously individualized that it is difficult to specify precisely how hormones affect sexual motivation.

PSYCHOSOCIAL FACTORS

Although hormones can influence human sexual motivation, they are far from the only important factor. Psychological and cultural conditions probably play a greater role in human sexual arousal and expression. Two sources of evidence are firsthand experience and cross-cultural studies.

Firsthand Experience   Some of the best evidence of psychological influences on sexual motivation come from our own experiences and observations. Ask yourself, for instance, what motivates your own or others' sexual behavior and what are the most important restrictions on sexual behavior?

The majority of people continue to express sexuality throughout most of their lives because sexual activity is reinforcing. This reinforcement takes many forms, including a sense of self-esteem that comes from being loved, erotic pleasure and gratification, reduction of feelings of anxiety, and a sense of closeness to another person. Our discussion of the sensation-seeking motive indicates that sexual expression even provides a way of relieving boredom and raising arousal levels.

Such reinforcers suggest that our incentives for sexual expression are largely psychosocial. They also reveal the basically social nature of humans, a propensity that greatly influences the manner in which we express our sexuality. In contrast to other animals, humans' sexual behaviors are not strongly correlated with reproductive cycles and related biological events.

Just as many of the factors that motivate sexual expression are psychosocial, so are many of its constraints. In all societies, such limits result primarily from psychosocial conditioning, which often inhibits sexual arousal and response through the creation of negative emotions such as fear, guilt, and shame. Our sexual *mores* (firmly established customs or folkways of a given culture) are also critical in shaping sexual motivation and behavior. That is why children in one culture may openly engage in sexually motivated play while young people in a more restrictive society may inhibit their sexual feelings. Cultural mores also tend to limit sexual expression to certain "acceptable" behaviors (Crooks & Baur, 1987).

Of course, there are also physiological restraints, such as disease and anatomical pathology. However, there seem to be no consistent biological restraining factors in humans. Other animals stand in sharp contrast: Female sexual receptivity is governed by the reproductive cycle; biological cues (such as odors) are often necessary to instigate sexual activity; and hormone levels are much more closely tied to the ability to respond sexually. Some social restraints on sexual behavior exist among nonhuman animals, but biological restraints are of primary importance.

Cross-Cultural Evidence   Social scientists have recorded in detail the tremendous variation that occurs in human sexual behavior in different societies (Crooks & Baur, 1987; Ford & Beach, 1951). Societies exist in which individuals in their 60s are more active sexually than the typical 30-year-old American. In many societies, the marked gender differences in adolescent sexual behaviors that typify our own society are totally lacking. Such widespread fluctuations in sexual norms and behavior cannot be attributed to the influence of hormones.

Nor can they be attributed to geographical factors. No other animal species have different sexual behaviors in different parts of the world. Rats in Ethiopia copulate the same way and are triggered by the same stimuli as rats in Dillon, Montana. The sexual patterns of dogs, cows, fowl, and higher primates are all highly similar, regardless of where they live. Thus, humans are unique in creating highly localized patterns of sexual behavior. This is perhaps the strongest evidence for the preeminence of psychosocial factors in human sexual motivation and expression.

COMPLEX PSYCHOSOCIAL MOTIVES: THE NEED FOR ACHIEVEMENT

Human sexual motivation is influenced by both biological and psychosocial factors, but another group of motives do not reflect biological drives. The complex psychosocial motives are determined by learning and experience. There are a variety of psychosocial motives, ranging from socially based motives, such as the need for affiliation and the need for social approval, to psychologically induced motives such as the need to achieve, power needs, and the need for competence. We will examine one psychosocial motive, the need for achievement.

If you are the kind of person who is not content unless you make top grades, and who is committed to being highly successful in your chosen career, psychologists would say that you have a high **need for achievement.** The concept of achievement motivation was first defined in 1938 by Henry Murray as the need to ". . . accomplish something difficult. To overcome obstacles and attain a high standard. To rival and surpass others. To increase self regard by the successful exercise of talent" (p. 164). Murray developed the *Thematic Apperception Test* (TAT) to measure the need for

TABLE 9.3 *Characteristics of High nAch Individuals*

1. Are optimistic about personal prospects for success; feel personally in control of their destinies, and are willing to delay gratification for the sake of achieving long-term goals (for example, willingness to extend education into postgraduate studies rather than going for the immediate economic rewards of a lesser job) (Kulka, 1972).
2. Tend to seek higher levels of socioeconomic success than parents, and are more often successful in achieving this than people with low nAch scores (McClelland et al., 1976).
3. Are inclined to set realistic career goals that are neither too easy nor too difficult for their skills, whereas low nAch scorers tend to select career goals that are either too easy or unrealistic in light of their abilities (Mahone, 1960; Morris, 1966).
4. Attain higher grades in academic courses related to career goals than do low need achievers (Raynor, 1970).
5. Tend to be relatively independent and more concerned with succeeding on tasks than with how they affect other people (McClelland, 1976).

achievement and other human motives. Not until the 1950s, however, was the TAT sufficiently refined (McClelland et al., 1953) to be an effective tool for assessing the need for achievement (abbreviated as *nAch*). The TAT asks people to make up stories about a series of ambiguous pictures, the idea being that people will project into the stories their own motives, interests, and values. We will have more to say about the TAT in Chapter 13.

A number of studies show that people who score high in need for achievement differ notably from those with moderate or low nAch scores. Table 9.3 summarizes some of the traits characteristic of people who have a high need for achievement.

HOPE OF SUCCESS VERSUS FEAR OF FAILURE

What determines whether we avoid a difficult task or try our best to achieve it? A number of researchers have theorized that our achievement motive is the result of a complex interaction between our *hope of success* and *fear of failure* (Atkinson, 1957; Atkinson & Litwin, 1960; Atkinson & Raynor, 1974). According to this interpretation, we may want to become involved in a task because we would like to succeed in it, but at the same time we may be repelled by a fear of failure. Overall, our net achievement motivation is seen as a result of the combination of these two interacting forces.

EXPLAINING HOW FEAR OF FAILURE INFLUENCES TASK SELECTION

The conceptualization that two opposite processes are involved in achievement motivation leads to a number of predictions. For example, when people are more interested in avoiding failure than in striving for success, they will pursue goals that are either very easy or very difficult. Can you think of a commonsense basis for this prediction? Give it some thought before reading on.

Logically, we might predict that people who are driven primarily by fear of failure will be equally comfortable tackling a very easy or a very difficult task because they probably think that they will succeed at the simple job and that failure on the tough task will be no disgrace, since most people fail such assignments. Thus, it is the tasks of moderate difficulty that are most likely to be avoided by people motivated by fear of failure. In contrast, people who are motivated by the hope or expectation of success are likely to set more realistic goals and to become involved in tasks of intermediate difficulty that offer a moderate degree of challenge. Available research data provide strong support for the first of these predictions and moderate but not totally consistent support for the second (Geen et al., 1984; Houston, 1985).

INFLUENCING ACHIEVEMENT MOTIVATION IN CHILDREN

Since the achievement need is a psychosocial motivation, it is highly influenced by learning and experience. Indeed, ample evidence demonstrates that the way in which we raise our children may significantly influence their need to achieve (McClelland, 1985; McClelland & Pilon, 1983). One way to help instill a desire to achieve is to encourage children to set reasonable goals and to provide ample reinforcements for their successes. Being realistic about goals is especially important because reasonable goals are likely to be achieved, thus allowing children to experience success.

Of equal importance is fostering independence. In one study, Marion Winterbottom (1958) found that children who demonstrated high achievement motivation usually had parents who expected them to master their own environments and to show independent behavior (by doing things such as earning their own spending money) well before their teenage years. Little things like expecting a child to pick out what he or she is going to wear to school or letting children have a vote in certain family decisions encourage a sense of independence and a desire to achieve success.

THE NATURE OF EMOTIONS

As we saw earlier in this chapter, motivation and **emotion** (subjective feelings and moods) are closely connected. Emotions often motivate our actions, as when a child's anger causes her to kick a bedroom wall or when fear of failure motivates a student to withdraw from a class. The expectation of pleasant emotions also serves as an incentive, in that many of our purposeful, motivated behaviors are designed to induce feelings of happiness, joy, excitement, and pride.

Emotions do more than motivate behavior. They provide the zing and zest to our existence. They can be confusing and difficult to identify, but can you imagine what life would be like without them? In the remainder of this chapter we explore emotions in the effort to find out more about what they are and how they come about.

THE COMPONENTS OF EMOTION

Although the terms *emotion* and *feelings* are often used interchangeably, a careful analysis reveals that feelings are only one of four integral components of human emotions: cognitive processes, subjective feelings, physiological arousal, and behavioral reactions. Take a moment to read the following first-person account. It illustrates all of these components.

First Person 9.3

My 10-year-old daughter has been testing me to the limit lately, to see what she can get away with. She went too far the other day. While she was at school, I went into her room to leave some clean laundry on her bed, and I could hardly believe what I saw. My new white sweater, which she had admired greatly, was crumpled up under the bed, partly visible from where I stood. When I pulled it out to make sure it was what I thought it was, I could see a large stain where nail polish had been spilled on it. She had borrowed my sweater without asking, carelessly ruined it, and then had hidden the evidence!

My initial reaction was fury. It is lucky she wasn't there, since I am not sure how I might have responded in those first few moments—the juices were flowing and I was ready to become a child abuser! I threw the sweater down, muttered something very unmotherly about my child, and started rummaging furiously through her drawers, looking for a favorite item of hers that *I* could ruin. Then I began to think more clearly. Rather than stooping to the level of a 10-year-old, I thought I stood a better chance of teaching her a lesson by dealing rationally with the incident. I neatly folded the sweater with the stain showing, wrote a brief note requesting that my daughter meet me in my room at 5:00 for a talk, and left the note on top of the sweater, in the middle of her bed. (*Authors' files*)

Cognitive Processes Psychologists differ in the extent to which they emphasize the role of cognitive processes in the arousal and expression of emotions. There is a general consensus, however, that perception, thinking, and memory are very much involved in emotional expression. In the first-person account, the mother would not have experienced anger had she been unable to perceive and understand the implications of what she found in her daughter's room.

Subjective Feelings All emotions include subjective feelings that involve both a general affective or emotional state that is positive or negative, and a specific feeling tone such as joy, anger, fear, or disgust. The emotions recorded in the first-person account reflected both a general state of negativity and the specific feeling of intense anger. When psychologists attempt to ascertain a person's emotional state, they typically ask the individual to describe the emotions he or she is experiencing. Most people respond by describing their feelings—"I am depressed"; "I am extremely happy"; "I feel nervous and apprehensive." Thus, for most individuals, these subjective feelings constitute emotion.

Physiological Arousal The mother described her anger by saying "the juices were flowing." Actually, the "juices" probably were flowing, in the form of epinephrine and other hormones associated with the arousal of anger. One might also guess that for a few minutes, until she calmed down, her heart rate increased dramatically, her blood pressure probably increased significantly, and her breathing may have become rapid and uneven.

Emotions are typically associated with mild to extreme changes in the physiological processes occurring within our bodies. In addition to the changes listed above, these processes may include metabolic changes, altered muscle tension, changes in activity of the salivary and sweat glands, modified digestive processes, and changes in the levels of certain neurotransmitters in the brain. (Recall from Chapter 3 that the autonomic nervous system is involved in most of the physiological changes associated with emotional arousal.)

Behavioral Reactions Emotions often cause us to act out our feelings. These expressions may range from crying, screaming, or verbal outbursts ("muttering something unmotherly") to smiling or laughing. Facial expressions, tone of voice, posture, and other kinds of body language are all common signals of emotion. In addition to being expressive, behavioral reactions to emotions may also be instrumental. An example of this is running away from a dangerous situation.

THE RANGE OF HUMAN EMOTIONS

Adoration, amazement, amusement, anger, anxiety, contempt, disgust, distress, ecstasy, embarrassment, envy, fear, guilt, humiliation, interest, jealousy, joy, loathing, rage, reverence, sadness, shame, sorrow, surprise, terror—these are just a few of the emotions we recognize. Some of these emotions overlap: ecstasy and joy, for instance, clearly share certain elements. Thus, differences between emotions are often more a matter of degree than of kind. Furthermore, many emotional experiences may represent a blending of more basic emotions. The mother in the previous example may have felt a combination of anger and anxiety about her daughter's behavior.

Some psychologists have attempted to identify a number of primary emotions, combinations of which provide the building blocks for more com-

FIGURE 9.7 PLUTCHIK'S EMOTION WHEEL

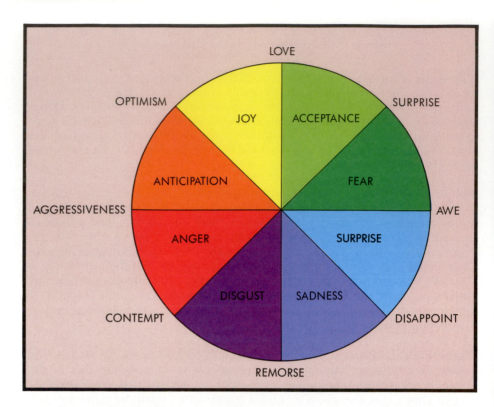

According to Robert Plutchik, there are eight primary, or basic, human emotions, which consist of four pairs of opposites: acceptance and disgust, fear and anger, surprise and anticipation, and sadness and joy. Plutchik maintains that adjacent emotions, such as joy and acceptance, blend to form more complex feelings, such as love, which are listed on the outer rim of the emotion wheel.

plex emotions. One of the best known schemes was developed a few years ago by Robert Plutchik.

Plutchik's Emotion Wheel   According to Plutchik (1980), there are eight primary or basic human emotions, which consist of four pairs of opposites: acceptance and disgust, fear and anger, surprise and anticipation, and sadness and joy. Plutchik adopted the unique approach of arranging these eight primary emotions on an "emotion wheel" (see Figure 9.7). He maintains that all human emotions are variations or derivations of these eight. The closer emotions are on the wheel, the more they have in common. For example, anticipation and joy both share an element of expectation, whereas fear and surprise share the quality of the unknown. Plutchik maintains that adjacent emotions blend to form the more complex feelings listed on the outer rim of the emotion wheel. Many of us would probably agree that love does involve, at least to some degree, elements of joy and acceptance, and that contempt certainly involves components of both anger and disgust.

EMOTIONS: THEORIES AND CONTROVERSIES

We have learned that emotional expression is a complex process involving cognitions, subjective feelings, physiological arousal, and behavioral reactions. How do these processes interact to produce an emotional response? What is the usual sequence of events? Is it necessary to think before we feel, or do we feel an emotion and then later interpret it as fear, happiness, and so forth? Psychologists have proposed contradictory answers to these questions, in a controversy that sometimes resembles the well-known debate about whether the chicken or the egg came first. We will examine the evidence.

THE JAMES-LANGE THEORY

Imagine that after having trouble sleeping, you decide to take a midnight walk. It is dark and still; no one else is in sight. Suddenly, you hear a rustling in the bushes behind you, followed by rapidly approaching footfalls. Your response will probably be one of terror: you are likely to run for your life. What would activate your fear in this situation? Is it triggered by the sounds you hear, which in turn induce you to run? Or is it more likely that your awareness of danger causes your heart to beat faster and your legs to carry you away, and that these physical responses trigger your emotional response of fear?

When these questions are put to students, the vast majority answer that hearing noises in the dark causes fear, which in turn triggers a flood of physical reactions. This "commonsense" interpretation of the activation of emotion seems quite logical (see Figure 9.8). We perceive and interpret a particular stimulus, in this case threatening noises, and these cognitive processes give rise to an emotion (fear), which triggers certain physiological reactions and body movements. Along these lines, we would also conclude that we cry because we feel sad, rather than becoming sad because we cry, and that we laugh because we are happy, rather than being happy because we laugh.

However, the American psychologist William James (1884), and the Danish physiologist Carl Lange (1885), writing independently of each other, both questioned this commonsense view. Their interpretation, referred to as the **James-Lange theory,** suggests that environmental stimuli trigger physiological responses from viscera (the internal organs such as the heart and lungs). For instance, heart rate and respiration both increase. At the same time, the body may also respond with muscle movements, as when we jump at an unexpected noise. These visceral and muscular responses then activate emotional states. Thus, James and Lange would argue that your fear stems from your awareness of specific body reactions that you associate with fear—a pounding heart, rapid breathing, running legs, and so forth—rather than from your cognitions about noises in the dark.

Although it might seem to contradict common sense, the James-Lange theory makes sense at some level. We have all encountered unexpected situations in which we seemed to respond automatically, before we had a chance to experience emotion. For example, if a car suddenly veered onto the sidewalk and threatened to run you down, you would no doubt leap out of the way. You might not label your heightened arousal and reactive state as one of "fear" until the danger had passed and you had become aware of your weak knees and pounding heart. In such situations, the emotions seem to follow the bodily changes and behavioral reactions. James and Lange argued that we often encounter situations in which behavioral and physiological reactions occur too quickly to be triggered by emotions.

Some intriguing evidence collected from human subjects with spinal cord injuries provides some support for the James-Lange theory. If feedback from the internal organs through the autonomic nervous system is important, we might expect that individuals with damage high on the spinal cord (quadraplegics) would experience emotional feelings of lower intensity than those with low injury (paraplegics), because a high injury would cut off feedback from a greater portion of the body. This is exactly what research has revealed. The higher the injury to the spinal cord, and consequently the less sensory feedback received, the less intense the emotional feelings reported by an individual (Hohmann, 1966). One quadraplegic with high injury describes these altered feelings:

> Now, I don't get a feeling of physical animation. It's sort of cold anger.
> Sometimes I act angry when I see some injustice. I yell and cuss and raise

The expectation of pleasant emotions serves as an incentive, in that many of our purposeful, motivated behaviors are designed to induce feelings of happiness, joy, excitement, and pride.

The "Common Sense" View of Emotion. We perceive and interpret a particular stimulus and these cognitive processes give rise to an emotion which triggers certain physiological reactions and body movements. "I see a bear, feel fear, experience a flood of physiological reactions, and run because I am afraid."

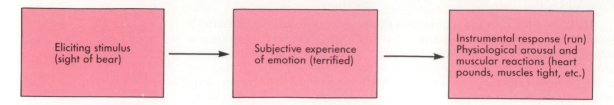

The James-Lange Theory. Environmental stimuli triggers physiological responses and bodily movements, and emotion occurs when the individual interprets his or her visceral and muscular responses. "I must be afraid because my heart is pounding and I am running like crazy."

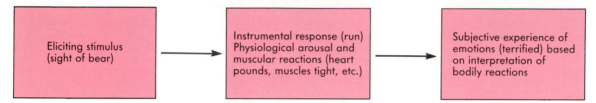

The Cannon-Bard Theory. Emotion is a cognitive event that is enhanced by bodily reactions. Bodily reactions do not cause emotion but rather occur simultaneously with the experience of emotion. "I am afraid because I know bears are dangerous."

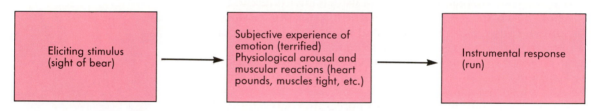

The Schachter-Singer Theory. Emotions depend upon a kind of double cognitive interpretation: we appraise the emotion-causing event while also evaluating what is happening with our bodies. "I am afraid because I know bears are dangerous and because my heart is pounding."

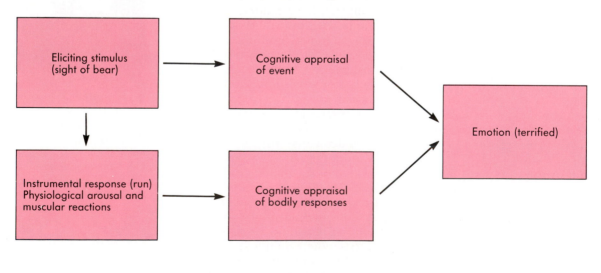

FIGURE 9.8   THEORIES OF EMOTION

hell, because if you don't do it sometimes, I've learned people will take advantage of you, but it just doesn't have the heat to it that it used to. It's a mental kind of anger. (Hohmann, 1966, p. 151)

The James-Lange theory has also been challenged, however. Prominent American physiologist Walter Cannon (1927) and his student, Philip Bard, objected to the idea that different emotions have distinct patterns of visceral and muscular responses that we recognize and then interpret in our emotional reactions. Cannon and Bard collected laboratory evidence indicating that physiological changes associated with happiness, sadness, and anger were quite similar. All of these emotions are typically accompanied by increased breathing and heart rate, secretion of epinephrine, and pupil dilation. How can people distinguish between different emotions that are accompanied by very similar physiological responses?

Psychologists today hesitate to reject the notion that people are able to discriminate between subtle differences in visceral and muscular patterns associated with specific emotions. Recent research has demonstrated that although different emotions are associated with similar physiological changes, these changes are not identical. For example, subtle distinctions have been demonstrated between emotions such as anger, fear, happiness, and sadness. These include variations in heart rate, resistance of the skin to the passage of a weak electrical current (galvanic skin response), temperature of the hands, patterns of activity in facial muscles, and neural activity in the frontal lobes of the brain (Davidson, 1984; Ekman et al., 1983; Schwartz, 1982).

Certainly, these more recent findings do not prove the James-Lange theory. There is little concrete evidence that people are able to make the fine discrimination between the varied, often highly similar, patterns of physiological and muscular responses to determine what emotions they are experiencing. However, it is possible that we are sensitive to a wide variety of these responses and that enough of these changes occur sufficiently quickly to serve as the basis for feelings of emotion.

THE CANNON-BARD THEORY

Walter Cannon followed his criticism of the James-Lange theory by proposing that physiological and muscular changes are not the cause of emotion, but rather that emotional experiences and physical changes occur simultaneously. This viewpoint, as modified by Philip Bard (1934), is known as the **Cannon-Bard theory.**

Cannon and Bard theorized that the thalamus (see Chapter 3) plays a key role in our emotional responses. It not only channels sensory input to the cerebral cortex, where it is interpreted, but at the same time it sends activation messages through the peripheral nervous system to the viscera and skeletal muscles. These activation messages trigger the physiological and behavioral reactions that typically accompany emotions (see Figure 9.8).

Cannon and Bard would explain your emotional response to being approached in the dark in the following manner: The sensory input of the sounds you heard in the dark were relayed simultaneously to your cerebral cortex and your internal organs and muscles. This allowed you to perceive fear at the same time that your internal organs and muscles were reacting to the stimulus. Cannon and Bard would contend that your fear was enhanced by your pounding heart, rapid breathing, and flight from the source of the noise, rather than resulting from these physical changes, as James and Lange would suggest.

Subsequent research has revealed that the hypothalamus and certain other structures in the limbic system (see Chapter 3) are the brain centers most directly involved in integrating emotional responses—not the thalamus. However, the Cannon-Bard theory points out the important role of the brain in our emotional responses.

A major shortcoming of both the Cannon-Bard theory and the James-Lange theory is that neither adequately recognizes that emotions are more than automatic reactions to stimuli, and that they are often influenced by how we interpret feedback from our bodies. The Schachter-Singer theory presents an interesting assessment of the role of appraisal or judgment (cognitions) in the activation of emotion.

THE SCHACHTER-SINGER THEORY

In the early 1960s, Stanley Schachter and Jerome Singer (1962) developed the **Schachter-Singer theory** of emotions, which combined elements from both the James-Lange and the Cannon-Bard theories. Schachter and Singer believed that emotion follows behavioral and physiological reactions, as suggested by James and Lange, but they also agreed with Cannon and Bard that cognitive processes are central to emotional experiences.

Instead of viewing emotion as a joint effect of both physical reactions and cognitive appraisal, Schachter and Singer maintained that emotions depend on a kind of double cognitive interpretation: we appraise the emotion-causing event while also evaluating what is happening with our bodies. The key process in emotional arousal is how we interpret feedback from our bodies in light of our present situation.

For example, suppose you have just run several blocks across campus to avoid being late to a class. You will probably note that you are panting and sweating and that your heart is pounding, but you are unlikely to experience an emotional response to these heightened physical reactions. If you experienced these same physical responses under different circumstances, however—for example, while running across a farmer's field to escape an enraged bull—you would probably interpret your arousal as fear.

The James-Lange view proposed that a given state of bodily reaction and arousal produces a specific emotion. Schachter and Singer suggested that a given body state could produce a variety of emotions, depending upon the context within which they occur. From this point of view, we might interpret highly similar patterns of arousal as reflecting distinctly different emotions in different contexts.

Schachter and Singer (1962) designed an ingenious experiment to test this theory. Male college student volunteers were told they would be participating in an experiment dealing with vision. All were given an injection of a substance the experimenters called "Suproxin," which was described as a vitamin compound that would temporarily affect vision. In reality, some subjects were injected with the hormone epinephrine, which is known to increase heart and respiration rates and blood pressure, produce muscle tremors, and generally cause a "jittery" feeling. Other subjects, the control group, were merely injected with a placebo that produced no physical effects. The experimenters manipulated their subjects' cognitions about the cause of their arousal by providing accurate or inaccurate information about the connection between their symptoms and the earlier injection. Some of these subjects (the *informed group*) were told that some people react to Suproxin with the side effects just described. A second group of subjects (the *uninformed group*) received no information about side effects, and a third group (the *misinformed group*) received false information, such as that the drug might cause itching or facial numbness.

Next, all subjects experienced certain staged social cues during a 20-minute "waiting period" before the vision test (which never actually took place). Subjects were placed, one at a time, in the waiting room with another person who was introduced as a fellow subject, but who was actually a confederate of the experimenters. Half of the waiting subjects were exposed to a euphoria condition in which the accomplice behaved in a happy manner, engaging in such playful activity as shooting baskets with paper wads and a trashcan. These subjects were repeatedly asked to join in the good fun. In contrast, the other half of the subjects were assigned to an anger condition. They and the accomplice were asked to fill out a questionnaire, to which the accomplice reacted by grumbling loudly, tearing up the questionnaire, and eventually storming out of the room in a state of high anger. During these staged waiting periods, the subjects' behavior was observed through a one-way mirror; each subject was also questioned about his emotional state.

PREDICTING THE RESULTS OF THE SCHACHTER-SINGER EXPERIMENT

Assuming that Schachter's and Singer's view of emotional arousal is correct, what pattern of results would you predict in this experiment? Were the subjects' assessments of their emotional state influenced by the confederate's antics? Were there differences between the informed, uninformed, and misinformed groups? Before reading on, take some time and attempt to predict the probable outcome of this experiment.

Schachter and Singer predicted that subjects in the informed group, who knew that the injected drug was the cause of their physical arousal, would not experience any strong emotion. It was assumed they would observe their trembling hands and pounding heart and conclude that the drug was really doing its stuff. In contrast, subjects in the uninformed and misinformed groups would be aware of their arousal but have no obvious explanation for it. Therefore, it was assumed that they would conduct a cognitive appraisal of their environments for a logical explanation and a suitable label for their arousal (see Figure 9.9).

This is essentially what occurred. The subjects who had been uninformed or misinformed tended to use the confederate's behavior as a relevant cue for identifying and labeling their own unexplained arousal as either anger or euphoria. In contrast, subjects in the informed group or the control group, who either were not aroused or who had an appropriate explanation for their arousal, tended not to share the confederate's emotional state.

The Schachter-Singer theory has directed the attention of psychologists to the important role of cognitive interpretation in emotional experi-

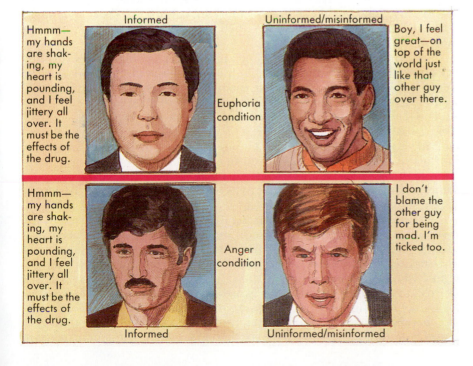

FIGURE 9.9 A SIMPLIFIED POR-TRAYAL OF THE RESULTS OF THE SCHACHTER AND SINGER STUDY

ence. However, Schachter's and Singer's theory and supporting research are not without their critics. Several researchers have criticized the design of the classic 1962 experiment, and some attempts to replicate its findings have produced somewhat inconsistent results (Leventhal & Tomarken, 1986; Marshall & Zimbardo, 1979; Maslach, 1979). Furthermore, our own everyday experiences suggest that many emotions, particularly those that are triggered spontaneously and instantly by sudden stimuli, do not appear to result from interpreting and labeling unexplained arousal. For example, if you heard screeching tires as you were walking across a street, you would probably experience fear long before you have cognitively assessed why your heart was in your throat.

TOMKINS' FACIAL FEEDBACK THEORY

Still another explanation of emotions relates directly to some studies conducted by Charles Darwin in the late nineteenth century (1872). Darwin believed that many of our emotional expressions, particularly patterns of facial display, result from inherited traits that are universal in the human species. Enlisting the aid of missionaries and other people from all over the world, he conducted the first recorded study of facial expression of emotions. Darwin asked his recruits to observe and record the facial expressions of the local population in a variety of emotional contexts. Comparing their observations, he found a remarkable consistency in the facial expressions associated with such emotions as anger, fear, disgust, and sadness.

Darwin's findings have been borne out a century later in studies by Paul Ekman and his associates (Ekman, 1982; Ekman & Friesen, 1984). These researchers demonstrated not only that people in various parts of the world show emotion with similar facial expressions; they also interpret these expressions in the same way. Ekman and his colleagues took photographs of American faces depicting happiness, sadness, surprise, anger, fear, and disgust. They then asked people from several different cultures (including the United States, Japan, Brazil, Chile, Argentina, and the Fore and Dani tribes in remote regions of New Guinea) to observe and identify the emotions shown in the photographs. People from all of these cultures were able to identify the emotion from the facial expression with better than 80 percent accuracy. Furthermore, American college students who viewed videotapes of emotions expressed facially by members of the Fore society were also able to correctly identify these basic emotions, although they sometimes confused fear and surprise. Figure 9.10 shows photographs of these six emotions.

A number of researchers have argued that facial muscles respond very rapidly and with sufficient differentiation to account for a wide range of emotional experience; some have theorized that feedback from our own facial expressions determines our emotional experiences. Perhaps the most influential proponent of this **facial feedback theory** is Sylvan Tomkins (1962, 1963). Like James and Lange, Tomkins argues that different kinds of physical actions precede different emotional experiences, with genetically determined brain mechanisms linked to the emotions of fear, anger, happiness, sadness, surprise, interest, disgust, and shame. Tomkins also argues that a specific facial display is universally associated with each of these neural programs.

Tomkins' notion of universal facial expressions was supported by the cross-cultural research just discussed; and further support has been provided by an intriguing two-part experiment conducted by Paul Ekman and his associates (1983). Here, professional actors were employed as subjects. In the first part of the experiment, each subject was coached, with the aid of a mirror, to assume a specific facial expression corresponding to each of the six emotions in Figure 9.10. They were told exactly which muscles to contract, but they were not asked to feel or express a particular emotion. As a control measure, some actors were coached to move muscles not involved in

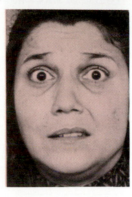

FIGURE 9.10   FACIAL EXPRES-
SIONS OF SIX EMOTIONS USED
IN RESEARCH CONDUCTED BY
PAUL EKMAN

Actors were coached, with the aid of a mirror, to assume a facial expression corresponding to each of the six emotions portrayed in this figure. Can you identify these emotions
before you read on? From left to right and top to bottom, the faces express happiness,
anger, sadness, surprise, disgust, and fear.

a particular emotional expression. As the subjects molded their facial
expressions, several physiological responses were measured, including
heart rate, galvanic skin response, temperature of the hands, and muscle
tension in the arms. In the second phase of this experiment, subjects were
simply asked to think of emotional experiences in their own lives that produced each of the six emotions. For example, subjects might recall a recent
encounter that made them angry.

Two major findings emerged from this study. First, the researchers
noted that each of the four negative emotions of anger, fear, disgust, and
sadness, whether induced by facial modeling or thinking of an emotional
experience, was accompanied by a distinct physiological "fingerprint" or
pattern of physical responses. For example, heart rate was much greater in
anger than in disgust and the hands were colder in fear than in anger.
Ekman's findings seem to support James's and Lange's assertion that different emotions produce distinct physiological fingerprints.

The second and perhaps the most intriguing finding in this experiment is that when the subjects simply followed instructions to move their
facial muscles to mirror a given emotion, they also experienced patterns of
physiological arousal that were comparable to those recorded when they
relived an actual emotional experience. In some instances, the physiological
signs of emotion were more pronounced when the subjects merely moved
their facial muscles than when they thought of an emotional experience.

This research has some practical implications. We have all heard the
sage advice to "keep our chins up" or "to put on a happy face" when we are
feeling sad or depressed. Ekman's findings suggest that there may be some
validity to this advice. Subjects felt happy just by contracting the facial muscles associated with happiness. Therefore, if we act cheerfully, smile, and

laugh when we feel down, perhaps the emotion of happiness will replace our feelings of sadness.

This advice should be taken with some caution, however. Masking our true feelings may not always be helpful, and in some instances it may actually impede our ability to deal effectively with our feelings. Nevertheless, all of us experience circumstances in which we would like to feel just a bit more cheerful. Perhaps in these circumstances, masquerading the desired emotion may be helpful.

Some experimental support for this speculation was obtained in a study in which subjects were instructed to either suppress or exaggerate the facial expression associated with the fear and discomfort of receiving electric shocks. The researchers monitored physiological arousal during the course of shock administration and also obtained written self-reports of the subjects' feelings. The results revealed that subjects who had been told to suppress their facial expression demonstrated lower physiological arousal and reported less negative feelings than the participants who were not told to conceal their facial reactions (Lanzetta et al., 1976).

In concluding our discussion of theories of emotion, we must acknowledge that many questions remain to be answered. Instead of one comprehensive theory that encompasses all human emotional expression, we have several diverse theories, each of which helps explain at least a part of the process whereby emotions are activated and all of which are supported to some degree by research.

SUMMARY

THE NATURE OF MOTIVATION

1. Motivation can be defined as any condition that might energize and direct our actions.
2. Motivation not only energizes or activates us to behave in a certain way; it also directs or defines the direction of the resulting behavior. Motivation also has a direct impact upon how vigorous or intense our behaviors are.

EXPLAINING MOTIVATION: THEORETICAL PERSPECTIVES

3. One of the earliest attempts to explain motivation was based on the notion of instincts—innate patterns of behavior that occur in every normally functioning member of a species under certain set conditions.
4. The flaw in instinct theory is that instincts do not explain behavior; they simply provide another way of labeling it.
5. Contemporary psychologists agree that our behaviors are so profoundly influenced by learning that it is essentially impossible to find one example of human behavior that fits the literal definition of instincts.
6. According to the drive-reduction theory, motivation originates with a need or drive, experienced as an unpleasant aversive condition, that motivates us to act in a way that will reduce the aversive condition.
7. While the drive-reduction theory explains some aspects of motivation, it is limited in scope by three facts: first, many events that serve as reinforcers for behavior do not reduce any known drive; second, psychologists have demonstrated that external stimuli (incentives) can motivate behavior even when no internal drive state exists; and third, in contrast to the drive-reduction hypothesis, many motivated behaviors do not grow weaker as they are expressed.
8. Maslow proposed that human needs exist on a multilevel hierarchy consisting of five stages ranging from the "lowest," most basic biological needs to the "highest" need for self-actualization.
9. Criticisms of Maslow's hierarchy of needs theory include the fact that there is little evidence that human motives or needs are ordered in the sequence that Maslow proposed and that many of his major precepts, particularly the concept of self-actualization, are so vague that it is virtually impossible to define them operationally.
10. According to the cognitive perspective, our cognitions—thoughts, beliefs, expectations, and other mental processes—play an important role in motivating our actions.

THE RANGE OF HUMAN MOTIVATION

11. It is useful to classify human motives under four categories: biologically based motives rooted primarily in body tissue needs; sensation-seeking motives expressed as a need for certain levels of stimulation; multifactor motives that are based on a combination of biological, psychological, and cultural factors; and complex psychosocial motives that seem to demonstrate little or no relationship to biological needs.

HUNGER AND EATING

12. Research has ruled out the hypothesis that the hunger motive is primarily caused by stomach contractions.
13. According to the dual hypothalamic control theory, two regions within the hypothalamus may possibly serve as control centers for eating. According to this view the ventromedial hypothalamus (VMH) seems to act as a satiety center that signals when an organism has had enough to eat, while the lateral hypothalamus (LH) seems to act as an "on switch" that instigates eating.
14. The glucostatic theory proposes that levels of glucose are monitored by glucoreceptors (cells sensitive to glu-

cose in the bloodstream). Hunger results whenever the glucoreceptors detect that glucose is unavailable. According to the best evidence, it appears that glucoreceptors in the liver, and possibly the duodenum, detect changes in blood glucose levels and then send this information through the nervous system to specialized control centers within the hypothalamus.

15. The lipostatic theory of long-term control of hunger and eating suggests that our bodies monitor the amount of fat they contain and use this as a barometer to regulate food intake so that fat levels are held relatively constant.

16. Many researchers believe that our bodies may be programed in some fashion to maintain a preferred level of body weight for each individual, a phenomenon known as set point.

17. By midlife, more than half the people in this country are overweight. Obesity places a person at risk for developing one or more serious health problems such as high blood pressure, heart disease, and depression.

18. Research demonstrates that between 75 percent and 95 percent of people who lose weight through dieting regain most if not all of their lost weight.

19. Genetic factors, conditions of early development, emotional stress, and metabolic factors have all been suggested as possible causes of obesity.

20. Two eating disorders common among certain segments of society, particularly young women, are anorexia nervosa, a form of self-starvation, and bulimia, in which a person may eat a full meal and then purge the stomach and intestines of food by inducing vomiting or using a laxative.

21. Suggested causes for anorexia nervosa and bulimia include a disturbed body image, depression, anxiety, and possibly physical abnormalities involving the hypothalamus or endocrine system.

SENSATION-SEEKING MOTIVES

22. The need to manipulate and explore the environment and the need for sensory stimulation both fall under the category of sensation-seeking motives.

23. Psychologists have theorized that people have an optimum level of arousal which is the level at which their performance will be most efficient. According to the Yerkes-Dodson law, the optimum level of arousal for peak performance varies depending on the nature of the task.

24. Level of arousal is also related to how we feel. It has been suggested that most people prefer intermediate levels of arousal most of the time.

25. Subjects exposed to prolonged sensory deprivation appear to develop a strong need for sensory stimulation. Prolonged sensory deprivation also frequently reduces a person's performance on a variety of mental tasks.

SEXUAL MOTIVATION

26. In humans, sexual interest and expression are controlled less by hormones and more by the cerebral cortex, reflecting a complex combination of biological, psychological, and cultural factors.

27. While it is difficult to distinguish the effects of sex hormones and of learning experiences on sexual arousal, research does indicate that androgens appear to facili-

tate sexual interest in males. The relationship between female sexuality and hormones, if one exists, is very difficult to pinpoint.

28. Psychological and cultural conditions probably play a greater role than hormones in human sexual motivation. This is reflected in the role of reinforcement and psychosocial conditioning, which maintain and constrain sexual expression, respectively.

29. Humans are unique among living creatures in our propensity to create geographically localized patterns of sexual behavior. This is perhaps the strongest evidence for the preeminence of psychosocial factors in human sexual motivation and expression.

COMPLEX PSYCHOSOCIAL MOTIVES: THE NEED FOR ACHIEVEMENT

30. A good example of a complex psychosocial motive that is determined by learning and experience is the need for achievement—the need to excel and to accomplish something difficult.

31. Researchers have theorized that our achievement motive is the result of a complex interaction between our hope of success and fear of failure.

32. One way to help instill a desire to achieve is to encourage children to set reasonable goals and to provide ample reinforcements for their successes.

THE NATURE OF EMOTIONS

33. Motivation and emotion are closely connected. Emotions often motivate our actions.

34. Emotions are composed of four integral components: cognitive processes, subjective feelings, physiological arousal, and behavioral reactions.

EMOTIONS: THEORIES AND CONTROVERSIES

35. According to the James-Lange theory, environmental stimuli trigger physiological responses from the viscera and muscle movements. These visceral and muscular responses then activate emotional states.

36. Recent evidence has demonstrated that different emotions are associated with similar, but not identical, physiological changes. However, there is little concrete evidence that people are able to make fine discriminations between the varied, often highly similar, patterns of physiological and muscular responses to determine what emotions they are experiencing.

37. The Cannon-Bard theory suggests that internal physiological changes and muscular responses are not the cause of emotion, but rather that emotional experiences and physical changes occur simultaneously.

38. The Schachter-Singer theory combines elements from both the James-Lange and Cannon-Bard theories. Schachter and Singer maintained that emotions depend on a kind of double cognitive interpretation: we appraise the emotion-causing event while also evaluating what is happening physiologically with our bodies.

39. According to the facial feedback theory, facial muscles respond very rapidly and with sufficient differentiation to account for a wide range of emotional experience. Feedback from our own facial expressions helps determine our emotional experiences.

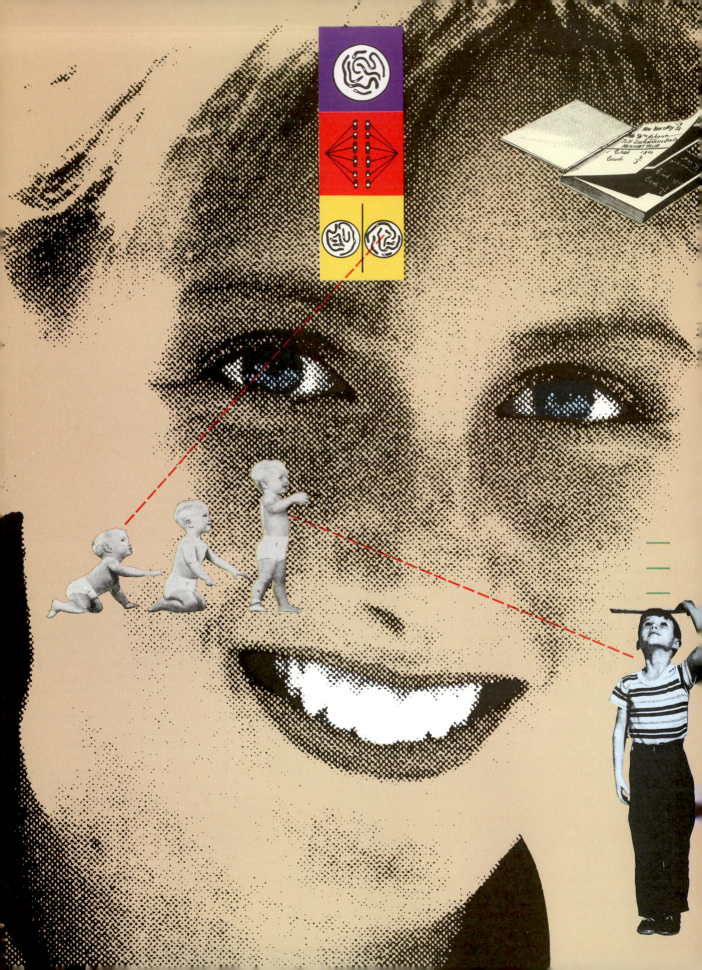

PART 4

DEVELOPMENTAL PROCESSES AND INDIVIDUAL DIFFERENCES

10

DEVELOPMENT FROM CONCEPTION
TO THE END OF CHILDHOOD

11

DEVELOPMENT FROM ADOLESCENCE
TO THE END OF LIFE

12

INTELLIGENCE

13

PERSONALITY

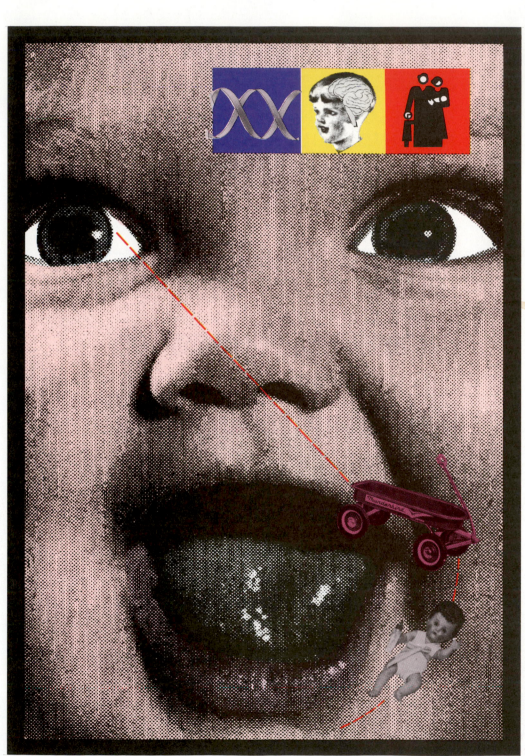

10 Development from Conception to the End of Childhood

We are constantly changing, growing, and developing throughout our lives, from conception to old age. At some periods, these changes are very rapid and clear to anyone who is there to observe them; at others, particularly later in life, they may not be so obvious. This chapter begins at the beginning as it explores conception, *prenatal* (before birth) development, and childhood. Chapter 11 continues where this chapter leaves off, exploring adolescence and the adult years. First, we will outline some key issues that have been the center of debate among developmental psychologists and examine typical ways in which development is studied.

SOME DEVELOPMENTAL ISSUES

A number of issues have influenced developmental theory and research; we now look at three of the most important. The first is the ongoing "nature versus nurture" controversy: What are the relative impacts of heredity and environment in shaping development? A second question has to do with the way in which development proceeds: Do changes take place in a continuous fashion throughout our lives, or do they occur in stages, with qualitatively different changes taking place at different points in our lives? A third issue has to do with critical periods in development: Do certain experiences have to take place during a specific window of time in our lives in order for development to proceed normally, or can later experiences make up for earlier deficiencies? We provide an overview of each of these issues in the following paragraphs, and we will revisit them all at different points in this chapter and Chapter 11.

ARE WE PRODUCTS OF HEREDITY OR ENVIRONMENT?

Some individuals are capable of prodigious intellectual feats, while others have only average ability. Some of us are extroverted and outgoing, while others are introverted and shy. A few of us are leaders, while most are followers. Are such differences due to inheritance or are they learned?

One answer to this question is that we are products of the experiences that *nurture* our development from conception to death. This view was expressed by the seventeenth-century English philosopher John Locke, who proposed that an infant's mind at birth is a *tabula rasa* or blank slate

Did Mary Lou Retton's ability in gymnastics result primarily from the environment in which she was raised, or was it influenced to a greater extent by genetically determined attributes?

upon which virtually anything can be written by experience. The behaviorist John Watson updated this view:

> Give me a dozen healthy infants, well-formed and my own specific world to bring them up in and I'll guarantee to take any one at random and train him to become any type of specialist I might select—a doctor, lawyer, artist, merchant-chief and, yes, even beggar-man and thief, regardless of his talents, penchants, tendencies, abilities, vocations and race of his ancestors (1926, p. 10).

The opposing point of view in the **nature-nurture controversy** is that our genetic endowment, or *nature*, is what makes us who we are. The eighteenth-century French philosopher Jean Jacques Rousseau saw human development as simply the unfolding of genetically determined attributes; and in this century developmental psychologist Arnold Gesell (1928) stated that "It is the hereditary ballast which conserves and stabilizes the growth of each individual infant" (p. 378).

Neither the nature nor the nurture position is supported today in its extreme form. Instead, contemporary theorists are interested in how genetics and experience interact. Although heredity predisposes us to behave in certain ways (and also sets limits on what we can do), environment is also critical. For example, a child might have the intellectual potential of an Einstein but end up an educational failure in the absence of intellectual stimulation or encouragement. (Chapter 12 explores the relative influences of heredity and environment on intelligence.)

Thus, human traits develop within the context of our environments. Some behaviors or attributes, such as the style of clothing you prefer, are largely, if not exclusively, determined by experience. Others seem to develop without any specific experience or practice, as long as environmental conditions stay within a typical or normative range. An example is the early stages of language acquisition, as we saw in Chapter 8. Another is the universal developmental sequence through which babies progress from sitting without support to crawling and ultimately to walking. Virtually all babies crawl, commencing at around 10 months, before they begin to walk at about 13 or 14 months. (Throughout this chapter, we will quote average ages for different developmental milestones. Please note that there is a wide range of individual variation around these norms.) This biologically determined sequence occurs even if children are not encouraged to sit, crawl, or walk. Both language acquisition and walking are examples of **maturation,** the orderly unfolding of certain patterns of behavior in accordance with genetic blueprints.

Some behaviors seem to develop without any specific experience or practice, such as the universal developmental sequence through which babies progress from sitting without support to crawling and, ultimately, to walking.

IS DEVELOPMENT CONTINUOUS OR DOES IT OCCUR IN STAGES?

A second issue confronting developmental psychologists concerns the nature of changes that occur over the span of our lives. We all know that adolescents are quite different from infants and that most elderly people are noticeably different from young adults. Are these differences created by a gradual, cumulative growth, with each new developmental change building upon earlier developments and experiences in a fashion characterized by *continuity*, or do these changes exhibit *discontinuity*—that is, are the behaviors expressed at each new stage of development qualitatively different from those of the previous stage?

In general, psychologists who emphasize the role of learning have tended to view development as a gradual, continuous process. According to this view, the mechanisms that govern development are constant throughout a person's life: Because individuals accumulate experiences, development is seen as a *quantitative* change (change due to increases in the amount or quantity of experiences). Developmental psychologists who embrace this perspective believe that the only important difference between young people and those who are older is that the latter have experienced more in life

Stage theorists see adults as being better problem solvers than children, not just because they know more, but also because they think in a more logical and systematic fashion.

and are likely to know more. In contrast, many developmentalists who emphasize maturation view development as a discontinuous process that occurs in a series of steps or stages. A *stage* is a concept used to describe how a person's manner of thinking and behavior is organized and directed during a particular period.

Stage theorists are inclined to interpret the differences between children and adults as being *qualitative* in nature (differences due to distinctions in the kind or nature of experiences). For instance, adults are viewed as better problem solvers than children not just because they know more, but also because they think in a more logical and systematic fashion. In this chapter and Chapter 11 we discuss two influential stage theories: Jean Piaget's theory of cognitive development and Erik Erikson's theory of psychosocial development.

An important aspect of the continuity-discontinuity issue is the question of whether development from infancy to old age is characterized more by stability than by change. For instance, will an introverted, withdrawn child grow up to be reclusive as an adult? How much can we rely on a person's present behavior to predict what that person will be like in the future? Many of us do grow up to be older versions of our earlier selves. Stability is not inevitable, however, and at least some people develop into persons quite different from their earlier selves.

ARE THERE CRITICAL PERIODS IN DEVELOPMENT?

A third developmental issue is the relative importance of different periods of development. Is the timing of training essential for optimal acquisition of certain skills—and is timing also necessary for the development of behavioral traits? Is it necessary to have certain experiences early in life to ensure normal later development?

According to one point of view, there are **critical periods** during which an infant or child must experience certain kinds of social and sensory experiences: If the proper experiences are not provided at the right time, later experiences will not be able to make up for the deficit. An alternative view suggests that while certain early experiences are important, the timing is not absolutely crucial, and later experience can often make up for earlier deficiencies.

Psychologists who argue for critical periods often cite animal research for support. One widely quoted source of evidence is the research

FIRST PERSON 10.1

Of all my high-school classmates, the one whose later success amazed me the most is a fellow I played football with. This guy was the classic jock who was into partying and having a good time—the heck with studies. He was real tough, ready to fight at the slightest provocation, and totally indifferent to the feelings of others. If they had held an election for "least likely to succeed," this joker would have had my vote. Therefore, you can imagine my amazement when this guy showed up 20 years later as an interviewee on a local TV newscast. He had just been appointed to the top administrative position in a major state agency. He appeared to be highly articulate and very well informed; he also came across as a pretty sensitive person. If he hadn't looked like a weathered version of my old football teammate, I would have sworn it was someone else with the same name. Later I read a newspaper article indicating he had had a distinguished academic career in college and graduate school. It was hard to believe this was the same bum who never cracked a book in high school. (**Authors' files**)

In a series of experiments, Konrad Lorenz demonstrated that newly hatched ducklings will begin to follow the first moving thing they see, whether it be their own mother or Lorenz himself.

of biologist Konrad Lorenz (1937), who was curious about why baby ducks begin to follow their mothers shortly after they are hatched. In a series of experiments he demonstrated that newly hatched ducklings will begin to follow the first moving thing they see—their mother, a member of another species like a goose, or even Lorenz himself (see the photo on this page). Lorenz labeled this phenomenon **imprinting.**

Another famous study was conducted by psychologist Harry Harlow and his associates at the University of Wisconsin. Harlow found that when baby monkeys are deprived of "contact comfort" with their mothers during early development, the result is emotional and social impairments. For instance, infant monkeys who were reared in isolation for the first six months or more showed severely disturbed behavior such as incessant rocking, timidity, and inappropriate displays of aggression—behaviors that persisted into adulthood, even after the imposed isolation was ended (Suomi & Harlow, 1978). We will discuss this research in more detail later in this chapter.

ARE THERE CRITICAL PERIODS IN HUMAN DEVELOPMENT?

We have considered some of the evidence for critical periods in animals such as ducks and monkeys, but what about humans? If an infant is deprived of warm human contact (touching, cuddling, etc.) during the first months or years of life, is it inevitable that the child will grow into an adult who is unable to have warm, loving relationships? Do you think that the timing of some early experiences is so essential that their absence results in inevitable and irreversible impairment of later development? Take some time to consider this question before reading on.

The evidence of critical stages in human development is inconsistent. One widely quoted early study reported that institutionalized infants who were deprived of loving, responsive care during their first six months were significantly more likely to be emotionally and socially maladjusted than infants who were institutionalized after they had experienced a period of close contact with responsive caregivers during the early months of their lives (Goldfarb, 1945). Some psychologists saw this study as evidence that the first six months are a critical period for starting a child on the proper path toward healthy emotional and social adjustment.

However, other studies have had very different findings. In one, for example, infants who had been subjected to a profoundly impoverished orphanage environment for most of their first two years were then transferred to another institution where they received extensive one-on-one contacts with loving caregivers. Despite the early lack of love and stimulation, these infants developed into well-adjusted adults without identifiable behavioral problems (Skeels, 1966—see Chapter 12 for a more detailed discussion of this classic study). Numerous other investigations have shown that children adopted after infancy and raised by loving parents can overcome early disadvantages associated with severely deprived environments (Kagan et al., 1978; Maccoby, 1980; Yarrow et al., 1973).

Even Harlow's monkey studies cast doubt on the critical-period theory. If monkeys who had been deprived of contact comfort during infancy were later provided extensive contact with "therapist monkeys" (infant monkeys, still in the clinging stage, who provided extensive contact comfort to the older monkeys—see Figure 10.1), their behavioral deficits could be almost entirely overcome. Monkeys exposed to longer periods of isolation (12 months instead of 6 months) also responded to this unusual therapy, but their recovery was not as complete (Novak & Harlow, 1975; Suomi & Harlow, 1972).

Another question related to the critical-period issue is whether bonding between parent and infant must take place at a certain point. Most nonhuman mammals lick and groom their offspring during the first hours after birth, often rejecting their young if this early "getting acquainted" session is somehow prevented. Some child specialists have suggested that a similar critical period exists for humans in the first hours after birth, and that if contact is prevented, mother-infant bonding will not develop adequately (Klaus & Kennell, 1982). This notion has received little support from research, however (Goldberg, 1983; Lamb, 1982; Myers, 1984). Instead, the parent-child relationship seems to be malleable, with plenty of opportunity to establish attachment throughout development.

In all, the evidence suggests that most effects of adverse early experiences can be modified if not overcome by later experiences. Certainly the kinds of experiences we have during our early development may strongly influence our feelings about ourselves and others, our styles of relating to people, our mode of expressing emotions, the degree to which we realize our intellectual potential, and countless other aspects of our psychological adjustment. Most contemporary psychologists agree, however, that the concept of critical periods in infant development, at least when applied to emotional, intellectual, and behavioral traits, lacks supporting evidence.

FIGURE 10.1

A young monkey still in the clinging stage acts as "therapist" for an older monkey

HOW DEVELOPMENT IS STUDIED

The task of developmental psychology is to describe and attempt to explain the nature of psychological and behavioral changes that occur throughout the life span. To realize this aim, researchers need to gather information about people at different points in their development. Three research designs have been developed for this purpose: the cross-sectional, longitudinal, and cross-sequential methods.

THE CROSS-SECTIONAL DESIGN

The most widely used research method in developmental psychology is the **cross-sectional design.** Here, groups of subjects of different ages are assessed and compared at one point in time, and the researcher draws conclusions about behavior differences that may be related to age differences. For example, suppose we want to determine whether there are age differences in television-viewing habits. Using the cross-sectional method, we might attach program-monitoring devices to the television sets of a sample population ranging from young adults to retirees, then analyze several months of viewing records. The result would be a profile of viewing habits of different age groups.

The cross-sectional study gives an accurate "snapshot" of one point in time, but it leaves an important question unanswered: do its findings reflect developmental differences or changes in the environment? For instance, suppose we discover that young adults watch very few comedies while older adults spend most of their television time viewing comedies. Does this mean that when the young people in our sample grow older, they will spend more time viewing comedies, or does it simply reflect the fact that the older subjects developed their viewing habits in an era when situation comedies were featured in television programming? One way to find out if a behavioral change is related to development is to conduct a longitudinal study.

THE LONGITUDINAL DESIGN

The **longitudinal design** evaluates behavior in the same group of people at several points in time, to assess what kinds of changes occur over the long term. To apply this method to the study of age-related television preferences, we might begin by monitoring the viewing habits of a group of young adults at age 20. The same subjects might then be repeatedly observed at five-year intervals over the next 50 years. This method would allow us to assess reliably whether or not the television consumption habits of our subjects actually change with age, and if so, in what direction.

A famous example of a longitudinal investigation is Lewis Terman's long-term study of gifted children with IQs above 135. (You may recall our brief discussion of this study in Chapter 1.) A Stanford University psychologist, Terman began his research in the early 1920s with a sample of 1,528 gifted boys and girls of grade-school age. These subjects were evaluated and tested at regular intervals, first to see if they would maintain their intellectual superiority, and later to see how well they adjusted to life. Although Terman died in 1956, his research was continued by Stanford psychologists Robert Sears and Pauline Sears. The Terman "whiz kids" are now in their seventies.

This classic study has provided a wealth of information about the impact of superior intelligence on life satisfaction and on the course of development. Over time, Terman's gifted subjects have been shown to be healthier, happier, more socially adept, and more successful in their careers than are comparably aged people of average intelligence. They have also exhibited a much lower than average incidence of emotional disorders, substance abuse, suicide, and divorce (Sears, 1977; Sears & Barbee, 1977; Terman, 1925, 1954). These findings have helped dispel the common myth that people of very high intelligence are more likely to exhibit severe behavior disorders than are people of average intelligence.

Unlike the cross-sectional design, the longitudinal approach allows researchers to track an individual's changes over time. However, the longitudinal approach does have some drawbacks. One is the large investment of time that it requires: relatively few researchers are ready to embark on a Terman-like study whose results will not be evident for years. Another problem is the "shrinking sample." Over time, subjects may lose contact as they move away, die, or simply lose interest.

Finally, environmental factors still play a role in longitudinal studies, and so researchers must be cautious in generalizing their findings. For example, suppose that as part of a longitudinal study you interview a group of subjects during the 1950s and then again in the 1980s, asking them their opinions about abortion. You might find that as middle-aged adults these subjects expressed more support for a woman's right to choose abortion than they did as young adults. Does this mean that attitudes toward abortion become more liberalized in the period between early and mature adulthood? Such a conclusion would overlook the dramatic social changes that have taken place in the last 10 to 20 years. The attitudinal changes in our study group might well reflect social changes rather than a normal developmental change.

THE CROSS-SEQUENTIAL DESIGN

In an attempt to overcome some of the drawbacks of both the cross-sectional and longitudinal designs, researchers have combined the best features of each in a **cross-sequential design.** Here, subjects in a cross-sectional sample are observed more than once, but over a shorter span of time than is typical of longitudinal studies. Subjects in cross-sequential studies with the same year of birth are said to belong to the same *birth cohort*. Developmental psychologists who use this research design generally choose cohorts whose ages will overlap during the course of the study. This helps to avoid both the longitudinal shortcoming of limited generalizability of findings and the potential cross-sectional problem of confusing the effects of growth with those of societal conditions.

THE BEGINNINGS OF LIFE

For all of us, life begins in the same way. Shortly after a ripened ovum is released from one of our mother's ovaries, a sperm cell penetrates the ovum, fertilizing it. The sperm and ovum, collectively called **gametes** or **germ cells,** normally unite in the upper portion of the *fallopian tube*. The resulting new cell, called a **zygote,** then travels downward through the fallopian tube to the *uterus* or womb (see Figure 10.2).

The nuclei of the sperm and ovum each contain 23 rodlike structures called chromosomes, 22 of which are autosomes (not sex determining) and one of which is a sex chromosome. After fertilization, the zygote contains a

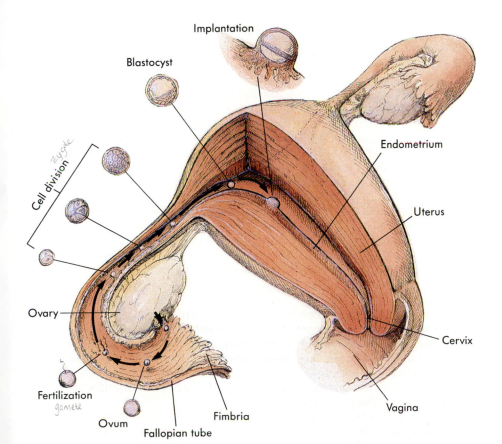

FIGURE 10.2 FROM OVULA-TION TO FERTILIZATION AND IMPLANTATION

The egg travels into the fallopian tube where fertilization occurs. The fertilized ovum divides as it travels toward the uterus where it implants on the wall.

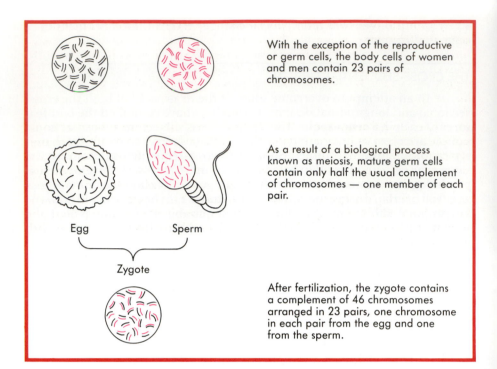

FIGURE 10.3 CHROMOSOME COMPLEMENT OF THE ZYGOTE AFTER FERTILIZATION

With the exception of the reproductive or germ cells, the body cells of women and men contain 23 pairs of chromosomes.

As a result of a biological process known as meiosis, mature germ cells contain only half the usual complement of chromosomes—one member of each pair.

After fertilization, the zygote contains a complement of 46 chromosomes arranged in 23 pairs—one chromosome in each pair from the egg and one from the sperm.

Figure labels: Egg   Sperm   Zygote

With the exception of the reproductive or germ cells, the body cells of women and men contain 23 pairs of chromosomes.

As a result of a biological process known as meiosis, mature germ cells contain only half the usual complement of chromosomes — one member of each pair.

After fertilization, the zygote contains a complement of 46 chromosomes arranged in 23 pairs, one chromosome in each pair from the egg and one from the sperm.

complement of 46 chromosomes arranged in 23 pairs, one chromosome in each pair from the sperm and one from the egg (see Figure 10.3).

THE MECHANISMS OF HEREDITY

Chromosomes are composed of thousands of **genes,** the chemical blueprints of all living things. Genes determine physical traits such as eye color, blood type, and bone structure; they also have a significant impact on behavioral traits such as intelligence, temperament, and sociability.

Genes are made of **DNA (deoxyribonucleic acid)** molecules. Under high amplification, a DNA molecule looks like a long double strand arranged in a spiraling, staircase fashion. Although DNA molecules are composed of the same chemical bases, the exact arrangement of chemicals varies, causing different DNA molecules to have different effects. A person's genetic code thus consists of a variety of patterns of DNA molecules arranged in gene groupings on specific chromosomes within a cell's nucleus. Each individual's genetic code is unique.

The exception, of course, is **identical twins** (also called **monozygotic** or **one-egg twins**), who share the same genetic code. Identical twins originate from a single fertilized ovum that divides into two separate entities with identical genetic codes. Identical twins are always same-sex individuals who physically appear to be carbon copies of each other. Since they have the same genes, any differences between them must be due to environmental influences.

In contrast, **fraternal twins** (also known as **dizygotic** or **two-egg twins**) occur when the woman's ovaries release two ova, each of which is fertilized by a different sperm cell. Since fraternal twins result from the fusion of different germ cells, their genetic makeup is no more alike than that of any other siblings. Physical and behavioral differences between fraternal twins may be due to genetic factors, environmental influences, or a combination of the two.

Psychologists who seek to understand the relative roles of genetics and environment in determining behavioral traits often compare the degree to which a particular trait is expressed by both members of a twin pair.

When identical twins are more alike (**concordant**) than fraternal twins in a particular trait, we can assume that the attribute has a strong genetic basis. Conversely, when a trait shows a comparable degree of concordance in both types of twins, we can reasonably assume that environment is exerting the greater influence. We will have more to say about twin studies throughout this text.

Genotypes and Phenotypes The assortment of genes we inherit at conception is known as our **genotype;** the characteristics that result from the expression of various genotypes are known as **phenotypes.** Sometimes genotypes and phenotypes are consistent, as when a person with brown eyes (phenotype) carries only genes for brown eye color (genotype). However, genotype and phenotype are often inconsistent, so that a person with brown eyes may carry a blue-eye as well as a brown-eye gene. This happens because genes occur in pairs, one of which is contributed by the mother and one by the father.

If your genetic blueprint contains different genes for a trait, you are said to be **heterozygous** for that trait. In contrast, if you inherit identical genes from both your parents, you are **homozygous** for that trait. What determines how a phenotype will be expressed when a person is heterozygous for a particular trait?

Dominance and Recessiveness Suppose you received a gene for brown eyes from one parent and a gene for blue eyes from the other. The principles of *dominance* and *recessiveness* would allow us to predict that the actual color of your eyes would be brown. We know this because genes for brown eyes are dominant over blue-eye genes. A **dominant gene** is one that is always expressed in the phenotype; it is the gene that prevails when paired with a subordinate or recessive gene. A **recessive gene** is one that may be expressed only in the absence of a dominant gene, or when it is paired with a similar recessive gene. Table 10.1 lists some dominant and recessive traits.

Not all human traits can be predicted as easily as can eye color. Several traits, such as growth or metabolic rate, result from gene pairs working in consort with each other. This more complicated form of genetic transmission, in which several gene pairs interact, is called **multifactorial inheritance.**

Sex-Linked Inheritance You may be aware that certain undesirable traits, such as red-green color blindness and hemophilia (abnormal bleeding) are far more common among males than females. Have you ever wondered why males are more susceptible to these and other diseases that demonstrate

TABLE 10.1 *Some Common Dominant and Recessive Traits*

Dominant Traits	Recessive Traits
Dark hair	Light hair
Nonred hair (brunette or blond)	Red hair
Normal hair growth	Baldness
Curly hair	Straight hair
Brown eyes	Blue, green, hazel, or gray eyes
Normal color vision	Red-green color blindness
Normal visual acuity	Nearsightedness
Normal protein metabolism	Phenylketonuria (inability to convert phenylalanine into tyrosine)
Type A or type B blood	Type O blood
Normal blood clotting	Hemophilia
Normal blood cells	Sickle-cell anemia
Normal skin coloring	Albinism (lack of pigment)
Double-jointedness	Normal joints
Huntington's disease	Normal health
Abnormal digits in fingers or toes (extras, fused, stumps, etc.)	Normal digits

FIGURE 10.4 THE SEX-LINKED INHERITANCE OF HEMOPHILIA

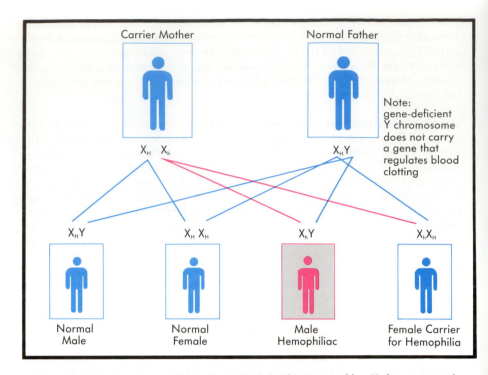

A female can carry a recessive gene for hemophilia (h) on one of her X chromosomes but nevertheless have blood that clots normally due to the presence of a dominant H on the other member of XX pair. A male, however, will be a bleeder if he inherits only one h gene from his mother, since the gene-deficient Y chromosome does not carry a gene that regulates blood clotting. The odds for each male child of this union are 50/50: (1) 50 percent risk of inheriting the hemophilia gene and developing the disease; (2) 50 percent chance of inheriting a normal clotting gene and not developing the disease. For each female child the odds are: (1) 50 percent risk of inheriting one hemophilia gene, to be a carrier like her mother; (2) 50 percent chance of inheriting no faulty gene.

Folk singer Woody Guthrie died from Huntington's disease, an incurable disorder that progressively destroys brain cells. Common symptoms include jerky, uncontrollable movements, loss of balance, intellectual impairment, and emotional disturbance.

sex-linked inheritance? The answer lies in the fact that the smaller Y chromosome carries fewer genes than the much larger X chromosome. (The sex chromosome pair in males is XY, whereas in females it is XX.) The genes that determine whether or not a person develops these diseases are carried only on the X chromosome.

In the case of hemophilia, as long as a person has at least one dominant gene for normal blood clotting (which we designate as H: geneticists use upper-case letters to denote dominant genes and lower-case letters for recessive genes), the disease will not be expressed. Thus, a female can carry the recessive gene for hemophilia (h) on one of her X chromosomes but nevertheless have blood that clots normally due to the presence of a dominant H on the other member of her XX pair. A male, however, will be a bleeder if he inherits only one h gene from his mother, since the gene-deficient Y chromosome does not carry a gene that regulates blood clotting.

A woman who carries the hemophilia trait can pass her defective gene to her children. If the offspring is a male, there is a 50 percent probability that he will inherit the disease since there is no dominant H gene present on the smaller Y chromosome to block the expression of the disorder. Figure 10.4 illustrates the sex-linked inheritance of hemophilia.

PROBLEMS IN INHERITANCE

Perhaps the greatest hope of most expectant parents is that their baby will be born healthy and normal. Thankfully, the odds are very high, about 95 percent, that this wish will be granted. This means, however, that about 5 percent of all babies born each year in the United States have some gene defect or chromosomal abnormality that produces a physical and/or mental handicap (March of Dimes Birth Defects Foundation, 1983). Some of these defects are apparent at birth or shortly thereafter; others do not show up until later in life. The following paragraphs describe some inherited abnormalities.

Huntington's Disease **Huntington's disease,** or Huntington's chorea, is one of the cruelest of all genetic diseases. This incurable disorder, which killed folk singer Woody Guthrie, progressively destroys brain cells (Ferrante et al., 1987; Mazziotta et al., 1987). Common symptoms include jerky, uncontrollable movements, loss of balance, intellectual impairment, and emotional disturbance (depression, irritability, etc.). Not uncommonly the disease is confused with disorders such as Parkinson's disease, Alzheimer's disease, and schizophrenia.

Huntington's disease is caused by a dominant gene that does not produce symptoms until a person is 35 to 45 years old. Unfortunately, by that age a person is likely to have already had children, unaware that each child has a 50 percent chance of inheriting the illness. (Figure 10.5 illustrates the genetic transmission of Huntington's disease.)

The National Huntington's Disease Association has reported that at least 25,000 Americans have the illness, and that an additional 50,000 to 100,000 people may have inherited the disease but do not yet know that they have. Until recently there was no way to identify people who had inherited the gene until symptoms began to appear. However, in 1983 Harvard molecular biologist and geneticist James Gusella and his colleagues announced that they had located a genetic marker for Huntington's disease on chromosome 4.

Gusella made his discovery by applying **recombinant DNA technology,** sometimes called gene splicing. This extremely complex technique allows researchers to examine microscopic strands of genetic material for indicators of disease. Researchers use chemicals called restriction enzymes to cut apart and reassemble sections of DNA strands in different ways so they can look at genetic information that is passed along in a family. Analysis of these DNA fragments has revealed many variations in DNA scattered throughout the chromosomes. Some of these DNA variants are close enough to a defective gene to travel along with it and can be used as genetic markers of the disease (Breakerfield & Cambi, 1987; Martin, 1987).

Since individual differences in DNA patterns run in families, Gusella reasoned that a particular DNA pattern might be linked with Huntington's disease. He tested his theory on blood samples from 25 living members of

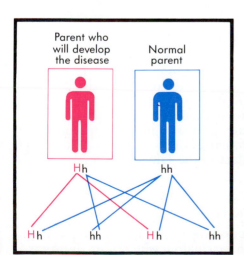

FIGURE 10.5 THE GENETIC TRANSMISSION OF HUNTINGTON'S DISEASE

One parent who will eventually develop Huntington's disease by age 35–45 has a single faulty gene for the disorder (H) that *dominates* its normal counterpart (h).

The odds for each child of this union are 50/50: (1) 50 percent risk of inheriting the dominant Huntington's gene and developing the disease; (2) 50 percent chance of inheriting the normal gene and not being afflicted with the disorder.

When my husband and I decided to begin our family in the 1950s both of us felt it was important to look into our family backgrounds to see if there was anything that might be a matter of concern from the standpoint of heredity. There seemed to be nothing unusual in my family pedigree, but one thing about my husband's background concerned me. His father had been institutionalized in a mental hospital where he eventually died. We were told, however, that mental illness was not inherited, so rather than obtaining his medical records we dismissed this information as inconsequential. Over the next 10 years we had four healthy children.

A few years later, when my husband was in his early 40s, the world fell in on us. He began to lose his balance and to be plagued with uncontrollable muscle twitches. At first physicians thought he might have a brain tumor. Eventually he was diagnosed as having Huntington's chorea. Apparently, his father's case of Huntington's chorea had been misdiagnosed when he was placed in a mental institution. Now each of our dear children have a 50/50 chance of going through the same agony they watched their father endure. (*Authors' files*)

In 1983, Harvard molecular biologist and geneticist James Gusella and his colleagues discovered a genetic marker for Huntington's disease on chromosome 4.

an American family known to have a high incidence of the disease. Gusella quickly located a marker for the disease, and his findings were later corroborated in a much larger sample of over 500 people from a small community in Venezuela where the disease is rampant (Miller, 1983). Now that scientists have found a marker for this gene, they hope eventually to be able to isolate it and develop a test to determine whether a person has inherited it before symptoms appear. Thus far, however, such a breakthrough has eluded researchers (Kohler, 1987). Medical geneticists are also hopeful that once they have isolated the Huntington's gene they will be able to alter its deadly message through a process of genetic engineering or gene therapy, discussed later in this chapter.

Phenylketonuria   Phenylketonuria (PKU) is another potentially devastating genetic disease. PKU is caused by a recessive gene that, when present in a double dose, results in the absence of an enzyme necessary to metabolize the protein phenylalanine found in milk. A newborn with phenylketonuria cannot convert phenylalanine from milk. Unmetabolized phenylalanine converts to phenylpyruvic acid. The consequence is an excessive accumulation of phenylpyruvic acid, which damages the baby's developing nervous system and can lead to mental retardation and a variety of other disruptive symptoms.

Fortunately, a routine screening process can be used to test levels of phenylpyruvic acid shortly after birth. Infants who show high levels of phenylpyruvic acid test positive for PKU, and they can be placed on milk substitutes. They must remain on the diet for several years until their brains have developed to the point that they can no longer be damaged by the acid.

There are many other examples of diseases caused by genetic defects. These include such conditions as *muscular dystrophy*, *cystic fibrosis*, *sickle-cell anemia* (a blood disorder that primarily affects blacks), and *Tay-Sachs disease* (a disorder characterized by progressive degeneration of the central nervous system that occurs primarily in Jewish people of Eastern European origins). However, many inherited diseases are caused not by the transmission of faulty genes but rather by chromosomal abnormalities. One of the best-known conditions caused by chromosomal abnormalities is Down's syndrome.

Down's Syndrome   Down's syndrome is the most common chromosomal disorder. It is characterized by a distinctive physical appearance—short stature, small round head, flattened skull and nose, oval-shaped eyes with an extra fold of skin over the eyelid, a short neck, a protruding tongue, and sometimes webbed fingers or toes. People with this syndrome also demonstrate marked mental retardation. Down's syndrome children tend to be cheerful, affectionate, and sociable. Most are educable, and some acquire simple skills that allow them to earn an income and live independently in special environments.

Down's syndrome is an autosomal chromosome disorder in which the 21st chromosome pair has an additional chromosome attached to it. A person with Down's syndrome thus has 47 chromosomes rather than the normal 46. Although this disorder is occasionally hereditary, it is usually caused by a chromosomal accident (Smith & Wilson, 1973). Older women are at greater risk of bearing Down's syndrome children, a fact that has led many researchers to attribute this disorder primarily to deterioration of the mother's ova with age. However, recent evidence suggests that the syndrome may also be caused by a defect in the father's sperm (Abroms & Bennett, 1981).

GENETIC COUNSELING AND GENETIC ENGINEERING

The idea behind **genetic counseling** is that it is often possible to estimate the odds that a couple will have children with certain disorders. A

Most Down's children, like this young man with his arm raised in a "mainstream" classroom, tend to be cheerful, affectionate, sociable, and educable.

genetic counselor, who may be a genetic specialist, obstetrician, pediatrician, or family practice physician, can often make such predictions based on a detailed study of family histories and medical examinations of both partners. Laboratory investigations may use urine, blood, and skin samples. Often, chromosomes obtained from tissue samples are photographed, and the photos are cut and rearranged so that the chromosomes are organized according to size and structure on a chart called a **karotype.** A karotype often reveals any chromosomal abnormalities that may exist.

A genetic counselor can only estimate the probability of having children with a disorder. The couple must decide if the risks are great enough to elect not to have children. In such a case, many alternatives are available. The partner with the defective gene may choose to be sterilized, and the couple may wish to consider adoption or a variety of other alternatives. For example, if the man carries the genetic defect, the woman can be artificially inseminated with a donor's semen. If the problem lies with the woman, the man's sperm may be used to fertilize a female donor's ovum. In this process, called **artificial embryonation,** a female volunteer is artificially inseminated with sperm, and approximately five days after fertilization the tiny embryo is removed from the woman donor and transferred surgically into the uterus of the mother-to-be, who then carries the pregnancy. "Test-tube babies" and surrogate mothers are two other options that have received considerable media attention. (See photos on p. 339.)

The recent development of several revolutionary techniques for assessing fetal development and diagnosing birth defects in utero, together with the legalization of abortion, have encouraged some couples with a history of genetic disease to take a chance on a pregnancy.

One of these techniques is a reliable and accurate method of prenatal screening known as **amniocentesis.** If a woman and her physician have some reason to suspect that there may be fetal abnormalities, amniocentesis can help establish whether a problem exists. The test is done during the 14th to 16th week of pregnancy. As Figure 10.6 indicates, a needle is inserted through the woman's abdominal wall and into the uterus to draw out a sample of the *amniotic fluid* (fluid surrounding the fetus). Fetal cells from the fluid are cultured for chromosome analysis and the fluid is then tested, using procedures that take two to three weeks.

Another technique for detecting birth defects is **chorionic villi sampling (CVS).** The chorionic villi are threadlike protrusions on a membrane

I was convinced that my career was more important than having a family. Consequently, I elected not to get pregnant while I focused my energies on being a success. By the time I decided that I wanted to have a child, I was in my late 30s. Considering that my age put me in a much higher risk group for having a child with birth defects, it is doubtful I would have risked a pregnancy without the knowledge that amniocentesis was available to detect Down's syndrome and other defects. I realize that not all problems can be detected by amniocentesis, but any pregnancy has some element of risk attached to it. At least prenatal screening shifted the odds to my favor. So I went for it and my reward was a healthy boy who is the joy of my life! (*Authors' files*)

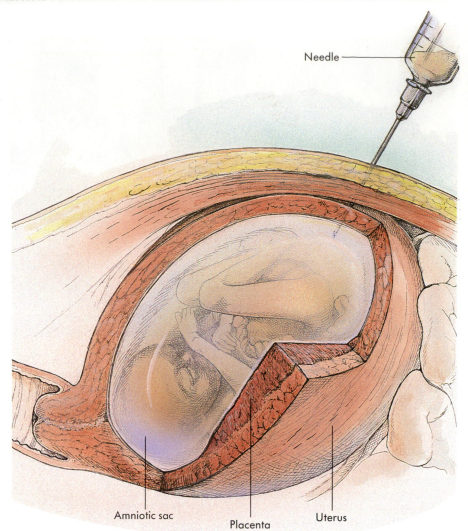

Needle

Amniotic sac   Placenta   Uterus

FIGURE 10.6   AMNIOCENTESIS

This procedure consists of inserting a needle through the woman's abdominal wall into the uterine cavity to draw out a sample of the amniotic fluid (fluid surrounding the fetus). Fetal cells from the fluid are cultured for chromosome analysis, and the fluid is then tested in procedures that take two to three weeks.

A genetic counselor will analyze different factors and estimate the odds that a couple will have children with certain disorders. Chromosomes obtained from tissue samples are often photographed, and the photos are cut and rearranged so that the chromosomes are organized according to size and structure on a chart.

surrounding the fetus. This test involves inserting a thin catheter through the vagina and cervix into the uterus and taking a small sample of the chorionic villi. This procedure has several advantages over amniocentesis: It can be done as early as the eighth week instead of the 14th, and the results are available in 6 to 24 hours rather than two to three weeks (Cadkin et al., 1984). Both amniocentesis and CVS involve some risks, including damage to the fetus, induced miscarriage, and infection. For this reason, the procedures are not used unless there is a likelihood of a problem.

Prenatal screening through either amniocentesis or CVS cannot detect all birth defects. However, rapidly improving technologies for detecting faulty genes—such as the recombinant DNA procedure for marking the presence of the Huntington's gene—suggest that prenatal screening will prove increasingly helpful in the years to come.

The most controversial new technology is the developing science of **genetic engineering,** sometimes called **gene therapy** (Caskey, 1987; Hirschhorn, 1987). Genetic engineering involves using recombinant DNA techniques both to identify gene defects and to insert a new gene into cells to alter and correct a defective genetic code. The artificially introduced gene instructs the recipient cells to begin manufacturing a substance they might not otherwise produce because of a genetic error. Most of the genetic engineering research to date has been conducted with nonhuman subjects such as mice and monkeys. For example, scientists recently reported success using this technique to treat an inherited disorder in mice that is characterized by violent shivering, convulsions, and death within three to four months of birth (Readhead et al., 1987). At the present time, human

A case of surrogate motherhood: who is "Baby M's" real mother? Elizabeth Stern (left) contracted with Mary Beth Whitehead (right) to act as a surrogate mother and have her baby by being artificially inseminated by her husband, Mr. Stern (center, holding "Baby M"). After giving birth, Mary Beth Whitehead claimed the baby was hers, since she was the natural mother. What about the father's claim to the child, and what of the original contract? In subsequent court hearings, these were some of the many issues that the jury had to consider. Until legal matters surrounding surrogate parents are clarified, everyone involved in such a transaction is at risk of litigation.

research efforts are focused on the *somatic* or nonreproductive body cells so that any genetic changes that do occur will not be passed on to children. Thus, while a person might be cured of an inherited disease, he or she would still have to contend with the risk of passing the defect on to children. To prevent this from occurring, genetic engineers would have to alter the reproductive cells—a procedure that for ethical reasons is probably still years away (Young, 1985).

PRENATAL DEVELOPMENT

The nine months or approximately 266 days of prenatal development takes place in three stages: germinal, embryonic, and fetal. These stages of prenatal development are not to be confused with the customary convention of dividing pregnancy into three-month segments called *trimesters*.

During the **germinal** or **zygote stage** (the first two weeks after fertilization), the zygote develops rapidly as it becomes attached to the walls of the uterus. By the end of the second week, various auxiliary structures—the amniotic sac, umbilical cord, and placenta—are well established and the cell mass is called an **embryo**.

The second stage, the **embryonic stage**, lasts from the beginning of the third week to the end of the eighth. It is characterized by very fast growth and differentiation of the heart, lungs, pancreas, and other vital organs as well as the major body systems. During this stage, the embryo is extremely vulnerable to negative environmental influences such as faulty nutrition, drugs, or maternal disease. Because any of these environmental insults may have devastating, irreversible effects on the developing baby, the embryonic period is viewed as a critical stage of development. The vast majority of environmentally induced prenatal development defects, as well as most spontaneous abortions (miscarriages), occur during this period. (The Health Psychology and Life discussion, "Health Risks During Prenatal Development," outlines several known hazards.) By the end of the embry-

FIGURE 10.7 PRENATAL DEVELOPMENT AT FIVE WEEKS

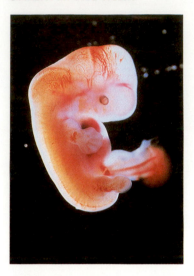

FIGURE 10.8 PRENATAL DEVELOPMENT AT 14 WEEKS

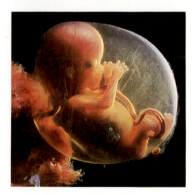

onic stage almost all of the baby's structures and organs are formed and a few organs, like the heart, are already functioning. By the end of eight weeks the baby, now called a **fetus,** has clearly discernible features and a prominent head.

During the final **fetal stage,** which extends from the beginning of the third month to birth, bone and muscle tissue form and the various organs and body systems continue to mature and develop. By the end of four months external body parts, including fingernails, eyebrows, and eyelashes, are clearly formed. Fetal movement may be felt at this time. Future prenatal development consists primarily of growth in size and refinement of the features that already exist. (Figures 10.7 and 10.8 portray prenatal development at five and 14 weeks, respectively.)

Throughout pregnancy, the fetus depends upon the mother for nutrients, oxygen, and waste elimination as substances pass through the placenta and the umbilical cord to the fetus. Fetal and maternal blood do not mix: Fetal blood circulates independently within the closed system of the fetus and inner part of the placenta; maternal blood flows in the uterine walls and outer part of the placenta. All exchanges between fetal and mater-

---

HEALTH PSYCHOLOGY AND LIFE

HEALTH RISKS DURING PRENATAL DEVELOPMENT

Because fetal blood and maternal blood do not mix directly, the placenta protects the fetus from many types of bacterial infection. However, many substances ingested by the mother easily cross through the placenta and can damage the developing fetus. Drugs, alcohol, and tobacco as well as certain medications are all potentially dangerous, and there have been many tragic cases in which children have been damaged by medications taken by their pregnant mothers. The drug *thalidomide*, prescribed as a sedative to pregnant women during the early 1960s, was absorbed into the circulatory system of fetuses, causing severe deformities to the extremities. Another drug, Accutane, which is used to treat severe acne, creates almost as high a risk of major malformation as did thalidomide (Lammer et al., 1985). In the last few years, some children of women who took diethylstibestrol (DES) while pregnant have developed cancer of the vagina or testicles. Tetracycline, a commonly used antibiotic, can damage an infant's teeth and cause stunted bone growth if taken during pregnancy. In animal studies, even nonprescription drugs such as aspirin have been linked to fetal abnormalities.

Some substances known to cause harm to the mother also pose serious hazards to a developing fetus. The babies of mothers who regularly use addictive drugs such as heroin, codeine, or morphine during pregnancy are often born addicted. Because withdrawal can be fatal to a newborn, the drug must often be continued until the infant is strong enough to be taken off it. Another health hazard for the fetus is cigarette smoking. Smoking reduces the amount of oxygen in the bloodstream, which may slow the fetus's growth. Infants of mothers who smoked during pregnancy often weigh less and are in poorer general condition than infants of mothers who do not smoke (Spady, 1986). In addition, smoking increases the chances of spontaneous abortion and of pregnancy complications that can result in fetal or infant death.

The leading cause of developmental disabilities and birth defects in the United States is **fetal alcohol syndrome (FAS)** (Centers for Disease Control, 1984). Heavy alcohol use can cause fetal death and spontaneous abortion, premature birth, congenital heart defects, damage to the brain and nervous system, and numerous physical malformations. Most FAS babies are eventually shown to have below-normal IQs. Infants may be born addicted to alcohol, and consequently experience alcohol withdrawal symptoms for several days after birth (Clarren & Smith, 1978). In 1981, the Food and Drug Administration advised women to abstain completely from alcohol use during pregnancy. Research also indicates that heavy marijuana use may cause problems similar to fetal alcohol syndrome (Hingson et al., 1982).

Although the extent of our knowledge about the effects of most substances on a fetus is very limited, we do know that the more we learn, the more potential hazards are being discovered. For this reason, *no drugs should be used during pregnancy unless they are absolutely necessary and are taken under close medical supervision.*

nal blood systems take place as substances pass through the walls of the blood vessels.

PHYSICAL DEVELOPMENT FROM BIRTH TO THE END OF CHILDHOOD

The period from *infancy* (birth to roughly the toddler stage) through *childhood* (toddler to the onset of adolescence) is marked by many important developmental changes. The remainder of this chapter deals with various aspects of physical, cognitive, and psychosocial development that occur during the first 12 or 13 years. We begin by discussing physical development, including development of the brain, physical growth, and motor development.

BRAIN DEVELOPMENT

A newborn's brain has most if not all of the neurons it ever will have. However, it is still far from mature. At birth, the brain is only about 25 percent of its adult weight, and the complex neural networks that form the basis for our skills and memories are just beginning to form. Growth occurs rapidly: By six months the brain is 50 percent of its adult weight; at two years, 75 percent; and at five years, 90 percent of its final weight. At age 10, the figure is 95 percent. These figures stand in sharp contrast to the weight of the entire body, which at birth is only about 5 percent of adult weight and at 10 years is only about 50 percent (Peacock, 1986). During this period of rapid growth (and to a lesser extent in the years that follow), neural networks become increasingly complex as changes take place in the size, shape, and density of interconnections among neurons (see Figure 10.9).

The brain develops in an orderly fashion after birth. In the first few months the primary motor area of the cerebral cortex develops rapidly as the infant progresses from involuntary reflexive activity to voluntary control over motor movements. The cortical areas that control vision and hearing develop somewhat more slowly. By three months of age, however, these sensory areas, particularly those controlling visual perception, are more fully developed, so that infants can reach out and touch objects that they see. In the ensuing months, further development and refinement of sensory and motor capabilities are closely linked to changes in the brain and the rest of the nervous system.

Recall from Chapter 3 that certain cognitive functions tend to be localized in one of the cerebral hemispheres. At one time it was believed that much of this hemispheric specialization or localization of cortical functions occurs gradually throughout childhood (Lenneberg, 1967). Recent evi-

FIGURE 10.9   DEVELOPMENT OF BRAIN TISSUES AFTER BIRTH

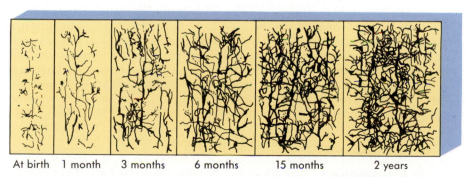

At birth   1 month   3 months   6 months   15 months   2 years

As these drawings of human brain tissues from the cerebral cortex illustrate, during the period of rapid early growth after birth, neural networks become increasingly complex.

FIGURE 10.10 DO ENRICHED AND IMPOVERISHED ENVIRONMENTS HAVE DIFFERENT EFFECTS ON THE DEVELOPMENT OF RATS' BRAINS?

Mark Rosenzweig and his colleagues found that rats reared in enriched environments, replete with "toys" and other rats, developed heavier brains with thicker cerebral cortexes than animals reared in sterile, solitary environments.

Impoverished environment

Enriched environment

dence suggests, however, that this specialization begins very early (Bryden & Saxby, 1985; Hahn, 1987). One study demonstrated that most newborns are better able to process speech syllables in their left than right hemispheres (Molfese & Molfese, 1979). (Remember that verbal functions tend to be localized in the left hemispheres of most people.) By age three, nine out of ten children show this specialization for verbal processing. Left- or right-handedness also develops early, providing further evidence of hemispheric specialization during infancy (Bryden & Saxby, 1985; Hawn & Harris, 1983).

Early Experiences and Brain Development   Do the kinds of experiences we have during our early years influence the way our brains develop? Some experiments performed in the late 1960s indicate that they do. Mark Rosenzweig and his colleagues at the University of California at Berkeley conducted a series of experiments to compare how being raised in enriched as opposed to impoverished environments affected rats (Rosenzweig, 1966). Some of the rats were reared in sterile, dimly lit, individual cages with solid side walls that prevented them from seeing or touching other animals; others were raised in a large cage with 10 to 12 other rats and plenty of "toys" such as ladders, wheels, and boxes (see Figure 10.10).

   The researchers were not originally looking for significant brain differences: most psychologists at the time had not considered that experience might alter brain anatomy. However, Rosenzweig and his associates routinely recorded brain weights as part of their research. Two years into their research they realized that the brains of the rats reared in the enriched environments were heavier than those of rats raised in solitary confinement. These variations were most pronounced in the cerebral cortex, where the average weight difference was four percent. Rats raised in the impoverished, sterile environments tended to develop a lighter and thinner cortex, with smaller-than-normal neurons (Rosenzweig et al., 1972).

   More recent evidence provided by researchers at the University of Illinois has supported these findings, linking enriched early experiences with expanded dendritic networks in the precise areas of the brain where the experiences are processed (Greenough & Green, 1981). The increased number of dendrites seems to preserve newly established neural networks. More branches mean more synapses, suggesting that greater amounts of information can be transmitted more efficiently in these animals' brains.

Early experience seems to affect brain biochemistry as well as anatomy. In the enriched rats, Rosenzweig and his colleagues also found a significant increase in the activity of two enzymes, acetylcholinesterase and cholinesterase, both of which play an important role in the synaptic transmission of neural messages (Rosenzweig & Bennett, 1970).

In both the Berkeley and University of Illinois studies, the anatomical and biochemical effects were not restricted to the earliest periods of development. Rats who were reared under normal laboratory conditions in their early days and then subjected to either impoverished or enriched environments showed similar weight and biochemical changes in their brains. Although the effects of environmental stimulation may be greater during early development, these findings indicate that the brains of rats, and possibly humans, are malleable throughout development.

PHYSICAL GROWTH

Changes that take place in the brain are only part of the picture of what happens during development. Another significant change is physical growth. Children grow more rapidly during the first few years than at any other time. During the first six months, in fact, infants more than double their weight, and by their first birthday most infants have tripled their birth weight (the average newborn weighs seven pounds) and increased their birth height by 50 percent. In the next two years they gain another eight inches and 10 pounds, on the average. After their third birthday, this early growth spurt levels off somewhat to a more steady two to three inches per year, until the adolescent growth spurt.

Both physical growth and motor development follow two basic patterns. The first pattern is **cephalocaudal** (that is, from head to foot); the second pattern is **proximodistal** (inner to outer) [Hall, 1987]. The cephalocaudal pattern of development occurs first and most rapidly in the head and upper parts. This is why newborns have large heads; it is also why a one-year-old's brain weighs approximately two-thirds of its eventual adult size while the rest of the body is a much smaller proportion of its adult size. The cephalocaudal principle also explains why babies can track things with their eyes before they can effectively move their trunks, and why they can do many things with their hands before they can use their legs. Because development is also proximodistal, infants gain control over the upper portions of their arms and legs, which are closer to the center of the body, before they can control their forearms and forelegs. Control of the hands, feet, fingers, and toes comes last.

MOTOR DEVELOPMENT

Another basic rule of development is that we move from the simple to the more complex. This is particularly apparent in the acquisition of motor skills. The motor movements of young babies are dominated by a number of involuntary reflexes that offer either protection or help in securing nourishment. An example is the *rooting reflex*: When babies are stroked on the cheek, they turn their heads toward the sensation, vigorously "rooting" for a nipple (see Figure 10.11). Other common reflexes are listed in Table 10.2. As development progresses, voluntary, cortex-controlled movements begin to take over, and the primitive reflexes disappear according to the timetable shown in the table. Some reflexes, such as coughing, sneezing, gagging, and the eyeblink, remain with us throughout our lives.

As the nervous system and muscles mature, more complicated motor movements and skills begin to emerge. There is wide variation in the ages at which babies are able to roll over, sit without support, stand, and walk, but

FIGURE 10.11   THE "ROOTING REFLEX"

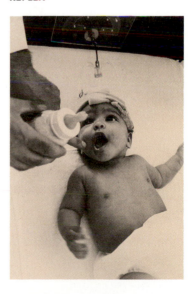

When babies are stroked on the cheek, they turn their heads toward the sensation, vigorously "rooting" for a nipple to suck on.

TABLE 10.2 *Primitive Reflexes in Human Infants*

Name of Reflex	Stimulation	Behavior	Age of Dropping Out
Rooting	Cheek stroked with finger or nipple	Head turns, mouth opens, sucking movements begin	9 months
Moro (startle)	Sudden stimulus such as gunshot or being dropped	Extends legs, arms, and fingers, arches back, draws back head	3 months
Darwinian (grasping)	Palm of hand stroked	Makes such a strong fist that baby can be raised to standing position if both fists are closed around a stick	2 months
Swimming	Put in water face down	Well-coordinated swimming movements	6 months
Tonic neck	Laid down on back	Turns head to one side, assumes "fencer" position, extends arms and legs on preferred side, flexes opposite limbs	2 months
Babinski	Sole of foot stroked	Toes fan out, foot twists in	6–9 months
Walking	Held under arm, with bare feet touching flat surface	Makes steplike motions that look like well-coordinated walking	2 months
Placing	Backs of feet drawn against edge of flat surface	Withdraws foot	1 month

Source: Papilia and Olds, 1986.

the sequence of these developments is universal. Figure 10.12 shows the average age at which some milestones in motor development occur.

Can different environmental experiences influence the rate at which we acquire motor skills? A number of studies have explored this question, and within a normal range of experiences, the answer seems to be no. As long as children are well fed, healthy, and free to initiate motor skills when they are ready, the role of environmental influences on motor development is quite limited (Clarke-Stewart, 1977; Ridenour, 1982). For example, regardless of the amount of "training" or encouragement children receive, they will not walk until the cerebellum has matured enough to create a readiness or capacity (an event that occurs at about age one).

WHAT HAPPENS WHEN INFANTS ARE PREVENTED FROM WALKING?

In certain Indian cultures, infants are wrapped in swaddling clothes and bound to cradleboards during most of their waking hours for the first 12 or more months of their lives. We have just seen that children will not walk until they reach a certain level of biological readiness. Is the converse true? Will children begin to walk when their biological clock reaches a certain point, even if they have not had earlier opportunities to crawl and otherwise move about on their own? Make a reasoned prediction before reading on.

In the discussion of maturation earlier in this chapter (see "Are We Products of Heredity or Environment?"), we noted that certain biologically determined sequences occur even if children do not receive encouragement. In fact, studies have shown that babies who have been virtually immobilized on cradleboards during their first year typically begin to walk at about the same age as infants from other cultures who are free to practice sitting, crawling, and pulling themselves up on furniture (Orlansky, 1949). This does not mean that the environment has no influence at all. Studies of children raised with insufficient love, stimulation, or proper nutrition often show profound physical and mental retardation.

If early training does not significantly accelerate the rate at which children master motor skills such as standing or walking, does the same rule apply to other physical skills such as bowel and bladder control? A classic early study assessed the effect of differential toilet training on twin boys. One was placed on a toilet once on the hour every day from two months of

FIGURE 10.12   SOME MILESTONES IN HUMAN MOTOR DEVELOPMENT

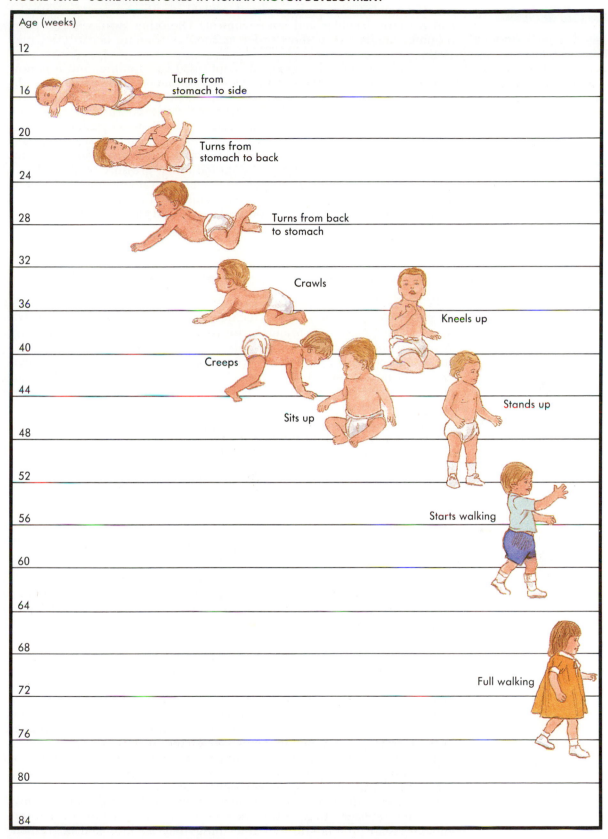

There is wide variation in the ages at which babies are able to sit without support, stand up, and so forth, but the sequence of these developments is universal. The age norms given here are averages.

age, while the other was not toilet trained until age 23 months. The first twin did not demonstrate any control until 20 months, but by 23 months he had mastered bladder and bowel control. The other twin, with no prior training, caught up in short order as soon as training began (McGraw, 1940).

Later research has generally confirmed this finding, and it is now widely recognized that no amount of encouragement, rewards, punishments, or pleading will induce successful toilet training until the necessary muscular and neurological maturation has occurred (usually sometime between 15 and 24 months of age). Unfortunately, toilet training is often begun long before an infant can contract the sphincter muscles to retain waste. While this does not hasten toilet training, it may result in extra emotional strain, particularly if parents put too much pressure on a child.

Although the milestones are no longer so dramatic, motor development continues beyond infancy and early childhood. Parents are sometimes amazed to realize one day that the awkward child they observed banging around the house has been transformed into a coordinated athlete who performs with distinction.

COGNITIVE DEVELOPMENT FROM BIRTH TO THE END OF CHILDHOOD

Cognitive development refers to the development of various mental activities such as perceiving, remembering, reasoning, and problem solving. When do children begin to remember? How do they categorize experiences? When can they see things from another's perspective, reason logically, and think symbolically? Most efforts to answer such questions lead inevitably to the writings of the late Swiss psychologist Jean Piaget.

PIAGET'S THEORY OF COGNITIVE DEVELOPMENT

No one has provided more insights into cognitive development than Jean Piaget (1970, 1972). Piaget became interested in how children's minds work in the early 1920s, when he was working with Alfred Binet in Paris on standardizing children's intelligence tests. At first, his goal was to find certain questions that the average child of a specific age could answer correctly. However, Piaget soon became intrigued with another finding: The mistakes made by many children of the same age were often strikingly similar (and strikingly different from those made by children of other ages). It occurred to Piaget that children's cognitive strategies are age related, and that the way children think about things changes with age regardless of the specific nature of what they are thinking about. These observations led Piaget to refocus his research. From this point until his death in 1980, he devoted his efforts to understanding how cognitive abilities develop. Piaget's theory gradually evolved from years of carefully observing and questioning individual children, including his own three offspring. The following paragraphs provide an overview of his major themes.

Schemas According to Piaget, the impetus behind human intellectual development is an urge to make sense out of our worlds. To accomplish this goal, he theorized, our maturing brains form mental structures or **schemas** which assimilate and organize processed information. These schemas guide future behavior while providing a framework for making sense out of new information.

Newborns are equipped with only primitive schemas that guide certain basic sensorimotor sequences such as sucking, looking, and grasping. According to Piaget, these early schemas become activated only when certain objects are present—for example, things that can be looked at, grasped, or sucked. However, as an infant evolves into a child and later an adult, these schemas become increasingly complex, often substituting symbolic representations for objects that are physically present (Piaget, 1977).

By the time we reach adulthood, our brains are filled with countless schemas or ways of organizing information that range from our knowledge of how to play a tune to the fantasies we concoct when we are bored. To Piaget, cognitive growth involves a constant process of modifying and adapting our schemas to account for new experiences. This adaptation takes place through two processes: assimilation and accommodation.

Assimilation and Accommodation   **Assimilation** is the process by which we interpret new information in accordance with our existing knowledge or schemas. In this ongoing process, we may find it necessary to modify the information we assimilate in order to fit it into our existing schemas. At the same time, however, we adjust or restructure what we already know so that new information can fit in better—a process Piaget called **accommodation.**

For instance, an infant who is accustomed to taking its nourishment from the breast uses a simple "suck and swallow" schema to guide this basic sensorimotor sequence. When it is switched from the breast to the bottle, the infant assimilates this new experience into the existing schema and continues to suck and swallow. What happens when the parents introduce a notable variation by filling the formula bottle with apple juice instead of milk? The baby's initial reaction may be to spit out the strange new substance. With time, the infant may come to like apple juice but dislike other types of juice. Basically the infant has accommodated the new information by modifying the "suck and swallow" schema to one of "suck, taste, and swallow (maybe)."

Piaget believed that we learn to understand our world as we constantly adapt and modify our mental structures through assimilation and accommodation. As we develop, assimilation allows us to maintain important connections with the past while accommodation helps us to adapt and change as we gain new experiences.

Four Stages of Cognitive Development   Piaget viewed cognitive growth as a four-stage process with qualitatively different kinds of thinking occurring in each of these stages. Although all people progress through these stages in the same sequence, Piaget noted that the speed of this progression may vary from person to person. Table 10.3 outlines these four stages: the sensorimotor, preoperational, concrete operations, and formal operations.

Sensorimotor Stage (Birth to about 24 Months)   During the **sensorimotor stage,** infants learn about their worlds primarily through their senses and actions. Instead of thinking about what is going on around them, infants discover by sensing (sensori-) and doing (motor). They learn by their actions, which gradually evolve from reflexes to more purposeful behaviors. For example, an infant might learn that shaking a rattle produces a sound or that crying at night produces parents. Thus, some of the schemas that develop during this stage are organized around the principle of causality, as the infant begins to perform cognitively organized goal-directed behaviors.

Another key aspect of the sensorimotor stage is the gradual development of **object permanence**—the realization that objects (or people) continue to exist even when they are not immediately in view. Up to about the age of four months, an object ceases to exist for the infant when it is out of sight (see Figure 10.13). After four months, babies begin to look for objects they no longer see, and sometime between eight and 12 months they begin to manually retrieve objects they see being hidden. By age two, most children are able to incorporate into their schemas symbolic representations of objects, which are clearly independent of their perception of these articles. This is the point in development when toddlers will gleefully and systematically search all kinds of possible hiding places for objects they have not

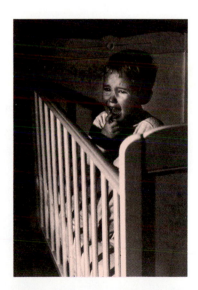

Infants in the sensorimotor stage learn by their actions, which gradually evolve from reflexes to more purposeful behaviors. For example, this infant has learned that crying at night results in the appearance of his parents.

TABLE 10.3 *Piaget's Four Stages of Cognitive Development*

Cognitive Development Stage	Approximate Age	General Characteristics
Sensorimotor	Birth to about 24 months	Infants experience world primarily by sensing and doing. They learn by their actions, which gradually evolve from reflexes to more purposeful behaviors. Cognitive growth marked by improving ability to imitate behavior and gradual development of object permanence.
Preoperational	2–7 years	The child begins to acquire the ability to use symbols to represent people, objects, and events. However, the child cannot reason logically and thought tends to be limited by the inability to take into account more than one perceptual factor at the same time and to perceive the world from any perspective other than one's own.
Concrete operations	7–12 years	The child makes a major transition in cognitive development by shifting from a single-dimensional emphasis on perception to a greater reliance on logical thinking about concrete events. During this stage children master the principle of conservation.
Formal operations	12 years and older	Abstract reasoning emerges during this stage. Teenagers acquire the ability to make complex deductions and solve problems by systematically testing hypothetical solutions.

seen hidden. (Recent research suggests that object permanence in infants may occur as early as age 3½ months [Baillargeon, 1987].)

Another important cognitive skill of the sensorimotor stage is *imitation*. Even a tiny baby may try to imitate the facial expression of an older person: Under controlled laboratory conditions, researchers have found that attempts at imitation are clearly present even among newborns seven to 72 hours old (Meltzoff & Moore, 1983). For example, when an experimenter stuck his tongue out at a newborn, the infant responded in kind! This cognitive skill continues to be refined so that by the end of the sensorimotor period children imitate all kinds of behaviors.

FIGURE 10.13   LACK OF OBJECT PERMANENCE DURING FIRST MONTHS OF LIFE

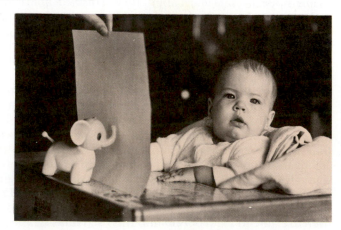

Up to about the age of four months, an object ceases to exist for an infant when it is out of sight. After four months, babies begin to look for objects they no longer see, and sometime between 8 and 12 months they begin to retrieve objects manually that they see being hidden.

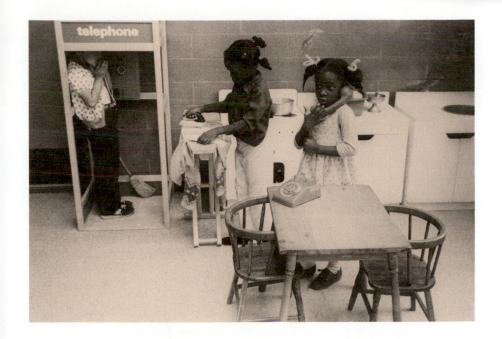

After their second birthday, children's play activities become increasingly focused on make-believe. Three- and four-year-olds begin to imitate another person's behavior and to demonstrate an increasing mental sophistication.

Preoperational Stage (Ages Two to Seven) As children move beyond their second birthday, they increasingly use symbolic thought. Having mastered object permanence, they are now ready to think representatively, using symbols rather than depending on what they see or touch. The ability to use words to represent people, objects, and events allows children to make giant steps in cognitive development. Imagination becomes important as children's play activities become increasingly focused on make-believe. Three- and four-year-olds can now imitate another person's behavior after a lapse of time—a qualitative change from the immediate imitation that took place during the sensorimotor stage. The use of language, imaginative play, and delayed imitation all demonstrate an increasing mental sophistication.

Despite these advances, however, preoperational thought remains somewhat limited, for it depends largely on how things appear or seem to be. Children at this stage have yet to master logical reasoning processes based on rules and concepts. This is why Piaget used the term **preoperational stage:** Young children are only able to develop immature concepts, or *preconcepts*, in their effort to understand the world. For example, an adult has no problem distinguishing between a sports car and a sedan, or a new versus an old car. However, a small child has only a ill-defined, immature concept of a car—something that has wheels and doors and goes vrooooom!

Another limitation of preoperational thought is apparent in the phenomenon of **centration**—the inability to take into account more than one perceptual factor at the same time. (The ability to evaluate two or more physical dimensions simultaneously, a process called **decentration,** does not emerge until the end of the preoperational period.)

Piaget demonstrated centration and decentration in a simple experiment. When he poured equal amounts of liquid into two identical glasses, five-, six-, and seven-year-old children all reported that the glasses contained equal amounts. However, when the liquid from one glass was poured into a taller, narrower glass, the children had different opinions about which of the two glasses contained the most liquid. The five- and six-year-olds knew that it was the same liquid, but they were unable to generalize beyond the central perceptual factor of greater height, which normally indicates "more." Thus, they indicated that the tall glass had more juice. In contrast, the seven-year-olds generally reported there was no difference, a fact they knew to be true since they were able to decentrate, or simultaneously take into account the two physical dimensions of height and width.

In a reenactment of Piaget's liquid conservation test, the experimenter poured equal amounts of liquid into two identical glasses. Both children reported that the glasses contained equal amounts. However, when the liquid from one glass was poured into a taller, narrower glass, the five-year-old boy thought the taller glass held more water, but the seven-year-old girl reported that there was no difference.

The ability to decentrate enables children to master **conservation,** the understanding that changing something's form does not necessarily change its essential character. Research conducted by Piaget and others has demonstrated that children do not understand the principle of conservation until the concrete-operations stage of cognitive development.

Piaget also stressed the egocentric nature of preoperational thinking. *Egocentrism* does not imply selfishness, but rather the inability to perceive the world from any perspective other than one's own. In essence, Piaget said that preoperational children view life as though everyone else were looking at it from their perspective.

Piaget demonstrated egocentrism using the "three-mountain problem." Here, a child is seated at a table upon which three mountains are

FIGURE 10.14 THE THREE-MOUNTAIN PROBLEM

While seven- or eight-year-olds understand that the teddy bear sees the mountains from a different perspective than their own, a younger preoperational child does not.

placed (see Figure 10.14). A teddy bear occupies another chair on a different side of the table. The child is asked to decide what the teddy bear would see, and to indicate this by selecting the appropriate scene from a set of drawings. Piaget found that children of age seven or eight are likely to choose the correct drawing, while younger preoperational children typically choose a depiction of what they see from their own chair (Piaget & Inhelder, 1967).

In recent years, Piaget's conclusions about the degree of egocentric thinking in young children have been challenged (Ford, 1985; Moore et al., 1987). Did his young subjects perform poorly because their thinking was egocentric, or because the problem was simply too difficult? Some later studies have shown that even three- and four-year-olds can successfully manipulate movable versions of simple scenes to show another's view (Borke, 1975). Researchers have also noted that four-year-olds seem to understand that two-year-olds perceive things differently, since they change their way of speaking when conversing with the toddlers (Shatz & Gelman, 1973).

Although preoperational children are not necessarily incapable of viewing things from the perspective of others, it is generally agreed that young children tend to be egocentric, as Piaget suggested. This explains why children, who see themselves as central to all events in their worlds, often view themselves as causing certain outcomes. For example, young children of divorcing parents may think that they are the cause of the estrangement. Needless to say, children in such highly vulnerable situations may require a great deal of assurance that they are not the cause of calamitous events such as divorce.

Sometimes young children of divorcing parents think that they are the cause of the estrangement. These children require a great deal of assurance that they are not the cause of such a calamitous event.

Concrete-Operations Stage (Ages Seven to 12) Between ages seven and 12, children again make a qualitative leap as they learn to engage in decentration and to shed their egocentrism. Whereas the preoperational stage is characterized by intuitive thinking and a dependence on imagination and the senses, children in the **concrete-operations stage** begin to use logical *mental operations* or rules. This shift from a single-dimensional emphasis on perception to a greater reliance on logic is a major transition in cognitive development.

As we saw earlier, Piaget viewed mastery of the concept of conservation as a milestone of the concrete-operations stage. Children master different aspects of conservation at various times during the concrete-operations stage. For example, a child who understands conservation of substance will realize that a ball of clay rolled into the shape of a hot dog still has the same amount of clay. However, when the same child sees two identical clay balls weighed on a balance scale, and then watches as one of the balls is rolled into a hot-dog shape, a strange thing may happen. Although the child understands conservation of substance, he or she may not yet understand the more abstract principle of conservation of weight—and thus does not realize the hot dog and ball will weigh the same. By the end of the concrete-operations stage, children typically master all of the various dimensions of conservation: substance, length, number, weight, and volume.

Throughout this stage, thinking is still somewhat restricted by a tendency to limit the use of logical operations to concrete situations and objects in the visible world. For example, if you played "20 questions" with an eight-year-old, the child would be likely to stick with concrete questions that, if correct, would solve the problem ("Is it a carrot?" "Is it a rabbit?"). In contrast, older children in the final stage of cognitive development might approach the problem more abstractly, asking general questions such as "Is it vegetable?" or "Is it animal?" before making specific guesses.

In the concrete-operations stage, children are not yet able to deal with completely hypothetical problems of a "what if" nature in which they must compare what they know to be true with what may be true. For instance, if you ask children in this stage what it would be like if people could fly, their answers will probably reflect what they have actually seen (in cartoons and movies as well as in real life) rather than total abstractions. Thus, you might be told that people would look funny with wings or that people cannot fly. In contrast, older children are more able to imagine things beyond their own experiences. Thus, a teenager might tell you that if people could fly, department stores would no longer need elevators, or that no one would need to take drugs to "get high."

Formal-Operations Stage (Age 12 and Older) In the **formal-operations stage,** individuals acquire the ability to make complex deductions and solve problems by systematically testing hypothetical solutions. Adolescents can now think about abstract problems. For example, younger children in the concrete-operations stage would indignantly reject the syllogism, "People are faster than horses, and horses are faster than cars; therefore people are faster than cars" because it runs counter to concrete, observable facts: they *know* cars are faster than humans. In contrast, adolescents in the formal-operations stage are able to evaluate the logic of this syllogism separately from its content.

Although Piaget originally believed that the formal-operations stage almost always began at about the age of 12, he later revised this position to allow for a variety of situations that could either postpone or prevent the arrival of this stage. Piaget did maintain that once children enter the stage of formal operations, there are no longer any qualitative differences between their thought processes and those of older teenagers or adults. Any further advances in cognitive functions are merely refinements in the ability to think logically and reason abstractly. We will have more to say about this final stage of cognitive development in Chapter 11.

Piaget's theory of cognitive development has been criticized for placing too much emphasis on the maturation of biologically based cognitive structures while understating the importance of environment and experience. He has also been criticized for ignoring individual differences in his attempt to portray developmental norms. Despite these criticisms, however, his theory has had a profound impact upon developmental psychology and on educational procedures in the Western world. Its basic tenets have been repeatedly tested and largely supported. Particularly noteworthy is recent research revealing that the occurrence of growth spurts in the development of human cerebral hemispheres tends to overlap with the timing of the major developmental stages described by Piaget (Thatcher et al., 1987). These findings add credibility to Piaget's assertion that biological maturation and cognitive development are closely associated. In conclusion, Piaget's theory has provided immense insights into understanding the development of thought, stimulating more research than any other developmental theory and providing the impetus for many valuable changes in both education and child care.

PSYCHOSOCIAL DEVELOPMENT FROM INFANCY TO THE END OF CHILDHOOD

Children's physical and cognitive growth are accompanied by psychosocial development—changes in the way they think, feel, and relate to their world and the people in it. This section first describes two areas of psychosocial development—the establishment of attachment and the impact of parenting styles—then concludes with Erik Erikson's theory of psychosocial development.

ATTACHMENT

You may have observed babies at the age of seven or eight months and up to a year and a half who are content as long as a parent is nearby, but who are virtually inconsolable as soon as the parent leaves the room. Many a babysitter has spent frustrating hours cuddling, bouncing, and singing to a baby who refuses to take comfort from anyone but the "real thing"—mom or dad.

Such experiences demonstrate one of the earliest and most profound aspects of early psychosocial development: **attachment.** Attachment is the term applied to the intense emotional tie that develops between two individuals, in this case an infant and a parent. Attachment has clear survival value in that it motivates infants to remain close to their parents or other caregivers who protect them from danger. Infants may establish intense, affectionate, reciprocal relationships with their parents, older siblings, grandparents, or any other consistent caregiver. However, the most intense attachment relationship that typically occurs in the early stages of development is between mother and child, and most of the available research has focused on the development of this bond (Cohn & Tronick, 1987; Field et al., 1987; Rutter & Durkin, 1987).

Attachment develops according to a typical sequence (Ainsworth, 1963; Schaffer & Emerson, 1964). During the first few months, babies exhibit **indiscriminate attachment:** Social behaviors such as smiling, nestling, and gurgling are typically directed to just about anyone. This pattern continues for about six to seven months, when babies begin to develop selective, **specific attachments.** At this time, they often show increased responsiveness to their parents or other regular caregivers by smiling more, holding out their arms to be picked up, and vocalizing more than to other people. This specific attachment is likely to become so strong that infants will show great distress when separated from their parents. Nurturing approaches by strangers may be merely tolerated or perhaps overtly rejected.

Fortunately for the countless babysitters, grandparents, and friends who are distressed at being rejected, most infants progress to a third stage of **separate attachments** by about 12 to 18 months. During this final stage they take an active social interest in people other than their mothers or fathers. Fear of strangers also typically diminishes during this period.

How Attachment Forms   How do babies form attachments to primary caregivers? A number of early developmental theorists believed that feeding was the key ingredient in the development of attachment: Because the mother provides nourishment, the baby learns to associate mother with a sense of well-being and consequently wants her to remain close at hand. This idea was popular until a series of landmark studies were released by Harry Harlow and his associates (Harlow & Zimmerman, 1958; Harlow & Harlow, 1966; Harlow et al., 1971).

Harlow's research began as the study of learning abilities in rhesus monkeys. To eliminate the possible variable input of early experiences, he separated baby monkeys from their mothers shortly after birth and raised them in individual cages which were equipped with soft blankets. Unexpectedly, the monkeys became intensely attached to the blankets, showing extreme distress when they were removed for laundering. The behavior was comparable to that of baby monkeys when they are separated from their mothers.

Harlow and his colleagues were intrigued, for this finding contradicted the notion that attachment develops through feeding. The researchers decided to conduct some experiments to find out whether contact comfort is more important than food in developing attachment. They separated infant monkeys from their mothers, rearing them in cages containing two artificial "mothers." One "mother" was made of a wire mesh cylinder; the other was a similar wire cylinder wrapped with foam rubber and covered with terry cloth to which the infant could cling. A bottle could be attached to either artificial mother so that it could serve as the monkey's source of food.

If attachment were linked to feeding, we would expect the monkeys

When my granddaughter was born, I took care of her for a few weeks because my daughter became ill shortly after coming home from the hospital. I loved caring for my granddaughter, and there seemed to be a strong bond between us. Eventually my daughter was well enough to assume full-time mothering, and I had to return to my job. Since I live in a different part of the country, I was unable to return for another visit until my granddaughter was almost 11 months old.

I couldn't believe the change in her. It was as if our first month together hadn't even happened. Every time I tried to cuddle her, she would struggle and cry for her mother. It was very distressing. Even by the end of my week's visit, she would cry and cry when left with me while my daughter and son-and-law went out for the evening. I couldn't understand why she had changed so much from a baby who obviously once loved all the attention I had given her. (*Authors' files*)

to form attachments consistently to the "mother" with the bottle. This was not what happened, however. Monkeys who were reared with a nourishing wire mother and a nonnourishing cloth mother clearly preferred the latter, spending much more time clinging to their "contact-comfort" mother. Even while they were obtaining nourishment from the wire mother, the monkeys often maintained simultaneous contact with the cloth mother (see Figure 10.15). The cloth mother also provided the baby monkeys with some degree of confidence in exploring new situations. When novel stimuli were introduced, the monkeys would gradually venture away from their cloth "mothers" to explore, often returning to receive some contact comfort before exploring further. When a fear stimulus (such as a toy bear beating loudly on a drum) was introduced, the frightened infants would rush to their cloth mothers for security. If their cloth mothers were absent, the babies would freeze into immobility or cry and dash aimlessly around the cage.

The researchers concluded that the satisfaction of contact comfort was more important in establishing attachment than was the gratification of being fed. When other qualities were added to the cloth mother, such as warmth, mechanical rocking, and feeding, the bonding was even more intense. Clearly, there is a strong parallel between this artificial situation and what often occurs when human infants have contact with the warm bodies of parents who cuddle, rock, and feed them. Harlow's demonstration that attachment does not depend upon feeding should be reassuring to fathers of breast-fed babies.

Effects of Attachment Deprivation   Although Harlow's experiments were aimed at determining whether food was the crucial element in forming attachments, they also provided some valuable information about emotional and social development. One particularly interesting finding has to do with the long-term effects of being raised without a real mother.

Although the young monkeys in Harlow's experiments seemed to develop normally at first, a different picture emerged when the females reached sexual maturity. Despite elaborate efforts to create ideal mating circumstances, most of them rejected the advances of male monkeys, and only four of 18 conceived as a result of natural insemination (many more were artificially inseminated). Most of these "unmothered mothers" rejected their young; some were merely indifferent, while others pushed their babies away. In spite of this rejection, the babies persisted in their attempts to establish a bond with their mothers (and in some situations, they actually succeeded). In subsequent pregnancies, these deprived mothers became more adept at nurturing their offspring.

How does this relate to human behavior? Do human infants deprived of attachment with nurturing caregivers develop in a similar way, and if so, are the emotional scars permanent? Up until the 1970s most developmental psychologists were inclined to answer yes to both of these questions, citing numerous studies of infants raised from birth in orphanages (Bowlby, 1965; Goldfarb, 1945; Ribble, 1943; Spitz, 1945). In these studies, orphanage children who were provided adequate physical care and nutrition but were deprived of close nurturing relationships with adult caregivers often developed problems such as physical diseases of unknown origin, retarded physical and motor development, and impaired emotional and social development. In one study of 91 orphanage infants in the United States and Canada, over a third died before reaching their first birthday, despite good nutrition and medical care (Spitz & Wold, 1946).

These studies clearly demonstrate that an early lack of nurturance can have devastating effects. More recent evidence, however, adds some significant corollaries. Several studies conducted in the 1970s indicate that damage associated with emotional and social deprivation in early infancy can be overcome if the child later receives plenty of loving nurturance (Clarke & Clarke, 1976). Furthermore, as we saw earlier in this chapter, Harlow found that he could reverse, or at least moderate, the effects of early

FIGURE 10.15

Infant monkeys in Harry Harlow's classic experiment maintained contact with the terry-cloth contact-comfort "mother" even when obtaining nourishment from the wire mesh "mother."

environmental impoverishment by providing deprived monkeys with extensive contact with "therapist monkeys" (Novak & Harlow, 1975).

One of the most impressive indications that there is hope for babies deprived of early bonding was provided by evidence collected by Harvard University's Jerome Kagan and his associates. This research team studied a Guatemalan Indian society in which infants routinely spend the first year of their lives confined to small, windowless huts. (Their parents believe that sunlight and fresh air are harmful to babies.) Since the parents are occupied with subsistence tasks, they rarely cuddle, play with, or talk to their babies. The infants are listless, unresponsive, and intellectually retarded, as judged by standards of normal development. However, when they emerge from the dark huts shortly after their first birthdays, they rapidly evolve into youngsters who play, laugh, explore, and become attached just like youngsters who have not been similarly deprived (Kagan & Klein, 1973).

We do not mean to suggest that the effects of early deprivation are always transitory. There is a big difference between being raised from infancy to childhood in a sterile orphanage environment and receiving loving care at age six months, one year, or two years. It is also important to note that all infants who do establish early attachments do not necessarily express this bonding in the same manner. As the following discussion points out, some attachments are more secure than others.

Secure and Insecure Attachments In the effort to find out more about infants' attachments, developmental psychologist Mary Ainsworth (1979) used a laboratory procedure that she labeled the "strange situation." In this procedure, a one-year-old infant's behavior in an unfamiliar environment is assessed under various circumstances—with the mother present, with the mother and a stranger present, with only a stranger present, and totally alone.

Ainsworth discovered that infants react differently to these strange situations. Some, whom she labeled *securely attached*, would use their mothers as a safe base for happily exploring the new environment and playing with the toys in the room. When separated from their mothers they expressed moderate distress, and when reunited they would seek contact, and subsequently stay closer to their mothers. *Insecurely attached* infants reacted differently. They showed more apprehension and less tendency to leave their mothers' sides to explore. They were severely distressed when their mothers left, often crying loudly, and when she returned they often seemed angry, behaving with hostility or indifference.

What accounts for these differences? The answer probably lies in a combination of two factors: parenting practices and the inborn differences among infants themselves. There is good evidence that some infants may be innately predisposed to form more secure attachments than others, just as some newborns seem to respond more positively to being held and cuddled (Thomas & Chess, 1977). A second factor in the babies' different reactions was the way in which their mothers responded to them at home. Mothers of the securely attached babies were inclined to be sensitive and responsive to their babies, noticing what they were doing and responding accordingly. For example, they would feed their infants when they were hungry, rather than following a set schedule. They also tended to cuddle their babies at times other than when feeding and diapering. In contrast, mothers of insecurely attached babies tended to be less sensitive and responsive. For example, they might feed their babies when they felt like it and perhaps ignore the child's cries of hunger at other times. These mothers also tended to avoid close physical contact with their babies. Recent research has also shown that mothers of anxious, insecurely attached children are less likely to become actively involved in the play of their offspring than are mothers of securely attached children (Roggman et al., 1987; Slade, 1987).

The establishment of a trusting, secure attachment between child and parent appears to have demonstrable effects on a child's later development. Several studies have indicated that children who are securely attached by age 18 months are likely to demonstrate much greater social competence as two- to five-year-olds than are insecurely attached babies. In general, securely attached children are more enthusiastic, persistent, cooperative, curious, outgoing, socially involved, competent, and appropriately independent (Arend et al., 1979; Matas et al., 1978; Sroufe, 1985; Sroufe et al., 1983; Waters et al., 1979).

Father-Child Attachment   We have seen that most investigations of attachment have focused on the mother-child bond. This tendency to overlook fathers probably reflects, at least in part, a general societal conception of fathers as less interested in or capable of providing quality child care. In recent years, however, these attitudes have begun to change, and researchers have turned their attention to the role of fathers in their children's early lives.

They have discovered that many fathers form close bonds with their offspring shortly after birth (Greenberg & Morris, 1974), and that most infants form specific attachments to their fathers at about the same time as they establish these relationships with their mothers. This seems to be true even in families where fathers play only a minor role in child care (Lamb, 1979). In one study of interactions between babies aged 12 months or older and their parents, almost half of the infants were equally or more attached to their fathers than to their mothers (Kotelchuck, 1976).

Fathers tend to interact with their children somewhat differently than do mothers. They often spend less time with their children, and that time is more likely to be devoted to play, often of a boisterous nature, than to providing care (Clarke-Stewart, 1978; Lamb, 1979). The differences between maternal and paternal parenting styles seem to be much more related to societal roles than to biologically based sex differences (Lamb, 1981). In fact, when fathers become the primary caregivers, they interact with their babies in the nurturing, gentle fashion typical of mothers (Field, 1978).

PARENTING STYLES AND SOCIAL/EMOTIONAL DEVELOPMENT

Most parents naturally want their children to grow up to be socially and emotionally competent. Certainly there is no shortage of "expert" child-rearing advice, from talk shows, writers of how-to books, parents and in-laws, and well-meaning friends. Unfortunately, much of this advice is based

Fathers tend to interact with their children in a more boisterous manner than do mothers.

on armchair logic rather than solid empirical evidence. However, a good deal of psychological research provides important insights into how different parenting styles affect a child's social and emotional development. In the next few paragraphs we will briefly summarize the evidence.

Research conducted by Stanley Coopersmith (1967) and Diana Baumrind (1971) has identified three specific styles of parenting: permissive, authoritarian, and authoritative. **Permissive** parents are inclined not to control their children, preferring instead to adopt a "hands off" policy. They make few demands and are reluctant to punish inappropriate behavior. Permissiveness sometimes stems at least in part from the parents' indifference or preoccupation with other functions. More commonly, however, permissive parents hope that providing their children with plenty of freedom will encourage the development of self-reliance and initiative.

In sharp contrast to the permissive style of parenting, **authoritarian** parents rely on strictly enforced rules as they try to make their children adhere to their standards. Authoritarian parents tend to be autocratic, leaving little room for discussions of alternative points of view and often using punishments to ensure compliance. Authoritarian parents generally direct minimal warmth, nurturance, or communication toward their children.

The third type of parents, **authoritative** parents, also have definite standards or rules that children are expected to meet. Unlike authoritarian parents, however, they typically solicit their children's opinions during open discussions and rule-making sessions. Although children understand that certain standards of behavior are expected, they are also encouraged to think independently, and they acquire a sense that their viewpoints carry some weight. Both authoritarian and authoritative parenting styles seek to control children's behaviors. However, the former tries to achieve this goal through restrictive control without open communication, while the latter establishes reasonable rules in an atmosphere of warmth and open dialogue.

There is convincing evidence that neither the permissive nor the authoritarian parenting styles are conducive to developing social and emotional competence in children. Children of permissive parents tend to be immature, impulsive, dependent on others, and low in self-esteem. Since they have received so little guidance, they are often indecisive in new situations. Children from authoritarian homes may also have difficulty deciding how to behave, because they are worried about their parents' reactions. Authoritarian-reared children are also less likely to express curiosity and positive emotions, and they tend to have few friends.

It is probably no surprise to you that the most well-adjusted children in these studies tended to be those of authoritative parents. This style of parenting provides a structure reflecting parent's reasonable expectations and realistic standards within an overall atmosphere of love and trust. Perhaps one of the primary reasons why this style is clearly more advantageous is that it provides children the greatest sense of control over their lives. Their participation in family discussions means that the rules that ultimately emerge have been negotiated, rather than being arbitrarily imposed. Also, since authoritative parents tend to enforce rules with consistent, predictable discipline, children are more likely to acquire a sense of control over the consequences of their actions.

A SECOND LOOK AT PARENTING PRACTICES

The evidence presented above suggests that parenting styles influence the social and emotional development of children. While this is likely to be true, there are other conclusions that might be drawn from the data. Can you think of other explanations for why authoritative parenting is associated with social and emotional competence in children? Consider this issue for a few minutes before reading on.

FIRST PERSON 10.6

When I was growing up, my father ruled me and everyone else in the family with an iron hand. When he said to do something, you jumped right to it or suffered the consequences. When I was little, I did everything he said, but I hated his domineering, facist style of expecting unquestioning obedience. I always felt like he was lurking somewhere in the background, ready to pounce if I showed the least signs of independence or nonconformity with his views. My teenage years were really rough as a result of my rebelling against my father's arbitrary authority. It seemed like we were always locking horns. (*Authors' files*)

We have seen that parenting styles seem to influence the behaviors children express as they develop. The evidence is of a correlational nature, however, and, as we learned in Chapter 2, correlation does not necessarily imply cause and effect. Perhaps authoritatively reared children are more socially and emotionally competent because of the manner in which they have been reared. However, it is also possible that some other characteristic coincidentally associated with authoritative parents may be the key factor. For example, parents who raise children in such a reasonable fashion may also have better relationships with one another; thus their children's emotional/social development is likely to progress in a healthy fashion free of the stresses imposed by family conflicts.

It has also been suggested that some of Baumrind's findings could reflect child-to-parent effects rather than parent-to-child effects (Lewis, 1981). Perhaps children who are socially and emotionally well adjusted, for reasons other than parenting practices, may elicit more reasonable, democratic responses from their parents than do children who are less competent and more belligerent.

In all, we cannot conclude with absolute certainty that child-rearing practices influence the social and emotional competence of children. Nevertheless, the evidence certainly indicates a high probability that this is the case.

THE FORMATION OF GENDER IDENTITY AND GENDER ROLES

Gender identity refers to each person's subjective sense that "I am a male" or "I am a female"—an identity that most of us form in the first few years of life. The development of gender identity has been the subject of much research and discussion. How do we come to think of ourselves as male or female? This question has at least two answers. The first centers on biological factors: the most obvious reason we think of ourselves as male or female is our biological sex. The second answer is based on social-learning theory, which says that our identification as either masculine or feminine results primarily from social and cultural influences during our early development.

It seems clear that both biology and social learning help form our gender identity. Certainly there is a wealth of evidence implicating the important role of multiple biological factors in shaping our sense of maleness or femaleness. The chromosomes, gonads, hormones, internal reproductive structures, external genitals, and even the brain all differ from male to female. Under normal circumstances, these factors interact to determine a person's biological sex and, later, to influence the formation of his or her gender identity. However, there is also extensive evidence supporting the important role of social learning in shaping our gender identity, and today virtually all researchers and theorists support an *interactional model* which sees gender identity as the product of a complex interplay of biological and social-learning factors. A discussion of the biological side of this model involves a complexity and quantity of data beyond the scope of this text. However, in the next few pages we will consider some of the evidence pertaining to social-learning factors in gender identity and the socialization of gender roles.

Social-Learning Factors in Gender Identity   At birth, parents label their children male or female with the announcement "It's a boy!" or "It's a girl!" From this point on, people react to children according to their gender-role expectations. Parents typically dress boys and girls differently, decorate their rooms differently, provide them with different toys, and even respond to them differently. For instance, it is common for a child to be told "You are a sweet little girl" or "You are a bright little boy." While small children may not comprehend what makes them biologically male or female, they definitely are not confused about whether they are boys or girls. Just try calling a two-year-old boy a girl, or vice versa, and observe the indignant manner in which you are set straight!

Further evidence supporting the social-learning interpretation is provided by anthropological studies of other cultures. Perhaps the most noteworthy is Margaret Mead's study of three societies in New Guinea (*Sex and Temperament in Three Primitive Societies,* 1963), which reveals that the differences between the sexes that we often assume are innate are not necessarily found in other societies. Among the Mundugumor, Mead reported that both males and females exhibit aggressive behaviors that would be considered masculine in our society. In another society, the Arapesh, both sexes are nonaggressive and nurturing—behaviors that many Americans would judge feminine. In a third society, the Tchambuli, Mead observed a reversal of our typical masculine and feminine gender roles. Tchambuli females tend to be very much in charge, while males are nonassertive and emotionally dependent. Since there is no evidence that people in these societies are biologically different from Americans, it seems that their different masculine and feminine behaviors must result from different social learning.

Some of the most impressive support for the social-learning viewpoint has come from investigations of children whose external genitals represent such a mixture of male and female characteristics that biological sex identification is difficult. (Differentiation of the internal and external sex structures occurs under the influence of timed biological cues. When these signals deviate from normal patterns, the end result can be ambiguous biological sex. People with ambiguous or contradictory sex characteristics are sometimes called *hermaphrodites.*) John Money and his colleagues at Johns Hopkins University have found that in most of the cases they have evaluated, children whose assigned sex did not match their chromosomal sex developed a gender identity consistent with the manner in which they were reared (Money, 1965; Money & Ehrhardt, 1972; Money et al., 1955).

The Socialization of Gender Roles   The issue of gender goes beyond the processes by which we acquire a male or female identity. Society dictates a set of behaviors that are considered normal and appropriate for each sex. These standards are typically labeled **gender roles** or sex roles. How do gender roles arise? At least some behavioral differences between males and females may be related to biological factors such as muscle mass, hormonal variations, and brain differences (Bloom et al., 1985; Diamond, 1977, 1979; Karlen, 1980). Nevertheless, most theorists believe that gender roles are largely the result of socialization (Archer & Lloyd, 1985; Doyle, 1985; Hyde, 1985). **Socialization** refers to the process by which society conveys behavioral expectations to the individual. There are many agents of this socialization process, including parents, peers, textbooks, and television.

Parents have certain preconceived ideas about how boys and girls differ, and they communicate these views to their children from the very beginning. For example, in one study (Rubin et al., 1974) parents were asked to describe their infants within 24 hours of birth. All babies included in this sample were of approximately the same height, weight, and muscle tone. Yet parents of girls tended to describe their daughters as soft, sweet, fine-featured, and delicate. On the other hand, parents of boys used terms like strong, well-coordinated, active, and robust. Such perceptions may well influence the way children learn to think of themselves.

Parents tend to interact differently with boys and girls, also. Baby girls are often treated as if they were more fragile than boys (Doyle, 1985; Fagot, 1978; Tauber, 1979) and they may receive more attention than boy babies (Thoman et al., 1972). Parents often encourage boys to suppress emotion and to be independent and aggressive, while girls are expected to display the opposite characteristics (Armentrout & Burger, 1972; Gagnon, 1977; Hyde, 1985). Although parents are becoming more sensitive to the kinds of toys children play with, many still choose different toys and play

Although parents are becoming more sensitive to the kinds of toys children play with, many still choose different toys and play activities for boys than for girls. Tea sets, dolls, and dollhouses are still common girls' toys, while trucks, toy guns, and footballs are common boys' toys.

activities for boys than for girls (Archer & Lloyd, 1985; Fein et al., 1975). Tea sets, dolls, and dollhouses are still common girls' toys, while boys often receive trucks, toy guns, and footballs. Such parental influences may combine to produce men who are comfortable being assertive and competitive and women who are inclined to be nonassertive and nurturing.

The peer group is another agent of socialization, particularly during late childhood and adolescence (Adams, 1973; Doyle, 1985; Hyde, 1985). Most youths have fairly rigid views of what is gender appropriate and what is not. For girls, being popular and attractive may be very important. In contrast, boys may try to prove their worth on the athletic field. Individuals who do not conform to these traditional roles may be subjected to considerable peer pressure.

Psychologist Eleanor Maccoby (1985) notes another aspect of the peer-group structure among American children that helps perpetuate traditional gender roles. She has observed a pronounced segregation between the sexes that begins very early in life. Research conducted by Maccoby and Carol Jacklin suggests that even preschool children select same-sex playmates about 80 percent of the time. By the time they enter the first grade, children voluntarily select other-sex playmates only about five percent of the time.

Textbooks and television also help develop and perpetuate gender roles. Two major investigations of children's textbooks conducted in the early 1970s found that girls were typically depicted as domestic, dependent, fearful, unambitious, not very successful or clever. In contrast, boys were brave, strong, independent, ambitious, very active (even aggressive), successful, and in charge of their fates (Saario et al., 1973; Women on Words and Images, 1972). In recent years publishers have begun to make an effort to avoid gender stereotypes. For example, one recent study reported that men played the dominant roles in about two out of every three stories in American reading texts in the early 1980s, in contrast with approximately four of five stories featuring men as the key characters in the early 1970s (Britton & Lumpkin, 1984).

There is nothing subtle about the way television portrays gender roles. In a major investigation of the mid-1970s, commercials were found to depict men as authoritative sources on most topics (McArthur & Resko, 1975). A study of prime-time shows also found that women were commonly portrayed as seductive sex objects who were incompetent, domestically inclined, passive, and even unintelligent. In contrast, men were typically shown as competent, intelligent, brave, adventurous, active, and in charge (Women on Words and Images, 1975). There have been few notable changes in the last few years (Atkin, 1982; Kalisch & Kalisch, 1984). However, the relatively recent emergence of several television series that portray women in active, assertive roles (such as "Cagney and Lacey," and "L.A. Law") may signal a slight shift in traditional gender-role programming.

We have seen how family and friends, textbooks, and television all contribute to the development of traditional gender-role assumptions and behavior. Of course, not all people are influenced to the same degree. To some extent, however, we are all affected by gender-role conditioning, and our assumptions about males and females may affect many aspects of our lives.

ERIKSON'S THEORY OF PSYCHOSOCIAL DEVELOPMENT

Our discussion of development would not be complete without a brief outline of Erik Erikson's theory of psychosocial development (1963). Erikson has proposed the only theory of normal development that covers the entire life span. He outlined eight stages of psychosocial development, each of which involves specific personal and social tasks that must be accomplished if development is to proceed in a healthy fashion. Each of the eight stages is defined by a major crisis or conflict, suggesting that an individual's personality is greatly influenced by the success with which each of these sequential conflicts is resolved.

Only the first four stages in Erikson's theory apply strictly to the years of infancy and childhood. We will briefly outline all eight stages here, however, providing a look ahead to Chapter 11.

Stage 1: Trust versus Mistrust During the first stage, which covers the first 12 to 18 months of life, infants acquire either a sense of *basic trust* or a sense of *mistrust*. In this stage, infants acquire a feeling of whether the world is to be trusted, a conclusion that is shaped largely by the manner in which their needs are satisfied. If they are cuddled, comforted, talked to, and fed when hungry, infants are likely to learn to trust their world, but if these interactions are not provided, they will probably become fearful and mistrusting.

Stage 2: Autonomy versus Shame and Doubt Erikson's next major stage occurs between 18 months and three years, when children who have developed a basic trust become ready to assert some of their independence and individuality. How well this task is accomplished determines whether the child will achieve a sense of *autonomy* or a sense of *shame and doubt*.

During this stage, children learn to walk, talk, and do other things for themselves. Parents who encourage and reinforce these efforts can foster a sense of autonomy and independence. In contrast, when parents are overprotective, or when they disapprove of a child's initiative, the child is likely to become doubtful, hesitant, and perhaps ashamed.

Stage 3: Initiative versus Guilt Between about age three and five, children broaden their horizons by exploring new situations and meeting new people. During this stage, a conflict exists between children's taking the *initiative* to strike out on their own, and the potential *guilt* they will feel if this offends their parents. Parents who encourage inquisitiveness make it easier for a child to express such healthy behaviors, while those who actively discourage such actions may contribute to their children's ambivalence or even guilt about striking out on their own.

Stage 4: Industry versus Inferiority The next stage extends from about age six to 11. At this point, children are much more involved in learning to master intellectual, social, and physical skills. The peer group becomes much more important during this time, as children constantly evaluate their abilities and compare them to those of their peers. If their assessments are positive, they may contribute to a sense of *industry* or achievement. In contrast, a poor self-assessment is likely to induce feelings of *inferiority*. Parents and other adult caregivers can help a child develop a sense of industry by encouraging participation in a variety of tasks that are challenging without being too difficult, and by reinforcing a child for completing such tasks.

Stage 5: Identity versus Role Confusion The next conflict occurs during adolescence, from approximately ages 12 to 18. Now an individual's major task is to secure a stable *identity*. According to Erikson, this is the time when we must integrate all of our experiences in order to develop a sense of "who I am." Young people who are unable to reconcile all of their various roles (as a dependent child, independent initiator of industrious actions, and so forth) into one enduring, stable identity experience *role confusion*.

Stage 6: Intimacy versus Isolation As adolescents emerge into young adulthood, they now face the task of achieving *intimacy*. According to Erikson, an adult who has previously achieved a stable identity is often able to form close, meaningful relationships in which intimacy can be shared with significant others. Failure to achieve intimacy is likely to result in a sense of *isolation* in which the young adult may be reluctant to establish close ties with anyone else.

Erik Erikson

Stage 7: Generativity versus Stagnation The middle years of adulthood are characterized by still another conflict, this one between *generativity* and *stagnation*. Here, our central task is to determine our purpose or goal in life, and to focus on achieving aims and contributing to the well-being of others, particularly children. People who successfully resolve this conflict establish clear guidelines for their lives and are generally productive and happy with this directive framework. In contrast, individuals who fail to accomplish these goals by the middle years of life are likely to become self-centered and stagnated in personal growth.

Stage 8: Ego Integrity versus Despair Erikson's final stage extends into the older years of life. This phase of development is characterized by extensive reflection on our past accomplishments and failures. According to Erikson, individuals who can reflect on a lifetime of purpose, accomplishments, and warm, intimate relationships will find *ego integrity* in their final years. In contrast, people whose lives have been characterized by lack of purpose, disappointments, and failures are likely to develop a strong sense of *despair*.

Erikson's theory has been praised for recognizing the importance of sociocultural influences on development, and because it encompasses the entire life span. However, many of Erikson's assertions are so nebulous that they are virtually impossible to test.

SUMMARY

SOME DEVELOPMENTAL ISSUES

1. Contemporary developmental theorists believe that humans are the products of both nature and nurture, and they are interested in how genetics and experience interact to shape development and the expression of human behavior.

2. Psychologists who emphasize the role of learning have tended to view development as a gradual, continuous process in which individuals undergo qualitative changes over the life span as they accumulate experiences. In contrast, psychologists who emphasize maturation (the orderly unfolding of certain genetically determined behaviors) view development as a discontinuous process that occurs in a series of stages.

3. Most contemporary psychologists agree that the concept of critical periods in infant development, at least when applied to emotional, intellectual, and behavioral traits, lacks supporting evidence.

HOW DEVELOPMENT IS STUDIED

4. Three research designs have been widely used in the study of development: the cross-sectional, longitudinal, and cross-sequential methods.

5. In the cross-sectional design, groups of subjects of different ages are assessed and compared at one point in time, and the researcher draws conclusions about behavior differences that may be related to age differences.

6. The longitudinal design evaluates behavior in the same group of people at several points in time, to assess what kinds of changes occur over the long term.

7. Subjects in a study employing the cross-sequential design are observed more than once, but over a shorter span of time than is typical of longitudinal studies.

THE BEGINNINGS OF LIFE

8. Life begins when the germ cells (sperm & ovum) unite to produce a zygote. The zygote contains a complement of 46 chromosomes arranged in 23 pairs, one chromosome in each pair from the sperm and one from the egg.

9. Chromosomes are composed of thousands of genes, the chemical blueprints that determine physical characteristics and influence behavioral traits.

10. The assortment of genes we inherit at conception is known as our genotype; the characteristics that result from expression of various genotypes are known as phenotypes.

11. A dominant gene is one that is always expressed in the phenotype; a recessive gene is one that may be expressed only in the absence of a dominant gene, or when it is paired with a similar recessive gene.

12. Many sex-linked diseases are more common in males than females because only a single dose of the defect-causing gene on the X chromosome is necessary to cause the disease. (The gene-deficient Y chromosome does not carry a gene that may counteract this adverse factor.)

13. About five percent of babies born each year in the United States have some gene defect or chromosomal abnormality that produces a physical and/or mental handicap.

14. Huntington's disease is caused by a dominant gene that does not cause symptoms until a person is 35 to 45 years old.

15. Recombinant DNA technology allows researchers to map microscopic strands of genetic material for indicators of disease.

16. Phenylketonuria (PKU) is a potentially devastating genetic disease, characterized by mental retardation and other disruptive symptoms, that is caused by a recessive gene.

17. Down's syndrome, the most common chromosomal disorder, is an autosomal chromosome disorder in which the 21st chromosome pair has an additional chromosome attached to it.

18. The idea behind genetic counseling is that it is often

possible to estimate the odds that a couple will have children with certain disorders.

19. Techniques for assessing fetal development and diagnosing birth defects in utero include amniocentesis and chorionic villi sampling (CVS).

20. Genetic engineering, sometimes called gene therapy, involves using recombinant DNA techniques to insert a new gene into cells to alter and correct a defective genetic code.

PRENATAL DEVELOMENT

21. The approximately nine months of prenatal development takes place in three stages: germinal (the first two weeks after fertilization), embryonic (beginning of the third week to the end of the eighth), and fetal (from the beginning of the third month to birth).

22. Addictive drugs, alcohol, tobacco, and a multitude of medications can cross through the placenta and damage the developing fetus. No drugs should be used during pregnancy unless absolutely necessary and taken under close medical supervision.

PHYSICAL DEVELOPMENT FROM BIRTH TO THE END OF CHILDHOOD

23. Brain growth is very rapid in the early years of life. At age six months the brain is 50 percent of its adult size; by age five it has reached 90 percent of its adult size.

24. Hemispheric specialization begins very early during infancy.

25. Research has revealed anatomical and biochemical brain changes associated with improved cortical functioning in animals exposed to environmental enrichment.

26. Children grow more rapidly during the first few years than at any other time.

27. Both physical growth and motor development follow two basic patterns: cephalocaudal (that is, from head to foot), and proximodistal (inner to outer).

28. Motor development follows a pattern of progression from the simple to the more complex.

29. Within a normal range of experiences, the role of environmental influences on motor development is quite limited.

COGNITIVE DEVELOPMENT FROM BIRTH TO THE END OF CHILDHOOD

30. Piaget formulated the concepts of schemas, assimilation, and accommodation to explain how we organize incoming information (schemas), interpret it in accordance with existing schemas (assimilation), and restructure it to fit better with already existing schemas (accommodation).

31. Piaget viewed cognitive growth as a four-stage process with qualitatively different kinds of thinking occurring in each of these four stages: the sensorimotor, preoperational, concrete operations, and formal operations.

32. During the sensorimotor stage (birth to about 24 months), infants learn about their worlds primarily through their senses and actions.

33. The preoperational stage (ages two to seven) is characterized by an increasing use of symbolic thought, language, and imaginative play. However, children at this stage have yet to master logical reasoning processes based on rules and concepts and have difficulty taking into account more than one perceptual factor at the same time.

34. Between ages seven and 12 children in the concrete-operations stage again make a qualitative leap as they begin to use logical mental operations or rules. However, children in this stage are not yet able to deal with completely hypothetical problems.

35. In the formal-operations stage (ages 12 and older) individuals acquire the ability to think abstractly and to make complex deductions and solve problems by systematically testing hypothetical solutions.

PSYCHOSOCIAL DEVELOPMENT FROM INFANCY TO THE END OF CHILDHOOD   *Erikson*

36. Attachment is the term applied to the intense emotional tie that develops between infants and their parents or other consistent caregiver. The most intense attachment relationship that typically occurs in the early stages of development is between mother and child.

37. Research suggests that satisfaction of contact comfort is more important in establishing attachment than is gratification of being fed.

38. Infants deprived of early attachment with nurturing caregivers may suffer serious developmental difficulties. However, there is evidence that damage associated with deprivation in early infancy can be overcome by ample loving nurturance during childhood.

39. In general children who are securely attached to their mothers or other caregivers demonstrate a more healthy picture of psychosocial adjustment than children who are insecurely attached.

40. Research has shown that most infants form specific attachments to their fathers at about the same time as they establish these relationships with their mothers.

41. The authoritative style of parenting is much more conducive to developing social and emotional competence in children than either the permissive or authoritarian parenting style.

42. The formation of gender identity—each person's subjective sense of maleness or femaleness—occurs in the first few years of life as the result of a complex interplay of biological and social-learning factors.

43. Society dictates a set of behaviors that are considered normal and appropriate for each sex. These standards are typically labeled gender roles or sex roles.

44. Socialization refers to the process by which society conveys behavioral expectations to the individual. The many agents of this socialization process include parents, peers, textbooks, and television.

45. Erik Erikson's theory of psychosocial development outlines eight stages that people pass through during their journey through life: trust versus mistrust (birth to 18 months); autonomy versus shame and doubt (18 months to three years); initiative versus guilt (age three to five); industry versus inferiority (age six to 11); identity versus role confusion (ages 12 to 18); intimacy versus isolation (early adulthood); generativity versus stagnation (middle years of adulthood); and ego integrity versus despair (older years).

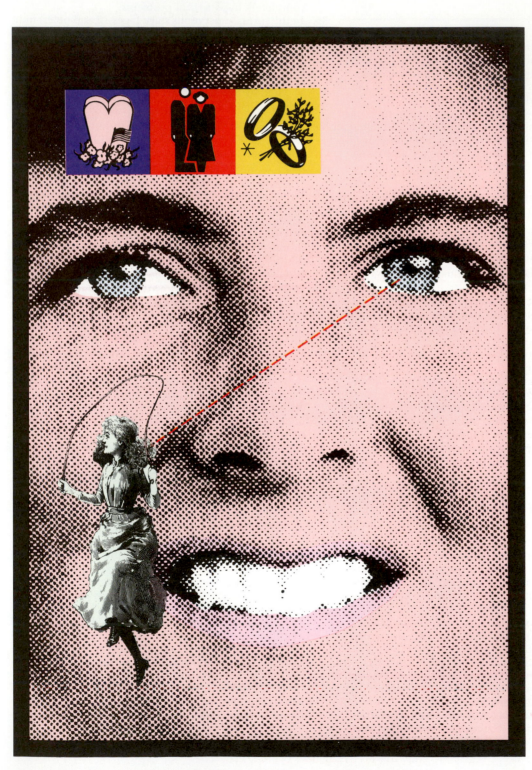

11 Development from Adolescence to the End of Life

Although the experiences expressed in the first-person account in the margin are not common to all adolescents in our society (we will see in this chapter that there is no such thing as a "typical adolescence"), it is probably fair to say that most of us have some painful memories of our teenage years. It is also a fair prediction that most of us will experience a certain degree of conflict at other transitions in our lives, for the ages of 30, 40, 60 and so on are all milestones that may seem to us to mark the closing of one phase of our lives or the entrance into another.

Whether the transition be the entrance into adulthood, middle age, or the older years, much of the conflict we experience has to do with our images or expectations for the "new era" we are entering. How accurate are these images? Certainly not all adolescents go through a period of "storm and stress," nor do all young adults embark on a career and start a family. For that matter, not all older adults fit our society's characterizations of old age. As we explore adolescent and adult development in this chapter, one of the most interesting findings will be the diversity with which individuals experience various "ages and stages." Perhaps the most striking diversity occurs during adolescence, and we begin by examining this transitional period.

ADOLESCENCE

Adolescence is a time of dramatic physiological change and social-role development. In Western societies, it is the transition between childhood and adulthood that typically spans ages 12 to 20. Although most major physical changes take place during the first few years of adolescence, important and often profound changes in behavior and expectations occur throughout the period.

By cross-cultural standards, the prolonged period of adolescence in America and other modern Western societies is unusual. In many nonindustrial societies, adolescence is considered to be either nonexistent or nothing more than a period of rapid physical changes leading to sexual maturity. In such societies, the transition from child to adult is often marked by some sort of "rite of passage" (Dunham et al., 1986). Even in our own society, adolescence is a relatively recent phenomenon. Before schooling requirements were extended through high school early in this century, children were often expected to join the work force when they became teenagers.

Our society has no single initiation rite that signals passage into adulthood. Instead, a variety of signposts may herald this transition, including graduation from high school or college, moving away from home, securing a full-time job, or establishing an intimate, monogamous relationship.

Just as there is no one rite of passage into adulthood, in many ways there is no "typical" adolescence. Much has been written about the many conflicts and dilemmas faced by teenagers. However, the teenage years can also be a rewarding, relaxing, and exciting time of life, free from the stresses and responsibilities that come with adulthood. For most of us, adolescence probably varied between a time of anxiety and stress and a time of freedom and optimism—depending on what day we were asked. Although we cannot describe a "typical" adolescence, we can describe some of the common physical, cognitive, and psychosocial changes that most teenagers experience.

PHYSICAL DEVELOPMENT DURING ADOLESCENCE

Puberty (from the Latin *pubescere*, to be covered with hair) describes the approximately two-year period of rapid physical changes that culminate in sexual maturity. In our society, the onset of puberty in girls generally occurs sometime between ages 7 and 14, with the average about age 10. Boys typically enter puberty two years later at about age 12, with a normal range of 9 to 16 (Chumlea, 1982).

Physical Changes during Puberty   As we saw in Chapter 10, the first few years of life are marked by rapid growth. With adolescence, children enter a second period of accelerated growth, often called the **adolescent growth spurt,** which usually runs its course in the two years following the onset of puberty. Sexual maturity is reached soon after the growth spurt ends.

The physical changes that occur during puberty are quite dramatic and rapid. Suddenly the body a person has inhabited for years undergoes a mysterious transformation. What causes these changes? One important factor is a genetically determined timetable that causes the pituitary gland to trigger the rapid growth that takes place at the start of adolescence (Brodzinsky et al., 1986). The hypothalamus also increases production of chemicals that stimulate the pituitary to release larger amounts of **gonadotropins**—hormones that stimulate production of testosterone in men and estrogen in women. The resulting developments (breasts, deepened voice, and facial, body, and pubic hair) are called **secondary sex characteristics.** The timetable that governs these processes may also be influenced by environmental factors as well as by an individual's health.

EXPLAINING THE DECLINING AGE OF PUBERTY

In many societies throughout the world, young people are entering puberty and achieving sexual maturity sooner than their parents did. There has also been an upward trend in overall height and weight of these populations. This trend has not been observed in many preindustrial societies. Why do you suppose children in the United States and many other societies are maturing earlier and growing bigger than their ancestors? What factors might account for these trends? Give this question some thought before reading on.

We cannot be certain about what causes **secular growth trends,** changes in human physical growth patterns (including height, weight, and rates of maturation) measured in sample populations of people throughout the world. However, the most likely cause is the improved standard of living in societies where these changes have been observed. Over the last several decades, children in such diverse places as Japan, New Zealand, China, the United States, and Western Europe have experienced increasingly better nourishment and improved health care during their childhood years. The fact that physical and sexual maturity is taking place at a later age in many preindustrial societies today tends to support the view that secular growth trends in the West are related to improved nourishment and health care (Eveleth & Tanner, 1976).

Effects of Early and Late Maturation Adolescents are often very concerned with what other people think of them, and anything that sets them apart from the crowd is likely to have a notable impact on their psychosocial adjustment. Thus, it is not surprising that being either the first or the last to go through puberty can cause a good deal of self-consciousness. The timing of physical and sexual maturity may also have an important influence on psychosocial adjustment, especially for males.

A number of studies have shown that early maturation often holds some advantages for boys. Males who mature early tend to be more poised, easygoing, and good-natured; they are also more likely to be school leaders, better at sports, more popular, and more successful academically (and later vocationally). However, early maturers may find it difficult to live up to expectations that they should act mature just because they happen to have adultlike bodies. In addition, being thrust into adolescence at such an early age shortens the period of transition from childhood. Early maturers tend to be more bound by rules and routines, more conventional in career and lifestyle choices, more cautious, and more inclined to worry about what other people think of them (Jones, 1957, 1958; Mussen & Jones, 1957; Peskin, 1973; Siegel, 1982).

In general, late-maturing boys are more likely to be inappropriately aggressive and rebellious against adult authority; they may also lack self-confidence, feeling inadequate and insecure. On the other hand, late-maturing males tend to be more flexible during their youth and more insightful, independent, and less bound to conventional lifestyles and routines later on (Livson & Peskin, 1980; Musen & Jones, 1957; Peskin, 1967, 1973; Siegel, 1982). A few of the differences between early and late maturers may persist into the adult years, but most disappear or are compensated for by the development of other traits.

For girls, early maturation generally seems to be less advantageous than for boys (Brooks-Gunn & Petersen, 1983; Peterson, 1979). Early-maturing girls are bigger than practically all the boys their age; they also look more grown-up than most of the girls their age. As a consequence, they may feel terribly conspicuous at a time of life when they would most like to blend in with the crowd. Because they are so advanced physically, they are

FIRST PERSON 11.3

A man remembers his adolescence: I was the first one to get hair on my chest. At first I would cut it off so I wasn't different from everyone else in the shower room. (*Authors' Files*)

A woman remembers her adolescence: All my friends had started menstruating a long time before and I still had not. I started wearing pads and a belt once a month so I wouldn't feel so out of it. (*Authors' files*)

Early-maturing girls are bigger than practically all the boys their age, and they may feel terribly conspicuous at a time of life when they would most like to blend in with the crowd.

often shunned by their peers. As a result, many early-maturing girls tend to be more introverted and less sociable than girls who mature at a later age (Jones, 1958; Peskin, 1973). They also may have to deal with parents and other caregivers who react to their early sexual development by being overly restrictive. However, these disadvantages are short-lived, and early-maturing girls often are as well (or even better) adjusted in their adult years as are girls who mature later (Jones & Musen, 1958; Livson & Peskin, 1980; Peskin, 1973).

COGNITIVE DEVELOPMENT DURING ADOLESCENCE

Although the most obvious changes of adolescence are physical, significant changes also take place in the way we think. With adolescence, individuals acquire the ability to think abstractly. Teenagers can engage in hypothetical reasoning, imagining all kinds of possibilities in a given situation. They also begin to approach problems more systematically and logically rather than relying upon trial-and-error strategies.

Formal Operations As we saw in Chapter 10, Piaget maintained that most people enter the formal-operations stage sometime around age 12. This stage of cognitive development is marked by the emergence of the capacity to manipulate objects mentally, even when they are not physically present, and by the ability to engage in deductive reasoning. Deductive reasoning requires mental manipulations of complex thoughts and concepts. Piaget devised the *pendulum problem* to illustrate deductive reasoning in the formal-operations stage. Here, a child is shown a pendulum consisting of an object suspended from a string. The child is then shown how to manipulate four variables: the length of the string, the weight of the suspended object, the height in the pendulum arc from which the object is released, and the force with which the object is pushed. Then the child is instructed to determine which of these factors, singly or in combination, influences how fast the object swings.

Piaget discovered that typical seven- or eight-year-olds try to solve the problem by physically manipulating the four variables in a random fashion. For instance, they might release a light weight from high in the arc, then release a heavy weight from a low point in the arc. Because they did not systematically test each variable, these younger children often arrived at erroneous conclusions (and then insisted that their answers were correct!). At age 10 or 11, children are more systematic in their approach, but they still lack the capacity to engage in careful hypothesis testing and deductive logic.

By adolescence, perhaps as early as age 12, children's strategies change radically. Now they systematically keep one variable constant while manipulating the others. In this fashion, they can deduce that only one factor (the length of the string) determines how fast the pendulum swings. Formal-operations adolescents also tend to work out a plan or strategy for approaching the pendulum problem before commencing their tests. The ability to think a problem through mentally before actually performing any concrete physical manipulations represents a major qualitative change in cognitive functioning.

Some Implications of Formal-Operations Thinking These new-found cognitive abilities have important implications for the way adolescents perceive their world. With their increased ability to think logically and abstractly, teenagers often detect what they consider to be logical inconsistencies in other people's thinking, and they may be impatient with the thought processes and decisions of others. Adolescents also may question their own judgments, and the result of this is often confusion.

Adolescence is also a time when individuals begin to ponder and debate such complex issues as social justice, the meaning of life, the validity

---

FIRST PERSON 11.4

I remember going through a period of disillusionment with my parents when I was about 14 or 15. All of a sudden it dawned on me that they were far from perfect. In fact, I realized that some of their actions were quite hypocritical. For example, my Dad and Mom were always harping on honesty as a virtue. But one day they received a bill for several pieces of furniture in which the store had made an error by not including one item in the billing. I remember them gleefully saying that there was some justice in the world after all since the store had made too big a profit on the other furniture they were billed for. This is how they rationalized ripping the furniture company off. Some lesson in honesty, huh? Here were two people who were obviously not practicing what they preached. (*Authors' files*)

of religious dogma, and the value of material wealth. No longer constrained by personal experiences and concrete reality, teenagers can mentally explore all kinds of "what if" possibilities. They may feel compelled to contribute to ending human misery, poverty, social injustice, and war. During this time of zealous, idealistic thinking, many adolescents are vulnerable to charismatic leaders with utopian solutions to the world's problems. This is why some extreme religious movements, communal societies, and political philosophies gain so many adolescent converts. As adolescents grow older, however, much of their idealism is replaced with a more pragmatic or practical view.

In Chapter 10 we explored some criticisms of Piaget's theory, but we did not specifically discuss criticisms of his formal-operations stage. A number of developmentalists have challenged Piaget's ideas about when this stage occurs. Researchers have found that the transition to formal operations does not necessarily occur rather abruptly at the onset of adolescence, for even relatively young children often demonstrate rudiments of logical thinking (Ennis, 1982; Keating, 1980). In addition, adolescents (and even adults) often revert to nonlogical thinking as they deal with issues and problems. Thus, unlike the sudden and dramatic physical changes of adolescence, the shift to formal operations is often gradual, spanning late childhood and adolescence and perhaps even extending into the adult years.

Some critics have also argued that many adolescents and adults never attain the level of formal operations logic (Kohlberg & Gilligan, 1971; Scribner, 1977). Piaget anticipated this criticism by noting that even though adolescents may attain the level of brain maturation necessary for abstract reasoning and logical thinking, they may never achieve the formal operations stage unless they are provided with adult models of formal reasoning and schooled in the principles of logic. Thus both neurological maturation and specific training may be necessary for higher cognitive development. As we will see in the following section, whether we reach formal operations or not may have a profound influence on another area of development, moral development.

MORAL DEVELOPMENT DURING ADOLESCENCE

When we begin life, we are all *amoral*: We do not yet have even the rudiments of moral judgment. By the time we become adults, however, most of us possess a complex notion of *morality*. Morality is a system of personal values and judgments about the fundamental rightness or wrongness of acts, and of our obligations to behave in just ways that do not interfere with the rights of others. How do we evolve from amoral to moral, from a total lack of understanding our responsibilities to others to a complex perception of right and wrong?

Kohlberg's Theory of Moral Development   This question has occupied the attention of a number of developmental theorists, most notably Lawrence Kohlberg (1964, 1968, 1969, 1981, 1984). Kohlberg was more interested in the ways in which thinking about right and wrong change with age than the specific things that children might consider to be right or wrong. For example, whether we are 8, 16, or 32, most of us would say that it is wrong to break society's laws. However, our reasons for not breaking the law, as well as our views about whether we might be justified in breaking the law under some circumstances, might change drastically as we develop.

To learn how this change takes place, Kohlberg devised a series of moral dilemmas that typically involved a choice between two alternatives, both of which would generally be considered unacceptable by society's standards. Heinz's dilemma is an example:

> In Europe a woman was near death from a special kind of cancer. There was one drug that the doctors thought might save her. It was a form of radium that a druggist in the same town had recently discovered. The

drug was expensive to make, but the druggist was charging ten times what the drug cost him to make. He paid $200 for the radium and charged $2,000 for a small dose of the drug. The sick woman's husband, Heinz, went to everyone he knew to borrow the money, but he could only get together $1,000 which is half of what it cost. He told the druggist that his wife was dying and asked him to sell it cheaper or let him pay later. But the druggist said, "No, I discovered the drug, and I am going to make money from it." So Heinz got desperate and broke into the man's store to steal the drug for his wife. (1969, p. 379)

What is your reaction to this story? Kohlberg would not be interested in whether you thought Heinz was right or wrong. (In fact, either answer could demonstrate the same level of moral development.) Instead, Kohlberg was interested in the process you used to reach your judgment, for your reasoning would indicate how advanced your moral thinking is.

Kohlberg asked his subjects a series of questions about each moral dilemma, then used a complex scoring system to assign a subject to a particular category or stage of moral reasoning. This approach led him to formulate a theory of moral development in which he proposed that we move through as many as six stages of moral reasoning that traverse three basic levels: preconventional, conventional, and postconventional.

According to Kohlberg, most children between ages four and 10 have a **preconventional morality,** a kind of self-serving approach to right and wrong. In *stage 1* of preconventional morality, children behave in certain ways in order to avoid being punished; during *stage 2,* they behave in certain ways to obtain rewards. At this lowest level of moral development, children have not internalized a personal code of morality. Rather, they are molded by the standards of adult caregivers and the consequences of adhering to or rejecting these rules.

By late childhood or early adolescence, a person's sense of right and wrong typically matures to the level of **conventional morality.** Here, the motivating force behind behaving in a just or moral fashion is the desire either to help others and gain their approval (*stage 3*) or to help maintain the social order (*stage 4*). As children and young adolescents progress through these stages, they begin to internalize the moral standards of valued adult role models.

A few individuals, particularly those who become adept at the abstract reasoning of formal operational thought, may progress to the final level of **postconventional morality.** *Stage 5* of postconventional morality affirms values agreed upon by society, including individual rights and the need for democratically determined rules; in *stage 6,* individuals are guided by universal ethical principles in which they do what they think is right as a matter of conscience, even if their acts conflict with society's rules. Table 11.1 summarizes Kohlberg's six stages of moral reasoning and illustrates how an individual at each stage might respond to the story about Heinz.

A person may progress from conventional to postconventional morality any time during adolescence. However, Kohlberg maintained that only about 25 percent of adults in our society progress beyond stage 4, and that most of these individuals do so sometime during their adult years.

Evaluating Kohlberg's Theory Kohlberg's theory is an impressive attempt to account systematically for the development of moral reasoning. His writings have also provided some guidelines for implementing moral education for children and adolescents. He suggests that people are often encouraged to advance to higher, more mature levels of moral reasoning through exposure to the more advanced moral reasoning of others, and that moral reasoning may develop at a faster rate and achieve a higher pinnacle if children have frequent opportunities to confront moral challenges. Parents and educators might take a cue from these suggestions by arranging for frequent moral consciousness-raising experiences during the developmental years of childhood and adolescence.

TABLE 11.1 *Kohlberg's Levels and Stages of Moral Development with Stage-Graded Answers to the Story of Heinz*

Stage Description	Examples of Moral Reasoning Favoring Heinz's Thievery	Examples of Moral Reasoning Opposing Heinz's Thievery
Level One—Preconventional Morality		
Stage 1: Punishment and Obedience Orientation (the consequences of acts determines if they are good or bad)	He should steal the drug because he offered to pay for it and because it is only worth $200 and not the $2,000 the druggist was charging. He should steal it because if he lets his wife die he would get in trouble.	He shouldn't steal the drug because it is a big crime. He shouldn't steal the drug because he would get caught and sent to jail.
Stage 2: Instrumental Orientation (an act is moral if it satisfies one's needs)	It is all right to steal the drug because his wife needs it to live and he needs her companionship. He should steal the drug because his wife needs it and he isn't doing any harm to the druggist because he can pay him back later.	He shouldn't steal the drug because he might get caught and his wife would probably die before he gets out of prison, so it wouldn't do him much good. He shouldn't steal it because the druggist was not doing a bad thing by wanting to make a profit.
Level Two—Conventional Morality		
Stage 3: Good Person Orientation (an action is moral if it pleases or helps others and leads to approval)	He should steal the drug because society expects a loving husband to help his wife regardless of the consequences. He should steal the drug because if he didn't his family and others would think he was an inhuman, uncaring husband.	He shouldn't steal the drug because he will bring dishonor on his family and they will be ashamed of him. He shouldn't steal the drug because no one would blame him for doing everything that he could legally. The druggist, and not Heinz, will be considered to be the heartless one.
Stage 4: Maintaining the Social Order Orientation (moral people are those who do their duty in order to maintain the social order)	He should steal the drug because if he did nothing he would be responsible for his wife's death. He should take it with the idea of paying the druggist back. He should steal the drug because if people like the druggist are allowed to get away with being greedy and selfish, society would eventually break down.	He should not steal the drug because if people are allowed to take the law into their own hands, regardless of how justified such an act might be, the social order would soon break down. He shouldn't steal the drug because it's still always wrong to steal and his law-breaking would cause him to feel guilty.
Level Three—Postconventional Morality		
Stage 5: Social Contract and Individual Rights Orientation (a moral person carefully weighs individual rights against society's need for consensus rules)	The theft is justified because the law is not set up to deal with circumstances in which obeying it would cost a human life. It is not reasonable to say the stealing is wrong, because the law should not allow the druggist to deny someone's access to a life-saving treatment. In this case it is more reasonable for him to steal the drug than to obey the law.	You could not really blame him for stealing the drug, but even such extreme circumstances do not justify a person taking the law into his own hands. The ends do not always justify the means. He shouldn't steal the drug because eventually he would pay the price of loss of self-respect for disregarding society's rules.
Stage 6: Universal Ethical Principles Orientation (the ultimate judge of what is moral is a person's own conscience operating in accordance with certain universal principles. Society's rules are arbitrary and they may be broken when they conflict with universal moral principles.)	He must steal the drug because when a choice must be made between disobeying a law and saving a life, one must act in accordance with the higher principle of preserving and respecting life. Heinz is justified in stealing the drug because if he had failed to act in this fashion to save his wife, he would not have lived up to his own standards of conscience.	Heinz must consider the other people who need the drug just as much as his wife. By stealing the drug he would be acting in accordance with his own particular feelings with utter disregard for the value of all the lives involved. He should not steal the drug because even though he would probably not be blamed by others he would have to deal with his own self-condemnation because he had not lived up to his own conscience and standards of honesty.

I have always believed that next to developing a unlimited capacity for love and compassion, a child should be encouraged to develop a clear sense of moral justice. Consequently, from the time my children were able to sit down and have a reasonable conversation, I have tried to convey my moral values whenever the right situations occur. For example, I recall a time when I was shopping with both my son and daughter, ages 8 and 10. When we got back to the car I realized that the cashier had given me too much change. I told my kids what had happened and asked what they thought I should do. My son thought I should keep it because it was the store's mistake; also, they would never know they had given me too much money. My daughter said that I should give it back because they might realize later they had given me too much change and my not returning it could make me look bad. My daughter had the right answer but the wrong reason. We sat in the car for a couple of minutes as I explained that keeping the money, while not quite like stealing, was still dishonest. We also talked about how "getting away with something" that was not right would ultimately make us feel bad: we can sometimes fool someone else but we can never fool ourselves. I also pointed out that if we kept the money it might hurt someone else, for the cashier might have to make up the cash shortfall at the end of the day. When we went back to the store and returned the money, the cashier's positive response helped to reinforce this lesson in morality. (*Authors' files*)

Recently, John Snarey (1987) reported his evaluation of data obtained from 45 studies conducted in 27 diverse world cultures that "provide striking support for the universality of Kohlberg's first four stages" (p. 8). However, Snarey did find some cultural diversity in the expression of moral principles beyond stage 4.

Kohlberg's theory has been criticized for a number of reasons. Some critics argue that a high level of moral reasoning does not necessarily go hand in hand with moral actions, especially if a person is under strong social pressure (Blasi, 1980; Kurtines & Greif, 1974). This was demonstrated in an experiment conducted by Stanford's David Rosenhan (1973). At the first stage of this study, Kohlberg's assessment procedures were used to classify subjects according to their level of moral reasoning. Next, each subject became the "teacher" in a replication of Stanley Milgram's classic study of obedience (see Chapter 2), in which "teacher"-subjects administered what they thought were electric shocks to learners who gave incorrect answers. Rosenhan found that even some subjects who scored at the highest level of moral development, stage 6, still delivered the full 450 volts to learners who gave incorrect responses. (In all fairness to Kohlberg, we must point out that stage 6 subjects were less likely to continue to the maximum of 450 volts than were subjects at the lowest stages of Kohlberg's scheme.)

Other critics take issue with Kohlberg's assertion that postconventional morality is somehow preferable to conventional morality. Since most adults in our society never reach these stages, these critics argue that widespread moral education programs designed to take people to the sixth stage of moral development could have disastrous results. They ask, where would we be if most people chose to act according to individual moral principles with little regard for society's rules? (Shweder, 1982)

PSYCHOSOCIAL DEVELOPMENT IN ADOLESCENCE

In addition to the physical, cognitive, and moral developments of adolescence, there are also significant social and psychological changes. During this period, relationships with parents may be under stress, the peer group may become of paramount importance in influencing behavior, and there is an increased interest in sexual behavior. Perhaps the most important task an adolescent faces is to answer the question, "Who am I"?

Identity Formation Considering the tremendous diversity of possible answers to questions such as "Who am I?" and "Where am I headed?" it is understandable that a great deal of experimentation takes place during adolescence. This experimentation often takes the form of trying out different roles or "selves"—which explains the unpredictability of many teenagers who behave in different ways from one day to the next.

By experimenting with different roles, many adolescents eventually forge a functional and comfortable sense of self. For some, this process takes place with little conflict or confusion. Parents of these young people may wonder why such a fuss is made over the supposedly rebellious teenage years. Other parents may feel like tearing out their hair as their adolescent children blaze their own trails in unexpected directions.

The rapid social changes in contemporary society have greatly complicated the task of achieving a sense of identity. Not only traditional gender roles, but also values associated with religion, marriage, and patriotism are being challenged in society today. Perhaps as a result, several recent studies have found that contemporary adolescents continue to struggle with their identity crises well into their college years (Archer, 1982; Waterman, 1982). In fact, as we shall see in this chapter, our sense of identity is likely to be modified and recast throughout our lives. However, it is during the glorious and confusing years of our adolescence that most of us first acquire a genuine appreciation of who we are and what we might become.

The Role of Parents and the Peer Group An important part of establishing an identity is gaining independence from parents (Douvan, 1986). Although this process begins long before adolescence, it is accelerated during the teenage years. As parental influence diminishes, the peer group's influence grows (Brown et al., 1986a, 1986b). This does not necessarily mean that relationships between parents and their teenage children will take a nose dive. The popular image of the teenage years as a time of rebellion and intergenerational warfare is more myth than fact, and most teen-

FIRST PERSON 11.6

I never know from day to day which of my daughter's personalities I will be dealing with. She is like a chameleon—one day sweet, philosophical, and interested in "adult" conversation about things like religion and the purpose of life. And then the next day she will bring chums home from school and suddenly she is transformed into an obnoxious person whose attitude toward me can be summarized by two words: "get lost." Another thing that drives me crazy is the way she changes her hair style or the way she dresses about as often as the wind changes direction. I hope she figures out who she is pretty soon so that her behavior will at least take on some semblance of consistency. (*Authors' files*)

HEALTH PSYCHOLOGY AND LIFE

MAINTAINING HEALTHY PARENT-TEEN RELATIONSHIPS

While most readers are probably not yet parents, the odds are that many of you will have teenage children at some future point. Perhaps at that time you may recall some of the following potentially helpful suggestions for maintaining good communication and positive relationships. Some of these guidelines are adapted from a publication of the National Institute of Mental Health (1981) and some are our own suggestions.

1. Teenagers need to question the values and viewpoints of their parents and other adults as part of their search for identity. At the same time, however, they want and need consistency in the rules and standards established by their parents. Although parents may be tempted to compromise their own rules of behavior in order to defuse conflicts temporarily, this is likely to magnify problems in the long run by increasing teenagers' role confusion and perhaps forcing them to look for more outrageous ways to rebel.

2. Parents often complain that their teenage children never talk to them. This may stem from their own negative responses when their children try to communicate. Since adolescence is a time for testing one's wings, it is not surprising that at least some of the ideas and opinions that teens express may be difficult to hear. Nevertheless, it is important to listen calmly, attentively, and in a nonjudgmental fashion.

3. Sometimes it is useful for parents to try to put themselves in their teenagers' shoes (and vice versa). Parents who have difficulty with this can ask their children for help ("I am having some trouble seeing this from your perspective—can you help me out?"). If you find that this process better helps you understand your child's viewpoint, by all means say so. Indicating that you see how reasonable another viewpoint must seem is a process called *validating* (Gottman et al., 1976). Validating does not mean that you will give up your position; you are simply admitting that another point of view may make sense, given some assumptions that

you may not share with the other person. Sometimes the process of trying to see the validity of another viewpoint may lead to new perspectives that can reduce conflicts between parents and teenagers.

4. It is always a good rule to talk with significant others, children as well as adults, as courteously and pleasantly as we would to a respected stranger. When parents begin conversing with their children with anger, sarcasm, or irritation in their voices it is like waving a red flag. However, when teenagers experience calm, courteous, and attentive reactions from their parents, they are greatly encouraged to keep channels of communication open. Their identity as unique individuals with worthwhile opinions is validated when parents treat them as people worthy of respect and attention.

5. Parents can encourage their children to test new ideas by not belittling these viewpoints. If they disagree, they can listen carefully and then offer their own perspective in an honest, caring, and nonpompous fashion. As part of achieving their own identity, teenagers often need to challenge the opinions and acts of their parents. If parents react calmly to these assertions of independence, teenagers are less likely to feel compelled to engage in extreme acts of rebelliousness.

This is not to say that all acts of independence should be treated with nonchalance. Teenagers expect disapproval if they engage in behavior they know is contrary to family values. Parents who fail to react to the "little rebellions" may inadvertently nudge their children toward more dramatic acts of rebellion. Therefore, wise parents indicate their disapproval or discomfort but nevertheless accept their children's rights to assert their independence within limits.

6. Finally, and perhaps most importantly, parents are encouraged to love their children openly, with no strings attached, and to administer plenty of appropriate praise. We all need to be loved and to receive recognition for our good deeds. Teenagers in particular need reinforcement from their parents at a time when they are likely to be feeling emotionally vulnerable.

I used to harass my mother to let me do things I was really a little afraid of doing. Although I would feel inner relief when she said no, I would belligerently tell her how mean she was. (*Authors' files*)

agers and parents resolve their conflicts with a minimum of fireworks. The Health Psychology and Life discussion on the previous page, "Maintaining Healthy Parent-Teen Relationships," provides some insights into ways that conflicts can be kept to a minimum.

The process of becoming a separate, unique individual is a natural part of the transition from child to adult. Certainly most parents would be distressed if their grown children still depended upon them for their sense of self and direction in life. However, the process of separation may give rise to difficulties. Parents may feel that their values are being rejected, and adolescents may be torn between the need to be dependent and the need to be independent.

When conflicts increase, family tension often rises. Culturally defined "adult" behaviors, such as driving, drinking, and smoking, are sometimes used by adolescents as symbols of maturity or as a form of rebellion. Adolescents may reason that they are not children anymore as they seek to become increasingly independent of their parents' authority. However, they still need support from others. This need may be greater now than ever before, considering the profound physical and psychological changes they are experiencing. In a sense it is paradoxical that adolescents' driving needs for independence force them to retreat from the very people who are likely to be the most supportive and nurturing. To satisfy their needs for both support and independence from their family, teenagers typically turn to other people who are in the same boat—namely, their peers.

Adolescent friendships are typically much closer and more intense than at any previous time in development (Fischer et al., 1986). American teenagers spend over half their waking hours talking to and doing things with friends of the same age group (see Figure 11.1). They tend to identify more with their peers than with adults, and most rate themselves as happiest when they are with their friends. Adolescents are also more inclined to share intimate information with peers than with parents or other adults (Berndt, 1982; Csikszentmihalyi & Larson, 1984; Csikszentmihalyi et al., 1977). The important role of peers in adolescent development appears to be a worldwide phenomenon (Newman, 1982).

There are good reasons why this is so. Young people may find it reassuring to be with friends who are experiencing the same kinds of awkward physical changes. Having friends the same age to go to for advice allows teenagers to get support and counsel without short-circuiting their independence from their parents. The peer group also provides a sounding

During adolescence, the peer group may become of paramount importance and may markedly influence dress, attitude, and other behavior. Most adolescents rate themselves as happiest when they are with their friends.

Adolescents often use culturally defined "adult" behaviors, such as driving, drinking, and smoking, as symbols of maturity or as a form of rebellion.

FIGURE 11.1   WITH WHOM DO ADOLESCENTS SPEND THEIR TIME?

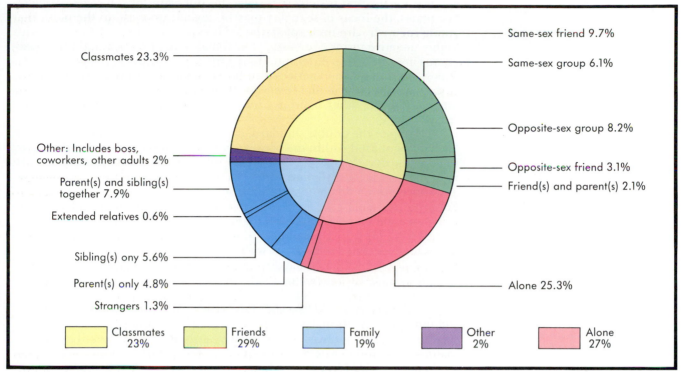

Classmates 23.3%

Same-sex friend 9.7%

Same-sex group 6.1%

Opposite-sex group 8.2%

Opposite-sex friend 3.1%

Friend(s) and parent(s) 2.1%

Other: Includes boss, coworkers, other adults 2%

Parent(s) and sibling(s) together 7.9%

Extended relatives 0.6%

Sibling(s) ony 5.6%

Parent(s) only 4.8%

Strangers 1.3%

Alone 25.3%

| Classmates 23% | Friends 29% | Family 19% | Other 2% | Alone 27% |

(*Source:* Adapted from Csikszentmihalyi & Larson, 1984)

board for trying out new ideas and behaviors. Finally, it is comforting for teenagers to feel they belong to a world of their own rather than being minor players in the adult world.

It is not surprising, then, that adolescents are strongly inclined to conform to the standards of their peer group in order to gain approval. This conformity may sometimes be taken to extremes in which they radically change their manner of dress, hair styles, and behaviors. If they identify with a group whose values and behavioral styles are dramatically different from those of their parents, considerable strife and stress may result (Newman, 1982). Of course, parents' horrified responses are often welcomed by teenagers as evidence that their rebellion has succeeded!

Despite the increased influence of peers and occasionally extreme acts of independence, however, the so-called "generation gap" between parents and teens is rather small. Parents continue to exert a strong influence upon their teenagers' attitudes and values, and in fact, adolescents are often more inclined to accept their parents' values and opinions than those of their peers (Brittain, 1963; Emmerick, 1978; Offer & Offer, 1975). Peer influence is greatest in matters of dress and hair styles, problems related to school and dating, and minor day-to-day concerns, but teenagers appear to be more influenced by their parents in issues of politics, religion, morality, and major decisions such as career choices (Emmerick, 1978; Gallatin, 1980; Lerner & Spanier, 1980).

Sexual Development   It is impossible to explore the psychosocial development of adolescence without taking notice of the changes that take place in sexual behavior. While much of teenage sexuality represents a progression from childhood behavior, a new significance is often attached to sexual expression. Two pervasive influences on adolescent sexuality are the male-female double standard and "sexual liberation."

The Double Standard during Adolescence   Although children have been exposed to gender-role socialization since infancy, the emphasis on

Adolescents sometimes engage in extreme acts of independence that may reflect markedly different behavioral standards than those of their parents while, at the same time, they demonstrate conformity to the standards of their peer group.

gender-role differentiation often increases during adolescence. In our society, this means that teenagers receive the full brunt of the *double standard*. For males, the focus of sexuality may be sexual conquest, to the point that young men who are nonexploitative or inexperienced may be labeled with highly negative terms like "sissy." For females, the message and the expectations are often very different. Many girls learn to appear "sexy" to attract males, yet they often experience ambivalence about overt sexual behavior. If they do not have sexual relations, they worry that a boy friend will lose interest. On the other hand, having sex might make a boy think they are "easy."

Despite the double standard, early sexual experiences are now more likely to be shared within the context of an ongoing relationship than they were a few decades earlier. It appears that contemporary adolescents are most likely to be sexually intimate with someone they love or feel emotionally attached to, and changes in both sexes are narrowing the gender gap. For instance, adolescent females seem to be more comfortable in having sex with someone they feel affection for rather than feeling they need to "save themselves" for a love relationship, while adolescent males are becoming increasingly inclined to have sex with someone they feel close to rather than engaging in sex with a casual acquaintance or stranger (Delamater & MacCorquodale, 1979; Sorenson, 1973; Zabin et al, 1984).

Peer Pressure and "Sexual Liberation"   While the double standard is still influential, both males and females today are also affected by another societal influence: increasingly permissive attitudes toward sex. The greater tolerance for and increased expectation of sexual behavior sometimes goes by the label *sexual liberation.* A dimension of this so-called liberation is considerable pressure to be sexually active. Teenagers who resist the pressure to become sexually experienced run the risk of being labeled "up tight" or old-fashioned. On the other hand, teenagers who become sexually active may feel anxious, confused, guilty, or inadequate.

In view of these kinds of pressures, how appropriate is the term "sexual liberation"? It is our belief that true liberation means promotion of choice rather than coercion to say yes to sexual intercourse or other activities. Given the current pressure in some peer groups, however, saying no is often difficult.

Nevertheless, even today many adolescents have not experienced premarital sexual intercourse, although the results of four major nationwide surveys of adolescent sexual behaviors reveal a strong upward trend over the last four decades (see Table 11.2). In broad terms, we can briefly summarize the major changes in adolescent coital activities as follows. First, while there has been an increase in the percentages of both young men and young women who have experienced coitus, these increases have been considerably larger for females than for males. Second, fewer teenage women than men experience premarital intercourse, but the difference between the sexes has been diminishing rapidly. Unfortunately there have been no recent large-scale national surveys that would allow us to determine if the upward trend in premarital coitus rates among teenage women has continued in the 1980s. However, some relatively small-scale studies have indicated a possible leveling off of this trend, with only small increases occurring in the early 1980s (Ostrov et al., 1985).

TABLE 11.2 *Percentage of Adolescents Who Reported Having Premarital Intercourse by Age 19*

	Females	Males
Kinsey (1948, 1953)	20%	45%
Sorenson (1973)	45%	59%
Zelnik and Kantner (1977)	55%	No males in survey
Zelnik and Kantner (1980)	69%	77%

ADULTHOOD

You may have either recently entered young adulthood or are presently making this important transition. What lies ahead in the remaining 70 percent of your life? Will you continue to grow and change, or has the die already been cast? Will you be the same person at age 40, or age 70, that you are now at age 19 or 20?

It is now widely acknowledged that development continues throughout life, and that this growth is not limited merely to physical changes. Contemporary developmentalists have been amazed at the extent of psychosocial changes, and to a lesser degree cognitive development, that continue during the adult years. In all, we can say with some confidence that you will not be the same person at age 40 that you are at 19 or 20.

Most developmentalists divide the adult years into three periods: early adulthood (roughly 20 to 40), middle adulthood (40 to about 65), and late adulthood (after 65). Although these categories are convenient, they are somewhat arbitrary and carry the danger of promoting the notion of *age-based expectations* (the tendency to associate certain developmental tasks or appropriate behaviors with each phase of adult life). Young adults may be expected to marry and start families, and people in the middle adult years are often expected to reach the top of their careers. However, as we noted at the beginning of this chapter, not all of us experience the phases of our lives in the same orderly fashion.

In fact, many age-based expectations in our society have begun to break down (Neugarten & Neugarten, 1987). People often postpone marriage or decide not to marry at all; in addition, many people are becoming first-time parents in middle adulthood, and gray-haired retirees are now a common sight in many college classrooms. In all, "we seem to be moving in the direction of what might be called an age-irrelevant society; and it can be argued that age, like race or sex, is diminishing in importance as a regulator of behavior" (Neugarten & Hagestad, 1976, p. 52).

One reason for this is that age per se is not the cause of changes in our lives. A 30-year-old advertising executive is not more mature than she was as a college student simply because she is older. Rather, her increased maturity reflects the experiences she has encountered in her personal and professional life. Thus, instead of measuring development only by age categories, many of us find it useful to define our phase of adult development in terms of *perceived age*:—how old we feel (Brodzinsky et al., 1986).

In keeping with this reduced emphasis on age, the following sections describe physical, cognitive, and social development in fairly general terms during the years between the twenties and the sixties. We begin with the physical changes that take place during adulthood.

Gray-haired retirees are now a common sight in many college classrooms, which is helping to break down some of the age-based expectations in our society.

PHYSICAL DEVELOPMENT IN EARLY AND MIDDLE ADULTHOOD

During early adulthood—the twenties and thirties—people reach the peak of their biological efficiency. These are typically years of good health and high energy, which is fortunate considering that this is the time of life when most of us are busy establishing careers, adjusting to marriage, and perhaps responding to the boundless needs of small children.

Physical Capacities   A number of physical attributes are likely to reach their high point during early adulthood. During this period most of us reach the peak of our reproductive capacities and enjoy the best health of any time of our lives. The speed with which we can react to complex stimuli is fastest at around age 20, then gradually declines from the mid–twenties on. However, simple reflex time (such as the jerk of the knee when tapped with a mallet) remains relatively constant from age 20 to 80 (Brodzinsky et al., 1986; Hodgkins, 1962). Vision and hearing are at their best at around age 20; as we move into our middle adult years, we can expect to become

Changes over time in our physical strength, stamina, and cardiac output are probably influenced more by our lifestyle and exercise habits than they are by aging alone. Many men and women in their forties and fifties who regularly run, swim, bicycle, or play racquet sports are considerably more fit than many teenagers and young adults who live more sedentary lives.

gradually more farsighted and to lose our ability to hear higher notes. Smell, taste, and tactile sensitivity, however, remain relatively unchanged until age 50 or older.

Physical strength also tends to peak sometime in the mid- to late twenties. It then declines gradually, dropping about 10 percent between ages 30 and 60 (Bischoff, 1976; Troll, 1975). Unless you happen to compete in swimming, running, or some other athletic endeavor requiring peak performance, you may hardly notice the barely perceptible decline in physical strength, stamina, and cardiac output over the third and fourth decades of your life. However, sometime in your late forties or early fifties you may note that your body is beginning to show indications of wear.

These changes are closely related to our lifestyle and exercise habits, which probably influence physical strength and stamina much more than does aging alone. Many men and women in their forties and fifties who regularly run, swim, bicycle, or play racquet sports are considerably more fit than many teenagers and young adults who live more sedentary lives.

Over time, however, middle adulthood brings a gradual decline in physical functioning and perhaps a corresponding increase in health problems. We may begin to notice that it is not so easy to rebound the morning after a late party, or that the body protests more after a hard workout on the tennis courts. Some of the most notable changes, particularly for women, have to do with changing hormonal patterns that, among other things, alter reproductive capacity.

Hormonal Changes and the Climacteric   The term **climacteric** refers to the physiological changes that occur during a woman's transition from fertility to infertility. **Menopause,** one of the events of the female climacteric, refers to the cessation of menstruation. Menopause results from certain physiological changes, most notably a reduction in estrogen levels. It can take place any time between 40 and 60, but most commonly occurs between ages 45 and 50 (Crooks & Baur, 1987). Many women consider the cessation of menstruation and fertility to be the most significant biological change related to aging. Its physical impact, however, is often less significant than its psychological impact, for menopause signals an end of childbearing years, a time of liberation from contraceptive worries and fear of pregnancy, and sometimes a perceived loss of femininity.

Do men also undergo a climacteric? Not in the same sense as women. For one thing, men often retain their reproductive capacity well into the older years (although with declining fertility). The hormonal changes men undergo are much more gradual. Male hormone levels usually reach their peak sometime between ages 17 and 20, then steadily but slowly decline until around age 60, when they level off. Middle-aged and older men are somewhat more likely than younger men to experience depression, irritability, headaches, and insomnia, but researchers have found no links between these changes and altered hormone levels (Doering et al., 1975; Henker, 1981).

The Double Standard of Aging   In a society that places a premium on youth, it can be difficult for both men and women to grow older. This process is usually more difficult for women than for men because of another double standard of our society—this one related to aging. Although a woman's erotic and orgasmic capabilities continue after menopause, it is not uncommon for her to be considered past her "sexual prime" relatively early in the aging process. This is because the cultural image of an erotically appealing woman is commonly one of youth. As a woman grows away from this image, she is usually considered less and less attractive. Cosmetics, specially designed clothing, and even surgery are often used to maintain a youthful appearance for as long as possible.

In contrast, men's physical and sexual attractiveness is often considered to be enhanced by the aging process. Gray hair and wrinkles may be thought to look "distinguished" on men, signs of accumulated life experience and wisdom. Likewise, while the professional achievements of women may be perceived as threatening to some males, a man's sexual attractiveness is often closely associated with his achievements and social status, both of which may increase with age.

It is our opinion that exaggerated attempts at remaining perpetually youthful are both a losing battle and a denial of a woman's full humanity. Susan Sontag (1972) presents an alternative:

> Women have another option. They can aspire to be wise, not merely nice; to be competent, not merely helpful; to be strong; not merely graceful; to be ambitious for themselves; not merely themselves in relation to men and children. They can let themselves age naturally and without embarrassment, actively protesting and disobeying the conventions that stem from this society's double standard about aging. Instead of being girls, girls as long as possible, who then age humiliatingly into middle-aged women and then obscenely into old women, they can become women much earlier—and remain active adults, enjoying the long, erotic career of which women are capable, for longer. Women should allow their faces to show the lives they have lived. (p. 38)

COGNITIVE DEVELOPMENT IN EARLY AND MIDDLE ADULTHOOD

At one time, intellectual ability was believed to peak in young adulthood just as do most aspects of physical functioning. This view was supported by an early large-scale study which administered standardized intelligence tests to large samples of adults of varying ages. Young adults were found to score higher than middle-aged adults, who in turn outperformed older adults (Jones & Conrad, 1933). A more recent cross-sectional study reported a somewhat later peak of intelligence, in the late twenties or early thirties, but it also showed middle-aged and older subjects scoring lower than younger adults (Schaie, 1975).

DOES INTELLIGENCE DECLINE WITH AGE?

Both of the previous studies, which reported a decline in intelligence with age, employed a cross-sectional design. Can we assume that the IQ differences between age groups in these two sample populations were due solely to aging? Are there other factors that might account for these differences? As you think about this question, you may wish to review the methodological shortcomings of the cross-sectional design outlined in Chapter 10.

The cross-sectional design involves evaluating people of different ages at one point in time. As we saw in Chapter 10, the major shortcoming of this method is that it cannot rule out a possible generational influence: Subjects were born at different times and thus have experienced varied cultural conditions (Flynn, 1987). For example, the older group may have experienced less formal education, poorer nutrition, less childhood exposure to intellectually stimulating events, or even fewer experiences with this kind of standardized test than the younger subjects. Unless we know what 60-year-olds scored when they were 40 and 20, we cannot determine that intelligence declines with age.

In fact, a number of longitudinal studies have generally contradicted the results of the cross-sectional studies, suggesting that people retain their intellect well into middle age. In two well-designed longitudinal studies, subjects actually achieved slightly higher scores in middle age than in early adulthood (Eichorn et al., 1981; Nisbet, 1957). One recent cross-sequential study showed no significant declines in most areas of intellectual functioning until age 60 or older (Schaie and Hertzog, 1983).

Crystallized versus Fluid Intelligence Some changes in specific kinds of intelligence do appear to be age related, however. Psychologists distinguish between crystallized and fluid intelligence (Horn, 1982). **Crystallized intelligence** results from accumulated knowledge, including a knowledge of how to reason, language skills, and understanding of technology; it is linked closely to education, experience, and cultural background. Crystallized intelligence is measured by tests of general information, reasoning ability, vocabulary, mechanical knowledge, and social judgment. Research indicates that crystallized intelligence increases with age, and that people tend to continue improving their performance on tests of this form of intelligence until near the end of their lives (Horn, 1982; Horn & Donaldson, 1980).

Fluid intelligence allows us to perceive and draw inferences about relationships among patterns of stimuli, to conceptualize abstract information, and to solve problems. It is measured by various kinds of test problems that people are unlikely to have been previously exposed to, such as grouping numbers and symbols according to some abstract principle. Fluid intelligence seems to be relatively independent of education and cultural influences. It peaks sometime between ages 20 and 30 and declines steadily thereafter (Horn, 1982; Horn & Donaldson, 1980).

It is possible that these age-related differences may somehow be an artifact of the research strategy used, since much of the basic research on crystallized and fluid intelligence has relied on the cross-sectional approach. However, since fluid intelligence depends more on optimal neurological functioning than does crystallized intelligence, it seems likely that it is more adversely influenced by age-associated neurological declines.

A Fifth Stage of Cognitive Development? Recall that Piaget saw formal operations as the highest level of cognitive functioning. Some critics disagree, maintaining that many adults progress beyond formal operations to what might be called a fifth stage of intellectual development. One theorist, P. A. Arlin (1975, 1977), believes that adults develop cognitively to the level of **problem finding.** Someone at the problem finding stage is concerned with posing new questions about the world and trying to discover novel solutions to old problems. Arlin believes that problem finding allows intellectually maturing adults to progress beyond Piaget's formal operations to the level of creative thinking.

Klaus Riegel (1973) offers another interpretation of the fifth stage of cognitive development. Riegel believes that the mature mind appreciates the dialectical process that results when two or more incompatible viewpoints oppose one another. Have you ever discussed contradictory religious philosophies or political views with friends? If so, you have engaged in what Riegel would label **dialectic operations.** For Riegel, this dialectic-operations stage represents the final stage of cognitive development, when the mature adult thinker realizes and accepts that conflict and contradiction in such areas as morality, politics, and religion are natural consequences of living.

Neither Arlin's problem finding nor Riegel's dialectic operations are widely recognized as a fifth stage of adult cognitive development. However, there is increasing evidence of changes in adult thinking that are not easily accounted for within Piaget's framework (Commons et al., 1982; Kramer, 1983). The way in which we think about things, whether it be defining new problems or dealing with contradictions, continues to change well into our adult years.

PSYCHOSOCIAL DEVELOPMENT IN EARLY AND MIDDLE ADULTHOOD

We saw in Chapter 10 that Erik Erikson described two primary developmental tasks in early and middle adulthood: first the establishment of intimacy, and then the achievement of generativity through commitments to family, work, and future generations. The two major topics in this section, "Single and Married Lifestyles" and "Commitments to Parenting and Work," explore some of the ways in which people respond to these challenges.

Single and Married Lifestyles   As we make the transition from adolescent to young adult, the central focus of our psychosocial adjustment is likely to shift from wanting to be liked by people to needing a loving relationship with someone special. Establishing an intimate relationship requires courage, moral fiber, and a certain amount of self-abandon and willingness to compromise personal preferences. In Erikson's view, two people who achieve true intimacy are able to fuse their identities while at the same time retaining a sense of self. Too much independence may prevent the establishment of intimacy and result in a state of isolation.

Erikson emphasized traditional marriage as a vehicle for fulfilling intimacy needs, but there is plenty of statistical evidence that the commitment to marriage is changing in our society. Can the decision to remain single or cohabit also provide a satisfactory adjustment? The following discussions explore the evidence.

Single Living   Increasing numbers of young and middle-aged adults in our society live alone, many out of choice. This increase is most pronounced among people in their twenties and early thirties. For example, in 1970 17.1 percent of all American households were one-person households, compared to 23.7 percent in 1985 (U.S. Bureau of the Census, 1987a). The proportion of adults in their late twenties and early thirties who have never married has approximately doubled since 1970 (U.S. Bureau of the Census, 1987a).

Although single life is still often seen as the period before, in between, or after marriage, these societal attitudes may be changing. Until recently in the United States a stigma was often attached to remaining single, especially for women. Today it seems quite possible that more and more people will remain single, either as an option to first marriage or following divorce. If this happens, there may also be a reduction in the number of people who marry primarily for convention's sake.

Various factors contribute to the increasing numbers of single adults. These include people marrying at a later age, more women placing career objectives ahead of marriage, high divorce rates, a greater emphasis on advanced education, and an increase in the number of women who need not depend on marriage to ensure economic stability (Glick & Norton, 1979; U.S. Bureau of the Census, 1987a).

A recent survey of 482 single Canadian adults in several major population centers tells us something about why people choose to remain single and also how satisfied they are with single life (Austrom & Hanel, 1985). In this study, almost half of the subjects said they were single by choice. The vast majority denied that they were single because they were reluctant to be committed to an exclusive relationship, because they lacked desire for sexual relations with the other sex, or because high divorce rates made them apprehensive about marriage. Instead, most were unmarried "simply because they had not met the right person and also because their expectations of a marriage partner were very high" (p. 17).

Many of these single subjects were able to fulfill their intimacy needs, at least to some extent, without either living with someone or marrying. The study linked satisfaction with single life to the number and types of friendships described by the respondents. Those who reported having socially and emotionally supportive relationships were especially inclined to value their lifestyle. This observation provides us food for thought when we compare it to Erikson's emphasis on traditional marriage for fulfilling intimacy needs.

Although single living is becoming more acceptable in our society, most adults still choose to enter into a long-term relationship with a partner, even though it may not be a lifelong bond. There are several kinds of long-term intimate relationships; we will look at the most common, cohabitation and marriage.

Cohabitation Attitudes toward **cohabitation** (living together in a sexual relationship without being married), have only recently begun to undergo change. The past few decades have seen a significant increase in both the number of people choosing this living arrangement and societal acceptance of what was once an unconventional practice. U.S. Census Bureau figures reveal that by 1985 the number of unmarried couples living together in the United States numbered 1,983,000—nearly triple the number in 1970 (U.S. Bureau of the Census, 1986). It appears that cohabitation is now well established as a social phenomenon. In 1980 the U.S. Census Bureau formally acknowledged it by announcing a new category, POSSLQ ("person of opposite sex sharing living quarters").

This dramatic increase in cohabitation has been attributed to a growing inclination to question traditional mores, particularly those pertaining to marriage. Today many people believe that sexuality is an important part of life, and that marriage is not the only lifestyle that legitimizes sexual relations.

IS LIVING TOGETHER GOOD "PRACTICE" FOR MARRIAGE?

Does the experience of living together have a measurable effect upon the longevity and happiness of a subsequent marriage? At the present time there are two opposing views, one arguing that living together has a positive effect on marriage and the other arguing just the opposite, that cohabitation leads to less stable marriages. What do you think? Can you think of supportive arguments for each of these opposing viewpoints? Consider these questions before reading on.

The more popular point of view among college students is that cohabitation will result in happier and more stable marriages. Trial experiences with the struggles and joys of an everyday relationship allow individuals to identify their own needs and expectations. In this view, cohabiting allows the couple to explore their compatibility before making a long-term commitment.

The opposing view suggests that living together will have an overall negative impact on the institution of marriage, particularly its long-term stability. Faced with conflict, a couple who are living together may find it easier to end the relationship than to make a grand effort to resolve their problems. Once the pattern of breaking up has been established, people may be more likely to respond to marital conflict in the same way.

Perhaps neither of these views is correct, and cohabitation has no demonstrable effect upon marriage. There is some limited evidence supporting this contention. In one study, couples who had cohabited before marriage were just as likely to divorce as those who did not (Newcomb & Bentler, 1980). Another study of university students examined whether cohabitation (with either the future spouse or someone else) had any influence on subsequent marital happiness. It found no differences on several measures, including indicators of relationship stability, sexual satisfaction, physical intimacy, and openness of communication (Jacques & Chason,

---

FIRST PERSON 11.8

When I was a college student in the early 1960s, the possibility of living with someone dear to me, without the sanctity of marriage, simply never entered my mind. When I met a very special person and found myself wishing for the intimacy of sharing a home together, marriage was my only option. Although we were sexual prior to marriage, we never even took a weekend trip together. The topic of unmarrieds living together was never discussed, although I did occasionally hear a hushed reference to someone "living in sin." (*Authors' files*)

TABLE 11.3 *Number of Marriages and Divorces per 1,000 Resident Population, 1970–1985*

	1970	1971	1972	1973	1974	1975	1976	1977	1978	1979	1980	1981	1982	1983	1984	1985
Marriages	10.6	10.6	10.9	10.8	10.5	10.0	9.9	9.9	10.3	10.4	10.6	10.6	10.6	10.5	10.5	10.2
Divorces	3.5	3.7	4.0	4.3	4.6	4.8	5.0	5.0	5.1	5.3	5.2	5.3	5.0	5.0	4.9	5.0

Source: From U.S. Bureau of the Census, 1987b.

1979). In contrast to these two studies, however, a more recent survey of over 300 couples linked cohabitating with a future spouse to a significantly lower perceived quality of communication for wives and significantly lower marital satisfaction for both partners (DeMaris & Leslie, 1984). Clearly, further research is necessary to clarify what impact, if any, cohabitation has on marriage.

Marriage   In spite of rapidly changing mores, people do not seem to be permanently substituting single living, cohabitation, or other alternative lifestyles for traditional marriage. About nine out of every 10 adults in the United States marry, some more than once. Statistics released in 1987 show that the number of new marriages each year per 1,000 resident U.S. population remained relatively constant between 1970 and 1985 (see Table 11.3).

There are good reasons why the institution of marriage is found in virtually every society, for it serves several personal and social functions. It provides societies with stable family units that help to perpetuate social norms, as children learn society's rules and expectations from parents or kinship groups. It also structures an economic partnership that ties child support and subsistence tasks into one family unit. Marriage regulates sexual behavior and also provides a framework for fulfilling people's needs for social and emotional support.

Historically, the function of marriage has been to provide a stable economic unit in which to raise children. In many societies, and in some groups within our own society in the past, marriages were arranged through contracts between parents; "romance" was not expected to play a part. Today, however, most people expect more from the marriage relationship, seeking fulfillment for their social, emotional, financial, and sexual needs. Happiness itself is sometimes thought to be an automatic outcome of marriage. These are high expectations, and they are difficult to meet. As one observer states, "Marriage was not designed as a mechanism for providing friendship, erotic experience, romantic love, personal fulfillment, continuous lay psychotherapy or recreation" (Cadwallader, 1975, p. 134). However, many modern couples expect all these benefits from the marital relationship.

While people's expectations for marriage have increased, our society's supportive network for marriage has decreased. In a mobile, urban society in which a couple often settle down far from their extended families, many married couples are isolated from their families and neighbors. This places further demands on the marriage, for there is often no place else to turn for such things as child-care assistance, emotional support, and financial or household help.

Another development that is influencing marital patterns is increased longevity. "Till death do us part" now means many more years than it did in the past. This raises the question of how long even the best marriage can be expected to fulfill so many functions.

Despite all these pressures, marriage still succeeds in fulfilling many people's needs for intimacy. What makes a successful marriage? Francine Klagsbrun (1985) recently conducted in-depth interviews with 90 couples married 15 years or more who rated their marriages as happy and successful. Some of the traits she found to be associated with good marriages included spending focused time together, sharing values (more important than sharing interests), and flexibility (that is, a willingness to accept change both in one's partner and in the nature of the relationship). Other studies link marital happiness to positive communication, high levels of physical intimacy, and perceptions of emotional closeness and mutual empathy (Laurer & Laurer, 1985; Tolstedt & Stokes, 1983; Zimmer, 1983).

Commitments to Parenting and Work   We have been looking at the task of establishing intimacy, but another important challenge of adulthood is to focus on things beyond self. This is most often expressed as a commitment to family and work during our thirties and forties. Erikson suggested that the most important expression of generativity involves molding and nurturing our own children, but he also acknowledged the great potential of work for satisfying this need. In the following paragraphs we consider each of these areas.

Having Children   Until recently parenthood was an expected consequence of marriage, and most married couples still have one or more children. Today, however, effective birth control methods give adults more choice about becoming parents, and more married people are deciding not to have children at all. How does either having or not having children affect psychosocial development? There is too little evidence to reach a clear-cut answer. Investigations of parenthood have traditionally focused almost exclusively on the question of how parenting styles affect children. Only recently have they begun exploring the reverse question—how having children influences an adult.

We do know of many potential advantages to having children. Parenthood may enhance a couples' love and intimacy as they share in the experiences of raising their offspring. Managing the challenge of parenthood can also be a source of self-esteem, providing a sense of accomplishment. Many parents believe that their children provide them not only with reciprocal love but also with a sense of purpose (Hoffman & Manis, 1979).

Parenthood is often an opportunity for discovering new and untapped dimensions of oneself that can give life greater meaning and satisfaction. Many parents say that they have become better people through parenthood, and according to at least one major study, most indicate that being a parent is a major source of satisfaction (Veroff et al., 1981). Children offer ongoing stimulation and change, and they may also provide financial or emotional support in their parents' older years (Mayleas, 1980).

Some people prefer not to have children, however. These individuals and couples have much more time for themselves and do not have to worry about providing for the physical and psychological needs of children. Recreational and social patterns can be more spontaneous, and adults can more fully pursue careers that also provide challenge and fulfillment. Couples without children usually have more time and energy for companionship, and there is often less stress on their marriages. Some studies show that marriages without children are happier and more satisfying than marriages with children (Campbell, 1975).

Children absorb time as well as emotional and financial resources—strains that often increase over time (Feshbach, 1985; Rollins & Galligan, 1978). The result may be a decrease in marital happiness that commences with the birth of the first child, but is likely to reverse itself when all the children have reached adulthood and left the home (Datan & Thomas, 1984; Reinke et al., 1985).

In all, there are no guarantees that the benefits of either children or childless living will meet one's expectations. Still, it is important to assess the choice of parenthood carefully, for it is a permanent and major life decision.

The World of Work   If you were to pick at random any young or middle-aged adult today and ask "who are you?" the chances are good that most would reply "I am a teacher" (or computer programmer, medical technologist, or some other profession). Adults are inclined to define or identify who they are by what they do. This has probably always been true of men; now it is also true of most women, since the majority of adult American women have occupations outside the home. Beyond the sense of competence that successful parenting can provide, much of what people do to fulfill generativity needs involves their work.

During late adolescence, many individuals struggle with developing a career track—one reason why so many college students change their majors one or more times. By young adulthood, most of us accomplish the crucial task of choosing a career. In some ways, careers have become more accessible to both sexes than at any previous time in history. Earlier in this century advanced education was a privilege enjoyed mostly by the affluent, but today almost any motivated high school graduate can attend college. Traditional pressures for sons to follow in their fathers' footsteps and for women to become homemakers are diminishing, and new fields of specialization provide many more potential careers for both sexes.

This increased freedom has also been the source of new frustrations and anxieties, however. As we saw in the discussion of decision making in Chapter 8, virtually unlimited opportunities can seem overwhelming, and young adults are often unsure what to do about their careers. This uncertainty may carry over into the work situation and contribute to a tendency of young workers to be less satisfied with their jobs than middle-aged or older adults (Bass & Ryterband, 1979; Janson & Martin, 1982; Quinn et al., 1974).

How many Americans are satisfied with their jobs? According to one major survey, almost nine out of ten respondents answered yes to the question, "Are you satisfied with your job?" However, when the same subjects were asked, "If you could start over, would you seek the same job you have now?" less than half of those with white-collar jobs and only a quarter of the blue-collar workers said yes (Weaver, 1980). These findings indicate that job statisfaction is something less than optimal for many if not most workers. People who are generally satisfied with their jobs also tend to be satisfied with their lives (Keon & McDonald, 1982).

JOB SATISFACTION AND AGE

On the whole, job satisfaction tends to be lower among young adults than middle-aged or older workers. Can you think of possible explanations for this finding? Do young people's work expectations differ significantly from those of older workers, or are there other generational factors that might account for this difference? Think about these questions before reading on.

One common explanation is that young adults earn less money, have fewer responsibilities, and are less challenged than their older counterparts. Certainly these factors may contribute to lower job satisfaction, but other factors may also play a role. One is the "reality shock" many individuals feel when they discover that their initial career choice is not at all what they expected. For example, individuals who have chosen a college major in a "practical field" like accounting or nursing because these professions seemed to fit their self-concept may find that the nature of the work does not match up at all with their expectations, interests, or self-concept. Such a circumstance often contributes to higher job turnover and lower satisfaction among younger workers (Havinghurst, 1982; Ritzer, 1977). Presumably, most people eventually figure out what they want to do and find more suitable jobs as they grow older, and thus experience improved job satisfaction.

Another possible explanation is that many young, newly hired workers have had little or no prior experience with working 40 or more hours per week, with no end in sight. Young people who have not yet adjusted to this routine may be dissatisfied with any job, regardless of its potential to fulfill their expectations or promote a positive self-identity.

Finally, since most of the research in this area is cross-sectional, it is possible that generational effects may contribute to age-graded differences in job satisfaction. The greater emphasis that is placed on education and careers today may influence both sexes to have higher career expectations and feel more pressure to succeed—a setup for stress and disillusionment. Also, since young adults today tend to be better educated than older generations, they may be harder to please.

Roughly two out of three women aged 25–44 work outside the home, a figure that has doubled since the early 1950s. A few factors contribute to this increase: (1) traditional social taboos against mothers working outside the home have largely disappeared; (2) a higher percentage of women have a college education; and (3) women have greater accessibility to once male-dominated professions.

FIGURE 11.2   PERCENTAGE OF WOMEN IN THE LABOR FORCE WHO HAVE CHILDREN UNDER 18

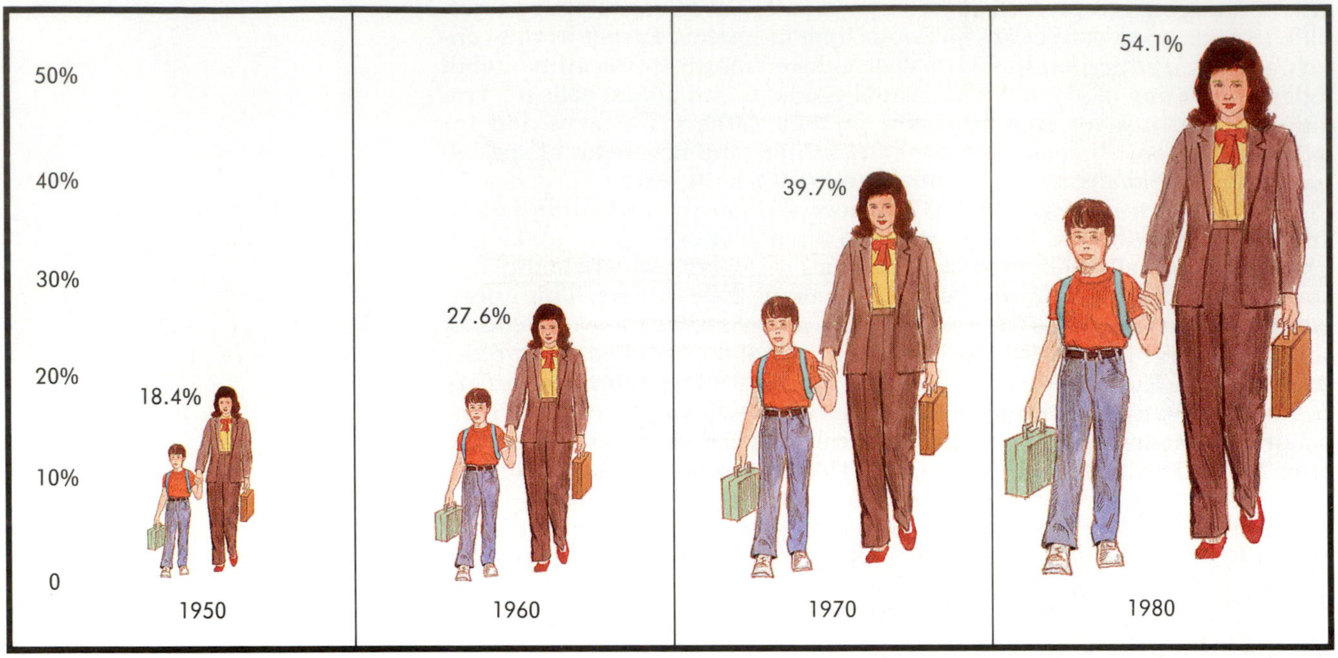

(*Source:* Adapted from Schaie, 1977–1978)

One of the most noteworthy recent trends is the dramatic increase in the number of women in the work force. Today roughly two out of every three women aged 25 to 44 work outside the home, a figure that has doubled since the early 1950s. More than half of mothers with children under 18 are participating in the labor force, more than triple the number three decades ago (see Figure 11.2) (U. S. Department of Labor, 1984).

A number of social trends contribute to this increase. For one, traditional social taboos against mothers working outside the home have largely disappeared. Another factor is that more women are now attending college, and higher education tends to create a desire to apply one's accumulated wisdom in a career. Furthermore, many professions once considered the domain of men are now more accessible to women.

There are also important practical benefits to working. A job provides a way to broaden social networks, as well as an escape from the sense of isolation that many nonworking women experience. Another benefit is the increased financial security provided by two incomes. Dual-career families are better able to afford the "extras" that add to enjoyment of life and are less likely to be confronted with the stress of financial crises. Finally, Erikson's assertion that a man's sense of identity and self-worth is strongly influenced by his work also applies to women. A number of studies have shown that women who enjoy their work have higher self-esteem, a greater sense of pride and power, better emotional and physical health, and a greater sense of overall life satisfaction than do women who do not work outside of the home (Baruch et al, 1983; Hoffman, 1974, 1979).

Dual-provider families also face some potential disadvantages, however. One of the biggest problems is finding enough time for everything. At the end of the day the couple must face mundane tasks such as paying the bills, doing housework, washing clothes, and preparing meals. If they have children, there are additional demands that may make it difficult to spend quality time together or to enjoy leisure activities (Moen, 1982). This can exact a high price both in diminished energy levels and downgraded quality of a relationship. Unfortunately, women seem to bear the brunt of these increased pressures, and they often must contend with *role overload* if husbands neglect to share domestic duties equally (Pleck, 1977; Slocum & Nye, 1976).

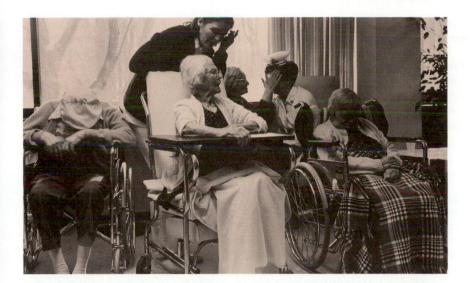

Do you think of elderly people as being forgetful, cranky, depressed, frail, unhealthy, and dependent upon others (left), or, do you think of elderly people as being like George Abbott, famous Broadway producer and director who celebrated his 100th birthday on June 29, 1987, and who is still actively writing and directing for the theater?

THE OLDER YEARS

What kinds of associations or images come to your mind when you hear the words *old people* or *old age*? If you are like most Americans, young and old alike, you are likely to think of old people as forgetful, cranky, touchy, depressed, frail, unhealthy, poorly coordinated, and not as smart as when they were younger. You are also likely to view the older years as a time when people become more dependent on others, less interested in sex, obsessed with physical complaints, more isolated from friends and family, mentally unreliable, and likely to be institutionalized in "rest homes." Are these stereotypes more myth than fact? In the remaining pages of this chapter we explore the evidence about the physical, cognitive, and psychosocial developments that accompany older adulthood.

THE GRAYING OF AMERICA

People today are living longer and retaining their health and vigor longer than previous generations. In fact, the proportion of older people in the American population has increased quite dramatically in recent years. Whereas in 1900 the average life expectancy was slightly less than 50 years, by the mid–1980s it had increased to approximately age 75. Only four percent of the American populace were over 65 in 1900, but in the mid-1980s this figure had tripled to approximately 12 percent. Over the last few decades, the proportion of American people 65 and older has grown at twice the rate of the rest of our population. By the year 2030, more than 20 percent of the American population will be 65 and older (Horn & Meer, 1987).

The so-called graying of America may be attributed to a number of factors. To some extent, it is a function of an increased birth rate that commenced around the turn of the century, combined with higher immigration rates early in this century. However, much of this trend is caused by technological changes since 1900 that have resulted in longer life spans and lower mortality rates for the elderly. Improved medications and medical procedures prolong the lives of many older people. A sharp reduction in death rates from heart disease and strokes in the last two decades has also been a prime factor in lowering mortality rates among the elderly.

The graying of America has significant implications for changing family patterns, employment trends, social policies, and political trends, but our concern is with the individuals who are experiencing longer life spans. Does a longer life mean a welcome prolongation of life's "golden years," or has technology merely expanded the pain and travail of life on a downward slide?

PHYSICAL DEVELOPMENT IN THE OLDER YEARS

We noted earlier that physical decline in such things as muscle strength, vision, and hearing begins in early to middle adulthood. While many of these changes are barely noticeable in the middle years, they often are disturbingly obvious as one grows older. One area in which there are often sharp declines is vision. Older people may become more farsighted; they may also have trouble perceiving color and depths and adapting to changes in lighting. (It is common to have difficulty seeing at night.)

Hearing loss is also common: Many older people have difficulty following a conversation, particularly when there is competing noise from television, radio, or other background sound. This can increase a sense of isolation and perhaps even contribute to mild paranoia if they assume that people are trying to hide something from them by whispering (Zimbardo et al., 1981). Other frequent accompaniments to aging are a reduction in taste and smell sensitivity (which explains why food often does not taste as good to older people) and a diminution of the body senses of kinesthesis and equilibrium (see Chapter 4), which may be one reason why older people are more likely to lose their balance and fall.

The organ systems also show a decline in functional efficiency with age. When we are young, our hearts, lungs, kidneys and other organs have the potential to increase their outputs to a level several times greater than normal under emergency conditions, a capacity that is known as **organ reserve**. For example, strenuous physical activity can cause a young heart to work six times harder than normal. As we grow older, organ reserve is reduced. The heart's ability to pump blood declines by about one percent per year from the early twenties on, and by age 60 blood flow from the arms to the legs is slower than at age 25 (Brody, 1986). By age 75 there has been an average decline in lung capacity of approximately 50 percent in men and 30 percent in women. Furthermore, muscle fibers decrease in number at an average rate of three to five percent per decade after age 30 (Brody, 1986).

Although this may seem to be a rather depressing picture, there is a brighter side to the story. Many of the visual and hearing difficulties of older people can be adequately compensated for by glasses, hearing aids, and other medical procedures. There is also evidence that regular exercise can significantly reduce deterioration of many bodily functions that accompanies aging. It has been estimated that disuse accounts for about half of the functional decline that occurs between ages 30 and 70 (Brody, 1986). It would appear that the advice "use it or lose it" has some validity.

Despite the declines associated with the older years, widespread evidence indicates that most older people enjoy reasonably good health, some virtually to the end of their lives (Horn & Meer, 1987; Neugarten & Neugarten, 1987). While it is true that people over 65 are more subject to chronic long-term ailments, such as arthritis, rheumatism, and hypertension, they are also less likely than younger people to be troubled by short-term acute ailments like colds, flu, and digestive problems (Palmore, 1981). According to a 1983 survey by the U.S. Census Bureau, four out of five people over 65 report their health to be good or excellent.

Why Do People Age? People have long wondered why our bodies lose their capacity to function efficiently as we grow older. Most investigators

Regular exercise can significantly reduce deterioration of many bodily functions that accompany aging. These four people have entered a skiing competition for seniors who are over 70.

agree that aging is influenced by several factors, including heredity, physical activity, nutrition, disease, and a host of environmental factors. However, science has yet to discover exactly why body cells age and cease to function properly.

Over the years there have been two major theories of aging. One, the **genetic clock** or **programmed theory**, maintains that life itself is a terminal disease: Aging is built into every organism through a genetic code that instructs the body cells when it is time to call it a day. Support for this theory was provided by research conducted by Leonard Hayflick (1974), whose investigations of cellular processes in a variety of species revealed that body cells will divide only a preordained number of times (about 50 in the case of humans). The fact that identical twins have very similar life spans seems to support the genetic clock theory. Furthermore, we know that a number of rare human conditions involving accelerated aging are the result of defective genes (Eckholm, 1986).

An alternative theory sees aging as a consequence of **accumulating damages** that emerge from the **wear-and-tear** of living (Holiday, 1987). Our bodies, like machines, eventually wear out as a result of accumulated insults and damages from continued, nonstop use. As we grow older, our worn-out body cells eventually lose their ability to repair or replace damaged components, and thus they eventually cease to function.

These two theories have different implications for those who are interested in counteracting the ravages of aging. People who believe we age only because things wear out might focus on reducing the stresses that produce damage and on avoiding harmful substances that might aggravate the wearing-out process. Those who lean toward the genetic clock view are probably less optimistic about our ability to alter the aging process. However, thanks to recent advances in genetic engineering (see Chapter 10), it now seems possible that genetic alterations might lead to prolonged life spans. Recently a molecular biologist at the University of California at Irvine was able to increase markedly the life span of a species of roundworm by altering a single gene (Johnson, 1986).

A complete understanding of why we age will probably eventually involve aspects of both the genetic clock and accumulated damages theories, with a gradual blurring of the distinction between the two. This seemed to be the consensus of researchers attending a conference on "Modern Biological Theories of Aging" at Mount Sinai Medical Center in New York in 1986.

COGNITIVE DEVELOPMENT IN THE OLDER YEARS

It is often said that old people have poor memories and that intelligence declines sharply in the older years. How accurate is this picture? For most people, the ability to learn and retain meaningful information declines only slightly in the older years (Labouvie-Vief & Schell, 1982; Perlmutter, 1983). The characterization of old age as a time of mental decline may be related to a few conditions: one of these is a decline of fluid intelligence that usually does accompany aging; another is the highly visible condition of senility that affects a relatively small percentage of older people. Let us look at both of these factors.

Intelligence and Aging   As we saw earlier in this chapter, there seem to be two types of intelligence. Crystallized intelligence tends to hold steady or perhaps even improve somewhat in the older years—a finding that is consistent with our tendency to continue to add to our storehouse of knowledge as we grow older, often up to the end of our lives. In contrast, fluid intelligence declines with age, a process that may be related to reduced efficiency of neurological functioning.

There is another possible explanation for the discrepancy between crystallized and fluid intelligence in the older years. People may be more likely to maintain crystallized abilities because they are exercised or used on a regular basis, whereas older people are less likely to be challenged to use their fluid abilities (Denney & Palmer, 1981). This suggestion presents another version of the "use it or lose it" concept mentioned earlier.

Senile Dementia For a small number of people, old age brings a nightmare of deteriorating mental functions known commonly as senility or more technically as **senile dementia** (a collective term that describes a variety of conditions characterized by memory deficits, forgetfulness, disorientation for time & place, declines in ability to think, impaired attention, altered personality, and difficulties in relating to others). Dementia has many causes, some treatable and some that cannot be remedied at the present time. Occasionally the mental confusion characteristic of dementia can be attributed to improper use of medications, hormonal abnormalities, infectious diseases, or metabolic disorders. (Dementia resulting from these causes may often be remedied by medical treatment.) More commonly it is associated with a series of small strokes, brain tumors, or chronic alcoholism, all of which can result in irreversible loss of brain neurons.

The most common form of senile dementia is **Alzheimer's disease**, a currently incurable condition that robs individuals of the capacity to remember, think, relate to others, care for themselves, and even to be aware of their own existence. In the mid–1980s, the National Alzheimer's Disease and Related Disorders Association estimated that roughly 2.5 million Americans, most of whom are over 60, have this dreadful illness. Current estimates suggest that approximately five percent of people over 65 years of age are victims of Alzheimer's disease (Anderton, 1987).

A tremendous amount of research is currently underway to determine the cause(s) of this disease, and some clues have been uncovered. One line of evidence suggests that victims of Alzheimer's disease may lack a specific brain enzyme necessary for the successful function of brain cells that produce the neurotransmitter acetylcholine (Taminga et al., 1987). Research has also linked Alzheimer's disease to the presence of a protein substance referred to as β amyloid protein (DeLabar et al., 1987; Kang et al., 1987; Tanzi et al., 1987). Amyloid proteins duplicate themselves to such an excessive extent in people with Alzheimer's disease that they create tangled webs, known as *amyloid webs*, which produce massive neurological damage and ultimately choke the life out of infected brain cells. Amyloid webs have been detected in the brain cells of people who die of Alzheimer's disease and some other brain-destroying ailments (Perlman, 1985).

Another line of research has looked for genetic clues. About one out of 10 cases of Alzheimer's disease are hereditary, and recently members of a research team headed by Peter St. George-Hyslop (1987) have identified the location of a defective gene that causes the familial or inherited form of Alzheimer's disease. This genetic defect is located on chromosome 21— interestingly, the same chromosome that exists in triplicate in Down's syndrome (see Chapter 10). (People with Down's syndrome typically develop a brain pathology that is indistinguishable from Alzheimer's disease by the time they reach age 60 [Anderton, 1987].) The genetic defect in Alzheimer's disease is located on the same region of chromosome 21 that contains the gene coding for the β amyloid protein (Barnes, 1987a; St. George-Hyslop, 1987; Tanzi et al., 1987).

What about the nine out of 10 cases of Alzheimer's disease that are not familial? Another research team, led by Dmitry Goldgaber (1987), has located a genetic defect that appears to be linked with nonfamilial cases of Alzheimer's disease. This defect is located in the same region of chromosome 21 as the defect associated with the familial form of the disease, suggesting that both forms of Alzheimer's disease may result from a defect of the same gene that contains the coding for the β amyloid protein.

Researchers continue to study the relationship between the defective genetic coding on chromosome 21 and the brain pathology associated with

Will I be the same 20 years from today as I am now? How will I change in appearance, in mental ability, and in interpersonal relationships? These are questions that most of us have asked ourselves at one time or another.

Alzheimer's disease. Scientists hope that this ongoing research will eventually unravel the mystery of Alzheimer's disease and lead to the development of effective preventive or treatment procedures.

Continuing Cognitive Development in the Older Years   Despite the wide publicity received by Alzheimer's disease in recent years, 90 percent or more of people over 65 show little or no cognitive deterioration (National Institute on Aging Task Force, 1980). Research conducted by Marion Diamond (1978) of the University of California at Berkeley suggests that loss of brain neurons is likely to be very minimal in most human brains until very late in life, if then—and that even in old age the neurons of the cerebral cortex seem capable of responding to enriched conditions by forming additional functional connections with other neurons. In a recent interview, Diamond commented on the implications of her research by observing that "Nerve cells can grow at any age in response to intellectual enrichment of all sorts: travel, crossword puzzles, anything that stimulates the brain with novelty and challenge" (in Goleman, 1985, p. 2).

This viewpoint is echoed by University of California at Los Angeles researcher Lissy Jarvik, who has conducted longitudinal research on the aging process in humans. She has found that older people in her studies who maintain their cognitive abilities at high levels are those who keep mentally active. However, mental activity will not ward off conditions that produce dementia such as Alzheimer's disease.

PSYCHOSOCIAL DEVELOPMENT IN THE OLDER YEARS

We have seen that the popular stereotype of old age as a time of rapidly deteriorating physical and cognitive functioning is much more myth than fact—but what about the psychological and social health of older people? Is aging associated with depression, despair, dissatisfaction, unhappiness, and a breakdown of interpersonal relationships? Fortunately, this is true of only a small proportion of aging people.

In reality, the older years do tend to be the "golden years" for a large number of individuals. Several major national surveys have found that satisfaction with life in general, feelings of well-being, and marital satisfaction actually tend to be higher among the aged than among younger adults (Dickie et al., 1979; Herzog et al., 1982). Despite the common misconception that many older people end up in institutions for the aged, only about five percent of America's aged population live in institutions. For most, old age is a time of continued independence, with the additional freedom from the burdens of job and family obligations.

This is not always the case, however. Some older people who are widowed, isolated from friends, in poor health, economically disadvantaged, or resentful of being forced to retire, may find the older years to be far from golden. Admittedly, some of these factors are beyond most individuals' control, but in many ways our satisfaction in old age is the product of our own attitudes and behaviors.

Successful Aging   Many Americans see continued active involvement in life as the best road to successful aging. Older people are encouraged to remain active and not to "retire from their lives" when they retire from their jobs, but might there not also be advantages to cutting back, relaxing, and gracefully withdrawing from the bustle of life?

These descriptions summarize two popular theories of successful aging that have generated considerable discussion and research. According to the **activity theory**, the more involved and active older people remain, the more happy and fulfilled they will be. Thus, older people should pursue hobbies, travel, do volunteer work, engage in "active grandparenting," or involve themselves in other endeavors that help to sustain a relatively high level of activity. In contrast, the **disengagement theory** suggests that we are more likely to be happy in our older years if we cut back on the stresses associated with an active life, taking time to relax, reduce social obligations, and enjoy the tranquility of peaceful reflections.

Which of these prescriptions should a person follow? In general, we can safely say that neither lifestyle is a guarantee of successful, happy aging. There is evidence that people's happiness may have little connection with how active they happen to be (Lemon et al., 1972). Furthermore, the process of disengagement, at least when carried to the extreme, seems to be more related to preparation for imminent death than it does to successful aging (Lieberman & Coplan, 1970). Just as happiness for you or us is not strongly correlated with a particular lifestyle, the same is true for older people. Some are happiest when they are busy and socially involved, while others may enjoy indulging in plenty of relaxation, perhaps for the first time in their lives (Neugarten, 1972; Neugarten et al., 1965; Reichard et al., 1962). Bernice Neugarten (1972) has suggested that most older people tend to select a lifestyle that reflects their personality and the kinds of activities they engaged in while they were younger.

Recall that Erik Erikson viewed successful aging as conditioned upon achieving integrity. He believed that people who are able to view their lives retrospectively with a sense of satisfaction and accomplishment are likely to achieve a sense of unity or integrity. In contrast, people who view their lives as a series of disappointments and failures are likely to experience unhappiness and despair. Robert Butler (1961) agrees that older people often conduct a **life review** in which they reminisce about their past, sorting out their accomplishments and their disappointments. In addition to allowing older people to achieve a state of integrity, this life review may also provide a new focus for the future. Remember Ebenezer Scrooge in Charles Dickens' *A Christmas Carol*, whose "forced" life review produced a dramatically more optimistic focus to his life in his remaining years.

The importance of security and close relationships in successful aging should also be noted. Research indicates that those individuals who make the best psychosocial adjustments to the older years tend to be in good health, to be financially secure, and to have close ties with family and friends (Herzog et al., 1982; Dickie et al., 1979). Furthermore, evidence suggests that the process of finding meaning and purpose in life in the older years can help promote health and wellness, whereas, in contrast, experiencing a sense of meaninglessness may lead to the onset of such negative conditions as anxiety, depression, and/or physical decline (Reker et al., 1987).

FIRST PERSON 11.9

Recently I was talking with my 18-year-old son and somehow we got onto the topic of dying. I remarked that my life was over half gone and that really set him off. He asked some pointed questions about life expectancy, religious interpretations of the afterlife, and nuclear holocaust. The entire discussion seemed to have a profound impact upon him. It was as though he had never before encountered the prospect of his own death. He went off to bed shaking his head and saying that he couldn't get it out of his mind—that he was going to die someday, in his words, "the ultimate bummer." (*Authors' files*)

FACING DEATH

Most adolescents and young adults rarely think about dying—it is an event far removed in time and profoundly antithetical to the health and optimism of youth. Some people may even engage in what has been called an "illusion of immortality" (Barrow & Smith, 1979), completely avoiding confronting the fact that their own days are numbered.

This illusion may be a relatively recent phenomenon. Not many generations ago, death was very much a part of most people's daily lives. Even small children were likely to confront death early in life. Today, however, people are less likely to succumb to illnesses at an early age, and when they do, death usually occurs in the antiseptic isolation of hospitals. As a result of this as well as our society's avoidance of issues of death and dying, many people neither confront the realities of death nor come to terms with the knowledge that they are going to die.

In recent years, however, there has been an increasing emphasis on research and dialogue about death, and a strong interest in **thanatology**—the study of death and dying—has emerged. The infant field of thanatology bears the indelible stamp of its most influential pioneer, Elizabeth Kübler-Ross, who described five stages that most dying people pass through in her immensely influential book, *On Death and Dying* (1969). Kübler-Ross based

In Charles Dickens' *A Christmas Carol,* Ebenezer Scrooge gets a visit from the "Ghost of Christmas Past," who takes him back to important moments of his life. After this review of his life, Scrooge emerges from an existence of unhappiness and despair to one with a much more optimistic focus.

her stage theory on interviews conducted with hundreds of dying patients, both young and old.

According to Kübler-Ross, the first stage of coming to terms with death is *denial*. People often refuse to confront the reality that they are dying. ("There must be some mistake." "This can't be happening to me.") During this phase, individuals may simply ignore the evidence or perhaps seek out other medical opinions to correct a "misdiagnosis." (Aside from the issue of denial, a second opinion is generally a good idea when one is confronted with catastrophic illness.)

Eventually, however, reality catches up and many people progress to the second stage of *anger* and outrage about the injustice of their death. ("Why me?" "I don't deserve this!") Family and health professionals may become targets of angry outbursts as the dying person expresses resentment for being ill (and perhaps envy of others' good health).

In the third stage, *bargaining*, many people take a last shot at regaining health or at least extending the time that remains ("Please God, if you let me live I will go to church or synagogue every Sabbath"; or "I will be a better person if you will just let me live long enough to get my business back on its feet.") Eventually, however, bargaining gives way to the fourth stage, *depression*. Depression comes from an often overwhelming sense of loss—loss of relationships, a future, life itself. ("I won't be able to see my children grow up." "How will my wife cope with being alone in her older years?")

The final stage, *acceptance*, is hopefully reached after working through the feelings of denial, anger, and despair. According to Kübler-Ross, this last stage is often a peaceful time of quiet resignation when individuals are able to achieve a state of serene acceptance. ("My time is near, and it's okay.")

Not everyone goes through these five stages in the same sequence, and a dying person may experience more than one stage at a time. Some of Kübler-Ross' critics have argued that her theory is too pat, denying the fact that just as we all live our lives in unique ways, we are also unique in our manner of dying (Kastenbaum & Costa, 1977; Schulz & Aderman, 1974). For example, some people may cope best with death by denying it, whereas others may choose to do battle right up to the final round. Age may also influence how people face death: older people are generally less inclined to view their own dying with as much grief or anger as are younger people (Wass et al., 1978).

Hospices are facilities that are designed to care for the special needs of the dying, including love and support, pain control, and maintaining a sense of dignity.

Some critics of Kübler-Ross' theory express concern that it be seen as prescriptive. A proliferation of books and courses on death and dying present Kübler-Ross' theory as though it were carved in stone. Critics express fear that her theory will be held up as the model for the "good death," with the result that dying people are analyzed or manipulated according to Kübler-Ross' scheme rather than being treated as individuals.

The thanatology movement has helped raise society's consciousness about the needs of dying people and to encourage us to take steps toward humanizing death. Perhaps one of the brightest new developments in this area is the recent spread of hospices. **Hospices** are facilities designed to care for the special needs of the dying, including love and support, pain control, and maintaining a sense of dignity (Buckingham, 1983). Recognizing that many people prefer to live their final days in the comfort of their homes, many hospices arrange for staff and volunteer workers to provide care in a dying person's own home. One of the best features of the hospice movement is its emphasis on involving family members in the care and support of the dying person.

Hopefully these steps will help reduce the isolation often experienced by people who die in hospitals that emphasize preserving life rather than humanizing death. It is likely that death will be unwelcome to most of us, but at least there is reason to be optimistic that we may be able to complete our lives in a state of dignity, close to people we love.

SUMMARY

ADOLESCENCE

1. In America and other modern Western societies the period of adolescence is prolonged and, unlike many nonindustrial societies, our society has no single initiation rite that signals passage into adulthood.
2. Puberty is the approximately two-year period of rapid physical changes that culminate in sexual maturity. The adolescent growth spurt usually runs its course in the two years following the onset of puberty.
3. Secular trends refer to changes in human physical growth patterns in many societies around the world that appear to be caused by improved standards of living.
4. In general, research has shown that early maturation holds some advantages for boys and some disadvantages for girls.
5. The onset of adolescence is marked by the emergence of the capacity to manipulate objects mentally that are not physically present and by the ability to engage in deductive reasoning, both traits Piaget associated with the formal-operations stage of cognitive development.
6. According to Lawrence Kohlberg's theory of moral development most children ages four to 10 exhibit a preconventional morality in which they behave in certain ways to avoid being punished or to obtain rewards. By late childhood or early adolescence one achieves the level of conventional morality exemplified by either the desire to help others or to help maintain the social order. Some adults progress to the final level of postconventional morality, in which they affirm individual rights and perhaps are guided by universal moral principles that may conflict with society's rules.
7. It is during our adolescence that most of us first acquire an identity or sense of self. An important part of establishing an identity is gaining independence from parents. As parental influence diminishes, the peer group's influence grows.
8. American teenagers spend over half their waking hours with friends of the same age, they tend to identify more with their peers, and they rate themselves as happiest when they are with friends.
9. Adolescent sexuality in America is marked by the double standard, considerable pressure to be sexually active, and not infrequently, anxiety, confusion, guilt, and feelings of inadequacy.
10. Over the last four decades there has been a strong upward trend in the numbers of adolescents who experience sexual intercourse. These increases have been considerably larger for females than males. Fewer adolescent women than men experience premarital intercourse, but the difference between the sexes has been diminishing rapidly.

ADULTHOOD

11. Many age-based expectations—the tendency to associate certain developmental tasks or appropriate behaviors with each phase of adult life—have begun to break down in contemporary society. We appear to be moving in the direction of an age-irrelevant society in which such attributes as age, race, or sex are diminishing in importance as regulators of behavior.
12. During early adulthood—the twenties and thirties—people reach the peak of their biological efficiency. During this time most of us enjoy the best health of any time in our lives.
13. Middle adulthood—the forties and fifties—brings a gradual decline in physical functioning and perhaps a corresponding increase in health problems.
14. Our society has a double standard of aging that tends to regard postmenopausal women as past their sexual prime, whereas men's physical and sexual attractiveness is often considered to be enhanced by the aging process.
15. Research has shown that people retain their intellectual abilities well into middle age and beyond. Some changes in specific kinds of intelligence do appear to be age

related. Crystallized intelligence, which results from accumulated knowledge, tends to increase with age. In contrast, fluid intelligence, or the ability to conceptualize abstract information and to solve problems, tends to decline after age 30.

16. Two primary developmental tasks in early and middle adulthood are the establishment of intimacy and the achievement of generativity through commitments to family, work, and future generations.

17. Erik Erikson emphasized traditional marriage as the avenue for fulfilling intimacy needs; however, an increasing number of people remain unmarried today, many of whom are also able to fulfill their intimacy needs through close friendships and/or cohabitation relationships.

18. Further research is necessary to clarify what impact, if any, cohabitation has on marriage.

19. Over the years the expectations Americans have for marriage have increased while society's supportive network for marriage has decreased.

20. Studies have linked marital happiness to positive communication, high levels of physical intimacy, mutual empathy, spending focused time together, sharing values, and flexibility.

21. Having children may be associated with both positive and negative consequences. On the positive side, parenthood may enhance a couple's love and intimacy and provide them with a sense of accomplishment and a chance to discover untapped personal dimensions and resources. On the debit side, children often sap energy, reduce time for each other, and place a drain on emotional and financial resources.

22. Aside from parenting, much of what people do to fulfill generativity needs involves their work.

23. Young workers generally tend to be less satisfied with their jobs than middle-aged or older adults. People who are satisfied with their jobs also tend to be satisfied with their lives.

24. One of the most noteworthy trends in the world of work is the dramatic increase in the number of women in the work force.

25. Studies have shown that women who enjoy their work have higher self-esteem, better emotional and physical health, and a greater sense of overall life satisfaction than do women who do not work outside the home.

THE OLDER YEARS

26. Over the last few decades, the proportion of American people 65 and older has grown at twice the rate of the rest of our population.

27. In the older years people experience a decline in all sensory functions together with a reduction in organ reserve (the capacity of organs like the heart & lungs to increase their outputs under emergency conditions).

28. There is ample evidence that regular exercise can significantly reduce the deterioration of many bodily functions that accompanies aging.

29. The two major explanations of why people age are the genetic clock theory, which maintains that aging is built into the body cells through a genetic code, and the accumulating damages interpretation which suggests that our bodies eventually wear out as a result of accumulated insults and damages from continued, nonstop use.

30. For most people, the ability to learn and retain meaningful information declines only slightly in the older years.

31. Only a small number of older people experience the ravages of senile dementia associated with such things as strokes, brain tumors, or chronic alcoholism.

32. The most common form of senile dementia is Alzheimer's disease, which has been linked with a deficiency of the neurotransmitter acetylcholine. Research has also linked this disease to the presence of a protein that creates tangled amyloid webs that destroy brain cells. Finally, both familial and nonfamilial Alzheimer's disease are associated with a genetic defect on chromosome 21.

33. Even in old age the neurons of the cerebral cortex seem capable of forming additional functional connections with other neurons.

34. Studies have shown that satisfaction with life in general and feelings of well-being tend to be higher among the aged than among younger adults.

35. Happiness in the older years does not appear to be correlated with a particular lifestyle. Some older people are happiest when they are busy and socially involved, while others may enjoy indulging in plenty of relaxation. Most older people tend to select a lifestyle that reflects their personality and the kinds of activities they engaged in while they were younger.

36. In recent years there has been a strong interest in thanatology, the study of death and dying.

37. Elizabeth Kübler-Ross has described five stages that most dying people pass through: denial, anger, bargaining, depression, and, finally, acceptance.

38. Not everyone goes through these five stages in the same sequence, and a dying person may experience more than one stage at a time.

39. Hospices are facilities designed to care for the special needs of the dying, including love and support, pain control, and maintaining a sense of dignity.

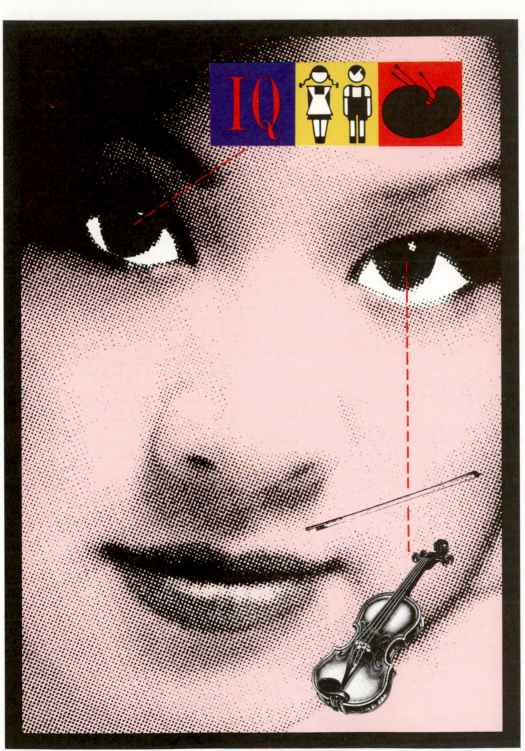

12 Intelligence

P eople have always been aware of differences in intelligence between individuals, but not until the closing decades of the 1800s were any efforts made to quantify or measure people's intelligence. The story of how and why the intelligence testing movement began is an interesting one, and it is a good place to start this chapter.

The story centers around Sir Francis Galton (1822–1911), a British biologist who also happened to be the cousin of Charles Darwin. Galton was very much influenced by his cousin's theory of natural selection (see Chapter 1), and he saw the process of "survival of the fittest" at work in British society. He declared that among humans, the "most fit" were those with high intelligence. How could we tell who these superior people were? Independently wealthy himself, Galton assumed that those individuals in the upper stratum of society must be the most intelligent. The very fact that they had risen to the top was evidence that they had adapted most successfully to their environment. (No matter that the upper classes were born with a head start denied to the rest of society! Since Galton believed that intelligence was inherited, this detail was of minor importance, for a son would inherit his father's intelligence as well as his hard-earned wealth.) Galton also believed that men were intellectually superior to women, and that Caucasians were superior to other races.

Galton was not satisfied merely to assume that the upper classes were intellectually superior to the rest of society. As biologist Stephen Jay Gould has noted, "quantification was Galton's god" (1981, p. 76), and Galton would not rest until he had proven his theory by measuring people's intelligence. Galton designed a number of procedures (including simple tests of sensory acuity and reaction time as well as some very precise skull measurements) to measure attributes that he thought were the basis of human intelligence. The 1884 International Exposition was taking place in London, and so Galton set up a laboratory there. For threepence, visitors could expose themselves to Galton's procedures and find out how they rated.

Thus, the first intelligence test was conducted on some 10,000 visitors to the Exposition. The results may have disappointed Galton, for they documented neither the superiority of the upper classes nor even the superiority of the white Caucasian male. However, this episode marked the beginning of scientific efforts to determine what intelligence is and how to measure it. Although our understanding of intelligence and our ability to measure it have come a long way since Galton's time, we will see in this

Sir Francis Galton

chapter that intelligence is still an elusive concept. (We will also meet up with Francis Galton a few more times, for several of his observations about intelligence are still relevant today.)

We begin by trying to determine what intelligence is, then move on to explore some of the methods that are used to measure people's intelligence. We also discuss one of psychology's most debated controversies: To what degree is intelligence a product of heredity, and to what degree is it a product of environment? Finally, the chapter ends with a discussion of the relationship between intelligence and creativity.

WHAT IS INTELLIGENCE?

Virtually all of us have used the term "intelligent" to describe friends and acquaintances, but what is intelligence? What attributes must a person display to earn the label intelligent? Consider the personal traits ascribed to the following two hypothetical people and decide which person sounds most intelligent to you:

Person A	*Person B*
1. Speaks clearly and articulately	1. Displays a good vocabulary
2. Sees all aspects of a problem	2. Is intellectually curious
3. Is a good source of ideas	3. Learns rapidly
4. Deals effectively with people	4. Thinks deeply
5. Makes good decisions	5. Solves problems well
6. Deals with problems resourcefully	6. Displays logical reasoning
7. Is sensitive to other people's needs and desires	7. Displays interest in the world at large
8. Thinks before speaking and doing	8. Is verbally fluent

Admittedly, making a judgment based on this limited information is not easy. Nevertheless, there is reason to believe that you may have found yourself favoring person A. This prediction is based on research conducted a few years ago by psychologist Robert Sternberg and his colleagues (Sternberg et al., 1981). Sternberg's group surveyed several hundred laypeople representing a broad spectrum of society as well as over 100 psychologists with a special interest in intelligence. Both the nonpsychologists and the specialists were asked to list specific kinds of behavior that they thought were indicative of intelligence or the lack of intelligence. A list of 170 indicators emerged from this study.

Most of these behaviors fall into one of three categories: *verbal ability* (speaks clearly and articulately; is verbally fluent), *practical problem-solving ability* (sees all aspects of a problem; is able to apply knowledge to problems at hand), and *social competence* (is sensitive to other people's needs and desires; thinks before speaking and doing). The nonpsychologists and the experts had remarkably similar views, with one major difference: Laypeople were much more inclined than the research psychologists to include dimensions of social competence as attributes of intelligence. Since social competence traits were ascribed only to person A (items 4, 7, and 8), we predicted that you would be likely to consider person A more intelligent than person B.

SOME THEORETICAL MODELS OF INTELLIGENCE

Sternberg is interested in more than simply the attributes that people associate with intelligence. He has also studied the ways in which people process information, and his conclusions form the basis of one theoretical model of intelligence. We will look at Sternberg's model of intelligence as a process, as well as some structural models that conceptualize intelligence as a combination of several abilities.

Sternberg's Information-Processing Approach Sternberg's theory of intelligence (1979, 1981, 1982) focuses on how people process information in order to solve problems and deal effectively with their environment. Sternberg conducted a number of experiments to study the steps that people go through when solving the kinds of problems that are typically encountered on intelligence tests. He has identified six steps:

1. *Encoding*: Identifying the key terms or concepts in the problem and retrieving any relevant information from long-term memory.
2. *Inferring*: Determining the nature of relationships that exist between these terms or concepts.
3. *Mapping*: Clarifying the relationship between previous situations and the present one.
4. *Application*: Deciding if the information about known relationships can be applied to the present problem.
5. *Justification*: Deciding if the answer can be justified.
6. *Response*: Providing the answer that seems best based on proper information processing at each of the previous stages.

One of Sternberg's most interesting findings is that good problem solvers who score high on intelligence tests spend more time analyzing a question, particularly in the encoding stage, than do those who score lower. He determined this by presenting a subject with a problem, such as "Washington is to one as Lincoln is to ___," and then measuring how long it took a person to indicate comprehension of the question. Then he showed the subject the answer choices—(a) 5; (b) 10; (c) 15; (d) 50—and recorded how long it took to obtain an answer. If you remembered that George Washington's picture is on a one-dollar bill, and Abraham Lincoln's on a five, you may have realized that the correct answer is 5. Sternberg discovered that his highly intelligent subjects spent longer than average analyzing a question before signaling that they understood it, but were able to recognize the correct answer more quickly than subjects with average intelligence (Sternberg, 1984).

Perhaps you have noticed that students who earn top grades are often among the last to finish an exam. These slow finishers sometimes express embarrassment or concern that their slowness reflects some intellectual inadequacy. Now, thanks to Sternberg's model, we have evidence that intelligence does not necessarily equal speed, and that people who score highest on tests often take a sufficient amount of time to analyze problems carefully.

Sternberg's research has some practical implications. If we can analyze how people use the various steps to process information and solve problems, it may be possible to teach them strategies for improving their performances. For example, a common factor in low test scores is the tendency of some students to rush through a test without carefully analyzing each question and considering a range of options. Such people have a tendency merely to grab on to the first answer that seems halfway reasonable. We have found that the exam scores of these speedy test takers can sometimes be improved by suggesting that they take their finished exams back to their desks and spend the remainder of the test period carefully considering their answers.

By learning to think about how they approach problems and how to function more effectively, Sternberg believes, people can be taught to construct their own problem-solving strategies. In this sense, people's intelligence, at least as it is measured by intelligence tests, can be increased by

A common factor in low test scores is the tendency of some students to rush through a test without carefully analyzing each question and considering a range of options. People who score highest on tests often take a sufficient amount of time to analyze problems carefully.

teaching them to apply problem-solving strategies more effectively. A good deal of formal education seems to focus on teaching people lots of facts rather than teaching them how to think; perhaps with more emphasis on the latter, we might increase the intelligence scores of our students.

Spearman's Two-Factor Theory Sternberg's model of the *process* of intelligence represents a different approach from some other models of intelligence. Many theorists have been more concerned with the *structure* of intelligence—that is, the skills and abilities that it consists of.

This is true of the first widely influential theory of intelligence, proposed in 1904 by Charles Spearman. Spearman's view of intelligence reflected his use of *factor analysis,* a statistical procedure that enables researchers to identify groupings of test items that seem to tap a common ability or factor. For example, people who are quickly able to assemble colored blocks to match pictures of complex designs also tend to perform well when asked to assemble pieces of a puzzle. We could view these two behaviors, as well as other behaviors that reflect an ability to visualize and manipulate patterns and forms in space, as defining a spatial ability factor. Spearman developed his model of intelligence by applying factor analysis to the scores of a large number of subjects on diverse tests that assessed many different intellectual skills and abilities. This approach allowed him to assess which of these skills were related to each other.

Spearman noted that some subjects consistently scored high on all of the various tests, regardless of what they were supposed to be measuring, and that a roughly equal number could be counted on to score low. People who scored high (or low) on one kind of test also tended to score at a similar level on other tests, but their scores on various skill tests did tend to differ somewhat.

These observations prompted Spearman to propose that intelligence is made up of two things: a **g-factor**, or general intelligence, and a collection of specific intellectual abilities that he labeled **s-factors**. According to this view, we all have a certain level of general intelligence (g-factor), probably genetically determined, that underlies all of our intelligent behavior. We also have specific abilities (s-factors) that are more useful on some tasks than on others. This theoretical perspective leads to the prediction that a person with a high g-factor will score higher on most skill tests than will a person with an average level of general intelligence. It would not be particularly

TABLE 12.1 *L. L. Thurstone's Seven Primary Mental Abilities*

Ability	Brief Description
Verbal comprehension	The ability to understand the meaning of words, concepts, and ideas.
Numerical ability	The ability to use numbers quickly to compute answers to problems.
Spatial relations	The ability to visualize and manipulate patterns and forms in space.
Perceptual speed	The ability to grasp perceptual details quickly and accurately and to determine similarities and differences between stimuli.
Word fluency	The ability to use words quickly and fluently in performing such tasks as rhyming, solving anagrams, and doing crossword puzzles.
Memory	The ability to recall information such as lists of words, mathematical formulas, definitions, etc.
Inductive reasoning	The ability to derive general rules and principles from presented information.

surprising, however, for individuals with average general intelligence to score higher on some specific skills because of a particular strength in their s-factors.

Thurstone's Primary Mental Abilities   One of Spearman's strongest critics was L. L. Thurstone (1938). Thurstone used factor analysis on the scores of a large number of subjects on over 50 different ability tests, but he found no evidence for a general intelligence ability as Spearman had proposed. Instead, he declared that human intelligence is a composite of seven **primary mental abilities**: verbal comprehension, numerical ability, spatial relations, perceptual speed, word fluency, memory, and inductive reasoning. Table 12.1 provides a summary.

Thurstone considered each mental ability to be independent, so that it could be measured separately from other abilities. Unlike Spearman, Thurstone did not believe that a person's intelligence can be expressed as a single score. Rather, assessing any person's intelligence would require measuring all seven of these primary abilities.

Guilford's Structure of Intellect   Since Thurstone's time, there have been many attempts to isolate different kinds of intellectual attributes. One of the most ambitious efforts is that of J. P. Guilford (1967, 1977, 1982) who also bases his model of intelligence on factor analysis. Guilford proposes that intelligence consists of 150 separate abilities, with no overall general intelligence factor.

Guilford believes that any intellectual task can be analyzed in terms of three major intellectual functions: the mental **operations** that are used (how we think); the **content** upon which those operations are performed (what we think about); and the **products** of applying a particular operation to a particular content. Each of these three functions is divided into a number of subfunctions, and there are 150 possible interactions or combinations of these subfunctions. Guilford thus maintains that he has isolated 150 kinds of intelligence.

DEFINING INTELLIGENCE

The theoretical models we have just discussed help us understand the processes as well as the specific skills associated with intelligence, but it is unwieldy to define **intelligence** with an exhaustive list of attributes. How can all this information be distilled into a succinct and concise definition? Several psychologists have risen to this challenge. Lewis Terman (1921), an influential pioneer in intelligence research and testing, defined intelligence as *the ability to think abstractly*. David Wechsler (1944), who developed tests that are today widely used to measure intelligence, considered intelligence to be *the ability to act purposefully, to think rationally, and to deal effectively with the environment*. More recently, Robert Sternberg and William Salter (1982) reported that most experts view intelligence as *a person's capacity for goal-directed adaptive behavior*.

All of these definitions seem reasonable and they are acceptable to many people, including many psychologists. However, they each pose additional problems. For example, what does it mean to "think abstractly," "act purposefully," or engage in "goal-directed adaptive behavior"? Because these descriptions are ambiguous, these definitions may mean different things to different people.

CAN INTELLIGENCE BE DEFINED OPERATIONALLY?

Virtually all intelligence researchers agree that intelligence is not a precisely measurable commodity that we possess. Rather, it is a concept or label invented to explain why some people behave in a more effective and adaptive manner than others. If you wanted to conduct research in which intelligence would be one of your key variables (for example, a study of the relationship between birth order and intelligence) you would need to define intelligence operationally. An imprecise concept such as the ability to think abstractly would be unworkable, for how do you measure abstract thinking? How would you develop a precise operational definition of intelligence that would allow you to quantify and measure this variable? Can intelligence be defined operationally? Take a couple of minutes to consider this question before reading on. (You may wish to review the information about operational definitions in Chapter 2.)

Unfortunately, the only operational definition of intelligence that psychologists have agreed upon to date may be stated as follows: *Intelligence is that which intelligence tests measure*. Virtually all intelligence research to date, whether it be of a correlational or experimental nature, has used test scores to measure intelligence. To make a reasonable judgment about how sound this practice is, you need more information about how intelligence is measured.

MEASURING INTELLIGENCE

We saw at the beginning of this chapter that Sir Francis Galton's early intelligence testing efforts were somewhat disappointing. The story did not end there, however. Over a period of many years, procedures for measuring intelligence have evolved considerably, so that today there are a number of highly regarded devices for measuring intelligence. This section will provide a brief overview of what has happened in the interim.

BINET AND INTELLIGENCE TESTING

The so-called modern intelligence testing movement was launched around the turn of the century by French psychologist Alfred Binet in response to an urgent need to ease problems of overcrowding in French schools. The French government had recently made education compulsory for all children, but it had not anticipated two outcomes of this edict. First, the classrooms were filled to the overflow point, and second, teachers now had to cope with a much wider range of differences in students' abilities than ever before. It soon became apparent that a sizable number of children needed special classes.

How could these children be identified? Since Binet was the leading French psychologist at the time, he was asked to develop an objective test to identify pupils who needed special classes. With a number of collaborators,

Alfred Binet

most notably Theodore Simon, Binet set out to devise a test to measure children's intellectual skills.

Binet and his collaborators reasoned that virtually all children follow essentially the same course of intellectual development, but that some progress more rapidly than others. Thus, children of subnormal intelligence were presumed to be merely "retarded" in their development.

Taking this reasoning one step further, Binet theorized that a child of low intelligence should perform on tests of intellect as would a normal child of a younger age—and conversely, that a precocious child should perform like an older child of average intelligence. Binet coined the term *mental level* to express a child's composite test score. This term, later referred to as **mental age**, corresponds to the chronological (calendar) age of children who, on the average, receive a similar test score. Thus, a six-year-old who scored as well as an average eight-year-old would be said to have a mental age of eight. Binet and his collaborators reasoned that it would be possible to obtain accurate estimates of children's abilities to profit from the standard school curriculum by comparing their mental age to their chronological age (Binet & Simon, 1905).

Guided by this theoretical perspective, Binet and his associates developed a series of subtests covering a range of reasoning and problem-solving abilities. (Subtests are discrete groups of test items used to measure a particular skill or aptitude, which when evaluated together form an entire test.) The end result was a fairly elaborate test that first appeared in 1905, followed by a major revision three years later. Unlike Galton's attempt to differentiate between "superior" and "inferior" people, the Binet test was quite successful in evaluating the intellectual level of Parisian school children, and it was generally reliable as a predictor of children's success in regular schoolwork.

The Intelligence Quotient A few years after Binet's pioneering efforts, the German psychologist L. Wilhelm Stern devised a simple formula to avoid the problem of needing to deal with fractions that arose when mental age was compared to chronological age. His formula, MA (*mental age*) ÷ CA (*chronological age*) × 100, yielded an **intelligence quotient** or **IQ** score, which provided a rough index of how dull or bright a child was compared to her or his peers. For example, a child with a mental age of seven and a chronological age of five has an IQ of 140 ($7 \div 5 \times 100 = 140$).

IS THE ORIGINAL IQ FORMULA APPLICABLE TO ADULTS?

Do you think that the original IQ formula (MA ÷ CA × 100) is applicable to adults? Why or why not? Can you think of an alternative approach to calculating adult IQs? Give these questions some thought before reading on.

An average six-year-old can do certain things—like telling the difference between a slipper and a boot—that most four- and five-year-olds cannot do. Consequently, items like this became six-year-level subtest items. In similar fashion, Binet and later Lewis Terman (discussed in the next section) were able to select items that differentiated between average seven- and eight-year-olds, nine- and ten-year-olds and so forth. However, as they moved up the chronological age scale, it became increasingly difficult to find items that would demonstrate proportionate age differences while maintaining the integrity of the IQ formula.

The credibility of the original formulation completely breaks down in the adult age range. Consider, for example, a 20-year-old who performs on an IQ test as well as an average 36-year-old. Would it be logical to conclude that the younger person has an IQ of 180 ($36 \div 20 \times 100 = 180$)? The fact that this conclusion is clearly not justifiable indicates why psychologists needed to come up with an alternative method for computing adult IQs. As we will see shortly, they resolved the problem by designing adult intelligence tests in which IQ scores are based on how subjects compare to the average performance of others in the same age bracket.

THE STANFORD-BINET INTELLIGENCE SCALE

Stanford University psychologist Lewis Terman imported Binet's test to America shortly after Binet's death in 1911. Terman discovered that the age norms developed for French students did not work very well with American children. Consequently, he revised Binet's scale as he translated many of the original items, added some new questions, and established new age norms using Caucasian California pupils to evaluate how effective test items were for measuring age-related changes. Terman labeled the revised test the **Stanford-Binet**, a name it still retains over 60 years and several revisions later.

The Stanford-Binet test has undergone a number of revisions since it first appeared in 1916. In 1937, Terman and his associates introduced two alternate forms of the test, and later revisions in 1960 and 1985 updated some items and introduced a change in the scoring scheme. The individually administered Stanford-Binet test is made up of a series of subtests that are graded by age level.

The concept of designing different test items or questions for different age levels reflects Binet's original conception that average children of different ages can do different things. Although the test is used primarily for children, there are also some subtests for adults.

The Stanford-Binet has been widely used for a longer period of time than any other test of intelligence, and it is still highly regarded by most specialists in the testing field. It possesses impressive predictive ability, providing reasonably good estimates of a child's ability to do well in school. A number of studies have shown substantial positive correlations between Stanford-Binet IQ scores and grade-school, high-school, and college grades. The correlations are generally stronger at the lower grade levels.

THE WECHSLER ADULT INTELLIGENCE SCALE

Since the early days of its use, one of the most frequent criticisms of the Stanford-Binet test has been that it places too much emphasis on verbal abilities such as word knowledge, sentence interpretation, and so forth. In so doing, the test discriminates against people for whom English is a second language as well as members of American subcultures (such as economically disadvantaged blacks) who have their own unique style of verbal communication. Another criticism of the Stanford-Binet test has been that it was originally designed for children and still remains far more applicable to children than adults.

In the late 1930s, psychologist David Wechsler developed a new kind of intelligence test to avoid these two problems. His initial product, published in 1939, was a test designed exclusively for people in late adolescence or adulthood. This test, now called the **Wechsler Adult Intelligence Scale (WAIS),** includes 11 subtests which are arranged according to the aptitude being tested rather than by age level. These subtests are grouped into two major categories or scales: a *verbal scale* made up of six subtests, and a *performance (nonverbal) scale* comprising the other five subtests. (Table 12.2 provides examples of subtests from the 1981 revision of the WAIS.) This division allows for the calculation of separate verbal and performance IQ scores as well as an overall IQ, a feature that was warmly received by professionals in the testing field. For the first time, it was possible to identify individuals with special strengths in nonverbal areas and to detect superior intelligence even in people who might have had limited opportunities to develop verbal skills.

TABLE 12.2 *Verbal and Performance Subtests from the Wechsler Adult Intelligence Scale (WAIS-R, 1981)*

Verbal Subtests	Performance Subtests
1. *Information:* "What is the capital of the United States?" "Who was Shakespeare?"	7. *Digit Symbol:* Learning and drawing meaningless figures that are associated with numbers.
2. *Comprehension:* "Why do we have zip codes?" "What does 'A stitch in time saves nine' mean?"	8. *Picture Completion:* Pointing to the missing part of a picture.
3. *Arithmetic:* "If 3 candybars cost 25 cents, how much will 18 candybars cost?"	9. *Block Design:* Copying pictures of geometric designs using multicolored blocks.
4. *Similarities:* "How are good and bad alike?"	10. *Picture Arrangement:* Arranging cartoon pictures in sequence so that they tell a meaningful story.
5. *Digit Span:* Repeating series of numbers forwards and backwards	11. *Object Assembly:* Putting pieces of a puzzle together so that they form a meaningful object
6. *Vocabulary:* "What does canal mean?"	

Items for subtests 1, 2, 3, 4, and 6 are similar but not identical to actual test items.

GROUP VERSUS INDIVIDUAL INTELLIGENCE TESTS

Both the Stanford-Binet test and the Wechsler Intelligence Scale are individual intelligence tests: they are administered to one subject at a time by a specially trained tester who can use clinical insight in evaluating the subject's performance.

Many other intelligence tests are administered collectively to a group of subjects. These group IQ tests originated in the early 1900s in this country with mass intelligence testing of World War I recruits. The American Psychological Association developed two group IQ tests: the **Army Alpha test** (for recruits who could read) and the **Army Beta test** (for illiterates and non-English-speaking). The original purpose of these two tests was to enable the Army to assign soldiers to appropriate jobs, but their real value (to the field of psychology, at least) lay in the mass of data they generated from approximately three million subjects. These tests were enormously helpful both as models for group intelligence tests and as an impetus to developing more effective tests.

Dozens of group intelligence tests are in use today, primarily in educational settings. The name most commonly associated with the development of group IQ tests is Arthur Otis, a former student of Stanford's Lewis Terman. The **Otis-Lennon School Ability Test (OLSAT)**, appropriate for children of all school ages, is widely used. Another group intelligence test popular in many school systems is the **Cognitive Abilities Test (CAT)**, which is actually a series of tests, each appropriate for a specific age level from kindergarten through high school.

Group tests have certain obvious advantages over individual tests. They are cheaper, quicker, and easier to administer. Since good norms are available for the widely used group intelligence tests, they may be scored quickly and accurately, with no need for the kind of clinical interpretation by trained testers that individual tests demand. On the other hand, group tests also have potential limitations. When many people take a test in a group setting, such as a full classroom, it is impossible for the tester to be certain that all subjects understand directions, feel comfortable with the testing situation, and are motivated to do their best. Thus, a child or adult who is not feeling well or whose mind is preoccupied may perform well below her or his potential. Although individual tests take more time to administer and score, they allow for the establishment of rapport and they also are more likely to encourage the best performance from subjects.

APTITUDE VERSUS ACHIEVEMENT TESTS

We live in a society that places a good deal of emphasis on intelligence and aptitude testing (Linn, 1986). Whether or not you have taken any of the tests specifically mentioned above, the odds are that you have experienced plenty of tests, mostly in educational settings.

Many students are confused about the difference between aptitude tests and achievement tests. IQ tests and college entrance exams are generally classified as **aptitude tests**—tests designed to predict your ability to learn new information or a new skill. In contrast, **achievement tests** are intended to measure what you have already learned. Examples of achievement tests are final exams that test what you have learned in your various courses.

Although most psychologists distinguish between aptitude and achievement tests, they are quick to acknowledge that the differences are far from clear-cut. For example, it is reasonable to assume that your scores on the achievement exams given in this course will reflect not only your mastery of general psychology but also your aptitude for learning. The reverse is also true. A test such as the Wechsler Adult Intelligence Scale contains many subtests that measure a range of specific skills or aptitudes, a composite of which presumably reflects overall intelligence. However, many of the items also measure what one has already learned or achieved. For example, a person's ability to define words (vocabulary) or figure out what is missing from a picture (picture completion) is related to how much has been learned by exposure to previous information. Unfortunately, most items on widely used IQ tests reflect, at least to some degree, what we have already learned. Furthermore, since intelligence test constructors are typically middle- and upper-middle-class whites, these items also reflect cultural biases. As we will see later in this chapter, this raises some fundamental questions about their applicability for members of racial minorities or lower socioeconomic levels.

There have been several attempts to design tests to measure a kind of "pure" intelligence—that is, a person's basic capacity to behave intelligently rather than a reflection of how much that person has learned from previous experiences. Unfortunately, these efforts have fallen short of expectations, and to date there is still no clear measure of people's aptitudes as distinct from what they have already learned.

EVALUATING INTELLIGENCE TESTS

Earlier in this chapter we asked whether intelligence could be defined operationally, and had to settle for the operational definition that intelligence is "that which intelligence tests measure." We now know something about intelligence tests, but we still do not have enough information about the dependability of these tests to evaluate our operational definition.

To be a good measure of intelligence, a test must be well designed, reliable, and a valid instrument for assessing the particular abilities that indicate intelligence. A look at the processes by which IQ tests are constructed and evaluated can help us determine how effective modern intelligence tests are.

HOW INTELLIGENCE TESTS ARE DEVELOPED

The process by which IQ tests (as well as other psychological assessment methods) are developed can be simplified into four steps: developing test items, evaluating these test items, standardizing the test, and establishing norms. We now take a brief look at this process.

Developing a Pool of Test Items   Test constructors generally begin by developing a large pool of potential test items that seem to fit their partic-

The fact that Winston Churchill failed one grade in secondary school tells us little or nothing about his intelligence. People fail for many reasons: lack of interest, low drive, personality conflicts, and so on. Sometimes people of only average intelligence emerge as leaders who have an ability to speak eloquently.

ular testing needs. For example, the developers of the original Stanford-Binet scales started out with many items that seemed capable of differentiating between the intellect of children of different ages. These items were based on such things as common sense and direct observation. Since children's abilities to construct things out of blocks were known to improve with age, for instance, several kinds of block-building tasks of varying complexity were included in the original test-item pool. And since the ability to repeat digits from memory also reflected age-graded differences in intellect, measures of these abilities were also included in the test-item pool. Test constructors today may invent new test items, or they may modify existing ones from other tests.

Evaluating the Test Items   The next step in test construction is to separate the effective test items from those that are ineffective or misleading. To do this, all the items in the test pool are administered to large numbers of subjects who are representative of the intended test population. For example, since the developers of the Stanford-Binet were trying to differentiate between high, average, and low intelligence among a broad spectrum of children, they administered their pool of items to thousands of preschool and school-age children. They found that some items were effective in reliably differentiating between children of different age levels, while others were not. The test items that were ineffective were discarded.

Standardizing the Test   As test items are being evaluated and selected, test constructors must also develop **standardization procedures**—uniform and consistent procedures for both administering and scoring a test. Why are uniform procedures so crucial?

Suppose you are developing a Binet-type intelligence test and one of your subtests evaluates the ability of young children to build a bridge out of wooden blocks, guided only by a pictorial model. An average six-year-old can master this task, but it is too difficult for the average five-year-old—unless the examiner provides some hints or directives. If testers administered this kind of item in an inconsistent fashion, providing additional hints to some subjects but not to others, two kinds of errors might result. First, during the development stage the test designers might make errors in age-grading the difficulties of the item, assuming that younger children were able to perform the task. Later, after the test had already been developed, errors could be made in assessing the intellect of a child subject.

The purpose of standardization procedures is to avoid these kinds of errors. A standardized test includes instructions that spell out precisely how it should be administered and scored, so that the testing situations are as identical as possible for all subjects. This means all testers are required to use the same demonstrations, impose the same time limits, and provide the same directions (no random "helpful hints"). Testers who provide hints that other testers do not provide can give their subjects an edge over other testers' subjects.

Establishing Norms   Once the items for an intelligence test have been selected and standardization procedures implemented, the final step is to establish norms. A **norm** reflects the normal or average performance of a particular group of people. For example, if you developed an intelligence test for adults and found that the average score of 20- to 25-year-olds was 185 points, a score of 185 would become your basic norm or standard of performance for people in this age category. Similarly, if 40- to 45-year-olds scored 169 on the average, this would be your norm for this age group. The frequency and magnitude of scores that deviate from these norms are then analyzed to provide a basis for evaluating other levels of performance.

Most intelligence tests assign IQ scores of 85 and 115 to performances that fall one standard deviation below or above the norm for a particular age group. (See the Statistics Appendix for a discussion of *stan-*

What kind of a test would be capable of differentiating between the intellect of children of different ages? Developers of the Stanford-Binet scales decided to include several kinds of block-building tasks in the original test-item pool as one way to make this distinction.

FIRST PERSON 12.2

I vividly remember my first genuine IQ test. I was 17 at the time. The youth director at my church was in graduate school, working on an advanced degree in psychology, and as part of a course in intelligence testing, he was required to administer an IQ test to several subjects. I was one of his selected "volunteers," although I was also a friend. I remember wondering later about whether or not he had given me an unfair advantage on the test. He often responded to my asking for clarification by going into great detail while explaining a particular kind of question. I wondered if my score would be comparable to that of another person who was tested by someone who was not so generous about clarifying items. (*Authors' files*)

FIGURE 12.1   A TYPICAL BELL-SHAPED OR NORMAL CURVE DISTRIBUTION OF IQ SCORES

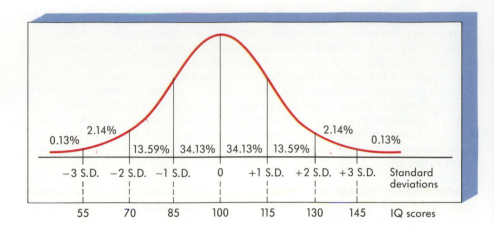

dard deviation, a statistical measure that indicates the degree to which scores are dispersed around the average.) Approximately 68 percent of people who take an IQ test achieve scores within a narrow range of about 85 to 115. About 95 percent of IQ scores fall between 70 and 130, and almost all (99.7 percent) are within a range of 55 to 145.

This method of assigning IQ scores is based on the concept of a normal distribution. Recall from Chapter 2 that a normal distribution forms a bell-shaped or normal curve. Many human attributes, including intelligence, are distributed along a normal or bell-shaped curve. Figure 12.1 demonstrates a typical normal distribution curve of IQ scores. This curve provides the basis for determining where a particular score falls relative to other scores. Thus, if you achieved an IQ of 130 on the test that provided the basis for the curve shown in the figure, approximately 98 percent of subjects would achieve an IQ score lower than you on the test. That is because only a fraction over two percent of subjects scored higher than 130. Similarly, if you scored 85, you might expect that about 84 percent of subjects would score higher than you.

TEST RELIABILITY AND VALIDITY

The procedures we have just described are designed toward one end: developing a test that will provide a sound, accurate measure of intelligence for the intended subjects. A test that meets this criterion is said to possess two qualities, reliability and validity, and psychologists use a number of methods to check for these qualities.

Determining Test Reliability   A good test must measure with dependable consistency. This quality is called **reliability**. Since a person's intelligence does not fluctuate widely over time, developers of IQ tests hope to achieve a quantitative consistency in the scores people obtain on their tests. This consistency may be assessed in a variety of ways.

One common method for evaluating test reliability is to give the same person or group of people the same test more than once. This procedure yields a measure of **test-retest reliability**. However, this method may itself be unreliable, for people often score better the second time they take a test because of familiarity with the test items or the test routine. One way to minimize this problem is to use an **alternate-forms reliability** check. Here, subjects take two different forms of a test that are as similar as possible, but not identical, in content and level of difficulty. This approach eliminates the possibility that a subject will score higher because of familiarity with specific test items, but it does not avoid score improvements that might result from practice taking a particular kind of test. Even practice effects can be averted, however, by calculating **split-half reliability.** Here, the reliability of a subject's performance on a single administration of a test is assessed by comparing performance on half of the test items compared to the other half (most commonly, scores for the odd- and even-numbered questions are compared). If the two scores obtained by any of these three methods generally agree, a test is considered to be reliable.

Assessing Test Validity   Suppose that you design a simple test of intelligence based on manual dexterity. You design a pegboard task in which subjects' scores are based on the speed with which they insert pegs of varied diameters into holes with comparable dimensions. Assume further that you design two alternate forms of this test that are comparable in format and level of difficulty. You administer both forms of the test to several hundred children and adults and determine that the alternate-forms reliability is very high. Does this mean that you have made an important breakthrough in intelligence testing?

The answer is: not necessarily. Just because a test is reliable does not necessarily mean that it also has **validity**. A test is considered valid if it accurately measures what it is supposed to measure. All you have measured in your test is the speed with which people can fit pegs into holes—a skill that may be completely unrelated to their level of intelligence.

MEASURING TEST VALIDITY

How would you go about finding out if fast peg fitters are more intelligent than slow peg fitters? In other words, how do you measure the validity of your test (or any other test for that matter)? Take a few moments to see what ideas you can come up with before reading on.

One of the simplest ways to assess if a test measures what it is supposed to measure is to compare peoples' test scores with their scores on other measures or *criteria* that are known to be good indicators of the skill or trait being assessed. This is called **criterion-related validity**.

There are two types of criterion-related validity: concurrent and predictive. **Concurrent validity** involves comparing test performance to other criteria that are currently available. For example, you might compare subjects' scores on your peg task to their IQ scores as assessed by established intelligence tests whose validity is recognized. If you found that high, average, and low scores on your manual dexterity task consistently matched up with correspondingly high, average, or low IQ scores, you might reasonably conclude that your test is a valid measure of intelligence.

Predictive validity is assessed by determining the accuracy with which tests predict performance in some future situation—for example, how well the Stanford-Binet scores of grade-school children predict their high-school grades or how precisely Scholastic Aptitude Test (SAT) scores predict a student's scholastic standing after one year of college.

CULTURAL BIAS IN IQ TESTS

Despite the care taken in designing a test, evaluating test items, and assessing validity and reliability, it is virtually impossible to avoid some built-in biases that may favor some subjects and place others at a disadvantage (Snyderman & Rothman, 1987). This is because any intelligence test is bound to reflect the cultural experiences of the test constructors. Subjects who are not from the dominant cultural segment of the population that a test is primarily designed to serve may be at some disadvantage in their abililty to understand and interpret test items.

Since IQ tests are typically constructed by white, middle-class city dwellers, it is not surprising that test questions often reflect the mainstream values and experiences of this segment of American culture. For example, a

Robert Williams, who designed the Black Intelligence Test of Cultural Homogeneity (BITCH)

WAIS question such as "Why do people buy fire insurance?" may have no relevance for minority group members raised in poor central city or rural environments.

This type of cultural bias is not unique to American tests or subcultures. Anne Anastasi (1976), a renowned specialist in psychological testing, reported an interesting situation in Israel in which Oriental immigrant children were asked to decide what was missing from a picture of a face with no mouth. Since their cultural background had not provided them opportunities to consider a drawing of a head as a complete picture, they typically answered "incorrectly" that the body was missing. This "mistake" did not mean they were less intelligent than native-born Israeli children who typically responded that the mouth was missing. Instead, it indicates how difficult it is to avoid cultural bias in designing intelligence tests.

What are the implications of this kind of bias? In an effort to demonstrate how the white, middle-class slant of mainstream American IQ tests affects minority subjects, two concerned social scientists decided to turn the tables. They designed black alternative IQ tests that drew primarily upon black experience. One test, designed by Robert Williams (1972), is titled the Black Intelligence Test of Cultural Homogeneity (BITCH). The average BITCH score for a group of 100 black teenagers was 30 points higher, on the average, than that for a group of same-age whites. Adrian Dove (1968) created a similar test, the Counterbalanced General Intelligence Test.

Sample questions from each of these tests are included in Figure 12.2. See how you fare on these items. If you are a white member of the middle class, you will probably perform like most college students in this category—not very well. Neither of these tests has been seriously considered as a substitute for traditional IQ testing among black populations. However, the publicity associated with their introduction has dramatically highlighted the problems associated with cultural bias in IQ testing. As one observer noted, "By showing educated whites an intellectual task on which they do poorly, BITCH challenges whites to defend the functional worth of other tests loaded with culture-specific tasks" (Cronbach, 1978, p. 250).

WHAT DETERMINES INTELLIGENCE?

Although we may disagree with many of Sir Francis Galton's early ideas about intelligence, most of us would probably agree with one of his observations—that it tends to run in families. You may have noticed that some of your brightest friends seem to have intelligent parents, while those with more average abilities often are products of families in which the parents seem to be of average intelligence.

The degree of relationship or correlation between the IQs of parents and their children has been shown to be approximately +.35 (see Table 12.3. (Recall from Chapter 2 that a coefficient of correlation always falls between −1.00 and +1.00, and that the closer it is to 1.00, the stronger is the relationship between two variables.) Researchers have found that parents with high IQs tend to have children with high IQs, and parents with low IQs are somewhat prone to have children with relatively low IQs. This finding lends credence to the widespread assumption that intelligence does indeed run in families.

Was Galton correct in saying that intelligence is largely inherited? From our previous discussions of the nature–nurture controversy (see Chapters 1 and 10), you are probably aware that environment as well as heredity contributes to most individual traits. Indeed, nowhere does the "nature" versus "nurture" controversy rage more actively than in the question of intellect.

According to the *hereditarian* view, genetics determine the structural and functional efficiency of the brain, which in turn clearly influences intellectual functioning. In contrast, the *environmentalist* view says that environment plays a greater role than genes in shaping human intellect, and that

FIGURE 12.2   IQ TESTS AND THE BLACK EXPERIENCE

1. "Boogie Jugie" means the same as
   (a) tired   (b) worthless   (c) old   (d) well put together

2. Black Draught is a
   (a) winter's cold wind   (b) laxative   (c) black soldier
   (d) dark beer

3. An alley apple is a
   (a) brick   (b) piece of fruit   (c) dog   (d) horse

4. "Boot" refers to
   (a) a cotton farmer   (b) a Black   (c) an Indian
   (d) a Vietnamese citizen

5. If you throw the dice and 7 is showing on the top, what is facing down?
   (a) 7   (b) "snake eyes"   (c) "Boxcars"   (d) "Little Joes"
   (e) 11

6. Jazz pianist Ahmad Jamal took an Arabic name after becoming really famous. Previously, he had some fame with what he called his "slave name." What was his previous name?
   (a) Willie Lee Jackson   (b) Le Roi Jones
   (c) Wilber McDougal   (d) Fritz Jones   (e) Andy Johnson

7. A "gas-head" is a person who has a
   (a) fast-moving car   (b) stable of "lace"   (c) process
   (d) habit of stealing cars   (e) long jail record for arson

8. A handkerchief head is
   (a) a cool cat   (b) a porter   (c) an Uncle Tom   (d) a hoddi
   (e) a preacher

Answers: 1. b 2. b 3. a 4. b 5. a 6. d 7. c 8. c

To illustrate that performance on Mainstream IQ tests depends largely upon exposure to white middle-class experiences, two concerned social scientists decided to "turn the tables" by designing tests culturally biased toward the black experience. The first four items are from the BITCH test designed by Robert Williams (1972), and the final four items are examples of questions from the Counterbalanced General Intelligence Test authored by Adrian Dove (1968). Try your hand at these tests and then check your performance against the answers listed below.

the positive relationship in parent-child IQs reflects the fact that adults tend to create home environments that are similar to those they experienced in their own childhood. With comparable sources of intellectual stimulation, an environmentalist would argue that it is not surprising that children develop a level of intelligence similar to that of their parents.

Which point of view is more accurate? Even after years of research, we still are not certain exactly what relative influences heredity and environment have upon intelligence.

DESIGNING RESEARCH TO ISOLATE HEREDITARY AND ENVIRONMENTAL CONTRIBUTIONS TO INTELLIGENCE

How can we determine to what extent intelligence (or any other human trait) is influenced by heredity or by environment? Take a moment to consider what research strategies might effectively be used to answer this question before reading on.

If ethics were not a consideration, an obvious choice might be to take people with clearly different genetic makeups (for example, unrelated children) and raise them in identical environments. If we could accomplish this, and all our identically reared children developed similar IQs, we could then conclude with confidence that genetic differences have little or no influence on intelligence, and that environment is the major determinant of intellect.

For obvious reasons, such an experiment has never been conducted. Most parents would not permit their children to be removed from them at an early age so that they might be raised in a controlled environment. Even if we were able to obtain a sample group and create a special environment for them, it is impossible to ensure that two people's experiences are identical. Even identical twins who grow up together do not have exactly the same environments—for each twin may relate differently to other family members and to individuals outside the home.

Since psychologists must work within both ethical and practical constraints, research into the relative impact of heredity and genetics has taken several forms other than the hypothetical method described above. The following paragraphs highlight what researchers have been able to discover through a number of studies of twins, adopted children, orphanage and environmental enrichment programs, birth-order studies, and even some animal research.

TWIN STUDIES

The intellectual differences that exist among all of us are a product of only two factors: genes and environment. Identical twins are unique in that only one of these factors, environment, contributes to differences in intelligence between members of a twin pair. Thus, a considerable amount of attention has focused on studies of twin pairs.

A hereditarian who discounts the role of environment in determining intelligence would predict a very high positive correlation between the IQs of identical twins, no matter whether they were raised together or in separate environments. Environmentalists, in contrast, would predict a much lower IQ correlation for separated identical twins than for twins reared together, since they place greater weight on environment in determining IQ scores.

What has the evidence shown? Table 12.3 presents the median IQ correlation coefficients for a variety of relationships as determined by a number of studies. You can see that identical twins reared together are highly similar in tested intelligence (.86), and that the second highest degree of correlation is demonstrated by identical twins reared separately (.72).

The slight decline in the degree of IQ correlation among sets of separated identical twins provides some evidence for the environmentalist prediction that IQ correlation will be reduced by differences in the environ-

TABLE 12.3 *Approximate Correlation Coefficients Between IQ Scores of Persons with Different Amounts of Genetic and Environmental Similarity*

Relationship	Median Correlation
Identical (monozygotic) twins	
reared together	.86
reared apart	.72
Fraternal (dizygotic) twins	
reared together	
same sex	.62
opposite sex	.62
reared apart	(no data available)
Siblings	
reared together	.38
reared apart	.24
Parent and child	
live together	.35
separated by adoption	.31
Genetically unrelated persons	
unrelated children reared together	.25
adoptive parent and adopted child	.15

These data were obtained from a variety of studies, most of which were relatively recent investigations. The correlations in the table reflect the median of a range of correlations obtained from several individual studies. You will note that as the degree of genetic similarity decreases, so does the magnitude of obtained correlations. It is also noteworthy that a shared environment increases the IQ correlations in all cases where applicable.

Source: Adapted from Henderson, 1982, and Plomin & Defries, 1980.

ment. However, identical twins reared separately are still more similar in IQ than are fraternal twins of the same sex who are reared together (.62). This finding seems to undermine the environmentalist view that fraternal twins reared together should have a higher degree of IQ correlation than identical twins raised apart.

For years, many psychologists viewed such findings as evidence that heredity plays an exceedingly large role in determining intelligence. The most widely quoted and best known of these studies was conducted by the late English psychologist Sir Cyril Burt (1966), who reported remarkable IQ similarities between 53 pairs of separated identical twins purportedly reared in totally different environments. In the early 1970s, however, American psychologist Leon Kamin (1974) became suspicious when he noticed several peculiarities in Burt's data and procedures. Shortly after, an investigative reporter for the *London Sunday Times* discovered that two of Burt's collaborators who had supposedly collected much of his data never existed (Gillie, 1976). By the end of the 1970s, even Burt's most staunch supporters conceded that his research was fraudulent and that he had succeeded in perpetrating a massive hoax on the world scientific community (Hearnshaw, 1979). (The spurious data from Burt's "research" are not included in Table 12.3.)

This unfortunate episode seriously weakened the case of the hereditarians. However, other studies of identical twins reared apart have reported similarly high IQ correlations. Investigations conducted by James Shields (1962) and Horatio Newman and his colleagues (1937) are representative of other research in this area. Both studies reported very high IQ correlations among sets of identical twins reared apart. In many instances, however, the environments of the separated twins were not very different. In some cases, twin sets were raised by relatives and had considerable contact with each other during their development. Furthermore, the more similar were the twins' family environments, the more alike were their IQ scores.

Psychologists continue to study twins in the hope that such research will lead to a better understanding of the relative contributions of heredity. One major ongoing study at the University of Minnesota, under the direction of Thomas Bouchard, may eventually provide some highly reliable data. Preliminary findings on several sets of identical and fraternal twins reared apart indicate a much greater degree of similarity in identical than fraternal twins in a wide range of intellectual, emotional, and behavioral attributes (Bouchard, 1984; Bouchard & McGue, 1981). This evidence seems to support the view that genetic factors are important in producing differences in intelligence between people—but again, environmentalists can also find some support in these same data. For example, preliminary findings have revealed that when identical twins were reared in dramatically different environments, the spread between their respective IQs widened to as great as 20 points in one case. Thus, the debate rages on. Hopefully, when enough reliable data are collected, psychologists may be able to reach some consensus on the implications of twin study findings.

ADOPTION STUDIES

Other evidence concerning the influence of nature and nurture on intelligence is provided by studies of adopted children. Here, a few research approaches have been used. One is to measure the degree of correlation between the IQs of children adopted in infancy and those of their adoptive parents. This measure is then compared with a similar correlation statistic from studies of children raised by their biological parents. Whereas children reared by their natural parents may be similar to them because of both genetic and environmental factors, similarities between adopted children and their genetically unrelated parents can only be explained by environmental factors.

An environmentalist would predict that the relationship between the IQs of children and the parents who raise them would be similar regardless of whether or not a biological relationship exists. However, a number of studies have found that children are significantly more similar in intelligence to their biological parents who rear them than are adopted children to their adoptive parents. Several studies have also shown that adopted children's IQ scores are more similar to those of their biological parents than of their adoptive parents (Scarr & Carter-Saltzman, 1983).

One problem with adoption studies is the difficulty in assessing the degree of similarity between the home environments of adoptive and biological parents. When major discrepancies exist, there is some indication that environment may play a greater role than otherwise. For example, when children of poor, undereducated parents are adopted into a family of high socioeconomic status, the children may exhibit very large increases in IQ scores, a finding that suggests that environment has a major impact on intelligence (Scarr & Weinberg, 1976). When the socioeconomic status of both biological and adoptive parents is about equal, however, the IQs of adopted children tend to be much more similar to those of their biological parents than of their adoptive parents (Scarr & Weinberg, 1978). This latter finding suggests the importance of heredity in determining intelligence.

ORPHANAGE AND ENVIRONMENTAL ENRICHMENT STUDIES

Some of the strongest support for the environmentalist position has come from studies of children reared in orphanages. The classic experiment in this area was begun in the 1930s under the guidance of H. M. Skeels (1966). Thirteen apparently retarded two-year-olds, who were living in an orphanage in Iowa, were transferred to an institution that housed mentally retarded women. Each child was placed in the care of a young woman resident who spent much of her time "mothering," loving, and caring for her foster child. Within a relatively brief period of four years, these children had gained an average of about 30 IQ points—compared to a control group of 12 children remaining in the orphanage, who had lost an average of 20 IQ points. Twenty years later, Skeels reevaluated these children and found that the differences between the two groups were still profound. Most of the 13 raised by the retarded foster mothers had graduated from high school, found jobs, and married. The 12 reared in the orphanage did not fare so well: most were grade-school dropouts and several were either still institutionalized or not self-supporting.

In a more recent study, psychologist J. McVicker Hunt (1982) assessed the effects of environmental enrichment on 11 children living in an Iranian orphanage. Before entering the enrichment program as infants, all of these children were developmentally and emotionally retarded, passive, and unresponsive to their environments. In the program, trained caregivers provided special attention to the infants, playing vocal games with them, responding to any signs of distress, and so forth. As in the Skeels study, the impact of this environmental enrichment was dramatic. All 11 infants demonstrated marked acceleration in acquiring language skills. They also became much more animated in their reactions to people and events, and in general began to behave in a more intelligent fashion typical of children raised in natural home environments.

In the United States, the most extensive educational and environmental enrichment program has been Project Head Start, a federally funded program launched in 1965 to provide special intellectual and social skills training for children from disadvantaged environments. Typically, a child enrolled in the Head Start program is provided one to two years of compensatory education and environmental enrichment beginning at age four.

The program has been closely watched, and hundreds of research studies have been conducted. Initial findings showed significant short-term

IQ gains, generating a great deal of optimism among researchers and educators connected to the program. Unfortunately, however, later follow-up studies revealed that the earlier IQ gains did not hold up over longer periods after children had entered the mainstream educational system.

The program has continued, however, and the consensus today is that Project Head Start has been a qualified success. Although Head Start children typically do not exhibit large, enduring IQ gains, they do fare better on many other measures of success than disadvantaged children who do not participate in the program. For example, Head Start children are less likely to require special remedial classes and are less likely to fail grades. They also tend to adjust better to the school environment, exhibit better social skills, and, perhaps most importantly, enjoy more positive self-esteem (Collins, 1983, 1984; McKey et al., 1985; Zigler & Berman, 1983).

In evaluating the Head Start program, it is important to remember that unlike the studies of Skeels and Hunt, in which children were "rescued" from the damaging effects of impoverished orphanage environments in the first year or two of their lives, the children who enter the Head Start program have already experienced four years of impoverished environment. Hunt (1982) believes that much intellectual and emotional damage has already been incurred by age four, and that enrichment programs such as Head Start should be implemented at birth. This bold approach would surely be controversial, but perhaps it might result in more pronounced and enduring IQ gains as well as other benefits.

The Head Start studies and the orphanage studies provide evidence of the role environment plays in intellectual development. In most of these cases, however, the children had previously been subjected to less than optimal environmental conditions. Many researchers believe that the impact of environment on intelligence is far less pronounced among children who experience adequate human contact and normal exposure to environmental stimulation (Scarr, 1984). This suggests that special enrichment programs are likely to have less impact upon the intellectual development of children reared in "normal" environments than on children from disadvantaged environments. This is not to say, of course, that outside of marked neglect, parenting patterns have no impact on children's intellectual growth. The Health Psychology and Life discussion, "Maximizing Children's Intellectual Potential," suggests several strategies for structuring a home environment to help children reach their intellectual potential.

Children enrolled in Head Start programs are less likely to require special remedial classes, tend to adjust better to the school environment, exhibit better social skills, and enjoy more positive self-esteem.

BIRTH-ORDER STUDIES

For still further evidence on the influence of heredity and environment, we return to our friend Sir Francis Galton. Galton made still another intriguing observation that we have not yet discussed. He noted a connection between the order in which children were born and intelligence, noting that an unusual number of eminent British scientists were first-born children. In the years following Galton's observation, a number of studies have revealed that first-born children do in fact tend to score higher on IQ tests than those born later (Zajonc & Markus, 1975).

BIRTH ORDER AND INTELLIGENCE

How would you explain the fact that first-borns typically score higher on IQ tests than their later-born siblings? What is the implication of this evidence for the nature-nurture controversy? Take a moment to consider your answers before reading on.

While the meaning of birth-order data is not clear-cut, some psychologists believe that family size influences the amount of stimulation available in the home environment, and that this is reflected in the relationship

MAXIMIZING CHILDREN'S INTELLECTUAL DEVELOPMENT

Both heredity and environment exert an important influence on the development of intelligence. Occasionally people have incorrectly interpreted evidence indicating that IQ is largely inherited, and concluded that there is little a parent or other caregiver can do beyond making sure that children are not exposed to severely impoverished environments. Most psychologists agree that this is not the case. A substantial body of evidence suggests that people's experiences, particularly during the early years, can significantly influence the development of intelligence. The following noninclusive list of parental and family characteristics have been shown to foster intellectual growth (Belsky, 1981; Carew, 1980; Estrada et al., 1987; Gottfried, 1984; Maziade et al., 1987; McCall, 1983; Trickett et al., 1983).

1. Parents of children who are high achievers at school and who score well above average on intelligence tests tend to be very warm and loving toward their children. This love is often of the unconditional variety, rather than the type that conveys the message "I will love you if you. . . ."

2. You may have heard it said that rigorous discipline contributes to strong mental discipline and "strength of character." Research has shown that this is not necessarily the case. Children are much more likely to thrive intellectually in homes where parents encourage their offspring to explore and express themselves in a wide range of activities, while continually expressing acceptance of these exploratory behaviors. This is not to say that children should be raised in homes that are entirely devoid of limits. Some degree of structure should be provided to establish reasonable limits, but at the same time children should be permitted wide latitude in expressing their curiosity and creativity.

3. Children should be encouraged to be independent. Parents can begin to implement independency training at a very early age, as indicated by the following account:

My husband and I decided that it was important for children to begin to make independent choices at a very young age. We have seen too many children who seem indecisive and unable to make the simplest decision without consulting their parents. How can you expect children to grow up to be successful achievers if they are always hanging back, waiting for someone else to take the lead in decision making? We decided to introduce our strategy in non-stressful ways with our first-born daughter. When she started preschool, I would make certain she had an ample supply of clean clothes, but it was her responsibility to decide what to wear each day. If she ended up with different socks or an atrocious color match, we didn't intervene. This is not to say that we didn't offer suggestions if she asked for advice. But the final decision was left up to her. As she grew older, we extended this independency training to areas of more importance—for example, what classes to take in school or what was a reasonable time she should return home from a date. I am pleased to report that this tactic paid off with both our daughters and our younger son. Each has been remarkably successful in their lives, and in most instances they have made very good decisions. (*Authors' Files*)

4. Closely related to the benefit of independency training is the opportunity for children to acquire a sense of control over their environments. Children who learn early that their actions count are encouraged to think creatively and learn to make intelligent, informed decisions. Here again, the sense of control can be accomplished early on by giving children a voice in family decisions. For example, when planning a vacation, parents can ask their children's opinions about possible destinations and can provide them with an equal vote in making the actual choice. Children can also be included in other family decisions, such as whether or not to change residences, what television program to watch, how household chores should be divided, and so forth.

5. Parents or other caregivers who provide children with plenty of quality attention help promote both a sense of personal warmth and a desire to maximize one's potential. Unfortunately research shows that a typical American child spends considerably more time watching television (not the greatest enhancer of intellect) than interacting with his or her parents.

6. Beyond providing ample attention, a few specific patterns of parent-child interaction may help to maximize a child's intellectual growth. One is reading. It can be helpful to read thought-provoking literature to a child, both fiction and nonfiction, and to discuss reactions to the content. Reading to a child is an excellent vehicle for establishing an early interest in books, thus encouraging an enduring relationship with the storehouses of human knowledge. Other helpful types of interaction include engaging in creative leisure activities, from cooking or art projects to constructing a new toy with an erector set, and playing stimulating and

challenging games with children. Consider the following account:

Many years ago, when my children were still young, a friend presented me with an interesting problem to solve. It was sort of a riddle. It went something like this. A man is watching a funeral procession. He turns to another man in the crowd of onlookers and asks who the deceased is. The stranger responds, "Brothers and sisters had he none, but that man's father was my father's son." I brought the riddle home to my children and they really got a bang out of it. We had to talk and argue a long time before they agreed on the correct answer.

I discovered something that day. Kids love to be challenged by a tough but solvable problem. From that point on it became a custom around our house that Dad would bring home a riddle or problem every few days. As the kids got older I tried to find increasingly challenging problems. Several of my

friends at work helped me out by supplying some good material. A common question at coffee breaks was "Got any new riddles?" Today my children are adults and they still like a good riddle. Now it is they that bring them home during visits with my wife and me. (Authors' Files)

(By the way, the answer to the riddle is that the dead man is the speaker's own son.)

7. There is ample evidence that stressful environments can significantly retard intellectual development. Conversely, home environments that are largely free of the tensions and conflicts associated with relationships turmoil, financial pressures, and related stresses are more conducive to the realization of one's full intellectual potential.

Perhaps you can expand upon this list of potentially enriching environmental factors. Remember, however, that while there is much that we can do to help children reach the upper limits of their intelligence potential, nothing is more important than nurturing them with abundant and unconditional love.

between birth order and intelligence. According to this view, first-borns do not have to compete with other siblings for parental attention. Thus, they experience a more stimulating environment with extensive individual attention. In contrast, their later-born siblings receive less parental attention, for they must compete with brothers and sisters. If this line of reasoning is valid, one might infer that second-born children will tend to have higher IQs than third-born, third higher than fourth, and so on, for the more siblings there are, the greater the competition is. In fact, some research has supported this interpretation.

Some psychologists believe that first-born children score higher on IQ tests than their siblings because they do not have to compete for parental attention. Thus, they experience a more stimulating environment with extensive individual attention. Later-born siblings receive less parental attention, for they must compete with brothers and sisters.

Robert Zajonc and Gregory Markus (1975) studied a wide range of children from families of different sizes. Overall, they found a close agreement between birth order and the average IQs of children in their sample groups, with IQs dropping commensurate with a decline in intellectual climate with each subsequent child. (Interestingly, the progressive reduction in IQs of later-born siblings reversed itself commencing with the eighth child. This is because as older siblings approach or enter their teenage years, they are able to contribute to a more intellectually stimulating environment for the youngest brothers or sisters.) It is important to note that Zajonc and Markus were dealing with average values. As you might expect, many younger children had IQs higher than their older siblings.

Other research has reported findings similar to those of Zajonc and Markus. A major Israeli study of about 200,000 subjects from large families found that first-borns had higher IQs than second children, who in turn exceeded third children and so on to the seventh child. At this point, the trend reversed itself. Eighth-born children demonstrated higher IQs than seventh children, ninth higher than eighth, and tenth slightly higher still (Davis et al., 1977).

These studies of birth order and intelligence support the importance of environment in the fostering of intellectual growth. Of course, one might argue that children who are born later might show lower IQ scores as a result of other effects. For instance, an older mother's uterus might be less conducive to optimal prenatal growth than might have been the case during earlier pregnancies when she was younger and perhaps healthier. However, this biologically based argument does not explain the apparent reversal in the trend that occurs from the eighth child on. In balance then, studies of the relationship between birth order and intelligence suggest the importance of environment in determining intellectual development.

ANIMAL RESEARCH

Another source of evidence on the influence of environment and heredity has been animal studies. The most notable research is a classic selective-breeding experiment conducted by Robert Tryon (1940) of the University of California at Berkeley. Tryon developed a kind of IQ test for rats in which he measured their ability to learn a complicated maze. Rats who performed very well on this task were mated with other animals who performed similarly, while rats who made many errors were mated with animals that also performed poorly. After many generations of selective breeding (with careful attention to make sure that environments were identical for all rats), the result was two strains of rats that demonstrated substantial differences in the number of errors they made while negotiating the maze. Tryon labeled these distinct strains *maze-bright* and *maze-dull*.

This study seems to support the view of geneticists, for despite comparable environments, the rats differed substantially in at least this one measure of intelligence. However, other studies with Tryon's maze-bright and maze-dull rats have shown that the former are not necessarily superior to the latter in all learning tasks. Thus, just as with the other studies we have explored in this section, we must be cautious in interpreting this important evidence.

NATURE VERSUS NURTURE: EVALUATING THE EVIDENCE

We have looked at a considerable range of evidence in the previous discussions, some of which seems to support each side of the nature-nurture controversy. Many of the twin, adoption, and selective-breeding studies provide strong indications of the role of heredity in determining intelligence. However, some of these investigations, plus evidence from orphanage and birth-order studies, suggest that environment is also important. We could continue exploring this controversy by examining still more evidence.

No matter how much more research we study, however, most of us would still reach the same conclusion: It is simply not possible, in light of our current state of knowledge, to determine precisely what percentage of our IQs is attributable to genes and what percentage is the product of experience.

Today it is widely recognized that nature and nurture interact in determining intelligence; the continuing controversy focuses on an attempt to ascertain the relative contributions of each. In a recent survey of several hundred psychologists and educational specialists with expertise in areas related to intelligence testing, these experts believed the *heritability* of intelligence to be roughly 60 percent (Snyderman & Rothman, 1987). Heritability is a statistical concept which estimates the relative contribution of genetic factors to variability in measures of a particular trait found among members of a sample population. Even if this estimate is accurate, we should not conclude that heredity accounts for 60 percent of our intelligence and environment the rest. Rather than estimates of the percent of our intellects that is due to heredity, heritability percentages provide estimates of the amount of variation in intelligence that may be attributed to heredity among individuals within a population.

Some researchers have provided somewhat higher estimates of the heritability of intelligence. Arthur Jensen, an educational psychologist and hereditarian, is probably the most controversial advocate of the viewpoint that IQ differences are due primarily to heredity. In 1969 he published an article in the *Harvard Education Review* concluding that heredity accounts for approximately 80 percent of the differences in IQ scores among individuals—an extreme position that has not been supported by the mainstream of psychologists. Many of his arguments have been sharply criticized (Loehlin et al., 1975).

Jensen took his argument one step further. He reasoned that if IQ differences between people were largely due to genetic factors, this might also be true for IQ differences between races. This perspective led him to assert that differences in IQ scores between blacks and whites are very likely attributable to genetic factors. Needless to say, this controversial view has been challenged by members of both the scientific community and the general public. The following section of this chapter describes evidence pertinent to this controversial issue.

RACIAL DIFFERENCES IN INTELLIGENCE: FACT OR FICTION?

Numerous studies conducted over the last 50 to 60 years have found that American blacks score an average of about 15 IQ points below American whites on standard tests of intelligence. However, as Figure 12.3 reveals, the scores of significant numbers of both black and white individuals fall at all points in the distribution, and there is a great deal of overlap between the two races on IQ scores. Furthermore, the fact that the range of scores for both groups extends from very low to very high indicates that IQ differ-

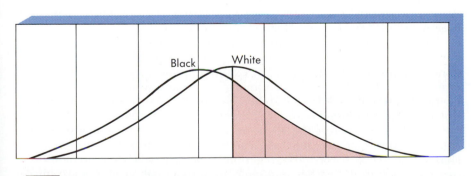

Blacks with IQ's exceeding average IQ's for whites

FIGURE 12.3 THE LARGE DEGREE OF OVERLAP BETWEEN DISTRIBUTIONS OF IQ SCORES OF AMERICAN BLACKS AND WHITES

(*Source:* From Anastasi, 1958)

ences among individuals within one racial group are profoundly greater than differences between average scores of the two groups. Finally, a substantial number of blacks have IQs that far exceed the average IQ for whites.

In view of the comparably wide distribution of IQ scores in both populations and the great overlap between each, we must conclude that knowing if a person is white or black provides little basis for predicting his or her IQ. Even Arthur Jensen conceded that all levels of human intellect are present among both races. Still, we are left with the puzzling matter of a 15-point spread between the two races.

RACIAL DIFFERENCES IN IQ SCORES

Psychologists do not dispute the fact that blacks, on the average, score lower than whites on IQ tests. The question is, why? We have already seen evidence that most of the IQ tests commonly used today place blacks at a disadvantage. Can you think of any other factors that might contribute to this difference, or do you agree with Jensen that these differences reflect genetic factors? Consider these questions before reading on.

One of the saddest aspects of American culture is the irrefutable fact that blacks are socioeconomically and educationally disadvantaged in comparison with whites. Blacks have been subjected to discrimination and deprivation dating to the time they were first forceably brought to this country, and it is impossible to discount the influence of this experience on their intellectual development. Perhaps what is truly remarkable is that so many brilliant blacks have emerged from less than advantageous environments.

Today a widespread opinion among psychologists is that intelligence differences between racial groups are largely if not exclusively the result of environmental factors. The findings on which this conclusion is based come from a variety of research studies.

One research direction is educational differences between blacks and whites. Many years ago, researchers noted that IQ scores of black children from the rural South increased after they moved to northern cities, and that the extent of their IQ improvement was positively correlated with the number of years they spent in northern schools (Klineberg, 1935; Lee, 1951). Presumably, this improvement was a direct result of exposure to educational environments that were far superior to the notoriously limited environments of southern country schools for blacks only.

Interestingly, a similar argument has been used to explain another racial difference that has been noted in IQ scores—that children in Japan tend to outscore American white children by several IQ points (Mohs, 1982). Although a few researchers suggest that these differences may be due to genetic factors, most believe this gap is attributable to the superior Japanese school system (Stevenson, 1983). The academic year for Japanese elementary school students lasts 30 percent longer than that of the typical American school system, and Japanese pupils average about twice the homework of American students.

As you might expect, numerous studies have shown a relationship between IQ scores and socioeconomic status similar to that between intelligence and quality of education. For example, James Coleman (1966) found that children from low socioeconomic groups score well below the national average on tests of intellectual ability. Needless to say, blacks are disproportionately overrepresented among families of low socioeconomic status.

Efforts to correct the social and educational deficits in the lives of blacks through such programs as Head Start, as we have already seen in this chapter, as well as school desegregation, have achieved some qualified success. In general, the earlier in a child's life that such attempts are implemented, the more successful they are (Cook, 1984). There is some evidence

Children educated in Japan tend to outscore American white children by several IQ points. Although a few researchers suggest that these differences may be due to genetic factors, most believe that this gap is attributable to the superior Japanese school system.

that as socioeconomic and educational conditions continue to improve for blacks—a painfully slow process—IQ differences between the races are beginning to shrink (Jones, 1984).

There is evidence that an enriched environment can have a significant positive impact on IQ scores. The work of Sandra Scarr and Richard Weinberg (1976) was mentioned earlier in the discussion of adoption studies, and it is also relevant here. These researchers studied 99 black children in Minneapolis who were adopted by white middle-class parents and raised in environments more affluent and advantaged than the ones they were born in. The average IQ of these black children was about 106, which is equivalent to the typical IQ of white children adopted into similar privileged families and above the average for white children in general. In contrast, the average of 106 is significantly higher than the average IQ of 90 for black children reared in their own homes in the Minneapolis area.

Note that this difference of 16 IQ points is approximately equal to the gap between white and blacks in general. Such a finding provides strong evidence for the role of environment in racial IQ differences. Scarr and Weinberg found that the younger the children were at the age of adoption, the higher their IQs tended to be—a finding that underscores the importance of early experiences in fostering intellectual growth.

This latter finding is not surprising in view of evidence that IQ differences between very young black and white children are minimal, but as the children grow older the gap substantially widens (Osborne, 1960). It appears that the negative effects of disadvantaged, impoverished environments have a cumulative effect on intellectual growth, and that these effects are much more adverse for black children whose environments tend to be more impoverished than those of white children.

Even Arthur Jensen provided some evidence supporting environmental explanations for racial IQ differences. In 1977 he reported the results of an investigation of IQ scores of white and black children in a rural area of Georgia where blacks were greatly disadvantaged, both educationally and socioeconomically. He found evidence of a steady and substantial decline in the IQ scores of black children as they grew older, from age five to 16. Comparable declines for whites were not observed. Jensen admitted that this "cumulative deficit" found only among blacks could not be accounted for by genetic factors. Rather, this finding provides clear evidence that impoverished educational and economic environments severely curtail the opportunities for intellectual growth.

INTELLIGENCE AND CREATIVITY

As you may recall from our earlier discussion of Lewis Terman's long-term study of intellectually gifted individuals (see Chapters 2 and 10), people with high IQs tend to be healthier, happier, more socially adept, and more successful in their careers than comparably aged people of average intelligence. Do high intelligence and creativity also go hand in hand? In order to answer this question, we must first define creativity.

Most definitions of **creativity** focus on the products of creative activity. From this perspective, we can define creativity as the ability to produce outcomes that are novel as well as useful or valuable (Matlin, 1983; Amabile, 1983). This definition applies regardless of whether these creative products are unique solutions to engineering problems, a novelist's or poet's prose, or paintings.

Although most of us recognize the element of originality or novelty in creative acts, the criterion of usefulness or value is sometimes overlooked. However, it is this aspect of our definition that distinguishes between nonsensical or meaningless acts and genuine creativity. For example, suppose someone suggests that you wash your car by driving it into the nearest river. This suggestion, while certainly novel, fails to meet the criterion of usefulness.

Most definitions of creativity focus on the products of creative activity. Walt Disney certainly fits this definition of a creative person. Some of the products of his creativity include his famous animated characters and his fantasyland, Walt Disney World.

Do high intelligence and creativity go hand in hand? Creative people do tend to have above average IQs, but they do not differ in level of intelligence from their less creative peers.

In an attempt to measure creativity psychologists have designed tests that measure **divergent thinking**, which is the ability to come up with unusual but appropriate responses to questions such as "How many uses can you think of for a newspaper?" Divergent thinking is distinct from **convergent thinking** in which a person responds to the information presented by eliminating possibilities and narrowing his or her response down to the single best solution to a problem. Most intelligence tests focus primarily on convergent thinking by utilizing well-defined problems that have a single best solution (Guilford, 1967).

People have been shown to differ in their capacity to engage in divergent thinking, but research efforts to demonstrate a relationship between this ability and creativity have been inconsistent (Hayes, 1978; Suler, 1980). Furthermore, psychologists have had considerable difficulty developing measurement procedures that reliably predict real-life occurrences of creativity in either the sciences or the arts (Jensen, 1980).

With these limitations in mind, let us return to our original question about whether or not intelligence and creativity are related. In general, research has demonstrated only a moderate correlation between creativity and IQ (Anastasi & Schaefer, 1971; Barron & Harrington, 1981; Getzels & Jackson, 1963; Kershner & Ledger, 1985). Creative people do tend to have above-average IQs, but they do not differ in level of intelligence from their less creative peers. For example, research has shown that exceptionally creative biologists, mathematicians, architects, and engineers tend to score no higher on IQ tests, on the average, than less creative persons in their fields (Barron & Harrington, 1981; Mackinnon & Hall, 1972).

These findings suggest that intelligence is perhaps only one of several components of creativity. Other traits that have been linked with creativity include independence and nonconformity (Conger & Petersen, 1984; Getzels & Jackson, 1962); a tendency to be motivated more by intrinsic factors, such as a desire for self-expression, than by extrinsic rewards, such as public recognition of work (Amabile, 1985); flexibility, originality, and constructiveness in approaching problems (Cross et al., 1967; Guilford, 1959); and the inclination to express rather than inhibit feelings (Getzels & Jackson, 1962).

SUMMARY

WHAT IS INTELLIGENCE?

1. Sternberg's information-processing model of intelligence identifies six steps that people generally go through when solving problems typically encountered on intelligence tests. These steps are encoding, inferring, mapping, applications, justification, and response.
2. Sternberg has found that people who score high on intelligence tests typically spend more time analyzing a question than do those who score lower.
3. Spearman has proposed that intelligence is made up of two things: a g-factor, or general intelligence, and a collection of specific intellectual abilities that he labeled s-factors.
4. Thurstone proposed that human intelligence is a composite of seven primary mental abilities: verbal comprehension, numerical ability, spatial relations, perceptual speed, word fluency, memory, and inductive reasoning.
5. Guilford proposes that intelligence consists of 150 separate abilities, with no overall general intelligence factor.
6. The only operational definition of intelligence that psychologists have agreed upon is that intelligence is that which intelligence tests measure.

MEASURING INTELLIGENCE

7. The modern intelligence testing movement was launched by Alfred Binet and his associates, who devised a test to measure French children's intellectual skills.
8. Terman revised the original Binet test to make it applicable to American children. The revised test is called the Stanford-Binet, most recently revised in 1986.
9. The Stanford-Binet is an individually administered IQ test that is made up of a series of subtests that are graded by age level.
10. Studies have demonstrated substantial positive correlations between Stanford-Binet IQ scores and school grades.
11. The Wechsler Adult Intelligence Scale (WAIS) is an individually administered IQ test for people in late adolescence or adulthood that includes 11 subtests grouped into two major categories or scales: a verbal scale and a performance scale.
12. Group intelligence tests, which are widely used today, are cheaper, quicker, and easier to administer than individual tests like the Stanford-Binet or WAIS. However, group tests are limited by the inability of the tester to determine accurately testees' level of comprehension of directions and motivation to perform well.
13. Aptitude tests are designed to predict one's ability to learn new information or a new skill, whereas achievement tests are intended to measure what one has already learned. Intelligence tests tend to measure both aptitudes and achievement.

EVALUATING INTELLIGENCE TESTS

14. The process by which IQ tests are developed can be simplified into four steps: developing test items, evaluating these test items, standardizing the test, and establishing norms.
15. Good tests of IQ (or any other psychological assessment device) must possess both reliability and validity. Reliability refers to measuring a trait with dependable consistency. A test that possesses validity is able to measure accurately what it is supposed to measure.
16. Thus far it has been impossible to eliminate cultural bias from IQ tests. Test questions often reflect the mainstream values and experiences of white middle-class city dwellers.

WHAT DETERMINES INTELLIGENCE?

17. Evidence from twin, adoption, and selective-breeding studies provide strong indications of the role of heredity in determining intelligence. However, certain aspects of these investigations, together with evidence from orphanage and birth-order studies, suggest that environment is also important.
18. It is simply not possible, in light of our current state of knowledge, to determine precisely what percentage of our IQs is attributable to genes and what percentage is the product of experience.
19. A survey of several hundred professionals with expertise in the field of intelligence revealed that the experts believe that the heritability of intelligence is roughly 60 percent. Heritability percentages provide estimates of the amount of variation in intelligence that may be attributed to heredity.

RACIAL DIFFERENCES IN INTELLIGENCE: FACT OR FICTION?

20. Significant numbers of both blacks' and whites' scores fall at all points in distributions of IQ scores, and there is a great deal of overlap between the two races on IQ scores.
21. The fact that blacks score somewhat lower on IQ tests, on the average, than whites may be attributed to the higher incidence of socioeconomic and educational disadvantages in the black versus white population.
22. When social and educational deficits in the lives of blacks are corrected (through such things as geographical relocation and adoption into more socioeconomically advantaged environments) IQ differences between the races shrink.

INTELLIGENCE AND CREATIVITY

23. Most definitions of creativity focus on the products of creative activity, emphasizing that such outcomes must be both novel and useful or valuable.
24. Psychologists attempt to measure creativity by designing tests that measure divergent thinking, which is the ability to come up with unusual but appropriate responses to questions.
25. In general, research has demonstrated only a moderate correlation beween creativity and IQ. Creative people do tend to have above-average IQs, but they do not differ in level of intelligence from their less creative peers.

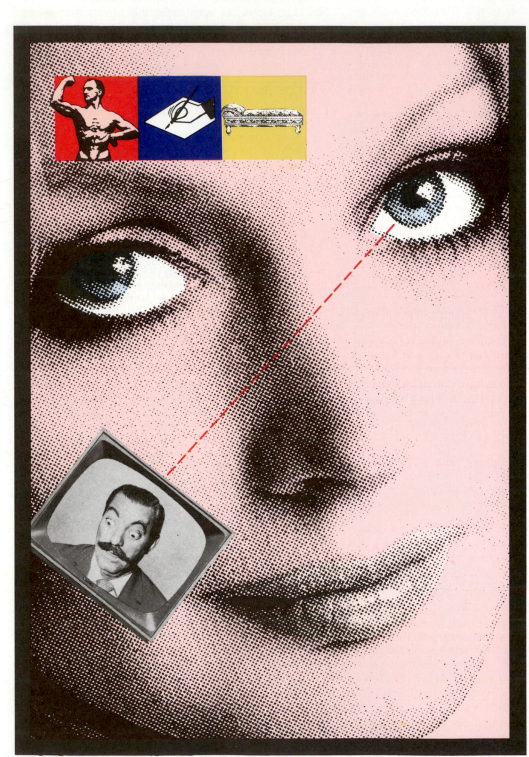

13 Personality: Theories and Assessment

Hippocrates

What makes people different from one another? The ancient Greeks thought the answer had something to do with the four basic body fluids or *humors*: blood, phlegm, black bile, and yellow bile. According to the Greek physician Hippocrates (460–371 B.C.), there were four possible personality types. *Sanguine* individuals had an abundance of blood; they tended to be cheerful, optimistic, and active. *Phlegmatic* people were listless, sluggish, and tired because they had too much phlegm. Sad, brooding, *melancholic* temperaments resulted from too much black bile, and *choleric* (excitable, easy to anger) personalities resulted from an excess of yellow bile.

Although Hippocrates' terminology still survives as descriptive adjectives we use today, both the typologies psychologists use to distinguish personalities and the explanations of what causes personality differences have changed considerably in the last 2,300 years. In this chapter we look at some more contemporary conceptions of personality, including both theories that describe personality traits and the psychoanalytic, behavioral, and humanistic explanations of what makes each of us unique. Like Chapter 12, this chapter also describes assessment techniques, although here our interest is in assessing people's personalities instead of their intelligence. We begin by trying to define personality.

WHAT IS PERSONALITY?

You have often heard statements like "Mary has a lot of personality" or "John has no personality at all." Such descriptions imply that personality is an attribute that people possess in varying amounts. However, personality is not something we possess in large or small quantities, nor is it a concrete thing that is easily observable, such as blue eyes or blond hair. Rather, personality is what we are, a collection of all our many traits and attributes, the sum total of which constitutes a unique person unlike anyone else.

Although personality psychologists have not reached a general consensus on a formal definition of **personality,** a common theme can be found in most definitions. A leading personality theorist of our time, Columbia University's Walter Mischel (1986), notes this common theme by observing that "personality usually refers to the distinctive patterns of behavior (including thoughts and emotions) that characterize each individual's adaptation to the situations of his or her life" (p. 4). We will use this summary as a working definition in this chapter.

Personality is what we are, a collection of all our many traits and attributes, the sum total of which constitutes a unique person unlike anyone else.

A key aspect of virtually all definitions of personality is their emphasis on the individual. In contrast to the study of perception, learning, memory, motivation, and other topics we have previously considered in this text, the field of personality psychology does not look for general principles that apply to all people. Instead, it focuses on the individual. We may best describe *personality psychology* as the study of individuals—their distinctive characteristics and traits and the manner in which they integrate all aspects of their psychological functioning as they adapt to their environments.

Since for most personality theorists the focus of personality research is nothing less than the total person, it is not surprising that personality psychology has a broader topic area than any other field within psychology. You will find that many of the discussions in the following pages relate closely to other chapters in this book, particularly discussions of development, learning, psychological disorders, and assessment techniques.

In view of the far-reaching nature of personality psychology, it is common for personality theorists to attempt to integrate most or all aspects of human behavior into a single theoretical framework. A number of theories have been developed in the attempt to do this. Virtually all of these theoretical perspectives share a focus on the whole person, although they take different approaches. The *trait* theories are primarily descriptive, attempting to identify specific dimensions or characteristics that are associated with different personalities. Other theories make a more thorough attempt to explain these differences. Predictably, the three major viewpoints are the *psychoanalytical* theory of Sigmund Freud and his followers, with its emphasis on the role of unconscious motivation in personality; the attempts of the *behavioral* and *social-learning* theorists to explain how our personalities are shaped by interacting with our environments; and the *humanistic* psychologists' view of personality as molded by our capacities for personal growth and self-actualization. Because the trait theories help describe personality, we begin with them.

TRAIT THEORIES

A number of theorists have tried to identify the behavioral traits that are the building blocks of personality (Buss & Finn, 1987). How do these trait theorists determine what traits are relevant in describing personality? A few different approaches have been used. One approach, known as the *idio-*

graphic approach, defines traits by studying individuals in depth and focusing on the distinctive qualities of their personalities. A second approach, known as the *nomothetic* approach, studies groups of people in the attempt to identify personality traits that tend to appear in clusters. This approach employs the factor analysis technique we learned about in Chapter 12. We will look at one representative of each method: first, the idiographic approach of Gordon Allport; and next, the nomothetic approach of Raymond Cattell.

ALLPORT'S CARDINAL, CENTRAL, AND SECONDARY TRAITS

Gordon Allport (1897–1967) considered patterns of traits to be unique attributes of individuals. Thus, Allport conducted thorough and detailed studies of individuals in depth, often through long-term case studies. His research led him to conclude that all people have certain *traits* or personal dispositions that are the building blocks of personality (1937, 1961, 1965, 1966). He described these traits as "predispositions to respond" or "generalized action tendencies." He further maintained that it is these "bona fide mental structures in each personality that account for the consistency of its behavior" (1937, p. 289).

Why do traits produce consistencies in behavior? According to Allport, traits are both enduring and broad in scope, and so they act to unify a person's responses to a variety of stimulus situations. For example, a person with the trait of friendliness might be expected to be pleasant and sociable when meeting strangers, helpful and supportive on the job, and warm and sensitive when relating to family members (see Figure 13.1). Allport believed that our personality traits determine our unique patterns of response to environmental events. Thus, the same stimuli might be expected to have quite a different impact on different people. For example, a person with a trait of shyness might react to meeting strangers by acting withdrawn and noncommunicative—a very different reaction from that of the person with the friendliness trait.

Allport described three types of traits that operate to provide a person's own unique personality structure. A **cardinal trait** is a powerful, dominating behavioral predisposition that seems to provide the pivot point in a person's entire life. For example, if you are the kind of person who organizes your entire life around competitiveness—beating classmates on exams, being the fastest down the ski slope, and so forth—we might say that competitiveness is your cardinal trait. Allport recognized that only a very small number of people have cardinal traits. Some famous and infamous examples that come to mind are Adolf Hitler (hatred), the Marquis de Sade (cruelty), Don Juan (lust), and Albert Schweitzer (reverence for life).

All of us have the second kind of trait, the **central trait.** These traits are major characteristics of our personalities, such as sensitivity, honesty, and generosity. While less pervasive than cardinal traits, central traits are quite generalized and enduring, and it is these traits that form the building blocks of our personalities. Allport found that most people could be characterized by a fairly small number (usually five to 10) of central traits.

Gordon Allport

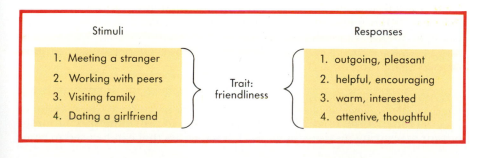

Stimuli		Responses
1. Meeting a stranger		1. outgoing, pleasant
2. Working with peers	Trait: friendliness	2. helpful, encouraging
3. Visiting family		3. warm, interested
4. Dating a girlfriend		4. attentive, thoughtful

FIGURE 13.1 HOW A PERSONALITY TRAIT UNIFIES A PERSON'S RESPONSES TO A VARIETY OF STIMULUS SITUATIONS

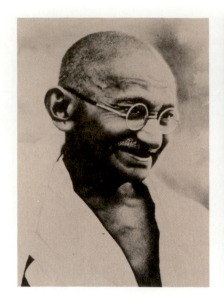

According to Allport, few people have cardinal traits—powerful, dominating behaviorial predispositions that seem to provide the pivotal point in a person's entire life. How would you describe the cardinal traits of Mahatma Gandhi and Adolf Hitler?

Finally, we also have a number of less generalized and far less enduring **secondary traits** that affect our behaviors in specific circumstances. Examples of secondary traits might include our dress style preferences or patterns of exercise, both of which are quite changeable and thus not central or enduring aspects of personality.

CATTELL'S SIXTEEN PERSONALITY FACTORS

Raymond Cattell (1905–present) took just the opposite approach from Allport, studying groups of people rather than individuals. He began his work by identifying certain obvious personality traits such as integrity, friendliness, and tidiness (1950, 1965, 1973, 1982). He called these dimensions of personality **surface traits.** He then used both direct observations of behavior in everyday situations (what he called *life records*) and a variety of questionnaires to obtain extensive data about surface traits from a large number of people. Statistical analysis of this data revealed that certain surface traits seemed to occur in clusters, and Cattell theorized that these clusters probably indicated the operation of a single underlying trait. Cattell applied factor analysis to determine what the surface trait clusters had in common. This analysis yielded a list of 16 primary or **source traits** which he considered to be at the center or core of personality. He listed each of these traits as a pair of polar opposites, such as trusting vs. suspicious.

Cattell and his colleagues developed a questionnaire called the *16 Personality Factor Questionnaire* (or the *16 PF*) to measure these source traits. Figure 13.2 shows samples of these profiles for subjects from three different occupational groups: writers, artists, and airline pilots. As you might expect, Cattell and his associates found that writers and artists have more in common than either group has with pilots.

Cattell demonstrated a number of potential applications of his trait theory and the questionnaire he designed to measure source traits. For example, in one study of 180 married couples, he found that the most satisfied couples were those that were most alike in their personality profiles derived from the 16 PF (Cattell, 1973).

EVALUATING THE TRAIT THEORIES

Trait theories offer the distinct advantage of providing specific methods for measuring or assessing basic characteristics that can be used in com-

Raymond B. Cattell

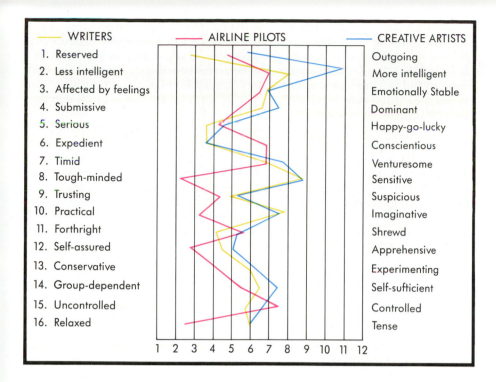

	WRITERS	AIRLINE PILOTS	CREATIVE ARTISTS	
1. Reserved				Outgoing
2. Less intelligent				More intelligent
3. Affected by feelings				Emotionally Stable
4. Submissive				Dominant
5. Serious				Happy-go-lucky
6. Expedient				Conscientious
7. Timid				Venturesome
8. Tough-minded				Sensitive
9. Trusting				Suspicious
10. Practical				Imaginative
11. Forthright				Shrewd
12. Self-assured				Apprehensive
13. Conservative				Experimenting
14. Group-dependent				Self-sufficient
15. Uncontrolled				Controlled
16. Relaxed				Tense

1 2 3 4 5 6 7 8 9 10 11 12

FIGURE 13.2 PERSONALITY PROFILES, VIA CATTELL'S 16 PF QUESTIONNAIRE, FOR THREE OCCUPATIONAL GROUPS: WRITERS, AIRLINE PILOTS, AND ARTISTS

paring individuals. While they often disagree about which basic traits are needed to describe personality, these theories share a common assumption that traits may be used to explain consistencies in behavior and to explain why different people tend to react differently to the same situations (Mischel, 1986).

HOW DO DESCRIPTIONS DIFFER FROM EXPLANATIONS?

A trait theorist such as Allport might observe that a woman who returns excess change to a cashier, admits to damaging a fixture in a motel, and refuses to accept help from a classmate during an exam behaves in these ways because she has the trait of honesty. What is the problem with this kind of reasoning? Think about it before reading on.

How do we know that the woman just described has the trait of honesty and that it causes her behavior? The only answer Allport or other trait theorists might provide is "because she is honest in much of her behavior." If you have taken any logic courses, you may recognize this as circular reasoning: we first deduce the existence of a trait from observing a behavior, then use our deduction to explain the behavior. For this reason, most psychologists insist that traits are only descriptions, not explanations.

Related to this point are criticisms of the view that traits produce consistent behavior from one situation to the next. Cattell went so far as to contend that a person's 16 PF Questionnaire scores can be used to predict such diverse things as success in school, accident-proneness, or marital happiness (Cattell, 1973).

A number of psychologists, most notably Water Mischel (1968, 1979, 1984), have argued that while people may possess certain enduring behavioral predispositions, they do not act with consistency from one situation to the next. You may have noticed that you are shy in some kinds of situations and more assertive in others. Such inconsistencies are common to many of us, and a considerable body of research indicates that many personality "traits" may be situationally dependent.

Sometimes I make myself mad. When I am with someone I would like to impress, or with people who are really impressive themselves, it's like I change into another person who is awkward, tongue-tied, and ill at ease. People who know me sometimes ask what is wrong with me in these situations. I guess they assume something must be wrong for me to be transformed from my usual relaxed, conversational self. I know from what others have said that I am basically fun to be around and that people enjoy talking to me. Why can't I act like this when it really counts? (*Authors' files*)

My boyfriend says I am an aggressive person. I don't think this is a fair assessment. I may seem aggressive to him because he is so laid back that if I waited for him to make decisions our relationship would be consistently on hold. So I guess the fact that I run the show gets translated by him into the idea that I am aggressive. He should talk to my boss, who is constantly encouraging me to be more assertive with obnoxious customers, or to my brother who says I am a real pushover. (*Authors' files*)

One early study observed over 10,000 children who were given opportunities to steal, cheat, or lie in a variety of contrived situations at home, in the classroom, and on the playground (Hartshorne & May, 1928). It found very little consistency in the behavior of subjects: most of the children would lie, steal, or cheat in some circumstances, but not in others. The researchers thus concluded that the "trait" of honesty was actually a collection of *situation-specific habits*.

Later studies have reported similar inconsistencies in behavior. For example, a study of punctuality among several hundred college students revealed virtually no consistency in their time of arrival at a variety of college-related events (Dudycha, 1936). Walter Mischel's (1968) more recent investigation of college students' conscientiousness (turning in assignments on time, arriving before a lecture begins, and so forth) revealed a similar lack of situational consistency. Mischel went on to examine the research literature on this topic, and found very little evidence that behavior is consistent across different circumstances.

A number of personality psychologists have objected to this criticism, however. As one observer notes, trying to predict a person's behavior in a specific situation, based on either a questionnaire score or past observations, is like trying to predict how carefully you will check your next English composition for errors, based on the care you took in reviewing your answers on a previous psychology exam (Epstein, 1983). A person's behavior in any given situation depends on many factors, from the amount of sleep they have had, to whether they are in a good mood, to their past experiences in similar situations.

Some of the debate over the consistency issue may stem, at least in part, from the fact that some people may be more consistent than others. According to one observer, if you think of yourself as a person who behaves according to your true feelings and attitudes, you will be inclined to act consistently in different situations. In contrast, if you perceive yourself as acting like a different person in different circumstances, your behavior is more likely to be inconsistent (Snyder, 1983). Thus, if you perceive yourself as an honest person, you are more likely to demonstrate this trait consistently than if you do not have a clear sense of yourself as honest. It is also possible that people may be consistent in some traits and not in others—that people show situational consistency only in those trait behaviors in which they perceive themselves as being consistent (Bem, 1983).

Despite situational variance in behavior, however, our tendency to be honest (or happy, shy, outgoing, or any other quality) over a variety of situations is somewhat predictable. If we average out our behaviors across a range of situations, at least some of our most distinctive personality traits contribute to a consistency that tends to be enduring over the life span. For example, a child who is gregarious during her early developmental years is likely to remain friendly and outgoing throughout her life. Research indicates that threads of behavioral continuity do emerge when people are examined over long time spans (Arend et al., 1979; Block, 1971).

Where did these traits come from in the first place? This leads to a final criticism of trait theories—that they offer essentially no understanding of how personality develops. Instead of telling us about the origin of traits, how they are learned, how they may be changed, and how they interact with each other to shape behavior, these theories offer a rather static view of personality as a collection of characteristics or behaviors. For answers to the question of where traits come from, we must turn to the psychoanalytic, behavioral, and humanistic theories.

PSYCHOANALYTIC THEORY

The most influential, most comprehensive and systematic, and most widely studied personality theory of all time is the psychoanalytic theory of the Viennese physician Sigmund Freud (1856–1939). It is impossible to do justice in a few pages to Freud's theoretical interpretations, originally published in 24 volumes between 1888 and 1939. However, we will attempt at least to acquaint you with some of the most important features of his theory.

THE HISTORICAL CONTEXT OF FREUD'S THEORY

Although Freud presented the Western world with a bold new vision of human nature, his views also reflected his own upbringing in the Victorian climate of nineteenth-century Austria. Freud was the first-born child in a large, middle-class Jewish family. Almost his entire life was spent in Vienna where, as a young man, he received a medical degree and entered private practice as a neurologist.

Freud's interest was in nervous disorders, but early in his medical career he noticed that many of his patients showed no evidence of nervous-system pathology. A patient might be unable to walk, see, or hear—but no neurological impairment could be found. Freud suspected that such symptoms might be psychological rather than physical. After observing neurologists such as Jean Charcot and Freud's colleague Joseph Breuer, both of whom were using hypnosis to treat cases similar to his own, Freud incorporated Breuer's *cathartic* method into his treatment regimen. This approach involved hypnotizing patients, then encouraging them to recall the first time their symptoms were experienced and to talk freely about the circumstances surrounding this occurrence. When such experiences could be relived, the effect was often a release of bottled-up emotions in a kind of cathartic experience, followed by a marked reduction of the symptoms. Eventually Freud dispensed with hypnosis, expanding the cathartic technique into a method known as **free association.** Here, Freud encouraged patients to relax and to say whatever came to their minds, no matter how embarrassing, painful, or trivial.

Sigmund Freud developed the psychoanalytic theory—the most influential, comprehensive, and systematic personality theory of all time.

PERSONALITY AND THE UNCONSCIOUS

Through listening to his patients free-associate about their early experiences, fears, and concerns, Freud gradually began to formulate a concept of the **unconscious mind,** which ultimately became central to his personality theory. He envisioned the mind as like an iceberg, with most of it hidden beneath the surface in the vast reservoir of the unconscious. He theorized that memories and feelings are repressed or submerged into the unconscious because they are too painful or anxiety-producing to be tolerated in conscious thoughts. Free association was able to open a door to the unconscious, allowing a person to release or express its contents.

Freud used the term **psychoanalysis** to describe his interpretation of a patient's revelations of normally unconscious cognitions. The psychoanalytic theory of personality gradually evolved from his attempts to explain certain recurrent themes that emerged from his use of psychoanalysis. Thus, the psychoanalytic perspective is both a theory of personality and a method for treating psychological disorders. (We will discuss the therapy side of psychoanalysis in Chapter 15.)

The more Freud listened to his patients, the more convinced he became that unconscious thoughts and feelings are powerful molders of personality. He believed that these ever-present forces emerge into consciousnessness in disguised form, influencing our relationships with others, the kind of work we do, the beliefs we hold, and the symptoms of emotional disorders. Freud believed that the workings of the unconscious can be seen in the kinds of dreams we have. As you may recall from Chapter 5, he was particularly fond of analyzing dreams, which he considered to be a major outlet for unconscious wishes. Freud also believed that slips of the tongue or pen can provide insights into the unconscious. For example, the woman who describes her father as kind, generous, and "insensitive" (instead of "sensitive") may be expressing thinly disguised, repressed hostility.

Freud's training in physiology and medicine led him to conclude that we are biological organisms dominated by biological needs, especially sexual, that must be controlled if we are to become civilized human beings. In his view, our perpetual struggle to tame these impulses leads to the emotional conflicts that so profoundly shape our personalities. Considering the extreme sexual repression of the Victorian period, it is not surprising that Freud's initial theories of personality placed such an emphasis on conflicts surrounding sexual urges. Many years later, the death of millions of people in World War I also had a profound impact on Freud, and he modified his theory to include an equally strong emphasis on aggressive urges in molding personality. Thus the **psychoanalytic theory** of personality depicts people as being shaped by an ongoing conflict between their primary drives, particularly sex and aggression, and the social pressures of civilized society.

Freud also theorized that early childhood experiences play a major role in molding personality. After listening to countless revelations of what he considered to be profoundly significant events in his patients' early years, he concluded that such experiences place an indelible stamp on personality and behavior. In the next several paragraphs, we will look at Freud's view of the structure, dynamics, and development of personality.

THE STRUCTURE OF PERSONALITY

One of the best known aspects of Freud's theory is his conceptualization of human personality as composed of three interacting systems or structures: the id, ego, and superego. These structures are not physically present in the brain; they are psychological concepts or constructs that Freud invented to help explain certain aspects of human behavior. These three systems are interrelated and interactive, but each has its own characteristics, as Table 13.1 illustrates.

The Id According to Freud, the **id** is basically the biological component of personality. It consists of a vast reservoir of instinctual drives which Freud called the *life instincts* (such as hunger, thirst, and sex); it also includes the *death instinct*, which is responsible for aggressiveness and destruction. The id is fueled primarily by a form of energy called **libido** that motivates all behavior. It operates according to the **pleasure principle,** seeking immediate gratification of all instinctive drives regardless of reason, logic, or the impact that the behaviors it motivates will have. Freud believed that only the id is present at birth; thus, a newborn's behaviors are dominated by the id. This viewpoint has a ring of truth for anyone who has observed a hungry infant's demanding cry for attention regardless of what important tasks Mom or Dad are engaged in.

The id cannot tolerate any tension, and so it seeks immediate gratification. However, since it operates essentially at an unconscious level, it is not able to interact effectively with external reality to achieve gratification.

TABLE 13.1 *Mental Structure According to Freud*

Structure	Consciousness	Contents and Function
Id	Unconscious	Basic impulses (sex and aggression); seeks immediate gratification regardless of consequences; impervious to reason and logic; immediate, irrational, impulsive
Ego	Predominantly conscious	Executive mediating between id impulses and superego inhibitions; tests reality; seeks safety and survival; rational, logical taking account of space and time
Superego	Both conscious and unconscious	Ideals and morals; strives for perfection; observes, dictates, criticizes, and prohibits; imposes limitations on satisfactions; becomes the conscience of the individual

Thus the newborn is largely helpless, driven by basic instincts but dependent upon others for fulfilling these needs. Freud believed that the id seeks to discharge tension by conjuring up mental images of the object it desires. Thus a hungry baby might form an internal image of the mother's breast, or we might dream about sex. Freud called this wish-fulfilling mental imagery **primary process thinking.**

In sum, the id is the storehouse of largely unconscious, biologically based, instinctive drives that provide the basic energy source for the entire personality system. It is also the foundation from which the ego and superego later evolve.

The Ego   A newborn's world is not designed to serve his or her every need. No matter how much crying or carrying on might occur, a mother's breast or a bottle does not always appear magically, and so infants soon come to realize that immediate gratification is not always possible. According to Freud, such discoveries prompt the development of the **ego as an outgrowth of the id.** The ego develops gradually as the infant learns to cope with the real world. It functions as an intermediary between the instinctual demands of the id and the reality of the world. Freud's concept of the ego explained how the id-dominated infant who might lie helplessly crying for food gradually evolves into a toddler who is able to reach into the cookie jar or say the word "milk."

The ego operates by the **reality principle,** seeking to satisfy the id's wants and needs in ways that are consistent with reality. To accomplish this, the ego must be largely conscious and in direct contact with the external world. Furthermore, to carry out its "executive" functions of screening the id's impulses, the ego system must include our abilities to perceive, think, learn, and remember. Thus what psychologists now call cognitive processes were considered by Freud to be functions of the ego.

The Superego   In the early years of life, the ego only needs to check out external reality to determine if a particular id impulse may be expressed: morality has no influence at all. Thus if a toddler is hungry and a freshly baked cake that Mom baked for the school fund-raiser is within reach, the outcome is predictable even though such behavior is "wrong."

As the infant becomes a child, however, Freud theorized that a third system of personality emerges. The **superego** is a composite of the moral values and standards of parents and society that we incorporate into our personalities as we develop.

While the id is driven to seek pleasure and the ego to test reality, the superego is concerned with striving for perfection. The superego makes the task of the ego much harder by forcing it to consider not just what is real, but also what is right.

According to Freud, the superego includes two distinct subsystems. The first, the *conscience*, consists of the moral inhibitions or "should nots" of behavior that stem from punishments (either parental punishments or punishing ourselves through guilt). The second subsystem, the *ego-ideal*, is the "shoulds" of behavior for which we receive approval and/or rewards, and to which we aspire. Freud believed that emotions such as guilt and pride are essential in the functioning of our superegos. He particularly emphasized the role of guilt both in inhibiting id impulses and in contributing to many personality disorders.

The superego, then, is the moral arm of personality that tries to prevent the id from expressing its primitive impulses. Even though the superego shares some characteristics with the id (it is nonrational) and the ego (it is controlling), it nevertheless stands in opposition to both of them. Unlike the ego, which merely suppresses the id long enough to find a rational way to satisfy its needs, the superego tries to block id impulses totally. In this sense, it is the original "spoilsport." If the superego is too successful in its task, the end result is a rigid, guilt-ridden, inhibited personality. But if

The superego makes the task of the ego much harder by forcing it to consider not just what is real but also what is right.

According to Freud, the conscience consists of the moral inhibitions or "should nots" of behavior that stem from punishments (either parental punishments or self-punishment through guilt).

the superego consistently plays a weak hand, the result is a self-centered, self-indulgent, antisocial personality.

PERSONALITY DYNAMICS

Personality theorists use the term *dynamics* to refer to the forces that shape personality. According to Freud, the dynamics of personality reside in the continuous interaction and clash between the impulse-driven id, the guilt-inducing superego, and the ego, which acts as mediator by reconciling reality with the demands of both the id and the superego. The interplay among these personality forces requires a delicate balance that is difficult to achieve. No matter how well we have adjusted to external reality and integrated a system of morality into our daily lives, Freud maintained that the id's primitive urges will inevitably create conflicts that upset this balance. A severe breakdown of this balance may result in various forms of behavioral disorders, such as psychological amnesia, paralysis, or blindness—just the kinds of symptoms that aroused Freud's interest in the first place.

When the ego is faced with conflicts that threaten to disrupt the balance among the systems of personality, it sounds an alarm in the form of anxiety which, in turn, induces it to fall back on a variety of mechanisms designed to control this anxiety.

Anxiety and the Defense Mechanisms   **Anxiety** is a kind of free-floating fear with no easily identifiable source. Since its source is abstract, a person with anxiety cannot act to eliminate the cause. This is why anxiety can be such a devastating emotion. Freud maintained that anxiety stems primarily from an unconscious fear that our id will cause us to do something that will result in punishment or guilt. (In terms of the three systems of personality, the ego experiences anxiety when an impulse that is unacceptable to the superego threatens to be expressed in overt behavior.) When the ego is not able to relieve this anxiety through rational, problem-solving methods, Freud suggested that it resorts to certain less rational maneuvers called **defense mechanisms.** The purpose of the defense mechanisms is to shield the ego from some of the harsh aspects of reality (see Figure 13.3).

All defense mechanisms share two characteristics. First, they protect the ego from anxiety by denying or distorting reality. Second, they operate unconsciously so that we are not aware that a distortion of reality has taken

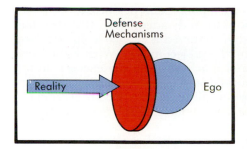

FIGURE 13.3   THE PURPOSE OF THE DE-FENSE MECHANISMS

The defense mechanisms serve to shield the ego from some of the harsh aspects of reality. (*Source:* Adapted from Bruno, 1983)

place. Thus, defense mechanisms are not subject to the normal checks and balances of rational, conscious reasoning—a limitation that causes people who are using defense mechanisms to be absolutely convinced of the correctness of their viewpoint.

People often assume that using a defense mechanism is a sign of a weakness or a disturbed personality. In fact, all of us, well-adjusted and otherwise, use the common defense mechanisms in our everyday lives. Therefore, if you recognize yourself in some of the examples of defense mechanisms in the following paragraphs, do not conclude that you are "weak." Most of us would not do very well if we were prevented from occasionally resorting to such defensive maneuvers. In fact, in some situations the ability to deceive ourselves by using repression or some other defense mechanism may actually be helpful (Goleman, 1987). Because they are beyond the reality checks of conscious awareness, however, the potential danger exists that one or more of these defenses may become habitual. We will look here at a number of defense mechanisms, including repression, rationalization, projection, displacement, regression, and reaction formation.

Repression   The ego's first line of defense against anxiety is often **repression.** This defense mechanism involves holding back or banishing from consciousness a variety of unacceptable impulses and disturbing memories. For example, you might repress the aggressive impulses you feel toward a teacher or employer because these feelings are unacceptable and therefore anxiety-provoking.

Freud believed that all defensive reactions to anxiety first begin with a massive inhibition or repression of id urges: We first attempt to fend off anxiety-arousing thoughts and feelings by blocking them out. Repression is the most basic and pervasive of the defenses against anxiety, and it underlies all other defense mechanisms. Since the id has such an overwhelming number of disruptive urges, however, this primary defense mechanism is unable to contain them all. Thus we use other secondary defense mechanisms.

Many students confuse repression with a similar term, suppression. The two processes are quite distinct. When we repress an impulse or feeling, such as hostility toward a parent, we block it from our conscious awareness because it is too painful or threatening to face directly. This mechanism is involuntary and we are unaware of the process. In contrast, when we suppress something, such as an urge to hit back after being slapped, we are fully aware of our impulse, and we voluntarily hold it in check. Although the end result of each process may be the same—namely, blockage of a particular behavior—there is a considerable difference between the two.

Rationalization   Another widely used defense mechanism is **rationalization, in which we substitute self-justifying excuses or explanations for the real reasons for our behaviors.** For example, the parent who severely disciplines a child with physical punishment may rationalize this behavior with the saying "sparing the rod will spoil the child," although the real motive may be to vent repressed aggression and hostility.

College students often rationalize a poor exam performance by stating that they had too many distractions to study adequately, that they had worked hard all semester and that they deserved a chance to have a little fun, or that they just could not get into the subject matter. What is the harm in these excuses? Probably there is not much harm, if the excuses do not become a habit: It would be a grim world if we had to come away from every unsuccessful event with a deep sense of failure. However, an overdependence on rationalization, or any other defense mechanism, may lead to serious problems.

Consider the case of a student we know who began and dropped an introductory psychology class four times. Each time he had a "legitimate" excuse. One term he had to drop out because of a sick mother who needed extra attention; another time financial problems caused him to lighten his class load so he could work longer hours. A look into his background revealed that quitting was a common occurrence. When this pattern was called to his attention, he denied that he was a drop-out by choice; instead, he was a victim of circumstances, and it is likely that he truly believed in his own excuses. In-depth counseling revealed that the student had a deeply rooted fear of failure, and that he had been withdrawing from challenging situations to avoid the profoundly disturbing possibility of failing.

Projection A third defense mechanism, **projection,** occurs when we reduce the anxiety created by our own unacceptable impulses by attributing these impulses to someone else. An example is the married woman who blames an extramarital sexual affair on the man who "led me on." In addition to allowing us to project our unacceptable impulses onto another, projection provides a mechanism for blaming others for our own shortcomings. For example, a student might project the blame for a poor exam performance onto a "devious professor who purposely writes ambiguous questions just to make students squirm."

Displacement In the defense mechanism known as **displacement,** individuals divert their impulse-driven behavior from primary targets to secondary ones that will arouse less anxiety. Thus, a student who does not want to risk expressing anger toward a professor may come home and pick a fight with her roommate.

In the defense mechanism known as displacement, individuals divert their impulse-driven behavior from primary targets to secondary ones that will arouse less anxiety. Perhaps you can think of an incident when someone made you angry and you "took it out" on a friend or a loved one.

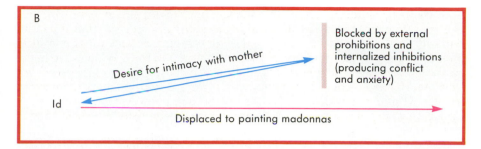

B

Desire for intimacy with mother

Blocked by external prohibitions and internalized inhibitions (producing conflict and anxiety)

Id

Displaced to painting madonnas

FIGURE 13.4   THE PSYCHODYNAMIC TRANSFORMATION OF MOTIVES: DISPLACEMENT IN THE FORM OF SUBLIMATION

Displacement can sometimes produce a socially valued accomplishment. When it does, it is called **sublimation.** Freud believed that sublimation is a mechanism that provides a major impetus for the development of culture and the production of artistic endeavors. He suggested that Leonardo da Vinci's paintings of madonnas resulted from a displacement or redirection of da Vinci's impulse to achieve intimacy with his mother, from whom he had been separated in early childhood (see Figure 13.4). Freud also maintained that many repressed sexual urges of youth, particularly those centered on masturbation, are transformed or sublimated into such socially acceptable activities as athletics, music, art, or horseback riding.

Regression   Sometimes people may attempt to cope with anxiety-producing situations by retreating to an earlier stage of development in an effort to recapture the security they remember. This defense mechanism of **regression** may be expressed in such familiar behavior as a child returning to the infantile pattern of thumb sucking on the first day of school or a newlywed running home to Mom and Dad after the first serious argument with the new spouse.

Reaction Formation   In **reaction formation,** the ego unconsciously replaces unacceptable impulses with their opposites. Thus, a person with a barely controllable fascination with obscene literature and films may become involved in an obscenity-fighting group that actively reviews and censors sexually explicit literature and movies. In this fashion the id impulses may be expressed, but in a disguised form that is acceptable to the ego.

PERSONALITY DEVELOPMENT

Freud's experiences in conducting psychotherapy convinced him that personality is essentially formed within the first few years of life. He believed that most of his patients' symptoms stemmed from unresolved conflicts, particularly conflicts involving sexual themes that emerged in the early years.

Psychosexual Development   At the time Freud formulated his theory, it was traditional to view childhood as a period when sexuality remains unexpressed. Freud challenged this thinking, asserting that a child is very aware of the sexual pleasure inherent in body stimulation. His concept of this sexual urge was quite broad, dealing with several different parts of the body (called *erogenous zones*) that play key roles in the arousal and gratification of sexual drive. Freud theorized that a child progresses through a series of stages of **psychosexual development** in which the focus of sexual gratification shifts from one body site to another. The manner in which a child goes through these stages, said Freud, is a major determinant of the personality that emerges as development progresses.

Freud theorized that during the third phase of psychosexual development, a child may feel sexual attraction to the parent of the other sex. This is called the Electra complex and Oedipus complex in girls and boys, respectively.

The first phase of psychosexual development is the **oral stage,** spanning the first 12 to 18 months of life. During this stage, the lips and mouth are the erogenous zone and the id's pleasure-seeking energies find an outlet in sucking, chewing, and biting. Thus, babies suck not just because they are hungry, but also because they find such activity to be sensually pleasurable.

At some point during the second year of development the erogenous zone shifts from the mouth to the anal area. This shift coincides with the neurological development of the anal sphincter muscles, and it marks the beginning of the **anal stage** (12–18 months to three years). Freud believed that the nature of toilet training during this stage could have serious ramifications for later adult personality. (We will elaborate on this point later.)

The third phase of psychosexual development, the **phallic stage,** occurs from the age of three to age five or six. During this time the focus of sexual gratification shifts to genital stimulation. At the same time, the "family romance" may emerge in which a child feels sexual attraction to the parent of the other sex, and also experiences jealousy of the same-sex parent. Freud coined the terms **Oedipus complex** and **Electra complex** to describe this reaction in boys and girls, respectively. He believed that most children find this situation stressful, so they resolve it by repressing their feelings of sexual attraction and identifying with the same-sex parent.

The fourth stage of psychosexual development, the **latency period,** extends from age five or six to puberty. Freud believed that sexual drives remain unexpressed or latent during this period. Finally, during the last phase of sexual development, the **genital stage** (from puberty on), sexual feelings that were dormant during the latency period reemerge in full force. Adolescents and later adults seek to gratify these drives through sexual relations with people outside the family.

Fixation   Freud believed that a child may experience an arrest in development at one of the early stages of psychosexual development as a result of being exposed to too little or too much gratification. This is called **fixation,** and it can influence adult personality. For example, children thwarted from experiencing oral stimulation (sucking, biting, eating) may be inclined to eat excessively or smoke as adults. Frustration during the oral stage might also lead to a later lack of trust of others or to certain aggressive oral behaviors such as verbal hostility. Excessive gratification can also affect personality, so that infants who are always given a bottle or pacifier may be overly dependent as adults, or toddlers who are subjected to very early and stressful toilet training may as adults be obsessively concerned with cleanliness and orderliness.

Freud never explained clearly the precise mechanism whereby fixation occurs, and few of the predictions stemming from this concept have been supported by research.

EVALUATING FREUD'S PSYCHOANALYTIC THEORY

Freud based his theory on his own analysis of his patients' free associations and dreams. Therefore it is not surprising that perhaps the most serious shortcoming of Freud's theory is the difficulty in testing it empirically. As we saw in Chapter 2, a good scientific theory contains terms that may be defined operationally and is constructed in such a way that it generates hypotheses or predictions about behavior that can be confirmed or disproven by empirical tests. Freud's vague pronouncements about personality meet neither of these requirements; and terms such as "primary process thinking" and "oral dependent personality" are virtually impossible to define operationally. Although many experiments have attempted to prove or disprove Freud's basic ideas, the collective results have been ambiguous (Fisher & Greenberg, 1977; Ross, 1987).

Another difficulty that critics have pointed out has to do with predicting behavior. Psychoanalytic theory provides no clear-cut predictions about how a particular collection of experiences will affect personality and behavior. For example, punitive toilet training might produce a compulsively neat personality—but then again, it could also result in an excessively sloppy individual. Freud did recognize this limitation of his theory, particularly as it related to predicting adult personality from childhood experiences. He admitted that "we never know beforehand which of the determining factors will prove the weaker or the stronger. We can only say at the end that those which succeeded must have been the stronger" (1933, p. 227).

Another criticism has to do with Freud's sample. Freud based virtually his entire theory on his observations of a relatively small number of troubled patients, primarily middle- and upper-class Austrian women. Perhaps Freud's failure to appreciate the strengths of healthy personalities resulted in a theory that tended to emphasize the negative and irrational components of human behavior. Freud's patients were also the products of a sexually repressed Victorian society. Thus, it seems likely that this group of people collectively experienced a far greater number of sexual conflicts than we might expect to find in a sample of contemporary Austrian or American people. Today there is widespread agreement among Freud's supporters as well as his detractors that his theory placed far too much emphasis on sex as a dominant motivating force throughout life.

Another area of criticism is Freud's emphasis on the importance of early experience. As we saw in Chapters 10 and 11, behavior and personality are shaped throughout the life cycle. Freud did teach us, however, to recognize the importance of childhood experiences in molding personality and influencing our thoughts, feelings, and behaviors at later points in our development.

Freud also incorrectly assumed that women are inferior to men in a number of ways: sexually (because they do not have a penis and because they often lack the "maturity" to transfer their erotic sensitivity from the clitoris to the vagina); morally (because the Oedipus complex creates a more severe conflict than the Electra complex, thus stimulating development of a stronger superego in males than females); and culturally (because women's weaker superegos result in less sublimation of primitive urges into creative endeavors).

These criticisms are all valid, and from the perspective of the 1980s it is relatively easy to recognize Freud's shortcomings. We must keep in mind,

Although Freud presented the Western world with a bold new vision of human nature, his views also reflected his own upbringing in the sexually repressed climate of nineteenth-century Austria.

however, that Freud developed his theory in virtually a vacuum of psychological data about human development, thinking, emotions, and social behavior. From this perspective, it is remarkable that several of his theoretical perspectives continue to be supported by mainstream psychology today. We have Freud to thank for the concept of the unconscious. (Although most modern theorists do not believe that the unconscious plays a much greater role than the conscious mind in shaping behavior, at least some of our actions are influenced by unconscious forces.) We also must credit Freud for the understanding that unresolved conflicts are central to many psychological problems; for making sexuality, from childhood through adulthood, a legitimate topic for psychological research; and for introducing the concept of defense mechanisms.

In all, Freud created a theory of momentous proportions that has irrevocably influenced our view of human nature. While few people today agree with all of Freud's basic premises, no one suggests that his ideas were anything less than bold, creative, and highly courageous, considering the cultural context within which he worked. We can expect that Freud's personality theory will continue to influence the views of future generations, primarily because psychology has emerged from years of storm and controversy over Freudian doctrine with the somewhat pragmatic conclusion that psychoanalytic theory "is not an entity that must be totally accepted or rejected as a package. It is a complex structure consisting of many parts, some of which should be accepted, others rejected, and the rest at least partially reshaped" (Fisher & Greenberg, 1977, p. 28).

BEHAVIORAL AND SOCIAL-LEARNING THEORIES

Whereas the psychoanalytic perspective looks to internal mechanisms to explain personality, behavioral and social-learning theories take a distinctly different approach. These theories emphasize the role of external events in personality formation. We look first at the behaviorist position, then at the perspective of social-learning theory.

THE BEHAVIORIST APPROACH

We have discussed the views of B. F. Skinner (1904–present) and other behaviorists in previous chapters, so it should come as no surprise that these theorists reject the psychoanalytic notion that internal forces are the primary instigators of behaviors. To the extent that an individual has identifiable characteristics, behaviorists maintain, they are merely products of external environmental forces in the form of reinforcing stimuli.

According to Skinner, we do not need to assume that a man is a nonstop smoker because he was fed irregularly during infancy. His behavior can be explained, says Skinner, by noting the reinforcements that have been associated with it. Not only is it a waste of time to search for personality structures in the form of internal forces, argues Skinner; it may also impede our efforts to understand the true causes of personality:

> The practice of looking inside the organism for an explanation of behavior has tended to obscure the variables which are immediately available for a scientific analysis. These variables lie outside the organism, in its immediate environment and in its environmental history. (1953, p. 31)

To Skinner, our personalities are the sum total of our overt and covert responses to the world around us. Furthermore, our patterns of responding to environmental stimuli are a direct outgrowth of the reinforcements we have experienced in the past. We are unique individuals because no two people share identical reinforcement histories. Thus, from the perspective of behaviorism, conditioning (defined in Chapter 6) is responsible for the development of personality. The reason why two people act differently in the same situation is not because they have different traits, as trait theorists would argue, or because they have stronger or weaker superegos, as Freud would argue, but rather because of their own unique histories of operant and classical conditioning.

Skinner and other behaviorists challenge the notion that enduring traits are evidence of some underlying behavioral predisposition, as trait theorists would claim. Instead, they suggest that the reason some so-called "traits" appear to be stable is because the environment is itself relatively stable: people are often subjected to a consistent pattern of reinforcement contingencies.

Behaviorists are probably more interested in changes in behavior than they are in behavioral consistencies. If sufficient changes are made in the environment, they note that certain "enduring" aspects of personality may undergo dramatic change. For example, suppose you become the new foster parent of an 11-year-old boy who is remarkably submissive and *introverted* (socially withdrawn and emotionally reserved). You check with the child welfare agency who placed the child with you, and find that these behavioral patterns were first noted in his case file record several years ago. Does this mean that you can expect these qualities to endure? The behaviorists would say no. If you change the boy's environment by rewarding even the slightest indications of sociability (for instance, smiling at you) and assertiveness (such as his meekly saying he likes his eggs scrambled rather than fried), you will probably be able to increase the frequency of these behaviors gradually, using the operant principle of shaping (see Chapter 6). These changes in his environment are likely to change his personality by replacing his introversion and submissiveness with more sociable and assertive behavior patterns. As we shall see in Chapter 15, some of the most effective methods for changing the behaviors of "unhealthy personalities" have evolved out of the behavioral approach.

THE SOCIAL-LEARNING PERSPECTIVE

Like behaviorists, social-learning theorists believe that external events are important determiners of personality. However, they part company with Skinner and other behaviorists on the issue of cognitive processes. Whereas Skinner asserts that internal cognitive processes such as thinking, perceiving, and feeling are only incidental to behavior and personality, social-learning theorists emphasize our cognitive interpretations of external events to fit our memories, beliefs, and expectations.

A basic tenet of the social-learning approach is that cognitive processes greatly influence the molding of personality by mediating between external environmental events and behavior. Thus, unlike the more traditional behaviorist approach, the social-learning perspective stresses the role of our thoughts, perceptions, and feelings in acquiring and maintaining our behavior patterns (which in the final analysis represent our personalities). Thus, instead of emphasizing how we are controlled by our environments, they focus on the interaction between cognitions and environments in shaping personality.

Because of its emphasis upon cognitive processes, the social-learning approach is sometimes referred to as the *social-cognitive perspective*. The following paragraphs outline the key tenets of Albert Bandura, the most influential representative of this perspective.

Bandura's Social-Cognitive Perspective   Albert Bandura (1925–present) is perhaps the most eloquent spokesman for the viewpoint that observational learning strongly influences our behaviors (1982, 1983, 1986). Recall from Chapter 6 that observational learning is the process whereby we learn patterns of behavior simply by observing people *(models)*. This process allows us to acquire cognitive representations of the behaviors of others, which may then serve as models for our own actions. Bandura maintains that throughout both childhood and adulthood, our observations of which

Albert Bandura

behaviors are rewarded and which are punished or ignored provide us with many such cognitive representations. Accordingly, our own consistent patterns of responding to various situations—in other words, our personality styles—reflect our observational learning.

Bandura has conducted numerous experiments that he believes demonstrate that children may learn "personality traits" through observation. Chapter 6 discussed his famous BoBo doll study, in which he demonstrated that children may learn to be more aggressive simply by observing an aggressive model. Another of Bandura's more interesting experiments concerned the ability to delay gratification, a propensity that many people would consider to be a basic personality trait.

Bandura and Walter Mischel (1965) conducted an experiment with nine- and 10-year-olds to see whether this trait can be manipulated by observational learning. The experimenters wanted to see if they could modify children's inclinations to prefer immediate or delayed gratification by exposing them to adult models. Their first step was to determine each subject's preference for high or low delay of rewards. They accomplished this by providing each child with a series of test situations in which they could choose between small, immediate rewards or larger payoffs that they had to wait for. The next step was to assign a child to one of three conditions: a live adult that modeled behavior opposite to the child's demonstrated preference; a symbolic model (written information) supporting a contrary position; or no model at all. After this phase was completed, the children's preferences were again evaluated by a second series of test situations. Finally, one month later their preferences were again evaluated to see if any effects of the modeling persisted. The results, presented in Figure 13.5, reveal that both live and symbolic models were effective in causing children to change their preferences, and that these "personality changes" tended to persist for at least a month.

Another keystone of Bandura's social-cognitive perspective is his concept of **reciprocal determinism.** According to this principle, our behaviors and thus our personalities are shaped by the interaction between cog-

FIGURE 13.5 THE IMPACT OF MODELS AS CHANGE AGENTS FOR A PERSONALITY TRAIT

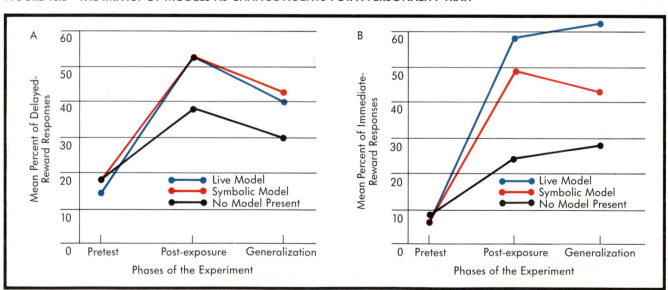

Graph A demonstrates the average change of response in children who initially preferred immediate rewards. Graph B shows average change of response in children who initially preferred delayed rewards. The graphs reveal that both live and symbolic models were effective in causing children to change their behavior. (*Source:* From Bandura & Mischel, 1965)

nitive factors (such as thoughts, feelings, and perceptions) and environmental factors. For example, our response to first meeting our sweetheart's family is likely to be influenced not only by environmental factors (such as whether we meet at their home or in an environment we are familiar with, like the campus) but also by personal-cognitive factors such as our past experiences meeting strangers, our degree of anxiety about making a good impression, and our sense of self-worth.

Each of these two sets of factors can influence and change the other, and the direction of change is typically *reciprocal* rather than one-way. If we have a history of reinforcing experiences of meeting people for the first time, we are likely to perceive our present situation in a positive way and thus act in a sociable manner. Our actions might also have a decided effect on the environment—for instance, if our sweetheart's parents are so charmed by our friendliness that they quickly shift from aloofness to warm sociability. Thus, environmental stimuli, internal cognitive factors, and behavior all operate as reciprocal determinants of each other.

One final element of the social-cognitive perspective deserves mention. In recent years Bandura has made the concept of **self-efficacy** a central component of his theory. Self-efficacy is described as our belief that we can perform adequately and deal effectively with a particular situation. Bandura believes that our sense of self-efficacy greatly influences personality development by affecting whether or not we will even try to behave in a certain way. For example, if we think that we are socially inept and boring, we are inclined to avoid social interactions with people. This may cause others to view us as aloof or withdrawn, even further reducing our sense of social self-efficacy.

The concept of self-efficacy is sometimes confused with self-esteem, but Bandura does not equate the two. He views self-efficacy as a collection of specific evaluations that we make about our sense of adequacy in a variety of situations. Thus, a person who feels socially inept may at the same time have a strong sense of artistic self-efficacy.

Self-efficacy arises from a variety of experiences, including our past successes or failures, our observations of the performances of others ("Gee, I think I can do that" or "That looks too hard for me"), and our own particular feelings as we contemplate a task. (Anxiety or depression lowers self-efficacy, while excitement and anticipation tend to elevate expectations of good performances.)

Besides influencing what activities or situations we become involved in, our self-efficacy judgments are likely to influence the amount of effort we exert. For instance, if you perceive yourself as a good student, you will probably be more likely to persist in your efforts to understand a difficult intellectual concept than will someone with a lower sense of self-efficacy as a student.

In summary, Bandura's social-cognitive perspective stresses the reciprocal interaction between environmental conditions and our beliefs and expectations. Bandura views people not as slaves to environmental stimuli, but rather as individuals capable of assessing situations based on previous experiences, judging their own capability to deal effectively with these situations, and choosing their behavior accordingly.

EVALUATING THE BEHAVIORAL AND SOCIAL-LEARNING THEORIES

Both the behavioral and social-learning approaches focus on the important role of external events in shaping and molding our personalities. Bandura's social-cognitive theory extends this focus to include the reciprocal influence of behaviors and external stimuli.

An important contribution of behavioral and social-learning theories to the field of personality research is their emphasis on rigorous experimental research in testing personality theory. These two perspectives have

If you perceive yourself as a good student who will eventually graduate, you will probably be more likely to persist in your efforts to understand more difficult concepts and to exert more effort in making passing grades in order to reach your goal than will someone with a lower sense of self-efficacy as a student.

helped foster a climate of empirical science that is sorely lacking in many other areas of personality theory.

Behaviorists and social-learning theorists have also provided important insights into why behavior may change from situation to situation, and why certain presumably enduring aspects of personality may not be so enduring after all. As we will see in Chapter 15, this latter perspective has been the basis of some of our most effective models for altering maladaptive behavior. Finally, we cannot overstate the profound impact of the social-cognitive perspective in sensitizing personality psychologists to the important role of personal-cognitive factors in the interactions of behavior and environmental stimuli.

The behavioral and social-learning theories have also generated a considerable amount of criticism, however, particularly Skinner's behaviorist approach. Skinner argues that personality is essentially the result of environmental experiences, a perspective that ignores extensive evidence that infants differ noticeably in temperament just after birth (indicating the possible role of genetic predisposition) and that at least some of these distinctive traits appear to be long-lasting (Garrison et al., 1984; Hewitt, 1984; Thomas et al., 1970). Some critics have responded to Skinner's behaviorism by noting that it just does not match up very well with the world as we know it:

> If one really believes that situations determine behavior, then there is no reason to test or interview prospective employees for jobs such as police officer; it is only necessary to structure the job situation properly. Picking a mate would simply be a matter of finding someone whose physical characteristics appeal to you. In a properly managed class all students would work up to their abilities. Do you know anyone who believes these things? Obviously not. (Rorer & Widiger, 1983, p. 445)

A related criticism is that since learning theories focus so much on the external situation, they fail to recognize that inner forces also influence our behaviors. Certainly no one argues with the contention that events in our external environments influence our behaviors, but what about unconscious motives and conflicts? Also, what about traits such as a tendency to be moody and introverted or sociable and outgoing? These elements also shape our personalities, say critics.

Finally, it has been suggested that their emphasis on external reinforcements, observational learning, and imitation causes both behaviorist and social-learning theorists to ignore the truly human dimensions of our personalities—creativity, spontaneity, joy, love, and strivings for fulfillment. This criticism has emerged primarily from the humanist psychologists, whose viewpoints we turn to next.

HUMANISTIC THEORIES

The humanistic personality theorists—so-called because of their emphasis on the unique characteristics of humanity and their rejection of animal models of behavior—emerged in the late 1950s and early 1960s as a third force in personality theorizing. This movement grew in part out of the humanists' dissatisfaction with the idea that personality is molded by either unconscious drives or the environment. The alternative view presented by the humanists is a much more optimistic interpretation of human nature.

Although the humanistic perspective encompasses a range of viewpoints, its theorists agree on several points. First, virtually all humanistic theorists agree that a primary motivation for behavior comes from each person's strivings to develop, change, and grow in pursuit of the full realization of human potential (recall Maslow's concept of self-actualization, discussed in Chapter 9). Second, humanists collectively reject the notion that personalities are significantly influenced by the kinds of baser impulses postulated by Freud and his followers. Third, humanistic theories also tend to be *phenomenological*, emphasizing a subjective view of reality as seen from the individual's own frame of reference. We can learn more about personality from understanding what it is like to be "in the other person's shoes," argue the humanists, than from objectively observing and analyzing what people say and do. For humanists, the "stuff" of personality consists of our own subjective, personal view of the world, including our attitudes, beliefs, and feelings. The theories of the two most influential humanists, Carl Rogers and Abraham Maslow, both illustrate these features.

ROGERS AND THE SELF

Carl Rogers (1902–1987) began his professional career as a practicing psychotherapist in the late 1920s. Like Freud, his eventual emergence as a personality theorist was stimulated by what he observed in his patients' revelations. However, Rogers' reading was quite different from that of Freud. Instead of seeing people as driven by sexual and aggressive impulses, Rogers saw the inherent potential for good in each of us (1961, 1977, 1980). Through listening to his clients, he became convinced that the most enduring, driving force in people's lives is their constant striving toward self-fulfillment and the realization of their own unique potential. He considered this striving to be a positive, constructive force that motivates us to engage in healthy behaviors that enhance our sense of self.

Central to Rogers' theory of personality is the concept of **self**, the basic core of our beings that glues the elements of our personalities together. It is the central organizing, all-encompassing structure that accounts for the coherence and stability of our personalities. Rogers did not claim to have invented the concept of self—it was the Greeks who first provided us with the mandate "know thyself." What Rogers did was sensitize psychology to the role of this ancient maxim in the evolution and expression of human personality. "At bottom, each person is asking, Who am I, really? How can I get in touch with this real self, underlying all my surface behavior? How can I become myself?' " (1961, p. 108).

Carl Rogers

I remember a period of about six months several years ago when I was out of work. I lost my job through no failing of my own—my company went under and all of us had to join the unemployment lines. Nothing about the experience was fun, but the worst part of all was the roller-coaster ride my emotions took. Once in a while a prospect looked good and I'd be so excited I couldn't sit still. But most of the time my self-confidence was shredded. Not only did I doubt my own professional skills, but I was so anxious that I had trouble sleeping, lost my appetite, and withdrew from my friends. The funny thing was that on a logical level I *knew* that my skills were excellent, but without the daily feedback that comes with a regular job, I couldn't really believe it. (*Authors' files*)

In response to the question, "Who am I?" Rogers maintains that we derive a self-concept, or image of ourselves, that determines how we perceive and respond to the world. If we see ourselves as being likeable and attractive, we are likely to approach the intriguing person we see at a party. If, on the other hand, we see ourselves as boring and unattractive, we are less likely to make overtures.

Rogers believes that the key to healthy adjustment and happiness is a consistency or *congruence* between our self-concept and our experiences. Thus, if you consider yourself to be likeable and easy to get along with, this image will be bolstered by your good relationship with your friends. The opposite is true when your experiences are not congruent with your self-concept. For instance, if you find one year that you cannot seem to get along with either your roommate or neighbors, you will probably feel anxious and troubled. In Rogers' view, such incongruence between self-concept and experiences is often an important factor in maladjustment. To regain a sense of congruence, you must either change your behaviors or your self-concept.

In addition to the interrelationship between the self and the outside world, Rogers suggests that all of us are possessed of a sense of the *ideal self*, what we would like to be. Just as maladjustment can be caused by experiences that contradict our self-concept, it can also be caused by a discordance between the ideal self and the *real self*, our perception of ourselves as we really are.

Since Rogers' primary endeavor was as a psychotherapist, he was involved in treating the maladjustment that results from poor fits between either the self and external reality or between the ideal self and the real self. His therapy strategy was to help people initiate behavior changes where necessary, and ultimately to come to know, accept, and be true to themselves. We will have more to say about Rogers' therapeutic rationale in Chapter 15.

MASLOW AND SELF-ACTUALIZATION

Abraham Maslow's (1908–1970) initial training as a psychologist was in the behaviorist tradition. However, early in his career he began to question the idea that human actions can be explained solely in terms of rewards and punishments. This attitude eventually led him to move in the direction of humanistic psychology, which he named the "third force" (with psychoanalytic theory and behaviorism being the other two forces) (1968, 1970, 1971).

Most of Maslow's life was spent developing and expanding a theory of motivation and personality that emphasized people's positive strivings toward intimacy, joy, love, a sense of belonging, self-esteem, and fulfillment of their highest potential. As we saw in Chapter 9, Maslow proposed that we are motivated by a hierarchy of needs (see Figure 9.1). When our basic needs for things like food, warmth, and security are met, we are then motivated toward higher needs—first for love and self-esteem, and then, for some people, for self-actualization.

Maslow derived his ideas about human motivation and personality from the study of healthy people rather than disturbed people observed in clinical settings. Perhaps it was his intense interest in creative, vibrant, well-adjusted people that led him to place a strong emphasis on such positive human qualities as joy, love, enthusiasm, creativity, and humor while largely ignoring other forces like guilt, anger, shame, conflict, and hostility. Maslow was influenced and inspired by his study of a number of historical and contemporary public figures who he believed exemplified his concept of self-actualization. In 1950 he identified 38 people he assessed as having reached their fullest potential. This select group included a number of lesser known people Maslow knew personally, as well as many historical luminaries such as Ludwig van Beethoven, William James, Abraham Lincoln, Jane Addams, Albert Schweitzer, Albert Einstein, and Eleanor Roosevelt. Maslow identified 16 individual characteristics of the self-actualized person. If you would like to see how closely you fit his conception of a completely fulfilled person, take a look at his characteristics as listed below.

The self-actualized person:

1. Is accepting of self and others.
2. Takes a realistic, nonfanciful view of life.
3. Is inclined to appreciate people and new ideas, and is not inclined to view them in a stereotypical fashion.
4. Enjoys intimate and loving relationships with a few people.
5. Has a lively sense of humor.
6. Is disinclined to go along with tradition just for the sake of conformity.
7. Shows the ability to expand and improve the environment rather than merely adjust to it.
8. Is creative.
9. Has democratic values.
10. Is problem-centered rather than self-centered.
11. Is independent and able to function on one's own without being hindered by the opinions of others.
12. Is open and spontaneous.
13. Is inclined to seek privacy and is content in one's own company.
14. Feels a strong identification with the plight of all human beings.
15. Has the ability to separate means from ends.
16. Has a history of "peak experiences" (moments of profound intellectual insight or intense appreciation of music or art).

EVALUATING THE HUMANISTIC THEORIES

Humanistic theories of personality have inspired psychologists and laypersons alike to consider the positive dimensions of human personality. Their approach provides a welcome focus on the healthy personality that has helped to broaden our perspectives on human nature. The humanistic view of the self or self-concept as a central component of human personality has added a valuable dimension in our understanding of personality. The current emphasis on fostering personal growth and a positive sense of self that we see in such diverse areas as counseling, education, child-rearing, and even occasionally in management policies is due at least in part to the pervasive influence of Rogers and Maslow. A number of valid criticisms have challenged the humanistic perspective, however.

One key objection has to do with the vague, subjective nature of many humanistic concepts. The humanists have been criticized for basing their theories on subjective, nonverifiable observations of people in clinical or natural settings. Rogers' concept of *self* and Maslow's principle of *self-actualization* are both terms that defy objective, operational descriptions. If you cannot describe something operationally, how can you conduct empirical research to test its validity? The fact that many humanists are demonstrably unconcerned about putting their ideas to empirical tests does not add to their credibility among psychologists who value verifiable evidence. Critics also claim that a theoretical perspective centered on such nebulous concepts as self-perception, the individual's subjective assessment of the world, and the meaning of his or her experiences does not add to our ability to explain behavior. "In the last analysis, explaining personality on the basis of hypothesized self-tendencies is reassuring doubletalk, not explanation" (Liebert & Spiegler, 1982, p. 411).

The humanists have also been criticized for focusing so closely on the individual and the role of the self that they have largely ignored the impact of environmental factors in shaping behavior. Finally, a few psychologists have expressed concern that the humanistic perspective places so much emphasis on being in touch with self, being true to the self, and striving to fulfill one's potential, that it promotes a kind of "me first" philosophy that encourages selfishness and self-indulgence (Campbell & Specht, 1985; Wallach & Wallach, 1983, 1985).

PERSONALITY ASSESSMENT

In our overview of trait theories and the psychoanalytic, behavioral, and humanistic perspectives, we have seen a variety of descriptions and explanations of human personality. Thus, it should come as no surprise that *personality assessment*, the measurement or assessment of personality, has been approached in a variety of ways.

Indeed, personality assessment is far from an exact science, and the reason has to do with the difficulty in pinpointing the subject matter. If psychologists limited their interests in human personality only to those overt behaviors that can be directly observed, the task of personality assessment would be relatively straightforward. However, as we have learned, personality theorists are also interested in the unconscious mechanisms, behavioral predispositions, and traits that presumably underlie our actions. How can such abstract things as repression, anxiety, introversion, dominance, the self, and self-actualization be measured? Psychologists have devised a variety of methods for at least obtaining glimpses of these seemingly intangible dimensions. We will comment on how well they have succeeded as we outline four of the most important methods: behavioral observation, interviews, paper-and-pencil questionnaires, and projective tests.

BEHAVIORAL OBSERVATION

If you notice that a classmate always sits alone and appears flustered when a question is directed his way, you will probably infer that he is shy and withdrawn. Similarly, if a roommate always remembers to deliver phone messages and clean up after herself, you may conclude that she is a responsible person. Virtually all of us develop impressions of people by observing how they act. This is the essence of one personality assessment method, **behavioral observation**. The assumption underlying this technique is that personality is best assessed within the environment in which behavior occurs. This method is favored by behavioral and social-learning theorists who emphasize people's interactions with their environments. In their view, this technique is the best and most logical procedure for identifying the stimulus events associated with particular types of behaviors.

Clinical psychologists, clinical social workers, and psychiatrists also use this method to gain insight into their clients' personalities. For example, a client's gestures, manner of speaking, facial expressions, and reactions to the clinician's questions can all provide important information.

As logical and practical as this technique may seem, however, it also can be misleading. Certainly all of us have discovered from time to time that our initial conclusions about people do not always hold up over time. For example, you might be surprised to observe your shy, introverted classmate talking animatedly and dancing up a storm at a party. Our observations of people can be misleading because they typically provide an opportunity to observe behavior in only a limited range of circumstances. However, the behavior we happen to observe in any given situation may not be at all typical of an individual's personality.

HOW CAN BEHAVIORAL OBSERVATION BE MADE MORE RELIABLE?

Can you think of any techniques that could make the behavioral observation method a more reliable tool for assessing personality? Take a moment to consider this question before reading on.

Psychologists sometimes go to considerable lengths to engage in more structured observations of behavior in a variety of situations. For example, a child psychologist interested in studying personality development in small children might observe a child's behavior in the natural setting of the classroom, playground, and at home with family. By carefully recording the times and places certain behaviors occur (such as sharing things with others, engaging in aggressive behavior, acting in a submissive manner, or displaying dependency behaviors), important information might be obtained about the role of the environment in shaping certain personality traits.

This more structured approach to behavioral observation improves the reliability and precision of measurement. As we saw in Chapter 2, it is also limited by the fact that an observer's presence may influence the subject's behavior, and that any one observer's interpretation of behavior may reflect his or her own biases. Furthermore, as a matter of practicality, any observer is generally able to sample only a relatively limited range of a subject's behaviors in only a few situations.

As a remedy to these shortcomings, psychologists have developed *rating scales*. A rating scale is a device, like the one shown in Figure 13.6, that several people who know a subject can use to indicate the degree to which particular traits are evident in her or his personality. Thus, researchers studying personality development by observing child subjects in a few natural settings might also expand their database by asking parents, teachers, older siblings, and adult friends to fill out scales rating such traits as sociability, aggression, submission, and dependency.

Although rating scales can provide valuable insights into an individual's personality, there is no guarantee that all observers will provide unbiased records. For example, a teacher who does not like a child may exaggerate her negative traits, whereas the child's parents may do exactly the opposite. As a safeguard against the biases of individual raters, psychologists who use this technique try to secure as many ratings as possible.

INTERVIEWS

Another valuable method of learning about an individual's personality is to ask that person questions. Freud relied heavily upon the **interview** approach, and today it is used by advocates of all the theoretical perspectives we have considered, including the behaviorists. Interviews range from informal, unstructured exchanges in which an interviewer asks a few broad questions and encourages the subject to talk extensively, to much more structured procedures in which very specific questions are asked in a prescribed sequence.

An important advantage of the interview technique is its flexibility. If some questions are confusing, the interviewer can clarify them; their sequence can also be varied to meet the subject's needs. A competent interviewer can establish a sense of rapport that may encourage more candor than that produced by more impersonal assessment methods such as questionnaires. This technique also allows interviewers to delve into whatever areas of personality interest them. Unstructured interviews also provide the option of pursuing or dropping a particular line of questioning depending on the amount of useful information that is being produced. Furthermore,

FIGURE 13.6   A HYPOTHETICAL EXAMPLE OF A RATING SCALE FOR A CANDIDATE FOR EMPLOYMENT

	Below Average (Lowest 50%)	Average (Right in the Middle)	Above Average (Next Highest 25%)	Very Good (Next Highest 15%)	Unusually High (Top 10%)	No Basis for Judgment
Academic Performance						
General Intellectual Ability						
Initiative and Resourcefulness						
Communication Skills: Written						
Communication Skills: Oral						
Maturity						
Creativity						
Capacity for Self-Growth						
Leadership Potential						
Self-Discipline						
Sociability (Effective Inter-Personal Skills						
Ability to Act Independently						

an interview allows an interviewer to assess not only what a subject says, but also how it is said.

The interview method also has its limitations. The basic data of interviews—what people say about themselves—is virtually impossible to quantify. This means that what get recorded are largely the interviewer's impressions and inferences, and these are subject to observer bias. Secondly, since there is no standard way of conducting an interview, an interviewer's personal style may significantly influence the subject's responses. The same subject may respond gregariously to a warm, affable interviewer but hold back information when interviewed by someone with a less approachable style. Extensive clinical evidence suggests that an interviewer's approach may also influence the subject. It is noteworthy that interviewers who have a strong theoretical perspective on personality may influence subjects to respond in ways that are supportive of the interviewer's position (Feshbach & Weiner, 1982).

PAPER-AND-PENCIL QUESTIONNAIRES

While the observational and interview methods have strengths, neither is as standardized or objective as personality psychologists would like them to be, and while both techniques allow psychologists to observe what people do or say, there is always the concern that knowing how people behave may not reveal what they are thinking or feeling. To compensate for these shortcomings, psychologists have developed a number of **paper-and-pencil questionnaires**: objective, self-report inventories designed to measure scientifically the variety of characteristics or traits that make up personality.

Most paper-and-pencil questionnaires ask subjects to rate as true or false a collection of statements about their thoughts, feelings, and behaviors. Some of these questionnaires are designed to measure a very limited range of traits or only a single personality characteristic such as anxiety, self-concept, or introversion-extroversion. Others are designed to provide more global measures of personality. Two noteworthy examples of questionnaires are the Minnesota Multiphasic Personality Inventory and the California Psychological Inventory.

Minnesota Multiphasic Personality Inventory   The best known and most widely used objective personality inventory is the *Minnesota Multiphasic Personality Inventory (MMPI)* (Hathaway & McKinley, 1942). Originally designed to help diagnose and classify persons with psychological disorders, its developers started with a pool of 1,000 possible test-item statements describing mood states, attitudes, and overt behavior. These statements were drawn from such sources as existing tests and psychiatry and psychology textbooks. Following a test development procedure similar to that described in Chapter 12 (see "How Intelligence Tests Are Developed"), the researchers administered these items to a standardization group of approximately 200 psychiatric patients with a variety of diagnosed disorders and to roughly 1,000 so-called "normal" individuals recruited from university applicants, hospital visitors, and residents of Minneapolis.

This procedure resulted in a final version of the MMPI that consisted of 566 statements about behavior, thoughts, or emotional reactions that subjects rate as "true" of themselves, "false," or "cannot say" (undecided about the truth of the statement). Examples of the kinds of items found on the MMPI include, "I am basically a happy person"; "I believe people are plotting against me"; "Sometimes I disobey laws"; and "I worry a lot about sex." (These are not exact replicas of MMPI items.)

The MMPI is referred to as a **criterion-keyed test** because each of the 566 items is referenced to one of the original criterion groups that were used in developing the test—either the 1,000 nonpatients or the subjects who had been diagnosed as having a particular psychiatric disorder. For example, most people would respond "false" to an item like "I believe people are plotting against me." On the other hand, a person with a *paranoid disorder* (delusions of persecution and/or grandeur) would be more likely to respond "true." Thus, this item is referenced to the paranoid criterion group. It is not possible to make a diagnosis based on just one item, so the developers of the MMPI used statistical procedures to group together items which clearly relate to a particular clinical condition or criterion group. For

TABLE 13.2   *MMPI Scales and Descriptions*

Scale	Abbreviation	Definition
Validity Scales		
Question	?	Corresponds to number of items left unanswered
Lie	L	Lies or is highly conventional
Frequency	F	Exaggerates complaints, answers haphazardly
Correction	K	Denies problems
Clinical Scales		
Hypochondriasis	Hs	Expresses bodily concerns and complaints
Depression	D	Is depressed, pessimistic, guilty
Hysteria	Hy	Reacts to stress with physical symptoms, lacks insight
Psychopathic deviate	Pd	Is immoral, in conflict with the law, involved in stormy relationships
Masculinity femininity	Mf	Has interests characteristic of stereotypical sex roles
Paranoia	Pa	Is suspicious, resentful
Psychasthenia	Pt	Is anxious, worried, high-strung
Schizophrenia	Sc	Is confused, disorganized, disoriented
Hypomania	Ma	Is energetic, active, easily bored, restless
Social Introversion	Si	Is introverted, timid, shy, lacking self-confidence

example, a paranoia scale contains items that people with diagnosed paranoia respond to differently than either normal subjects or subjects with other diagnosed disorders.

The MMPI contains 10 clinical scales designed to measure such conditions as depression, social introversion, schizophrenia, paranoia, and psychopathic personality. It also includes four validity scales designed to assess whether subjects have falsified or faked their answers. Table 13.2 lists all 14 clinical and validity scales on the MMPI.

The MMPI is widely used for its original purpose of diagnosing psychological disorders. Many clinical psychologists today find it to be helpful as an aid to the diagnostic process, and personality psychologists have also found it to be a useful source of information about the personalities of normal people. However, the MMPI has been widely criticized for a number of reasons.

First, some psychologists have expressed reservations about the original sample group of disturbed individuals because it was severely limited in both size and geographic representation. Recall that the standardization sample included only 200 disturbed patients, and that the "normal" group was drawn from a limited population within Minneapolis.

Of even greater concern are questions about the reliability and validity of clinical diagnoses of the original psychiatric sample used in standardizing the MMPI (Ross, 1987). Since the decision process by which these diagnoses were made has not been well documented, we cannot be certain that all or the great majority of the patients in these criterion groups were correctly diagnosed. To the extent that at least some members of the original patient population were misdiagnosed, the validity of the MMPI itself would need to be questioned. The MMPI has also been criticized because some of its items, particularly those dealing with sex and religion, represent an invasion of privacy, and because its excessive length causes at least some subjects to get sloppy in their haste to get the process over with. In addition, low test-retest reliability has also been a problem.

The MMPI has been shown to be a good device for differentiating disturbed and normal people, but it lacks the capacity to differentiate reliably between people within each of these categories (Kleinmuntz, 1982; Ross, 1987). This major limitation renders the MMPI less than useful to personality researchers interested in assessing individual differences.

California Psychological Inventory   A few global personality question-naires have been designed specifically for use with normal populations. Perhaps the most exemplary of this group is the **California Psychological Inventory (CPI)** (Gough, 1957, 1975). The format of this questionnaire is similar to that of the MMPI, and it also is criterion keyed, but here, the criteria are 15 "normal" personality traits: dominance, sociability, self-acceptance, social presence, self-control, achievement via conformance, achievement via independence, responsibility, intellectual efficiency, flexibility, socialization, femininity, capacity for status, psychological minded-ness, and tolerance.

The CPI was developed by selecting test items from a pool of statements administered to people known to differ on some personality trait. For example, if an item differentiated between people known to have high or low levels of self-acceptance (based on self-reports and the ratings of others who knew them well), it was included in a final self-acceptance scale. In this manner, a total of 15 "normal" personality traits and three response-bias scales were included in the final instrument.

The CPI has a much larger standardization group (7,000 females and 6,000 males) than does the MMPI, and much greater care was taken in controlling for factors such as social status, geographical locale, and age. Furthermore, in contrast to the relatively low test-retest reliability of the MMPI, the CPI has a test-retest reliability of approximately .90 (Ross, 1987). Finally, this questionnaire has been shown to have good predictive validity for a variety of purposes such as predicting school and job success, leadership, conformity, and reactions to stress (Megargee, 1972; Ross, 1987). From an overall perspective then, the CPI is in many ways a more valid instrument than the MMPI, even though it is much less widely used.

PROJECTIVE TESTS

Paper-and-pencil questionnaires such as the MMPI and CPI are relatively easy to standardize, administer, and score because they are highly structured and empirically constructed. Their tight structure, however, can also be a liability, particularly in view of the fact that subjects must limit responses to "true," "false," or "cannot say." Partly in response to this limitation and partly out of a desire to tap unconscious thoughts and feelings, psychologists have developed **projective tests**.

Projective tests are collectively distinguished by a loose structure and unclear or ambiguous stimuli that allow respondents a wide latitude of response. Because the tests do not have obviously correct or socially more or less desirable responses, it is assumed that subjects "project" their own thoughts or feelings into their responses—hence the name projective tests, or techniques. The underlying rationale, manner of development, and application of projective techniques is based primarily on psychoanalytic theory, which predicts that people will resort to hidden or inner processes to "project" structure onto ambiguous stimuli. A trained examiner then applies subjective clinical judgment to draw inferences about such dimensions of personality as unconscious conflicts, repressed impulses, hidden fears, and ego defenses. The two most commonly used projective techniques are the Rorschach ink-blot test and the Thematic Apperception Test.

The Rorschach Ink-blot Test   The **Rorschach ink-blot test**, developed in 1921 by the Swiss psychiatrist Hermann Rorschach, consists of 10 cards showing ink blots, such as the one in Figure 13.7. Blots are presented to a subject one at a time in an order prescribed by Rorschach. The subject is asked to examine each of the blots and say what it looks like or brings to mind.

Scoring of the Rorschach is highly complex, involving extensive training in one of several systems by which the responses are coded, scored, and interpreted. However, all of the various systems agree that the major

FIGURE 13.7   A SAMPLE ROR-SCHACH INK BLOT

What does this look like or bring to mind?

scoring categories for each response include its *location* (where the subject focuses attention), its *determinants* (color, implied movement, shading, particular form, etc.), and its *content* (human, nonhuman animal, or object). Various interpretations may be assigned to a subject's responses. For example, if a person focuses on only a small portion of a blot, this might indicate that this person pays attention to the little details and likes things to be neat and orderly. A person who gives very unusual or unique responses might be considered to be overly concerned with asserting independence and individuality, whereas someone who gives many obvious and common responses might be considered to be conventional and anxious to blend in with the crowd. These interpretations are very subjective, however, and even the experts who work with the Rorschach all the time do not always agree on how various responses should be interpreted.

The fact that clinicians who regularly use the Rorschach often disagree in their interpretations raises serious doubts about its validity as a diagnostic instrument. One of the problems in assessing the validity of the Rorschach test is that most clinicians use it along with several other diagnostic procedures. Thus, they typically interpret a person's Rorschach responses in the context of information obtained from such sources as interviews, family members, and other kinds of tests. As a result, it is very difficult to assess the capacity of this instrument by itself to provide valid personality assessments and accurate predictions of behavior. When researchers have attempted to study the diagnostic and predictive accuracy of Rorschach scores considered in isolation from other sources of information, they have found them to have little or no predictive validity (Kleinmuntz, 1982).

Despite this liability, the Rorschach continues to be one of the most widely used instruments for clinical diagnosis and personality assessment. Many clinical practitioners point out that the validity studies are not a fair representation of the manner in which they use the Rorschach in their practices. Many claim, rightfully so, that the Rorschach is just one of many assessment methods they use to evaluate their clients, and as such it continues to be a valuable source of important insights into the inner workings of the psyche.

The Thematic Apperception Test   You may recall being introduced to the **Thematic Apperception Test (TAT)** in Chapter 9, where we discussed its application in assessing achievement needs. The TAT consists of 30 cards that depict various scenes and one blank card. While recognizable, all the pictures are vague and ambiguous (see Figure 13.8). In the standard admin-

FIGURE 13.8 A SAMPLE THEMATIC AP-PERCEPTION TEST CARD

What is going on in this scene, what are the characters thinking and feeling, what led up to the portrayed situation, and what will its outcome be?

istration of the TAT, the tester selects 20 cards on the basis of the sex and age of the subject, who is then shown the cards one at a time and asked to describe what is going on in each scene, what the characters are thinking and feeling, what led up to the portrayed situation, and what its outcome will be.

Like the Rorschach ink-blot test, the TAT is based on the assumption that when people are asked to respond to unstructured stimuli, they will reveal certain aspects of their inner selves that they normally keep under wraps. As one of the developers of the TAT observed, "The test is based on the well-recognized fact that when a person interprets an ambiguous social situation he is apt to expose his own personality as much as the phenomenon to which he is attending" (Murray, 1938, p. 530).

Formal systems for scoring and interpreting TAT responses are available. However, most clinicians tend to disregard these systems, relying instead on their own impressionistic, subjective assessments. Typically clinicians look for common themes that run through the stories (hence the term, *thematic*). For example, if a person told several stories with themes of loneliness or isolation, an examiner might interpret this as a sign of depression or alienation.

How valid is the TAT for clinical diagnosis? Many examiners use only a few cards that they think will be most productive in revealing aspects of a particular client's personality. This preselection compromises efforts to assess the test's validity because the clinician is likely to draw upon other sources of information in making the initial judgment about which cards to use. Furthermore, scoring tends to be highly subjective, based on an examiner's experience and clinical judgment which has already been influenced by knowledge of the subject. However, when the TAT has been used as a research tool in controlled experiments, it has demonstrated very good validity. An example is the research discussed in Chapter 9 that measured the relationship between need to achieve and various behaviors, in which the TAT was used to measure achievement motivation.

In all, although a wide range of methods are used to assess personality, none is without limitations. Most psychologists agree, however, that it is important to continue our efforts to understand the distinctive needs, values, and patterns of behavior that characterize individuals' adaptations to the situations of their lives. Therefore we can expect that personality assessment devices will continue to evolve.

SUMMARY

WHAT IS PERSONALITY?

1. Personality is not an attribute that people possess in varying amounts. Rather, personality is what we are, a collection of all our many traits and attributes, the sum total of which constitutes a unique person unlike anyone else.

2. We may best describe personality psychology as the study of individuals—their distinctive characteristics and traits and the manner in which they integrate all aspects of their psychological functioning as they adapt to their environments.

TRAIT THEORIES

3. Trait theorists attempt to identify the behavioral traits that are the building blocks of personality.

4. Two approaches to determining personality traits are the idiographic approach, which defines traits by studying individuals in depth to determine the distinctive qualities of their personalities, and the nomothetic approach which studies groups of people in the attempt to identify personality traits that tend to appear in clusters.

5. Allport's application of the idiographic approach led to a description of three types of traits that operate to provide a person's own unique personality structure. A cardinal trait is a dominating behavioral predisposition that provides the pivotal point in a person's life. Central traits are major characteristics of someone's personality, such as honesty or generosity. Finally, secondary traits are less enduring behavioral tendencies such as dress style preference.

6. Cattell's nomothetic approach has yielded a list of 16 primary or source traits which he considers to be the center or core of personality. He lists each of these traits as a pair of polar opposites, such as trusting vs. suspicious.

7. Critics of trait theories have suggested that traits are only descriptions, not explanations, that personality "traits" may be situationally dependent, and that trait theories offer essentially no understanding of how personality develops.

PSYCHOANALYTIC THEORY

8. Freud's psychoanalytic theory of personality evolved from his attempts to explain certain recurrent themes that emerged from his psychoanalysis of patients.

9. The psychoanalytic theory of personality depicts people as being shaped by an ongoing conflict between their primary drives, particularly sex and aggression, and the social pressures of civilized society. Freud also theorized that early childhood experiences play a major role in molding personality.

10. According to Freud the dynamics of personality reside in the continuous interactions of the impulse-driven id, the guilt-inducing superego, and the ego, which acts as mediator by reconciling reality with the demands of both the id and the superego.

11. Freud maintained that the ego experiences anxiety when an impulse that is unacceptable to the superego threatens to be expressed in overt behavior. When the ego is not able to relieve this anxiety through rational methods, it resorts to certain less rational maneuvers called defense mechanisms, which include repression, rationalization, projection, displacement, sublimation, regression, and reaction formation.

12. Freud theorized that a child progresses through a series of stages of psychosexual development in which the focus of sexual gratification shifts from one body site (erogenous zone) to another. During the first phase, the oral stage (birth to 12–18 months) the lips and the mouth are the erogenous zone. During the second phase or anal stage (12–18 months to three years) the erogenous zone shifts from the mouth to the anal area. During the third phase of psychosexual development, the phallic stage (ages three to five or six), the focus of sexual gratification shifts to genital stimulation. The latency period (age five or six to puberty) is characterized by unexpressed or latent sexual drives. Finally, during the genital stage (from puberty on), sexual feelings are expressed in sexual relations with people outside the family.

13. Too much or too little gratification can result in a child becoming arrested or fixated at an early stage of psychosexual development.

14. Criticisms of psychoanalytic theory include concern about the inability to define operationally and test some of its basic tenets, its lack of clear-cut predictions about how specific experiences will affect personality and behavior, its failure to appreciate the strengths of healthy personalities, its overemphasis on the importance of early experiences, and the inherent assumption that women are inferior to men in a number of ways.

BEHAVIORAL AND SOCIAL-LEARNING THEORIES

15. To Skinner, our personalities are the sum total of our overt and covert responses to the world around us.

16. From the perspective of behaviorism, each person's own unique history of operant and classical conditioning is responsible for the development of his or her personality.

17. Social-learning theorists also believe that external events are important determiners of personality. However, unlike traditional behaviorists, social-learning theorists emphasize our cognitive interpretations of external events to fit our memories, beliefs, and expectations.

18. According to Bandura, our own consistent patterns of responding to various situations—in other words, our personality styles—reflect our observational learning (the process whereby we learn patterns of behavior simply by observing people).

19. Another keystone of Bandura's social-cognitive perspective is his concept of reciprocal determinism, which suggests that our personalities are shaped by the interaction between cognitive factors and environmental factors.

20. Bandura also believes that self-efficacy, or our belief that we can perform adequately and deal effectively with situations, greatly influences personality development by affecting whether or not we will even try to behave in a certain way.

21. Critics of Skinner's behaviorist approach have suggested that such a strong focus on the external environment leads to a failure to recognize the role of both

inner forces and innate predispositions that influence behavior and lead to differences among individuals. It has also been suggested that their emphasis on external reinforcements, observational learning, and imitation causes both behaviorist and social-learning theorists to ignore the truly human dimensions of our personalities such as creativity, spontaneity, and love.

HUMANISTIC THEORIES

22. The humanistic personality theorists agree that a primary motivation for behavior comes from each person's strivings to develop, change, and grow in pursuit of the full realization of human potential.

23. Central to Rogers' theory of personality is the concept of the self, the basic core of our beings that is the central organizing, all-encompassing structure that accounts for the coherence and stability of our personalities.

24. Rogers believes that the key to healthy adjustment and happiness is a consistency or congruence between our self-concept and our experiences.

25. Maslow's theory of motivation and personality emphasizes people's positive strivings toward intimacy, joy, love, a sense of belonging, self-esteem, and fulfillment of their highest potential.

26. Critics have objected to the vague, subjective nature of many humanistic concepts, and the humanists have been criticized for basing their theories on subjective, nonverifiable observations of people in clinical or natural settings. The humanists have also been criticized for focusing so closely on the individual and the role of the self that they have largely ignored the impact of environmental factors in shaping behavior.

PERSONALITY ASSESSMENT

27. Four of the most important methods for assessing personality include behavioral observation, interviews, paper-and-pencil questionnaires, and projective tests.

28. The assumption underlying behavioral observation is that personality is best assessed within the environment in which behavior occurs. Limitations of this method include the fact that an observer's presence may influence the subject's behavior, and that any one observer's interpretations of behavior may reflect his or her own

biases. To remedy these shortcomings, psychologists use rating scales that several people who know a subject can use to indicate the degree to which particular traits are evident in her or his personality.

29. Interviews, which range from informal, unstructured exchanges to much more structured procedures, have the important advantage of flexibility (questions can be clarified, sequence varied, etc.). However, it is virtually impossible to quantify the basic data of interviews that consist of the interviewer's impressions and inferences, both of which are subject to observer bias.

30. Paper-and-pencil questionnaires are objective self-report inventories that typically ask subjects to rate as true or false a collection of statements about their thoughts, feelings, and behaviors.

31. The best known and most widely used objective personality inventory is the Minnesota Multiphasic Personality Inventory (MMPI), which is designed to measure a variety of clinical conditions such as depression and paranoia. The MMPI is widely used for diagnosing psychological disorders. Concerns about the MMPI include questions about its original standardization group, its reliability and validity, and its tendency to invade one's privacy.

32. The most exemplary of the global personality questionnaires designed for use with normal populations is the California Psychological Inventory (CPI), which is designed to measure 15 "normal" personality traits such as sociability and self-control. This questionnaire has been shown to have good predictive validity for a variety of purposes such as predicting school and job success.

33. Projective tests are collectively distinguished by a loose structure and ambiguous stimuli that allow respondents to "project" their own thoughts or feelings into their responses.

34. The Rorschach ink-blot test, which consists of 10 cards showing ink blots, has been shown to have little or no predictive validity when considered in isolation from other sources of information.

35. The Thematic Apperception Test (TAT), which consists of a series of cards that depict various scenes, allows clinicians to look for common themes that run through the stories that subjects tell about each scene. When the TAT has been used as a research tool in controlled experiments, it has demonstrated very good validity.

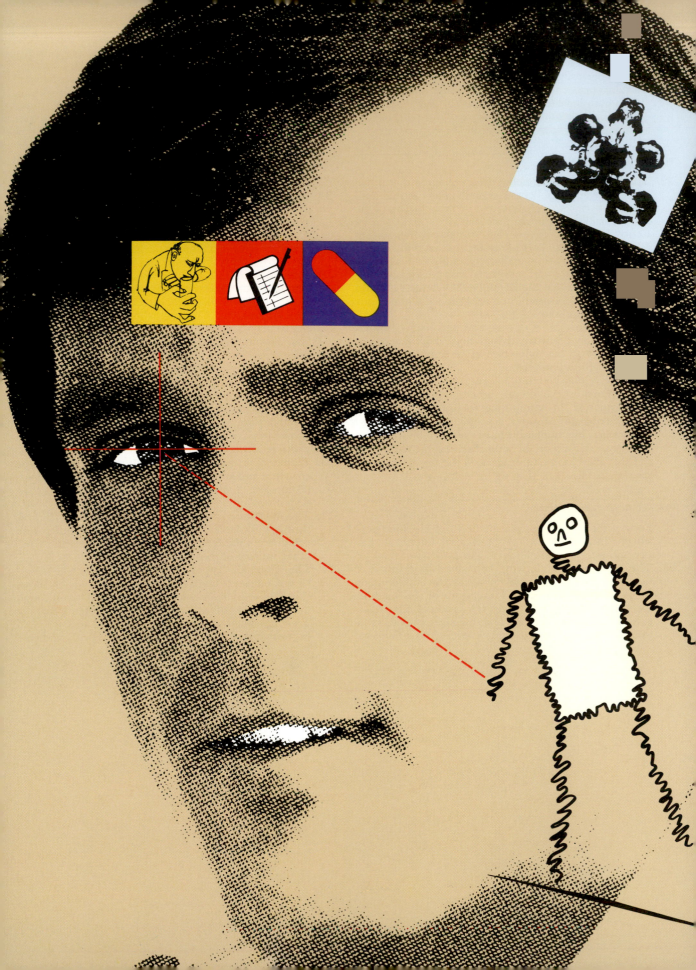

PART 5

THE NATURE AND TREATMENT OF PSYCHOLOGICAL DISORDERS

14

PSYCHOLOGICAL DISORDERS

15

THERAPY

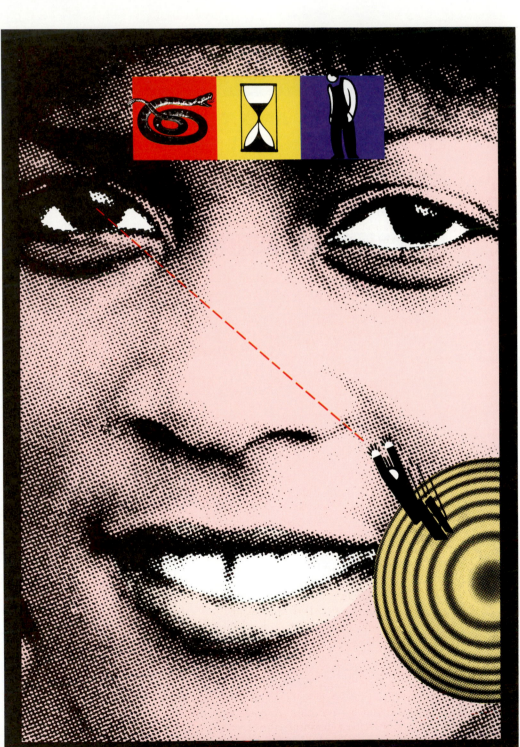

14 Psychological Disorders

On admission [to the mental hospital] she slapped the nurse, addressed the house physician as God, made the sign of the cross, and laughed loudly when she was asked to don the hospital garb. This she promptly tore into shreds. She remained nude for several hours before she was restrained in bed. She sang at the top of her voice, screamed through the window, and leered at the patients promenading in the recreation yard. She was very untidy and incontinent. . . . Frequently she would utter the words, "God, Thou Holy One," cross herself, laugh, and then give vent to vile expletives while she carried out suggestive movements of the body. She yelled for water, and, when this was proffered, she threw the tin cup across the room." (Karnosh & Zucker, 1945, p. 78)

It is not difficult to tell that the person just described is severely disturbed, or, stated another way, that her behavior is *abnormal*. When someone's behavior deviates so extremely from the way people customarily behave, no one would question the label abnormal. (This woman was in fact diagnosed as having a mood disorder, one of several types of psychological disorders discussed in this chapter.)

But what about the schoolteacher who functions well in her everyday life but confides in a friend that sometimes she hears the voice of her deceased child? or the person who seems normal but refuses to ride in elevators? Are these also examples of abnormal behavior? Defining abnormality is not always an easy task. There are shades of gray on the continuum from normal to abnormal, and it is often difficult to know where to draw the line.

Psychology and psychiatry have a long history of debate in the interrelated areas of defining abnormality and classifying psychological disorders. However, after extensive discussions and many changes, clinicians are beginning to reach some consensus about what constitutes disordered behavior. In this chapter we first look at the criteria for defining abnormality and the classification of psychological disorders, then look more closely at some specific psychological disorders.

Most people would consider talking to a statue to be an example of abnormal behavior in that it represents a marked deviation from the way people customarily behave.

DEFINING ABNORMALITY

There is no universally accepted definition of abnormality. However, psychologists who specialize in studying abnormal behavior tend to emphasize a common core of four criteria that may be used to distinguish between normal and **abnormal behavior**: atypicality, maladaptivity, psychological discomfort, and social unacceptability.

The behavior of the person described in the opening account is certainly *atypical*, and indeed all of the psychological disorders that we will consider in this chapter are atypical in a statistical sense. However, rarity alone is not a sufficient criterion for determining that a behavior is abnormal or disordered. If it were, we would have to conclude that people like Albert Einstein and Leonardo da Vinci were psychologically disordered. More important from a psychological perspective is the fact that the behaviors associated with psychological disorders are often *maladaptive*; that is, the person's ability to function adequately in everyday social and occupational roles is impaired. The degree of maladaptivity in psychological disorders varies from relatively minor to so severe that a person may need to be hospitalized. Some psychologists believe that maladaptivity may be the most important criterion for distinguishing psychologically abnormal behavior (Coleman et al., 1984).

Despite the myth that severely disordered people are "in their own little worlds" that may be more comforting than the real world, people with psychological disorders often experience a great deal of *psychological discomfort*. This third criterion may take the form of anxiety, depression, or agitation. Finally, the behaviors of psychologically disordered people are often judged to be *socially unacceptable*. We would not consider tearing up a hospital robe and screaming out the window to be acceptable behavior.

It is important to note that perspectives on what is normal are both culturally based and era dependent. For example, while we consider talking to oneself or hallucinating imaginary visions to be clear signs of a serious psychological disorder, these same behaviors are viewed by people in certain Polynesian and South American societies as indications of a great gift or special status among deities.

All four characteristics of abnormality are not necessarily evident in all psychological disorders. Aside from the fact that they are all atypical or uncommon, any given disorder may reflect only one or a combination of the characteristics of maladaptivity, psychological discomfort, and social unacceptability. Specific symptoms also vary according to the disorder, and these symptoms form the basis for classifying disorders.

CLASSIFYING PSYCHOLOGICAL DISORDERS

The first widely accepted system for classifying psychological disorders was published in 1952 by the American Psychiatric Association in the *Diagnostic and Statistical Manual of Mental Disorders*, conveniently shortened to *DSM-I*. This scheme, which listed the symptoms of 60 disorders, was poorly organized and widely criticized. An improved version, *DSM-II*, was published in 1968. DSM-II attempted to provide more definitive diagnostic categories, delineating 145 types and subtypes of disorders.

Both DSM-I and DSM-II divided mental disorders into two broad categories: neuroses and psychoses. Freud had used the term **neurosis** to describe anxiety disorders, and from Freud's time until the publication of the third *Diagnostic and Statistical Manual (DSM-III)* in 1980, the term *neurosis* was widely used to describe a range of psychological disorders that are distressing and often debilitating, but that are not characterized by a loss of contact with reality, severe thinking disturbances, or inability to carry on the tasks of daily living. The term **psychosis** was used to describe more severe disorders that involve disturbances of thinking, reduced contact with reality, loss of ability to function socially, and other bizarre behaviors.

DSM-I and -II's general division between neuroses and psychoses was widely criticized, mainly because such extremely varying conditions were grouped together under the labels "neurosis" and "psychosis." Therefore, when DSM-III was published in 1980, it dispensed with this broad division and used more specifically defined diagnostic categories instead.

In 1987 the American Psychiatric Association published a revision of DSM-III which incorporates recent research findings and provides even more precise behavioral criteria for diagnosing a broad array of psychological disorders. Like its predecessors, DSM-III-R is the most widely used scheme today for classifying and diagnosing psychological disorders throughout the world. This chapter's coverage of psychological disorders is based on DSM-III-R's categories. We have elected to discuss a few major categories in depth rather than presenting many groups superficially. The conditions we have included—anxiety, somatoform, associative, mood, schizophrenic, and personality disorders—were selected either because they are among the most common of the psychological disorders or because they are unusual.

It is possible that some of the behaviors described in this chapter may not be all that different from those of your friends, loved ones, or even yourself. Does this mean that people you know who share some of these symptoms are disordered? Although we all have times when we are depressed, anxious, or somewhat disorganized in our thinking, the key to diagnosis of a psychological disorder is the possession of a cluster of symptoms that are persistent rather than transitory. Therefore, do not be too hard on yourself (or your friends). It has been estimated, however, that as many as 70 million U.S. citizens now living will experience a diagnosable psychological disorder at some point in their lives (Goldstein et al., 1986).

We end our discussion of each major category of disorder with an overview of theoretical explanations. Space limitations prevent us from considering all explanations. Therefore, each discussion includes a brief summary of the three most well-known etiological (explanatory) perspectives: psychoanalytic theory, the behavioral/learning model, and biological explanations. Chapter 15 discusses therapeutic intervention techniques for treating psychological disorders.

ANXIETY DISORDERS

Anxiety may be descibed as a generalized feeling of dread or apprehension, typically accompanied by a variety of physiological reactions including increased heart rate, rapid shallow breathing, sweating, muscle tension, and drying of the mouth. Anxiety differs from fear in one important respect.

FIRST PERSON 14.1

Things have been going all to hell for me lately. It seems like I am tense and nervous all the time. I have trouble sleeping and my head aches a lot. I can't seem to shake a sense of dread or foreboding, as if something terrible is going to happen to me. The worst part is that I can't figure out what is causing these feelings. (*Authors' files*)

Fear has an obvious cause, and once that cause is eliminated, the fear will subside. In contrast, anxiety is less clearly linked to specific events or stimuli. Therefore, it tends to be more pervasive and less responsive to changes in the environment.

We all experience occasional episodes of anxiety. For approximately one out of every 10 to 15 Americans, however, anxiety is such a pervasive condition that they are said to suffer from an **anxiety disorder** (Freedman, 1984; Regier et al., 1984). Anxiety is also present in many of the other psychological disorders we will discuss in this chapter, but it is typically most pronounced in the various anxiety disorders.

DSM-III-R proposes several categories of anxiety disorders: *panic disorder (with or without agoraphobia)*, *agoraphobia without history of panic disorder*, *social phobia*, *simple phobia*, *obsessive-compulsive disorder*, *posttraumatic stress disorder*, and *generalized anxiety disorder*.

PANIC DISORDER (WITH OR WITHOUT AGORAPHOBIA)

Have you had an experience in which everything was fine one moment, and then for no apparent reason you suddenly felt an intense apprehension and overwhelming terror that caused your heart to pound, your breathing to become labored, and your hands to tremble? If your answer is yes, you have probably experienced a *panic attack*. There is good evidence that many people have occasional panic attacks. In one recent survey of college students, about one in three had experienced one or more panic attacks in the preceding year (Norton et al., 1985).

Having an occasional panic attack does not necessarily mean that you suffer from a **panic disorder**. DSM-III-R stipulates that a person who experiences four or more attacks in a four-week period suffers from a panic disorder. Approximately one out of every 100 Americans fall into this category (Myers et al., 1984; Robins et al., 1984). A recent research report revealed that panic disorder led the list of psychological disorders for which people in five American urban centers sought mental-health services (Boyd, 1986).

The panic attacks associated with a panic disorder may be so overwhelmingly terrifying that a person may feel driven to attempt suicide. During an attack, people may think they are going crazy or that death from a heart attack is likely. Sometimes people have a sense of *derealization* (the feeling that the world is not real), or *depersonalization* (a sense of being outside one's body). Physical symptoms include erratic or pounding heartbeats, labored breathing, dizziness, chest pain, sweating and trembling, and feelings of choking and suffocating. The following account provides a vivid description of a panic attack:

> I remember walking up the street, the moon was shining and suddenly everything around me seemed unfamiliar, as it would be in a dream. I felt panic rising inside me, but managed to push it away and carry on. I walked a quarter of a mile or so, with the panic getting worse every minute. . . . By now, I was sweating, yet trembling; my heart was pounding and my legs felt like jelly. (Melville, 1977, p. 1)

In the majority of cases of panic disorder seen by clinicians, the person also exhibits symptoms of agoraphobia (American Psychiatric Association, 1987). **Agoraphobia** is characterized by intense fear of being in places or situations from which escape might be difficult or in which help might not be available in the event of a panic attack. Common focal points for agoraphobic fear are being outside the home alone or being in open, public places such as stores, theaters, buses, and trains. To avoid these situations, individuals with this disorder may stay away from all public places and, in extreme cases, become virtual prisoners in their own homes.

Less commonly, people may suffer a panic disorder without related symptoms of agoraphobia. Conversely, in some people agoraphobia exists

Crowds or public places can be particularly terrifying for someone who is afflicted with agoraphobia. Agoraphobia is characterized by intense fear of being in places or situations from which escape might be difficult or in which help might not be available in the event of a panic attack.

without any symptoms or prior history of panic disorder (American Psychiatric Association, 1987). Agoraphobia is but one of several kinds of **phobias**, which are characterized by a persistent fear of and consequent avoidance of a specific object or situation. People with phobic disorders may be terrified of spiders, snakes, heights, open spaces, being alone, or numerous other objects or situations. Although they usually realize that their fear is far out of proportion to any actual danger, this does little to reduce the fear.

Phobias are among the most common psychological disorders; approximately 14 percent of the general population have been estimated to have a phobia (Robins et al., 1984). This estimate is inexact, however. Since less than 10 percent of these phobias are serious enough to be considered significantly disruptive (Duke & Nowicki, 1986), most go untreated. A person who is afraid of heights may be more inclined simply to avoid climbing ladders or hiking along high mountain trails than to seek professional help. In addition to agoraphobia, DSM-III-R provides diagnostic categories for social phobias and simple phobias.

SOCIAL PHOBIAS

A **social phobia** is a persistent, irrational fear of performing some specific behavior, such as talking, writing, eating, drinking, or using public lavatories, in the presence of other people. People with social phobias are compelled to avoid situations in which they may be observed behaving in an ineffective or embarrassing manner. Many social phobics are particularly fearful of interaction with authority figures such as teachers, employers, or police officers. Some social phobics have a poor self-image of their physical appearance, and they may seek to correct what they perceive to be defects in their anatomy, even to the extent of using plastic surgery.

SIMPLE PHOBIAS

In **simple phobias** the source of the irrational fear is a specific situation or object, such as heights, small closed places, various living things (particularly dogs, cats, snakes, mice, and spiders), transportation (flying, cars, trains), thunder, and darkness (see Table 14.1). Although the simple phobias are the most common phobic disorders, they are also the least disruptive. Therefore, they are only infrequently seen in clinical settings.

OBSESSIVE-COMPULSIVE DISORDER

If you have ever had the experience of not being able to get a catchy, repetitious jingle out of your mind, or of needing to go back and make sure you have locked all the doors even though you are sure you have, you should have a sense of what an **obsessive-compulsive disorder** is like. Here, a person's profound sense of anxiety is reflected in persistent, unwanted, and unshakable thoughts and/or irresistible, habitual repeated actions.

TABLE 14.1 *Some Varieties of Phobias*

Name	Object(s) Feared	Name	Object(s) Feared
Acrophobia	High places	Hematophobia	Blood
Agoraphobia	Open places	Monophobia	Being alone
Ailurophobia	Cats	Mysophobia	Contamination
Algophobia	Pain	Nyctophobia	Darkness
Anthropophobia	Men	Ocholophobia	Crowds
Aquaphobia	Water	Pathophobia	Disease
Astraphobia	Storms, thunder, and lightning	Pyrophobia	Fire
		Syphilophobia	Syphilis
Claustrophobia	Closed places	Thanatophobia	Death
Cynophobia	Dogs	Xenophobia	Strangers
		Zoophobia	Animals or a single animal

When Lady Macbeth washed her hands after helping to murder the king, she was engaging in one of the most common compulsions of obsessive-compulsive behavior.

Although the approximately 2.5 percent of Americans who have this disorder (Robins et al., 1984) usually know that their obsessive thoughts or compulsive actions are irrational, they still cannot block out their thoughts or keep themselves from performing the repetitious act, often an extreme number of times. There is one report of a woman who washed her hands over 500 times per day (Davison & Neale, 1986). (The hand-washing compulsion—which Lady Macbeth acquired after helping her husband murder the king of Scotland—is one of the most common compulsions reported.) The senseless, repetitious behavior seems to ward off a flood of overwhelming anxiety that would result if the compulsive acts were terminated.

In the classic manifestation of this disorder, obsessive thoughts lead to compulsive actions. The following case illustrates this connection:

> Shirley K, a twenty-three-year-old housewife, came to the clinic with a complaint of frequent attacks of headaches and dizziness. During the preceding three months she had been disturbed by recurring thoughts that she might harm her two-year-old son, Saul, either by stabbing or choking him (the obsessive thought). She constantly had to go into his room, touch the baby and feel him breathe in order to reassure herself that Saul was still alive (the compulsive act); otherwise she became unbearably anxious. If she read a report in the daily paper of the murder of a child, she would become agitated, since this reinforced her fear that she too might act on her impulse. Shirley turned to the interviewer and asked, with desperation, whether this meant that she was "going crazy." (Goldstein & Palmer, 1975, p. 155)

In this case, it appears that by constantly checking on her son's well-being this woman was able to relieve temporarily the anxiety caused by her thoughts about harming her son. Obsessive thoughts also commonly occur without being accompanied by a compulsive act.

POSTTRAUMATIC STRESS DISORDER

People who experience a profoundly traumatic event, such as an assault, accident, or wartime combat, often exhibit a range of severely distressing symptoms as an aftermath to the occurrence. For example, a rape survivor may have vivid flashbacks of the attack in which she reexperiences all the terror of the assault. Many Vietnam veterans also had flashbacks of traumatic war experiences as an aftermath of their participation in this war (Solomon et al., 1987). A similar kind of reliving the trauma often occurs among survivors of severe accidents. In one study, all 10 survivors of a plane crash that left 127 dead relived the tragedy over and over again in the form of dreams, nightmares, or panic attacks (Krupnick & Horowitz, 1981).

These symptoms are typical of **posttraumatic stress disorder (PTSD).** According to DSM-III-R, PTSD develops after a person experiences a psychologically traumatic event (or events) outside the normal range of human experience. Characteristic symptoms include "reexperiencing the traumatic event, avoidance of stimuli associated with the event or numbing of general responsiveness, and increased arousal" (American Psychiatric Association, 1987, p. 247). If these symptoms persist for less than one month, the diagnosis of PTSD does not apply.

Posttraumatic stress disorder differs from other anxiety disorders in that it can be explained solely on environmental grounds. An examination of the life histories of people who have conditions such as phobias or obsessive-compulsive disorders does not reveal a consistent pattern of background factors. In contrast, all victims of PTSD, while certainly different from one another in many ways, share experiences with a profoundly traumatizing event(s).

GENERALIZED ANXIETY DISORDER

Generalized anxiety disorder is a chronic state of anxiety so pervasive that it is often referred to as "free-floating anxiety." The anxiety is so omnipresent across a wide range of situations that many clinicians think it is fruitless to try to pin it down to specific eliciting stimuli. Thus, the individual is unable to take any concrete avoidance actions to cope with it. This condition has been compared to what it must be like to be a soldier who is on the alert for attack: there is a constant sense of danger, but its source cannot be identified (Goldstein et al., 1986).

Psychological symptoms associated with generalized anxiety disorder include a persistent state of apprehension, or worry about impending disaster; constant scanning or checking out of the environment, as though looking for danger signs; poor concentration, high distractibility, and indecision; impatience and irritability; mild depression; hypersensitivity to criticism; and insomnia. Physical symptoms may include heart palpitations, clammy hands, sweating, shakiness, upset stomach, dry mouth, fatigue, muscle aches, and diarrhea.

THEORETICAL PERSPECTIVES ON ANXIETY DISORDERS

How can anxiety disorders be explained? Psychoanalytic theory, the behavioral/learning perspective, and biological explanations all provide some insight into these disorders. We look briefly at each perspective.

Psychoanalytic Perspective   Freud (1936) explained the anxiety disorders as a result of internal conflicts, particularly those involving sexual or aggressive impulses. Recall from Chapter 13 that Freud saw the ego's primary function as protecting a person from severe anxiety. It does this by mediating among the id's impulses, the superego's demands, and reality, often relying on the ego defense mechanisms. According to psychoanalytic theory, anxiety and the symptoms of anxiety disorders will appear when these defenses are overused or rigidly applied, or when they fail.

This perspective explains generalized anxiety disorders as the result of unacceptable impulses that the ego has blocked. These impulses are powerful enough to produce a constant state of tension and apprehension, but since they are unconscious, the person is unaware of the source of the anxiety.

Phobias may occur if the individual *displaces* this anxiety to some object, situation, or social function which can be avoided (Nemiah, 1981). This is illustrated in one of Freud's most famous cases, that of a five-year-old boy known as Little Hans, whose phobic fear of horses kept him from going outside his house. Freud concluded that Hans' fear of horses was an expression of anxieties related to an Oedipal complex: he unconsciously feared and hated his father (whom he perceived as a rival for his mother's affections), and he displaced this fear onto horses, which he could avoid more easily than his father.

Psychoanalytic theory has a different explanation for panic disorders and agoraphobia. According to this view, these disorders may both be rooted in an unresolved separation anxiety (a fear of being separated from parents) early in life (Klein & Rabkin, 1981). People who have learned during childhood to protest intensely when they are threatened with separation from a parental figure may experience panic attacks later in life when they either perceive a threat of or actually experience separation from a significant other.

Still another explanation is suggested for obsessive-compulsive disorder, which is seen as the result of a fixation at the anal stage of psychosexual development. Freud believed that when children are subjected to harsh toilet-training experiences, they react with anger and aggressive urges that must be controlled if punishment is to be avoided. The persistent thoughts or repetitive behavioral rituals associated with this disorder serve to dissipate angry feelings before they can be translated into aggressive acts. The fact that compulsive behavior rituals often involve cleanliness themes lends support to Freud's contention that such neurotic acts reflect fixation during the anal period, a time focused on mastering "unclean" bowel and bladder functions.

Behavioral/Learning Perspective   During the 1960s several behavioral theorists (Wolpe & Rachman, 1960; Bandura, 1969) carefully analyzed Freud's published account of Little Hans and noted that his phobic response occurred only in the presence of a large horse pulling a heavily loaded cart at high speed. They further noted that Hans' phobia originally appeared after he had witnessed a terrible accident involving a horse pulling a cart at high speed. Not surprisingly, these observations led behaviorists to a different explanation: Hans' phobia was a classically conditioned fear that had nothing to do with Oedipal complexes or displacement. Behaviorists see conditioning, discussed in Chapter 6, as the source of the anxiety disorders.

On the surface, the classical-conditioning model seems to provide a logical explanation: Phobias are the result of chance pairings between previously neutral stimuli and frightening events. Thus we might argue that a person develops a fear of heights after falling off a ladder, or a fear of riding in cars after being in a bad automobile accident. This model is expanded by the *two-factor theory*, which sees anxiety disorders as resulting from a blending of classical and operant conditioning (Mowrer, 1947). (In two-process or two-factor conditioning, a person is first classically conditioned to fear a stimulus, then learns to reduce this conditioned fear by using the operant response of avoiding the fear stimulus.)

DOES CLASSICAL CONDITIONING EXPLAIN ALL PHOBIAS?

Although both classical conditioning and two-factor conditioning seem plausible, these models leave some questions unanswered. How can we explain the fact that many people who have phobias have had no frightening experiences with the object or situation that they fear so greatly? Furthermore, although there are quite a few different kinds of phobias, the objects of these phobias tend to be limited to a fairly narrow range of stimuli (Goldstein et al., 1986). By far the most common phobias are *zoophobias* (fear of particular animals, such as snakes or mice). Yet in our own society today, we are exposed far more to motor vehicles and machines than we are to snakes. Why don't we develop proportionately more phobias to these objects?

How can we explain the fact that many people who have phobias have had no frightening experiences with the object or situation that they fear?

Different theorists have approached this question in different ways; two answers are particularly interesting. The first has been proposed by Martin Seligman (1971), who suggests that evolution has built into humans a biological predisposition to react fearfully to certain classes of potentially dangerous stimuli, such as snakes and spiders. It is not difficult to believe that a natural wariness can have some adaptive advantage to humans, but is there any objective evidence to support this notion? The answer is a tentative yes. One series of experiments attempted to classically condition fear responses to both "evolutionarily prepared stimuli" such as spiders and snakes, and to innocuous stimuli such as mushrooms. It found not only that fear responses to evolutionarily prepared stimuli were much easier to establish (often in only one trial), but that these responses were very difficult to extinguish (Ohman, 1979).

Not all theorists agree with Seligman's explanation of biological predispositions. Social-learning theorist Albert Bandura (1969) believes that modeling, or imitating the behavior of others, provides a more likely explanation for how some anxiety disorders are acquired. For example, a child who observes a parent reacting anxiously to dogs or thunderstorms may also acquire a phobic fear of dogs or thunder. In this manner phobias may be transmitted from one generation to the next (see Figure 14.1). This interpretation is supported by evidence that animal phobias typically occur in children who are about age five and whose mothers have the same phobia (Klein, 1981). Thus, the fact that a relatively narrow range of stimuli become phobic objects may be due to social-learning mechanisms rather than biological predispositions.

How do behavioral and learning theorists explain other anxiety disorders? Posttraumatic stress disorders, as we have seen, are clearly linked to traumatizing experiences. The behavioral explanation of obsessive-compulsive disorders is more complex. Here, some behaviorists look to operant conditioning, arguing that compulsive, repetitious acts such as hand washing occur repeatedly because they provide a temporary reduction in anxiety, which is in turn negatively reinforcing.

The Biological Perspective   While psychoanalytic and behavioral theory look to conflicts and experiences in explaining anxiety disorders, the bio-

FIGURE 14.1

Phobias can be learned through modeling or imitating the behavior of others.

TABLE 14.2 *Risk for All Types of Anxiety-Based Disorders in Siblings and Parents of Agoraphobics, Panic-Disordered, and Nonanxious Controls*

	Patient Status		
	Agoraphobia	Panic	Controls
Incidence (%) in first degree relatives for the disorders:			
Agoraphobia	8.6	1.9	4.2
Panic disorder	7.7	20.5	4.2
Generalized anxiety	5.1	6.5	5.3
Atypical anxiety	2.6	3.7	0.0
Social phobia	3.4	0.0	1.1
Simple phobia	2.6	0.0	0.0
Obsessive-compulsive	1.7	0.0	0.0
Total of all anxiety-based disorders	31.7	32.6	14.8

Source: From Harris, E. L., Noyes, R., Crowe, R. R., and Chaudhry, D. R. (1983). Family study of agoraphobia. *Archives of General Psychiatry, 40,* 1061–1069.

logical perspective looks for clues in the biological or genetic makeup of individuals who develop these disorders. Some of these clues are intriguing.

The best place to start is with a notion that has been suggested by several researchers—that some people with unusually responsive nervous systems may be biologically predisposed to develop anxiety disorders. There is some evidence that the autonomic nervous systems of people with anxiety disorders are more easily aroused by environmental stimuli, a condition referred to as *autonomic lability.* This condition might contribute to a tendency to be "jumpy," anxious, or apprehensive (Ciesielski et al., 1981; Lacey, 1967; Turner et al., 1985). There is also evidence that some people may be biochemically predisposed to at least some types of anxiety disorders (Liebowitz et al., 1984).

If certain people are biologically predisposed to some anxiety disorders, it follows that there may be a genetic basis for these disorders. In fact, extensive evidence seems to support this conjecture. One recent study measured the incidence of anxiety disorders among siblings, mothers, and fathers of three groups of subjects: agoraphobics, panic-disordered individuals, and a control group with no diagnosed anxiety disorders. As Table 14.2 shows, the relatives of both groups of anxiety-disordered subjects showed more than double the incidence of anxiety disorders that were found among relatives of the control group (Harris et al., 1983). Other research has also reported a higher than normal incidence of anxiety disorders among relatives of people with diagnosed panic disorders (Cloninger et al., 1981).

A GENETIC LINK FOR ANXIETY DISORDERS?

The studies described above suggest a genetic component in anxiety disorders. But does the evidence they provide point clearly to a hereditary explanation, or is there another possible explanation for these findings? What other types of research besides family studies might provide more clear-cut evidence? Give these questions some thought before reading on.

As we noted in Chapter 12, the fact that a particular trait or condition runs in a family does not prove it has a genetic basis. Another interpretation might be that environmental factors that give rise to a disorder in one person are likely to have a similar effect on relatives who share the same environment.

A more reliable source of evidence about the role of genetic transmission is twin studies; so far, the information gathered from this source points to a genetic link for anxiety disorders. A major study conducted recently in Norway reported a much higher concordance rate among identical twins (45 percent) than among fraternal twins (15 percent) for a grouping of anxiety disorders that included agoraphobia, panic disorders, obsessive-compulsive disorders, and social phobias (Torgersen, 1983). Other studies have reported similar concordance rates for anxiety disorders among identical and fraternal twins (Rosenthal, 1970; Katsching & Shepherd, 1978). Slater & Shields (1969) reported a concordance rate for generalized anxiety disorders of 49 percent for identical twins and only four percent for fraternal twins. Thus, there does seem to be strong evidence that genetic factors play a role in the various anxiety disorders.

SOMATOFORM DISORDERS

Whereas the primary symptom of anxiety disorders is psychological distress, the **somatoform disorders** are expressed through *somatic* or physical symptoms. Dizziness, stomach pain, vomiting, breathing difficulties, difficulty in swallowing, impaired vision, inability to move the legs, and numbness of the hands are common symptoms of somatoform disorders. In all cases, however, the symptoms have no physiological basis.

The somatoform disorders affect a much smaller percent of the population than do anxiety disorders—less than one percent (Robbins et al., 1984). DSM-III-R classifies several types of somatoform disorders. We will look at three: *somatization disorder*, *hypochondriasis*, and *conversion disorder*.

SOMATIZATION DISORDER

A person with **somatization disorder** typically has multiple and recurrent physical symptoms for which medical attention is repeatedly sought, but which have no physical cause. People who have this disorder commonly complain about chest, stomach, and back pain, headaches, heart palpitations, vomiting, dizziness and fainting, and genitourinary symptoms. Table 14.3 indicates the type and frequency of symptoms reported by a sample of people with somatization disorder. Patients typically present their complaints in such a convincing fashion that medications and medical procedures are provided, including unnecessary surgery in some cases. This

TABLE 14.3 *Various Symptoms and Their Frequncy as Reported by a Sample of Patients with Somatization Disorder*

Symptom	Percent Reporting	Symptom	Percent Reporting	Symptom	Percent Reporting
Dyspnea (labored breathing)	72	Sudden fluctations in weight	16	Back pain	88
Palpitation	60	Anorexia	60	Joint pain	84
Chest pain	72	Nausea	80	Extremity pain	84
Dizziness	84	Vomiting	32	Burning pains in rectum, vagina, mouth	28
Headache	80	Abdominal pain	80	Other bodily pain	36
Anxiety attacks	64	Abdominal bloating	68	Depressed feelings	64
Fatigue	84	Food intolerances	48	Phobias	48
Blindness	20	Diarrhea	20	Vomiting all nine months of pregnancy	20
Paralysis	12	Constipation	64	Nervous	92
Anesthesia	32	Dysuria (painful urination)	44	Had to quit working because felt bad	44
Aphonia (loss of voice above a whisper)	44	Urinary retention	8	Trouble doing anything because felt bad	72
Lump in throat	28	Dysmenorrhea (painful menstruation, premarital only)	4	Cried a lot	70
Fits or convulsions	20	Dysmenorrhea (prepregnancy only)	8	Felt life was hopeless	28
Faints	56	Dysmenorrhea (other)	48	Always sickly (most of life)	40
Unconsciousness	16	Menstrual irregularity	48	Thought of dying	48
Amnesia	8	Excessive menstrual bleeding	48	Wanted to die	36
Visual blurring	64	Sexual indifference	44	Thought of suicide	28
Visual hallucination	12	Inability to experience orgasm	24	Attempted suicide	12
Deafness	4	Dyspareunia (painful sexual intercourse)	52		
Olfactory hallucination	16				
Weakness	84				
Weight loss	28				

Source: From Perley & Guze, 1962.

disorder typically begins in the late teenage years, and is more common among women than men (Kroll et al., 1979). Recent data suggest that approximately one person in 250 falls victim to this disorder (Swartz et al., 1986).

HYPOCHONDRIASIS

Like somatization-disordered individuals, people with **hypochondriasis** also complain about a variety of physical difficulties (most commonly stomach and heart problems). The primary difference between the two conditions is that people with this disorder are fearful that their symptoms indicate a serious disease(s), while people with somatization disorder typically do not progress beyond a concern with the symptoms themselves. A hypochondriac who notices a minor heart palpitation may be convinced it is a sign of severe cardiac disease, or may interpret a cough as a sign of lung cancer. Hypochondriacs have also been shown to be excessively fearful about death and often to spend an inordinate amount of time consulting with physicians about imaginary symptoms of physical illness (Kellner et al., 1987).

The following excerpt from a letter written by a hospitalized woman to her relatives illustrates a severe case of hypochondriasis:

Dear Mother and Husband:
I have suffered terrible today with drawing in my throat. My nerves are terrible. My head feels queer. . . . I've been on the verge of a nervous chill all day, but I have been fighting it hard. It's night and bedtime, but, Oh, how I hate to go to bed. Nobody knows or realizes how badly I feel because I fight to stay up and outdoors if possible.
I haven't had my cot up for two days, they don't want me to use it.
These long afternoons and nights are awful. There are plenty of patients well enough to visit with but I'm in too much pain.
The nurses ignore any complaining. They just laugh or scold.
Eating has been awful hard. They expect me to eat like a harvest hand. Every bite of solid food is agony to get down, for my throat aches so and feels so closed up. . . .
I haven't slept well since I've been here. My heart pains as much as when I was at home. More so at night. I put hot water bottle on it. . . .
I had headache so badly in the back of my head last night and put hot water bottle there. My nurse said not to.

Annie

(Menninger, 1945, pp. 139–140)

CONVERSION DISORDER

A third somatoform disorder, **conversion disorder**, is typically manifested as a sensory or motor-system disturbance for which there is no known organic cause. Unlike the two previous categories of somatoform disorders, conversion disorders are seldom confused with genuine physical disease because their symptom patterns do not make anatomical sense. In the condition known as *sensory conversion*, for example, people may lose sensitivity in specific parts of their bodies in which the loss-of-feeling pattern is neurologically impossible (see Figure 14.2). Other kinds of sensory conversions may be reflected in loss of sensitivity to pain, impaired vision or hearing, and in some cases, heightened sensitivity to touch. In another related condition, *motor conversion*, people may experience paralysis in some part of their bodies, usually a limb, or experience uncontrollable tremors or twitches.

Conversion disorders typically surface after a person has experienced serious stress or conflict, and the symptoms appear to allow the person to escape from or avoid that stress and conflict. This is apparent in the following case, in which a man developed a sensory conversion to escape from a nagging wife and mother-in-law:

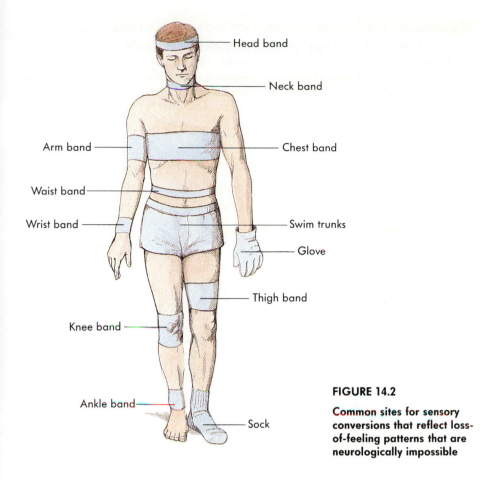

Head band

Neck band

Arm band

Chest band

Waist band

Wrist band

Swim trunks

Glove

Thigh band

Knee band

Ankle band

Sock

FIGURE 14.2

Common sites for sensory conversions that reflect loss-of-feeling patterns that are neurologically impossible

Phil, forty years of age, had a history of marginal work adjustment since his discharge from the Army at age twenty-five. In the fifteen years since discharge, he had depended on public assistance and financial aid from relatives to get by. He painted a very dismal picture of his married life, as one of almost constant harassment from his wife and mother-in-law. He had a history of minor illnesses involving his eyes, none of which had grossly affected his visual acuity.

During the Christmas season his wife and mother-in-law were being more demanding than usual, requiring him to work nights and weekends at various chores under their foremanship. Three days before Christmas, while shopping with his wife and mother-in-law, Phil suddenly became blind in both eyes.

Neurological and ophthalmological exams were essentially negative in accounting for his blindness, and a diagnosis of conversion disorder was made. At this time, Phil did not seem greatly alarmed by his loss of sight, but instead had an attitude of patient forbearance. Observers in the hospital noticed that Phil could get about in the ward better than expected for a totally blind man. He was not concerned with this, but felt hurt and unjustly accused when other patients pointed out the discrepancy to him. (Adapted from Brady & Lind, 1965, p. 762)

Phil's apparent lack of concern about his condition is fairly common among people with conversion disorders. The French psychiatrist Pierre Janet (1929) labeled this blasé attitude *la belle indifference,* or the noble lack of concern. Observers may incorrectly assume that a person with a conversion disorder is *malingering,* or deliberately faking symptoms. However, unlike malingerers, who tend to be cautious about discussing their symptoms for fear that they will be discovered, people with a conversion disorder appear eager to talk at great length about their symptoms.

THEORETICAL PERSPECTIVES ON SOMATOFORM DISORDERS

Recall from Chapter 13 that Freud was profoundly influenced by experiences with patients whose physically manifested symptoms had no neurological basis. Freud thought such problems stemmed from unresolved sexual impulses, particularly Oedipal and Electra complexes. These unresolved incestuous yearnings, said Freud, produce intense anxiety, which the individual may then convert into physical symptoms. This conversion reduces the anxiety associated with repressed id impulses, a process Freud called *primary gain*. Freud also noted that such disorders might also produce some *secondary gain*, allowing the person to avoid or escape from some currently stressful life situation.

Freud's concept of secondary gain is similar to the interpretation of somatoform disorders offered by some behavioral theorists. According to this viewpoint, the symptoms of a somatoform disorder are reinforced if they allow a person to escape from or avoid the negative reinforcer of anxiety. There is little evidence that biological predispositions or genetic factors play a noteworthy role in the somatoform disorders.

DISSOCIATIVE DISORDERS

In the **dissociative disorders**, the thoughts and feelings that generate anxiety are separated or *dissociated* from conscious awareness by memory loss or a change in identity. These uncommon disorders usually take the form of *psychogenic amnesia*, *psychogenic fugue*, or *multiple personality*.

PSYCHOGENIC AMNESIA

The most common dissociative disorder is **psychogenic amnesia**. Here, a person experiences sudden loss of memory, usually after a particularly stressful or traumatic event. The most typical manifestation of this disorder is loss of memory for all events for a specified period of time. For example, a person involved in a terrible accident might block out all memory of the accident as well as everything that happened just before or after it. Less commonly, a person may develop total amnesia for all prior experiences, and will be unable to recognize relatives, friends, and familiar places. (In these cases, the individual usually retains reasoning and verbal abilities, talents such as the ability to play a musical instrument, and general knowledge.) Episodes of psychogenic amnesia may last from several hours to many years. They typically disappear as suddenly as they appeared, and they rarely recur.

Memory loss may also result from organic brain disease associated with such things as chronic alcoholism and Alzheimer's disease, as we saw in Chapters 7 and 11. However, *physiogenic* amnesia is easily distinguished from psychogenic amnesia in that memory loss due to organic causes is generally a gradual process that is not connected with traumatic events.

PSYCHOGENIC FUGUE

While a person with amnesia escapes from a stressful situation by blocking it out of awareness, **psychogenic fugue disorder** combines amnesia with a more radical defensive maneuver—a "flight" away from an intolerable situation. Typically, the fugue state is of relatively brief duration in which a person travels from place to place in an apparently purposeful fashion but has little social contact with other people. It is likely that many of the "amnesia victims" who end up in police reports or local newspaper accounts are experiencing psychogenic fugue disorder.

Less frequently, a person may relocate to another part of the country and assume a new identity complete with new name, job, and perhaps a new family. All this may be accomplished without the individual ever seriously questioning her or his inability to remember the past.

MULTIPLE PERSONALITY

Multiple personality is a very uncommon form of dissociative disorder. A person with this disorder alternates between an original or primary personality and one or more secondary or subordinate personalities. Usually the subordinate personality is aware of the primary personality but not vice versa.

In a sense, we are all multiple personalities in that we have conflicting tendencies—for instance, between the part of us that is socially conforming and the part that likes to cut loose. Most of us are able to find appropriate outlets for expressing different aspects of our personalities. However, not everyone is able to achieve a satisfactory synthesis. Multiple personality disorder seems to provide an outlet for these different aspects, by separating the conflicting parts and elaborating each into an essentially autonomous personality system. Frequently the separated personalities represent two extremes, from responsible and conforming to irresponsible and "naughty."

Perhaps the most famous case of multiple personality on record was that of "Eve," who was treated by psychiatrists Corbett Thigpen and Harvey Cleckley and was the subject of their book, *The Three Faces of Eve* (1954). The original personality, Eve White, was a retiring, conventional person who was receiving psychotherapy because of amnesia, severe headaches, and marital problems. After several months of treatment, another personality emerged during a therapy session. Thigpen and Cleckley describe this startling change:

> As if seized by sudden pain, she put both hands to her head. After a tense moment of silence, both hands dropped. There was a quick, reckless smile, and in a bright voice that sparkled, she said, "Hi there Doc!" The demure and constrained posture of Eve White had melted into buoyant repose. . . . This new and apparently carefree girl spoke casually of Eve White and her problems, always using she or her in every reference, always respecting the strict bounds of a separate identity. . . . When asked her name, she immediately replied, "Oh, I'm Eve Black." (p. 137)

Apparently Eve Black, with her propensity to be seductive, wear expensive clothes, and act in a frivolous and fun-loving manner, allowed Eve White to gratify the desires of her "bad self" without conscious knowledge or guilt. As therapy progressed, a third personality, Jane, appeared as an apparent synthesis of the opposites represented by Eve White and Eve Black. The real Eve White, Chris Sizemore (see Figure 14.3), later revealed that 12 more personalities emerged, in addition to the initial three (Sizemore & Pitillo, 1977). (The clinical literature has reported as many as 23 distinct personalities in one individual [Coons & Bradley, 1985].)

Multiple personality disorder seems to occur more frequently in women than men (Duke & Nowicki, 1986). It has been widely assumed that multiple personality is very rare: according to one estimate, only about 300 cases had been reported in the world's professional literature prior to 1970 (Bliss, 1984). In recent years, however, the reported incidence of this disorder has been on the rise (Boor, 1982). One clinician reported seeing more than 100 cases of multiple personality between 1980 and 1984 (Bliss, 1984).

Are all these cases real? Caution should be exercised in diagnosing a multiple personality disorder, especially when the diagnosis may produce secondary gains (Thigpen & Cleckley, 1984). This issue was brought to public attention recently by the case of Kenneth Bianchi (the Los Angeles "Hillside Strangler") who manifested what appeared to be a multiple personality disorder. The primary personality of Kenneth claimed no awareness of two underlying or subordinate personalities: "Steve," who claimed

FIGURE 14.3

The real Eve White, Chris Sizemore, shown with one of her paintings entitled *Three Faces in One*

responsibility for a number of rape-murders, and "Billy," who was allegedly responsible for thefts and forgeries. At first, examining clinicians diagnosed Bianchi as having a genuine multiple personality disorder that would make him legally insane (Watkins, 1984). However, later findings (including a lack of consistency in the structure and content of the personalities over time and the inability of Bianchi's acquaintances to support his claims) led to the conclusion that Bianchi was simulating a multiple personality in order to avoid the death penalty (Orne et al., 1984). Bianchi was diagnosed as having an antisocial (psychopathic) personality with sexual sadism, and the court held him responsible for his actions.

THEORETICAL PERSPECTIVES ON DISSOCIATIVE DISORDERS

Dissociative disorders are among the least understood of all psychological disorders. Thus, explanations are highly speculative. In some ways, all three of the dissociative disorders we have discussed—amnesia, fugue, and multiple personality—seem to provide some of the best support for Freud's view that excessive application of the defense mechanisms can lead to serious disorders.

Psychoanalytic theory sees all of these conditions as resulting from massive reliance on repression to ward off unacceptable impulses, particularly those of a sexual nature. These yearnings increase during adolescence and adulthood, until they are finally expressed, often in a guilt-inducing sexual act. Normal forms of repression are not effective in blocking out this guilt, and so the person blocks the acts and related thoughts entirely from consciousness by developing amnesia or acquiring a new identity for the dissociated "bad" part of self.

Behavioral/learning theory does not offer a well-developed and cohesive explanation for dissociative disorders. A number of theorists within this perspective suggest, however, that the dissociative reactions may involve operant avoidance responses that are reinforced because they allow an individual to avoid anxiety associated with highly stressful events. There is no evidence that genetic factors or biological predispositions play a significant role in the development of dissociative disorders.

MOOD DISORDERS

> I do not care for anything. I do not care to ride, for the exercise is too violent. I do not care to walk, walking is too strenuous. I do not care to lie down, for I should either have to remain lying, and I do not care to do that, or I should have to get up again, and I do not care to do that either . . . I do not care at all. (Kierkegaard, 1844)

This account was written by the nineteenth-century Danish philosopher Sören Kierkegaard, who was subject to recurring bouts of severe depression. It provides a firsthand description of some of the characteristics of depression, the primary symptom of the **mood disorders**.

We have all experienced depression on occasion, as a natural response to setbacks such as failing an exam, ending a relationship, or being rejected by a potential employer. Fortunately, for most of us depression is a transitory state that generally lifts in short order as life goes on. However, when feelings of sadness, dejection, and hopelessness persist longer than a few weeks and when these feelings are severe enough to disrupt everyday functioning, the depression is considered to be an abnormal psychological state.

The common symptoms or signs of depression include a variety of psychological, psychomotor, and physical manifestations such as severe and prolonged feelings of sadness, hopelessness, and despair; low self-esteem; a sense of worthlessness; eating disturbances (either undereating or overeating); sleep disturbances (either insomnia or excessive sleep); psychomotor disturbance characterized by a marked shift in activity level; a variety of somatic or bodily complaints; lack of energy with accompanying fatigue; loss of interest in and enjoyment of everyday activities; indecisiveness; difficulty in concentrating; and persistent thoughts of suicide and death.

Like anxiety, depression is associated with many varieties of psychological disorders, including the anxiety and somatoform disorders, addictive disorders such as alcoholism (discussed in Chapter 5), and schizophrenia, which we will discuss later in this chapter. In these and related conditions, depression is secondary to other symptoms. In contrast, depression is the primary problem in the mood disorders.

The DSM-III-R distinguishes two major mood disorders, **major depression (unipolar disorder)** and **bipolar (manic-depressive) disorder**. Major depression is a mood disorder characterized by deep depression. It is sometimes referred to as a unipolar disorder because there is just one "pole" or extreme. In contrast, bipolar disorder is characterized by intermittent episodes of both depression and *mania*, highly energized behavior characterized by euphoria and excessive mental and physical activity. These two extremes give rise to the label manic-depressive disorder.

The distinction between major depression and bipolar disorder is an important one that is based on both different symptomatology and etiology. Bipolar disorder generally appears during a person's twenties, whereas major depression is more likely to develop later, often in a person's thirties. However, major depression may occur in children, adolescents, or young adults, and recent research provides evidence of an increased rate in younger people (Weissman, 1987). Symptoms of depression may vary somewhat according to the illness. The depression associated with bipolar disorder typically causes a person to become lethargic and sleep more. In contrast unipolar depression is characterized by insomnia and agitation (Wehr et al., 1987). These two different types of mood disorders also respond quite differently to various treatments.

Whereas major depression is the most common of the serious psychological disorders that may warrant hospitalization in our society (Regier et al., 1984), bipolar disorder is much more rare. As many as one out of five Americans may experience severe depression at any point in time (Boyd & Weissman, 1981), but only about one percent of the population have been

When feelings of sadness, dejection, and hopelessness persist longer than a few weeks, and when these feelings are severe enough to disrupt everyday functioning, the depression is considered to be an abnormal psychological state.

diagnosed with bipolar disorder (Davison & Neale, 1986). Evidence suggests that the incidence of mood disorders has been progressively increasing over the last few decades (Gershon et al., 1987). We look first at major depression, then at bipolar disorder.

MAJOR DEPRESSION (UNIPOLAR DISORDER)

People diagnosed as having a major depression disorder typically manifest their symptoms over an extended period, from several months to a year or longer, and their ability to function effectively may be so impaired that hospitalization is warranted. The following brief case study illustrates some of the common symptoms of severe depression:

> On admission to the hospital, the patient sat slumped in a chair, frowning deeply, staring at the floor, his face looking sad and drawn. When questioned he answered without looking up, slowly and in a monotone. Sometimes there was such a long pause between question and reply that the patient seemed not to have heard. Every now and then he shifted his position a little, sighed heavily and shook his head from side to side. His first verbal response was, "It's no use. I'm through. All I can think is I won't be any good again." In response to further inquiries he made the following comments, relapsing into silence after each short statement until again asked a question. "I feel like I'm dead inside . . . like a piece of wood . . . I don't have any feeling about anything, its not like living anymore . . . I'm past hope . . . there's nothing to tell." (Cameron, 1947, p. 508)

Earlier we mentioned that the depression in unipolar disorder is more likely to be accompanied by agitation than it is in manic-depressive disorder. This state may cause people to pace, wring their hands, or cry out and moan loudly. Depressed people who express this heightened motor activity continue to feel worthless and without hope.

Not surprisingly, people with major depression almost inevitably experience a breakdown in interpersonal relationships. Most of us do not enjoy being around irritable people, and since many depressed people are irritable, it is understandable that friends, associates, and even family members may eventually gravitate away from such people. In addition, depressed people often seek guidance and support from others, and it can be very frustrating for friends to observe that their efforts to provide help often seem to have no effect. Sometimes people may avoid depressed people because such interactions often make them feel gloomy or depressed (Hammen & Peters, 1978).

Although often incapacitating and sometimes even life-threatening (people who contemplate suicide are often deeply depressed), episodes of major depression are generally transitory in nature. In most cases the depression lifts over a period of months, regardless of whether or not it is treated. However, most people with diagnosed unipolar disorder experience one or more recurrences of major depression later on in their lives (Duke & Nowicki, 1986). Women are more likely than men to experience major depression (Nolen-Hoeksema, 1987).

BIPOLAR (MANIC-DEPRESSIVE) DISORDER

In contrast to major depression, bipolar disorder is characterized by extreme mood swings, from immobilizing depression to euphoria and frantic activity. In some cases, episodes of depression and elation may alternate regularly, with months or years of symptom-free normal functioning between the disordered mood states. Other cases may be characterized by a series of intermittent manic episodes followed by a period of depression. Unlike the normal highs and lows most of us experience in response to life events, the depression and mania associated with bipolar disorder do not seem to be triggered by identifiable events. In some manic-depressives, depressive symptoms may occur concurrently with classic manic features, a condition referred to as *mixed mania* (Secunda et al., 1987).

About one in 100 people suffer from bipolar disorder, a rate comparable to that of schizophrenia but far lower than the incidence of major depression (Kolata, 1987; Robertson, 1987). Men and women are equally likely to develop bipolar disorder. Since the depression experienced by bipolars is quite similar to that previously described of unipolars (with noteworthy differences in sleep and activity level), we focus here on the manic side of the disorder.

According to DSM-III-R, manic episodes are characterized by "inflated self-esteem or grandiosity (which may be delusional), decreased need for sleep, pressure of speech, flight of ideas, distractibility, increased involvement in goal-directed activity, psychomotor agitation, and excessive involvement in pleasurable activities which have a high potential for painful consequences that the person often does not recognize" (American Psychiatric Association, 1987, pp. 214–15). Manic episodes often begin suddenly and rapidly escalate, as revealed in the following case:

> Mr. M., a thirty-two-year-old postal worker, had been married for eight years. He and his wife lived comfortably and happily in a middle-class neighborhood with their two children. In retrospect there appeared to be no warning for what was to happen. On February the twelfth Mr. M. let his wife know that he was bursting with energy and ideas, that his job as a mail carrier was unfulfilling, and that he was just wasting his talent. That night he slept little, spending most of the time at a desk, writing furiously. The next morning he left for work at the usual time but returned home at eleven A.M., his car filled to overflowing with aquaria and other equipment for tropical fish. He had quit his job and then withdrawn all the money from the family's savings account. The money had been spent on tropical fish equipment. Mr. M. reported that the previous night he had worked out a way to modify existing equipment so that fish ". . . won't die anymore. We'll be millionaires." After unloading the paraphernalia, Mr. M. set off to canvass the neighborhood for possible buyers, going door to door and talking to anyone who would listen.

The following bit of conversation from the period after Mr. M. entered treatment indicates his incorrigible optimism and provocativeness.

Therapist: Well, you seem pretty happy today.

Client: Happy! Happy! You certainly are a master of understatement, you rogue! (Shouting, literally jumping out of his seat.) Why I'm ecstatic, I'm leaving for the West coast today, on my daughter's bicycle. Only 3100 miles. That's nothing, you know. I could probably walk, but I want to get there by next week. And along the way I plan to contact a lot of people about investing in my fish equipment. I'll get to know more people that way—you know, Doc, "know" in the biblical sense (leering at therapist seductively). Oh, God, how good it feels. (Davison & Neale, 1986, p. 196)

A manic episode often follows a three-stage course of accelerating intensity (Carlson & Goodwin, 1973). In the first stage, *hypomania*, people typically retain their capacity to function in their daily lives, and they may even exhibit high levels of productivity. However, as they progress through the second and third stages of *mania* and *severe mania*, their thinking becomes more disorganized and their behavior often takes on a bizarre psychotic-like quality. These advanced stages may be accompanied by both **delusions** (exaggerated and rigidly held beliefs that have little or no basis in fact, such as Mr. M's belief that he had found a way to keep tropical fish alive forever) and **hallucinations** (false perceptions that lack a sensory basis, such as hearing or seeing imaginary voices or images). Bizarre symptoms such as those described in this chapter's opening case are not often manifested, since modern drugs are quite effective in controlling such behaviors.

A number of studies have shown a disproportionately high incidence of bipolar disorder among creative individuals (see Figure 14.4). One of the first studies to demonstrate this apparent connection found almost five

FIGURE 14.4

Studies have shown a disproportionately high incidence of manic-depressive disorder among creative people. Four famous examples are poets Robert Lowell (top left) and Anne Sexton (top right), and novelists Virginia Woolf (lower left) and Ernest Hemingway (lower right).

times the incidence of mood disorder in a sample of American creative writers as in a matched control group (Andreasen & Carter, 1974). A more recent study of 47 award-winning British writers and artists revealed that 38 percent had been treated for mood disorders (Jamison, reported in Goodwin & Jamison, 1986).

Episodes of either mania or depression tend to last only a few weeks or months. When they lift, the person recovers and returns to a symptom-free life. Unfortunately, however, the symptoms tend to recur, and many people with this disorder require periodic treatment and sometimes maintenance medication throughout their lives. This takes its toll in the form of alienated friends and loved ones, financial problems, and careers that remain on hold due to the unpredictable nature of symptoms. One of the most devastating aspects of this disorder is the high risk of suicide associated

TABLE 14.4 Suicide Facts

1. Approximately 30,000 people in the United States take their own lives each year (although this is probably an underestimation, since many suicides are not officially recorded).
2. For every successful suicide, there are at least eight attempts. This translates to approximately a quarter of a million suicide attempts each year in this country.
3. Somewhere between 50 and 80 percent of people who complete suicides have made one or more previous attempts.
4. Two to three times more men than women succeed in committing suicide, although over three times as many women as men attempt suicide. Men often use absolute and irreversible methods, such as guns and hanging, to kill themselves, whereas women are more likely to use drugs, gas, or poison.
5. Suicide rates by age group rise steadily from adolescence, peaking in the 45+ group. Recent evidence indicates a rising incidence of suicide among adolescents and young adults.
6. Suicide ranks as the tenth leading cause of death among all American adults, but it is second only to accidents as a cause of death among college students.
7. Divorced people, particularly men, are more likely to commit suicide than married people.
8. Suicide is found among all socioeconomic levels, but certain professions, including physicians (particularly psychiatrists), psychologists, and attorneys, have a disproportionately high incidence.
9. In the United States and many other countries, May and October are times of peak incidence of suicides. These findings are consistent with seasonality data for mood disorders, particularly bipolar disorders.
10. About 80 percent of people who kill themselves provide ample verbal or other behavior clues beforehand.
11. It is believed that more than half of the people who commit suicide are seriously depressed at the time of the act. However, many people who kill themselves do not have a diagnosable psychological disorder.
12. Surveys of people who have survived suicide attempts indicate a range of motives, including loneliness, powerlessness, a feeling that no one can help to ease the pain, depression, poor health, conflicts involving spouses or other people, unhappiness, and loss of a close relative or a friend.

Sources: Davison & Neale, 1986; Dorpat & Ripley, 1967; Duke & Nowicki, 1986; Goldstein et al., 1986; Goodwin & Jamison, 1986; Holinger, 1979, 1980; Kaprio et al., 1987; Michel, 1987; Miles, 1977; Schneidman, 1987, 1974; Schneidman et al., 1970; Seiden, 1974.

with it (see Table 14.4). Available evidence indicates that people with bipolar disorders are more likely to kill themselves than any other group of people with a psychological disorder (Goldstein et al., 1986). The following Health Psychology and Life discussion, "Strategies for Preventing Suicide," outlines what actions can be most helpful if someone you know threatens suicide.

THEORETICAL PERSPECTIVES ON MOOD DISORDERS

Psychoanalytic theory, the behavioral/learning perspective, and biological explanations provide different insights into the causes of mood disorders. We look at each in turn.

The Psychoanalytic Perspective   The first detailed theoretical interpretation of depression was offered by Karl Abraham (1911), a psychoanalyst who was once a student of Freud. Abraham suggested that mood disorders are rooted in an oral fixation. Frustrated in their efforts to achieve gratification at the oral stage of psychosexual development, individuals develop ambivalent feelings toward their mothers, which eventually transfer to other loved ones so that they are unable to relate successfully to people they love. The consequence is a regression back to the oral level, where these individuals can direct their original love/hate ambivalence toward the self. At times they overly love themselves (mania), whereas at other times they experience excessive self-hatred (depression).

In addition to emphasizing the love/hate ambivalence suggested by Abraham, Freud (1917) theorized that the fixation also causes a person to depend too heavily on others for gratification of basic needs and for main-

STRATEGIES FOR PREVENTING SUICIDE

Sometime during our lifetimes most of us will know someone—an acquaintance, friend, or loved one—who threatens suicide. Although highly trained clinicians are best able to intervene and treat a suicidal person, it is caring friends that are often the first line of defense. The following comments offer suggestions that may prove helpful should someone you know seem bent on self-destruction.

1. A person who is despondent should be encouraged to seek help from qualified clinicians. Be particularly alert for factors that indicate a high risk for suicide: prolonged depression, sleep disturbances, increased use of alcohol or other drugs, loss of interest and reduced performance in school or on the job, reduced communication with others, markedly diminished participation in favorite activities, deteriorating health, and giving valued possessions away (Schneidman, 1987). People who are considering suicide often drop hints by saying things like "What's the use" or "Sometimes I wonder if it's really all worth it."

2. If you perceive symptoms such as those described above, do not hesitate to ask directly if the person is thinking about suicide. Many people shy away from this question because they are afraid to open up a problem they feel unqualified to deal with, or because they fear they will put the idea into their friend's mind. There is ample evidence that talking about suicide does not increase the risk. Quite the contrary, a caring inquiry may be the first important step in successful therapeutic intervention (Beck et al., 1979).

3. If a person acknowledges considering suicide, even if he or she tries to make light of it, it is important to continue your efforts to see that this crisis is resolved on the "side of life." If the person denies considering suicide even though his or her actions indicate otherwise, it is still wise to pursue the matter. Encourage the individual to talk about the source of the depression. You do not need to be a trained psychotherapist to provide a caring ear and a sense of genuine empathy.

4. A suicidal person should be placed in the care of qualified mental health professionals. Phone-in suicide prevention centers are located in virtually every large city and many smaller towns, and they are excellent resources for a suicidal person or for someone who is concerned about that person. Paraprofessional volunteers (people trained by clinicians) who answer the phones at such centers are often able to assess the severity of a person's suicidal feelings, and they can make referrals for appropriate treatment. In

A caring friend often can be the first line of defense in helping a suicidal person.

addition, they sometimes are able to actively intervene to prevent suicide.

5. Consider accompanying your friend to a counselor. If the person refuses to seek help or to accompany you to a treatment facility, do not give up; the stakes are too high to take a "hands-off" approach. Contact others that you think might be of help—teachers, professors, a physician that may have treated the person for other problems, even family members. (Sometimes family members are unaware of the problem or do not comprehend its magnitude.)

6. If all else fails, and you find yourself standing alone between a person you care for and that person's death urge, remember that the resolve to commit suicide may often last only a brief time (Duke & Nowicki, 1986). People do not sit in a dark room with a gun to their head, or stand on a high bridge poised to leap, for hours or days on end. Thus, any stop-gap tactics that might get them past this critical period will increase their chances of surviving until more effective therapy can be provided. You might even suggest that suicide is a postponable option that a determined person continues to retain—"Let's at least talk now, and if you are still bent on ending your life tomorrow or a week from now, no one can stop you."

7. A person on the brink of suicide may be so overwhelmed with sadness and hopelessness that there may seem to be no other avenue of escape. It is not wise to respond to this attitude by pointing out how irrational it is or how crazy the person is to have settled on such a disastrous solution. A better response would be to "tune in" to the person's feelings, expressing empathy for his or her obvious pain. Having done this, you may then take a more positive, active stand, encouraging the individual to talk about family, hopes, or plans for the future. Most would-be suicides are ambivalent about dying; try to direct your probes to the part of the person that wants to live.

8. Do whatever you can to help reduce the person's pain. If at all possible, intervene with whatever or whoever is causing the suffering—academic or job situations, lovers, friends, or family members. Edwin Schneidman, a researcher and clinician who has treated and studied hundreds of suicidal people over 40 years, recently observed "I have found that if you reduce these pressures and lower the level of suffering, even just a little, suicidal people will choose to live" (1987, p. 56).

9. Finally, it may be helpful to talk about how family members and friends will respond to their suicide. Sometimes people become so caught up in their own despair that they fail to consider how their act will affect those who love them. The message is that people who live on are victims themselves (Rudestam & Agnell, 1987).

We hope that you will never have to do battle with that part of a friend or loved one that seeks self-destruction. However, if you find yourself in this situation, we hope that at least some of the previous guidelines will serve you well.

---

taining self-esteem. Freud thought mood disorders were rooted in relationships involving overdependency and ambivalent feelings of love and hate. When a person experiences loss (or even the threat of loss) of such a relationship, the unconscious hostility toward the lost person surfaces as anger that is turned back against oneself. This anger takes the form of despair that may be so intense as to motivate suicide, the ultimate form of aggression turned inward.

Many critics ask why only the hate component of a person's love/hate ambivalence is turned inward. Presumably, if the positive feelings were turned inward, a person would emerge from mourning with happy memories. Psychoanalytic theorists explain this paradox by arguing that loss of a loved one through death or separation is likely to be interpreted as rejection by a person who already feels ambivalent and emotionally dependent. Accordingly, an intense negative emotional state is a more likely consequence than are happy memories.

What little research there is does not support Freud's speculations. Researchers have analyzed the dreams of depressed people and found that they reflect themes of disappointment, failure, and loss rather than anger, hostility, and aggression (Beck & Ward, 1961). Furthermore, if depressed people do turn their anger inward, we should not expect to find much evidence of overt hostility to others. In fact, studies have revealed that depressed people often direct excessive amounts of hostility toward people who are close to them (Weissman & Paykel, 1974; Weissman et al., 1971). Finally, there is a lack of direct evidence that depressed people interpret the death of a loved one as rejection of themselves (Davison & Neale, 1986).

The Behavioral/Learning Perspective   Behavioral and learning theorists tend to view depression in a different light. Behaviorists note that death of or separation from a loved one means the loss of a primary source of positive reinforcement from the external environment (Ferster, 1965, 1966). Thus, a person whose spouse has recently died or who has recently divorced may sit at home alone. With no one there to provide ongoing positive reinforcements, he or she may fall into a rut, participating in fewer social and leisure activities that would normally function as primary sources of reinforcement.

Peter Lewinsohn (1974) has expanded this behavioral explanation, noting that depressed behaviors themselves may be reinforced by friends' concern, sympathy, increased attention, and perhaps lowered expectations for the person's performance. Lewinsohn also suggests that people who lack social skills are prime candidates for depression, because their social ineptness is not likely to produce much positive reinforcement from others. Lewinsohn's model of depression (see Figure 14.5) takes into account both the reduction of positive reinforcements that result from decreased activi-

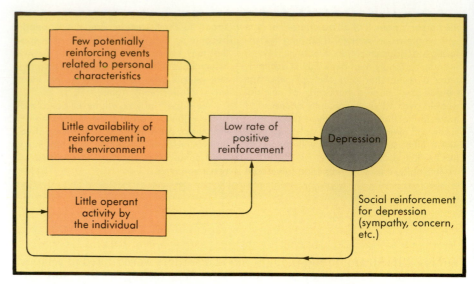

FIGURE 14.5

Lewinsohn's model of depression takes into account both the reduction of positive reinforcements that result from decreased activities, such as going out with friends, and increased expressions of concern from others, which he sees as a reinforcement for depression. (*Source:* From Lewinsohn, 1974)

ties, such as going out with friends, and also increased expressions of concern from others, which he sees as a reinforcement for depression.

Behavioral/learning theory suggests that there are other sources of depression besides the loss of a loved one. Loss of a job, a move to a different geographic area that cuts one off from a primary circle of friends (for example, going away to college), or a prolonged illness can all substantially reduce positive reinforcements; thus, all may be linked to depression.

Support for the behavioral explanation has been inconsistent. Contrary to Lewinsohn's view, depressed people seem more likely to elicit negative responses than expressions of concern from people they interact with (Coyne, 1976; Hammen & Peters, 1978; Gotlib & Robinson, 1982). The behavioral model of depression has some support, however, from findings that depressed people indicate having fewer pleasant experiences than do nondepressed people (MacPhillamy & Lewinsohn, 1974), and that the more depressed a person is, the fewer pleasant experiences are likely to be reported (Lewinsohn & Libet, 1972). The evidence does not rule out the possibility that depression precedes rather than follows a reduction in pleasant experiences, however, and it certainly seems plausible that people who become depressed may curtail their participation in reinforcing events. Thus, we are left with the chicken-and-egg question: which comes first?

Another theoretical perspective on depression that places more emphasis on the cognitive components of learning is Martin Seligman's theory of **learned helplessness** (Garber & Seligman, 1980; Peterson & Seligman, 1984; Seligman, 1975). This theory, which suggests that people become depressed when they believe that they have no control over the rewards and punishments in their lives, evolved out of a series of experiments with nonhumans. For example, in one study Seligman and Steven Maier (1967) used dogs as subjects which were assigned to one of three groups. Subjects in one group, the escape group, quickly learned to escape from repeated electric shocks by using their noses to press a panel. In contrast, animals in the inescapable group were exposed to the same pattern of shocks but were not provided with an escape response, and termination of the shock was independent of their actions. Dogs in a third control group were placed in the same apparatus but not shocked. Animals in the inescapable group appeared to acquire a sense of passive resignation to the unavoidable shock.

In a later phase of the experiment, dogs from all three groups were placed in another circumstance in which they could easily learn to avoid a shock by merely jumping over a hurdle to a safe compartment after hearing a warning signal. This avoidance task was easily mastered by dogs previously assigned to either the escape or control conditions. Animals in the inescapable group, however, merely sat passively, making no efforts to escape the pain. Seligman and his colleagues labeled this phenomenon learned helplessness.

What does this have to do with human depression? Seligman argues that humans, like the dogs in his experiment, develop a sense of helplessness as a result of previous experiences which produce an expectancy that they are unable to produce desirable changes in their environments by their actions. People thus become depressed when they feel helpless to influence their encounters with pleasure and pain. According to Seligman, people are most inclined to become depressed if they attribute their helplessness and failure to internal inadequacies (such as a lack of ability, social incompetence, etc.) that are unlikely to change in the future instead of external environmental conditions that are changeable.

Support for Seligman's cognitive-learning perspective on depression has been somewhat inconsistent. Some studies have demonstrated that mildly depressed people do tend to express defeatist, helpless cognitions (Peterson & Seligman, 1984). However, other studies of people hospitalized with severe depression demonstrate that although helpless cognitions often accompany depressive episodes, once patients' depressive episodes end they are no different from never-depressed control subjects in the tendency for their interpretations of negative events to be colored by an attitude of helpless resignation (Hamilton & Abramson, 1983; Fennell & Campbell, 1984). This finding suggests that an attitude of helplessness may be a symptom rather than a cause of depression.

The Biological Perspective   Whereas the evidence for both the psychoanalytic and behavioral explanations is ambiguous, considerable evidence points toward biological factors. Most of these findings concentrate in two areas, genetics and brain biochemistry. We first look at the evidence suggesting the role of genetics.

Genetics   Some of the most compelling evidence linking genetics to mood disorders comes from that old standby of nature-nurture research, the twin method. Table 14.5 provides an overview of concordance rates among identical and fraternal twins found in several studies. The average concordance rate for identical twins in these studies (65 percent) is almost five times that for fraternal twins (14 percent). The concordance rates in this table include both unipolar and bipolar forms of mood disorders. If the data are further broken down according to type of disorder, the concordance rates for identical twins are much higher for bipolar than unipolar disorders—72 percent versus 40 percent. Concordance rates for fraternal twins are approximately equal for the two disorders (Allen, 1976). It has also been

TABLE 14.5   *Concordance of Affective Disorders in Identical and Fraternal Twins*

Investigator	Number of Pairs in Sample	Concordance among Identical Twins	Number of Pairs in Sample	Concordance among Fraternal Twins
Luxenberger (1930)	4	75%	13	0%
Rosanoff et al. (1935)	23	70%	67	16%
Slater (1953)	7	57%	17	24%
Kallman (1954)	27	93%	55	24%
Harvald & Hauge (1965)	15	67%	40	5%
Allen et al. (1974)	15	33%	34	0%
Bertelsen (1979)	55	58%	52	17%
Totals	146	65%	278	14%

Source: Adapted from Nurnberger & Gershon, 1982.

demonstrated that concordance rates among identical twins are higher in severe than in milder forms of mood disorders (Nurnberger & Gershon, 1982).

For the last several years genetic researchers have been applying a recently developed technology involving the use of DNA markers to pinpoint the location of genes that induce a variety of diseases. The idea behind this approach is to trace the inheritance of a given disease within large high-risk families and to look for a DNA segment that is inherited along with a predisposition to develop the disease. This technique has been successful in finding markers for several major diseases, including Huntington's disease (see Chapter 10) and Alzheimer's disease (Chapter 11).

Recently a team of researchers headed by Janice Egeland (1987) has located two genetic markers for bipolar disorder. The subjects were 81 people selected from four high-risk families, all part of an Old Order Amish community in Pennsylvania. Of the total group of 81, 14 were diagnosed as having a bipolar disorder, and all 14 were shown to have the genetic markers on chromosome 11. Although Egeland and her colleagues were not able to identify a specific bipolar gene, they found it noteworthy that another gene located in the same region of chromosome 11 is known to be involved in the synthesis of neurotransmitters known as the catecholamines (including norepinephrine, epinephrine, and dopamine). Disturbances in the function of these neurotransmitters have also been implicated in a broad array of psychological disorders.

Other research teams have attempted to corroborate this finding in two other subject populations in which bipolar disorder appears to be inherited—a group of three large Icelandic families (Hodgkinson, 1987), and a group of three North American families (Detera-Wadleigh, 1987). Neither study found evidence of chromosome 11 linkage. This does not cast doubt on the Amish data reported by Egeland and her associates. Instead, it suggests that there are at least two or more different genes that produce predispositions to bipolar disorder (Kolata, 1987b; Robertson, 1987).

Numerous other family studies have shown that siblings and parents of people with mood disorders are from two to five times more likely to have unipolar and bipolar disorders than are normal subjects (Nurnberger & Gershon, 1982; Weissman, 1987; Weissman et al., 1982). Adoption studies provide further support: in one study, adoptees who had a biological parent or parents diagnosed as having mood disorder were much more likely to develop the illness themselves than were adoptees whose biological parents were free of the disorder (Cadoret, 1978). Another study of adoptees with diagnosed bipolar disorders found a considerably higher incidence among biological than adoptive parents (Mendlewicz & Rainer, 1977).

Virtually all researchers studying the causes of mood disorders currently agree that the data from twin, family, and adoption studies present compelling evidence for a strong genetic factor in vulnerability to mood disorders. The exact mode of transmission is unknown, but it is presumed to be quite complex, considering the wide variation in the degree of severity and manner of expression of the mood disorders.

Brain Biochemistry If mood disorders can be genetically transmitted, this trait must be expressed through some physiological mechanism that makes a person vulnerable to mood disorders. Present evidence strongly suggests that this physiological expression takes the form of altered levels of neurotransmitters in the brain. Recall from Chapter 3 that neurotransmitters are chemical messengers that make it possible for nerve impulses to move from one neuron to another. The level of certain critical neurotransmitters is strongly linked to mood disorders.

The search for a link between neurotransmitters and mood disorders began in the 1950s, when it was learned that two classes of drugs, the *monoamine oxidase inhibitors* (*MAO inhibitors*) and the *tricyclics*, often alleviated the symptoms of depression. Subsequent studies of nonhuman subjects revealed that both of these drugs act to increase the brain levels of two neurotransmitters, *norepinephrine* and *serotonin*. Thus, it seemed that low levels of these neurotransmitters might contribute to depression. This and other research led to the first formal biochemical theory of mood disorders, known as the *norepinephrine theory* (Schildkraut, 1970). This theory proposed that depression is related to too little norepinephrine, while the manic side of bipolar disorder results from an excess of this neurotransmitter.

The norepinephrine theory was supported by a number of studies. In addition to the evidence that drugs that increase norepinephrine levels often reduce depression (Maas et al., 1972; Teuting et al., 1981), lower than normal levels of norepinephrine were found in the urine of depressed people, while abnormally high levels were found in the urine of manic patients (Kety, 1975). In one interesting series of studies, researchers monitored urinary levels of norepinephrine in a sample of bipolar patients as they cycled through the stages of depression, normalcy, and mania. They found that the norepinephrine levels decreased as the subjects entered depression and increased when they became manic (Bunney et al., 1970, 1972). The drug lithium carbonate, now widely used to treat the manic side of bipolar disorder, has been shown to reduce norepinephrine levels significantly at certain synapses in the brain (Teuting et al., 1981).

Abnormalities in serotonin levels also seem to be related to mood disorders, but in a different way. Studies have found low serotonin levels in depressed people (Goodwin et al., 1978; Shaw et al., 1967) as well as in manic people (Coppen, 1972; Van Praag, 1981).

The *permissive theory* of mood disorders (Kety, 1975; Prange et al., 1974) attempts to integrate the different patterns of norepinephrine and serotonin into a cohesive explanation. According to this theory, serotonin places limits on the range of variations possible in norepinephrine levels. When serotonin levels are normal, norepinephrine levels also remain within a normal range, and the person experiences only normal highs and lows. However, a deficiency in serotonin causes a breakdown in its stabilizing functions, allowing norepinephrine levels to fluctuate beyond the normal high and low boundaries. This can result in deep depression or excessive mania (see Figure 14.6).

The permissive theory seems to make sense, but how does it stand up to research? As with the other disorders we have discussed in this chapter, the evidence is not entirely conclusive. Recall the two drugs, tricyclics and MAO inhibitors, that were discovered in the 1950s to alleviate depression.

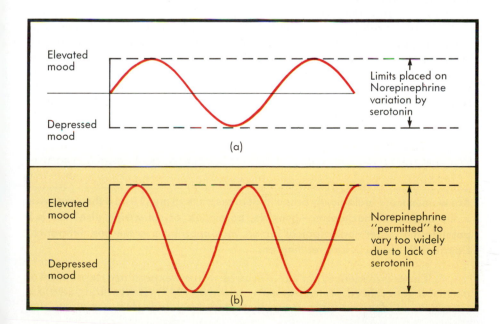

FIGURE 14.6

A schematic representation of the permissive theory of affective disorders. Normal levels of serotonin limit fluctuations in norepinephrine level, but when levels of serotonin are too low, norepinephrine fluctuates beyond the normal highs and lows.

We reported earlier that these drugs act to increase the brain levels of norepinephrine and serotonin. However, this effect occurs only in the period immediately after the drug therapy begins: within a few days, these two neurotransmitters return to their level prior to drug therapy.

This finding would not present a problem for the permissive theory if the antidepressant effect of the drugs also occurred during the brief period when transmitter levels are elevated, but such is not the case. Both tricyclics and MAO inhibitors generally take from one to two weeks to relieve depression. Contrary to the permissive theory, then, it appears that the effectiveness of these drugs in alleviating depression is not due merely to a change in neurotransmitter levels (Heninger et al., 1983). Then what is it due to? Researchers have speculated that the MAO inhibitors and tricyclic drugs may reduce depression by increasing the sensitivity of both norepinephrine and serotonin receptors in receiving neurons. The increased sensitivity would allow receptors to utilize better what limited supplies of neurotransmitters are available, thus relieving the depression (Charney et al., 1984; Heniger et al., 1983). Although we still do not know exactly why antidepressant drugs are effective, it is clear that biochemical factors are strongly implicated in mood disorders.

Looking Beyond the Three Theoretical Perspectives   As persuasive as the biological evidence is, can we explain mood disorders solely in terms of genetics and brain biochemistry? Many psychologists now believe that vulnerability to mood disorders involves an interaction of biological predispositions and psychosocial factors, and a number of studies support this interactive model.

In one fascinating study, monkeys were subjected to a range of developmental conditions including being raised by their mothers, removed from mothers and raised with peers with no separations from these peers, and raised with peers with intermittent separations of variable frequency. At a later stage of development, the monkeys were given variable doses of a drug known to reduce norepinephrine levels in the brain; then their behaviors were monitored to see if they would exhibit signs of depression (such as decreased activity or huddling behaviors). The researchers found that monkeys who had remained with their mothers required up to eight times as much drug to produce depression symptoms as monkeys reared only with peers. And of the two groups of peer-reared monkeys, those that had experienced frequent separations from their companions were more susceptible to the depressant effects of the drug than were those who experienced few or no separations (Kraemer & McKinney, 1979).

This study suggests that both environment and biological factors interact to determine susceptibility to depression. But how does this finding relate to humans, many of whom develop depression despite stable home lives? One interesting finding, for instance, is that as many as six times more women than men in this country are diagnosed as suffering from depression (Duke & Nowicki, 1986), a finding that has been corroborated in other societies as well (Goldstein et al., 1986).

EXPLAINING THE INCIDENCE OF DEPRESSION IN FEMALES AND MALES

Are women more biologically prone to depression than men? And if they are, what is the biological mechanism—genetics, hormones, or something else? Or is it possible that other nonbiological factors may contribute to this sex difference? Consider this issue before reading on.

There is evidence that a minority of women experience depression as part of a generalized premenstrual syndrome (PMS) (Boyle et al., 1987), a term used to identify a myriad of physical and psychological symptoms that

precede each menstrual period and are occasionally severe enough to interfere with some aspects of daily functioning. Some studies have also shown
an increase in depression in women taking oral contraceptives (Hatcher et
al., 1986). However, even if we inflate the estimate of the incidence of
depression related to PMS or pill use, there is no good evidence that hormones account for the magnitude of the differences in depression rates
between the sexes (Weissman & Klerman, 1977).

A number of theorists have looked into the role of cultural conditioning. When this issue is put to students, many of them speculate that the
high incidence of depression among women has something to do with the
housewife role, which may cause them to feel isolated from the "mainstream" of life. However, there is evidence not only that married women
with careers are no less depressed than housewives, but also that married
women with careers have much higher rates of depression than do married
men with careers (Radloff, 1975).

P. Susan Penfold (1981) proposes a broader explanation. She argues
that the higher rate of depression among women is largely a function of the
nature of gender role socialization. The roles commonly assigned to women
in most contemporary societies may contribute to a sense of powerlessness,
resentment, boredom, and fatigue—fertile ground for a major depression
disorder. Lenore Radloff (1975) also suggests that depression among
women may reflect a kind of learned helplessness that evolves directly out of
proscribed roles in society. Support for this view is provided by evidence
that many little girls may actually be trained to be helpless (Broverman et
al., 1970). Radloff maintains that the higher incidence of depression and
some other psychological disorders among women stems directly from their
lack of personal and political power—and from the fact that stereotypical
female roles do not encourage women to feel competent.

Penfold's and Radloff's viewpoints are only hypotheses, and we must
be cautious about attributing the greater incidence of depression among
women largely to psychosocial factors. Perhaps future evidence will reveal
that genetic programing and/or biological predispositions are somehow
linked to sex differences in depression. The psychosocial interpretation,
however, certainly seems quite plausible. It will be interesting to see if our
society's shift toward more equal gender roles will eventually reduce the
different depression rates among males and females.

The roles commonly assigned to
women in most contemporary societies may contribute to a sense of
powerlessness, resentment, boredom, and fatigue—fertile ground
for a major depression disorder.

SCHIZOPHRENIC DISORDERS

When my first episode of schizophrenia occurred, I was 21, a senior in
college. . . . Everything in my life was just perfect. I had a boyfriend
whom I liked a lot, a parttime job tutoring Spanish, and was about to run
for the Ms. Senior pageant.

All of a sudden things weren't going so well. I began to lose control of my
life and, most of all, myself. I couldn't concentrate on my schoolwork, I
couldn't sleep, and when I did sleep, I had dreams about dying. I was
afraid to go to class, imagined that people were talking about me, and on
top of that I heard voices. . . . I moved [off campus to live] . . . with my
sister, [but] things got worse. I was afraid to go outside and when I
looked out of the window, it seemed that everyone outside was yelling,
"kill her, kill her. . . . " I imagined that I had a foul body odor and I
sometimes took up to six showers a day. . . . I couldn't remember a thing.
I had a notebook full of reminders telling me what to do on that particular day. I couldn't remember my schoolwork, and I would study from
6:00 P.M. until 4:00 A.M., but never had the courage to go to class on the
following day. I tried to tell my sister about it, but she didn't understand.
She suggested that I see a psychiatrist, but I was afraid to go out of the
house to see him.

One day I decided that I couldn't take this trauma anymore, so I took an
overdose of 35 Darvon pills. At the same moment, a voice inside me said,
"What did you do that for? Now you won't go to heaven." At that instant

I realized that I really didn't want to die, I wanted to live, and I was afraid. I got on the phone and called the psychiatrist. . . . I told him that I had taken an overdose of Darvon and that I was afraid. He told me to take a taxi to the hospital. . . . Somehow I just couldn't accept the fact that I was really going to see a psychiatrist. I thought that psychiatrists were only for crazy people, and I definitely didn't think I was crazy yet. As a result, . . . I left the hospital and ended up meeting my sister on the way home. She told me to turn right back around, because I was definitely going to be admitted. (O'Neal, 1984, pp. 109–110)

The young woman who related this account was diagnosed as having a **schizophrenic disorder**. Schizophrenia is one of the most severe and disabling of all mental disorders, characterized by extreme disruptions of perceptions, thoughts, emotions, and behavior. At any point in time it affects about one percent of people throughout the world, and it is estimated that as many as three out of every 100 people may experience this disorder at some time during their lives (Regier et al., 1984). Approximately 600,000 people receive treatment for schizophrenia annually in the United States. This disorder occurs with equal frequency in both sexes.

Schizophrenia was once called *dementia praecox* (Kraeplin, 1918), a term derived from the fact that the disorder typically has an early onset (*praecox*) in the teenage or young adult years and that it is characterized by a progressive intellectual deterioration (*dementia*). The term *schizophrenia* was later coined by Eugene Bleuler (1950) to describe what he saw as the primary symptom of this disorder: a dissociation of thoughts from appropriate emotions caused by a splitting off (Greek *schizo* for "split") of parts of the mind (Greek *phrenum* for "mind"). Laypersons often confuse schizophrenia with the entirely different disorder, multiple personality. Although the split in multiple personality disorder is between different personalities, all of which are capable of maintaining contact with reality, the split in schizophrenia is between thoughts and feelings. The result is often bizarre behavior that is highly dysfunctional.

Schizophrenic disorders are distinguished from other disorders primarily by the characteristically extreme disturbances in thinking that cause people to behave in maladaptive ways. In addition to these thought disturbances, however, a constellation of other symptoms are used to diagnose this disorder. People diagnosed as schizophrenic may show considerable diversity of symptoms. They typically exhibit most but not necessarily all of

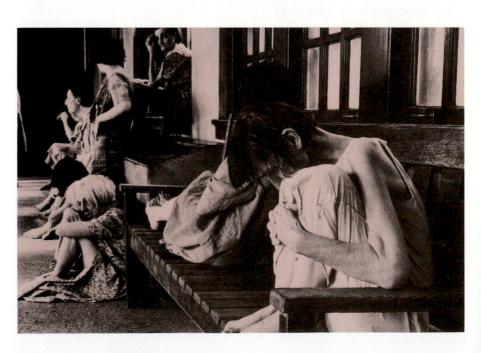

Schizophrenia is one of the most severe and disabling of all mental disorders and is characterized by extreme disruptions of perceptions, thoughts, emotions, and behavior.

a *primary* core of symptoms as well as one or more *secondary* symptoms that are used to assign the individual to a particular subtype of schizophrenia. We will look at the primary symptoms that typify all forms of schizophrenia, then at the secondary symptoms of each subtype.

PRIMARY SYMPTOMS OF SCHIZOPHRENIA

The collection of primary or core symptoms that are characteristic of many forms of schizophrenia include disturbances in thought, perception, emotional expression, and speech, together with social withdrawal and diminished motivation.

Disturbances of Thought   Thought disturbances associated with schizophrenia tend to be of two basic types: disturbances of *content* (that is, the actual ideas that are expressed), and disturbances of *form* (the manner in which ideas are organized).

Most people with schizophrenia demonstrate marked disturbances in the content of their thoughts. These disturbances may be evident from a few characteristic symptoms. One is a lack of awareness of some of the basic realities of life, such as what is going on around them and the nature of their condition. Another disturbance in the content of thoughts is delusions. Table 14.6 describes several varieties of delusional thoughts that may be associated with schizophrenia.

Disturbances in the form of thought may be evident in the incoherence of the ideas a person verbalizes. This is illustrated in the following account of a conversation between a schizophrenic patient and a clinician:

> "How old are you?"
> "Why I am centuries old, sir."
> "How long have you been here?"
> "I've been now on this property on and off for a long time. I cannot say the exact time because we are absorbed by the air at night, and they bring back people. They kill up everything: they can make you lie; they can talk through your throat."
> "Who is this?"
> "Why, the air."
> "What is the name of this place?"
> "This place is called a star."
> "Who is the doctor in charge of your ward?"
> "A body just like yours, sir. They can make you black and white. I say good morning, but he just comes through there. At first it was a colony. They said it was heaven. These buildings were not solid at the time,

TABLE 14.6   *Several Varieties of Delusional Thoughts That May Be Associated with Schizophrenia*

Delusion of influence	A belief that others are influencing one by means of wires, TV, and so on, making one do things against one's will.
Delusion of grandeur	The belief that one is in actuality some great world or historical figure, such as Napoleon, Queen Victoria, or the President of the United States.
Delusion of persecution	The belief that one is being persecuted, hunted, or interfered with by certain individuals or organized groups.
Delusion of reference	The belief that others are talking about one, that one is being included in TV shows or plays or referred to in news articles, and so on.
Delusion of bodily change	The belief that one's body is changing in some unusual way—for example, that the blood is turning to snakes or the flesh to concrete.
Delusion of nihilism	The belief that nothing really exists, that all things are simply shadows; also common is the idea that one has really been dead for many years and is observing the world from afar.

and I am positive that this is the same place. They have others just like it. People die, and all the microbes talk over there, and prestigitis you know is sending you from here to another world. . . . I was sent by the government to the United States to Washington to some star, and they had a pretty nice country there. Now you have a body like a young man who says he is of the prestigitis."

Who was this prestigitis?"

Why, you are yourself. You can be prestigitis. They make you say bad things; they can read you; they bring back Negroes from the dead." (White, 1932, p. 228).

It is common for schizophrenics to invent new words, or **neologisms**, like the word "prestigitis" in the passage above. Another anomaly in the form of schizophrenic thoughts is *loose associations,* in which ideas shift from one topic to another so that it is very difficult for a listener to follow the train of thought.

Disturbance of Perception A second primary symptom, disturbed perception, may include such things as changes in how the body feels (numbness, tingling, or burning sensations, or the feeling that organs are deteriorating or that parts of the body are too large or small), or a feeling of depersonalization that makes a person feel separated from his or her body. Many schizophrenics report changed perceptions of their external environment. For some, everything may appear two dimensional and colorless; others report that they are hypersensitive to light, sounds, or touch.

The most common form of altered perception in schizophrenia are hallucinations. Hallucinations may occur in any of the sense modalities, but most often a schizophrenic person hears voices that seem to be coming from outside the person's head. It has been suggested that at least some of the auditory hallucinations experienced by schizophrenics may be projections of their own thoughts (Bick & Kinsbourne, 1987). These voices may give commands ("take off your clothes"; "kill corrupting prostitutes") that are sometimes obeyed with disturbing or tragic consequences. More commonly the imagined voices may make insulting comments about the person's character or behavior. This is illustrated in the following account:

A forty-one-year-old housewife heard a voice coming from a house across the road. The voice went on incessantly in a flat monotone describing everything she was doing with an admixture of critical comments. "She is peeling potatoes, got hold of the peeler, she does not want that potato, she is putting it back, because she thinks it has a knobble like a penis, she has a dirty mind, she is peeling potatoes, now she is washing them . . . " (Mellor, 1970, p. 16)

Disturbance in Emotional Expression A third common symptom of schizophrenia is a disturbance in emotional expression. This may take the form of a *blunted or flat affect,* in which there is a dramatic lack of emotional expression. The person may stare vacantly with listless eyes, speak in a monotone, and show no facial expression. Differing theories have been offered to explain this lack of affect, including the possibility that schizophrenic people may be so absorbed in responding to internal stimuli that they are unresponsive to outside stimuli (Venables & Wing, 1962). It has also been suggested that by "turning themselves off," schizophrenics are able to protect themselves from stimuli which they feel incapable of coping with (Mednick, 1958).

Perhaps even more common than flat affect are inappropriate emotional responses, in which the emotional expression is incongruous with its context. For example, a schizophrenic person may laugh upon hearing of the death of a loved one, or may fly into a rage when asked an innocuous question such as "Did you enjoy your dinner?" Mood states may shift rapidly for no discernible reason.

Schizophrenic people may be so absorbed in responding to internal stimuli that they are unresponsive to outside stimuli. This is called *blunted* or *flat effect.*

Disturbances in Speech   In addition to abnormal speech patterns (such as incoherence and loose associations) that result from thought disturbances, two verbal dysfunctions may be viewed as primary examples of speech disturbances. In **mutism**, the person may not utter a sound for hours or days regardless of how much encouragement or prodding may be provided. In the other disturbance, **echolalia**, a person might answer a question by repeating it verbatim or might repeat virtually every statement he or she hears uttered.

Social Withdrawal   A fifth primary symptom of schizophrenia is the inclination to withdraw from the company of others. In the early stages of the disorder, people with schizophrenia may go into their bedroom, close the door, and remain alone for extended periods. As the illness advances they become progressively more isolated and emotionally detached, and friends and family members may complain that they seem to be living in their own world. This alienation is often intensified in a hospital setting. The person may be aware of this isolation, as the account below illustrates, but may be unwilling or unable to rectify it:

A common symptom of schizophrenia is the inclination to withdraw from the company of others. As the illness progresses, people with schizophrenia become more isolated and emotionally detached, and friends and family members may complain that they seem to be living in their own world.

> During the visit I tried to establish contact with her, to feel that she was actually there, alive and sensitive. But it was futile. Though I certainly recognized her, she became part of the unreal world. I knew her name and everything about her, yet she appeared strange, unreal, like a statue. I saw her eyes, her nose, her lips moving, heard her voice and understood what she said perfectly, yet I was in the presence of a stranger. To restore contact between us I made desperate efforts to break through the invisible dividing wall but the harder I tried, the less successful I was. . . . (Torrey, 1983, p. 17)

Diminished Motivation   People with schizophrenia almost inevitably show a markedly diminished level of motivation. Like social withdrawal, this symptom may show up early in the course of the disorder. It is also one of the most persistent symptoms, lingering on even after an individual is well on the road to recovery.

These six primary symptoms do not typically appear suddenly in full-blown form. In most cases, the illness progresses gradually over three stages or phases. The first signs that something is not quite right appear during the *prodromal stage*, usually during late adolescence or early adulthood. Early symptoms often include diminished interest in work, school, and leisure activities; lowered productivity; social withdrawal; and a deterioration in health and grooming habits. The prodromal phase may last for months or even years.

The major symptoms of schizophrenia appear during the second phase, the *active stage*. The duration of this phase is highly variable, ranging from months to most of a lifetime. When and if the active phase subsides, either spontaneously or as a result of treatment, the person enters the third, or *residual phase*, in which the major symptoms are absent or markedly diminished. During this gradual recovery, residual symptoms such as continued difficulty establishing social contacts, low motivation, somewhat blunted or inappropriate affect, and unusual perceptual experiences may linger.

SUBTYPES OF SCHIZOPHRENIA

Although the primary symptoms of schizophrenia are common in all the various subtypes of this disorder, the secondary symptoms make these subtypes appear very different from one another. DSM-III-R distinguishes five subtypes or varieties of schizophrenia: *disorganized (hebephrenic)*, *catatonic*, *paranoid*, *undifferentiated*, and *residual*.

Personality disintegration is generally most severe in disorganized schizophrenia. Emotional moods change constantly, with wild swings from fits of crying to episodes of uncontrollable giggling.

Disorganized (Hebephrenic) Schizophrenia Personality disintegration is generally most severe in **disorganized schizophrenia**. This subtype is characterized by marked disorganization and regression in thinking and behavioral patterns. Hallucinations and delusions are very common, often with sexual, religious, or hypochondriacal themes. Emotional moods change constantly, with wild swings from fits of crying to episodes of uncontrollable giggling. A person with disorganized schizophrenia often behaves in an infantile manner, neglecting personal hygiene and sometimes even engaging publicly in bladder and bowel functions. Speech is often incoherent, marked by stringing together similar sounding or rhyming words or phrases (this thinking distortion is called a *clang*) and neologisms. The term *word salad* has been used to describe the bombastic, illogical flood of words that stream forth from the mouths of disorganized schizophrenics.

Catatonic Schizophrenia The distinguishing symptoms of **catatonic schizophrenia** are extreme psychomotor disturbances, which may range from stuporous immobility to wild excitement and agitation. In the stuporous state of catatonic immobility, a person may adopt a strange posture that is held for prolonged periods of time, sometimes even after the limbs become stiff, blue and swollen from lack of movement. The person's limbs often exhibit a kind of *waxy flexibility*, so that another person can move them about and put them in new positions which are then maintained. Although people in this state appear totally oblivious to what is going on around them, interviews with recovered catatonics show that many have excellent recall for what occurred around them during their episodes of stupor.

Agitated catatonia is characterized by extreme motor excitement in which the person thrashes about, shouts, talks continuously and incoherently, or runs about wildly. Sometimes stuporous catatonics will suddenly, without warning, blast out of their immobility into frenzied activity. During this state of great agitation an individual can do considerable damage to the self, nearby objects, and other people. These bizarre motor symptoms are fairly uncommon today, due to effective drug therapy.

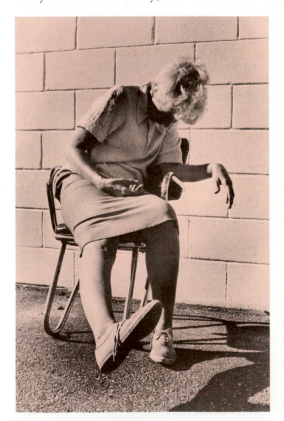

In the stuporous state of catatonic immobility, a person may adopt a strange posture that is held for prolonged periods of time, sometimes even after the limbs become stiff, blue, and swollen from lack of movement.

Paranoid Schizophrenia Of all the subtypes of schizophrenia, people with **paranoid schizophrenia** demonstrate the highest level of awareness and the least impairment of ability to carry out daily functions. However, this disorder is also a profound disturbance. Its dominant symptom is the presence of well-organized delusional thoughts, such as those described earlier in Table 14.6. Vivid auditory, visual, or olfactory hallucinations are also common in this condition. Paranoid schizophrenics often appear agitated, angry, argumentative, and sometimes violent. They may become particularly dangerous if they decide to destroy their "persecutors."

Undifferentiated and Residual Schizophrenia **Undifferentiated schizophrenia** is a kind of "catch-all" category that schizophrenics are assigned to if they do not manifest the specific symptom patterns of disorganized, catatonic, or paranoid forms of the disorder. However, the primary core of symptoms, such as disturbance of thought, perception, and emotional expression, are present. The final category, **residual schizophrenia**, is a label used for schizophrenics in the residual stage, described earlier.

THEORETICAL PERSPECTIVES ON SCHIZOPHRENIC DISORDERS

Schizophrenia has spawned more research into causes and treatments than any other psychological disorder. We will look at the psychoanalytic, behavioral/learning, and biological perspectives, then present a model that accounts for both biological and psychological factors.

The Psychoanalytic Perspective Freud believed that schizophrenia occurs when a person's ego either becomes overwhelmed with id demands or is besieged by unbearable guilt. In both cases, the ego elects to retreat rather than attempt to set things straight, and the person undergoes a massive regression back to the oral stage of psychosexual development. In the first phase of this retreat, *regressive symptoms* demonstrate a return to the infantile. A person may return to primary process thinking (see Chapter 13) and may experience delusions of self-importance. Eventually the regression becomes so extensive that all contact with reality is lost. At this point, the schizophrenic begins a struggle to regain reality. *Restitutional symptoms* appear, such as hallucinations, delusions, and bizarre speech patterns that reflect an effort to reestablish verbal communication with other people. Today only a very few psychoanalytic theorists place much credibility in Freud's explanation of schizophrenia.

The Behavioral/Learning Perspective It is difficult to apply basic learning-theory principles such as reinforcement and modeling to people who are as out of touch with reality as schizophrenics are. However, learning theorists Leonard Ullman and Leonard Krasner (1975) propose one explanation—that schizophrenics either have not been reinforced adequately for responding to normal social stimuli, or perhaps have even been punished for such responses. As a consequence, normal patterns of attending to or reacting to appropriate social cues are extinguished or suppressed. To fill the resulting void, they begin to respond to inappropriate stimuli, such as imaginary voices emanating from the coffee pot. Other people's responses to these bizarre behaviors may then further reinforce these patterns.

The Biological Perspective A stronger explanation for schizophrenia is provided by the biological perspective. As with mood disorders, substantial clues point toward both genetics and brain biochemistry.

Genetics An extensive body of research indicates that certain people are genetically predisposed to develop schizophrenia (Barnes, 1987b; Gottesman et al., 1987). Table 14.7 summarizes some of these data, from a number of twin studies: note that the concordance rate for identical twins

TABLE 14.7 *Concordance Rates of Schizophrenia among Identical and Fraternal Twins*

Investigator	Country	Identical Twins		Fraternal Twins	
		Number of pairs in sample	Percentage concordance rate	Number of pairs in sample	Percentage concordance rate
Gottesman & Shields	England	22	40–50*	33	9–19
Pollin et al.	U.S.A.	95	14–27	125	4–8
Fischer	Denmark	21	24–48	41	10–19
Kringlen	Norway	55	25–38	90	4–10
Tienari	Finland	17	0–36	20	5–14

*The range in the concordance rate figures reflects different estimates of what would constitute a concordant pair, which vary depending on how narrowly or broadly schizophrenia is defined. The lower figure is for the narrower definition, which requires a majority of the major symptoms of schizophrenia to be present.

Source: Adapted from Gottesman & Shields, 1982.

runs two to four times higher than that reported for fraternal twins. Studies have also demonstrated that concordance rates among identical twins are higher in severe than in milder forms of schizophrenia (Gottesman & Shields, 1982).

Family studies have shown a substantially higher incidence of schizophrenia among relatives of schizophrenics than among the general population (Kendler et al., 1985; Mayer-Gross et al., 1969; Rosenthal, 1971; Slater & Cowie, 1971). Adoption studies have provided further evidence: Several investigators have found that adoptees whose biological parent or parents were diagnosed as schizophrenic were considerably more likely to develop the disorder than were adoptees whose biological parents were free of the illness (Kety et al., 1975; Rosenthal, 1977; Rosenthal et al., 1971).

Thus, there is abundant evidence that genetics is an important factor in the development of schizophrenia. We cannot conclude that genes alone cause this disorder, however, for if that were the case, the concordance rate between identical twins would be virtually 100 percent. Furthermore, even when both parents have schizophrenia, the odds are better than 50:50 that their offspring will not develop the disorder. Several schizophrenia researchers explain this discrepancy by theorizing that a genetic predisposition toward schizophrenia is by no means a sufficient condition to produce this disorder, and that certain environmental stresses must also be present (Kessler, 1980; Mirsky & Duncan, 1986). We will return to this interaction hypothesis after considering some additional evidence of biological factors.

Brain Biochemistry   As with the mood disorders, researchers studying schizophrenia have focused considerable attention on biochemical abnormalities. Two major hypotheses have been proposed. The first, the *inborn error of metabolism hypothesis*, suggests that an error of metabolism causes the body to produce certain chemicals that cause altered states of perception, thought, and feeling. The other major theory, the *dopamine hypothesis*, suggests that schizophrenia is caused either by abnormally high levels of the neurotransmitter dopamine or by above normal reactivity to this chemical due to an increased number of receptors for dopamine (Barnes, 1987b; Wong et al., 1986).

Unfortunately, efforts to test these hypotheses have been limited by the inability to perform useful animal research. As we saw earlier, it has been possible to study depression-like symptoms in monkeys, but nonhuman animals do not appear to manifest symptoms of schizophrenia. Thus, scientists have been limited to analyzing *metabolites* (the products of metabolism) of brain chemicals that show up in the blood and urine, and in some cases to analyzing samples of cerebrospinal fluid from subjects with schizophrenia. Although the study of metabolites has become more precise in recent years, it is complicated by the fact that a variety of factors (including ingested drugs, diet, smoking, and even emotional states) may affect the composition of metabolites. Despite these limitations, however, the evidence is intriguing.

According to the inborn error of metabolism hypothesis, a genetically determined error of metabolism causes the body to break down naturally occurring chemicals into toxic ones that cause many of the symptoms of schizophrenia. Researchers have long noted that certain hallucinogenic drugs like LSD, mescaline, and psilocybin produce distortions of perception, thought, and mood similar to those typical of schizophrenia. It seems possible that schizophrenia might also result from certain internally produced hallucinogenic substances (Bowers, 1980; Osmond & Smythies, 1953; Rosengarten & Friedhoff, 1976).

Interestingly, the chemical structures of both norepinephrine and dopamine are very similar to that of mescaline, a known hallucinogen (see Figure 14.7). Thus even a slight alteration in these two major neurotransmitters could induce a continuous "trip" or schizophrenic disorder. Although it has not been easy to find traces of hallucinogen-like chemicals, one study not only found the hallucinogen dimethyltryptamine (DMT) in the urine of schizophrenics but also observed that the clinical symptoms of these patients were somewhat alleviated when DMT levels decreased (Murray et al., 1979). Other researchers have found small amounts of hallucinogen-like chemicals in the cerebrospinal fluid of schizophrenics (Christian et al, 1975; Smythies, 1976). Thus, it appears that there may be some kind of relationship between internally produced hallucinogens and the symptoms of schizophrenia.

The dopamine hypothesis offers a different explanation. It suggests that schizophrenia results from abnormalities in the availability of the neurotransmitter dopamine in various areas of the brain, particularly the limbic system. These abnormalities may be reflected in either a hypersensitivity of neurons to dopamine (Langer et al., 1981) or to an excessive amount of the neurotransmitter (Carlsson, 1977).

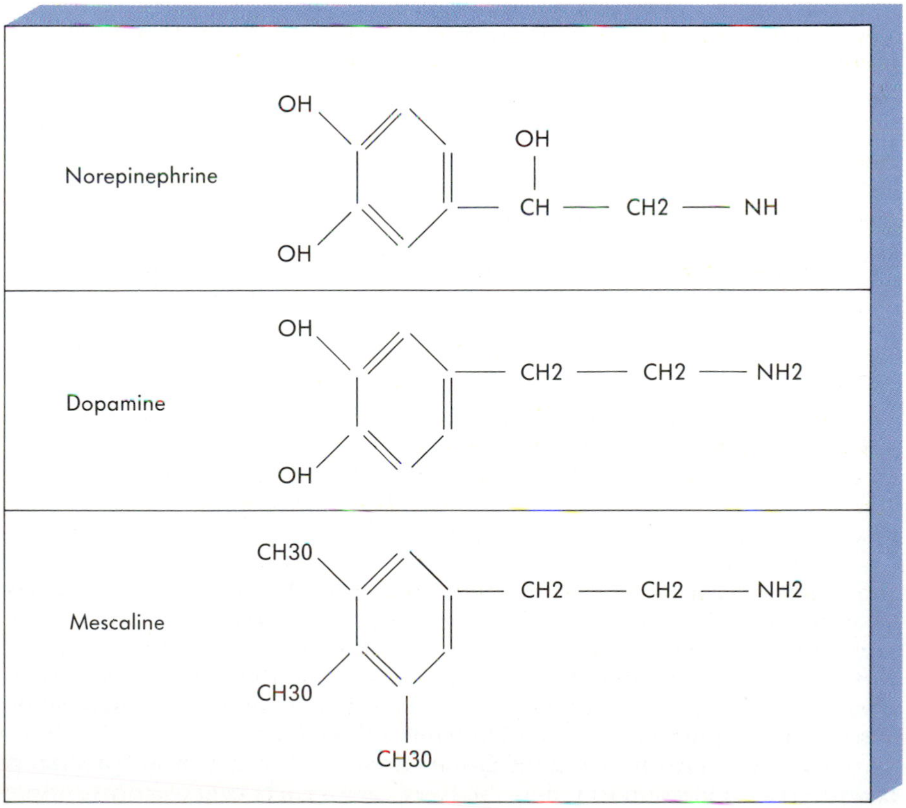

FIGURE 14.7

Similarities in molecular structure between two neurotransmitters, norepinephrine and dopamine, and mescaline, a known hallucinogen.

This hypothesis is also supported by research. For example, it is known that the *phenothiazines* (drugs that alleviate some of the symptoms of schizophrenia) reduce the activity of dopamine by blocking postsynaptic dopamine receptors. In addition, postmortem brain analyses have found an abnormal number of dopamine receptors in the brains of some schizophrenics (Crow et al., 1978), as well as abnormally high levels of dopamine in certain areas of schizophrenic brains (Bird et al., 1979; Stein & Wise, 1971). Considered together, these findings provide strong evidence linking either excessive dopamine levels or abnormal sensitivity to dopamine (or perhaps both) to schizophrenia.

An Interactional Model   As strong as the biological evidence is, the fact remains that not everyone who is genetically predisposed toward schizophrenia becomes schizophrenic. The *diathesis-stress model* ("diathesis" means biological vulnerability) attempts to integrate both psychological and biological factors into one integrated theory of schizophrenia (Gottesman & Shields, 1976; Rosenthal, 1970; Zubin & Spring, 1977). According to this model, two factors are necessary for schizophrenia to develop. The first is a biological vulnerability to schizophrenia; the second is severe life stresses such as those found in disturbed family environments with constant hostility and conflicts, bizarre patterns of communication, and distorted role relationships. The *vulnerability-stress model* (Nuechterlein & Dawson, 1984) builds on the diathesis-stress model by specifying certain genetically determined traits that can make a person particularly vulnerable to schizophrenia. These traits include information processing deficits, hyperactivity of the autonomic nervous system, low social competence, and poor coping skills.

We hope that continued research will eventually provide a clearer explanation of schizophrenia. Until that time, theorists will continue their attempt to build a comprehensive model that explains how biological predispositions and psychological stresses interact to cause one of the most debilitating of all the psychological disorders.

PERSONALITY DISORDERS

We end our discussion of psychological disorders with a look at a diverse array of disorders grouped under the category of **personality disorders**. The diagnosis of these disorders is based on a perspective derived from the trait approach to personality (see Chapter 13). DSM-III-R describes the personality disorders as follows:

> It is only when personality traits are inflexible and maladaptive and cause either significant functional impairment or subjective distress that they constitute Personality Disorders. The manifestations of Personality Disorders are often recognized by adolescence or earlier and continue throughout most of adult life, though they often become less obvious in middle or old age. . . .
>
> Many of the features characteristic of the various Personality Disorders . . . may be seen during an episode of another mental disorder, such as Major Depression. The diagnosis . . . should be made only when the characteristic features are typical of the person's long-term functioning and are not limited to discrete episodes of illness (p. 335).

DSM-III-R lists a total of 11 personality disorders that are grouped into three clusters, outlined in Table 14.8. The disorders in the first cluster are all characterized by odd and/or eccentric behavior; those in the second cluster share a common denominator of dramatic, emotional, or erratic behavior; and those in the third cluster are all characterized by anxious or fearful behavior.

The various personality disorders are linked by a number of shared characteristics. First, most tend to show up at an early age, usually no later

TABLE 14.8 *Personality Disorders*

Cluster A: Disorders of Odd or Eccentric Behavior	Cluster B: Disorders of Dramatic, Emotional, or Erratic Behavior	Cluster C: Disorders Involving Anxious or Fearful Behavior
Paranoid Personality Disorder Extreme and pervasive suspiciousness, mistrust, and envy of others; hypersensitivity and difficulty in getting along with others; restricted expression of emotion; inclined to avoid intimacy.	*Antisocial Personality Disorder* A continuous pattern of utter disregard for the rights of others and the rules of society; antisocial acts usually commence before age 15; often unable to perform adequately on the job or in relationships; a strong tendency to engage in exciting, impulsive behavior with little attention to the consequences.	*Avoidant Personality Disorder* Hypersensitive to the possibility of being rejected by others; a desire for close social relationships but unable to reach out to others because of fear of rejection; very low self-esteem.
Schizoid Personality Disorder Very cold, aloof, and socially isolated; unable to form close relationships; humorless; appears to be indifferent to praise or criticism.	*Borderline Personality Disorder* This condition is not associated with a characteristic pattern of behavior that is invariably present, and it is often associated with other personality disorders (hence the label "borderline"); instability in several areas including mood, self-image, behavior, and interpersonal relationships; a chronic inclination to be indecisive and uncertain about a variety of important life issues.	*Dependent Personality Disorder* Extremely poor self-image and a lack of self-confidence; depends upon others to make all major decisions; subordinates personal needs to avoid alienating people depended upon; unable to tolerate being alone.
Schizotypal Personality Disorder Oddities or eccentricities in thought, perception, speech, or behavior not severe enough to be diagnosed as schizophrenic; extreme social isolation; strong tendency toward egocentrism.	*Histrionic Personality Disorder* Overly dramatic behavior, frequently expressed as drawing attention to oneself and/or overreacting to minor events of small consequence; self-centered, self-indulgent, vain, manipulative, and inconsiderate; tendency to be dependent on others but poor interpersonal skills.	*Obsessive-Compulsive Personality Disorder* Excessive preoccupation with rules and regulations and the need to do things "by the book"; inflexible, stiff workaholic; limited ability to express tender emotions such as warmth, caring, and love.
	Narcissistic Personality Disorder Grandiose sense of self-importance; preoccupied with fantasies of great achievements; childish demands for constant attention and special favors; little empathy for others.	*Passive-Aggressive Personality Disorder* Expresses indirect or passive resistance to demands of others for adequate performance at work or in personal relationships through such actions as dawdling, procrastinating, inefficiency, and forgetfulness; tendency to be a complainer or whiner.

Source: Adapted from DSM-III-R, American Psychiatric Association, 1987.

than adolescence, and the characteristic maladaptive behaviors often tend to become more deeply ingrained over the years. Another common feature is that very few individuals diagnosed as having a personality disorder ever seem to believe that there is something wrong with the way they are functioning. Third, there is a strong tendency for the various personality-disordered behaviors to be rigidly ingrained, highly repetitive, and ultimately self-defeating. Finally, the prognosis for overcoming any of the personality disorders is rather poor. This may be due, at least in part, to the fact that individuals with personality disorders are generally more inclined to refuse therapy than are people with the other psychological disorders outlined in this chapter (Vallant & Perry, 1985). The antisocial personality disorder has been the subject of more research and theorizing than any of the other 10 personality disorders; therefore, we focus our remaining discussion on this disorder.

ANTISOCIAL PERSONALITY DISORDER

From the point of view of society at large, the most disruptive of the personality disorders is the **antisocial personality disorder**, also referred to as psychopathic or sociopathic personality disorder. Recent estimates indicate that almost three percent of the population have antisocial personalities, with six times as many men as women included in this diagnostic category (Robins, 1987). Perhaps the best clinical description of this disorder was provided by Hervey Cleckley in his book, *The Mask of Sanity* (1976). The following list summarizes some of the most prominent characteristics of an antisocial personality as outlined by Cleckley and as described in DSM-III-R:

1. A history dating back to before age 15 that demonstrates a pattern of chronic and continuous disregard for the rights of others and the rules of society. Commonly occurring behavior includes such things as truancy, expulsion from school, delinquency, persistent lying, substance abuse, thievery, vandalism, and assault. Much of this antisocial behavior appears to be highly impulsive, inadequately motivated, and poorly planned.

2. Lack of remorse, guilt, or a sense of shame pertaining to antisocial acts.

3. Repeated failures to achieve lasting success in school, on the job, or in personal relationships. Particularly irresponsible in marital and parental roles.

4. Poor decision making, failure to learn from experience, and an inability to see self as others do (lack of insight).

5. Intelligent, superficially charming and likable; but underneath this facade there is a profound poverty of deep and lasting emotions, particularly those involving tenderness and nurturance.

6. Often combines intelligence and charm to con and manipulate others for personal gain.

7. Absence of any of the classic symptoms of other psychological disorders such as excessive anxiety, depression, irrational thought processes, or hallucinations.

8. Extremely egocentric and self-centered. Can pretend to love or care for others but appears to be lacking in genuine capacity to love.

A number of these characteristics are apparent in the following account of an interview with a man diagnosed as having an antisocial personality disorder:

In the early 1950s, I interviewed a 20-year-old man on the prison ward at Bellevue Psychiatric Hospital who had planned, conspired, and helped commit a double murder with ruthless disregard for the consequences of his actions. In a very businesslike way he had persuaded a companion, a schizophrenic who was the only son of two physicians, to poison them by having them both drink champagne, which the instigator had filled with arsenic, on the parents' wedding anniversary night at a "celebration" by this foursome. The police listed their deaths as a double suicide for more than a year. Meanwhile, a life insurance policy of $150,000 was shared by the two youths. The reason for their eventual arrest was my patient's need to impress his girlfriend by constantly boasting of his role in killing his friend's parents; she eventually informed the police about the crime. As a result, both young men were placed on the prison ward for examination and observation. The couple's son was diagnosed as a schizophrenic and my patient as a "psychopathic personality."

During my psychiatric interviews with him, he neither showed conscious remorse, guilt, shame, nor anxiety, nor did he admit feeling any of these emotions. He admitted readily to his part in the murder which he said was, to him, an experience similar to Oscar Wilde's "In Search of a New Experience." He did not have any remorse about his actions, except for the regret he felt about being apprehended and imprisoned. He admitted seeing nothing wrong with murder, stealing, or any other immoral or amoral actions, provided he or anyone else could "get away with it." He showed no psychotic illness or symptoms. (Hott, 1979)

Theoretical Perspectives on Antisocial Personality Disorder   In spite of several decades of extensive research, we still do not have a clear understanding of the origins of the antisocial personality disorder. The following paragraphs briefly consider the psychoanalytic, learning, and biological perspective on the etiology of this condition.

The psychoanalytic perspective looks to the childhood development of personality dynamics. Recall that Freud and his followers maintained that our sense of right and wrong emerges with the development of the superego sometime during the childhood years. It is the superego that places moral and ethical restraints on one's actions. Theorists with a psychoanalytic orientation suggest that because of some aberration in the normal course of early personality development, a person with an antisocial personality disorder fails to acquire a superego. Consequently, he or she acts to satisfy id instincts without regard for social mores and unhindered by guilt or shame.

Learning theorists propose a number of interpretations; perhaps the most prominent is the view that people with antisocial personality disorder act impulsively and repeatedly manifest antisocial misbehavior because they have not learned to avoid punishment. Such inappropriate behaviors persist despite repeated social and/or legal sanctions.

What is the source of this apparent indifference to punishment? Psychologist David Lykken (1957) reasoned that people with antisocial personality disorder may have far less anxiety about the possible consequences of punishment than do most people. To test this hypothesis, Lykken devised a complex learning task in which three groups of male subjects—imprisoned sociopaths, nonsociopathic inmates, and college students—were told that electric shocks would be randomly administered for incorrect responses as a stimulant for good performance. Successful mastery of the task was not made contingent on avoiding shocks and subjects were not told that avoiding shock was desirable or even possible. (In actuality, it was possible to learn to avoid shocks while mastering the task.) Although all three groups performed equally well on the learning task, there were considerable differences in the way they responded to the shocks. The college men eventually figured out how to respond in such a way as to decrease their chance of receiving a shock, but individuals with antisocial personality disorder demonstrated little or no such learning. (The nonsociopathic inmates exhibited shock-avoidance behavior that fell between these two extremes.) Lykken's findings have been supported by other research (Chesno & Kilman, 1975; Schachter & Latone, 1964); and other studies have also shown that antisocial personalities demonstrate considerably less emotional responsiveness to threatened pain than do nondisordered people (Borkovec, 1970; Hare, 1975; Hare et al., 1978; Mednick et al., 1982). Considered collectively, such findings suggest that punishments may have little meaning for people with antisocial personality disorder. Perhaps because of their lower degree of anticipatory anxiety, such people seem to express the attitude "you can't hurt me because I have little fear of pain."

Finally, we turn to the biological perspective on antisocial personality disorder. Several investigations have shown that 50 to 60 percent of people with antisocial personality disorder exhibit abnormal brain waves, compared to 10 to 15 percent of nondisordered people (Hare, 1970; Mednick et al., 1982; Syndulko, 1978). The most frequent of these aberrations in electroencephalogram (EEG) readings is an abnormally excessive amount of very slow brain-wave activity (5–8 cycles/second) (Mednick et al., 1981). Since this pattern is more typical of children than adults, some theorists have suggested that higher brain centers mature more slowly in antisocial personalities. One consequence of this might be reduced cortical control over impulsive actions.

The biological perspective is also supported by evidence linking this disorder to genetic factors. For example, some investigators have reported a much higher concordance rate for antisocial personality disorder among identical than among fraternal twins (Slater & Cowie, 1971). A number of studies have also shown that adoptees whose biological parent or parents were diagnosed as having an antisocial personality disorder were considerably more likely to develop the disorder than were adoptees whose biological parents were free of psychological disorders (Cadoret et al., 1987;

One theory suggests that those suffering from antisocial personality disorder act impulsively and repeatedly manifest antisocial misbehavior because they have not learned to avoid punishment.

Crowe, 1974; Hutchings & Mednick, 1974; Mednick et al., 1984; Schulsinger, 1972).

SUMMARY

DEFINING ABNORMALITY

1. While there is no universally accepted definition of abnormality, psychologists emphasize a common core of four criteria that distinguish between normal and abnormal behavior: atypicality, maladaptivity, psychological discomfort, and social unacceptability.
2. Any given psychological disorder may reflect only one or a combination of these four criteria.

CLASSIFYING PSYCHOLOGICAL DISORDERS

3. DSM-III-R is the most widely used scheme today for classifying and diagnosing psychological disorders throughout the world.

ANXIETY DISORDERS

4. A panic disorder is characterized by episodes of intense apprehension and overwhelming terror that occur as often as four or more times in a four week period.
5. Most people who have a panic disorder also exhibit symptoms of agoraphobia. Agoraphobia is characterized by intense fear of being in places or situations from which escape might be difficult or in which help might not be available in the event of a panic attack.
6. Less commonly people may suffer a panic disorder without symptoms of agoraphoria. In some people, agoraphobia exists without any symptoms or prior history of panic disorder.
7. Phobias, characterized by a persistent fear of and consequent avoidance of a specific object or situation, are among the most common psychological disorders.
8. A social phobia is a persistent, irrational fear of performing some specific behavior in the presence of other people.
9. A simple phobia is an irrational fear of a specific situation or object such a closed places or spiders.
10. An obsessive-compulsive disorder is characterized by a profound sense of anxiety that is reflected in persistent, unwanted, and unshakable thoughts and/or irresistible habitual actions in which one repeatedly engages in some ritualistic act.
11. Posttraumatic stress disorder occurs after a person experiences a psychologically traumatic event (or events) outside the normal range of human experience. PTSD is characterized by vivid flashbacks and avoidance of stimuli associated with the traumatic event or numbing of general responsiveness.
12. Generalized anxiety disorder is characterized by a chronic state of anxiety that is omnipresent across a wide range of situations.
13. Freud explained the anxiety disorders as a result of internal conflicts, particularly those involving sexual or aggressive impulses.
14. Behaviorists see conditioning as the source of the anxiety disorders.
15. The biological perspective on anxiety disorders includes evidence that genetic factors play a role in these disorders and that some people with unusually responsive nervous systems may be biologically predisposed to develop anxiety disorders.

SOMATOFORM DISORDERS

16. A person with somatization disorder typically has multiple and current physical symptoms for which medical attention is repeatedly sought, but which have no physical cause.
17. People with hypochondriasis also complain about a variety of physical difficulties. The primary difference between hypochondriasis and somatization disorder is that people manifesting the former are fearful that their symptoms indicate a serious disease(s), while people with somatization disorder typically do not progress beyond a concern with the symptoms themselves.
18. Conversion disorder is typically manifested as a sensory or motor system disturbance for which there is no known organic cause.
19. Freud believed that somatoform disorders stem from unresolved sexual impulses, particularly Oedipal and Electra complexes. According to the behavioral/learning perspective, a somatoform disorder allows a person to escape from or avoid the negative reinforcer of anxiety. There is little evidence that biological factors play a role in these disorders.

DISSOCIATIVE DISORDERS

20. A person with psychogenic amnesia experiences sudden loss of memory, usually after a particularly stressful or traumatic event.
21. Psychogenic fugue disorder combines amnesia with a more radical defensive maneuver—a "flight" away from an intolerable situation.
22. A person with a multiple personality disorder alternates between an original or primary personality and one or more secondary or subordinate personalities.
23. Psychoanalytic theory considers all dissociative disorders to be the result of massive reliance on repression to ward off unacceptable impulses, particularly those of a sexual nature. Behavioral/learning theory suggests that dissociative reactions may involve operant avoidance responses that are reinforced because they allow an individual to avoid anxiety associated with stressful events. There is no evidence that biological factors are involved in the development of these disorders.

MOOD DISORDERS

24. DSM-III-R distinguishes two major mood disorders: major depression (unipolar disorder) and bipolar (manic-depressive) disorder.
25. Major depression is characterized by deep depression. In contrast, bipolar disorder is characterized by intermittent episodes of both depression and mania (highly energized behavior reflective of euphoria and excessive mental and physical activity).

26. People with major depression typically manifest their symptoms over an extended period (from months to a year or longer), are unable to function effectively, and experience a breakdown in interpersonal relationships.

27. In some cases of bipolar depression, episodes of depression and mania may alternate regularly, with months or years of symptom-free normal functioning between the disordered mood states.

28. A manic episode often follows a three-stage course of accelerating intensity (mania, hypomania, and severe mania) in which an afflicted person's thinking and behavior become progressively more disorganized and psychotic-like.

29. According to the psychoanalytic perspective, mood disorders are rooted in relationships involving overdependency and ambivalent feelings of love and hate. When a person experiences loss (actual or threatened) of such a relationship, the unconscious hostility toward the lost person surfaces as anger that is turned back against oneself in the form of depression.

30. Behavioral and learning theorists see depression as emerging from the loss of a primary source of positive reinforcement through such things as separation from or death of a loved one or loss of a job.

31. Seligman's cognitive learning perspective on depression suggests that people become depressed when they believe that they have no control over the rewards and punishments in their lives.

32. There is compelling evidence linking genetics to mood disorders.

33. Present evidence strongly suggests that genetic predispositions toward mood disorders are expressed physiologically in the form of altered neurotransmitters in the brain. The permissive theory of mood disorders suggests that a deficiency in serotonin causes a breakdown in its stabilizing functions, allowing norepinephrine levels to fluctuate beyond the normal high and low boundaries. This can result in deep depression or excessive mania.

34. Many psychologists now believe that vulnerability to mood disorders involves an interaction of biological predispositions and psychosocial factors.

SCHIZOPHRENIC DISORDERS

35. The collection of primary or core symptoms that are characteristic of many forms of schizophrenia include disturbances in thought, perception, emotional expression, and speech, together with social withdrawal and diminished motivation.

36. Disorganized schizophrenia is characterized by marked disorganization and regression in thinking and behavioral patterns. A person with this disorder often behaves in an infantile manner and expresses wild swings in mood from fits of crying to episodes of uncontrollable giggling.

37. The distinguishing symptoms of catatonic schizophrenia are extreme psychomotor disturbances, which may range from stuporous immobility to wild excitement and agitation.

38. The dominant symptom of paranoid schizophrenia is the presence of well-organized delusional thoughts.

39. Freud believed that schizophrenia occurs when a person's ego either becomes overwhelmed with the id demands or is besieged by unbearable guilt. In both cases, the person undergoes a massive regression back to the oral stage of psychosexual development.

40. Ullman and Krasner provide a behavioral/learning perspective that suggests that schizophrenics either have not been reinforced adequately for responding to normal social stimuli, or perhaps have even been punished for such responses. As a consequence, normal patterns of responding to environmenal cues are extinguished or suppressed and the schizophrenic begins to respond to inappropriate stimuli, such as imaginary voices, to fill the resulting void.

41. An extensive body of research indicates that certain people are genetically predisposed to develop schizophrenia.

42. On the biochemical side, there is evidence that schizophrenia may be caused by errors of metabolism that cause the body to produce certain chemical that cause altered states of perception, thought, and feeling. There is also extensive evidence that schizophrenia is triggered either by abnormally high levels of the neurotransmitter dopamine or by above normal reactivity to this chemical.

43. According to the interactional model of schizophrenia, two factors are necessary for this disorder to develop. The first is a biological vulnerability to schizophrenia; the second is severe life stresses.

PERSONALITY DISORDERS

44. Personality disorders are grouped into three clusters. Disorders in the first cluster are characterized by odd and/or eccentric behavior; those in the second cluster share a common denominator of dramatic, emotional, or erratic behavior; and those in the third cluster are all characterized by anxious or fearful behavior.

45. Common characteristics of antisocial disorder include a history dating back to before age 15, lack of remorse or guilt over antisocial acts, repeated academic, vocational, and relationship failures, lack of insight, superficial charm, manipulative behavior, and extreme egocentricity.

46. Psychoanalytic theorists associate antisocial personality disorder with the failure to acquire a superego during early childhood development. Learning theorists suggest that people with antisocial personality disorder manifest antisocial behavior because they have not learned to avoid punishment. The biological perspective is based both on the speculation that higher brain centers may mature more slowly in antisocial personalities and evidence linking this disorder to genetic factors.

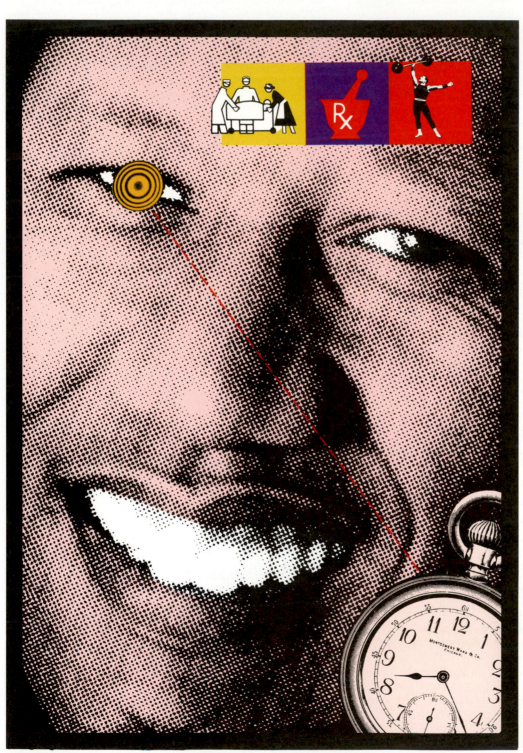

15 Therapy

Chapter 14 discussed a variety of psychological disorders. It did not deal with how these disorders are treated, however. That is the topic of this chapter, which describes the kinds of therapeutic interventions used to help people overcome or at least better cope with psychological problems. Although the final segment of this chapter deals with biomedical treatments such as drug therapy, our primary focus will be **psychotherapy**—any nonbiological, noninvasive psychological technique or procedure designed to improve a person's adjustment to life. *Noninvasive* means that no attempt is made to alter body physiology or function, as occurs with biomedical therapies. We will discover that psychotherapy takes many different forms; we will also see that these varied approaches share many common themes. Today psychotherapy is provided by a variety of clinicians, including clinical psychologists; clinical social workers; psychiatrists; and family, marital, school, and pastoral counselors.

In the following pages we discuss several different forms of psychotherapy, including psychoanalytic, humanistic, cognitive, behavior, and group therapies. We begin our discussion with an overview of psychoanalysis.

PSYCHOANALYSIS

The first formal model of psychotherapy was developed by Sigmund Freud at the end of the last century. Freud's technique, which became known as psychoanalysis, spawned a vast collection of observations and insights into the human condition which were eventually organized in the psychoanalytic theory of personality discussed in some detail in Chapter 13.

Psychoanalysis is based on a number of assumptions, the most fundamental of which is that disordered behavior results from unconscious conflicts and repressed urges, most of which are rooted in childhood experiences. A primary theme in many of these conflicts is the struggle between the id's sexual and aggressive impulses and the superego's moralistic commands. These conflicts generate anxiety, which the ego defense mechanisms may not be able to ward off. As the individual tries more desperate strategies for coping with anxiety, symptoms of psychological disturbance such as phobias and conversion disorders begin to appear. At this point the person is likely to seek psychotherapy.

Freud believed that the only way to help people gain true relief from severe anxiety was to enter their unconscious, search out the anxiety-causing conflict(s), and help them gain *insight* or conscious awareness of the repressed conflict. Only then can the conflict be resolved. Put another way, the aim of psychoanalysis is to make the unconscious conscious (Kutash & Wolf, 1986). To accomplish this goal, Freud developed a number of therapeutic techniques.

TECHNIQUES OF PSYCHOANALYSIS

Classical Freudian psychoanalysis was organized around several major techniques. Probably the most important of these are free association, dream analysis, and interpretations of resistance and transference (Blum, 1986; Kutash & Wolf, 1986).

Free Association   If you visited Freud as a patient, you would be asked to lie down on a comfortable couch. Freud would sit behind you, out of your line of vision—a practice that Freud believed helped to reduce distractions that might interfere with his patients' concentration. Freud would encourage you to say whatever came into your mind, no matter how silly or frivolous it might seem. As we saw in Chapter 13, Freud believed that through the process of free association, he could obtain glimpses of the unconscious conflicts and desires boiling just below the surface of conscious awareness. He also believed that the actual process of venting repressed feelings (*catharsis*) can result in at least a temporary reduction in tension. Freud realized that free association is not an easy process, and that it often takes several sessions before a person begins to open up.

Dream Analysis   Freud placed great emphasis on **dream analysis,** or interpretation of dreams. He believed that dreams are the "royal road to the unconscious" and thus a rich source of information about the hidden aspects of personality. Freud provided his patients with suggestions on how to remember their dreams. During a session of analysis patients were encouraged to report the apparent or *manifest* content of their dreams, then to work with Freud to uncover the hidden or *latent* content that often revealed the workings of the unconscious mind. Manifest and latent content of dreams are discussed in Chapter 5.

Resistance   Freud believed that what a patient does not say is as important as what is verbalized. He noted that his patients often exhibited **resistance,** or an unwillingness to discuss freely some aspects of their lives. This might show up as disrupting a session or changing the subject whenever a certain topic came up, consistently joking about something as though it were unimportant (or avoiding the topic altogether), or missing appointments or arriving late. Freud believed that it was only natural to resist delving into certain areas, because it is often very painful to bring unconscious conflicts into conscious awareness. Resistance was thus viewed as a sign that the therapist was getting close to the problem and the unconscious was struggling to avoid giving up its secrets. One of the major goals of Freudian psychoanalysis was to detect and break through these resistances.

Transference   People who undergo long-term psychotherapy often begin to relate to their therapists in much the same way as to a parent, lover, or some other important person in their lives. Thus, feelings such as anger, love, hostility, and dependency that characterize a person's relationships with other important people might be transferred to the therapist. Freud believed that this process of **transference** exposes long-repressed feelings, which the patient can then work through with the help of the analyst.

Freud used transference as a model to gain insight into the significant relationships of his patients. He wrote extensively about the benefits of

If you visited Freud as a patient, you would be asked to lie down on this comfortable couch. Freud would sit behind you, out of your line of vision—a practice that Freud believed helped to reduce distractions that might interfere with his patients' concentration.

transference as a way to make a patient's strong feelings more accessible and thus easier to interpret and work through. (He also wrote about the potential dangers of therapists doing the same thing—of letting their relationships with their patients become complicated by their own past experiences and emotional histories, a process he called *countertransference*.)

Interpretation To Freud it was important for analysts to interpret for patients the underlying meaning of their experiences, resistances, transferences, and dreams. He believed that such interpretations would help break through patients' defenses, providing them with insight into the causes of their neurotic behavior. This insight was also viewed as an excellent motivator to encourage a patient's active and willing participation in the therapeutic process. In the words of a contemporary psychoanalyst, "the acquisition of insight, the experiences of new and affectively meaningful understanding, has a powerful impact on the patient's continuing interest and investment in the analytic process" (Blum, 1986, p. 5). An example of psychoanalytic interpretation is provided in the following excerpt from a psychoanalytic therapy session:

> The patient is a middle-aged businessman whose marriage had been marked by repeated strife and quarrels. His sexual potency has become tenuous. At times he has suffered from premature ejaculation. At the beginning of one session, he began to complain about having to return to treatment after a long holiday weekend. He said, "I'm not so sure I'm glad to be back in treatment even though I didn't enjoy my visit to my parents. I feel I just have to be free." He then continued with a description of his home visit, which he said had been depressing. His mother was bossy, aggressive, manipulative, as always. He feels sorry for his father. . . . "She has a sharp tongue and a cruel mouth. Each time I see my father he seems to be getting smaller; pretty soon he will disappear and there will be nothing left of him. She does that to people. I always feel that she is hovering over me ready to swoop down on me. She has me intimidated just like my wife.
>
> I was furious this morning. When I came to get my car, I found that someone had parked in such a way that it was hemmed in. . . . I feel restrained by the city. . . . I hate the feeling of being stuck in an office from nine until five."

At this point, the therapist called to the patient's attention the fact that throughout the material, in many different ways, the patient was describing how he feared confinement, that he had a sense of being trapped.

The patient continued, "You know I have the same feeling about starting an affair with Mrs. X. She wants to and I guess I want to also. Getting involved is easy. It's getting uninvolved that concerns me . . . ."

In this material, the patient associates being trapped in a confined space with being trapped in the analysis and with being trapped in an affair with a woman.

At this point, the analyst is able to tell the patient that his fear of being trapped in an enclosed space is the conscious derivative of an unconscious fantasy in which he imagines that if he enters the woman's body with his penis, it will get stuck; he will not be able to extricate it; he may lose it.

The analyst goes on to say that one important goal of therapy would consist of making the patient aware of childhood sexual strivings towards his mother, of a wish to have relations with her, and of a concomitant fear growing out of the threatening nature of her personality, and that, like a hawk, she would swoop down upon him and devour him. These interpretations would give him insight into the causes of his impotence and his stormy relations with women, particularly his wife. (Arlow, 1984, pp. 37–39)

PRESENT STATUS OF PSYCHOANALYSIS

Earlier in this century psychoanalysis was the only form of psychotherapy available, and it remained the dominant force in psychotherapy until the early 1950s. Since that time, however, its popularity and influence have steadily declined, and today very few psychotherapists practice classical psychoanalysis as developed by Freud. Instead, psychoanalytically oriented therapists are likely to practice a modified version in which patients sit in a chair and face the therapist rather than lie on a couch. In addition, treatment tends to be briefer in duration, with less emphasis on restructuring a person's entire personality and more attention directed to the patient's current life and relationships. Contemporary psychoanalysts still attempt to help people gain insights into the unconscious roots of their problems, but early childhood conflicts are not emphasized as much. One thing that has not changed from the time of Freud is the fact that psychoanalysis simply does not work with severely disturbed or noncommunicative people. The best candidates for this type of therapy seem to be relatively young, intelligent, successful, and highly verbal individuals. As you might guess, the same observation might be made for several other forms of psychotherapy.

HUMANISTIC THERAPIES

Whereas the psychoanalytic perspective tends to take a pessimistic view of humans, viewing people who seek treatment as sick "patients" in need of a doctor's care, humanistic therapists are much more optimistic about the individual's potential for self-examination, personal growth, and self-fulfillment. People undergoing humanistic therapy are considered "clients" rather than patients, and they are treated as partners in the endeavor of therapy. Responsibility for the success of therapy is placed more on the shoulders of the client than on the therapist. Humanistic therapists see their primary goal as fostering psychological growth. This is accomplished in a special supportive environment that permits the client to achieve greater self-awareness, self-acceptance, personal fulfillment, and self-actualization. Therapists who operate within this theoretical framework tend to focus on the present rather than the past, and on conscious thoughts and feelings rather than repressed conflicts. They also believe that clients can take charge of their lives and be responsible for their actions rather than be victimized by obstacles outside of their awareness or control.

This philosophical framework has given rise to a number of specific therapeutic models. We will consider two: the person-centered approach of Carl Rogers, and Gestalt therapy, founded by Frederick Perls.

PERSON-CENTERED THERAPY

Person-centered therapy, a continually evolving and changing approach to psychotherapy, was first introduced in the 1940s by Carl Rogers. Rogers originally called his approach "client-centered therapy," but in 1974 he and his colleagues changed the name to "person-centered therapy," in order to focus more clearly on the human values that this approach emphasizes (Meador & Rogers, 1984). The central premise of this approach may be summarized by Rogers' own words:

> It is that the individual has within himself or herself vast resources for self-understanding, for altering his or her self-concept, attitudes, and self-directed behavior—and that these resources can be tapped if only a definable climate of facilitative psychological attitudes can be provided. (1986, p. 197)

This "definable climate" consists of three major elements: genuineness, a deep caring expressed as unconditional positive regard, and an empathic understanding.

Genuineness **Genuineness** is the ability of therapists to be in touch with their own current feelings or attitudes, and to allow these inner experiences to be apparent to the client. Therapists are closely attuned to what the client is expressing from moment to moment, and they openly share their immediate responses with the client. With such an approach to therapy, it is impossible for the therapist to put on a professional facade and play the "objective observer."

Unconditional Positive Regard The second essential ingredient in creating a climate for change is an attitude of **unconditional positive regard** on the part of person-centered therapists. This means that therapists experience a genuine, unconditionally accepting attitude toward whatever the client is at the moment, regardless of what the client may say or do. Therapists do not express approval or disapproval, only acceptance. Rather than offering interpretations or advice, therapists trust their clients' ability to draw upon inner resources for self-understanding, and to initiate positive changes for self-growth. The theory is that if clients can clearly see that someone else believes in their ability to grow, they may begin to believe in themselves (Meador & Rogers, 1984).

Empathic Understanding The third key element in the therapeutic environment is **empathic understanding** of the world as experienced by the client. This involves more than merely understanding the client's words. The therapist, in effect, tries to get "under the skin" of the client, to the point where the therapist may be aware even of feelings or meanings that the client is not yet aware of. To do this, the therapist uses a special listening technique known as **active listening.** Rogers called active listening "one of the most potent forces for change that I know" (1986, p. 198). It is used to indicate therapists' acceptance and understanding of what the client is saying, and it involves restating or responding to feelings the client is expressing but may not be fully aware of.

Active listening accomplishes a dual purpose. First, it may help clients better understand or clarify their feelings. Secondly, it lets the client know that the therapist both understands and accepts what he or she is saying. A person-centered therapist may ask for clarification now and then, but does not offer direct advice or interpretations. Rogers trusts the individual to discover his or her own capacity to resolve difficulties and experience self-growth: What is necessary is not someone to tell clients how to accomplish this, but simply the provision of a special environment in which clients may tap into their own resources.

A brief excerpt from one of Rogers' therapy sessions with a client called Jan illustrates his technique of active listening. At this point in the session, Jan is expressing concern about growing older, an issue that appears to involve impressions about how her mother lived and died and Jan's own fear of marriage:

JAN: Well my mother died at fifty-three, [CARL: Mm-hmm.] and she was a very young and very bright woman in many ways. But I think maybe that has something to do with it. I don't know.

CARL: You sort of felt that if your mother died at that early age, that was a possibility for you, too. [Pause] And time began to seem a lot shorter.

JAN: Right! When I look at my mother's life—and she had many talents—she unfortunately, towards the end, became a bitter woman. The world owed her a living. Now I don't want ever to be in that situation. And at this point in time, I'm not. I've had a very full life—both very exciting and very sad at times. I've learned a lot and I've a lot to learn. But—I *do* feel that what happened to my mother is happening to me.

CARL: So that remains sort of a specter. Part of your fear is: "Look what happened to my mother, and am I following in the same path [JAN: Right.] and will I feel that same fruitlessness, perhaps?"

JAN: [Long pause] Do you want to ask me some more questions, because I think that will help you to draw information out of me? I just can't—everything is a whirlwind, [CARL: Mm-hmm.] going around in circles.

CARL: Things are just going around so fast inside of you, you don't quite know where to [JAN: Where to begin.] take hold. I don't know whether you want to talk anymore about your relationship to your mother's life, your fear of that, or what?

(A long pause)

JAN: The older I get, though, the stronger I feel about the marriage situation. Now whether the two are related, I don't know. But the fear of getting married, and being committed, and children—I find very, very frightening. And it's getting stronger as I get older—

CARL: It's a fear of commitment, and a fear of having children? And all that seems to be a growing fear, all those fears seem to keep increasing.

JAN: Yes. I'm not afraid of commitment. For instance, when it comes to my work, to friendship, to doing certain things. But to me marriage is very—

CARL: So you're not a person who's irresponsible or anything like that— [JAN: No, not at all.] you're committed to your work, you're committed to friends. It's just that the notion of being tied into marriage—that's scary as hell. (Rogers, 1986, pp. 200–202)

GESTALT THERAPY

Frederick (Fritz) Perls (1948, 1973) took a somewhat different approach to therapy than Rogers. He believed that psychological problems often stem from people's inability to integrate the various parts of their personalities (such as thoughts, feelings, and actions) into a healthy, well-organized whole. His **Gestalt therapy** borrows the term *Gestalt* from perception psychology, for this collection of therapeutic techniques is designed to help a person bring together the alienated fragments of self into an integrated, unified whole. (Recall from Chapter 4 that Gestalt refers to the fact that the whole is different from the sum of its parts.)

Frederick (Fritz) Perls believed that psychological problems often stem from people's inability to integrate the various parts of their personalities into a healthy, well-organized whole.

Perls was originally trained as a Freudian psychoanalyst, and some of this tradition is reflected in his emphasis on bringing unconscious feelings and unresolved conflicts into awareness. However, unlike the psychoanalysts, he believed that therapy should focus on the present rather than the past, and, therefore, whatever unresolved conflicts might linger in a person's unconscious should be uncovered and brought to bear on the here and now.

The primary focus in Gestalt therapy is on moment-to-moment awareness of oneself (Simkin et al., 1986). The therapist's role is one of active *coexplorer* with clients, encouraging them to break through whatever defenses are preventing them from fully experiencing their feelings and thoughts. Gestalt therapists use a number of techniques to help people to become aware of who they are and what they are feeling. In *role playing,* for example, clients might act out feelings about significant others in their lives, or perhaps the therapist may assume the role of someone who is integral to a conflict in the client's life. Another common technique to help clients recognize and take responsibility for their own feelings is to train them to speak in the first person. For example, a client who says "Sometimes people are afraid to take that first step in initiating a relationship for fear of being rejected," would be encouraged to restate this concern by saying something like "I am afraid to reach out to another because I am afraid of being rejected."

As in person-centered therapy, the goal of Gestalt therapy is to help the person become his or her true self. However, the Gestaltists tend to be much more direct in their effort to achieve this end. They will not hesitate to point out an incongruence or discrepancy between what the client says and does. For instance, if a client protests that he is not angry even though his face is flushed and fists are clenched, the therapist might say something like "Get serious. Look at your clenched fists. Your face is red. I know an angry person when I see one, and you are angry. In fact, you're steaming!" Gestalt therapists are also not opposed to interpreting a client's verbal and nonverbal expressions, and they provide considerably more feedback than the person-centered therapists.

The following brief excerpt from a therapy session illustrates some of the important features of Gestalt therapy, including interpretation and phrasing feelings in the first person. The therapist is James Simkin, a respected Gestalt therapist who directed the Simkin Training Center in Gestalt Therapy up to his death in 1984. The client, Florence, is a 51-year-old marriage counselor who was previously married to an alcoholic. We pick up the therapy at a point where Florence is dealing with feeling old, lonely, and useless:

FLORENCE: I would like to be more comfortable.

JIM: What would you like me to do as you're getting yourself more comfortable?

FLORENCE: I, let's see, what do I want from you? I would like to explore with you inner structure—which procedure or structure or program to use—[Sighs] I'm split. [Sounds teary] *I don't want to do what I am doing.*

JIM: Right now?

FLORENCE: Right now, which is crying, [Sighs] and that other split part of me, I want to—I will get on and listen.

JIM: Uh-huh. If this feels right to you, I want you to say: "I don't want to cry and I am crying."

FLORENCE: I don't want to cry and I am crying.

JIM: "And I want to get on with living."

FLORENCE: And I want to get on with living. I don't want to cry and I am crying, and I want to get on with living.

JIM: How can I be useful, or how do you want to use me in this process?

FLORENCE: When I think of getting on with living, I think of Chet and I start to cry. When I am away from here. That is the only time I cry.

JIM: When you think of getting on with living and you think of Chet, you start to cry. Does Chet have anything to do with living, getting on with living?

FLORENCE: No. Well, nothing that comes to my head, I guess.

JIM: Chet, I am interested in getting on with living, and when I think of you, I start to cry.

FLORENCE: "And crying is part of my living," I would say to finish that sentence. (Simkin et al., 1986, p. 211)

COGNITIVE THERAPIES

The **cognitive therapies** (often called *cognitive-behavioral therapies*) are based on the premise that most psychological disorders result from distortions in a person's cognitions or thoughts. Psychotherapists who operate within the cognitive framework attempt to demonstrate to their clients how their distorted or irrational thoughts have contributed to their difficulties, and they use a variety of techniques to help them change these cognitions to more appropriate ones. Thus, while the goal of therapy may be to change people's maladaptive behavior and feelings, the method is to change what they think.

Over the last two decades, many psychotherapists have incorporated a cognitive orientation into their therapy practices. The primary models for the cognitive focus are provided by Albert Ellis' rational emotive therapy and by Aaron Beck's cognitive restructuring therapy.

RATIONAL-EMOTIVE THERAPY

Rational-emotive therapy (RET) was developed in the 1950s by Albert Ellis (1962, 1984, 1986), who was originally trained as a psychoanalyst. After years of "being allergic to the passivity of psychoanalysis" (1986, p. 277) and frustrated in his efforts to "reform" the Freudian approach to therapy, Ellis began experimenting with new methods. His efforts eventually culminated in his highly influential RET approach.

Rational-emotive therapy is based on the premise that psychological problems result when people interpret their experiences on the basis of certain self-defeating, irrational beliefs. The therapist's approach is to help people find the flaws in their thinking, to challenge or dispute these maladaptive cognitions (in Ellis' words, to "make mincemeat" of them), and then to guide clients to substitute more logical or realistic thoughts. Ellis provides a brief summation of this model in the following quote:

Rational-emotive therapy (RET) . . . holds that when a highly charged emotional consequence (C) follows a significant activating event (A), A may seem to, but actually does not, cause C. Instead, emotional consequences are largely created by B—the individual's *belief system*. When an undesirable emotional consequence occurs, such as severe anxiety, this can usually be traced to the person's irrational beliefs, and when these beliefs are effectively disputed (at point D), by challenging them rationally, the disturbed consequences disappear and eventually cease to recur. (Ellis, 1984, p. 196)

Figure 15.1 summarizes this model. A number of self-defeating, irrational beliefs that Ellis has found to be particularly disruptive are listed in Table 15.1.

Ellis and other RET therapists take a much more active or directive role than either the psychoanalytic or humanistic therapists. To minimize a client's self-defeating outlook, RET therapists employ an eclectic, or highly varied, collection of therapeutic techniques, including such things as con-

Albert Ellis

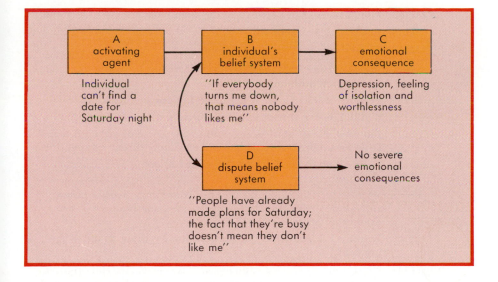

FIGURE 15.1 ELLIS' MODEL OF HOW PSYCHOLOGICAL PROBLEMS ARISE

frontation, persuasion, role playing, interpretation, behavior modification, and reflection of feelings. The focus of therapy is on the here-and-now, rather than on the client's history. In Ellis' words, rational-emotive therapists do not "spend a great deal of time . . . encouraging long tales of woes, sympathetically getting in tune with emotionalizing, or carefully and incisively reflecting feelings" (Ellis, 1984, p. 214). All of these methods may be used occasionally and briefly, but RET therapists shy away from what Ellis calls "long-winded dialogues," viewing them as indulgent. Rather than helping the client *feel* better during a therapy session, Ellis is more interested in helping clients *get* better.

In most cases rational-emotive therapists use a rapid-fire directive approach, quickly pinning the client down to a few irrational beliefs. This is demonstrated in the following excerpt from an initial session with a 25-year-old single woman who manages a computer-programming department.

> ELLIS: [reading from the biographical information form that the clients at the Institute for Rational-Emotive Therapy in New York City fill out before their first session]: Inability to control emotions; tremendous feelings of guilt, unworthiness, insecurity; constant depression; conflict between inner and outer self; overeating; drinking; diet pills. All right, what would you like me to start on first?

TABLE 15.1 *Some Self-Defeating Beliefs (According to Albert Ellis' Rational-Emotive Perspective)*

1. The idea that you can give yourself a global rating as a human and that your general worth and self-acceptance depend upon the goodness of your performances and the degree that people approve of you.
2. The idea that you must have sincere love and approval almost all of the time from all the people you find significant.
3. The idea that emotional misery comes from external pressures and that you have little ability to control your feelings or rid yourself of depression and hostility.
4. The idea that people and things should turn out better than they do; and that you have to view it as awful and horrible if you do not quickly find good solutions to life's hassles.
5. The idea that life proves awful, terrible, horrible, or catastrophic when things do not go the way you would like them to go.
6. The idea that your past remains all-important and that because something once strongly influenced your life, it has to keep determining your feelings and behavior today.

Source: Adapted from Ellis, 1962, 1975; Ellis & Harper, 1975

CLIENT: I don't know. I'm petrified at the moment!

ELLIS: You're petrified—of what?

CLIENT: Of you!

ELLIS: No, surely not of me—perhaps of yourself!

CLIENT: [laughs nervously]

ELLIS: Because of what I am going to do to you?

CLIENT: Right! You are threatening me, I guess.

ELLIS: But how? What am I doing? Obviously, I'm not going to take a knife and stab you. Now, in what way am I threatening you?

CLIENT: I guess I'm afraid, perhaps, of what I'm going to find out— about *me*.

ELLIS: Well, so let's suppose you find out something *dreadful* about you—that you're thinking foolishly, or something. Now why would that be awful?

CLIENT: Because I, I guess I'm the most important thing to me at the moment.

ELLIS: No, I don't think that's the answer. It's, I believe, the opposite! You're really the *least* important thing to you. You are prepared to beat yourself over the head if I tell you that you're acting foolishly. If you were not a *self-blamer*, then you wouldn't care what I said. It would be important to you—but you'd just go around correcting it. But if I tell you something really negative about you, you're going to beat yourself mercilessly. Aren't you?

CLIENT: Yes, I generally do.

ELLIS: All right. So perhaps *that's* what you're really afraid of. You're not afraid of me. You're afraid of *your* own self-criticism.

CLIENT: [sighs] All right.

ELLIS: So why do you have to criticize yourself? Suppose I find you're the worst person I ever met? Let's just suppose that. All right, now *why* would you have to criticize yourself?

CLIENT: [pause] I'd have to. I don't know any other behavior pattern, I guess, in this point of time. I always do. . . .

ELLIS: Yeah. But that, that isn't so. If you don't know how to ski or swim, you could learn. You can also learn not to condemn yourself, no matter what you do.

CLIENT: I don't know.

ELLIS: Well, the answer is: you don't know how. . . . Now, what are you *mainly* putting yourself down for right now?

CLIENT: I don't seem quite able, in this point of time, to break it down very neatly. The form gave me a great deal of trouble. Because my tendency is to say *everything*. I want to change everything; I'm depressed about everything.

ELLIS: Give me a couple of things, for example.

CLIENT: What I'm depressed about? I, uh, don't know that I have any purpose in life. I don't know what I—what I am. And I don't know in what direction I'm going.

ELLIS: Yeah. But that's—so you're saying "I'm ignorant!" [client nods] Well, what's so awful about being ignorant? It's too bad you're ignorant. It would be nicer if you weren't—if you *had* a purpose and *knew* where you were going. But just let's suppose the worst: for the rest of your life you didn't have a purpose, and you stayed this way. Let's suppose that. Now, why would *you* be so bad?

CLIENT: Because everyone *should* have a purpose!

ELLIS: Where did you get the *should*?

CLIENT: 'Cause it's what I believe in. [silence for a while]

ELLIS: I know. But think about it for a minute. You're obviously a bright woman; now, where did that *should* come from?

CLIENT: I, I don't know! I'm not thinking clearly at the moment. I'm too nervous! I'm sorry.

ELLIS: Well, but you *can* think clearly. "What [an idiot] I am for not thinking clearly!" You see you're blaming yourself for *that*. (Ellis, 1984, pp. 215–216)

You can see in this account that Ellis attempts to get the client to recognize her irrational ideas, such as the belief that it would be terrible if someone did not like her, and the idea that she is an inadequate person for not having a clear purpose in life. It is also apparent that Ellis is attempting to break down her tendency to be a self-blamer, and to get her to realize that even if her behavior is not what she would like it to be, this in no way reduces her value as a person.

Aaron Beck

COGNITIVE RESTRUCTURING THERAPY

Like rational-emotive therapy, **cognitive restructuring therapy** approaches therapy with the premise that psychological problems stem primarily from a few irrational beliefs that cause people to behave and emote in maladaptive ways. Aaron Beck, who developed cognitive restructuring therapy, believes that disturbed people typically have very negative self-images based on highly negative self-labels (1976).

For example, a recent college graduate may be depressed and plagued with a defeatist, "What's the use" attitude that is based on the belief that he is a mediocre person who is boring and unattractive to the other sex. Beck believes that people who do not value themselves have a tendency to overgeneralize from their experiences, and unconsciously to seek out other experiences that will confirm their poor self-image. Thus, if our hypothetical graduate were turned down on his first job interview and rebuffed by the attractive woman he met at a recent party, he may go on to apply for jobs that he is clearly not qualified for and perhaps to approach women that he senses are not interested in him—efforts that will validate his poor self-image because he will be rejected. Such people are likely to continue to be victimized by their own self-defeating behaviors unless salvaged through therapeutic intervention.

Like Ellis, Beck's aim is to get his clients to restructure their thinking, particularly their negative self-labels. His methods, however, tend to be less confrontative and more experiential. A common strategy is for the therapist and client to make a list of the client's misguided self-impressions (although, at this point, the client is not likely to consider them to be "misguided"), and then to agree on some "experiments" to test these assumptions. For example, a therapist working with our college graduate might suggest that he obtain several job interviews for positions well within his level of expertise. Since the therapist is interested in setting up experiments that will disprove rather than confirm the client's negative self-image, some time might be spent providing guidance on how to conduct himself effectively in an interview session. Some efforts might also be made to change the client's thoughts about unsuccessful interviews from such things as "I'll never get a good job," or "This rejection proves I am a mediocre person," to "Looks like I may have some difficulty getting the job I want," or "How annoying to be turned down."

BEHAVIOR THERAPIES

Traditional models of psychotherapy have emphasized the underlying causes of psychological disorders, which are viewed as distinct from those that mold so-called "normal behavior." **Behavior therapy** departs from this traditional conception. Its central thesis is that maladaptive behavior has been learned, and that it can be unlearned. Furthermore, the same principles that govern the learning of normal behavior also determine the acquisition of abnormal behaviors. Operating within this perspective, many behavior therapists believe that it is reasonable to describe many of the psychological disorders outlined in Chapter 14 as "behavior disorders." Behavior therapy draws heavily upon the extensive body of laboratory research on learning to devise strategies for helping people to unlearn maladaptive behavior patterns at the same time that they learn more adaptive behaviors.

Behavior therapy focuses on the person's current behaviors (or inaction) that are creating problems. These maladaptive patterns are considered to be the problem: Behavior therapists are not interested in restructuring personalities or searching for repressed conflicts. To change these disruptive behaviors, they enact appropriate changes in the interaction between the client and his or her environment (Kuehnel & Liberman, 1986).

For example, a person with a phobic fear of hospitals and medical personnel might be helped to gain exposure gradually to these feared situations until the anxiety is reduced to manageable levels. Parents of children who fight and squabble incessantly might be shown how to extinguish these inappropriate behaviors by no longer providing the inadvertent reward of paying attention to such activities. A person who responds sexually to inappropriate stimuli, such as small children, might be treated through repeated exposures to an aversive stimulus paired with the stimuli that elicit the deviant arousal pattern. The following paragraphs outline some of the more commonly employed behavior therapies.

CLASSICAL CONDITIONING THERAPIES

You may recall Chapter 6's account of the woman who was afraid of the biology laboratory. Her fear had been classically conditioned. Fears may often be acquired as a result of a traumatic classical conditioning experience. It follows, then, that classical conditioning principles should also be able to help people unlearn fears—and this is the basic premise of classical conditioning therapy.

For example, suppose you are afraid of the dark as a result of a particularly frightening experience in a darkened room that occurred some years ago. Before this experience, darkness (the conditioned stimulus) was a neutral or nonfrightening stimulus, but now, due to the pairing of the CS with the frightening event (an unconditioned stimulus), fear has been learned as a conditioned response.

We know that repeated exposures to darkness without the association of a frightening experience will eventually cause the conditioned fear response to extinguish. However, you would probably be unwilling to expose yourself to solitary darkness long enough for the fear response to be extinguished. In view of this limitation, behavior therapists have devised a number of *counterconditioning* strategies, in which a client is taught to substitute a new response—one that is incompatible with fear—to the threatening stimulus.

Systematic Desensitization   Perhaps the most widely used behavioral therapy technique is **systematic desensitization,** a strategy developed in the late 1950s by Joseph Wolpe (1958, 1982) to treat people who respond to specific stimulus situations with excessive anxiety or phobic fear. Wolpe's therapy method is based on the premise that people cannot be both relaxed and anxious at the same time. Therefore, he reasoned, if people can be trained to relax when confronted with fear-inducing stimuli, they will be able to overcome their anxiety. The key to his procedure is to proceed slowly and systematically.

For instance, in one case known to the authors, a young woman in her middle 20s sought treatment at the urging of her husband, who was tired of sleeping "with a searchlight on every night." The woman had a deeply rooted phobic fear of darkness that had generalized to situations

TABLE 15.2 *An Anxiety Hierarchy in Descending Order of Intensity*

1. At home at night, alone in bed, no light
2. Outside at night, alone, walking in a poorly lighted residential area
3. At home, at night, alone, not in bed, power failure
4. At home at night, in bed with husband, no light
5. Outside at night, with a friend or husband, walking in a poorly lighted residential area
6. At home at night, husband present, not in bed, power failure
7. Outside at night, alone, walking in a well-lighted commercial area
8. Outside at night, with a friend or husband, walking in a well-lighted commercial area
9. Outside at dusk, walking alone in a residential area
10. Outside at dusk, with a friend or husband, walking in a residential area
11. Outside at dusk, with a friend or husband, walking in a commercial area

other than just being in bed with the lights off. She was afraid to go anywhere it was likely to be dark, particularly if she had to go alone.

The first step in treating Anne (not her real name) was to analyze her problem carefully, step by step. The goal of treatment was determined to be for the client to be unafraid of the dark no matter where she might encounter it—at home in bed, outside at night walking to a friend's house, and so forth. The next step was to construct a hierarchy of situations that triggered her fear of darkness, with the most intense fear-inducing situation at the top of the list and the least at the bottom. As Table 15.2 shows, this woman's fear hierarchy ranged from a mildly anxiety-provoking situation of walking in a commercial area at dusk with a companion to the intensely frightening situation of being in bed alone with no lights on.

The next phase of treatment was to teach the client how to relax by first training her to recognize muscle tension in various parts of her body and then how to relax all of the various muscle groups in a progressive fashion until she was in a state of complete, tranquil relaxation. Finally, when the woman was in a state of complete relaxation, she was told to imagine as vividly as possible the scene at the bottom of her anxiety hierarchy. If at any time she found herself becoming anxious, she was instructed to signal by raising a finger, to switch the image off immediately, and to concentrate again on becoming deeply relaxed. When she was able to imagine this mildly threatening situation repeatedly without experiencing any anxiety, her attention was directed to the next image in the hierarchy. In this fashion, she was able to move up the hierarchy gradually and systematically until, after several sessions, she could imagine any of the scenes on her list with no discomfort.

The final phase of treatment was to instruct the client to confront the anxiety-producing stimuli in the real world. Here again, she was encouraged to move slowly, starting with situations at the bottom of her anxiety hierarchy. As she received firsthand evidence that she was able to apply her newly acquired ability to relax in real life, she was encouraged to expose herself gradually to even the most fearful situation listed in the hierarchy. The treatment was successful: several months after therapy was terminated, there was still no "searchlight" in the couple's bedroom at night.

Research has shown that systematic desensitization is often effective in dealing with specific fears and anxieties, such as those that occur in many phobic disorders. It is less effective in treating the diffuse fear that accompanies conditions such as generalized anxiety disorder. Compared with other therapeutic approaches to dealing with specific fears and phobias, systematic desensitization often fares best. For example, in one study systematic desensitization was found to be considerably more effective in alleviating stage fright than psychoanalytically oriented insight therapy or a placebo condition in which people were provided kind attention and a fake "tranquilizer" (Paul, 1966). Table 15.3 summarizes these findings.

Joseph Wolpe

TABLE 15.3 *Percentage of Clients Who Demonstrate Various Levels of Improvement in Their Stage-Fright Condition after Being Exposed to One of Three Treatment Conditions or No Treatment at All*

Treatment	Number of Cases	Unimproved	Slightly Improved	Improved	Much Improved
Desensitization	15	0%	0%	14%	86%
Insight (psychoanalytic)	15	7%	47%	27%	20%
Attention (placebo)	15	20%	33%	47%	0%
No treatment (control)	29	55%	28%	17%	0%

Source: From Paul, 1966.

Aversive Conditioning   Aversive conditioning is another variety of classical conditioning behavior therapy that is quite different from systematic desensitization. Here, the goal is to substitute a negative (aversive) response for a positive response to an inappropriate or harmful stimulus such as nicotine or alcohol. For example, an alcoholic's behavior is normally characterized by excessive attraction to the stimulus of alcoholic drinks. However, suppose a chronic drinker is given a drug that induces nausea and vomiting when combined with alcohol. The drug alone will not make the person sick, but immediately after alcohol enters the system, the person experiences violent nausea and vomiting. It does not take many pairings of the CS, alcohol, and the UCS, sickness, before the alcohol begins to elicit an aversive fear response (CR). This conditioned aversion response may generalize to a variety of alcohol-related stimuli including the taste and smell of alcohol and visual displays of containers of alcohol. (Effective therapeutic intervention using this strategy actually combines both classical and operant conditioning. Once the classically conditioned fear of alcohol is established, an alcoholic person is inclined to avoid future contact with alcohol [operant response] to alleviate his or her fear of this substance [negative reinforcement]. This is a form of two-process learning, described in Chapter 6.)

Aversive conditioning is not a pleasant experience, and you may wonder why anyone would undergo it voluntarily. The answer is that people who are desperate to overcome their alcohol dependency, or highly motivated to stop smoking, may consider continuation of the undesired behavior to be more aversive than the treatment. Clearly, aversive conditioning is not an appropriate treatment strategy unless the client consents to it.

AVERSIVE THERAPY: DOES IT WORK?

Aside from any ethical issues that may have been raised in your mind by our discussion of aversive conditioning, can you think of any pragmatic issues, related to persistence of therapeutic effects, that this approach to therapy raises? Think a moment before reading on.

Common sense might suggest that any beneficial effects associated with aversive therapy would only be short-lived. People have the cognitive ability to discriminate between the clinical situation in which the aversive condition occurs and situations in the real world. Thus, why not expect clients to resume the harmful behavior as soon as treatment ends?

To answer that question, let us consider a hypothetical example. If you have ever overindulged yourself in a favorite food and then become violently ill, the odds are good that you acquired an aversion for the food even though you knew that you got sick only because you ate too much. Such a classically conditioned fear or aversion response is often highly resistant to extinction, and that is one reason why this treatment is effective. (Nevertheless, when the desire to engage in the inappropriate behavior is very strong, it is still possible to overcome the aversive conditioning effect.)

A number of studies have provided encouraging findings about the use of this therapeutic intervention in treating alcohol or nicotine addiction. For example, one study of 685 alcoholics who underwent an intensive aversive therapy program, followed by several booster treatments over a period of several months, showed that 63 percent still avoided alcohol one year later. Three years later this figure had changed to approximately one third still abstaining (Wiens & Menustik, 1983). A 30 percent success rate over a period of four years is significant in an area of treatment characterized by high recidivism rates.

OPERANT CONDITIONING THERAPIES

We learned in Chapter 6 that behaviors under our voluntary control are strongly influenced by their consequences. Reinforcers are powerful molders of behavior, and by manipulating reinforcers, behavior therapists are often able to exert a strong influence upon behavior. Three versions of **operant conditioning therapies** (sometimes called *behavior modification* techniques) include attempting to induce desired behavior through *positive reinforcement,* or striving to eliminate undesirable or maladaptive behavior through either *extinction* or *punishment.*

Positive Reinforcement The **positive reinforcement therapy** technique is based on the fact that people are strongly inclined to behave in ways that produce positive consequences or rewards. This approach to behavior therapy involves identifying the behavior that is desired and determining one or more rewards that will be effective motivators, then providing the reward contingent upon the client's voluntarily manifesting the desired behavior.

For instance, in one case reported by Arthur Bachrach and his associates (1965), a young anorexic woman had so drastically curtailed her eating that she was hospitalized, in danger of dying. When all else had failed, behavior therapy was applied to the woman, who now weighed only 47 pounds. In the first step of treatment, the therapist determined an appropriate reinforcer that could be made contingent upon eating. A social reinforcer was chosen: the therapist sat with her when a meal was delivered, and each time she swallowed a bite of food, she was rewarded by the therapist talking to her and generally being attentive. If she refused to eat, the therapist left the room and she remained alone until the next meal was served. In this manner her eating behavior was gradually increased and other rewards were introduced contingent upon her continuing to eat and gain weight. For example, other people joined her at mealtime or she was rewarded by having her hair done after an appropriate gain in weight. This positive reinforcement method succeeded in inducing a dramatic gain in weight, and she was eventually discharged from the hospital. Her parents were instructed in ways to continue reinforcing her for appropriate eating behaviors, and a follow-up almost three years later revealed that she was maintaining an adequate weight.

Positive reinforcement is also a powerful tool for shaping desirable behaviors in everyday life. For example, a parent who wishes a child to use better table manners, or to be more responsible about room-cleaning chores, will probably find that reinforcing positive efforts in this direction will be a more effective agent of behavior change than punishment. As we saw in Chapter 6, the most effective approach is often *shaping*, which involves systematically rewarding closer and closer approximations to the final desired behavior. For example, a child who picks up only a few toys might at first be provided some little reward or praise, then later the reward may be made contingent upon picking up more and more toys until eventually only a complete room cleaning is rewarded.

Extinction Technique Just as positive reinforcement may be used to establish appropriate behaviors, it may also be possible to eliminate unde-

Positive reinforcement is a powerful tool for shaping desirable behaviors in everyday life. How might these parents shape this child's behavior so that he becomes more involved in the day-to-day responsibilities of his family?

sired behaviors by eliminating the reinforcers that maintain them. For this technique to be effective, the behavior therapist must be able both to identify and to eliminate the reinforcer(s) that is maintaining the maladaptive behavior. This may not always be as easy as it sounds. An example is the case of Norma (not her real name), a 20-year-old woman known to the authors. Norma reluctantly sought help for a problem described by her parents as "compulsive face picking." According to both her parents and fiancé, Norma could not seem to keep her hands off her face. Whenever she found some little blemish or pimple, she would pick and scratch at it until it became a bleeding sore. As a result, her face was marked by several unsightly sores. This situation greatly distressed everybody but Norma, who seemed remarkably unconcerned. Both the parents and the fiancé had tried several tactics to get Norma to stop picking her face, including appealing to her vanity ("You are such an attractive person when your face is clear"), pleading ("I can't stand to see you do that to yourself"), and threats ("I won't be seen with you in public with your face in such a bad state").

What possible reinforcers could be maintaining Norma's behaviors? As we learned in Chapter 6, attention can be a powerful reinforcer for behavior, even when the actual form of the attention may be negative. In this case, too, the therapist determined that Norma's face picking was maintained by the great deal of attention that both her parents and her fiancé directed toward this behavior. As long as Norma continued picking her face, the pattern of inadvertent reinforcements was maintained, and she would likely remain the center of attention.

Realizing this, the therapist instructed Norma's parents and fiancé to ignore her face picking entirely. They were cautioned that it would probably get worse before improving. (At the beginning of extinction training, people and other animals typically increase the intensity of no-longer-reinforced behaviors before discarding them.) True to prediction, Norma did exhibit a temporary increase in her face picking. However, when it was clear that this behavior would no longer generate attention, it was quickly extinguished. (To prevent it from reappearing, the therapist encouraged both the parents and the fiancé to provide plenty of loving attention and support to Norma contingent upon a variety of healthy, adaptive behaviors.)

Punishment   We have previously learned how the use of a negative stimulus such as an electric shock can be used in aversion therapy to classically condition a negative response to an attractive but harmful stimulus. Aversive stimuli can also be used to punish voluntary maladaptive responses.

An example is the case of a nine-month-old infant, whose life was endangered by a chronic pattern of vomiting and regurgitating food (Lang & Melamed, 1969). From a six-month weight of 17 pounds, the infant had dropped to an emaciated 12 pounds. Attempts to feed him through a tube inserted through his nasal passage were a losing cause, since he continued to regurgitate his food within minutes. The behavior therapists assigned to this case carefully evaluated the vomiting behavior. Using electrical recordings of muscular activity, they found they could detect when the infant was about to vomit. On this basis they designed a treatment strategy. Each time electrical recordings signaled that the infant was about to vomit, the therapists delivered a brief shock to his leg. This electrical shock was immediately effective in reducing the vomiting, and after a few short training sessions the undesirable behavior had completely ceased. Within a relatively short period the child had gained considerable weight and was well enough to be discharged from the hospital (see Figure 15.2). A follow-up one year later revealed a continuation of healthy development, with no recurrences of the vomiting behavior.

Students are often disturbed by this case, on two counts. The first is ethical: Many people cringe at the prospect of a helpless infant getting electric shocks. It is true that there are ethical implications of using punish-

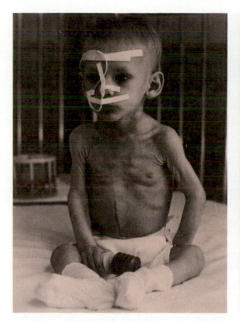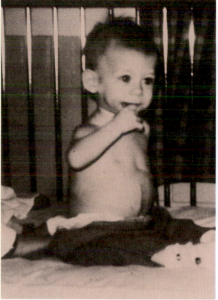

FIGURE 15.2 THE APPEARANCE OF A NINE-MONTH-OLD INFANT BEFORE AND AFTER APPLICATION OF ELECTRIC SHOCK TO PUNISH VOLUNTARY, MALADAPTIVE VOMITING AND REGURGITATION OF FOOD

(*Source:* From Lang & Melamed, 1969; courtesy of Peter Lang)

ment to modify behavior, and such an approach should only be given consideration as a last resort. Nevertheless, in view of the fact that the infant was dangerously close to dying, we believe that this drastic approach to treatment was justified.

The second reservation expressed by many students is a practical one. We have learned that punishment generally produces only a temporary suppression of undesirable behavior, and that it is unlikely to have a lasting effect unless another, reinforcement-inducing behavior pattern is substituted for the suppressed behavior. Why was punishment so effective in this case? We can assume that the infant's reduced hunger and improved physical well-being provided adequate reinforcement to maintain the new behavior pattern. Thus, there was no return to the vomiting behavior even after the electric shocks ceased.

MODELING

As we saw in Chapter 6, the social-learning theorists have convincingly demonstrated that some kinds of learning cannot be explained solely by classical or operant conditioning. One kind of alternative learning discussed by Albert Bandura (1986) and other social-learning theorists is behavior change through *modeling* or observing others. Modeling can be a helpful therapy technique for extinguishing irrational fears or for establishing new, more adaptive behaviors.

For example, suppose you are deathly afraid of snakes. Although this phobia might be treated by systematic desensitization, modeling might also be effective: You might observe others handling snakes with no visible adverse results. Modeling may be *live*, or it may take place through films or videotapes. The beneficial, antiphobia effects of this modeling technique may be enhanced even further if relaxation training is also used to ensure the client is in a calm, tranquil state while observing the models.

Modeling has wide application in treating people with phobias. In one study, children who were extremely fearful about undergoing a dental exam were first exposed to a 10-minute videotape in which a child model appeared to be happy and relaxed while experiencing several dental procedures (X-rays, oral exam, etc.). These children exhibited markedly fewer signs of distress during the actual exam than a matched control group of children who were not exposed to the modeling procedure (Crooks, 1969).

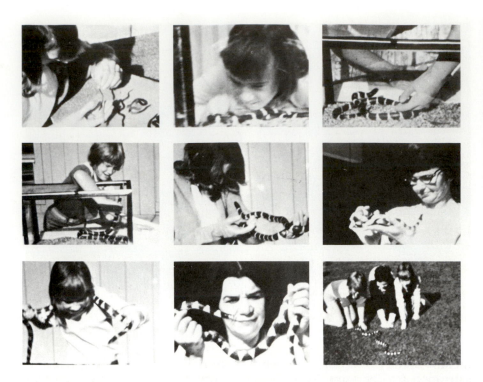

Suppose you are deathly afraid of snakes. You might overcome this aversion by observing others handling snakes with no visible adverse results.

Modeling may also be helpful in establishing new, more appropriate responses. For example, people who are shy or nonassertive may observe live or filmed vignettes of models acting out scenes in which people effectively initiate social contacts or behave in an appropriately assertive way. Ideally, these behaviors are shown to produce rewards, so that the observers may achieve a kind of vicarious reinforcement by identifying with the model. Clients are often asked to participate actively in the desired behavior after viewing the models. In one study, modeling and active role playing were found to be considerably more effective than insight-oriented therapy in establishing appropriate assertive behaviors (Gormally et al., 1975).

GROUP THERAPY

To this point in the chapter, we have been discussing individual therapy in which one client meets alone with a therapist. However, virtually all the major schools of psychotherapy also treat people in groups of 3 or more. This form of therapy, known as **group therapy,** varies widely according to group composition. Large groups may consist of one or two group leaders and five to seven clients, who may represent a heterogeneous mix of different problems or a more homogeneous group of people with the same basic problems (such as drug abusers, people with eating disorders, or shy people). Groups may also be composed of entire families or a couple being treated as a collective unit, usually by only one therapist.

> ### WHAT BENEFITS OF GROUP THERAPY ARE NOT TYPICALLY OBTAINED IN INDIVIDUAL THERAPY?
>
> **Psychologists and their clients often prefer group over individual therapy for a number of reasons. Can you think of some benefits that you might achieve from participating in group therapy that are less likely to occur in individual therapy? See how many advantages you can think of before reading on.**

One of the greatest advantages of group therapy is simply that it operates in a group setting. Many of the problems that lead people to seek

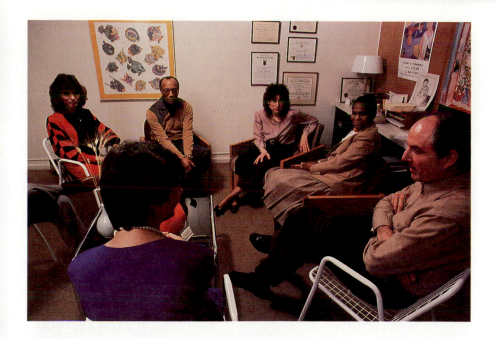

What do you think are the benefits you might achieve in group therapy that are less likely to occur in individual therapy? Why do you think some people prefer individual therapy over group therapy?

therapy in the first place involve getting along with others, and these problems can often be brought out into the open more easily within a group environment.

This setting also has advantages for individual members of a group. Many participants in groups are immediately struck by the realization that they are not alone—a "my gosh, other people are just as fouled up as me" awareness. This sense of solidarity with others, together with feelings of safety and support, can be very comforting, encouraging participants to open up and share their problems more readily than they might in individual therapy.

Group-therapy participants have the advantage of receiving feedback not only from the group leader, but also from other members of the group, whose insights and observations can be very beneficial. Groups can provide a much more true-to-life environment than individual therapy for trying out new behaviors and ways of relating to others. The feedback from other group members, which is often considerably more direct than in the outside world, may be extremely helpful in modifying flaws in interpersonal skills.

In addition to receiving advice and suggestions from other members, group members also have an opportunity to observe how others work out their problems. Participants in groups may also experience a boon to their self-esteem as a result of helping other members.

A final advantage of group therapy is a practical one. Therapy can be expensive, particularly when it extends over many months: Six months of weekly individual sessions with a psychologist or psychiatrist may cost as much as $1,200 to $2,400. The cost of group therapy, shared across several clients, is likely to be considerably less than this amount. Furthermore, since groups typically meet once a week for one and a half to two hours, the amount of time spent in a therapeutic setting is increased by 50 to 100 percent over individual therapy. (Of course, it is also true that the amount of individual attention will be considerably less than in one-on-one therapy.)

All kinds of problems may be effectively treated in a group setting, including substance abuse, eating disorders, child abuse, the effects of sexual victimization, problems expressing feelings to others, shyness and lack of assertiveness, social incompetence, compulsive gambling, and difficulties in being intimate with others. People most likely to benefit from group therapy are those who can communicate thoughts and feelings and who are motivated to be active participants. Poor candidates are people who are withdrawn, uncommunicative, combative, antisocial, or so depressed or unreachable that they are likely to frustrate other group members (Bloch, 1979). We now look at two different forms of group therapy: family therapy and couple therapy.

FAMILY THERAPY

Family therapy has gained steadily in popularity and respect over the last few decades. Family therapy differs from therapy with groups of unrelated individuals in that family units bring to therapy a shared history of patterns of interrelationships. The family therapist is more likely to take an active role as model or teacher than are other group leaders, who frequently define their role as facilitator rather than director (Yalom, 1975).

Family therapy is based on the premise that an individual's psychological adjustment is profoundly influenced by patterns of social interaction within the family unit. Families characterized by strife, poor communication, and pathological interaction patterns can foster psychological difficulties in one or more individual members. The assumption that individual pathology has its roots in a disturbed family leads to the logical deduction that changing patterns of interaction in a disturbed family will affect those family members who have adjustment problems (Kutash & Wolf, 1986). The task of the family therapist is to alter maladaptive relationship patterns, so that symptoms of disturbed behavior diminish or disappear (Foley, 1984).

Family therapists use a number of techniques to change maladaptive patterns in a disturbed family. One strategy may be to alter patterns of alliances that are damaging to one or more family members. For instance, suppose an alliance has formed between a mother and her son, so that the father feels left out, angry, and depressed—feelings that may cause the father to act hostilely toward his son and to withdraw from his wife. The therapist may seek to restructure patterns of family interaction by encouraging the father to take a more active interest in his son's experiences and to be more involved in making decisions that directly affect his son (Kendall & Norton-Ford, 1982).

Family therapists also aim to have all family members redefine problems as a family responsibility rather than projecting the blame onto only one member. For example, a teenage daughter's school truancy and drug use might be viewed as reflecting problem behavior of all family members. Perhaps she has reasoned that if she acts bad enough, her feuding parents will be forced to focus on her problems and thus stop battling with each other.

In summary, family therapists treat the entire family as the patient as they seek to educate all members about what kinds of maladaptive patterns are occurring within the family unit, how each member contributes to these problems, and what can be done to change the disruptive patterns to a more healthy system of interrelationships. Family therapy often tends to be relatively short-term, consisting of once-a-week sessions for several weeks or a few months. The family may always be seen as an entire unit, although occasionally separate sessions may be scheduled for one or more members.

COUPLE THERAPY

Assume that you are having serious conflicts with your spouse. Perhaps you are struggling with role definitions, a breakdown in communication, financial decisions, or matters related to expressing intimacy. You are determined to get help but do not know whether you should seek treatment as an individual, encourage your partner to get help (maybe you think the problem is primarily his or hers), or go for treatment together. Therapists who practice couple therapy agree with the underlying premise of family therapy, that difficulties that exist within a primary unit, in this case a couple, are best treated within the context of the unit rather than through individual therapy. Today conjoint or **couple therapy**—working with the two partners together—has become the most common approach for treating relationship problems within a primary couple, married or unmarried (Sager, 1986).

Because unclear, ambiguous, or mixed messages often contribute to relationship conflicts, couple therapists often focus on improving communication between partners. However, the fact that a couple knows how to communicate effectively is no guarantee that they will apply this knowledge in their relationship. Therapists often need to probe for "hidden agendas" or underlying reasons why one or both partners seem unwilling or unable to explore ways to improve the level of verbal, emotional, and physical intimacy between them.

EVALUATING PSYCHOTHERAPY

We have discussed several approaches to psychotherapy without stopping to evaluate them or discuss whether one approach is more effective than another. This section first deals with this issue, addressing the questions of whether psychotherapy is better than no therapy at all and whether one type of psychotherapy is better than another. It concludes by describing common features that are shared by the various approaches to psychotherapy.

IS PSYCHOTHERAPY MORE BENEFICIAL THAN NO THERAPY?

You may have heard people criticize psychotherapy, saying that with a little bit of gumption, people can get well on their own. Even though many people who have gone through therapy swear by it, these critics answer that it is normal for people to defend an investment of so much time and money. Indeed, it has been shown that clients may work very hard to find something positive to say about their therapists (Zilbergeld, 1983). What does the record say—are people with adjustment problems just as well off if they do not see a therapist?

In the effort to answer this question, a number of controlled research studies have attempted to evaluate psychotherapy. The first of these studies was published in 1952 by an English psychologist, Hans Eysenck. Eysenck was well aware that many people with psychological problems get well on their own without any formal treatment—a process called *spontaneous remission*. Therefore he compared the success rates of psychotherapy reported in 24 studies with spontaneous remission rates among untreated psychologically disturbed individuals. (To determine this, he collected data such as the number of people on waiting lists for treatment who spontaneously improved and therefore removed themselves as candidates for psychotherapy.) Eysenck reported that approximately two out of every three people treated with psychotherapy improved markedly. However, he also reported approximately the same two-thirds improvement rate among disturbed people who received no treatment.

Critics questioned the criteria Eysenck used to assess therapy outcomes; they also argued that people in Eysenck's untreated control group differed in important ways from individuals who received treatment. In the late 1970s, researchers reanalyzed his clinical data and discovered that his reported spontaneous remission rate of almost 70 percent was actually closer to 40 percent (Bergin & Lambert, 1978). Thus, Eysenck's research was eventually discredited.

Clinical researchers then set out to design better studies. More effective criteria of success were developed, including scores on psychological tests, self-ratings, ratings by clinicians not involved in treating subjects, and

FIGURE 15.3 NORMAL DISTRIBUTION CURVES SHOWING IMPROVEMENT OUTCOMES FOR PSYCHOTHERAPY CLIENTS AS OPPOSED TO UNTREATED PATIENTS

(*Source:* Adapted from Smith et al., 1980)

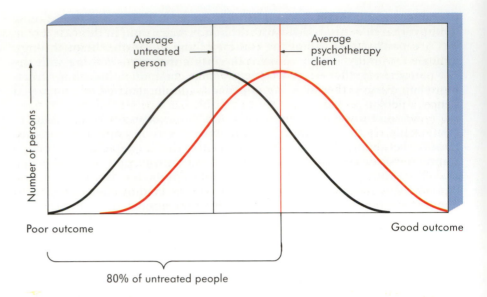

recidivism rates (such as whether or not additional therapy was sought in a given period of time after initial treatment ended, or what percentage of hospitalized patients were readmitted after discharge). Drawing upon data from these better designed comparison studies, Lester Luborsky and his associates (1975) reported that 80 percent of the studies found significant benefits associated with psychotherapy. In most cases, these improvement rates were markedly better than those for untreated individuals.

Several years later the most ambitious evaluation of psychotherapy outcomes to date was reported by Mary Lee Smith, Gene Glass, and Thomas Miller (1980). These researchers applied a complex statistical procedure called *meta-analysis* to combine and collectively analyze data from 475 psychotherapy outcome studies. Their findings confirmed those of the Luborsky group. On the average, clients treated by psychotherapy were found to score higher on a number of outcome measures than untreated people with similar problems and characteristics. As Figure 15.3 shows, however, there is a considerable overlap in the outcomes reported for the untreated or control samples and the treatment groups. The fact that many untreated people do experience spontaneous improvement with time is testimony to people's great capacity for self-growth and health.

IS ONE TYPE OF PSYCHOTHERAPY MORE EFFECTIVE THAN ANOTHER?

The Smith study discussed in the preceding section also looked at the success rates of different types of therapy. Its finding: that no particular type of therapy is *significantly* superior to others. From an overall perspective, only slight differences emerged—for instance, psychoanalytic and person-centered approaches were approximately equal in effectiveness, and both were slightly less effective than the cognitive and behavior therapies. Furthermore, whether therapy took place in individual or group settings, over the short term or the long term, seemed to have little impact on its effectiveness.

If all psychotherapies are roughly equal in effectiveness, does it follow that most therapists are equally effective? The answer is no. As in any other profession, most psychotherapists continue to improve and grow more effective as they accumulate experience. There is just so much that one can learn in graduate school or from books. Most therapists are in agreement that on-the-job training is the best way to acquire effective therapeutic skills. Research supports the assumption that, all things being equal, experienced psychotherapists in any of the major theoretical frameworks tend to achieve better results than do novice therapists (Gurman & Raxin, 1977; Russell, 1981). This does not mean that all novice therapists have questionable skills, nor that some relatively inexperienced therapists may not be more effective in treating a particular individual than some other, more experienced therapist. We are only suggesting that based on the evidence, a person seeking a therapist probably has a better chance of achieving good results with someone with several years of experience.

Research also indicates that the most effective psychotherapists are people who genuinely care about their clients and who are able to establish a warm, empathic relationship that helps to foster respect, trust, and the feeling of being cared for (Strupp, 1984). A clinician who is reserved, aloof, and emotionally detached is not likely to provide the kind of warm, supportive atmosphere that is essential to therapeutic progress.

COMMON FEATURES OF PSYCHOTHERAPEUTIC APPROACHES

One reason why researchers have found so little difference in the effectiveness of the various psychotherapy methods may be the fact that certain common features are shared by almost all styles of therapy. It is possible that the equivalency of their healing power stems from these commonalities. Researchers Jerome Frank (1982) and Marvin Goldfield (Goldfield & Padawer, 1982) have extensively analyzed the commonalities of different psychotherapies, and we will explore some of their findings.

Combating the Client's Demoralization   People who seek the services of a psychotherapist are typically demoralized by anxiety, depression, and a poor self-image, and they often have little hope for escaping from their misery. By inspiring expectations of help, providing new learning experiences, and enhancing people's sense of self-worth and efficiency, psychotherapists may be powerful morale builders. Virtually all effective psychotherapists, regardless of their particular methodology, tend to inspire in their clients a sense of hope and a belief that things will get better. These morale-boosting expectations may well contribute to a reduction in symptoms and an improved sense of well-being (Jacobson, 1968; Prioleau et al., 1983).

Providing a Rationale for Symptoms and Treatment   Regardless of their theoretical orientation, virtually all therapists provide their clients with a plausible explanation for their symptoms and a logical scheme for alleviating them. As clients rethink the nature of their problems and possible solutions, they often acquire a new perspective on themselves as well as some new ideas about how to respond to their world more effectively. Acquiring a better understanding of oneself and one's problems, along with developing possible solutions, may contribute greatly to the healing process.

Providing a Warm, Supportive Relationship   Effective therapists are individuals who are able to establish a caring, trusting, and empathic relationship with their clients. In one study, clients rated their personal relationship and interaction with their therapist as the most important part of their treatment (Sloane et al., 1975). Another study demonstrated that even paraprofessionals (lay people trained by professionals) who were versed in how to engage in empathic listening were quite effective in helping people overcome psychological problems (Berman & Norton, 1985). Thus, it would seem that the nature of the client-therapist relationship has much to do with the success of the treatment (Henry et al., 1986). The fact that most therapists attempt to establish a warm, confiding, and empathic relationship with their clients may account, at least in part, for the comparable success rate reported for each method.

Providing a Professional Setting Good therapy does not usually take place over a cup of coffee, in the room of a private home that does double duty as a family room, or over the telephone. Instead, it usually takes place in a dignified, professional setting in a mental health clinic, hospital, or private office. This kind of setting may contribute much to the therapeutic process. An office that is quiet and professional looking is likely to provide a sense of security and safety that people may not experience in an informal setting, where the possibility of being overheard or interrupted may inhibit spontaneity. In addition, such a setting is likely to enhance the therapist's prestige and, by inference, to heighten the client's expectations for effective treatment.

In view of the widespread and extensive nature of psychological problems, it is likely that at some point in our lives many of us will think seriously about seeking professional help in the form of psychotherapy. The Health Psychology and Life discussion, "Guidelines for Seeking Professional Help," offers some suggestions that may facilitate the process of finding a psychotherapist.

BIOMEDICAL TREATMENT OF PSYCHOLOGICAL DISORDERS

We have been dealing exclusively with verbal and behavioral approaches to treating psychological disorders. There are also, however, a number of biological or medical therapies. Biomedical approaches to treatment are based on one or both of two assumptions: that psychological problems result from biological abnormalities, and that physiological intervention will alleviate or significantly reduce the symptoms of emotional disorders.

Only clinicians with medical degrees may use biomedical treatments. However, psychologists often refer clients to a psychiatrist or other medical practitioner when they feel that biomedical treatment might be helpful. In this section we examine three types of biomedical treatment: psychosurgery, electroconvulsive (shock) therapy, and psychoactive drugs.

PSYCHOSURGERY

In the early decades of this century mental hospitals throughout the Western world overflowed with severely disturbed patients, and there was a shortage of both professional staff and effective treatment strategies. During this time many mental-health professionals became frustrated with what they perceived to be a general practice of using mental hospitals as little more than warehouses for severely disordered patients. In the effort to alleviate patient suffering and reduce problems of overcrowding, a number of psychiatrists were motivated to experiment with a variety of often radical biological interventions.

One such person was a Portuguese neuropsychiatrist, Antonio de Egas Moniz. In 1935 Moniz attended a professional conference in London and was impressed by a report describing brain surgery on two chimpanzees in which the prefrontal areas (forwardmost portion of the frontal lobes) of their cerebral cortexes were removed. The effect of this surgery was to abolish the violent outbursts that both animals had been prone to prior to surgery. On the basis of this single instance of chimpanzee brain surgery, Moniz persuaded a colleague, Almeida Lima, to experiment with surgery on the frontal lobes of schizophrenics and other severely disturbed patients. The surgical procedure was to sever the nerve tracts connecting the frontal cortex to lower regions in the brain that mediate emotional responses, most notably the thalamus and hypothalamus. Essentially, the idea was to disconnect thought (mediated by the cortex) from emotion (mediated by lower brain centers). Such a procedure was expected to have a calming effect on patients troubled by severely disruptive emotional patterns.

This operation, known as a **lobotomy,** was originally performed by a very crude surgical procedure in which a hole was drilled through the skull

GUIDELINES FOR SEEKING PROFESSIONAL HELP

Many people are reluctant to seek professional help because they incorrectly believe that taking this step is an admission that they are weak and incapable of helping themselves. Quite the contrary, people who seek professional help demonstrate a high level of self-awareness and emotional maturity by recognizing that there are limitations to their ability to help themselves when faced with seriously disruptive psychological problems. If some day you find yourself entering into a therapeutic relationship with a psychotherapist, give yourself credit for having the wisdom to recognize that a skilled therapist can offer useful information, emotional support, a perspective other than your own, and specific problem-solving techniques, all of which may help you make the desired changes in your life.

As we have seen in this text, however, not all therapists are equally effective in providing successful treatment. How do you go about selecting a therapist? Assuming that your symptoms are not so acute that they demand immediate attention, we suggest you shop as carefully for a therapist as you might when making a major purchase such as a car or a Caribbean cruise. Yet many people do not know where to start in making this kind of decision.

A good first step in locating a psychotherapist is to seek referrals from people you know who are likely to be familiar with your community's mental health resources—your psychology instructor, your health care practitioner, or perhaps your minister, rabbi, or priest. (The clergy often deal with people who have psychological problems, and they are quite familiar with community mental-health resources.) Do not hesitate to talk with friends who have experienced psychotherapy in the past. Sometimes firsthand recommendations can be especially helpful. You may also want to see if your college or university has a counseling center or clinic for students. Such a service may be free or at very low cost. In addition, city, county, and state psychological associations can provide names of licensed clinical psychologists in your area, and county medical societies have lists of names of psychiatrists.

We recommend that you contact several sources and then pool the information. This process may leave you with several choice options. To narrow down your choices, consider the professional backgrounds of your prospective therapists: Remember that many so-called "professional" counselors have little or no professional training. Many states now license practicing clinical psychologists, and you may inquire as to whether or not a therapist is licensed. It is highly appropriate for you to inquire about the specific training and credentials or certification of a prospective therapist; you may also wish to inquire as to the number of years a therapist has practiced. These inquiries may be made over the phone. If a prospective therapist is reluctant to provide this information, go elsewhere.

Cost may also be an issue as you seek to narrow your choices. Fees vary considerably, from no charge to $100 or more per 45–50-minute session. Psychiatrists are usually on the upper end of the fee scale, psychologists are in the middle, and social workers and counselors are usually on the lower end. A higher fee does not necessarily indicate better therapy skills. Some mental-health agencies and private practitioners offer sliding fee schedules based on the client's income. Many health insurance companies now provide partial to full coverage for psychotherapy services, but note that they may have certification or licensing requirements.

To help determine if a specific therapist will meet your needs, you may wish to establish the following points at your first meeting:

1. What do you want from therapy? You and your therapist should reach an agreement on your and his or her goals. This agreement is sometimes referred to as the therapy contract.
2. What is the therapist's approach and what kind of participation is expected of you? You can ask about the general process (what the therapist will do) during therapy sessions.
3. How do you feel about talking with the therapist? Therapy is not intended to be a light social interaction. It can be difficult. At times it may be quite uncomfortable for a client to discuss personal concerns. However, for therapy to be useful, you will want to have the sense that the therapist is open and willing to understand you.

While these suggestions may not ensure that you find a therapist who is a "perfect fit" for your needs, it is likely that they will increase the odds that you will select a qualified counselor.

FIGURE 15.4

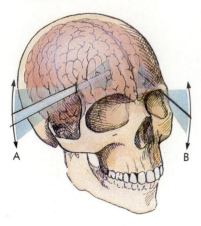

The idea behind the lobotomy was to produce a calming effect on patients troubled by severely disruptive emotional patterns by disconnecting thought from emotion. In an effort to accomplish this, a procedure was developed whereby a blunt instrument was inserted through holes drilled in each side of the skull and used to sever the nerve tracts connecting the frontal cortex to lower brain regions (see A). In a later refinement of this procedure, a similar therapeutic effect was sought by inserting an icepicklike instrument into the brain through an eye socket and rotating it back and forth (see B).

covering on each side of the head, and a blunt instrument was then inserted and rotated in a vertical arc. The procedure was later refined by the *transorbital lobotomy* technique, in which an icepicklike instrument called a leucotome is inserted into the brain through an eye socket and rotated back and forth. Figure 15.4 illustrates both procedures.

The lobotomy rapidly became popular in Europe as a treatment for a wide variety of disorders including schizophrenia, severe depression, and occasionally anxiety disorders. Moniz enthusiastically claimed that the procedure was very effective in calming severely disturbed psychotics, and that many lobotomized patients were able to leave the hospital. (Strangely, though, his claims were even more widely influential after he was partially paralyzed by a gunshot inflicted by one of his lobotomized patients [Valenstein, 1973].) Neurosurgeons Walter Freeman and James Watts (1950) introduced lobotomy to the United States, where it flourished until the late 1950s. By the time the popularity of lobotomies had begun to wane, over 40,000 people are thought to have been recipients of this surgical intervention (Kalinowsky, 1975).

Lobotomized patients seemed more tranquil or calm after the operation, and thus more manageable. However, some observant clinicians began to raise questions. They suggested that the "calming" effect was actually more a conversion of emotionally labile patients into lethargic, vegetative patients. In addition, it was noted that very little research evidence had substantiated the effects of this treatment.

Once researchers began to investigate seriously the effects of lobotomies, they found that the claims of pronounced improvements in behavior had been greatly exaggerated. True, lobotomized patients had slightly higher rates of discharge from hospitals than did matched controls, but this was counterbalanced by higher rates of recidivism or return to hospitals. Furthermore, these studies provided some profoundly disturbing evidence—that some lobotomized patients had been transformed into lethargic, unmotivated, robotlike personalities that were hollow remnants of what they had once been. This effect was dramatized in Ken Kesey's novel, *One Flew over the Cuckoo's Nest* (1962). Other irreversible side effects were uncovered, including memory loss, inability to plan ahead, seizures, and even death. Furthermore, lobotomies were found to produce no changes in the major manifestations of severe mental illness other than reduction of emotional agitation (Barahal, 1958; Robbin, 1958, 1959).

Such findings prompted several critics to call for a ban on all forms of psychosurgery. Although no formal prohibition was enforced, medical practitioners have drastically curtailed their use of this method. (This movement away from psychosurgery gained momentum with the emergence of calming psychoactive drugs, whose effects are temporary rather than permanent, as was the case with lobotomies.)

Psychosurgery did not die out completely. In fact, since the early 1970s there has been a growing interest in using surgical techniques to alter behavior when all other reversible treatment methods have failed. Newer surgical techniques produce only a small fraction of the brain damage associated with older procedures. For example, highly refined methods are now available for disconnecting the frontal cortex from lower brain centers, destroying less than 10 percent of the amount of brain tissue destroyed by the transorbital technique (Shevitz, 1976). Other contemporary psychosurgery techniques involve destruction of limited amounts of tissue in precisely located sites within such brain structures as the amygdala, thalamus, and hypothalamus. These refined procedures are often effective in alleviating symptoms of severe depression, uncontrollable rage attacks, extreme anxiety, obsessive-compulsive disorders, schizophrenia, uncontrollable seizures, and severe pain—all of which may have resisted more conventional forms of therapy—with very few serious side effects (Corkin, 1980; Donnelly, 1980; Mirsky & Orzacki, 1980; Valenstein, 1980). Although these newer techniques are clearly an improvement over the lobotomies of the 1940s

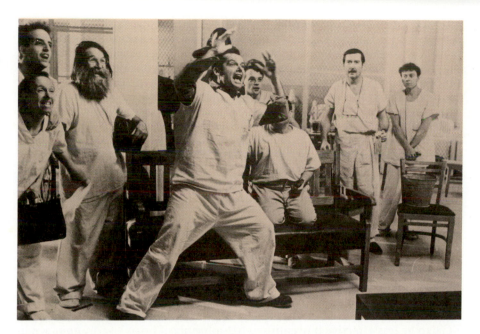

The effects of the lobotomy were dramatized in the movie based on Ken Kesey's novel, *One Flew Over the Cuckoo's Nest*. Here, actor Jack Nicholson plays the part of a vivacious, outgoing personality. After his lobotomy, he becomes lethargic, unmotivated, robotlike—a hollow remnant of what he had been before the surgery.

and 1950s, most contemporary clinicians believe that their use should be limited to patients whose problems are severe, persistent, and resistant to all other treatments.

ELECTROCONVULSIVE THERAPY

Electroconvulsive therapy (ECT) is a biomedical intervention in which electrical current applied to the brain induces a convulsive seizure. Many students wonder how such a technique ever became part of the psychiatric arsenal. The answer is an interesting story.

In the early 1930s a Hungarian physician, Lazlo Von Meduna, noticed that hospitalized psychiatric patients often seemed to experience a remission or lessening of their psychotic symptoms after undergoing a spontaneous seizure of the type that occurs in epilepsy. Excited by this discovery, Von Meduna began to experiment with different techniques for artificially inducing convulsions. He first used intramuscular injections of camphor oil to elicit seizures. Although several patients were made physically ill by the injections, a number showed remarkable improvement. Von Meduna soon substituted a synthetic camphor, metrazol, which seemed to lessen the side effect of physical illness. The use of *pharmacoconvulsive therapy* (drug-induced seizures) quickly gained a worldwide foothold among psychiatrists desperate for a way to combat severe psychological disorders.

Unfortunately, pharmacoconvulsive therapy was not without problems. Although the symptoms of psychological disorders were often reduced, the procedure had other severe side effects, including painful preseizure spasms and uncontrollable convulsions that sometimes resulted in fractures and even death (Weiner, 1985). In the late 1930s two Italian neuropsychiatrists, Ugo Cerletti and Lucino Bini (1938), introduced a safer, better controlled method for inducing seizures using electric shock. By 1940 electroconvulsive therapy had become a major component of psychiatric treatment strategies worldwide.

Early ECT sessions resembled something out of a horror movie. A wide-awake and often terrified patient was strapped to a table, electrodes were attached to each side of his or her forehead, and a current of roughly 100 volts was then passed between the electrodes for a fraction of a second, producing severe convulsions and a temporary loss of consciousness. Upon regaining consciousness the patient often seemed confused, distressed, and unable to remember events that happened both before and immediately

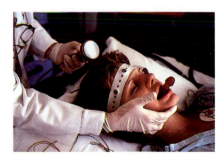

Electroconvulsive therapy (ECT) is used to treat 80,000 Americans each year. The most common and successful application is for severely depressed patients who have not responded to antidepressant drugs or who cannot tolerate waiting for the slower acting drugs to take effect.

after the procedure. In addition, the seizures induced by the electric current often produced such a rapid and intense contraction of skeletal muscles that bone fractures, bruises, and other injuries sometimes resulted. Altogether, not a pretty picture—but one that was repeated countless thousands of times due to compelling evidence that ECT was often amazingly effective in reducing symptoms of severe psychological distress, particularly depression.

Since the early days of the development of ECT, several modifications have been introduced to make this treatment safer and more humane. Today patients are first put to sleep and administered a powerful muscle relaxant before the shock is delivered. General anesthesia circumvents the terror many patients experienced in the early years of this treatment. The patient typically wakes up in a half hour or so, with no recollection of the treatment. ECT is now often applied to only one of the cerebral hemispheres, usually the one that is not dominant. This unilateral treatment has significantly reduced the confusion and memory loss associated with ECT.

There is extensive evidence that ECT often produces a rapid and sometimes dramatic reduction of the symptoms of major depression (Kalinowsky, 1980; Kramer, 1987; Scovern & Kilmann, 1980; Weiner, 1985; Yudofsky, 1982), and the treatment is sometimes effective in counteracting bipolar disorder (Berman & Wolpert, 1987). Research has generally shown ECT to be less effective in treating schizophrenia. The most common application of ECT today is for severely depressed patients who have not responded to antidepressant drugs or who cannot tolerate waiting for the slower acting drugs to take effect (Weiner, 1985). Recently, a review panel commissioned by the National Institutes of Health concluded that while ECT is not without problems, it is nevertheless a relatively effective treatment for severe depression that has not responded to psychotherapy or drug therapy (Kolata, 1985).

Not everyone agrees with this favorable assessment of ECT, however. One outspoken critic is psychiatrist Peter Breggin, who wrote the book *Electroshock: Its Brain-Disabling Effects* (1979). Breggin asserts that the effects of ECT on the brain are often "catastrophic." While acknowledging that some depressed patients experience short-term benefits from the procedure, he believes that there is plenty of evidence that extended treatment can lead to "complete neurological collapse." Breggin's evidence suggests that psychiatrists who do not use ECT have success rates comparable with those who use ECT extensively. In his opinion, it is reckless and unconscionable to use a treatment that may have devastating effects on the brain when other equally effective and safer strategies are available.

Some of Breggin's concerns have been shared by other researchers. Some have issued warnings about the possibility of permanent memory impairment, which has been observed among some recipients of extensive ECT therapy (Rouche, 1980). Psychiatrist Richard Weiner (1985), an advocate of ECT as a "second-line treatment modality" (a treatment to be used if first-choice measures fail) acknowledges that ECT patients typically have some difficulty in retaining newly learned material following a course of ECT treatments. Controlled studies in his own laboratory have revealed a persistent memory deficit as long as six months after ECT. Furthermore, "there have been a number of complaints by patients and their families of more persistent losses. . . ." (p. 463).

This finding is in line with other research, discussed in Chapter 2, which assessed the proactive (forward-acting) effects of a series of electroconvulsive shocks on the long-term memories of laboratory rats (Crooks, 1972). Here, long-term memory formation was found to be markedly impaired after ECT treatment. Of course, rats are not humans, but more recent evidence of ECT-induced memory deficits should be viewed as an indicator to exercise caution in the use of ECT. The shift to unilateral ECT, which tends to reduce memory deficits and other negative side effects of the treatment, may be viewed as a welcome change in ECT methodology.

One of the most perplexing aspects of electroconvulsive therapy is that no one is sure how the treatment works. We know that ECT alters the electrochemical processes in many central nervous system structures, but we still have not been able to determine which of these changes, if any, are linked with the antidepressant effects of ECT. One popular theory is that ECT increases the availability of the neurotransmitters norepinephrine and serotonin at the synapses in certain brain sites in a fashion similar to the chemical antidepressants (Kety, 1975; Weiner, 1985). Another hypothesis is that depression is associated with overactivity in selective brain sites, and that the brain becomes less active after ECT treatments in a kind of compensation for the hyperactivity associated with the seizures (Sackheim, 1985). It has even been suggested that the antidepressant effects of ECT can be explained by operant conditioning. According to this interpretation, a patient learns the operant response of not being depressed in order to avoid the aversive stimulus of ECT (Costello, 1976).

The questions and concerns raised by ECT will no doubt continue to be debated, and we can expect that ECT will continue to be used to treat approximately 80,000 Americans per year (Sackheim, 1985; Thompson & Blaine, 1987). Researchers hope eventually to clarify how ECT works and whether or not its potential beneficial effects are outweighed by disruptive or disabling side effects.

PSYCHOACTIVE DRUGS

The use of chemicals to control symptoms of psychological disorders became a primary part of psychiatric practices during the 1950s. Since then, therapy with **psychoactive drugs** has become by far the most common biomedical treatment. The use of psychoactive drugs has contributed both to a decline in the number of people hospitalized for psychological disorders and to a significant reduction in the average duration of hospitalization. "Now, hospitalization of the mentally ill is seldom measured in terms of years but is more often a matter of months or even weeks" (Avison & Speechley, 1987). Drugs are often so effective in controlling disruptive symptoms that many patients who might previously have required restraints or close observation in locked wards are now able to function reasonably effectively outside of a hospital setting. Even patients who still require hospitalization typically need less supervision than did their counterparts in the days before drugs were introduced.

The four major categories of psychoactive drugs that are used to control or alleviate symptoms of psychological disorders are *antipsychotics, antidepressants, antimanics,* and *antianxiety drugs.* Table 15.4 lists several commonly used drugs in these categories. As we shall see, the various widely used psychoactive drugs differ considerably in their effects: some calm, some energize, and some provide an emotional lift. However, they all share one common feature. Generally speaking, all psychoactive drugs merely help to *control* or manage symptoms rather than *cure* the disorder. When people cease taking these medications, symptoms tend to recur.

Besides dramatically enhancing the ability of psychiatrists to treat severely disordered patients, biomedical drug therapy has stimulated an abundance of research, resulting in some important new hypotheses linking several disorders to possible neurochemical factors (Lipper, 1985).

Antipsychotics   The **antipsychotic drugs,** sometimes called *neuroleptics* or *major tranquilizers,* were first used in the early 1950s to treat schizophrenia. As Table 15.4 shows, there are several varieties of these drugs. The most commonly employed are the *phenothiazine* derivatives. The most widely used drug in this group is chlorpromazine, sold under the name Thorazine. Chlorpromazine has been the number-one medication for treating schizophrenia since it was introduced to American psychiatry in 1952 (Duke & Nowicki, 1986). The effects of this drug and other antipsychotic drugs is to

TABLE 15.4 *The Major Categories of Psychoactive Drugs*

Category	Chemical Group	Generic Name	Trade Name
Antipsychotics	phenothiazines	chlorpromazine	Thorazine
Schizophrenia		thioridazine	Mellaril
		trifluoperazine	Stelazine
	butyrophenones	haloperidol	Haldol
	thioxanthenes	chorprothixene	Taractan
	dihydroindolones	molindone	Moban
Antidepressants	tricyclics	doxepin	Sinequan
		amitriptyline	Elavil
		imipramine	Tofranil
		nortriptyline	Aventyl
		protriptyline	Vivactyl
	monoamine oxidase (MAO) inhibitors	phenelzine	Nardil
		tranylcypromine	Parnate
	newer agents	isocarboxazid	Marphan
		amoxapine	Asendin
		maprotiline	Ludiomil
		trazodone	Desyrel
Antimanics	inorganic salts	lithium carbonate	Lithane, Lithonate
Antianxiety drugs	propanediols	meprobamate	Miltown, Equanil
	benzodiazepines	chlordiazepoxide	Librium
		diazepam	Valium
		alprazolam	Xanax
		clorazepate	Tranxene
		halazepam	Paxipam
		lorazepam	Ativan
		oxazepam	Serax
		prazepam	Centrax

calm and quiet patients, reducing their responsiveness to irrelevant stimuli. This therapeutic effect is believed to result from the fact that antipsychotic drugs block dopamine receptor sites in the brain, thus reducing brain activity (Davison & Neale, 1986; Lipper, 1985).

Although the antipsychotic drugs are used to treat a variety of severe disorders, they have generally proven to be most effective in managing the symptoms of schizophrenia. In one important study conducted in the mid-1970s (May et al., 1976), researchers assigned first-admission schizophrenics (people who had not previously been hospitalized) to one of five treatment groups: (1) individual psychoanalytic-type psychotherapy, (2) phenothiazine drugs and nothing else, (3) psychoanalytic psychotherapy plus phenothiazines, (4) ECT, and (5) *milieu therapy* (a method of treatment that attempts to make the total environment of a disturbed patient, including all personnel and other patients, a therapeutic community). Improvement was assessed by ratings of nurses and clinicians, together with data on release rates and duration of hospitalization. The results showed the two most effective treatment modalities to be drugs alone and psychotherapy plus drugs. (Psychotherapy seemed to add little or no tangible effects, for the success rate of these two treatment conditions were essentially the same.)

Antidepressants The **antidepressant drugs,** also introduced in the 1950s, consist of two main groups, the *tricyclics* and the *monoamine oxidase (MAO) inhibitors,* and a group of more recently introduced "newer" antidepressant agents listed in Table 15.4. As we saw in Chapter 14, these drugs are used to treat major depression (unipolar disorder), and they are often very effective in lifting the spirits of severely depressed patients. While it has been widely believed that these drugs act to increase levels of the neurotransmitters norepinephrine and serotonin in certain areas of the brain (Colasanti, 1982a), it is possible that their antidepressant effects may be related to increased sensitivity of the receptors for those two neurotransmitters. Hopefully, further research will clarify how and why the antidepressants are so effective.

A number of studies comparing tricyclic drugs with other treatments have yielded mixed findings. One study (Murphy et al., 1984) compared improvement rates among four matched groups of depressives who received one of the following treatments: (1) cognitive therapy alone, (2) cognitive therapy plus tricyclics, (3) tricyclics alone, and (4) a placebo drug. All treatments were equally effective—a finding that indicates that expectations of getting better have a lot to do with whether people improve. Another study comparing tricyclics alone to cognitive therapy alone found the psychotherapy to be more effective (Rush et al., 1977). In still two other studies, tricyclics combined with psychotherapy provided the best treatment results (DiMascio et al., 1979; Weissman et al., 1981). More recently, a study of 59 unipolar depressives who were treated with a combination of tricyclics and psychotherapy revealed that the relapse rate among these patients after eight weeks of recovery was only 8.5 percent. (Kupfer & Frank, 1987). This compares with a relapse rate of approximately 22 percent reported for another group of patients treated solely with drugs (Prien & Kupfer, 1986). Considered together, these various findings seem to suggest that a combination of antidepressant drugs and psychotherapy may be the most effective approach to treating major depression, although additional research is still needed.

The MAO inhibitors have been shown to be generally less effective than the tricyclics, although some people who do not respond to the tricyclics do benefit from MAO inhibitors. In recent years there has been a marked reduction in the use of these antidepressants because of their serious side effects.

Antimanics   In 1970 lithium carbonate was approved by the Food and Drug Administration for use as an **antimanic** medication. This drug, a simple inorganic salt, has been found to be the most effective drug for controlling the manic symptoms of bipolar disorder and has even been shown to help reduce depression associated with this disorder (Giannini et al., 1986). Lithium therapy appears to be less effective when applied to patients experiencing a state of mixed mania (Secunda et al., 1987). Its greatest benefit, however, seems to be as a prophylactic, reducing the frequency and severity of manic episodes or perhaps preventing them altogether (Lipper, 1985; Prien et al., 1984). Lithium is believed to accomplish its antimanic effects by increasing the reuptake of norepinephrine and serotonin, thus reducing the available amount of these neurotransmitters at various synaptic sites in the brain (Colasanti, 1982b).

Antianxiety Drugs   The **antianxiety drugs,** sometimes called minor tranquilizers, are used to reduce symptoms of anxiety and tension in people whose psychological disturbances are not severe enough to warrant hospitalization. These medications are particularly helpful in reducing the symptoms of generalized anxiety disorders. Like most of the drugs we have discussed in this section, the antianxiety medications were introduced in the 1950s.

There are two major categories of minor tranquilizers: *propanediols* and *benzodiazepines.* The first to be introduced were the propanediols, the most common of which is meprobamate (Miltown). These drugs accomplish their antianxiety effect by reducing muscular tension. They also have a tendency to produce drowsiness. When people stop taking propanediol medications after a long course of fairly large doses, a severe withdrawal syndrome may be precipitated. This withdrawal can produce such effects as tremors, convulsions, hallucinations, and severe anxiety.

Over the years the propanediols have become gradually less popular, and they have been largely replaced by the more recently developed benzodiazepines. The most widely used of these medications, chlordiazepoxide (Librium) and diazepam (Valium), are among the most frequently prescribed medications in the United States (Duke & Nowicki, 1986).

Like the propanediols, the benzodiazepines also seem to accomplish their antianxiety effects by relaxing the skeletal muscles. A specific benzodiazepine receptor has been discovered in the CNS, which suggests that these drugs may accomplish their therapeutic effect by mimicking or blocking a naturally produced substance, although such a substance has not yet been found (Lipper, 1985).

SUMMARY

PSYCHOANALYSIS

1. Psychoanalysis is based on a number of assumptions, the most fundamental of which is that disordered behavior results from unconscious conflicts and repressed urges, most of which are rooted in childhood experiences.
2. Major techniques of psychoanalysis include free association, dream analysis, and interpretations of resistance and transference.
3. Freud believed that it is important to break through patients' defenses and to provide them with insight by interpreting the underlying meaning of their experiences, resistances, transferences, and dreams.
4. Psychoanalysis as practiced today tends to be briefer in duration and less focused on restructuring a person's entire personality than was the case in Freud's time.

HUMANISTIC THERAPIES

5. Humanistic therapists, who see their goal as fostering psychological growth, place more responsibility for the success of therapy on the client than on the therapist and tend to focus on the present rather than the past.
6. Rogers' person-centered therapy emphasizes creating a therapeutic environment characterized by three dimensions or characteristics expressed by the therapist: genuineness, unconditional positive regard, and empathic understanding.
7. Gestalt therapy strives to help a person bring together the alienated fragments of self into an integrated, unified whole.
8. Techniques employed by Gestalt therapists to help people become aware of who they are and what they are feeling include role playing, encouraging people to speak in the first person, and pointing out incongruities or discrepancies between what the client says and does.

COGNITIVE THERAPIES

9. Cognitive therapies are based on the premise that most psychological disorders result from distortions in a person's cognitions or thoughts.
10. Rational-emotive therapy (RET) is based on the belief that psychological problems result when people interpret their experiences based on certain self-defeating, irrational beliefs. The goal of therapy is to "make mincemeat" of these maladaptive cognitions.
11. Like RET, cognitive restructuring therapy also aims to get clients to restructure their thinking, particularly negative self-labels, by arranging certain experiences that will disprove rather than confirm the client's negative self-image.

BEHAVIOR THERAPIES

12. The central thesis of behavior therapy is that maladaptive behavior has been learned and that it can be unlearned; furthermore, that the same principles that govern the learning of normal behavior also determine the acquisition of abnormal behavior.
13. The classical conditioning therapies, which include systematic desensitization and aversive conditioning, apply classical conditioning principles to help people to overcome maladaptive behavior.
14. Systematic desensitization involves training people to relax when confronted with fear-inducing stimuli.
15. In aversive therapy the goal is to substitute a negative (aversive) response for a positive response to an inappropriate or harmful stimulus such as nicotine or alcohol.
16. The operant conditioning therapies, which include positive reinforcement, extinction, and punishment, focus on manipulating reinforcers as a way to overcome behavioral problems.
17. In positive reinforcement therapy the therapist first identifies desirable behavior and then provides appropriate rewards contingent upon the client voluntarily manifesting the desired behavior.
18. The extinction technique involves eliminating undesired behaviors by eliminating the reinforcers that maintain them.
19. In the punishment technique aversive stimuli are used to punish voluntary maladaptive responses.
20. Behavior change through modeling or observing others can be a helpful therapy technique for extinguishing irrational fears or for establishing new, more adaptive behaviors.

GROUP THERAPY

21. Potential benefits associated with participating in group therapy include a sense of solidarity with others, feedback from other group members as well as the group leader, opportunities to observe how others work out their problems, the satisfaction of helping others, and lower cost.
22. Family therapy with entire family units is based on the premise that an individual's psychological adjustment is profoundly influenced by patterns of social interaction within the family unit.
23. Today conjoint or couple therapy—working with two partners together—has become the most common approach for treating relationship problems experienced by a primary couple, married or unmarried.

EVALUATING PSYCHOTHERAPY

24. Research has clearly demonstrated that in most cases improvement rates for people undergoing psychotherapy are markedly better than those for untreated individuals.

25. Research has also shown that no particular type of therapy is significantly superior to others.

26. All things being equal, experienced psychotherapists in any of the major theoretical frameworks tend to achieve better results than do novice therapists.

27. Certain common features shared by almost all styles of therapy include combating the client's demoralization, providing a rationale for the client's symptoms and their treatment, providing a warm, supportive relationship, and providing a professional setting.

BIOMEDICAL TREATMENT OF PSYCHOLOGICAL DISORDERS

28. Lobotomy was originally performed as a very crude surgical procedure designed to improve a patient's mental state by severing the nerve tracts connecting the frontal cortex to lower regions in the brain that mediate emotional responses.

29. Lobotomies eventually fell into disrepute when research revealed that they produced no changes in the major manifestations of severe mental illness other than reduction of emotional agitation, and that many lobotomized patients had been transformed into lethargic, unmotivated, robotlike personalities.

30. Newer psychosurgery techniques, which produce only a small fraction of the brain damage associated with the older and more crude lobotomies, have been shown to have some value in alleviating symptoms of severe disorders that have resisted more conventional forms of therapy.

31. There is extensive evidence that electroconvulsive therapy (ECT) often rapidly alleviates the symptoms of major depression. Some researchers believe that extended ECT treatment may damage the brain and produce severe memory deficits. No one is sure how ECT accomplishes its therapeutic effect.

32. Therapy with psychoactive drugs, by far the most common biomedical treatment, has contributed to both a decline in the number of people hospitalized for psychological disorders and a significant reduction in the average duration of hospitalization.

33. The four major categories of psychoactive drugs that are used to control or alleviate symptoms of psychological disorders are antipsychotics, antidepressants, antimanics, and antianxiety drugs.

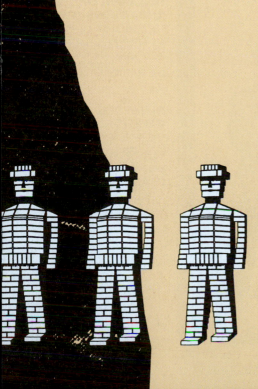

PART 6

SOCIAL AND
APPLIED PSYCHOLOGY

16
SOCIAL PSYCHOLOGY

17
APPLIED PSYCHOLOGY

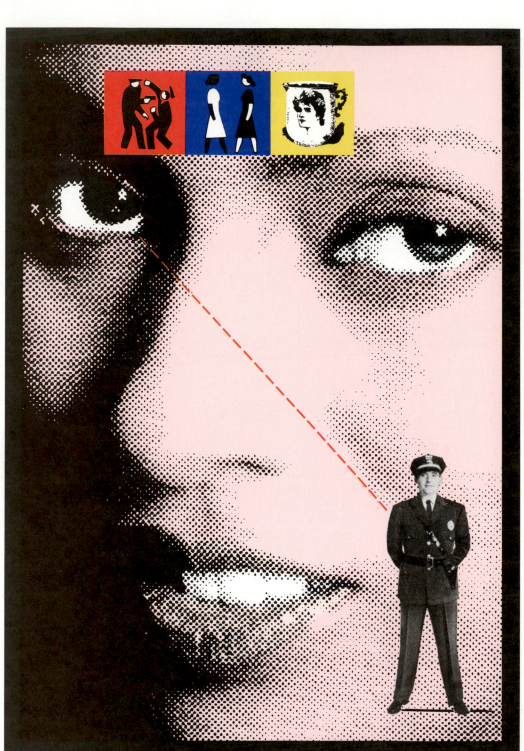

16 Social Psychology

Imagine that you have volunteered to participate in a study in which you and several other students will discuss personal problems caused by the pressures of university life. You are told that to avoid embarrassment, you and five (or perhaps two or one, depending on which group you are placed in) other participants will not see one another; instead, you will sit in individual cubicles and talk over an intercom system. Participants' microphones will be activated only when it is their turn to speak, and to preserve anonymity, the experimenters will not listen.

The experiment begins and the first voice you hear is that of a young man. Haltingly, he explains that he is having a great deal of difficulty adjusting to the pressures he is experiencing. He also states, with obvious embarrassment, that he is prone to epileptic-like seizures when he is under stress. You and the other participants talk in turn about your own reactions to stress. Now it is the first young man's turn to speak again. After a very short time, it is apparent that he is in trouble: he seems to fumble for words, then begins choking and pleading for help. He is clearly experiencing a seizure. What will you do?

We have just described an experiment conducted by two social psychologists, John Darly and Bibb Latané (1968). In the actual experimental design, the researchers had prerecorded all "participants'" voices so that only one subject actually took part in each group discussion, and that subject's reactions were the focus of the study. The results might surprise you. When subjects thought that they alone were aware of the emergency, Darly and Latané found that 85 percent sought help. In contrast, only 62 percent of subjects sought help when they thought there were two other bystanders, compared to a mere 31 percent of subjects who thought there were five others in the group.

Social psychologists use the term **diffusion of responsibility** to explain Darly and Latané's findings. Our own sense of responsibility is diminished by the presence of other bystanders. Because we assume that they have as much responsibility to act as we have, we are less likely to intervene to give aid. Diffusion of responsibility helps to explain some other disturbing incidents. One is the widely reported 1964 stabbing murder of a woman named Kitty Genovese as at least 38 residents of a Queens, New York apartment complex looked on, making no move to intervene or call for help. These bystanders showed signs of extreme anxiety as a result of their experience (as did the subjects of Darly and Latané's experiment), but

At 3:20 A.M. March 13, 1964, Kitty Genovese (left) drove into the parking lot and parked (1). Noticing a man in the lot, she became nervous and walked in the street toward a police telephone box. The man caught and attacked her with a knife (2). She got away, but the man caught and attacked her again (3) and again (4). During this gruesome murder, at least 38 residents in the nearby apartment complex looked on, making no move to help.

they still made no move, counting instead on the probability that someone else would call for help.

Such incidents illustrate an important fact that we have not yet fully explored in this text—that our actions are greatly influenced by social processes and our perception of our social environments. *Social psychology* is the field of psychology that is concerned with how social influences affect our thoughts, beliefs, feelings, and behaviors, and it asks a number of questions that we will attempt to answer in this chapter. How, for instance, do we form impressions of people, and how do these impressions influence our behavior? Why is it that some individuals have the ability to persuade other people to change their attitudes, while others of us have so little influence? Why do we like some people the first time we meet them? How likely are we to resist pressures to change our beliefs or behavior so that they conform with those of other people even when we disagree with their actions or opinions? Why do some people perform aggressive acts against other people?

The scope of social psychology is far too broad to cover comprehensively in one chapter. Instead of taking a shotgun approach that covers many topics with little depth, we have limited our discussion to the broadly researched areas of social perceptions, attribution, attitudes, social influence, prejudice, interpersonal attraction, and aggression. We begin with social perception.

SOCIAL PERCEPTION

We encounter many people each day, from the clerk at the grocery store to the classmate sitting behind us to the mechanic who is servicing our car.

Even if our interactions with these people are very brief, we form impressions or perceptions of them. The term **social perception** describes the ways we perceive, evaluate, categorize, and form judgments about the qualities of people we encounter.

These social perceptions have a critical influence on our interactions. In fact, they are more important in guiding our feelings, thoughts, and behaviors than are the actual traits or attitudes of the people around us. Thus, the subjects in Darly and Latané's diffusion of responsibility experiment did not intervene because they *perceived* that others would probably seek help. Likewise, you may withdraw from a friend because you perceive that she is annoyed with you. Whether she actually is annoyed is not as significant in determining your response as your own perceptions.

Since these readings of other people are so important, it is worthwhile knowing how we form them. Three factors that influence our social perceptions are first impressions, schemas, and implicit personality theories.

FIRST IMPRESSIONS

First impressions are the initial judgments we make about people, and they play an important role in social perceptions. We are more likely to form opinions of others quickly, based on first impressions, than to refrain from forming opinions until we have more information. These first impressions may change as we get to know a person better, but we often tend to hang on to them even in the face of contradictory evidence. Thus, initial opinions may have a strong impact on our future interactions with people.

For example, if you first meet a new tenant in your apartment building at a party at which he appears to be loud and egotistical, it will probably be hard for you to perceive him as a sensitive, caring person when you later see him comforting a small child who has scraped his knee. The first information we receive about a person often seems to count the most, a phenomenon referred to as the **primacy effect.**

This effect was demonstrated in an experiment in which two lists of traits describing a person were read to two separate groups of subjects (Asch, 1946). In one group, subjects heard a description that began with positive characteristics (such as intelligent and industrious) followed by negative ones (impulsive, stubborn, and so forth). Their overall assessments of this person were positive. Subjects in the other group heard the same list, but in reverse order. The result: Their assessments were far more negative.

SCHEMAS

What determines whether our first impression of a person will be positive or negative? For instance, are you drawn to the person shown in the photo on the following page, or is your impression less favorable? Your answer will depend in large part on the *schema* you have developed for people who adopt punk conventions.

Recall from Chapter 7, "Memory," that schemas are the conceptual frameworks we use to make sense out of our world. The concept of schemas helps explain how we perceive the people we meet. For example, you might have schemas of lawyers as aggressive and intelligent, and of professors as studious and somewhat introverted. Social psychologists refer to these generalized assumptions about certain classes of people as *person schemas.*

Person schemas provide a structure for evaluating the people we meet, allowing us to take shortcuts by concentrating on some facts and ignoring others. When we assess others for the first time, we tend to pick up only the information that fits our existing schemas, ignoring the rest. This process is cognitively efficient, but, unfortunately, it is not always the most accurate way of forming impressions (Brigham, 1986). For example, you

FIRST PERSON 16.1

When I think about how wrong first impressions can be, I remember one student I met for the first time a few years ago. He was a man in his late 20s, and when I first saw him he was wearing a short-sleeved T-shirt that displayed an incredible musculature—I mean, it looked like he spent most of his time pumping iron! The fact that he flexed several times during class (while supposedly scratching his back) added to the general impression of a brawny, physical type who was probably much more interested in developing his body than his mind. But this first impression could not have been more wrong. He got a perfect score on the first exam, placing him well above the rest of his classmates. And later, during several after-class conversations, it was easy to see that this man was a highly intelligent, thoughtful, and inquisitive person who was as interested in good books and stimulating conversations as he was in maintaining his physique. (*Authors' files*)

Are you drawn to the person shown in this photo, or is your impression less favorable? Your answer will depend in large part on the schema that you have developed for people who adopt punk conventions.

may have completely discounted the possibility that the punk-type person shown in the photo is a successful author of short stories.

Once we fit a person into a schema, we tend to use that schema as a general organizing principle for interpreting further information about the person. For example, if our first impression of a new neighbor is that she is unfriendly, we are likely to evaluate her failure to comment on our shiny new car as further evidence of unfriendliness. If she then acts in a way that does not fit the schema (for example, picking up our garbage after it has been scattered by a storm), we may dismiss that act by concluding that she picked up the mess only because she was worried that it would blow onto her lawn.

IMPLICIT PERSONALITY THEORIES

Just as person schemas guide us in fitting people into preexisting categories, we also make implicit assumptions about personality traits that usually go together. For instance, if we meet a person whom we perceive as intelligent, we may expect that person also to be skillful and imaginative. These assumptions about how traits are related to each other in people's personalities are called **implicit personality theories** (Bruner & Tagiuri, 1954; Cantor & Mischel, 1979). We may not be aware of many of our implicit assumptions. However, since these associations may be firmly rooted in our minds, they are likely to be activated when we meet people for the first time. In one study researchers graphically plotted clusters of associations among 60 character traits. The results are shown in Figure 16.1 (Rosenberg et al., 1968).

Our implicit personality theories are often organized around **central traits**—traits that we tend to associate with many other characteristics. For example, many people associate the trait of coldness with unsociability, humorlessness, and lack of popularity. Even a single central trait may play an important role in organizing our implicit personality theories about others. In an early study, Solomon Asch (1946) presented two groups of subjects with a list of seven traits describing a hypothetical person. The list for each group differed on only one central trait dimension—*warm* versus *cold*—yet this difference significantly influenced the subjects' predictions about other traits of the hypothetical person. Thus, subjects who had been provided a trait list that included *warm* were more likely to predict that the hypothetical person was generous or had a good sense of humor than were those subjects whose list contained the word *cold*.

Psychologists use the term **halo effect** to describe our tendency to infer other positive (or negative) traits from our perception of one central trait. The halo effect was demonstrated in a study in which subjects observed two versions of an interview with a Belgian professor in which he appeared to be either likable or unlikable. Not only did subjects prefer the "likable" person in the interview; they also responded more positively to seemingly unrelated qualities such as his accent and physical appearance (Nisbett & Wilson, 1977).

ATTRIBUTING CAUSES TO BEHAVIORS

An important part of social perceptions are the judgments we make about why people behave as they do. Our responses to other people are strongly influenced by these attributions, and we are constantly attempting to understand the reasons for other people's behavior. Attributions allow us to make sense out of other people's actions, figure out their attitudes and personality traits, and, ultimately, gain some control over subsequent interactions with them through our increased ability to predict their behaviors.

According to **attribution theory** (Heider, 1958; Jones, 1979; Kelley, 1971; Ross & Fletcher, 1985), we tend to attribute people's behavior either to *dispositional* (internal) causes, such as motivational states or personality

FIGURE 16.1 A GRAPHIC PORTRAYAL OF ASSOCIATIONS AMONG 60 CHARACTER TRAITS

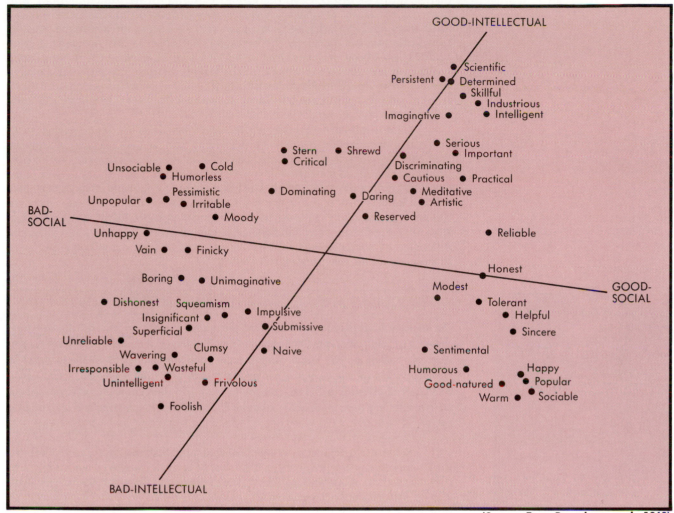

(Source: From Rosenberg et al., 1968)

traits, or to *external* causes, such as environment or situational factors. This distinction can have important effects on our relationships with people. For example, suppose you have recently begun dating someone you like very much, and the two of you spend a weekend visiting your date's parents. Much to your dismay, your friend acts like a different person—restrained, impersonal, and physically unresponsive. What has caused the change? If you attribute it to external factors (that your date is ill at ease around his or her parents) you are unlikely to feel that the relationship is seriously threatened. However, if you attribute the change to an internal cause (that your partner no longer feels responsive to you), you may seriously reevaluate the relationship.

Clearly, our attributions of the causes of people's behaviors have an important impact on relationships. How do we make these attributions? Two theories that attempt to explain this process are the *correspondent inference theory* and the *covariation principle*.

THE CORRESPONDENT INFERENCE THEORY

The **correspondent inference theory** (Jones, 1979; Jones & McGillis, 1976) attempts to explain the attributions we make about people's behaviors by looking at the conditions under which we make those attributions. Theorists Edward E. Jones and his colleagues use the term *correspondent inference* to describe cases in which we attribute a person's behavior to an underlying disposition. For instance, in the earlier example of the new neighbor who behaved raucously at a party, you may have inferred that the person had a loud and unpleasant disposition. However, we do not always make dispositional attributions based on the behaviors we observe. If you watch a television game-show emcee acting solicitous and charming to guest participants, you are unlikely to infer that the host is a genuinely warm and caring person. Why do we make correspondent inferences about people's dispositions in some cases but not in others? Jones and his associates suggest several factors.

One important variable is the *social desirability* or "expectedness" of behaviors we observe. Some common behaviors are so socially acceptable that they reveal virtually nothing about a person. For example, we expect politicians running for office to smile and shake hands with strangers. This expected behavior fits in nicely with our schema of a politician, but it does not tell us very much about the politician's true disposition. True, the candidate might actually be a warm and friendly person, but it is equally possible that the smiles, handshakes, and baby-kissing are due instead to the influence of social norms. Thus, we are unlikely to draw correspondent inferences about the politician.

ATTRIBUTIONS AND SOCIALLY UNDESIRABLE BEHAVIOR

Do socially undesirable actions have the same impact on our attribution processes as socially acceptable behaviors? For instance, if you observe a tennis pro slam his racket on the court after a bad call, are you more likely to make a correspondent inference about his or her disposition than if you observed polite and controlled behavior? If so, can you explain why unacceptable behavior would be more telling than desirable behavior? Consider this question before reading on.

Several experiments have demonstrated that we are more likely to make correspondent inferences from socially undesirable or norm-deviant behaviors than from socially desirable behaviors (Skowronski & Carlston, 1987). For example, in one study subjects listened to various versions of tapes of a man being interviewed for a job in which the interviewer opened the interaction by specifying the personality traits required for the job—traits such as independence and self-reliance. In one version, the applicant described himself in a way that closely matched the desired attributes, while in another version he described his traits as entirely different from those the interviewer was seeking. Most subjects indicated they were able to make confident judgments about the applicant's true character only when he had described himself as being the opposite of what the job demanded (Jones et al., 1961).

Such findings are consistent with the correspondent inference theory. Apparently, when a person's behavior fits external social expectations, we tend to discount it as a clue to a person's true nature. It is the unexpected behavior, which deviates from social desirability norms, that influences us to attribute actions to internal dispositions.

A second variable that determines whether we make correspondent inferences about a person's disposition is the degree to which his or her behavior is focused on achieving unique outcomes (or *noncommon effects*) that would be unlikely to occur as a result of some other behavior. For example, suppose a friend of yours, a physics major, signs up for a course in quantum mechanics. Will you be unimpressed, or will your image of your friend change? If you find out that the course is required for a degree in physics, you are likely to attribute your friend's action to external causes, since it accomplishes the unique or noncommon outcome of obtaining a degree, a goal that could not have been achieved in any other way. If, on the other

What correspondent inferences do you make about John McEnroe's disposition when he slams down his tennis racket after a bad call? If he acted politely, would your inferences change? Why do you think people tend to make more correspondent inferences about disposition based on socially unacceptable rather than socially acceptable behavior?

hand, you discover that this course is an obscure offering that is neither required nor recommended for a physics major, you are more likely to make a dispositional attribution about your friend's great intellectual curiosity.

A third variable that influences correspondent inferences is whether or not we perceive a person's behavior to result from *free choice.* If we know that a person freely chose to behave in a particular manner, we probably assume that these actions reflect underlying dispositions. On the other hand, if that person was pressed to act in a certain way by situational forces, we are more inclined to attribute the behavior to external than internal causes. For example, if one of your friends told you while you were eating lunch together that she strongly supported a conservative political group, you would probably be more inclined to attribute a conservative political attitude to her than if she were to say the same things during a dinner hosted by a politically conservative dean at your college.

THE COVARIATION PRINCIPLE

A second theory of how people make attributions builds on the principle that when we try to figure out the causes and effects of particular events, we generally begin with the premise that cause and effect go together. Thus, if a cause is altered, the effect will also be changed—that is, that causes and effects will *covary.* According to Howard Kelley (1967, 1971, 1973), when we make attributions about people's behavior (the effect) we tend to look at three potential causes: the *situations* or context in which the behavior occurs, the *persons* involved, and the *stimuli* or objects toward which the behavior is directed.

Kelley's theory is known as the **covariation principle.** To illustrate, suppose you enroll in an art appreciation class, and on your first visit to a gallery you observe one member of the class, an intense-looking young man, lingering at each oil painting, staring with apparent rapture. Observing this behavior, you might wonder about this person. Your attribution of causes for this young man's behavior will depend on factors inherent in the *situation* or context in which the behavior occurred (the art gallery), the *persons involved* (the intense young man and other classmates), and the *stimuli* or objects toward which the observed behavior is directed (the oil paintings).

Kelley suggests that as we seek additional information to aid our interpretation of the causes of a person's behavior we act like social scien-

What attributions would you make about this person's behavior? What variables would you take into account when you make these judgments?

tists, carefully analyzing the data, paying particular attention to variations in situation, persons, and stimuli on each of three separate dimensions:

1. *Distinctiveness:* The degree to which other stimuli are capable of eliciting the same behavior from the young man. Does he behave in the same way at other art galleries or museums that your class visits, or does the behavior occur only at this gallery? (We tend to attribute highly distinctive actions to external causes.)

2. *Consistency:* The degree to which the young man exhibits the same behavior in response to the same stimulus on other occasions. Does the person behave in essentially the same way on other visits to this art gallery? (Consistency is important for both internal and external attribution.)

3. *Consensus:* The degree to which other people exhibit the same response to the stimulus as does the actor. Do other people react to the art in this gallery in the same or similar fashion? (We tend to attribute low consensus responses to internal causes.)

According to Kelley, we take in information about all of these dimensions and use it to determine whether the behavior we have observed is caused by an internal dispositional trait or by external forces. Thus, you might create the following mental checklist concerning the young man:

Distinctiveness: low. The young man behaves the same way at other galleries.

Consistency: high. When you return to the same gallery on another occasion, the young man still displays high interest.

Consensus: low. Other visitors do not show the same remarkable interest.

Based on this assessment, you will probably attribute the young man's behavior to the internal cause of a genuine interest in art. Had you noted a pattern of high consistency, high consensus, and high distinctiveness, you would probably have attributed the young man's behavior to an external cause, such as a curiosity about the particular artist displayed at the first gallery.

BIASES IN ATTRIBUTION PROCESSES

Both the correspondent inference theory and the covariation principle suggest that we make attributions in a rational, methodical way. Unfortunately, this does not mean that our judgments are always accurate. We often make errors in the inferences we draw from other people's behavior, and these errors can usually be traced to a few common attribution biases. We will look at a few of these biases, including the fundamental attribution error, false consensus bias, and the illusion of control.

Fundamental Attribution Error One of the most common attribution biases is a tendency to overestimate dispositional causes and to underestimate external causes when accounting for the behavior of others. (Interestingly, we tend to do exactly the opposite when accounting for our own behaviors.) This inclination is so pervasive that it has been labeled the **fundamental attribution error** (Baron & Byrne, 1987; Ross, 1977). For example, when a casual acquaintance complains that she has just failed a history exam, do you attribute her poor performance to a "tricky test" or a lack of adequate preparation time (both external causes), or are you more inclined to assume she is not very bright (dispositional cause)? If you are like most of us, you will probably tend to overestimate the latter cause and discount the former. Had you failed the same exam, however, the odds are good that you would look for external causes.

Research provides evidence of our tendency to make fundamental attribution errors. In one study, for instance, male college students were asked why they had chosen their majors and why they liked their current girl friend; they were also asked the same questions about their best male friend (Nisbett et al., 1973). Their answers indicated a strong tendency to attribute their best friends' choices to dispositional qualities ("He is the kind of person who likes . . ."), whereas they described their own choices in terms of environmental conditions such as characteristics of their majors or their girl friends ("Chemistry is a high-paying field"; "She is attractive and intelligent").

Why are we so quick to attribute other people's behavior to their inner dispositions? At least part of the answer lies in the fact that while we know what situational factors affect our own behavior, we have far less information about how such factors affect other people. Thus, we take the easiest path and assume that they acted in a particular way because "that is the kind of people they are." It is easier to draw conclusions from the behaviors we can observe than to look for hidden reasons.

False Consensus Bias   Another common attributional bias is the assumption that most people share our own attitudes and behaviors. This assumption is known as **false consensus bias,** and it influences us to judge any noteworthy deviations from our own standards as unusual or abnormal.

For example, suppose you note that someone living in your apartment complex never laughs or even cracks a smile while listening to a certain television comedian that you find hilarious. Consequently, you make a dispositional attribution: You assume that the other person has no sense of humor. This bias may be so strong that you do not stop to think that there are probably a number of people with good senses of humor who do not enjoy this comedian.

Illusion of Control   Have you ever had a bad experience such as being in an auto accident, and then later lamented that if only you had left at a different time you could have avoided the situation? People often blame themselves or others for events that are beyond their control. This attributional bias, called the **illusion of control,** is the belief that we control events in our lives—even those that are actually influenced primarily or solely by external causes. The illusion of control is reflected in the behavior of many gamblers such as the slot player who thinks she can tell when a machine is ready to get "hot" by observing its payoff patterns with other players.

Why do we hold on to the illusion that we are in control of such events? Most of us want to be in control of our own lives, and the feeling of being out of control can be very distressing, even when the uncontrollable event is highly negative. Thus, it may actually be less stressful to blame ourselves for losing a job in a round of company layoffs ("I should have seen it coming") than to acknowledge that there was nothing we could do.

The illusion-of-control bias was demonstrated in an interesting experiment in which some subjects were given lottery tickets and others were allowed to pick their own numbers. On the day of the lottery all subjects were individually urged to resell their tickets. Subjects who had not been permitted to choose their own tickets were more inclined to resell them. Furthermore, those subjects who had selected their own tickets and decided to resell them tended to demand higher resale prices than those who had not chosen their lottery numbers (Langer, 1975).

We have been talking about social perceptions and the inferences we make about other people's behavior. These perceptions all contribute to our attitudes about people, groups, and situations. Attitudes have been the subject of more research than any other topic in social psychology, for they guide not only our social interactions but also our thoughts, feelings, and behaviors. In the following section we explore this topic.

ATTITUDES

The term *attitude* is so commonly used in everyday language that we all have some idea what it means. If you were asked to define what an attitude is, you might reply "a person's feelings about something." This definition is not far off the mark. One of the pioneers in attitude measurement, L. L. Thurstone, defined an attitude as "the intensity of positive or negative affect for or against a psychological object" (1946, p. 39). Thurstone's interpretation allows us to define people's attitudes operationally as the favorableness or unfavorableness of their feelings toward any given object or situation.

More recently, social psychologists Martin Fishbein and Icek Ajzen (1975) have built upon the Thurstone definition to describe **attitudes** as learned, relatively enduring predispositions to respond in consistently favorable or unfavorable ways to certain people, groups, ideas, or situations. We will use this definition because it points out that attitudes are learned, that they tend to endure, and that they involve feelings and actions.

Of course, our feelings are rooted in our thoughts or cognitions, and therefore we might also define attitudes as a composite of cognition, affect, and behavior. Many social psychologists, particularly those with a cognitive bent, use this definition of attitudes. Figure 16.2 portrays this three-component (or *tripartite*) model of attitudes. To illustrate this model, suppose you have a friend who has a strong aversion to dogs. This negative attitude is based on certain *cognitions* or beliefs—that dogs are dirty, and that they are also dangerous. These beliefs lead naturally to negative affect or *feelings* such as disgust and fear, and these cognitions and feelings induce specific *behaviors:* If your friend sees a dog while walking in the neighborhood, she reverses her route to avoid contact.

HOW WE ACQUIRE ATTITUDES

How do we develop attitudes? As you might guess, attitudes are shaped by experiences, including our observations of behavior (both other people's and our own); classical and operant conditioning; and direct experiences with the *attitude object* (the people, ideas, or things we hold attitudes about).

Observing Other People's Behavior   As we saw in Chapter 6, we learn some behaviors by observing and imitating influential role models (Bandura, 1986). Attitudes can be learned by the same process. Parents and peers have an especially strong influence on our attitudes. Thus, young people whose friends view adult authority figures with mistrust are likely to acquire this attitude, particularly if it serves a social adjustment function for them.

Observing Our Own Behavior   Although it is commonly believed that attitudes cause behavior, the reverse is sometimes true, too. Social psychologist Daryl Bem (1972) has proposed what he describes as a *self-perception theory* which maintains that when we are not sure how we feel toward a particular attitude object, we sometimes infer our attitudes from our behavior. An example is a man known by the authors who commented that he could tell when he was really attracted to someone because "my body gets turned on and my tongue freezes!"

Classical Conditioning   Some of our attitudes are acquired through the simple associative process of classical conditioning, described in Chapter 6. Whenever positive or negative experiences (elicited by the unconditioned stimulus, or UCS) are paired with an attitude object (the conditioned stimulus, or CS), new attitudes are likely to be formed. For example, you may have a fairly neutral opinion about rice: It goes nicely with a variety of foods, but you cannot get very excited about it. Now assume that you are

My 11-year-old plays on a YMCA-sponsored basketball team. One of his teammates is unbelievably aggressive. When a game starts he treats his opponents like they are enemies. The way he throws his elbows around, and sometimes even his fists, you would think he was in a war instead of a children's game. He was even thrown out of one game for unsportsmanlike conduct. Recently I discovered where this attitude came from. His dad plays on a city league team sponsored by a local business. The other day, I attended a game and there was the little menace, tagging along with his father. He looked like a younger version of his dad, but they had more in common than looks. The old man played just like the kid, only with a nastier attitude toward his opponents. And all the time, the kid was drinking it all in. Well, as the saying goes, like father, like son. (*Authors' files*)

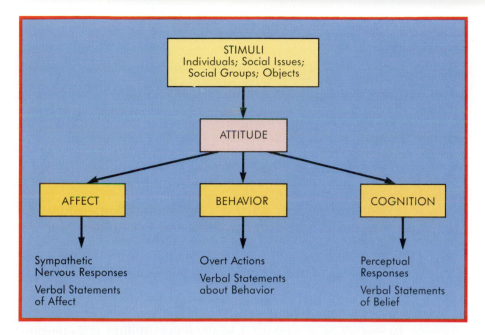

FIGURE 16.2 **THE THREE-COMPONENT (TRIPARTITE) MODEL OF ATTITUDES**

(*Source:* From Breckler, 1954)

kidnapped by terrorists, and that for weeks you are given nothing to eat but rice. You may well come out of this conditioning experience with a strong negative attitude toward rice.

Advertisers employ classical conditioning techniques in their efforts to sway our attitudes toward a particular product. For example, at the time of this writing a manufacturer of a popular brand of men's shirts is running television commercials in which a presumably neutral object (a dress shirt) is worn by attractive women with the implied suggestion that the shirt is all they are wearing. The expectation is that the women will serve as a UCS, eliciting positive associations on the part of the viewer. Although the average male viewer may logically realize that the shirt has nothing to do with attractive women, the association may nevertheless be strong enough to influence his buying habits.

Operant Conditioning We also acquire attitudes by receiving praise, approval, or acceptance for expressing them, and we may be punished for expressing other attitudes. When attitudes produce punishment (or when they fail to elicit social approval), they tend to be weakened; when they are reinforced, they tend to be strengthened (Insko & Melson, 1969). For instance, a child who discovers that making derogatory comments about a different racial group will earn a nod of approval from her parents is likely to develop a strong racial prejudice.

Direct Experience with the Attitude Object Finally, we learn many of our attitudes through direct contact with the attitude object. For instance, you may test-drive an auto with a revolutionary new suspension system and as a result of this experience develop a very favorable attitude toward the new design. Attitudes acquired through direct experience are likely to be more deeply ingrained and held more confidently than those learned through observation (Fazio et al., 1983; Fazio & Zanna, 1981; Wu & Shaffer, 1987). Thus, trying the new suspension system yourself is likely to influence your attitude much more strongly than is watching a television commercial or even hearing about the design from friends who have tried it.

THE FUNCTIONS OF ATTITUDES

Whether we learn them from our own experiences or from observing others, attitudes serve a number of important functions in our lives

Operant conditioning helps to explain how and why many socially unacceptable attitudes and behaviors continue for generations. This infant child of a KKK member will probably earn a nod of approval from her parents when she makes racially derogatory comments and, thus, will be encouraged to engage in similar behavior in the future.

(Brigham, 1986; DeBono, 1987). One is an **understanding function:** Attitudes provide a frame of reference that helps us structure and make sense out of the world and our experiences. For example, your attitudes about what personal attributes you favor in a date provide you with a frame of reference for evaluating prospective romantic interests. If a person possesses traits you evaluate positively, you are likely to respond favorably to that individual.

Just as we rely on our own attitudes to evaluate unfamiliar situations or objects, we also rely on the attitudes of others. For instance, suppose a friend has just attended the first lecture in a class you are thinking about signing up for. Your first question to her will probably be something like "Well, how did you like the class and the instructor?" If her attitude is positive, you will be more likely to sign up as well.

A second function of attitudes is a **social identification function.** The attitudes of others provide us with important information about what they are like, just as the attitudes we express tell others about us. That is why, when you date a person for the first time, you usually exchange information about favorite activities, food preferences, music interests, and so forth. Our overall assessment of other people is often strongly influenced by what we perceive to be their likes and dislikes.

A third function of attitudes is a **social adjustment function.** The attitudes we express sometimes allow us to identify with or gain approval from our peers. For instance, if your very attractive date expresses a deep enthusiasm for great Russian literature, you may also immerse yourself in Tolstoy, Dostoevsky, and Turgenev. Of course, attitudes that serve a social adjustment function in one setting may have quite a different effect in a different environment. For example, if you begin describing your favorite passage from *Crime and Punishment* to some acquaintances during the next Saturday night dance, you might soon find yourself standing alone. This brings up the concept of **impression management,** which describes our tendency to select carefully what information we reveal about our attitudes, depending on how we think such information will affect our image in the eyes of others. Figure 16.3 provides a classic example of impression management in action.

Attitudes may also serve a **value-expressive function,** expressing values that have central importance in our lives. For instance, if you are strongly opposed to aggression or violence, you may speak out against family violence, lobby for more humane prison systems, or join a political action group picketing a local producer of components in nuclear weaponry.

Finally, attitudes may sometimes have adverse consequences, especially when they serve an **ego-defensive function.** An example of this is the person who feels powerless and oppressed, and attempts to restore his or her self-esteem by developing negative attitudes about a group of people to

FIGURE 16.3   IMPRESSION MANAGEMENT IN ACTION

(*Source:* From The Des Moines Register, 1980)

SOCIAL ADJUSTMENT AND EXPRESSED ATTITUDES

John Connally, a candidate for the Republican presidential nomination in 1980, glibly revises his position on the Equal Rights Amendment in order to impress a voter. Impression management in action.

The Very Republican Lady from Columbus, Ohio, looked sternly at former Texas Gov. John Connally and asked: "What are your views on the ERA?" "I'm for it," Connally shot back. "I've been for it since 1962."

The Very Republican Lady, obviously no fan of the Equal Rights Amendment, glared. After a short, pained silence, Connally began to revise and extend his remarks. "Actually, I have mixed feelings," he said. "If the amendment would weaken or destroy family life, I'd have to take another look. . . . I wouldn't have voted to extend the time for ratification. That was wrong. . . . So for all practical purposes I guess you could say I'm against it today."

whom he or she can feel superior. This is one of the underlying causes of human prejudice. People who are prejudiced against other ethnic or religious groups may experience ego-enhancement by elevating themselves to a position where they view such groups as "beneath" them. We will have more to say about prejudice later in this chapter.

ATTITUDES AND BEHAVIOR

Whether attitudes serve a positive or negative function, it seems natural to assume that they influence our behavior. If you like jazz, you will be likely to attend a local concert where good jazz is being played, and if you believe strongly that formal religion is important, you will probably participate actively in your church or temple. Do our attitudes, however, always guide our actions? Consider the student who is strongly opposed to cheating but finds at exam time that she is doing so poorly in one course that her chances of being accepted into a graduate program are jeopardized. In this situation, her motive to succeed coupled with her perceived failure may well have a stronger influence on her behavior than her attitude toward cheating.

To what extent do attitudes determine behavior? Sociologists began investigating the relationship between attitudes and behavior over 50 years ago, with surprising results. One widely known study was conducted by sociologist Richard LaPiere (1934) in the early 1930s, a time when there was considerable prejudice against Chinese people in the United States. LaPiere traveled extensively throughout the West and Midwest with a Chinese couple he described as "personable" and "charming." Considering the national attitude toward Chinese, LaPiere expected to be turned away at many hotels and restaurants. However, his traveling companions were served at all of the 184 restaurants they visited, and were rejected at only one of 67 lodging places. Approximately six months later, LaPiere wrote to each of the places he and the Chinese couple had patronized and asked whether they would accept members of the Chinese race as guests at their establishment. Of those restaurants and hotel proprietors who responded (51 percent of the total), over 90 percent said they would not. Many social scientists interpreted these results as indicating that there is little or no relationship between attitudes and behavior.

In the years following publication of LaPiere's findings, dozens of other studies further tested the relationship between attitudes and actions with similar results. These studies asked people to express their attitudes about a variety of objects such as racial minorities, church attendance, and cheating, then compared their actual behavior in a measurable situation related to those attitudes. The measured relationship between attitudes and behavior in such areas and many others was shown to be so small that one social psychologist concluded that ". . . it [seems] considerably more likely that attitudes will be unrelated or only slightly related to behavior than that attitudes will closely be related to action" (Wicker, 1969, p. 65).

DO ATTITUDES HAVE NO IMPACT ON BEHAVIOR?

Intuitively, it seems obvious that attitudes influence behavior, yet the findings of LaPiere and other early researchers lead to just the opposite conclusion. Can you explain this discrepancy? Try to answer this question before reading on, considering the design of LaPiere's experiment and the other early studies.

LaPiere and other early researchers employed a single instance of behavior (such as the yes or no responses to LaPiere's letter) as an indication of the relationship between attitudes and behavior. In contrast, more recent studies have measured a variety of behaviors relevant to the attitude (Brigham, 1986). The results have been significant.

For example, in one study researchers measured people's attitudes toward environmental issues such as pollution control and conservation, and then observed subjects' behaviors over the next two months. Fourteen environmentally relevant behaviors were recorded, including recycling paper, picking up litter, and circulating petitions pertaining to clean environment issues. Considered individually, any one of these behaviors showed only a relatively small or moderate correlation with the subjects' environmental attitudes, but when these actions were treated collectively, attitudes and behaviors were strongly correlated (Weigel & Newman, 1976). A clear implication of this finding is that to make an accurate judgment about someone's attitude toward a particular object, issue, or situation, we should observe as many attitude-reflective behaviors as possible.

When Do Our Attitudes Predict Our Behavior? Studies using multiple behavior indices have suggested that, as we suspected from the start, attitudes are strong predictors of behavior. As the earlier example of attitudes toward cheating illustrated, however, our attitudes do not always predict our behaviors. What determines how influential our attitudes will be?

One important variable is the degree to which other factors influence our behavior. As long as other influences are minimized, our attitudes are likely to guide our behaviors. One influence that is particularly likely to mask the predictive relationship between attitudes and behavior is social expectations. For example, a teenager who has a negative attitude toward drinking alcoholic beverages will usually say no when offered a drink. On the other hand, what if he attends a party at the college where he plans to enroll in the fall, and several of the college students in attendance encourage him to "join the party and drink up"? In this situation, the need to conform to social expectations is particularly strong, and he may well have a beer despite his attitude toward alcohol consumption.

Another variable that influences how closely our behaviors will reflect our attitudes is the relevance of an attitude to the behavior being considered. People may be less inclined to behave consistently with broad attitudes. For example, you may know people who say they support equality of the sexes but refuse to share equally in household chores. In contrast, when there is a close association between an expressed attitude and a particular situation, the picture is often quite different. For instance, our attitudes about the relative skills of several friends who play tennis is probably a good predictor of whom we would ask to team with us in a doubles tournament.

A third condition that affects how well our attitudes can predict our behaviors is simply how conscious we are of our attitudes when we act. We often act without stopping to think about what we are doing. You may believe it is very important to eat a healthy diet, for instance, but if someone passes around a plate of sweet rolls at work, you may pick one up and start eating without even stopping to think. If you are with someone who is also very health conscious when the sweet rolls are passed around, however, that person's abstinence may make you much more aware of your attitude. Then you will be more likely to behave in a way that is consistent with your commitment to health.

A number of studies have shown that attitudes are more strongly related to behavior when subjects are reminded to consider their attitudes before they act (Snyder & Swann, 1976), or when they are made particularly self-conscious (Carver & Scheier, 1978; Diener & Wallbom, 1976). Studies in which subjects have repeatedly reminded themselves of their attitudes (for example, by filling out a series of attitude rating scales) have found that attitudes are more likely to guide behaviors (Fazio, 1986; Powell & Fazio, 1984).

Does Our Behavior Affect Our Attitudes? We have seen that our attitudes often guide our behavior. The reverse is also often the case, for our behaviors may shape our attitudes (Chaiken & Stangor, 1987). For instance, many a college student has looked with amusement or perhaps mild disdain upon those young executive types who dress up in their natty business suits and tuck their *Wall Street Journals* under their arms as they commute to impressive high-rise buildings. These attitudes often change quickly, however, after the students graduate and join the ranks of the employed.

A classic demonstration of the impact of actions upon attitudes was provided by an experiment whose subjects were Duke University women students (Gergen, 1965). Initially, all subjects filled out a questionnaire rating their degree of self-esteem. Some time later, each was separately interviewed. Those in the first group were encouraged to provide honest and accurate self-descriptions; those in the second were urged to present themselves in a very positive light. Some time later, all the women again filled out the self-esteem questionnaire. Of those subjects who had provided presumably inflated descriptions of themselves, most showed a marked enhancement of their self-esteem. In contrast, the self-images of the women in the first group were unchanged. Apparently, even the brief experiences of role-playing a positive self-assessment actually boosted their attitudes about themselves.

CHANGING ATTITUDES

We have just seen that experiences such as taking a job or writing a glowing self-evaluation can produce a change in attitude, but how and why does this attitude change take place? Part of the answer lies in our need for consistency. Just as we attempt to fit new acquaintances into preexisting person schemas in order to minimize the differences between the familiar and the unfamiliar, we also are most secure when our attitudes are consistent both with other attitudes we hold and with our behaviors. This is the basic idea behind the *consistency theories,* which see attitude change as "an attempt on the part of the individual to achieve cognitive equilibrium" (Penrod, 1986, p. 257). We will consider two noteworthy consistency theories: balance theory and cognitive dissonance theory.

Balance Theory **Balance theory** emerges from the writings of Fritz Heider (1946, 1958), who argued that people are inclined to achieve consistency in their attitudes by balancing their beliefs and feelings about a particular issue, object, event, or situation against their attitudes about other people. According to this theory, the attitudes of other people play a significant role in determining whether we maintain our attitudes or change them. For instance, suppose you are strongly opposed to busing as a way to achieve a better racial balance in schools. Now, suppose a person you know named John also has a strong opinion about busing. According to balance theory, if you like John, and he also is opposed to busing, you will feel no need to change your attitude because a "balanced" cognitive state will exist. Similarly, if you dislike John and he supports busing, you will still be in a balanced state because your dislike of John will cause you to discount his opinions.

In contrast, you will be in an unbalanced state if you like John and discover that he supports busing, or if you dislike John and find that he is dead set against busing. To restore balance, you might: (1) decide that John is not such a good guy after all (which will then allow you to reject his opinions); (2) become a supporter of busing so that you will not be identified with the viewpoint of someone you dislike; or (3) decide John is not such a bad guy after all.

Cognitive Dissonance Theory Like balance theory, **cognitive dissonance theory** is concerned with the ways in which beliefs and attitudes are consistent or inconsistent with one another (Festinger, 1957). The cognitive dissonance model, however, focuses more closely on the internal psychological

FIRST PERSON 16.4

One of my really good buddies in college is an older guy that I met in one of my classes. Over the last several months we have spent a lot of time together, studying, hanging out, going to ball games—the kinds of things good friends do together. All this time he said very little about his background. Then one day in sociology class, we were discussing the criminal justice system and my buddy ups and says that he is an ex-con and that he believes that if more emphasis were placed on rehabilitation through jobs and education, there would be a lot fewer parolees returning to prison. He went on to say how he got an early release from prison conditioned upon his going to college and keeping his grades up. All the time I had been hanging out with him, and not a word.

Before his "revelation" I had considered convicts and ex-cons as the dregs of society—people that I would never associate with. Now I'm not so sure anymore. Obviously, there are some exceptions judging from the actions of my friend. Maybe he is right that many ex-cons would turn out to be okay citizens if given half a chance. (Authors' files)

comfort or discomfort of the individual. According to this theory, a person experiences a state of discomfort, or *dissonance,* whenever two related cognitions (thoughts or perceptions) are in conflict. For example, imagine that you have always considered yourself a supporter of busing, but you find yourself protesting when it is announced the next year your daughter will be bused to a school in an economically disadvantaged area. There is a discrepancy between what you believe and the way you perceive yourself acting, and if you become aware of it (it is quite possible that you will not), you will experience dissonance.

Like hunger, dissonance is an unpleasant state that motivates its own reduction, but while hunger requires a person to interact with the environment to achieve its reduction, dissonance may be reduced merely by realigning the key cognitive elements to restore a state of *consonance,* or psychological comfort. Thus, you may reduce your dissonance over the busing issue by changing your attitude to oppose busing, so that it will be consistent with your behavior. You might also restore consonance by philosophically aligning yourself with the notion that if you believe in something you should support it with your actions even at the risk of personal hardship.

The cognitive dissonance theory has been supported by numerous studies. An example is a study of Princeton University men who had all indicated that they were opposed to banning alcohol from campus (Croyle & Cooper, 1983). These subjects were all asked to write a letter that forcefully argued *in favor of* banning alcohol from campus. Half of these writers were reminded that their participation in this effort was purely voluntary; the other half were authoritatively ordered to register their arguments. At a later point, after the letter-writing process was completed, the researchers again assessed the subjects' attitudes toward the proposed ban.

PREDICTING THE RESULTS OF THE PRINCETON STUDY

Based on cognitive dissonance theory, would you predict that subjects in either of these groups demonstrated noteworthy changes in their attitudes toward banning alcohol on campus? Only one group or both? Why? Think about these questions and make your predictions before reading on.

As predicted by the cognitive dissonance theory, writing a letter in favor of something they opposed created cognitive dissonance in the Princeton subjects, most of whom reduced this dissonance by changing their attitudes. This shift in attitudes was more pronounced for those subjects who saw their participation as voluntary in nature. Apparently, if we act contrary to our prevailing attitudes, and if we cannot attribute our actions to coercion, we are more likely to see the rationale for what we are doing and to come to believe in it.

This phenomenon is believed to have accounted, at least in part, for the success of certain "brainwashing" tactics on some American prisoners during the Korean conflict. The captors began by persuading prisoners to make some minor statement like "America is certainly not perfect." Next, prisoners might be asked to write down some flaws in the United States system of government. Eventually, they might be encouraged to develop a speech denouncing America. The inducement to take these actions might be something quite minor, such as a few extra privileges, more food, and so forth. In the end, the prisoner's awareness that his actions were not induced by coercion and that others were aware of his unpatriotic statements might actually cause him to change his attitude toward his homeland to be consistent with his behavior, thus reducing dissonance (Schein, 1956).

Persuasion The balance theory and the cognitive dissonance theory help explain why we change our attitudes about things. They do not explain how a speaker can persuade members of an audience to change their attitudes, or why a talk with someone we respect can be enough to convert us to supporters of a particular cause.

We know that some persuasive efforts are more effective than others. What makes the difference? Carl Hovland and his colleagues at Yale University tackled this question in the 1950s, and found three elements to be particularly important in persuasive communication: the source of the message, the way in which the message is stated, and the characteristics of the message recipients (the audience).

The Communicator If a close friend whom you respect and trust becomes involved in a fringe religious movement and tries to persuade you to join, you are more likely to reevaluate your attitude toward such movements than if a person you did not like approached you. Research demonstrates that the source or origin of a persuasive communication is a very important determinant of whether or not we change our attitude. The probability that persuasion will succeed is highest when the source of persuasion is seen as possessing any or all of the qualities of credibility, power, and attractiveness.

A communicator with the quality of *credibility* is more likely to succeed in changing our attitude. Two important elements of credibility are perceived expertise and trustworthiness. Our perception of expertise involves our assessment of the communicator's knowledge about a topic and of his or her experience, education, and competence to speak authoritatively about it. For instance, when you watch the Super Bowl on television, you are less likely to dispute the views of a commentator who was once a football pro than if the same comment were offered by a friend with no athletic experience.

A second important element of credibility is trustworthiness—our perception of a communicator as being basically honest. Trustworthiness is important because we typically make attributions about why a person is advocating a particular position. As we might predict from the correspondent inference theory, discussed earlier in this chapter, our perception of trustworthiness is enhanced when the communicator seems to be arguing against his or her own best interests, or when the content of the message is not what we expect. For example, one investigation found that university students were more inclined to be persuaded by arguments against pornography if they perceived that the communicator was opposed to censorship than if the communicator favored censorship (Wood & Eagly, 1981). In another study, a convicted felon who argued that police should have fewer legal constraints placed upon their efforts to deal with crime produced significantly greater attitude changes than a criminal who argued that police power should be restrained (Walster et al., 1966). In still another study, listeners were more persuaded by a proenvironmental speech if they perceived that the speaker either had a probusiness background or had tailored his or her speech to a probusiness group than if they perceived the opposite to be true (Eagly et al., 1978).

A second factor that influences how persuasive a communicator will be is *power.* At least as it is measured by overt expression, attitude change is particularly likely to occur when three conditions are met: (1) the communicator has the power to administer rewards or punishments to the target; (2) the communicator very much wants his or her message to have the desired effect on the target; and (3) the target knows the communicator will be able to evaluate whether or not she or he conforms to the message (McGuire, 1969; Rosenbaum & Rosenbaum, 1975). In view of these findings, it is not surprising that children often express attitudes similar to those of their parents, and that low-level management people may mirror the attitudes of higher level executives.

A third strong influence on a communicator's effectiveness is attractiveness. A physically attractive communicator is often more effective than one whose appearance is either average or unattractive (Kelman, 1965;

Mills & Aronson, 1965). Attractiveness is influenced not only by physical looks, however, but also by likability, pleasantness, and perceived similarity to the audience. A communicator who does not have these qualities is usually less effective in changing people's attitudes than one who does.

The Message Just as the source of a message has a strong influence on whether we are persuaded to change our attitude, the message itself is also a critical factor. Researchers have found that several message characteristics may be particularly important. One factor is the degree of discrepancy between the message and the audience's viewpoint. If the discrepancy is too great, the audience may discount or dismiss the message, especially if the communicator has low credibility. On the other hand, too little discrepancy may result in the audience failing to perceive any difference of opinion or persuasive intent (Hovland et al., 1957; Peterson & Koulack, 1969). Thus, attitude change is often greatest at moderate levels of discrepancy.

In some cases, messages will be more effective if they appeal to emotion (particularly the emotion of fear) than if they appeal to logic. However, people who are well informed and personally concerned about a particular issue may be persuaded more effectively by logic than by emotional appeals (Petty et al., 1983). Although appeals to fear are sometimes effective, the relationship between fear and persuasion is very complex and difficult to generalize about.

For example, in one early study researchers used three separate messages to sway attitudes about oral hygiene. Subjects in the high-fear group were shown horrific color slides of rotting teeth and diseased gums, and were told that these terrible conditions were the direct result of poor oral hygiene. Those in the moderate-fear condition heard a message about the importance of good oral hygiene illustrated by pictures of mild gum infections and tooth decay. Finally, those in the low-fear group were simply told that failure to brush regularly can lead to tooth decay and gum disease; no pictures were used. The high-fear message was found to be the least effective in changing behavior (and presumably attitudes), whereas the low-fear message produced the greatest change in dental habits (Janis & Feshback, 1953). How can this result be explained? Researchers interpreted the results as indicating that fear may promote attitude change only up to a certain point: When tension becomes too great, people may attempt to reduce their anxiety by blocking out or discounting the message (McGuire, 1968a).

Several later studies have demonstrated that, under some conditions, messages with moderate-fear appeal may be effective in changing attitudes and behavior. If the source has high credibility and if the fear-arousing message contains clear information about what to do to avoid the fearful consequences, people are more likely to be persuaded by the message (Leventhal & Nerenz, 1983; Rogers & Mewborn, 1976).

Novelty is another message characteristic that can make a difference. Generally speaking, a message that is presented in an unusual or novel fashion is more effective than timeworn arguments. People tend to tune out messages they have heard too many times before. Also, the expectation of something new or novel makes a message more attractive (Sears & Freedman, 1965).

Still another quality that helps determine how influential a message will be is whether it presents one or both sides of the issue. Interestingly, the effect of this variable seems to depend on the characteristics of the audience. A one-sided argument seems to be more effective if the audience is poorly educated and/or unfamiliar with the issue (Chu, 1967; Hovland et al., 1949), while a two-sided presentation works better with a well-educated, well-informed audience (Lumsdaine & Janis, 1953). In fact, well-informed people may react strongly against one-sided arguments in order to protect their sense of free will or as a reaction against feeling coerced into adopting a particular view—a process called *psychological reactance* (Jones & Brehm, 1970).

The Audience   We have just seen that an audience's intelligence and knowledgeability can make a difference in the effectiveness of tactics such as presenting one or both sides of an issue. A variety of other personality factors also seem to influence people's susceptibility to persuasion. For one, the age of an audience seems to make a difference. Researchers have found that teenagers and young adults, whose attitudes and opinions are not yet as well defined as those of older people, are more likely to shift their attitudes in response to a persuasive communication (Sears, 1979).

Another factor that may make a difference is the self-esteem of listeners in the audience. Studies conducted in the late 1960s indicated that people with high self-esteem seem generally less likely to yield to persuasion than those with low self-esteem (Cook, 1970; McGuire, 1969), a finding that was interpreted as indicating that people with a very positive self-image have confidence in their opinions, which they may view as being more credible than those of the communicator. A more recent investigation, however, reported that people with high self-esteem are just as easily persuaded as those with a low self-image (Baumeister & Covington, 1985). More research is needed to clarify these mixed findings.

Research has also been unclear on the impact of listeners' intelligence on attitude change. For a persuasive message to be effective, an audience must both comprehend it and be willing to yield to the views of another. High intelligence tends to increase comprehension, but it may also reduce a person's inclination to yield to persuasion. Therefore it is difficult to draw any definitive conclusion about the relationship between intelligence and persuadability. One researcher, William McGuire (1968b), has theorized that attitude change may be greatest among listeners with moderate levels of intelligence, since their likelihood of both understanding a message and yielding to it are relatively strong. Research support for this commonsense interpretation has been mixed (Eagly, 1981; Eagly & Warren, 1976).

When the persuader is able to get the audience to think seriously about the points he or she is making, the chances of attitude change are enhanced (Petty & Cacioppo, 1986). To the extent that the audience members are open to a particular viewpoint, getting them to think about and elaborate upon the message in their own minds is likely to increase the probability of attitude change.

SOCIAL INFLUENCE

We have seen how our feelings about certain people, groups, ideas, or situations may be changed by people we come in contact with. However, **social influence**—the efforts by others to alter our feelings, beliefs, and behavior—extends beyond merely changing how we feel about something. In this section we will examine conformity, compliance, and obedience, all of which are forms of social influence that seek to change our behavior and/or beliefs.

CONFORMITY

Conformity refers to a tendency to change or modify our own beliefs or behaviors so that they are consistent with those of other people. Often these shifts in opinion or actions are accompanied, at least to some degree, by a perceived social pressure to conform.

Our outward conformity to group standards may or may not mean that we have accepted the group's position. Morton Deutsch and Harold Gerald (1955) suggest that we should make a distinction between **informational social influence,** in which we accept a group's beliefs or behaviors as providing accurate information about reality, and **normative social influence,** in which we conform not because of an actual change in our beliefs, but because we think that we will benefit in some way, such as gaining approval or avoiding rejection. It is helpful to keep this distinction between

FIGURE 16.4 RESULTS OF CON-FORMITY STUDY JUDGING MOVEMENT OF A LIGHT

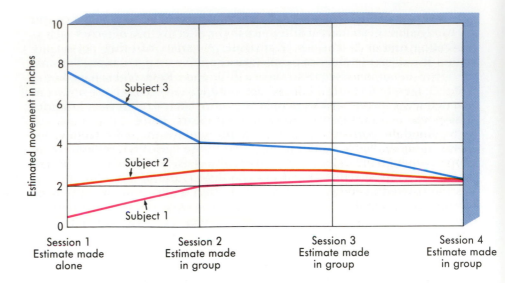

informational and normative social influence in mind as we explore what we have learned about conformity.

One of the first investigations of social influence explored how norms develop in small groups (Sherif, 1937). During an initial session, each subject was seated alone in a dark room and asked to stare at a tiny pinpoint of light about 15 feet away. The subject was then asked to estimate how far the light moved from its original position. (Actually, the light was stationary, but it appeared to move due to a perceptual illusion.) There was considerable variation in these initial estimates. During a second session, the subject was joined by two other participants; all three repeated the procedure of the first session, voicing their estimates in the presence of each other. This procedure was repeated in two more group sessions. Figure 16.4 shows what happened in the second, third, and fourth sessions. As you can see, the estimates of the three participants progressively converged until by session four they were essentially identical.

DISTINGUISHING INFORMATIONAL SOCIAL INFLUENCE FROM NORMATIVE SOCIAL INFLUENCE

In the study just discussed, do you think that the subjects' final estimates reflected a genuine belief that this was the correct estimate (informational social influence), or do you think they felt pressured to conform even though they privately disagreed with the consensus group estimate (normative social influence)? How would you find out which form of social influence was operative in this case? Give these questions some thought before reading on.

The researchers provided an answer to the question by conducting additional solo sessions after the group norms had been established. In these sessions, subjects' solo estimates continued to reflect the group norm rather than corresponding to their initial estimates in the first individual sessions. The fact that subjects continued to express group estimates clearly demonstrates that they were responding to informational and not normative social influence.

In the study we have been discussing, subjects were faced with an ambiguous situation in which it was difficult to distinguish between reality and imagination. In such a circumstance, it is understandable that they relied on others as sources of information. What about situations, however, in which people clearly know what is correct but still experience pressure to conform to group norms that deviate from the truth? For instance, what if you were asked which of the three comparison lines in Figure 16.5 was equal to the standard line—and although you knew that the answer was B, everyone else answered C? This was the situation that Solomon Asch (1951) presented to subjects in a classic experiment.

In the experiment, seven men sat around a table and were asked to make a series of 18 line-comparison judgments such as the one just described. Six of the men were confederates of the experimenter; the one subject was unaware that he was being set up. None of the 18 tasks was ambiguous; the correct answer was always readily apparent. The experimental design called for each group member to provide his response in turn as Asch sequentially solicited answers from each man, moving from his left to right around the table. The naïve subject was always located so that he was the sixth of the seven subjects to make his judgment (see Figure 16.6). On the first two trials, all seven chose the correct line. On 12 of the remaining 16 trials, however, the confederates unanimously chose the wrong comparison line.

How did the subjects respond? Many showed signs of strain, leaning forward, straining, double-checking, and glancing around at the other group members. Nevertheless, about one in every three subjects adjusted his responses to match the incorrect judgments of the confederates in half or more of the 12 conformity trials. Only 25 percent of the subjects completely resisted group pressure by making the correct response on all 12 of the conformity trials.

Since the correct answers were so obvious, Asch's experiment seems to be a clear example of normative social influence. Just to make sure, Asch interviewed the subjects after the experiment was completed. He found that in some cases the answers had been the result of normative social influence: these subjects had gone along with the group consensus against their better judgment because they did not want to appear different from the others. However, some of the conforming subjects stated that they had thought that the majority opinion was probably correct and that their own perceptions were inaccurate. If this explanation is taken at face value, we must conclude

FIGURE 16.5 ASCH'S LINE-COMPARISON TASK

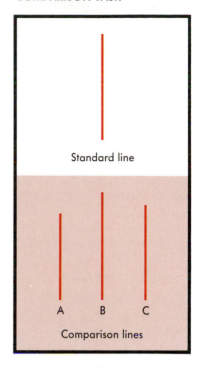

Which of the three comparison lines is/are equal to the standard line?

FIGURE 16.6 SUBJECTS IN ASCH'S CONFORMITY EXPERIMENT

In the classic study of conformity, Solomon Asch had subjects sit around a table and judge which of three lines was equal in length to a standard line they had seen earlier. The only real subject in the situation depicted in this photo was number 6; the others were paid confederates of Asch. Although the task was very easy, on some of the trials the confederates all lied about which line was correct. When it was number 6's turn to respond, he usually showed signs of conflict (straining, double-checking) over whether to conform to the group judgment or give the response that he perceived was correct.

that informational social influence occurs even in unambiguous situations where conformity goes clearly contrary to reality. (Of course, it is also possible that subjects who claimed they thought the majority was right might have only been attempting to justify their submission to the influence of the group [Berkowitz, 1986].)

When Are We Most Likely to Conform: In the years since Asch's study, there have been numerous additional experiments on conformity. In general these studies have found that our tendency to conform will be increased in situations in which some conditions are met. We list these conditions briefly as a conclusion to this discussion of conformity:

1. *Unanimity of the majority group.* We are much more likely to conform if the majority group is unanimous (Allen, 1965; Allen & Levine, 1969); even one dissenter greatly reduces our inclination to conform. Asch found that if one dissident agreed with the subject, the subject was almost 18 percent less likely to conform (Asch, 1951).

2. *Perception that majority group members act independently.* If we perceive that the other members of a group are acting independently of one another, we are more likely to conform than if we sense some collusion among them (Wilder, 1978).

3. *Majority group size.* The size of the group makes a difference. If there are at least three or four other people in the group, we are more likely to conform. Further increases in group size generally do not increase the likelihood of conformity, and may even decrease it (Gerald et al., 1968; Tanford & Penrod, 1984).

4. *Familiarity with the attitude object.* If we have no preconceived notions about the attitude object, we are more likely to act in a conforming manner than if this is not the case (Berkowitz, 1986).

5. *Low self-esteem.* People whose sense of personal self-worth is low (Santee & Maslach, 1982) or who are especially concerned about social relationships (Thibaut & Strickland, 1956; Mullen, 1983) are more likely to conform than are people with a higher self-esteem or less regard for social relationships.

6. *Perceptions about other group members.* We are more likely to conform if we consider the other group members to be of higher status than ourselves (Forsyth, 1983; Giordano, 1983), or if we have high regard for the other group members (Berkowitz, 1954, 1986). We are also more likely to conform if we perceive other group members as having power over us (in the sense of being able to administer rewards or punishments) (Berkowitz, 1986) or if we know that other group members will be able to observe our actions (Berkowitz, 1954).

COMPLIANCE

Although both conformity and compliance involve yielding to some pressure exerted by others, **compliance** involves an element of coercion as well in that it takes place in situations where we alter our behavior in response to direct requests from others. Compliance is a very common form of social influence. We all experience a barrage of requests daily—ranging from friends, lovers, or family members asking us to change certain aspects of our behavior to requests by politicians or salespersons for votes or purchase of goods. Social psychologists have noted a number of techniques or forms of pressure that people use to increase the likelihood of compliance with their requests. Two of these methods are the foot-in-the-door technique and the door-in-the-face technique.

The Foot-in-the-Door Technique   Researchers have demonstrated that sometimes the best road to compliance is to begin by getting a person to agree to a relatively minor or trivial request that serves as a set-up for a second, more major request (which is the actual goal). This so-called **foot-in-the-door technique** (Freedman & Fraser, 1966) is widely used by salespeople who attempt to produce a favorable attitude toward their product. For example, if a car salesperson can get you to comply with an initial request to "come in the office and we will run some numbers," you are more likely to develop the attitude that "I need that car." It has been suggested that the success of the foot-in-the-door technique is related to the fact that when people comply with a request, they begin to perceive themselves as "the kind of person who does this sort of thing" and thus are inclined to make even greater commitments to a particular line of requests in order to be consistent with their perceived self-image (Pliner et al., 1974).

The Door-in-the-Face Technique   Suppose you are moving to another apartment and you want your husky neighbor to help you move your piano. Anticipating a likely negative response to your request, you first ask if he would mind spending the afternoon helping you move all your stuff. As expected, he begs off, claiming a heavy study load. Next, you ask if he would have just a few minutes to help with the piano. How can he say no to such a reasonable request after he has already "slammed the door in your face" in response to the larger request? While some people might say no to both requests, research demonstrates that we are often more inclined to comply with a moderate request if we have already refused a larger one than if the smaller request is presented alone.

This **door-in-the-face technique,** which is essentially the opposite of the foot-in-the-door method, was demonstrated in an interesting study in which a group of college students were asked to serve as unpaid counselors to delinquent youth for two years at the rate of two hours per week. Predictably, none complied with this request. However, when presented with a second, far more moderate request to take the delinquents on a short outing to the zoo, 50 percent complied with this request. In contrast, only 17 percent of a control group of students agreed to this smaller request when it was presented alone (Cialdini et al., 1975).

OBEDIENCE

All of us routinely succumb to social influence by conforming to behavioral standards established by others or by complying with the requests of associates. Less commonly, social influence takes the form of **obedience,** in which we alter our behavior in response to commands or orders from people we may perceive as having power or authority.

The most dramatic study of obedience was conducted by social psychologist Stanley Milgram (1963). As you may recall from Chapter 2, Milgram sought to determine if subjects would inflict considerable pain on others merely because an authority figure instructed them to do so. His all-male subjects thought they were participating in a study of the effects of punishment on learning. They were told to use an intercom system to present problems to another person (a total stranger who was actually an accomplice of the experimenter) who was strapped in a chair in another room, and to administer a shock each time the "learner" gave the wrong answer to a problem. Labeled switches on the "shock apparatus" ranged from a low of 15 volts to a high of 450 volts; subjects were instructed to increase the voltage with each successive error the learner made.

According to design, the learner made many errors. The result was a progressive escalation of shock intensity that posed a serious dilemma for the subjects, virtually all of whom exhibited high levels of stress and discomfort as they administered the shocks. Should they continue subjecting the learner to pain, or should they refuse to go on? Whenever they hesitated or protested, the experimenter pressured them to continue by such commands as "It is absolutely essential that you continue," or "You have no other choice, you must go on."

Despite the fact that all subjects were volunteers, paid in advance, and obviously distressed, only a minority failed to exhibit total obedience. In fact, fully 65 percent proceeded to the final 450-volt level! A number of subsequent studies conducted with different research populations reported findings similar to those of Milgram (Kilham & Mann, 1974; Shanab & Yahya, 1977).

Why do people succumb to such destructive instances of obedience? This question has been explored and debated by both social scientists and laypersons. Social psychologists Robert Baron and Donn Byrne (1987) have outlined three reasons why people may respond to social influence in the form of destructive obedience. First, many people seem to believe that their personal accountability for their actions is somehow diminished or relieved by those authority figures who issue the commands. In Milgram's research, subjects were told at the outset that the experimenter rather than the participants was responsible for the learner's well-being. Thus, one can see how they may have felt less responsible for their own actions. It is disheartening, however, that this same logic has been employed by people like Nazi war criminal Adolf Eichmann, who committed unimaginable atrocities against the Jewish people during Hitler's reign of terror, and Lieutenant William Calley, who was court-martialed for the 1968 massacre of Vietnamese civilians at My Lai, both of whom justified their acts by claiming "I was only following orders."

A second factor contributing to obedience is that authority figures often possess highly visible symbols of their power or status that make it difficult to resist their dictates (symbols such as the white coat and title of a researcher, or the uniform and rank of a military officer). The impact of these external trappings of power was demonstrated in one experiment in which people were randomly stopped on the street and ordered to give a dime to a person in need of parking meter change. Subjects were decidedly more inclined to obey this order if it was issued by someone wearing a fire fighter's uniform than if the source of the command was dressed in a business suit or laborer's clothes (Bushman, 1984).

Finally, people often comply with orders, even orders that are potentially destructive in nature, because they are "sucked in" by a series of graduated demands, beginning with seemingly innocuous or harmless orders that gradually escalate to orders of a more serious or potentially destructive nature. For example, a corporate executive might request that a "loyal" employee, who has a friend who works at a competitor company, ask the friend if his or her employer plans to introduce a new product line. Later, such requests might escalate to orders to ask specific questions about the nature of the products on the drawing board, followed by commands to conduct outright industrial espionage. In a sense, this is what occurred with Milgram's subjects, who were first required to deliver only mild shocks followed by progressively more intense punishment. The problem with such a gradual escalation of demand intensity is that a person is often unable to distinguish a definite point at which disobedience is clearly a more appropriate course of action than obedience.

PREJUDICE

Consider the following conversation overheard recently by the authors. The speakers are a third-year medical student and a college psychology teacher.

> STUDENT: Homosexuals may not be the only people who get AIDS, but they are certainly the major reason why all of us now have to live in fear of this disease.

TEACHER: The vast majority of AIDS cases in Central Africa have occurred among heterosexuals.

STUDENT: Well, if that is true, then it probably just indicates that the
Africans will not tolerate promiscuous relationships among
homosexuals like what occurs in places like New York and
San Francisco.

TEACHER: Many epidemiologists are now predicting that in a few years
America will be just like Central Africa, with the majority of
AIDS cases reported among heterosexuals.

STUDENT: Well, if this occurs it will be further evidence of what is already clearly obvious—homosexuals are so indiscriminant and
promiscuous in their sexual practices that they don't care who
they put at risk.

This AIDS literature was published
to inform people that not all AIDS
victims are white and homosexual.
Stereotypes such as this can be
very dangerous and could ultimately harm the person holding
such a stereotype.

The medical student's point of view is an excellent example of **prejudice,** a negative, unjustifiable, and inflexible attitude toward a group and
its members that is based on erroneous information. This definition contains three important elements. First, prejudice is usually characterized by
very negative or hostile feelings toward all members of a group, often a
minority, without any attention to individual differences among members
of that group. Second, prejudice is based on inaccurate or incomplete information. For instance, the medical student in our example incorrectly
assumed that AIDS is a disease of homosexuals and that heterosexuals who
get AIDS are victims of the promiscuity of homosexual people. Finally,
prejudice demonstrates great resistance to change even in the face of compelling contradictory evidence. The medical student was not about to revise
his opinion that AIDS is inextricably linked to the sexual practices of homosexuals, despite contradictory evidence.

Prejudice is built upon **stereotypes,** preconceived and oversimplified
beliefs and expectations about the traits of members of a particular group
that do not account for individual differences. These stereotyped beliefs,
coupled with hostile feelings, often predispose people to act in an abusive
and discriminatory fashion toward members of a disliked or hated minority.
The widespread incidence of **discrimination** (the behavioral consequence
of prejudice in which victims of prejudice are treated differently from other
people) throughout the world reveals what a profoundly adverse impact
prejudice has upon human society.

To believe that black people are lazy, that women are low in ambi-
tion, that overweight people are gluttonous, or that homosexuals are promiscuous is to stereotype all members of a group. To devalue or feel
contempt for blacks, women, overweight people, or homosexuals is to be
prejudiced. To avoid hiring, associating with, renting to, or acknowledging
the contributions of such people is to discriminate. Thus, prejudice, like all
other attitudes is composed of three basic components: beliefs, feelings,
and behavior. How can prejudice be explained? We turn to that question
next.

OUTGROUPS, INGROUPS, AND THE CAUSES OF PREJUDICE

Central to any explanation of prejudice is our inclination to define
ourselves at least partly according to the particular group we belong to. We
all tend to categorize ourselves according to race, age, education, creed,
economic level, and so forth—a process that inevitably leads us to categorize
people who do not belong to these groups as "different." The result is that
we divide our world into two groups: "us" and "them" (Baron & Byrne,
1987). The very process of being in the "us" or **ingroup** category tends to
create an **ingroup bias** (a tendency to see one's own group in a favorable
light) while at the same time inducing a negative attitude or prejudice
against the **outgroup.**

A number of studies have demonstrated that ingroup bias and prejudice toward the outgroup often occur when experimental subjects are sep-

arated into we-they groups based on trivial factors that bear no relationship to real-life social categories (Tajfel, 1982; Tajfel & Turner, 1979; Turner, 1984; Wilder, 1981). By perceiving their ingroup as superior to an out-group, people seem to be attempting to enhance their self-esteem.

Competition between Groups   If we already tend to view the world in terms of "us" and "them," the addition of another ingredient—competition for jobs, power, or other limited resources—adds to the likelihood that hostility and prejudice will develop. In such circumstances the more dominant group may exploit and discriminate against a less powerful group. This was demonstrated during the development of this country, when competition for land between European settlers and native Americans led to prejudice, mistreatment, and extreme acts of discrimination against the minority native Americans (Brigham & Weissbach, 1972). Today in our country, competition for jobs has been viewed as a source of prejudice between whites and Hispanics, native Americans and German immigrants, Chinese and whites, Cuban immigrants and white Floridians, and whites and blacks (Aronson, 1980).

The manner in which intergroup competition can produce hostility, conflict, and prejudice was demonstrated in a classic experiment conducted by Muzafer Sherif and his colleagues (1961), who set up a summer camp for a group of all white, middle-class, bright, well-adjusted boys, ages 11 and 12, near Robbers' Cave, Oklahoma. Initially, the boys lived together in harmony as they worked on a number of cooperative projects such as building a rope bridge and conducting cookouts. However, the researchers soon divided the boys into two separate groups, the Eagles and the Rattlers. After several days of living, playing, and working in separate groups, both the Eagles and the Rattlers developed strong senses of ingroup solidarity.

The next phase of the experiment was to engage the Eagles and Rattlers in a series of competitions, such as touch football games and a tug-of-war, in which prizes were awarded to the winning teams. As the competition became very intense, so did stereotyping, hostility, and overt conflicts between the groups. Thus, the introduction of competition between two clearly defined groups transformed a harmonious atmosphere into one of prejudice and hostility. What happened to the Eagles and the Rattlers? The Health Psychology and Life discussion, "Reducing Prejudice," describes how Sherif and his associates were able to undo what they had done; it also contains suggestions for minimizing prejudice in other situations.

Frustration, Scapegoating, and Prejudice   Just as competition can lead to hostility and prejudice under certain conditions, so can frustration. People who are frustrated by their lack of accomplishments or by adverse living conditions often vent their frustrations on scapegoats whom they perceive as being less powerful than themselves, such as members of a minority group. An example of how frustration may be tied to prejudice is provided by data relating economic conditions in the South from 1882 to 1930 to violence of whites toward blacks. Research has shown that whenever the price of cotton decreased during this period, the number of lynchings of blacks by whites increased (Hovland & Sears, 1940).

The relationship between frustration and prejudice was demonstrated in an experiment in which researchers first measured subjects' attitudes toward a variety of minority groups, then frustrated the subjects by denying them a chance to see a good movie and making them complete a series of difficult tasks instead. The subjects' attitudes toward the same minority groups were measured a second time, after this frustrating experience. This time they demonstrated a marked increase in prejudice not exhibited by control subjects who had not experienced the frustrating condition (Miller & Bugelski, 1948). In related experiments, students who are made to feel like failures have demonstrated an increased tendency to

HEALTH PSYCHOLOGY AND LIFE

REDUCING PREJUDICE

The text discussion of the causes of prejudice looks at the Robbers' Cave study, in which researchers created an atmosphere of prejudice and hostility at a boys' camp by creating groups and then encouraging intergroup competition. The final phase of the study was a prejudice-reduction phase. How did the researchers undo what they had done? Their strategy, as well as techniques used in some other experiments, provides a valuable lesson on how to reduce and in some cases prevent prejudice.

To reduce the prejudice they had created between the two camp groups, the Eagles and the Rattlers, researchers created situations in which the members of the two groups had to cooperate to achieve goals beneficial to all. For example, in one situation the two groups had to pool their money to rent a movie, and in another the two groups had to work together to fix a water supply that had been sabotaged by the experimenters. After several days of cooperative efforts, the hostility between the two groups dissolved, intergroup friendships were formed, and a pattern of cooperative work and play was established.

A number of other studies have demonstrated that prejudice and intergroup hostility can be reduced by encouraging cooperation between groups. An example is the *jigsaw technique,* designed by Elliot Aronson and his colleagues (1978) to encourage classroom cooperation among children of different ethnic and racial backgrounds. Here teachers assign different aspects of a common project to children belonging to different ingroups. The children soon discover that by consulting and cooperating with others, they can complete the project more quickly and more successfully than if they work by themselves or only with children of their own group. Such cooperative efforts have been shown to improve the participants' attitudes toward themselves and other children (regardless of race or ethnic background), as well as toward school itself. Other researchers have placed students in cooperative learning situations where individual outcomes depend on group efforts, with similar results (Johnson et al., 1984; Sharan, 1980). Such methods have even been used to bring together members of extremely hostile groups, such as the Israelis and Egyptians (Kelman & Cohen, 1979).

Social integration is another strategy for reducing prejudice. One study of whites and blacks in a neighborhood that had been integrated in the early 1970s revealed that after one year, the whites living in this neighborhood expressed considerably less prejudice toward blacks than did a comparable group of whites living in a segregated neighborhood (Hamilton & Bishop, 1976). The important factor contributing to the reduction in prejudice was a *disconfirmation of expectancies*—that is, a failure to confirm a number of fears and apprehensions that the white residents had held. When they discovered that increased violence, reduced property values, and other anticipated consequences of integration did not come to pass, their attitude toward blacks changed in a more positive direction. A follow-up study several years later showed that this positive attitude change demonstrated remarkable staying power (Hamilton et al., 1984).

School integration has also been shown to have a positive influence on both attitudes and behavior. For example, one study combined integration with concerted efforts to get blacks and whites to work together toward common goals. The result was improved racial attitudes and many interracial friendships (Patchen 1982). In another study, the cooperative method was applied to newly integrated fifth- and sixth-grade classrooms. Racially mixed study groups were set up in which each member contributed part of the lesson, and all parts had to be completed if the students were to pass their exams. The effects of this "forced" cooperation were profound. Within one week, most children had set aside their racial prejudices (Aronson & Osherow, 1980). Numerous other students provide additional evidence that school desegregation often results in reduced prejudice and better interracial relationships (Cook, 1984a, 1984b; Miller & Brewer, 1984).

Cooperative efforts among children have been shown to improve the participants' attitudes toward themselves and other children (regardless of race or ethnic background).

Social integration is an effective way to reduce prejudice. When people of different racial or ethnic groups associate with each other they often experience a *disconfirmation of expectancies*, that is, the failure to confirm a number of fears and apprehensions that members of different groups hold toward each other.

Interracial sports activities are particularly effective in reducing racial prejudice. This was demonstrated in two separate studies in which the experience of playing on a racially mixed team was found to reduce racial prejudice significantly among both blacks and whites (McConahay, 1978; Slavin & Madden, 1979).

Prejudice can often be prevented from developing in the first place through effective child-rearing practices. If parents allow children to express their frustrations and even anger, such children may not feel the need to suppress their hostility and later displace it onto minority group members. Also, since low self-esteem seems to be related to prejudicial attitudes (Crocker et al., 1987), parents may help counteract prejudice by creating a home environment in which children feel that they are loved and respected and that their opinions count for something.

People who like themselves are inclined to like others and not to feel the need to find some group to put down so they can inflate their own feelings of worth.

In view of the powerful connection between parents' racial attitudes and those of their children, we strongly urge parents to avoid passing prejudicial attitudes to their children. Many of us may be aware that we harbor some deep-seated negative attitudes toward people that we perceive as being different than ourselves. Although we may struggle a lifetime to overcome these prejudicial attitudes, we can free our children from the need to wage similar battles by not sharing our negative attitudes with them. Who knows, perhaps in the process of changing our behaviors for the sake of our children, we may find that our own prejudicial attitudes will also become diminished.

express negative attitudes toward others (Amabile & Glazebrook, 1982; Cialdini & Richardson, 1980).

Social Learning and Prejudice   We have seen that many of our attitudes are acquired by observing and emulating other people, particularly respected role models. Prejudice can also be learned by this process. Racism, sexism, and other negative prejudicial attitudes are often passed directly from parents to children (Katz, 1976a, 1976b; Stephan & Rosenfield, 1978). For example, research has shown that children's racial attitudes are often closely aligned with those of their parents (Ashmore & Del Boca, 1976). Children may internalize the prejudices they observe in their parents and, in some cases, learning this lesson may earn the reward of approval from their parents or others. Even children whose parents are relatively free of prejudice may acquire prejudicial attitudes from other influential sources such as peers, books, and the television and movie media, which often promote stereotypical beliefs and disparaging assessments of minority group members.

A "PREJUDICED PERSONALITY"?

We all have experienced competition and frustration, and most of us have probably observed incidents of prejudice and discrimination. Nevertheless, prejudice is not an attitude that we all adopt. What kinds of qualities predispose a person to develop prejudices? Some reasearch in the late 1940's at the University of California at Berkeley sheds some light on this question. Here, researchers investigated the dynamics of *anti-Semitism* (prejudice against Jewish people) and *ethnocentrism* (general prejudice toward all outgroups). Their findings led them to describe a personality characterized by intolerance, emotional coldness, rigidity, unquestioning submission to higher authority, stereotyped thinking, and identification with power as particularly prone to developing prejudicial attitudes. A person possessing this cluster of characteristics was labeled an **authoritarian personality** (Adorno et al., 1950). These researchers developed a rating scale to detect people with authoritarian personalities, called the *Potentiality for Fascism Scale*, or *F Scale*. Table 16.1 presents some items from the F Scale that an authoritarian personality would be likely to agree with.

How does an authoritarian personality develop? The researchers examined the backgrounds of subjects who scored high on the F Scale and

TABLE 16.1 *Selected Items from the F Scale*

3. America is getting so far from the true American way of life that force may be necessary to restore it.
31. Homosexuality is a particularly rotten form of delinquency and ought to be severely punished.
35. There are some activities so flagrantly un-American that, when responsible officials won't take the proper steps, the wide-awake citizen should take the law into his own hands.
50. Obedience and respect for authority are the most important virtues children should learn.

Source: Adapted from Adorno et al., 1950.

found that such individuals shared certain common features in the manner in which they were reared. Their parents tended to be harsh disciplinarians who used threats, physical punishment, and fear of reprisals to enforce desired behavior. Children were not permitted to express aggressive behaviors themselves, and love was often withheld or made contingent on "being good." As a result, the children were inclined to grow up feeling hostile toward their parents but at the same time dependent upon them. They were also fearful of authority figures and generally insecure. The researchers saw these attitudes and feelings as prime breeding ground for the development of extreme prejudice and displaced hostility.

Although research on the so-called authoritarian personality has provided some important insights into the causes of prejudice, we must be cautious in concluding that there is a cause-and-effect relationship between the patterns of child-rearing just described and the development of prejudicial attitudes. Parents who raise their children in a harsh, authoritarian fashion may be strongly inclined to be prejudiced themselves, with the result that their children may acquire these same prejudices through social learning.

INTERPERSONAL ATTRACTION: LIKING AND LOVING

We have been exploring how we form perceptions of people, how our attitudes affect our behavior, and how people influence us. The most influential people in our adult lives are the people we are closest to—our good friends and our partners in long-term intimate relationships. In this section we first analyze why we feel attracted to certain people as friends and lovers, and then we explore the nature of love.

FACTORS THAT CONTRIBUTE TO INTERPERSONAL ATTRACTION

Have you ever had the experience of meeting a total stranger—at a party, on the first day of school, or in a bookstore—and feeling immediately that you liked one another? If so, you may have wondered what it was that made you feel close to the other person. This question has been the topic of research for some four decades, and the answers that social psychologists have found center on three primary variables: proximity, similarity, and physical attractiveness.

Proximity Although most people overlook **proximity,** or geographical nearness, in listing factors that attracted them to a particular person, this is one of the most important variables. We often develop close relationships with people whom we see frequently in our neighborhoods, in school, at work, or at church or synagogue.

The classic study of the effect of proximity on attraction was conducted by Leon Festinger and his colleagues (1950), who evaluated friendship patterns among married MIT students living in a housing development consisting of 17 two-story buildings with five apartments per floor. All of the residents were asked to name their three best friends among residents of the housing development. These friends almost invariably lived in the

FIGURE 16.7 THE MERE EXPO-
SURE EFFECT

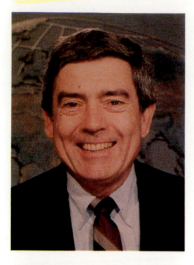

Which of these images do you prefer? Chances are you picked the
top photo, since this is the Dan
Rather you are accustomed to seeing. However, Dan Rather would
probably be inclined to express
preference for the bottom photo,
since this is the image he sees every day in the mirror. Most of us
are seldom satisfied with photographs of ourselves because our
faces do not look quite right. This
is because we are accustomed to
seeing reflected images of ourselves in which left and right are
reversed. Others are more likely to
prefer the natural, nonreversed image of our face.

same building, with next-door neighbors being the most likely to be named
as a friend and the next most likely living two doors away. When the friendship ratings of all participants were pooled, certain people emerged as being
widely liked (that is, included in the lists of many of the residents). The
people who were most often listed as friends lived in apartments close to
heavily trafficked areas such as mailboxes, stairway entries, and exits. Not
coincidentally, people with the fewest friends lived in more out-of-the-way
apartments.

The profound impact of proximity on interpersonal attraction has
been confirmed by other research (Saegert et al., 1973; Segal, 1974). Why is
it such a powerful factor? Social psychologists have offered a number of
plausible explanations. One is simply that familiarity breeds liking. Research has shown that when we are repeatedly exposed to novel stimuli—
whether they be unfamiliar musical selections, nonsense syllables, works of
art, or human faces—our liking for such stimuli increases (Zajonc, 1968,
1970; Moreland & Zajonc, 1982). This phenomenon, called the **mere exposure effect,** explains in part why we are attracted to people in close proximity to us.

The mere exposure effect even seems to influence our view of ourselves. Many of us are seldom satisfied with photographs of ourselves; our
faces do not look quite right. One of the reasons for this may be that the face
we see in the photo is not the one we see staring back at us in the mirror.
Since left and right are reversed in mirror images, the face we see looking
back at us is always slightly different from what others see (Figure 16.7).
Thus we prefer the mirror image of our faces, whereas others will prefer the
natural version. The mere exposure effect was supported by a study in
which women subjects were shown two photos of themselves—one a normal
photo and the other a mirror-image photo—and asked to indicate which
one they preferred. A close friend of each subject also indicated photo preferences. The results: while most subjects preferred the mirror-image photographs, most of their friends preferred the normal photos (Mita et al.,
1977).

Another likely reason why proximity influences attraction is the fact
that the more we see others, the more familiar we become with their ways
and thus the better able we are to predict their behavior. If you have a
good idea of how someone is likely to behave in any given situation, you will
probably be more comfortable with this person. It is also possible that when
we know we shall be seeing a lot of a person, we may be more motivated to
see his or her good traits and to keep our interactions as positive as possible.

Similarity A second factor attracting people to one another is similarity.
Contrary to the old adage that "opposites attract," people who are attracted
to one other often share similar beliefs, values, attitudes, interests, and intellectual ability (Byrne, 1971; Byrne & Griffitt, 1973; Byrne et al., 1966, 1968;
Judd et al., 1983; Moreland & Zajonc, 1982; Wetzel & Insko, 1982). This
was demonstrated in one study in which 13 men independently expressed
their attitudes on 44 separate issues prior to being housed together for 10
days in the close quarters of a fallout shelter. At intervals of one, five, and
nine days of confinement, each subject was asked to list the three men in the
group he would most like to remain and the three he would most like to see
removed from the shelter. The results provided consistent and clear indications that the participants wanted to keep the men who were most like
them (judged by the earlier attitude assessments) and to get rid of those who
were least like them (Griffitt & Veitch, 1974).

Why do we feel drawn to people who are like us? For one thing,
people with similar attitudes and interests are often inclined to enjoy participating in the same kinds of leisure activities. Even more important, however, we are more likely to communicate well with people whose ideas and
opinions are similar to ours, and communication is a very important aspect

of enduring relationships. It is also reassuring to be with similar people, for they confirm our view of the world, validate our own experiences, and support our opinions and beliefs (Arrowood & Short, 1973; Sanders, 1982).

Physical Attractiveness   Physical attraction may profoundly influence our impressions of the people we meet. In general, research reveals that physically attractive people are more likely to be sought as friends, to impress potantial employers favorably, to be treated better, and to be perceived as more likable, sensitive, poised, happy, sexy, competent, and socially skilled than people of average or unattractive appearance (Cash & Janda, 1984; Dion & Dion, 1987; Dion & Berscheid, 1974; Hatfield & Sprechler, 1986; Lerner & Lerner, 1977; Snyder et al., 1977).

A fascinating, recent study that was conducted by Judith Langlois and her colleagues (1987) at the University of Texas at Austin revealed that infants from two to eight months old demonstrated marked preferences for attractive faces. When they were shown pairs of color slides of the faces of adult women previously rated by other adults for attractiveness, the infants demonstrated a marked inclination to look longer at the most attractive face in the pair. These findings "challenge the commonly held assumption that standards of attractiveness are learned through gradual exposure to the current cultural standard of beauty and are merely 'in the eye of the beholder'" (p. 363).

Why is physical beauty such a powerful factor in attracting us to others? One answer has to do with aesthetics. We all enjoy looking at something or someone that we consider to be beautiful. Another factor is that many people apparently believe that beautiful people have more to offer in terms of desirable personal qualities than do those of us who are less attractive. As pointed out earlier, we also may be attracted to beautiful people because they offer us the possibility of status by association. There is also the possibility that beautiful people, by virtue of having been treated very well by others over the course of their lives, may be very secure and comfortable with themselves, a fact which may translate into particularly satisfying relations with others.

Although physical attractiveness profoundly influences our impressions of the people we meet, our standards of attractiveness vary widely, as can be seen in these five photos of beautiful women from around the world.

THE NATURE OF LOVE

Whether we are attracted to people by familiarity, similarity, stunning looks, or some other quality, the mutual feelings sometimes progress from liking to love. Love has intrigued people throughout history; it is one of the most pervasive themes in the art and literature of many cultures. Each of our own lives has likely been influenced in some significant way by love; indeed, our best and worst moments may be tied to a love relationship. As important as love is to us, however, we know relatively little about it. Although we know that love is a special kind of attitude with strong emotional and behavioral components, it eludes easy definition or explanation. One investigation revealed that two out of three queried students were not sure they knew what love was (Kephart, 1967).

Measuring Love   As difficult as love is to define, can it be meaningfully measured? Some social scientists have attempted to do so, with interesting results. Perhaps the most ambitious attempt to measure love was undertaken some years ago by psychologist Zick Rubin (1973). He administered a questionnaire to several hundred dating couples at the University of Michigan and used their responses to develop a 13-item measurement device that he called a love scale. On this scale, people are asked to indicate if a particular statement accurately reflects their feelings about another person, usually someone they are interested in romantically.

As measured by Rubin's scale, love has three components: attachment, caring, and intimacy. *Attachment* refers to a person's desire for the physical presence and emotional support of the other person. *Caring* refers to an individual's concern for the other's well-being. *Intimacy* is the desire for close, confidential communication with the other.

Some people may argue that it is simply not possible to measure such an unfathomable emotion as love, particularly with a paper-and-pencil measurement device. However, Rubin did obtain some evidence supporting the validity of his scale. For example, the scale was used to investigate the popular belief that lovers spend a great deal of time looking into one another's eyes. Couples were observed through a one-way mirror while they waited to participate in a psychological experiment. The findings revealed that "weak lovers" (couples who scored below average on the love scale) made significantly less eye contact than did "strong lovers" (those with above-average scores) (Rubin, 1970).

TYPES OF LOVE

One of the problems in defining as well as measuring love is that we use the term broadly to describe different kinds of feelings, from the excitement of going steady in high school to the closeness of a couple who have been married for 50 years. Recognizing this fact, a number of social scientists have focused more narrowly on trying to define and understand different types of love. One of the most useful divisions is between *passionate love* and *companionate love*.

Passionate Love   **Passionate love,** also known as romantic love or infatuation, is a state of extreme absorption in another person. It is characterized by intense feelings of tenderness, elation, anxiety, sexual desire, and ecstasy. Along with a feeling of great excitement, passionate love is often accompanied by generalized physiological arousal, complete with increased heart beat, perspiration, blushing, and sometimes even a churning stomach. Strong sexual desire is typically a major component.

Certain types of situations may serve to heighten our feelings of passion, although different people seem to have different ideas about what is romantic. Common romantic themes include walking on a moonlit beach, having a quiet dinner at home, kissing in public, or making love all weekend. For many, romance is typified by heightened emotions arising from unusual sex—outside during a storm, for example, or in the bathtub. For some others, the intense, painful emotions in unrequited love or betrayal, of being separated from a loved one, or of love doomed to failure seem very romantic (Rubinstein, 1983).

Intense passionate love typically occurs early in a relationship. It sometimes seems as if the less one knows the other person, the more intense is the passionate love. In passionate love, people often overlook faults and avoid conflicts. Logic and reasoned consideration are swept away by excitement.

Unfortunately, love that is based on ignorance about a person's full character is bound to change with increased familiarity. Many couples make a commitment, such as becoming engaged, moving in together, or marrying, in the excitement of passionate love, only to feel disillusioned later on when the relationship becomes routine and everyday annoyances begin to surface. Some couples ultimately succeed in working through this period to build a lasting relationship of mutual love; others are not so successful. Because of this, it is often wise for a couple to allow their relationship to develop over several months or even years before making a commitment. Time often provides the opportunity to see whether a passionate love relationship can develop into a long-term commitment.

Companionate Love   While many people who experience the lessening of passion believe this is the end of love, others look forward to a different kind of relationship. Erich Fromm once commented, "Romantic love is a delicious art form but not a durable one. In the end, its most persistent practitioners confess that they would like to escape from its patterned illusion into the next more realistically satisfying stage of an enduring relationship" (1965, p. 252).

This more enduring type of love is known as **companionate love.** Companionate love is less intense than passionate love (Walster & Walster, 1978), characterized by friendly affection and deep attachment based on extensive familiarity. It involves a thoughtful appreciation of one's partner. Companionate love often encompasses a tolerance for another's shortcomings along with a desire to overcome difficulties and conflicts in a relationship. This kind of love is committed to ongoing nurturing of a partnership. In one survey on love and romance, respondents said that the three most important ingredients of love were friendship, devotion, and intellectual compatibility. These qualities, which typify companionate love, rated higher than the passionate love characteristics of sexual "electricity" and longing (Rubenstein, 1983).

The term *mutative relationship* (from the Latin *mutare,* to change) has been used to describe an enduring companionate relationship (Goethals, 1980), for both the partners and the relationship itself continually generate change. This kind of relationship has a dynamic quality that helps satisfy the often contradictory human desires for both security and excitement. Partners in mutative relationships grow and change, sometimes in response to individual challenges and sometimes in response to the relationship itself.

INTERPERSONAL AGGRESSION

All of us have been victimized by the aggressive behavior of others, whether it be someone who knowingly initiates a false rumor about us, a parent who strikes us in a fit of anger, or a teammate who ridicules our athletic ability. Sometime during our lives, more than a few of us may become victims of violent crime such as rape, mugging, or murder—a grim prediction substantiated by evidence that well over a million Americans are victimized annually by violent crimes (Federal Bureau of Investigation, 1986). Criminal violence is an extreme form of **interpersonal aggression**—that is, any

FIRST PERSON 16.5

I just don't feel the same excitement and the same passion for my lover as I used to feel. I used to feel overwhelmed waiting for her to meet me. I still look forward to seeing her, but not with breathless anticipation. I guess that I must not be in love anymore. (*Authors' files*)

physical or verbal behavior intended to hurt another person. Many instances of interpersonal aggression may not qualify as criminal acts, but they can nevertheless be very hurtful. Why do people behave aggressively? Explanations have focused on biological mechanisms as well as psychosocial influences. We look briefly at the evidence.

THE BIOLOGY OF AGGRESSION

The biological perspective has been championed in recent years by a number of **sociobiologists,** researchers and theorists who seek to understand the biological factors that underlie social behaviors in all animal species, including humans. Many sociobiologists believe that aggressive behavior may be at least partly related to biological mechanisms. Among the prominent spokespersons for this viewpoint are Harvard biologist Edward O. Wilson (1975, 1978) and Nobel prize winner Konrad Lorenz (1974).

Lorenz's interpretation is particularly intriguing. He maintains that all animals, humans included, have a "fighting instinct" directed toward their own kind. Lorenz believes that this aggressive inclination has great survival value and evolutionary significance for the species. For example, when the males of many species fight for mates, the strongest prevail, ensuring that the more fit will reproduce. An innate inhibition prevents most animals from killing members of their own species, but Lorenz believes that humans never developed this inhibition, probably because with neither lethal claws nor sharp teeth, they were unlikely to inflict serious damage on one another. Today, however, our guns and bombs make us the most dangerous of all living creatures. Lorenz suggests that the situation is worsened by social norms that suppress our fighting instincts, thus causing our aggressive urges to build up to the point that they are sometimes explosively released in acts of extreme violence.

As you might predict from Chapter 9's discussion of instinct-based explanations of human behavior, most contemporary psychologists are not very receptive to the idea that aggression is an instinctive drive. This does not mean that they reject offhand the possibility that biology may contribute to aggression. In fact, there is considerable evidence that aggressive tendencies may be influenced by biological factors (Bell & Hepper, 1987). One study demonstrated that boys and girls who were exposed to high levels of androgens before birth were found to be significantly more aggressive than their same-sexed siblings who had had normal hormonal exposure (Reinisch, 1981). Other research has provided convincing evidence that aggressive behavior often results when certain regions within the limbic systems of the brains of humans and other animals are stimulated through implanted electrodes, lesions, or other abnormal physiological processes (Moyer, 1983).

Some researchers have also linked genetic factors with aggression. For example, Finnish psychologist Kirsti Lagerspetz (1979) selected out the most and least aggressive animals from a large sample of mice, and then bred the fighters with one another and the nonaggressive mice with one another. After 25 generations, she had two distinct strains of mice: a vicious, superaggressive strain and a docile, passive strain. Although such experiments suggest that human aggression may have a link with heredity, we must remember that behavioral patterns in nonhuman animals frequently show a stronger influence of nature than of nurture. Efforts to link heredity to human aggression have proved tenuous at best.

THE PSYCHOSOCIAL BASES OF AGGRESSION

All of the various biological explanations of aggresion suffer from one serious shortcoming: they fail to account for the widespread variation in the extent to which different people display aggression. To explain this diversity, most psychologists look to the psychosocial bases of aggression.

Three major areas of focus are the frustration-aggression hypothesis, social-learning theory, and the influence of mass media violence.

The Frustration-Aggression Hypothesis   Almost 50 years ago John Dollard and his colleagues (1939) proposed that there is a consistent link between frustration, the negative emotional state that results when something interferes with obtaining a goal, and aggression. In their widely influential **frustration-aggression hypothesis,** Dollard and his associates asserted that "aggression is *always* a consequence of frustration" and that "frustration *always* leads to aggression" (p. 1). According to this theory, we might expect that anytime we are thwarted in our efforts to finish a job, find the proper ingredients for a midnight sandwich, or win in a game of basketball, we become aggressive. This does not mean that we always vent our frustration on the object of our frustration, such as our opponents on the basketball court. Rather, Dollard suggested that aggression may be delayed, disguised, or even displaced from its most obvious source to a more acceptable outlet. For instance, we may go home and yell at our dog after losing our basketball game. In spite of these possible modifications in the mode of expression, the frustration-aggression hypothesis maintained that when we are frustrated, some kind of aggressive reaction is inevitable.

This theory is intuitively appealing, and certainly all of us have had the experience of lashing out against something or someone when we are frustrated. Does it seem reasonable to assume, however, that every time we are frustrated we respond with aggressive actions? A number of critics of the frustration-aggression hypothesis did not think so, and psychologist Neal Miller (1941) proposed a revision of the original hypothesis. Miller suggested that frustration can produce a number of possible responses, only one of which is aggression. Other responses to frustration may include withdrawal, apathy, hopelessness, and even increased efforts to achieve a goal.

If aggression is only one of several possible responses to frustration, then what circumstances will cause frustration to produce aggression? Social psychologist Leonard Berkowitz (1978) suggested that two conditions act together to instigate aggression. One is a *readiness* to act aggressively, which is often associated with the emotion of anger. The second is the presence of *environmental cues,* such as the presence of others who are perceived as accepting aggressive behavior, the availability of weapons, and the presence of an acceptable target for aggression. Thus, Berkowitz suggests that while we may respond to frustration by becoming angry, our anger is not likely to be translated into aggression unless suitable environmental cues are present. A number of studies in which subjects experience frustration in either the presence or absence of suitable aggression cues have supported Berkowitz's prediction (Berkowitz & Geen, 1966; Berkowitz & Lepage, 1976; Frodi, 1975; Leyens & Parke, 1975).

The frustration-aggression hypothesis, as first modified by Miller and later by Berkowitz, provides one important theoretical perspective on the psychosocial causes of aggression. Frustration often does cause anger, which in turn may be released in the form of aggression if suitable cues are present in the environment. However, is frustration the only cause of aggression? What about the grade-school student who hits the schoolyard weakling because he has seen another admired classmate do the same thing? Social-learning theory helps to explain some other instances of aggression.

Social-Learning Theory   Social psychologists are generally in agreement that human aggressive behavior is learned. We have discussed Albert Bandura's (1986) social-learning theory in several sections of this book, and this approach also helps us understand aggression. As you recall, Bandura emphasizes the processes of reinforcement and imitation of models. Anyone who has observed a child using aggression to take a desired toy away from another has seen the power of reinforcement as a shaper of aggres-

If children learn to behave aggressively by observing their parents, other adults, and their peers, what is the impact of violence in the mass media on their behavior?

sion. If we learn that acting aggressive will produce rewards, it is only natural that such actions will become part of our behavioral repertoire. Even nontangible reinforcements, such as praise for "being tough" or "not taking guff from anybody," may increase a child's inclination to repeat such behaviors.

People may also learn to be aggressive by observing the behavior of others. A child who sees an adult or friend behave aggressively may imitate this behavior. As we saw in Chapter 6, Bandura demonstrated this process in a classic experiment in which three-, four-, and five-year olds observed an adult beating on a five-foot Bobo doll, then behaved in a similar way when given a chance to "play" with the doll (see Figure 16.8). Subsequent research revealed that imitation of aggression tends to be most pronounced when the aggressive acts are observed to produce rewards, or at least not to result in punishment (Bandura, 1965; Bandura et al., 1963; Walters & Willows, 1968). Of course, it might be argued that children who observe aggression and then imitate it in a laboratory setting are not necessarily inclined to model such aggressive behavior in the real world. This argument is countered, however, by extensive evidence that children who are raised by parents who behave aggressively are strongly inclined to be aggressive themselves (Bandura, 1960; Bandura & Walters, 1959; and that children who are victimized by physically abusive parents often tend to behave in the same fashion toward their own children.

Mass Media Violence   If children learn to behave aggressively by observing their parents, other adults, and their peers, what is the impact of mass media violence on their behavior? Most children in our society observe thousands upon thousands of murders and other senseless acts of violence and mayhem as part of the normal television fare. The question of whether viewing television violence actually increases a person's inclination to act

FIGURE 16.8   OBSERVATIONAL LEARNING OF AGGRESSIVE BEHAVIOR: THE BOBO DOLL EXPERIMENT

Bandura and his colleagues (1963) demonstrated that when children observe an adult model beating on a Bobo doll (top row) they tend to behave in a similar way when given a chance to "play" with the doll (bottom two rows).

aggressively has been the center of a lively debate. On one side of the issue, some psychologists have argued that observing violence may be *cathartic,* for when we watch other people behaving violently we vicariously vent some of our own frustration and anger, so that we are less likely to behave aggressively.

Research evidence has not been very supportive of the catharsis hypothesis (Brigham, 1986; Evans, 1974; Tavris, 1982). Most psychologists who are familiar with the extensive body of findings are convinced that exposure to media violence increases the odds that the viewer will behave aggressively (Berkowtiz, 1986; Friedrich-Cofer, 1986; Penrod, 1986). In 1982 the National Institutes of Mental Health released an extensive analysis of the research literature on the effects of television viewing on behavior, in which they concluded that:

> The consensus among most of the research community is that violence on television does lead to aggressive behavior by children and teenagers who watch the programs. This conclusion is based on laboratory experiments and on field studies. Not all children become aggressive, of course, but the correlations between violence and aggression are positive. In magnitude, television violence is as strongly correlated with aggressive behavior as any other behavioral variable that has been measured. (p. 6)

Not all psychologists support this interpretation. One dissenter, Jonathan Freedman (1984), has argued that laboratory studies provide an artificial environment that influences subjects' behavior. Since they have been given permission to act aggressively and because they have no fear of retaliation or punishment, subjects are more likely to imitate aggressive acts they have viewed in experimental studies. Freedman further argues that laboratory studies typically involve isolating subjects and exposing them to a concentrated dose of violence, a situation which is quite different from the real world in which our exposure to violence is tempered by much more extensive exposure to nonviolent human interaction. Furthermore, Freedman suggests that even those studies that have demonstrated a positive relationship between viewing violence and aggressive behavior in a natural setting (Eron et al., 1972; Milavsky et al., 1982) do not necessarily demonstrate a cause-and-effect relationship. He suggests an alternate explanation: that aggressive persons are inclined to select television programs with high violence content.

Freedman's critique should not be dismissed lightly. We must note, however, that while his criticisms of mass media violence studies may be accurate, the fact still remains that virtually all of these studies reach the same general conclusion that filmed violence spawns aggressive behavior. It seems reasonable to conclude that the effect of viewing filmed aggressive acts must be fairly substantial to show consistently across so many diverse research designs.

Many parents are concerned about the link between television and aggression, but are not sure how to combat this potentially damaging influence in their children's lives. One answer is to get rid of their television sets altogether, or to limit severely what their children view. Both of these options may seem rather unrealistic in an era when the average American household has its television set on for close to eight hours a day. Throughout history, however, families have been able to survive and even thrive without television, and this option is still possible today.

If television is to be a part of your family's routine, it might be helpful to discuss with your children their feelings and your feelings about television violence. A recent study investigated the effects of an innovative educational program in which 170 children were taught that (1) television does not portray the world as it really is, (2) aggression is considerably less common and effective than portrayed on television, and (3) aggression is wrong (Eron & Huesmann, 1984). A two year follow-up revealed that the children exposed to this training were less inclined to model television violence than were children in an untrained control group.

FIRST PERSON 16.6

Throughout most of my life I have not been a fan of violence in movies or on TV. However, an exception to this was the years when I was in graduate school. These were very difficult times, filled with frustration and suppressed hostility toward the often inane dictates of my major professors. Unable to strike out against the source of my anger, I found myself developing a craving for James Bond thrillers and spaghetti Westerns, both very violent types of movies. It was amazing how much better I felt after watching the figures on the screen bash heads for two hours of almost nonstop violence. It was as though all my pent-up frustration and anger was purged, at least temporarily, by identifying with the actions of the violent aggressors featured in the films. (*Authors' files*)

SUMMARY

SOCIAL PERCEPTION

1. The term social perception describes the ways we perceive, evaluate, categorize, and form judgments about the qualities of people we encounter. Three factors that influence our social perceptions are first impressions, schemas, and implicit personality theories.

2. The first information we receive about a person often seems to count the most, a phenomenon referred to as the primacy effect.

3. Person schemas, which are generalized assumptions about certain classes of people, provide a structure for evaluating the people we meet.

4. Implicit personality theories allow us to draw conclusions about what people are like based on certain implicit assumptions about personality traits that usually go together. Implicit personality theories often tend to be organized around central traits—traits that we tend to associate with other characteristics. For example, if we meet a person that we perceive as being warm, we may expect that person also to be generous and to have a good sense of humor.

5. The term halo effect is employed to describe our tendency to infer other positive (or negative) traits from our perception of one central trait.

ATTRIBUTING CAUSES TO BEHAVIORS

6. Attributions are the judgments we make about why people behave as they do. We tend to attribute people's behavior either to dispositional (internal) causes, such as motivational states or personality traits, or to external causes, such as environmental or situational factors.

7. Two theories that attempt to explain the process of making attributions in a rational, methodical manner are the correspondent inference theory—which suggests that we attribute a person's behavior to an underlying disposition—and the covariation principle that maintains that we make attributions by analyzing the manner in which causes and effects covary.

8. Biases in attribution processes include the fundamental attribution error (a tendency to overestimate dispositional causes and to underestimate external causes when accounting for the behavior of others), false consensus bias (the assumption that most people share our own attitudes and behaviors), and the illusion of control (the belief that we control events in our lives).

ATTITUDES

9. Attitudes are learned, relatively enduring predispositions to respond in consistently favorable or unfavorable ways to certain people, groups, ideas, or situations.

10. Attitudes are shaped by experiences, which include our observations of behavior (both other people's and our own), classical and operant conditioning, and direct experiences with the attitude object (the people, ideas, or things we hold attitudes about).

11. Attitudes serve a number of important functions in our lives, including an understanding function, a social identification function, a social adjustment function, a value-expressive function, and an ego-defensive function.

12. Studies which have measured a variety of behaviors relevant to a given attitude have revealed a strong correlation between attitudes and behavior.

13. Attitudes are particularly strong predictors of behavior when other factors influencing our behavior are minimized, when an attitude is highly relevant to the behavior being considered, and when we are quite conscious of our attitudes when we act.

14. Consistency theories have been proposed as an attempt to explain why we sometimes change our attitudes in an effort to maintain consistency among attitudes we hold and between our attitudes and our behaviors.

15. Two noteworthy consistency theories of attitude change are Heider's balance theory and Festinger's cognitive dissonance theory. Balance theory argues that people are inclined to be consistent in their attitudes by balancing their beliefs and feelings about a particular issue, object, or situation against their attitudes about other people. According to cognitive dissonance theory, people experience an unpleasant state of dissonance whenever they perceive a discrepancy between their actions and their attitudes. In such a situation, attitudes may be changed to be more consistent with behaviors, thus resulting in a state of consonance or psychological comfort.

16. Three elements are particularly important in persuasive communication: the source of the message, the way the message is stated, and the characteristics of the message recipients.

17. The probability that persuasion will succeed is highest when the source of persuasion is seen as possessing any or all of the qualities of credibility, power, and attractiveness.

18. Persuasive messages may be most effective when there is a moderate level of discrepancy between the message and the audience's viewpoint. When the message appeals to fear, it may be most effective in inducing attitude change when it elicits moderate fear and when it contains clear information about what to do to avoid the fearful consequences.

19. A message that is presented in an unusual or novel fashion is often more effective than timeworn arguments.

20. A one-sided argument seems to be more effective if the audience is poorly educated and/or unfamiliar with the issue, whereas a two-sided argument tends to work better with a well-educated, well-informed audience.

21. Teenagers and young adults are generally more susceptible than older people to persuasive communication. Research has been unclear about the impact of listeners' self-esteem and intelligence on their inclination to yield to persuasion.

SOCIAL INFLUENCE

22. The realm of social influence—the efforts by others to alter our feelings, beliefs, and behavior—encompasses the related phenomena of conformity, compliance, and obedience.

23. Conformity refers to a tendency to change or modify our own beliefs or behaviors so that they are consistent with those of other people.

24. Social psychologists make a distinction between conformity that results from informational social influence, in which we accept a group's beliefs or behaviors as providing accurate information about reality, and confor-

mity via normative social influence, in which we conform not because of an actual change in our beliefs but because we think that we will benefit in some way, such as gaining approval or avoiding rejection.

25. Compliance is somewhat different from conformity in that while both involve yielding to some pressure exerted by others, compliance involves an element of coercion as well, in that it takes place in situations where we alter our behavior in response to direct requests from others.

26. Two methods employed by people who wish to increase the probability of compliance in others is the foot-in-the-door technique and the door-in-the-face technique.

27. Social influence in the form of obedience occurs in situations in which people alter their behavior in response to commands or orders leveled by people they may perceive as having power or authority.

28. Psychologists have suggested three reasons why people may respond to social influence in the form of destructive obedience. First, many people seem to believe that their personal accountability for their actions is somehow diminished or relieved by those authority figures who issue the commands. Second, authority figures often possess highly visible symbols of power or status that make it difficult to resist their dictates. Finally, people often comply with potentially destructive orders because they have first been "sucked in" by seemingly harmless commands.

PREJUDICE

29. Prejudice is a negative, unjustifiable, and inflexible attitude toward a group and its members that is based on erroneous information, often in the form of stereotypes (preconceived and oversimplified beliefs and expectations about the traits of members of a particular group that do not account for individual differences).

30. Prejudice often stems from a marked tendency for people to categorize themselves as belonging to an ingroup (based on race, age, education, creed, economic level, etc.) and to have a negative attitude or prejudice against people in outgroups who do not possess the ingroup characteristics. By perceiving their ingroup as superior to an outgroup, people seem to be attempting to enhance their self-esteem.

31. People who are frustrated by their lack of accomplishments or by adverse living conditions often vent their frustration in the form of prejudice against members of a minority group that they perceive as being less powerful than themselves.

32. Racism, sexism, and other prejudicial attitudes are often passed directly from parents to children through the social learning mechanisms of observation and emulation.

33. There is some evidence that people raised in a harsh, authoritarian fashion may be strongly inclined to de- velop a prejudiced personality characterized by intolerance, emotional coldness, rigidity, unquestioning submission to higher authority, stereotyped thinking, and identification with power.

INTERPERSONAL ATTRACTION: LIKING AND LOVING

34. Factors known to contribute strongly to interpersonal attraction include proximity, similarity, and physical attractiveness. We often develop close relationships with people that we see frequently, with those that share similar beliefs, and with individuals that we perceive as being physically attractive.

35. Social scientists have made a distinction between passionate love and companionate love. Intense, passionate love, characterized by extreme absorption in and strong sexual desire for another person, is typically a transitory state that occurs early in a relationship. Passionate love often gives way to the more enduring form of companionate love, which is characterized by friendly affection and deep attachment based on extensive familiarity.

INTERPERSONAL AGGRESSION

36. Explanations for why people engage in interpersonal aggression—that is, any physical or verbal behavior intended to hurt another person—range from a focus on biological mechanisms to a discussion of psychosocial influences.

37. The biological perspective, championed by the sociobiologists, maintains that people inherit an instinctive aggressive drive. While most psychologists do not reject the notion that biological factors may be linked with aggressive behavior, they are quick to note that efforts to connect heredity to human aggression have proved tenuous at best.

38. On the psychosocial side, research has revealed that frustration often causes anger, which in turn may be released in the form of aggression if suitable cues are present in the environment.

39. Social-learning theorists suggest that aggressive behavior is often learned via a process of receiving reinforcements for aggressive acts and by observing and imitating the aggressive behavior of others.

40. Some psychologists have argued that observing mass media violence may be cathartic, for when we watch other people behaving violently we vicariously vent some of our own frustration and anger, so that we are less likely to behave aggressively. Research evidence has not been very supportive of the catharsis hypothesis and most psychologists who are familiar with the research findings are convinced that exposure to media violence increases the odds that the viewer will behave aggressively.

17 Applying Psychology

The eager young Canadian researcher Hans Selye was conducting research that he hoped would lead to the discovery of a new sex hormone. The leads were promising so far. When he injected rats with extracts of ovary tissue, the results were consistent: bleeding ulcers in the stomach and small intestine, enlargement of the adrenal cortex, and shrinkage of the thymus gland. Since no hormone was known to produce these effects, Selye was convinced that he was on the track of identifying a new one. His elation was quickly dampened, however, for when he injected extracts from other tissues, the effects were identical. Furthermore, the same thing occurred when he injected toxic fluids that were not derived from tissues.

Selye was devastated by this turn of events. But instead of giving up, he tried to figure out what had happened. The answer occurred to him only when he stopped trying to relate his findings to the discovery of a new sex hormone. In his own words: "it suddenly struck me that one could look at [my ill-fated experiments] from an entirely different angle. . . . [Perhaps] there was such a thing as a single nonspecific reaction of the body to damage of any kind. . . ." (1976, p. 26).

Selye went on to study how animals responded to a wide range of stressful events other than injections. He exposed rats to a variety of adverse conditions such as extreme cold and fatigue, electric shock, immobilizing restraint, and surgical trauma—and noted the same physiological response pattern as he had originally observed with injections of tissue extracts. As we shall see later in this chapter, Selye also learned that humans respond to stress with fairly consistent physiological patterns (1936, 1956, 1974, 1976). From the awareness that stress can have harmful effects on our bodies have come many more studies, as well as techniques for reducing the impact of stress on our own lives.

We have chosen Selye's story as the starting point for this chapter because it illustrates *applied psychology*. In the course of their research, psychologists often learn things that may be applied directly to improving the quality of our lives. We have already seen many such applications throughout this text, as we have explored topics such as weight control, memory improvement techniques, ways to cope with sleep disorders, using reinforcements to modify behavior, and strategies for making decisions. In this chapter we continue this theme by examining three additional areas in which psychologists have been able to apply knowledge about behavior and mental functioning in a beneficial manner: environmental psychology,

Hans Selye

industrial and organizational psychology, and health psychology. These three topics are not meant to represent the extent of practical applications of psychology in improving our lives. There are many important applications that we do not have space to discuss in this chapter, including consumer behavior, education, forensic work, and sports. Instead, we have elected to discuss these three major areas in some depth. We begin with a look at how psychology can be applied to helping us adapt to our environment and to structuring our environment to suit our needs.

ENVIRONMENTAL PSYCHOLOGY

In Chapter 16, we learned how our thoughts, feelings, and attitudes are influenced by our social context. Psychologists have also confirmed that our physical environment can have a profound effect on our functioning. This is the focus of **environmental psychology,** which explores how our physical environment (both natural features and those that have been created by humans) affects psychological processes. Environmental psychologists have a wide range of interests (Holahan, 1986). Two of the most interesting are the impact of adverse environmental conditions on our behavior and the way in which we use space.

ADVERSE ENVIRONMENTAL CONDITIONS

Most of us have experienced moments when we could not concentrate because the radio blaring in the next room distracted us. We have also had days when we had a list of things to accomplish but got almost nothing done because it was simply too hot. Environmental psychologists are interested in how both noise and heat affect our functioning (and what can be done to minimize negative effects); they are also interested in another adverse condition that we are often less aware of—environmental toxins. We look first at the effect of noise.

Noise We learned in Chapter 4 that very loud sounds may result in permanent damage to the neural mechanisms involved in hearing. But noise has other effects that may be less obvious. Research has linked excessive noise to high levels of stress as well as anxiety reactions, increased aggression, impaired intellectual functioning, and reduced worker productivity (Bell et al., 1978; Cohen et al., 1981; Donnerstein & Wilson, 1976; Glass & Singer, 1972).

Psychologists have been particularly interested in the question of how loud sounds affect cognitive functioning. Some of the most interesting research in this area has dealt with children. In one study, Sheldon Cohen and his associates (1980) compared a group of children who attended schools located near the Los Angeles Airport with a matched group of children with similar backgrounds whose school was located in a quieter neighborhood. They found that the children whose schools were near the airport performed more poorly at proofreading a printed paragraph; they were also more easily distracted and were quicker to give up on solving difficult puzzles. These children also had higher blood pressure than children from quieter schools.

In another study, Cohen and his colleagues (1973) explored how a noisy home environment affects children's cognitive skills. The subjects were children who lived in a 32-story high-rise apartment complex in a noisy urban area. The higher a child's apartment was located, the lower were the noise levels. As Figure 17.1 shows, tested reading performance was found to be positively correlated with how high a child lived in the building.

Still another study compared the reading skills of children whose classrooms were located on the loud side of a school building adjacent to elevated railroad tracks with those of students on the quiet side of the build-

Research has linked excessive noise to high levels of stress, as well as to anxiety reactions, increased aggression, impaired intellectual functioning, and reduced worker productivity.

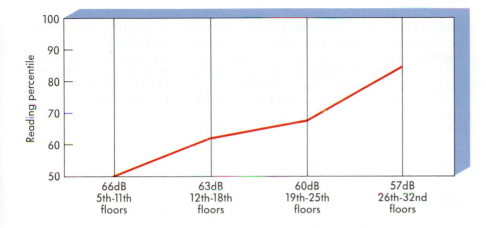

FIGURE 17.1 HOW NOISE LEVELS AFFECTED READING PERFORMANCE ON DIFFERENT FLOORS OF A HIGH-RISE APARTMENT BUILDING

Noise level, in decibels, on different floors. (*Source:* From Cohen et al., 1973)

ing. The children on the quieter side tested significantly better than those from the noisy side (Bronzaft & McCarthy, 1975).

Such findings have been applied in efforts to reduce excess noise in industrial settings, with the result of improved worker morale and higher productivity (Broadbent & Little, 1960). Awareness of the adverse effect of loud sounds has also made urban planners more mindful of the need to locate schools, hospitals, and other such structures in areas where noise is minimal. Public officials are also more likely to consider the effects of excessive noise as they make decisions about where to construct industrial plants, roads, and freeways. In response to one plan to build a major new highway near a school, for instance, researchers used tape recordings of traffic noise to simulate conditions students would be subjected to once the highway was constructed. Their demonstration showed that learning would be impaired, prompting officials to reroute the highway (Ward & Suedfeld, 1973).

Heat Just as noise affects our ability to function, so do a variety of weather-related variables such as barometric pressure, climatic changes, and temperature. Temperature is the most widely researched of these variables. Both extreme cold and extreme heat can adversely affect behavior and thought, although heat seems to be the most disruptive since it is not as easily compensated for. The effect of heat upon performance varies somewhat depending on the task performed and an individual's heat tolerance. However, most of us perform best at moderate temperatures, ideally somewhere between 69–74 degrees (Baron, 1977; Hickish, 1955). When we are too warm, we are likely to work less efficiently (Calvert-Boyanowsky et al., 1976).

HEAT AND AGGRESSION

In addition to the impact of excessive heat on productivity, environmental psychologists have also been concerned with another possible effect of heat: its influence on aggressive behavior. It is commonly believed that riots and other acts of violence increase during the hot days of summer. Do you believe that this assumption is supported by hard data, and if so, would you expect the relationship between heat and aggression to be linear (in other words, the higher the temperature, the greater the incidence of aggressive acts)? To the extent that a correlation exists between heat and violence, do you think it is a cause-and-effect relationship? Give some thought to these questions before reading on.

Considerable evidence has been cited to support the notion that people act more aggressively when outside temperatures rise (Anderson, 1987; Penrod, 1986). For example, Steven Penrod (1986) conducted an analysis of the annual crime reports issued by the FBI over a 10-year period. The

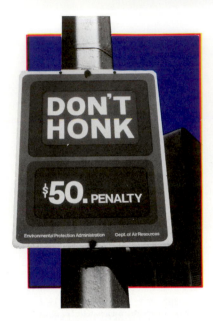

Urban planners have become more aware of the adverse effect of loud sounds and, as a result, have become more mindful of the need to locate schools, hospitals, and other such structures in areas where noise is minimal. "No Honking" signs and fees for ignoring these signs are becoming more popular in urban areas, where noise is most bothersome and where the effects of noise are most harmful.

results of his analysis, shown in Figure 17.2 clearly demonstrate that the incidence of murder, rape, and aggravated assault increase notably during the third quarter of the year (July–September), a time when temperatures are likely to peak.

We must use caution when interpreting these findings, however. Although it is possible that a direct cause-and-effect relationship exists between heat and violence, other factors may also be associated with this correlation. For example, people are more likely to be out and about during the summer months, which increases the frequency of their contact with potential perpetrators or victims. Other factors that might influence this relationship include seasonal unemployment, which is highest in summer; more leisure time for children and adolescents during summer vacation; and the increased accessibility to homes in the summer, when doors and windows are more likely to be left open.

If the incidence of violent acts increases during periods of hot weather, is this relationship linear, or is there a point at which it becomes so hot that people are too sapped and uncomfortable to do anything, including behaving violently? This question was addressed by researchers Robert Baron and Victoria Ransberger (1978), who assessed the relationship between temperature and 102 riots that took place in American cities during the late 1960s and early 1970s. They found that up to a point, the probability of riots increased as temperatures rose. When temperatures continued to rise beyond 81–85 degrees, however, the probability of riots seemed to decrease. The researchers concluded that whereas moderately high heat encourages aggression, very hot weather discourages any activity that requires energy, including aggression.

This conclusion is intuitively appealing, for at one time or another we have all probably felt drained and lethargic in very high temperatures. However, some observers questioned Baron and Ransberger's interpretation. J. Merrill Carlsmith and Craig Anderson (1979) suggested that the apparent reduction in riots at high temperatures had a far simpler expla-

FIGURE 17.2 SEASONAL TRENDS IN MURDER, RAPE, AND AGGRAVATED ASSAULT

The graphic portrayal of data supplied by the FBI over a 10-year period clearly demonstrates that the incidence of murder, rape, and aggravated assault increases notably during the third quarter of the year (July–September), a time when temperatures are likely to peak. (*Source:* From Penrod, 1986. Data from Uniform Crime Reports for the United States, Federal Bureau of Investigation, U.S. Department of Justice, 1980)

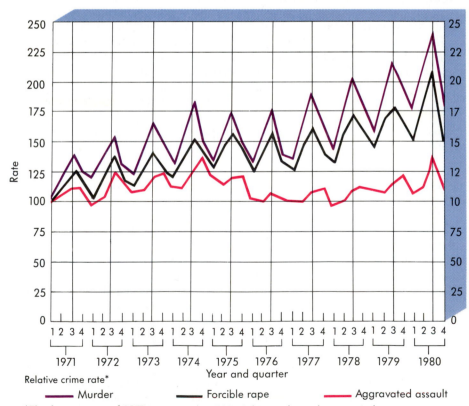

nation: there are fewer days in the year when temperatures are extremely hot. When they factored this discrepancy into the analysis, they found that the probability of riots increased proportionately to outside temperatures, with no decline above 85 degrees (see Figure 17.3). Note, however, that the same cautions we suggested in interpreting correlational data on heat and violent acts should be applied to the results of investigations of heat and riots.

Environmental Toxins   A third adverse environmental condition, the literally hundreds of toxic chemicals that are part of modern life, is perhaps the most disquieting. These hazardous substances are present in our air, in the water and food we consume, in the paint on our walls, in the substances we handle at work, in the clothes we wear—quite literally, everywhere (Anderson, 1982; Belger et al., 1987; Fein et al., 1983; Weiss, 1983). Many of these environmental poisons are classified as *neurotoxins* because of their damaging impact on our nervous systems. Often the initial signs of exposure to such toxins are subtle changes in behavior rather than physical symptoms. As a consequence, environmental psychologists have become increasingly involved in assessing how these environmental toxins affect behavior, and in diagnosing psychological problems related to such pollutants. This is the focus of **behavioral toxicology.** Research in this field is producing an ever-expanding database that clearly demonstrates that many neurotoxins, even in small doses, may have adverse emotional and behavioral consequences (Fein et al., 1983).

Some of the best publicized findings have linked lead to cognitive and behavioral abnormalities. Lead is pervasive in our environment. Airborne lead from exhaust fumes has been a long-standing problem in congested inner-city areas, although the use of unleaded gas has improved this situation significantly in recent years. Another source of lead contamination is lead-based wall paint and plumbing. These problems are more pronounced in inner-city areas and poor residential districts, where buildings and houses were built before the danger of lead in construction materials was recognized. The water and dust in such structures often contains lead, cadmium, and other toxic metals.

There is clear evidence that when concentrated in sufficient quantities in the human body, lead can impair the functioning of the nervous system and interfere with our ability to learn. In one study, for instance,

One of the main sources of lead in our environment is found in lead-based wall paint and plumbing. When concentrated in sufficient quantities in the human body, lead can impair the functioning of the nervous system and interfere with our ability to learn. One study estimates that at least 20 percent of inner-city black children have been contaminated with levels of lead sufficient to impede their intellectual functioning.

FIGURE 17.3   THE RELATIONSHIP BETWEEN TEMPERATURE AND RIOTS

The probability of street riots increased proportionately to outside temperatures. (*Source:* From Carlsmith & Anderson, 1979)

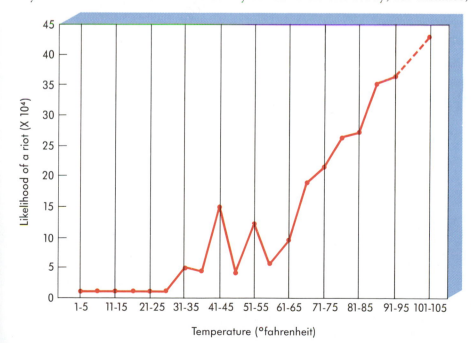

Temperature (°fahrenheit)

Carbon monoxide (CO) is plentiful in areas of heavy traffic, since it is present in heavy concentration in exhaust from automobiles. Prolonged exposure to this gas has been linked to a variety of serious consequences, including reduced attention span; memory deficits; impaired thinking, vision, and hearing; and severe psychotic-like symptoms.

researchers analyzed hair samples to assess the level of lead in children. They found that children with higher levels of lead in their bodies were more prone to serious learning problems than those with lower levels (Pihl & Parkes, 1977). Children who live in poverty receive the brunt of this serious environmental hazard. For example, one estimate suggests that at least 20 percent of inner-city black children have been contaminated with levels of lead sufficient to impede their intellectual functioning (Raloff, 1982).

Another environmental toxin, carbon monoxide (CO), affects many workers employed in industries that use combustion processes. CO is odorless and invisible. Prolonged exposure to this gas has been linked to a variety of serious consequences, including reduced attention span; memory deficits; impaired thinking, vision, and hearing; and severe psychotic-like symptoms (Anderson, 1982; Garland & Pierce, 1967). CO is plentiful in areas of heavy traffic, since it is present in heavy concentration in automobile exhaust. (A common method of suicide is by CO poisoning.) One particularly disturbing study demonstrated that subjects exposed to air collected from an area of high motor-vehicle traffic showed markedly poorer performance than a matched control group on tests measuring such things as concentration and reaction time (Lewis et al., 1970).

Table 17.1 provides some selected examples of common neurotoxins and their impact on mental functioning and behavior. An examination of this list may give you a better sense of why the field of behavioral toxicology is becoming an increasing important area of psychology.

THE EFFECTS OF SPACE ON BEHAVIOR

Many students who are first entering college expect to encounter a certain amount of stress as a result of academic pressure, feeling "at sea"

TABLE 17.1 *Some Selected Neurotoxins and Their Impact on Mental Functioning and Behavior*

Substance	Common Source	Effect(s)
Lead	Smelters, motor vehicle emissions, lead-based paint and plumbing	Impaired learning ability, convulsions, lack of coordination, visual disturbances, behavioral disorders
Carbon monoxide	Industries using combustion processes and automobile emissions (leaded gas)	Impaired performance on information-processing tasks
Carbon disulfide	Rubber vulcanization	Psychotic-like symptoms, nerve damage in hands and feet
Mercury (organic and inorganic)	Chemical research and hat manufacturing	Loss of appetite, convulsions, speech impairments, tremors in face, hands, and legs, visual impairment, headaches, lack of coordination, impaired learning ability, behavioral disorders
Carbon tetrachloride	Dry-cleaning industry	Constriction of visual field
Trichloroethylene	Dry-cleaning and industries that use degreasing agents	Impaired memory and attention span, loss of facial sensation, tremors
Dieldrin	Pesticides	Impaired coordinations, visual disturbances, convulsions
Toluene	Paints and explosives	Impaired coordination, tremors, emotional instability, bizarre behavior
Methylene chloride	Solvents—multiple uses	Delusions and hallucinations

Source: Adapted from Anderson, 1982; Weiss, 1983.

among people they have never met before, and simply adjusting to being on their own, away from their parents. For those who live in dorms, there is often a more subtle form of stress that they may not have counted on (and may not even be aware of)—the feeling of crowding and lack of privacy that is imposed by the design of their living quarters.

To illustrate, look at the floor plans of corridor and suite designs for the two dormitories shown in Figure 17.4. In the corridor-design shown in the top portion of the figure, a large group of 34 residents are housed, two to a room, along a long, narrow corridor; they share one bathroom and one lounge area. In contrast, the dormitory with the suite design, shown at the bottom, creates small groups of six residents whose bedrooms are clustered around each suite's bathroom and lounge area.

These two dormitory designs were the subject of a classic series of studies at the State University of New York at Stony Brook. Researchers Andrew Baum and Stuart Valins (1977, 1979) were interested in determining how the architectural design of college dormitories influenced student residents. The actual floor density (the number of students per unit of space) was comparable in both types of dormitories. However, extensive interviews with residents as well as observations of their behavior revealed that the two different architectural designs had quite different impacts. Compared to those who lived in suites, students who lived in corridor dormitories reported that they felt more stress, crowding, lack of privacy, and overexposure to unwanted social interaction. Many also felt that they had little control over events in their dorm, and they reported that they often tried to avoid encounters with others, both friends and strangers alike. In contrast, suite residents felt more in control of events in their living environments, and they were much less inclined to avoid contact with others.

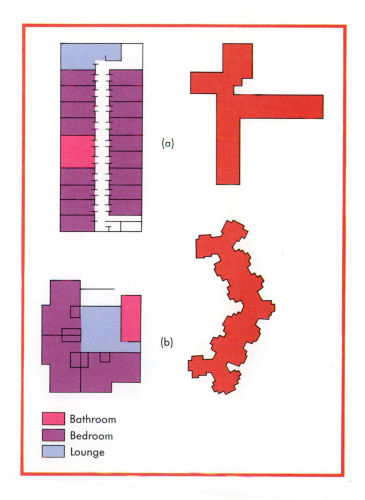

Bathroom
Bedroom
Lounge

FIGURE 17.4   FLOOR PLANS OF CORRIDOR (A) AND SUITE (B) DORMITORIES

(*Source:* From Baum and Valins, 1977)

FIGURE 17.5 AN ARCHITECTURAL SOLUTION FOR CROWDING IN A TRADITIONAL, CORRIDOR-STYLE DORM

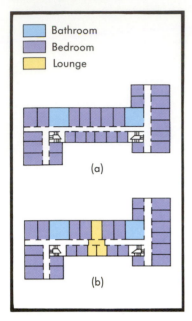

■ Bathroom
■ Bedroom
■ Lounge

(a)

(b)

In the modified dorm (b), the only difference from the traditional long-corridor dorm (a) was that unlocked doors were used to divide the long hallway in half, and three centrally located bedrooms were converted into a lounge area. (*Source:* Adapted from Baum & Davis, 1980)

Observational data supported these subjective reports. Residents of the traditional corridor dorms were more likely to spend time in their bedrooms where they could avoid social interaction, while students who lived in suites spent more time in their lounge areas. Corridor dorm residents also sought health services at the campus health center more often than did their counterparts in suite dorms.

A later experiment demonstrated that even a relatively small change in the architectural design of a dorm can yield a marked reduction in feelings of being crowded and stressed (Baum & Davis, 1980). In this study, the thoughts and behaviors of students living in the fairly traditional long-corridor dorm shown in Figure 17.5a were compared with those of students who lived in the slightly altered dorm shown in Figure 17.5b. In the modified dorm, the only difference was that unlocked doors were used to divide the long hallway in half, and three centrally located bedrooms were converted into a lounge area. Interviews and direct observation revealed that students living in dorm a reported less stress from crowding than residents of dorm b. In addition, residents of the modified dorm b felt more open to social interaction than did occupants of the long-corridor dorm, and developed more friendships with other residents.

These studies illustrate a few applications of **architectural psychology,** the study of the behavioral implications of building design. Architectural psychology is only one subspecialty of environmental psychology. Some other areas of interest are territoriality, personal space, and crowding.

Territoriality Why does the layout of a dormitory (or office, or home study area) have such an effect on our functioning? The answer is complex, but one factor is our tendency to stake out certain areas that we consider to be "our turf" that can be entered only at our invitation. **Territoriality** refers to visual boundaries of a given space or territory that we consider to be a special domain for our own use, whose boundaries are relatively fixed (Bell et al., 1978).

Most of the research on territoriality has focused on nonhuman animal behavior. It has revealed that many different animal species establish and defend specific geographical territories for securing food, mating, and rearing their young (Lorenz, 1969). For example, wolves will traverse very large territories, marking the boundaries with urine scents that serve as warnings to other wolves that are not part of the primary unit to stay out of

Why are humans and other animals territorial creatures? When animals, such as the wolves pictured in the photo, perceive a threatened or actual invasion of their territory, they may defend it vigorously. Similarly, humans may also defend their territories by engaging in the ritualistic posturing of military exercises along their borders when they perceive a threat from neighboring countries.

this area. When animals perceive a threatened or actual invasion of their territory, they may defend it vigorously. Sometimes ritualistic posturing and threats of aggression are sufficient to ward off invaders; in other cases combat takes place. Humans may also defend their territories with ritualistic posturing. Examples range from street gangs parading along the boundaries of their turf to nations engaging in military exercises along their borders when they perceive a threat from neighboring countries.

Why are we territorial creatures? Territoriality provides us with a way to achieve a degree of privacy. As we saw earlier, this may be particularly important in areas such as college dormitories, or in large families where many people use the same space. Having a room that is clearly off limits to others may provide a sanctuary of quiet order that restores psychological equilibrium and makes life easier to cope with. We are often at our best on our home turf. This shows up in improved performance, better communication, and a higher quality of social interaction with others (Altman, 1975). (Other possible functions of territoriality include physical and psychological protection, freedom of action, and provision of a sense of identity.)

Irwin Altman's (1975) review of the literature on human territoriality led him to distinguish between primary and secondary territories. A *primary territory* is an area such as a bedroom, a workshop in the basement, or an office at work, that we define as ours and nobody's else's. In a sense we are saying that "This is my space and you had better stay out of it unless I specifically invite you in." Humans don't scent-mark their private territories, but they do fence their yards, place locks on their doors, and put signs on their office desks—all behaviors that are designed to stake a claim to a private space. Like other animals, we may be quite upset when our primary territory is entered without invitation, and we may act aggressively to repel such intrusions.

Altman suggests that we also have *secondary territories* that are less well defined. We often set aside such areas for social interaction with friends. For example, you and your friends may have a particular table at a local cafe where you like to hang out and socialize. Although it can be upsetting to discover that someone else is using "our table," we generally tend to be much less protective of secondary territories, both because we do not own them and because they are relatively inconsequential to our personal identities.

Personal Space   Suppose you are riding on an almost empty bus when a stranger sits down right next to you. You will probably feel uneasy, anxious, and perhaps angry; you might get up and move to another seat. This motivation to keep our distance from other people, especially people we do not know, is not quite the same thing as territoriality, for instead of fixed spaces or locations it involves a space we carry around with us. **Personal space** is the invisible boundary or imaginary circle of space with which we all surround ourselves, and into which others are not supposed to enter without an invitation. Like territoriality, personal space is another area of interest to environmental psychologists.

According to this concept, we each maintain a different degree of *interpersonal distance* between ourselves and other people. Unlike the territory we stake out, this interpersonal distance is not always the same; it varies from situation to situation according to the nature of our actual or desired relationship, the context within which the interaction occurs, our age, and the age and sex of the other person (Aiello & Aiello, 1974; Evans & Howard, 1973; Hall, 1966; Hewitt & Henley, 1987; Young & Guile, 1987). For instance, imagine that the stranger who sits next to you on the empty bus happens to be an attractive member of the other sex. In these circumstances, you might feel considerably less uneasy. If the stranger turned out to be an old childhood friend whom you had failed to recognize at first, you would be even less inclined to feel that your personal space had been violated.

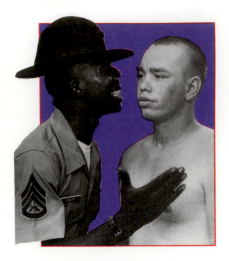

This marine drill instructor is purposely invading the personal space of a new recruit. Why do you think he is doing this, and how do you think you might respond to this invasion if you were in the recruit's position?

Context also exerts a powerful influence on personal space. For instance, you would respond differently if a stranger sat right next to you on a full bus, for you would adjust your personal space to take into account the crowded conditions. On a broader scale, our cultural context also influences personal space. In France, Greece, Japan, and certain Latin American and Middle Eastern countries, people are likely to stand much closer to one another and have much more physical contact when they interact than is common in countries like England, Sweden, and the United States (Hall, 1966; Sommer, 1969).

Anthropologist Edward Hall (1966) has studied personal space extensively, and he suggests that in our culture we maintain various gradations of distances depending on the type of social interaction we are participating in. According to Hall, when we interact with lovers and close friends, it is common to be either very close or in direct physical contact. This *intimate distance* is somewhere between actual contact and approximately 18 inches away from the other person. If a person we are not very close to enters this very restricted area, we are likely to feel uncomfortable and intruded upon.

Our interactions with friends and acquaintances with whom we are less intimate take place at a greater distance, from about 18 inches to approximately four feet. Hall calls this extended personal space boundary *personal distance.* Thus, when you find yourself chatting with friends and acquaintances between classes, at parties, or at other gatherings of small groups, you are likely to adjust your circle of personal space to keep others at roughly arm's length. If someone crosses this line, you may back off to a more comfortable distance. A third gradation is *social distance*, ranging from four to twelve feet. According to Hall, we typically maintain social distance when we interact with people we do not know very well. For example, when you drop by a professor's office or consult with your physician, you will probably note that at least a body length or more separates the two of you. Sometimes a physical barrier such as a desk adds to the atmosphere of separateness.

Although we are likely to feel uncomfortable if any of these distances are violated, it is important to distinguish between voluntary and involuntary invasions of personal space. In our earlier example, for instance, we would be much less likely to feel invaded if a stranger came too close on a crowded bus than if the same thing happened when the bus was almost empty (Murphy-Berman & Berman, 1978). If we think our personal space has been voluntarily invaded, we may experience some kind of bodily reaction or physiological arousal. This response is likely to be strongly influenced by how we assess the situation. If we interpret the invasion as hostile and dangerous, we may withdraw or flee from the invader. If we assess the intrusion as rude and thoughtless, we may respond with anger and perhaps take action to repel the invader. Figure 17.6 shows some ways in which our cognitive assessments of violations of personal space may affect our behaviors.

Crowding Knowing what we now do about territoriality and personal space, we can pose a question that is of great concern to environmental psychologists. Given that even conservative estimates predict that the world population will double in 35 to 40 years if current trends continue, how will the resulting crowded conditions affect human behavior?

One of the most widely discussed studies of crowding explored the effects of overpopulation on rats, not humans. It was conducted by John Calhoun (1962) who housed 80 rats in a $10' \times 14'$ room divided into four pens (see Figure 17.7). The rats were provided with unlimited food and water and allowed to mate at will; all they lacked was adequate space. Connecting ramps allowed the rats to circulate among the pens, but two ramps led to pens 2 and 3 while only one ramp led to pens 1 and 4. Thus, pens 2 and 3 became overcrowded, an effect that was increased further by the

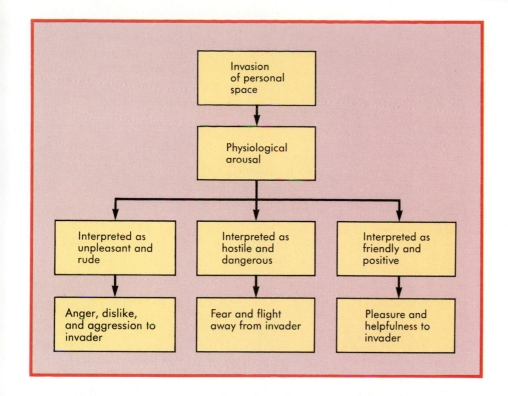

FIGURE 17.6   HOW WE RE-SPOND TO AN INVASION OF PERSONAL SPACE DEPENDS IN LARGE PART ON OUR COGNITIVE APPRAISAL OF THE INTRUSION

(*Source:* From Baron & Byrne, 1984)

actions of two dominant males, who staked out private territory in pens 1 and 4.

How did the crowding affect the rats? Calhoun observed pathological behavior in both male and female rats, especially in pens 2 and 3. Many of the males in these crowded pens displayed hypersexuality (mounting other animals indiscriminantly regardless of sex, age, or receptivity), extreme agitation, unusually high levels of aggression, and even cannibalistic behavior. Other rats displayed the other extreme of behavior, showing withdrawal and sexual passivity. Infant mortality rate was abnormally high. Many of the rats died during the course of the study, apparently as the result of stress-related physical disorders.

OVERCROWDING: HOW MUCH CAN WE LEARN FROM RATS?

The results of the Calhoun study are disquieting, especially when we consider recent statistics showing high levels of human violence and socially disruptive behaviors in crowded inner-city areas. Do the same destructive forces of overcrowding affect humans similarly? If so, can we view Calhoun's findings as a broad metaphor for our own fate as world population continues to increase?

It is true that some studies have reported a correlation between urban population density and high delinquency and crime rates, behavioral disorders, and stress-related illnesses (Altman, 1975; Freedman, 1975, 1979). Although crowding may contribute to these effects, we must be cautious in applying Calhoun's findings to humans. For one thing, we cannot rule out the possibility that other correlates of inner-city life, such as noise pollution, environmental toxins, the threat of crime, and educational, nutritional, and economic disadvantages, may also be to blame. Furthermore, the disadvantages that we often associate with crowded city life may be offset by better access to health care facilities, systems for handling emergencies, and various cultural and entertainment centers (Barker, 1968; Creekmore, 1985).

FIGURE 17.7

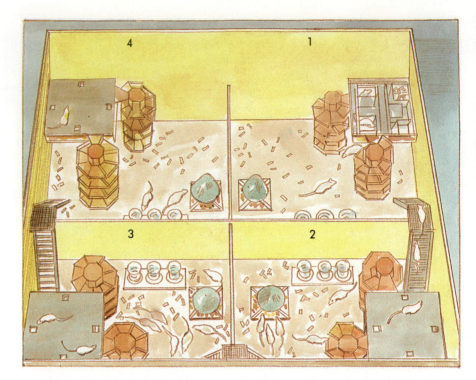

John Calhoun housed 80 rats in this 10′ × 14′ room divided into four pens. The rats were provided with unlimited food and water. (The four conical objects in the center are food hoppers, and the four adjacent trays contain three bottles for drinking.) The elevated sleeping areas or nests, shown exposed in pen 1, could be reached by climbing the winding staircases. Connecting ramps allowed the animals to circulate among the pens. However, the lack of a direct connection between pens 1 and 4 resulted in overcrowding in pens 2 and 3. (*Source:* From Calhoun, 1962).

FIRST PERSON 17.3

My Dad has a real thing about peace and quiet and solitude, particularly during family vacations, so we usually end up in some remote mountain hideaway where the nearest people are miles away. My idea of a fun vacation is crowded beaches, bodies everywhere, tuneboxes jamming, and people rapping. One Christmas we went to Hawaii. The beaches were packed and I had a ball. My Dad got sick. I guess the stress of too many people got to him. (*Authors' files*)

Contrary to a popular misconception, research shows that many of the urban poor living in inner-city slums and ghettos are not necessarily disenchanted with their lives. This may be due to a very strong network of social relationships that exists among neighbors and relatives who live in these densely populated urban centers (Fried & Gleicher, 1961; Hagedorn, 1983). The group cohesiveness that results from widespread social interaction in local parks, restaurants and bars, stores, and on the sidewalks and streets in front of apartment buildings is very different from the aloofness and impersonality that often characterizes more affluent and less densely populated suburban communities.

Although we cannot clearly demonstrate a cause-and-effect relationship between crowding and adverse behavioral consequences in humans, this does not necessarily mean that crowding has no effect on behavior. We have all probably felt uncomfortable and distressed in situations in which we have been crowded together with others, but the context in which we experience crowding has a strong influence on whether or not we interpret crowded conditions to be aversive. For example, if you had to share a small, 600-square-foot apartment with 10 other people, you would probably feel terribly stressed by the crowded conditions. Likewise, crowding into a car with a half-dozen people is also likely to make you feel uncomfortable and stressed. However, you may not feel crowded at all when sharing a 600-square-foot classroom with 10 other people or cramming into a coliseum with 15,000 fans to watch a basketball game.

Observations such as these have led environmental psychologists to distinguish between density and crowding. **Density** is a physical attribute that is reflected in the number of people in a given amount of space. **Crowd-**

The context in which we experience crowding has a strong influence on whether or not we interpret crowded conditions to be aversive. For example, if we were walking down a crowded street in downtown Tokyo in the middle of a rainstorm, we would most likely interpret the situation as being terribly stressful. However, we may not feel at all uncomfortable or stressed if we were crammed into a coliseum with thousands of spectators.

ing refers to a psychological response to a lack of space characterized by subjective feelings of overstimulation, distress, and discomfort.

As you might guess from your own experiences, environmental psychologists have found that high densities do not always produce feelings of crowding and psychological discomfort. In some situations, such as home environments, prisons, or vehicles of transportation, high densities may be very stressful. At musical concerts, athletic events, popular beaches, or parties, however, dense concentrations of people may not be a source of discomfort and may actually add to the subjective pleasures of the people involved (Freedman, 1975). Thus, population density interacts with other situational and environmental variables in exerting an influence upon behavior.

INDUSTRIAL/ORGANIZATIONAL PSYCHOLOGY

A second area in which psychology has been effectively applied is **industrial/organizational (I/O) psychology,** the application of psychological principles to improve the functioning of businesses and industrial organizations. I/O psychology can be traced back to the work of Hugo Munsterberg in the early 1900s, and to the time-motion studies of the 1920s and 1930s, in which the movements of workers were carefully analyzed to detect ways of eliminating inefficiency and increasing productivity. Its scope has expanded dramatically since those early studies: I/O psychology now encompasses such diverse activities as analyzing organizational structures, assessing the effectiveness of varied management strategies, increasing communication among workers and management personnel, devising effective personnel selection procedures, improving employee satisfaction, reducing employee stress and turnover, and devising ways to improve the efficiency of human/machine interactions. We will explore three major focuses of I/O psychologists: personnel selection, worker satisfaction and productivity, and organizational structure and management styles. A more extensive overview of I/O psychology, written by Professor William Titus of Arkansas Tech University, is provided in Appendix B.

PERSONNEL SELECTION

Suppose you have just purchased a business that consists of a chain of four physical fitness centers. You have some information suggesting that the clubs have been poorly managed under the previous ownership, and you are convinced that good management will result in a profitable operation. Your first priority is to hire four top-notch managers. How do you proceed? One application of I/O psychology has been to help make the process of personnel selection more effective (Hakel, 1986). Personnel selection consists of two phases: analyzing the job itself so that you know what qualifications are required, and selecting the candidate who comes closest to meeting those qualifications.

Job Analysis   A *job analysis* is a specific description of the exact nature of a job and the tasks that must be performed. For instance, you may analyze your management job and determine that employees will be required to:

1. Demonstrate and repair all types of exercise equipment.
2. Communicate to customers the relationship between various exercises and the development of specific areas of the physical anatomy.
3. Present to the public a personal image that reflects physical fitness.
4. Communicate effectively with both employees and consumers.
5. Keep accurate records of all financial transactions.
6. Demonstrate previous management-level employment experience.
7. Administer cardiopulmonary resuscitation (CPR) in the event of exercise-induced cardiac arrest.

A job analysis is a necessary basis for determining *job specifications,* specific measurable characteristics that the employee you hire needs to possess in order to fulfill his or her job. For your manager position, for instance, these job specifications would include mechanical aptitude (equipment repair), knowledge of human anatomy, excellent physical fitness, good communication skills, mathematical/bookkeeping skills, previous managerial experience, and knowledge of CPR.

The Selection Process   Once you know what traits and skills your employees must have, how do you determine which job applicants possess them? Employers use a number of techniques, including *application forms, interviews, tests,* and *assessment center* data.

Application Forms   An application form is a questionnaire that asks candidates for information about themselves, their past experiences, and often their reasons for applying for a specific position. Application forms are useful as rough screening devices that employers can use to weed out candidates who do not meet minimum requirements such as educational level, specific skills, or previous work experience. Extensive application forms such as those typically required by most major corporations (as well as many smaller businesses) may provide a wealth of *biodata* (detailed biographical data that are often very helpful in predicting future job success) (Eberhardt & Muchinsky, 1982; Landy, 1985; Owens & Shoenfeldt, 1979). Biodata may include information about past academic achievement and attitudes toward school, participation in extracurricular activities, previous employment experience (especially the length of time spent at previous jobs and reasons for leaving), and any special educational or training experiences. If a candidate for your manager position indicated previous extensive participation in sports, years of involvement in active exercise programs, and several years' employment in a management position involving extensive public contact, you would have a good basis for predicting the success of the candidate in your business.

Interviews   A second assessment method, the *personal interview*, is still one of the most popular ways of selecting employees: candidates who are not screened out by the application form are almost certain to be subjected to at least one interview. Despite its widespread use, however, validity studies have indicated that the interview is a "dismal" predictor of ultimate job success (Tenopyr, 1981).

The effectiveness of interviews may be seriously compromised by a few factors. Both the interviewer's biases and the halo effect (discussed in Chapter 16) are often very influential. Even interviewers who pride themselves on being objective may nevertheless fall victim to the halo effect when interviewing an applicant who happens to have graduated from their alma mater. Interviews may also provide inaccurate impressions. The highly stressful nature of a job interview might cause a person who is usually comfortable in interpersonal situations to appear tongue-tied, while a superficially charming candidate who is very good at projecting the image the interviewer is looking for may seem right for the job despite poor qualifications. Research has demonstrated that job candidates may achieve very high ratings from interviewers simply by speaking fluently, remaining composed, and maintaining eye contact (Hollandsworth et al., 1979; Tessler & Suschelsky, 1978).

Can interviews be made more effective? I/O psychologists have researched this question and have introduced a number of modifications to the interview method, including developing much more structured interview formats, training interviewers to be aware of the impact of personal biases and the halo effect, and combining evaluations from two or more interviewers. Such procedures may lead to moderate improvements in the validity of the interview as a predictor of future job success. Nevertheless, the current state of the art suggests that people involved in personnel selection should be very cautious in interpreting interview data, and that they should avoid placing undue emphasis on interviewer assessments (Cronbach, 1984).

Tests   Literally hundreds of different kinds of tests are used to assess the suitability of applicants for specific jobs. These tests include *vocational interest tests*, such as the Strong-Campbell Interest Inventory or the Kuder Occupational Interest Survey, *personality tests*, a multitude of which are available (see Chapter 13), and a wide range of *aptitude tests*. I/O psychologists may recommend specific tests for a particular selection task.

How valuable are these tests in predicting employee performance? Their effectiveness depends on so many variables—from the selection task, to what tests are employed, to who interprets them—that it is impossible to answer this question definitively. In general, however, the more specific a test is in measuring the skills or attributes for a specific job, the more helpful it is as a selection device (Cronbach, 1984). Aptitude tests that measure specific traits, such as clerical or mechanical aptitude, may be relatively effective predictors (Schultz, 1979). This is especially true of somewhat simple jobs: if you are selecting an applicant for a word-processing position, you can be fairly confident that his or her score on a word-processing test will be a fairly good measure of ability to do the job. In contrast, tests that measure either levels of interest in different vocations or general personality traits tend to be far less effective in predicting job success (Borman et al., 1980).

Assessment Centers If interviews have a poor track record and tests are most effective for measuring specific skills, how do employers make decisions about candidates for more demanding jobs, such as managerial or executive-level positions? One approach taken by hundreds of large corporations (including IBM, Ford Motor Company, Sears, Bell Telephone, and Kodak) in recent years is to use **assessment centers.** If you plan to pursue a career in business or industry, the odds are good that you will encounter such a selection procedure.

Although assessment centers may conduct interviews and tests, the truly unique feature of these centers is their use of simulated work situations in which applicants may be observed in conditions typical of the actual work environment—often including moderate levels of stress. One widely used assessment-center method is called the *in-basket technique*. In this exercise, an applicant is instructed to read through, sort out, prioritize, and then deal with a basket full of memos, assignments, and requests of the type that might be encountered during a typical day on the job. Observing how well a candidate is able to accomplish this task may provide important clues to his or her ability to function in the actual job.

Another assessment-center technique, known as the **leaderless group discussion,** places several applicants in a group where they are asked to solve a realistic business problem related to the position for which they are applying. As they struggle with the problem, they are periodically interrupted by "clerks" who bring in information about shipment delays, price changes, and other data that complicate the task at hand. Observing candidates' performance provides useful information about their leadership skills as well as their ability to cope effectively with stress.

How reliable are such techniques in predicting actual job performance? According to some recent data, assessment centers have been quite effective in predicting performance in a variety of civilian and military jobs (Borman et al., 1983). For example, one study used assessment-center techniques to predict the management potential of a sample of women. When a follow-up was conducted seven years later, a strong relationship was found between assessment-center predictions and actual career progress (Ritchie & Moses, 1983). Some researchers are skeptical about claims of assessment-center successes, however, and they urge personnel officials to use the same caution in interpreting this kind of information as they use in evaluating data from interviews and other assessment techniques (Landy, 1985; Zedeck & Cascio, 1984).

A concluding comment regarding employee selection techniques is in order. American businesses and corporations operate under federal laws mandating that all selection techniques used to determine which applicants are most qualified must fairly measure the knowledge and skills required to perform well in a specific job. Furthermore, it is the employers' responsibility to demonstrate that the selection procedures they use (including tests, interviews, and so forth) do measure knowledge and skills needed for successful job performance (Bersoff, 1981). These legal constraints are sometimes overlooked in practice. In these times of escalating civil litigation, however, we might anticipate eventual clarification of the legal environment within which employers conduct personnel selection processes. It seems likely that corporations and businesses will experience an increasing pressure to demonstrate the validity of their employee selection procedures.

WORKER SATISFACTION AND PRODUCTIVITY

One of the central questions in I/O research has been what factors contribute to job satisfaction. This question is important because low job satisfaction is associated with high rates of employee absenteeism and turnover, which in turn reduce productivity. The relationship between low job satisfaction and high turnover rates is particularly strong (Beck, 1986).

Job satisfaction may be defined as "the attitude one has toward his or her job" (McCormick & Ilgen, 1980, p. 303). This definition is deceptively simple, however, in that a particular employee's level of satisfaction may vary significantly depending on what aspect of the job is in question. For instance, your love of books may motivate you to get a job as a librarian. You may be extremely satisfied with the work you do at the library, pleased with your co-workers, more than satisfied with the hours you work, and satisfied with the fringe benefits. At the same time, you may think your salary is inadequate and that opportunities for advancement are limited. Your over-all job satisfaction would thus reflect a blending of all of these various aspects, each of which would weigh differently in your overall feelings about your job.

Since job satisfaction is a state of mind, it cannot be observed directly. Instead, I/O psychologists use questionnaires and rating scales to measure it. The result has been a legion of studies of job satisfaction—over 3,000 were conducted between 1935 and 1976, an average of one publication every five days! (Locke 1976). After all this research, we have a much better understanding of at least some of the contributors to job satisfaction. We have also learned, however, that job satisfaction is an exceedingly complex cognitive reaction. Table 17.2 provides a brief summary of some of the factors that contribute to job satisfaction.

Different people would prioritize the items in Table 17.2 differently. Some consider wages to be a top priority for job satisfaction. However, the substantial majority of surveys show that most workers rate a variety of other factors, including autonomy, challenging work, good social relations with co-workers, and opportunities to influence corporate policy, as more important than money.

One instrument that is often used to measure job satisfaction is the **job description index (JDI)** (Smith, Kendall, & Hulin, 1975). The JDI assesses five dimensions of job satisfaction that exist in virtually any job: supervision, co-workers, promotions, pay, and the work itself. These dimensions apply to jobs in a wide variety of organizations, but the JDI attempts to be sensitive to the fact that each employee's frame of reference is important when evaluating various aspects of his or her job. Employees completing the JDI use personal criteria to decide about each dimension.

By comparing an individual's score for each dimension to overall norms, one can use the JDI to evaluate how satisfied an employee is on a particular dimension relative to other workers. The norms of the JDI have been stratified as a function of a number of different variables, such as income level, age, sex, and tenure on the job; thus, it is possible to get quite a close match between each employee and the JDI norms.

TABLE 17.2 *Factors Related to Job Satisfaction*

1. The work is rated as interesting.
2. Work performance receives adequate recognition
3. The work contributes to positive self-esteem.
4. Opportunities for promotion or advancement are present.
5. The job provides at least some degree of autonomy and independence.
6. There are opportunities to influence company policy and procedures by participating in decision making.
7. Adequate information, help, and equipment are available to accomplish the job.
8. A worker has enough authority to ensure that a job is successfully completed.
9. The end results of a work endeavor may be seen.
10. Pay is perceived as being adequate and equitable.
11. Job security is high.
12. There are good communication and positive relationships with supervisory personnel.
13. There are opportunities for enjoyable social interaction with other employees.
14. There is a positive attitude toward the work environment (safety, health, and physical environment).
15. The work is perceived to be challenging.
16. There are opportunities to apply one's own judgment, intelligence, and skills.

Source: Adapted from Davis & Cherns, 1975; Lawler, 1982; Locke, 1976; McCormick & Ilgen, 1980; Schultz, 1979; Tuttle, 1983; Work in America, 1973.

Two cautions should be remembered in using job satisfaction instruments such as the JDI. First, the JDI produces relative, not absolute, information about job attitudes. Any individual's score must be assessed in the context of other scores. Second, it is often tempting to make conclusions about other aspects of a worker's behavior based on his or her job satisfaction. A number of studies have explored the relationship between job satisfaction and variables such as productivity, turnover rates, and absences; their findings should be considered before using information about job satisfaction as the basis for predicting a worker's effectiveness.

IS A HAPPY WORKER A PRODUCTIVE WORKER (AND VICE VERSA)?

How do you think job satisfaction and productivity are related? Does good worker performance occur as a result of high job satisfaction, or is it the other way around? Give these questions some consideration before reading on.

A widely held belief among management personnel and corporate executives is that a satisfied worker is a productive worker, and this belief leads naturally to the assumption that procedures that increase job satisfaction will inevitably yield increased profits through greater productivity. Almost 60 years of research has revealed, however, that things are just not that simple. A large number of studies have demonstrated a relationship between these two variables, but this relationship is far from perfect (Beck, 1986; Tuttle, 1983). As we learned in Chapter 2, a positive correlation does not necessarily demonstrate cause and effect. Thus, to argue that if we do things to make our workers happier they will inevitably perform better is to assume a causal relationship that may not exist. For example, it may be that good productivity on the job might lead to job satisfaction rather than vice versa. Furthermore, research has shown that increasing a worker's satisfaction does not necessarily yield improvements in productivity (Howell & Dipboye, 1982).

An important factor in the equation of job satisfaction and productivity is each individual's personal priorities. For some people, other aspects of life are far more important than what they do when they are on the job. You may have friends or acquaintances who like their jobs because so few demands are placed upon them. For people like this, low productivity may be associated with high job satisfaction. At the opposite extreme are people who react to job dissatisfaction by working all the harder to earn a promotion to a more satisfying position. For such individuals, low job satisfaction may be associated with high productivity. Increasing productivity may also lead some people to feel personal pride in a job well done, which translates into increased job satisfaction. This may backfire, however, for workers might also perceive that they are being exploited by management. In sum, the relationship between job satisfaction and productivity is exceedingly complex.

A few major findings have been well supported, however. One is that high job satisfaction is related to low turnover rates (Beck, 1986). This finding is important for business and industrial organizations who wish to reduce the high costs of selecting and training new employees. Table 17.2's list of conditions that contribute to job satisfaction might serve as a useful guide for businesses plagued by high turnover rates.

The other major finding is that absenteeism is also related to job satisfaction. I/O psychologists have been especially concerned with this finding, since job absenteeism costs American business many billions of dollars in lost revenue each year (Steers & Rhodes, 1978). Of course other factors, such as health problems and injuries, can contribute to absenteeism as well as low job satisfaction. Research clearly shows, however, that employees who are unhappy with their jobs are more likely to take days off from work with

FIRST PERSON 17.4

A few months ago I began working for a corporation that really believes in learning the business from the ground up. I have a college degree, and they have me primarily doing manual labor. I hate doing menial tasks that could be performed by virtually anybody. But from talking to other employees who have good management-level positions, I know that they also started virtually at the bottom. If I work very hard and demonstrate that I have what it takes, I hope to eventually be able to move through a series of promotions to an excellent position. For now, I'll keep my dissatisfaction to myself, grit my teeth, and go for the brass ring. But if I see no signs of better work in the next year or so, I'll begin looking for another job. (*Authors' files*)

no legitimate reason (Jones & Nicholson, 1982). During the course of one study of job satisfaction among Sears Roebuck employees in Chicago, a severe snowstorm created havoc with Chicago's transportation system. Sears employees were told they need not come to work unless they wanted to. As you might predict, those employees who came to work despite the offer of a no-penalty day off were predominantly the same employees who had been assessed as having high job satisfaction (Smith, 1977).

One recent innovation in the world of work has had a marked impact on absenteeism. This approach, known as **flextime,** allows workers to have some flexibility in picking their starting and quitting times as long as they are present during a core work period (Owen, 1976). Thus, a given business might allow its employees to arrive anytime between 7:00 A.M. and 10:00 A.M., and to depart between 3:00 P.M. and 6:00 P.M. I/O psychologists were prime movers behind this innovation, which was designed to boost morale by giving workers increased control over their working conditions, allowing them to avoid rush-hour traffic, and helping them accommodate family responsibilities. Research has linked flextime to reduced absenteeism, increased job satisfaction, increased productivity, and improved relations between management and line workers (Narayan & Nath, 1982; Orpen, 1981).

ORGANIZATIONAL STRUCTURE, MANAGEMENT STYLES, AND WORKER RESPONSE

In small businesses with only two or three workers, there may be little formal organization, and affairs are often conducted on a simple "I will do this and you do that" basis. Larger businesses and corporations simply cannot function in this fashion. One of the first things that many employees discover when they join the ranks of corporate workers is that they must work within the company's formal structure. This often means going to their supervisor when they wish to get something done or writing a formal memo when they want to modify a procedure.

Is the organizational hierarchy that seems inevitable in larger companies necessary for efficient functioning, or can large businesses be run effectively (and perhaps with greater worker satisfaction) without this type of structure? This question has been explored by I/O psychologists, with some interesting results. Some companies have applied a strategy known as **participant management,** in which all levels of employees are included in decision making.

A classic example of this process is the Honda plant in Maryville, Ohio (Abrams, 1983). In this large industrial complex, every employee has a say in important decisions that relate to such things as plant safety and quality control. Daily departmental meetings allow workers to share their thoughts with managers and to participate in making policy decisions; and the organizational structure allows for two-way communication between managers and line workers. Status differences between employees are minimized. Regardless of job level, every employee holds the same title of associate and wears an identical white uniform; and instead of working in private offices, executives work alongside employees. The result has been high productivity, low employee turnover and absenteeism, and a remarkable absence of the labor-management clashes that have typified the automobile industry over the last several decades. Some other studies have also linked participant management to greater job satisfaction, improved work climate, and greater productivity (Jackson, 1983).

Participant management is but one application of a management style known as employee-centered management or **Theory Y** management (McGregor, 1960). The idea behind this approach is that workers are willing to accept responsibility, and that they will be more productive in an atmosphere that allows them a certain degree of autonomy and independence. Therefore, workers are allowed considerable latitude and personal discretion in the manner in which they carry out job functions. Employee-centered managers are concerned with the *psychological efficiency* of workers, who they believe will function more effectively if they are provided with support and permitted to develop a sense of pride and personal involvement in policy setting.

In contrast to Theory Y is the **Theory X** management style, also known as job-centered or scientific management. This management style tends to emphasize production, placing primary emphasis on improving *work efficiency* (defined as maximum output at the lowest possible cost). Managers operating within this framework watch workers closely to be certain they are meeting quotas and working at peak efficiency. Scientific management also usually emphasizes policies and procedures that are believed to improve worker output, such as time-motion studies, job specialization, work quotas, bonuses tied to productivity, and rigid time schedules. Organizational structures tend to be very tight and communication one-directional, with instructions flowing from the top down through a rigid chain of command that offers little or no opportunity for employee involvement in decision making.

Which approach is more effective? Research clearly indicates that in most work situations the employee-centered management style is considerably more effective in inducing both increased productivity and job satisfaction (Anastasi, 1979; Beck, 1986; Dessler, 1980; Likert, 1961).

HEALTH PSYCHOLOGY

A revolution in medicine occurred over a century ago when medical researchers made a series of important discoveries. These discoveries led to the so-called germ theory of illness, which proposed that many diseases are caused by infectious organisms. This theory was applied in the development of many new means for controlling and treating illness, including sterilization, pasteurization, immunization, and antibiotic drugs. As a direct result of germ theory, what were once the leading causes of death in the world—tuberculosis, influenza, intestinal infections, pneumonia, and diphtheria—no longer pose a serious threat in areas of the world where modern health care is available.

This revolution has improved the quality and duration of our lives. However, with its toxic substances, dietary excesses, environmental stressors, and sedentary lifestyles, contemporary civilization has not yet abolished serious illness. We have reason to be hopeful, however, that a second revolution in medicine may offer the very real prospect that during our lifetimes we will see a dramatic reduction in some catastrophic illnesses. The primary impetus of this second revolution is an explosion of information about how psychological, social, and behavioral factors contribute to physical illness. Our lifestyles, our interpersonal relationships, and our state of mind all play a role in our health.

The idea that our state of mind can influence physical as well as mental health is by no means a new concept. In fact, *psychosomatic medicine*—a subfield of psychiatry that emerged in the early 1900s—has long stressed the interplay of the mind and the body in producing illness. Until relatively recently, psychosomatic medicine focused narrowly on particular illnesses that were thought to reflect mind-body interaction, such as migraine headaches, asthma, ulcers, rheumatoid arthritis, and hypertension. Recently, however, psychosomatic medicine has broadened its scope, joining with other disciplines to form the field of **behavioral medicine.** This enormously important new area of medicine encompasses professionals from many disciplines, including psychology, psychiatry, sociology, anthropology, epidemiology, physiology, pharmacology, nutrition, neuroanatomy, endocrinology, immunology, nursing, social work, health education, and public health (Miller, 1983).

Thanks to the combined efforts of these approaches, we are moving very rapidly toward a much more comprehensive understanding of how behavior affects physical disease processes. To gain a sense of the extent to which behavior factors are linked to serious illness, we need only refer to widely quoted estimates that between 50 and 70 percent of mortality from the 10 leading causes of death in the United States is largely behaviorally determined (Heffernan & Albee, 1985; National Academy of Sciences Institute of Medicine, 1982; Richmond, 1979). The connection is particularly strong between behavioral influences and two leading causes of death in America, cardiovascular disorders and cancers.

HOW IS BEHAVIOR LINKED TO PHYSICAL ILLNESS?

Take a few moments to consider what aspects of people's behavior you think might be strongly linked to physical illness and disease. It might help for you to think about the lifestyles of people you have known who have suffered from serious illnesses or medical conditions like coronary heart disease, hypertension, cancer, and so forth. See how many of the key behavioral factors you can identify before reading on.

Many of the diseases of contemporary civilization are not caused by germs but rather by the way we live our lives and interact with our social environments. Among the factors that have been identified as particularly influential in the etiology of disease are cigarette smoking, poor nutrition, inadequate exercise, obesity, maladaptive responses to stress, excessive alcohol consumption, use of illicit drugs, and failure to comply with physicians' recommendations (Kranz et al., 1985; Taylor, 1986). The more we can translate our escalating knowledge of the behavioral causes of serious illness into effective strategies for changing these maladaptive behaviors, the further we will progress in the second revolution in medicine.

In recent years psychologists have become increasingly involved in both researching the relationship between psychological factors and physical health and applying their findings to real-life problems. The result, **health psychology,** is one of the most dynamic of the new emerging specialties in psychology. Recently, the American Psychological Association formally acknowledged the importance of psychology's link with behavioral medicine by creating a distinct health psychology division within the APA. Health psychology is concerned with psychological aspects of health and illness, including such things as the etiology and correlates of health and illness, health promotion and maintenance, prevention and treatment of illness, and efforts to formulate health policy and improve the health care system (Taylor, 1986).

The Health Psychology and Life discussions throughout the preceding chapters have provided you with a sense of the wide-ranging scope of this topic. It is our perspective that any application of the principles and discoveries of psychology that improve our mental or physical health may be appropriately classified under the general rubric of health psychology.

One of the major research areas of health psychology, and behavioral medicine in general, has been the relationship between stress and illness. The remainder of this chapter explores this important topic.

THE NATURE OF STRESS

We began this chapter by talking about the Canadian researcher Hans Selye and his discovery that his laboratory rats responded to stressful laboratory conditions with consistent bodily reactions. From the headaches, upset stomachs, muscle tension, sleeplessness, and other responses most of us have experienced as a result of everyday situations like being caught in a traffic jam, it is clear that it takes far less than a laboratory experiment to produce symptoms of stress.

Although we are all familiar with stress, it is an elusive concept to define. One of the reasons for this is that stress means so many different things to different people, researchers and laypersons alike. Some of us think of stress as sweaty palms, a fast-beating heart, gritted teeth, and a churning stomach; and, following Selye's lead, researchers have for many years focused on the physiological changes that accompany stress. More recently, however, the study of stress responses has been expanded to include emotional, cognitive, and behavioral changes as well as physical reactions. Another focus of research explores the stressful environmental events, called *stressors,* that induce stress reactions. When we are feeling stressed we may be more inclined to describe our condition as being unprepared for an exam, feeling crowded in our dorms, or being harassed by a supervisor on the job, rather than focusing on our bodily or psychological responses.

Most contemporary researchers believe that an adequate definition of stress must take into account the interplay between external stressors and our physical and psychological responses. This relationship is neither simple nor predictable, for it varies from person to person and from day to day. As we will see later in this chapter, this variation occurs because stress is inextricably connected to our cognitive appraisals of events. Health psychologist Shelley Taylor (1986) has integrated all of these aspects of stress— stressors, responses to stress, and cognitive appraisal—into one definition. According to Taylor, **stress** is "the process of appraising events (as harmful, threatening, or challenging), of assessing potential responses, and of responding to those events" (1986, p. 146). Taylor notes that those responses may include not just physiological but also cognitive and behavioral changes. In the following paragraphs we examine physiological and psychological responses to stress as well as the situations that produce stress; we will then explore what we know about the role stress plays in some common illnesses.

PHYSIOLOGICAL RESPONSES TO STRESS

Hans Selye's observations of how his rats responded to stressors led him to formulate the concept of the **general adaptation syndrome (GAS).** According to this notion, when an organism is confronted with a stressor, its body mobilizes for action. This mobilization effort is mediated by the sympathetic nervous system, as we saw in Chapter 3, and it works primarily through the action of specific stress hormones on the body's muscles and organ systems. The response to stress is *nonspecific,* for the same physiological reactions occur regardless of the stressor. Selye also noted that repeated or prolonged exposure to stress that is not adequately managed or reduced will result in tissue damage (such as bleeding ulcers), increased susceptibility to disease, and even death in extreme cases.

Alarm, Resistance, and Exhaustion   Selye described three phases of the general adaptation syndrome: alarm, resistance, and exhaustion (see Figure 17.8). When an organism is exposed to a stressful event, it first experiences an *alarm* reaction in which it mobilizes to meet the threat. A sudden arousal of the sympathetic nervous system produces a flood of stress hormones— corticosteroids from the adrenal cortex and epinephrine (often called adrenalin) and norepinephrine from the adrenal medulla.

These hormones prepare the body for "fight or flight" by producing a number of physiological reactions. First, our heart rate is likely to increase, as is our blood pressure. This forces blood to parts of the body that may need it for strenuous physical activity such as flight away from danger. We experience this response as a pounding heart, like the rapid-fire thumping you may have felt after barely avoiding an accident on the freeway. Sugars

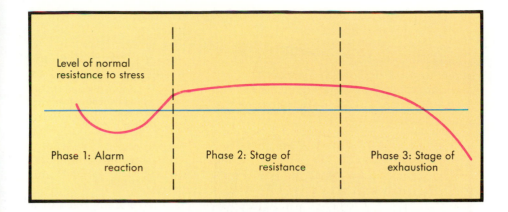

Level of normal resistance to stress

Phase 1: Alarm reaction

Phase 2: Stage of resistance

Phase 3: Stage of exhaustion

FIGURE 17.8   THE THREE PHASES OF SELYE'S GENERAL ADAPTATION SYNDROME

(*Source*: Adapted from Selye, 1956)

and fats also flood the blood to provide fuel for quick energy. This emergency response provides extra reserves, with the result that people are often able to perform seemingly "superhuman" feats (such as lifting a heavy beam off a person trapped in a mine cave-in) that they could not otherwise perform. Digestion slows or ceases during the alarm stage, making more blood available to the muscles and brain.

Our breathing rate also accelerates to supply increased oxygen to muscles poised for greater than normal output. This is why people often have difficulty catching their breath after a severe fright. Still another response to stress is a tensing of the muscles in preparation for an adaptive response. This explains the stiff neck, sore back, and painful aching in our legs that many of us experience after a long, hard exam or a rough day at work.

We also tend to perspire more when under stress—a response that acts as a kind of built-in air conditioner that cools our energized bodies. It also allows us to burn more energy (which produces heat) when we are faced with emergency situations. This is why many people find themselves drenched with perspiration after giving a speech or undergoing a stressful interview.

Finally, clotting agents are released into the blood when we are under stress, so that our blood will clot more rapidly if we are injured. One reason why we may not notice an injury we receive during an accident or fight is because the wound may have bled very little. Figure 17.9 summarizes these responses to stress.

We are not able to maintain the alarm phase's high level of bodily response or sympathetic activity for very long. Eventually the parasympathetic nervous system comes into play, providing a braking mechanism for the organs activated by the sympathetic system. At this point the organism enters into the second stage of *resistance*. Now the body continues to draw upon resources at an above-normal rate, but it is less aroused than in the alarm state. If the stress is prolonged or repeated, an organism is likely to enter the third stage of *exhaustion*. As a direct result of the continued drain on resources, the body tissues may begin to show signs of wear and tear during the exhaustion stage. Susceptibility to disease also increases, and continued exposure to the stressor is likely to deplete the organism's adaptive energy. The symptoms of the initial alarm reaction are likely to reappear, but resistance is now decreased and the alarm reaction is likely to continue unabated. If the organism is unable to develop strategies to overcome or cope with the stress, serious illness or even collapse and death may result.

Selye's model has had a profound impact on our understanding of stress and its links to illness. It not only provides a way of conceptualizing our physiological response to environmental events, but it also provides a plausible explanation for the relationship between stress and disease. Few medical experts today disagree with Selye's basic contention that prolonged

We tend to perspire more when we are under stress. Perhaps you can think of a situation (an interview, an audition, a speech) in which you were drenched with perspiration. This response acts as a sort of built-in air conditioner that cools our energized bodies. It also allows us to burn more energy when we are faced with emergency situations.

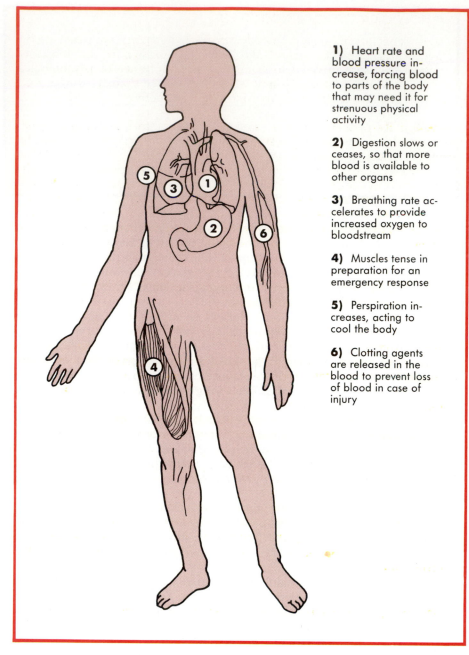

1) Heart rate and blood pressure increase, forcing blood to parts of the body that may need it for strenuous physical activity

2) Digestion slows or ceases, so that more blood is available to other organs

3) Breathing rate accelerates to provide increased oxygen to bloodstream

4) Muscles tense in preparation for an emergency response

5) Perspiration increases, acting to cool the body

6) Clotting agents are released in the blood to prevent loss of blood in case of injury

FIGURE 17.9   SOME PHYSIOLOGICAL RESPONSES TO STRESS

stress will often produce bodily wear and tear and erode our ability to resist disease if it is not effectively coped with. However, Selye's theory has also been criticized on a few counts. One criticism is that Selye failed to acknowledge the important role of psychological factors in stress responses (for example, the significant role of cognitive appraisal in determining the extent to which we assess a particular environmental event as stressful). Furthermore, some newer evidence suggesting that particular stressors may be associated with distinctly different physiological responses calls into question Selye's assumption of nonspecificity in reaction to stress (Mason, 1974, 1975). Although these criticisms have had little impact on Selye's cornerstone position in the field of stress research, health psychologists have become increasingly interested in other aspects of the experience of stress.

PSYCHOLOGICAL RESPONSES TO STRESS

Most of Selye's work focused on endocrinological responses to stress in non-human animals, most notably rats. In recent years, however, increased attention has been directed to assessing the importance of psychological factors in stress reactions. It is now widely recognized that stress affects not only our bodies but also how we think, feel, and behave.

Cognitive Responses to Stress If you think back to a situation in which you were under a great deal of stress—after breaking up with a partner, for instance, or perhaps receiving a rejection letter from a special school your heart was set on—it is quite possible that your cognitive responses stand out more clearly in your memory than do your physiological responses. Typical cognitive responses may include reduced ability to concentrate, higher than normal levels of distractability, impaired performance on cognitive tasks (such as reading or doing your homework), and sometimes a tendency to be plagued by disruptive or morbid thoughts (Cohen, 1980; Taylor, 1986; Zajonc, 1965). People who are under a great deal of stress often find that their minds wander and that they are easily distracted. It is also common to be troubled by intrusive, repetitive thoughts such as "I'm worthless" or "I just don't have what it takes," especially after experiencing a setback such as the loss of a job.

We often react to stressful events by employing one or more of the defense mechanisms outlined in Chapter 13. For example, we may seek to minimize the harm or threat of a stressful event by blocking it from our conscious awareness (repression), engaging in rationalization ("I didn't have a chance to prepare adequately and that is why I failed the test"), projecting blame ("I had to cheat to keep up with the rest of the cheaters in the class"), and so forth.

Stressful events may also result in positive cognitive responses, as we learn new ways to cope with or neutralize the stressful event. For example, you may learn to cope with the stress of getting caught in rush-hour traffic by leaving for class earlier or not scheduling courses at times that coincide with heavy commuter traffic, or you may take a basic course in auto mechanics to avoid the stress of a car that does not operate properly.

Why do some stressful situations produce negative effects while others have a positive outcome? Psychologists Richard Lazarus and Susan Folkman (1984a, 1984b) propose that our cognitive appraisal of a stressor makes a difference in our immediate response as well as our ability to cope with the stressor in the long run. Lazarus and Folkman maintain that when we confront situations that may be potentially stressful, we first engage in a process of *primary appraisal* to determine if the event is positive, neutral, or negative. If we consider an event to be negative, we further appraise it to determine how harmful, threatening, or challenging it is.

For example, suppose the person you were engaged to just returned your ring and broke off your relationship. This is potentially a very stressful event that you might appraise according to the three dimensions of harm, threat, and challenge. *Harm* is your assessment of the damage inflicted immediately by the event, such as damaged reputation, lowered self-esteem, loss of intimacy, and so forth. *Threat* is your assessment of possible future damage that may result from the unpleasant occurrence, such as a reluctance to develop another close intimate relationship out of fear that the same painful experience will be repeated. Finally, you may appraise your broken engagement in terms of the *challenge* it provides to overcome and profit from the event. Perhaps you had second thoughts yourself about the relationship, and you may see your new unattached status as providing opportunities for other involvements.

Once we complete the process of primary appraisal of potentially stressful events, Lazarus and Folkman suggest that we engage in a *secondary appraisal* to determine whether or not our coping abilities and resources will

FIGURE 17.10 LAZARUS AND FOLKMAN'S PSYCHOLOGICAL MODEL OF STRESS

(*Source:* From Taylor, 1986)

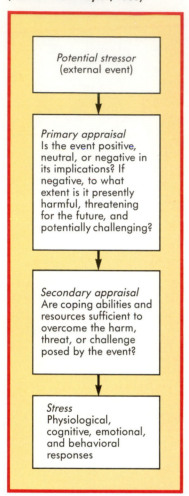

allow us to overcome the harm or threat and successfully meet the challenge. The end result, in terms of the amount of stress we actually experience, represents a blending or balance between these two processes of primary and secondary appraisal. If we perceive the harm and/or threat to be very high, we are likely to experience a high degree of stress. On the other hand, if we think we can cope with the situation, we are likely to experience far less stress. Figure 17.10 summarizes Lazarus and Folkman's psychological model of stress.

Emotional Responses to Stress Emotional responses to stress include such feelings as anxiety, irritability, anger, embarrassment, depression, helplessness, and hostility. Anxiety is potentially one of the most damaging emotional reactions. It is especially likely to develop when we perceive a marked imbalance between the threat posed by a stressor and our personal resources for coping with it. We have seen in previous discussions how devastating anxiety can be. People who are unable to cope effectively with anxiety become physically and psychologically taxed, making them susceptible to a variety of mental and physical disorders.

Behavioral Responses to Stress There are so many behavioral responses to stress that it is impossible to outline them all here. We have seen, however, that two general classes of adaptive behavioral responses are suggested by the "fight or flight" pattern. In some cases we take some kind of assertive action (*fight*) to confront stressors. For example, if you find that your home environment is stressful because of a parent who is constantly nagging at you, you may eventually confront the complaining parent. By confronting the source of your stress, you may be able to "clear the air" and find mutually acceptable ways of reducing or eliminating this stressor in your life. Sometimes, however, people prefer to withdraw from a threatening or harmful situation (*flight*). That is, you may decide you will experience less stress if you move into your own place.

Our strategies for coping with stress are not always either a clear confrontation or a clear withdrawal. A third alternative is to try to *adapt* to the stress. For example, assume you live near elevated train tracks and once every hour, at roughly the same time, you are disturbed by the loud noise caused by a passing train. If you are trying to study in your home, this intrusive noise could be a major source of stress in your life. You might neutralize this stressor simply by taking short hourly study breaks whenever a train passes. The Health Psychology and Life discussion "Managing Stress," proposes several physiological cognitive, and behavioral strategies for reducing the effects of stress.

STRESSORS

We have been looking at the ways we respond to stress, but so far we have said relatively little about the situations or events that produce stress in our lives. Are some kinds of events more likely to cause stress than others? Are stressors always negative events? We explore these questions next.

Factors That Contribute to Stress Our cognitive assessments have a lot to do with how much stress an event will produce in our lives, but it is not true to say that all events have the same potential for eliciting stress. What characteristics increase the likelihood that we will perceive an event as stressful?

Lack of Control One factor that contributes to the stressfulness of a situation is our lack of control over it. This is why it is much less stressful for you to stick a needle into yourself (for example, when removing a splinter) than to have a physician stick a needle into your arm. Research reveals that uncontrollable or unpredictable events are generally more stressful than

HEALTH PSYCHOLOGY AND LIFE

MANAGING STRESS

Mounting evidence linking stress with a variety of illnesses has prompted many health professionals to turn their attention to developing techniques for managing stress. These techniques take aim not only at our physiological, cognitive, and behavioral responses to stress but also at behaviors and thought patterns that may induce or increase stress. The following paragaphs summarize some of the strategies that have been successfully applied in various stress-management programs offered at hospitals, clinics, and corporations. For more information about these techniques or about stress-management programs, you may wish to check your library or bookstore for some of the many excellent self-help stress-management books currently available.

Managing Physiological Responses to Stress

Much of the physical damage associated with stress results from our bodies' physiological responses. Many techniques have been developed to minimize these reactions; three of the most effective are biofeedback, relaxation training, and exercise.

Biofeedback We are seldom aware of the subtle physiological changes that take place when we are under stress, such as rising blood pressure or increased heart rate. The theory behind **biofeedback** is that if we learn to recognize these destructive changes we can also learn to control them. Biofeedback provides individuals with information about their bodily processes that they can use to modify these processes. For instance, people who suffer from high blood pressure might be hooked up to a biofeedback apparatus that constantly monitors their blood pressure, sounding a tone whose pitch changes as their blood pressure rises or falls. Through this process, they may eventually learn to recognize symptoms of high blood pressure even when they do not hear a tone, so that they can apply techniques to control this response. Although biofeedback is not a panacea for all stress-related disorders, it has been helpful in treating migraine headaches, tension headaches, muscle tension, blood pressure abnormalities (both high and low), and chronic pain (Miller, 1985; King & Montgomery, 1980; Qualls & Sheehan, 1981; Turk et al., 1979).

Relaxation Training Virtually every formal stress-management program teaches some kind of relaxation technique. One of these is *progressive relaxation,* in which a person first tightens the muscles in a given area of the body (such as the legs), then relaxes them, then progresses systematically to other body areas until the entire body is relaxed. The idea that physical relaxation can lead to mental relaxation has been supported by experience, and progressive relaxation is now a key element in many stress-management programs. (Two other relaxation techniques, meditation and the relaxation response, are discussed in Chapter 5.)

How effective is relaxation in controlling

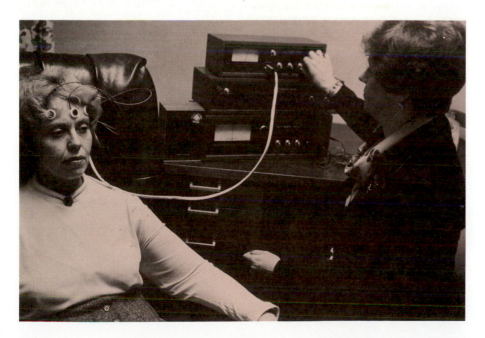

Biofeedback provides individuals with information about their bodily processes that they can use to modify these processes. For example, a person may be hooked up to a biofeedback apparatus and learn to recognize symptoms of high blood pressure (or whatever the particular problem may be) so that she or he can apply techniques to control this response.

Exercise helps to dissipate the pent-up energy and tension produced by stress; regular exercise can also help to moderate some potentially damaging physical effects of stress by lowering blood pressure, improving circulation, and strengthening the heart muscle. Many companies have become aware of the benefits of exercise and offer corporate fitness programs to their employees.

stress-induced effects such as muscle tension and high blood pressure? In one recent study, several hundred heart attack survivors were randomly assigned to one of two groups. One group received standard advice about proper diet and exercise; the other received the same advice, plus counseling on how to relax and slow down. In the ensuing three years, subjects in the group that received relaxation counseling experienced only half as many recurrent heart attacks as did those who had received the standard medical advice (Friedman & Ulmer, 1984).

Exercise Have you ever noticed that some types of exercise, such as jogging a few miles or playing tennis, can help to relieve stress? Exercise helps to dissipate the pent-up energy and tension produced by stress; regular exercise can also help to moderate some potentially damaging physical effects of stress by lowering blood pressure, improving circulation, and strengthening the heart muscle (Brown & Lawton, 1986; Roviario et al., 1984). Unfortunately, many people enthusiastically begin an exercise plan only to decide it "isn't for them" (Oldbridge, 1982). One way to avoid being an early quitter is to choose an exercise that is relatively pleasant. If you are bored with running or with riding a stationary bike, it may be easier to maintain an interest in racquetball, swimming, or aerobics.

Modifying Cognitive Antecedents of Stress

People involved in stress-management programs learn to pay attention to what they are thinking just before they experience stress. One of the benefits of this self-monitoring is the awareness of how frequently our own upsetting thoughts or negative self-talk trig-

gers our feelings of stress. Negative self-talk such as "I'll never be able to pass this exam" can make the difference between good performance and failure; it can also help to bring on the elevated physical reactions typical of stress responses (Schuele & Wiesenfeld, 1983).

To modify these common cognitive antecedents of stress, Canadian psychologist Donald Meichenbaum (1977) suggests a technique he calls *stress inoculation* in which we learn to replace negative self-statements with positive coping statements. For example, when faced with the stress of an exam we might use positive self-talk such as "There's no point in imagining the worst; I've prepared as well as anyone and I'll do the best I can." Although it may take some time to learn to alter negative self-talk successfully, the effect can be a reduction in anxiety and stress.

Modifying Behavioral Antecedents of Stress

Many of us bring stress on ourselves by certain maladaptive behaviors. For instance, we may use our time poorly and then suddenly find ourselves under pressure; or we may habitually take on too many tasks to accomplish in the time we have. Stress management programs offer a variety of techniques for modifying such stress-producing behaviors. The following abbreviated list illustrates a number of these behaviors as well as some strategies that are helpful in combating them.

Procrastination. Time-management training can help people pace themselves to avoid leaving too much for the last minute.

The "superperson syndrome." For some

people, an important part of stress management is learning to say "no" and to delegate tasks to others. Time-management training can also help people recognize their limits so that they do not commit to more work than they can complete.

Disorganization. Stress-management programs often help people deal with disorganization by providing training in how to set goals for each day, establish priorities, avoid wasting time, and become task-oriented.

Lack of assertiveness. People who have difficulty standing up for their rights may be "boiling inside," generating tremendous amounts of stress. To combat this tendency, many stress-management programs incorporate *assertiveness training,* which teaches people to confront such situations rather than tiptoe around them.

Going it alone. Facing stress alone is much more damaging than facing it with the support of people who care about us (Rook, 1987). Talking with others provides us with new perspectives; it may also boost our self-esteem and our sense that we are valued (Cohen & Wills, 1985). Thus, an important tactic in managing stress is to talk things over with someone. If friends or family members are not able to provide support, a campus counseling center, community health center, or private clinic may be a valuable resource.

those we can control or predict (Fleming et al., 1987; Frankenhaeuser, 1975; Glass & Singer, 1972; Singer et al., 1978; Suls & Mullen, 1981; Thompson, 1981). You might think that certain experiences, such as excessive noise, a nagging parent, or a series of painful rehabilitative exercises after a serious accident, would be stressful for anybody exposed to these events. This is not necessarily the case, however. When people believe that they can predict, modify, or end an unpleasant event, they are likely to experience it as being less stressful (even if they take no action to modify it). The knowledge that something can be done may be sufficient to reduce the stress.

Suddenness A second variable influencing how stressful we perceive an event to be is the suddenness with which it overtakes us. When people experience accidents, the sudden death of a loved one, or an unexpected pink slip at work, they may find it very difficult to mobilize adequate coping mechanisms. In general, it is easier to cope with challenges that we can foresee. Thus, a person who loses a loved one after a long, protracted illness or who loses a job after expecting to be terminated for months may be much less stressed by these aversive events.

People who experience the sudden death of a loved one may find it very difficult to mobilize adequate coping mechanisms. In general, it is easier for us to cope with challenges that we can foresee.

Ambiguity In general, a stressor that we perceive as ambiguous is likely to induce more stress than one that is clear-cut. This is because in clear-cut situations we may be able to determine an appropriate course of action (fight, flight, or adapt), but ambiguity forces us to spend a lot of resource-depleting energy trying to figure out the nature of the stressor. Research demonstrates that role ambiguity is a major cause of stress on the job (Cooper & Marshall, 1976). If you have a job in which your role is not clearly defined so that you do not know what is expected of you, you are likely to experience far more stress than if your employer's expectations are made clear.

Life Changes and Stress From our discussion so far, it may seem that all-stress is bad and that stressors are always negative events. This is not the case. Many of the happiest and most positive events in our lives—for instance, getting accepted to our first-choice college, getting married, having a baby, and receiving a promotion—can also be highly stressful. While such events often bring out the best in us by mobilizing our energies and providing opportunities for development, they may still place heavy demands on our resources. It is common to experience reactions such as loss of sleep, a feeling of confusion, and even an irritating lack of groundedness because we are too excited to function normally. Even though positive events may be stressful, however, events that we perceive as negative are much more likely to produce both physical and psychological manifestations of stress than are positive events (McFarlane et al., 1980; Sarason et al., 1978; Vinokur & Selzer, 1975).

Some psychologists have attempted to assess how various positive and negative changes in our lives may contribute to stress. An ambitious effort is the Social Readjustment Rating Scale (SRRS) published in the late 1960s (Holmes & Rahe, 1967). This scale, shown in Table 17.3, is based on the assumption "that any changes in our life situation, for either the better or the worse, can produce stress. The SRRS assigns different values to a number of life events. For instance, marriage is assigned a value of 50 stress points (called *life change units*). A person's score is obtained by adding the numbers associated with each event experienced in the last 12 months.

Early research reported positive correlations between SRRS scores and the incidence of physical illnesses. For example, scores in the 200s were linked with about a 50-percent chance of developing a physical illness within the next two years, while scores of 300 or higher were associated with about an 80-percent chance of illness (Holmes & Rahe, 1967; Rahe & Arthur, 1978). More recent research, however, has demonstrated that total scores on life-change scales such as the SRRS are not very accurate predictors of future problems with illness and disease (Krantz et al., 1985; McCrae, 1984; Schroeder & Costa, 1984).

One of the difficulties with trying to predict health problems from supposedly stressful life-change events is that merely adding up values assigned to each event does not take into consideration our cognitive appraisal of the potential stressfulness of events. For example, a marriage, divorce, a child leaving home, or retirement might dramatically increase stress for one person while significantly lowering it for another. As we have seen, the amount of stress an event produces is not inherent in the event

One of the most difficult job situations I've ever experienced was when I was working for a manager who kept changing his mind about what he wanted from me. One day he would call me into his office and tell me what a good job I was doing; two weeks later he would chew me out. I hadn't done anything different; he had just dreamed up some new policy that I wasn't following because I didn't know anything about it. My friends at work felt the same way I did: with a boss who ran hot and cold depending on factors they couldn't understand, they never knew where they stood either. (*Authors' files*)

Even the happiest and most positive events in our lives can also be highly stressful. Although such events often bring out the best in us by mobilizing our energies and providing opportunities for development, they may still place heavy demands on our resources.

TABLE 17.3 *Social Readjustment Rating Scale*

Rank	Life Event	Mean Value	Rank	Life Event	Mean Value
1	Death of spouse	100	23	Son or daughter leaving home	29
2	Divorce	73	24	Trouble with in-laws	29
3	Marital separation	65	25	Outstanding personal achievement	28
4	Jail term	63	26	Spouse begin or stop work	26
5	Death of close family member	63	27	Begin or end school	26
6	Personal injury or illness	53	28	Change in living condition	25
7	Marriage	50	29	Revision of personal habits	24
8	Fired at work	47	30	Trouble with boss	23
9	Marital reconciliation	45	31	Change in work hours or conditions	20
10	Retirement	45	32	Change in residence	20
11	Change in health of family member	44	33	Change in schools	20
12	Pregnancy	40	34	Change in recreation	19
13	Sex difficulties	39	35	Change in church activities	19
14	Gain of new family member	39	36	Change in social activities	18
15	Business readjustment	39	37	Mortgage or loan less than $10,000	17
16	Change in financial state	38	38	Change in sleeping habits	16
17	Death of close friend	37	39	Change in number of family get-togethers	15
18	Change to different line of work	36	40	Change in eating habits	15
19	Change in number of arguments with spouse	35	41	Vacation	13
20	Mortgage over $10,000	31	42	Christmas	12
21	Foreclosure of mortgage or loan	30	43	Minor violations of the law	11
22	Change in responsibilities at work	29			

Source: From Holmes & Rahe, 1967.

itself. Instead, our perception of an event as stressful determines how much stress we actually experience.

In addition, as Richard Lazarus (1981) has pointed out, it is not just the major life changes that produce stress. Everyday stressors such as traffic jams, arguments with a partner, or a car that does not operate properly may well have a much greater impact on us than the major life-change events listed in scales such as the SRRS.

STRESS AND ILLNESS

Stress is widely recognized as a major factor in a wide range of physical illnesses (Maddi et al., 1987). It has been estimated that as many as three out of four visits to physicians are prompted by stress-related problems (Charlesworth & Nathan, 1982). In this final section we explore the evidence linking stress with four common physical disorders: coronary heart disease, hypertension, malfunctioning of the immune system, and cancer.

Coronary Heart Disease   Coronary heart disease (CHD) is a general label for illnesses that cause a narrowing of the coronary arteries, the vessels that supply the heart with blood. CHD accounts for nearly half of all deaths in the United States each year (American Heart Association, 1984), many of which occur when people are still in the prime of life. Millions of Americans also experience reduced quality of life as a result of the ravages of CHD.

While factors such as smoking, obesity, diabetes, family history, diets high in fat, high serum cholesterol levels, physical inactivity, and high blood pressure are all linked to CHD, these risk factors considered together account for less than half of all diagnosed cases of CHD (American Heart Association, 1984). Something else besides diet, exercise, and general health habits must be a factor in CHD; and research over the last three decades has strongly implicated stress.

The story of how stress was first linked with heart disease begins with an unexpected discovery by cardiologists Meyer Friedman and Ray Rosenman (1974). In the late 1950s, Friedman and Rosenman were studying the relationship between eating behavior and disease among a sample of San Francisco couples. They found that although the women consumed amounts of cholesterol and animal fat equal to that consumed by their husbands, the women were dramatically less susceptible to heart disease than the men in the study. Since most of the men were employed and their wives were not, Friedman and Rosenman began to suspect that job-related stress might be implicated in the sex differences in CHD. Following up on this hunch, they mailed questionnaires to hundreds of physicians and business executives, asking them to speculate about what had caused the heart attacks of their patients, friends, and colleagues. Their responses overwhelmingly blamed job-related stress.

The next step was to conduct a field study. A sample of 40 tax accountants were studied over several months, commencing with the first of the year. During the first three months, laboratory measures of two warning indicators, blood-clotting speed and serum cholesterol levels, were generally within the normal range. This changed, however, as the April 15 tax-filing deadline approached. During these few weeks the accountants were under a great deal of pressure to finish their clients' tax returns, and both blood-clotting measures and serum cholesterol rose to dangerous levels. Once the tax-filing crunch passed, both measures returned to normal.

Convinced that responses to stress may be a major contributor to coronary heart disease, Friedman and Rosenman embarked on a nine-year study of several thousand men, ages 35–39, who were physically healthy at the outset of their investigation. Each subject was asked specific questions about his work and eating habits and his usual ways of responding to stressful situations. Using subjects' responses as well as observations of their behavior, the researchers divided participants into two groups roughly equal in size. Subjects in the **Type A** group tended to be hard-driving, ambitious, very competitive, easily angered, very time conscious, and demanding of perfection in both themselves and others. In contrast, **Type B** subjects were relaxed, easygoing, not driven to achieve perfection, happy in their jobs, understanding and forgiving, and not easily angered (Friedman & Rosenman, 1974; Friedman & Ulmer, 1984).

By the end of the long-term study, it was clear that Type A subjects were far more prone to heart disease than their Type B counterparts. Over the nine-year period, 257 subjects in the total research population had suffered heart attacks, and approximately 70 percent of these subjects were Type As. In other words, Type A men were more than twice as vulnerable as Type Bs. Subsequent studies by other researchers have also linked Type A behavior to CHD risk, a relationship that seems to be true of women as well as men (Baker et al., 1984; Haynes et al., 1980).

More recent studies have also confirmed that there are noteworthy differences between Type A people and Type B people. For example, research comparing Type A and Type B individuals has revealed that the former demonstrate a greater time urgency (Glass et al., 1974), a stronger tendency to think negative thoughts (Henly & Williams, 1986), greater competitive achievement strivings (Glass, 1977; Van Egeren et al., 1982; Vega-Lahr & Field, 1986), a stronger tendency to suppress symptoms of fatigue (Schlegel et al., 1980), a greater probability of experiencing an occupational injury (Cooper & Sutherland, 1987; Niemcryk et al, 1987), and more expression of aggression and hostility (Carver & Glass, 1978; Van Egeren et al., 1982). While all of these behaviors may increase the risk of CHD, hostility and an aggressively reactive temperament seem to play an especially important role (Dembroski et al., 1985; Spielberger et al., 1985). Thus, it may be that people who are inclined to lash out at others may also be striking at themselves, placing their own health in jeopardy.

We still do not understand exactly how Type A behavior is linked to coronary heart disease, but a few possibilities have been explored. First, it is possible that Type A people are more likely to engage in behaviors that are known risk factors in CHD, such as drinking more caffeine-containing beverages, sleeping less, exercising less, smoking more, and eating more fatty fast foods (Hicks et al., 1983; Hicks & Pellegrini, 1982). A second possibility is that the temperaments and physiological responses to stress of Type A people may also contribute to their proneness to heart disease. Several studies have shown Type As to be much more physiologically reactive than are Type Bs to potentially stressful situations (Dembroski et al., 1978; Krantz & Manuck, 1984; Manuck et al., 1978). It is also possible that both of these suggested tendencies may interact in some complex fashion to induce heart disease.

Still another line of research suggests that Type A behavior may represent a *response* to rather than a *cause* of excessive physiological reactivity (Krantz & Durel, 1983). One intriguing study revealed that even when unconscious, Type A patients undergoing surgery manifested a greater elevation of blood pressure than Type B patients experiencing the same procedure (Kahn et al., 1980). Since subjects were not able to respond cognitively and emotionally when they were unconscious, the greater response of the Type A subjects suggests a possible predisposition to greater than normal physiological responses to stress. If this is the case, it seems possible that Type A behavior may represent a coping response to heightened sympathetic nervous system activity, rather than a cause of this activity.

Hypertension Hypertension, commonly referred to as high blood pressure, occurs when blood flow through the vessels is excessive, a condition that may cause both hardening and general deterioration of tissue in the vessel walls. It has been estimated that roughly 30 million Americans suffer from hypertension and that annually about 16,000 die as a direct result of this disease (Taylor, 1986).

A number of physical factors may contribute to hypertension, including such things as obesity, excess salt intake, and genetic predispositions (Shapiro & Goldstein, 1982). However, there is also substantial evidence linking stress to increased blood pressure (Harrell, 1980; Obrist, 1976; Shapiro & Goldstein, 1982). For instance, one study identified areas of high and low stress within the city of Detroit, Michigan (high-stress locales were characterized by high poverty, high population density, high crime rates, and high divorce rates), and measured the blood pressures of a representative sample from each area. The highest blood pressure readings were recorded among residents of the high-stress areas (Harburg et al., 1973).

It has been suggested that a variety of personality factors may be linked to hypertension. Most frequently mentioned are a tendency to deal with anger by suppressing it (Gentry et al., 1982; Harrell, 1980) and the Type A behavior pattern discussed in the preceding section.

Some people may also be physically predisposed toward hypertension. Many hypertensive people show a more pronounced blood pressure response to a range of stressors (such as exposure to cold water or participation in a challenging mental task) than do people without hypertension (Harrell, 1980), an excess reactivity that may to some extent be genetically programed. In a recent study, 30 nonhypertensive subjects with a strong family history of hypertension were exposed to a variety of stressful tasks. Most exhibited an elevation of heart and blood pressure rates well above the norms for these tasks, a finding which suggests that a genetically based overreactivity of the sympathetic nervous system to stress may play a role in chronic hypertension (Jorgensen & Houston, 1981).

Stress and the Immune System The immune system is an exceedingly complex surveillance system that guards the body by recognizing and removing bacteria, viruses, cancer cells, and other hazardous foreign substances (Pomerleau & Rodin, 1986). When such substances are detected, our immune systems respond by stimulating *lymphocytes* (white blood cells) to attack and destroy these invaders. The action of the lymphocytes as well as other immune-system responses are delicately regulated in an extremely complex process. If the immune system is suppressed, we become more vulnerable to a variety of infectious organisms and cancers, a fact that has been made painfully clear in recent years with the unfolding story of

Acquired Immune Deficiency Syndrome (AIDS). Conversely, a breakdown in the body's system of checks and balances may cause the immune system to become overreactive, turning on itself to attack and destroy healthy body tissues. (This occurs in autoimmune disorders such as rheumatoid arthritis.) While diet, age, heredity, and general health all affect the functioning of the immune system, stress also exerts a marked influence on *immunocompetence*—the immune system's ability to defend our bodies successfully (Arnetz et al., 1987; Irwin et al., 1987; Jemmott & Locke, 1984; Martin, 1987).

For instance, many studies of nonhuman animals have demonstrated that experimentally manipulated stressors, such as separation from mother, isolation from peers, exposure to loud noise, and electric shock, can reduce immunocompetence by suppressing the activity of the lymphocytes (Borysenko & Borysenko, 1982; Esterling & Rabin, 1987; Laudenslager et al., 1982; Monjan & Collecter, 1977; Rogers et al., 1979). Research with human subjects has revealed similar results. Lymphocyte production has been shown to be suppressed following death of a spouse (Bartrop et al., 1977; Schleifer et al., 1983); and studies of Apollo and Skylab astronauts revealed immunological deficiencies immediately after the stress of reentry and splashdown (Fisher et al., 1972; Kimzey, 1975; Kimzey et al., 1976). High-stress periods such as final exam week have also been linked to reduced immunocompetence—a finding which helps explain why people may be more likely to become ill during finals (Jemmott et al., 1983). Research with children has revealed an increased incidence of infectious disease when the family is under stress, suggesting a suppression of the immune system (Boyce et al., 1977; Meyer & Haggerty, 1962). Research on adult subjects has also linked symptoms of a variety of infectious diseases, including colds, influenza, herpes, and mononucleosis, to stressful events (Jemmott & Locke, 1984).

We still do not know exactly how stress suppresses immunocompetence. However, several lines of evidence suggest that endocrine responses to stress may play a primary role (Authur, 1987; Martin, 1987). Recall from our earlier discussion of Selye's general adaptation syndrome that stress arouses the sympathetic nervous system, triggering the release of stress hormones. There is good reason to believe that these stress hormones—corticosteroids, epinephrine, and norepinephrine—function to suppress the immune system. It seems possible that this process may play a major role in increasing our susceptibility to disease during difficult times. It is also possible, however, that further research will reveal a relationship between immune-system suppression and some mechanism that we are not yet aware of (Jemmott & Locke, 1984; Taylor, 1986).

Cancer Evidence linking stress to cancer is less conclusive and certainly more controversial than that for CHD, hypertension, or immune-system suppression. However, many specialists in the field of behavioral medicine strongly suspect there is a connection. Cancer is a collection of many diseases (over 100), all of which result from a DNA malfunctioning that produces runaway cell growth. Although researchers are still a long way from understanding all the mechanisms and agents involved in cancer, compelling evidence suggests a relationship between stress and cancer (Baltrusch & Waltz, 1985).

Studies of cancer patients often reveal that they have experienced a higher than normal rate of stressful life events prior to the onset of their disease (Sklar & Anisman, 1981). Several studies have also found a high incidence of cancer among people who have experienced prolonged episodes of depression, grieving, or helplessness (Sklar & Anisman, 1981). Stress associated with lack of social support has also been linked to cancer. For example, the lack of close family relations during childhood and the absence of a social support network of friends and family members during adulthood has been linked to a higher than normal cancer incidence (Shaffer et al., 1982; Thomas et al., 1979; Thomas & Duszynski, 1974). In accord with this, cancer has been found to occur more often among widowed, divorced, or separated adults than among those who are married (Tache et al., 1979).

Animal studies provide information not available in human research. For example, rats who are inoculated with cancerous cells and then exposed to inescapable electric shocks are less able to reject the cancerous cells than are rats who are subjected to escapable shocks (Visintainer et al., 1983). This suggests that the greater stress associated with an uncontrollable event may have reduced the animals' resistance to cancer. Other studies, in which animals have been exposed to stressors such as crowding, have also reported higher incidences of malignancies than among nonstressed animals (Amkraut & Solomon, 1977).

Another promising line of research has explored the idea of a *cancer-prone personality*. Researchers have long suspected that people who are inhibited, compliant, conforming, inclined to depression, calm, passive, and with strong tendencies to suppress their emotions are particularly prone to develop cancer (Bahnson, 1981; Renneker, 1981). A major methodological problem with many of these studies, however, is that it is often not possible to determine whether this pattern of personality traits triggers cancer or whether it develops as a consequence of the disease.

A CANCER-PRONE PERSONALITY? DIFFERENTIATING CAUSE FROM EFFECT

Assume you are a health psychologist studying the relationship between personality variables and cancer. You find an unusually high incidence of traits such as passivity, compliance, and suppression of emotion among a sample of cancer patients. While these traits may have existed before the cancer and played a role in its development, you suspect that at least some of the traits may have developed as a consequence of the disease. What kind of research design would you use to clarify whether these personality traits are more likely to be a cause or a consequence of cancer? Consider this issue for a moment before reading on, reviewing the research methods discussed in Chapter 10 if necessary.

To differentiate between potential cause and consequence, you would need to apply the longitudinal research design. Here, you would begin by identifying personality factors in a population of cancer-free people, then follow up over a period of years to determine whether those who subsequently develop cancer had different personality profiles from those who do not. One study that used this methodology did find evidence supporting the idea of a cancer-prone personality. In this investigation, researchers compared personality profiles of patients who had cancer with those who did not, based on scores from a widely used personality inventory, the MMPI (see Chapter 13), which had been administered several years earlier. Those subjects who became cancer patients had been shown to be significantly more inclined to suppress their emotions than were those who did not develop this disease (Dattore et al., 1980).

Research also suggests a possible link between personality factors and the course of cancer once it is diagnosed (Levy, 1983). People who are polite, acquiescent, and not emotionally reactive tend to experience a rapid course of illness leading to early death, in contrast to the slower progression of the disease experienced by many people who exhibit anger and combativeness (Derogatis et al., 1979; Rogentine et al., 1979). Research linking personality factors to both the etiology and course of cancer does not necessarily provide evidence that cancer is linked to stress. However, it is quite possible that people who fit the cancer-prone personality profile may be inclined to direct their responses to stress and frustration inwardly.

Researchers have also speculated about the biological mechanisms linking stress to cancer, and several have implicated an impaired immune system (Levy, 1983). As we have just seen, the immune system guards against invaders and foreign tissue of all kinds, including cancerous or pre-cancerous cells. In fact, the immune system may produce tumor-specific chemicals that attack and destroy cancerous growth (Rogers et al., 1979). Since we know that prolonged or severe stress can suppress immune response, it follows that stress may also allow cancer cells to proliferate more rapidly than might otherwise occur.

SUMMARY

ENVIRONMENTAL PSYCHOLOGY

1. Environmental psychology explores how our physical environment affects psychological processes. Two areas of special interest are the impact of adverse environmental conditions on our behavior and the way in which we use space.
2. Research has linked excessive noise to high levels of stress, anxiety reactions, increased aggression, impaired intellectual functioning, and reduced worker productivity.
3. Both extreme cold and extreme heat may have an adverse impact on behavior. This is particularly true of heat. Most of us perform best at moderate temperatures, ideally somewhere between 59–74 degrees.
4. The incidence of violent interpersonal crimes increases, notably during the third quarter of the year (July–September), a time when temperatures are likely to peak.
5. Research has shown that the probability of riots increases proportionately to outside temperatures, with no decline above 85 degrees.
6. Research in behavioral toxicology has revealed that a variety of environmental neurotoxins, even in small doses, may have adverse emotional and behavioral consequences.
7. There is clear evidence that excess bodily concentrations of lead can impair the functioning of the nervous system and interfere with the ability to learn.
8. Prolonged exposure to carbon monoxide has been linked to such adverse consequences as reduced attention span, memory deficits, impaired thinking, vision, and hearing, and severe psychotic-like symptoms.
9. Research has shown that only slight modifications in the architectual design of college dormitories may have a profound effect on students' feelings of privacy, stress, control over social interaction, and so forth.
10. Territoriality refers to visual boundaries of a given space or territory that we consider to be a special domain for our own use, the boundaries of which are relatively fixed.
11. A distinction has been made between primary and secondary territories. A primary territory is an area such as an office or bedroom that we define as ours and nobody else's. We may respond with aggression to unsolicited intrusions into our primary territories. In contrast, we are generally much less protective of secondary territories, such as a special table in the college cafeteria, where we like to socialize with friends.
12. Personal space is the invisible boundary or imaginary circle of space with which we all surround ourselves, and into which others are not supposed to enter without an invitation. Unlike the fixed spaces of territoriality, personal space involves a space we carry around with us.

13. The size of our personal space preferences, or the interpersonal distance we wish to maintain between ourselves and other people, varies from situation to situation according to the nature of our actual or desired relationship, the context within which the interaction occurs, our age, and the age and sex of the other person.
14. Environmental psychologists distinguish between density and crowding. Density is a physical attribute that is reflected in the number of people in a given amount of space. Crowding refers to a psychological response to a lack of space characterized by feelings of overstimulation, distress, and discomfort.
15. Research has shown that high densities do not always produce feelings of crowding and psychological discomfort. In situations such as homes or vehicles, high densities may be very stressful. However, in some situations such as musical concerts or parties, dense concentrations of people may contribute to subjective pleasure.

INDUSTRIAL/ORGANIZATIONAL PSYCHOLOGY

16. Industrial/organization (I/O) psychology involves the application of psychological principles to improving the functioning of businesses and industrial organizations.
17. Personnel selection consists of two phases: analyzing the job itself to determine the necessary qualifications of a candidate, and selecting the candidate who comes closest to meeting those qualifications. The first phase is typically accomplished via a job analysis—a specific description of the job and its required tasks—which leads to the establishment of job specifications—specific measurable characteristics that successful job applicants must possess. In the second phase or selection process, employers use a number of techniques including application forms, interviews, tests, and assessment-center data.
18. A central question in I/O research has been what factors contribute to job satisfaction. This question is important because low job satisfaction is strongly associated with high rates of employee absenteeism and turnover.
19. The factors that contribute to job satisfaction are difficult to assess, due largely to the fact that job satisfaction itself, which is essentially a state of mind, cannot be observed directly.
20. There is, however, substantial evidence that most workers rate factors such as autonomy, challenging work, good social relations with co-workers, and opportunities to influence corporate policy as more important than money.
21. The relationship between job satisfaction and productivity is exceedingly complex. Increasing a worker's satisfaction does not necessarily yield improvements in productivity. However, research has clearly demon-

strated that high job satisfaction is related to low absenteeism and employee turnover rates.

22. Research has attempted to assess the relationship between two distinct management styles and worker response. The idea behind Theory Y or employee-centered management is that workers are willing to accept responsibility and that they will be more productive in an atmosphere that allows them a certain degree of autonomy and independence. In contrast, the theory X management style, also known as job-centered or scientific management, tends to emphasize production and improving work efficiency (defined as maximum output and lowest possible cost).

23. Research indicates that in most work situations, the employee-centered management style is considerably more effective than job-centered management in inducing both increased productivity and job satisfaction.

HEALTH PSYCHOLOGY

24. Psychosomatic medicine—a subfield of psychiatry—has long stressed the interplay between the mind and the body in producing illness. Recently psychosomatic medicine has broadened its scope by joining the broad interdisciplinary field of behavioral medicine which seeks to apply the knowledge of many disciplines to understanding how behavior affects physical disease processes. Health psychology is the branch of psychology that has joined ranks with the behavioral medicine team.

25. It has been estimated that 50 percent to 70 percent of mortality from the 10 leading causes of death in the United States is largely behaviorally determined.

26. Among the behavioral factors that have been linked with the etiology of disease are cigarette smoking, poor nutrition, inadequate exercise, obesity, maladaptive responses to stress, excessive alcohol consumption, use of illicit drugs, and failure to comply with physicians' recommendations.

27. There is a powerful relationship between stress and illness. Stress may be defined as the process of appraising events (as harmful, threatening, or challenging), of assessing potential responses, and of responding to those events.

28. Selye's observation of organisms' physiological responses to stress led him to formulate the general adaptation syndrome (GAS), composed of three phases: alarm, resistance, and exhaustion. The alarm phase is characterized by a flood of stress hormones that pre-

pare the body for "fight or flight." In the resistance stage the body returns to a less aroused state, but one in which it continues to draw upon resources at an above-normal rate. If the stress is not alleviated, an organism is likely to enter the third state of exhaustion in which its body tissues begin to show signs of wear and tear and susceptibility to disease increases.

29. In recent years there has been increased attention directed to assessing not only how our bodies react to stress, but also how we think, feel, and behave in stressful situations.

30. Typical cognitive responses to stress include reduced ability to concentrate, distractibility, impaired performance on cognitive tasks, and a tendency to be plagued by disruptive or morbid thoughts.

31. Emotional responses to stress include such feelings as anxiety, irritability, anger, embarrassment, depression, and hostility.

32. There are a myriad of possible behavioral responses to stress including some kind of assertive action to confront stressors, withdrawal from a stressful situation, and adapting to the source of stress.

33. Factors that contribute to the stressfulness of a situation include our lack of control over it, a sudden onset, and a degree of ambiguity that forces us to spend a lot of resource-depleting energy trying to figure out the nature of the stressor.

34. Research has demonstrated that total scores on life change scales are not very accurate predictors of future problems with illness and disease.

35. Responses to stress may be a major contributor to coronary heart disease. Type A people, who tend to be hard-driving, ambitious, competitive, and perfectionists, are much more prone to CHD than are Type B people, who are more relaxed, easygoing, and not driven to achieve perfection.

36. People who deal with anger by suppressing it and those who exhibit Type A behavior may be particularly predisposed to develop hypertension.

37. Stress appears to exert a pronounced negative effect on immunocompetence—the immune system's ability to defend our bodies successfully against hazardous substances.

38. There is evidence that stress increases susceptibility to cancer. There are also some indications of the existence of a cancer-prone personality characterized by an inclination to be inhibited, compliant, conforming, depressed, calm, passive, and with strong tendencies to suppress emotions. Research indicates that such people may be particularly prone to develop cancer.

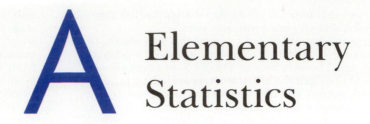

A Elementary Statistics

The single most commonly used tool in psychology is statistics. All areas of psychology rely on one or both of the two basic types of statistics: (1) *descriptive statistics*, which are used to summarize the results of research, and (2) *inferential statistics*, which are used to draw conclusions about the results.

DESCRIPTIVE STATISTICS

MEASURES OF CENTRAL TENDENCY

Suppose a teacher gives an IQ test to 10 students. How would he or she describe the test results? One way would be to name all students and list their IQ scores—10 names and 10 scores. That would probably work nicely in a small class. But it would certainly be inefficient and confusing with a class of 500. Moreover, a listing of numbers does not indicate much of anything about the group as a whole. It also would be helpful to know the average, typical, or most representative score. What is needed is a measure of *central tendency* in the group of scores, a number that represents the average. We shall describe three commonly used measures.

The Mean   The *mean* (short for arithmetic mean) is computed by adding up all the scores and dividing by the number of scores. We can express that in notational form in the following formula:

$$\overline{X} = \frac{\Sigma X}{N}$$

This formula introduces some elementary statistical symbols. The letter X refers to the variable, which can take on many different values. The variable is measured by the researcher. It could be anything—IQ, anxiety, height. The researcher measures the variable for each subject and assigns a score to each subject to represent the level of the variable in that subject. The capital Greek letter sigma (Σ) in the formula is a shorthand symbol for "add up these scores." We then divide this sum by the number of scores (symbolized by N) to arrive at the mean which is symbolized by $\overline{X}$ (read "X bar").

We have made up a set of 10 IQ scores and computed their mean in Table A-1. To compute the mean, we add up the 10 scores and divide by 10. Table A-1 also gives the height of each student in inches. To keep the

TABLE A.1   Computation of the Mean IQ and Height of a Class of 10 Students

Student's Name	X (IQ)	Y (Height in Inches)
Rita	125	65
Norma	120	60
Lyle	105	66
Bruce	100	68
John	130	72
Jane	95	64
Linda	90	62
Ralph	110	74
Frank	85	70
Polly	125	67
	$\Sigma X = 1085$	$\Sigma X = 668$
	$N = 10$	$N = 10$

Then, the mean of the X scores is

$$\overline{X} = \frac{\Sigma X}{N}$$

or

$$\overline{X} = \frac{1085}{10} = 108.5$$

Likewise, the mean of the Y scores is

$$\overline{Y} = \frac{\Sigma Y}{N}$$

or

$$\overline{Y} = \frac{668}{10} = 66.8$$

variable of height distinct from IQ, we signify height by Y. So ΣY tells us to add up the heights, which is also done in Table A-1. Dividing this total by the number of scores gives us the mean height of the students (66.8 inches). Just as above, we can express these steps in a shorthand formula.

$$\overline{Y} = \frac{\Sigma Y}{N}$$

Now if we ask the teacher how the class performed on the IQ test, the teacher could simply report the value of $\overline{X}$; if we ask how tall the students are, the teacher could report $\overline{Y}$. This is obviously much simpler than listing all the X and Y scores and gives a better idea of the students' general level of ability and the students' typical height.

The Median   The *median* is the *middle score* in a list of scores that have been arranged in increasing order. If there is an odd number of scores, then there will be one score exactly in the middle. Thus, if the class had 11 students, the score of the sixth student in order would be the median—there would be 5 scores higher and 5 scores lower. With an even number of scores, there is no single middle score; instead, there are two scores that determine the middle (one is above and one is below the theoretical midpoint). In our example of 10 IQ scores, the middle two scores are the fifth and sixth scores. Table A-2 shows the 10 IQ scores from Table A-1, but this time we have arranged them in order. The middle point is between the fifth and sixth score (105 and 110). We average these two scores to obtain the median (107.5).

The mean and the median are typically close, but not usually the same. They will be very close when the distribution of scores is symmetrical or equally balanced around the mean.

Now consider the set of salary scores in Table A-3. Here we note that most of the 10 people working for the Zappo Cereal Company are not making a lot of money, though one employee, presumably the president, is making a bundle. This distribution of scores is asymmetrical and unbalanced. Technically, we call it *skewed*. The distribution in Table A-3 is skewed to the high end (positively skewed). The mean weekly salary for Zappo employees is $1,395, which might lead us to believe that the company pays very well. But the median is only $425, which would make us think a little differently about Zappo. The median will be unaffected if the president

TABLE A.2 Computation of Median IQ Score of a Class of 10 Students

Name	X	
John	130	
Polly	125	
Rita	125	
Norma	120	
Ralph	110	←—— The median is the average of these
Lyle	105	←—— two middle scores (105 and 110).
Bruce	100	
Jane	95	
Linda	90	
Frank	85	

The average of 105 and 110 is 107.5.

$$\frac{105 + 110}{2} = 107.5$$

Note that the median would not change if we changed John's score from 130 to 160, but the mean would change. What would the mean be in this case?

gives himself or herself a big raise, but the mean will go up. Note that, in this case, the median is more representative of the group as a whole than the mean. Furthermore, the median is *unaffected* by extreme scores such as the president's salary.

The Mode The **mode** is the *most frequently occurring* score. In a small set of scores as in Tables A-1, 2, and 3, there is the possibility that no score will occur more than once and, thus, there is no mode. But suppose a psychologist gives an anxiety test to a group of 200 mental patients. With such a large group, it is convenient to set up a *frequency distribution* showing the various possible scores on the test and, for each possible score, how many people (*f* or frequency) actually got that score. We have set up in Table A-4 such a frequency distribution for the anxiety scores from the 200 mental patients. Looking down the frequency column in Table A-4, we see that 27 is the highest frequency—27 people obtained a score of 15. Therefore, 15 is the *mode* or the *modal score*. Note that the sum of all the frequencies in the *f*

TABLE A.3 Comparison of the Mean and Median Weekly Salaries of the Zappo Cereal Company Employees

Employee Number	Weekly Salary X (in Dollars)	
1	10,000	
2	600	
3	550	
4	500	
5	450	←—— midpoint
6	400	
7	375	
8	375	
9	350	
10	350	
	$\Sigma X = \overline{13,950}$	
	$N = 10$	

We can see from the midpoint that the median salary is the mean of 400 and 450, which is $425.

Yet the mean salary is

$$\overline{X} = \frac{X}{N} = \frac{13950}{10} = \$1,395$$

Which value, the mean or the median, do you think is more representative of Zappo's wages?

TABLE A.4 *A Frequency Distribution of the Anxiety Scores of 200 Mental Patients*

Score (X)	f or Frequency
20	10
19	10
18	12
17	15
16	20
15	27
14	15
13	21
12	22
11	12
10	10
9	8
8	7
7	5
6	3
5	0
4	2
3	1
2	0
1	0
	$\Sigma f = \overline{200} = N$

The mode, the score that occurs most frequently, is equal to 15.

column is equal to N, the number of people taking the test—in this case, 200.

Frequency distributions can also be represented graphically. Figure A-1 shows the graphic representation of the frequency distribution from Table A-4. The horizontal axis of the graph represents the values of the variable X (the anxiety score) and the vertical axis represents the frequency.

MEASURES OF VARIABILITY

There are differences among people; not everyone gets the same score on a test or has the same height; these **individual differences** among people are a fact of life. The variability among people may be large when it comes to anxiety or IQ scores, but small when it comes to the number of fingers they have. How do we quantify the degree of variability in the scores?

The quickest and least informative measure of the variability in a set of scores is the range. The **range** is defined as the *highest score minus the lowest score.* In Table A-4, we see that the patients' anxiety scores range from a high of 20 to a low of 3, and so the range would be $20 - 3 = 17$. Although the range as a measure of variability is easy to compute, it is based on only two scores (the highest and the lowest) and, therefore, tells us little about the variability in the entire distribution. Better measures of variability are the *variance* and *standard deviation,* both of which reflect the degree of spread or fluctuation of scores *around the mean.*

Suppose we have a set of 10 scores with a mean of 20. Two such sets are shown in Table A-5. All but two of the scores in Set A cluster close to the mean. In Set B, we have the same mean, but the variability is higher, with several scores a long way from the mean. If we described both sets with a central tendency measure (such as the mean), the two sets would appear to be similar. If we described the variability of each set using the range, again the two sets would appear to be similar. To reflect the differences between the sets more accurately, we need a measure of variability which takes into account all the scores (not just the highest and lowest).

The *variance* and the *standard deviation* are both measures of variability that are based on all of the scores in the sample. The **variance** is essen-

FIGURE A.1 A GRAPHIC REPRE-SENTATION OF A FREQUENCY DISTRIBUTION BASED ON THE DATA IN TABLE A.4

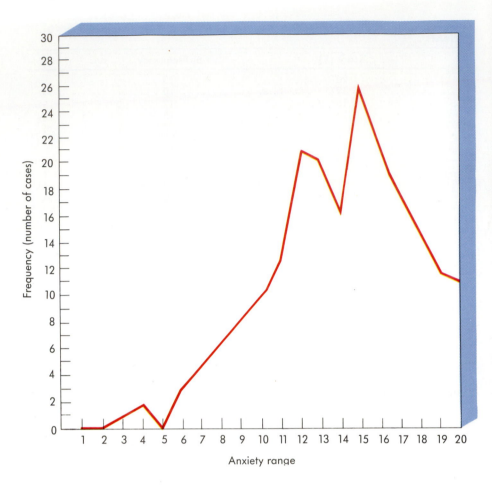

tially the *average of the squared distances of the scores from the mean.* It is symbolized by s^2. To compute the variance, we first subtract the mean from each score as we have done in Table A-6. These differences are measures of each score's distance from the mean. Now why not just calculate the mean of these distance scores? The reason is that the mean of these distance scores will always be equal to zero regardless of how variable the scores are. Instead, we square each score before adding them. These squared distance scores are also shown in Table A-6. Now we can add these scores up and

TABLE A.5 *Two Sets of Scores That Have the Same Mean but Differ in Variability*

Set A	Set B
36	36
22	32
21	28
21	24
20	20
20	20
19	16
19	12
18	8
4	4
$\Sigma X = 200$	$\Sigma X = 200$
$N = 10$	$N = 10$
$\bar{X} = \dfrac{200}{10} = 20$	$\bar{X} = \dfrac{200}{10} = 20$
Range = 36 − 4 = 32	Range = 36 − 4 = 32

TABLE A.6 *Computation of the Variance and Standard Deviation for Two Sets of Scores*

	Set A			Set B	
X	$(X - \bar{X})$	$(X - \bar{X})^2$	X	$(X - \bar{X})$	$(X - \bar{X})^2$
36	16	256	36	16	256
22	2	4	32	12	144
21	1	1	28	8	64
21	1	1	24	4	16
20	0	0	20	0	0
20	0	0	20	0	0
19	−1	1	16	−4	16
19	−1	1	12	−8	64
18	−2	4	8	−12	144
4	−16	256	4	−16	256
SUMS	0	524		0	960

SET A

$s^2 = $ variance $= \dfrac{\Sigma(X - \bar{X})^2}{N} = \dfrac{524}{9} = 58.22$

$s = $ standard deviation $= \sqrt{s^2} = \sqrt{58.22} = 7.63$

Range $= 36 - 4 = 32$

SET B

$s^2 = $ variance $= \dfrac{\Sigma(X - \bar{X})^2}{N} = \dfrac{960}{9} = 106.67$

$s = $ standard deviation $= \sqrt{s^2} = \sqrt{106.67} = 10.33$

Range $= 36 - 4 = 32$

divide by the number of scores minus 1[1]. These steps are expressed in notational form below.

$$\text{Variance} = s^2 = \frac{\Sigma(X - \bar{X})^2}{N - 1}$$

The **standard deviation** is simply the *square root of the variance.* As we will see shortly, the standard deviation is often a convenient measure of variability.

$$\text{Standard Deviation} = s = \sqrt{s^2} = \sqrt{\frac{\Sigma(X - \bar{X})^2}{N - 1}}$$

The standard deviation and the variance are better measures of variability than the range because they take all of the scores into account, not just the highest score and lowest score. If we compare the two data sets in Table A-6, we see that, even though the range is the same in the two sets, both the variance and the standard deviation reflect the smaller average spread of scores in Set A relative to Set B—unlike Set B, most of the scores in Set A cluster close to the mean of 20. The variance in Set A is 58.22 and in Set B is 106.67. The standard deviation in Set A is 7.63 and in Set B is 10.33. The range is 32 (36 − 4) in both data sets.

THE NORMAL FREQUENCY DISTRIBUTION

Earlier in this appendix, we introduced the *frequency distribution* and showed how it could be represented graphically. Figure A-2 presents the

[1]The formula given in the text is shown as the *unbiased* formula for the variance. Dividing by $N - 1$ instead of by N corrects for a small bias that would be present if we were to use simply the average squared deviation from the mean as the variance. Unfortunately, the logic behind this correction is beyond the scope of this appendix.

graph of what is called the ***normal distribution*** (or *normal curve*). This figure is not a graph of an actual data set (as in Figure A-1). Instead, this is a theoretical distribution defined by a mathematical equation. A normal distribution is symmetric; if you fold it over at the mean, the two halves will overlap each other. Moreover, it is a bell-shaped curve (meaning it looks like a bell); scores near the mean are most common, and the frequency drops off smoothly as we move to the extremes. The normal distribution is very useful in psychology because so many psychological variables are "normally distributed" in the population—that is, the graph of the distribution of the variable would be very similar in shape to the graph in Figure A-2. The variable of IQ is a good example. IQ is normally distributed with a mean of 100 and a standard deviation of 15; if we obtained IQ scores for everybody, the mean IQ would be 100 and the standard deviation would be 15. Furthermore, if we drew a graph representing the frequency of each of the possible IQ scores, it would show the characteristic bell shape of a normal distribution.

If we know that a variable such as IQ is normally distributed and if we know the mean and the standard deviation, we can use the mathematical properties of the normal distribution to deduce more information about the variable. We can do this because, in any normal distribution, the standard deviation can be used to divide the distribution into sections containing fixed percentages of the scores. Figure A-3 shows a normal distribution divided up in this way for the variable of IQ. The fixed percentages are printed in the various sections of the curve. For example, about 34 percent of the IQ scores lie between the mean and a score of 115—that is, 34 percent of the people have IQs between the mean and one standard deviation above the mean. The standard deviation is a distance measure, and the "distance" from 115 to the mean of 100 is one standard deviation unit. An IQ of 130 would be two standard deviation units above the mean; an IQ of 145 would be three standard deviations above the mean. One standard deviation below the mean would be an IQ of 85; two standard deviations below the mean would be an IQ of 70; three standard deviations below the mean would be an IQ of 55. Regardless of the variable being measured, almost all of the scores will fall in the range from three standard deviation units below the mean on up to three standard deviation units above the mean (for IQ scores, from 55 up to 145). Although it is theoretically possible to obtain scores outside of this range, scores more than three standard deviations from the mean are very rare. It is often convenient to convert the scores into standard deviation scores, called z scores, using the following formula:

$$z = \frac{X - \overline{X}}{s}$$

A major advantage of the z score is that it can be used as a common yardstick for all tests, allowing us to compare scores on different tests. For example, suppose you receive 80 on an English test, which has a class mean of 70 with a standard deviation of 10. On your psychology test, you got a 90, and the class mean was 85 with a standard deviation of 5. We also know that the distribution of test scores was normal in each class. On which test did you do better? These test scores are not immediately comparable, but if you change each score into a z score using the mean and standard deviation for each test, you will discover that you did equally well on both tests in terms of where you stood in the class distribution (obtaining a z score of +1.00 on each test). Using the information in Figure A-3, we can infer that your score on each test puts you at approximately the 84th percentile—34 percent of the class scored between your score and the mean and another 50 percent of the class scored below the mean.

Figure A-4 again shows the IQ normal distribution, but this time we have two horizontal axes displayed. The upper one shows IQ scores, and the lower one shows the equivalent z scores. This figure shows that an IQ score of 115 is 1 standard deviation above the mean, and so the z score corre-

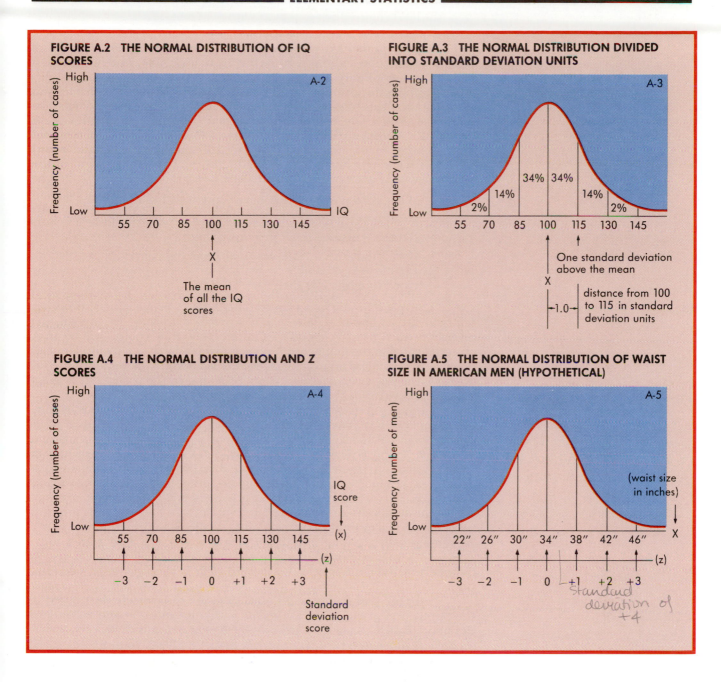

FIGURE A.2   THE NORMAL DISTRIBUTION OF IQ SCORES

FIGURE A.3   THE NORMAL DISTRIBUTION DIVIDED INTO STANDARD DEVIATION UNITS

FIGURE A.4   THE NORMAL DISTRIBUTION AND Z SCORES

FIGURE A.5   THE NORMAL DISTRIBUTION OF WAIST SIZE IN AMERICAN MEN (HYPOTHETICAL)

sponding to 115 is +1.0. If your friend tells you that his z score in IQ is +2.0, you can see that he has an IQ of 130. If he tells you that his z score is +4.0, he is either very brilliant or he is pulling your leg.

From Figure A-4, suppose we ask you to figure out what percentage of the people have IQs between 85 and 115, which is the same as asking how many people have z scores between −1.0 and +1.0. The answer is 68 percent; 34 percent between 85 and 100, and another 34 percent between 100 and 115. If we know that the scores are distributed normally and we know the mean and standard deviation of the distribution, we can find the percentage of scores between *any* two points by using a simple table (the *Standard Normal table*) that can be found in almost any statistics textbook. An important thing to remember is that these percentages and the z score procedure apply to *any normal distribution,* not just the IQ distribution. The only difference between the IQ distribution and any other normal distribution of scores is that the other distributions probably have different means and different standard deviations. But if you know that something has a normal distribution and if you know the mean and standard deviation of it, you can set up a figure like the one in Figure A-4.

Suppose, for example, that we told you that waist size in American men is normally distributed with a mean of 34 inches and a standard deviation of 4. You could now set up a normal frequency distribution as in Figure A-5. Almost all American men have a waist size within the range of 22 inches (z score of −3; 22 is 3 standard deviation units below the mean) and 46 (z score of +3; 3 units above the mean). Now can you fill in the percentages and answer the following questions?

1. What percentage of men have waist sizes less than 30 inches?
2. What percentage of men have waist sizes greater than 38?
3. If Joe's waist size is 47, is he unusual?
4. If we randomly selected one man from the American population, what is the probability (how likely is it?) that his waist size will be equal to or greater than 38?

This last question brings us to the notion of probability. **Probability** refers to the *proportion of cases that fit a certain description.* In general, the probability of A (the likelihood that a randomly drawn object will be an A object) is equal to the number of A objects divided by the total number of all possible objects. The number of A objects divided by the total number of objects is the *proportion* of objects that are A, and so the probability is just a proportion.

Suppose, as in question 4 above, we wanted to know the probability that a randomly selected American man will have a waist size equal to or greater than 38. To find the probability of selecting at random such an individual, we have to know what proportion of all men have waist sizes of 38 or greater. In Figure A-5, we can see that 14 percent of the men have waist sizes between 38 and 42 inches and an additional 2 percent are greater than 42, and so we add 14 percent and 2 percent and find that 16 percent of American men have waist sizes of 38 or greater. In proportion terms, this becomes .16 (we move the decimal point two places to the left to translate a percentage into a proportion). In summary, the probability of selecting a man with a waist size equal to or greater than 38 is .16. This means that 16 out of every 100 random selections would yield a man who fits this description.

Suppose that scores on an anxiety scale are normally distributed in the population of all American people with a mean of 50 and a standard deviation of 10. Calculate the probability that a randomly drawn person has an anxiety score that is equal to or less than 40. Check your answer at the end of the appendix.

CORRELATION

The **correlation coefficient** was introduced in Chapter 2. The correlation coefficient does not describe a single variable as the mean or standard deviation does. Instead, it describes the degree of relationship between two variables. It is basically a measure of the degree to which the two variables vary together, or *covary.* Scores can vary together in one of two ways: (1) a *positive covariation,* in which high scores in one variable tend to go with high scores in the other variable (and low scores go with low scores), or (2) *negative covariation*, in which high scores in one variable tend to go with low scores in the other variable (and low scores go with high scores). When there is a positive covariation, we say that the two variables are *positively correlated,* and when there is a negative covariation, we say they are *negatively correlated.* A common example of positive correlation is the relationship between height and weight—the taller you are, the more you will tend to weigh. A common example of negative correlation might be the relationship between

TABLE A.7 *The Correlation between Anxiety and Happiness*

Name	Anxiety (X)*	Happiness (Y)
Joan	1	10
Larry	2	9
Ralph	3	8
Clint	4	7
Sue	5	6
Sharon	6	5
Sam	7	4
Bonnie	8	3
Marsha	9	2
Harry	10	1

*Here we have arranged the anxiety scores in order. Note that the happiness scores are in reverse order. When these data are graphed in a scatter plot (see Figure A-6), all the points fall on a straight line, which indicates that the correlation is perfect (in this case, −1.00).

the amount of alcohol a person has drunk in an evening and his or her ability to drive an automobile—the more the person has drunk, the lower his or her ability to drive will be.

Note that we used "tend to go with." Correlations are almost never perfect—not all tall people are particularly heavy, and not all short people are lightweights. In some cases, there may be a *zero correlation* between two variables—that is, no relationship between the variables. We might expect, for example, there to be a zero correlation between your height and your ability to learn psychology. So two variables can be *positively* or *negatively correlated* or *not correlated at all,* and the degree of correlation can be great or small. What we need is a statistic that conveniently measures the degree and the direction (positive or negative) of the correlation between two variables, and this is what the correlation coefficient does.

Table A-7 shows the scores of 10 people on two tests—a test of anxiety and a test of happiness. The possible scores on each test ranged from one to 10. Larger scores represent more of the variable being measured. Hence, a high score on the anxiety measure represents a high level of anxiety; a low score represents a low level of anxiety. Intuitively, we would expect a negative correlation between the two variables of anxiety and happiness—the less anxious you are, the more happy you will be, and vice versa.

Table A-7 presents the anxiety and happiness scores for each of the 10 subjects. These data can be more easily visualized in a *scatter plot,* which we have set up in Figure A-6. In this scatter plot, the horizontal axis indicates the anxiety score, and the vertical axis indicates the happiness score. Each person is represented by a point on the graph that locates him or her on the two tests. For example, Clint had an anxiety score of 4 and a happiness score of 7. So we go over (to the right) to 4 on the anxiety scale and then up to 7 on the happiness scale, and we place a dot at that point to represent Clint's scores. The scores from all 10 people are represented in the graph. In this case, the 10 points all fall on a straight line, which means that the correlation is perfect. Further, the line slopes down to the right, which means that the correlation is negative in direction—high anxiety scores go with low happiness scores, and vice versa.

As we have said, however, correlations are almost never perfect. More often, the points are likely to be scattered all over the graph, hence the term *scatter plot.* The closer the points are to lying on a straight line, the higher the degree of correlation. If the points seem to cluster about a line that slopes downward to the right, then the correlation will be negative as in Figure A-6. If the points seem to cluster about a line that slopes upward to the right, the correlation will be positive. Figure A-7 shows four scatter plots. In panel A the two variables in question are negatively correlated; the points all seem to cluster about a straight line which slopes downward to the right. In panel B there is a positive correlation; the points again all seem to cluster about a line, but this time the line slopes upward to the right. In

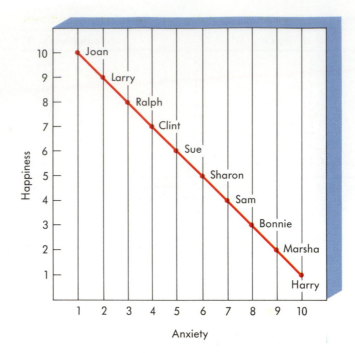

FIGURE A.6 "SCATTER PLOT" OF THE DATA FROM TABLE A.7, RELATING ANXIETY TO HAPPINESS

panel C there is no correlation; the points are scattered all over, and there is no line that fits them very well. Panel D presents an interesting case. The points do seem to cluster about a line, but it is a curved rather than a straight line. The scatter plot does suggest that there is a relationship between the variables, but it is not a simple relationship. Most correlation coefficients are designed to quantify a simple straight-line relationship and will give misleading results when applied to a complex relationship such as the one in panel D.

The **Pearson product-moment correlation coefficient** (symbolized r_{xy}) is the most often used of several measures of correlation. It can take on any numerical value from -1.0 through 0.0 up to $+1.0$. A perfect negative product-moment correlation, as shown in Figure A-6, is equal to -1.0, and a perfect positive correlation is equal to $+1.0$. Correlations close to zero mean there is little or no relationship between the two variables, X and Y. The size of the correlation (ignoring the sign) represents the degree of relationship. The sign of the correlation (positive or negative) tell us the direction of the relationship between the variables, but not the degree of the relationship. Thus, a correlation of $-.77$ is just as strong a correlation as is a correlation of

FIGURE A.7   SCATTER PLOTS OF FOUR RELATIONSHIPS

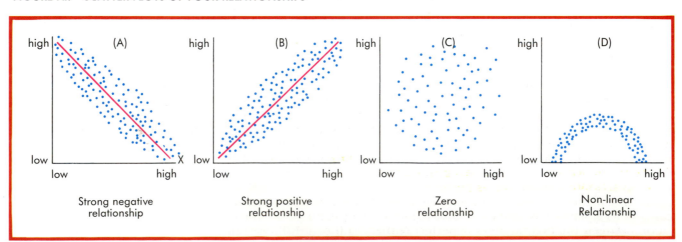

TABLE A.8 *Calculating the Pearson Product-Moment Correlation Coefficient*

Name	Anxiety (X)	X²	Happiness (Y)	Y²	XY (X times Y)
John	2	4	9	81	18
Ralph	5	25	6	36	30
Mary	9	81	4	16	36
Sue	1	1	3	9	3
Jan	3	9	2	4	6
Harvey	7	49	2	4	14
Jane	8	64	4	16	32
Joanne	6	36	5	25	30
N = 8 people	$\Sigma X = 41$	$\Sigma X^2 = 269$	$\Sigma Y = 35$	$\Sigma Y^2 = 191$	$\Sigma XY = 169$

$$r_{XY} \text{ (the correlation between X and Y)} = \frac{N\Sigma XY - (\Sigma X)(\Sigma Y)}{\sqrt{[N\Sigma X^2 - (\Sigma X)^2][N\Sigma Y^2 - (\Sigma Y)^2]}}$$

For these data:
$$r_{\text{ANXIETY} \cdot \text{HAPPINESS}} = \frac{(8)(169) - (41)(35)}{\sqrt{[(8)(269) - (41)^2][(8)(191) - (35)^2]}} = \frac{1352 - 1435}{\sqrt{(2152 - 1681)(1528 - 1225)}}$$

$$= \frac{-83}{\sqrt{(471)(303)}} = \frac{-83}{\sqrt{142713}} = \frac{-83}{377.77} = -.219$$

+.77; the only difference is the direction. Table A-8 shows the steps for calculating the Pearson product-moment correlation coefficient in case you want to see exactly how it is done.

In all the examples so far, we have been correlating the scores of a person on two different tests, but we can use correlations in other ways. We might correlate the scores of a person on the same test taken at two different times. If the test measures a variable that should be stable, then the correlation between two administrations of the test would indicate an aspect of the reliability of the test—that is, how consistent are a person's scores on the same test given on two different occasions? A good test should be reliable (see Chapter 12). Another common use of correlation is to determine the test's validity—does the test measure what it is supposed to measure? For example, a test of intelligence should correlate positively with performance in school. If it did, it would help us argue that the test really did measure intelligence. (See Chapter 12 for a discussion of validity.)

REGRESSION

One important use of the correlational statistics is in a procedure called **regression.** A correlation coefficient tells us the degree to which a person's scores on two tests are related. Suppose, for example, that we try to predict your weight. We have no idea what to guess, because all we know about you is that you are reading this book. If we knew that the average person reading this book weighs 142 pounds, then that would be our best guess, and we would make the same guess for every reader. But if we knew your height, and we also knew the correlation between weight and height, then we could make a much more accurate guess of your weight. For example, if we knew that you were 6 feet, 6 inches tall, we would hardly guess 142 pounds. Someone that tall would almost certainly weigh more than 142 pounds. Likewise, if we knew you were 4 feet, 2 inches, 142 pounds would also be an inappropriate guess. We would adjust our prediction of your weight according to what we knew about your height. Regression is a fancy, complex, but accurate way of making this adjustment and allowing us to make as accurate a prediction as possible.

The higher the correlation between height and weight, the better we can predict a person's weight from knowing his or her weight. If the correlation between the two variables is perfect (either +1.0 or −1.0), we can predict perfectly the value of one of the variables if we know the value of the other. But, because correlations are almost never perfect, our predictions are normally close, but usually not exactly correct. The lower the correlation is, the greater will be the average error in prediction.

Regression is used in many different settings. Many of you probably took the College Board examinations for getting into college. From past research we know there is a positive correlation between one's score on the College Boards and one's success in college. Therefore, the College Board tests can now be given to college applicants and, on the basis of their scores, we can predict approximately how a person will do in college. These predictions are used to help decide whom to admit. Similar procedures are used to process applications for law school, medical school, graduate school, or a job. Using regression techniques, the psychologist predicts the applicant's success on the job or in school, and these predictions are used to determine whether or not to hire or admit the applicant. It is a serious business, and the decisions made on this basis are extremely important to the people involved.

The simplest type of regression (known as *linear regression*) is based on a mathematical equation for a straight line (hence the term *linear*). What we are looking for is the straight line that comes closest to the most points on a scatter diagram (see Figure A-8). Figure A-8 shows two different hypothetical scatter plots relating scores on the College Boards (SAT scores) to grade point average in college (GPA). Each point in the diagram represents the SAT score and college GPA for one student. With data on SAT scores and college GPAs, we can proceed to use regression to make predictions for future students. First, we solve the equation for the best-fitting straight line (known as the *regression line*), a complex procedure we need not describe here. Then we draw the line on the scatter plot. Now we can use the line as a way to predict the GPA given a student's SAT score. For example, consider a student who scores 700 on the SAT; we draw a vertical line up from 700 until it intersects the regression line, and then we draw a horizontal line from this point to the Y axis and read off the predicted GPA. In this case, we come up with a prediction of 3.6 for the student's GPA.

This procedure will not give us perfect predictions. Not all students scoring 700 had 3.6 averages in college; some were higher than 3.6 and some lower. As we have said, the main factor in determining the accuracy of

FIGURE A.8   SCATTER PLOTS FOR HIGH (A) AND LOW (B) DEGREES OF RELATIONSHIP BETWEEN COLLEGE GPAS AND SAT SCORES (HYPOTHETICAL)

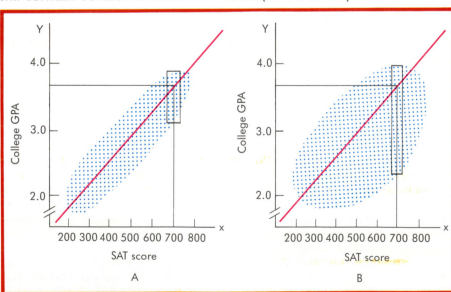

In the regression procedure, we try to predict what a person's score on one test will be using his or her score on another test as a basis.

the predictions is the degree of correlation between the two variables. If the variables are highly correlated, as depicted in panel A, all the points will cluster close to the regression line, and none of the predictions is likely to be far off. In fact, if the correlation were perfect, all the points would be right on the line, and there would be no error. (All students with 700 SATs would get 3.6 GPAs.) On the other hand, with low correlations, the points will be widely scattered, and many of them will be a long way from the regression line, as depicted in panel B of Figure A-8. In such a case, the predictions can sometimes be way off. Take a look at the GPAs of the students who scored around 700 on the SATs in the two panels; these points are boxed in on the graphs. In the left panel, which depicts a high correlation, you can see that all the students ended up with high college GPAs, and all were fairly close to 3.6, the average we would predict using the regression line. In contrast, in the right panel, the students with 700 on the SATs varied widely in their GPAs, with some as low as 2.2 and others as high as 3.95. Regression would have predicted 3.6 for all of them, but this prediction would have been way off for some students. *The lower the correlation is between the two variables, the less precise will be our predictions.* In fact, if the correlation drops to zero, a regression equation will not improve our prediction at all—once again, our best guess would be the mean. Given some degree of correlation, however, we can do better using regression than by simply guessing the mean, and the higher the correlation is, the better our predictions will be.

Often there is more than one variable that is correlated with the criterion (the number we are trying to predict). In such cases, a procedure called *multiple regression* can be used to improve and maximize the accuracy of our predictions. For example, in addition to SAT scores, we might also know each student's high-school GPA and rank in his or her high-school class. Rank, GPA, and SAT scores all could then be combined by using multiple regression to predict the college GPA.

INFERENTIAL STATISTICS

Inferential statistics are used to make inferences from data, to draw conclusions, and to test hypotheses. Two of the basic concepts in inferential statistics are *estimation* and *hypothesis testing*.

ESTIMATION

One use of inferential statistics is to estimate the actual value of some population characteristic. Suppose, for example, we wanted to know how knowledgeable, on average, American adults are about current events. We could construct a test of current events with carefully worded questions covering as many areas of current news as possible. Since we are interested in the population of all adult Americans, we could test every American age 18 and older (the entire population) and compute a mean score on our test. But it would be handy to have a shortcut method that did not require testing the entire population.

In order to estimate the mean and standard deviation of a variable in a population, we take a *sample* of the population and measure the variable in each member of the sample. We then compute the statistics on the sample scores and use these statistics to estimate what the mean and standard deviation would be if we could test every member of the population. For example, we might sample 200 American adults and use their scores on our current events test to estimate what the whole population of adults is like. Public opinion polls and the TV rating services use this sampling approach and estimation procedure.

It is important that the sample is *representative* of the population. This is usually done by making the sample a random selection from all possible members of the population. A **random sample** is one in which everyone in the specified population has the same chance of being in the sample. For example, it would not be a fair sample for estimating Americans' knowledge of current events if we measured only white female citizens of La Mirada, California. The second factor in sampling is sample size. Generally, the larger the sample is, the more accurate the estimates will be. If you randomly chose one person from the phone book, scheduled him or her for our test of current events, got a score, and then estimated that this score was the mean for all American adults, you would almost certainly be off the mark. A sample larger than a single person is needed. But how many should there be in the sample? The amazing thing about sampling is that the size of the sample necessary to get a fairly accurate idea of the population is much smaller than you might guess. A sample of 30 or 40 American adults out of 100 million, if properly drawn, would give a very accurate estimate of the entire population. There are ways of estimating how big a sample you need for a given level of accuracy. Of course, if the sample is not properly drawn so that it is not representative, then increasing the sample size will not improve the accuracy of estimation.

HYPOTHESIS TESTING

When we set out to do an experiment in psychology, we always begin with a hypothesis. For our brief discussion, we shall use the example of a psychologist who wants to know if Zappo cereal increases endurance in the people who eat it. The psychologist carefully devises a test of physical endurance that gives a consistent score (i.e., it is a reliable measure) and accurately predicts endurance in real life situations (i.e., it is a valid measure). The working hypothesis in the study is "People who eat Zappo will show greater endurance than people who eat Brand X." The psychologist gets 60 subjects to volunteer for the experiment and randomly assigns them to one of two groups, 30 per group. The random assignment is designed to create two groups that are equal in average endurance at the start of the experiment. The Zappo group eats Zappo for 1 year and the Brand X group eats Brand X for 1 year. At the end of this time, the psychologist tests all 60 subjects on the test of endurance and finds that the mean endurance score of Zappo eaters is 105 and the mean endurance score of Brand X eaters is 100. What can the psychologist conclude or infer about the initial hypothesis? If the Zappo group and the Brand X group were very close—say 99.5 and 100.1 were the means—the psychologist would probably conclude that Zappo does not increase endurance; if they were very far apart—say 125 for Zappo eaters and 85 for Brand X eaters—the conclusion would probably be that eating Zappo increases endurance. But what do we conclude about results that fall between these extremes?

There has to be an objective way to decide whether or not the psychologist's hypothesis can be accepted. We cannot leave it up to intuition, especially not the intuition of the owner of Zappo Cereal Company. This is what inferential statistics can provide. There are many different kinds of inferential statistics. Here we shall consider the *t-test.*

We want to decide whether the difference between 100 (the mean of the Brand X eaters) and 105 (the mean of the Zappo eaters) is a real difference. Is it a *statistically significant difference*? A difference is said to be statistically significant if it is very unlikely that it would happen by chance. The difference in endurance scores between the Zappo and Brand X groups is 5.0 points. We say the *mean difference* is 5.0 (105 − 100 = 5.0). Could this be just a chance difference or could this be a real difference that we would see again and again if we were to repeat the study—not necessarily with the same scores, but with the same consistent finding that Zappo eaters show greater endurance than people who eat the Brand X cereal?

For a moment, let's assume that Zappo has no effect on endurance. This is called the *null hypothesis*. Note that the null hypothesis predicts no difference, whereas our working hypothesis (that Zappo increases endurance) does predict a difference. Specifically, the null hypothesis predicts that the variable being manipulated (the independent variable) will have no effect on the behavior being measured (the dependent variable). It is the null hypothesis that is actually tested with inferential statistics. We then draw conclusions about our working hypothesis on the basis of our findings regarding the null hypothesis.

What we need to know is, *if the null hypothesis is true* (Zappo does not affect endurance), what is the probability that the two samples will differ by 5 points or more on our endurance measure? If Zappo is not different from Brand X, then any difference we find between our two groups will be just a chance difference. After all, we would not expect two random groups of 10 people to have exactly the same means. Sample means will differ, and every once in a while there will be a difference of 5 or more points by chance alone, with no help from Zappo. The question is, how often will we get a difference this large? Or what is the probability of the difference occurring by chance alone?

In order to answer this question, we must know not only the mean values, but also the standard deviations in the two samples. We have to know how much natural variability between people there is in the endurance scores. To understand this, look at the three panels in Figure A-9. Each panel shows two frequency distributions, one for a Zappo group and one for a Brand X group. Note that in each panel, the mean of the Zappo group is 105 and the mean of the Brand X group is 100, but the three panels display quite different pictures in terms of variability among people within each group on the endurance measure. In the top panel, the variability is very small (all Zappo eaters score about the same, near 105, and all Brand X eaters are close to 100). The two distributions do not overlap at all (all Zappo eaters have higher endurance scores than all Brand X eaters do). In this case, it looks as though the 5-point difference between the means is a significant one.

In the middle panel, there is a great deal of variability between people within each group on the endurance measure. There is a lot of overlap in the two distributions. Some Zappo eaters have lower endurance scores than do some Brand X eaters, and some Brand X eaters have higher endurance scores than do some Zappo eaters. In fact, there is so much overlap in the two distributions that we would probably question whether the difference between 100 and 105 (the two means), which is very small compared to the variability, is just a chance difference. The two distributions look almost identical.

Situations like those depicted in the top panel are very rare indeed. Unfortunately, the middle panel is a more common outcome of an experiment—the means are so close together and there is so much overlap of scores that the groups appear to be indistinguishable on the dependent variable. The bottom panel represents the most common outcome of all. Here, the conclusion is less clear. The two distributions overlap somewhat, much more than in the top panel, but much less than in the middle panel. There is a moderate amount of variability among subjects within each group. Can we conclude whether the 105-to-100 mean difference is a real one? Stated differently, "Is there a statistically significant difference between the means?"

The *t*-test is designed to answer this question in a systematic and precise way. It is basically a ratio, the ratio of the mean difference to an error term. A primary factor in the error term is the variability of scores within each group. In the top panel the difference is 5 units, but the variability of scores within each group is very small. Therefore, the error term will be small. So if we divide the mean difference by this very small error term, we shall get a large number for the *t* ratio, and we then declare the difference to be significant. In the middle panel, the same 5-point mean difference will be divided by a very large error term, giving us a very small *t* ratio. We declare the difference insignificant. In the bottom panel, we have the borderline

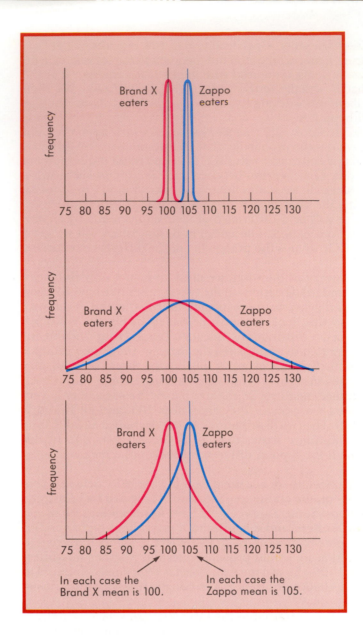

**FIGURE A.9 THREE EXPERIMEN-
TAL OUTCOMES DIFFERING IN
VARIABILITY AND OVERLAP, BUT
EACH WITH THE SAME MEANS
(100 AND 105) AND THE SAME
MEAN DIFFERENCE (105–100)**

case. We divide the mean difference by a moderate-sized error term, and
the *t* value obtained will be moderately large. What do we conclude? Fortunately for us, statisticians have prepared tables of the probability of various values of *t* occurring by chance. We compute the *t* ratio and then look it
up in the statistical tables to find the chance probability of a *t* as large as the
one we found. If the table tells us that the observed *t* ratio is *unlikely to happen
by chance,* we conclude that what we have is not a chance effect but a real
difference. By convention, we use a cutoff probability of .05. This means
that if our obtained *t* ratio is likely to happen only 5 percent of the time or
less by chance, then it is unlikely to be just a chance event and probably
reflects a real difference between the groups. In other words, the data suggest a statistically significant difference between the groups.

The null hypothesis says, "There is no difference between Zappo and
Brand X." If we obtain a significant *t* ratio, we conclude that the null
hypothesis is wrong. Statistical inference is basically a procedure for drawing conclusions about the null hypothesis. Of course, our inference about
the null hypothesis has implications for our working hypothesis. If we reject
the null hypothesis and conclude that the observed difference between the

TABLE A.9 _Type I and Type II Errors in Decisions Based on Experimental Data_

	Based on the experiment you conclude	
	Zappo improves endurance	Zappo does not improve endurance
	Type I Error	_Correct Decision_
Zappo does not improve endurance	Reject the null hypothesis when it is, in fact, true.	Do not reject the null hypothesis when it is, in fact, true.
The truth of the matter is:		
	Correct Decision	_Type II Error_
Zappo improves endurance	Reject the null hypothesis when it is, in fact, false.	Failing to reject the null hypothesis when it is, in fact, false.

groups is significant, then we can further conclude that Zappo does improve endurance because the people in our study who ate Zappo showed _significantly greater endurance_ than the Brand X control subjects.

We shall not go into the details of actually calculating a _t_ ratio. You can find that information in any elementary statistics book. Simply remember that when an experiment is done, the results will usually indicate some differences between the conditions in the study. The _t_-test, as well as many other types of inferential statistics, are used to help the experimenter decide whether the differences are large enough, relative to the variability, to allow rejection of the null hypothesis and support for the working hypothesis.

It is important to realize that statistical decisions are not always perfect; sometimes we make an incorrect decision on the basis of the data even though we have done everything correctly. There is always the chance, for example, that the samples are not truly representative of the populations from which they were drawn. There are two types of errors that can occur when we draw conclusions from experimental data, and these are depicted in Table A-9. A _Type I error_ is made when we conclude that the independent variable has an effect on the dependent variable, when the truth of the matter is that it has no effect. A _Type II error_ is made when we conclude that the independent variable has no effect on the dependent variable when, in fact, it does. Each type of error has a certain probability of occurring in any given experiment. By tradition, we require strong evidence for an effect of the independent variable on the dependent variable before we accept that such an effect exists. What this means is that we try to minimize the level of Type I error. However, you should note that Type I error and Type II error have an inverse relationship to one another—as one increases, the other decreases. Therefore, minimizing Type I errors will normally result in an increase in Type II errors. The task for the researcher is to balance these two types of errors, which requires a thorough understanding of research design and statistical procedures.

ADVANCED STATISTICAL TECHNIQUES

ANALYSIS OF VARIANCE

The _t_-test is used when testing the difference between two groups. But most experiments have more than two groups, and so the _t_-test is not used in such cases. Instead, a statistical procedure called _analysis of variance_ is used. Although the name may imply otherwise, analysis of variance is conceptually similar to the _t_-test. The size of the mean difference between groups is compared to an error term which is, in part, a function of the variability within each group. In fact, the analysis of variance procedure and the _t_-test will lead to exactly the same decision in the special case where there are just two groups. The test in analysis of variance is known as the *F* test, named after the famous English statistician R. A. Fisher. Basically, the procedure is just like that for the *t*-test. It allows the experimenter to make inferences or draw conclusions about the differences among a set of means. It is a very common technique now, and so you are likely to encounter the *F* test if you read any modern psychology journal.

FACTOR ANALYSIS

Factor analysis is a highly sophisticated correlational procedure that is used to identify the basic factors underlying a psychological phenomenon. The technique boils down to finding clusters of tests that correlate with one another. Suppose we administer the following six tests to 100 young men: (1) vocabulary, (2) ability to play basketball, (3) ability to write an essay on philosophy, (4) speed at running the 100-yard dash, (5) ability to understand statistics, and (6) ability to climb trees. Each man takes all six tests, and then we intercorrelate the tests. We correlate test 1 with 2, 1 with 3, 1 with 4, and so on. Suppose we find that tests 1, 3, and 5 correlate highly with one another and that 2, 4, and 6 correlate highly with one another, but that 1, 3, and 5 show little or no correlation with 2, 4, and 6. Why would this be the case? Look at the tests; tests 1, 3, and 5 all involve thinking or knowledge—they all require "mental ability." On the other hand, tests 2, 4, and 6 all require "physical ability." So probably 1, 3, and 5 all are measuring something in common, which we might call Factor A. Would you guess that Factor A has something to do with intelligence? Tests 2, 4, and 6 also seem to be measuring something in common. We will call it Factor B. Because tests 1, 3, and 5 do not correlate with tests 2, 4, and 6, we conclude that Factor A, which we now have decided to call *intelligence,* is not the same thing as Factor B, which we might label *athletic ability.*

In short, we have isolated two factors that are involved in performance on our six tests; one we call intelligence, and the other we call athletic ability. Factor analysis is basically a correlational technique that allows us to separate performance on a large number of tests into factors, by isolating clusters of tests (even when the clustering is not as obvious as it is in the foregoing example). Correlations between tests are high within a cluster but low among clusters. We assume that the clusters then "represent" and measure psychological factors.

This technique has been used extensively in two areas of psychology, intelligence testing and personality assessment (see Chapters 12 and 13). Intelligence consists of many factors, as does personality. With factor analysis we can identify these factors and hope to learn more about intelligence and personality.

Answer to Probability Question: Probability = .16

B Industrial/ Organizational Psychology

The application of psychological principles, knowledge, methods, and perspectives has increased at a rapid pace in recent years. Chapter 17 explored a few areas of applied psychology, touching briefly on *industrial/ organizational (I/O) psychology*—the branch of psychology that studies human behavior in industrial and business settings. In this appendix, we will look more closely at several key areas of this field, including the selection and evaluation of personnel, employee motivation, leadership, and human factors or ergonomics. We start with a look at the origins of I/O psychology:

THE ORIGINS OF I/O PSYCHOLOGY

The field of I/O psychology has its roots in three important areas of research that were explored early in this century. This research included the studies of F. W. Taylor and Hugo Münsterberg, and the landmark research conducted at the Hawthorne plant of the Western Electric Company in Cicero, Illinois.

F. W. Taylor (1911) was an industrial engineer who extended engineering principles to work behavior. Taylor studied workers at a steel factory and noted many extraneous movements that wasted employee energy and reduced the efficiency of their task performance. Based on these observations, Taylor made suggestions for modifying both tools and work situations, with the result of increasing productivity manyfold and at the same time reducing worker fatigue. His work became the basis for scientific management systems aimed at making workers and work situations more efficient.

Hugo Münsterberg's book, *Psychology and Industrial Efficiency* (1913), marked the beginning of I/O psychology as a recognizable branch of psychology. This book established the foundation for an empirical approach to studying applied problems such as the testing of prospective employees to make sure they are suited to a job.

The major impetus to the field of I/O psychology, however, came from a series of studies conducted during the 1920s at the Hawthorne plant of the Western Electric Company (Roethlisberger & Dickson, 1939). Here, researchers operating from Taylor's scientific management perspective were attempting to establish a relationship between productivity and illumination levels. Expecting to find that better lighting consistently improved worker output (and that poorer illumination had the opposite effect), the researchers were puzzled to discover that adjusting the lighting in either direction caused increased productivity. In fact, some of the highest productivity for the fine, detailed work of assembling small electrical components occurred at illumination levels equivalent to moonlight!

What explained this puzzling finding? Clearly, something other than lighting was responsible for the changes in output. The researchers concluded that "from [an] attempt to set the proper conditions for the experiment, there arose indirectly a change in human relations which came to be of great significance" (1939, pp. 58–59)—and that it was this change, not the lighting levels, that explained their findings. This conclusion led to the recognition that work behavior is influenced not only by physical conditions but also by psychological variables.

Because of their explicit recognition that psychological factors are central to workers' behavior, the Hawthorne studies are viewed today as the beginning of "modern" I/O psychology. These studies have additional importance because the researchers identified several issues that are still core areas of research, including the effects of group formation, the influence of leadership style, and the relative influence of intrinsic versus extrinsic motivation on task performance.

PERSONNEL SELECTION AND EVALUATION

I/O psychology has probably had the greatest impact on business and industry in personnel-related applications. We looked briefly at the topic of personnel selection in Chapter 17; here, we will explore that topic more fully and also find out how I/O psychology is applied to evaluating job performance. Of course, the concerns of personnel departments range far beyond selecting and evaluating employees, including such things as legal issues, recruitment, training programs, and ethics. The two topics we discuss here, however, are both representative of the goal of all personnel functions: to provide an organization with the best possible human resources.

SELECTING EMPLOYEES

Employee selection involves deciding which potential employee or group of employees will function best in an organization, if given the chance. "Best" in this case can be defined in a number of ways, including most production, highest quality output, or fewest absences. Typically, employers prefer to hire individuals who are the most productive per unit of time.

How can productivity be empirically determined? I/O psychology can be applied in a series of steps to determine what variable or combination of variables will distinguish potential employees who will perform successfully from those who will not. The first step, as we saw in Chapter 17, is to conduct a job analysis to determine what duties a particular job entails and what individual characteristics are necessary to perform those duties successfully. For example, suppose you need to hire five new employees for your garment factory. A partial specification of the new employees' duties might include three tasks: cutting material from a pattern, sewing material according to the pattern, and maintaining the machinery used for cutting and sewing.

Although these specifications describe what activities an employee is expected to perform, the list does not indicate what types of skills, characteristics, or attributes are necessary to perform the job. These qualifications, collectively referred to as *job specifications* or personnel specifications, are the predictors used to decide which potential employees will be successful. If you were to compile a list of job specifications for garment factory workers, you would probably include the ability to read sewing plans or patterns, reasonable command of the English language, good hand-eye coordination, good finger dexterity, and the ability to follow sequential instructions.

Once you have compiled a list of job specifications, the next step is to determine the degree to which each of your current employees possesses each job specification. This is done by using reliable tests to measure hand–eye coordination, finger dexterity, and so forth. Next, a measure of each employee's job performance is obtained. In this case, the number of garments that pass inspection sewn per unit of time would probably provide a valid indicator of employee performance. Each job specification is then correlated with the job performance measure. (See Appendix A on statistics for a discussion of correlations.)

If a strong correlation exists between a particular job specification (such as hand–eye coordination) and the job performance of successful current employees, then you may reasonably conclude that that specification is a good *predictor* of job performance. In statistical terms, we can say that *concurrent validity* exists between the predictor and the *criterion* (that is, current job performance as measured by the number of garments completed per unit of time).

Let us assume that you do in fact find that a strong positive correlation exists between the scores obtained by your current employees on a test of hand–eye coordination and the number of properly sewn garments each is able to produce in a set period of time. (In other words, the faster each worker sews. the higher she or he tends to score on the coordination test.) Such a process would establish concurrent validity and lead you to predict that the better a prospective employee's hand–eye coordination, the more garments he or she will be able to produce in a given time frame.

Once you have established the strength of the correlational relationship between hand–eye coordination and sewing rate, the regression method described in Appendix A could be used to provide a basis for predicting a given individual's sewing rate from the score obtained on the hand–eye coordination test. With this information in hand, you might then hire several employees whose coordination scores are predictive of better than average sewing speed.

Next, after a reasonable period of time for job training, each new worker's average output of sewn garments (their criterion score) could be compared with the performance prediction derived from your application of regression analysis. If the job performance of your new workers generally reflects a close match to your predicted outputs, then *predictive validity* is said to exist. Note that it is possible to have concurrent validity without having predictive validity. Therefore, both concurrent validity and predictive validity must always be assessed to ensure the validity of tests used to evaluate prospective employees.

EVALUATING WORKER PERFORMANCE

Another central function of personnel departments is the evaluation of current employees' performance. This aspect of personnel work is highly sensitive, for it is an important basis for salary increases, promotions, terminations, and the selection of workers for special training programs. Both subjective and objective techniques are used to assess employee performance; we will look at each.

Subjective Techniques for Evaluating Performance Subjective assessments of current employees are probably most frequently conducted by supervisors, who rate their subordinates on job-related dimensions such as motivation or enthusiasm, ability to get along with supervisors or fellow workers, and perceived quality of job performance. Typically, supervisors are asked to rate each subordinate on a questionnaire that contains rating scales designed to assess various aspects of each employee's job performance. For example:

Rate this employee's enthusiasm for his or her job: ____ (excellent = 1, above average = 2, average = 3, below average = 4, poor = 5)

Such subjective assessments rely on human judgment, and as a result they have several potential problems. One is the *halo effect*, discussed in Chapter 16. If a worker is good or bad on one attribute, the supervisor may tend to rate that individual as good or bad on other attributes that are actually unrelated. For instance, a supervisor who believes that motivation is an important quality may give a highly motivated worker high ratings on other qualities such as leadership ability, ability to get along with other workers, and dedication to the company—even though the evidence for these other qualities is inconsistent with the supervisor's high ratings. Such errors in judgment may ultimately lead to incorrect or costly decisions about who will be trained, promoted, or terminated.

Another potential problem associated with subjective techniques is *personal bias*. In general, supervisors tend to give subordinates who are similar to themselves (for instance, in gender, ethnicity, age, or attitudes) higher ratings than subordinates who are dissimilar (Palukos & Wexley, 1983). As with the halo effect, the result may be inaccurate information that can lead to inappropriate personnel decisions.

Objective Techniques for Evaluating Performance   Objective measures of employee evaluation avoid pitfalls such as the halo effect and personal bias. These measures typically evaluate actual job performance. For example, an objective measure of an electronics-component assembler's performance would be the number of components assembled per unit of time.

There are two main types of objective measures: direct measures of production or service (such as the number of customers served, amount produced per unit of time, or quality of production), and measures of behaviors (such as absences, injuries, and tardiness) that are critical to an employee's functioning even though they are not directly related to production or service. Both types of objective measures avoid the errors associated with subjective evaluations. However, objective measures cannot be easily applied to all employee situations. For instance, how could such measures be used to evaluate the performance of a therapist or a manager? In cases where objective measures are inappropriate and it is necessary to use subjective measures, special precautions should be taken to control potential bias.

WORKER MOTIVATION

A second important concern of I/O psychology is employee motivation. If employees are properly motivated, it stands to reason that there will be greater output per unit of time, higher quality output, more organizational loyalty, and higher job satisfaction. As we saw in Chapter 9, *motivation* can be defined as any condition that might energize and direct our actions. Several major theoretical perspectives have attempted to explain human motivation, but our concern in this appendix is with two theoretical perspectives that have had popular applications in business and industry: Maslow's need theory, and Herzberg's two-factor theory.

APPLYING NEED THEORY TO MOTIVATING WORKERS

One of the most popular theories used in organizations was proposed by Abraham Maslow (1954). In his original writings, Maslow argued that human needs are arranged according to a hierarchy of five levels: physiological needs, safety or security needs, belongingness needs, esteem needs, and, finally, self-actualization needs.

Maslow theorized that while all five levels of needs exist within everyone, these needs are not uniformly motivating. For example, in one person at one point in time, level-one needs may comprise 10 percent of motivational output, level-two needs 15 percent, level-three needs 55 percent, level-four needs 12 percent, and level-five needs 8 percent. This person's dominant level-three needs for belongingness and affection will provide motivation to behave in ways that meet those needs. In another individual, level-two security needs may occupy 60 percent of motivational output. This person's behavior will clearly be different from that of the person who is dominated by belongingness needs.

How can the notion of individual need hierarchies be applied to business and industry? Employers who adopt Maslow's perspective are concerned with understanding which needs are most relevant to which employees (Wexley & Yukl, 1984), for this information should logically provide the key to motivating employees to the greatest work performance. If level-two needs such as job security or pay are critical to certain workers, for instance, then employers need to fulfill those needs.

Although individual needs may be a key to motivating employees, Maslow's theory also presents a problem for employers: If each worker has a different hierarchy of needs, how can an employer motivate *all* of its employees? One answer that shows sensitivity to different worker needs is to offer "cafeteria benefits." Here, a range of different benefits is provided, and each worker is given *x* amount of dollars to spend on his or her choice of benefits. Thus, if one worker has a spouse and three children, this worker may choose health insurance to cover the entire family as well as life insurance for both adults. An older worker whose children are grown may not need as much health insurance; he or she may allocate most of their benefit dollars instead to a retirement plan, disability insurance, or increased vacation time.

Although Maslow's need theory continues to influence motivational programs, its empirical status has been questioned; indeed, some research findings have directly contradicted some of its underlying assumptions (Hall & Nougaim, 1968; Lawler & Suttle, 1972). Thus, while several of Maslow's more general propositions provide a useful perspective for motivating employees, most contemporary I/O psychologists do not consider his theory to be representative of an optimal model for employee motivational programs.

APPLYING TWO-FACTOR THEORY TO MOTIVATING WORKERS

Another approach to employee motivation, F. Herzberg's **two-factor theory** (Herzberg, Mausner, & Snyderman, 1959; Herzberg, 1966) has been one of the more popular theories in business and industry over the past 15 years (Landy & Trumbo, 1980). According to this theory, individuals have two types of needs: hygiene needs and motivator needs. *Hygiene needs* are system-maintenance needs; in the workplace, they translate into variables such as job security, a pleasant and safe work environment, equitable pay, and fair company policies. Employees expect hygiene needs to be met in a work situation, and these needs are very much related to the context in which the job is performed.

Simply meeting hygiene needs, however, may not be sufficient to motivate workers. Paying employees what they perceive to be appropriate wages does not ensure that they will be highly motivated. From their perspective, their pay simply meets their expectations. Alternatively, *not* meeting hygiene needs can act as a dismotivator, for employees who are not receiving what they perceive as adequate pay will be dissatisfied and therefore will not be motivated to perform.

In contrast to hygiene needs, *motivator needs* reflect what Herzberg believes are "human" qualities or traits. These needs are manifested in a desire for challenge, stimulation, autonomy, and recognition. Whereas hygiene needs are related to job *context,* motivator needs must be satisfied primarily through job *content*—that is, what a worker actually does, Herzberg sees workers as seeking both hygiene and motivator needs.

In general, it is in the interest of an organization for workers to be motivator seeking rather than hygiene seeking. The reason for this has to do with the difference between extrinsic and intrinsic motivation. Hygiene needs are extrinsic motivators because they are met primarily through sources outside the person. Motivator needs, on the other hand, are intrinsic motivators, for they are met primarily within the person. Intrinsically motivated behavior is self-induced; it tends to last longer, be more intense, and require less monitoring than extrinsically motivated behavior. An employee who is intrinsically motivated works for the sake of doing work. This is clearly advantageous to an organization.

Herzberg's theory has had a tremendous impact on business and industry. It is the primary basis for *job enrichment* or *job enlargement* programs that attempt to make a job more intrinsically motivating by associating it with more responsibility, autonomy, and recognition for achievements. Redesigning jobs to fulfill motivator needs can increase employee commitment, so that workers view their jobs as extensions of themselves. The net result is improved productivity and work quality.

Although we have considered only two motivational theories in this discussion, many other theoretical perspectives have also been applied to business and industry. These include ERG theory (Alderfer, 1969, 1972); expectancy theory (Vroom, 1964; Porter & Lawler, 1968), and need theory (McClelland, 1953, 1955, 1961).

LEADERSHIP

It has been argued that probably the single most important factor in determining the success or failure of any business or industry is its leadership. In general, **leadership** is viewed as a series of behaviors an individual performs that coordinate the actions of others to accomplish a goal or goals. From the perspective of I/O psychology, a leader's overall goal is to produce goods and services in a profitable manner.

What makes a leader a good leader? According to one theoretical perspective, certain personality traits predispose an individual to be a successful leader. Research based on this *trait approach* attempts to discover which traits or characteristics distinguish successful leaders from unsuccessful leaders, or what traits are common to successful leaders (Ghiselli, 1963, 1971; Stodgill, 1948). Another theoretical perspective argues that a leader's personal characteristics interact with situations, so that an individual may be a good leader in certain situations but a poor leader in others (Fiedler, 1967). Research based on this *contingency approach* attempts to identify which leadership styles work best in particular types of situations.

WHAT MAKES A LEADER SUCCESSFUL? THE TRAIT APPROACH

Early leadership research focused primarily on identifying personality traits that were strongly correlated with being a successful leader (Bellingrath, 1930; Dunkerley, 1949). Since informal observation of successful leaders had indicated a number of common qualities (such as above-average intelligence, assertiveness, and motivation), this approach seemed logical. However, we have seen throughout this text that commonsense assumptions are not always supported by research; and here, too, that is the case. Several reviews of the literature have failed to identify traits that are consistent among either successful or unsuccessful leaders (Hollander & Julian, 1969; Mann, 1959; Stodgill, 1948).

WHAT MAKES A LEADER SUCCESSFUL? THE CONTINGENCY APPROACH

A currently popular approach to explaining leadership is based on F. E. Fiedler's contingency approach (Fiedler, 1967; Fiedler & Chemers, 1984). Basically, the *contingency approach* looks at the relationship between leadership styles and situational factors to explain why an individual is successful or unsuccessful as a leader in a particular situation.

Leadership Style *Leadership style* is a measure of how a leader perceives his or her subordinates; it is assessed using a test known as the *least-preferred co-worker (LPC)*. The LPC measures how a leader describes the co-worker with which he or she has the most difficulty in accomplishing a task. The results of the LPC are then coded to determine whether a leader is high-LPC or low-LPC.

High-LPC leaders (also referred to as relationship- or person-motivated leaders) describe their least-preferred co-worker in a relatively positive manner, using terms such as "friendly" or "cooperative." According to Fiedler, high-LPC leaders seem able to separate workers' characteristics or traits from the quality or level of their job performance. High-LPC leaders are likely to be concerned with their subordinates' feelings, and they are highly motivated to have positive interpersonal relationships with their subordinates. In fact, the self-esteem of high-LPC leaders tends to be a direct function of how others perceive and relate to them.

In contrast, *low-LPC leaders* (also known as task-motivated leaders) describe their least-preferred co-worker in negative terms such as "unfriendly" or "uncooperative." These leaders seem unable to separate their subordinates' personality traits from the quality of their job performance. Low-LPC leaders are much less concerned with the feelings and job satisfaction of their subordinates; their primary motivation is to ensure that the organization's goals are met.

Which leadership style is more effective? Although it is tempting to predict that high-LPC leaders are more effective, Fiedler argues that the answer depends on the situation. The situational variable that determines a leader's effectiveness is seen as the level of situational control a leader enjoys.

Situational Control *Situational control* refers to the climate in which a leader operates. It is composed of three dimensions: leader-member relations, task structure, and position power.

The term *leader-member relations* refers to how well a leader is liked, respected, and trusted by subordinates. If a leader enjoys this esteem, then he or she is said to have high leader-member relations; if the opposite is true, the leader has low leader-member relations. A leader with high leader-member relations has an easier time leading. Because subordinates are eager to follow directives, the leader can be confident that his or her instructions will have the intended impact. Leaders with low leader-member relations, in contrast, lack their subordinates' respect, loyalty, and trust; they cannot be confident that their directives will be carried out. According to Fiedler, leader-member relations is the most important of the three dimensions determining situational control.

The second most important dimension of situational control is *task structure:* the clarity of subordinates' task goals, task procedures for reaching those goals, and measures for evaluating task outcomes. In general, it is easier to lead workers when jobs have a clear task structure than when task goals, procedures, and outcome evaluation are ambiguous.

A third dimension of situational control is *position power*—the degree of "fate control" a leader has over subordinates. A leader who has the authority to present or withdraw rewards, who can influence subordinates' tenure within the organization, and who has access to needed resources has high position power; one who lacks this control has low position power, and has little "formal" power to influence subordinates. According to Fiedler, position power is a less important determinant of situational control than either leader-member relations or task structure.

The overall degree of situational control can be assessed by determining the relative amounts of leader-member relations, task structure, and position power that a leader possesses within a particular situation. Fiedler's model does not predict that any leader will always be more effective when all three dimensions of situational control are high, for as we saw earlier, lead-

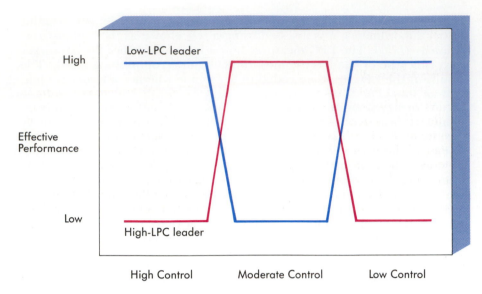

FIGURE B.1   HYPOTHESIZED RELATIONSHIP BETWEEN SITUATIONAL CONTROL AND LEADERSHIP EFFECTIVENESS AS A FUNCTION OF LEADERSHIP STYLE

(*Source:* Adapted from Fiedler & Chemers, 1984, p. 166)

ership effectiveness is a joint function of both situational control and leadership style. In general, high-LPC leaders operate most effectively in situations of moderate control, whereas low-LPC leaders are most effective in situations of high or low situational control (see Figure B.1).

What explains this difference? If leadership style is a part of one's personality, as Fiedler argues, then it not only directs how a leader interacts with subordinates; it also determines what motivates or challenges that leader. For example, a low-LPC leader would react very differently from a high-LPC leader to a work situation that provides high leader-member relations, task structure, and position power. This situation removes many of the variables that are likely to make the low-LPC leader's job more difficult; as a result, this leader can function in a relaxed manner, knowing that tasks will be accomplished effectively and efficiently. The low-LPC leader will be more free to demonstrate concern for subordinates' problems, and may even solicit suggestions on how to accomplish organizational goals.

A high-LPC leader is likely to react very differently to the same work situation. This leader is not as concerned with employee support or with worries that tasks won't be accomplished, but is motivated more by the desire to maintain good interpersonal relations—something not necessary in this situation. This leader is likely to find a high-control situation boring and unchallenging, to the extent that he or she may look to other activities, such as revising procedures that do not need revision or supervising the petty details of subordinates' activities. Such actions may be viewed by others as unnecessary or even capricious. Thus, the high-control situation that brings out the best in a low-LPC leader seems likely to bring out the worst in a high-LPC leader.

How accurate are such predictions? That question has generated a great deal of research and debate. Whereas one recent review (Strube & Garcia, 1981) supports Fiedler's theories about leadership, these conclusions are contradicted by another study (Vecchio, 1983).

Fiedler has developed a leadership-training program designed to train leaders to understand how their own leadership style interacts with the degree of situational control that exists in their work situation, so that they may adjust their work situation to make it more compatible with their style of leadership. In general, Fiedler reports good success with his program (Fiedler & Chemers, 1984; Csoka & Bons, 1978).

HUMAN FACTORS

A final area of I/O psychology that we discuss in this appendix is **human factors** or **ergonomics** (Willems, 1984). This subfield focuses primarily on the interface between human characteristics and the equipment, products, or systems that humans use on the job. The main objective of human factors research is fairly straightforward: to design tools, equipment, products, and systems to be as efficient and as effective as possible, taking into account human capabilities and limitations. Of all the areas of study in I/O psychology, human factors research has most clearly shown the importance of the interaction between humans and their environments in determining what we are capable of accomplishing.

The current approach to human factors research is primarily a *systems approach* that involves four basic functions of the human system: sensing, information storage, information processing and decision making, and action (McCormick & Sanders, 1982).

SENSING FUNCTIONS

Sensing refers to the registering of information by the human system. We know that information enters our systems through our sensory apparatus—our auditory, olfactory, and visual processes, and so forth. Human factors research regarding this function is concerned with learning how to present information to individuals in such a manner that it will be most easily sensed and retained.

One goal of human factors research is to design displays to ensure that the information that people need to perform their jobs will in fact be sensed. An important aspect is the question of which sensory channels are most effective for transmitting information in different situations (Deatherage, 1972). As Table B-1 shows, the selection of either auditory or visual channels for transmitting information depends not only on the nature of the message but also on the context in which the message is presented and the nature of the action that an individual must perform.

Since vision is so important to humans, another crucial area of sensory research focuses on the best way to design visual displays to ensure that visual information is sensed. To determine whether visual displays are effective, such research must take into account not only the content of the message but also the rate at which information is presented.

TABLE B.1   *When to Use the Auditory or Visual Form of Presentation*

Use auditory presentation if:	Use visual presentation if:
1. The message is simple.	1. The message is complex.
2. The message is short.	2. The message is long.
3. The message will not be referred to later.	3. The message will be referred to later.
4. The message deals with events in time.	4. The message deals with location in space.
5. The message calls for immediate action.	5. The message does not call for immediate action.
6. The visual system of the person is overburdened.	6. The auditory system of the person is overburdened.
7. The receiving location is too bright or dark-adaptation integrity is necessary.	7. The receiving location is too noisy.
8. The person's job requires him to move about continually.	8. The person's job allows him to remain in one position.

Source: From Deatherage, 1972, p. 124, table 4-1.

A standard approach to designing visual displays is to compare various displays and determine which is the most efficient. In designing the control panel of an airplane, for instance, what is the most effective and least confusing placement of gauges for altitude, speed, danger signals, and so forth? It has been found that many "system failures," ranging from inefficiency to fatal errors, have resulted from overloading the visual sensory system: The individuals using a particular display were simply not capable of processing all the information provided by the display (Landy, 1985). Such findings have led researchers to design guidelines for developing displays that transfer some sensing duties to other sensory modalities (McCormick & Sanders, 1982).

INFORMATION STORAGE, PROCESSING, AND DECISION-MAKING FUNCTIONS

The second basic function studied by the systems approach is *information storage:* the placing of information in memory for later use. Not only must information be stored in memory; it also must be stored in such a manner that it is easily retrieved for later use. Chapter 7's discussion of memory explored the cognitive processes involved in information storage and retrieval; human factors research seeks to determine how information can be placed in the system to make it easiest to store and later to recall.

The third function, *information processing and decision making,* also focuses on human cognitive processes. Here, researchers are concerned with finding out how information can be stored in the system so that it is most easily retrieved and subsequently used to make sound decisions. The nature of these decisions will vary according to the purpose of a particular decision-making process.

Research into information storage, processing, and decision-making functions has focused on the cognitive processing capacities of humans—their information storage and retrieval systems as well as the thinking processes that lead to correct decisions. The goal of research in this area is to facilitate cognitive processing by providing workers with the necessary information with which to make accurate judgments, evaluations, or conclusions.

ACTION FUNCTIONS

The final area of systems research, *action functions,* is concerned with the consequences of implementing decisions. In general, the consequences of an action function can be physical (for instance, plugging a silicon chip into a computer memory board) or communicative (as when a worker records that the action has been performed). Research into action functions is directed toward determining what actions are most compatible with human abilities. Such research may investigate the ease of use of different devices, such as control panels, machines, or tools, for performing different types of actions. This issue is crucial, because an inefficiently built device this is antagonistic to human capabilities may lead to accidents and injury. Imagine the potential for danger in an electric knife whose on-off switch is located too close to its blade!

Research into action functions has resulted in the development of products and tools that are less fatiguing to use and that result in fewer errors. Tools have been reshaped to be more compatible with human capabilities. The reshaping of tools is based on extensive research into ways of taking advantage of human sensory and physiological capabilities.

Any discussion of the systems approach to human factors should note that the distinctions made among the four functions just outlined is somewhat arbitrary (McCormick & Ilgen, 1985). The stages tend to blend into one another, and in practice the distinctions are often blurred. For example, to have information available to make correct decisions (functions two and three) requires that the information be presented in a manner that facilitates its incorporation into memory structures (function one). In all, the individual components of the systems approach are highly inter-dependent.

C Sexuality

Our sexuality is a richly varied, highly individualized, and potentially profoundly enriching aspect of our lives. We express our sexuality in many ways, and the feelings, thoughts, and attitudes we bring to this area of human experience also vary widely. Space constraints do not allow us to explore the broad gamut of human sexual behavior. Instead, we will endeavor to present a brief overview of selected topics which provide an introduction to certain biological, psychosocial, behavioral, and cultural aspects of sexuality.

We begin by outlining a four-phase model of human sexual response followed by discussions of sexual behavior patterns, sexual orientation, and cross-cultural variations in sexual expression. For those of you interested in a more comprehensive exploration of sexuality, we recommend enrolling in a course in human sexuality (typically offered by most colleges and universities in psychology, sociology, health, or biology departments) and/or one of the many excellent books dealing with various aspects of sexuality. (An annotated list of suggested readings concludes this appendix.)

A FOUR-PHASE MODEL OF SEXUAL RESPONSE

Human sexual response is highly individual, involving physical, emotional, and mental processes. Nevertheless, the sexual response cycle follows a general pattern of common physiological changes.

Masters and Johnson (1966) distinguish four phases in the sexual response patterns of both men and women: **excitement, plateau, orgasm, and resolution.** In addition, they include a **refractory period** (a recovery stage during which there is a temporary inability to reach orgasm) in the male resolution phase. Figures C-1 and C-2 illustrate these four phases of sexual response in women and men. These charts provide basic "maps" of common patterns—although a few cautions should be used in interpreting them.

First, these diagrams are highly simplified, obscuring the wide individual variations that occur in real life. Masters and Johnson charted only the physiological responses to sexual stimulation. Although our biological reactions may follow a relatively predictable course, there is tremendous variability in our subjective responses to sexual arousal.

A second caution has to do with a too-literal interpretation of the so-called plateau stage of sexual response. Within the behavioral sciences,

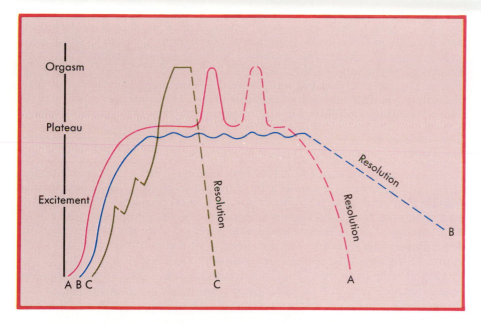

FIGURE C.1 FEMALE SEXUAL
RESPONSE CYCLE

Masters and Johnson identified three basic patterns in female sexual response. Pattern A most closely resembles the male pattern, with the exception of the possibility of one or more orgasms without dropping below plateau level of sexual arousal. Variations may include an extended plateau with no orgasm (line B), or a rapid rise to orgasm (line C) with no definitive plateau and a very quick resolution. (*Source:* From Masters & Johnson, 1966)

the term *plateau* is typically used to describe a leveling-off period where there are no observable changes in behavior. For example, it might refer to a flat spot in a learning curve where no new behaviors occur for a certain period of time. It has been diagramed in just this manner in the male chart and in pattern A of the female chart. Actually, the plateau level of sexual arousal involves a powerful surge of sexual tensions that can be measured by increased heart and breathing rates as well as other functions.

The phases of the response cycle follow the same general patterns regardless of the method of stimulation. Masturbation, manual stimulation

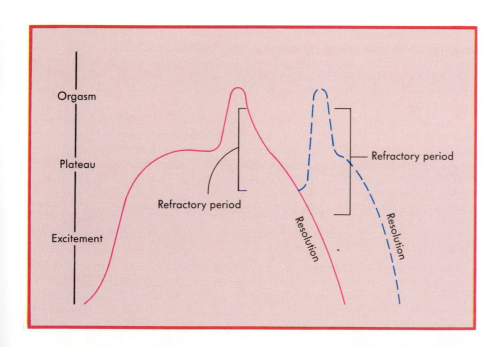

**FIGURE C.2 MALE SEXUAL RE-
SPONSE CYCLE**

Only one male response pattern was identified by Masters and Johnson. However, men do report considerable variation in their response patterns. Note the refractory period: Males do not have a second orgasm immediately after the first. (*Source:* From Masters & Johnson, 1966)

by one's partner, oral stimulation, penile-vaginal intercourse, dreaming, fantasy, and, in some women, breast stimulation can all result in completion of the response cycle. The intensity and rapidity of response may vary according to the kind of stimulation.

The next several paragraphs outline the major physiological reactions that occur during each of the four phases of the sexual response cycle. Note the strong similarities in the response patterns of men and women.

EXCITEMENT

The first phase of the sexual response cycle is the excitement phase. It is characterized by a number of common responses, including muscle tension and some increase in heart rate and blood pressure. In both women and men, several areas of the sexual anatomy become engorged with blood, a physiological response known as *vasocongestion*. The most obvious manifestations of this response are the erection of the penis in men and lubrication of the vagina in women. In addition, other body areas may become engorged—the labia, testicles, clitoris, nipples, and even the earlobes. The appearance of a *sex flush* (a pink or red rash on the chest or breasts) occurs among both sexes, but is more common with women.

PLATEAU

During the plateau phase, sexual tension continues to heighten until it reaches the extreme level that leads to orgasm. It is difficult to define clearly the point at which the plateau phase begins. Unlike the excitement phase, there is no clear external sign such as lubrication or erection to indicate its onset. Instead, a number of these physiological reactions become more pronounced. Heart rate and blood pressure continue to rise; breathing grows faster; and sex flushes become more noticeable. Muscle tension continues to build up, and the face, neck, hands, and feet may undergo involuntary contractions and spasms in both the plateau and the next phase, orgasm. Among women, plateau phase is also distinguished by development of the "orgasmic platform" (a term used to describe the markedly increased engorgement of the outer third of the vagina).

ORGASM

As stimulation continues, many individuals move from plateau to orgasm. This stage is marked by reduction in voluntary muscle control, with involuntary muscle spasms throughout the body; a peak in blood pressure, heart rate, and rate of breathing; rhythmic contractions of the vagina and usually the uterus in women; and expulsion of semen in men. The experience of orgasm can be an intense mixture of sensations that are highly pleasurable.

Do women and men experience orgasm differently? This question was evaluated in an analysis of orgasm descriptions provided by college students (Wiest, 1977). Using a standard psychological rating scale, this study found that women's and men's subjective descriptions of orgasm were indistinguishable. Similar results were obtained in an earlier study, when a group of 70 judges were unable to reliably distinguish between reports of orgasms written by men and women (Proctor et al., 1974).

RESOLUTION

During the final phase of the sexual response cycle, the sexual systems return to their nonexcited state. Heart rate, blood pressure, and breathing all return to normal, as does muscle tension. If no additional stimulation occurs, resolution begins immediately after orgasm. Some of the changes take place rapidly, while others occur more slowly.

There is one significant difference in the response of men and women during this phase. That is their physiological readiness for further sexual stimulation. After orgasm, men typically experience a refractory period when no amount of additional stimulation will result in orgasm. The length of this period ranges from minutes to days, depending on a variety of factors such as age, the frequency of previous sexual activity, and the degree of emotional closeness and sexual desire. Women typically experience no refractory period. They are physiologically capable of returning to another orgasmic peak from anywhere in the resolution phase. However, a woman may or may not desire to do so.

SEXUAL EXPRESSION

The four phases of the sexual response cycle present a clinical analysis of human sexual behavior. People express their sexuality in many ways, however, and the response cycle cannot help us understand this diversity. The remainder of this appendix deals with some of these variations—in sexual behavior patterns, in sexual orientations (the sex to which an individual is attracted), and in variations in sexual expression in different societies.

SEXUAL BEHAVIOR PATTERNS

There are many forms of sexual behavior that provide absorbing discussion. In this appendix, however, we have space only to explore briefly four common types of sexual expression: masturbation, erotic fantasy, oral-genital stimulation, and coitus.

Masturbation *Masturbation,* or self-stimulation of the genitals for sexual pleasure, has been a source of social concern and censure for hundreds of years, resulting in both misinformation and considerable personal shame and fear.

Many of the negative attitudes toward masturbation are rooted in the early Judeo-Christian view that the only legitimate purpose of sexual behavior was procreation (Bullough, 1986). Since masturbation could not result in conception, it was condemned. The "evils" of masturbation received a great deal of publicity during the mid-eighteenth century, due largely to a European physician named Tissot who write vividly about the mind- and body-damaging effects of "self-abuse." This view of masturbation became part of social and medical attitudes that persisted well into the twentieth century.

Freud and most other early psychoanalysts recognized that masturbation is not physically harmful. They saw it as normal during childhood, but believed that it could result in "immature" sexual development and the inability to form good sexual relationships as an adult.

Today there are conflicting views of masturbation. Much of the traditional condemnation still exists: In 1976 the Vatican issued a "Declaration on Certain Questions Concerning Sexual Ethics," which described masturbation as an "intrinsically and seriously disordered act." On the other hand, many writers today view masturbation as a positive aspect of sexuality (Crooks & Baur, 1987). People masturbate for a variety of reasons, not the least of which is arousal and orgasm. Some people also find that the independent release available through masturbation can help them make better decisions about relating sexually with other people. Within a relationship, too, masturbation can help to even out the effects of dissimilar sexual interest. Finally, masturbation can be a means of self-exploration that can help some women learn to have orgasms and can sometimes help men increase ejaculatory control (Crooks & Baur, 1987).

Erotic Fantasy Another common form of sexual experience, *erotic fantasy,* occurs within a person's mind, either with or without accompanying sexual behavior. Fantasies are mental experiences that may arise from our imagi-

TABLE C.1 *Male and Female Sexual Fantasies during Masturbation*

Fantasy Content	% Men	% Women
Intercourse with loved one	75	70
Intercourse with strangers	47	21
Sex with more than one person of the other sex	33	18
Sexual activities that would not be done in reality	19	28
Forcing someone to have sex	13	3
Being forced to have sex	10	19
Homosexual activity	7	11

Source: From Hunt, 1974.

nation or from memories of previous experiences. They may also be stimulated by literature, drawings, or photographs.

Erotic fantasies are common. In the classic studies of Alfred Kinsey and his associates (1948, 1953), 84 percent of men and 67 percent of women reported having sexual fantasies. A more recent survey of college students found that 60 percent of both men and women reported fantasizing during intercourse (Sue, 1979). Greater sexual experience may contribute to increased sexual fantasizing. In one study, for example, women with the greatest amount of sexual experience reported having more sexual fantasies than women with little or no sexual experience (Knafo & Jaffe, 1984).

The content of sexual fantasies varies greatly, ranging from pleasant, romantic images to graphic representations of real or imagined experiences. This diversity is illustrated in Tables C-1 and C-2.

Erotic fantasies serve many functions. First, they can be a source of pleasure and arousal. Erotic thoughts may enhance sexual arousal during masturbation or sexual sharing with a partner. The ability to fantasize appears to be an important component of sexual interest and arousal; a deficit of erotic fantasy is often associated with problems of low sexual desire and arousal (Nutter & Condron, 1983). Some sexual fantasies allow for tolerable expression of "forbidden wishes." Indeed, the fact that sexual activity in a fantasy is "forbidden" may make it more exciting.

Both masturbation and fantasy are individual forms of sexual expression. Other sexual behaviors take place as interactions between people. Two of the most common forms of shared sexual behavior are oral-genital stimulation and coitus.

Oral-Genital Stimulation Both the mouth and genitals are *primary erogenous zones* (areas highly responsive to stimulation due to dense concentrations of nerve endings). Therefore, couples who are psychologically comfortable with *oral-genital stimulation* often find both giving and receiving to be highly pleasurable.

TABLE C.2 *Male and Female Sexual Fantasies during Intercourse*

Fantasy Content	% Males	% Females
Sex with a former lover	43	41
Sex with an imaginary lover	44	24
Oral-genital sex	61	51
Group sex	19	14
Being forced into a sexual relationship	21	36
Being observed engaging in sexual intercourse	15	20
Being found sexually irresistible by others	55	53
Being rejected or sexually abused	11	13
Forcing others to have sexual relations with you	24	16
Having others give in to you after resisting	37	24
Observing others engaging in sex	18	13
Sex with a member of the same sex	3	9
Sex with animals	1	4

Source: From Sue, 1979.

Some people may have reservations about oral-genital stimulation. These views come from a number of sources. As we have seen, sexual behaviors that do not have the potential of resulting in pregnancy within marriage have been historically labeled immoral, and many people believe that oral sex is wrong. This notion of immorality has been institutionalized into law, and sexual behaviors other than coitus are still illegal in many states.

Another reason some people object to oral sex is the belief that it is a "homosexual act"—even when experienced by heterosexual couples. Although many homosexual people do engage in oral sex, the activity is not homosexual by nature. Its "homosexuality" or "heterosexuality" depends on the sexes of the partners involved.

Despite these negative attitudes, oral-genital contact is quite common and has become even more so in recent years. It seems to have gained more acceptance throughout a cross-section of educational levels. Kinsey's research in the late 1940s and early 1950s revealed that 60 percent of college-educated couples, 20 percent of high-school-educated couples, and 10 percent of grade-school-educated couples had experienced oral-genital stimulation in marital sex. A survey in the early 1970s of over 2,000 men and women in a broad range of urban centers revealed that 90 percent of married couples under 25 years of age had experienced oral-genital sex, regardless of educational level. Surveys of several thousand college students over the last few years show that approximately 81 percent of women and 79 percent of men have experienced both giving and receiving oral stimulation (Crooks, 1986).

Coitus As we have seen, a long-standing sexual legacy in most Western cultures is the idea that the only legitimate purpose of sexual activity is reproduction. In our culture, one of the most prominent expressions of this theme is in the notion that sex is synonymous with *coitus* (penile-vaginal intercourse).

Certainly coitus can be a very fulfilling part of sexual expression. However, excessive emphasis on intercourse often has negative consequences (Crooks & Baur, 1987). For one, it perpetuates the notion that sexual response and orgasm are supposed to occur during penetration. Such a narrow focus can place tremendous performance pressure on both women and men.

This tendency to focus on coitus as the "main event" may also result in devaluing other forms of sexual behavior. Some activities—for instance, affectionate kisses, body caresses, and manual or oral stimulation—are often relegated to the secondary status of *foreplay* (usually considered to be any activity before intercourse), to be followed by the "real sex" of coitus.

HOMOSEXUALITY

Different people have different views of what is sexually exciting and sexuality can be expressed in a variety of ways. One way in which sexual expression varies from person to person is in **sexual orientation**—that is, the sex to which an individual is attracted. Attraction to partners of the same sex is a homosexual orientation, and attraction to partners of the other sex is a heterosexual orientation. Bisexuality refers to attraction to partners of both sexes.

Defining Homosexuality Most people think of homosexuality as sexual contact between individuals of the same sex. However, this definition is limited in that it does not encompass all of the meanings of the term *homosexual,* which can refer to (1) sexual behavior, (2) emotional affiliation, and (3) a definition of self. The following definition incorporates a broader spectrum of elements: A homosexual person is an individual "whose primary erotic, psychological, emotional, and social interest is in a member of the same sex, even though that interest may not be overtly expressed" (Martin & Lyon, 1972, p. 1).

A homosexual person's gender identity agrees with his or her biological sex; that is, homosexual people perceive themselves as male or female, respectively, and are attracted toward people of the same sex.

A word commonly used for homosexual is *gay*. Gay was initially used as a code word between homosexuals, but has since moved into popular usage to describe men, women, and social concerns related to homosexual orientation. Gay women are often referred to as lesbians.

A Continuum of Sexual Orientations In our society, we tend to make clear-cut distinctions between homosexuality and heterosexuality. The delineation is not so clear-cut, however.

On one end of a broad spectrum, a relatively small percentage of people consider themselves exclusively homosexual; on the other end, a greater number think of themselves as exclusively heterosexual. Between the two groups exist varying degrees of preference and experience, as shown in Figure C-3 (Kinsey, 1948). The scale ranges from 0 (exclusive contact with and erotic attraction to the other sex) to 6 (exclusive contact with and attraction to the same sex). Category 3 represents equal homosexual and heterosexual attraction and experience; in between are varying degrees of homosexual and heterosexual orientation.

How many people in our society fall into the exclusively homosexual category? According to Kinsey, this group comprises two percent of women and four percent of men. Although this percentage appears small, slightly less than three percent of the population of the United States would be almost seven million people. Some gay-rights advocates believe that the actual number of predominantly homosexual people is 10 percent of the population. This higher estimate is based partly on the assumption that social pressures cause many homosexual people to conceal their orientation (a behavior that is commonly known as being "in the closet").

Between the extremes on the continuum are many individuals who have experienced sexual contact with or been attracted to people of the same sex. Kinsey's estimate of this group's number was quite high: 37 percent of males and 13 percent of females in his research populations reported having had overt homosexual experiences at some point in their lives, and even more had been erotically attracted to the same sex.

Societal Attitudes toward Homosexuality A monumental survey of 190 societies throughout the world, conducted by an anthropologist and a psychologist (Ford & Beach, 1951), found that homosexuality was accepted in

FIGURE C.3 CONTINUUM OF SEXUAL ORIENTATION

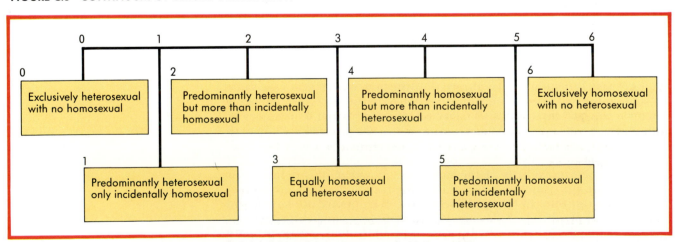

(*Source:* Adapted from Kinsey et al., 1948, p. 638)

approximately two-thirds of these societies. Homosexuality has also been widely accepted in many earlier cultures. For example, over half of 225 Native American tribes accepted male homosexuality, and 17 percent accepted female homosexuality (Pomeroy, 1965).

Our own Judeo-Christian tradition has had a far more negative view of homosexuality. Many religious scholars believe that the condemnation of homosexuality stems from a reformation movement beginning in the seventh century B.C., through which Jewish religious leaders wanted to develop a distinct, closed community that was different from others of the time. Homosexual activities were a part of the religious services of many groups of people, including the Jewish people in that era. Rejecting religious rituals involving homosexual activities that had previously been considered sacred was one way of establishing the uniqueness of a religion. Homosexual behaviors were condemned as a form of pagan worship (Kosnik et al., 1977). Strong prohibitive biblical scriptures were written. For example, "You shall not lie with a man as one lies with a female, it is an abomination" (Leviticus 18:22).

In recent years there has been a shift in attitudes toward homosexuality. The view that homosexuality is immoral has been replaced to some degree by a common belief that homosexuality is a sickness. Most current research, however, contradicts this notion. Studies comparing nonpatient heterosexual and homosexual individuals have found no significant differences in adjustment between the two groups (Hooker, 1957; Wilson, 1984). Two noted researchers in this area, Allan Bell and Martin Weinberg, state that ". . . homosexual adults who have come to terms with their homosexuality, who do not regret their sexual orientation and who can function effectively sexually and socially, are no more distressed psychologically than are heterosexual men and women" (1979, p. 216).

How Does Homosexuality Develop? A variety of theories have attempted to explain how homosexuality develops. There is still no single clear answer, but recent research conducted by Alan Bell, Martin Weinberg, and Sue Hammersmith (1981) helps shed some light on the question. Bell and his colleagues used a sample of 979 homosexual people matched to a control group of 477 heterosexual people. All subjects were questioned about their childhood, adolescence, and sexual practices, and their responses were analyzed using sophisticated statistical techniques. Much of the information presented in this discussion is based on this study's findings. We will refer to it as we evaluate both psychosocial and biological explanations of how homosexuality develops.

Psychosocial Theories Many theories seek to explain homosexuality as the result of learned or psychological factors—experiences, parenting patterns, or the individual's own psychological attributes. For instance, one explanation for homosexuality is that it may be the result of unhappy heterosexual experiences or the inability to attract partners of the other sex.

HOMOSEXUALITY AS A LEARNED RESPONSE

It is often assumed that lesbianism is caused by a resentment, dislike, fear, or distrust of men rather than attraction toward women. Do you think this explanation is sound? Consider this question, as well as your reasons for answering yes or no, before reading on.

Perhaps the best way to evaluate this explanation of homosexuality is to turn the argument around: Is female heterosexuality caused by a dislike and fear of women? The answer is no, just as lesbianism is not caused by unhappy experiences with men. In fact, research indicates that up to 70 percent of lesbian women have had sexual experiences with men, and many report having enjoyed them. However, they prefer to be sexual with women (Klaich, 1974; Lyon, 1972).

According to Bell and his colleagues' study, lesbianism is not related either to unpleasant heterosexual experiences or to a lack of such experiences (1981, p. 176). This study revealed that homosexual and heterosexual people dated about equally in high school—a finding that contradicts the notion that a lack of heterosexual opportunity causes homosexuality. Both male and female homosexual subjects did tend, however, to feel differently about dating than did heterosexual subjects—few of them reported enjoying it. These feelings probably indicate that these subjects were less interested in heterosexuality. For example, although the homosexual males dated as much as the heterosexual males in the study, they tended to have fewer sexual encounters with females. The researchers concluded that "unless heterosexual encounters appeal to one's deepest sexual feeling, there is likely to be little about them that one would experience as positive reinforcement for sexual relationships with members of the opposite sex" (p. 108).

Another myth dispelled by the Bell research team is that young men and women become homosexual because they have been seduced by older homosexuals. In reality, most subjects (both male and female) had their first homosexual encounter with someone about the same age as themselves. In fact, homosexual subjects were less likely than heterosexual subjects to have had initial sexual encounters with a stranger or an adult.

Some people may believe that homosexuality can be "caught" from someone else—for instance, that a homosexual teacher, especially one that is well liked and respected, will become a role model for students. However, homosexual orientation appears to be established even before school age, and modeling is not a relevant factor (Marmor, 1980).

Another theory links homosexuality to certain patterns in family background. Sigmund Freud (1905) maintained that children's relationships with their fathers and mothers was a crucial factor. Although Freud viewed men and women as innately bisexual, he thought that individuals normally passed through a "homoerotic" phase in the course of heterosexual development. Certain people could become "fixated" at the homosexual phase if some kinds of life experiences occurred, especially if a boy had a poor relationship with his father and an overly close relationship with his mother.

Freud's theory that family background is related to homosexuality is often cited, but it has not been established by research. In fact, Bell and his colleagues reported that no particular phenomenon of family life can be singled out as especially consequential in the development of either heterosexual or homosexual orientations.

Biological Theories If psychosocial causes cannot explain homosexuality, does biology provide any more reliable answers? In the effort to answer this question, researchers have investigated a number of possible biological factors. The two most promising lines of research have been genetic factors and hormonal causes.

According to one argument, a person's homosexuality may be determined by his or her genetic makeup. One study conducted by Franz Kallman (1952a, 1952b) tested this theory by comparing sexual orientations in both fraternal and identical twins. In all cases, the twins had been reared together, so their prenatal and postnatal environments were virtually identical. The primary difference between the two groups lay in their genetic makeup, which was identical for the identical twins but not for the fraternal twins.

Kallman reported an approximately 95 percent *concordance rate* for homosexuality among the identical twins. In contrast, the concordance rate for fraternal twins was only 12 percent. A more recent investigation reported concordance rates for homosexuality of approximately 75 percent and 19 percent respectively among identical and fraternal twins (Whitman & Diamond, 1986). However, other research has failed to find evidence of hereditary factors in homosexuality (Heston & Shields, 1968). Additional research is needed before we can conclude that genetic makeup determines sexual orientation.

Other research has tested the theory that homosexuality results from hormonal imbalances, both before birth and during adulthood. One explanation supported by some research is that prenatal hormone imbalances alter the masculine and feminine development of the fetal brain, thus contributing to homosexuality (Murphy & Fain, 1978). When prenatal androgen deficiencies are produced experimentally in animals, males will later show female mating behavior (Dörner, 1976; Money & Ehrhardt, 1972). If there is a critical period during which the fetus is particularly sensitive to levels of sex hormones, it seems possible that a prenatal androgen deficiency in human males could contribute to homosexuality. One big question left unanswered by this theory, of course, is whether or not such sensitivity is a factor in human development.

Hormone levels may be a factor in adulthood as well as in prenatal development. Some researchers have compared hormone levels in adult homosexual men and women with those in heterosexual adults, with contradictory results. Some studies report that homosexual males have less androgen than heterosexual males; others indicate just the opposite; and still others reveal no difference (Meyer-Bahlburg, 1977; Tourney, 1980). Only a few studies have explored hormone levels in lesbians. Just as in male homosexual studies, the results of these studies have been inconsistent (Gaitwell et al., 1977; Griffiths et al., 1974).

Although Bell and his co-workers did not measure hormone levels in their study, they suggest that biology may be a factor in the development of homosexuality. They believe that individuals are predisposed to be either heterosexual or homosexual, and they see homosexuality as "a pattern of feelings and reactions within the child that cannot be traced back to a single social or psychological root" (p. 192).

In conclusion, while research seems to suggest that some people may be biologically predisposed to homosexuality, the exact causes are still speculative. At this point, it seems most appropriate to think of sexual orientation as influenced by a variety of psychosocial and biological factors that are unique for each person, rather than trying to find a single cause.

CROSS-CULTURAL VARIATIONS IN SEXUAL EXPRESSION

Many of us have our own ideas about what is "normal" sexual behavior and what is not, but often the meaning of a given act (sexual or otherwise) cannot be fully understood without also understanding its cultural context. For example, in North American society, we may attribute sexual overtones to the act of two men embracing each other. In Iran, however (and in many other societies), it is completely normal (and nonsexual) for men to hug one another.

There is such diversity among the cultures of the world that the very definition of what is sexually arousing may vary greatly. For example, exposed female breasts may trigger sexual interest in men of one society while inducing little or no erotic interest in a different society. Furthermore, the acceptability of certain sexual activities varies widely from culture to culture. In some societies, such as the Mangaians of Polynesia, sex is highly valued and almost all manifestations of it are considered beautiful and natural. Other societies, such as the Manus of New Guinea, view any sexual act as undesirable and shameful (Crooks & Baur, 1987).

Almost any sexual behavior is viewed in widely different ways in different societies. For example, masturbation by children may be overtly condemned in one society, covertly supported in another, openly encouraged in still another, and even occasionally initiated by parental example.

The diversity of sexual expression throughout the world tends to mask a fundamental generalization that can be applied without exception to all social orders. This is the fact that within the **cultural mores** (established customs and beliefs) of all societies the conduct of sexual behavior is regulated in some way. The rules vary from one society to the next, but no social order allows sexuality to remain unregulated.

The best way to understand the diversity of sexual expression in different societies is through examples. We will look briefly at three societies with very different views of sexuality: the Polynesian society of the island Mangaia, the inhabitants of an island off the coast of Ireland known as Inis Beag, and the Dani of New Guinea. (These social groups have all been studied at some time during the last few decades. However, they may have undergone cultural change since they were observed.)

Mangaia Mangaia is the southernmost of the Polynesian Cook Island chain. Its inhabitants were studied in the 1950s by anthropologist Donald Marshall (1971), whose accounts of Mangaian sexual practices have been widely quoted.

When Marshall visited Mangaia, he observed a society in which sexual pleasure and activity is a principal concern, starting in childhood (Marshall, 1971). Children have extensive exposure to sexuality: They hear folk tales containing detailed descriptions of sex acts and sexual anatomy, and they watch provocative ritual dances. At the onset of puberty, both sexes receive detailed sex instruction.

Once their instruction is completed, boys begin to seek girls. Sex occurs in "public privacy," as young males engage in a practice called *night-crawling,* where boys enter their chosen lover's house at night and have sexual relations while other family members sleep nearby. (In the 1950s, when Marshall conducted his research, most Mangaian houses had only a single sleeping area.) If awakened, the other 5 to 15 family members politely pretend to sleep. Parents approve of this practice and listen for sounds of laughter as a sign that their daughter is pleased with her partner. They also encourage their daughters to have a variety of lovers so that they may find a sexually compatible marriage partner. Young men gain social prestige through their ability to please their partners. These patterns persist on a daily basis throughout the adolescent years for unmarried men and women.

Sexual relations continue to occur frequently after marriage. A wide range of sexual activity is approved, including oral-genital sex and a considerable amount of touching before and during intercourse. Among the Mangaians, then, sexual activity is not only condoned but is actively encouraged.

Inis Beag A sharp contrast to Mangaian practices is provided by the community of the Irish island known as Inis Beag (a pseudonym used to protect the privacy of these people). Anthropologist John Messenger (1971) studied this society between 1958 and 1966. He observed that sexual expression is discouraged from infancy on: Mothers avoid breast-feeding their children, and after infancy parents seldom kiss or fondle them. Children learn to abhor nudity. They learn that elimination is "dirty" and that bathing must be done only in absolute privacy. Any kind of childhood sexual expression is punished.

As they grow older, children usually receive no information about sex from their parents. Young girls are often shocked by their first menstruation, and they are never given an adequate explanation of what has happened. Priests and other religious authorities teach that it is sinful to discuss premarital sexual activity, masturbation, or sex play. Religious leaders on the island have denounced even *Time* and *Life* magazines as pornographic.

Marriage partners generally know little or nothing about precoital sex play, like oral or manual stimulation of the breasts and genitals. Beyond intercourse, sexual activity is usually limited to mouth kissing and rough fondling of the woman's lower body by the man. Men invariably initiate sex, using the man-on-top coital position, and both partners usually wear night clothes during coitus. Female orgasm is unknown or considered a deviant response.

Sexual misconceptions continue through adulthood. For example, many women believe that menopause causes insanity, and some women confine themselves to bed from menopause to their death. During menstruation and also during the months following childbirth, men consider intercourse to be harmful to them. Many men also believe coitus to be debilitating, avoiding sex the night before a strenuous job. In general, sexual expression in Inis Beag is marked by anxiety-laden attitudes and rigid restrictions.

The Dani of New Guinea   In both Mangaia and Inis Beag, sexuality receives a great amount of attention, albeit in different ways. This is not characteristic of all societies, however. The Dani people of West New Guinea seem to be largely indifferent to sexuality (Heider, 1976). Sexual activity is infrequent among adults. Although courtship covers an extended period (marriages are held only during a certain feast that occurs every four to six years), there is almost no premarital sex. After marriage, a couple abstains from sex for at least two years and then has infrequent coitus. Following the birth of a child, husband and wife do not have sex for four to six years. During this time there is no reported masturbation, and extramarital sex is rare.

According to Karl Heider, who studied this society in the 1960s, the Dani culture does not overtly enforce these behavior patterns. Heider also observed no indications of hormonal or physiological deficiencies that could result in low sexual interest. In general, the Dani are relaxed, physically healthy people who live in a moderate climate and have an adequate food supply. They appear to be very calm, only rarely expressing anger. Heider believes that the apparent infrequency of sexual activity reflects the Dani's relaxed life style and their low level of emotional intensity.

SUGGESTED READINGS

Marshall, Donald, & Suggs, Robert (Eds.). (1971). *Human Sexual Behavior: Variations in the Ethnographic Spectrum.* Englewood Cliffs, NJ: Prentice Hall. A superb collection of eight articles that detail the sexual attitudes, behaviors, and mores of societies around the world.

Boston Women's Health Book Collective. (1984). *Our Bodies, Ourselves* (3rd ed.). New York: Simon & Schuster. A thorough exploration of female sexuality, anatomy, and physiology. The book has a strong emphasis on health care and covers such topics as sexual relationships, rape, sexually transmitted diseases, birth control, parenthood, and menopause.

Zilbergeld, Bernie. (1978). *Male Sexuality: A Guide to Sexual Fulfillment.* Boston: Little, Brown. An exceptionally well-written and informative treatment of male sexuality, including such topics as sexual functioning, self-awareness, and overcoming difficulties.

Fromm, Erich. (1963). *The Art of Loving.* New York: Bantam Books. A classic on the topic of love. Fromm elucidates the power of love to develop human potential within oneself and within a relationship.

Hanckel, Frances, & Cunningham, John. (1979). *A Way of Love, A Way of Life.* New York: Lothrop, Lee & Shepard. This book is written to inform people about what it means to be gay. It discusses how young people who are gay can know that they are, how to develop positive attitudes about themselves, how to tell family and friends, where to go for help, the history of gay rights, and variations in lifestyles.

Hatcher, Robert, et al. (1986). *Contraceptive Technology: 1986–1987.* New York: Irvington. A comprehensive up-to-date book about birth control, which includes a section about birth control and nutrition. A must for anyone who wants the latest information about the technology and effects of contraception.

Herzfeld, Judith. (1985). *Sense and Sensibility in Childbirth.* New York: Norton. A book that offers insights and advice on childbirth concerns.

Calderone, Mary, and Ramey, James. (1982). *Talking With Your Child About Sex.* New York: Random House. This excellent book provides practical and wise advice for parents who wish to raise sexually healthy children.

Blumstein, Philip, & Schwartz, Pepper. (1983). *American Couples.* New York: Morrow. This highly acclaimed book provides a wealth of information about current trends in relationships among couples—married and cohabiting, heterosexual and homosexual.

Kaplan, Helen. (1983). *The Evaluation of Sexual Disorders.* New York: Brunner/Mazel. A thorough and scholarly presentation of information about psychosexual and medical evaluation of sexual problems.

Lumiere, Richard, & Cook, Stephani. (1983). *Healthy Sex and Keeping It That Way*. New York: Simon & Schuster. A valuable resource guide to genital health and disease for the layperson.

Colao, Flora, & Hosansky, Tamar. (1983). *Your Children Should Know*. New York: Bobbs-Merrill. A very fine book written in an engaging syle that provides a wealth of information about preventing child sexual abuse and strategies for coping with such occurrences. Children, parents, educators, and health professionals all might profit from reading this excellent text.

The following four selections represent comprehensive human sexuality textbooks, written for the college student population, all of which provide excellent coverage of a broad spectrum of relevant topics.

Crooks, Robert, & Baur, Karla. (1987). *Our Sexuality* (3rd ed.). Menlo Park, CA: Benjamin/Cummings.

Allgeier, Elizabeth, & Allgeier, Albert. (1987). *Sexual Interactions* (2nd ed.). Lexington, MA: D.C. Heath.

Hyde, Janet. (1986). *Understanding Human Sexuality* (3rd ed.). New York: McGraw-Hill.

Masters, William, Johnson, Virginia, & Kolodny, Robert. (1985). *Human Sexuality* (2nd ed.). Boston: Little, Brown.

Abnormal behavior Behavior that is atypical, maladaptive, socially unacceptable, and produces psychological discomfort.

Absolute threshold The minimum physical intensity of a stimulus that can be perceived by an observer 50 percent of the time.

Accommodation In vision, the focusing process in which the lens adjusts its shape, depending on the distance between the eye and the object viewed, in order to project a clear image consistently onto the retina. In the theory of Jean Piaget, the process of adjusting existing knowledge so that new information can fit more readily.

Accumulating damages theory Theory that explains aging as a consequence of the accumulated insults and damages that result from an organism's continued use of its body. Also known as wear-and-tear theory.

Achievement need See Need for achievement.

Achievement test A test designed to measure an individual's learning (as opposed to the ability to learn new information).

Acquisition In classical conditioning, the process of learning to associate a conditioned stimulus with an unconditioned stimulus.

Acronym A meaningful arrangement of letters that provides a cue for recalling information; a mnemonic device.

Acrostics Sentences whose first letters serve as cues for recalling specific information; a mnemonic device.

Action potential The electrical signal that flows along the surface of the axon to the terminal buttons, initiating the release of neurotransmitters.

Active listening A key element of person-centered therapy, active listening is a technique in which therapists indicate their acceptance and understanding of what clients say.

Activity theory Theory that the more involved and active older people remain, the more happy and fulfilled they will be.

Adaptation In perception, the decrease in the response of sensory receptors to stimuli when exposed to continual, unchanging stimulation.

Additive color mixing Color mixing that occurs when lights of different wavelength simultaneously stimulate the retina, so that color perception depends on the adding or combining of these wavelengths. *See Subtractive color mixing.*

Adolescent growth spurt A period of accelerated growth that usually occurs within about two years after the onset of puberty.

Adrenal glands Glands within the endocrine system, located just above the kidneys, that influence emotional state, energy levels, and responses to stress.

Aerial perspective See Atmospheric perspective.

Afferent neuron See Sensory neuron.

Age regression A phenomenon reported to be associated with hypnosis, in which the hypnotized subject appears to move back in time to reenact events that occurred in earlier years. Age regression seems to be role-playing of the subject's current conception of his or her past.

Agoraphobia An anxiety disorder characterized by an intense fear of being in places or situations from which escape might be difficult or in which help might not be available, such as stores, theaters, and trains. Agoraphobia often accompanies panic disorder.

Alcohol A depressant drug that acts to impair motor coordination, reaction time, thinking, and judgment.

Algorithm Problem-solving strategy that involves a systematic exploration of every possible solution; computers use algorithms to find the correct answer.

All-or-none law An action potential will be passed through a neuron's axon as long as the sum of graded potentials reaches a threshold. The strength of an action potential does not vary according to the degree of stimulation.

Altered state of consciousness A nonnatural state of consciousness resulting from deliberate efforts to change one's state of consciousness, as through drugs, meditation, or hypnosis.

Alternate-forms reliability A method of assessing test reliability in which subjects take two different forms of a test that are very similar in content and level of difficulty.

Alternative state of consciousness A natural state of consciousness, such as sleep or daydreaming, that differs from normal conscious awareness. *See also Normal and altered states.*

Alzheimer's disease A currently incurable condition that destroys the capacity to remember, think, relate to others, and care for oneself.

Amniocentesis Method of prenatal screening for fetal

abnormalities in which a small sample of amniotic fluid is extracted from the uterus for chromosome analysis.

Amphetamines A group of powerful stimulants, including Benzedrine, Dexedrine, and Methedrine, that dramatically increase alertness and promote feelings of euphoria.

Amygdala A small limbic-system structure located next to the hippocampus in the brain that plays an important role in the expression of anger, rage, and aggressive behavior.

Anal stage In Freud's theory of psychosexual development, the period between about 12 months and 3 years, during which the erogenous zone shifts from the mouth to the anal area.

Androgens Male sex hormones, the most common of which is testosterone.

Anorexia nervosa Eating disorder characterized by prolonged refusal to eat adequate amounts of food.

Anterograde amnesia Memory loss for information an individual is exposed to after experiencing brain trauma, as through injury or chronic alcoholism.

Antiandrogens Drugs that have the effect of drastically reducing the amount of testosterone circulating in the bloodstream.

Antianxiety drugs Sometimes called minor tranquilizers, drugs in this class are used to reduce symptoms of anxiety and tension in disorders that are not severe enough to warrant hospitalization.

Antidepressant drugs Drugs that are used to treat major depression (unipolar disorder).

Antimanic drugs Drugs that are used for controlling the manic symptoms of bipolar disorder.

Antipsychotic drugs Any of a class of drugs that have the effect of calming and quieting patients with some psychotic disorders, most notably schizophrenia.

Antisocial personality disorder Personality disorder characterized by disregard for rights of others, lack of remorse or guilt for antisocial acts, irresponsibility in job or marital roles, failure to learn from experience, and a profound poverty of deep and lasting emotions.

Anxiety A free-floating fear with no easily identifiable source.

Anxiety disorder Any of a number of disorders that produce pervasive feelings of anxiety.

Aptitude test Test designed to predict an individual's ability to learn new information or skills.

Architectural psychology The study of the behavioral implications of building design.

Army Alpha and Beta tests Group IQ tests developed early in this century by the American Psychological Association to assist the Army in making job assignments for soldiers.

Arousal The state of mind and body, in which an individual is able to process information effectively and to engage in motivated behavior.

Artificial embryonation Procedure in which a female volunteer is artificially inseminated, and in about five days the embryo is transferred to the uterus of another woman who carries the baby through the remaining course of pregnancy.

Assessment centers Centers that conduct interviews and tests as well as simulate work situations in order to determine how well-suited job candidates are for managerial or executive-level positions.

Assimilation In Jean Piaget's theory, the process by which individuals interpret new information in accordance with existing knowledge or schemas.

Association cortex The largest portion of the cerebral cortex (about 75 percent), involved in integrating sensory and motor messages as well as processing higher mental functions such as thinking, interpreting, and remembering.

Associative learning Learning by making a connection or association between two events, through either classical conditioning or operant conditioning.

Atmospheric perspective A monocular distance cue based on the fact that distant objects tend to appear more fuzzy and less clear than those close to the viewer, due to dust and haze. Also known as aerial perspective.

Attachment An intense emotional tie between two individuals, such as an infant and a parent. *See also Indiscriminate attachment and Specific attachment.*

Attention A psychological selection mechanism that determines which stimuli an organism perceives.

Attitude Any learned, relatively enduring predisposition to respond in consistently favorable or unfavorable ways to certain people, groups, ideas, or situations.

Attribution theory Theory that we attempt to make sense out of other people's behavior by attributing it to either dispositional (internal) causes or external causes.

Auditory cortex The region of the temporal lobe located just below the lateral fissure that is involved in responding to auditory signals, particularly the sound of human speech.

Auditory localization The ability to locate the origins of sounds by differences from ear to ear in variables such as intensity and the time the sound arrives at each ear.

Auditory memory See Echoic memory.

Authoritarian Style of parenting in which parents rely on strictly enforced rules, leaving little room for children to discuss alternatives.

Authoritarian personality Personality characterized by intolerance, emotional coldness, rigidity, submission to higher authority, stereotyped thinking, and identification with power.

Authoritative Style of parenting in which parents enforce clear rules and standards but also show respect for children's opinions.

Autonomic nervous system The division of the peripheral nervous system that transmits messages between the central nervous system and the glands as well as the smooth muscles of the heart, lungs, stomach and other internal organs that operate without intentional control.

Availability heuristic Approach to decision making based on information assessed from memory. It assumes that the probability of an event is related to how frequently it occurred in the past, and that events that occur more frequently are easier to remember.

Aversive conditioning A classical conditioning behavior therapy approach which substitutes a negative response for positive responses to inappropriate stimuli.

Avoidance conditioning In operant conditioning, the learning of a response to a discriminative stimulus that allows an organism to avoid exposure to an unpleasant stimulus.

Awareness One's subjective sense of oneself, one's actions, and one's environment.

Axon Extension of a neuron that transmits an impulse from the cell body to terminal buttons on the tip of the axon.

Backward conditioning In classical conditioning, presenting the unconditioned stimulus prior to the conditioned stimulus.

Balance theory Theory that people are inclined to achieve consistency in their attitudes by balancing their beliefs and feelings about a particular issue, object, event, or situation against their attitudes about other people.

Basic level In a concept hierarchy, the classification that people naturally use when they think about an object. (For instance, a yellow-throated warbler is simply "a bird.")

Basilar membrane The membrane in the cochlea of the inner ear that vibrates in response to pressure waves, causing auditory hair cells on the adjoining Organ of Corti to release neurotransmitters that activate neurons of the auditory nerve.

Behavior therapy Therapy based on the assumption that maladaptive behavior has been learned and can therefore be unlearned.

Behavioral geography An application of cognitive map theory based on people's perceptions or internal representations of relationships between geographical locations.

Behavioral medicine The study of how behavior and state of mind can influence physical as well as mental health.

Behavioral observation Personality assessment method that involves observing an individual's behavior as he or she interacts with the environment.

Behavioral toxicology The study of how environmental toxins affect behavior, and how psychological problems are related to environmental pollutants.

Behaviorism The approach to psychology that focuses on the relationship between environmental events (stimuli) and an organism's response to them, emphasizing objectively verifiable phenomena.

Belief-bias effect The tendency to accept conclusions that conform to one's beliefs (and reject conclusions that do not conform) regardless of how logical these conclusions are.

Binocular cues Visual cues for depth or distance, such as binocular disparity and convergence, that depend on both eyes working together.

Binocular disparity The difference in the retinal image of an object as seen from each eye, due to the difference in viewing angles, that provides an important binocular cue for depth. Also known as retinal disparity.

Biofeedback Technique providing individuals with information about their bodily processes that they can use to modify those processes.

Biologically based motives Motives such as hunger and thirst that are rooted primarily in body tissue needs; sometimes referred to as drives.

Bipolar (manic-depressive) disorder A mood disorder characterized by intermittent episodes of both depression and mania (highly energized behavior).

Body senses A term used to describe the two interrelated sensory systems of kinesthesis and equilibrium.

Brain stimulation A technique for studying the brain that involves stimulating precise regions with a weak electric current.

Brightness The intensity of light, measured by the number of photons, or particles of electromagnetic radiation, emitted by a light source.

Brightness constancy An element of perceptual constancy: we perceive objects that we see at night or in poor lighting to be the same brightness as they appear during the day.

Broca's area The region of the left frontal lobe that is the primary brain center for controlling speech.

Bulimia Eating disorder characterized by periodic episodes of binge eating followed by deliberate purging using either vomiting or laxatives.

Caffeine A stimulant found in coffee, tea, and chocolate that acts to increase heart rate and blood pressure.

California Psychological Inventory (CPI) A global personality assessment test designed specifically for use with normal populations.

Cannon-Bard theory Theory that emotions occur simultaneously with physiological changes, rather than deriving from body changes as the James-Lange theory suggests.

Cardinal trait In Gordon Allport's trait theory of personality, a powerful, dominating behavioral predisposition that is an organizing principle in a small number of people's lives. *See also Central trait* and *Secondary trait.*

Case study A method of research that involves in-depth study of one or more subjects who are examined individually using direct observation, testing, experimentation, and other methods.

Catatonic schizophrenia Subtype of schizophrenia characterized by extreme psychomotor disturbances, which may range from stuporous immobility to wild excitement and agitation.

Cell body The largest part of a neuron, containing the nucleus as well as structures that handle metabolic functions.

Central nervous system (CNS) The part of the nervous system that consists of the brain and the spinal cord.

Central trait In Gordon Allport's trait theory of personality, a major characteristic such as honesty or sensitivity. *See also Cardinal trait* and *Secondary trait.*

Centration In Jean Piaget's theory of cognitive development, centration (the inability to take into account more than one perceptual factor at a time) is characteristic of the preoperational stage of development.

Cephalocaudal Pattern of physical and motor development that is normal among humans, in which the head and upper portion of the body develops first and most rapidly.

Cerebellum A brain structure located beneath the overhanging back part of the cerebral hemispheres which functions to coordinate and regulate motor movements.

Cerebral cortex The thin outer layer of the brain's cerebrum (sometimes called the "gray matter") that is responsible for higher mental processes, including perceiving, thinking, and remembering.

Cerebral hemispheres The two sides (right and left) of the cerebrum.

Cerebrum The largest part of the brain, consisting of two cerebral hemispheres.

Chorionic villi sampling (CVS) Method of prenatal screening for fetal abnormalities in which threadlike protrusions on the membrane surrounding the fetus are extracted and cultured for chromosome analysis.

Chunk A meaningful unit of short-term memory. *See also Chunking.*

Chunking The process of grouping items into longer meaningful units to make them easier to remember.

Classical conditioning Learning that takes place when a neutral stimulus (the CS) is paired with a stimulus (UCS) that already produces a response (UCR). The organism then responds to the neutral stimulus in the same way (CR) as to the UCS.

Climacteric The physiological changes, including menopause, that occur during a woman's transition from fertility to infertility.

Clinical psychology An area of specialization involved in the diagnosis and treatment of psychological problems.

Closure The perceptual organizing principle that we tend to perceive incomplete figures as complete.

Clustering A mnemonic device involving grouping items into categories.

Cocaine A powerful central nervous system stimulant derived from the leaves of the coca shrub.

Cochlea A coiled, fluid-filled chamber in the inner ear with two flexible surfaces, the oval window and the round window.

Coefficient of correlation The statistic used to describe the amount and type of relationship between variables. Positive correlations indicate that variables vary together in the same direction, while negative correlations indicate the opposite.

Cognitive abilities test (CAT) A group intelligence test widely used in many school systems.

Cognitive dissonance theory Theory that people experience psychological discomfort or dissonance whenever two related cognitions are in conflict.

Cognitive learning Learning that involves complex processes such as thinking, reasoning, and memory.

Cognitive learning theory The theoretical perspective that attempts to clarify the role of mental processes in learning.

Cognitive map A mental picture of the relationship between events or spatial elements.

Cognitive psychology The approach to psychology that focuses on mental processes such as thinking, language, problem solving, and creativity that intervene between stimuli and responses, and on the ways in which organisms process information.

Cognitive restructuring therapy A cognitive therapy aimed at restructuring irrational thinking patterns such as the tendency to use negative self-labels.

Cognitive therapies Approaches to therapy that are based on the premise that most psychological disorders result from distortions in cognitions or thoughts.

Cohabitation Living together in a sexual relationship without being married.

Color constancy An element of perceptual constancy: we perceive objects that we see in the dark to be the same color as they appear during the day even though their retinal images change.

Companionate love Type of love characterized by friendly affection and deep attachment based on extensive familiarity. *See also Passionate love.*

Compensatory model Decision-making model such as the additive model and the utility-probability model in which the desirable potential outcomes of alternative choices are weighed against undesirable potential outcomes. Compare with *Noncompensatory model.*

Complex psychosocial motives Motives that demonstrate little or no relationship to biological needs, but are determined by learning.

Compliance A form of social influence in which a person alters his or her behavior in response to direct requests from others, which usually involve a degree of coercion.

Computerized axial tomography (CAT) A technique used to locate brain abnormalities that involves rotating an X-ray scanner around the skull to produce an accurate image of a living brain.

Concepts Cognitive categories for grouping events, objects, or processes.

Concordance The degree to which twins share a trait.

Concrete operations stage The third stage of cognitive development in Jean Piaget's theory (ages 7–12), during which children begin to use logical mental operations or rules, mastering the concept of conservation.

Concurrent validity A type of criterion-related validity that involves comparing test performance to other criteria that are currently available. *See also Predictive validity.*

Conditioned reinforcer See Secondary reinforcer.

Conditioned response (CR) In classical conditioning, a learned response to a stimulus.

Conditioned stimulus (CS) In classical conditioning, a stimulus that an organism learns to respond to in a certain way.

Conduction hearing loss Hearing loss caused by the failure of the outer and middle ear to conduct sound energy to the inner ear's receptors, sometimes due to infection or to build-up of ear wax.

Cones Photoreceptor cells distributed across the inner layer of the retina that play an important role in the perception of color.

Confirmation bias In problem solving, the tendency to seek out evidence that confirms a hypothesis and to overlook contradictory evidence.

Conformity The tendency to change or modify beliefs and behaviors so that they are consistent with those of other people.

Consciousness The mental state of awareness of processes that are going on inside or outside one's own body.

Conservation The understanding that changing the form of an object does not necessarily change its essential character. Conservation is a key achievement in Piaget's theory of cognitive development. *See also Concrete operations stage.*

Consolidation The process by which information is transferred from short-term electrical activation of neuronal circuits to a longer-term memory coded by physical cell changes in the brain.

Content One of three major intellectual functions in J. P. Guilford's structure of intellect model, content refers to what we think about. *See also Operations and products.*

Continuous reinforcement schedule In operant conditioning, the reinforcement of a behavior every time it occurs.

Control group In experimental psychology, a group of subjects who experience all the same conditions as subjects in the experimental group except for the key factor the researcher is evaluating.

Controlled drinking Technique for overcoming alcoholism through teaching skills that allow a person to drink in moderation.

Conventional morality The second level in Lawrence Kohlberg's theory of moral development, consisting of stages 3 and 4, in which the motivating force for moral behavior is the desire either to help others or to gain approval.

Convergence The binocular distance cue based on the fact that the two eyes must converge or rotate toward the inside to perceive objects closer than about 25 feet. The closer the object, the more rotation is necessary and the more muscle tension is created.

Convergent thinking Thinking in which an individual responds to information presented in a problem by eliminating possibilities and narrowing his or her responses down to the single best solution.

Conversion disorder A somatoform disorder that is manifested as a sensory or motor-system disorder for which there is no known organic cause.

Coronary heart disease (CHD) Any illness that causes a narrowing of the coronary arteries.

Corpus callosum A broad band of nerve fibers that connects the left and right hemispheres of the cerebral cortex.

Correlation coefficient See Coefficient of correlation.

Correlational method A research method that uses statistical techniques to determine relationships between variables.

Correspondent inference theory Theory that the attributions we make about other people's behavior are influenced by a variety of conditions, such as the social desirability of that behavior or whether the behavior results from free choice.

Counseling psychology An area of specialization involved in the diagnosis and treatment of problems of adjustment. Counseling psychologists tend to focus on less serious problems than clinical psychologists; they often work in settings such as schools.

Couple therapy Therapy in which partners meet together with a therapist.

Covariation principle Theory that our attributions about people's behavior are influenced by the situations in which the behavior occurs, the persons involved, and the stimuli or objects toward which the behavior is directed.

Crack Street name for a processed form of cocaine that takes effect more rapidly and is available at a cheaper price than powdered cocaine.

Creativity The ability to produce outcomes that are novel as well as useful or valuable.

Credibility The quality of trustworthiness and perceived expertise that increases the likelihood that a communicator will persuade an individual to change his or her attitude.

Criterion-keyed test An assessment test in which each test item is referenced to one of the original criterion groups that were used in developing the test.

Criterion-related validity A method of assessing test validity that involves comparing peoples' test scores with their scores on other measures already known to be good indicators of the skill or trait being assessed.

Critical periods According to one point of view, periods in the developmental sequence during which an infant or child must experience certain kinds of social or sensory experiences in order for normal development to take place.

Cross-sectional design Research design in which groups of subjects of different ages are assessed and compared at one point in time, so that conclusions may be drawn about behavior differences that may be related to age differences.

Cross-sequential design Research design which combines elements of the cross-sectional and longitudinal designs. Here, subjects in a cross-sectional sample are observed more than once over a period of time.

Crowding A psychological response to a lack of space, characterized by subjective feelings of overstimulation, distress, and discomfort.

Crystallized intelligence Intelligence that results from accumulated knowledge, including knowledge of how to reason, language skills, and understanding of technology. *See also Fluid intelligence.*

Cultural mores Established customs or beliefs in a particular culture.

Cumulative curve A measure of the strength of operant conditioning; the more frequently an operant response takes place, the steeper the curve.

Dark adaptation The process by which an organism's vision gradually becomes more sensitive to minimal levels of light, due to a chemical change in the rods and cones of the retina.

Decentration The ability to evaluate two or more physical dimensions simultaneously. *See also Centration.*

Declarative memory Recall of specific facts, such as information read in a book. *See also Procedural memory, Episodic memory,* and *Semantic memory.*

Deductive reasoning Reasoning that begins with a general premise that is believed to be true, then draws conclusions about specific instances based on this premise. *See also Inductive reasoning.*

Defense mechanism In Freud's psychoanalytic theory, an unconscious maneuver that shields the ego from anxiety by denying or distorting reality.

Delayed conditioning In classical conditioning, learning that takes place when the conditioned stimulus is presented just before the unconditioned stimulus is presented and continues until the organism begins responding to the unconditioned stimulus.

Delusion An exaggerated and rigidly held belief that has little or no basis in fact.

Dendrite Branchlike extension from a neuron with the specialized function of receiving messages from surrounding neurons.

Density In environmental psychology, a physical attribute measured by the number of people in a given space.

Dependent variable In experimental research, the behavior that results from manipulation of an independent variable.

Depressant drugs Psychoactive drugs, including opiates, sedatives, and alcohol, that have the effect of slowing down or depressing central nervous system activity.

Descriptive statistics A mathematical method for reducing statistical data to a form that can be readily understood.

Developmental psychology A field of specialization in psychology concerned with factors that influence development and shape behavior throughout the life cycle, from conception through old age.

Dialectic operations A fifth stage of cognitive development (after Piaget's fourth stage of formal operations) proposed by Klaus Riegel, in which an individual realizes and accepts that conflict and contradiction are natural consequences of living.

Difference threshold The minimum difference in intensity that we can distinguish between two stimuli 50 percent of the time. Also known as the just noticeable difference (jnd).

Diffusion of responsibility The tendency for an individual to feel a diminished sense of responsibility to assist in an emergency when other bystanders are present.

Discrimination In classical conditioning, the process by which generalized responses are restricted to specific conditioned stimuli. In social psychology, the behavioral consequence of prejudice in which one group is treated differently from another group.

Discriminative stimulus In operant conditioning, a stimulus that controls a response by signaling the availability of reinforcement.

Disengagement theory Theory that maintains that individuals are more likely to experience happiness in older age if they cut back on the stresses of active life, taking time to relax instead.

Disorganized schizophrenia A subtype of schizophrenia characterized by marked disorganization and regression in thinking and behavioral patterns, accompanied by sudden mood swings and often hallucinations. Also known as hebephrenic schizophrenia.

Displacement Defense mechanism in which a person diverts his or her impulse-driven behavior from a primary target to secondary targets that will arouse less anxiety.

Dissociative disorders The group of disorders, including psychogenic amnesia, psychogenic fugue, and multiple personality, in which the thoughts and feelings that generate anxiety are separated or dissociated from conscious awareness.

Divergent thinking Thinking in which an individual comes up with unusual but appropriate responses to questions, often associated with creativity.

Dizygotic twins See Fraternal twins.

DNA (deoxyribonucleic acid) Chemical substance whose molecules, arranged in varying patterns, are the building blocks of genes.

Dominant gene A gene that prevails when paired with a recessive gene, so that it is always expressed in the phenotype.

Door-in-the-face technique Method for encouraging compliance in which an unreasonable request is followed by a more minor, reasonable request (which is the requester's goal in the first place).

Down's syndrome A chromosomal disorder characterized by marked mental retardation as well as distinctive physical traits including short stature, a flattened skull and nose, and an extra fold of skin over the eyelid.

Dream analysis Psychoanalytic technique involving the interpretation of dreams to learn about hidden aspects of personality.

Drive A term commonly used to describe motives that are based on tissue needs, such as hunger and thirst.

Dual-code model of memory The theory that memories may be stored either in sensory codes or in verbal codes.

Dual hypothalamic control theory Theory that the ventromedial hypothalamus and the lateral hypothalamus operate together to maintain a relatively constant state of satiety.

Echoic memory Auditory sensory memory; fleeting impressions of what we hear. Also known as auditory memory.

Echolalia A speech disturbance characteristic of some forms of schizophrenia in which a person repeats virtually every statement he or she hears uttered.

Educational psychology The field of specialization in psychology concerned with the study and application of learning and teaching methods, focusing on areas such as improving educational curricula and training teachers.

Efferent neuron See Motor neuron.

Ego In Sigmund Freud's psychoanalytic theory, the component of personality that acts as an intermediary between the instinctual demands of the id and the reality of the real world. *See also Id, Superego,* and *Reality principle.*

Ego-defensive function Negative function served by prejudicial attitudes which bolster a person's self-esteem by letting him or her feel superior to another group of people.

Eidetic imagery Also known as photographic memory, the very rare ability to retain large amounts of visual material with great accuracy for several minutes.

Elaborative rehearsal A system for remembering that involves using mnemonic devices; it is more effective than maintenance rehearsal.

Electra complex According to Sigmund Freud, the sexual attraction that a girl may feel toward her father (and jealousy toward her mother) during the phallic stage of psychosexual development.

Electrical recording A technique for studying the brain in which tiny wires implanted in the brain are used to record neural electrical activity.

Electroconvulsive therapy (ECT) Biomedical intervention in which electrical current applied to the brain induces a convulsive seizure.

Electroencephalography (EEG) A technique used to measure and record electrical activity of the cortex.

Embryonic stage The second stage of prenatal development, lasting from the beginning of the third week to the end of the eighth week after fertilization, characterized by fast growth and differentiation of the major body systems as well as vital organs.

Emotions An individual's subjective feelings and moods that are expressions of complex cognitive and physiological states.

Empathic understanding A key element of person-centered therapy, referring to therapists' ability to see the world as the client sees it.

Encoding In memory, the process of perceiving information, then categorizing or organizing it in a meaningful way so that it can be more easily stored and recalled.

Endocrine system The system of ductless glands, including the pituitary, thyroid, parathyroids, adrenals, pancreas, and gonads, that secrete hormones directly into the bloodstream or lymph fluids.

Endogenous opiates Morphinelike substances occurring naturally in the brain that act as neurotransmitters and also act to inhibit or increase the activity of other transmitters.

Engineering psychology Sometimes called human factors psychology, engineering psychology is concerned with creating optimal relationships among people, the machines they operate, and the environments they work in.

Environmental psychology The field of specialization in psychology concerned with assessing the effects of environmental factors such as noise, pollution, or overcrowding on behavior.

Episodic memory Autobiographical memories about one's own experiences.

Equilibrium The sense of balance, localized within the inner ear and comprising two sensory receptors: the semicircular canals and the vestibular sacs.

Ergonomics See Human factors.

Escape conditioning In operant conditioning, learning that takes place when an organism performs a response that will terminate an unpleasant stimulus.

Estrogens Hormones that influence female sexual development.

Excitatory postsynaptic potentials (EPSPs) The effects that occur when excitatory neurotransmitters cause a graded potential to be released in the dendrite or cell body of a receiving neuron when they come in contact with the postsynaptic membrane.

Excitement The first phase in the sexual response pattern of men and women, characterized by increased muscle tension, heart rate, and blood pressure.

Exemplar theory Theory that the natural concepts we form in everyday life are structured around prototypes or typical representatives of categories (such as robins and jays as prototypes of the concept "bird").

Experimental groups In experimental research, groups of subjects who are exposed to different varieties of independent variables, so that resulting behaviors can be compared.

Experimental psychology The field of specialization in psychology in which the primary activity is conducting research.

Experimental research Research conducted in precisely controlled laboratory conditions in which subjects are confronted with specific stimuli and their reactions are carefully measured to discover relationships among variables.

Extinction In classical conditioning, the process by which a conditioned stimulus is extinguished through repeated presentation of the conditioned stimulus without the unconditioned stimulus.

Facial feedback theory Theory that specific facial displays are universally associated with the expression of the emotions of fear, anger, happiness, sadness, surprise, interest, disgust, and shame.

False consensus bias Attribution bias caused by the assumption that most people share our own attitudes and behaviors.

Family therapy Therapy in which family members meet together with a therapist.

Fetal alcohol syndrome (FAS) A variety of developmental complications including spontaneous abortion, premature birth, infants born addicted to alco-

hol, and numerous developmental disabilities which are related to the mother's use of alcohol during pregnancy.

Fetal stage The third and final stage of prenatal development, extending from the beginning of the third month to birth, during which bone and muscle tissue form and the organs and body systems continue to develop.

Fetus The name used to describe an unborn infant during the period from the beginning of the third month after fertilization until birth.

Figure In perception, the part of an image on which we focus our attention.

Fixation In Freud's theory of psychosexual development, arrested development that results from exposure to either too little or too much gratification.

Fixed interval (FI) schedule A partial reinforcement schedule in operant conditioning wherein reinforcement is provided for the first response after a specified period of time has elapsed.

Fixed ratio (FR) schedule A partial reinforcement schedule in operant conditioning wherein reinforcement occurs after a fixed number of responses.

Flashbulb memory Vivid recall for an extremely emotional event, such as the assassination of a president or the death of a relative.

Flextime An approach to scheduling work hours in which employees have some flexibility in picking starting and quitting times, as long as they are present during core work hours.

Fluid intelligence The ability to perceive and draw inferences about relationships among patterns of stimuli, to conceptualize abstract information, and to solve problems. *See also Crystallized intelligence.*

Foot-in-the-door technique Technique for encouraging compliance in which a person is first encouraged to agree to a relatively minor request that serves as a set-up for a more major request.

Forensic psychology The field of specialization in psychology that works with the legal, court, and correctional systems for purposes such as developing personality profiles of criminals, making decisions about disposition of convicted offenders, and helping law enforcers understand behavioral problems.

Formal concepts Logical, clearly defined concepts with unambiguous rules specifying what features belong to that category.

Formal-operations stage The fourth and final stage in Jean Piaget's theory of cognitive development (ages 12+), during which individuals acquire the ability to make complex deductions and solve problems by systematically testing hypotheses.

Fraternal twins Twins produced when two ova are fertilized by two different sperm cells, so that their genetic codes are no more similar than those of any other siblings.

Free association Psychoanalytic technique developed by Sigmund Freud in which patients relax and say whatever comes to their minds.

Frequency theory of pitch discrimination The theory that perception of low tones depends on the frequency with which auditory hair cells in the inner ear's organ of Corti trigger the firing of neurons in the auditory nerve. *See also Volley theory.*

Frontal lobe The largest lobe in the cerebral cortex; an important center for both the association and motor cortex.

Frustration-aggression hypothesis Theory that aggression is always a consequence of frustration, and that frustration always leads to aggression.

Functional fixedness The tendency to be so set in our perception of the proper function of a given object that we are unable to think of using it in a novel way to solve a problem.

Functionalism The approach to psychology that emphasized the functional, practical nature of conscious mind. Influenced by Darwin's theory of natural selection, functionalists attempted to learn how mental processes such as thinking and perceiving helped people adapt.

Fundamental attribution error A tendency to overestimate dispositional, or internal, causes and to underestimate external causes for other people's behavior.

G-factor One of the two factors in Charles Spearman's conceptualization of intelligence, the g-factor consists of general intelligence, which is largely genetically determined. *See also S-factor.*

Gamete The reproductive cells, or sperm and ovum. Also known as germ cells.

Gate-control theory The theory that neural "gates" in the spinal cord allow passage of pain signals to the brain; these gates may be closed by the simultaneous firing of nonpain nerve fibers, so that pain is not perceived.

Gender identity An individual's subjective sense of being male or female.

Gender role The set of behaviors that is considered normal and appropriate for each sex in a society.

Gene The "chemical blueprints" of all living things. Genes are made of DNA molecules, and each chromosome contains thousands of genes.

Gene therapy See Genetic engineering.

General adaptation syndrome (GAS) The response to stress described by Hans Selye, in which when an organism is confronted with a stressor, its body mobilizes for action.

Generalization The process by which an organism responds to stimuli that are similar to the conditioned stimulus, without undergoing conditioning for each similar stimulus.

Generalized anxiety disorder A chronic state of free-floating anxiety that is omnipresent.

Genetic clock theory Theory of aging that maintains that aging is built into every organism through a genetic code that preprograms the body cells to stop functioning at a certain point. Also known as programed theory.

Genetic counseling Counseling that uses information about family histories as well as medical and laboratory investigations to predict the likelihood that a couple will have children with certain disorders.

Genetic engineering Also known as gene therapy, a process that uses recombinant DNA techniques to insert a new gene into cells to alter and correct a defective genetic code.

Genital stage The fifth and final stage in Freud's theory of psychosexual development, beginning with puberty, during which sexual feelings that were dormant during the latency stage reemerge.

Genotype The assortment of genes each individual inherits at conception.

Genuineness An important element of person-centered therapy, referring to therapists' ability to be in touch with their own current feelings or attitudes.

Germ cell See Gamete.

Germinal stage The first of three stages in prenatal development of a fetus. The germinal stage spans the first two weeks after fertilization. Also known as the zygote stage.

Gestalt psychology The approach to psychology that argues that the whole of an experience is different from the sum of its parts. Gestalt psychology is an active force in current investigations of perceptual processes and learning as well as therapy, where it emphasizes the "whole person."

Gestalt therapy Therapy approach that attempts to help individuals bring the alienated fragments of their personalities into an integrated, unified whole.

Glia cells Specialized cells that form insulating covers called myelin sheaths around the axons of some neurons, increasing conductivity.

Glucostatic theory Theory that hunger results when glucoreceptors detect a lack of availability of glucose, either because blood levels of glucose are low or because insulin is not available in sufficient quantity.

Gonadotropins Hormones released by the pituitary gland that stimulate production of testosterone in men and estrogen in women.

Gonads Glands within the endocrine system (ovaries in females and testes in males) that produce sex hormones that influence development of sexual systems and secondary sex characteristics as well as sexual motivation.

Good continuation The perceptual grouping principle that we are more likely to perceive stimuli as a whole or single group if they flow smoothly into one another than if they are discontinuous.

Graded potential Voltage change in a neuron's dendrites that is produced by receiving an impulse from another neuron or neurons.

Ground In perception, the background against which the figure that we focus on stands. *See also Figure.*

Group therapy Therapy in which three or more clients meet simultaneously with a therapist.

Gustation The sense of taste, which like olfaction is activated by chemical senses in the environment.

Hallucination False perception that lacks a sensory basis.

Hallucinogens A class of psychoactive drugs, including LSD and PCP, that alter sensory perceptions, thinking processes, and emotions, often causing delusions, hallucinations, and altered sense of time and space.

Halo effect The tendency to infer other positive or negative traits from our perception of one central trait in another person.

Health psychology The area of specialization in psychology concerned with the interaction between psychological factors and physical health.

Height on a plane An important monocular depth cue based on the fact that objects that are highest on one's plane of view appear to be farthest away.

Heterozygous Genotype that contains different genes for a trait (for instance, both brown-eye and blue-eye genes).

Heuristics Rule-of-thumb ("quick-fix") problem-solving strategies, such as means-ends analysis and working backward.

Higher order conditioning In classical conditioning, the process by which a conditioned stimulus is used to condition the same response to other stimuli.

Hippocampus A structure in the brain's limbic system that seems to play an important role in memory.

Homozygous Genotype that consists of the same genes for a trait (for instance, brown-eye genes inherited from both parents).

Hormones Chemical messengers secreted by the endocrine glands that act to regulate the functioning of specific body organs.

Hospice A facility designed to care for the special needs of the dying, including love and support, pain control, and maintaining a sense of dignity.

Hue The color we perceive, determined partly by the wavelength of light and partly by the complex process by which an organism's visual system mixes wavelengths.

Human factors The area of research related to I/O psychology that focuses on the interface between human characteristics and the equipment, products, environments, and systems that humans use in the performance of their jobs.

Humanistic psychology The approach to psychology that emphasizes the role of free choice and our ability to make conscious rational decisions about how we live our lives.

Huntington's disease Also known as Huntington's chorea, a genetically transmitted disease that progressively destroys brain cells in adults.

Hypertension Commonly referred to as high blood pressure; a condition of excessive blood flow through the vessels that can result in both hardening and general deterioration of the walls of the vessels.

Hypnosis A state of altered consciousness characterized by a deep relaxation and detachment as well as heightened suggestibility to the hypnotist's directives.

Hypochondriasis A somatoform disorder in which the individual is excessively fearful of contracting a serious illness or of dying.

Hypogonadism A state of androgen deprivation resulting from certain diseases of the endocrine system.

Hypothalamus A small structure located below the thalamus in the brain which plays an important role in motivation and emotional expression, as well as controlling the neuroendocrine system and maintaining the body's homeostasis. The hypothalamus is part of the limbic system.

Hypothesis A statement proposing the existence of a relationship between variables, typically as a tentative explanation for psychological events. Hypotheses are often designed to be tested by research.

Iconic memory Visual sensory memory, including fleeting impressions of what we see. Also known as visual memory.

Id In Freud's psychoanalytic theory, the biological component of personality consisting of life instincts and death instincts. See also ego, superego, libido, and pleasure principle.

Identical twins Twins who share the same genetic code. Also known as one-egg or monozygotic twins.

Illusion A false or inaccurate perception that differs from the actual physical state of the perceived object.

Illusion of control Attributional bias caused by the belief that we control events in our own lives that are beyond our control.

Implicit personality theories Assumptions people make about how traits usually occur together in other people's personalities.

Impression management The tendency of individuals to select carefully what information they reveal about their attitudes, depending on how they think such information will affect their image in the eyes of others.

Imprinting The process by which certain infant animals, such as ducklings, learn to follow or approach the first moving object they see. *See also Critical period.*

Incentive Any external stimulus that can motivate behavior even when no internal drive state exists.

Independent variable A condition or factor that the experimenter manipulates in a psychological experiment in order to determine whether changes in behavior (the dependent variable) result.

Indiscriminant attachment The attachment typically displayed by human infants during the first few months, when social behaviors are directed to virtually anyone. *See also Specific attachment* and *Separate attachment.*

Inductive reasoning Reasoning that draws broad conclusions by generalizing from specific instances. *See also Deductive reasoning.*

Industrial/organizational (I/O) psychology The field of specialization in psychology that is concerned with using psychological concepts to make the workplace a more satisfying environment for employees and management.

Inferential statistics The process of using mathematical procedures to draw conclusions about the meaning of statistical data.

Information processing An emerging approach to understanding psychology that uses computers to help develop models of cognitive processing of information.

Informational social influence One basis of conformity, in which we accept a group's beliefs or behaviors as providing accurate information about reality. *See also Normative social influence.*

Ingroup In social psychology, the group in which people include themselves when they divide the world into "us" and "them."

Ingroup bias The tendency to see one's own group in a favorable light.

Inhibitory postsynaptic potentials (IPSPs) These effects occur when inhibitory neurotransmitters that inhibit the postsynaptic membrane of a receiving neuron from releasing a graded potential.

Insight A sudden recognition of relationships that leads to the solution of a complex problem.

Insomnia Sleep disorder characterized by a consistent inability to get to sleep or by frequent awakenings during sleep.

Instincts Innate patterns of behavior that occur in every normally functioning member of a species under certain set conditions.

Intelligence An operational definition states simply that intelligence is that which intelligence tests measure, although intelligence is commonly understood to include the abilities to think rationally and abstractly, act purposefully, and deal effectively with the environment.

Intelligence quotient (IQ) Intelligence measurement derived by dividing an individual's mental age by the chronological age, then multiplying by 100.

Interneurons Neurons of the central nervous system that function as intermediaries between sensory and motor neurons.

Interpersonal aggression Any physical or verbal behavior intended to hurt another person.

Interposition See Overlap.

Interview Method used in psychological studies in which an individual is asked questions. Interviews may be informal and unstructured or they may be highly structured.

James-Lange theory Theory that explains emotional states (such as fear) as resulting from an organism's awareness of bodily responses to a situation, rather than from cognitions about that situation.

Just noticeable difference (jnd) See Difference threshold.

Karotype Chart in which photographs of an individual's chromosomes are arranged according to size and structure.

Kinesthesis The body sense that provides information about perceptions of the location of various body parts in relation to other parts and about the position of the body in space.

Language acquisition device (LAD) In the genetic or nativist view, the "prewiring" that gives humans the innate ability to learn language.

Latency period The fourth stage of psychosexual development in Sigmund Freud's theory, extending from about age five to puberty, during which sexual drives remain unexpressed or latent.

Latent content In psychoanalytic theory, the hidden content or true meaning of dreams.

Latent learning Learning that is not demonstrated by an immediately observable change in behavior.

Lateral hypothalamus (LH) One of two areas in the hypothalamus that seem to act as a control center for eating. Destruction of the LH causes dramatic reduction in feeding behavior, while stimulation causes overeating. *See also Ventromedial hypothalamus; Dual hypothalamic control theory.*

Lateralization of function The degree to which a particular function, such as the understanding of speech, is controlled by one rather than both cerebral hemispheres.

Law of effect The theory proposed by Edward Thorndike that is the foundation of operant conditioning theory, that behavior followed by a satisfying consequence will be strengthened.

Leaderless group discussion Technique used in some assessment centers that places several job applicants in a group and asks them to solve a business problem while many realistic emergencies and interruptions occur.

Leadership A series of behaviors an individual performs that coordinate the actions of others to accomplish a goal or goals.

Learned helplessness The belief that an individual has no

control over the rewards and punishments in his or her life.

Learning A relatively enduring change in potential behavior that results from experience.

Lesion production A technique for studying the brain that involves surgical damage to a precise region of the brain.

Libido In Freud's psychoanalytic theory, the energy that fuels the id and motivates all behavior.

Life review Process by which older people may retrospectively view their past, sorting out their accomplishments from their disappointments.

Light adaptation The process by which an organism's vision adjusts to bright lighting, due to a chemical change within the rods and cones of the retina.

Limbic system A collection of structures located around the central core of the brain that play a critical role in emotional expression as well as motivation, learning, and memory. Key structures of the limbic system include the amygdala, the hippocampus, the septal area, and parts of the hypothalamus.

Linear perspective An important monocular distance cue based on the fact that parallel lines converge when stretched into the distance.

Lipostatic theory Theory that explains long-term eating control as a result of a constant monitoring of levels of body fat, which is used as a barometer to regulate food intake. *See also Set point.*

Lobotomy Surgical procedure which severs the nerve tracts connecting the frontal cortex to lower brain areas that mediate emotional responses.

Longitudinal design Research design that evaluates a group of subjects at several points in time, over a number of years, to assess how certain characteristics or behaviors change during the course of development.

Long-term memory (LTM) The third memory system in the three-system model of memory. Information transferred from short-term to long-term memory may be stored for periods of time from minutes to years.

Loudness In hearing, the intensity of a sound as measured by decibels. Loudness is determined by the amplitude of a sound wave.

LSD (Lysergic acid diethylamide) Hallucinogenic drug derived from a fungus that grows on rye grass that produces profound distortions of sensations, feelings, time, and thought.

Lucid dreaming The process of being aware that one is dreaming and of influencing the content of one's own dreams.

Maintenance rehearsal A system for remembering that involves repeatedly rehearsing information without attempting to find meaning in it. *See also Elaborative rehearsal.*

Major depression (unipolar disorder) A type of mood dis-

order characterized by deep and persistent depression.

Manic-depressive disorder See Bipolar disorder.

Manifest content In psychoanalytic theory, the disguised version of the latent content, or true meaning, of dreams.

Marijuana Drug derived from the hemp plant *Cannabis sativa,* containing the chemical THC (delta 9-tetrahydrocannabinol), which is commonly classified as a hallucinogen although it also may have depressant and stimulant effects.

Maturation The orderly unfolding of certain patterns of behavior, such as language acquisition or walking, in accordance with genetic blueprints.

MDMA Common name for 3,4-methylenedioxymethamphetamine (also known as "ecstasy"); a "designer drug" chemically related to amphetamines that acts as a central nervous system stimulant.

Mean In descriptive statistics, the arithmetic average obtained by adding scores and dividing by the number of scores.

Means-ends analysis A common heuristic problem-solving strategy that involves identifying the difference between an original state and a desired goal, then progressing through a series of subgoals to reach the solution.

Measure of central tendency In descriptive statistics, a value that reflects the middle or central point of a distribution of scores. The three measures of central tendency are the mean, the median, and the mode.

Measure of variability In descriptive statistics, a measure that indicates whether distribution scores are clustered closely around their average or widely spread out. Three measures of variability are the range, variance, and the standard deviation.

Median In descriptive statistics, the score that falls in the middle of a distribution of numbers arranged from the lowest to the highest.

Meditation The practice of deliberately altering one's state of consciousness in an effort to achieve a state of deep relaxation. Meditation is characterized by alpha brain waves as well as other physiological measures such as lowered respiration and heart rate.

Medulla A structure low in the brain that controls vital life-support functions such as breathing, heartbeat, and blood pressure; it also regulates many reflexive functions such as coughing or sneezing.

Memory (1) The process or processes of storing newly acquired information for later recall; (2) recall for a specific experience, or the total collection of remembered experiences stored in our brains.

Menopause The cessation of menstruation that takes place during the climacteric.

Mental age In IQ testing, the chronological age of children who on the average receive a test score similar to that of the subject. For instance, a six-year old whose composite score is equivalent to that of a nine-year old has a mental age of 9.

Mental set In problem solving, a tendency to approach a problem or situation in a predetermined way, regardless of the requirements of the specific problem.

Mere exposure effect The phenomenon by which repeated exposure to novel stimuli tends to increase an individual's liking for such stimuli.

Mnemonic device A memory system, such as clustering or acrostics, that organizes material in a meaningful way to make it easier to remember.

Mode In descriptive statistics, the score that occurs most frequently in a distribution of numbers.

Modeling A learning process wherein an individual acquires a behavior by observing someone else performing that behavior. Also known as observational learning.

Monocular cues Distance cues such as linear perspective and height on a plane that can be used with just one eye.

Monozygotic twins See Identical twins.

Mood disorders A class of disorders including major depression and bipolar disorder that are characterized by persistent depression (which in bipolar disorder is accompanied by intermittent episodes of mania).

Morpheme The smallest unit of meaning in a given language.

Motion parallax See Relative motion.

Motivation Any condition that might energize and direct an organism's actions.

Motor cortex The region of the cerebral cortex that transmits messages to muscles. The motor cortex controls virtually all intentional body movement.

Motor neuron Neuron that transmits messages from the central nervous system to muscles or glands.

Multifactor motive Motive that is based upon a combination of biological, psychological, and cultural factors.

Multifactorial inheritance Genetic transmission in which several gene pairs interact to produce a trait.

Multiple personality A form of dissociative disorder in which a person alternates between a primary personality and one or more secondary or subordinate personalities.

Mutism Speech disturbance characteristic of schizophrenia in which an individual may not utter a sound for hours or days at a time.

Myelin sheath Insulating cover around some axons that increases a neuron's ability to transmit impulses quickly. Myelin sheaths are made of specialized cells called glia cells.

Narcolepsy A sleep disorder characterized by falling asleep suddenly and uncontrollably.

Narcotics Also known as opiates, a class of depressant drugs that include opium, morphine, codeine, and heroin.

Natural concepts Concepts that are commonly used in thinking about events and experiences, but that are more ambiguous than formal concepts.

Naturalistic observation Psychological research using the observational method that takes place in a natural setting, such as a subject's home or school environment.

Nature-nurture controversy The controversy over whether individual personalities and traits are the result of genetic endowment (nature) or of learning (nurture).

Need for achievement A complex psychosocial motive to accomplish difficult goals, attain high standards, surpass the achievements of others, and increase self-regard by succeeding in exercising talent.

Negative reinforcer In operant conditioning, any stimulus that increases the probability of a response through its removal when the desired response is made.

Neodissociation theory Ernest Hilgard's explanation of hypnosis as a state in which a subject operates on more than one level of consciousness, so that some behaviors are dissociated from conscious awareness.

Neologisms Literally, new words. Invention of neologisms is characteristic of schizophrenic disorder.

Neuron Type of cell that is the basic unit of the nervous system. Neurons transmit and receive messages.

Neuropsychology Also known as physiological psychology. The study of the brain and the rest of the nervous system.

Neurosis Term originally used by Freud to describe anxiety disorders, and widely used until publication of DSM-III to describe a range of disorders that are distressing and often debilitating, but are not characterized by a loss of contact with reality.

Neurotransmitter A chemical messenger that transmits an impulse across the synaptic gap from one neuron to another.

Nicotine A stimulant found in tobacco that acts to increase heart rate, blood pressure, and stomach activity and to constrict blood vessels.

Night terror A sleep disorder in which a person suddenly awakens from Stage 4 sleep in a panic, typically with no recollection of a bad dream.

Nightmare A bad dream that occurs during REM sleep.

Node of Ranvier A small gap or exposed portion of the axon of a neuron between the glia cells that form the myelin sheath.

Noncompensatory model Decision-making model, such as the maximax, minimax, and conjunctive strategies, which involves evaluating some rather than all features of the various alternative choices. Compare with *compensatory model.*

Nonconsciousness A classification used to describe a person's subjective sense of events that cannot be called into conscious awareness, such as the flow of blood through one's own veins.

Norm A standard that reflects the normal or average performance of a particular group of people on a measure such as an IQ test.

Normal distribution In descriptive statistics, a distribution in which scores are distributed similarly on both sides of the middle value, so that they have the appearance of a bell-shaped curve when graphed.

Normal state (of consciousness) The state of consciousness in which a person is alert and aware of his or her environment, as contrasted to alternative or altered states of consciousness.

Normative social influence Social influence in which we conform not because of an actual change in our beliefs, but because we think that we will benefit in some way (such as gaining approval). *See also Informational social influence.*

NREM sleep (Non-rapid eye movement sleep) Stages of sleep during which rapid eye movements typically do not occur. Dreaming occurs far less frequently during NREM sleep than during REM sleep.

Nuclear magnetic resonance (NMR) A procedure for studying the brain that uses radio waves to excite hydrogen protons in the brain tissue, creating a magnetic field change.

Obedience Social influence in which we alter our behavior in response to commands or orders from people perceived as having power or authority.

Obese Condition in which an individual weighs 20 percent or more above the desirable weight for his or her height.

Object permanence The realization that objects continue to exist even when they are not in view. Piaget sees this awareness as a key achievement of the sensorimotor stage of development.

Observational learning See Modeling.

Observational method A method of psychological research in which subjects are observed as they go about their usual activities. The observational method provides descriptive information. *See also Naturalistic observation.*

Observer bias The tendency of an observer to read more into a situation than is actually there or to see what he or she expects to see. Observer bias is a potential limitation of the observational method.

Observer effect The tendency of subjects to modify behavior because they are aware of being observed.

Obsessive-compulsive disorder Anxiety disorder characterized by persistent, unwanted, and unshakeable thoughts and/or irresistible, habitual repeated actions.

Occipital lobe A region at the rear of the cerebral cortex that consists primarily of the visual cortex.

Oedipus complex In Freud's theory of psychosexual development, the attraction a male child feels toward his mother (and jealousy toward his father) during the phallic stage.

Olfaction The sense of smell, which like taste is activated by chemical substances in the environment.

One-egg twins See Identical twins.

Operant conditioning The learning process also known as instrumental conditioning by which an organism learns to associate its own behavior with consequences.

Operant conditioning therapies Behavior modification techniques that attempt to influence behavior by manipulating reinforcers.

Operational definition A definition that specifies the operations that are used to measure or observe a variable, such as a definition of obesity specifying a certain weight-height relationship.

Operations In J. P. Guilford's model of intelligence, operations, or how we think, is one of the three major intellectual functions. *See also Content and Products.*

Opiates See Narcotics.

Opponent-process theory of color vision Theory that explains color vision based on six primary colors which are grouped into three pairs (red-green, blue-yellow, black-white). Receptors in the eye are sensitive to specific pairs, and the presence of one member of a pair inhibits vision of the other. *See also Trichromatic theory.*

Optimum level of arousal The level of arousal at which an individual's performance is most efficient.

Oral stage According to Freud, the first stage of psychosexual development spanning birth through 12–18 months, during which the lips and mouth are the primary erogenous zone.

Organ of Corti A structure in the inner ear located directly above the basilar membrane, consisting of auditory hair cells, a tectoral membrane, and cilia.

Organ reserve The potential ability of organs such as the heart, lungs, and kidneys to increase their output to a level several times greater than normal under emergency conditions.

Organic amnesia Memory deficits caused by altered physiology of the brain, as might result from an accident or certain physical illnesses.

Orgasm The third phase in the human sexual response pattern, characterized by reduction in voluntary muscle control; peaks in blood pressure, heart rate, and respiration rate; and pleasurable sensations.

Ossicles The set of three tiny linked bones (the malleus, incus, and stapes) in the middle ear that receives a sound stimulus from the tympanic membrane and transfers it to the oval window of the inner ear.

Otis-Lennon School Ability Test (OLSAT) A group IQ test for children of all ages that is widely used in schools.

Outgroup The "them" group when individuals divide the world into "us" and "them."

Overlap An important monocular distance cue based on the fact that objects close to us tend to block out parts of objects that are farther away. Also known as interposition.

Overlearning Technique for memorizing material that involves rehearsing information after it has already been learned.

Panic disorder An anxiety disorder in which an individual experiences numerous (four or more in a four-week period) panic attacks, which are characterized by overwhelming terror and often a feeling of unreality or of depersonalization.

Paper-and-pencil questionnaire In personality testing, an objective, self-report inventory designed to measure scientifically the variety of characteristics or traits that make up personality.

Paranoid schizophrenia Subtype of schizophrenic disorder characterized by the presence of well-organized delusional thoughts.

Parasympathetic nervous system The division of the autonomic nervous system that functions to conserve energy, returning the body to normal from emergency responses set in motion by the sympathetic nervous system.

Parietal lobe A region of the cerebral cortex located just behind the central fissure and above the lateral fissure. The parietal lobe contains the somatosensory cortex as well as association areas that process sensory information received by the somatosensory cortex.

Partial reinforcement effect Behaviors that are acquired on partial instead of continuous reinforcement schedules tend to be established more slowly, but are more persistent when no reinforcement is provided.

Partial reinforcement schedule In operant conditioning, the reinforcing of a behavior only part of the time, as on ratio or interval schedules.

Participant management A management strategy in which all levels of employees are included in decision making

Passionate love Also known as romantic love; this form of love is a state of extreme absorption in another person.

PCP (Phencyclidine hydrochloride) A drug commonly known as "angel dust" that produces sensory distortions and hallucinations as well as having stimulant, depressant, and painkilling properties. Side effects include unpredictable violent behavior.

Pearson product-moment correlation coefficient The most frequently used measure of correlation, ranging from -1.0 to $+1.0$. Correlations close to 0 indicate little or no relationship between two variables, while correlations close to $+1.0$ or -1.0 indicate more significant positive or negative relationships.

Percentile Numbers from a range of data that indicate percentages of scores that lie below them.

Perception The process of interpreting, organizing, and often elaborating on sensations.

Perceptual constancy The fact that objects are normally perceived to be constant in size, color or brightness, and shape despite the fact that their retinal images change according to different conditions.

Perceptual grouping The tendency to organize patterns of stimuli into larger units according to proximity, similarity, and good continuation.

Perceptual organization The process by which we structure elementary sensations (such as lines, brightness, and points we see) into the objects we perceive.

Perceptual set The tendency to see, hear, smell, feel, or taste what we expect or what is consistent with our preconceived notions.

Peripheral nervous system (PNS) The portion of the nervous system that transmits messages to and from the central nervous system. The peripheral nervous system consists of the somatic nervous system and the autonomic nervous system.

Permissive Parenting style in which parents adopt a "hands off" policy, making few demands and showing reluctance to punish inappropriate behavior.

Personal space The invisible boundary or imaginary circle of space with which individuals surround themselves, and into which others are not supposed to enter without invitation.

Personality The distinctive patterns of behavior, emotions, and thoughts that characterize an individual's adaptations to his or her life.

Personality disorders A diverse class of disorders that is collectively characterized by inflexible and maladaptive personality traits that cause either functional impairment or subjective distress.

Personality psychology The field of psychology that focuses on exploring the uniqueness of the individual, describing the elements that make up human personality, and investigating how personality develops and how it influences people's activities.

Person-centered therapy Therapeutic approach designed to help the client tap his or her own inner resources within a climate of genuineness, unconditional positive regard, and empathic understanding.

PET scan See Positron emission tomography.

Phallic stage According to Freud, the third phase of psychosexual development, spanning age three through age five or six, during which the focus of sexual gratification is genital stimulation.

Phenotype Characteristics that result from the expression of various genotypes (for instance, brown eyes or blond hair).

Phenylketonuria (PKU) A disease caused by a recessive gene that results in the absence of an enzyme necessary to metabolize the milk protein phenylalanine.

Phobia Any of a number of anxiety disorders which are characterized by a persistent fear of and consequent avoidance of a specific object or situation.

Phonemes Individual sounds (such as "s" and "sh") that are the basic structural elements of language.

Physiological dependence Addiction to a chemical substance in which withdrawal of that substance results in physiological symptoms such as cramps, nausea, tremors, headaches, or sweating.

Physiological psychology Also known as neuropsychology. The branch of psychology that studies the relationship between physiological processes and behavior.

Pitch The dimension of hearing that determines how high or low a sound is, measured in hertz. Pitch is determined by frequency of a sound wave.

Pituitary gland Gland in the endocrine system, located directly below the hypothalamus, that produces a number of hormones, many of which trigger other endocrine glands to release hormones.

Place theory of pitch discrimination The theory that we discriminate different pitches because sound waves of different frequency displace different regions on the cochlea's basilar membrane.

Plateau The second stage in the human sexual response pattern, characterized by the pronounced physiological reactions that directly precede orgasm.

Pleasure principle According to Freud, the principle guiding the id which seeks immediate gratification of all instinctive drives regardless of reason, logic, or the possible impact of behaviors.

Pons A brain structure located just above the medulla, which functions in fine-tuning motor messages, "programming" species-typical behaviors, processing sensory information, and controlling respiration.

Positive reinforcement therapy Behavior therapy technique which identifies the desired behavior, then uses rewards to motivate this behavior.

Positive reinforcer In operant conditioning, any stimulus presented after a response that increases the probability of the response.

Positron emission tomography (PET scan) A technique for studying the brain that involves injecting a subject with a glucoselike sugar tagged with a radioactive isotope that accumulates in brain cells in direct proportion to their activity level.

Postconventional morality The third and highest level in Lawrence Kohlberg's theory of moral development, in which individuals are guided by values

agreed upon by society (stage 5) or by universal ethical principles (stage 6).

Posttraumatic stress disorder (PTSD) Anxiety disorder that typically follows a traumatic event or events, and is characterized by a reliving of that event, avoidance of stimuli associated with the event or numbing of general responsiveness, and increased arousal.

Preconscious The mental state describing thoughts and memories that exist on the fringe of awareness, and which can be readily brought into consciousness.

Preconventional morality The lowest level of moral development in Lawrence Kohlberg's theory, comprising stage 1 and stage 2, in which individuals have not internalized a personal code of morality.

Predictive validity A type of criterion-related validity assessed by determining the accuracy with which tests predict performance in some future situation. *See also Concurrent validity.*

Prejudice A negative, unjustifiable, and inflexible attitude toward a group and its members, based on erroneous information.

Premack principle For any given individual, any behavior in a reinforcement hierarchy may reinforce any behaviors that are located below it in the hierarchy; and any behavior may be reinforced by behaviors above it in the hierarchy.

Premenstrual syndrome (PMS) A term used to describe a myriad of physical and psychological symptoms that precede each menstrual period for some women.

Preoperational stage According to Piaget, the second major stage of cognitive development (ages 7–12). Preoperational children can develop only limited concepts, and they are unable to evaluate simultaneously more than one physical dimension. *See also Centration.*

Primacy effect Term used to describe the phenomenon that the first information we receive about a person often has the greatest influence on our perceptions of that person.

Primary mental abilities In L. L. Thurstone's theory of the structure of intelligence, the separate and measurable attributes (for instance, numerical ability) that make up intelligence.

Primary process thinking According to Freud, wish-fulfilling mental imagery used by the id to discharge tension.

Primary reinforcer In operant conditioning, a stimulus that satisfies a biologically based drive or need (such as hunger or sleep).

Proactive interference In memory, the phenomenon that occurs when earlier learning disrupts memory for later learning.

Probability In statistics, the proportion of cases that fit a certain description.

Problem finding A fifth stage of cognitive development (beyond Piaget's fourth stage of formal operations) proposed by P. A. Arlin, in which individuals pose new questions about the world and try to discover novel solutions to old problems.

Procedural memory Recall for how to perform skills such as bicycle riding or swimming. *See also Declarative memory.*

Products In J. P. Guilford's theory of intelligence, products (the result of applying a particular operation to a particular content) are one of the three major intellectual functions. *See also Operations* and *Content.*

Programed theory See Genetic clock theory.

Projection Defense mechanism in which an individual reduces anxiety created by unacceptable impulses by attributing those impulses to someone else.

Projective test Personality tests that consist of loosely structured, ambiguous stimuli that require the subject's interpretation.

Proximity The perceptual grouping principle that, all else being equal, we tend to organize perceptions by grouping elements that are the nearest to each other. In social psychology, the geographical nearness of one person to another, which is an important factor in interpersonal attraction.

Proximodistal Pattern of development normal to humans in which infants gain control over areas that are closest to the center of their bodies (so that, for instance, control is gained over the upper arms before the fingers).

Psychoactive drugs Drugs that have the effect of altering perceptions and behavior by changing conscious awareness.

Psychoanalysis Technique developed by Sigmund Freud in which an individual's revelations of normally unconscious cognitions are interpreted.

Psychoanalytic approach The approach to psychology developed by Sigmund Freud, which emphasizes the dynamics among the three forces of personality, the id, ego, and superego; the importance of defense mechanisms; and the importance of dreams as the "royal road to the unconscious."

Psychoanalytic theory Theory of personality that views people as shaped by ongoing conflicts between primary drives and the social pressures of civilized society.

Psychogenic amnesia A type of dissociative disorder characterized by sudden loss of memory, usually after a particularly stressful or traumatic event.

Psychogenic fugue disorder A type of dissociative disorder characterized by a loss of memory accompanied by a fugue state in which the individual travels from place to place with little social contact with other people.

Psycholinguistics The psychological study of how sounds and symbols are translated to meaning, and of the cognitive processes that are involved in the acquisition and use of language.

Psychological dependence Dependence on a chemical substance in which a person finds the substance so pleasurable or helpful in coping with life that he or she becomes addicted to its use.

Psychology The scientific study of the behavior and mental processes of humans and other animals.

Psychophysics The study of the relationship between the physical aspects of external stimuli and our own perceptions of these stimuli.

Psychosexual development Stages of development, in Freud's perspective, in which the focus of sexual gratification shifts from one body site to another.

Psychosis A term used until publication of DSM-III in 1980 to describe severe disorders that involve disturbances of thinking, reduced contact with reality, loss of ability to function socially, and often bizarre behaviors.

Psychotherapy Any nonbiological, noninvasive psychological technique or procedure designed to improve a person's adjustment to life.

Puberty The approximately two-year period of rapid physical changes that occur sometime between ages seven and 16 in our society and culminate in sexual maturity.

Punishment A consequence that decreases the probability that a given response will occur.

Quantitative psychology The field of specialization in psychology that uses mathematical techniques and computer science to aid in understanding human behavior.

Random sample A sample group of a larger population that is selected by randomization procedures. A random sample differs from a representative sample.

Range In descriptive statistics, a measure of variability that indicates the difference between the highest and lowest scores.

Rational-emotive therapy (RET) Approach to therapy based on the premise that psychological problems result when people interpret their experiences based on self-defeating, irrational beliefs.

Rationalization Defense mechanism in which an individual substitutes self-justifying excuses or explanations for the real reasons for behaviors.

Reaction formation Defense mechanism in which the ego unconsciously replaces unacceptable impulses with their opposites.

Reality principle According to Freud, the tendency to behave in ways that are consistent with reality. The reality principle governs the ego.

Recall In memory tests, a subject's ability to reproduce information that he or she was previously exposed to. Fill-in-the-blank and essay questions test recall.

Recessive gene A gene that is expressed in the phenotype only in the absence of a dominant gene, or when it is paired with a similar recessive gene.

Reciprocal determinism According to Albert Bandura, the principle that individual behaviors and thus personalities are shaped by the interaction between cognitive factors and environmental factors.

Recognition In memory tests, a subject's ability to recognize whether he or she has been previously exposed to information. Multiple-choice and true/false questions test recognition.

Recombinant DNA technology A complex technique sometimes called gene splicing that researchers use to cut apart and reassemble sections of DNA strands to locate genetic information.

Refractory period In the male resolution phase of the human sexual response cycle, a recovery stage characterized by a temporary inability to reach orgasm.

Regression Defense mechanism in which an individual attempts to cope with an anxiety-producing situation by retreating to an earlier stage of development. In statistics, a procedure for predicting the size of one variable based on a knowledge of the size of a correlated variable and the coefficient of correlation between the two variables.

Reinforcement In operant conditioning, any event that increases the probability that a response will occur.

Relative motion A monocular distance cue based on the fact that moving objects appear to move a greater distance when they are close to the viewer than when they are far away. Also known as motion parallax.

Relative size A monocular distance cue based on the fact that objects of the same size appear to be smaller the farther they are from the viewer.

Relaxation response A state of deep relaxation similar to meditation.

Relearning A technique for testing memory that involves measuring how much more quickly a person can relearn material that was learned at some previous time.

Reliability In testing, the dependable consistency of a test.

REM sleep A stage of sleep characterized by rapid eye movements, and often associated with dreaming.

Replication studies Research conducted for the purpose of verifying previous findings.

Representative heuristic Strategy for categorizing an object or situation based on one's preconceived notion of characteristics that are typical of that category.

Representative sample A sample in which critical subgroups are represented according to their incidence in the larger population that the researcher wishes to draw conclusions about. *See also Survey.*

Repression In psychoanalytic theory, the defense mechanism by which ideas, feelings, or memories that are too painful to deal with on a conscious level are banished to the unconscious.

Residual schizophrenia Term used to describe the residual phase of schizophrenic disorder, which is a recovery phase during which major symptoms are absent or markedly diminished.

Resistance In psychoanalysis, a patient's unwillingness to describe freely some aspects of his or her life.

Resolution The fourth stage in human sexual response. Directly following orgasm, body responses and sexual systems return to their nonexcited state.

Resting potential The state in which a neuron is not transmitting a nerve impulse. A neuron in this state has a net negative charge relative to its outside environment, and this state of potential energy prepares it to be activated by an impulse from an adjacent neuron.

Reticular activating system (RAS) See Reticular formation.

Reticular formation The set of neural circuits extending from the lower brain up to the thalamus that play a critical role in controlling arousal and alertness, also known as the reticular activating system.

Retina The thin membrane at the back of the eye containing photoreceptors called rods and cones. The retina functions to record images.

Retinal disparity See Binocular disparity.

Retrieval The process by which information stored in memory is accessed.

Retroactive interference In memory, the phenomenon that occurs when a later event interferes with the recall of earlier information.

Retrograde amnesia Memory loss for certain details or events that occurred prior to experiencing brain trauma; a form of organic amnesia.

Rods Photoreceptor cells distributed across the inner layer of the retina that are important in peripheral vision as well as helping us to see in dim light.

Rorschach ink-blot test A commonly used projective test in which the subject is asked to examine ink blots and say what they look like or bring to mind.

S-factor In Charles Spearman's two-factor theory of the structure of intelligence, s-factors are specific abilities or skills. *See also G-factor.*

Sample A selected segment of a larger population that is being studied in psychological research using the survey method. Two kinds of samples are the representative sample and the random sample.

Saturation The proportion of colored or chromatic light to noncolored or nonchromatic light, which determines how colorful light appears.

Schachter-Singer theory Theory that a given body state can be linked to a variety of emotions depending on the context in which the body state occurs.

Schema In reference to memory, schemas are conceptual frameworks that individuals use to make sense out of stored information. In the theory of Jean Piaget, schemas are the mental structures we form to assimilate and organize processed information.

Schizophrenic disorder A class of severe and disabling mental disorders that are characterized by extreme disruptions of perceptions, thoughts, emotions, and behavior. Types of schizophrenia identified by DSM-III-R include disorganized, catatonic, paranoid, undifferentiated, and residual schizophrenia.

School psychology The field of specialization in psychology concerned with evaluating and resolving learning and emotional problems.

Secondary reinforcer A stimulus that acts as a reinforcer by virtue of its association with one or more primary reinforcers. Also known as a conditioned reinforcer.

Secondary sex characteristics Physical characteristics typical of mature males or females (such as facial, body, and pubic hair) that develop during puberty as a result of the release of testosterone or estrogen.

Secondary trait In Gordon Allport's trait theory of personality, any of a variety of less generalized and often short-term traits that affect people's behavior in specific circumstances. *See also Cardinal trait* and *Central trait.*

Secular growth trends Changes in human physical growth patterns (including height, weight, and rates of maturation) measured in sample populations throughout the world.

Sedatives A class of depressant drugs including tranquilizers, barbiturates, and nonbarbiturates that induce relaxation, calmness, and sleep.

Selective perception A form of perceptual set; the tendency to perceive stimuli that are consistent with expectations and to ignore those that are inconsistent.

Self The central organizing, all-encompassing structure that accounts for the coherence and stability of each individual's personality.

Self-efficacy An individual's belief that he or she can perform adequately and deal effectively with a particular situation.

Semantic memory General, nonpersonal knowledge about the meaning of facts and concepts.

Semantics The study of meaning in language.

Semicircular canals Three ring-shaped structures in the inner ear that provide information about the body's equilibrium or balance.

Senile dementia A collective term describing a variety of conditions sometimes associated with aging, including memory deficits, forgetfulness, disorientation for time and place, declining ability to think, and so forth.

Sensations The basic, immediate experiences that a stimulus such as a sound elicits in a sense organ such as the ear.

Sensation-seeking motive An innate need for certain levels of stimulation. Sensation-seeking motives include the need to explore the environment and the need for sensory stimulation.

Sensorimotor stage In Jean Piaget's theory, the period of development between birth and about two years during which infants learn about their worlds primarily through their senses and actions.

Sensorineural hearing loss Hearing loss caused by damage to either the hair cells of the inner ear or the auditory nerve.

Sensory cortex The region of the cerebral cortex that is involved in receiving sensory messages.

Sensory deprivation Experimental situation used to study sensation-seeking motives, in which subjects lie motionless and are deprived of tactile, visual, and auditory sensations.

Sensory memory (SM) The first system in the three-system model of memory, in which brief impressions from any of the senses are stored fleetingly, disappearing within a few seconds if they are not transferred to short-term memory. *See also Iconic* and *Echoic memory.*

Sensory neuron Neuron or nerve cell that carries messages to the CNS from receptors in the skin, ears, nose, eyes, and other receptor organs. Also known as afferent neuron.

Separate attachment Attachment typically displayed by infants by about 12–18 months, when fear of strangers diminishes and interest in people other than primary caregivers develops. *See also Indiscriminant attachment* and *Specific attachment.*

Septal area A structure in the brain's limbic system that plays a role in the experiencing of pleasure.

Serial position effect The tendency to remember items at the beginning and end of a list more readily than those in the middle.

Set point Physiologically preferred level of body weight for each individual.

Sex-linked inheritance Genetic transmission involving genes that are carried only on the X chromosome. (Females carry the XX chromosome pair while males carry the XY pair.)

Sexual orientation The sex to which an individual is attracted.

Shape constancy An element of perceptual constancy: we perceive objects as maintaining the same shape even though their retinal images change when we view them from different angles.

Shaping An operant technique wherein responses that are increasingly similar to the desired behavior are reinforced, step by step, until the desired behavior occurs.

Short-term memory (STM) The immediate recollection of stimuli that have just been perceived; unless it is transferred to long-term memory, information in this memory system is usually retained only momentarily.

Similarity In perception, the principle that we tend to group elements that are similar to each other.

Simple phobia Anxiety disorder characterized by an irrational fear of a specific situation or object, such as heights, small closed places, or spiders.

Simultaneous conditioning In classical conditioning, learning that takes place when the conditioned stimulus is presented at the same time as the unconditioned stimulus.

Size constancy One form of perceptual constancy: although the retinal image of an object becomes smaller as it recedes into the distance (or larger as it approaches), the viewer adjusts for this change and perceives the object to be constant in size.

Skewed In descriptive statistics, the term *skewed* describes an unbalanced distribution of scores.

Skill training intervention Technique for treating alcoholism that teaches subjects positive coping behaviors for responding to stress.

Sleep A natural, periodically occurring state of rest characterized by reduced activity, lessened responsiveness to stimuli, and distinctive brain wave patterns.

Sleep apnea A sleep disorder characterized by irregular breathing during sleep.

Sleep disorders A class of disorders that interfere with sleep, including insomnia, sleep apnea, night terrors, nightmares, and sleepwalking.

Sleepwalking A sleep disorder, also known as somnambulism, characterized by walking in one's sleep during Stage 3 or 4 of NREM sleep.

Social adjustment function One of the most important functions of our attitudes, which is to allow us to identify with or gain approval from our peers.

Social identification function One of the most important functions served by the attitudes of other people, which is to provide us with information about what those individuals are like.

Social influence The efforts by others to alter our feelings, beliefs, and behavior.

Social-learning theory Learning theory that emphasizes the role of observation in learning.

Social perception The way in which we perceive, evaluate, categorize, and form judgments about the qualities of other people.

Social phobia An anxiety disorder characterized by a persistent, irrational fear of performing some specific behavior (such as talking or eating) in the presence of other people.

Social psychology The field of specialization in psychology concerned with understanding the impact of social environments and social processes on individuals.

Socialization The process by which society conveys behavioral expectations to an individual, through various agents such as parents, peers, and school.

Sociobiologist A researcher or theorist who seeks to understand the biological factors that underlie social behaviors in all animal species, including humans.

Soma See Cell body.

Somatic nervous system The division of the peripheral nervous system that transmits messages to and from major skeletal muscles as well as from sensory organs to the CNS.

Somatization disorder A type of somatoform disorder characterized by multiple and recurrent physical symptoms which have no physical cause.

Somatoform disorder A class of disorders including somatization disorder, hypochondriasis, and conversion disorder that are manifested through somatic or physical symptoms.

Source traits In Raymond Cattell's trait theory of personality, basic, underlying traits that are the center or core of an individual's personality. *See also Surface traits.*

Specific attachment Highly selective attachment often displayed by human infants sometime between 6 and 18 months, when increased responsiveness is displayed toward primary caregivers and distress may be displayed when separated from parents. *See also Indiscriminant attachment* and *Separate attachment.*

Split-half reliability Measure of test reliability in which a subject's performance on a single administration of a test is assessed by comparing performance on half of the test items with performance on the other half of the test items.

Spontaneous recovery In classical conditioning, the spontaneous reappearance of a conditioned response after extinction has taken place.

Stage 1 sleep The light sleep that occurs just after dozing off, characterized by brain waves called theta waves.

Stage 2 sleep The stage of sleep that typically follows Stage 1 sleep, characterized by brief bursts of brain activity called sleep spindles as well as K complex responses to stimuli such as noises.

Stage 3 sleep The stage of sleep that typically follows Stage 2 sleep, characterized by an EEG tracing 20–50 percent of which consists of delta waves. There are virtually no eye movements during Stage 3 sleep.

Stage 4 sleep The deepest level of sleep, characterized by an EEG tracing exceeding 50 percent delta waves. There are virtually no eye movements during Stage 4 sleep.

Standard deviation In descriptive statistics, a measure of variability that indicates the average extent to which all the scores in a distribution vary from the mean.

Standard score In descriptive statistics, a measure that indicates how far a score deviates from the average in standard units.

Standardization procedures Uniform and consistent procedures for administering and scoring tests, such as IQ or personality tests.

Stanford-Binet IQ test developed by Lewis Terman by revising Binet's scale and adapting questions to American pupils.

State-dependent memory The phenomenon wherein recall of particular events, experiences, or information is aided by being in the same context or mood in which the information was first encoded.

Statistical significance A term used to describe research results in which changes in the dependent variable can be attributed with a high level of confidence to the experimental condition (or independent variable) being manipulated by the researcher.

Statistics Mathematical methods for describing and interpreting data. Two kinds of statistics are *descriptive* and *inferential statistics*.

Stereotypes Preconceived and oversimplified beliefs and expectations about the traits of members of a particular group that do not account for individual differences.

Stimulants Psychoactive drugs, including caffeine, nicotine, amphetamines, and cocaine, that stimulate the central nervous system by increasing the transmission of neural impulses.

Storage The process by which encoded material is retained over time in memory.

Stress The process of appraising events or situations as harmful, threatening, or challenging, of assessing potential responses, and of responding to those events.

Structuralism An approach to psychology that attempted to break down experience into its basic elements or structures, using a technique called introspection in which subjects provided "scientific" reports of perceptual experiences.

Sublimation A form of the defense mechanism displacement in which impulse-driven behaviors are channeled toward producing a socially valued accomplishment.

Subtractive color mixing The color mixing process that occurs when pigments are mixed, so that when light falls on the colored object some wavelengths are absorbed (or subtracted) and others are reflected. *See also Additive color mixing.*

Superego According to Freud, the third system of personality which consists of an individual's conscience as well as the ego-ideal (the "shoulds" of behavior). *See also Id, Ego.*

Surface traits In Raymond Cattell's trait theory of personality, dimensions or traits that are usually obvious (such as integrity or tidiness) and which tend to be grouped in clusters that are related to source traits.

Survey A research method in which a representative sample of people are questioned about their behaviors or attitudes. The survey provides descriptive information. *See also Sample.*

Syllogism An argument consisting of two or more premises, followed by a statement of conclusion that may or may not follow logically from the premises.

Sympathetic nervous system The division of the autonomic nervous system that functions to produce emergency responses such as increased heart rate, pupil dilation, and inhibited digestive activity; the sympathetic nervous system works in tandem with the parasympathetic nervous system.

Synapse The space between transmitting and receiving neurons, including a portion of the presynaptic and postsynaptic membranes, that is involved in transmitting an impulse between neurons.

Syntax The set of language rules that govern how words can be combined to form meaningful phrases and sentences; grammar.

Systematic desensitization Behavior therapy technique that pairs the slow, systematic exposure to anxiety-inducing situations with relaxation training.

Temporal lobe The region of the cerebral cortex located below the lateral fissure that contains the auditory cortex.

Terminal buttons Swollen bulblike structures on the ends of a neuron's axon that release chemical substances known as neurotransmitters.

Territoriality The tendency to stake out certain areas with relatively fixed boundaries that others can enter only on invitation.

Testing hypotheses Problem-solving strategy that involves formulating specific hypotheses that generate relatively efficient approaches to solving a problem, then testing these hypotheses in a systematic fashion.

Test-retest reliability Method for evaluating test reliability by giving a subject (or subjects) the same test more than once.

Texture gradients A monocular distance cue based on the fact that textured surfaces (such as a grassy lawn) appear to be smoother, denser, and less textured when they are far from the viewer than when they are close.

Thalamus A structure located beneath the cerebrum in the brain that functions as a "relay station," routing incoming sensory information to appropriate areas in the cerebral cortex. The thalamus also seems to play a role in regulating sleep cycles.

Thanatology The study of death and dying.

Thematic Apperception Test (TAT) Projective test for personality assessment in which the subject is shown cards depicting various scenes and is asked to describe what is happening in each scene.

Theory X A term used to describe job-centered or scientific management, which places primary emphasis on improving maximum work output at the lowest possible cost. Contrast with Theory Y.

Theory Y A term used to describe employee-centered management, which is based on the idea that workers will be more productive in an atmosphere that allows them a certain degree of autonomy, responsibility, and independence. Contrast with Theory X.

Thought Any cognitive processes directed toward problem solving, understanding language, memory retrieval, and perceiving patterns in sensory inputs.

Threshold The minimum level of intensity or strength of a stimulus that is sufficient to activate a sensory process (for instance, the minimum number of molecules that must be present in the air for us to smell a substance).

Thyroid gland A gland in the endocrine system, located in the neck, that influences metabolism, mood states, and behavior.

Timbre A quality of complex sound that is a product of the combination of fundamental frequency and additional frequency components called overtones.

Trace conditioning In classical conditioning, learning that takes place when presentation of the conditioned stimulus begins and ends before the unconditioned stimulus is presented.

Transduction The process by which sensory organs transform mechanical, chemical, or light energy into the electrochemical energy that is generated by neurons firing.

Transference In psychotherapy, a process in which a patient begins to relate to the therapist in much the same way as to another important person in his or her life (such as a parent).

Trial and error Problem-solving strategy that involves trying possible solutions, one by one, to see which one is correct.

Trichromatic theory of color vision Also known as the Young-Helmholtz theory, the postulation that the human eye contains three types of color receptors (for red, green, and blue), which form the basis for our perception of all colors. *See also Opponent-process theory.*

Two-egg twins See Fraternal twins.

Two-factor theory An influential theory in I/O psychology that says that employees are motivated by two types of needs: extrinsic hygiene needs for job security, adequate pay, and so forth; and intrinsic motivator needs for challenge, autonomy, and recognition.

Two-process learning Learning that combines both classical and operant conditioning.

Tympanic membrane Also known as the eardrum, the tympanic membrane stretches across the end of the auditory canal and vibrates in response to sound waves.

Type A Individuals who are hard-driving, ambitious, competitive, easily angered, time conscious, and demanding of both themselves and others, as described by Friedman and Rosenman in their study of coronary heart disease.

Type B Individuals who are relaxed, easygoing, not driven to achieve perfection, happy in their jobs, understanding, and not easily angered, as described by Friedman and Rosenman in their study of coronary heart disease.

Unconditional positive regard In person-centered therapy, the therapist's attitude of unconditional acceptance toward the client.

Unconditioned response (UCR) In classical conditioning, an unlearned response to a stimulus.

Unconditioned stimulus (UCS) In classical conditioning, a stimulus that elicits an unlearned response.

Unconscious A level of mental awareness describing ideas, feelings, and memories that cannot easily be brought into consciousness.

Unconscious mind According to Freud's theory, the vast reservoir of the mind which holds countless memories and feelings that are repressed or submerged because they are anxiety-producing.

Understanding function One of the most important functions of attitudes—to provide a frame of reference for structuring and making sense out of the world and our experiences.

Undifferentiated schizophrenia A "catch-all" category that individuals with schizophrenia are assigned to if they do not manifest specific symptoms of disorganized, catatonic, or paranoid schizophrenia.

Validity In testing, the ability of a test to measure accurately what it is supposed to measure.

Value-expressive function One of the most important functions of attitudes, to express values that have central importance in our lives.

Variable interval (VI) schedule A partial reinforcement schedule in operant conditioning wherein opportunities for reinforcement occur at variable time intervals.

Variable ratio (VR) schedule A partial reinforcement schedule in operant conditioning wherein reinforcement is provided after an *average* of a specific number of responses occur.

Variance In descriptive statistics, a measure of variability that is the average of the squared distances of the scores from the mean.

Ventromedial hypothalamus (VMH) One of two regions of the hypothalamus that seems to act as a control center for eating. Stimulation of the VMH inhibits feeding and destruction of the VMH may result in extreme overeating. *See also Lateral hypothalamus; Dual hypothalamic control theory.*

Vestibular sacs Structures at the junction of the semicircular canals and cochlea of the middle ear that provide information about the head's position in space.

Visual cortex The portion of the occipital lobe that integrates sensory information received from the eyes into electrical patterns that the brain translates into vision.

Visual memory See Iconic memory.

Volley theory Related to the frequency theory of pitch discrimination, this theory postulates that since single auditory neurons cannot fire rapidly enough to enable us to perceive tones in the 1000–4000 Hz range. Pitch perception in this range is made possible by groups of interrelated neurons firing in concert.

Wear-and-tear theory See Accumulating damages theory.

Weber's Law One of the major principles of sensation, based on the fact that for various stimulus intensities, the difference threshold tends to be a constant fraction of the stimulus. As the strength of the original stimulus increases, the magnitude of the change must also increase in order for a just noticeable difference to be perceived.

Wechsler Adult Intelligence Scale (WAIS) Intelligence test developed by David Wechsler in the 1930s with subtests grouped by aptitude rather than age level.

Wernicke's area An area of the left temporal lobe that is the brain's primary area for understanding speech.

Working backward A common heuristic problem-solving strategy that starts with defining the goal, then defines the step that directly precedes that goal, and works backward in this manner until the steps needed to reach the goal are defined.

Yerkes-Dodson law Principle that the optimum level of arousal for peak performance will vary somewhat depending on the nature of the task.

Young-Helmholtz theory See Trichromatic theory.

Zygote The cell produced by the uniting of a sperm cell with an egg cell.

Zygote stage See Germinal stage.

Abel, E. (1984). Opiates and sex. *Journal of Psychoactive Drugs, 16*, 205–216.

Abraham, K. (1911). Notes on the psychoanalytical investigation and treatment of manic-depressive insanity and allied conditions. Originally written in 1911 and later published in E. Jones (Ed.), *Selected Papers of Karl Abraham, M.D.* London: Hogarth Press.

Abrams, A. (1983). Honda Ohio plant transplants Japan methods, harmony. *Los Angeles Times,* January 7, Part IV, 1–2.

Abroms, K., & Bennett, J. (1981). Changing etiological perspectives in Down's syndrome: Implications for early intervention. *Journal of the Division for Early Childhood, 2*, 109–112.

Abu-Mostafa, Y., & Psaltis, D. (1987). Optical neural computers. *Scientific American, 256*, 88–95.

Adam, K., & Oswald, I. (1977). Sleep is for tissue restoration. *Journal of the Royal College of Physicians, 11*, 376–388.

Adams, J. (1973). *Understanding Adolescence.* Boston: Allyn & Bacon.

Ader, R., & Cohen, N. (1982). Behaviorally conditioned immunosuppression and murine systemic lupus erythematosus. *Science, 215*, 1534–1536.

Adorno, T., Frenkel-Brunswick, E., Levinson, D., & Sanford, R. (1950). *The Authoritarian Personality.* New York: Harper & Row.

Aiello, J., & Aiello, T. (1974). The development of personal space: Proxemic behavior of children 6 through 16. *Human Ecology, 2*, 177–189.

Ainsworth, M. (1963). The development of infant-mother interaction among the Ganda. In B. Foss (Ed.), *Determinants of Infant Behavior* (Vol. 2). New York: Wiley.

Ainsworth, M. (1979). Infant-mother attachment. *American Psychologist, 34*, 932–937.

Alderfer, C. (1969). An empirical test of a new theory of human needs. *Organizational Behavior and Human Performance, 4*, 142–175.

Alderfer, C. (1972). *Existence, Relatedness, and Growth: Human Needs in Organizational Settings.* New York: Free Press.

Aldrich, M., Alessi, A. Beck, R., & Gilman, S. (1987). Cortical blindness: Etiology, diagnosis, and prognosis. *Annals of Neurology, 21*, 149–158.

Allen, M. (1976). Twin studies of affective illness. *Archives of General Psychiatry, 33*, 1476–1478.

Allen, V. (1965). Situational factors in conformity. In L. Berkowitz (Ed.), *Advances in Experimental Social Psychology* (Vol. 2). New York: Academic Press.

Allport, G. (1937). *Personality: A Psychological Interpretation.* New York: Holt, Rinehart and Winston.

Allport, G. (1961). *Pattern and Growth in Personality.* New York: Holt, Rinehart and Winston.

Allport, G. (1965). *Letters from Jenny.* New York: Harcourt, Brace & World.

Allport, G. (1966). Traits revisited. *American Psychologist, 21*, 1–10.

Allport, G., & Postman, L. (1947). *The Psychology of Rumor.* New York: Holt, Rinehart and Winston.

Almli, C. (1978). The ontogeny of feeding and drinking behavior: Effects of early brain damage. *Neuroscience and Behavioral Reviews, 2*, 281–300.

Altman, I. (1975). *The Environment and Social Behavior.* Monterey, CA: Brooks/Cole.

Altman, J. (1986). Images in and of the brain. *Nature, 324*, 405.

Amabile, T. (1983). The social psychology of creativity: A componential conceptualization. *Journal of Personality and Social Psychology, 45*, 357–376.

Amabile, T. (1985). Motivation and creativity: Effects of motivational orientation on creative writers. *Journal of Personality and Social Psychology, 48*, 393–399.

Amabile, T., & Glazebrook, A. (1982). A negativity bias in interpersonal evaluation. *Journal of Experimental Social Psychology, 18*, 1–22.

American Heart Association. (1984). *Heart Facts.* Dallas: American Heart Association.

American Psychological Association. (1981). Ethical principles of psychologists. *American Psychologist, 36*, 633–638.

American Psychological Association. (1985). *Directory of the American Psychological Association* (1985 edition). Washington, DC: American Psychological Association.

American Psychiatric Association. (1987). *Diagnostic and Statistical Manual of Mental Disorders* (3rd ed. rev.). Washington, DC: American Psychiatric Association.

Amit, Z., & Galina, H. (1986). Stress-induced analgesia: Adaptive pain suppression. *Physiological Reviews, 66*, 1091–1120.

Amkraut, A., & Solomon, G. (1977). From the symbolic stimulus to the pathophysiologic response: Immune mechanisms. In Z. Lipowski, D. Lipsitt, & P. Whybrow (Eds.), *Psychosomatic Medicine: Current Trends and Clinical Applications.* New York: Oxford University Press.

Amoore, J. (1970). *Molecular Basis of Odor.* Springfield, IL: Thomas.

Amoore, J. (1982). Odor theory and odor classification. In E. Theimer (Ed.), *Fragrance Chemistry—The Science of the Sense of Smell.* New York: Academic Press.

Anand, B., & Brobeck, J. (1951). Hypothalamic control of food intake in rats and cats. *Yale Journal of Biological Medicine, 24*, 123–140.

Anastasi, A. (1958). *Differential Psychology* (3rd ed.). New York: Macmillan.

Anastasi, A. (1976). *Psychological Testing* (4th ed.). New York: Macmillan.

Anastasi, A. (1979). *Fields of Applied Psychology* (2nd ed.). New York: McGraw-Hill.

Anastasi, A., & Schaefer, C. (1971). Note on concepts of creativity and intelligence. *Journal of Creative Behavior, 3*, 113–116.

Anderson, A. (1982). "Neurotoxic follies." *Psychology Today,* July, 30–42.

Anderson, C. (1987). Temperature and aggression: Effects on quarterly, yearly, and city rates of violent and nonviolent crimes. *Journal of Personality and Social Psychology, 52*, 1161–1173.

Anderson, J. (1983a). *The Architecture of Cognition.* Cambridge, MA: Howard University Press.

Anderson, J. (1983b). A spreading activation theory of memory. *Journal of Verbal Learning and Verbal Behavior, 22*, 261–295.

Anderson, K. (1983). Crashing on cocaine. *Time,* April 13.

Anderton, B. (1987). Alzheimer's disease: Progress in molecular pathology. *Nature, 325*, 658–659.

Andreasen, N., & Canter, A. (1974). The creative writer: Psychiatric symptoms and family history. *Comprehensive Psychiatry, 15*, 125–131.

Archer, J., & Lloyd, B. (1985). *Sex and Gender.* New York: Cambridge University Press.

Archer, S. (1982). The lower age boundaries of identity development. *Child Development, 53*, 1551–1556.

Arehart-Treichel, J. (1977). The science of sleep. *Science News,* March 26, 203.

Arend, R., Gove, F., & Sroufe, L. (1979). Continuity of individual adaptation from infancy to kindergarten: A predictive study of ego-resiliency and curiosity in pre-schoolers. *Child Development, 50*, 950–959.

Arlin, P. (1975). Cognitive development in adulthood: A fifth stage? *Developmental Psychology, 11*, 602–606.

Arlin, P. (1977). Piagetian operations in problem finding. *Developmental Psychology, 13*, 297–298.

Arlow, J. (1984). Psychoanalysis. In R. Corsini (Ed.), *Current Psychotherapies.* Itasca, IL: Peacock.

Armentrout, J., & Burger, G. (1972). Children's reports of parental child-rearing behavior at five grade levels. *Developmental Psychology, 7*, 44–48.

Armstrong, S., Gleitman, L., & Gleitman, H. (1983). What some concepts might not be. *Cognition, 13*, 263–308.

Arnetz, B., Wasserman, J., Petrini, B., Brenner, S., Levi, L., Eneroth, P., Salovaara, H., Hjelm, R., Salovaara, L., Theorell, T., & Petterson, I. (1987). Immune function in unemployed women. *Psychosomatic Medicine, 49*, 3–12.

Aronson, E. (1980). *The Social Animal* (3rd ed.). New York: W. H. Freeman.

Aronson, E., & Osherow, N. (1980). Cooperative, prosocial behavior, and academic performance: Experiments in the desegregated classroom. In L. Bickman (Ed.), *Applied Social Psychology Annual* (Vol. 1). Beverly Hills, CA: Sage.

Arrowood, J., & Short, J. (1973). Agreement, attraction, and self-esteem. *Canadian Journal of Behavioral Science, 5*, 242–252.

Arthur, A. (1987). Stress as a state of anticipatory vigilance. *Perceptual and Motor Skills, 64*, 75–85.

Asch, S. (1946). Forming impressions of personality. *Journal of Abnormal and Social Psychology, 41*, 258–290.

Asch, S. (1951). Effects of group pressure upon the modification and distortion of judgments. In H. Guetzkow (Ed.), *Groups, Leadership, and Men.* Pittsburgh: Carnegie Press.

Aserinsky, E., & Kleitman, N. (1953). Regularly occurring periods of eye motility and concomitant phenomena during sleep. *Science, 118*, 273–274.

Ashmore, R., & Del Boca, F. (1976). Psychological approaches to understanding intergroup conflicts. In P. Katz (Ed.), *Towards the Elimination of Racism.* New York: Pergamon.

Aslin, R., Pisoni, D., & Jusczyk, P. (1983). Auditory development and speech perception in infancy. In M. Harth & J. Campos (Eds.), *Handbook of Child Psychology: Infancy and Developmental Psychobiology* (Vol. 2). New York: Wiley.

Athanasiou, R., Shaver, P., & Tavris, C. (1970). Sex. *Psychology Today,* July, 39–52.

Atkin, C. (1982). Changing male and female roles. In M. Schwarz (Ed.), *TV and Teens: Experts Look at the Issues.* Reading, MA: Addison-Wesley.

Atkinson, J. (1957). Motivational determinants of risk-taking behavior. *Psychological Review, 64*, 359–372.

Atkinson, J., & Litwin, G. (1960). Achievement motive and test anxiety conceived as motive to approach success and motive to avoid failure. *Journal of Abnormal and Social Psychology, 60*, 52–63.

Atkinson, J., & Raynor, J. (1974). *Motivation and Achievement.* Washington, DC: Winston.

Atkinson, R., & Shiffrin, R. (1968). Human memory: A proposed system and its control processes. In K. Spence and J. Spence (Eds.), *The Psychology of Learning and Motivation: Advances in Research and Theory* (Vol. 2). New York: Academic Press.

Atkinson, R., & Shiffrin, R. (1971). The control of short-term memory. *Scientific American, 224*, 83–89.

Austrom, D., & Hanel, K. (1985). Psychological issues of single life in Canada: An exploratory study. *International Journal of Women's Studies, 8*, 12–23.

Avison, W., & Speechley, K. (1987). The discharged psychiatric patient: A review of social, social-psychological, and psychiatric correlates of outcomes. *American Journal of Psychiatry, 144*, 10–18.

Bachrach, A., Erwin, W., & Mohn, J. (1965). The control of eating behavior in an anorexic by operant conditioning techniques. In L. Ullman & L. Krasner (Eds.), *Case Studies in Behavior Modification.* New York: Holt, Rinehart and Winston.

Backlund, E., Grandberg, P., Hamberger, B., Knutsson, E., Martensson, A., Sedvall, G., Seiger, A., & Olson, L. (1985). Transplantation of adrenal medullary tissue to striatum in Parkinsonism: First clinical trials. *Journal of Neurosurgery, 62*, 169–173.

Bahnson, C. (1981). Stress and cancer: The state of the art. *Psychosomatics, 22*, 207–220.

Baillargeon, R. (1987). Object permanence in 3½- and 4½-month-old infants. *Developmental Psychology, 33*, 655–664.

Bakay, R. (1985). Paper presented at the World Congress of Neurosurgery, Toronto, Canada.

Baker, L., Dearborn, M., Hastings, J., & Hamberger, K. (1984). Type A behavior in women: A review. *Health Psychology, 3*, 477–497.

Bale, J., Bell, W., Dunn, V., Afifi, A., & Menezen, A. (1986). Magnetic resonance imaging of the spine in children. *Archives of Neurology, 43*, 1253–1256.

Balota, D., & Lorch, R. (1986). Depth of automatic spreading activation: Medicated primary effects in pronunciation but not in lexical decision. *Journal of Experimental Psychology: Learning, Memory, and Cognition, 12*, 336–345.

Baltrusch, H., & Waltz, E. (1985). Cancer from a biobehavioral and social epidemiological perspective. *Social Science and Medicine, 20*, 789–794.

Bancroft, J. (1984). Hormones and sexual behavior. *Journal of Sex and Marital Therapy, 10*, 3–21.

Bandura, A. (1960). *Relationship of Family Patterns to Child Behavior Disorders.* Progress Report, Project M-1734, Stanford University, Stanford, CA: U.S. Public Health Service.

Bandura, A. (1965). Influence of model's reinforcement contingencies on the acquisition of imitative responses. *Journal of Personality and Social Psychology, 1*, 589–595.

Bandura, A. (1969). *Principles of Behavior Modification.* New York: Holt, Rinehart and Winston.

Bandura, A. (1971). *Social Learning Theory.* Morristown, NJ: General Learning Press.

Bandura, A. (1977). *Social Learning Theory.* Englewood Cliffs, NJ: Prentice-Hall.

Bandura, A. (1982). Self-efficacy mechanism in human agency. *American Psychologist, 37*, 122–147.

Bandura, A. (1983). Temporal dynamics and decomposition of reciprocal determinism: A reply to Phillips and Orton. *Psychological Review, 90*, 166–170.

Bandura, A. (1986). *Social Foundations of Thought and Action: A Social Cognitive Theory.* Englewood Cliffs, NJ: Prentice-Hall.

Bandura, A., & Mischel, W. (1965). Modification of self-imposed delay of reward through exposure to live and symbolic models. *Journal of Personality and Social Psychology, 2*, 698–705.

Bandura, A., Ross, D., & Ross, S. (1961). Transmission of aggression through imitation of aggressive models. *Journal of Abnormal and Social Psychology, 63*, 575–582.

Bandura, A., Ross, D., & Ross, S. (1963). Imitation of film-mediated aggressive models. *Journal of Abnormal and Social Psychology, 66*, 3–11.

Bandura, A., & Walters, R. (1959). *Adolescent Aggression.* New York: Ronald Press.

Barahal, H. (1958). 1000 prefrontal lobotomies: Five-to-ten-year follow-up study. *Psychiatric Quarterly, 32*, 653–678.

Barber, T. (1975). Responding to "hypnotic" suggestions: An introspective report. *American Journal of Clinical Hypnosis, 18*, 6–22.

Barber, T., & Wilson, S. (1977). Hypnosis suggestions and altered states of consciousness: Experimental evaluation of a new cognitive-behavioral theory and the traditional trance-state therapy of "hypnosis." *Annals of the New York Academy of Sciences, 296,* 34–47.

Bard, P. (1934). On emotional expression after decortization with some remarks on certain theoretical views. *Psychological Review, 41,* 309–329.

Baribeau, J., Braun, C., & Dubé, B. (1986). Effects of alcohol intoxication on visuo-spatial and verbal-contextual tests of emotion discrimination in familial risk for alcoholism. *Alcoholism: Clinical and Experimental Research, 10,* 496–499.

Barker, R. (1968). *Ecological Psychology.* Stanford, CA: Stanford University Press.

Baron, J. (1977). What we might know about orthographic rules. In S. Dornic (Ed.), *Attention and Performance.* Hillsdale, NJ: Erlbaum.

Baron, R., & Byrne, D. (1984). *Social Psychology* (4th ed.). Boston: Allyn and Bacon.

Baron, R., & Byrne, D. (1987). *Social Psychology: Understanding Human Interaction* (5th ed.). Boston: Allyn & Bacon.

Baron, R., & Ransberger, V. (1978). Ambient temperature and the occurrence of collective violence. The "long, hot summer" revisited. *Journal of Personality and Social Psychology, 36,* 351–360.

Barnes, D. (1987a). Defect in Alzheimer's is on chromosome 21. *Science, 23,* 846–847.

Barnes, D. (1987b). Biological issues in schizophrenia. *Science, 235,* 430–433.

Barron, F., & Harrington, D. (1981). Creativity, intelligence, and personality. *Annual Review of Psychology, 32,* 439–476.

Barrow, G., & Smith, P. (1979). *Aging, Ageism, and Society.* St. Paul, MN: West.

Bartlett, F. (1932). *Remembering: A Study in Experimental and Social Psychology.* Cambridge, England: Cambridge University Press.

Bartrop, R., Lockhurst, E., Lazarus, L., Kiloh, L., & Penny, R. (1977). Depressed lymphocyte function after bereavement. *Lancet, 1,* 834–836.

Bartusiak, M. (1980). Beeper man. *Discover,* November, 57.

Bass, B., & Ryterband, E. (1979). *Organizational Psychology* (2nd ed.). Boston: Allyn & Bacon.

Baum, A., & Davis, G. (1980). Reducing the stress of high-density living: An architectual intervention. *Journal of Personality and Social Psychology, 38,* 471–481.

Baum, A., & Valins, S. (1977). *Architecture and Social Behavior: Psychological Studies of Social Density.* Hillsdale, NJ: Erlbaum.

Baum, A., & Valins, S. (1979). Architectural mediation of residential density and control: Crowding and regulation of social contact. In L. Berkowitz (Ed.), *Advances in Experimental Social Psychology,* Vol. 12. New York: Academic Press.

Baumeister, R., & Covington, M. (1985). Self-esteem, persuasion, and retrospective distortion of initial attitudes. *Electronic Social Psychology, 1,* 1–22.

Baumrind, D. (1964) Some thoughts on ethics of research after reading Milgram's "Behavioral study of obedience." *American Psychologist, 19,* 421–423.

Baumrind, D. (1971). Current patterns of parental authority. *Developmental Monographs, 4,* 1–103.

Baylis, G., Rolls, E., & Leonard, C. (1985). Selectivity between faces in the responses of a population of neurons in the cortex in the superior temporal sulcus of the monkey. *Brain Research, 342,* 91–102.

Beck, A. (1976). *Cognitive Therapy and Emotional Disorders.* New York: International Universities Press.

Beck, A., Kovacs, M., & Weissman, A. (1979). Assessment of suicidal ideation: The Scale for Suicide Ideation. *Journal of Consulting and Clinical Psychology, 47,* 343–352.

Beck, A., & Ward, C. (1961). Dreams of depressed patients: Characteristic themes in manifest content. *Archives of General Psychiatry, 5,* 462–467.

Beck, R. (1986). *Applying Psychology* (2nd ed.). Englewood Cliffs, NJ: Prentice-Hall.

Begleiter, H., Porjesz, B., Bihari, B., & Kissin, B. (1984). Event-related brain potentials in boys at risk for alcoholism. *Science, 225,* 1993–1996.

Belger, A., Blehm, K., & Buchan, R. (1987). The determination of ambient air quality within an environmental care unit. *Journal of Environmental Health, 49,* 288–293.

Belicki, D., & Belicki, K. (1982). Nightmares in a university population. *Sleep Research, 11,* 116–121.

Belko, A., Van Loan, M., Barbieri, T., & Mayclin, P. (1987). Diet, exercise, weight loss, and energy expenditure in moderately overweight women. *International Journal of Obesity, 11,* 93–104.

Bell, A., & Weinberg, M. (1978). *Homosexualities: A Study of Diversity Among Men and Women.* New York: Simon and Schuster.

Bell, A., Weinberg, M., & Hammersmith, S. (1981). *Sexual Preference: Its Development in Men and Women.* Bloomington, IN: Indiana University Press.

Bell, P., Fisher, J., & Loomis, R. (1978). *Environmental Psychology.* Philadelphia: Saunders.

Bell, R., & Hepper, P. (1987). Catecholamines and aggression in animals. *Behavioural Brain Research, 23,* 1–21.

Bellingrath, G. (1930). Qualities associated with leadership in extra curricular activities of the high school. *Teachers College, Contributions to Education, 399,* Columbia University.

Bem, D. (1972). Self-perception theory. In L. Berkowitz (Ed.), *Advances in Experimental Social Psychology* (Vol. 6). New York: Academic Press.

Bem, D. (1983). Further *deja vu* in the search for cross-situational consistency: A response to Mischel and Peake. *Psychological Review, 90,* 390–393.

Bemis, K. (1978). Current approaches to the etiology and treatment of anorexia nervosa. *Psychological Bulletin, 85,* 593–617.

Benbow, C. (1987). Possible biological correlates of precocious mathematical reasoning ability. *Trends in Neurosciences, 10,* 17–20.

Benson, H. (1977). Systematic hypertension and the relaxation response. *The New England Journal of Medicine, 296,* 1152–1156.

Benson, H., Kotch, J. Crassweller, K., & Greenwood, M. (1977). Historical and clinical considerations of the relaxation response. *American Scientist, 65,* 441–445.

Bergin, A., & Lambert, M. (1978). The evaluation of therapeutic outcomes. In S. Garfield & A. Bergin (Eds.), *Handbook of Psychotherapy and Behavior Change: An Empirical Analysis* (2nd ed.). New York: Wiley.

Berkowitz, L. (1954). Group standards, cohesiveness, and productivity. *Human Relations, 7,* 509–519.

Berkowitz, L. (1978). Whatever happened to the frustration-aggression hypothesis? *American Behavior Scientist, 21,* 691–708.

Berkowitz, L. (1986). *A Survey of Social Psychology* (3rd ed.). New York: Holt, Rinehart and Winston.

Berkowitz, L., & Geen, R. (1966). Film violence and cue properties of available targets. *Journal of Personality and Social Psychology, 3,* 525–530.

Berkowitz, L., & Lepage, A. (1976). Weapons as aggression-eliciting stimuli. *Journal of Personality and Social Psychology, 7,* 202–207.

Berlyne, D. (1970). Novelty, complexity, and hedonic value. *Perception and Psychophysics, 8,* 279–286.

Berlyne, D. (1971). *Aesthetics and Psychobiology.* New York: Appleton, Century, Crofts.

Berman, E., & Wolpert, E. (1987). Intractible manic-depressive psychosis with rapid cycling in an 18-year-old woman successfully treated with electroconvulsive therapy. *The Journal of Nervous and Mental Disease, 175,* 236–239.

Berman, J., & Norton, N. (1985). Does professional training make a therapist more effective? *Psychological Bulletin, 98,* 401–407.

Berndt, T. (1982). The features and

effects of friendships in early adolescence. *Child Development, 53,* 1447–1460.

Bersoff, D. (1981). Testing and the law. *American Psychologist, 36,* 1047–1056.

Besson, J., & Chaouch, A. (1987). Peripheral and spinal mechanisms of nociception. *Physiological Reviews, 67,* 67–186.

Bexton, W., Heron, W., & Scott, T. (1954). Effects of decreased variation in the sensory environment. *Canadian Journal of Psychology, 8,* 70–76.

Bick, P., & Kinsbourne, M. (1987). Auditory hallucinations and subvocal speech in schizophrenic patients. *American Journal of Psychiatry, 144,* 222–225.

Binet, A., & Simon, T. (1905). *The Development of Intelligence in Children.* Baltimore: Williams & Wilkins.

Bingol, N., Fuchs, M., Diaz, V., Stone, R., & Gromisch, D. (1987). Teratogenicity of cocaine in humans. *Journal of Pediatrics, 110,* 93–96.

Bird, E., Spokes, E., & Iversen, L. (1979). Brain norepinephrine and dopamine in schizophrenia. *Science, 204,* 93–94.

Bischof, L., (1976). *Adult Psychology* (2nd ed.). New York: Harper & Row.

Bitterman, M. (1975). The comparative analysis of learning. *Science, 188,* 699–709.

Black, I., Adler, J., Dreyfus, C., Friedman, W., LaGamma, E., & Roach, A. (1987). Biochemistry of information storage in the nervous system. *Science, 236,* 1263–1268.

Blaney, P. (1986). Affect and memory: A review. *Psychological Bulletin, 99,* 229–246.

Blasi, A. (1980). Bridging moral cognition and moral action: A critical review of the literature. *Psychological Bulletin, 88,* 1–45.

Bleuler, E. (1950). *Dementia Praecox or the Group of Schizophrenias.* New York: International Universities Press.

Bliss, E. (1984). Spontaneous self-hypnosis in multiple personality disorder. *Psychiatric Clinics of North America, 7,* 135–148.

Bloch, S. (1979). Group psychotherapy. In S. Bloch (Ed.), *An Introduction to the Psychotherapies.* Oxford, England: Oxford University Press.

Block, J. (1971). *Lives Through Time.* Berkeley, CA: Bancroft.

Bloom, F., Lazerson, A., & Hofstadter, L. (1985). *Brain, Mind, and Behavior.* New York: W. H. Freeman.

Bloom, L., & Capatides, J. (1987). Sources of meaning in the acquisition of complex syntax: The sample case of causality. *Journal of Experimental Child Psychology, 43,* 112–128.

Blum, H. (1986). Psychoanalysis. In I. Kutash & A. Wolf (Eds.), *Psychotherapist's Casebook.* San Francisco: Jossey-Bass.

Blum, K. (1984). *Handbook of Abusable Drugs.* New York: Gardner Press.

Boffey, P. (1982). Panel clears 2 accused of scientific fraud in alcoholism study. *The New York Times,* November 5, A12.

Bolles, R. (1979). *Learning Theory* (2nd ed.). New York: Holt, Rinehart and Winston.

Bolter, A., Heminger, A., Martin, G., & Fry, M. (1976). Outpatient clinical experience in a community drug abuse program with phencyclidine abuse. *Clinical Toxicology, 9,* 593–600.

Boor, M. (1982). The multiple personality epidemic: Additional cases and inferences regarding diagnosis, etiology, dynamics, and treatment. *Journal of Nervous and Mental Disease, 170,* 302–304.

Borke, H. (1975). Piaget's mountains revisited: Changes in the egocentric landscape. *Developmental Psychology, 11,* 240–243.

Borkovec, T., (1970). Autonomic reactivity to sensory stimulation in psychopathic, neurotic, and normal juvenile delinquents. *Journal of Consulting and Clinical Psychology, 35,* 217–222.

Borman, W., Eaton, N., Bryan, J., & Rosse, R. (1983). Validity of army recruits behavioral assessment. Does the assessor make a difference? *Journal of Applied Psychology, 68,* 415–419.

Borman, W., Rosse, R., & Abrahams, N. (1980). An empirical construct validity approach to studying predictor-job performance links. *Journal of Applied Psychology, 65,* 662–671.

Borysenko, M., & Borysenko, J. (1982). Stress, behavior, and immunity: Animal models and mediating mechanisms. *General Hospital Psychiatry, 4,* 59–67.

Bouchard, T. (1984). Twins reared together and apart: What they tell us about human diversity. In S. Fox (Ed.), *Individuality and Determinism.* New York: Plenum.

Bourne, L., Dominowski, R., Loftus, E., & Healy, A. (1986). *Cognitive Processes* (2nd ed.). Englewood Cliffs, NJ: Prentice-Hall.

Bourne, L., Ekstrand, B., & Dominowski, R. (1971). *The Psychology of Thinking.* Englewood Cliffs, NJ: Prentice-Hall.

Bousfield, W. (1953). The occurrence of clustering in the recall of randomly arranged associates. *Journal of General Psychology, 49,* 229–240.

Bower, G. (1981). Mood and memory. *American Psychologist, 36,* 129–148.

Bower, G., & Clark, M. (1969). Narrative stories as mediators for serial learning. *Psychonomic Science, 14,* 181–182.

Bower, G., & Mayer, J. (1985). Failure to replicate mood-dependent retrieval. *Bulletin of the Psychonomic Society, 23,* 39–42.

Bowers, M. (1980). Biochemical processes in schizophrenia: An update. *Schizophrenia.* Washington, DC: NIMH.

Bowlby, J. (1965). *Child Care and Growth of Love* (2nd ed.). Baltimore: Penguin.

Boyd, J. (1986). Use of mental health services for the treatment of panic disorder. *American Journal of Psychiatry, 143,* 1569–1574.

Boyd, J., & Weissman, M. (1981). Epidemiology of affective disorders. *Archives of General Psychiatry, 38,* 1039–1046.

Boyle, C., Berkowitz, G., & Kelsey, J. (1987). Epidemiology of premenstrual symptoms. *American Journal of Public Health, 77,* 349–350.

Bradburn, N., Rips, L., & Shevell, S. (1987). Answering autobiographical questions: The impact of memory and inference on surveys. *Science, 236,* 157–161.

Brady, J., & Lind, D. (1965). Experimental analysis of hysterical blindness. In L. Ullman and L. Krasner (Eds.), *Case Studies in Behavior Modification.* New York: Holt, Rinehart and Winston.

Breakefield, X., & Cambi, F. (1987). Molecular genetic insights into neurological diseases. *Annual Review of Neuroscience, 10,* 535–594.

Brecher, R., & Brecher, E. (1966). *An Analysis of Human Sexual Response.* New York: New American Library.

Breckler, S. (1984). Empirical validation of affect, behavior, and cognition as distinct components of attitude. *Journal of Personality and Social Psychology, 47,* 1191–1205.

Breggin, P. (1979). *Electroshock: Its Brain-Disabling Effects.* New York: Springer.

Bremer, J. (1959). *Asexualization.* New York: Macmillan.

Brewer, W., & Nakamura, G. (1984). The nature and functions of schemas, In R. Wyer and T. Srull (Eds.), *Handbook of Social Cognition* (Vol. 3). Hillsdale, NJ: Erlbaum.

Briddell, D., & Wise, G. (1976). Effects of alcohol and expectancy set on male sexual arousal. *Journal of Abnormal Psychology, 85,* 225–234.

Brigham, J. (1986). *Social Psychology.* Boston: Little, Brown.

Brigham, J., & Weissbach, T. (Eds.). (1972). *Racial Attitudes in America: Analyses and Findings of Social Psychology.* New York: Harper & Row.

Brittain, C. (1963). Adolescent choices and parent-peer cross-pressures. *American Sociological Review, 28,* 385–391.

Britton, G., & Lumpkin, M. (1984). Battle to imprint for the 21st century. *Reading Teacher, 37,* 724–733.

Broadbent, D., & Little, E. (1960). Effects of noise reduction in a work situation. *Occupational Psychology, 34,* 133–140.

Brodbeck, A., & Irwin, O. (1946). The

speech behavior of infants without families. *Child Development, 17,* 145–156.

Brody, J. (1985). Federal panel issues warning of obesity peril. *The Oregonian,* February 14, A1.

Bronzaft, A., & McCarthy, D. (1975). The effects of elevated train noise on reading ability. *Environment and Behavior, 7,* 517–527.

Brooks-Gunn, J., & Peterson, A. (1983). *Girls at Puberty: Biological and Psychosocial Perspectives.* New York: Plenum.

Brouilette, R., Fernbach, S., & Hunt, C. (1982). Obstructive sleep apnea in infants and children. *Journal of Pediatrics,* 31–40.

Broverman, J., Broverman, D., & Clarkson, F. (1970). Sexual stereotypes and clinical judgments of mental health. *Journal of Consulting and Clinical Psychology, 34,* 1–7.

Brown, B., Clasen, D., & Eicher, S. (1986a). Perceptions of peer pressure, peer conformity dispositions, and self-reported behavior among adolescents. *Developmental Psychology, 22,* 521–530.

Brown, B., Lohr, M., & McClenahan, E. (1986b). Early adolescent's perceptions of peer pressure. *Journal of Early Adolescence, 6,* 139–154.

Brown, J. (1958). Some tests of the decay theory of immediate memory. *Quarterly Journal of Experimental Psychology, 10,* 12–21.

Brown, J., & Lawton, M. (1986). Stress and well-being in adolescence: The moderating role of physical exercise. *Journal of Human Stress, 12,* 125–131.

Brown, R. (1973). *A First Language: The Early Stages.* Cambridge, MA: Howard University Press.

Brown, R., & Kulik, J. (1977). Flashbulb memories. *Cognition, 5,* 73–99.

Bruch, H. (1961). Transformation of oral impulses in eating disorders: A conceptual approach. *Psychiatric Quarterly, 35,* 458–481.

Bruner, J., Goodnow, J., & Austin, G. (1956). *A Study of Thinking.* New York: Wiley.

Bruner, J., & Tagiuri, R. (1954). The perception of people. In G. Lindzey (Ed.), *Handbook of Social Psychology* (Vol. 2). Reading, MA: Addison-Wesley.

Bruno, F. (1983). *Adjustment and Growth.* New York: Wiley.

Bryden, M., & Saxby, L. (1985). Developmental aspects of cerebral lateralization. In J. Obrzat & G. Hynd (Eds.), *Child Neuropsychology, Vol. 1: Theory and Research.* Orlando, FL: Academic Press.

Buchsbaum, M., Wu, J., DeLisi, L., Holcomb, H., Hazlett, E., Cooper-Langston, K., & Kessler, R. (1987). Positron emission tomography studies of basal ganglia and somatosensory cortex neuroleptic drug effects: Differences between normal controls and schizophrenic patients. *Biological Psychiatry, 22,* 479–494.

Buckingham, R. (1983). Hospice care in the United States: The process begins. *Omega, 13,* 159–171.

Bullough, V. (1986). Sexuality and religion. Paper presented at the Western Region Annual Conference of the Society for the Scientific Study of Sex, Scottsdale, Arizona, January.

Bunney, W., Goodwin, F., & Murphy, D. (1972). The "Switch Process" in manic-depressive illness. *Archives of General Psychiatry, 27,* 312–317.

Bunney, W., Murphy, D., Goodwin, F., & Borge, G. (1970). The switch process from depression to mania: Relationship to drugs which alter brain amines. *Lancet, 1,* 1022.

Burbach, J., Kovacs, G., de Wied, D., van Nispen, J., & Greven, H. (1983). A major metabolite of arginine vasopressin in the brain is a highly potent neuropeptide. *Science, 221,* 1310–1312.

Bureš, J., Burešova, O, & Bolhuis, J. (1987). Processing temporally discontiguous information is neither an exclusive nor the only function of the hippocampus. *Behavioral and Brain Sciences, 10,* 154–156.

Burt, C. (1966). The genetic determination of differences in intelligence: A study of monozygotic twins reared together and apart. *British Journal of Psychology, 57,* 137–153.

Buschke, H. (1977). Two-dimensional recall: Immediate identification of clusters in episodic and semantic memory. *Journal of Verbal Learning and Verbal Behavior, 16,* 201–215.

Bushman, B. (1984). Perceived symbols of authority and their influence in compliance. *Journal of Applied Social Psychology, 14,* 501–508.

Buss, A., & Finn, S. (1987). Classification of personality traits. *Journal of Personality and Social Psychology, 52,* 432–444.

Butler, R. (1961). Re-awakening interests. *Nursing Homes: Journal of American Nursing Home Associations, 10,* 8–19.

Byrne, D. (1971). *The Attraction Paradigm.* New York: Academic Press.

Byrne, D., Clore, G., & Worchel, P. (1966). The effect of economic similarity-dissimilarity on interpersonal attraction. *Journal of Personality and Social Psychology, 4,* 220–224.

Byrne, D., & Griffitt, W. (1973). Interpersonal attraction. *Annual Review of Psychology, 24,* 317–336.

Byrne, D., London, O., & Reeves, K. (1968). The effects of physical attractiveness, sex, and attitude similarity on interpersonal attraction. *Journal of Personality, 36,* 259–271.

Byrne, J. (1987). Cellular analysis of associative learning. *Physiological Reviews, 67,* 329–439.

Cadoret, R. (1978). Evidence for genetic inheritance of primary affective disorder in adoptees. *American Journal of Psychiatry, 135,* 463–466.

Cadoret, R., Troughton, E., & O'Gorman, T. (1987). Genetic and environmental factors in alcohol abuse and antisocial personality. *Journal of Studies on Alcohol, 48,* 1–8.

Cadwallader, M. (1975). Marriage as a wretched institution. In J. DeLora & J. DeLora (Eds.), *Intimate Lifestyles: Marriage and Its Alternatives.* Pacific Palisades, CA: Goodyear.

Cain, W. (1981). Educating your nose. *Psychology Today,* July, 49–56.

Calhoun, J. (1962). Population density and social pathology. *Scientific American, 206,* 139–148.

Calvert-Boyanowsky, J., Boyanowsky, E., Atkinson, M., Gaduta, D., & Reeves, J. (1976). Patterns of passion: Temperature and human emotions. In D. Krebs (Ed.), *Readings in Social Psychology: Contemporary Perspectives.* New York: Harper & Row.

Cameron, N. (1947). *The Psychology of Behavior Disorders.* Boston: Houghton Mifflin.

Campbell, A. (1975). The American way of mating: Marriage Si, children only maybe. *Psychology Today,* May, 37–43.

Campbell, C., & Davis, J. (1974). Licking rate of rats is reduced by intraduodenal and intraportal glucose infusion. *Physiology and Behavior, 12,* 357–365.

Campbell, D., & Specht, J. (1985). Altruism: Biology, culture, and religion. *Journal of Social and Clinical Psychology, 3,* 33–42.

Campbell, S. (1987). Evolutions of sleep structure following brief intervals of wakefulness. *Electroencephalographic Clinical Neurophysiology, 66,* 175–184.

Campos, J., Hiatt, S., Ramsay, D., Henderson, C., & Svejda, M. (1978). The emergence of fear on the visual cliff. In M. Lewis and L. Rosenblum (Eds.), *The Development of Affect.* New York: Plenum.

Cannon W. (1927). The James-Lange theory of emotions: A critical examination and an alternative. *American Journal of Psychology, 39,* 106–124.

Cannon, W. (1934). Hunger and thirst. In C. Murchison (Ed.), *Handbook of General Experimental Psychology.* Worcester, MA: Clark University Press.

Cannon, W., & Washburn, A. (1912). An exploration of hunger. *American Journal of Physiology, 29,* 441–454.

Cantor, N., & Mischel, W. (1979). Prototypes in person perception. In L. Berkowitz (Ed.), *Advances in Experimental Social Psychology* (Vol. 12). New York: Academic Press.

Carelli, M., & Benelli, B. (1986). Linguistic development of twins. *Eta Evolutiva*, 24, 107–116.

Carew, J. (1980). Experience and the development of intelligence in young children at home and in day care. *Monographs of the Society for Research in Child Development*, 45, 6–7.

Carew, T., & Sahley, L. (1986). Invertebrate learning and memory: From behaviorism to molecules. *Annual Review of Neuroscience*, 9, 435–487.

Carlen, P., Penn, R., Fornazzari, L., Bennett, J., Wilkinson, D., Phil, D., & Wortzman, G. (1986). Computerized tomographic scan assessment of alcoholic brain damage and its potential reversibility. *Alcoholism: Clinical and Experimental Research*, 10, 226–232.

Carlsmith, J., & Anderson, C. (1979). Ambient temperature and the occurrence of collective violence. A new analysis. *Journal of Personality and Social Psychology*, 37, 337–341.

Carlson, B., & Goodwin, F. (1973). The stages of mania. *Archives of General Psychiatry*, 28, 221–228.

Carlson, N. (1981). *Physiology of Behavior* (2nd ed.). Boston: Allyn & Bacon.

Carlsson, A. (1977). Does dopamine play a role in schizophrenia? *Psychological Medicine*, 7, 583–595.

Cartwright, R. (1978). Happy endings for our dreams. *Psychology Today*, December, 66–77.

Carver, C., & Glass, D. (1978). Coronary-prone behavior pattern and interpersonal aggression. *Journal of Personality and Social Psychology*, 36, 361–366.

Carver, C., & Scheier, M. (1978). Self-focusing effects of dispositional self-consciousness, mirror presence, and audience presence. *Journal of Personality and Social Psychology*, 36, 324–332.

Cash, T., & Janda, L. (1984). The eye of the beholder. *Psychology Today*, December, 46–52.

Casper, C., Eckert, E., Halmi, K., Goldberg, S., & Davis, J. (1980). Bulimia: Its incidence and clinical importance in patients with anorexia nervosa. *Archives of General Psychiatry*, 37, 1030–1035.

Castillo, M., & Butterworth, G. (1981). Neonatal localization of a sound in visual space. *Perception*, 10, 331–338.

Cattell, R. (1950). *A Systematic Theoretical and Factual Study*. New York: McGraw-Hill.

Cattell, R. (1965). *The Scientific Analysis of Personality*. Baltimore: Penguin Books.

Cattell, R. (1973). Personality pinned down. *Psychology Today*, July, 40–46.

Cattell, R. (1982). *The Inheritance of Personality and Ability*. New York: Academic Press.

Cattell, R., Saunders, D., & Stice, G. (1950). *The 16 Personality Factor Questionnaire*. Champaign, IL: Institute for Personality and Ability Testing.

Centers for Disease Control. (1984). Fetal alcohol syndrome: Public awareness week. *Morbidity and Mortality Weekly Report*, 33, 1–2.

Cerlitti, B., & Bini, L. (1938). L'elettroshock. *Archiva Generale Neurologia Psychiatria Psicoanalysia*, 19, 266.

Chadwick, D. (1986). "Grizz"—of men and the great bear. *National Geographic*, 169, 182–213.

Chaiken, S., & Stangor, C. (1987). Attitudes and attitude change. *Annual Review of Psychology*, 38, 575–630.

Chang, T. (1986). Semantic memory: Facts and models. *Psychological Bulletin*, 99, 199–220.

Charlesworth, E., & Nathan, R. (1982). *Stress Management: A Comprehensive Guide to Wellness*. Houston, TX: Biobehavioral Press.

Charney, D., Heninger, G., & Sternberg, D. (1984). Serotonin function and the mechanism of action of antidepressant treatment. *Archives of General Psychiatry*, 41, 359–365.

Chase, M. (1986). Overview of sleep research, circa 1985. *Sleep*, 9, 452–457.

Chase, M., & Morales, F. (1983). Subthreshold excitatory activity and motor neuron discharge during REM periods of active sleep. *Science*, 221, 1195–1198.

Chesno, F., & Kilmann, P. (1975). Effects of stimulation intensity on sociopathic avoidance learning. *Journal of Abnormal Psychology*, 84, 144–151.

Chomsky, N. (1965). *Aspects of the Theory of Syntax*. Cambridge, MA: MIT Press.

Chomsky, N. (1968). *Language and Mind*. New York: Harcourt Brace Jovanovich.

Chomsky, N. (1980). The linguistic approach. In M. Piatelli-Palmarini (Ed.), *Language and Learning*. Cambridge, MA: Harvard University Press.

Chorover, S., & Schiller, P. (1965). Short-term retrograde amnesia in rats. *Journal of Comparative and Physiological Psychology*, 59, 73–78.

Chozick, B. (1986). The behavioral effects of lesions of the amygdala: A review. *International Journal of Neuroscience*, 29, 205–221.

Christian, S., Bennington, F., Marin, R., & Corbett, L. (1975). Gas-liquid chromatographic separation of biologically important indolealkylamines from human cerebrospinal fluid. *Biochemical Medicine*, 14, 191–200.

Chu, G. (1967). Prior familiarity, perceived bias, and one-sided versus two-sided communication. *Journal of Experimental Social Psychology*, 3, 243–254.

Chumlea, W. (1982). Physical growth in adolescence. In B. Wolman (Ed.), *Handbook of Developmental Psychology*. Englewood Cliffs, NJ: Prentice-Hall.

Cialdini, R., & Richardson, K. (1980). Two indirect tactics of image management: Basking and Blasting. *Journal of Personality and Social Psychology*, 39, 406–415.

Cialdini, R., Vincent, J., Lewis, S., Catalan, J., Wheeler, D., & Darby, B. (1975). Reciprocal concessions procedure for inducing compliance: The door-in-the-face technique. *Journal of Personality and Social Psychology*, 31, 206–215.

Ciesielski, K., Beech, H., & Gordon, P. (1981). Some electrophysiological observations in obsessional states. *British Journal of Psychiatry*, 138, 479–484.

Cirignotta, F., Mondini, S., Zucconi, M., Lenzi, P., & Lugaresi, E. (1985). Insomnia: An epidemiological survey. *Clinical Neuropharmacology*, 8, Suppl. 1, 549–554.

Clarizio, H., & Yelon, S. (1974). Learning theory approaches to classroom management: Rationale and intervention techniques. In A. Brown & C. Avery (Eds.), *Modifying Childrens' Behavior: A Book of Readings*. Springfield, IL: Thomas.

Clark, D., & Teasdale, J. (1982). Diurnal variation in clinical depression and accessibility of memories of positive and negative experiences. *Journal of Abnormal Psychology*, 91, 87–95.

Clark, E. (1983). Meanings and concepts. In J. Flavell & E. Markman (Eds.), *Handbook of Child Psychology: Cognitive Development* (Vol. 3). New York: Wiley.

Clarke, A. M., & Clarke, A. D. (1976). *Early Experience: Myth and Evidence*. London: Open Books.

Clark-Stewart, A. (1977). *Child Care in the Family: A Review of Research and Some Propositions for Policy*. New York: Academic Press.

Clarke-Stewart, K. (1978). And daddy makes three: The father's impact on mother and young child. *Child Development*, 49, 466–478.

Clarren, S., & Smith, D. (1978). The fetal alcohol syndrome. *The New England Journal of Medicine*, 298, 1063–1067.

Cleckley, H. (1976). *The Mask of Sanity* (5th ed.). St. Louis: Mosby.

Cloninger, C., Martin, R., Clayton, P., & Guze, S. (1981). Blind follow-up and family study of anxiety neuroses. In D. Klein & J. Rabkin (Eds.), *Anxiety: New Research and Changing Concepts*. New York: Raven.

Cloninger, R., Bohman, M., & Sigvaardson, S. (1981). Inheritance of alcohol abuse: Cross-fostering analysis of adopted men. *Archives of General Psychiatry*, 38, 861–867.

Cohen, S. (1978). Marijuana as medicine. *Psychology Today*, April, 60–73.

Cohen, S. (1980). Aftereffects of stress on human performance and social behavior: A review of research and theory. *Psychological Bulletin*, 88, 82–102.

Cohen, S., & Callahan, J. (Eds.) (1986). *The Diagnosis and Treatment of Drug and Alcohol Abuse*. New York: Haworth Press.

Cohen, S., Evans, G., Krantz, D., & Stokols, D. (1980). Physiological, motivational, and cognitive effects of aircraft noise on children: Moving from the laboratory to the field. *American Psychologist*, 35, 231–243.

Cohen, S., Evans, G., Krantz, D., & Stokols, D. (1981). Cardiovascular and behavioral effects of community noise. *American Scientist*, 69, 528–535.

Cohen, S., Glass, D., & Singer, J. (1973). Apartment noise, auditory discrimination, and reading ability in children. *Journal of Experimental Social Psychology*, 9, 407–422.

Cohen, S., & Wills, T. (1985). Stress, social support, and the buffering hypothesis. *Psychological Bulletin*, 98, 310–357.

Cohn, J. & Tronick, E. (1987). Mother-infant face-to-face interaction: The sequence of dyadic states at 3, 6, and 9 months. *Developmental Psychology*, 23, 68–77.

Colasanti, B. (1982a). Anti-depressant therapy. In C. Craig & R. Stitzel (Eds.), *Modern Pharmacology*. Boston: Little, Brown.

Colasanti, B., (1982b). Anti-psychotic drugs. In C. Craig & R. Stitzel (Eds.), *Modern Pharmacology*. Boston: Little, Brown.

Coleman, J. (1966). *Equality of Educational Opportunity*. Washington, DC: U.S. Government Printing Office.

Coleman, J., Butcher, J., & Carson, R. (1984). *Abnormal Psychology and Modern Life* (7th ed.). Glenview, IL: Scott, Foresman.

Coles, C., Smith, I., Lancaster, J., & Falek, A. (1987). Persistence over the first month of neurobehavioral differences in infants exposed to alcohol prenatally. *Infant Behavior and Development*, 10, 23–37.

Collins, R. (1983). Head Start: An update on program effects. *Newsletter, Society for Research in Child Development*, Summer, 1–2.

Collins, R. (1984). Head Start: A review of research with implications for practice in early childhood education. Paper presented at the meeting of the American Education Research Association, New Orleans, Louisiana, April.

Collins, A., & Loftus, E. (1975). A spreading activation theory of semantic processing. *Psychological Review*, 82, 407–428.

Collins, A., & Quillian, M. (1969). Retrieval time from semantic memory. *Journal of Verbal Learning and Verbal Behavior*, 8, 240–247.

Colwill, R., & Rescorla, R. (1986). Associative structures in instrumental learning. In G. Bower (Ed.), *The Psychology of Learning and Motivation* (Vol. 20). New York: Academic Press.

Commons, M., Richard, F., & Armon, C. (1982). *Beyond Formal Operations: Late Adolescent and Adult Cognitive Development*. New York: Praeger.

Condon, W., & Sander, L. (1974). Neonate movement as synchronized with adult speech: Interactional participation in language acquisition. *Science*, 183, 99–101.

Conel, J. (1939–1963). *The Postnatal Development of the Human Cerebral Cortex* (Vols. I–VI). Cambridge, MA: Howard University Press.

Conger, J., & Peterson, A. (1984). *Adolescence and Youth: Psychological Development and a Changing World*. New York: Harper & Row.

Conrad, R. (1964). Acoustic confusions in immediate memory. *British Journal of Psychology*, 55, 75–84.

Conrad, R. (1972). Short-term memory in the deaf: A test for speech coding. *British Journal of Psychology*, 63, 173–180.

Cook, N. (1986). *The Brain Code: Mechanisms of Information Transfer and the Role of the Corpus Callosum*. New York: Methuen.

Cook, S. (1970). Motives in a conceptual analysis of attitude-related behavior. In W. Arnold and D. Levine (Eds.), *Nebraska Symposium on Motivation, 1969*. Lincoln, NE: University of Nebraska Press.

Cook, S. (1984a). The 1954 social science statement and school desegregation: A reply to Gerard. *American Psychologist*, 39, 819–832.

Cook, S. (1984b). Cooperative interaction in multiethnic contexts. In N. Miller & M. Brewer (Eds.), *Groups in Contact: The Psychology of Desegregation*. New York: Academic Press.

Coons, P., & Bradley, K. (1985). Group psychotherapy with multiple personality patients. *Journal of Nervous and Mental Disease*, 173, 515–521.

Cooper, C., & Marshall, J. (1976). Occupational sources of stress: A review of the literature relating to coronary heart disease and mental ill health. *Journal of Occupational Psychology*, 49, 11–28.

Cooper, J., Bloom, F., and Roth, R. (1986). *The Biochemical Basis of Neuropharmacology*. Fairlawn, NJ: Oxford University Press.

Coopersmith, S. (1967). *Antecedents of Self-Esteem*. San Francisco: W. H. Freeman.

Coppen, A. (1972). Indoleamines and affective disorders. *Journal of Psychiatric Research*, 9, 163–171.

Coren, S., Porac, C., & Ward, L. (1984). *Sensation and Perception* (2nd ed.). New York: Academic Press.

Corkin, S. (1980). A prospective study of cingulotomy. In E. Valenstein (Ed.), *The Psychosurgery Debate*. San Francisco: W. H. Freeman.

Costello, C. (1976). Electroconvulsive therapy: Is further investigation necessary? *Canadian Psychiatric Association Journal*, 21, 61–67.

Cowart, B. (1981). Development of taste perception in humans: Sensitivity and preference throughout the lifespan. *Psychological Bulletin*, 90, 43–73.

Cox, J. (1986). Cholecystokinin interacts with prefeeding to impair runway performance. *Behavioural Brain Research*, 21, 29–36.

Cox, V., Kakolewski, J., & Valenstein, E. (1968). Effect of ventromedial hypothalamic damage in hypophysectomized rats. *Journal of Comparative and Physiological Psychology*, 65, 145–148.

Coyne, J. (1976). Toward an interactional description of depression. *Psychiatry*, 39, 28–40.

Craik, F., & McDowd, J. (1987). Age differences in recall and recognition. *Journal of Experimental Psychology: Learning, and Cognition*, 13, 474–479.

Craik, F., & Tulving, E. (1975). Depth of processing and the retention of words in episodic memory. *Journal of Experimental Psychology: General*, 104, 268–294.

Creekmore, C. (1985). Cities won't drive you crazy. *Psychology Today*, 19, 46–53.

Crick, F. (1982). Do dendritic spines twitch? *Trends in Neuroscience*, February, 44–46.

Crick, F., & Mitchison, G. (1983). The function of dream sleep. *Nature*, 304, 111–114.

Crocker, J., Thompson, L., McGraw, K., & Ingerman, C. (1987). Downward comparison, prejudice, and evaluations of others: Effects of self-esteem and threat. *Journal of Personality and Social Psychology*, 52, 907–916.

Cronbach, L. (1978). Review of the BITCH test. In O. Buros (Ed.), *The Eighth Mental Measurements Yearbook* (Vol. 1). Highland Park, NJ: Gryphon Press.

Cronbach, L. (1984). *Essentials of Psychological Testing* (4th ed.). Cambridge, MA: Harper & Row.

Crooks, R. (1969). Alleviation of fear in a dental setting via film-modeling. In American Association of Dental Schools, *Report of Dental Education Summer Internship Program*. Chicago: American Association of Dental Schools.

Crooks, R. (1972). Differential proactive effects of ECS on massed versus spaced-trial learning. Unpublished Ph.D. Dissertation.

Crooks, R. (1986). Sexual attitudes and behaviors among a population of college students. Unpublished research.

Crooks, R., & Baur, K. (1987). *Our Sexuality* (3rd ed.). Menlo Park, CA: Benjamin/Cummings.

Cross, P., Cattell, R., & Butcher, H.

(1967). The personality patterns of creative artists. *British Journal of Educational Psychology*, 1967, 37, 292–299.

Crowder, R. (1970). The role of one's own voice in immediate memory. *Cognitive Psychology*, 1, 157–158.

Crowder, R. (1976). *Principles of Learning and Memory.* Hillsdale, NJ: Erlbaum.

Crowe, R. (1974). An adoption study of antisocial personality. *Archives of General Psychiatry*, 31, 785–791.

Croyle, R., & Cooper, J. (1983). Dissonance arousal: Physiological evidence. *Journal of Personality and Social Psychology*, 45, 782–791.

Csikszentmihalyi, M., & Larsen, R. (1984). *Being Adolescent: Conflict and Growth in the Teenage Years.* New York: Basic Books.

Csoka, L., & Bons, P. (1978). Manipulating the situation to fit the leader's style: Two validation studies of **Leader Match.** *Journal of Applied Psychology*, 63, 295–300.

Cunningham, C. (1986). Use of nuclear magnetic resonance spectroscopy to study the effects of ethanol consumption on liver metabolism and pathology. *Alcoholism: Clinical and Experimental Research*, 10, 246–250.

Cutting, J. (1987). Perception and information. *Annual Review of Psychology*, 38, 61–90.

Dale, P. (1976). *Language Development.* New York: Holt, Rinehart and Winston.

Darley, J., & Latané, B. (1968). Bystander intervention in emergencies: Diffusion of responsibility. *Journal of Personality and Social Psychology*, 8, 377–383.

Darwin, C. (1872). *The Expression of Emotion in Man and Animals.* New York: Philosophical Library [reprinted in 1955 & 1965 by the University of Chicago Press].

Datan, N., & Thomas, J. (1984). Late adulthood: Love, work and the normal transitions. In D. Offer & M. Sabshin (Eds.), *Normality and the Life Cycle.* New York: Basic Books.

Dattore, P., Shontz, F., & Coyne, L. (1980). Premarital personality differentiation of cancer and noncancer groups: A test of the hypothesis of cancer proneness. *Journal of Consulting and Clinical Psychology*, 48, 388–394.

Davidson, C. (1986). Changing concepts in the pathogenesis of alcoholic liver disease. *Alcoholism: Clinical and Experimental Research*, 10, supplement, 3–4.

Davidson, G. (1984). Hypnotic augmentation of terminal care chemoanalgesia. *Australian Journal of Clinical and Experimental Hypnosis*, 12, 133–134.

Davidson, J. (1984). Response to "Hormones and sexual behavior" by John Bancroft, M.D. *Journal of Sex and Marital Therapy*, 10, 23–27.

Davidson, R. (1984). Affect, cognition, and hemispheric specialization. In C. Izard,

J. Kagan, & R. Zajonc (Eds.), *Emotion, Cognition, and Behavior.* Cambridge, England: Cambridge University Press.

Davis, D., Cahan, S., & Bashi, J. (1977). Birth order and intellectual development: The confluence model in the light of cross-cultural evidence. *Science*, 196, 1470–1472.

Davis, H., & Silverman, S. (1960). *Hearing and Deafness.* New York: Holt, Rinehart and Winston.

Davis, J., Wheeler, W., & Willy, E. (1987). Cognitive correlates of obesity in a nonclinical population. *Psychological Reports*, 60, 1151–1156.

Davis, J., & Wirtshafter, D. (1978). Anorexia and body weight loss caused by intraventricular glyceral infusions. *Society for Neuroscience Abstracts*, 4, 173.

Davis, L., & Cherns, A. *The Quality of Working Life: Vol. I. Problems, Prospects, and the State of the Art.* New York: The Free Press.

Davis, P., & Schwartz, G. (1987). Repression and the inaccessibility of affective memories. *Journal of Personality and Social Psychology*, 52, 155–162.

Davison, G., & Neale, J. (1986). *Abnormal Psychology* (4th ed.). New York: Wiley.

Deater, T., & Tauber, R. (1987). Personal communication, April 20.

Deatherage, B. (1972). Auditory and other sensory forms of information presentation. In H. Van Cott and R. Kinkade (Eds.), *Human Engineering Guide to Equipment Design.* Washington, DC: U.S. Government Printing Office.

DeBono, K. (1987). Investigating the social-adjustive and value-expressive functions of attitudes: Implication for persuasion processes. *Journal of Personality and Social Psychology*, 52, 279–287.

DeCasper, A., & Fifer, W. (1980). Of human bonding: Newborns prefer their mothers' voices. *Science*, 208, 1174–1176.

Deci, E. (1980). *The Psychology of Self-Determination.* Lexington, MA: Lexington Books.

Delabar, J., Goldgaber, D., Lamour, Y., Nicole, A., Huret, J., De Grouchy, J., Brown, P., Gajdusek, D., & Sinet, P. (1987). β amyloid gene duplication in Alzheimer's disease and karyotypically normal Down syndrome. *Science*, 235, 1390–1392.

Delameter, J., & MacCorquodale, P. (1979). *Premarital Sexuality: Attitudes, Relationships, Behavior.* Madison, WI: University of Wisconsin Press.

Demaris, A., & Leslie, G. (1984). Cohabitation with the future spouse: Its influence upon marital satisfaction and communication. *Journal of Marriage and the Family*, 46, 77–84.

Dembroski, T., MacDougall, J., Shields, J., Petitto, J., & Lushene, R. (1978). Components of the Type A coronary-prone

behavior patterns and cardiovascular responses to psychomotor performance challenge. *Journal of Behavioral Medicine*, 1, 159–176.

Dembroski, T., MacDougall, J., Williams, B., & Haney, T. (1985). Components of Type A, hostility, and anger-in: Relationship to angiographic findings. *Psychosomatic Medicine*, 47, 219–233.

Dement, W. (1960). The effects of dream deprivation. *Science*, 131, 1705–1707.

Dement, W. (1972). *Some Must Watch While Some Must Sleep.* Stanford, CA: Stanford Alumni Association.

Dement, W., & Kleitman, N. (1957). Cyclic variations in EEG and their relation to eye movements, bodily motility and dreaming. *Electroencephalography Clinical Neurophysiology*, 9, 673–690.

Dempster, F. (1985). Proactive interference in sentence recall: Topic-similarity effects and individual differences. *Memory and Cognition*, 13, 81–89.

Dennerstein, L., Burrows, G., Wood, C., & Hyman, G. (1980). Hormones and sexuality: The effects of estrogen and progestagen. *Obstetrics and Gynecology*, 56, 316–322.

Denney, N., & Palmer, A. (1981). Adult age differences on traditional and practical problem-solving measures. *Journal of Gerontology*, 36, 323–328.

Derogatis, L., Abeloff, M., & Melasaratos, N. (1979). Psychological coping mechanisms and survival time in metastatic breast cancer. *Journal of the American Medical Association*, 242, 1504–1508.

Dessler, G. (1980). *Human Behavior: Improving Performance at Work.* Reston, VA: Reston Publishing Co.

Detera-Wadleigh, S., Berrettini, W., Goldin, L., Boorman, D., Anderson, S., & Gershon, E. (1987). Close linkage of c-Harvey-ras-I and the insulin gene to affective disorder is ruled out in three North American pedigrees. *Nature*, 325, 806–807.

Deutsch, J., & Folle, S. (1973). Alcohol and asymmetrical state-dependency: A possible explanation. *Behavioral Biology*, 8, 273–278.

Deutsch, M., & Gerard, H. (1955). A study of normative and informational influence upon individual judgment. *Journal of Abnormal and Social Psychology*, 51, 629–636.

DeValois, R., & DeValois, K. (1975). Neural coding of color. In E. Carterette & M. Friedman (Eds.), *Handbook of Perception* (Vol. 5). New York: Academic Press.

DeValois, R., & DeValois, K. (1980). Spatial vision. *Annual Review of Psychology*, 31, 309–341.

de Villiers, P., & de Villiers, J. (1979). *Early Language.* Cambridge, MA: Harvard University Press.

de Wied, D., van Wimersma Greidanus, T., Bohus, B., Urban, I., & Gispen, W. (1976). Vasopressin and memory consolidation. *Progress in Brain Research*, 45, 181.

Deykin, E., Levy, J., & Wells, V. Adolescent depression, alcohol and drug abuse. *American Journal of Public Health*, 77, 178–182.

Diamond, M. (1977). Human sexual development: Biological foundations for social development. In F. Beach (Ed.), *Human Sexuality in Four Perspectives*. Baltimore: Johns Hopkins University Press.

Diamond, M. (1978). The aging brain: Some enlightening and optimistic results. *American Scientist*, 66, 66–71.

Diamond, M. (1979). Sexual identity and sex roles. In V. Bullough (Ed.), *The Frontiers of Sex Research*. Buffalo, NY: Prometheus Press.

Dickie, J., Ludwig, T., & Blauw, D. (1979). Life satisfaction among institutionalized and non-institutionalized older adults. *Psychological Reports*, 44, 807–810.

Diener, E., & Wallbom, M. (1976). Effects of self-awareness on antinormative behavior. *Journal of Research in Personality*, 10, 107–111.

Dietz, W. (1986). Prevention of childhood obesity. *Pediatric Clinics of North America*, 33, 823–832.

DiMascia, A., Weissman, M., Prusoff, B., Neu, C., & Zwilling, M. (1979). Differential symptom reduction by drugs and psychotherapy in acute depression. *Archives of General Psychiatry*, 36, 1450–1456.

Dion, K., & Berscheid, E. (1974). Physical attractiveness and peer perception among children. *Sociometry*, 37, 1–12.

Dion, K. L., & Dion, K. K. (1987). Belief in a just world and physical attractiveness stereotyping. *Journal of Personality and Social Psychology*, 52, 775–780.

Dobelle, W. (1977). Current status of research on providing sight to the blind by electrical stimulation of the brain. *Journal of Visual Impairment and Blindness*, 71, 290–297.

Doering, C., Kraemer, H., Brodie, H., & Hamburg, D. (1975). A cycle of plasma testosterone in the human male. *Journal of Clinical Endocrinology and Metabolism*, 40, 492–500.

Dollard, J., Doob, L., Miller, N., Mowrer, O., & Sears, R. (1930). *Frustration and Aggression*. New Haven, CT: Yale University Press.

Donnelly, J. (1980). In H. Kaplan, A. Freedman, & B. Sadock (Eds.), *Comprehensive Textbook of Psychiatry*. Baltimore: Williams & Wilkins.

Donnerstein, E., & Wilson, W. (1976). Effects of noise and perceived control on ongoing and subsequent aggressive behavior. *Journal of Personality and Social Psychology*, 34, 774–781.

Dorfman, R., & Shipley, T. (1956). *Androgens: Biochemistry, Physiology, and Clinical Significance*. New York: Wiley.

Dorner, G. (1976). *Hormones and Brain Differentiation*. Amsterdam: Elsevier.

Dorpat, T., & Ripley, H. (1967). The relationship between attempted suicide and committed suicide. *Comprehensive Psychiatry*, 8, 74.

Dosher, B. (1984). Discriminating preexperimental (semantic) from learned (episodic) associations: A speed-accuracy study. *Cognitive Psychology*, 16, 519–555.

Douvan, E. (1986). Adolescence. In C. Tavris (Ed.), *Everywoman's Emotional Well-Being*. New York: Doubleday.

Dove, A. (1968). Taking the chitling test. *Newsweek*, July.

Dow, M., Hart, D., & Forrest, C. (1983). Hormonal treatments of unresponsiveness in post-menopausal women: A comparative study. *British Journal of Obstetrics and Gynecology*, 90, 361–366.

Doyle, J. (1985). *Sex and Gender*. Dubuque, IA: William C. Brown.

Dudycha, G. (1936). An objective study of punctuality in relation to personalities and achievement. *Archives of Psychology*, 204, 1–53.

Duke, M., & Nowicki, S. (1986). *Abnormal Psychology*. New York: Holt, Rinehart and Winston.

Dunham, R., Kidwell, J., & Wilson, S. (1986). Rites of passage at adolescence: a ritual process paradigm. *Journal of Adolescent Research*, 1, 139–154.

Dunkerley, M. (1940). A statistical study of leadership among college women. *Studies in Psychology and Psychiatry*, 4, 1–65.

Dusek, D., & Girdano, D. (1980). *Drugs: A Factual Account*. Reading, MA: Addison-Wesley.

Dywan, J., & Bowers, K. (1983). The use of hypnosis to enhance recall. *Science*, 222, 184–185.

Eagly, A. (1981). Recipient characteristics as determinants of responses to persuasion. In R. Petty, T. Ostrom, & T. Brock (Eds.), *Cognitive Responses in Persuasion*. Hillsdale, NJ: Erlbaum.

Eagly, A., & Warren, R. (1976). Intelligence, comprehension, and opinion change. *Journal of Personality*, 44, 226–242.

Eagly, A., Wood, W., & Chaiken, S. (1978). Causal inferences about communication and their effect on opinion change. *Journal of Personality and Social Psychology*, 36, 424–435.

Eberhardt, B., & Muchinsky, P. (1982). An empirical investigation of the factor stability of Owen's biographical questionnaire. *Journal of Applied Psychology*, 67, 138–145.

Echterling, L., & Emmerling, D. (1987). Impact of stage hypnosis. *American Journal of Clinical Hypnosis*, 29, 149–154.

Eckholm, E. (1986). Researchers dispute tolling of genetic clock. *The Oregonian*, June 19, F1–F2.

Egeland, J., Gerhard, D., Pauls, D., Sussex, J., Kidd, K., Allen, C., Hostetter, A., & Housman, D. (1987). Bipolar affective disorders linked to DNA markers on chromosome 11. *Nature*, 325, 783–787.

Eichorn, D., Hunt, J., & Honzik, M. (1981). Experience, personality, and IQ: Adolescence to middle age. In D. Eichorn, J. Clausen, N. Haan, M. Honzik, & P. Mussen (Eds.), *Present and Past in Middle Age*. New York: Academic Press.

Eimas, P. (1975). Developmental studies of speech perception. In L. Cohen & P. Salapatek (Eds.), *Infant Perception: From Sensation to Perception* (Vol. 7). New York: Academic Press.

Eimas, P. (1985). The perception of speech in early infancy. *Scientific American*, 252, 46–52.

Ekman, P. (1982). *Emotion and the Human Face* (2nd ed.). New York: Cambridge University Press.

Ekman, P., & Friesen, W. (1984). *Unmasking the Face* (2nd ed.). Palo Alto, CA: Consulting Psychologists Press.

Ekman, P., Levenson, R., & Friesen, W. (1983). Autonomic nervous system activity distinguishes among emotions. *Science*, 221, 1208–1210.

Elal-Lawrence, G., Slade, P., & Dewey, M. (1987). Treatment and follow-up variables discriminating abstainers, controlled drinkers, and relapsers. *Journal of Studies on Alcohol*, 48, 39–46.

Ellis, A. (1962). *Reason and Emotion in Psychotherapy*. Secaucus, NJ: Lyle Stuart/Citadel Press.

Ellis, A. (1975). *How to Live With a Neurotic*. N. Hollywood, CA: Wilshire Books.

Ellis, A. (1986). Rational-emotive therapy. In R. Corsine (Ed.), *Current Psychotherapies*. Itasca, IL: Peacock.

Ellis, A., & Harper, R. (1975). *A New Guide to Rational Living*. N. Hollywood, CA: Wilshire Books.

Emmerick, H. (1978). The influence of parents and peers on choices made by adolescents. *Journal of Youth and Adolescence*, 7, 175–180.

Ennis, R. (1982). Children's ability to handle Piaget's propositional logic: A conceptual critique. In S. Modgil & C. Modgil (Eds.), *Jean Piaget: Consensus and Controversy*. New York: Praeger.

Epstein, A. (1960). Reciprocal changes in feeding behaviors produced by intrahypothalamic chemical injections. *American Journal of Physiology*, 199, 969–974.

Epstein, A., & Teitelbaum, P. (1967). Specific loss of the hypoglycemic control of feeding in recovered lateral rats. *American Journal of Physiology*, 213, 1159–1167.

Epstein, L., & Wing, R. (1987). Behavioral treatment of childhood obesity. *Psychological Bulletin, 101*, 331–342.

Epstein, L., Wing, R., Koeske, R., & Valoski, A. (1987). Long-term effects of family-based treatment of childhood obesity. *Journal of Consulting and Clinical Psychology, 55*, 91–95.

Epstein, R., Lanza, R., & Skinner, B. (1980). Symbolic communication between two pigeons. *Science, 2*, 220–221.

Epstein, S. (1983). The stability of behavior across time and situations. In R. Zucker, J. Aronoff, & A. Robin (Eds.), *Personality and the Prediction of Behavior*. San Diego, CA: Academic Press.

Erikson, E. (1963). *Childhood and Society* (2nd ed.). New York: Norton.

Erlenmeyer-Kimling, L., & Jarvik, L. Genetics and intelligence. *Science, 142*, 1477–1479.

Erlich, S., & Itabashi, H. (1986). Narcolepsy: A neuropathologic study. *Sleep, 9*, 126–132.

Eron, L., & Huesmann, L. (1984). The control of aggressive behaviors by changes in attitudes, values and the conditions of learning. In R. Blanchard and C. Blanchard (Eds.), *Advances in the Study of Aggression* (Vol. 1). Orlando, FL: Academic Press.

Eron, L., Heusmann, L., Lefkovitz, M., & Walder, L. (1972). Does television violence cause aggression? *American Psychologist, 27*, 253–263.

Esterling, B., & Rabin, B. (1987). Stress-induced alteration of T-lymphocyte subsets and humoral immunity in mice. *Behavioral Neuroscience, 101*, 115–119.

Estes, W. (1972). An associative basis for coding and organization in memory. In A. Melton & E. Martin (Eds.), *Coding Process in Human Memory*. Washington, DC: Winston.

Estrada, P., Arsenio, W., Hess, R., & Holloway, S. (1987). Affective quality of the mother-child relationship: Longitudinal consequences for children's school-relevant cognitive functioning. *Developmental Psychology, 23*, 210–215.

Evans, F., & Orne, M. (1971). The disappearing hypnotist: The use of simulation subjects to evaluate how subjects perceive experimental procedures. *International Journal of Clinical and Experimental Hypnosis, 19*, 277–296.

Evans, G. (1980). Environmental cognition. *Psychological Bulletin, 88*, 259–287.

Evans, G., & Howard, R. (1973). Personal space. *Psychological Bulletin, 80*, 334–344.

Evans, J., Barston, J., & Pollard, P. (1983). On the conflict between logic and belief in syllogistic reasoning. *Memory and Cognition, 11*, 295–306.

Evans, R. (1974). A conversation with Konrad Lorenz about aggression, homosexuality, pornography, and the need for a new ethic. *Psychology Today,* November, 83ff.

Eveleth, P., & Tanner, J. (1976). *Worldwide Variation in Human Growth*. Cambridge, England: Cambridge University Press.

Eysenck, H. (1952). The effects of psychotherapy: An evaluation. *Journal of Consulting Psychology, 16*, 319–324.

Fagot, B. (1978). The influence of sex of child on parental reactions to toddler children. *Child Development, 49*, 459–465.

Fantino, E. (1973). Aversive control. In J. Nevin & G. Reynolds (Eds.), *The Study of Behavior: Learning, Motivation, Emotion, and Instinct*. Glenview, IL: Scott, Foresman.

Fantino, E. (1977). Conditioned reinforcement: choice and information. In W. Honig & J. Staddon (Eds.), *Handbook of Operant Behavior*. Englewood Cliffs, NJ: Prentice-Hall.

Fantino, E., & Logan, C. (1979). *The Experimental Analysis of Behavior: A Biological Perspective*. San Francisco: W. H. Freeman.

Farley, F. (1986). The big T in personality. *Psychology Today,* May, 44–52.

Fazio, R. (1986). How do attitudes guide behavior? In R. Sorrentino & E. Higgins (Eds.), *The Handbook of Motivation and Cognition: Foundations of Social Behavior*. New York: Guilford Press.

Fazio, R., Powell, M., & Herr, P. (1983). Toward a process model of the attitude-behavior relation: Assessing one's attitude upon mere observation of the attitude object. *Journal of Personality and Social Psychology, 44*, 723–735.

Fazio, R., & Zanna, M. (1981). Direct experience and attitude-behavior consistency. In L. Berkowitz (Ed.), *Advances in Experimental Social Psychology*. (Vol. 14). New York: Academic Press.

Federal Bureau of Investigation. (1986). *Uniform Crime Reports for the United States*. Washington, DC: Government Printing Office.

Fein, G., Johnson, D., Kesson, N., Stork, L., & Wasserman, L. (1975). Sex stereotypes and preferences in the toy choices of 20 month old boys and girls. *Developmental Psychology, 11*, 527–528.

Fein, G., Schwartz, P., Jacobson, S., & Jacobson, L. (1983). Environmental toxins and behavioral development. *American Psychologist, 38*, 1188–1197.

Fennell, M., & Campbell, E. (1984). The cognitive questionnaire: Specific thinking errors in depression. *British Journal of Clinical Psychology, 23*, 81–92.

Fernald, D. (1984). *The Hans Legacy*. Hillsdale, NJ: Erlbaum.

Ferrante, R., Kowall, N., Beal, M., Martin, J., Bird, E., & Richardson, E. (1987). Morphologic and histochemical characteristics of a spared subset of striatal neurons in Huntington's disease. *Journal of Neuropathology and Experimental Neurology, 46*, 12–27.

Ferster, C. (1965). Classification of behavior pathology. In L. Krasner & L. Ullman (Eds.), *Research in Behavior Modification*. New York: Holt, Rinehart and Winston.

Feshbach, N. (1985). Chronic maternal stress and its assessment. In J. Butcher & C. Speilberger (Eds.), *Advances in Personality Assessment* (Vol. 5). Hillsdale, NJ: Erlbaum.

Feshbach, S., & Weiner, B. (1982). *Personality*. Lexington, MA: D. C. Heath.

Festinger, L. (1957). *A Theory of Cognitive Dissonance*. Stanford, CA: Stanford University Press.

Festinger, L., Schachter, S., & Back, K. (1950). *Social Pressures in Informal Groups: A Study of Human Factors in Housing*. New York: Harper & Row.

Fiedler, F. (1967). *A Theory of Leadership Effectiveness*. New York: McGraw-Hill.

Fiedler, F., & Chemers, M. (1984). *Improving Leadership Effectiveness: The Leader Match Concept*. New York: Wiley.

Field, T. (1978). Interaction behaviors of primary versus secondary caretaker fathers. *Developmental Psychology, 14*, 183–184.

Field, T., Vega-Lahr, N., Goldstein, S., & Scafidi, F. (1987). Face-to-face interaction behavior across infancy. *Infant Behavior and Development, 10*, 111–116.

Fischer, C., Daniels, J., Levin, S., Kimzey, S., Cobb, E., & Ritzman, W. (1972). Effects of the spaceflight environment on man's immune system: II. Lymphocyte counts and reactivity. *Aerospace Medicine, 43*, 1122–1125.

Fischer, J., Sollie, D., & Morrow, B. (1986). Social networks in male and female adolescents. *Journal of Adolescent Research, 6*, 1–14.

Fishbein, M., & Ajzen, I. (1975). *Belief, Attitude, Intention, and Behavior: An Introduction to Theory and Research*. Reading, MA: Addison-Wesley.

Fisher, S., & Greenburg, R. (1977). *Scientific Credibility of Freud's Theories*. New York: Basic Books.

Flavell, J. (1985). *Cognitive Development* (2nd ed.). Englewood Cliffs, NJ: Prentice-Hall.

Flay, DPhil, B. (1987). Mass media and smoking cessation: A critical review. *American Journal of Public Health, 77*, 153–160.

Fleming, I., Baum, A., & Weiss, L. (1987). Social density and perceived control as mediators of crowding stress in high-density residential neighborhoods. *Journal of Personality and Social Psychology, 52*, 899–906.

Flynn, J. (1987). Massive IQ gains in

14 nations: What IQ tests really measure. *Psychological Bulletin*, 101, 171–191.

Foley, J. (1985). Binocular distance perception: Egocentric distance tasks. *Journal of Experimental Psychology: Human Perception of Performance*, 11, 133–149.

Foley, V. (1984). Family therapy. In R. Corsini (Ed.), *Current Psychotherapies*. Itasca, IL: Peacock.

Ford, C., & Beach, F. (1951). *Patterns of Sexual Behavior*. New York: Harper & Row.

Ford, M. (1985). Two perspectives on the validation of developmental constructs: Psychometric and theoretical limitations in research on egocentrism. *Psychological Bulletin*, 97, 497–501.

Forrester, W., & King, D. (1971). Effects of semantic and acoustic relatedness on free recall and clustering. *Journal of Experimental Psychology*, 88, 16–19.

Forsyth, D. (1983). *An Introduction to Group Dynamics*. Monterey, CA: Brooks/Cole.

Fosson, A., Knibbs, J., Bryant-Waugh, R., & Lask, B. (1987). Early onset anorexia nervosa. *Archives of Disease in Children*, 62, 114–118.

Foster, G., & Ysseldyke, J. (1976). Expectancy and halo effects as a result of artificially induced teacher bias. *Contemporary Educational Psychology*, 1, 37–45.

Foulkes, D., & Schmidt, M. (1983). Temporal sequence and unit composition in dream reports from different stages of sleep. *Sleep*, 6, 265–280.

Fox, P., Mintun, M., Raichle, M., Miezin, F., Allman, J., & Van Essen, D. (1986). Mapping human visual cortex with positron emission tomography. *Nature*, 323, 806–809.

Fox, S., Brown, C., Koontz, A., & Kessel, S. (1987). Perceptions of risks of smoking and heavy drinking during pregnancy: 1985 NHIS findings. *Public Health Representative*, 102, 73–79.

Frank, J. (1982). Therapeutic components shared by all psychotherapies. In J. Harvey & M. Parks (Eds.), *The Master Lecture Series: Vol. I. Psychotherapy Research and Behavior Change*. Washington, DC: American Psychological Association.

Frankenhaeuser, M. (1975). Sympathetic-adrenomedullary activity behavior and the psychosocial environment. In P. Venables and M. Christie (Eds.), *Research in Psychophysiology*. New York: Wiley.

Frankish, C. (1985). Modality-specific grouping effects in short-term memory. *Journal of Memory and Language*, 24, 200–209.

Freedman, D. (1941). Psychiatric epidemiology counts. *Archives of General Psychiatry*, 41, 931–934.

Freedman, J. (1975). *Crowding and Behavior*. San Francisco: W. H. Freeman.

Freedman, J. (1979). Reconciling apparent differences between the responses of humans and other animals to crowding. *Psychological Review*, 86, 80–85.

Freedman, J., & Fraser, S. (1966). Compliance without pressure: The foot-in-the-door technique. *Journal of Personality and Social Psychology*, 4, 195–202.

Freedman, S. (1984). Effects of television violence on aggression. *Psychological Bulletin*, 96, 227–246.

Freeman, W., & Watts, J. (1950). *Psychosurgery*. Springfield, IL: Thomas.

Freud, S. (1900). *The Interpretation of Dreams*. London: Hogart.

Freud, S. (1905). *Three Essays on the Theory of Sexuality* (J. Strachey, Ed. and translator). New York: Basic Books (1963: Originally published in 1905).

Freud, S. (1917). Mourning and melancholia. Originally written in 1917 and later published in *Collected Papers* (Vol. 4). London: Hogarth Press.

Freud, S. (1936). *The Problem of Anxiety*. New York: Norton.

Fried, M., & Gleicher, P. (1961). Some sources of residential satisfaction in an urban slum. *Journal of American Institute of Planners*, 27, 305–315.

Friedman, M., & Rosenman, R. (1974). *Type A Behavior and Your Heart*. New York: Knopf.

Friedman, M., & Ulmer, D. (1984). *Treating Type A Behavior—And Your Heart*. New York: Knopf.

Friedrich-Cofer, L. (1986). Television violence and aggression: the debate continues. *Psychological Bulletin*, 100, 364–371.

Frodi, A. (1975). The effect of exposure to weapons on aggressive behavior from a cross-cultural perspective. *International Journal of Psychology*, 10, 283–292.

Fromm, E. (1965). *The Ability to Love*. New York: Farrar, Straus and Giroux.

Frumkin, B., & Anisfeld, M. (1977). Semantic and surface codes in the memory of deaf children. *Cognitive Psychology*, 9, 475–493.

Fuchs, F. (1980). Genetic amniocentesis. *Scientific American*, 242, 47–53.

Fuhrer, M., & Baer, P. (1965). Differential classical conditioning: verbalizations of stimulus contingencies. *Science*, 150, 1479–1481.

Fukuda, M., Ono, T., Nishino, H., & Nakamura, K. (1986). Neuronal responses in monkey lateral hypothalamus during operant feeding behavior. *Brain Research Bulletin*, 17, 879–884.

Gage, D., & Safer, M. (1985). Hemisphere differences in the mood state-dependent effect for recognition of emotional faces. *Journal of Experimental Psychology: Learning, Memory, and Cognition*, 11, 752–763.

Gagnon, J. (1977). *Human Sexualities*. Glenview, IL: Scott, Foresman.

Gaito, J. (1974). A biochemical approach to learning and memory: Fourteen years later. In G. Newton and A. Riesen (Eds.), *Advances in Psychobiology* (Vol. 2). New York: Wiley.

Gaitwell, N., Loriaux, D., & Chase, T. (1977). Plasma testosterone in homosexual and heterosexual women. *American Journal of Psychiatry*, 134, 117–119.

Galef, B. (1970). Aggression and timidity responses to novelty in feral Norway rats. *Journal of Comparative and Physiological Psychology*, 70, 370–375.

Gallagher, W. (1986). The looming menace of designer drugs. *Discover*, August, 24–35.

Gallatin, J. (1980). Political thinking in adolescence. In J. Adelson (Ed.), *Handbook of Adolescent Psychology*. New York: Wiley.

Gallistel, C. (1986). The role of the dopaminergic projections in MFB self-stimulation. *Behavioural Brain Research*, 22, 97–105.

Galton, F. (1892). *Hereditary Genius* (2nd ed.). London: Macmillan.

Garber, J., & Seligman, M. (Eds.). (1980). *Human Helplessness: Theory and Application*. New York: Academic Press.

Gardner, R., & Gardner, B. (1969). Teaching sign language to a chimpanzee. *Science*, 165, 644–672.

Gardner, R., & Gardner, B. (1975). Early signs of language in child and chimpanzee. *Science*, 187, 752–753.

Garison, W., Earls, F., & Kindlon, D. (1984). Temperament characteristics and behavioral adjustment. *Journal of Clinical Child Psychology*, 13, 298–303.

Garland, J., & Pearce, J. (1967). Neurological complications of carbon monoxide poisoning. *Quarterly Journal of Medicine*, 36, 445–455.

Gawin, F., & Kleber, H. (1984). Cocaine abuse treatment. *Archives of General Psychiatry*, 41, 903–909.

Gazzaniga, M. (1970). *The Bisected Brain*. New York: Appleton, Century, Crofts.

Gazzaniga, M. (1987). Perceptual and attentional processes following callosal section in humans. *Neuropsychologia*, 25, 119–133.

Geen, R., Beatty, W., & Arkin, R. (1984). *Human Motivation*. Newton, MA: Allyn & Bacon.

Gehringer, W., & Engel, E. (1986). Effect of ecological viewing conditions on the Ames' distorted room illusion. *Journal of Experimental Psychology: Human Perception and Performance*, 12, 181–185.

Gentry, W., Chesney, A., Gary, H., Hall, R., & Harburg, E. (1982). Habitual anger-coping styles: I. Affect on mean blood pressure and risk for essential hypertension. *Psychosomatic Medicine, 44,* 195–202.

George, C., & Main, M. (1979). Social interactions of young abused children: Approach, avoidance, and aggression. *Child Development, 50,* 306–318.

Gerard, H., Wilhelmy, R., & Connolley, R. (1968). Conformity and group size. *Journal of Personality and Social Psychology, 8,* 79–82.

Gergen, K. (1965). The effects of interaction goals and personalistic feedback on the presentation of self. *Journal of Personality and Social Psychology, 1,* 413–424.

Gershon, E., Hamovit, J., Guroff, J., & Nurnberger, J. (1987). Birth-cohort changes in manic and depressive disorders in relatives of bipolar and schizoaffective patients. *Archives of General Psychiatry, 44,* 314–319.

Gesell, A. (1928). *Infancy and Human Growth.* New York: Macmillan.

Geshwind, N., & Levitsky, W. (1976). Left-right asymmetries in temporal speech region. *Science, 161,* 186–187.

Getchell, T. (1986). Functional properties of vertebrate olfactory receptor neurons. *Physiological Reviews, 66,* 772–818.

Getzels, J., & Jackson, P. (1962). *Creativity and Intelligence: Exploration with Gifted Students.* New York: Wiley.

Getzels, J., & Jackson, P. (1963). The highly intelligent and the highly creative adolescent: A summary of some research findings. In C. Taylor & F. Barron (Eds.), *Scientific Creativity: Its Recognition and Development.* New York: Wiley.

Ghiselli, E. (1963). Managerial talent. *American Psychologist, 16,* 632–641.

Ghiselli, E. (1971). *Explorations in Managerial Talent.* Pacific Palisades, CA: Goodyear Publishing Company.

Giannini, A., Pascarzi, G., Losiselle, R., Price, W., & Giannini, M. (1986). Comparison of clonidine and lithium in the treatment of mania. *American Journal of Psychiatry, 143,* 1608–1609.

Giardano, P. (1983). Sanctioning the higher-status deviant: An attributional analysis. *Social Psychology Quarterly, 46,* 329–342.

Gibbs, J., Young, R., & Smith, G. (1973). Cholescystokinin elicits satiety in rats with open gastric fistulas. *Nature, 245,* 323–345.

Gibson, E., & Spelke, E. (1983). The development of perception. In J. Flavell & E. Markman (Eds.), *Handbook of Child Psychology: Cognitive Development* (Vol. 3). New York: Wiley.

Gibson, E., & Walk, R. (1960). The visual cliff. *Scientific American, 202,* 64–71.

Giesser, B., Kurtzberg, D., Vaughan, H., Arezzo, J., Aisen, M., Smith, C., La-Rocca, N., & Scheinberg, L. (1987). Trimodal evoked potentials compared with magnetic resonance imaging in the diagnosis of multiple sclerosis. *Archives of Neurology, 44,* 281–284.

Gillam, B. (1980). Geometrical illusions. *Scientific American, 242,* 102–111.

Gilligan, C. (1982). *In a Different Voice: Psychological Theory and Women's Development.* Cambridge, MA: Howard University Press.

Gillie, O. (1976). Pioneer of IQ faked his research findings. *Sunday Times of London,* October 29, H3.

Glass, D. (1977). *Behavior Patterns, Stress, and Coronary Disease.* Hillsdale, NJ: Erlbaum.

Glass, D., & Singer, J. (1972). *Urban Stress.* New York: Academic Press.

Glass, D., Snyder, M., & Hollis, J. (1974). Time urgency and the Type A coronary-prone behavior pattern. *Journal of Applied Social Psychology, 4,* 125–140.

Glick, P., & Norton, A. (1979). *Update: Marrying, Divorcing, and Living Together in the U.S. Today.* Washington, DC: Population Reference Bureau.

Glucksberg, S., & Weisberg, R. (1966). Verbal behavior and problem solving: Some effects of labeling upon availability of novel functions. *Journal of Experimental Psychology, 71,* 659–664.

Goethals, G. (1980). Love, marriage, and mutual growth. In K. Pope (Ed.), *On Love and Loving.* San Francisco: Jossey-Bass.

Gold, P. (1987). Sweet memories. *American Scientist, 75,* 151–155.

Gold, R., Jones, A., Sawchenko, P., & Dapatos, G. (1977). Paraventricular area: Critical focus of a longitudinal neurocircuitry mediating food intake. *Physiology and Behavior, 18,* 1111–1119.

Goldberg, S. (1983). Parent-infant bonding: Another look. *Child Development, 54,* 1355–1382.

Goldberger, L. (1982). Sensory deprivation and overload. In L. Goldberger & S. Bresnitz (Eds.), *Handbook of Stress: Theoretical and Clinical Aspects.* New York: Free Press.

Golden, N., Sokol, R., Kuhnert, B., & Bottoms, S. (1982). Maternal alcohol use and infant development. *Pediatrics, 70,* 931–934.

Goldfarb, W. (1945). Psychological privation in infancy and subsequent adjustment. *American Journal of Orthopsychiatry, 15,* 247–255.

Goldfried, M., & Padawer, W. (1982). Current status and future directions in psychotherapy. In M. Goldfield (Ed.), *Converging Themes in Psychotherapy: Trends in Psychodynamic, Humanistic, and Behavioral Practice.* New York: Springer.

Goldgaber, D., Lerman, M., McBride, O., Saffiotti, U., Gajdusek, D. (1987). Characterization and chromosomal localization of a cDNA encoding brain amyloid of Alzheimer's disease. *Science, 235,* 877–880.

Goldstein, E. (1984). *Sensation and Perception* (2nd ed.). Belmont, CA: Wadsworth.

Goldstein, M., Baker, B., & Jamison, K. (1986). *Abnormal Psychology* (2nd ed.). Boston: Little, Brown.

Goldstein, M., & Palmer, J. (1975). *The Experience of Anxiety: A Casebook* (2nd ed.). New York: Oxford University Press.

Goleman, D. (1985). Stimulants keep brain "blooming" until late in life. *The Oregonian,* August 22, B2.

Goleman, D. (1987). A reward mechanism for repression. *Psychology Today,* March, 26–30.

Goodwin, D. (1981). *Alcoholism: The Facts.* Oxford, England: Oxford University Press.

Goodwin, D., Powell, B., & Brenner, D. (1969). Alcohol and recall: State-dependent effects in man. *Science, 163,* 1358–1360.

Goodwin, F., Cowdry, R., & Webster, M. (1978). Prediction of drug response in the affective disorders. In M. Lipton, A. Dimascio, & K. Killam (Eds.), *Psychopharmacology: A Generation of Progress.* New York: Raven.

Goodwin, F., & Jamison, K. (1986). *Manic-Depressive Illness.* New York: Oxford University Press.

Gordon, H. (1986). The cognitive laterality battery: Tests of specialized cognitive functions. *International Journal of Neuroscience, 29,* 223–244.

Gormally, J., Hill, D., Otis, M., & Rainey, L. (1975). A microtraining approach in assertion training. *Journal of Counseling Psychology, 22,* 340–344.

Gotlib, I., & Robinson, L. (1982). Responses to depressed individuals: Discrepancies between self-report and observer-rated behavior. *Journal of Abnormal Psychology, 87,* 322–332.

Gottesman, I., McGuffin, P., & Farmer, A. (1987). Clinical genetics as clues to the "real" genetics of schizophrenia. *Schizophrenia Bulletin, 13,* 23–47.

Gottesman, I., & Shields, J. (1976). A critical review of recent adoption, twin, and family studies of schizophrenia: Behavior genetics perspective. *Schizophrenia Bulletin, 2,* 360–398.

Gottesman, I., & Shields, J. (1982). *Schizophrenia: The Epigenetic Puzzle.* Cambridge, MA: Cambridge University Press.

Gottfredson, G. (1987). Employment setting, specialization, and patterns of accomplishments among psychologists. *Professional Psychology: Research and Practice* (in press).

Gottfried, A. (Ed.). (1984). *Home Environment and Early Cognitive Development: Longitudinal Research.* Orlando, FL: Academic Press.

Gottman, J., Notarius, C., Gonso, J., & Markham, H. (1976). *A Couple's Guide to Communication.* Champaign, IL: Research Press.

Gough, H. (1957/1975). *California Psychological Inventory: Manual* (rev. ed., 1975). Palo Alto, CA: Consulting Psychologists Press.

Gould, J., & Marler, P. (1987). Learning by instinct. *Scientific American, 256,* 74–85.

Gould, S. (1981). *The Mismeasure of Man.* New York: Norton.

Gray, C., & Gummerman, K. (1975). The enigmatic eidetic image: A critical examination of methods, data, and theories. *Psychological Bulletin, 82,* 383–407.

Greenberg, M., & Morris, N. (1974). Engrossment: The newborn's impact upon the father. *American Journal of Orthopsychiatry, 44,* 520–531.

Greenberg, R., & Pearlman, C. (1974). Cutting the REM nerve: An approach to the adaptive role of REM sleep. *Perspectives in Biology and Medicine, 17,* 513–521.

Greeno, J. (1980). Psychology of learning 1960–1980: One participant's observations. *American Psychologist, 35,* 713–728.

Greenough, W. (1984). Possible structural substrates of plastic neural phenomena. In G. Lynch, J. McGaugh, & N. Weinberger (Eds.), *Neurobiology of Learning and Memory.* New York: Guilford Press.

Greenough, W., & Green, E. (1981). Experience and the changing brain. In J. McGaugh, J. March, & S. Kiesler (Eds.), *Aging: Biology and Behavior.* New York: Academic Press.

Gregory, R. (1978). *Eye and Brain: The Psychology of Seeing* (3rd ed.). New York: McGraw-Hill.

Griffith, R., Miyago, O., & Tago, A. (1958). The universality of typical dreams: Japanese vs. Americans. *American Anthropologist, 60,* 1173–1179.

Griffiths, P., Merry, J., Browning, M., Eisinger, A., Huntsman, R., Lord, E., Polani, P., Tanner, J., & Whitehouse, R. (1974). Homosexual women: An endocrine and psychological study. *Journal of Endocrinology, 63,* 549–556.

Griffitt, W., & Veitch, R. (1974). Preacquaintance attitude similarity and attraction revisited. Ten days in a fall-out shelter. *Sociometry, 38,* 163–173.

Grossman, M., & Stein, I. (1948). Vagotomy and the hunger producing action of insulin in man. *Journal of Applied Physiology, 1,* 263–269.

Guilford, J. (1959). Traits of creativity. In H. Anderson (Ed.), *Creativity and Its Cultivation.* New York: Harper & Row.

Guilford, J. (1967). *The Nature of Human Intelligence.* New York: McGraw-Hill.

Guilford, J. (1977). *Way Beyond the I.Q.* Buffalo, NY: Creative Education Foundation and Bearly Unlimited.

Guilford, J. (1982). Cognitive psychology's ambiguities: Some suggested remedies. *Psychological Review, 89,* 48–59.

Guilleminault, C., & Dement, W. (Eds.) (1978). *The Sleep Apnea Syndrome.* New York: Liss.

Gurman, A., & Razin, M. (1977). *Effective Psychotherapy: A Handbook of Research.* New York: Pergamon.

Gusella, J., Wexler, N., Conneally, P., Naylor, S., Anderson, M., Tanzi, R., Watkins, P., Ottina, K., Wallace, M., Sakaguchi, A., Young, A., Shoulson, I., Bonilla, E., & Martin, J. (1983). A polymorphic DNA marker genetically linked to Huntington's disease. *Nature, 306,* 234–238.

Gwirtsman, H., & Gerner, R. (1981). Neurochemical abnormalities in anorexia nervosa: Similarities to affective disorders. *Biological Psychiatry, 16,* 991–995.

Haber, R. (1969). Eidetic images. *Scientific American, 220,* 36–44.

Hagedorn, R. (1983). *Sociology.* Dubuque, IA: William C. Brown.

Hakel, M. (1986). Personnel selection and placement. *Annual Review of Psychology, 37,* 351–380.

Halas, E. & Eberhardt, M. (1987). Blocking and appetitive reinforcement. *Bulletin of the Psychonomic Society, 25,* 121–123.

Hales, D. (1980). *The Complete Book of Sleep.* Reading, MA: Addison-Wesley.

Hall, D., & Nougaim, K. (1968). An examination of Maslow's need hierarchy in an organizational setting. *Organizational Behavior and Human Performance, 3,* 12–35.

Hall, E. (1966). *The Hidden Dimension.* New York: Doubleday.

Hall, J. (1986). The cardiopulmonary failure of sleep-disordered breathing. *Journal of the American Medical Association, 255,* 930–933.

Hall, W. (1987). Developmental psychobiology: Prenatal, perinatal, and early postnatal aspects of behavioral development. *Annual Review of Psychology, 38,* 91–128.

Halpern, D. (1984). (1984). *Thought and Knowledge: An Introduction to Critical Thinking.* Hillsdale, NJ: Erlbaum.

Hamilton, D., Carpenter, S., & Bishop, G. (1984). Desegregation of suburban neighborhoods. In N. Miller and M. Brewer (Eds.), *Psychology of Desegregation.* New York: Academic Press.

Hamilton, D., Katz, L., & Leirer, V. (1980). Memory for persons. *Journal of Personality and Social Psychology, 39,* 1050–1063.

Hamilton, E., & Abramson, L. (1983). Cognitive patterns and major depressive disorder: A longitudinal study in a hospital setting. *Journal of Abnormal Psychology, 92,* 173–184.

Hammen, C., & Peters, S. (1978). Interpersonal consequences of depression: Responses to men and women enacting a depressed role. *Journal of Abnormal Psychology, 87,* 322–332.

Hammer, C., & Peters, S. (1978). Interpersonal consequences of depression: Responses to men and women enacting a depressed role. *Journal of Abnormal Psychology, 87,* 322.

Hammond, K., & Arkes, H. (1986). *Judgment and Decision Making.* New York: Cambridge University Press.

Haney, C., & Zimbardo, P. (1977). The socialization into criminality: On becoming a prisoner and a guard. In J. Tapp & F. Levine (Eds.), *Law, Justice, and the Individual in Society: Psychological and Legal Issues.* New York: Holt, Rinehart and Winston.

Haney, D. (1983). Girth control. *The Oregonian,* November 21, B1.

Harburg, E., Erfurt, J., Havenstein, L., Chape, C., Schull, W., & Schork, M. (1973). Socio-ecological stress, suppressed hostility, skin color, and black-white male blood pressure: Detroit. *Psychosomatic Medicine, 35,* 276–296.

Hardy, J., Stolwijk, J., & Hoffman, D. (1968). Pain following step increase in skin temperature. In D. Kenshalo (Ed.), *The Skin Senses.* Springfield, IL: Thomas.

Hare, R. (1970). *Psychopathy: Theory and Research.* New York: Wiley.

Hare, R. (1975). Psychophysiological studies of psychopathy. In D. Fowles (Ed.), *Clinical Applications of Psychophysiology.* New York: Columbia University Press.

Hare, R., Frazelle, J., & Cox, D. (1978). Psychopathy and physiological responses to threat of an aversive stimulus. *Psychophysiology, 15,* 165–172.

Harlow, H., & Harlow, M. (1966). Learning to love. *American Scientist, 54,* 244–272.

Harlow, H., Harlow, M., & Meyer, D. (1950). Learning motivated by a manipulative drive. *Journal of Experimental Psychology, 40,* 228–234.

Harlow, H., Harlow, M., & Suomi, S. (1971). From thought to therapy: Lessons from a primate laboratory. *American Scientist, 59,* 538–549.

Harlow, H., & Zimmerman, R. (1958). The development of affectional responses in infant monkeys. *Proceedings of the American Philosophical Society, 102,* 501–509.

Harrell, J. (1980). Psychological factors and hypertension: A status report. *Psychological Bulletin, 87,* 482–501.

Harris, E., Noyes, R., Crowe, R., & Chaudhry, D. (1983). Family study of agoraphobia. *Archives of General Psychiatry, 40,* 1061–1069.

Hartmann, E. (1973). *The Functions of Sleep.* New Haven, CT: Yale University Press.

Hartmann, E., Russ, D., Oldfield, M.,

Sivan, I., & Cooper, S. (1987). Who has nightmares? *Archives of General Psychiatry*, 44, 49–56.

Hartmann, E., Russ, D., van der Kolk, B., Falke, R., & Oldfield, M. (1981). A preliminary study of the personality of the nightmare sufferer: Relationship to schizophrenia and creativity? *American Journal of Psychiatry*, 138, 794–797.

Hartshorne, H., & May, M. (1928). *Studies in the Nature of Character: Vol. I, Studies in Deceit.* New York: Macmillan.

Hatcher, R., Guest, F., Stewart, F., Stewart, G., Trussell, J., Cerel, S., & Cates, W. (1986). *Contraceptive Technology 1986–1987* (13th ed.). New York: Irvington.

Hatfield, E., & Sprecher, S. (1986). *Mirror, Mirror . . . The Importance of Looks in Everyday Life.* Albany: State University of New York Press.

Hathaway, S., & McKinley, J. (1942). *Minnesota Multiphasic Personality Inventory.* Minneapolis: University of Minnesota.

Havighurst, R. (1982). The world of work. In B. Wolman (Ed.), *Handbook of Developmental Psychology.* Englewood Cliffs, NJ: Prentice-Hall.

Hawn, P., & Harris, L. (1983). Laterality in manipulatory and cognitive related activity. In G. Young, S. Segalowitz, C. Corter, & S. Trehub (Eds.), *Manual Specialization and the Developing Brain.* New York: Academic Press.

Hayes, C. (1951). *The Ape in Our House.* New York: Harper & Row.

Hayes, J. (1978). *Cognitive Psychology: Thinking and Creating.* Homewood, IL: Dorsey Press.

Hayflick, L. (1974). The strategy of senescence. *The Gerontologist*, 14, 37–45.

Haynes, S., Feinleib, M., & Kannel, W. (1980). The relationships of psychosocial factors to coronary disease in the Framingham study. III. Eight-year incidence of coronary heart disease. *American Journal of Epidemiology*, 111, 37–58.

Hearnshaw, L. (1979). *Cyril Burt: Psychologist.* Ithaca, NY: Cornell University Press.

Heath, R. (1972). Pleasure and brain activity in man. *Journal of Nervous and Mental Disease*, 154, 3–18.

Hebb, D. (1949). *The Organization of Behavior.* New York: Wiley.

Hebb, D. (1955). Drives and the CNS. *Psychological Review*, 62, 243–254.

Heckel, R., Wiggins, S., & Salzberg, H. (1962). Conditioning against silences in group therapy. *Journal of Clinical Psychology*, 18, 216–217.

Heffernan, J., & Albee, G. (1985). Prevention perspectives. *American Psychologist*, 40, 202–204.

Heider, F. (1946). Attitudes and cognitive organization. *Journal of Psychology*, 21, 107–112.

Heider, F. (1958). *The Psychology of Interpersonal Relations.* New York: Wiley.

Heider, K. (1976). Dani sexuality: A low energy system. *Man*, 11, 188–201.

Heim, N. (1981). Sexual behavior of castrated sex offenders. *Archives of Sexual Behavior*, 10, 11–19.

Henderson, N. (1982). Human behavior genetics. *Annual Review of Psychology*, 33, 403–440.

Heninger, G., Charney, D., & Menkies, D. (1983). Receptor sensitivy and the mechanism of action of antidepressant treatment. In P. Clayton & J. Barrett (Eds.), *Treatment of Depression: Old Controversies and New Approaches.* New York: Raven.

Henker, F. (1981). Male climacteric. In J. Howells (Ed.), *Modern Perspectives in the Psychiatry of Middle Age.* New York: Bruner/Mazel.

Henly, A., & Williams, R. (1986). Type A and B subjects' self-reported cognitive/affective/behavioral responses to descriptions of potentially frustrating situations. *Journal of Human Stress*, 12, 168–174.

Henry, W., Schacht, T., & Strupp, H. (1986). Structural analysis of social behavior: Application to a study of interpersonal processes in differential psychotherapeutic outcome. *Journal of Consulting and Clinical Psychology*, 54, 27–31.

Herman, J., Ellman, S., & Roffwarg, H. (1978). The problem of NREM dream recall re-examined. In A. Arkin, J. Antrobus, & S. Ellman (Eds.), *The Mind in Sleep and Psychophysiology.* Hillsdale, NJ: Erlbaum.

Herman, J., & Roffwarg, H. (1983). Modifying aculomotor activity in awake subjects increases the amplitude of eye movement during REM sleep. *Science*, 220, 1074–1076.

Herrmann, D. (1987). Task appropriateness of mnemonic techniques. *Perceptual and Motor Skills*, 64, 171–178.

Herzberg, F. (1966). *Work and the Nature of Man.* Cleveland: World Publishing.

Herzberg, F., Mausner, B., & Snyderman, B. (1959). *The Motivation to Work.* New York: Wiley.

Herzog, A., Rogers, W., & Woodworth, J. (1982). *Subjective Well-Being Among Different Age Groups.* Ann Arbor, Mich: Institute for Social Research, University of Michigan.

Hess, W. (1957). *Functional Organization of the Diencephalon.* New York: Grune and Stratton.

Heston, L., & Shields, J. (1968). Homosexuality in twins. *Archives of General Psychiatry*, 18, 149–160.

Hetherington, A., & Ranson, S. (1940). Hypothalamic lesions and adiposity in the rat. *Anatomical Record*, 78, 149–172.

Hewitt, J. (1984). Normal components of personality variation. *Journal of Personality and Social Psychology*, 47, 671–675.

Hewitt, J., & Henley, R. (1987). Sex differences in reaction to spatial invasion. *Perceptual and Motor Skills*, 64, 809–810.

Hickish, D. (1955). Thermal sensations of workers in light industry in southern England. *Journal of Hygiene*, 53, 112–123.

Hicks, R., & Garcia, E. (1987). Levels of stress and sleep duration. *Perceptual and Motor Skills*, 64, 44–46.

Hicks, R., Kilcourse, J., & Sinnot, M. (1983). Type A-B behavior and caffeine use in college students. *Psychological Reports*, 52, 338.

Hicks, R., & Pellegrini, R. (1982). Sleep problems and Type A-B behavior in college students. *Psychological Reports*, 51, 96.

Hilgard, E. (1975). Hypnosis. *Annual Review of Psychology*, 26, 19–44.

Hilgard, E. (1977). *Divided Consciousness: Multiple Controls in Human Thought and Action.* New York: Wiley-Interscience.

Hilgard, E. (1979). *Personality and Hypnosis* (2nd ed.). Chicago: University of Chicago Press.

Hingson, R., Alpert, J., Day, N., Dooling, E., Kayne, H., Morelock, S., Oppenheimer, E., & Zuckerman, B. (1982). Effects of maternal drinking and marijuana use on fetal growth and development. *Pediatrics*, 70, 539–546.

Hinz, L. & Williamson, D. (1987). Bulimia and depression: A review of the affective variant hypothesis. *Psychological Bulletin*, 102, 150–158.

Hirsch, J. (1983). In NOVA. Fat chance in a thin world. Boston: WGBH Transcripts.

Hirsch, J., & Knittle, J. (1970). Cellularity of obese and nonobese human adipose tissue. *Federation Proceedings*, 29, 1516–1521.

Hirschhorn, R. (1987). Therapy of genetic disorders. *The New England Journal of Medicine*, 316, 623–624.

Hobson, J., & McCauley, R. (1977). The brain as a dream state generator: An activation-synthesis hypothesis of the dream process. *American Journal of Psychiatry*, 134, 1335–1348.

Hockett, C. (1960). The origin of speech. *Scientific American*, 203, 89–96.

Hodgkins, J. (1962). Influence of age on the speed of reaction and movement in females. *Journal of Gerontology*, 17, 385–389.

Hodgkinson, S., Sherrington, R., Gurling, H., Marchbanks, R., Reeders, S., Mallet, J., McInnin, M., Petersson, H., & Brynjolfsson, J. (1987). Molecular genetic evidence for heterogeneity in manic depression. *Nature*, 325, 805–806.

Hoebel, B., & Teitelbaum, P. (1966). Weight regulation in normal and hypothalamic hyperphagic rats. *Journal of Comparative and Physiological Psychology*, 61, 189–193.

Hoffman, L. (1974). Effects of maternal employment on the child—a review of the research. *Developmental Psychology, 10,* 204–228.

Hoffman, L. (1979). Maternal employment: 1979. *American Psychologist, 34,* 859–865.

Hoffman, L., & Manis, J. (1979). The value of children in the United States: A new approach to the study of fertility. *Journal of Marriage and the Family, 41,* 583–596.

Hogarth, R. (1981). Beyond discrete biases: Functional and dysfunctional aspects of judgmental heuristics. *Psychological Bulletin, 90,* 197–217.

Hohmann, G. (1966). Some effects of spinal cord lesions on experienced emotional feelings. *Psychophysiology, 3,* 143–156.

Holahan, C. (1986). Environmental psychology. *Annual Review of Psychology, 37,* 381–407.

Holden, C. (1981). Scientist convicted for monkey neglect. *Science, 214,* 1218–1220.

Holen, M., & Oaster, T. (1976). Serial position and isolation effects in a classroom lecture simulation. *Journal of Educational Psychology, 68,* 293–296.

Holiday, H. (1987). X-chromosome reactivation. *Nature, 327,* 661–662.

Holinger, P. (1979). Violent deaths among the young: Recent trends in suicide, homicides, and accidents. *American Journal of Psychiatry, 136,* 1144–1147.

Holinger, P. (1980). Violent deaths as a leading cause of mortality. *Journal of American Psychiatry, 137,* 472–476.

Hollander, E., & Julian, J. (1969). Contemporary trends in the analysis of the leadership process. *Psychological Bulletin, 71,* 387–397.

Hollandsworth, J., Kazelskis, R., Stevens, J., & Dressel, M. (1979). Relative contributions of verbal, articulative, and nonverbal communication to employment decisions in the job interview setting. *Personnel Psychology, 32,* 359–367.

Holmes, D. (1984). Meditation and somatic arousal reduction: A review of the experimental evidence. *American Psychologist, 39,* 1–10.

Holmes, D., & Jorgensen, B. (1971). Do personality and social psychologists study men more than women? *Representative Research in Social Psychology, 2,* 71–76.

Holmes, T., & Rahe, R. (1967). The social readjustment rating scale. *Journal of Psychosomatic Research, 11,* 213–218.

Holway, A., & Boring, E. (1941). Determinants of apparent visual sight with distant variant. *American Journal of Psychology, 54,* 21–37.

Hooker, E. (1957). The adjustment of the male overt homosexual. *Journal of Projective Techniques, 21,* 18–31.

Hopkins, B., & Palthe, T. (1987). The development of the crying state during infancy. *Developmental Psychobiology, 20,* 165–175.

Horn, J. (1982). The aging of human abilities. In B. Wolman (Ed.), *Handbook of Developmental Psychology.* Englewood Cliffs, NJ: Prentice-Hall.

Horn, J., & Donaldson, G. (1980). Cognitive development in adulthood. In O. Brim & J. Kagan (Eds.), *Constancy and Change in Human Development.* Cambridge, MA: Howard University Press.

Horn, J., & Meer, J. (1987). The vintage years. *Psychology Today,* May, 76–90.

Horton, D., & Mills, C. (1984). Human learning and memory. *Annual Review of Psychology, 35,* 361–394.

Hott, L. (1979). The antisocial character. *American Journal of Psychoanalysis, 39,* 235–249.

Houston, J. (1985). *Motivation.* New York: Macmillan.

Houston, J. (1986). *Fundamentals of Learning and Memory* (3rd ed.). New York: Harcourt Brace Jovanovich.

Hovland, C., Harvey, D., & Sherif, M. (1957). Assimilation and contrast effects in reactions to communication and attitude change. *Journal of Abnormal and Social Psychology, 55,* 244–252.

Hovland, C., Lumsdaine, A., & Sheffield, F. (1949). *Experiments on Mass Communication.* Princeton, NJ: Princeton University Press.

Hovland, C., & Sears, R. (1940). Minor studies in aggression, VI: Correlations of lynchings with economic indices. *Journal of Personality, 9,* 301–310.

Howard, A., Pion, G., Gottfredson, G., Flattau, P., Oskamp, S., Pfafflin, S., Bray, D., & Burstein, A. (1986). The changing face of American psychology. *American Psychologist, 41,* 1311–1327.

Howell, W., & Dipboye, R. (1982). *Essentials of Industrial and Organizational Psychology.* Homewood, IL: Dorsey Press.

Hubbard, J. (1975). *The Biological Basis of Mental Activity.* Reading, MA: Addison-Wesley.

Hubel, D., & Wiesel, T. (1979). Brain mechanisms of vision. *Scientific American, 241,* 150–162.

Hughes, J., Gust, S., & Pechacek, T. (1987). Prevalence of tobacco dependence and withdrawal. *American Journal of Psychiatry, 144,* 205–208.

Hughes, J., Smith, T., Kosterlitz, H., Fothergill, L., Morgan, B., & Morris, H. (1975). Identification of two related pentapeptides from the brain with potent opiate agonist activity. *Nature, 258,* 577–579.

Hull, C. (1920). Quantitative aspects of the evolution of concepts. *Psychological Monographs,* Whole No. 123.

Hull, C. (1943). *Principles of Behavior*

Theory. New York: Appleton, Century, Crofts.

Hulse, S., Egeth, H., & Deese, J. (1980). *The Psychology of Learning* (5th ed.). New York: McGraw-Hill.

Hunt, J. (1982). Toward equalizing the developmental opportunities of infants and preschool children. *Journal of Social Issues, 38,* 163–191.

Hunt, M. (1974). *Sexual Behavior in the 1970s.* Chicago: Playboy Press.

Hurvich, L. (1978). Two decades of opponent process. In F. Bilmeyer & G. Wyszecki (Eds.), *Color 77.* Bristol, England: Adam Hilger.

Hurvich, L. (1981). *Color Vision.* Sunderland, MA: Sinauer Associates.

Hutchings, B., & Mednick, S. (1974). Registered criminality in the adoptive and biological parents of registered male adoptees. In S. Mednick, F. Schulsinger, J. Higgins, & B. Bell (Eds.), *Genetics, Environment, and Psychopathology.* New York: Elsevier.

Hyde, J. (1985). *Half the Human Experience: The Psychology of Women.* Lexington, MA: Heath.

Insko, C., & Melson, W. (1969). Verbal reinforcement of attitude in laboratory and nonlaboratory contexts. *Journal of Personality, 37,* 25–40.

Irwin, D., & Yeomans, J. (1986). Sensory registration and informational persistence. *Journal of Experimental Psychology: Human Perception and Performance, 12,* 343–360.

Irwin, M., Daniels, M., Bloom, E., Smith, T., & Weiner, H. (1987). Life events, depressive symptoms, and immune function. *American Journal of Psychiatry, 144,* 437–441.

Jabbari, B., Gunderson, C., Wippold, F., Citrin, C., Sherman, J., Bartoszek, D., Daigh, J., & Mitchell, M. (1986). Magnetic resonance imaging in partial complex epilepsy. *Archives of Neurology, 43,* 869–872.

Jackson, S. (1983). Participation in decision making as a strategy for reducing job-related strain. *Journal of Applied Psychology, 68,* 3–19.

Jacobs, G. (1983). Colour vision in animals. *Endeavour, New Series, 7,* 137–140.

Jacobson, E. (1932). The electrophysiology of mental activities. *American Journal of Psychology, 44,* 677–694.

Jacobson, G. (1968). The briefest psychiatric encounter. *Archives of General Psychiatry, 18,* 718–724.

Jacques, J., & Chason, K. (1979). Cohabitation: Its impact on marital success. *Family Coordinator, 28,* 35–39.

James, W. (1884). What is an emotion? *Mind, 9,* 188–205.

James, W. (1890). *Principles of Psychology.* New York: Holt, Rinehart and Winston.

Janet, P. (1929). *The Major Symptoms of Hysteria* (2nd ed.). New York: Macmillan.

Janis, I., & Feshbach, S. (1953). Effects of fear-arousing communication. *Journal of Abnormal and Social Psychology, 48,* 78–92.

Janowitz, H., & Grossman, M. (1950). Hunger and appetite: Some definitions and concepts. *Journal of Mount Sinai Hospital, 16,* 231–240.

Janson, P., & Martin, J. (1982). Job satisfaction and age: A test of two views *Social Forces, 60,* 1089–1102.

Jemmott, H., & Locke, S. (1984). Psychosocial factors, immunologic mediation, and human susceptibility to infectious diseases: How much do we know? *Psychological Bulletin, 95,* 78–108.

Jensen, A. (1969). How much can we boost IQ and scholastic achievement? *Harvard Educational Review, 39,* 1–123.

Jensen, A. (1977). Cumulative deficit in IQ of blacks in the rural South. *Developmental Psychology, 13,* 184–191.

Jensen, A. (1980). *Bias in Mental Testing.* New York: Free Press.

Joe, G., & Simpson, D. (1987). Mortality rates among opioid addicts in a longitudinal study. *American Journal of Public Health, 77,* 347–348.

Joffe, R., & Brown, P. (1984). Clinical and biological correlates of sleep deprivation in depression. *Canadian Journal of Psychiatry, 29,* 530–536.

Johnson, D., Johnson, R., & Maruyama, G. (1984). Goal interdependence and interpersonal attraction in heterogeneous classrooms: A meta-analysis. In N. Miller and M. Brewer (Eds.), *Groups in Contact: The Psychology of Desegregation.* San Diego, CA: Academic Press.

Johnson, J., Adinoff, B., Bisserbe, J., Martin, P., Rio, D., Rohrbaugh, J., Zubovic, E., & Eckardt, M. (1986). Assessment of alcoholism-related organic brain syndromes with positon emisson tomography. *Alcoholism: Clinical and Experimental Research, 10,* 237–240.

Johnson, M., & Hasher, L. (1987). Human learning and memory. *Annual Review of Psychology, 38,* 631–638.

Johnson, M., & Magaro, P. (1987). Effects of mood and severity on memory processes in depression and mania. *Psychological Bulletin, 101,* 28–40.

Johnson, T. (1986). Paper presented at the Conference on Modern Biological Theories of Aging, Mount Sinai Medical Center, New York, June.

Johnston, W., & Dark, V. (1986). Selective attention. *Annual Review of Psychology, 37,* 43–75.

Jones, E. (1979). The rocky road from acts to dispositions. *American Psychologist, 34,* 107–117.

Jones, E., Davis, K., & Gergen, K. (1961). Role playing variations and their informational value on person perception.

Journal of Abnormal and Social Psychology, 63, 302–310.

Jones, E., & McGillis, D. (1976). Correspondent inferences at the attribution cube: A comparative reappraisal. In J. Harvey, W. Ickes, & R. Kidd (Eds.), *New Directions in Attribution Research* (Vol. I). Hillsdale, NJ: Erlbaum.

Jones, G., & Nicholson, N. (1982). The meaning of absence: New strategies for theory and research. In B. Staw & L. Cummings (Eds.), *Research in Organizational Behavior.* Greenwich, CT: JAI Press.

Jones, H., & Conrad, H. (1933). The growth and decline of intelligence: A study of a homogenous group between the ages of ten and sixty. *Genetic Psychology Monographs, 13,* 223–294.

Jones, L. (1984). White black achievement differences: The narrowing gap. *American Psychologist, 39,* 1207–1213.

Jones, M. (1957). The later careers of boys who were early- or late-maturing. *Child Development, 28,* 115–128.

Jones, M. (1958). A study of socialization patterns at the high school level. *Journal of Genetic Psychology, 93,* 87–111.

Jones, R., & Brehm, J. (1970). Persuasiveness of one- and two-sided communications as a function of awareness: There are two sides. *Journal of Experimental Social Psychology, 6,* 47–56.

Jones, W., & Anderson, J. (1987). Short- and long-term memory retrieval: A comparison of the effects of information load and relatedness. *Journal of Experimental Psychology: General, 116,* 137–153.

Jorgenson, R., & Houston, B. (1981). Family history of hypertension, gender and cardiovascular reactivity and stereotyping during stress. *Journal of Behavioral Medicine, 4,* 175–190.

Judd, C., Kenny, D., & Krosnick, J. (1983). Judging the positions of political candidates: Models of assimilation and contact. *Journal of Personality and Social Psychology, 44,* 952–963.

Kagan, J., Kearsley, R., & Zelazo, P. (1978). *Infancy: Its Place in Human Development.* Cambridge, MA: Harvard University Press.

Kahn, J., Kornfeld, D., Frank, K., Heller, S., & Hoar, P. (1980). Type A behavior and blood pressure during coronary artery bypass surgery. *Psychosomatic Medicine, 42,* 407–414.

Kahneman, D., & Tversky, A. (1984). Choices, values, and frames. *American Psychologist, 39,* 341–350.

Kalat, J. (1981). *Biological Psychology.* Belmont, CA: Wadsworth.

Kales, A., Caldwell, A., Preston, T., Healey, S., & Kales, J. (1976). Personality patterns in insomniacs: Theoretical implications. *Archives of General Psychiatry, 33,* 1128–1134.

Kales, A., Tan, T., Kollar, E., Naitoh, P., Preston, T., & Malmstrom, E. (1970). Sleep patterns following 205 hours of sleep deprivation. *Psychosomatic Medicine, 32,* 189–200.

Kales, J., Kales, A., Bixler, E., Soldatos, C., Cadieux, R., Kashurba, G., & Bela-Bueno, A. (1984). Biopsychobehavioral correlates of insomnia: Clinical characteristics and behavioral correlates. *American Journal of Psychiatry, 141,* 1371–1376.

Kalinowsky, L. (1975). Psychosurgery. In A. Freedman, H. Kaplan, & B. Sadock (Eds.), *Comprehensive Textbook of Psychiatry.* Baltimore: Williams & Wilkins.

Kalinowsky, L. (1980). Convulsive therapies. In H. Kaplan, A. Freedman, & B. Sadock (Eds.), *Comprehensive Textbook of Psychiatry.* Baltimore: Williams & Wilkins.

Kalisch, P., & Kalisch, B. (1984). Sex-role stereotyping of nurses and physicians on prime-time television. *Sex Roles, 10,* 533–554.

Kallman, F. (1952a). Comparative twin study on the genetic aspects of male homosexuality. *Journal of Nervous and Mental Disease, 115,* 283–298.

Kallman, F. (1952b). Twin and sibship study of overt male homosexuality. *American Journal of Human Genetics, 4,* 136–146.

Kamin, L. (1969). Predictability, surprise, attention, and conditioning. In B. Campbell & R. Church (Eds.), *Punishment and Aversive Behavior.* New York: Appleton, Century, Crofts.

Kamin, L. (1974). *The Science and Politics of IQ.* Potomac, MD: Erlbaum.

Kanellakos, D. (1978). Transcendental consciousness: Expanded awareness as a means of preventing and eliminating the effects of stress. In C. Spielberger & J. Sarason (Eds.), *Stress and Anxiety* (Vol. 5). New York: Wiley.

Kang, J., Lemaire, H., Unterbeck, A., Salbaum, J., Masters, C., Grzeschik, K., Multhaup, G., Beyreuther, K., & Müller-Hill, B. (1987). The precursor of Alzheimer's disease amyloid A4 protein resembles a cell-surface receptor. *Nature, 325,* 733–736.

Kaplan, B., & Weisberg, F. (1987). Sex differences and practice effects on two visual-spatial tasks. *Perceptual and Motor Skills, 64,* 139–142.

Kaplan, H. (1979). *Disorders of Sexual Desire.* New York: Bruner/Mazel.

Kaprio, J., Koskenvuo, M., & Rita, H. (1987). Mortality after bereavement: A prospective study of 95,647 widowed persons. *American Journal of Public Health, 77,* 283–287.

Karnosh, L., & Zucker, E. (1945). *Handbook of Psychiatry.* St. Louis: Mosby.

Kastenbaum, R., & Costa, P. (1977). Psychological perspectives on death. *Annual Review of Psychology, 28,* 225–249.

Katschnig, K., & Shepherd, M. (1978). Neurosis: The epidemiological perspective. In H. van Prang (Ed.), *Research in Neurosis*. New York: Spectrum Publications.

Katz, P. (1976a). The acquisition of racial attitudes in children. In P. Katz (Ed.), *Towards the Elimination of Racism*. New York: Pergamon.

Kaushall, P., Zetin, M., & Squire, L. (1981). A psychological study of chronic, circumscribed amnesia: Detailed report of a noted case. *Journal of Nervous and Mental Disorders,* 169, 383–389.

Keating, D. (1980). Thinking processes in adolescence. In J. Adelson (Ed.), *Handbook of Adolescent Psychology*. New York: Wiley-Interscience.

Keesey, R., Boyle, P., Kemnitz, J., & Mitchell, J. (1976). The role of the lateral hypothalamus in determining the body weight set point. In D. Novin, W. Wyrwicka, & G. Bray (Eds.), *Hunger: Basic Mechanisms and Clinical Implications*. New York: Raven.

Keesey, R., & Powley, T. (1986). The regulation of body weight. *Annual Review of Psychology,* 37, 109–133.

Keith-Lucas, T., & Guttman, N. (1975). Robust-single-trial delayed backward conditioning. *Journal of Comparative and Physiological Psychology,* 88, 468–476.

Kellerman, H. (Ed.). (1987). *The Nightmare: Psychological and Biological Foundations*. New York: Columbia University Press.

Kelley, H. (1967). Attribution theory in social psychology. In D. Levine (Ed.), *Nebraska Symposium on Motivation*. Lincoln, NE: University of Nebraska Press.

Kelley, H. (1971). *Attribution in Social Interaction*. Morristown, NJ: General Learning Press.

Kelley, H. (1973). The process of causal attribution. *American Psychologist,* 28, 107–128.

Kellner, R., Abbott, P., Winslow, W., & Pathak, D. (1987). Fears, beliefs, and attitudes in DSM-III hypochondriasis. *The Journal of Nervous and Mental Disease,* 175, 20–25.

Kellogg, W., & Kellogg, L. (1933). *The Ape and the Child*. New York: McGraw-Hill.

Kelman, H. (Ed.), (1965). *International Behavior: A Socio-psychological Analysis*. New York: Holt, Rinehart and Winston.

Kelman, H., & Cohen, S. (1979). Reduction of international conflict: An international approach. In W. Austin and S. Worchel (Eds.), *The Social Psychology of Intergroup Relations*. Monterey, CA: Brooks/Cole.

Kempler, D., & Van Lancker, D. (1987). The right turn of phrase. *Psychology Today,* April, 20–22.

Kendall, P., & Norton-Ford, J. (1982). *Clinical Psychiatry*. New York: Wiley.

Kendler, K., Gruenberg, A., & Tsuang, M. (1985). Psychiatric illness in first-degree relatives of schizophrenics and surgical control patients: a family study using DSM-III criteria. *Archives of General Psychiatry,* 42, 770–779.

Keon, T., & McDonald, B. (1982). Job satisfaction and life satisfaction: An empirical evaluation of their interrelationship. *Human Relations,* 35,167–180.

Kephart, W. (1967). Some correlates of romantic love. *Journal of Marriage and the Family,* 29, 470–474.

Kershner, J., & Ledger, C. (1985). Effects of sex, intelligence, and style of thinking on creativity: A comparison of gifted and average IQ children. *Journal of Personality and Social Psychology,* 48, 1033–1044.

Kessler, S. (1980). The genetics of schizophrenia: A review. *Schizophrenia Bulletin,* 6, 404–416.

Kety, S. (1975). Biochemistry of the major psychoses. In A. Freedman, H. Kaplan, & B. Sadock (Eds.), *Comprehensive Textbook of Psychiatry*. Baltimore: Williams & Wilkins.

Kety, S., Rosenthal, D., Wender, P., Schulsinger, F., & Jacobsen, B. (1975). Mental illness in the biological and adoptive families of adopted individuals who have become schizophrenic: A preliminary report based upon psychiatric interviews. In R. Fieve, D. Rosenthal, & H. Brill (Eds.), *Genetic Research in Psychiatry*. Baltimore: Johns Hopkins University Press.

Keys, A. (1983). In NOVA. Fat chance in a thin world. Boston: WGBH Transcripts.

Kierkegaard, S. (1844). *The Concept of Anxiety* (2nd ed.). Princeton, NJ: Princeton University Press (revised printing 1980).

Kilham, W., & Mann, L. (1974). Level of destructive obedience as a function of transmitter and executant roles in the Milgram obedience paradigm. *Journal of Personality and Social Psychology,* 29, 696–702.

Kim, E., & Haynie, T. (1987). *Nuclear Diagnostic Imaging*. New York: Macmillan.

Kimzey, S. (1975). The effects of extended spaceflight on hematologic and immunologic systems. *Journal of American Medical Women's Association,* 30, 218–232.

King, N., & Montgomery, R. (1980). Biofeedback-induced control of human peripheral temperature: A critical review of the literature. *Psychological Bulletin,* 88, 738–752.

Kingsbury, S. (1987). Cognitive differences between clinical psychologists and psychiatrists. *American Psychologist,* 42, 152–156.

Kinsey, A., Pomeroy, W., & Martin, C. (1948). *Sexual Behavior in the Human Male*. Philadelphia: Saunders.

Kinsey, A., Pomeroy, W., Martin, C., and Gebhard, P. (1953). *Sexual Behavior in the Human Female*. Philadelphia: Saunders.

Klagsbrun, G. (1985). *Married People: Staying Together in the Age of Divorce*. New York: Bantam Books

Klaich, D. (1974). *Woman Plus Woman: Attitudes Towards Lesbianism*. New York: Simon and Schuster.

Klaus, M., & Kennell, J. (1982). *Parent-Infant Bonding* (2nd ed.). St. Louis: Mosby.

Klein, D. (1981). Anxiety reconceptualized. In D. Klein & J. Rabkin (Eds.), *Anxiety: New Research and Changing Concepts*. New York: Raven.

Klein, D., & Rabkin, J. (1981). *Anxiety: New Research and Changing Concepts*. New York: Raven.

Kleinhauz, M., & Eli, I. (1987). Potential deleterious effects of hypnosis in the clinical setting. *American Journal of Clinical Hypnosis,* 29, 155–159.

Kleinmuntz, B. (1982). *Personality and Psychological Assessment*. New York: St. Martins Press.

Klineberg, O. (1935). *Negro Intelligence and Selective Immigration*. New York: Columbia University Press.

Knafo, D., & Jaffe, Y. (1984). Sexual fantasizing in males and females. *Journal of Research in Personality,* 19, 451–462.

Knittle, J., & Hirsch, J. (1968). Effect of early nutrition on the development of rat epididymal fat pads: Cellularity and metabolism. *Journal of Clinical Investigation,* 47, 2001–2098.

Kohlberg, L. (1964). The development of moral character and moral ideology. In M. Hoffman & L. Hoffman (Eds.), *Reviews of Child Development Research* (Vol. I). New York: Russell Sage Foundation.

Kohlberg, L. (1968). The child as a moral philosopher. *Psychology Today,* 2, 25–30.

Kohlberg, L. (1969). Stage and sequence: The cognitive-developmental approach to socialization. In D. Goslin (Ed.), *Handbook of Socialization Theory and Research*. Chicago: Rand McNally.

Kohlberg, L. (1981). *The Philosophy of Moral Development: Essays on Moral Development* (Vol. I). San Francisco: Harper & Row.

Kohlberg, L. (1984). *The Psychology of Moral Development: Essays on Moral Development* (Vol. II). San Francisco: Harper & Row.

Kohlberg, L., & Gilligan, C. (1971). The adolescent as a philosopher: The discovery of the self in a postconventional world. *Daedalus,* Fall, 1051–1056.

Kohler, R. (1987). Personal communication with Robert Kohler, Huntington's disease researcher and head of Medical Genetics Department, Oregon Health Sciences University, March 27.

Köhler, W. (1925). *The Mentality of Apes*. Translated by E. Winter. New York: Harcourt, Brace and World.

Kolata, G. (1985). A guarded endorsement for shock therapy. *Science, 228,* 1510–1511.

Kolata, G. (1987a). Metabolic catch-22 of exercise regimens. *Science, 236,* 146–147.

Kolata, G. (1987b). Manic-depressive gene tied to chromosome 11. *Science, 235,* 1139–1140.

Kolb, B., & Whishaw, I. (1985). *Human Neuropsychology.* New York: W. H. Freeman.

Kosnik, A., Carroll, W., Cunningham, A., Modras, R., & Schulte, J. (1977). *Human Sexuality: New Directions in American Catholic Thought.* New York: Paulist Press.

Kotelchuck, M. (1976). The infant's relationship to the father: Experimental evidence. In M. Lamb (Ed.), *The Role of the Father in Child Development.* New York: Wiley.

Kraemer, G., & Mckinney, W. (1979). Interactions of pharmacological agents which alter biogenic amine metabolism and depression. *Journal of Affective Disorders, 1,* 33–54.

Kraepelin, E. (1918). *Dementia Praecox.* London: Livingstone.

Kramer, B. (1987). Electroconvulsive therapy use in geriatric depression. *The Journal of Nervous and Mental Disease, 175,* 233–235.

Kramer, D. (1983). Post-formal operations? A need for further conceptualization. *Human Development, 26,* 91–105.

Krantz, D., & Durel, A. (1983). Psychobiological substrates of the Type A behavior pattern. *Health Psychology, 2,* 393–412.

Krantz, D., Grunberg, N., & Baum, A. (1985). Health psychology. *Annual Review of Psychology, 36,* 349–383.

Krantz, D., & Manuck, S. (1984). Acute psychophysiologic reactivity and risk of cardiovascular disease: A review and methodological critique. *Psychological Bulletin, 96,* 435–464.

Kripke, D., & Simons, R. (1976). Average sleep, insomnia, and sleeping pill use. *Sleep Research, 5,* 110.

Kripke, D., & Sonnenschein, D. (1978). A biologic rhythm in waking fantasy. In K. Pope & J. Singer (Eds.), *The Stream of Consciousness: Scientific Investigations into the Flow of Human Experience.* New York: Plenum.

Kroll, P., Chamberlain, P., & Halpern, D. (1979). The diagnosis of Briquet's syndrome in a male population. *Journal of Mental Disorders, 34,* 423–428.

Kronholm, W. (1985). Lower costs open high school doors to cocaine. *The Oregonian,* March 21, B1.

Krueger, H., & Bornstein, P. (1987). Depression, sex-roles and family variables: Comparison of bulimics, binge-eaters, and normals. *Psychological Reports, 60,* 1106.

Krupnick, J., & Horowitz, M. (1981). Stress response syndromes. *Archives of General Psychiatry, 38,* 428–435.

Kübler-Ross, E. (1969). *On Death and Dying.* New York: Macmillan.

Kuehnel, J., & Liberman, R. (1986). Behavior modification. In I. Kutash & A. Wolf (Eds.), *Psychotherapist's Casebook.* San Francisco: Jossey-Bass.

Kukla, A. (1972). Attributional determinants of achievement-related behavior. *Journal of Personality and Social Psychology, 21,* 166–174.

Kupfer, D., & Frank, E. (1987). Relapse in recurrent unipolar depression. *American Journal of Psychiatry, 144,* 86–88.

Kupperman, H., & Studdiford, W. (1953). Endocrine therapy in gynecologic disorders. *Postgraduate Medicine, 14,* 410–425.

Kurtines, W., & Greif, E. (1974). The development of moral thought: Review and evaluation of Kohlberg's approach. *Psychological Bulletin, 81,* 453–470.

Kutash, I., & Wolf, A. (Eds.). (1986). *Psychotherapist's Casebook.* San Francisco: Jossey-Bass.

Labbe, R., Firl, A., Mufson, E., & Stein, D. (1983). Fetal brain transplants: Reduction of cognitive deficits in rats with frontal cortex lesions. *Science, 219,* 470–472.

LaBerge, S., Nagel, L., Dement, W., & Zarcone, V. (1981). Lucid dreaming verified by volitional communication during REM sleep. *Perceptual and Motor Skills, 52,* 727–732.

Labouvie-Vief, G., & Schell, D. (1982). Learning and memory in later life. In B. Wolman (Ed.), *Handbook of Developmental Psychology.* Englewood Cliffs, NJ: Prentice-Hall.

Lacey, J. (1967). Somatic response patterning and stress: Some revisions of activation theory. In M. Appley & R. Trumball (Eds.), *Psychological Stress.* New York: McGraw-Hill.

Lamb, M. (1979). Paternal influences and the father's role. *American Psychologist, 34,* 938–943.

Lamb, M. (1981). The development of father-infant relationships. In M. Lamb (Ed.), *The Role of the Father in Child Development* (2nd ed.). New York: Wiley-Interscience.

Lamb, M. (1982). Second thoughts on first touch. *Psychology Today,* April, 9–11.

Lammer, E., Chen, D., Hoar, R., Agnish, N., Benke, P., Braun, J., Curry, C., Fernhoff, P., Grix, A., Lott, I., Richard, J., & Sun, S. (1985). Retinoic acid embryopathy. *The New England Journal of Medicine, 313,* 837–841.

Lancet, D. (1986). Vertebrate olfactory reception. *Annual Review of Neuroscience, 9,* 329–355.

Landy, F. (1985). *Psychology of Work Behavior.* Homewood, IL: Dorsey Press.

Landy, F., & Trumbo, D. (1980). *Psy-*

chology of Work Behavior. Homewood, IL: Dorsey Press.

Lang, P., & Melamed, B. (1969). Case report: Avoidance conditioning therapy of an infant with chronic ruminative vomiting. *Journal of Abnormal Psychology, 74,* 1–8.

Lange, C. (1885). *The Emotions.* Baltimore: Williams & Wilkins, 1922 (originally published in 1885).

Langer, D., Brown, G., & Docherty, J. (1981). Dopamine receptor supersensitivity and schizophrenia: A review. *Schizophrenia Bulletin, 7,* 273–280.

Langer, E. (1975). The illusion of control. *Journal of Personality and Social Psychology, 32,* 311–328.

Langerspetz, K. (1979). Modification of aggressiveness in mice. In S. Fesbach & A. Fruczek (Eds.), *Aggression and Behavior Change: Biological and Social Processes.* New York: Praeger.

Langlois, J., Roggman, L., Casey, R., Ritter, J., Rieser-Danner, L., & Jenkins, Y. (1987). Infant preferences for attractive faces: Rudiments of a stereotype? *Developmental Psychology, 23,* 363–369.

Lanzetta, J., Cartwright-Smith, J., & Kleck, R. (1976). Effects of nonverbal dissimulation on emotional experience and autonomic arousal. *Journal of Personality and Social Psychology, 33,* 354–370.

LaPiere, R. (1934). Attitudes vs. action. *Social Forces, 13,* 230–237.

Larsen, M. (1986). Normal developmental milestones, the significance of delayed milestones, and neurodevelopmental evaluations of infants and young children. In A. Raimondi, M. Choux, & C. DiRocco (Eds.), *Head Injuries in the Newborn and Infant.* New York: Springer-Verlag.

Lashley, K. (1929). *Brain Mechanisms and Intelligence.* Chicago: University of Chicago Press.

Lashley, K. (1950). In search of the engram. *Symposia of the Society for Experimental Biology, 4,* 454–482.

Laudenslager, M., Reite, M., & Harbeck, R. (1982). Suppressed immune response in infant monkeys associated with maternal separation. *Behavior and Neural Biology, 36,* 40–48.

Lauer, J., & Lauer, R. (1985). Marriages made to last. *Psychology Today, 19,* 22–26.

Lavie, P. (1987). Ultrashort sleep-wake cycle: Timing of REM sleep. Evidence for sleep-dependent and sleep-independent components of REM cycle. *Sleep, 10,* 62–68.

Lawler, E. (1982). Strategies for improving the quality of work life. *American Psychologist, 37,* 496–493.

Lawler, E., & Suttle, J. (1972). A causal correlational test of the need hierarchy concept. *Organizational Behavior and Human Performance, 7,* 265–287.

Lazarus, R. (1981). Little hassles can

be hazardous to health. *Psychology Today, 15,* 58–62.

Lazarus, R., & Folkman, S. (1984a). *Stress, Appraisal, and Coping.* New York: Springer.

Lazarus, R., & Folkman, S. (1984b). Coping and adaptation. In W. Gentry (Ed.), *The Handbook of Behavioral Medicine.* New York: Guilford.

Lechin, F., & Van der Dijs, R. (1984). Slow wave sleep (SWS), REM sleep (REMS), and depression. *Research Communication in Psychology, Psychiatry, and Behavior, 9,* 227–262.

Leconte, P., Hennevin, E., & Bloch, V. (1972). Increase in paradoxical sleep following learning in the rat: Correlation with level of conditioning. *Brain Research, 42,* 552–553.

LeDoux, J., Wilson, D., & Gassaniga, M. (1977). A divided mind: Observations of the conscious properties of the separated hemispheres. *Annals of Neurology, 2,* 417–421.

Lee, E. (1951). Negro intelligence and selective migration: A Philadelphia test of Klineberg's hypothesis. *American Sociological Review, 61,* 227–233.

Legros, J., Gilot, P., Seron, X., Claessens, J., Adam, A., Moeglen, J., Audibert, A., & Berchier, P. (1978). Influence of vasopressin on learning and memory. *Lancet, 1,* 41–42.

Lemon, B., Bengston, V., & Peterson, J. (1972). An exploration of the activity theory of aging: Activity types and life satisfaction among in-movers to a retirement community. *Journal of Gerontology, 27,* 511–523.

Lenneberg, E. (1967). *Biological Functions of Language.* New York: Wiley.

Leon, B., & Roth, L. (1977). Obesity: Psychological causes, correlations, and speculations. *Psychological Bulletin, 84,* 117–139.

Lerner, R., & Lerner, J. (1977). Effects of age, sex, and physical attractiveness on child-peer relations, academic performance, and elementary school adjustment. *Developmental Psychology, 13,* 585–590.

Lerner, R., & Spanier, G. (1980). *Adolescent Development: A Life-Span Perspective.* New York: McGraw-Hill.

Leventhal, H., & Cleary, P. (1980). *Adolescent Development: A Life-Span Perspective.* New York: McGraw-Hill.

Leventhal, H., & Cleary, P. (1980). The smoking problem: A review of the research and theory in behavioral risk modification. *Psychological Bulletin, 88,* 370–405.

Leventhal, H., & Nerenz, D. (1983). A model for stress research with some implications for the control of stress disorders. In D. Meichenbaum & M. Jaremko (Eds.), *Stress Reduction and Prevention.* New York: Plenum.

Leventhal, H., & Tomarken, A. (1986). Emotion: Today's problems. *Annual Review of Psychology, 37,* 565–610.

Levy, S. (1983). Death and dying: Behavioral and social factors that contribute to the process. In T. Burish and L. Bradley (Eds.), *Coping With Chronic Illness: Research and Application.* New York: Academic Press.

Lewin, J., & Gambosh, D. (1973). Increase in REM time as a function of the need for divergent thinking. In W. Koella and P. Lewin (Eds.), *Sleep: Physiology, Biochemistry, Psychology, Pharmacology, Clinical Implications.* Basel, Switzerland: Karger.

Lewin, R. (1987). Dramatic results with brain grafts. *Science, 236,* 245–247.

Lewinsohn, P. (1974). A behavioral approach to depression. In R. Friedman & M. Katz (Eds.), *The Psychology of Depression: Contemporary Theory and Research.* Washington, DC: Winston/Wiley.

Lewinsohn, P., & Libet, J. (1972). Pleasant events activity schedules and depression. *Journal of Abnormal Psychology, 79,* 291–295.

Lewis, C. (1981). The effects of parental firm control: A reinterpretation of findings. *Psychological Bulletin, 90,* 547–563.

Lewis, E., Baird, R., Leverenz, E., & Koyama, H. (1982). Inner ear: Dye injection reveals peripheral origins of specific sensitivities. *Science, 215,* 1641–1643.

Lewis, J., Baddeley, A., Bonham, K., & Lovett, D. (1970). Traffic pollution and mental efficiency. *Nature, 225,* 96.

Leyens, J., & Parke, R. (1975). Aggressive slides can induce a weapons effect. *European Journal of Social Psychology, 5,* 229–236.

Lieberman, M., & Coplan, A. (1970). Distance from death as a variable in the study of aging. *Developmental Psychology, 2,* 71–84.

Liebert, R., & Spiegler, M. (1982). *Personality: Strategies and Issues.* Homewood, IL: Dorsey Press.

Lieblich, I. (1979). Eidetic imagery: Do not use ghosts to hunt ghosts of the same species. *The Behavioral and Brain Sciences, 2,* 608–609.

Liebowitz, M., Fyer, A., Gorman, J., Dillon, D., Appleby, I., Levy, G., Anderson, S., Levitt, M., Palij, M., Davies, S., & Klein, D. (1984). Lactate provocation of panic attacks: I. Clinical and behavioral findings. *Archives of General Psychiatry, 41,* 764–770.

Likert, R. (1961). *New Patterns of Management.* New York: McGraw-Hill.

Linn, R. (1986). Educational testing and assessment. *American Psychologist, 41,* 1153–1160.

Lipper, S. (1985). Clinical psychopharmacology. In J. Walker (Ed.), *Essentials of Clinical Psychiatry.* Philadelphia: Lippincott.

Livson, N., & Peskin, H. (1980). Perspectives on adolescence from longitudinal research. In J. Adelson (Ed.), *Handbook of Adolescent Psychology.* New York: Wiley.

Locke, E. (1976). The nature and causes of job satisfaction. In M. Dunnette (Ed.), *Handbook of Industrial and Organizational Psychology.* Chicago: Rand-McNally.

Loehlin, J., Lindzey, G., & Spuhler, J. (1975). *Race Differences in Intelligence.* San Francisco: W. H. Freeman.

Loftus, E. (1975). Leading questions and the eyewitness report. *Cognitive Psychology, 7,* 560–572.

Loftus, E., & Burns, T. (1982). Mental shock can produce retrograde amnesia. *Memory and Cognition, 10,* 318–323.

Loftus, E., & Loftus, G. (1980). On the permanence of stored information in the human brain. *American Psychologist, 35,* 409–420.

Loftus, E., Miller, D., & Burns, H. (1978). Semantic integration of verbal information into a visual memory. *Journal of Experimental Psychology, 4,* 19–31.

Loftus, E., & Palmer, J. (1974). Reconstruction of automobile destruction: An example of interaction between language and memory. *Journal of Verbal Learning and Verbal Behavior, 13,* 585–589.

Loomis, A., Harvey, E., & Hobart, G. (1937). Cerebral status during sleep as studied by human brain potentials. *Journal of Experimental Psychology, 21,* 127–144.

Lorenz, K. (1937). The companion in the bird's world. *Auk, 54,* 245–273.

Lorenz, K. (1969). *On Aggression.* New York: Bantam Books.

Lorenz, K. (1974). *The Eight Deadly Sins of Civilized Man.* New York: Harcourt Brace Jovanovich.

Lovass, O. (1973). *Behavioral Treatment of Autistic Children.* Morristown, NJ: General Learning Press.

Luborsky, L., Singer, B., & Luborsky, L. (1975). Comparative studies of psychotherapies. *Archives of General Psychiatry, 32,* 995–1008.

Luce, G. (1965). *Current Research on Sleep and Dreams.* Health Service Publication No. 1389. U.S. Department of Health, Education and Welfare.

Luchins, A., & Luchins, E. (1959). *Rigidity of Behavior.* Eugene, OR: University of Oregon Press.

Lumsdaine, A., & Jones, I. (1953). Resistance to "counter-propaganda" produced by one-sided and two-sided "propaganda" presentations. *Public Opinion Quarterly, 17,* 311–318.

Lykken, D. (1957). A study of anxiety in the sociopathic personality. *Journal of Abnormal and Social Psychology, 57,* 6–10.

Lynch, G. (1984). A magical memory tour. *Psychology Today,* April, 70–76.

Lynch, G., & Baudry, M. (1984). The biochemistry of memory: A new and specific hypothesis. *Science, 224,* 1057–1063.

Maas, J., Fawcett, J., & Dekirmenjian, W. (1972). Catecholamine metabolism, depressive illness and drug response. *Archives of General Psychiatry, 26,* 252–262.

Maccoby, E. (1980). *Social Development: Psychological Growth and the Parent-Child Relationship.* New York: Harcourt Brace Jovanovich.

Maccoby, E. (1985). Address presented at a Symposium on Issues in Contemporary Psychology, Reed College, Portland, Oregon, May.

Mackinnon, D., & Hall, W. (1972). Intelligence and creativity. *Proceedings, XVIIth International Congress of Applied Psychology, 2,* 1883–1888.

MacPhillamy, D., & Lewinsohn, P. (1974). Depression as a function of levels of desired and obtained pleasure. *Journal of Abnormal Psychology, 83,* 651–657.

Maddi, S., Bartone, P., & Puccetti, M. (1987). Stressful events are indeed a factor in physical illness: Reply to Schroeder and Costa (1984). *Journal of Personality and Social Psychology, 52,* 833–843.

Maddison, S. (1977). Intraperitoneal and intracranial cholescystokinin depresses operant responding for food. *Physiology and Behavior, 19,* 819–824.

Madrazo, I., Drucker-Collin, R., Diaz, V., Martinez, J., Torres, C., & Becerril, J. Open microsurgical autograft of adrenal medulla to the right caudate nucleus in two patients with intractable Parkinson's disease. *The New England Journal of Medicine,* 316, 831–834.

Mahone, C. (1960). Fear of failure and unrealistic vocational aspiration. *Journal of Abnormal and Social Psychology, 60,* 253–261.

Malmstrom, P., & Silva, M. (1986). Twin talk: Manifestations of twin status in the speech of toddlers. *Journal of Child Language, 13,* 293–304.

Mann, R. (1959). A review of the relationships between personality and performance in small groups. *Psychological Bulletin, 56,* 241–270.

Manson, J., Stampfer, M., Hennekens, C., & Willett, W. (1987). Body weight and longevity. *Journal of the American Medical Association, 257,* 353–358.

Manuck, S., Craft, S., & Gold, K. (1978). Coronary-prone behavior patterns and cardiovascular response. *Psychophysiology, 15,* 403–411.

March of Dimes Birth Defects Foundation (1983). *Genetic Counseling.* Public Health Education Booklet.

Markman, E. (1987). How children constrain the possible meanings of words. In U. Neisser (Ed.), *Concepts and Conceptual Development: Ecological and Intellectual Factors in Categorization.* New York: Cambridge University Press.

Marler, P. (1967). Animal communication signals. *Science, 157,* 769–774.

Marlott, G. (1983). The controlled-drinking controversy: A commentary. *American Psychologist, 38,* 1097–1110.

Marlott, G. (1984). Relapse prevention with addictive behavior. Paper presented at Reed College, Portland, Oregon, Department of Psychology Colloquium, February 15.

Marmor, J. (Ed.). (1980). *Homosexual Behavior.* New York: Basic Books.

Marshall, D. (1971). Sexual behavior on Mangaia. In D. Marshall & R. Suggs (Eds.), *Human Sexual Behavior: Variations in the Ethnographic Spectrum.* Englewood Cliffs, NJ: Prentice-Hall.

Marshall, G., & Zimbardo, P. (1979). Affective consequences of inadequately explained physiological arousal. *Journal of Personality and Social Psychology, 37,* 970–988.

Martin, D., & Lyon, P. (1972). *Lesbian-Women.* New York: Bantam Books.

Martin, J. (1987). Genetic linkage in neurologic diseases. *The New England Journal of Medicine, 316,* 1018–1019.

Martin, P. (1987). Psychology and the immune system. *New Scientist,* April 9, 46–50.

Maslach, C. (1979). Negative emotional biasing of unexplained physiological arousal. *Journal of Personality and Social Psychology, 37,* 953–969.

Maslow, A. (1954). *Motivation and Personality.* New York: Harper & Row.

Maslow, A. (1968). *Toward a Psychology of Being* (2nd ed.). Princeton, NJ: Van Nostrand Reinhold.

Maslow, A. (1970). *Motivation and Personality* (2nd ed.). New York: Harper & Row.

Maslow, A. (1971). *The Farther Reaches of Human Nature.* New York: Viking.

Mason, J. (1974). Specificity in the organization of neuroendocrine response profiles. In P. Seeman and G. Brawn (Eds.), *Frontiers in Neurology and Neuroscience Research.* Toronto: University of Toronto Press.

Masters, W., & Johnson, V. (1966). *Human Sexual Response.* Boston: Little, Brown.

Matas, L., Arend, R., & Sroufe, L. (1978). Continuity of adaptation in the second year: The relationship between quality of attachment and later competence. *Child Development, 49,* 547–556.

Mater, P. (1980). Very rapid forgetting. *Memory and Cognition, 8,* 174–179.

Mathews, A. (1981). Treatment of sexual dysfunctions: psychological and hormonal factors. In J. Boulougouris (Ed.), *Learning Theory Application in Psychiatry.* New York: Wiley.

Matlin, M. (1983). *Cognition.* New York: Holt, Rinehart and Winston.

Mattson, M., Pollack, E., & Cullen, J. (1987). What are the odds that smoking will kill you? *American Journal of Public Health, 77,* 425–431.

Max, L. (1937). An experimental study of the motor theory of consciousness: IV. Action-curved responses in the deaf during awakening, kinaesthetic imagery and abstract thinking. *Journal of Comparative Psychology, 24,* 301–344.

May, P., Tuma, A., Yale, C., Potepan, P., & Dixon, W. (1976). Schizophrenia—A follow-up study of results of treatment: II. Hospital stay over two to five years. *Psychiatry, 33,* 481–486.

Mayer, J. (1955). Regulation of energy intake and body weight. The glucostatic and the lipostatic hypothesis. *Annals of the New York Academy of Science, 63,* 15–43.

Mayer, J. (1968). *Overweight: Causes and Control.* Englewood Cliffs, NJ: Prentice-Hall.

Mayer, R. (1982). Different problem-solving strategies for algebra word and equation problems. *Journal of Experimental Psychology: Learning, Memory, and Cognition, 8,* 448–462.

Mayer-Gross, W., Slater, E., & Roth, M. (1969). *Clinical Psychiatry* (3rd ed.). Baltimore: Williams & Wilkins.

Mayleas, D. (1980). The impact of tiny feet on love. *Self,* August, 105–110.

Maziade, M., Cote, R., Boutin, P., Bernier, H., & Thivierg, J. (1987). Temperament and intellectual development: A longitudinal study from infancy to four years. *American Journal of Psychiatry, 2,* 144–149.

Mazziotta, J., Phelps, M., Pahl, J., Huang, S., Baxter, L., Riege, W., Hoffman, J., Kuhl, D., Lanto, A., Wapenski, J., & Markham, C. (1987). Reduced cerebral glucose metabolism in asymptomatic subjects at risk for Huntington's disease. *The New England Journal of Medicine, 316,* 357–363.

McArthur, L., & Resko, B. (1975). The portrayal of men and women in American television commercials. *Journal of Social Psychology, 97,* 209–220.

McCall, R. (1983). Environmental effects on intelligence: The forgotten realm of discontinuous nonshared within-family factors. *Child Development, 54,* 253–259.

McCarthy, J. (1985). The medical complications of cocaine abuse. In D. Smith and D. Wesson (Eds.), *Treating the Cocaine Abuser.* Center City, MN: Hazelden.

McClelland, D. (1953). *The Achievement Motive.* New York: Appleton, Century, Crofts.

McClelland, D. (1955). *Studies in Motivation.* New York: Appleton, Century, Crofts.

McClelland, D. (1961). *The Achieving Society.* Princeton, NJ: D. Van Nostrand.

McClelland, D. (1985). *Human Motivation.* Glenview, IL: Scott, Foresman.

McClelland, D., Atkinson, J., Clark, R., & Lowell, E. (1976). *The Achievement Motive* (2nd ed.). New York: Irvington.

McClelland, D., & Pilon, D. (1983).

Sources of adult motives in patterns of parent behavior in early childhood. *Journal of Personality and Social Psychology, 44,* 564–574.

McCloskey, M., & Zaragoza, M. (1985a). Misleading postevent information and memory for events: Arguments and evidence against memory impairment hypothesis. *Journal of Experimental Psychology: General, 114,* 3–18.

McCloskey, M., & Zaragonza, M. (1985b). Postevent information and memory: Reply to Loftus, Schooler, and Wagenaar. *Journal of Experimental Psychology: General, 114,* 381–387.

McConahay, J. (1978). The effects of school desegregation upon students' racial attitudes and behavior: A critical review of the literature and a prolegomenon to future research. *Law and Contemporary Problems, 42,* 77–107.

McConnell, J. (1962). Memory transfer through cannibalism in planarians. *Journal of Neuropsychiatry, 3,* 542–548.

McConnell, J. (1983). *Understanding Human Behavior.* New York: Holt, Rinehart and Winston.

McCormick, E., & Ilgen, D. (1980). *Industrial Psychology* (7th ed.). Englewood Cliffs, NJ: Prentice-Hall.

McCormick, E., Ilgen, D. (1985). *Industrial and Organizational Psychology.* Englewood Cliffs, NJ: Prentice-Hall.

McCormick, E., & Sanders, M. (1982). *Human Factors in Engineering and Design.* New York: McGraw-Hill.

McCrae, R. (1984). Situational determinants of coping responses: Loss, threat, and challenge. *Journal of Personality and Social Psychology, 46,* 919–928.

McDonough, R., Madden, J., Falek, A., Shafer, D., Pline, M., Gordon, D., Bokos, P., Kuehnle, J., & Mendelson, J. (1980). Alteration of T and null lymphocyte frequencies in the peripheral blood of human opiate addicts: In vivo evidence for opiate receptor sites on T lymphocytes. *Journal of Immunology, 125,* 2539–2543.

McFarlane, A., Norman, G., Streiner, D., Roy, R., & Scott, D. (1980). A longitudinal study of the influence of the psychosocial environment on health status: A preliminary report. *Journal of Health and Social Behavior, 21,* 124–133.

McGaugh, J. (1983). Hormonal influences on memory. *Annual Review of Psychology, 34,* 297–323.

McGinty, D. (1969). Effects of prolonged isolation and subsequent enrichment on sleep patterns in kittens. *Electroencephalography and Clinical Neurophysiology, 26,* 335.

McGrath, M., & Cohen, D. (1978). REM sleep facilitation of adaptive waking behavior: A review of the literature. *Psychological Bulletin, 85,* 24–57.

McGraw, M. (1940). Neural maturation as exemplified in achievement of bladder control. *Journal of Pediatrics, 16,* 580–589.

McGregor, D. (1960). *The Human Side of Enterprise.* New York: McGraw-Hill.

McGuire, W. (1968a). Theory of the structure of human thought. In R. Abelson, E. Aronson, W. McGuire, T. Newcomb, M. Rosenberg, & P. Tannenbaum (Eds.), *Theories of Cognitive Consistency: A Sourcebook.* Chicago: Rand McNally.

McGuire, W. (1968b). Personality and susceptibility to social influence. In E. Borgatta & W. Lambert (Eds.), *Handbook of Personality Theory and Research.* Chicago: Rand McNally.

McGuire, W. (1969). The nature of attitudes and attitude change. In G. Lindzey and E. Aronson (Eds.), *The Handbook of Social Psychology* (2nd ed.). Reading, MA: Addison-Wesley.

McKey, R., Condelli, L., Ganson, H., Barrett, B., McConkey, C., & Plantz, M. (1985). *The Impact of Head Start on Children, Families, and Communities: Final Report of the Head Start Evaluation, Synthesis and Utilization Project* (NO. OHDS 85-31193). Washington, DC: U.S. Government Printing Office.

Mckoon, G., Ratcliff, R., & Dell, G. (1985). The role of semantic information on episodic retrieval. *Journal of Experimental Psychology: Learning, Memory, and Cognition, 11,* 742–751.

Mckoon, G., Ratcliff, R., & Dell, G. (1986). A critical evaluation of the semantic-episodic distinction. *Journal of Experimental Psychology: Learning, Memory, and Cognition, 12,* 295–306.

Mead, M. (1963). *Sex and Temperament in Three Primitive Societies.* New York: Morrow.

Meador, B., & Rogers, C. (1984). Person-centered therapy. In R. Corsini (Ed.), *Current Psychotherapies.* Itasca, IL: Peacock.

Medin, D., & Smith, E. (1984). Concepts and concept formation. *Annual Review of Psychology, 35,* 113–138.

Mednick, S. (1958). A learning theory approach to schizophrenia. *Psychological Bulletin, 55,* 316–327.

Mednick, S., Gabrielli, W., & Hutchings, B. (1984). Genetic influences in criminal convictions: Evidence from adoption cohort. *Science, 224,* 891–894.

Mednick, S., Pollock, V., Volavka, J., & Gabrielli, W. (1982). Biology and violence. In M. Wolfgang & N. Weiner (Eds.), *Criminal Violence.* Beverly Hills, CA: Sage.

Mednick, S., Volavka, J., Gabrielli, W., & Itil, T. (1981). EEG as a predictor of antisocial behavior. *Criminology, 19,* 219–231.

Mefford, I., Baker, T., Boehme, R., Foutz, A., Ciaranello, R., Barchas, J., & Dement, W. (1983). Narcolepsy: Biogenic amine deficits in an animal model. *Science, 220,* 629–632.

Megargee, E. (1972). *The California Psychological Inventory Handbook.* San Francisco: Jossey-Bass.

Meichenbaum, D. (1977). *Cognitive-Behavioral Modification: An Integrative Approach.* New York: Plenum.

Mellor, C. (1970). First rank symptoms of schizophrenia. *British Journal of Psychiatry, 117,* 15–23.

Meltzoff, A., & Moore, M. (1983). Newborn infants imitate adult facial gestures. *Child Development, 54,* 702–709.

Melville, J. (1977). *Phobias and Obsessions.* New York: Coward, McCann & Geoghegan.

Melzack, R. (1973). *The Puzzle of Pain.* New York: Basic Books.

Melzack, R. (1980). Psychological aspects of pain. In J. Bonica (Ed.), *Pain.* New York: Raven.

Melzack, R., & Wall, P. (1965). Pain mechanisms: A new theory. *Science, 150,* 971–979.

Melzack, R., & Wall, P. (1983). *The Challenge of Pain.* New York: Basic Books.

Mendlewicz, J., & Rainer, J. (1977). Adoption study supporting genetic transmission in manic-depressive illness. *Nature, 268,* 327–329.

Menninger, K. (1945). *The Human Mind* (3rd ed.). New York: Knopf.

Mervis, C., & Crisafi, M. (1982). Order of acquisition of subordinate, basic, and superordinate categories. *Child Development, 53,* 258–266.

Messenger, J. (1971). Sex and repression in an Irish folk community. In D. Marshall & R. Suggs (Eds.), *Human Sexual Behavior: Variations in the Ethnographic Spectrum.* Englewood Cliffs, NJ: Prentice-Hall.

Meyer-Bahlburg, H. (1977). Sex hormones and male homosexuality in comparative perspective. *Archives of Sexual Behavior, 6,* 297–325.

Michel, K. (1987). Suicide risk factors: A comparison of suicide attempters with suicide completers. *British Journal of Psychiatry, 150,* 78–82.

Milavsky, J., Kessler, R., Stipp, H., & Rubens, W. (1982). Television and aggression: results of a panel study. In D. Pearl, L. Bouthilet, and J. Lazer (Eds.), *Television and Behavior: Ten Years of Scientific Progress and Implications for the Eighties* (Vol. II. Technical Reviews). Rockville, MD: National Institute of Mental Health.

Miles, C. (1977). Conditions predisposing to suicide. *Journal of Nervous and Mental Disease, 164,* 231–246.

Milgram, S. (1963). Behavioral study of obedience. *Journal of Abnormal and Social Psychology, 67,* 371–378.

Milgram, S. (1964). Issues in the study

of obedience: A reply to Baumrind. *American Psychologist, 19,* 848–852.

Miller, G. (1956). The magic number seven plus or minus two: some limits on our capacity for processing information. *Psychological Review, 63,* 81–97.

Miller, G. (1981). *Language and Speech.* San Francisco: W. H. Freeman.

Miller, G., Galanter, E., & Pribram, K. (1960). *Plans and the Structure of Behavior.* New York: Holt, Rinehart and Winston.

Miller, J. (1983). Venezuelan connection. *Science News, 124,* 408–411.

Miller, L., & Branconnier, R. (1983). Cannabis: Effects on memory and the cholinergic limbic system. *Psychological Bulletin, 93,* 441–456.

Miller, N. (1941). The frustration-aggression hypothesis. *Psychological Review, 48,* 337–342.

Miller, N. (1983). Behavioral medicine: Symbiosis between laboratory and clinic. *Annual Review of Psychology, 34,* 1–31.

Miller, N. (1985). Rx: Biofeedback. *Psychology Today,* February, 54–59.

Miller, N., & Brewer, M. (Eds.). (1984). *Groups in Contact: The Psychology of Desegregation.* New York: Academic Press.

Miller, N., & Bugelski, R. (1948). Minor studies of aggression, II: The influence of frustrations imposed by the in-group on attitudes expressed toward out-groups. *Journal of Psychology, 25,* 437–452.

Miller, S. (1986). The treatment of sleep apnea. *Journal of the American Medical Association, 256,* 348.

Mills, J., & Aronson, E. (1965). Opinion change as a function of communicator's attractiveness and desire to influence. *Journal of Personality and Social Psychology, 1,* 173–177.

Milner, B. (1966). Amnesia following operation on the temporal lobes. In C. Whitty & O. Zangwill (Eds.), *Amnesia.* London: Butterworth.

Mirsky, A., & Duncan, C. (1986). Etiology and expression of schizophrenia: Neurological and psychosocial factors. *Annual Review of Psychology, 37,* 291–319.

Mirsky, A., & Orzack, M. (1980). Two retrospective studies of psychosurgery. In E. Valenstein (Ed.), *The Psychosurgery Debate.* San Francisco: W. H. Freeman.

Mischel, W. (1968). *Personality Assessment.* New York: Wiley.

Mischel, W. (1979). On the interface of cognition and personality. *American Psychologist, 34,* 740–754.

Mischel, W. (1984). Convergences and challenges in the search for consistency. *American Psychologist, 39,* 351–364.

Mischel, W. (1986). *Introduction to Personality* (4th ed.). New York: Holt, Rinehart and Winston.

Mishkin, M. (1982). A memory system in the monkey. *Philosophical Transactions of the Royal Society of London, 298,* 85–95.

Mishkin, M., Malamut, B., & Backevalier, J. (1984). Memories and habits: Two neural systems. In G. Lynch, J. McGaugh, & N. Weinberger (Eds.), *The Neurobiology of Learning and Memory.* New York: Guilford Press.

Mita, T., Dermer, M., & Knight, J. (1977). Reversed facial images and the mere-exposure hypothesis. *Journal of Personality and Social Psychology, 35,* 597–601.

Moen, P. (1982). The two-provider family: Problems and potentials. In M. Lamb (Ed.), *Nontraditional Families: Parenting and Child Development.* Hillsdale, NJ: Erlbaum.

Mohs, M. (1982). I.Q. *Discover,* September, 18–24.

Molen-Hoeksema, S. (1987). Sex differences in unipolar depression: Evidence and theory. *Psychological Bulletin, 101,* 259–282.

Molfese, D., & Molfese, V. (1979). Hemisphere and stimulus differences as reflected in the cortical responses of newborn infants to speech stimuli. *Developmental Psychology, 15,* 505–511.

Money, J. (1965). Psychosexual differentiation. In J. Money (Ed.), *Sex Research, New Developments.* New York: Holt, Rinehart and Winston.

Money, J., & Ehrhardt, A. (1972). *Man and Woman, Boy and Girl.* Baltimore: Johns Hopkins University Press.

Money, J., Hampson, J., & Hampson, J. (1955). An examination of some basic sexual concepts: The evidence of human hermaphrodism. *Bulletin of Johns Hopkins Hospital, 97,* 301–319.

Monjan, A., & Collector, M. (1977). Stress-induced modulation of the immune response. *Science, 196,* 307–308.

Monroe, L. (1967). Psychological and physiological differences between good and poor sleepers. *Journal of Abnormal Psychology, 72,* 255–264.

Moore, C., Williams, J., & Gorczynska, A. (1987). View specificity, array specificity, and egocentrism in young children's drawings. *Canadian Journal of Psychology, 41,* 74–79.

Moore, R. (1987). Parkinson's disease—a new therapy? *The New England Journal of Medicine, 316,* 872–873.

Mora, F., & Ferrer, J. (1986). Neurotransmitters, pathways and circuits as the neural substrates of self-stimulation of the prefrontal cortex: Facts and speculations. *Behavioural Brain Research, 22,* 127–140.

Moran, J., & Desimone, R. (1985). Selective attention gates visual processing in the extrastriate cortex. *Science, 229,* 782–784.

Morden, B., Mitchell, G., and Dement, W. (1967). Selective REM sleep deprivation and compensation phenomena in the rat. *Brain Research, 5* 339–349.

Moreland, R., & Zajonc, R. (1982). Exposure effects in person perception: Familiarity, similarity, and attraction. *Journal of Experimental Social Psychology, 18,* 395–415.

Morgan, C., & Morgan, J. (1940). Studies in hunger: The relation of gastric denervation and dietary sugar to the effect of insulin upon food-intake in the rat. *Journal of Genetic Psychology, 57,* 153–163.

Morris, J. (1969). Propensity for risk taking as a determinant of vocational choice: An extension of the theory of achievement motivation. *Journal of Personality and Social Psychology, 3,* 328–335.

Morrison, A. (1983). A window on the sleeping brain. *Scientific American, 248,* 94–102.

Mowrer, O. (1947). On the dual nature of learning—A reinterpretation of "conditioning" and "problem-solving." *Harvard Educational Review, 17,* 102–148.

Moyer, K. (1983). The physiology of motivation: Agression as a model. In C. Scheier & A. Rogers (Eds.), *G. Stanley Hall Lecture Series* (Vol. 3). Washington, DC: American Psychological Association.

Mullen, B. (1983). Operationalizing the effect of the group on the individual: A self-attentive perspective. *Journal of Experimental Social Psychology, 19,* 295–322.

Munsterberg, H. (1913). *Psychological and Industrial Efficiency.* Boston: Houghton-Mifflin.

Murdock, B. (1962). The serial position effect of free recall. *Journal of Experimental Psychology, 64,* 482–488.

Murdock, B. (1974). *Human Memory: Theory and Data.* New York: Wiley.

Murphy, G., Simons, A., Wetzcl, R., & Lustman, P. (1984). Cognitive therapy and pharmacotherapy: Singling out together in the treatment of depression. *Archives of General Psychiatry, 41,* 33–41.

Murphy, N., & Fain, T. (1978). Psychobiological factors in sex and gender identity. Paper presented to the AASECT Conference in Portland, OR, October 19.

Murray, H. (1938). *Exploration in Personality.* New York: Oxford University Press.

Murray, R., Oon, M., Rodnight, R., Birley, J., & Smith, A. (1979). Increased excretion of dimethyltryptamine and certain features of psychosis. *Archives of General Psychiatry, 36,* 644–649,

Murray, W. (1985). Hearing: Ears easy prey to onslaughts of noisy world. *The Oregonian,* April 18, C1–C2.

Murphy-Berman, V., & Berman, J. (1978). The importance of choice and sex in invasions of interpersonal space. *Personality and Social Psychology Bulletin, 4,* 424–428.

Mussen, P., & Jones, M. (1957). Self-conceptions, motivation, and interpersonal attitudes of late- and early-maturing boys. *Child Development, 28,* 243–256.

Muuss, R. (1985). Adolescent eating disorder: Anorexia nervosa. *Adolescence*, 79, 525–536.

Myers, B. (1984). Mother-infant bonding: The status of the critical period hypothesis. *Developmental Review*, 4, 240–274.

Myers, J. (1984). Right hemisphere language: Science or fiction? *American Psychologist*, 39, 315–320.

Myers, J., Weissman, M., Tischler, G., Holzer, C., Leaf, P., Orvaschel, H., Anthony, J., Boyd, J., Burke, J., Kramer, M., & Stoltzman, R. (1984). Six-month prevalence of psychiatric disorders in three communities: 1980–1982. *Archives of Abnormal Psychology*, 41, 959–967.

Naeser, M., Helm-Estabrooks, N., Haas, G., Auerbach, S., & Srinivasan, M. (1987). Relationship between lesion extent in "Wernicke's area" on computed tomographic scan and predicting recovery of comprehension in Wernicke's aphasia. *Archives of Neurology*, 44, 73–82.

Narayanan, V., & Nath, R. (1982). A field test of some attitudinal and behavioral consequences of flextime. *Journal of Applied Psychology*, 67, 214–218.

Nathans, J. (1987). Molecular biology of visual pigments. *Annual Review of Physiology*, 10, 163–194.

National Academy of Science's Institute of Medicine. *Marijuana and Health*. Washington, DC: National Academic Press.

National Institute of Mental Health. (1981). *Plain Talk About Adolescence*. Rockville, MD: U.S. Government Printing Office.

National Institute of Mental Health. (1982). *Television and Behavior: Ten years of Scientific Progress and Implications for the Eighties* (Vol. 1). Washington, DC: U.S. Government Printing Office.

National Institute on Aging Task Force. (1980). Senility reconsidered: Treatment possibilities for mental impairment in the elderly. *Journal of the American Medical Association*, 244, 259–263.

Nauta, W., & Feirtag, M. (1979). The organization of the brain. *Scientific American*, 241, 88–111.

Nebes, R. (1972). Dominance of the minor hemisphere in commissuratomized man in a test of figural unification. *Brain*, 95, 633–635.

Neely, J., & Durgunoglu, A. (1985). Dissociative episodic and semantic priming effects in episodic recognition and lexical decision tasks. *Journal of Memory and Language*, 24, 466–489.

Neill, J. (1987). "More than medical significance": LSD and American psychiatry 1953 to 1966. *Journal of Psychoactive Drugs*, 19, 39–45.

Neisser, U. (1967). *Cognitive Psychology*. New York: Appleton, Century, Crofts.

Neisser, U. (1982). Memory: What are the important questions? In U. Neisser (Ed.), *Memory Observed*. San Francisco: W. H. Freeman.

Nelson, K. (1981). Individual differences in language development: Implications for development and languages. *Developmental Psychology*, 17, 170–187.

Nemiah, J. (1981). A psychoanalytic view of phobias. *American Journal of Psychoanalysis*, 41, 115–120.

Neugarten, B. (1972). Personality and the aging process. *The Gerontologist*, 12, 9–15.

Neugarten, B., & Hagestad, G. (1976). Age and the life course. In H. Binstock and E. Shanas (Eds.), *Handbook of Aging and the Social Sciences*. New York: Van Nostrand Reinhold.

Neugarten, B., Havighurst, R., & Tobin, S. (1965). Personality and patterns of aging. In B. Neugarten (Ed.), *Middle Age and Aging*. Chicago: University of Chicago Press.

Neugarten, B., & Neugarten, D. (1987). The changing meanings of age. *Psychology Today*, May, 29–33.

Newcomb, M., & Bentler, P. (1980). Assessment of personality and demographic aspects of cohabitation and marital success. *Journal of Personality Development*, 4, 11–24.

Newell, A., & Simon, H. (1972). *Human Problem Solving*. Englewood Cliffs, NJ: Prentice-Hall.

Newman, H., Freeman, F., & Holzinger, K. (1937). *Twins: A Study of Heredity and Environment*. Chicago: University of Chicago Press.

Newman, P. (1982). The peer group. In B. Wolman (Ed.), *Handbook of Developmental Psychology*. Englewood Cliffs, NJ: Prentice-Hall.

Newsom, C., Favell, J., & Rincover, A. (1983). Side effects of punishment. In S. Axelrod & J. Apsche (Eds.), *The Effects of Punishment on Behavior*. New York: Academic Press.

Nicassio, P., Mendlowitz, D., Fussel, J., & Petras, L. (1985). The phenomenology of the pre-sleep state: The development of the pre-sleep arousal scale. *Behavior Research and Therapy*, 23, 263–271.

Nield, T. (1987). Lest you forget. *New Scientist*, May 7, 63.

Niemcryk, S., Jenkins, D., Rose, R., & Hurst, M. (1987). The prospective impact of psychosocial variables on rates of illness and injury in professional employees. *Journal of Occupational Medicine*, 29, 119–125.

Nisbet, J. (1957). Intelligence and age: Retesting with twenty-four years interval. *British Journal of Educational Psychology*, 27, 190–198.

Nisbett, R., Caputo, C., Legant, P., & Maracek, J. (1973). Behavior as seen by the actor and as seen by the observer. *Journal of Personality and Social Psychology*, 27, 154–164.

Nisbett, R., & Wilson, T. (1977). The halo effect: Evidence for unconscious alteration of judgments. *Journal of Personality and Social Psychology*, 35, 250–256.

Nordström, G., & Berglund, M. (1987). A prospective study of successful long-term adjustment in alcohol dependence: Social drinking versus abstinence. *Journal of Studies on Alcohol*, 48, 95–103.

Norman, D., & Bobrow, G. (1975). On data-limited and resource-limited processes. *Cognitive Psychology*, 7, 44–64.

Norman, D., & Rumelhart, D. (1975). *Explorations in Cognition*. San Francisco: W. H. Freeman.

Norman, R., Perlman, I., Kolb, H., Jones, J., and Daley, S. (1984). Direct excitatory interactions between cones of different spectral types in the turtle retina. *Science*, 224, 625–627.

Norton, G., Harrison, B., Hauch, J., & Rhodes, L. (1985). Characteristics of people with infrequent panic attacks. *Journal of Abnormal Psychology*, 94, 216–221.

NOVA. (1983). Fat chance in a thin world. Boston: WGBH Transcripts.

Novak, M., & Harlow, H. (1975). Social recovery of monkeys isolated for the first year of life: I. Rehabilitation and therapy. *Developmental Psychology*, 11, 453–465.

Novick, D., Stenger, R., Gelb, A., Most, J., Yancovitz, S., & Kreek, M. (1986). Chronic liver disease in abusers of alcohol and parenteral drugs: A report of 204 consecutive biopsy-proven cases. *Alcoholism: Clinical and Experimental Research*, 10, 500–505.

Novin, D. (1976). Visceral mechanisms in the control of food intake. In D. Novin, W. Wyrwicka, & G. Bray (Eds.), *Hunger: Basic Mechanisms and Clinical Implications*. New York: Raven.

Novin, D., Vanderweele, D., & Rezek, M. (1973). Infusion of 2-deoxy-D-glucose into hepatic portal system causes eating: Evidence for peripheral glucoreceptors. *Science*, 181, 858–860.

Nuechterlein, K., & Dawson, M. (1984). A heuristic vulnerability/stress model of schizophrenic episodes. *Schizophrenia Bulletin*, 10, 300–312.

Nurnberger, J., & Gershon, E. (1982). Genetics. In E. Paykel (Ed.), *Handbook of Affective Disorders*. New York: Guilford Press.

Nutter, D., & Condron, M. (1983). Sexual fantasy and activity patterns of females with inhibited sexual desire versus normal controls. *Journal of Sex and Marital Therapy*, 9, 276–282.

Obrist, P. (1976). The cardiovascular-behavior interaction—as it appears today. *Psychophysiology*, 13, 95–107.

O'Connor, R. (1972). Relative efficacy of modeling, shaping, and the combined procedures for notification of social withdrawal. *Journal of Abnormal Psychology*, 79, 327–334.

Oden, G. (1987). Concept, knowledge, and thought. *Annual Review of Psychology*, 38, 203–227.

Offer, D., & Offer, J. (1975). *From Teenage to Young Manhood*. New York: Basic Books.

Ohman, A. (1979). Fear relevance, autonomic conditioning and phobias: A laboratory model. In P. Sjoden, S. Bates, & W. Dockens (Eds.), *Trends in Behavior Therapy*. New York: Academic Press.

Ohtsuka, T. (1985). Relation of spectral types to oil droplets in cones of turtle retina. *Science*, 229, 874–877.

Oldbridge, N. (1982). Compliance and exercise in primary and secondary prevention of coronary heart disease: A review. *Preventive Medicine*, 11, 56–70.

Olds, J. (1956). Pleasure centers in the brain. *Scientific American*, 193, 105–116.

Olds, J. (1973). Commentary on positive reinforcement produced by electrical stimulation of septal areas and other regions of rat brain. In E. Valenstein (Ed.), *Brain Stimulation and Motivation: Research and Commentary*. Glenview, IL: Scott, Foresman.

Olds, M., & Forbes, J. (1981). The central basis of motivation: Intracranial self-stimulation studies. *Annual Review of Psychology*, 32, 523–574.

Olsen, G., Olson, R., & Kastin, A. (1986). Endogenous opiates: 1985. *Peptides*, 7, 907–933.

Woods, R. (1986). Brain assymmetries in situs inversus. *Archives of Neurology*, 43, 1083–1084.

Olton, D. (1979). Mazes, maps and memory. *American Psychologist*, 34, 583–596.

O'Neal, J. (1984). First person account: Finding myself and loving it. *Schizophrenia Bulletin*, 10, 109–110.

Oomura, Y. (1976). Significance of glucose insulin and free fatty acid on the hypothalamic feeding and satiety neurons. In D. Novin, W. Wyrwicka, & G. Bray (Eds.), *Hunger: Basic Mechanisms and Clinical Implications*. New York: Raven.

Oreskes, M. (1984). 10% of New York students "hooked" on alcohol. *The Oregonian*, October 23, B3.

Orlansky, H. (1949). Infant care and personality. *Psychological Bulletin*, 46, 1–48.

Orne, M. (1972). The stimulating subject in hypnosis research. In E. Fromm & R. Shor (Eds.), *Hypnosis, Research Developments and Perspectives*. Chicago: Aldine.

Orne, M., Dinges, D., & Orne, E. (1984). On the differential diagnosis of multiple personality in the forensic context. *International Journal of Clinical and Experimental Hypnosis*, 32, 118–169.

Orne, M., & Scheibe, K. (1964). The contribution of nondeprivation factors in the production of sensory deprivation effects: The psychology of the panic button. *Journal of Abnormal and Social Psychology*, 68, 3–12.

Ornstein, P., & Naus, M. (1978). Rehearsal processes in children's memory. In P. Ornstein (Ed.), *Memory Development in Children*. Hillsdale, NJ: Erlbaum.

Ornstein, R. (1977). *The Psychology of Consciousness* (2nd ed.). New York: Harcourt, Brace, Jovanovich.

Orpen, C. (1981). Effect of flexible working hours on employee satisfaction and performance: A field experiment. *Journal of Applied Psychology*, 66, 113–115.

Osborne, R. (1960). Racial differences in mental growth and school achievement: A longitudinal study. *Psychological Reports*, 7, 233–239.

O'Shea, R. (1987). Chronometric analysis supports fusion rather than suppression theory of binocular vision. *Vision Research*, 27, 781–791.

Osmond, H., & Smythies, J. (1953). Schizophrenia: A new approach. *The Journal of Mental Science*, 98, 309–315.

Ostrov, E., Offer, D., Howard, K., Kaufman, B., & Meyer, H. (1985). Adolescent sexual behavior. *Medical Aspects of Human Sexuality*, 19, 28–31; 34–36.

Owen, J. (1976). Flextime: Some problems and solutions. *Industrial and Labor Relations Review*, 29, 152–160.

Owens, W., & Schoenfeldt, L. (1979). Toward a classification of persons. *Journal of Applied Psychology Monograph*, 64, 569–607.

Palmore, E. (1981). The facts on aging quiz: Part two. *The Gerontologist*, 21, 431–437.

Palukos, E., and Wexley, K. (1983). The relationship among perceptual similarity, sex, and performance ratings in manager-subordinate dyads. *Academy of Management Journal*, 26, 129–139.

Panksepp, J. (1986). The neurochemistry of behavior. *Annual Review of Psychology*, 37, 77–107.

Parfit, M. (1984). Mapmaker who charts our hidden mental demons. *Smithsonian*, May, 123–131.

Parke, R. (1969). Effectiveness of punishment as an interaction of intensity, timing, agent nurturance and cognitive structuring. *Child Development*, 40, 213–235.

Parke, R., & Walters, R. (1967). Some factors determining the efficacy of punishment for inducing response inhibition. *Monographs of the Society for Research in Child Development*, 32, 1–45.

Patchen, M. (1982). *Black-White Contact in Schools: Its Social and Academic Effects*. West Lafayette, IN: Purdue University Press.

Paul, G. (1966). *Insight versus Desensitization in Psychotherapy: An Experiment in Anxiety Reduction*. Stanford, CA: Stanford University Press.

Peacock, D. (1983). Peacock's crusade. Paper presented at the Forestry Center, Portland, Oregon, January 5.

Peacock, W. (1986). The postnatal development of the brain and its coverings. In A. Raimondi, M. Choux, & C. DiRocco (Eds.), *Head Injuries in the Newborn and Infant*. New York: Springer-Verlag.

Pendery, M., Maltzman, I., & West, L. (1982). Controlled drinking by alcoholics? New findings and a reevaluation of a major affirmative study. *Science*, 217, 169–174.

Penfield, W., & Perrot, P. (1963). The brain's record of auditory and visual experience. *Brain*, 86, 595–696.

Penfold, P. (1981). Women and depression. *Canadian Journal of Psychiatry*, 26, 24–31.

Penrod, S. (1986). *Social Psychology* (2nd ed.). Englewood Cliffs, NJ: Prentice-Hall.

Perley, M., & Guze, S. (1962). Hysteria—the stability and usefulness of clinical criteria. *The New England Journal of Medicine*, 266, 421–426.

Perlman, D. (1985). Scientists unraveling secrets of thing that destroys brains. *San Francisco Chronicle*, April 23, A5.

Perls, F. (1948). Theory and technique of personality integration. *American Journal of Psychotherapy*, 2, 656–686.

Perls, F. (1973). *The Gestalt Approach*. Palo Alto, CA: Science and Behavior Books.

Permutter, M. (1983). Learning and memory through adulthood. In M. Riley, B. Hess, & K. Bond (Eds.), *Aging in Society: Selective Reviews of Recent Research*. Hillsdale, NJ: Erlbaum.

Peskin, H. (1967). Pubertal onset and ego functioning. *Journal of Abnormal Psychology*, 72, 1–15.

Peskin, H. (1973). Influence of the developmental schedule of puberty on learning and ego functioning. *Journal of Youth and Adolescence*, 2, 273–290.

Peterson, A. (1979). Female pubertal development. In M. Sugar (Ed.), *Female Adolescent Development*. New York: Bruner/Mazel.

Peterson, C., & Seligman, M. (1984). Causal explanations as a risk factor for depression: Theory and evidence. *Psychological Review*, 91, 347–374.

Peterson, J. (1979). Left-handedness: Differences between student artists and scientists. *Perceptual and Motor Skills*, 48, 961–962.

Peterson, L., & Peterson, M. (1959). Short-term retention of individual items. *Journal of Experimental Psychology*, 58, 193–198.

Peterson, P., & Koulack, D. (1969). Attitude change as a function of latitudes of acceptance and rejection. *Journal of Personality and Social Psychology,* 11, 309–311.

Petty, R., & Cacioppo, J. (1986). The elaboration likelihood model of persuasion. In L. Berkowitz (Ed.), *Advances in Experimental Social Psychology* (Vol. 19). Orlando, FL: Academic Press.

Petty, R., Cacioppo, J., & Schumann, D. (1983). Central and peripheral routes to advertising effectiveness: The moderating role of involvement. *Journal of Consumer Research,* 10, 135–146.

Phelps, M., Mazziotta, J., & Schelbert, H. (1986). *Positron Emission Tomography and Autoradiography.* New York: Raven.

Piaget, J. (1970). Piaget's theory. In P. Mussen (Ed.), *Carmichael's Manual of Child Psychology* (Vol. 1). New York: Wiley.

Piaget, J. (1972). Intellectual evolution from adolescence to adulthood. *Human Development,* 15, 1–12.

Piaget, J. (1977). *The Development of Thought: Equilibrium of Cognitive Structures.* New York: Viking Press.

Piaget, J., & Inhelder, B. (1967). *The Child's Conception of Space.* New York: Norton.

Pihl, R., & Parkes, M. (1977). Hair element content in learning disabled children. *Science,* 198, 204–206.

Pleck, J. (1977). The work-family role system. *Social Problems,* 24, 417–427.

Pliner, P., Hart, H., Kohl, J., & Saari, D. (1974). Compliance without pressure: Some further data on the foot-in-the-door technique. *Journal of Experimental Social Psychology,* 10, 17–22.

Plomin, R., & Defries, J. (1980). Genetics and intelligence: Recent data. *Intelligence,* 4, 15–24.

Plutchik, R. (1980). *Emotion: A Psychoevolutionary Synthesis.* New York: Harper & Row.

Pollock, V., Volavka, J., Goodwin, D., Mednick, S., Gabrielli, W., Knop, J., & Schulsinger, F. (1983). The EEG after alcohol administration in men at risk for alcoholism. *Archives of General Psychiatry,* 40, 857–861.

Pomerleau, O., & Rodin, J. (1986). Behavioral medicine and health psychology. In S. Garfield & A. Bergin (Eds.), *Handbook of Psychotherapy and Behavior Changes* (3rd ed.). New York: Wiley.

Pomeroy, W. (1965). Why we tolerate lesbians. *Sexology,* May, 652–654.

Pope, H., & Hudson, J. (1984). *New Hope for Binge Eaters: Advances in the Understanding and Treatment of Bulimia.* New York: Harper & Row.

Porter, L., and Lawler, E. (1968). *Managerial Attitudes and Performance.* Homewood, IL: Dorsey Press.

Posner, M. (1973). *Cognition: An Introduction.* Glenview, IL: Scott, Foresman.

Powell, M., & Fazio, R. (1984). Attitude accessibility as a function of repeated attitudinal expression. *Personality and Social Psychology Bulletin,* 10, 139–148.

Powley, T., & Keesey, R. (1970). Relationship of body weight to the lateral hypothalamic syndrome. *Journal of Comparative and Physiological Psychology,* 70, 25–36.

Prange, A., Wilson, I., & Lynn, C. (1974). L-tryptophan in mania: Contributions to a permissive amine hypothesis of affective disorders. *Archives of General Psychiatry,* 30, 56–62.

Premack, D. (1962). Reversibility of the reinforcement relation. *Science,* 136, 255–257.

Premack, D. (1965). Reinforcement theory. In M. Jones (Ed.), *Nebraska Symposium on Motivation.* Lincoln: University of Nebraska Press.

Premack, D. (1971). Language in chimpanzees. *Science,* 172, 808–822.

Prichard, J. (1986). NMR spectroscopy of brain metabolism in vivo. *Annual Review of Neuroscience,* 9, 61–85.

Prien, R., & Kupfer, D. (1986). Continuation drug therapy for major depressive episodes: how long should it be maintained? *American Journal of Psychiatry,* 143, 18–23.

Prien, R., Kupfer, D., Mansky, P., Small, J., Tuason, V., Voss, C., & Johnson, W. (1984). Drug therapy in the prevention of recurrences in unipolar and bipolar affective disorders. *Archieves of General Psychiatry,* 41, 1096–1104.

Prioleau, L., Murdock, M., & Brody, N. (1983). An analysis of psychotherapy versus placebo studies. *The Behavioral and Brain Sciences,* 6, 275–310.

Proctor, F., Wagner, N., & Butler, J. (1974). The differentiation of male and female orgasm: An experimental study. In N. Wagner (Ed.), *Perspectives on Human Sexuality.* New York: Behavioral Publications.

Pugh, E., & Miller, W. (1987). *Annual Review of Physiology,* 49, 711–714.

Qualls, P., & Sheehan, P. (1981). Electromyograph biofeedback as a relaxation technique: A critical appraisal and reassessment. *Psychological Bulletin,* 90, 21–42.

Quinn, R., Staines, G., & McCullough, M. (1974). *Job satisfaction: Is there a trend?* Washington, DC: U.S. Department of Labor, Manpower, & Research Monograph No. 30.

Rachman, S. (1966). Sexual fetishism: An experimental analogue. *Psychological Record,* 16, 293–296.

Rader, N., Bausano, M., & Richards, J. (1981). On the nature of the visual-cliff avoidance response in human infants. *Child Development,* 51, 61–68.

Radloff, L. (1975). Sex differences in depression: The effects of occupational and marital status. *Sex Roles,* 1, 249–265.

Rahe, R., & Arthur, R. (1978). Life changes and illness reports. In K. Gunderson and R. Rahe (Eds.), *Life Stress and Illness.* Springfield, IL: Thomas.

Raloff, J. (1982). Childhood lead: worrisome national levels. *Science News,* February 6, 88.

Raskin, M., Bali, L., & Peeke, H. (1980). Muscle biofeedback and transcendental meditation: A controlled evaluation of efficacy in the treatment of chronic anxiety. *Archives of General Psychiatry,* 37, 93–97.

Ratcliff, R., & Mckoon, G. (1986). More on the distinction between episodic and semantic memories. *Journal of Experimental Psychology: Learning, Memory, and Cognition,* 12, 312–313.

Raymond, C. (1986). Popular, yes, but jury still out on apnea surgery. *Journal of the American Medical Association,* 256, 439–441.

Raynor, J. (1970). Relationships between achievement-related motives, future orientation, and academic performance. *Journal of Personality and Social Psychology,* 15, 28–33.

Readhead, C., Popki, B., Takahashi, N., Shine, H., Saavedra, R., Sidman, R., & Hood, L. (1987). Expression of a myelin basic protein gene in transgenic shiverer mice: Correction of the dysmyelinating phenotype. *Cell,* 48, 703–712.

Rechler, M., Nissley, S., & Roth, J. (1987). Hormonal regulation of human growth. *The New England Journal of Medicine,* 316, 941–942.

Rechtschaffen, A., Gilliland, M., Bergmann, B., & Winter, J. (1983). Physiological correlates of prolonged sleep deprivation in rats. *Science,* 221, 182–184.

Regier, D., Myers, J., Kramer, M., Robins, L., Blazer, D., Hough, R., Eaton, W., & Locke, B. (1984). The NIMH epidemiologic catchment area program: Historical contact, major objectives, and study population characteristics. *Archives of General Psychiatry,* 41, 934–941.

Reichard, S., Livson, F., & Peterson, P. (1962). *Aging and Personality: A Study of 87 Older Men.* New York: Wiley.

Reinish, J. (1981). Prenatal exposure to synthetic progestin increases potential for aggression in humans. *Science,* 211, 1171–1173.

Reinke, B., Holmes, D., & Harris, R. (1985). The timing of psychosocial changes in women's lives: The years 25 to 45. *Journal of Personality and Social Psychology,* 48, 456–471.

Reker, G., Peacock, E., & Wong, P. (1987). Meaning and purpose in life and well-being: A life-span perspective. *Journal of Gerontology,* 42, 44–49.

Relman, A. (1982). Marijuana and health. *The New England Journal of Medicine,* 306, 603–604.

Renneker, R. (1981). Cancer and psychotherapy. In J. Goldberg (Ed.), *Psychother-*

apeutic Treatment of Cancer Patients. New York: Free Press.

Rescorla, R. (1965). Probability of shock in the presence and absence of CS in fear conditioning. *Journal of Comparative and Physiological Psychology, 66*, 1–5.

Rescorla, R. (1987). A Pavlovian analysis of goal-directed behavior. *American Psychologist, 42*, 119–129.

Restak, R. (1984). *The Brain*. New York: Bantam Books.

Rholes, W., Riskind, J., & Lane, J. (1987). Emotional states and memory biases: Effects of cognitive priming and mood. *Journal of Personality and Social Psychology, 52*, 91–99.

Ribble, M. (1943). *The Rights of Infants: Early Psychological Needs and Their Satisfaction*. New York: Columbia University Press.

Richards, J., & Rader, N. (1981). Crawling-onset age predicts visual cliff avoidance in infants. *Journal of Experimental Psychology: Human Perception and Performance, 7*, 382–387.

Richardson, A. (1986). Age trends in eidetikers. *Journal of Genetic Psychology, 147*, 303–308.

Richardson, J. (1983). Mental imagery in thinking and problem solving. In J. Evans (Ed.), *Thinking and Reasoning: Psychological Approaches*. London: Routledge and Kegan Paul.

Richmond, J. (1979). *Healthy People: The Surgeon General's Report on Health Promotion and Disease Prevention* (DHEW PHS Publication No. 79-5507). Washington, DC: U.S. Government Printing Office.

Ridenour, M. (1982). Infant walkers: Developmental tool or inherent danger. *Perceptual and Motor Skills, 55*, 1201–1202.

Riegal, K. (1973). Dialectic operations: The final period of cognitive development. *Human Development, 16*, 346–370.

Ries, W. (1973). Feeding behavior in obesity. *Proceedings of the Nutrition Society, 32*, 187–193.

Rips, L., Shoben, E., & Smith, E. (1973). Semantic distance and the verification of semantic relations. *Journal of Verbal Learning and Verbal Behavior, 12*, 1–20.

Riskind, J. (1983). Nonverbal expressions and the accessibility of life experience memories: A congruence hypothesis. *Social Cognition, 2*, 62–86.

Riskind, J., Rholes, W., & Eggers, J. (1982). The Velten Mood Induction Procedure: Effects on mood and memory. *Journal of Consulting and Clinical Psychology, 50*, 146–147.

Ritchie, R., & Moses, J. (1983). Assessment center correlates of women's advancement into middle management: A 7-year longitudinal analysis. *Journal of Applied Psychology, 68*, 227–231.

Ritzer, G. (1977). *Working: Conflict and Change* (2nd ed.). Englewood Cliffs, NJ: Prentice-Hall.

Robbin, A. (1958). A controlled study of the effects of leucotomy. *Journal of Neurology, Neurosurgery, and Psychiatry, 21*, 262–269.

Robbin, A. (1959). The value of leucotomy in relation to diagnosis. *Journal of Neurology, Neurosurgery, and Psychiatry, 22*, 132–136.

Roberts, M. (1987). No language but a cry. *Psychology Today*, June, 57–58.

Robertson, M. (1987). Molecular genetics of the mind. *Nature, 325*, 755.

Robins, L. (1986). The epidemiology of antisocial personality. In J. Cavenar (Ed.), *Psychiatry*. Philadelphia: Lippincott.

Robins, L., Helzer, J., Weissman, M., Orvaschel, H., Gruenberg, E., Burke, J., & Regier, D. (1984). Lifetime prevalence of specific psychiatric disorders in three sites. *Archives of General Psychiatry, 41*, 949–958.

Rock, I., & DiVita, J. (1987). A case of viewer-centered object perception. *Cognitive Psychology, 19*, 280–293.

Rodin, J. (1978). The puzzle of obesity. *Human Nature*, February.

Rodin, J. (1983). In NOVA. Fat chance in a thin world. Boston: WGBH Transcripts.

Roethlisberger, F., & Dickson, W. (1939). *Management and the Worker*. Cambridge, MA: Harvard University Press.

Rogentine, G., Van Kammen, D., Fox, B., Docherty, J., Rosenblatt, J., Boyd, S., & Bunney, W. (1979). Psychological factors in the prognosis of malignant melanoma: A prospective study. *Psychomatic Medicine, 41*, 647–655.

Rogers, C. (1961). *Becoming a Person: A Therapist's View of Psychotherapy*. Boston: Houghton Mifflin.

Rogers, C. (1977). *On Personal Power: Inner Strength and Its Revolutionary Impact*. New York: Delacorte.

Rogers, C. (1980). *A Way of Being*. Boston: Houghton Mifflin.

Rogers, C. (1986). Client-centered therapy. In I. Kutash and A. Wolf (Eds.), *Psychotherapist's Casebook*. San Francisco: Jossey-Bass.

Rogers, M., Dubey, D., & Reich, P. (1979). The influence of the psyche and the brain on immunity and disease susceptibility: A critical review. *Psychosomatic Medicine, 41*, 147–164.

Rogers, R., & Mewborn, D. (1976). Fear appeals and attitude change: Effects of a threat's noxiousness, probability of occurrence, and the efficacy of coping responses. *Journal of Personality and Social Psychology, 34*, 54–61.

Roggman, L., Langlois, J., & Hubbs-Tait, L. (1987). Mothers, infants, and toys: Social play correlates of attachment. *Infant Behavior and Development, 10*, 233–237.

Rogowitz, B. (1984). The breakdown of size constancy under stroboscopic illuminations. In L. Spillmann and B. Wooter (Eds.), *Sensory Experience, Adaptation, and Perception*. Hillsdale, NJ: Erlbaum.

Rohrbaugh, J. (1979). *Women: Psychology's Puzzle*. New York: Basic Books.

Rollins, B., & Galligan, R. (1978). The developing child and marital satisfaction of parents. In R. Levner & G. Spanier (Eds.), *Child Influences on Marital and Family Interaction: A Lifespan Perspective*. New York: Academic Press.

Rolls, E., Baylis, G., & Hasselmo, M. (1987). The responses of neurons in the cortex in the superior temporal sulcus of the monkey to band-pass spatial frequency filtered faces. *Vision Research, 27*, 311–326.

Rook, K. (1987). Social support versus companionship: Effects on life stress, loneliness, and evaluations by others. *Journal of Personality and Social Psychology, 52*, 1132–1147.

Rorer, L., & Widiger, T. (1983). Personality structure and assessment. Annual Review of Psychology, 34, 431–463.

Rosch, E. (1973). Natural categories. *Cognitive Psychology, 4*, 328–350.

Rosch, E. (1975). Cognitive representations of semantic categories. *Journal of Experimental Psychology: General, 104*, 192–253.

Rosch, E. (1977). Human categorization. In N. Warren (Ed.), *Advances in Cross-Cultural Psychology* (Vol. 1). London: Academic Press.

Rosch, E. (1978). Principles of categorization. In E. Rosch & B. Lloyd (Eds.), *Cognition and Categorization*. Hillsdale, NJ: Erlbaum.

Rosch, E., Mervis, C., Gray, W., Johnson, E., & Boyes-Braem, P. (1976). Basic objects in natural categories. *Cognitive Psychology, 8*, 382–439.

Rose, G., & Williams, R. (1961). Metabolic studies of large and small eaters. *British Journal of Nutrition, 15*, 1–9.

Rose, J., Brugge, J., Anderson, D., & Hind, J. (1967). Phase-locked responses to low-frequency tones in single auditory nerve fibers of the squirrel monkey. *Journal of Neurophysiology, 30*, 769–793.

Rose, J., & Fantino, E. (1978). Conditioned reinforcement and discrimination in second-order schedules. *Journal of the Experimental Analysis of Behavior, 29*, 393–418.

Rosenbaum, L., & Rosenbaum, W. (1975). Persuasive impact of a communicator where groups differ in apparent co-orientation. *Journal of Psychology, 89*, 189–194.

Rosenberg, S., Nelson, C., & Vivekananthan, P. (1968). A multidimensional approach to the structure of personality impressions. *Journal of Personality and Social Psychology, 9*, 283–294.

Rosengarten, H., & Friedhoff, A.

(1976). A review of recent studies of the bio-synthesis and excretion of hallucinogens formed by the methylation of neurotransmitters or related substances. *Schizophrenia Bulletin,* 2, 90–105.

Rosenhan, D. (1973). *Moral Development.* CRM–McGraw-Hill Films.

Rosenthal, D. (1970). *Genetic Theory and Abnormal Behavior.* New York: McGraw-Hill.

Rosenthal, D. (1971). *Genetics of Schizophrenia.* New York: McGraw-Hill.

Rosenthal, D. (1977). Searches for the mode of genetic transmission in schizophrenia: Reflections of loose ends. *Schizophrenia Bulletin,* 3, 268–276.

Rosenthal, D., Wender, P., Kety, S., Welner, J., & Schulsinger, F. (1971). The adopted away offspring of schizophrenics. *American Journal of Psychiatry,* 128, 307–311.

Rosenzweig, M. (1966). Environmental complexity, cerebral change, and behavior. *American Psychologist,* 21, 321–332.

Rosenzweig, M. (1984). Experience, memory, and the brain. *American Psychologist,* 39, 365–376.

Rosenzweig, M., Bennett, E., & Diamond, M. (1972). Brain changes in response to experience. *Scientific American,* 226, 22–29.

Ross, A. (1987). *Personality: The Scientific Study of Complex Human Behavior.* New York: Holt, Rinehart and Winston.

Ross, L. (1977). The intuitive psychologist and his shortcomings: Distortions in the attribution process. In L. Berkowitz (Ed.), *Advances in Experimental Social Psychology.* New York: Academic Press.

Ross, M., & Fletcher, G. (1985). Attribution and social perception. In G. Lindzey and E. Aronson (Eds.), *Handbook of Social Psychology.* New York: Random House.

Rotter, J. (1954). *Social Learning and Clinical Psychology.* Englewood Cliffs, NJ: Prentice-Hall.

Rotter, J. (1966). Generalized expectancies for internal versus external control of reinforcement. *Psychological Monographs,* 80, No. 601.

Rouche, B. (1980). *The Medical Detectives.* New York: Truman Talley Books.

Roviaro, S., Holmes, D., & Holmsten, R. (1984). Influence of a cardiac rehabilitation program on the cardiovascular, psychological, and social functioning of cardiac patients. *Journal of Behavioral Medicine,* 7, 61–81.

Rubenstein, C. (1983). The modern art of courtly love. *Psychology Today,* June, 39–49.

Rubin, J., Provenzano, F., & Luria, Z. (1974). The eye of the beholder: Parents' views on sex of newborns. *American Journal of Orthopsychiatry,* 44, 512–519.

Rubin, Z. (1970). Measurement of ro-mantic love. *Journal of Personality and Social Psychology,* 16, 265–273.

Rubin, Z. (1973). *Liking and Loving.* New York: Holt, Rinehart and Winston.

Rudel, R., Teuber, H., & Twitchell, T. (1974). Levels of impairment of sensorimotor function in children with early brain damage. *Neuropsychologia,* 12, 95–108.

Rudestam, K., & Agnelli, P. (1987). The effect of the content of suicide notes on grief reactions. *Journal of Clinical Psychology,* 43, 211–218.

Rugh, R., & Shettles, L. (1974). *From Conception to Birth: The Drama of Life's Beginning.* New York: Harper & Row.

Rumbaugh, D. (1977). *Language Learning by a Chimpanzee: The Lana Project.* New York: Academic Press.

Rush, A., Beck, A., Kovacs, M., & Hollon, S. (1977). Comparative efficacy of cognitive therapy and pharmacotherapy in the treatment of depressed outpatients. *Cognitive Therapy and Research,* 1, 17–39.

Russek, M. (1971). Hepatic receptors and the neurophysiological mechanisms controlling feeding behavior. In S. Ehrenpreis (Ed.), *Neurosciences Research* (Vol. 4). New York: Academic Press.

Russel, G. (1979). The present status of anorexia nervosa. *Psychological Medicine,* 7, 353–367.

Russell, R. (1981). Report on effective psychotherapy: Legislative testimony. Paper presented at a public hearing on the Regulation of Mental Health Practitioners, New York, March 5.

Rutter, D., & Durkin, K. (1987). Turn-taking in mother-infant interaction: An examination of vocalization and gaze. *Developmental Psychology,* 23, 54–61.

Rzewnicki, R., & Forgays, D. (1987). Recidivism and self-cure of smoking and obesity: An attempt to replicate. *American Psychologist,* 42, 97–100.

Saario, T., Jacklin, C., & Tittle, C. (1973). Sex role stereotyping in public schools. *Harvard Educational Review,* 43, 386–416.

Sackheim, J. (1985). The case for ECT. *Psychology Today,* June, 36–40.

SADAP Summary. (1986). Cocaine use: A growing concern. *Oregon State Alcohol and Drug Abuse Program Newsletter,* 6, 22–23.

Saegert, S., Snap, W., & Zajonc, R. (1973). Exposure, context, and interpersonal attraction. *Journal of Personality and Social Psychology,* 25, 234–242.

Sager, C. (1986). Couples therapy with marriage contracts. In I. Kutash and A. Wolf (Eds.), *Psychotherapist's Casebook.* San Francisco: Jossey-Bass.

Sanders, G. (1982). Social comparison as a basis for evaluating others. *Journal of Research in Personality,* 16, 21–31.

Sano, K. (1962). Sedative neurosurgery. *Neurologia,* 4, 112–142.

Santee, R., & Maslach, C. (1982). To agree or not to agree: Personal dissent amid social pressure to conform. *Journal of Personality and Social Psychology,* 42, 690–700.

Sarason, I., Johnson, J., & Siegel, J. (1978). Assessing the impact of life changes: Development of the Life Experiences Survey. *Journal of Consulting and Clinical Psychology,* 46, 932–946.

Satow, A. (1987). Four properties common among perceptions confirmed by a large sample of subjects: An ecological approach to mechanisms of individual differences in perception: II. *Perceptual and Motor Skills,* 64, 507–520.

Savage-Rumbaugh, E., Pate, J., Lawson, J., Smith, S., & Rosenbaum, S. (1983). Can a chimpanzee make a statement? *Journal of Experimental Psychology: General,* 112, 457–492.

Savage-Rumbaugh, E., Rumbaugh, D., & Boysen, S. (1980). Do apes use language? *American Scientist,* 68, 49–61.

Scarr, S. (1984). What's a parent to do? *Psychology Today,* May, 58–63.

Scarr, S., & Carter-Saltzman, L. (1983). Genetic differences in intelligence. In R. Sternberg (Ed.), *Handbook of Intelligence.* Cambridge, MA: Howard University Press.

Scarr, S., & Weinberg, R. (1976). IQ test performance of black children adopted by white families. *American Psychologist,* 31, 726–739.

Scarr, S., & Weinberg, R. (1978). Attitudes, interests, and IQ. *Human Nature,* April, 29–36.

Schachter, S. (1982). Don't sell habit-breakers short. *Psychology Today,* August, 27–33.

Schachter, S., & Latané, B. (1964). Crime, cognition, and the autonomic nervous system. In D. Levine (Ed.), *Nebraska Symposium on Motivation* (Vol. 12). Lincoln, NE: University of Nebraska Press.

Schachter, S., & Singer, J. (1962). Cognitive, social, and physiological determinants of emotional state. *Psychological Review,* 69, 379–399.

Schaeffer, J., Andrysiak, T., & Ungerleider, J. (1981). Cognition and long-term use of ganja (cannabis). *Science,* 213, 465–466.

Schaffer, H., & Emerson, P. (1964). The development of social attachments in infancy. *Monographs of the Society for Research in Child Development,* 20, Whole No. 94.

Schaie, J. (1977–78). Toward a stage theory of adult cognitive development. *International Journal of Aging and Human Development,* 8, 129–138.

Schaie, K. (1975). Age changes in intelligence. In D. Woodruff & J. Birren (Eds.), *Aging: Scientific Perspectives and Social Issues.* New York: Van Nostrand.

Schaie, K., & Hertzog, C. (1983). Fourteen-year-cohort-sequential analysis of adult intellectual development. *Developmental Psychology, 19,* 531–543.

Schare, M., Lisman, S., & Spear, N. (1984). The effects of mood variation on state-dependent retention. *Cognitive Therapy and Research, 8,* 387–408.

Schein, E. (1956). The Chinese indoctrination program for prisoners of war: A study of attempted brainwashing. *Psychiatry,* 19, 149–172.

Schell, R., & Hall, E. (1979). *Developmental Psychology Today* (3rd ed.). New York: Random House.

Schildkraut, J. (1970). *Neuropsychopharmacology of the Affective Disorders.* Boston: Little, Brown.

Schlegel, R., Wellwood, J., Copps, B., Gruchow, W., & Sharratt, M. (1980). The relationship between perceived challenge and daily symptom reporting in Type A vs. Type B postinfarct subjects. *Journal of Behavioral Medicine, 3,* 191–204.

Schleifer, S., Keller, S., Camerino, M., Thornton, J., & Stein, M. (1983). Suppression of lymphocyte stimulation following bereavement. *Journal of the American Medical Association, 250,* 374–377.

Schmitt, M. (1973). Influences of hepatic portal receptors on hypothalamic feeding and satiety centers. *American Journal of Physiology, 1973, 225,* 1089–1095.

Schon, M., & Sutherland, A. (1960). The role of hormones in human behavior. III. Changes in female sexuality after hypothysectomy. *Journal of Clinical Endocrinology and Metabolism, 20,* 833–841.

Schroeder, D., & Costa, P. (1984). Influence of life event stress on physical illness: Substantive effects or methodological flaws? *Journal of Personality and Social Psychology, 46,* 853–863.

Schuele, J., & Wisenfeld, A. (1983). Autonomic response to self-critical thought. *Cognitive Therapy and Research, 7,* 189–194.

Schulsinger, F. (1972). Psychopathy: Heredity and environment. *International Journal of Mental Health, 1,* 190–206.

Schultz, D. (1979). *Psychology in Use: An Introduction to Applied Psychology.* New York: Macmillan.

Schulz, R., & Aderman, D. (1974). Clinical research and the stages of dying. *Omega, 5,* 137–143.

Schvaneveldt, R., & Meyer, D. (1973). Retrieval and compassion processes in semantic memory. In S. Kornblum (Ed.), *Attention and Performance IV.* New York: Academic Press.

Schwartz, B. (1984). *Psychology of Learning and Behavior* (2nd ed.). New York: Norton.

Schwartz, G. (1982). Psychophysiological patterning and emotion revisited: A systems perspective. In C. Izard (Ed.), *Measuring Emotions in Infants and Children.* Cam-

bridge, England: Cambridge University Press.

Schwartz, J., & Greenberg, S. (1987). Molecular mechanisms for memory: Second-messenger induced modifications of protein kinases in nerve cells. *Annual Review of Neuroscience, 10,* 459–476.

Schwartz-Bickenbach, D., Schulte-Hobein, B., Abt, S., Plus, C., & Nau, H. (1987). Smoking and passive smoking during pregnancy and early infancy: effects on birth weight, lactation period, and cotinine concentrations in mother's milk and infant's urine. *Toxicology Letters, 35,* 73–81.

Scovern, A., & Kilmann, P. (1980). Status of electroconvulsive therapy: Review of the outcome literature. *Psychological Bulletin, 87,* 260–303.

Scribner, S. (1977). Modes of thinking and ways of speaking: Culture and logic reconsidered. In P. Johnson-Laird & P. Wason (Eds.), *Thinking: Readings in Cognitive Science.* New York: Cambridge University Press.

Seagall, M., Campbell, D., & Herskovits, M. (1966). *The Influence of Culture on Visual Perception.* New York: Bobbs Merrill.

Sears, D., & Freedman, J. (1965). Effects of expected familiarity of arguments upon opinion change and selective exposure. *Journal of Personality and Social Psychology, 2,* 420–425.

Sears, P., & Barbee, A. (1977). Career and life situations among Terman's gifted women. In J. Stanley, W. George, & C. Solano (Eds.), *The Gifted and the Creative: A Fifty-Year Perspective.* Baltimore: Johns Hopkins University Press.

Sears, R. (1977). Sources of life satisfaction of the Terman gifted men. *American Psychologist, 32,* 119–128.

Segal, M. (1974). Alphabet and attraction: An unobtrusive measure of the effect of propinquity in a field setting. *Journal of Personality and Social Psychology, 30,* 654–657.

Seiden, R. (1974). Suicide: Preventable death. *Public Affairs Report, 15,* 1–5.

Sekuler, R., & Blake, R. (1985). *Perception.* New York: Knopf.

Seligman, M. (1971). Phobias and preparedness. *Behavior Therapy, 2,* 307–320.

Seligman, M. (1975). *Helplessness: On Depression, Development and Death.* San Francisco: W. H. Freeman.

Seligman, M., & Maier, S. (1967). Failure to escape traumatic shock. *Journal of Experimental Psychology, 75,* 1–9.

Seligman, M., Maier, S., & Solomon, R. (1969). Unpredictable and uncontrollable aversive events. In F. Brush (Ed.), *Aversive Conditioning and Learning.* New York: Academic Press.

Selye, H. (1936). A syndrome produced by diverse nocuous agents. *Nature,* 138, 32.

Selye, H. (1956). *The Stress of Life.* New York: McGraw-Hill.

Selye, H. (1974). *Stress Without Distress.* Philadelphia: Lippincott.

Selye, H. (1976). *Stress in Health and Disease.* Woburn, MA: Butterworth.

Sem-Jacobsen, C. (1968). *Depth-Electrographic Stimulation of the Human Brain.* Springfield, IL: Thomas.

Semple, M., & Kitzes, L. (1987). Binaural processing of sound pressure level in the inferior colliculus. *Journal of Neurophysiology, 57,* 1130–1147.

Siegel, D. (1982). Personality development in adolescence. In B. Wolman (Ed.), *Handbook of Developmental Psychology.* Englewood Cliffs, NJ: Prentice-Hall.

Simkin, J., Simkin, A., Brien, L., & Sheldon, C. (1986). Gestalt therapy. In I. Kutash & A. Wolf (Eds.), *Psychotherapist's Casebook.* San Francisco: Jossey-Bass.

Simopoulos, A. (1987). Obesity and carcinogenesis: historical perspectives. *American Journal of Clinical Nutrition, 45,* 271–276.

Singer, J. (1975). Navigating the stream of consciousness. Research in daydreaming and related inner experience. *American Psychologist, 30,* 727–738.

Singer, J. (1978). Experimental studies of daydreaming and the stream of thought. In K. Pope and J. Singer (Eds.), *The Stream of Consciousness: Scientific Investigations into the Flow of Human Experience.* New York: Plenum.

Singer, J., Lundberg, V., & Frankenhaeuser, M. (1978). Stress on the train: A study of urban commuting. In A. Baum, J. Singer, and S. Valins (Eds.), *Advances in Environmental Psychology,* Vol. I, Hillsdale, NJ: Erlbaum.

Singh, S., Snyder, A., & Pullen, G. (1986). Fetal alcohol syndrome: Glucose and liver metabolism in term rat fetus and neonate. *Alcoholism: Clinical and Experimental Research, 10,* 54–58.

Sizemore, C., & Pittillo, E. (1977). *I'm Eve.* New York: Doubleday.

Shaffer, W., Duszynski, K., & Thomas, C. (1982). Family attitudes in youth as a possible precursor of cancer among physicians: A search for explanatory mechanisms. *Journal of Behavioral Medicine, 5,* 143–164.

Shanab, M., & Yahya, K. (1977). A behavioral study of obedience in children. *Journal of Personality and Social Psychology,* 35, 530–536.

Shapiro, C., Bortz, R., Mitchell, D., Bartel, P., & Jooste, P. (1981). Slow-wave sleep: A recovery after exercise. *Science,* 214, 1253–1254.

Sharan, S. (1980). Cooperative learning in small groups: Recent methods and effects on achievement, attitudes, and ethnic relations. *Review of Education Research,* 50, 241–271.

Sharpiro, D., & Goldstein, I. (1982). Biobehavioral perspectives on hypertension. *Journal of Consulting and Clinical Psychology, 50,* 841–858.

Shatz, C., & Sretavan, D. (1986). Interactions between retinal ganglion cells during the development of the mammalian visual system. *Annual Review of Neuroscience, 9,* 171–207.

Shatz, M., & Gelman, R. (1973). The development of communication skills: Modification in the speech of young children as a function of listener. *Monographs of the Society for Research in Child Development, 38,* Whole No. 5.

Shaw, D., Camps, F., & Eccleston, F. (1967). 5-Hydroxtryptamine in the hindbrain of depressive suicides. *British Journal of Psychiatry, 113,* 1407–1411.

Sheffield, F. (1966). A drive induction theory of reinforcement. In R. Haber (Ed.), *Current Research in Motivation.* New York: Holt, Rinehart and Winston.

Shepherd, R., & Cooper, L. (1982). *Mental Images and Their Transformation.* Cambridge, MA: MIT Press.

Sherif, M. (1937). An experimental approach to the study of attitudes. *Sociometry, 1,* 90–98.

Sherif, M., Harvey, O., White, B., Hood, W., & Sherif, C. (1961). *Intergroup Cooperation and Competition: The Robbers Cave Experience.* Norman, OK: University Book Exchange.

Sherif, M., & Sherif, C. (1969). *Social Psychology.* New York: Harper & Row.

Shettleworth, S. (1983). Memory in food-hoarding birds. *Scientific American, 248,* 102–110.

Shields, J. (1962). *Monozygotic Twins Brought Up Apart and Brought Up Together.* London: Oxford University Press.

Shiffrin, R., & Atkinson, R. (1969). Storage and retrieval processes in long-term memory. *Psychological Review, 76,* 179–193.

Shneidman, E. (1974). *Deaths of Man.* Baltimore: Penguin Books.

Shneidman, E. (1987). At the point of no return. *Psychology Today,* March, 55–58.

Shneidman, E., Faberow, N., & Litman, R. (Eds.) (1970). *The Psychology of Suicide.* New York: Jason Aronson.

Shweder, R. (1982). Liberation as destiny. *Contemporary Psychology, 27,* 421–424.

Skeels, H. (1966). Adult status of children with contrasting early life experiences: A follow-up study. *Monographs of the Society for Research in Child Development, 31,* Whole No. 105.

Skinner, B. (1953). *Science of Human Behavior.* New York: Macmillan.

Skinner, B. (1957). *Verbal Behavior.* Englewood Cliffs, NJ: Prentice-Hall.

Sklar, L., & Anisman, H. (1981). Stress and cancer. *Psychological Bulletin, 89,* 369–406.

Skowronski, J., & Carlston, D. (1987). Social judgment and social memory: The role of diagnosticity, positivity, and extremity biases. *Journal of Personality and Social Psychology, 52,* 689–699.

Skyrms, B. (1986). *Choice and Chance: An Introduction to Inductive Logic.* Belmont, CA: Dickinson.

Slade, A. (1987). Quality of attachment and early symbolic play. *Developmental Psychology, 23,* 78–85.

Slater, E., & Cowie, V. (1971). *The Genetics of Mental Disorders.* London: Oxford University Press.

Slater, E., & Shields, J. (1969). Genetic aspects of anxiety. In M. Lader (Ed.), *Studies of Anxiety.* Ashford, England: Headley Brothers.

Slavin, R., & Madden, N. (1979). School practices that improve race relations. *American Educational Research Journal, 16,* 169–180.

Sloane, R., Staples, F., Cristol, A., Yorkston, N., & Whipple, K. (1975). *Psychotherapy Versus Behavior Therapy.* Cambridge, MA: Harvard University Press.

Slocum, W., & Nye, F. (1976). Provider and housekeeper roles. In F. Nye (Ed.), *Role Structure and Analysis of the Family.* Beverly Hills, CA: Sage Foundations.

Smith, C., Almirez, R., Berenberg, J., & Asch, R. (1983). Tolerance develops to the disruptive effects of delta 9-tetrahydrocannabinal on primate menstrual cycle. *Science, 219,* 1453–1455.

Smith, D. (1986). Cocaine-alcohol abuse: Epidemiological, diagnostic and treatment considerations. *Journal of Psychoactive Drugs, 18,* 117–129.

Smith, D., & Wilson, A. (1973). *The Child With Down's Syndrome.* Philadelphia: Saunders.

Smith, F. (1977). Work attitudes as predictors of attendance on a specific day. *Journal of Applied Psychology, 62,* 16–19.

Smith, F. (1985). Physicians take a second look at hypnosis. *The Oregonian,* March 7, D1.

Smith, G., & Gibbs, J. (1976). Cholecystokinin and satiety: theoretic and therapeutic implications. In D. Novin, W. Wyrwicka, & D. Bray (Eds.), *Hunger: Basic Mechanisms and Clinical Implications.* New York: Raven.

Smith, K. (1947). The problem of stimulation deafness. Histological changes in the cochlea as a function of tonal frequency. *Journal of Experimental Psychology, 37,* 304–317.

Smith, M., Glass, G., & Miller, R. (1980). *The Benefits of Psychotherapy.* Baltimore: Johns Hopkins University Press.

Smith, S., Brown, H., Toman, J., & Goodman, L. (1947). The lack of cerebral effects of I-Tubercurarine. *Anesthesiology, 8,* 1–14.

Smythies, J. (1976). Recent progress in schizophrenia research. *Lancet, 2,* 136–139.

Snarey, J. (1987). A question of morality. *Psychology Today,* June, 6–8.

Snyder, M. (1983). The influence of individuals on situation: Implications for understanding the links between personality and social behavior. *Journal of Personality, 51,* 497–516.

Snyder, M., & Swann, W. (1976). When actions reflect attitudes: The politics of impression management. *Journal of Personality and Social Psychology, 34,* 1034–1042.

Snyder, M., Tanke, E., & Berscheid, E. (1977). Social perception and interpersonal behavior: On the self-fulfilling nature of social stereotypes. *Journal of Personality and Social Psychology, 35,* 691–712.

Snyder, S. (1984). Drug and neurotransmitter receptors in the brain. *Science, 224,* 22–31.

Snyder, S. (1986). *Drugs and the Brain.* San Francisco: W. H. Freeman.

Snyder, S., & Childers, S. (1979). Opiate receptor and opioid peptides. *Annual Review of Neuroscience, 2,* 35–64.

Snyderman, M., & Rothman, S. (1987). Survey of expert opinions on intelligence and aptitude testing. *American Psychologist, 42,* 137–144.

Sobell, M., & Sobell, L. (1973). Alcoholics treated by individualized behavior therapy: one year treatment outcome. *Behavior Research and Therapy, 11,* 599–618.

Sokolov, E. (1977). Brain functions: Neuronal mechanisms of learning and memory. *Annual Review of Psychology, 20,* 85–112.

Soloman, Z., Garb, R., Bleich, A., & Grupper, D. (1987). Reactivation of combat-related posttraumatic stress disorder. *American Journal of Psychiatry, 144,* 51–55.

Sommer, R. (1969). *Personal Space.* Englewood Cliffs, NJ: Prentice-Hall.

Sontag, S. (1972). The double standard of aging. *Saturday Review,* September 23, 29–38.

Sorenson, R. (1973). *Adolescent Sexuality in Contemporary America.* New York: World.

Spady, D. (1986). Effects of mothers' smoking on their infants' body composition as determined by total body potassium. *Pediatric Research, 20,* 716–719.

Spearman, C. (1904). General intelligence objectively determined and measured. *American Journal of Psychology, 15,* 201–293.

Sperling, G. (1960). The information available in brief visual presentations. *Psychological Monographs, 74,* 1–29.

Sperry, R. (1968). Hemispheric deconnection and the unity of conscious experience. *American Psychologist, 23,* 723–733.

Spielberger, C., Johnson, E., Russell, S., Crane, R., Jacobs, G., & Worden, T.

(1985). The experience and expression of anger. In M. Chesney, S. Goldston, & R. Rosenman (Eds.), *Anger and Hostility in Behavioral Medicine.* New York: Hemisphere/McGraw-Hill.

Spielman, A., Saskin, P., & Thorpy, M. (1987). Treatment of chronic insomnia by restriction of time in bed. *Sleep,* 10, 45–56.

Spiro, R. (1976). Remembering information from text: Theoretical and empirical issues concerning the state of schema reconstruction hypothesis. In R. Spiro and W. Montague (Eds.), *Schooling and the Acquisition of Knowledge.* Hillsdale, NJ: Erlbaum.

Spitz, R. (1945). Hospitalism: An inquiry into the genesis of psychiatric conditions in early childhood. *Psychoanalytic Study of the Child,* 2, 313–342.

Spray, D. (1986). Cutaneous temperature receptors. *Annual Review of Physiology,* 48, 625–638.

Squire, L., & Butters, N. (1984). *Neuropsychology of Memory.* New York: Guilford Press.

Sroufe, L. (1985). Attachment classification from the perspective of infant-caregiver relationships and infant temperament. *Child Development,* 56, 1–14.

Sroufe, L., Fox, N., & Pancake, V. (1983). Attachment and dependency in a developmental perspective. *Child Development,* 54, 1615–1627.

Stapp, J., & Fulcher, R. (1983). The employment of APA members: 1982. *American Psychologist,* 38, 1298–1320.

Stark, E. (1984). Hypnosis on trial. *Psychology Today,* February, 34–36.

Steers, R., & Rhodes, S. Major influences on employee attendance: A process model. *Journal of Applied Psychology,* 63, 391–407.

Stein, G. (1984). U.S. losing war against drugs; cocaine at all-time high. *The Oregonian,* June 3, A15.

Stein, J. (1986). Role of the cerebellum in the visual guidance of movement. *Nature,* 323, 217–221.

Stein, L., & Wise, C. (1971). Possible etiology of schizophrenia: Progressive damage to the noradrenergic reward system by 6-hydroxy dopamine. *Science,* 171, 1031–1036.

Stellar, E. (1954). The physiology of motivation. *Psychological Review,* 61, 5–22.

Stephan, W., & Rosenfield, D. (1978). Effects of desegregation on racial attitudes. *Journal of Personality and Social Psychology,* 36, 795–804.

Stern, D. (1986). *The Interpersonal World of the Infant.* New York: Basic Books.

Stern, J., Brown, M., Ulett, G., & Sletten, I. (1977). A comparison of hypnosis, acupuncture, morphine, valium, aspirin, and placebo in the management of experimentally induced pain. *Annals of the New York Academy of Sciences,* 296, 175–193.

Sternberg, R. (1979). The nature of mental abilities. *American Psychologist,* 34, 214–230.

Sternberg, R. (1981). Testing and cognitive psychology. *American Psychologist,* 36, 1181–1189.

Sternberg, R. (1982). Reasoning, problem solving, and intelligence. In R. Sternberg (Ed.), *Handbook of Human Intelligence.* New York: Cambridge University Press.

Sternberg, R. (1984). Testing intelligence without IQ tests. *Phi Delta Kappan,* 65, 694–698.

Sternberg, R., Conway, B., Ketron, J., & Bernstein, M. (1981). People's conceptions of intelligence. *Journal of Personality and Social Psychology,* 41, 37–55.

Sternberg, R., & Salter, W. (1982). Conceptions of intelligence. In R. Sternberg (Ed.), *Handbook of Human Intelligence.* New York: Cambridge University Press.

Sternberg, S. (1984). Smoking drug damages lungs. *The Oregonian,* May 22, C3.

Stevenson, H. (1983). *Making the Grade: School Achievement in Japan, Taiwan, and the United States.* Stanford, CA: Center for Advanced Study in the Behavioral Sciences, Annual Report.

Stewart, K. (1969). Dream theory in Malaya. In C. Tart (Ed.), *Altered States of Consciousness.* New York: Wiley.

ST George-Hyslop, P., Tanzi, R., Polinsky, R., Haines, J., Nee, L., Watkins, P., Myers, R., Feldman, R., Pollen, D., Drachman, D., Growdon, J., Bruni, A., Foncin, J., Salmon, D., Prommelt, P., Amaducci, L., Sorbi, S., Piacentini, S., Stewart, G., Hobbs, W., Conneally, M., Gusella, J. (1987). The genetic defect causing familial Alzheimer's disease maps on chromosome 21. *Science,* 20, 885–890.

Stine, E., & Bohannon, J. (1983). Imitation, interactions, and language acquisition. *Journal of Child Language,* 10, 589–603.

Stogdill, R. (1948). Personal factors associated with leadership. *Journal of Psychology,* 25, 35–71.

Straus, E., & Yalow, R. (1979). Cholecystokinin in the brains of obese and nonobese mice. *Science,* 203, 68–69.

Striegel-Moore, R., Silberstein, L., & Rodin, J. (1986). Toward an understanding of risk factors for bulimia. *American Psychologist,* 41, 246–263.

Strube, M., & Garcia, J. (1981). A meta-analytic investigation of Fiedler's contingency model of leadership effectiveness. *Psychological Bulletin,* 90, 307–321.

Strupp, H. (1984). Psychotherapy research: Reflections on my career and the state of the art. *Journal of Social and Clinical Psychology,* 2, 3–24.

Stunkard, A. (1980). *Obesity.* Philadelphia: Saunders.

Stunkard, A. (1983). In NOVA. Fat chance in a thin world. Boston: WGBH Transcripts.

Stunkard, A., Sorenson, T., Hanis, C., Teasdale, T., Chakraborty, R., Schall, W., & Schulsinger, F. (1986). An adoption study of human obesity. *The New England Journal of Medicine,* 314, 193–198.

Sue, D. (1979). Erotic fantasies of college students during coitus. *The Journal of Sex Research,* 15, 299–305.

Suler, J. (1980). Primary process thinking and creativity. *Psychological Bulletin,* 88, 144–165.

Suls, J., & Mullen, B. (1981). Life change in psychological distress: The role of perceived control and desirability. *Journal of Applied Social Psychology,* 11, 379–389.

Suomi, S., & Harlow, H. (1972). Social rehabilitation of isolate-reared monkeys. *Developmental Psychology,* 6, 487–496.

Suomi, S., & Harlow, H. (1978). Early experience and social development in Rhesus monkeys. In M. Lamb (Ed.), *Social and Personality Development.* New York: Holt, Rinehart and Winston.

Swanson, J., & Kinsbourne, M. (1976). Stimulant-related state-dependent learning in hyperactive children. *Science,* 192, 1354–1357.

Swartz, M., Blazer, D., George, L., & Landerman, R. (1986). Somatization disorder in a community population. *American Journal of Psychiatry,* 143, 1403–1408.

Syndulko, K. (1978). Electrocortical investigations of sociopathy. In R. Hare and D. Schalling (Eds.), *Psychopathic Behavior: Approaches to Research.* Chichester, England: Wiley.

Tache, J., Selye, H., & Day, S. (1979). *Cancer, Stress, and Death.* New York: Plenum.

Tajfel, H. (1982). *Social Identity and Intergroup Relations.* New York: Cambridge University Press.

Tajfel, H., & Turner, J. (1979). An integrative theory of intergroup conflict. In W. Autin & S. Worchel (Eds.), *The Social Psychology of Intergroup Relations.* Monterey, CA: Brooks/Cole.

Tamminga, C., Foster, N., Fedio, P., Bird, E., & Chase, T. (1987). Alzheimer's disease: Low cerebral somatostatin levels correlate with impaired cognitive function and cortical metabolism. *Neurology,* 37, 161–165.

Tanford, S., & Penrod, S. (1984). Social influence model: A formal integration of research on majority and minority influence processes. *Psychological Bulletin,* 95, 189–225.

Tanzi, R., Gusella, J., Watkins, P., Bruns, G., ST George-Hyslop, P., Van Keuren, M., Patterson, D., Pagan, S., Kurnit, D., & Neve, R. (1987). Amyloid B protein gene: cDNA, mRNA distribution, and genetic linkage near the Alzheimer locus. *Science, 235,* 880–884.

Tarpy, R. (1983). *Principles of Animal Learning and Motivation.* Glenview, IL: Scott, Foresman.

Tarter, R., Hegedus, A., Goldstein, G., Shelley, C., & Alterman, A. (1984). Adolescent sons of alcoholics: neuropsychological and personality characteristics. *Alcoholism: Clinical and Experimental Research, 8,* 216–222.

Tartter, V. (1986). *Language Processes.* New York: Holt, Rinehart and Winston.

Tauber, M. (1979). Sex differences in parent-child interaction styles in a free-play session. *Child Development, 50,* 981–988.

Tavris, C. (1982). *Anger: The Misunderstood Emotion.* New York: Simon & Schuster.

Taylor, F. (1911). *Principles of Scientific Management.* New York: Harper & Row.

Taylor, S. (1986). *Health Psychology.* New York: Random House.

Tenopyr, M. (1981). The realities of employment testing. *American Psychologist, 36,* 1120–1127.

Terman, L. (1921). In Symposium: Intelligence and its measurement. *Journal of Educational Psychology, 12,* 127–133.

Terman, L. (1925). Mental and physical traits of a thousand gifted children. In L. Terman (Ed.), *Genetic Studies of Genius.* Stanford, CA: Stanford University Press.

Terman, L. (1954). Scientists and nonscientists in a group of 800 gifted men. *Psychological Monographs, 68,* 1–44.

Terman, L., & Merrill, M. (1960). *Stanford-Binet Intelligence Scale: Manual for the Third Revision, Form L–M.* Boston: Houghton Mifflin.

Terrace, H. (1979). How Nim Chimsky changed my mind. *Psychology Today,* November, 63–91.

Terrace, H., Petitto, L., Sanders, R., & Bever, T. (1979). Can an ape create a sentence? *Science, 206,* 891–902.

Tessler, R., & Sushelsky, L. (1978). Effects of eye contact and social status on the perception of a job applicant in an employment interviewing situation. *Journal of Vocational Behavior, 13,* 338–347.

Teuting, P., Rosen, S., & Hirschfeld, R. (1981). *Special Report on Depression Research.* Washington, DC: NIMH-DHHS Publication No. 81–1085.

Thibaut, J., & Strickland, L. (1956). Psychological set and social conformity. *Journal of Personality and Social Psychology, 25,* 115–129.

Thigpen, C., & Cleckley, H. (1954). *The Three Faces of Eve.* Kingsport, TN: Kingsport Press.

Thigpen, C., & Cleckley, H. (1984). On the incidence of multiple personality disorder. *The International Journal of Clinical and Experimental Hypnosis, 32,* 63–66.

Thoman, E., Liderman, P., & Olsen, J. (1972). Neonate-mother interaction during breast feeding. *Developmental Psychology, 6,* 110–118.

Thomas, A., & Chess, S. (1977). *Temperament and Development.* New York: Bruner/Masel.

Thomas, A., Chess, S., & Birch, H. (1970). The origin of personality. *Scientific American, 223,* 102–109.

Thomas, C., Duszynski, K., & Shaffer, J. (1974). Closeness to parents and the family constellation in a prospective study of five disease states: Suicide, mental illness, malignant tumor, hypertension, and coronary heart disease. *Johns Hopkins Journal, 134,* 251–270.

Thomas, C., Duszynski, K., & Shaffer, J. (1979). Family attitudes reported in youth as potential precursors of cancer. *Psychosomatic Medicine, 41,* 287–302.

Thompson, C., Hamlin, V., & Roenker, D. (1972). A comment on the role of clustering in free recall. *Journal of Experimental Psychology, 94,* 108–109.

Thompson, D., & Campbell, R. (1977). Hunger in humans induced by 2-deoxy-D-glucose: Glucoprivic control of taste preference and food intake. *Science, 198,* 1065–1068.

Thompson, J., & Blaine, J. (1987). Use of ECT in the United States in 1975 and 1980. *American Journal of Psychiatry, 144,* 557–562.

Thompson, J., Jarvie, G., Lahey, B., & Cureton, K. (1982). Exercise and obesity: Etiology, physiology, and intervention. *Psychological Bulletin, 91,* 55–79.

Thompson, R. (1985). *The Brain.* San Francisco: W. H. Freeman.

Thompson, S. (1981). Will it hurt less if I can control it? A complex answer to a simple question. *Psychological Bulletin, 90,* 89–101.

Thorndike, E. (1911). *Animal Intelligence.* New York: Macmillan.

Thorndyke, P. (1984). Applications of schema theory in cognitive research. In J. Anderson & S. Kosslyn (Eds.), *Essays in Honor of Gordon Bower.* San Francisco: W. H. Freeman.

Thorngate, W. (1980). Efficient decision heuristics. *Behavioral Science, 25,* 219–225.

Thurstone, L. (1938). *Primary Mental Abilities.* Chicago: University of Chicago Press.

Thurstone, L. (1946). Comment. *American Journal of Sociology, 52,* 39–40.

Tokunaga, K., Fukushima, M., Kemnitz, J., & Bray, G. (1986). Comparison of ventromedial and paraventricular lesions in rats that become obese. *American Journal of Physiology, 251,* R1221–R1227.

Tolman, E., & Honzik, C. (1930). Introduction and removal of reward and maze performance in rats. *University of California Publications in Psychology, 4,* 257–275.

Tolman, E., Ritchie, B., & Kalish, D. (1946). Studies in spatial learning: II. Place learning versus response learning. *American Psychologist, 34,* 583–596.

Tolstedt, B., & Stokes, J. (1983). Relation of verbal, affective, and physical intimacy to marital satisfaction. *Journal of Counseling Psychology, 30,* 573–580.

Tomkins, S. (1962). *Affect, Imagery, and Consciousness: The Positive Effects* (Vol. 1). New York: Springer.

Tomkins, S. (1963). *Affect, Imagery, and Consciousness: The Negative Effects* (Vol. 2). New York: Springer.

Torgerson, S. (1983). Genetic factors in anxiety disorder. *Archives of General Psychiatry, 40,* 1085–1089.

Torrey, E. (1983). *Surviving Schizophrenia: A Family Manual.* New York: Harper & Row.

Tourney, G. (1980). Hormones and homosexuality. In J. Marmor (Ed.), *Homosexual Behavior.* New York: Basic Books.

Travers, J., Travers, S., & Norgen, R. (1987). Gustatory neural processing in hindbrain. *Annual Review of Neurosciences, 10,* 595–632.

Treisman, A. (1960). Contextual cues in selective listening. *Quarterly Journal of Experimental Psychology, 12,* 242–248.

Treisman, A. (1964). Monitoring and storage of irrelevant messages in selective attention. *Journal of Verbal Learning and Verbal Behavior, 3,* 449–459.

Trickett, P., Apfel, N., Rosenbaum, L., and Zigler, E. (1983). A five year follow-up of participants in the Yale Child Welfare Research Program. In E. Zigler & E. Gordon (Eds.), *Day Care: Scientific and Social Policy Issues.* Boston: Auburn House Publishing.

Troll, L. (1975). *Early and Middle Adulthood.* Monterey, CA: Brooks/Cole.

Tryon, R. (1940). Genetic differences in maze-learning ability in rats. In the *39th Yearbook, National Society for the Study of Education.* Chicago: University of Chicago Press.

Tulving, E. (1972). Episodic and semantic memory. In E. Tulving & W. Donaldson (Eds.), *Organization of Memory.* New York: Academic Press.

Tulving, E. (1977). Cue-dependent forgetting. In I. Janis (Ed.), *Current Trends in Psychology.* Los Altos, CA: Kaufmann.

Tulving, E. (1983). *Elements of Episodic Memory.* New York: Oxford University Press.

Tulving, E. (1986). What kind of a hypothesis is the distinction between episodic and semantic memory? *Journal of Experimental Psychology: Learning, Memory, and Cognition, 12,* 307–311.

Turk, D., Meichenbaum, D., & Berman, W. (1979). Application of biofeedback for the regulation of pain: A critical review. *Psychological Bulletin, 86,* 1322–1338.

Turk, D., & Rudy, T. (1986). Assessment of cognitive factors in chronic pain: A worthwhile enterprise? *Journal of Consulting and Clinical Psychology, 54,* 760–768.

Turner, J. (1984). Social identification and psychological group formation. In H. Tajfel (Ed.), *The Social Dimension.* Cambridge, England: Cambridge University Press.

Turner, S., Beidel, D., & Nathan, R. (1985). Biological factors in obsessive-compulsive disorders. *Psychological Bulletin, 97,* 430–450.

Tuttle, T. (1983). Organizational productivity: A challenge for psychologists. *American Psychologist, 38,* 479–486.

Tversky, A. (1972). Elimination by aspects: A theory of choice. *Psychological Review, 79,* 281–299.

Tversky, A., & Kahneman, D. (1973). On the psychology of prediction. *Psychological Review, 80,* 237–251.

Udry, J., Billy, J., Morris, N., Groff, T., & Raj, M. (1985). Serum androgenic hormones motivate sexual behavior in adolescent boys. *Fertility and Sterility, 43,* 90–94.

Ullman, L., & Krasner, L. (1975). *A Psychological Approach to Abnormal Behavior* (2nd ed.). Englewood Cliffs, NJ: Prentice-Hall.

Underwood, B. (1983). "Conceptual" similarity and accumulated proactive inhibition. *Journal of Experimental Psychology: Learning, Memory, and Cognition, 9,* 456–461.

U.S. Bureau of the Census. (1983). *America in transition: An aging society. Current Population Reports,* Series P–23, No. 128. Washington, DC: U.S. Government Printing Office.

U.S. Bureau of the Census. (1986). *Marital status and living arrangement: March 1985. Current Population Reports,* Series P–20, No. 410. Washington, DC: U.S. Government Printing Office.

U.S. Bureau of the Census. (1987a). *Population profile of the United States: 1984, 1985. Current Population Reports,* Series P–23, No. 150. Washington, DC: U.S. Government Printing Office.

U.S. Bureau of the Census. (1987b). *U.S.A. Statistics in Brief.* Washington, DC: U.S. Government Printing Office.

U.S. Department of Labor. (1984). Working mothers reach record number in 1984. *Monthly Labor Review,* December, 31–34.

Vaillant, G., & Perry, J. (1985). Personality disorders. In H. Kaplan & B. Sadock (Eds.), *Comprehensive Textbook of Psychiatry* (4th ed.). Baltimore: Williams & Wilkins.

Valenstein, E. (Ed.) (1980). *The Psychosurgery Debate.* San Francisco: W. H. Freeman.

Valian, V. (1986). Syntactic categories in the speech of young children. *Developmental Psychology, 22,* 562–579.

Vanderweele, D. & Sanderson, J. (1976). Peripheral glucosensitive satiety in the rabbit and the rat. In D. Novin, W. Wyrcicka, & G. Bray (Eds.), *Hunger: Basic Mechanisms and Clinical Implications.* New York: Raven.

Van Egeren, L., Sniderman, L., & Roggelin, M. (1982). Competitive two-person interaction of Type-A and Type-B individuals. *Journal of Behavioral Medicine, 5,* 55–66.

Van Praag, H. (1981). Management of depression with serotonin precursors. *Biological Psychiatry, 16,* 291–310.

Vecchio, R. (1977). An empirical examination of the validity of Fiedler's model of leadership effectiveness. *Organizational Behavior and Human Performance, 19,* 180–206.

Vecchio, R. (1983). Assessing the validity of Fiedler's contingency model of leadership effectiveness: A closer look at Strube and Garcia. *Psychological Bulletin, 93,* 404–408.

Vega-Lahr, N., & Field, T. (1986). Type A behavior in preschool children. *Child Development, 57,* 1333–1348.

Veleber, D., & Templer, D. (1984). Effects of caffeine on anxiety and depression. *Journal of Abnormal Psychology, 93,* 120–122.

Velley, L. (1986). The role of intrinsic neurons in lateral hypothalamic self-stimulation. *Behavioural Brain Research, 22,* 141–152.

Venables, P., & Wing, J. (1962). Level of arousal and the subclassification of schizophrenia. *Archives of General Psychiatry, 7,* 114–119.

Veroff, J., Douvan, E., & Kulka, R. (1981). *The Inner American.* New York: Basic Books.

Vinigan, R., Dow-Edwards, D., & Riley, E. (1986). Cerebral metabolic alterations in rats following prenatal alcohol exposure: A deoxyglucose study. *Alcoholism: Clinical and Experimental Research, 10,* 22–26.

Vinokur, A., & Selzer, M. (1975). Desirable versus undesirable life events: Their relationship to stress and mental distress. *Journal of Personality and Social Psychology, 32,* 329–337.

Visintainer, M., Seligman, M., & Volpicelli, J. (1983). Helplessness, chronic stress, and tumor development. *Psychosomatic Medicine, 45,* 75–76.

Vogel, G. (1975). A review of REM sleep deprivation. *Archives of General Psychiatry, 32,* 749–761.

von Békésy, G. (1960). *Experiments in Hearing.* New York: McGraw-Hill.

von Frisch, K. (1974). Decoding the language of the bee. *Science, 185,* 663–668.

von Winterfelt, D., & Edwards, W. (1986). *Decision Analysis and Behavioral Research.* New York: Cambridge University Press.

Vroom, V. (1964). *Work and Motivation.* New York: Wiley.

Wadden, T., & Anderton, C. (1982). The clinical use of hypnosis. *Psychological Bulletin, 91,* 215–243.

Wagensteen, O., & Carlson, A. (1931). Hunger sensation after total gastrectomy. *Proceedings of the Society of Experimental Biology, 28,* 545–547.

Wahba, N., & Bridwell, L. (1976). Maslow reconsidered: A review of research on the need hierarchy theory. *Organization Behavior and Human Performance, 15,* 212–240.

Wall, H., & Routowicz, A. (1987). Use of self-generated and others' cues in immediate and delayed recall. *Perceptual and Motor Skills, 64,* 1019–1022.

Wallace, R., & Benson, H. (1972). The physiology of meditation. *Scientific American, 226,* 84–90.

Wallach, M., & Wallach, L. (1983). *Psychology's Sanction for Selfishness: The Error of Egoism in Theory and Therapy.* New York: W. H. Freeman.

Wallach, M., & Wallach, L. (1985). How psychology sanctions the cult of the self. *Washington Monthly,* February, 46–56.

Wallis, C. (1984). Unlocking pain's secrets. *Time,* June 11, 58–66.

Walsh, B. Katz, J., Levin, J., Dream, J., Fukushima, D., Hellman, L., Weiner, H., & Zumoff, B. (1978). Adrenal activity in anorexia nervosa. *Psychosomatic Medicine, 40,* 499.

Walster, E., Aronson, E., & Abrahams, D. (1966). On increasing the persuasiveness of a low prestige communicator. *Journal of Experimental Social Psychology, 2,* 325–342.

Walster, E., & Walster, G. (1978). *A New Look at Love.* Reading, MA: Addison-Wesley.

Walters, G., & Grusec, J. (1977). *Punishment.* San Francisco: W. H. Freeman.

Walters, J., Apter, M., & Svebak, S. (1982). Color preference, arousal, and the theory of psychological reversals. *Motivation and Emotion, 6,* 193–215.

Walters, R., & Willows, D. (1968). Imitation of behavior of disturbed children following exposure to aggressive and nonaggressive models. *Child Development, 39,* 79–91.

Wang, M., & Freeman, A. (1987). *Neural Function.* Boston: Little, Brown.

Ward, L. & Suedfeld, P. (1973). Human responses to highway noise. *Environmental Research, 6,* 306–326.

Ward, T., & Lewis, S. (1987). The influence of alcohol and loud music on analytic and holistic processing. *Perception and Psychophysics, 41,* 179–186.

Warga, C. (1987). Pain's gatekeeper. *Psychology Today,* August, 51–56.

Wason, P. (1968). On the failure to eliminate hypothesis—a second look. In P. Wason & P. Johnson-Laird (Eds.), *Thinking and Reasoning.* Baltimore: Penguin.

Wass, H., Christian, M., Myers, J., & Murphy, M. (1978). Similarities and dissimilarities in attitudes toward death in a population of older people. *Omega,* 9, 337–354.

Waterman, A. (1982). Identity development from adolescence to adulthood: An extension of theory and a review of research. *Developmental Psychology,* 18, 341–358.

Waters, E., Wippman, J., & Sroufe, L. (1979). Attachment, positive affect, and competence in the peer group: Two studies in construct validation. *Child Development,* 50, 821–829.

Watkins, M., Ho, E., & Tulving, E. (1976). Context effects in recognition memory for faces. *Journal of Verbal Learning and Verbal Behavior,* 15, 505–518.

Watson, J. (1930). *Behaviorism.* New York: Norton.

Waxenberg, S., Drellich, M., & Sutherland, A. (1959). Changes in female sexuality after adrenalectomy. *Journal of Clinical Endocrinology,* 19, 193–202.

Weaver, C. (1980). Job satisfaction in the United States in the 1970s. *Journal of Applied Psychology,* 65, 364–367.

Webb, W. (1975). *Sleep the Gentle Tyrant.* Englewood Cliffs, NJ: Prentice-Hall.

Webb, W., & Bonnet, M. (1979). Sleep and dreams. In M. Meyer (Ed.), *Foundations of Contemporary Psychology.* New York: Oxford University Press.

Webb, W., & Campbell, S. Relationships in sleep characteristics of identical and fraternal twins. *Archives of General Psychiatry,* 40, 1093–1095.

Wechsler, D. (1944). *The Measurement of Adult Intelligence* (3rd ed.). Baltimore: Williams & Wilkins.

Wehr, T., Sack, D., & Rosenthal, N. (1987). Sleep reduction as a final common pathway in the genesis of mania. *American Journal of Psychiatry,* 144, 201–204.

Weiner, R. (1985). Electroconvulsive therapy. In J. Walker (Ed.), *Essentials of Clinical Psychiatry.* Philadelphia: Lippincott.

Weingartner, H., Gold, P., Bullenger, J., Smallberg, S., Summers, R., Rubinow, D., Post, R., & Goodwin, F. (1981). Effects of vasopressin on human memory functions. *Science,* 211, 601–603.

Weiss, B. (1983). Behavioral toxicology and environmental health science: Opportunity and challenge for psychology. *American Psychologist,* 38, 1174–1187.

Weiss, R. (1987). How dare we? *Science News,* 132, 57–59.

Weissman, M. (1987). Advances in psychiatric epidemiology: Rates and risks for major depression. *American Journal of Public Health,* 77, 445–451.

Weissman, M., Kidd, K., & Prusoff, B. (1982). Variability in rates of affective disorders in relatives of depressed and normal probands. *Archives of General Psychiatry,* 39, 1397–1403.

Weissman, M., & Klerman, G. (1977). Sex differences and the epidemiology of depression. *Archives of General Psychiatry,* 34, 98–111.

Weissman, M., Klerman, G., & Paykel, E. (1971). Clinical evaluation of hostility in depression. *American Journal of Psychiatry,* 128, 261–266.

Weissman, M., Klerman, G., Prusoff, B., Sholomskas, D., & Padian, N. (1981). Depressed outpatients. Results one year after treatment with drugs and/or interpersonal psychotherapy. *Archives of General Psychiatry,* 38, 51–56.

Weissman, M., & Paykel, E. (1974). *The Depressed Woman.* Chicago: University of Chicago Press.

Wetli, C., & Wright, R. (1979). Death caused by recreational cocaine use. *Journal of the American Medical Association,* 241, 2519–2522.

Wetzel, C., & Insko, C. (1982). The similarity-attraction relationship: Is there an ideal one? *Journal of Experimental Social Psychology,* 18, 253–276.

Wetzler, S. (1985). Mood state-dependent retrieval: A failure to replicate. *Psychological Reports,* 56, 759–765.

Wexley, K., & Yukl, G. (1984). *Organizational Behavior and Personnel Psychology.* Homewood, IL: Richard D. Irwin.

White, P. (1985). The poppy. *National Geographic,* 167, 143–188.

White, W. (1932). *Outlines of Psychiatry* (13th ed.). New York: Nervous and Mental Disease Publishing Company.

Whitham, T. (1977). Coevolution of foraging in *Bombus* and nectar dispensing in *Chilopsis:* A last dreg theory. *Science,* 197, 593–595.

Whitman, F., & Diamond, M. (1986). A preliminary report on the sexual orientation of homosexual twins. Paper presented at the Western Region Annual Conference of the Society for the Scientific Study of Sex, Scottsdale, Arizona, January.

Wicker, A. (1969). Attitudes versus actions: The relationship of verbal and overt behavioral responses to attitude objects. *Journal of Personality and Social Psychology,* 33, 793–802.

Wiens, A., & Menustik, C. (1983). Treatment outcome and patient characteristics in an aversion therapy program for alcoholism. *American Psychologist,* 38, 1089–1096.

Wiest, W. (1977). Semantic differential profiles of orgasm and other experiences among men and women. *Sex Roles,* 3, 399–403.

Wilder, D. (1978). Homogeneity of jurors: The majority's influence depends upon their perceived independence. *Law and Human Behavior,* 2, 363–376.

Wilder, D. (1981). Perceiving persons as a group: Categorization and intergroup relations. In D. Hamilton (Ed.), *Cognitive Processes in Stereotyping and Intergroup Behavior.* Hillsdale, NJ: Erlbaum.

Willems, P. (1984). Ergonomics. In P. Drenth, H. Thierry, P. Willems, & C. dWolff (Eds.), *Handbook of Work and Organizational Psychology.* Chichester: Wiley.

Williams, R. (1972). *The BITCH Test (Black Intelligence Test of Cultural Homogeneity).* St. Louis: Williams & Associates.

Williamson, D., Kelley, M., Davis, C., Ruggiero, L., & Blovin, D. (1985). Psychopathology of eating disorders: A controlled comparison of bulimic, obese, and normal subjects. *Journal of Consulting and Clinical Psychology,* 53, 161–166.

Williamson, P., Csima, A., Galin, H., & Mamelak, M. (1986). Spectral EEG correlates of dream recall. *Biological Psychiatry,* 21, 717–723.

Wilson, B., & Lawson, D. (1976). Effects of alcohol on sexual arousal in women. *Journal of Abnormal Psychology,* 85, 489–497.

Wilson, E. (1975). *Sociobiology: The New Synthesis.* Cambridge, MA: Harvard University Press.

Wilson, E. (1978). *On Human Nature.* Cambridge, MA: Harvard University Press.

Wilson, M. (1984). Female homosexuals' need for dominance and endurance. *Psychological Reports,* 55, 79–82.

Winograd, E., & Killinger, W. (1983). Relating age at encoding in early childhood to adult recall: Development of flashbulb memories. *Journal of Experimental Psychology,* 12, 413–422.

Winterbottom, M. (1958). The relation of need for achievement to learning experiences in independence mastery. In J. Atkinson (Ed.), *Motives in Fantasy, Action and Society.* Princeton, NJ: Van Nostrand.

Wirtshafter, D., & Davis, J. (1977). Body weight: Reduction by long-term glycerol treatment. *Science,* 198, 1271–1274.

Witelson, S. (1985). The brain connection: The corpus callosum is larger in left handers. *Science,* 229, 665–668.

Wolfe, J. (1936). Effectiveness of token rewards for chimpanzees. *Comparative Psychological Monographs,* 12, Whole No. 5.

Wolff, G. (1987). Body weight and cancer. *American Journal of Clinical Nutrition,* 45, 168–180.

Wolpe, J., & Rachman, S. (1960). Psychoanalytic "evidence." A critique based on Freud's case of Little Hans. *Journal of Ner-*

vous and Mental Disease, 131, 135–147.

Women on Words and Images. (1972). *Dick and Jane as Victims.* Princeton, NJ: Author.

Wong, D., Wagner, H., Tune, L., Dannals, R., Pealson, G., Links, J., Tamminga, C., Broussolle, E., Ravert, H., Wilson, A., Toung, J., Malat, J., Williams, J., O'Tuama, L., Snyder, S., Kuhar, M., & Gjedde, A. (1986). Positron emission tomography reveals elevated D_2 dopamine receptors in drug-naive schizophrenics. *Science,* 234, 1558–1563.

Wood, W., & Eagly, A. (1981). Stages in the analysis of persuasive messages: The role of causal attributions and message comprehension. *Journal of Personality and Social Psychology,* 40, 246–259.

Woody, C. (1982). *Conditioning: Representation of Involved Neural Functions.* New York: Plenum.

Woody, C. (1984). Studies of Pavlovian eyeblink conditioning in awake cats. In G. Lynch, J. McGaugh, & N. Weinberger (Eds.), *Neurobiology of Learning and Memory.* New York: Guilford Press.

Woody, C. (1986). Understanding the cellular basis of memory and learning. *Annual Review of Psychology,* 37, 433–493.

Wooley, S. (1983). In NOVA. Fat chance in a thin world. Boston: WGBH Transcripts.

Work in America (1973). Special Task Force, Department of Health, Education and Welfare. Cambridge, MA: MIT Press.

Wright, J, Waterson, E., Barrison, I., Toplis, P., Lewis, I., Gordon, M., MacRae, K., Morris, N., & Murray-Lyon, I. (1983). Alcohol consumption, pregnancy, and low birthweight. *Lancet,* 1, 663–665.

Wu, C., & Shaffer, D. (1987). Susceptibility to persuasive appeals as a function of source credibility and prior experience with the attitude object. *Journal of Personality and Social Psychology,* 52, 677–688.

Wyrwicka, W. (1976). The problem of motivation in feeding behavior. In D. Novin, W. Wyrwicka, & G. Bray (Eds.), *Hunger: Basic Mechanisms and Clinical Implications.* New York: Raven.

Yalom, I. (1975). *The Theory and Practice of Group Psychotherapy* (2nd ed.). New York: Basic Books.

Yarrow, L., Goodwin, M., Manheimer, H., & Milowe, I. (1973). Infancy, experience and cognitive and personality development at ten years. In L. Stone, H. Smith, & L. Murphy (Eds.). *The Competent Infant.* New York: Basic Books.

Yeomans, J., & Irwin, D. (1985). Stimulus duration and partial report performance. *Perception and Psychophysics,* 37, 163–169.

Yerkes, R., & Dobson, J. (1908). The relation of strength of stimulus to rapidity of habit formation. *Journal of Comparative Neurological Psychology,* 18, 459–482.

Yonas, A., Pettersen, L., & Granrud, C. (1982). Infants' sensitivity to familiar size as information for distance. *Child Development,* 53, 1285–1290.

Young, A., & Guile, M. (1987). Departure latency to invasion of personal space: Effects of status and sex. *Perceptual and Motor Skills,* 64, 700–702.

Young, P. (1985). Introduction of gene therapy likely to bring high hopes, ethical fears. *The Oregonian,* May 16, C1.

Yu, B., Zhang, W., Jing, Q., Peng, R., Zhang, G., and Simon, H. (1985). STM capacity for Chinese and English language materials. *Memory and Cognition,* 13, 202–207.

Yudofsky, S. (1982). Electroconvulsive therapy in the eighties: Techniques and technology. *American Journal of Psychiatry,* 36, 391–398.

Zabin, I., Hirsch, M., Smith, E., & Hardy, J. (1984). Adolescent sexual attitudes and behavior: Are they consistent? *Family Planning Perspectives,* 16, 181–185.

Zabin, J., & Barrera, S. (1941). Effect of electric convulsive therapy on memory. *Proceedings of the Society for Experimental Biology and Medicine,* 48, 596–597.

Zaidel, E. (1975). A technique for presenting lateralized visual input with prolonged exposure. *Vision Research,* 15, 283–289.

Zaidel, E. (1983). A response to Gazzaniga. *American Psychologist,* 38, 542–546.

Zajonc, R. (1965). Social facilitation. *Science,* 149, 269–274.

Zajonc, R. (1968). Attitudinal effects of mere exposure. *Journal of Personality and Social Psychology,* 9, Monograph Supplement No. 2, Part 2.

Zajonc, R. (1970). Brainwash: Familiarity breeds comfort. *Psychology Today,* February, 32–35, 60–62.

Zajonc, R., & Markus, G. (1975). Birth order and intellectual development. *Psychological Review,* 82, 74–88.

Zaragoza, M., McCloskey, M., & Jamis, M. (1987). Misleading postevent information and recall of the original event: Further evidence against the memory impairment hypothesis. *Journal of Experimental Psychology: Learning, Memory, and Cognition,* 13, 36–44.

Zedeck, S., & Cascio, W. (1984). Psychological issues in personnel decisions. *Annual Review of Psychology,* 35, 461–518.

Zelnick, M., & Kantner, J. (1977). Sexual and contraceptive experiences of young unmarried women in the United States, 1976 and 1971. *Family Planning Perspectives,* 9, 55–71.

Zelnick, M., & Kantner, J. (1980). Sexual activity, contraceptive use, and pregnancy among metropolitan-area teenagers: 1971–1979. *Family Planning Perspectives,* 12, 230–237.

Zhang, G., & Simon, H. (1985). STM capacity for Chinese words and idioms: chunking and acoustical loop hypotheses. *Memory and Cognition,* 13, 193–201.

Ziegler, J. (1984). Scientists ponder drinkers, drunks, differences. *The Oregonian,* July 5, B4–B5.

Zigler, E., & Berman, W. (1983). Discerning the future of early childhood intervention. *American Psychologist,* 38, 894–906.

Zilbergeld, B. (1983). *The Shrinking of America: Myths of Psychological Change.* Boston: Little, Brown.

Zimbardo, P. (1975). Transforming experimental research into advocacy for social change. In M. Deutsch and H. Hornstein (Eds.), *Applying Social Psychology: Implications for Research. Practice and Training.* Hillsdale, NJ: Erlbaum.

Zimbardo, P., Anderson, S., & Kabat, L. (1981). Induced hearing deficit generates experimental paranoia. *Science,* 212, 1529–1531.

Zimmer, D. (1983). Interaction patterns and communication skills in sexually distressed, maritally distressed, and normal couples: Two experimental studies. *Journal of Sex and Marital Therapy,* 9, 251–265.

Zimmerman, J., Stoyva, J., & Metcalf, D. (1970). Distorted visual feedback and augmented REM sleep. *Psychophysiology,* 7, 298.

Zubin, J., & Spring, B. (1977). Vulnerability—A new view of schizophrenia. *Journal of Abnormal Psychology,* 86, 103–126.

Zuckerman, M. (1979). *Sensation Seeking: Beyond the Optimal Level of Arousal.* Hillsdale, NJ: Erlbaum.

NAME INDEX

Abel, 162
Abraham, K., 481
Abrams, A., 599
Abramson, L., 485
Abroms, K., 336
Abu-Mostafa, Y., 14
Adams, J., 360
Ader, R., 183
Aderman, D., 393
Adorno, T., 568, 569
Agnell, P., 483
Aiello, J., 589
Aiello, T., 589
Ainsworth, M., 353, 355
Albee, G., 601
Alderfer, C., 642
Aldrich, M., 70
Allen, M., 485
Allen, V., 562
Allport, G., 232, 427–428, 429
Almli, C., 296
Altman, I., 589, 591
Altman, J., 79
Amabile, T., 421, 422, 568
Amit, Z., 122
Amkraut, A., 615
Amoore, J., 118
Anand, B., 156, 293
Anastasi, A., 410, 422, 600
Anderson, A., 585, 586
Anderson, C., 226, 583, 584
Anderson, J., 226
Anderson, K., 168
Anderton, B., 158, 390
Andreasen, N., 480
Anisfeld, M., 221
Anisman, H., 614
Apter, M., 304
Archer, J., 359
Archer, S., 360, 372
Arehart-Treichel, J., 150
Arend, R., 356, 430
Aristotle, 9, 10
Arkes, H., 266
Arlin, P. A., 380
Arlow, J., 508
Armentrout, J., 359
Armstrong, S., 253
Arnetz, B., 614
Aronson, E., 558, 566, 567
Arrowood, J., 571
Arthur, A., 610, 614

Asch, S., 543, 544, 561–562
Aserinsky, C., 142
Aslin, R., 274
Athanasiou, R., 26
Atkin, C., 360
Atkinson, J., 310
Atkinson, R., 215
Austrom, D., 381
Avison, W., 533

Bachrach, A., 519
Baer, P., 208
Bahnson, C., 615
Bakay, R., 61
Baker, L., 612
Bale, J., 80
Balota, D., 226
Baltrusch, H., 614
Bancroft, J., 308
Bandura, A., 29, 202, 209–210, 272, 290,
    441–443, 468, 469, 521, 550, 575–576
Barahal, H., 530
Barbee, A., 330
Barber, T., 161
Bard, P., 315–316
Baribeau, J., 164
Barker, R., 591
Barnes, D., 390, 495, 496
Baron, J., 583
Baron, R., 548, 564, 565, 584
Barron, F., 422
Barrow, G., 392
Bartlett, F., 231
Bartrop, R., 614
Bartusiak, M., 139
Bass, B., 385
Baudry, M., 241
Baum, A., 587, 588
Baumeiter, R., 559
Baumrind, D., 31, 357, 358
Baur, K., 307, 309, 378, 651, 653, 657
Baylis, G., 70
Beach, F., 309, 654
Beck, A., 482, 483, 512–515
Beck, R., 596, 598, 600
Begleiter, H., 164
Belger, A., 585
Belicki, D., 155
Belicki, K., 155
Belko, A., 300
Bell, A., 582, 655, 656, 657
Bell, R., 574

Bellingrath, G., 642
Bem, D., 430, 550
Bemis, K., 301
Benbow, C., 76
Benelli, B., 273
Bennett, E., 343
Bennett, J., 336
Benson, H., 156
Bentler, P., 382
Bergin, A., 525
Berglund, M., 165
Berkowitz, L., 562, 575, 577
Berlyne, D., 303
Berman, J., 527, 532, 590
Berman, W., 415
Berndt, T., 374
Berscheid, E., 517
Bersoff, D., 596
Besson, J., 121, 122
Bexton, W., 306
Bianchi, K., 475–476
Bias, L., 167
Bick, P., 492
Binet, A., 346, 402–403, 404
Bingol, N., 167
Bini, L., 531
Bird, E., 498
Bischoff, L., 378
Bitterman, M., 194
Blaine, J., 533
Blake, R., 91, 98, 108, 113, 116
Blasi, A., 372
Bleuler, E., 490
Bliss, E., 475
Block, J., 430
Bloom, F., 76, 99, 101, 243, 359
Bloom, L., 276
Blum, H., 506, 507
Blum, K., 166, 167, 168
Bobrow, G., 126
Boffey, P., 165
Bohannon, J., 272
Bolles, R., 209
Bolter, A., 170
Bonnet, M., 145, 153
Boor, M., 475
Boring, E., 130
Borke, H., 351
Borkovec, T., 501
Borman, W., 595
Bornstein, P., 301
Borysenko, J., 614

SUBJECT INDEX

Photo Credits (cont'd)

page 101, The Bettmann Archive; page 104, Four by Five; page 106, (Figure 4.12) American Optical Corporation from Their AO Pseudo Isochromatic Tests; page 109, (left) Museum of Modern Art/Film Stills Archive; (right) AP/Wide World Photos; page 115, AP/Wide World Photos; page 116, © Therese Frare/The Picture Cube; page 117, © Susan Johns/Photo Researchers, Inc.; page 118, © Topham/The Image Works; page 122, © Barbara Rios/Photo Researchers, Inc.; page 125, © Chris Gray/The Image Works; page 128, © B. Krueger, 1977/Photo Researchers, Inc.; page 129, (top) © Geopress/H. Armstrong Roberts, Inc.; (bottom) © Enrico Ferorelli/DOT; page 130, © Allsport—Vandystadt/Woodfin Camp & Associates; page 132, © Baron Wolman/Woodfin Camp & Associates; page 134, The Bettmann Archive

Chapter 5: page 140, © Conklin/Monkmeyer Press; page 147, Museum of Modern Art/Film Stills Archive; page 148, © David Krasnor/Photo Researchers, Inc.; page 151, © James Foote, 1978/Photo Researchers, Inc.; page 152, © John Fogle/The Picture Cube; page 156, (top) © Richard Hutchings/Photo Researchers, Inc.; (bottom) Photo Researchers, Inc.; page 158, © James D. Wilson/Woodfin Camp & Associates; page 161, © Arthur Tress/Photo Researchers, Inc.; page 163, © Hugh Rogers/Monkmeyer Press; page 164, (top) © Michael Hayman/Photo Researchers, Inc.; (bottom) © Alan Carey/The Image Works; page 166, © Van Bucher/Photo Researchers, Inc.; page 167, © Wesley Bocxe/Photo Researchers, Inc.; page 168, The Bettmann Archive; page 169, (left) © Omikron/Photo Researchers, Inc.; (center and right) Four by Five

Chapter 6: page 177, © Leonard Lee Rue, III/Photo Researchers, Inc.; page 178, Gatewood/The Image Works; page 179, (left) © Elfin Knight/The Picture Cube; (right) © Tom McHugh/Photo Researchers, Inc.; page 180, The Bettmann Archive; page 188, © Topham/The Image Works; page 191, © Barbara Alper/Stock Boston; page 195, (top) © Dave Schaefer, 1982/The Picture Cube; (bottom) Ralph Krubner/H. Armstrong Roberts, Inc.; page 196, © Topham/The Image Works; page 201, © Lionel J-M Delevingne/Stock Boston; page 205, The Picture Source; page 209, © Michael Heron/Woodfin Camp & Associates

Chapter 7: page 214, (top) © Michael Malyszko/Stock Boston; (bottom) H. Armstrong Roberts, Inc.; page 216, © Steven Baratz, 1985/The Picture Cube; page 220, © Frank Siteman, 1983/The Picture Cube; page 221, © George Mars Cassidy/The Picture Cube; page 222, (top) © Hervé Donnezan/Photo Researchers, Inc.; page 223, © Hazel Hankin/Stock Boston; page 228 (top) The Bettmann Archive, Inc.; (bottom) © Richard Wood, 1981/The Picture Cube; page 231, © Robert Azzi, 1986/Woodfin Camp & Associates; page 236, UPI/Bettmann Newsphotos

Chapter 8: page 247, The Bettmann Archive; page 248, (bottom) © Richard Hutchings/Photo Researchers, Inc.; page 250, The Bettmann Archive; page 252, © Jacques Chenet, 1984/Woodfin Camp & Associates; page 271, © Joseph Nettis, 1984/Photo Researchers, Inc.; page 272, © John Carter, 1986/Photo Researchers, Inc.; page 273, AP/Wide World Photos; (page 278, (top) © Frans Lanting/Photo Researchers, Inc.; (bottom) © Treat Davidson/Photo Researchers, Inc.; page 280, Language Research Center, Georgia State University; page 281, © Susan Kuklin/Photo Researchers, Inc.

Chapter 9: page 286, (top left) UPI/Bettmann Newsphotos; (top right) AP/Wide World Photos; (bottom) AP/Wide World Photos; page 287, (top) © 1984 Lewis Portnoy/The Stock Market; (bottom) © Francois Gohier/Photo Researchers, Inc.; page 288, © Frank Siteman, 1980/The Picture Cube; page 293, Photo courtesy of Neal E. Miller; page 297, © Peter Stion/Stock Boston; page 299, © 1987 Dave Schaefer/The Picture Cube; page 302, (top) © Ellis Herwig/Stock Boston; (bottom) © Patricia Beninger, 1982/The Image Works; page 304, (top) © Allsport-Vandystadt/Woodfin Camp & Associates; (bottom) Courtesy of McGill University; page 313, AP/Wide World Photos; page 319, Courtesy of Paul Ekman, Human Interaction Laboratory

Chapter 10: page 325, Michael Hayman/Stock Boston; page 326, (top) © Jerry Wachter/Photo Researchers, Inc.; (bottom) Four by Five; page 327, Jonathan L. Barkan/The Picture Cube; page 328, Nina Leen, Life Magazine © Time, Inc.; page 329, Harlow Primate Lab, University of Wisconsin; page 334, AP/Wide World Photos; page 336, UPI/Bettmann Newsphotos; page 337, © Richard Hutchings/Photo Researchers, Inc.; page 338, Alan Carey/The Image Works; page 339, (left and center) © Christopher Morris/Black Star; (right) © 1987 James Kamp/Black Star; page 340, (top) © Lennart Nilsson, from A Child Is Born, Dell Publishing Company, NY; (bottom) © Lennart Nilsson, from Behold Man, Little, Brown and Company, Boston; page 343, © 1986 Jason Laure/Woodfin Camp and Associates; page 347, © 1976 Suzanne Szasz/Photo Researchers, Inc.; page 348, George Zimbel/Monkmeyer Press; page 349, © Elizabeth Crews/Stock Boston; page 350, Eric Roth/The Picture Cube; page 351, © Erika Stone, 1981/Photo Researchers, Inc.; page 355, Harlow Primate Lab, University of Wisconsin; page 356, © L. Benedict Jones/The Picture Cube; page 360, (top) © Frank Siteman, 1979/The Picture Cube; (bottom) © Ellis Herwig/The Picture Cube; page 361, UPI/Bettmann Newsphotos

Chapter 11: page 367, Ellis Herwig/Stock Boston; page 374, (left) © Richard Hutchings/Photo Researchers, Inc; (right) © Rhoda Sidney/Monkmeyer Press; page 375, Arthur Grace/Stock Boston; page 377, © Jon L. Barkan/The Picture Cube; page 378, © Jerry Wachter/Photo Researchers, Inc.; page 385, © Pierre Kopp/Woodfin Camp & Associates; page 387, (left) © L. Starobin/The Picture Cube; (right) © 1982 Carol Bernson/Black Star; page 388, © Mark Antman/The Image Works; page 389, © Jean-Claude Lejeune/Stock Boston; page 390, © Michael Malysko, 1979/Stock Boston; page 393, (top) The Bettmann Archive; (bottom) Carl Glassman/The Image Works

Chapter 12 page 397, The Bettmann Archive; page 400, Owen Franken/Stock Boston; page 402, The Bettmann Archive; page 406, Culver Pictures; page 407, Judith D. Sedwick/The Picture Cube; page 410, UPI/Bettmann Newsphotos; page 415, Ellis Herwig/Stock Boston; page 417, © Bob Daemmrich/Stock Boston; page 420, © 1980 Elizabeth Hamlin/Stock Boston; page 422: (top left) Karsh, Ottawa/Woodfin Camp & Associates; (top right) © Akhtar Hussein/Woodfin Camp & Associates; (bottom) © 1981 Frank Siteman/The Picture Cube

Chapter 13: page 425, The Bettmann Archive; page 426, Rob Nelson/Stock Boston; page 427, Courtesy of the Harvard University News Office; page 428, (top 2 photos) The Bettmann Archive; (bottom) University of Illinois; page 433, Bob Kalman/The Image Works; page 434, Four by Five; page 436, Four by Five; page 437, The Bettmann Archive; page 438, Four by Five; page 439, The Bettmann Archive; page 441, Courtesy of Dr. Albert Bandura; page 444, © Barbara Alper/Stock Boston; page 445, Center for Studies of the Person, La Jolla, CA

Chapter 14: page 462, © 1981 Eunice Harris/Photo Researchers; Inc.; page 464, Jean-Marie Simon/Taurus Photos; page 466, The Bettmann Archive; page 468, Barbara Alper/Stock Boston; page 476, The Washington Post; page 477, Owen Franken/Stock Boston; page 478, J. R. Holland/Stock Boston; page 479, © Michael Weisbrot & Family; page 480, (top left) Henry Grossman/Black Star; (top right) UPI/Bettmann Newsphotos; (bottom left) The Bettmann Archive; (bottom right) © 1985 Hans Malmberg/Black Star; page 482, James H. Karales/Peter Arnold, Inc; page 489, © Arthur Tress/Photo Researchers, Inc.; page 490, © 1975 Jerry Cooke/Photo Researchers, Inc.; page 491, Dan Walsh/The Picture Cube; page 492, © Michael Weisbrot & Family; page 493, Michael Collier/Stock Boston; page 494, (top) © Mary Ellen Mark/Archive Pictures, Inc.; (bottom) Elinor S. Beckwith/Taurus Photos; page 501, John Running/Stock Boston

Chapter 15: page 507, courtesy of Edmund Engelman; page 512, courtesy of Dr. Albert Ellis; page 515, courtesy of Dr. Aaron Beck, University of Pennsylvania; page 517, courtesy of Dr. Joseph Wolpe; page 519, Four by Five; page 521, courtesy of Peter Lang; page 522, courtesy of Dr. Albert Bandura; page 523, Stacy Pick/Stock Boston; page 531, (top) Museum of Modern Art/Film Stills Archive; (bottom) Will McIntyre/Photo Researchers, Inc.

Chapter 16: page 542, AP/Wide World Photos; page 544, © Van Bucher, 1985/Photo Researchers, Inc.; page 546, AP/Wide World Photos; page 547, © Shepard Sherbell/Stock Boston; page 552, AP/Wide World Photos; page 561, William Vandivert and Scientific American; page 565, © Susan Van Etten/The Picture Cube; page 567, (top) © Alan Carey/The Image Works; (bottom) Four by Five; page 570, UPI/Bettmann Newsphotos; page 571, (clockwise) Taurus Photos; © George Holton, 1973/Photo Researchers, Inc.; Marcello Bertinetti/Photo Researchers, Inc.; © Nik Wheeler/Black Star; © Nik Wheeler/Black Star; page 576, (top) © Mark Antman/The Image Works; (bottom) courtesy of Dr. Albert Bandura

Chapter 17: page 581, AP/Wide World Photos; page 582, Edith G. Haun/Stock Boston; page 583, © Ginger Chih/Peter Arnold, Inc.; page 584, Mike Mazzaschi/Stock Boston; page 585, (top) © Frank Siteman/The Picture Cube; (bottom) Daniel S. Brody/Stock Boston; page 586, Jacques Jangoux/Peter Arnold, Inc.; page 588, (left) © Charlie Ott/Photo Researchers, Inc.; (right) Four by Five; page 590, © 1986 David H. Wells/The Image Works; page 593, Four by Five; page 603, © Dean Abramson/Stock Boston; page 607, Sybil Shelton/Monkmeyer Press; page 608, © S. Dapkiewicz/The Picture Cube; page 609, © John Coletti/Stock Boston; page 610, Four by Five

Copyright Acknowledgments

Fig. 1.1: Stapp, J., and R. Fulcher (1983). The employment of APA members: 1982. *American Psychologist 35*, 1298–1320. By permission of the American Psychological Association and the author.

Table 1.1: American Psychological Association (1985). Used by permission.

Table 1.2: Stapp, J., and R. Fulcher (1983). The employment of APA members: 1982. *American Psychologist 35*, 1298–1320. By permission of the American Psychological Association and the author.

Fig. 2.2: Zimbardo, P. (1985). The normal curve. In *Psychology and life*, 11th edition, p. 652. Published by Scott, Foresman. Reprinted by permission of the author.

Fig. 3.9: Geschwind, N. (1979). Specializations of the human brain. *Scientific american 241* (3), 180–199. From a drawing by Carol Donner. Copyright © 1979 by Scientific American, Inc. All rights reserved.

Fig. 3.10: LeDoux, J. E., D. H. Wilson and M. Gazzaniga (1977). A divided mind: Observation of the conscious properties of the separated hemispheres. *Annals of neurology 2*, 417–421. By permission of Michael S. Gazzaniga, M.D.

Fig. 3.12: Gazzaniga, M. (1970). *The bisected brain*. By permission of Plenum Press and Michael S. Gazzaniga, M.D.

Fig. 4.2: Papalia, D. E., and S. W. Olds (1985). *Psychology*, p. 69. By permission of McGraw-Hill Publishing Company.

Fig. 4.4: Hardy, J., J. Stolwijk and D. Hoffman (1968). Pain following step increase in skin temperature. In D. Kenshalo (ed.) *The skin senses*. Courtesy Charles C. Thomas Publisher, Springfield, Illinois.

Fig. 4.9: Cornsweet, T. N. (1970). *Visual perception*. Copyright © 1970 by Harcourt, Brace Jovanovich, Inc. Reprinted by permission of the publisher.

Fig. 4.11: Dobelle, W. (1977). Current status of research on providing sight to the blind by electrical stimulation of the brain. *Journal of visual impairment and blindness 71* (7), 290–297. Copyright © 1977 by American Foundation for the Blind, Inc., and reproduced by kind permission of American Foundation for the Blind, 15 W. 16th Street, New York, NY 10011.

Fig. 4.12: Dvorine Color Vision Test. Reproduced by permission. Copyright © 1944, 1953, 1958 by Isreal Dvorine. Published by the Psychological Corporation. All rights reserved.

Fig. 4.30: Gibson, E., and R. Walk (1960). The visual cliff. *Scientific American 202*, 64–71. Copyright © 1960 by Scientific American, Inc. All rights reserved.

Fig. 5.1: Courtesy of Dr. Wilse B. Webb.

Fig. 5.2: Hauri, P. (1977) *Sleep disorders*. By permission of The Upjohn Company and the author.

Fig. 5.4: Rechtschaffen, A., M. Gilliland, B. Bergmann and J. Winter (1983). Physiological correlates of prolonged sleep deprivation in rats. *Science 83 221* (8 July 1983), 182–184. Copyright 1983 by the American Association for the Advancement of Science.

Fig. 5.5: Griffith, R. M., O. Miyago and A. Tago (1958). The universality of typical dreams: Japanese vs. Americans. *American Anthropologist 60* (6), part 1, 1173–1179. Reproduced by permission of the American Anthropological Association. Not for further reproduction.

Fig. 6.3: Hulse, S. H., H. Egeth and J. Deese (1980). *The psychology of learning*. By permission of McGraw-Hill Book Company.

Fig. 7.1: Atkinson, R. C. and R. M. Shiffrin (1971). The control of short-term memory. *Scientific american 225*, 82–90. From an original drawing by Allen Beechel. Copyright © 1971 by Scientific American, Inc. All rights reserved.

Figs. 7.2, 7.3: Sperling, G. (1960). The information available in brief visual presentations. *Psychological monographs 74* (whole no. 11), 1–29. Copyright 1960 by the American Psychological Association. Reprinted by permission of the publisher and author.

Fig. 7.6: Craik, F. I. M. and E. Tulving (1975). Depth of processing and the retention of words in episodic memory. *Journal of experimental psychology: General 104*, 268–294. Copyright © 1975 by the American Psychological Association. Reprinted by permission of the author.

Fig. 7.9: Adapted from Hilen, M. and T. Oaster (1976). Serial position and isolation effects in a classroom lecture simulation. *Journal of educational psychology 68*, 293–296. By permission of the American Psychological Association and the author.

Fig. 7.10: Bartlett, F. (1932). *Remembering: A study in experimental social psychology*, pp. 65 and 72. Copyright © Cambridge University Press. Reprinted by permission of the publisher.

Fig. 7.11: Allport, G. W. and L. J. Postman (1958). The basic psychology of rumor. In E. E. Maccoby, T. M. Newcomb and E. L. Hartley (Eds.). *Readings in social psychology*, third edition. Copyright © 1947, 1952, 1958 by Henry Holt and Company. Reprinted by permission of Holt, Reinhart and Winston, Inc.

Fig. 7.12: Adapted from Loftus, E. and J. Palmer (1974). Reconstruction of automobile destruction: An example of interaction between language and memory. *Journal of verbal learning and verbal behavior 13*, 585–589. By permission of Academic Press and the author.

Fig. 8.3: Rosch, E. (1975). Cognitive representation of semantic categories. *Journal of experimental psychology: General 104*, 192–253. Copyright © 1975 by the American Psychological Association. Adapted by permission of the author.

Figs. 8.4, 8.5: Glucksberg, S. and R. W. Weisberg (1966). Some effects of labeling in a functional fixedness problem. *Journal of experimental psychology 71*, 659–664. Copyright © 1966 by the American Psychological Association. Adapted by permission of the author.

Fig. 8.6: Greeno, J. and J. C. Thomas (1974). An analysis of behavior in the hobbits-orcs problem. *Cognitive Psychology 6*, 270–292. By permission of Academic press and the authors.

Fig. 8.7: Luchins, A. and E. Luchins (1959). *Rigidity and behavior*. Adapted by permission of the authors.

Fig. 8.13: Von Frishc, K. (1974). Die Entschlussung der Bienensprache. Nobel lecture. Copyright © 1974 The Nobel Foundation.

Fig. 8.14: Premack, D. (1971). Language in chimpanzees. *Science 71 172*, 808–822 (figure on p. 812). Copyright 1983 by the American Association for the Advancement of Science.

Fig. 9.1: Maslow, A. (1970). *Motivation and personality*, second edition. Copyright © 1970 by Abraham H. Maslow. Reprinted by permission of Harper & Row, Publishers, Inc.

Fig. 9.8: Plutchik, R. (1980). A language for the emotions. *Psychology today* (February). Copyright © 1980 American Psychological Association.

Fig. 9.10: Schachter, S. and J. Singer (1962). Cognitive, social and physiological determinants of emotional state. *Psychological review 69*, 379–399. Copyright 1962 by the American Psychological Association. Adapted by permission of the author.

Table 9.2: Build Study, Society of Actuaries (1979) and Association of Life Insurance Medical Directors of America (1980). Courtesy of Metropolitan Life Insurance Co.

Fig. 10.9: Conel, J. L. (1939–1963). *The postnatal development of the human cerebral cortex*, vols. I–VI. Harvard University Press, publisher. Reprinted by permission.

Fig. 10.10: Rosenzweig, M. R., E. L. Bennett and M. C. Diamond (1972). Brain changes in response to experience. *Scientific american* (February), 22–29. Copyright © 1972 by Scientific American, Inc. All rights reserved.

Fig. 10.12: Rathus, S. A. (1987). *Psychology*, third edition. Copyright © 1987, 1984, 1981 by CBS College Publishing. Reprinted by permission of Holt, Rinehart and Winston, Inc.

Table 10.2: Papalia, D. E. and S. W. Olds (1986). *Human development*, third edition, p. 97. By permission of McGraw-Hill Book Company.

Fig. 11.1: Cskszentmihaly, M. and R. Larson (1984). *Being adolescent: Conflict and growth in the teenage years*. Copyright © 1984 by Basic Books, Inc. Reprinted by permission of the publisher.

Table 11.2: Crooks, R. L. and K. Baur (1987). *Our sexuality*, third edition. Copyright © 1980, 1983, 1987 by The Benjamin/Cummings Publishing Company, Inc., p. 440. Reprinted by permission.

Fig. 12.2: Adapted from Wechfler Adult Intelligence Scale. Reproduced by permission of the publisher, The Psychological Corporation, San Antonio, Texas. All rights reserved.

Fig. 12.3: Rathus, S. A. (1987). *Psychology*, third edition. Copyright 1987, 1984, 1981 by CBS College Publishing. Reprinted by permission of Holt, Rinehart and Winston, Inc.

Fig. 12.5: Anastasi, A. (1958). *Differential psychology*, third edition. Copyright © 1958 by Macmillan Publishing Company, Inc.

Table 12.3: Rathus, S. A. (1987). *Psychology*, third edition. Copyright © 1987, 1984, 1981 by CBS College Publishing. Reprinted by permission of Holt, Rinehart and Winston, Inc.

Fig. 13.1: Mischel, W. (1986). *Introduction to personality*, fourth edition. Copyright © 1986, 1981 by CBS College Publishing. Copyright © 1976 by Holt, Rinehart and Winston. Copyright © 1971 by Holt, Rinehart and Winston, Inc. Reprinted by permission of Holt, Rinehart and Winston, Inc.

Fig. 13.2: Rathus, S. A. (1987). *Psychology*, third edition. Copyright © 1987, 1984, 1981 by CBS College Publishing. Reprinted by permission of Holt, Rinehart and Winston, Inc.

Fig. 13.3: Bruno, F. J. (1983). *Adjustment and growth*. Copyright © 1983. Reprinted by permission of John Wiley & Sons, Inc.

Fig. 13.4: Mischel, W. (1986). *Introduction to personality*, fourth edition. Copyright © 1986, 1981 by CBS College Publishing. Copyright © 1976 by Holt, Rinehart and Winston. Copyright © 1971 by

Holt, Rinehart and Winston, Inc. Reprinted by permission of Holt, Rinehart and Winston, Inc.

Fig. 13.5: Bandura, A. and W. Mischel (1965). Modification of self-imposed delay of reward through exposure to live and symbolic models. *Journal of personality and social psychology 2,* 698–705. Copyright 1965 by the American Psychological Association. Adapted by permission of the author.

Fig. 13.7: Rorschach Psychodiagnostics Plate I. Copyright © Verlag Hans Huber, Bern.

Fig. 13.8: Sample Thematic Apperception Test Card. Copyright © 1943 by The President and Fellows of Harvard College; © 1971 by Henry A. Murray. Reprinted by permission of Harvard University Press.

Table 13.1: Mischel, W. (1986). *Introduction to personality,* fourth edition. Copyright © 1986, 1981 by CBS College Publishing. Copyright © 1976 by Holt, Rinehart and Winston. Copyright © 1971 by Holt, Rinehart and Winston, Inc. Reprinted by permission of Holt, Rinehart and Winston, Inc.

Table 13.3: Rathus, S. A. (1987). *Psychology,* third edition. Copyright © 1987, 1984, 1981 by CBS College Publishing. Reprinted by permission of Holt, Reinhart and Winston, Inc.

Fig. 14.2: Duke, M. and S. Nowicki (1986). *Abnormal psychology: A new look.* Copyright © 1986 by CBS College Publishing. Reprinted by permission of Holt, Rinehart and Winston, Inc.

Fig. 14.5: Lewinsohn, R. (1974). A behavioral approach to depression. In R. Friedman and M. Katz (Eds.). *The psychology of depression: Contemporary theory and resources,* fig. 1, p. 159. By permission of Hemisphere Publishing Corporation, a subsidiary of Harper & Row, Publishers, Inc.

Fig. 14.6: Duke, M. and S. Nowicki (1986). *Abnormal psychology: A new look.* Copyright © 1986 by CBS College Publishing. Reprinted by permission of Holt, Rinehart and Winston, Inc.

Fig. 14.7: Duke, M. and S. Nowicki (1986). *Abnormal psychology: A new look.* Copyright © 1986 by CBS College Publishing. Reprinted by permission of Holt, Rinehart and Winston, Inc.

Table 14.1: Duke, M. and S. Nowicki (1986). *Abnormal psychology: A New look.* Copyright © 1986 by CBS College Publishing. Reprinted by permission of Holt, Rinehart and Winston, Inc.

Table 14.3: Perley, M. and S. Guze (1962). Hysteria: the stability of usefulness of clinical criteria. *New England journal of medicine 266* (9), 421–426. Adapted by permission of the New England Journal of Medicine; Davison and Neale (1986). *Abnormal psychology.* Copyright © 1986. By permission of John Wiley & Sons.

Table 14.4: Nurnberger, J. I. and Gershon, E. S. (1982). Genetics. In E. S. Paykel (Ed.). *Handbook of affective disorders.* Adapted by permission of Guilford Press.

Table 14.5: Duke, M. and S. Nowicki (1986). *Abnormal psychology: A new look.* Copyright © 1986 by CBS College Publishing. Reprinted by permission of Holt, Rinehart and Winston, Inc.

Table 14.7: Gottesman, I. I. and J. Shields (1982). *Schizophrenia: The epigenetic puzzle.* Copyright © 1982 by Cambridge University Press. Reprinted with permission.

Quotes (MS 14–36): Davison G. and J. Neale (1986). *Abnormal psychology,* fourth edition. Copyright © 1986. Reprinted by permission of John Wiley & Sons, Inc.

Quotes (MS 14–56): O'Neal, J. (1984). First person account: finding myself and loving it. *Schizophrenia bulletin 10,* 109–110. By permission of the National Institutes of Mental Health, Schizophrenia Research Branch.

Fig. 15.3: Smith, M., G. Glass and R. Miller (1980). *The benefits of psychotherapy.* Adapted by permission of Johns Hopkins University Press.

Table 15.3: Paul, G. (1966). *Insight vs. desensitization in psychotherapy: an experiment in anxiety reduction.*

Quotes (MS 15–9, 15–10): Rogers, C. (1986). Client-centered therapy. In I. Kutash and A. Wolf (Eds.). *Psychotherapist's casebook.* Reprinted by permission of Jossey-Bass.

Quotes (MS 15–14): Simkin, J., A. Simkin, L. Brien and C. Sheldon (1986). Gestalt therapy. In I. Kutash and A. Wolf (Eds.). *Psychotherapist's casebook.* Reprinted by permission of Jossey-Bass.

Quotes (MS 15–16, 15–17, 15–18): Ellis, A. (1984). Rational-Emotive Therapy. In R. Corsini (Ed.). *Current psychotherapies.* Reprinted by permission of F. E. Peacock Publishers, Inc.

Quotes (MS 15–6, 15–7): Arlow, J. (1984). Psychoanalysis. In R. Corsini (Ed.). *Current psychotherapies.* Reprinted by permission of F. E. Peacock Publishers, Inc.

Fig. 16.1: Rosenberg, S., C. Nelson and P. S. Vivekananthan (1968). A multi-dimensional approach to the structure of personality impressions. *Journal of personality and social psychology 9* (4), 283–294. Copyright 1968 by the American Psychological Association. Reprinted by permission of the author.

Fig. 16.2: Breckler, S. (1984). Empirical validation of affect, behavior and cognition as distinct components of attitude. *Journal of personality and social psychology 47* (6), 1191–1205. Copyright © 1984 by the American Psychological Association. Reprinted by permission of the author.

Fig. 16.3: Copyright 1987, Des Moines Register and Tribune Company.

Fig. 16.4: Sherif, M. (1936). *The psychology of social norms.* Copyright 1936 by Harper & Row, Publishers, Inc. Reprinted by permission of the publisher.

Fig. 16.5: Asch, S. E. (1955). Opinions and social pressure. *Scientific american 193* (5), 31–35. Copyright © 1955 by Scientific American, Inc. All rights reserved.

Table 16.1: Adorno, T. W., E. Frenkel-Brunswick, D. J. Levenson and R. Nevitt Stanford (1950). *The authoritarian personality.* Copyright 1950 The American Jewish Committee. Reprinted by permission of Harper & Row, Publishers, Inc.

Fig. 17.1: Cohen, S., D. Glass and J. Singer (1973). Apartment noise, auditory discrimination and reading ability in children. *Journal of Experimental social psychology 9,* 407–422. Reprinted by permission of Academic Press and the authors.

Fig. 17.3: Carlsmith, J. and C. Anderson (1979). Ambient temperature and the occurrence of collective violence: a new analysis. *Journal of personality and social psychology 37,* 337–341. Copyright © 1979 by the American Psychological Association. Reprinted by permission of the author.

Fig. 17.4: Baum, A. and S. Valins (1977) *Architecture and social behavior: Psychological studies of social density.* By permission of Lawrence Erlbaum Associates, Inc.

Fig. 17.5: Baum, A. and G. Davis (1980). Reducing the stress of high-density living: an architectural intervention. *Journal of personality and social psychology 38,* 471–481. Copyright © 1980 by the American Psychological Association. Reprinted by permission of the author.

Fig. 17.6: Baron, R. and D. Byrne (1984). *Social psychology: Understanding human interaction,* fourth edition. Adapted by permission.

Fig. 17.7: Calhoun, J. B. (1962) Population density and social psychology. *Scientific american* 104–141. Copyright © 1962 by Scientific American, Inc. All rights reserved; Rathus, S. A. (1987). *Psychology,* third edition. Copyright © 1987, 1984, 1981 by CBS College Publishing. Reprinted by permission of Holt, Rinehart and Winston, Inc.

Figures A.1 through A.9: Bourne and Ekstrand (1985). *Psychology: Its principles and meanings,* fifth edition. Copyright © 1985 by CBS College Publishing. Reprinted by permission of Holt, Rinehart and Winston, Inc.

Tables A.1 through A.9: Bourne and Ekstrand (1985). *Psychology: Its principles and meanings,* fifth edition. Copyright © 1985 by CBS College Publishing. Reprinted by permission of Holt, Rinehart and Winston, Inc.

Fig. B.1: Fiedler, F. E. and M. M. Chemers (1984). *Improving leadership effectiveness: The leader match concept,* p. 166. Copyright © 1984. Reprinted by permission of John Wiley & Sons, Inc.

Fig. C.1 and C.2: Masters, W. and V. Johnson (1966). *Human sexual response.*

Fig. C.3: Kinsey, A. et al. (1948). *Sexual behavior in the human male,* p. 638. Reprinted by permission of the Kinsey Institute for Research in Sex, Gender and Reproduction, Inc.

Table C.1: Hunt, M. (1974). *Sexual behavior in the 1970's.* Copyright © 1974 by Morton Hunt. Reprinted by permission of Playboy Enterprises, Inc.

Table C.2: Sue, D. (1979). Erotic fantasies of college students during coitus. *Journal of sex research 15,* 299–305. Published by permission of *The Journal of Sex Research,* a publication of the Society for the Scientific Study of Sex.